United States Counties

For Ginger and Griff

United States Counties

Mark Dunn *and* Mary Dunn

McFarland & Company, Inc., Publishers
Jefferson, North Carolina, and London

LIBRARY OF CONGRESS ONLINE CATALOG

Dunn, Mark R.
United States counties / Mark Dunn and Mary Dunn.
p.   cm.
Includes index.

ISBN 0-7864-1515-0 (illustrated case binding : 50# alkaline paper)

1. United States — History, Local — Miscellanea.
2. United States — Administrative and political divisions — Miscellanea.
E180.D86   2003   917.3'003 22   2003014379

British Library cataloguing data are available

Cover image: *Cover art ©2003 Map Resources*

Manufactured in the United States of America

*McFarland & Company, Inc., Publishers
Box 611, Jefferson, North Carolina 28640
www.mcfarlandpub.com*

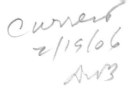

Acknowledgments

The authors offer special thanks to the following individuals without whose assistance this book would never have been completed:

Our editorial assistant, Laura Atlas, for her many hours of research.

Wayne Furman, director of the Office of Special Collections at the New York Public Library, for providing access to the Allen Room for scholars where much of the book was researched.

Warren Platt, general reference librarian at NYPL, for always going the extra mile for us.

Alice Hudson, chief of New York Public Library's Map Division, and her staff, for steering us to sources that were invaluable, and for facilitating easy access to the division's holdings.

Ruth Carr and the staff of the Division of U.S. History, Local History and Genealogy at NYPL.

Lorraine Wochna and Pat Gabridge, for their many helpful research suggestions.

Hank and Oliver Kranichfeld, for helping us to get all the professional sports teams assigned to their appropriate counties.

Gabor and SuzAnne Barabas, for setting our minds at ease about what publisher to approach.

And the hundreds of county librarians, historians and chambers of commerce officers and employees who offered material for this book.

Contents

Introduction

In November and December of 2000 America watched and winced as the closest presidential election in history spun itself into a political and judicial free-for-all. Through machine counts and hand counts, protests and contests, and the ubiquitous spin and counter-spin from the opposing political camps, this protracted historical soap opera offered Americans only one thing to agree on: It was a surprisingly good way to learn the names of the counties of Florida. But that wasn't the only thing about Florida that Americans were learning. Played out before the shifting backdrops of different Florida counties, the story took on a new hue each time the scenery changed. Each county had unique issues to resolve, its political makeup, character and history setting it apart as a separate but vital component in the political and social mix that is the state of Florida.

This extended national election may have been symptomatic of a flawed electoral process and the natural product of a troublingly divided electorate, but it was curiously framed by a geographical entity that has been holding this country together for the last 225 years: the *county*.

Borrowed along with a host of other government institutions and political traditions from our former landlords, the Brits, this political and geographical unit was far too useful to builders of a new nation not to be fully appropriated. And, in fact, long before independence was even a twinkle in our Founding Fathers' eyes, counties were already being carved out to serve the needs of toddling American colonists.

Over the years we have altered the original model (or in the case of Louisiana, given it a French accent). Alaska, to be different, joined the union eschewing the county concept altogether, and Connecticut and Rhode Island's counties were officially abolished a few years ago. (What remain within these two states today are geographical vestiges; we include these "shadow counties" with a nod toward their former days of function and glory.) And, to be fair, there

are other places in this country for which the county geographical unit was found to be an unsuitable vehicle for local governance. For this reason our book will include only through passing mention, and through Appendix I, the independent cities of St. Louis, Missouri; Baltimore, Maryland; Carson City, Nevada; and the forty other such municipalities in Virginia. These anomalies notwithstanding, we are, without doubt, a nation of counties — a great many counties — 3,071 to be exact, from Delaware's lonely trio to Texas's small army, 254 strong.

Our aim here is to take a look at our nation through a relatively underused lens, one too often simply taken for granted ... until, that is, the Palm Beach grannies move their ballot frustration to the streets; lovers commence to cuddle and coo among the bridges of Madison; until frogs take their marks in Calaveras ... or until it comes time to fund our county school system, upgrade a county road, elect a new county sheriff, or burnish the masonry of our inarguably favorite county courthouse — the one that stands proud and tall right in the middle of our very own county seat.

In the course of researching this book one of the librarians at the New York Public Library asked us how we could ever take on such a massive project. "You can't be serious," she noted, almost dismissive. "There are *hundreds* of counties."

"There are actually *thousands*," we laughed. "Nobody's ever compiled a book like this before. And we think it's time."

We have striven for accuracy throughout the book, but have often found ourselves at the mercy of fuzzy facts, variant spellings, and conflicting and sometimes outright erroneous sources, this sad reality making our task all the more laborious. (A well-known gazetteer in its very recent edition offers up national monuments that have long been national parks, streams that are actually rivers and vice versa, and products that haven't been made in significant numbers for years: LP record albums, dictaphones, and women's corsets, to name a few.) Trying to get it all right hasn't been easy. If you discover mistakes, please write us so that we may correct the error in the next edition of this book. And forgive the occasional discrepancy between what even our trustworthy sources have provided us with, and what you, perhaps the local expert on your county, know all too well to be the truth.

Likewise, we know that place names do change, colleges become universities, military bases close down. We have attempted to bring the information in this book as up to date as possible, but ask the reader to remember that this is a nation in the process of constant evolution, transition, and reinvention. Understand as well that as much as we regret it, we've had to leave a good deal of information out. To do a comprehensive survey of all of America's counties would result in a collection of volumes too expansive for even a large library's shelves. Los Angeles County alone would fill out a volume by itself. What we have done, instead, is include the following for every entry: name, county seat, population, land area, location and salient geographical features, name derivation, date of establishment, and products and industries. Selected entries will also include population and area rankings, name comparatives (31 counties are named for George Washington alone!), a sampling of famous residents, a smattering of historical facts, especially if the events that took place in a given county have national relevance, and a few facts that we found far too interesting or simply bizarre not to include. (Yes, you'll find mention of the world's largest ball of twine. It's in Mitchell County, Kansas.)

Information for each entry will be presented in this order:

Name • County seat • Population • Land area in square miles • Location & prominent geographical features • Name derivation • Date of establishment • History • Famous residents • Products & industries • Interesting facts

We have attempted to keep each entry as short as possible in order to meet our goal of offering the reader and researcher a compact, single volume encyclopedia. Since no volume of this scope has been compiled before, we were faced with a number of virginal concerns. Perhaps the most pressing was this: Should we be graciously democratic and grant each county's entry equal weight regardless of its population, or should we concede the enormous disparity between the macro-counties (Los Angeles, New York and Cook counties, for example) and the micro-counties (Loving County, Texas, pop. 67; Loup County, Nebraska, pop. 712) and make the necessary accommodations? While it

was our initial intent to celebrate the political and geographical diversity of our American counties by offering each entry relatively equal representation in this volume, reality and fairness have dictated that counties with 67 residents should be required to relinquish at least some portion of their claim for space in this book to a county, with, in the case of Los Angeles, 9.5 million. We think we have come up with a fair compromise: well-populated counties with their attendant rich histories and fertile profiles have been allotted slightly longer mention (although admittedly we can only scratch the surface with a toothpick here). We're hopeful that the residents of both Loving County, Texas, and Los Angeles County, California, will understand.

The counties are arranged alphabetically by state. We have included a master alphabetical index at the back of the book.

All population figures are drawn from the 2000 United States Census.

In researching the land area of each county we discovered enormous disparity among sources. We have chosen one source among the many and pronounced it definitive: the *Rand McNally Commercial Atlas and Marketing Guide*, 2002 Edition. Area square mileage figures are based on this source; we acknowledge that on occasion our figures may be open to some dispute. We believe that the reason for the widespread discrepancies rests in large part upon the various interpretations of area in terms of land and water. All areas noted here will refer to land area only.

We have tried to keep abbreviations to a minimum. Most state references, however, will use the familiar two-letter postal designations. For those of you who can't remember if AL stands for Alabama or Alaska, we've placed a reminder at the back of the book (Appendix III).

The official motto of each state is listed beneath the state's name.

And finally: having now visited by armchair, internet highway and library carrel all the counties in the United States, we will inevitably be asked if we have acquired a few favorites. We have. And at the risk of offending residents of those counties who did not make our somewhat quirky short list, we'll share them with you now:

Dunn County, North Dakota … *for obvious reasons.*
Dunn County, Wisconsin … *ditto.*
New York County, New York … *our urban home for the last fifteen years*
Travis County, Texas … *where we met and married, and where we worked as clerks for county justices of the peace from 1983 to 1987*
Hidalgo County, Texas … *where Mary was born*
Shelby County, Tennessee … *where Mark was born*

Woodbury County, Iowa ... *where we once won an eye-pop-*
ping $100 playing the riverboat slots
and the Montana counties of Musselshell, Petroleum, Rosebud and Sweet Grass ... *because, we confess, we just*
love the names.

We hope you find the book useful and entertain-
ing. Please feel free to write us with your corrections and
comments.

Mark and Mary Dunn
P.O. Box 40
Old Chelsea Station
New York, NY 10011

The Counties

ALABAMA

We Dare Defend Our Rights

Each of Alabama's sixty-seven counties is governed by a board of commissioners, officially known as county commission. The probate judge is the chief official in most of the state's counties. Other important county officials are the sheriff, district attorney, superintendent of education, engineer, tax assessor, and tax collector.

AUTAUGA *Prattville* • 43,671 • 596 • Central AL, bounded on the south by the Alabama River and on the west by the Mulberry River. The county lies in the Black Belt agricultural area. • Named for Autauga Creek • 1818, from Montgomery • Industrialist Daniel Pratt founded Prattville and based its design on a New England village. The cotton gin was first manufactured here by Pratt in the mid–1800s. • Cotton, hay, soybeans; textile and related industries • There has been cotton gin manufacturing in the county since 1838.

BALDWIN *Bay Minette* • 140,415 • 1,596 (the largest county in AL) • Southwestern AL, bounded on the west by the Tensaw River, on the southwest by Mobile and Bon Secour bays, on the northwest in part by the Alabama River, on the east in part by the Perdido River, on the southeast by Perdido Bay, on the south by the Gulf of Mexico, and on the north by the Little River. The Intracoastal Waterway crosses the county from Bon Secour Bay to Perdido Bay. Meaher and Historic Blakeley state parks are here, as is Baldwin State Forest. Several units of Bon Secour National Wildlife Refuge are found through the lower peninsula. Fort Mimms State Historic Site, Fort Morgan Historic Site, and William Weatherford Monument are also here. • One of two counties (the other in GA) named for Abraham Baldwin (1754–1807), American clergyman and U.S. senator from GA; founder of Franklin College (now University of Georgia) • 1809, from Washington • Soybeans, subtropical fruits, potatoes, sugar cane, pecans, vegetables, gladiolus bulbs; timber; crude oil and natural gas products; hunting and fishing; forest products, furniture, fabricated metal, clothing • Gulf State Park at Gulf Shores includes a 825-foot fishing pier on the Gulf of Mexico.

BARBOUR (one of two counties so named, the other in WV) *Clayton* • 29,038 • 885 • Southeastern AL, bounded on the east by the Chattahoochee River (forming Walter F. George Reservoir and the GA state line), on the northeast by the North Fork of the Cowikee, and on the west by the Pea River. Blue Springs and Lakepoint Resort state parks are here. Part of Eufala National Wildlife Refuge is in the northeast. • Named for James Barbour (1775–1842), governor of VA, minister to England and U.S. secretary of war • 1832, from Pike and territorial land • Politician George Wallace • Cotton, peanuts, corn, livestock; manufacture of textiles, carpet yarn, shoes, women's garments, doors, lumber, golf clubs; bauxite mining; paper milling.

BIBB *Centreville* • 20,826 • 623 • Central AL, crossed by the Cahaba River. Part of Talladega National Forest is in the south.

A plateau region is in the southeast and the Black Belt is in the southwest. Brierfield Ironworks Historic State Park is also here. • One of two counties (the other in GA) named for William Wyatt Bibb (1781–1820), U.S. senator from GA and first governor of AL • 1818 (prior to statehood) from Monroe and Montgomery • Hogs, cotton, peanuts, cattle; coal mining; manufacture of lumber, cabinets, toys, and clothing.

BLOUNT (one of two counties so named, the other in TN) *Oneonta* • 51,024 • 646 • North-central AL, bounded on the northwest by the Mulberry Fork of the Black Warrior River; drained by the Locust Fork of the Black Warrior River. The Sand and Blount mountains cross the county. • Named for Willie G. Blount (1768–1835), governor of TN • 1818 (prior to statehood) from Montgomery • Soybeans, wheat, corn, poultry, vegetables; coal, iron, limestone; millwork, manufacture of clothing, tire rims; meat packaging • Rickwood Caverns State Park includes 250-million-year-old limestone formations. Swann and Horton Mill covered bridges are in the county.

BULLOCK *Union Springs* • 11,714 • 625 • Southeastern AL. The county is watered by headstreams of the Conecuh and Pea rivers. • Named for Confederate colonel E. C. Bullock (1825–1861) • 1866 from Barbour, Pike, Macon and Montgomery • Livestock, pecans, peanuts • Chunnenuggee Garden, established in 1847 in Union Springs, was the state's first public garden. Union Springs hosts the largest amateur bird dog field trail competition in the U.S. each November.

BUTLER (one of eight counties so named) *Greenville* • 21,399 • 777 • Southern AL; drained by branches of the Sepulga River and Pigeon Creek • Named for William Butler (?–1818), GA legislator and soldier, killed by Indians • 1819 from Conecuh and Montgomery • Singer and guitarist Hank Williams • Soybeans, corn, pecans, peanuts, poultry; lumber milling, wood products; apparel, machinery, fertilizer.

CALHOUN *Anniston* • 112,249 • 608 • Northeastern AL, bounded on the west by the Coosa River, forming Neely Henry Lake reservoir. The Appalachians Mountains cross the county. Part of Talladega National Forest and Choccolocco State Forest are in the east. Anniston Army Depot is also here. • One of eleven counties named for John Caldwell Calhoun (1782–1850), U.S. statesman and champion of southern causes • Organized as Benton in 1832 from Creek cession; name changed 1858 • Anniston was settled in 1863; its first blast furnace supplied the Confederate Army. The old Cane Creek

Furnace, near Anniston, manufactured part of the iron used in the construction of the Confederate Battleship Merrimack. During World War II, nearly 500,000 men were trained at Fort McClellan, including a company of Japanese Americans. • Hay, soybeans, wheat, poultry, cattle; iron ore, limestone, bauxite, barites; manufacture of cast-iron pipe, textiles, and chemicals; education (Jacksonville State U.) • Fort McClellan is the site of the Women's Army Corps Museum.

CHAMBERS (one of two counties so named, the other in TX) *Lafayette* • 36,583 • 597 • Eastern AL, bounded on the east by the Chattahoochee River (forming the GA state line) and West Point Lake reservoir; drained on the northwest by the Tallapoosa River. • Named for Henry H. Chambers (1790–1826), physician and U.S. Senator • 1832 from Creek cession • Fort Tyler is the site of one of the last Civil War battles east of the Mississippi River (April 1865) • Livestock, hay; textile milling (towels, fabrics, yarns), manufacture of rubber; meat packing.

CHEROKEE *Centre* • 23,988 • 553 • Northeastern AL, bounded on the east by the GA state line and on the northwest by the Little River; drained by the Coosa, Chattooga, and Little Rivers. Weiss Lake reservoir dominates the center of the county. • One of eight counties named for the Cherokee Indians • 1836 from Cherokee cession • General William Tecumseh Sherman established the Tecumseh Furnace in southeastern Cherokee County after the Civil War, employing many former Union soldiers. • Soybeans, cotton, corn, livestock; lumber milling; iron, coal and limestone mining • Little River, located on Lookout Mountain in both Cherokee and DeKalb Counties, is the only river in the U.S. that runs its entire course on the top of a mountain. It forms the Little River Canyon (nature preserve). Known as the "Grand Canyon of the South," it is the deepest gorge east of the Mississippi River. • Bluffton had the first electricity in AL. • Weiss Lake proclaims itself the "Crappie Capital of the World" because of the size and number of crappie caught there.

CHILTON *Clanton* • 39,593 • 694 • Central AL, bounded on the east by the Coosa River, forming Lay Lake and Mitchell Lake reservoirs; drained by the Mulberry River. Part of Talladega National Forest is in the southwest. • Named for William Parish Chilton (1810–71), legislator, jurist, and member of the Confederate Congress • Organized as Baker in 1868 from Bibb, Perry, Autauga, and Shelby counties; name changed 1874 • Peaches (seventy-five percent of AL's crop is grown here), cotton, hay, livestock; meat and animal feed processing, cotton milling; lumber milling • Confederate Memorial Park is the site of AL's only Confederate retirement home (in operation from 1902–1939).

CHOCTAW *Butler* • 15,922 • 914 • Southwestern AL, bounded on the west by the Mississippi state line, on the east by the Tombigbee River. Choctaw National Wildlife Refuge, Bladen Springs State Park, and Coffeeville Lock and Dam are all located in the southeast. The county lies in the Black Belt.

• One of three counties named for the Choctaw Indians • 1847 from Sumter and Washington counties • Cotton, corn, peanuts, livestock; textiles; paper and lumber milling; crude oil production.

CLARKE (one of five counties so named) *Grove Hill* • 27,867 • 1,238 (the third largest county in AL) • Southwestern AL; bounded on the west by the Tombigbee River and on the southeast by the Alabama River. The county lies in the Black Belt. Coffeeville Lock and Dam on the Tombigbee River is in the northwest and the Claiborne Lock and Dam on the Alabama River is in the east. • Named for either Elijah Clarke (1733–1799), Revolutionary War general, or for John Clark (1766–1832), Governor of GA • 1812 (prior to statehood) from Washington County • Hay, corn, livestock; apparel manufacturing and lumber milling, woodworking; crude oil and natural gas products; artesian mineral wells.

CLAY (one of eighteen counties so named) *Ashland* • 14,254 • 605 • Eastern AL; part of Talladega National Forest is in the west and north. Cheaha Mountain (2,407 feet) in the Talladega Mountains, and on the Cleburne County line, is the highest point in the state. • One of fifteen counties named for the "Great Pacificator" Henry Clay (1777–1852), U.S. senator from KY, U.S. secretary of state, and candidate for presidency • 1866 from Talladega and Randolph • Supreme Court justice Hugo Black • Hay, hogs, poultry, corn; manufacture of apparel and furniture; food and plastics processing.

CLEBURNE *Heflin* • 14,123 • 553 • Eastern AL, bounded on the east by the GA state line and on the extreme southeast by the Little Tallapoosa River. The county is the Piedmont region and is crossed by the Tallapoosa River. Talladega National Forest covers much of the west. Cheaha State Park features many structures built by the Civilian Conservation Corps; it lies atop Cheaha Mountain (on the Clay county line), AL's highest point at 2,407 feet. • One of two counties (the other in AR) named for Confederate general Patrick R. Cleburne (1828–64) • 1855 from Calhoun and Randolph • Soybeans, corn, livestock (especially poultry); lumber milling, clothing manufacture.

COFFEE (one of three counties so named) *Elba* • 43,615 • 679 • Southeastern AL; drained by the Pea River. Part of Fort Rucker Military Reservation is on the eastern border. • One of two counties (the other in TN) named for Gen. John Coffee (1772–1833), TN surveyor and officer who served under Andrew Jackson • 1841 from Dale • Corn, peanuts, poultry, hogs; timber; manufacture of textiles and trailer trucks, forklifts, agricultural equipment; processing of meal products • A monument in Enterprise, which thanks the boll weevil for forcing the diversification of the local agriculture, is the only monument in the U.S. dedicated to a pest.

COLBERT *Tuscumbia* • 54,984 • 595 • Northwestern AL, bounded on the west by the MS state line, on the north by Pickwick Lake and Wilson Lake (both reservoirs on the Tennessee River), and on the east by Town River. The county is in the center of the Muscle Shoals region of TVA hydroelectric power development; the power industry has had a strong economic impact on the county's industrial growth. The Fall Line crosses the county north-south. • Named for brothers George and Levi Colbert, two Chickasaw Indian chiefs • 1867 from Franklin • In 1816, Andrew Jackson made speculative land purchases for an "industrial city" that was to become Sheffield. • Helen Keller was a county native. (*The Miracle Worker*, a play about Keller by William Gibson, is staged here each summer.) • Cotton, corn, soybeans, poultry and hogs; asphalt, bauxite, limestone, iron ore; light manufacturing • Over 100 coon dogs have been buried in the "Coon Dog Graveyard" since its creation here in 1937.

CONECUH *Evergreen* • 14,089 • 851 • Southern AL, bounded on the northeast by the Sepulga River and on the east in part by Pigeon Creek; drained by the Sepulga River, and Burnt Corn and Murder creeks. • Named for the Conecuh River • 1818 (prior to statehood) from Monroe • Corn, peanuts; crude oil and natural gas production; lumber milling; manufacture of fabricated metal products, apparel, textiles, motor vehicles, meat processing.

COOSA *Rockford* • 12,202 • 652 • East-central AL, bounded on the west by the Coosa River (forming Lay Lake and Mitchell Lake reservoirs); drained by Hatcher Creek. An arm of Lake Martin reservoir extends into the southeast corner. • Named for the Coosa River • 1832 from Creek cession • Itaba, an upper Creek Indian Village, located at Hatchet Creek, was visited by the De Soto expedition in 1540. • Hay, corn, livestock; marble, granite; lumber; textiles • Lay Dam, built in 1914, is Alabama Power Company's oldest hydroelectric plant in the state.

COVINGTON *Andalusia* • 37,631 • 1,034 • Southern AL, bounded on the south by the FL state line, on the west in part by Pigeon Creek and the Conecuh River, and on the north in part by the Conecuh River; drained by the Conecuh and Yellow rivers, and Patsaliga Creek. Part of Conecuh National Forest is in the south. Florala and Frank Jackson state parks are also here. • One of two counties (the other in MS) named for Leonard W. Covington (1773–1813), MD born legislator and army officer • Organized 1821 from Henry; name changed to Jones, 1868; name changed to original and present name 1868 • Hernando de Soto reputedly established a settlement on the Conecuh River near present day Andalusia. The site that would become Andalusia was crossed by the Three-Notched Trail, used by Andrew Jackson during his Creek Indian campaign (1813–14). • Cotton, corn, peanuts, soybeans, poultry, cattle, hogs; manufacture of textiles; trucking; lumber; crude oil production • Andalusia hosts the World Championship Domino Tournament every July.

CRENSHAW *Luverne* • 13,665 • 610 • South-central AL, bounded on the south, in part, by the Conecuh River; drained by the Conecuh River and Patsaliga Creek, both forming part of the county's eastern boundary. • Named for Anderson Crenshaw (1786–1847), lawyer and jurist • 1866 from Covington, Butler, Coffee, Lowndes, and Pike • Peanuts, corn, livestock (especially poultry); lumber milling; clothing manufacture, soft drink bottling.

CULLMAN *Cullman* • 77,483 • 738 • Northern AL, bounded on the east by the Mulberry Fork of the Black Warrior River. Lewis Smith Dam on the southwestern border forms Lewis Smith Lake reservoir. • Named for the city of Cullman, itself named for John G. Cullman, founder • 1877 from Blount, Morgan and Winston • Col. John Cullman developed the county in 1873 as a German colony; it ultimately attracted over 10,000 immigrants. Clarkson Covered Bridge, one of AL's largest covered truss bridges, was the site of the 1863 Battle of Hog Mountain. • Cotton, corn, peanuts, strawberries, sweet potatoes, poultry, cattle; lumber milling; coal; manufacture of electrical appliances, metal products, canned and frozen foods, apparel, and mattresses • The Ave Maria Grotto, known for its hand-crafted miniature reproductions of world famous buildings, is located at St. Bernard Abbey.

DALE *Ozark* • 49,129 • 561 • Southeastern AL; drained by the Choctawhatchee River and its west fork. Fort Rucker Military Reservation is here and includes the U.S. Army Aviation Museum. • Named for Samuel Dale (1772–1841), officer and scout in the Indian wars, and legislator in AL and MS • 1824 from Covington and Henry • Peanuts, corn, poultry, hogs; lumber • The Army Aviation Museum in Daleville displays one of the most comprehensive helicopter collections in the world.

DALLAS (one of five counties so named) *Selma* • 46,365 • 981 • South-central AL, bounded on the northeast in part by Mulberry Creek; drained by the Alabama and Cahaba rivers, and Cedar Creek. The county is in the Black Belt. Paul M. Grist State Park and part of Talladega National Forest are in the northwest. Old Cahawba Archaeological Park is also in the county. Part of William "Bill" Dannelly Reservoir is in the southwest. • Named for Alexander James Dallas (1759–1817), PA statesman and secretary of the treasury • 1818 (prior to statehood) from Montgomery • During the Civil War, Selma was a major Confederate supply depot. On April 2, 1865, it was captured by Union cavalry, which destroyed its military supply capability. On March 7, 1965, a planned march led by civil rights advocate Dr. Martin Luther King, Jr. from Selma to Montgomery was broken up by state police; on March 21, following a federal court ruling in their favor, the marchers proceeded to Montgomery, protected by the U.S. Army and federalized National Guard (National Voting Rights Museum). • Cotton, soybeans, dairy products, livestock; lumber; diversified industries.

DE KALB *Fort Payne* • 64,452 • 778 • Northeastern AL; bounded on the northeast by the GA state line and on the east in part by the Little River. The Sand Mountains extend throughout most of the county. De Soto and part of Buck's Pocket state parks and Sequoyah Caverns are also here. • One of six counties named for Johann, Baron de Kalb (1721–80), German-born French solder who fought with the Americans during the Revolutionary War • 1836 from Cherokee cession • In DeSoto State Park is the site of Will's Town, an Indian village where Sequoyah devised the Cherokee alphabet in 1809. • Corn, soybeans, hay, poultry, cattle, hogs; coal, iron, limestone, fuller's earth; light industry; tourism • The Little River, located on Lookout Mountain in both De Kalb and Cherokee Counties, is the only river in the U.S. that runs its entire course on the top of a mountain; it forms the Little River Canyon (nature preserve), the deepest gorge east of the Mississippi River.

ELMORE (One of two counties so named, the other in ID) *Wetumpka* • 65,874 (34% increase since 1990; second fastest growing county in AL) • 621 • East-central AL, bounded on the southwest by the Alabama River and on the east and south by the Tallapoosa River; drained by the Coosa River. The Fall Line crosses east-west. Part of Lake Martin and Lake Jordan reservoirs are here. The county has five hydroelectric plants wholly or partially within its borders. • Named for John Archer Elmore (1762–1834), an early settler and state legislator • Organized 1866 from Montgomery, Coosa, and Autauga, and from Tallapoosa in 1867 • Fort Toulouse/Jackson Park, erected by the French in 1717, was the site of the signing of the "Treaty of Fort Jackson," which forced the defeated Creek Nation to cede half of its land to the U.S. • Cotton, corn, livestock; textiles • A monument in Wetumpka honors the Crommelin brothers, members of the only family in AL to have sons all graduating from the U. S. Naval Academy and distinguishing themselves in military service.

ESCAMBIA (One of two counties so named, the other in FL) *Brewton* • 38,440 • 947 • Southern AL, bounded on the south by the FL state line, on the northeast in part by the Conecuh River, and on the northwest by the Little River; drained by the Conecuh (or Escambia) River, and Burnt Corn and Murder creeks. Part of Conecuh National Forest is in the east, and part of Little River State Forest is in the northwest. Poarch Creek Indian Reservation is in the county. • Named for the Escambia River • 1868 from Baldwin and Conecuh • Cotton, peanuts, corn; livestock, fruit; lumber milling, paper making, fence posts and piling; iron products, wire-bound boxes, containers, textiles, apparel; oil.

ETOWAH *Gadsden* • 103,459 • 535 (the smallest county in AL) • Northeastern AL; crossed by the Coosa River (forming Neely Henry Lake at the southern tip). Part of Blount and Lookout mountains cross the county. • The name of the county is of Cherokee origin, meaning unknown. • Organized as Baine, 1866; name changed 1868 • Corn, soybeans, cotton, beef, poultry, dairy; deposits of coal, iron, limestone, fuller's earth, manganese, barites; timber; iron and steel products; diversified manufacturing • Noccalula Falls, in Gadsden, is one of the few falls in the U.S. found entirely within a city limits.

FAYETTE (One of eleven counties so named) *Fayette* • 18,495 • 628 • Western AL; drained by the Sipsey and North rivers,

and Luxapillila Creek. The county is crossed north-south by the Fall Line. • One of seventeen counties named for the Marquis de Lafayette (1757–1834), French statesman and soldier who fought with Americans during the Revolutionary War • 1824 from Marion and Pickens • Cotton, corn, livestock; lumber milling, crude oil and natural gas products; deposits of coal, sandstone, fuller's earth; manufacture of apparel, yarn, tile, machinery.

FRANKLIN (one of twenty-five counties so named) *Russellville* • 31,223 • 636 • Northwestern AL; bounded on the west by the MS state line; drained by Bear Creek. The county is crossed north-south by the Fall Line. Part of William B. Bankhead National Forest is in the southeast. Cedar Creek and Bear Creek reservoirs are also here. • One of twenty-three counties named for Benjamin Franklin • 1818 (prior to statehood) from Cherokee cession • La Grange College, AL's first college, established here in 1830 and renamed Florence Wesleyan University in 1863, was burned to the ground by the 10th Missouri Cavalry during the Civil War. AL's iron industry originated on Cedar Creek near Russellville. • Soybeans, corn, poultry; deposits of coal, iron, limestone, bauxite; natural gas production.

GENEVA *Geneva* • 25,764 • 576 • Southeastern AL, bounded on the south by the FL state line; drained by the Pea and Choctawhatchee rivers. Geneva State Forest is in the west. • Named for the county seat, itself named for Geneva, Switzerland, home of many early settlers • 1868 from Coffee, Dale and Henry • The "Lincoln Flood" of 1865 forced the relocation of the entire town of Geneva to higher ground. • Poultry, peanuts, corn, soybeans • Designated as "Tree City, U.S.A." for several years, Geneva is the home of the landmark Constitutional Big Oak, one of the largest in the state.

GREENE *Eutaw* • 9,974 (the least populated county in AL) • 646 • Western AL; bounded on the north and northwest by the Sipsey River, on the west by the Tombigbee River, and on the east by the Black Warrior River. The county lies in the state's Black Belt • One of fourteen counties named for General Nathanael Greene (1742–86), hero of the Revolutionary War • 1819 from Marengo and Tuscaloosa • Almost completely surrounded by rivers, the county was spared destruction by the Union Army on its march from Tuscaloosa to MS. There was only one Civil War skirmish here, between Nathan Bedford Forrest and Union raiders in 1865. • Cattle, pecans, corn, soybeans, potatoes; timber.

HALE (one of two counties so named, the other in TX) *Greensboro* • 17,185 • 644 • West-central AL; bounded on the west by the Black Warrior River; drained by Big Brush Creek. The county lies in the Black Belt agricultural region. Part of Talladega National Forest is in the northeast. Part of Moundville Archaeological Park is also here. • Named for Stephen F. Hale (1816–62), lawyer, and Confederate army officer • 1867 from Greene, Marengo, and Perry • Cotton, cattle, corn, soybeans, grain; catfish; timber; food processing, manufacture of clothing and plastic bottles.

HENRY (one of ten counties so named) *Abbeville* • 16,310 • 562 • Southeastern AL; bounded on the east by the Chattahoochee River (forming the GA state line); drained by the Choctawhatchee River. The Walter F. George Lock and Dam forms its eponymous reservoir in the northeast. • One of ten counties named for Patrick Henry • 1819 from Conecuh. When established, Henry was the largest county in the newly created state; it is now among the smallest. • The first junior college in AL, Southeast Alabama Agricultural School, was established in 1889. • Peanuts, corn, hogs; bauxite; lumber • Abbeville is the oldest remaining colonial settlement in East AL.

HOUSTON (one of five counties so named) *Dothan* • 88,787 • 580 • Extreme southeastern AL, bounded on the east by the Chattahoochee River (forming the GA state line) and on the south by the FL state line. The county lies in the Wire Grass region of the state. Chattahoochee State Park is in the southeast. Landmark Park is also here. • Named for George Smith Houston (1811–79), U.S. senator and governor of AL • 1903 from Dale, Geneva, and Henry • Peanuts (the area produces over a quarter of all peanuts grown in the U.S.), corn, soybeans, hogs, cattle; diversified industries; education (Troy State U.–Dothan) • A giant gold peanut sculpture in Dothan proclaims the town "the Peanut Capital of the World." The National Peanut Festival is held here each October.

JACKSON (one of twenty-four counties so named) *Scottsboro* • 53,926 • 1,079 • Northeastern AL, bounded on the north by the TN state line and on the northeast by the GA state line; drained by the Tennessee (forming Guntersville Lake reservoir) and Paint Rock rivers. The Appalachian Mountains extend along the southeastern border. Fern Cave and Blowing Wind Cave national wildlife refuges are here. • One of twenty-two counties named directly or indirectly for President Andrew Jackson • 1819 from Cherokee cession • It was the scene in 1931 of the "Scottsboro Case," a trial at which nine African-American youths were convicted of raping two white women. U.S. Supreme Court reversals of the convictions became landmark civil rights rulings. • Soybeans, hay, corn, cattle, poultry; timber; deposits of coal and limestone • An almost continuous archeological record of human habitation (from at least 7000 BC to about AD 1650) is revealed in Russell Cave National Monument. Scottsboro is the site of two nuclear power plants and is an important component of the TVA.

JEFFERSON *Birmingham* • 662,047 (the most populated county in AL) • 1,113 (the fifth largest county in AL) • North-central AL, bound on the southwest in part by the Black Warrior River; drained by the Cahaba River and crossed by Locust Fork. Watercress Darter National Wildlife Refuge and Ruffner Mountain Nature Center are here. • One of twenty-six counties named directly or indirectly for President Thomas Jefferson • 1819 from Blount • The county, along with Walker, once accounted for sixty percent of AL's coal production. Lloyd Noland Hospital, founded in Fairfield in 1910, was an institutional pioneer in industrial medicine. Bessemer's Bell furnace produced the first basic iron in AL. In 1922, an explosion at a dolomite mine in the county killed 100 persons. Birmingham was the scene of black civil-rights and voter-registration drives led by the Reverend Martin Luther King, Jr. in the early 1960s. In 1971 it became the first U.S. city in which industrial plants were closed under federal law during an air pollution crisis. • Novelist Walker Percy; poet and playwright Sonia Sanchez; biologist Edward O. Wilson • Originally the iron and steel center of the south, the county's industries are now more diversified. Mining of coal, iron, and other minerals; iron and steel products; limestone quarrying; natural-gas production; manufacture of aircraft, acetylene, shellac, waxes, glycerine, other chemicals, wood blocks, fire extinguishers, bedding, bricks, cotton textiles; service industries; education (Samford U.; Miles College; U. of AL) • Annual events in Birmingham include the Festival of Arts in the spring and the State Fair in the fall. A fifty-five foot-tall cast-iron statue of Vulcan, the Roman god of fire, stands atop a 124 foot pedestal on Red Mountain overlooking Birmingham.

LAMAR (one of four counties so named) *Vernon* • 15,904 • 605 • Western AL, bounded on the west by the MS state line; drained by the Buttahatchee River, and Yellow and Luxapallila creeks. • One of three counties named for Lucius Q. C. Lamar (1825–93), U.S. senator and U.S. Supreme Court justice • Organized as Jones 1867 from Marion, Pickens, and Fayette counties; abolished the same year; recreated as Sanford 1868; renamed 1877 • Corn; timber; crude-oil and natural gas production; cotton-ginning, manufacture of clothing, furniture, electric heating elements, waste-handling and recycling equipment.

LAUDERDALE *Florence* • 87,966 • 669 • Extreme northwestern AL, bounded on the north by the TN state line, on the west by the MS state line, and on the south by the Tennessee River (here forming Pickwick Lake, Wilson Lake, Wheeler Lake, and Elk Lake reservoirs). Wilson and Wheeler dams provide hydroelectric power for industries at Florence. Joe Wheeler State Park and Key Cave National Wildlife Refuge are here. • One of three counties named for Col. James Lauderdale (?–1814), who fought in the Battle of Talladega • 1818 (prior to statehood) from Cherokee cession • Founded in 1830, La Grange College (now the University of North AL) was the first state-supported teachers college south of the Ohio River. • Composer W.C. Handy; labor organizer James T. Rapier • Cattle, poultry, corn, cotton, hay, soybeans, truck crops; manufacture of floor coverings, tiles, building materials, aluminum products; lumber; education (U. of Northern AL) • Florence hosts the W.C. Handy Music Festival every August. Indian Mound, in Florence, is the largest in the Tennessee Valley (42 feet high; base diameter 310 feet).

LAWRENCE (one of eleven counties so named) *Moulton* • 34,803 • 693 • Northwestern AL, bounded on the north by the Tennessee River (forming Wheeler Lake reservoir) and on the northwest by the Town River. Part of William B. Bankhead

National Forest is in the south, and includes Sipsey Fork (designated a National Wild and Scenic River). • One of nine counties named for Captain James Lawrence (1781–1813), U.S. Navy commander in War of 1812 • 1818 (prior to statehood) from Cherokee cession • Confederate General Joe Wheeler (homesite); athlete and Olympian Jesse Owens (memorial park) • Cotton, corn, soybeans, poultry, cattle; coal, limestone, asphalt; manufacture of clothing; lumber milling.

LEE (one of twelve counties so named) *Opelika* • 115,092 • 609 • Eastern AL, bounded on the east by the Chattahoochee River (forming the GA state line and Lake Harding and Lake Oliver reservoirs); drained by Sougahatchee Creek. Chewacla State Park is here. • One of eight counties named for Robert E. Lee • 1866 from Chambers and Macon • Pediatrician and virologist Frederick C. Robbins • Cotton, corn; granite, dolomite, manganese; lumber; education (Auburn U.); manufacture of textiles, recording tape, auto tires.

LIMESTONE (one of two counties so named, the other in TX) *Athens* • 65,676 • 568 • Northern AL, bounded on the north by the TN state line and on the southwest by the Tennessee River (forming Wheeler Lake reservoir); drained by the Elk River • Named for Limestone Creek, which flows through it • 1818 (prior to statehood) from Cherokee and Chickasaw cessions • Limestone was one of the first AL counties invaded by the Union in the Civil War (1862) and the scene of much fighting, especially in Athens. Confederate forces under General Nathan Bedford Forrest recaptured the city in 1864 when Col. Wallace Campbell surrendered his Federal forces. In 1934, Athens became the first city in AL to use electric power supplied by TVA. • President Andrew Johnson • Cotton (one of the top producing counties in the U.S.), corn, soybeans, livestock, hay, truck crops; timber; food-related industries; apparel manufacture; education (Athens State U.).

LOWNDES *Hayneville* • 13,473 • 718 • South-central AL, bounded on the north by the Alabama River; drained by its tributaries. The county is located in the Black Belt • One of three counties named for William J. Lowndes (1782–1822), SC legislator and U.S. representative • 1830 from Butler and Dallas • The town of Fort Deposit grew around a fort built here c. 1813 by Andrew Jackson • Cotton, corn, soybeans, dairying, poultry; lumber milling; manufacture of electrical components; pecan processing.

MACON *Tuskegee* • 24,105 • 611 • Eastern AL, bounded on the northwest by the Tallapoosa River. The county is in the Black Belt and contains Tuskegee National Forest. • One of six counties named for Nathaniel Macon (1758–1837), Speaker of the House and U.S. senator • 1832 from Creek cession • Tuskegee U. was founded here (as the Tuskegee Institute) by black leader and educator Booker T. Washington in 1881. It was here that scientist George Washington Carver discovered 300 useful by-products of the peanut plant. (Carver died in Tuskegee.) The school is also the home of the Center for Sweet Potato Research. • Civil rights activist Rosa Parks • Cotton, corn, soybeans, peanuts, sweet potatoes, cattle, dairying.

MADISON *Huntsville* • 276,700 (the third most populated county in AL) • 805 • Northern AL, bounded on the north by the TN state line, on the south by the Tennessee and Paint Rock rivers; crossed by the Flint River. Monte Sano State Park and part of Wheeler National Wildlife Refuge are here. • One of twenty counties named directly or indirectly for President James Madison • 1808 from Cherokee cession (prior to statehood) • Huntsville was the first community in AL to be granted a city charter (1811) by the territorial government. It was also the site (1819) of AL's first constitutional convention, and served briefly as the state capital. • Actress Viola Allen; Confederate guerrilla leader John H. Morgan • Cotton, corn, wheat, soybeans, hay, mules, cattle, poultry; textiles; aerospace related industries; education (AL A and M University; U. of AL–Huntsville; Oakwood College) • Huntsville, "Rocket City, U.S.A.," is the site of the Redstone Arsenal and the NASA Marshall Space Flight Center; scientists here developed many important rockets and space vehicles, including the Saturn 5 rocket system that carried the first astronauts to land on the moon.

MARENGO *Linden* • 22,539 • 977 • Western AL; bounded on the west by the Tombigbee River. The county lies in the state's agricultural Black Belt. Chickasaw State Park is located here. • The county's name commemorates Napoleon's victory over the Austrian army at Marengo, Italy (June 14, 1800) • 1818 (prior to statehood) from Choctaw cession • Demopolis was founded in 1817 by Bonapartist exiles and has fine Greek Revival homes built by cotton planters. • Corn, hay, cattle; lumber milling, manufacture of wood products, textiles and apparel, fertilizers, food and plastic products.

MARION *Hamilton* • 31,214 • 741 • Northwestern AL, bounded on the west by the MS state line; drained by the Buttahatchee and Sipsey rivers, and Bear Creek; crossed north-south by the Fall line • One of seventeen counties named for Gen. Francis Marion (?–1795), SC soldier and legislator • 1818 (prior to statehood) from Indian lands • The county had divided loyalties during the Civil War, with pro-Union independent farmers persecuted by pro-Confederate residents. Marion County is reputed to have provided as many troops for the Union as for the Confederacy. • Corn, soybeans, wheat, poultry; lumber, textiles; coal mines.

MARSHALL (one of twelve counties so named) *Guntersville* • 82,231 • 567 • Northeastern AL, bounded on the northwest by the Paint Rock and Tennessee rivers. Guntersville Dam, a major TVA installation on the Tennessee River, forms recreational Guntersville Lake reservoir, which dominates the county. Lake Guntersville and Cathedral Caverns state parks are also here. • One of eight counties named for John Marshall (1755–1835), who was the fourth Chief Justice of the U.S. and U.S. secretary of state • 1836 from Blount and Cherokee cession • Poultry, cattle, corn, soybeans, hay; manufacture of textiles, apparel, animal feeds, precision tools, concrete products; lumber.

MOBILE *Mobile* • 399,843 (the second most populated county in AL) • 1,233 (the fourth largest county in AL) • Extreme southwestern AL; bounded on the south by the Mississippi Sound, on the east by Mobile Bay, and the Mobile and Tensaw rivers, and on the west by the MS state line. The county includes Fort Gaines Historic Site and Big Creek Lake reservoir. The Intracoastal Waterway crosses through the Mississippi Sound, which separates Dauphin Island from the mainland. • Named for the city, bay and river • 1812 (prior to statehood) from Louisiana Purchase • Called the "City of Six Flags" because six governments have controlled it, Mobile is one of the nation's oldest cities, having been founded as Fort Louis de la Mobile by Sieur de Bienville in 1702. It was during Farragut's 1864 attack on the city that the Union Admiral said, "Damn the torpedoes! Full speed ahead!" Mobile was the last southern stronghold to fall to Federal forces. • Baseball player Hank Aaron; New York City socialite and suffragist Alva Belmont; U.S. army surgeon William C. Gorgas. Inventor William S. Burroughs and Confederate naval officer Raphael Semmes died here. • Corn, soybeans, pecans, berries, subtropical fruits; seafood; manufacture of lumber and paper products, fertilizer, chemicals, rayon; crude oil and natural-gas production; cotton processing; meat- and seafood packing; shipbuilding; education (U. of South AL; U. of Mobile) • The county is graced by thousands of azaleas each spring, both in the city's Azalea Trail festival and at Bellingrath Gardens (along with 65 acres of various other flowers). Mobile Bay is the retirement home of the World War II battleship, the USS Alabama; the World War II sub, the USS Drum; and the B-52 bomber, "Calamity Jane." The Bankhead Tunnel, built in 1940 under the Mobile River, was the first underwater tunnel built in the South.

MONROE *Monroeville* • 24,324 • 1,026 • Southwestern AL, bounded on the southwest by the Alabama River and on the south by the Little River. Part of Little River State Forest is on the southern border. Claude D. Kelley State Park and Claiborne Lock and Dam (on the Alabama River) are also here. • One of seventeen counties named for President James Monroe • 1815 (prior to statehood) from Creek cession • Cotton, peanuts, corn, soybeans, timber; crude-oil and natural gas production.

MONTGOMERY (one of eighteen counties so named) *Montgomery* • 223,510 (the fourth most populated county in AL) • 790 • East-central AL; bounded on the northwest by the Alabama River and on the north by the Tallapoosa River. The county lies in the Black Belt. Maxwell Air Force Base is also here. • Named for Lemuel P. Montgomery (1786–1814), officer in War of 1812 who died in combat against the Creek Indians • 1816 (prior to statehood) from Monroe • Known as the "Cradle of the Confederacy," Montgomery served as its first capital. Jefferson Davis occupied the First White House of the Confederacy here in 1861. It was also here that the Constitution of the Confederacy was drawn up. The first electric trolley streetcars in the U.S. began operating in Montgomery in

1866. In 1955, Rosa Parks refused to give up her seat on a city bus, resulting in a city-wide bus strike that led to a Supreme Court decision desegregating public transportation. • Singer Nat King Cole; football quarterback Bart Starr. Black planter and labor organizer James T. Rapier and political leader William L. Yancey died here. • Cotton, livestock, grain; manufacturing; education (AL State U.; Faulkner U.; others) • Maya Lin designed the Civil Rights Memorial to honor those who were killed in the struggle for equal rights. • F. Scott and Zelda Fitzgerald lived here between 1931–1932 while the novelist worked on *Tender is the Night.*

MORGAN (one of eleven counties so named) *Decatur* • 111,064 • 582 • Northern AL, bounded on the north by the Tennessee River (forming Wheeler Lake reservoir); drained by Flint Creek. Wheeler National Wildlife Refuge is in the north. • One of nine counties named for Daniel Morgan (1736–1802), general in the Revolutionary War • Organized as Cotaco, 1818 (prior to statehood) from Indian lands; name changed 1821 • Decatur was the eastern terminus of the first railroad in the U.S. west of the Appalachians. The town was occupied by both sides and nearly destroyed during the Civil War • Physician and astronaut Mae C. Jemison • Cotton, corn, soybeans, poultry, livestock; textiles; deposits of coal, sandstone, fuller's earth, asphalt; manufacture of hosiery, textiles, tire fabric, nylon, steel barges, chemicals, metal and rubber products • The Racing Horse Breeder's Association hosts the annual worldwide championship competitions in Decatur.

PERRY *Marion* • 11,861 • 719 • West-central AL; drained by the Cahaba River. The county lies in the Black Belt, with part of Talladega National Forest in the northeast. • One of ten counties named for Oliver H. Perry (1785–1819), U.S. naval officer during the War of 1812 • 1819 from Tuscaloosa • A resolution adopted by the Baptist State Convention meeting in Marion in 1845 separated the Baptists into Northern and Southern factions. • Civil rights activist Coretta Scott King • Soybeans, corn, hay, livestock; light industry; education (Judson College).

PICKENS *Carrollton* • 20,949 • 881 • Western AL, bounded on the west by the MS state line and on the southeast by the Sipsey River; drained by the Tombigbee River (forming Aliceville Lake reservoir on the western boundary), Lubbub Creek, and Sipsey River. The county lies in the Black Belt. • One of three counties named for Andrew Pickens (1739–1817), Revolutionary War general and U.S. representative from SC • 1820 from Tuscaloosa • Soybeans, corn, poultry; lumber milling; crude oil and natural gas production.

PIKE *Troy* • 29,605 • 671 • Southeastern AL, bounded on the southeast by the Pea River, on the northwest by Patsaliga Creek, and on the extreme southwest by the Conecuh River (which also drains the county). • One of ten counties named for Zebulon M. Pike (1779–1813), general in the War of 1812 and discoverer of Pikes Peak in CO • 1821 from Henry and Montgomery • Peanuts, pecans, corn, hay, poultry, cattle; lumber and wood products; manufacture of textiles, truck bodies, feed, plastic containers, food products; education (Troy State U.).

RANDOLPH (one of eight counties so named) *Wedowee* • 22,380 • 581 • Eastern AL, bounded on the east by the GA state line; drained by the Tallapoosa and Little Tallapoosa rivers, both forming R. L. Harris Reservoir. The county lies in the Piedmont. • One of four counties named for John Randolph (1773–1833), US congressman from VA and U.S. minister to Russia • 1832 from Creek cession • Livestock, poultry; manufacture of textiles and apparel, fertilizers, beverages; quarried products; lumber.

RUSSELL (one of four counties so named) *Phenix City* • 49,756 • 641 • Eastern AL, bounded on the east by the Chattahoochee River (forming the GA state line) and on the southwest by the North Fork of the Cowikee River. The county lies in the Black Belt region of the state. Remains of Fort Mitchell (erected in 1813 during the Creek War) are here, with Fort Mitchell National Cemetery located nearby. Part of Eufala National Wildlife Refuge is on the southern border. A portion of Fort Benning Military Reservation is also here. • Named for U.S. Col. Gilbert C. Russell (1782–1855) • 1832 from Creek cession • The last Civil War battle east of the Mississippi River was fought in Phenix City on April 16, 1865. The city was placed under martial law by the state of AL in 1954 following the assassination of anti-vice reformer Albert L. Patterson. A successful movement to clean up "sin city" was led by his son, John, who later became governor. • Peanuts, corn, cotton, livestock; manufacture of textiles, paperboard, bricks and tile, carpets, metal castings, recreation equipment.

SAINT CLAIR (one of four counties so named) *Ashville* • 64,742 • 634 • North-central AL, bounded on the east and southeast by the Coosa River (forming Neely Henry Lake and Logan Martin Lake reservoirs). Beaver Creek Mountains cross the county. • One of three counties named for Gen. Arthur St. Clair (1736–1818), delegate to the Continental Congress and governor of the Northwest Territory • 1818 (prior to statehood) from Shelby • Hay, livestock; sausage, manufacture of textiles, yarn, apparel, plastic products; iron ore, limestone; lumber.

SHELBY *Columbiana* • 143,293 (44% increase since 1990; fasting growing county in AL) • 795 • Central AL, bounded on the east by the Coosa River; drained by the Cahaba River, which roughly follows the northwestern boundary of the county. Oak Mountain State Park is in the northwest. • One of nine counties named directly or indirectly for General Isaac Shelby (1750–1826), officer in the Revolutionary War, NC legislator, and the first governor of KY • 1818 (prior to statehood) from Montgomery • Cotton, corn, hay, livestock; coal, limestone and iron ore; manufacture of textiles, wire; lumber milling and wood products; education (U. of Montevallo).

SUMTER *Livingston* • 14,798 • 905 • Western AL, bounded on the west by the MS state line and on the east by the Tombigbee River; drained by the Noxubee River. The county is located in the Black Belt. • One of four counties named for General Thomas Sumter (1734–1832), American Revolutionary officer and senator from SC • 1832 from Choctaw cession • Corn, soybeans, livestock; lumber milling; manufacture of paper products, clothing.

TALLADEGA *Talladega* • 80,321 • 740 • East-central AL, bounded on the west by the Coosa River (forming Logan Martin Lake reservoir in the northwest); drained by Talladega Creek. Parts of the Talladega Mountains and Talladega National Forest are in the east. De Soto Caverns are also here. • Named for the Battle of Talladega • 1832 from Creek cession • In 1813, Andrew Jackson's Tennessee Volunteers defeated a large force of Creek Indians at Talladega. • Soybeans, corn, poultry; iron mines; manufacture of textiles; education (Talladega College); cream-white marble quarrying and processing (beginning in 1840, with part of it used in the U.S. Supreme Court Building) • The Talladega County Courthouse, built in 1836, is the oldest courthouse in continual use in AL. The Talladega Superspeedway is recognized as "The World's Fastest Speedway."

TALLAPOOSA *Dadeville* • 41,475 • 718 • Eastern AL, bounded on the southwest in part by the Tallapoosa River, which dominates in the west; also drained by the Sougahatchee River and Lake Martin reservoir. Wind Creek State Park is located on the western shore of the reservoir. The county is in the Piedmont. • Named for the Tallapoosa River • 1832 from Chickasaw cession • On March 27, 1814, at the "horseshoe bend" in the Tallapoosa River, General Andrew Jackson's forces decimated the Upper Creek Indian Confederacy, thus facilitating white settlement in a large part of AL and GA (Horseshoe Bend National Military Park) • Cotton, livestock; timber and lumber products; manufacture of textiles, cast iron.

TUSCALOOSA *Tuscaloosa* • 164,875 (the fifth most populated county in AL) • 1,324 (the second largest county in AL) • West-central AL; drained by the Sipsey, North and Black Warrior rivers, the last forming part of the county's eastern boundary. Tuscaloosa County includes Lake Lurleen State Park and Reservoir, and Lake Tuscaloosa reservoir. Part of Talladega National Forest is in the southeast. • Tuscaloosa is an Indian name for the Black Warrior River • 1818 (prior to statehood) from Indian lands • Byler Road (now Main Avenue) in Northport was the first road laid in AL (1819). Tuscaloosa served as AL's first state capital from 1826 to 1846. Tannehill Ironworks Historic State Park is the site of one of the Confederacy's most important iron furnaces. • Physicist and inventor Robert Jemison Van de Graaff ; blues singer Dinah Washington ; Educator Julia Strudwick Tutwiler • Cotton, corn, soybeans, poultry; timber; coal, iron; manufacture of cast-iron, soil pipe, paper, rubber tires, chemicals, lumber products, cottonseed products; education (U. of AL; Stillman College).

WALKER (one of three counties so named) *Jasper* • 70,713 • 794 • North-central AL, bounded on the southeast by the

Black Warrior River and on the northeast by Lewis Smith Lake reservoir; crossed by Mulberry Fork and Lost Creek. • Named for John Walker (1783–1823), first U.S. senator from AL • 1823 from Marion and Tuscaloosa • William B. Bankhead, Speaker of the House of Representatives (1936–40) and his actress-daughter Tallulah Bankhead • Coal (Walker and Jefferson counties once accounted for sixty percent of AL's coal production, but the industry is now in decline); also natural gas; hay, corn, livestock, poultry; timber; manufacture of furniture, apparel, mattresses, golf bags, animal feeds.

WASHINGTON *Chatom* • 18,097 • 1,081 • Southwestern AL, bounded on the east by the Tombigbee River; drained by the Escatawpa River and on the west by the MS state line. St. Stephens Historic Site is in the northeast. • One of thirty-one counties named for President George Washington • Original county; organized 1800 (prior to statehood) • Soybeans, corn, poultry; timber; natural-gas production, petroleum processing; manufacture of raincoats.

WILCOX (one of two counties so named, the other in GA) *Camden* • 13,183 • 889 • Southwestern AL; drained by the Alabama River (Millers Ferry Lock and Dam, forming William "Bill" Dannelly Reservoir on the northern boundary). The county is located in the Black Belt. Roland Cooper State Park is also here. • Named for Lt. Joseph M. Wilcox (1791–1814), killed by Creek Indians • 1819 from Dallas and Monroe • Corn, cattle; lumber milling; manufacture of apparel.

WINSTON (one of two counties so named, the other in MS) *Double Springs* • 24,843 • 614 • Northwestern AL; drained by branches of Sipsey Fork. Sections of William B. Bankhead National Forest are scattered throughout the county. Several arms of Lewis Smith Lake extend into the southeast. Natural Bridge is also here. • Named for John A. Winston (1812–71), Confederate army officer and governor of AL • 1850 as Hancock from Walker; named changed 1858 • Corn, hay, melons, poultry; lumber milling.

ARIZONA

God Enriches

Arizona's fifteen counties are governed by either a three or five member board of supervisors, with each member elected to a four-year term. Most of Arizona's counties have either a county manager or an administrator who is guided by the board of supervisors. This individual conducts the daily business of the county.

APACHE *Saint Johns* • 69,423 • 11,205 (the third largest county in AZ and the sixth largest county in the U.S.) • Eastern and northeastern AZ, bounded on the east by the NM state line and on the north by the UT state line. The northeastern corner of the county is part of Four Corners Monument, the only point in the U.S. common to four states. The southern boundary is formed in part by the Black River. The county is crossed by the Zuni and Little Colorado rivers. Its northern half is occupied by Navajo Nation Indian Reservation. Part of Fort Apache Indian Reservation is in the southwest. The Zuni Reservation is northwest of St. Johns. Part of Apache National Forest is in the south. Also in the county are part of Petrified Forest National Park, a small part of Monument Valley Navajo Tribal Park, and all of Canyon de Chelly National Monument. Lyman Lake State Park is in the south. The Carrizo and Chuska mountains are in the northeast; the White Mountains are in the south. • Named for the Apache Indian tribe • 1879, from Mohave • Hay, alfalfa, cattle, sheep, grain sorghum; Native American crafts; logging • Window Rock is the capital of the large Navajo Nation Indian Reservation, which extends into several counties in AZ, NM and UT; it was established

in 1936 as the Central Agency Headquarters to consolidate many Indian agencies.

COCHISE *Bisbee* • 117,755 • 6,169 (the thirty-eighth largest county in the U.S.) • Southeastern AZ, bounded on the east by the NM state line, and on the south by the Mexican state of Sonora. The county's chief mountain ranges are the Chiricahua, Dos Cabezas, Dragoon and Mules. Chiricahua National Monument and Fort Bowie National Historic Site are in the east. Sections of Coronado National Forest are found throughout the county. San Pedro Riparian National Conservation Area is in the southwest. Fort Huachuca adjoins the city of Sierra Vista in the southwest. Kartchner Caverns and San Bernardino National Wildlife Refuge are also in the county. • Named for the Chiricahua Indian chief (?–1874) • 1881, from Pima • The first European exploration of the Southwest, by Francisco de Coronado, from 1540 to 1542, took place here near present day Hereford. In its wild and wooly days, Tombstone drew thousands of silver miners, gamblers and outlaws, including "Doc" Holliday and Johnny Ringo. The Earps fought the Clantons at O.K. Corral here; Boot Hill was named for many who "died with their boots on." Geronimo surrendered to U.S. forces at present-day Apache. In the Bisbee Deportation of 1917 more than 1,000 striking miners were forcibly transported to Columbus NM. • The county lies in one of the richest copper-producing regions in the U.S. Also, gold, silver, lead; tourism; cotton, alfalfa, hay, wheat, corn, sorghum, lettuce, cattle, hogs, dairying; some manufacturing • St. Paul's Episcopal Church in Tombstone is the oldest Protestant Church still in use in AZ.

COCONINO *Flagstaff* • 116,320 • 18,617 (the largest county in AZ and the second largest county in the U.S.) • Northern AZ, bounded on the north by the UT state line, on the northwest by Kanab Creek and the Colorado River which, along with the Little Colorado River, drain the county. Humphrey Peak (12,643 ft.), the highest peak in AZ, is located in one of the sections of Kaibab National Forest found in the county. Grand Canyon National Park and the Painted Desert, both of which lie in large part in the county draw over four million visitors each year. Grand Canyon National Park has some of the oldest exposed rock in the world, dating back 1.7 billion years. Also in the county are the national monuments of Sunset Crater Volcano, Vermilion Cliffs, Wupatki, and Walnut Canyon, as well as Meteor Crater Natural Landmark, which has been used as a training ground for astronauts. National forests here include parts of Kaibab, Coconino, and Sitgreaves. A number of plateaus and mesas, including Kaibito, Moenkopi, Mogollon, Coconino, Knaba, Kaibab and Paria raise the elevation of county terrain. Coconino is home to several Indian reservations, including part of the large Navajo Nation, part of Hopi, Havasupai, part of Hualapai, and part of Kaibab. Part of Glen Canyon National Recreation Area, including Glen Canyon Dam, is in the north. Camp Navajo is west of Flagstaff. • The county's name is a corruption of the Hopi Indian word for the Havasupai and Yavapai Indian tribes. • 1891, from Yavapai • Astronomers Percival Lowell and Vesto Melvin Slipher died here. • Lumber; sheep, cattle, hay; tourism; education (Northern Arizona U.) • Flagstaff is an astronomical center; Perkins and U.S. Naval observatories are here, as is Lowell Observatory, from which the planet Pluto was first observed in 1930.

GILA *Globe* • 51,335 • 4,768 • East-central AZ, bounded on the south by the San Carlos and Gila rivers, and on the northwest in part by the Verde River; drained by the San Carlos, Black, White and East Verde rivers. Mogollon Rim escarpment forms part of the northern boundary. Chief ranges here are the Sierra Ancha, Mazatzal and Pinal mountains. Theodore Roosevelt Dam and Reservoir on the Salt River, and Coolidge Dam and San Carlos Reservoir on the Gila River provide water for irrigation. The county includes a large part of Tonto National Forest, and part of San Carlos and Fort Apache Indian reservations, as well as Tonto Natural Bridge State Park and Tonto National Monument • Named for the Gila River • 1881, from Maricopa and Pinal • Tennis player Helen Hull Jacobs •

Copper, gold, silver, vanadium; cattle, hay; milling, lumbering; tourism.

GRAHAM *Safford* • 33,489 • 4,629 • Southeastern AZ; drained by the Gila and San Carlos (forming the northwestern boundary) rivers, and San Carlos Reservoir at their confluence on the western boundary. Part of the northern boundary is formed by the Black River. The chief mountain ranges here are the Gila, Pinaleno, Santa Teresa, and Galiuro. The county includes part of San Carlos Indian Reservation, sections of Coronado National Forest, part of Gila Box Riparian National Conservation Area, and Roper Lake State Park. • Named for its most prominent feature, Mount Graham, in the Pinaleno Mountains • 1881 (prior to statehood), from Apache and Pima • Cotton, hay, wheat, corn, sorghum, cattle; manufacture of paper products, machinery parts; printing and publishing • Mount Graham International Observatory is in the south.

GREENLEE *Clifton* • 8,547 (the least populated county in AZ) • 1,847 (the smallest county in AZ) • Southeastern AZ, bounded in part on the southwest by the crest of the Peloncillo Mountains and on the northwest by the Black River; drained by the Blue, Gila, and San Francisco rivers. Part of Apache National Forest covers the northern two-thirds of the county. Part of Gila Box Riparian National Conservation Area is in the south. • Named for Mason Greenlee (1835–1903), early prospector from VA • 1909 (prior to statehood) from Graham • Copper was discovered at Morenci in 1865 and first mined here in 1872. In 1937 the Phelps Dodge Corporation began excavating an open-pit copper mine, which is now one of the largest in the U.S. (7,920 feet across and more than 1,320 feet deep). Clifton is one of the oldest continuously producing copper-mining camps in the Southwest. • Apache leader Geronimo • Copper, silver, gems; alfalfa, hay, wheat, barley.

LA PAZ *Parker* • 19,715 • 4,500 • Western AZ, bounded on the west by the Colorado River (forming the CA state line) and on the north by the Bill Williams and Santa Maria rivers. Mountain ranges in the county include the Buckskin, Trigo, Harcuvar, Dome Rock, and part of the Harquahala. The county also includes part of Colorado River Indian Reservation, Cibola and Bill Williams River national wildlife refuges, and parts of Kofa and Imperial national wildlife refuges. Buckskin Mountain (with a population of desert bighorn sheep) and Alamo Lake state parks are in the extreme north. A portion of Yuma Proving Ground is in the southwest. • Named for La Paz, abandoned gold mining center • 1983 from Yuma • Cattle, alfalfa, hay • Harquahala Mountain Observatory is in the east.

MARICOPA *Phoenix* • 3,072,149 (the most populated county in AZ and the fourth most populated county in the U.S.) • 9,203 (the fifth largest county in AZ and the fourteenth largest county in the U.S.) • South central AZ. Part of the Mazatzal Mountains and part of Tonto National Forest are in the northeast. An irrigated agricultural area extends along the banks of the Salt, Gila, Santa Cruz, Verde, and Agua Fria rivers. The county is highly urbanized around Phoenix. A large portion of Sonoran Desert National Monument is in the south. A part of Barry M. Goldwater Air Force Range is in the extreme southwest. Luke Air Force Base is west of Phoenix. Fort McDowell, Salt River, and part of Gila River and Tohono O'odham Indian reservations are in the county. Painted Rocks Petroglyph Site in the southwest offers artistic-looking prehistoric imprints. • Named for the Indian tribe • 1871 (prior to statehood) from Yavapai and Yuma • Mesa was founded by Mormons in 1878. Phoenix became the capital of AZ in 1889. • Politicians Barry M. Goldwater and Carl T. Hayden. Actor Charles Boyer, author Erskine Caldwell, film studio president Harry Cohn, geophysicist and oceanographer Robert S. Dietz, philanthropist and businessman Frederick T. Gates, work efficiency expert Lilian Evelyn Gilbreth, baseball player Carl Hubbell, geologist and mining engineer Clarence King, magazine publisher Henry R. Luce, journalist and public figure Raymond Moley, biochemist John H. Northrop, architect Frank Lloyd Wright, salesman and manufacturer William Wrigley, Jr. all died here. • Long-staple cotton, citrus fruits, sugar beets, safflower, pecans, vegetables, hay, alfalfa, wheat, barley, cattle, sheep, hogs; government operations; manufacture of computers and electronic components, aircraft parts, heavy machinery, apparel, fabricated steel products; sugar refining; cutting and polishing of diamonds; food and cotton processing; aerial mapping; tourism; education (AZ State U.; Grand Canyon U.; American Graduate School of International Management). The county has a number of large retirement communities. • Thirteen Fortune 1000 companies have their corporate headquarters here. Phoenix's South Mountain Park, covering 16,000 acres, is the largest city park in the U.S. Frank Lloyd Wright's Taliesin West is located in Scottsdale. Williams Air Force Base was the home of the first jet air school in the U.S. Since 1971, Tempe has hosted the Fiesta Bowl. Scottsdale is the site of the four-day annual National Festival of the West and home to the Buffalo Museum of America. Several professional baseball teams hold spring training in the county. Phoenix is home to the Suns and Coyotes (America West Arena). The Arizona Diamondbacks and Cardinals play at Sun Devil Stadium in Tempe.

MOHAVE *Kingman* • 155,032 (66% increase since 1990; the fastest growing county in AZ) • 13,312 (the second largest county in AZ and the fifth largest county in the U.S.) • Northwestern AZ, bounded on the west by the Colorado River (forming here part of the NV and CA state lines), on the north by the UT state line, on the northeast by Kaibab Creek, and on the south by the Bill Williams and Santa Maria rivers; drained by the Big Sandy River. Lake Mead National Recreation Area, which follows part of the county's border with NV, is fed by the Colorado River, which crosses the county in the north, carving the western portion of the Grand Canyon (national park) along the way. The county includes parts of Hualapai and Kaibab (Pipe Spring National Monument here)

Indian reservations, as well as Fort Mojave Indian Reservation in the west. Also here are two sections of Havasu National Wildlife Refuge, Grand Canyon–Parashant National Monument, and Lake Havasu and Cattail Cove state parks. Mohave's diverse topography presents a tapestry of cliffs, plateaus, valleys, plains, and mountains. Ghost towns throughout attest to its earlier incarnation as a booming gold mining region • Named for the Indian tribe • 1864 (prior to statehood); in 1871 it annexed Pah-Ute County, which had been organized in 1865 • Copper, lead, silver, zinc, gold; cattle, alfalfa, wheat, barley, sorghum, lettuce, honeydews; tourism; light manufacturing, including chain saw production • Lake Mead, formed by Hoover Dam, was the first national recreation area established by act of Congress. Completed in 1831 over the Thames River in England, London Bridge was transplanted, re-erected, and finally dedicated in 1971 in its new home in the county, spanning a man-made inlet on the Colorado River at Lake Havasu City.

NAVAJO *Holbrook* • 97,470 • 9,953 (the fourth largest county in AZ and the eleventh largest county in the U.S.) • Eastern AZ, bounded on the north by the UT state line, on the extreme southeast by the Black River; crossed by the Little Colorado River. Rainbow and Shonto plateaus, and Black Mesa are in the north. Parts of Painted Desert are in north-center. A portion of Petrified Forest National Park is on the eastern border of the county. The northern half of the county is occupied by part of the Navajo Nation Indian Reservation (including two Navajo national monuments) and part of the Hopi Indian Reservation. The county also includes part of Mogollon Rim escarpment, which crosses it in the south and forms the border of Sitgreaves National Forest and Fort Apache Indian Reservation. Picturesque Monument Valley Navajo Tribal Park is in the extreme northeast. Also in the county is Homolovi Ruins State Park, AZ's first archeological park, representing one of the last prehistoric stopping places of the Hopi Indians. • Named for the Navajo Indian tribe • 1895 (prior to statehood) • Sheep, cattle, hogs, alfalfa, hay, corn; Native American handicrafts; Ponderosa pine lumber, planing and molding mills; railroad services • Walpi Indian pueblo is known for its antelope ceremony and snake dances, held in odd years in August; the original pueblo was founded around 1700.

PIMA *Tucson* • 843,746 (the second most populated county in AZ) • 9,186 (the fifteenth largest county in the U.S.) • Southern AZ, bounded on the south by the Mexican state of Sonora; drained by the Santa Cruz River. The Santa Catalina and Santa Rita mountains are in the east, the Growler and Agua Dulces in the west, the Baboquivaris in the south. Large parts of Coronado National Forest, a large part of Ironwood Forest National Monument, Organ Pipe Cactus National Monument, the eastern portion of Cabeza Prieta National Wildlife Refuge, Las Cienegas National Conservation Area, and Buenos Aires National Wildlife Refuge are all in the county. The western half of the county is dominated by Tohono O'odham Indian Reservation. Catalina State Park and

Mount Lemmon ski area are north of Tucson. Davis-Monthan Air Force Base is east of the city. The Sonoran Desert is the only place in the world where saguaro cactus grow; the largest concentration of this cactus is in Saguaro National Park, both west and east of Tucson. • Named for the Indian tribe • 1864 (prior to statehood) • Since being made a presidio by the Spanish army in 1776, Tucson's "Old Pueblo" has flown three additional flags: Mexican, Confederate, and American. Tucson lay in the territory that constituted the Gadsden Purchase from Mexico in 1854. The city served as territorial capital from 1867 to 1877. • Composer Ulysses Kay. Newspaper columnist Westbrook Pegler, birth control activist Margaret Sanger, research scientist Ralph Wycoff, dancer and choreographer Michael Bennett, astronomers Bart J. Bok and Andrew Douglass, anthropologist Emil W. Haury, naturalist Joseph W. Krutch, poet James Merrill, NATO commander Lauris Norstad, philanthropist John D. Rockefeller, Jr., paleontologist George G. Simpson, and photojournalist W. Eugene Smith all died here. • Cattle, cotton, sugar beets, barley, lettuce; mining of copper, gold, silver, and lead; manufacture of aircraft and missiles, electronics; tourism, including health resorts; research; education (U. of AZ). The county has a large retirement community. • Kitt Peak National Observatory houses the world's largest collection of telescopes. Biosphere 2 is in the county. The Arizona-Sonora Desert Museum is a living museum of desert wildlife and vegetation.

PINAL *Florence* • 179,727 (the third most populated county in AZ; 54% increase since 1990; the third fastest growing county in AZ) • 5,370 (the fiftieth largest county in the U.S.) • South-central AZ. The San Carlos Reservoir in the northeast holds water from the Gila and San Carlos rivers for irrigation. Indian reservations located fully or partially within the county are San Carlos, Tohono O'odham, Maricopa (Ak-Chin), and Gila River. Picacho Peak and Lost Dutchman state parks, McFarland State Historic Park, Boyce Thompson Arboretum (containing hundreds of plants from arid lands throughout the world), and Casa Grande Ruins National Monument are in the county, as are part of Sonoran Desert National Monument, Ironwood Forest National Monument, Coronado National Forest, and Tonto National Forest. The Tortilla Mountains are in the east, the Santa Catalinas in the southeast. • Named for either a local tribe, the Pinal Apaches, or for the Pinal Mountains • 1875 from Pima County • Florence is one of the oldest white settlements in the state (1866). • Lawyer and politician Ernest W. McFarland • Cotton, alfalfa, hay, wheat, barley, citrus fruits, figs, vegetables, sheep, hogs, cattle, poultry; copper, gold, silver mining; manufacture of clothing, furniture, fertilizer, fabricated steel products.

SANTA CRUZ *Nogales* • 38,381 • 1,238 • Southern AZ, bounded on the south by the state of Sonora in Mexico. The Patagonia Mountains are in the south, part of the Santa Rita Mountains in the north. There is irrigated farming along the Santa Cruz River. The county includes Tumacacori National Historic Park, Tubac Presidio State Historic Park (site of AZ's

first newspaper, first state park, and first European settlement) and sections of Coronado National Forest. Also found here are the Whipple Observatory, Patagonia Lake State Park, and Patagonia Sonoita Creek Preserve. • Named for the Santa Cruz River • 1899, from Pima • Nogales was the scene of fighting in 1916 between U.S. national guardsmen and forces of Pancho Villa, and in 1918 between town militias of Nogales, AZ and Nogales, Sonora, Mexico. • Jazz composer and musician Charles Mingus • Cattle, hay, alfalfa, cotton; mining of lead, zinc, and stone quarrying; border trade • Nogales is a port of entry on the Mexican border.

YAVAPAI *Prescott* • 167,517 (the fourth most populated county in AZ; 55% increase since 1990; the second fastest growing county in AZ) • 8,123 (the twenty-first largest county in the U.S.) • West-central AZ; crossed by the Verde, Santa Maria and Agua Fria rivers (the latter forming a small part of the southern boundary). The Juniper Mountains are in the northwest, the Weaver Mountains in the southwest. Part of Kaibab National Forest, part of Tonto National Forest, and Prescott National Forest (its headquarters in Prescott) are in the county, as are Agua Fria National Monument, Tuzigoot National Monument, Fort Verde State Historic Park, Montezuma Castle National Monument (one of the best preserved cliff dwellings in the U.S.), Dead Horse Ranch, Slide Rock, and Red Rock state parks, and Jerome State Historic Park. Yavapai-Prescott and Yavapai-Apache Indian reservations are here. • Named for the Indian tribe • 1864 • Prescott served as capital of the territory of AZ from 1864 to 1867, and from 1877 to 1889. The first rodeo to charge admission was held in the city on July 4, 1888. (The event grew into the annual three-day Prescott Frontier Days celebration.) • Film director Victor Fleming died here. • Gold, silver, copper, lead and zinc mining; alfalfa, hay, wheat, corn, fruit, cattle; education (Embry-Riddle Aeronautical U.; Prescott College); tourism.

YUMA *Yuma* • 160,026 (the fifth most populated county in AZ) • 5,514 (tied with San Juan County, NM for the forty-seventh largest county in the U.S.) • Southwestern AZ, bounded on the west by the Colorado river (forming the CA state line and part of the border with the Mexican state of Baja California), and on the south by the Mexican state of Sonora; drained by the Gila River. Part of Cabeza Prieta National Wildlife Refuge is in the south. Part of Kofa National Wildlife Refuge is in the north. Part of Yuma Proving Ground is in the county as is a part of the large Barry M. Goldwater Air Force Range. Cocopah Indian Reservation is in the southwest. There are alternating north-south mountain ranges and desert valleys in the south. The Castle Dome and Tank mountains are in the center of the county. The county receives much of its water through irrigation canals proceeding from All-American Canal. Yuma Desert is in the southwest. Yuma Territorial Prison State Historic Park is in Yuma. • Named for the Indian tribe. (It is one of two counties, the other in CO, named directly or indirectly for the Yuma Indians) • 1864 (prior to statehood) • Yuma played a key role in supplying the forts and soldiers of the southwestern U.S. during the late 19th century. • Railroad builder Mark Hopkins & migrant farm worker organizer Cesar Chavez died here. • Cotton, alfalfa, citrus fruits, dates, melons, vegetables, cattle, sheep, hogs; light manufacturing • The Yuma irrigation project along the Gila River is reclaiming a section of the Yuma Desert in the vicinity of Yuma. The Sahati Camel Farm and Desert Animal Breeding Center is near Somerton.

ARKANSAS

The People Rule

Each of Arkansas's seventy-five counties is administered by a county judge who handles county financial affairs. The judge also presides over the quorum court, a legislative body consisting of all the justices of the peace in the county. Other county officials include the assessor, clerk, coroner, sheriff, surveyor, treasurer, and tax collector. In some counties the sheriff serves as collector.

ARKANSAS *DeWitt and Stuttgart* • 20,749 • 988 (the third largest county in AR) • East-central AR, bounded on the south by the Arkansas River, on the southwest by Bayou Meto, and on the east by the White River; drained by La Grue Bayou and Bayou Meto. Part of the White River National Wildlife Refuge is in the east. Roth Prairie Natural Area is also here. • Named for the Quapaw, later called the Arkansas Indians • Original county, organized 1813 (prior to statehood) • Arkansas Post (National Memorial) is the site of the first white settlement in the present state of AR. Founded in 1686 by Henri de Tonty, it was an important trading post and the home of French and Spanish governors. John Law's "Mississippi Bubble" scheme for developing the area attracted settlers around 1719, but most left after the speculative bubble burst in 1720. Ceded to the U.S. as part of the Louisiana Purchase, Arkansas Post served as AR Territory's first capital from 1819 to 1821. Strong Confederate defenses here were reduced on January 11, 1863 by the combined assault of Federal forces under General John A. McClernand and a naval command under Adm. David D. Porter. • Cotton, rice, corn, oats, soybeans, hay, lespedeza, livestock; rice and cotton processing; lumbering; commercial fishing; pecan shipping.

ASHLEY *Hamburg* • 24,209 • 921 • Southeastern AR, bounded on the south by the LA state line and on the west by the Saline and Ouachita rivers; drained by Bayou Bartholomew. Overflow and part of Felsenthal national wildlife refuges are here. Felsenthal Lock and Dam impounds Lake Jack Lee. • Named for Chester Ashley (1790–1848), U.S. senator from AR • 1848 from Union and Drew • Pine and oak lumbering; cotton, rice, wheat, soybeans, hay, cattle; manufacture of chemicals, paper products, fabricated steel, apparel • The Armadillo Festival, which features an armadillo derby, is held in Hamburg every May.

BAXTER *Mountain Home* • 38,386 • 554 • Northern AR, bounded on the north by the MO state line, on the southwest by the White River (forming Bull Shoals Lake Dam and Reservoir in the northwest); drained by the North Fork (forming Norfolk Lake Dam and Reservoir in the east). The Norfolk National Fish Hatchery is the largest federal trout hatchery in the U.S. (Each year, over two million trout are raised here.) The county is situated in the Ozark region of the state and has become a major retirement center. Bull Shoals State Park is on both sides of Bull Shoals Dam (White River) in the west. Part of Ozark National Forest is in the south. A small part of Buffalo National River lies on the southwestern boundary. • Named for Elisha Baxter (1827–99), AR legislator, chief justice of the AR Supreme Court, and governor of AR • 1873 from Fulton • Hay, cattle, hogs, resorts, fishing.

BENTON (one of nine counties so named) *Bentonville* • 153,406 (57% increase since 1990; the fastest growing and third most populated county in AR) • 846 • Extreme northwestern AR, bounded on the west by the OK state line, and on the north by the MO state line; drained by the Illinois and White rivers (the latter forming Beaver Lake in the east). The county is in the Ozark Mountains, with a section of Ozark National Forest in the south. Beaver Lake State Park (including War Eagle Cavern) and Logan Cave National Wildlife Refuge are also here. • One of seven counties named for Thomas Hart Benton (1782–1858), long term U.S. senator • 1836 from Washington • Pea Ridge National Military Park memorializes one of the major Civil War engagements (March 7–8, 1862) west of the Mississippi River, leading to the Union's total control of MO. • Retail magnate Sam Walton • Chicken, turkeys, cattle, hogs, dairy products; timber, diversified manufacturing; mineral spring resorts; education (John Brown U.) • Bentonville is the headquarters of Walmart, a top ten Fortune 1000 company.

BOONE (one of eight counties so named) *Harrison* • 33,948 • 591 • Northern AR, bounded on the north by the MO state line; drained by the White River and Crooked Creek. The county lies in the Ozark Mountains region. Part of Bull Shoals Lake reservoir is in the northeast corner; a sliver of Table Rock Lake reservoir is in the northwest corner. Baker Prairie Natural Area is also here. • One of seven counties named for Daniel

Boone • 1869 from Carroll and Marion • Cattle, hogs, dairying, poultry; timber; lead and zinc, limestone, dolomite, marble, glass, sand; light manufacturing; tourism.

BRADLEY (one of two counties so named, the other in TN) *Warren* • 12,600 • 651 • Southern AR, bounded on the west by Moro Creek, on the southwest by the Ouachita River, and on the east in part by the Saline River; drained by the Saline River and L'Aigle Creek. Part of Felsenthal National Wildlife Refuge is in the south, Moro Bay State Park in the southwest. • Named for Hugh Bradley, captain under Andrew Jackson and territorial legislator • 1840 from Union • Truck farming, tomatoes, potatoes, vegetables, poultry, cattle; timber; manufacture of apparel and wood products • The pink tomato, AR's official fruit and vegetable, is celebrated during the Pink Tomato Festival, held each June in Warren, the "Pink Tomato Capital of the World."

CALHOUN *Hampton* • 5,744 (the least populated county in AR) • 628 • South-central AR, bounded on the southwest by the Ouachita River, on the east by Moro Creek, and on the northwest by Two Bayou; drained by Champagnolle Creek. • One of eleven counties named for John C. Calhoun (1782–1850), U.S. statesman and champion of Southern causes • 1850 from Dallas, Ouachita, and Union • Cattle; manufacture of apparel.

CARROLL (one of thirteen counties so named) *Berryville and Eureka Springs* • 25,357 • 630 • Northwestern AR, bounded on the north by the MO state line; drained by the White and King rivers, and Osage Creek. The county is located in the Ozark Mountains region. A small section of Hobbs Wildlife Management Area is in the southwest corner; Beaver Lake Dam (White River) is in the west; an arm of Table Rock Lake reservoir is in the eastern corner. • One of twelve counties named for Charles Carroll (1737–1832), signer of the Declaration of Independence, U.S. senator from MD and founder of the Baltimore and Ohio railroad • 1833 (prior to statehood) from Izard • Dancer Irene Castle died here. • Cattle, hogs, chickens, turkeys, dairying, fruits and vegetables; pine and oak timber, manufacture of machinery, electrical cable, harnesses; tourism, mineral spring health resorts • The state's premiere tourist town, Eureka Springs, is a sprawling Victorian village, an artists' colony (since the '30s), and a religious retreat. America's number one outdoor religious drama, the Great Passion Play (depicting Jesus Christ's last days on earth), is presented here for several months each year.

CHICOT *Lake Village* • 14,117 • 644 • Extreme Southeastern AR, bounded on the east by the Mississippi River (forming the MS state line) and on the south by the LA state line; drained by the Boeuf River and Bayou Macon. There are pockets of Chicot County on the MS side of the Mississippi River. • Named for Point Chicot on the Mississippi River • 1823 (prior to statehood) from Arkansas County • The Battle of Ditch Bayou was fought here in 1864. • Spanish explorer, Hernando de Soto, is reputedly buried in Lake Chicot. • Rice, cotton,

wheat, soybeans, cattle; lumber milling; catfish farming • Lake Chicot (at Lake Chicot State Park) is AR's largest natural lake and North America's largest oxbow lake. The park hosts programs for viewing rare storks, ibis and egrets. In 1923, Charles Lindbergh flew over the lake and the Mississippi River in the world's first night flight. New Hope Missionary Church in Lake Village is the oldest African-American church in the state.

CLARK (one of twelve counties so named) *Arkadelphia* • 23,546 • 865 • South-central AR, bounded on the south by the Little Missouri River and on the west in part by the Antoine River; drained by the Ouachita River (forming part of the eastern border), the Caddo River (forming De Gray Lake reservoir on the northern border), and Terre Noire Creek. Terre Noire Natural Area is also here. • One of three counties named for William Clark (1770–1838), explorer, and co-leader of the Lewis and Clark Expedition • 1818 (prior to statehood) from Arkansas County • Soybeans, cattle, hogs; timber; manufacturing; education (Henderson State U.; Ouachita Baptist U.) • DeGray Lake Resort State Park celebrates the migration of bald and golden eagles to the lake every January during Eagles Et Cetera Weekend.

CLAY (one of eighteen counties so named) *Corning and Piggott* • 17,609 • 639 • Extreme northeastern AR, bounded on the north and east by the St. Francis River (forming the MO state line) and on the west in part by the Current River; drained by the Black, Cache, and Little Black rivers. Crowley's Ridge intersects the county. • The county was originally called Clayton for AR legislator John M. Clayton. It is not clear if in shortening it to Clay, Mr. Clayton remained its honoree, or if the intended then became presidential candidate and KY senator Henry Clay (1777–1852). • 1873 from Randolph • Cotton, rice, wheat, soybeans, corn, fruits, sorghum, cattle, hogs; hardwood timber; manufacture of electrical equipment, wood products, fabricated metal products; fish hatchery • Ernest Hemingway wrote portions of *A Farewell to Arms* in Piggott.

CLEBURNE *Heber Springs* • 24,046 • 553 • North-central AR; drained by the Little Red River and its tributaries. The county lies in the Ozark region of the state. Part of Greers Ferry Lake reservoir dominates the county in the west. Greers Ferry Dam is in the center of the county on Little Red River. Big Creek Natural Area is also here. • One of two counties (the other in AL) named for General Patrick R. Cleburne (1828–64), major general in the Confederate Army • 1883 from White and Van Buren • Cattle, chickens, lumber milling; limestone; manufacture of wood products, machinery, building materials, leather products, medical equipment, consumer goods, tools.

CLEVELAND (One of three counties so named) *Rison* • 8,571 • 595 • South-central AR, bounded on the west by Moro Bayou; intersected by the Saline River. • One of two counties (the other in OK) named for President Grover Cleveland • Organized 1873 from Dallas County. Formerly Dorsey; name changed to Cleveland in 1885 • At Marks' Mills (Battleground Historic Monument) in the spring of 1864, Confederate soldiers captured a Union supply train. • Singer Johnny Cash • Cattle, hogs, chickens • Located at Rison, Pioneer Village is a restoration of a typical south Arkansas community during the late 1800s. • One of the few intact stands of virgin hardwoods still existing in AR is located in Moro Creek Bottoms. • The town of Rison sits on top of a 15 x 6 mile iron deposit, containing as much as forty-two percent magnetite, enough to cause magnetic disturbances for pilots flying over the area.

COLUMBIA (one of eight counties so named) *Magnolia* • 25,603 • 766 • Southwestern AR, bounded on the south by the LA state line; drained by Bayou Dorcheat (forming part of the western boundary). Lake Columbia reservoir is in the northwest. • Poetic and honorific reference to Christopher Columbus • 1852 from Lafayette • Cattle, hogs, chickens; timber; cotton ginning; oil wells, bromine; oil refining; light manufacturing; education (Southern AR U. Magnolia) • Logoly State Park is AR's first environmental education state park.

CONWAY *Morrilton* • 20,336 • 556 • Central AR, bounded on the south in part by the Arkansas River and on the east in part by Cadron Creek. Petit Jean State Park is in the southwest corner. A small part of Ozark National Forest lies in the northwest corner. • Named for Henry W. Conway (1793–1827), officer in the War of 1812 and delegate to Congress at the time of establishment • 1825 (prior to statehood) from Pulaski • Poultry, hogs, wheat, soybeans; timber; light manufacturing. • The Museum of Automobiles in Morrilton is one of the best museums of its kind in the country. Wincrock Farm was developed by AR governor Winthrop Rockefeller, and is noted for the breeding of Santa Gertrudis cattle.

CRAIGHEAD *Jonesboro and Lake City* • 82,148 • 711 • Northeastern AR, bounded on the northeast corner by the MO state line; intersected by Crowley's Ridge; drained by the St. Francis and Cache rivers, the latter forming part of the northwest boundary. • Named for Thomas B. Craighead, state senator who opposed the creation of the county • 1859 from Mississippi County • First woman elected to the U.S. Senate, Hattie Caraway; novelist John Grisham • Rice (Jonesboro is home to the world's largest rice milling facility, Riceland Foods), also cotton, soybeans, sorghum, fruit, cattle, hogs; gravel pits; manufacture of electric motors, shoes, machinery, plumbing fixtures; education (AR State U.).

CRAWFORD (one of eleven counties so named) *Van Buren* • 53,247 • 595 • Northwestern AR, bounded on the west by the OK state line, on the south by the Arkansas River, and on the east in part by the Mulberry River. Lock and Dam No. 13 (on Arkansas River) is in the south, Lake Fort Smith State Park in the northeast, the Ozarks in the north. Separate units of Ozark National Forest are in the county's northeast and northwest corners. • One of six counties named directly or indirectly for William H. Crawford (1772–1834) senator from GA, minister to France, U.S. secretary of war and U.S. secretary of treasury • 1820 (prior to statehood) from Pulaski • Van Buren developed as a trading post and "fitting-out" stop for settlers heading west. • Jewish educator Cyrus Adler; inventor and humorist Bob Burns • Cattle, hogs, poultry, wheat, soybeans; hardwood timber; food processing; shipping of vegetables, especially spinach; some manufacturing; mountain resorts.

CRITTENDEN (one of two counties so named, the other in KY) *Marion* • 50,866 • 610 • Eastern AR, bounded on the east by the Mississippi River (forming the TN state line); drained by the St. Francis River. Wapanocca National Wildlife Refuge is in the northeast. Porter Lake and Horseshoe Lake — backwater (oxbow) lakes of the Mississippi River — are in the far south. The county is traversed by the Tyronza River. • Named for Robert Crittenden (1797–1834), Arkansas Territory official • 1825 (prior to statehood) from Phillips • West Memphis began as a logging camp in 1910, near the site of Fort Esperanza, built by the Spanish in 1797. • Cotton, rice, soybeans, hay; timber; diversified industries; shipping point for liquid fertilizers, grain, coal, steel pipe, structural-steel products; greyhound-racing.

CROSS *Wynne* • 19,526 • 616 • Eastern AR; drained by the St. Francis and L'Anguille rivers; intersected by Crowley's Ridge. Part of Village Creek State Park (AR's largest) is in the south; Parkin Arch State Park is in the east. • Named for either David C. Cross, colonel in the Confederate Army; or for Edward Cross (1798–1887), jurist and U.S. representative from AR • 1862 from Crittenden, Poinsett, and Saint Francis • Hogs, cattle, rice, wheat, soybeans, peaches, cotton; hardwood timber; manufacture of footware, fabricated metal products; food processing.

DALLAS (one of five counties so named) *Fordyce* • 9,210 • 667 • South-central AR; drained by the Ouachita River (forming part of the western boundary) and the Saline River and Moro Creek (forming part of the eastern boundary). • One of three counties named for George Mifflin Dallas (1792–1864), U.S. statesman and U.S. vice president • 1845 from Clark and Hot Springs • Football coach Paul "Bear" Bryant • Cattle, poultry; timber, sawmilling; manufacture of wood products; hunting, fishing.

DESHA *Arkansas City* • 15,341 • 765 • Southeastern AR, bounded on the east by the Mississippi River (forming the MS state line); drained by the Arkansas and White rivers which form part of the northern boundary. Part of White River National Wildlife Refuge is in the far north. • Named for Captain Benjamin Desha (?–1835), officer in the War of 1812 • 1838 from Arkansas County • Magazine and book publisher John H. Johnson • Cotton, rice, wheat, soybeans, cattle; rice and lumber milling; light manufacturing, including apparel, paper.

DREW *Monticello* • 18,723 • 828 • Southeastern AR, bounded on the west by the Saline River; drained by the Bayou Bartholomew and Cut-Off Creek. Seven Devils Swamp reservoir and Warren Prairie Natural Area are in the county. • Named for Thomas S. Drew (1802–79), governor of AR • 1846 from Arkansas County • Cotton, rice, wheat, soybeans, cattle; timber; education (U. of AR–Monticello).

FAULKNER *Conway* • 86,014 (43% increase since 1990; the second fastest growing county in AR) • 647 • Central AR, bounded on the southwest by the Arkansas River; drained by Cadron Creek (which forms part of its western boundary). Toad Suck Lock and Dam (at Arkansas River) is in the southwest; Woolly Hollow State Park is in the north; Lake Conway reservoir and part of Camp Joseph T. Robinson National Guard Training Area are also in the county. • Possibly named for Sanford C. Faulkner (1803–1874), who wrote "The Arkansas Traveler," the state song • 1873 from Pulaski • Cattle, hogs, wheat, soybeans; timber; manufacture of steel bus bodies, refrigerator cabinets, pianos, furniture, shoes; education (U. of Central AR; Hendrix College; Central Baptist College).

FRANKLIN (one of twenty-five counties so named) *Charleston and Ozark* • 17,771 • 610 • Northwestern AR; intersected by the Arkansas River (forming part of the southern boundary); drained by the Mulberry River (a National Scenic and Recreational River; also forms part of the western boundary). The county is located in the Ozarks. Ozark Zeta Taylor Lock and Dam forms narrow Ozark Lake. Part of Fort Chaffee Maneuver Training Center is in the county's far southwest corner; part of Ozark National Forest is in the north. Also here are Cherokee Prairie Natural Area and Charleston Arkansas National Commemorative Site. • One of twenty-three counties named for Benjamin Franklin • 1837 from Crawford • Cattle, hogs, poultry, eggs; coal mining; timber; manufacture of bookcases, computer furniture, apparel, plywood, concrete, air-conditioner parts; food processing.

FULTON (one of eight counties so named) *Salem* • 11,642 • 618 • Northern AR, bounded on the north by the MO state line; drained by the Spring and Strawberry rivers. An arm of Norfolk Lake reservoir is in the southwest. Mammoth Spring, the focal point of Mammoth Spring State Park in the northeast, gushes nine million gallons of water an hour. • Named for William S. Fulton (1795–1844), last governor of the Arkansas Territory and U.S. senator • 1842 from Izard • Cattle, hogs; hardwood timber; manufacture of metal polishers, rubber regulating wheels, apparel.

GARLAND *Hot Springs* • 88,068 (the fifth most populated county in AR) • 677 • Central AR; intersected by the Ouachita River. Hot Springs National Park at Hot Springs is in the center of the county. Part of Ouachita National Forest is in the west. Lake Ouachita State Park is at the eastern end of Lake Ouachita reservoir (Ouachita River), the state's largest manmade lake. Lake Hamilton and part of Lake Catherine

reservoirs are also in the county. • Named for Augustus H. Garland (1832–99), U.S. senator from AR and governor of the state, and U.S. Attorney General • 1873 from Montgomery • The springs at Hot Springs were used by the Indians in the area for centuries, and were probably visited by Hernando de Soto in 1541. They were explored in the 1600s, and frequented by health seekers as early as the 1700s (in this case, by Spanish and French visitors). • President Bill Clinton. New York City mayor Fernando Wood died here. • Cattle, hogs; health (hydrotherapy), recreation and retirement resorts; light manufacturing, including aluminum products • The Hot Springs Documentary Film Festival, held here, is considered to be the premiere festival devoted exclusively to the documentary genre. From Hot Springs National Park's forty-seven thermal springs flow nearly one million gallons of water a day, with temperatures averaging 143 degrees F. Bill Shoemaker became the first jockey to win 100 stakes races worth $100,000 with his first place finish at Hot Springs's Oaklawn Park on March 30, 1974.

GRANT (one of fifteen counties so named) *Sheridan* • 16,464 • 632 • Central AR; drained by the Saline River (forming part of its southern boundary) and Hurricane Creek. • One of twelve counties named for President Ulysses S. Grant • 1869 from Jefferson • Jenkins' Ferry Battleground Historic Monument marks the site on which Confederate troops attacked General Steele's Union forces. • The county is known for the breeding of Arabian horses. Also cattle, hogs, catfish; timber; manufacture of laminated trailer floors, printing ink, metal wall panels, aircraft engine cowls, disposable paper bags, water faucets.

GREENE *Paragould* • 37,331 • 578 • Northeastern AR, bounded on the east by the St. Francis River (forming the MO state line); drained by the Cache River (forming part of the western boundary); intersected by Crowley's Ridge. The county includes Crowley's Ridge and Lake Frierson state parks. The latter is known for the blooms of its wild dogwoods. • One of fourteen counties named for Gen. Nathanael Greene (1742–86), hero of the Revolutionary War • 1833 (prior to statehood) from Lawrence • Cattle, hogs, sorghum, cotton, rice, wheat, soybeans; timber; gravel; diversified manufacturing • The official spelling of the county name is Green.

HEMPSTEAD *Hope* • 23,587 • 729 • Southwestern AR, bounded on the southwest by the Red and Little rivers, and on the north by the Little Missouri River and Hickory Creek. Part of Millwood Lake reservoir (Little River) is in the west; Old Washington Historic State Park in Washington is at the center of the county. • Named for Edward Hempstead (1780–1817), delegate to Congress from MO • 1818 (prior to statehood) from Arkansas County • The county's first county court was presided over by Stephen F. Austin, later known as the "Father of Texas," who temporarily resided in Washington along with other TX heroes Davy Crockett, Sam Houston, and Jim Bowie. Washington served as the Confederate capital of AR from 1863 to 1865. • President Bill Clinton •

Soybeans, cattle, poultry, eggs, hogs; timber; some manufacturing • Some of the largest watermelons in the world are displayed at the Hope Watermelon Festival. The famous Bowie knife is reputed to have been made here by James Black of Washington in 1831.

HOT SPRING *Malvern* • 30,353 • 615 • Central AR; drained by the Ouachita River and Caddo River. Remmel Dam forms Lake Catherine in the north; Lake Catherine State Park is on its southern shore. Part of De Gray Lake reservoir (Caddo River) lies along the county's southern boundary. • Named for the famous hot springs that were within the county's boundaries at the time of organization • 1829 (prior to statehood) from Clark • Cattle, hogs; diversified manufacturing; sand, gravel deposits; timber; rutile clay, bentonite, and barite (eighty percent of all barite used for oil drilling in the U.S. comes from the Magnet Cove area of the county). • The county is the birthplace of rural electrification; the Arkansas Power and Light Company of Malvern inaugurated service in 1913. The oldest chartered bank in AR was opened in Malvern in 1889. The oldest Methodist church west of the Mississippi is also located here. The first river bridge in AR was built over the Ouachita River at Rockport. Brickmaking, one of Malvern's oldest industries, is celebrated in the city's annual "Brickfest."

HOWARD (one of seven counties so named) *Nashville* • 14,300 • 587 • Southwestern AR; drained by the Saline (which forms most of western boundary) and Cassatot rivers, the latter a National Scenic and Recreational River. Part of Millwood Lake reservoir is in the extreme southwestern corner. Dierks Lake reservoir (Saline River) and Gillham Lake reservoir (Cassatot River) are also here. The county includes Cossatot River State Park and Natural Area, and Stone Road Glade Natural Area. • Probably named for James Howard, a state senator • 1873 from Pike • Cattle, hogs, grain, poultry (and processing of poultry products); cotton ginning; timber; sawmilling; manufacture of wood, plastic and cement products, consumer goods, building materials, machinery, beverages; cinnabar mines.

INDEPENDENCE *Batesville* • 34,233 • 764 • North-central AR, bounded on the east in part by the Black River; drained by the White River (forming part of the western boundary) and Departee Creek. Part of the Ozark Mountains are in the west. • The name of the county honors the Declaration of Independence • 1820 (prior to statehood) from Arkansas County • Rice, soybeans, wheat, cotton, cattle, hogs; poultry processing; lime, black marble quarries; timber; some manufacturing; education (Lyon College; U. of AR livestock and forestry experiment station).

IZARD *Melbourne* • 13,249 • 581 • Northern AR, bounded on the southwest by the White River; drained by the Strawberry River. North Central Correctional Unit is in the west. • Named for George Izard (1776–1828), general in the War of 1812 and governor of Arkansas Territory • 1825 (prior to state-

hood) from Independence • Cattle, hogs, chickens, hay, dairying; lumber milling; cotton ginning; glass sand, gravel pits; manufacture of aircraft parts, hardwood flooring, apparel.

JACKSON (one of twenty-four counties so named) *Newport* • 18,418 • 634 • Northeastern AR, bounded on the northwest by the Black River; drained by the White and Cache rivers, and by Departee Creek. Jacksonport State Park and part of Cache River National Wildlife Refuge are here. • One of twenty-two counties named directly or indirectly for President Andrew Jackson • 1829 (prior to statehood) from Independence • Wheat, sorghum, soybeans, rice, hogs; sand and gravel pits; manufacture of machinery, railroad equipment, aluminum, motor vehicles, food processing; lumber.

JEFFERSON *Pine Bluff* • 84,278 • 885 • Central AR, bounded on the east by Bayou Meto; drained by the Wabbaseka Bayou and Bayou Bartholomew; intersected by the Arkansas River, northwest to southeast. Lock and Dam No. 5 is in the northwest, Lock and Dam No. 4 near county center. Pine Bluff Arsenal is north of the city. • One of twenty-six counties named directly or indirectly for President Thomas Jefferson • 1829 (prior to statehood) from Arkansas and Pulaski counties • Football player Don Hutson • Cotton, hay, wheat, rice, soybeans, hogs, turkeys; timber; diversified manufacturing, including paper, archery supplies, cotton by-products; education (U. of AR at Pine Bluff) • The Band Museum, the only museum in the country devoted to band instruments and the history of the band movement in the U.S., is located in Pine Bluff. Grider Field, in Pine Bluff, is home to restored aircraft hangars, barracks, and WW II aircraft.

JOHNSON (one of twelve counties so named) *Clarksville* • 22,781 • 662 • Northwestern AR, bounded on the south by the Arkansas River (forming Lake Dardanelle reservoir in the southeast); drained by the Mulberry River (a National Scenic and Recreational River) and Big Piney Creek (National Scenic River). Part of Ozark National Forest covers the northern half of the county. • Named for Benjamin Johnson (1784–1849), a territorial judge • 1833 (prior to statehood) from Pope • Soybeans, cattle, cotton, fruit, hogs, turkeys, chickens; coal mines; timber, lumber milling; manufacture of machinery, shoes, fabricated metal products, hosiery, frozen foods, bricks; poultry processing; education (U. of the Ozarks). Clarksville is a major grocery distribution center.

LAFAYETTE (one of six counties so named) *Lewisville* • 8,559 • 527 (the smallest county in AR) • Southwestern AR, bounded on the south by the LA state line, on the west by the Red River, and on the east in part by Dorcheat Bayou; drained by Bodcau Creek. Lake Erling reservoir (Bodcau Creek) is in the southeast. • One of seventeen counties named for the Marquis de Lafayette (1757–1834), French statesman and soldier who fought with the Americans during the Revolutionary War • 1827 (prior to statehood) from Hempstead • James S. Conway, AR's first governor is buried here (Conway Cemetery

Historic State Park) • Wheat, soybeans, cattle, hogs, chickens; timber; gravel; oil and gas; manufacture of furniture, metal products • Writer Maya Angelou set her book *I Know Why the Caged Bird Sings* in Stamps.

LAWRENCE (one of eleven counties so named) *Walnut Ridge* • 17,774 • 587 • Northeastern AR, bounded on the east by the Cache River and on the north in part by the Spring River; drained by the Black and Strawberry rivers. Lake Charles State Park is in the county. • One of nine counties named for Captain James Lawrence (1781–1813), U.S. Navy commander in War of 1812 • 1815 (prior to statehood) from New Madrid County, MO. The county claims the title "Mother of Counties" because thirty-one of AR's present counties were carved from the original Lawrence County. • Cattle, hogs, rice, wheat, soybeans, sorghum, cotton; manufacture of mobile houses, apparel, fertilizer, shoe lasts; education (William Baptist College). • The Powhatan Courthouse (state park), built in 1888 and restored in 1970, is a regional archive containing some of the oldest records in the state.

LEE (one of twelve counties so named) *Marianna* • 12,580 • 602 • Eastern AR, bounded on the east by the Mississippi River (forming the MS state line); drained by the St. Francis and L'Anguille rivers and Big Creek. Part of St. Francis National Forest is in the southeast. Part of Louisiana Purchase Historical State Park is in the southwest corner. • One of eight counties named for Robert E. Lee • 1873 from Phillips and Monroe • Wheat, cotton, rice, soybeans, hogs; timber; manufacture of transportation equipment, fabricated metal products.

LINCOLN (one twenty-four counties so named) *Star City* • 14,492 • 561 • Southeastern AR, bounded on the northeast by the Arkansas River; drained by Bayou Bartholomew, claimed to be the world's longest bayou. Cane Creek State Park is found here. • One of eighteen counties named for President Abraham Lincoln • 1871 from Arkansas, Bradley, Desha, Drew and Jefferson • Cotton, soybeans, wheat, rice, fruit, watermelons, vegetables, cattle, hogs, poultry; manufacture of wood and plastic products.

LITTLE RIVER *Ashdown* • 13,628 • 532 • Southwestern AR, bounded on the west by the OK state line, on the south by the Red River (forming the TX state line), and on the northeast in part by the Little River. Millwood Lake reservoir (Little River) and State Park are in east. • Named for the Little River • 1867 from Hempstead • Wheat, soybeans, cattle, hogs; timber; lumber milling; manufacture of wood products, construction materials, paper, apparel; sand and gravel, limestone.

LOGAN (one of ten counties so named) *Booneville and Paris* • 22,486 • 710 • Western AR, bounded on the north by the Arkansas River (forming Lake Dardanelle reservoir in the northeast); drained by the Petit Jean River. Part of Ozark National Forest and Ouachita National Forest are here; part of Blue Mountain Lake reservoir (Petit Jean River) is in the south. The mesa-like summit of Magazine Mountain, at 2,753 feet, is the highest point in the state. • Named for James Logan (?–

1859), an early settler and member of the first AR legislature • Organized as Sarber 1871 from Franklin; name changed 1875 • US Air Force General John P. McConnell • Soybeans, chickens, cattle, hogs; timber; coal mining; sawmilling; cotton ginning; hunting (especially white-tail deer, turkey), fishing.

LONOKE *Lonoke* • 52,828 • 766 • Central AR, bounded on north by Cypress Bayou; drained by Wabbaseka, Meto and Two Prairie bayous (the last forming part of the eastern boundary). Toltec Mounds Archeology State Park (on Mound Lake) is in the southwest. • Variant spelling of lone oak, a former landmark at the county seat • 1873 from Pulaski and Jefferson • Lawyer and legislator Joseph T. Robinson • Rice, cotton, wheat, strawberries, soybeans, livestock; rice milling; manufacturing of wood products.

MADISON *Huntsville* • 14,243 • 837 • Northwestern AR; drained by White and Kings rivers and War Eagle Creek. Located in the Ozark region, the county includes Ozark National Forest along its southern border. Withrow Springs State Park is also here. • One of twenty counties named directly or indirectly for President James Madison • 1836 from Washington County • Cattle, hogs, chicken, turkeys; timber • Kings River was the first waterway in AR to receive legislative recognition and protection.

MARION *Yellville* • 16,140 • 598 • Northern AR, bounded on the north by the MO state line and on the east in part by the White River; drained by the Buffalo River and Crooked Creek; intersected by the White River (site of Bull Shoals Dam in the northeast). Bull Shoals State Park is at the dam. Bull Shoals Lake dominates the northern quarter of the county. Part of Buffalo National River is in the southeast. The county lies in the Ozark region of the state. • One of seventeen counties named for Revolutionary War general and SC legislator Francis Marion (?–1795) • Organized 1835 as Searcy (prior to statehood) from Izard; name changed to Marion 1836 • Cattle, hogs, turkeys; lead, zinc mines; timber; some manufacturing • The National Turkey Calling Contest is held in Yellville each October.

MILLER (one of three counties so named) *Texarkana* • 40,443 • 624 • Extreme southwestern AR, bounded on the west by the TX state line, on the south by the LA state line, and on the east and north by the Red River; drained by the Sulphur River. Sulphur River Wildlife Management Area is in the south. Miller County Sandhills Natural Area is in the southwest. • Named for General James Miller (1776–1851), first territorial governor of AR • 1820 (prior to statehood) • Wheat, soybeans, cattle, hogs, chickens (Texarkana is an agricultural marketing and distribution point); timber; oil and gas; diversified manufacturing • Miller County is inextricably linked to Bowie County, TX through the conjoined cities of Texarkana; the city, county, and state dividing line being State Line Avenue. The line runs through the middle of the shared post office/federal building, the only such anomaly in the U.S. It is appropriately constructed of Arkansas limestone and Texas pink granite. The two cities have separate municipal governments, but are linked economically and socially. The cities get their names from TEXas, ARKansas, and LouisiaANA (a few miles south). The Four States Fair and Rodeo is held in Texarkana (AR) every September.

MISSISSIPPI (one of two counties so named, the other in MO) *Blytheville and Osceola* • 51,979 • 898 • Northeastern AR, bounded on the north by the MO state line and on the east by the Mississippi River (forming the TN state line); drained by the East Hand and West Hand Chutes of the Little River. Hampson Museum State Park is at Wilson in the east. Big Lake National Wildlife Refuge and Herman Davis Memorial state parks are in the north. • Named for the Mississippi River • 1883 from Crittenden • Miller is the state's leading agricultural county: cattle, hogs, cotton, soybeans, sorghum, wheat, rice; timber; also diversified manufacturing, including farm equipment and ambulances; cotton and soybean processing; Blytheville Air Force Base (Strategic Air Command) is within the city limits of Blytheville. • Herman Davis Memorial State Park may be the only state park in the U.S. to honor an army private (local farm boy and World War I hero).

MONROE *Clarendon* • 10,254 • 607 • East-central AR; drained by the White (which forms the southwestern boundary) and Cache rivers. The county includes Pine City Natural Area. White River National Wildlife Refuge extends along the entire length of the river. • One of seventeen counties named for President James Monroe • 1829 from Phillips and Arkansas counties • Cotton, rice, wheat, soybeans, hogs; timber; commercial fishing; manufacturing.

MONTGOMERY (one of eighteen counties so named) *Mount Ida* • 9,245 • 781 • West-central AR; drained by the Ouachita, Caddo, and Little Missouri rivers. The county lies in the Ouachita Mountains. All of the county except for a narrow margin in the southeast falls within Ouachita National Forest. The western half of Lake Ouachita reservoir is in east. Little Missouri Falls is in the southwest. Blowout Mountain, Irons Fork, and Crystal Mountain scenic areas are also here. • One of sixteen counties named directly or indirectly for General Richard Montgomery (1738–1775), American Revolutionary War officer • 1842 from Clark • Cattle, hogs, chickens, dairying; food processing; cotton ginning; sawmilling; stone quarrying • The mineral-rich county has a world championship crystal dig in Mount Ida each fall.

NEVADA (one of two counties so named, the other in CA) *Prescott* • 9,955 • 620 • Southwestern AR, bounded on the northeast by the Little Missouri River; drained by Bayou Dorcheat, and Terre Rouge and Caney creeks. White Oak Lake State Park and Poison Spring State Forest are on the eastern boundary. • The county was given the name Nevada possibly because of its outline; viewed upside down, it roughly resembles the shape of the state of Nevada • 1871 from Hempstead • Chicken; lumber milling; oil and gas.

NEWTON (one of six counties so named) *Jasper* • 8,608 • 823 • Northwestern AR; drained by the Buffalo River (a National Wild and Scenic River) and its tributaries. The county lies in the Ozark region. Part of Ozark National Forest is in the south, a small unit to the north. The western part of Buffalo National River crosses the northern part of the county. Alum Cove Natural Bridge, Mystic Caverns, and Hurricane River Cave are also here. • Named for Thomas W. Newton (1804–53), AR legislator and U.S. representative • 1842 from Carroll • Cattle, hogs; lead and zinc; lumber milling.

OUACHITA (one of two county/parishes so named, the other in LA) *Camden* • 28,790 • 732 • Southern AR, bounded on the north in part by the Little Missouri river, on the south in part by Smackover Creek, and on the east in part by Two Bayou; drained by the Ouachita River (which forms part of the county's eastern boundary). White Oak Lake is surrounded by Poison Spring State Forest and includes White Oak Lake State Park. • Named for the Ouachita River • 1842 from Clark • The Battle of Poison Spring took place here on April 18, 1864 during the Camden Expedition of the Red River campaign (historic monument). Cattle, hogs, oil and gas, deposits of kaolin clay, lignite, sand and gravel, asphalt production; manufacture of timber products, including pulpwood and paper.

PERRY *Perryville* • 10,209 • 551 • Central AR, bounded on the northeast by the Arkansas River; drained by the Fourche La Fave River and its South Branch. Nimrod Dam in the Fourche La Fave River is on the western boundary. Part of Ouachita National Forest is in the southwestern half of the county, and includes South Fourche Scenic Area. • One of ten counties named for Oliver Hazard Perry (1785–1819), U.S. naval officer during the War of 1812 • 1840 from Pulaski • Soybeans, cattle, hogs, poultry; lumber milling.

PHILLIPS (one of three counties so named) *Helena* • 26,445 • 693 • Eastern AR, bounded on the east by the Mississippi River (forming the MS state line), on the west in part by the White River; drained by the St. Francis River and by Big Creek. The county includes part of Crowley's Ridge. Louisiana Purchase Historic State Park, part of the White River National Wildlife Refuge, and part of St. Francis National Forest are here. • Named for Sylvanus Phillips (1766–1831), who explored the area along the Arkansas River in the 1790s • 1820 (prior to statehood) from Arkansas County • Cotton, rice, wheat, soybeans, hogs; timber; gravel; manufacture of boxes, crates, plywood, cottonseed products, insecticides, fertilizers • The Delta Cultural Center is at Helena.

PIKE *Murfreesboro* • 11,303 • 603 • Southwestern AR, bounded on the south in part by the Little Missouri River, on the east by the Antoine River; drained by the Little Missouri and Caddo rivers. Lake Greeson is formed by Narrows Dam on the Little Missouri River here. Daisy State Park is on its northern shore. A small part of Ouachita National Forest is on the northern boundary of the county. • One of ten counties named for Zebulon M. Pike (1779–1813), U.S. army officer and discoverer of Pikes Peak in CO. • 1833 (prior to statehood) from Carroll and Clark • Cattle, hogs, chickens; manganese and quicksilver mines, gypsum quarries; lumbering • Crater of Diamonds State Park is the world's only publicly-operated diamond site open to rock hounds.

POINSETT *Harrisburg* • 25,614 • 758 • Northeastern AR; drained by the St. Francis and L'Anguille rivers and Left Hand and Right Hand Chutes of the Little River. The county is intersected by Crowley's Ridge. Lake Poinsett State Park is in the center of the county. • Named for Joel R. Poinsett (1779–1851), SC statesman and secretary of war who introduced the poinsettia flower to the U.S. from Mexico • 1838 from Greene • Cotton, rice, wheat, soybeans, alfalfa; hardwood timber; some manufacturing.

POLK (one of twelve counties so named) *Mena* • 20,229 • 859 • Western AR, bounded on the west by the OK state line; drained by the Ouachita, Saline, Little Missouri and Mountain Fork rivers. The county is located in the Ouachita Mountains with part of Ouachita National Forest in the north and southeast. Queen Wilhelmina Park is in the northwest. Part of Cossatot River State Park and Natural Area are also here. • One of eleven counties named for President James Knox Polk • 1844 from Montgomery • Lumbering, cattle, hogs, chickens, dairying; some manufacturing.

POPE (one of three counties so named) *Russellville* • 54,469 • 812 • North-central AR, bounded on the south by the Arkansas River; drained by Illinois Bayou and Big Piney Creek (a National Scenic River). The county is situated in the Ozark region. Part of Ozark National Forest is in the north and includes Pedestal Rocks. The Dardanelle Lock and Dam at Russellville forms Lake Dardanelle reservoir in the west. Dardanelle State Park is located on its northern shore. Holla Bend National Wildlife Refuge (on the south side of the Arkansas River bend and separated from the rest of the county by a new river channel) is in the south. • Named for John Pope (1770–1845), governor of Arkansas Territory and legislator from KY • 1829 (prior to statehood) from Pulaski • Wheat, soybeans, cattle, hogs, chickens; coal mines, some natural gas wells; timber; education (AR Tech. U.).

PRAIRIE (one of two counties so named, the other in MT) *Des Arc and De Valls Bluff* • 9,539 • 646 • East-central AR, bounded in the southwest by Two Prairie Bayou, bounded in part on the north by Bayou Des Arc and Cypress Bayou; drained by the White River. Part of White River National Wildlife Refuge is here. • Name for its open countryside • 1846 from Monroe • Rice, wheat, soybeans, hay, cattle, hogs; timber; lumber milling, commercial fishing.

PULASKI *Little Rock* • 361,474 (the most populated county in AR) • 771 • Central AR; drained by Bayou Fourche Creek and the Maumelle River. It is intersected northwest to southeast by the Arkansas River (David D. Terry Lock and Dam in the east, Murray Lock and Dam at center). The center of the county is highly urbanized around Little Rock, with agriculture in the southeast and northeast, and forest in the west. Pinnacle State Park is in the northwest on Lake Maumelle reservoir. Little Rock Air Force Base is in the northeast. • One of seven counties named for Count Casimir Pulaski (1748–79), Polish soldier who fought for America during the Revolutionary War • 1818 (prior to statehood) from Arkansas County • Before Union forces captured Little Rock in 1863, Confederate troops used the city as a supply center. The Old State Capitol, in use from 1836–1911, witnessed the historical vote for secession from the Union. Camp Joseph T. Robinson military reservation (built in 1917 as Camp Pike) was an important training center in both world wars. President Eisenhower ordered federal troops to Little Rock after Governor Orval Faubus prevented federally mandated school integration in September, 1957. • Black militant Eldridge Cleaver; general Douglas MacArthur; poet and critic John Gould Fletcher. Retail magnate Sam Walton and professional baseball player Bill Dickey died here. • Wheat, soybeans, cattle, hogs; oil and gas wells, stone quarries; distribution center for farm products; service industries, including government activities, health care and finance; diversified manufacturing; education (U. of AR at Little Rock; AR Baptist College; Philander Smith College) • Little Rock's Quapaw Quarter contains some of the city's oldest structures, including some that date from before the Civil War. The county contains abandoned bauxite mines.

RANDOLPH (one of eight counties so named) *Pocahontas* • 18,195 • 652 • Northeastern AR, bounded on the north by the MO state line and on the southwest by the Spring River; drained by the Black, Current, and Eleven Points rivers. Old Davidsonville State Park is in the south. • One of four counties named for John Randolph (1773–1833), U.S. congressman from VA and U.S. minister to Russia • 1835 (prior to statehood) from Lawrence • Rice, wheat, soybeans, cattle, hogs; timber • It is the only county in AR that has five rivers within its boundaries. • The largest meteorite to fall in the state of AR, weighing over 1,000 pounds, came to earth in the Black River bottoms in 1859, and is now on display at the courthouse in Pocahontas.

ST. FRANCIS *Forrest City* • 29,329 • 634 • Eastern AR; drained by the St. Francis and L'Anguille rivers. The county is intersected by Crowley's Ridge. Part of Village Creek, AR's largest state park, is in the north. • Named for the St. Francis River • 1827 (prior to statehood) from Phillips • Incorporated in 1871, Forrest City, the "Hub of Eastern AR," was built on the site of a camp located here during the construction of the Memphis to Little Rock Railroad, overseen by the eponymous Confederate general Nathan Bedford Forrest. • Boxer Sonny Liston • Cotton, rice, wheat, corn, peaches, soybeans, sweet potatoes, sorghum; timber (with planing mills); sand and gravel; manufacture of electrical equipment, farm machinery, television equipment, electric motors, textiles, materials-handling equipment.

SALINE (one of five counties so named) *Benton* • 83,529 • 723 • Central AR; drained by the Saline River and its tributaries, and Hurricane Creek. Ouachita National Forest (including Lake Winona reservoir) is in the northwest. • Named for local salt works • 1835 (prior to statehood) from Pulaski • Salt mining and pottery-making occupied early settlers. The lumbering of pine, oak and gum trees followed around 1900. The county's abandoned bauxite mines are a reminder of the importance of the high-grade ore to the thriving aluminum processing industry that served World War II needs. • Cotton, corn, cattle, hogs; manufacturing; gravel and clay pits; timber.

SCOTT (one of eleven counties so named) *Waldron* • 10,996 • 894 • Western AR, bounded on the west by the OK state line; drained by the Poteau and Fourche La Fave rivers. The Ouachita Mountains cross in the south. Most of the county, which includes part of Dutch Creek Mountain Scenic Area, lies within Ouachita National Forest. • Named for Andrew Scott (1788–1851), superior court justice for the Arkansas Territory • 1833 (prior to statehood) from Crawford and Pope • Lumbering; cattle, hogs, poultry, hay.

SEARCY *Marshall* • 8,261 • 667 • North-central AR; drained by the Middle Fork of the Little Red River. Buffalo National River (one of the few remaining unpolluted, free-flowing rivers in the lower forty-eight states) crosses the northern part of the county. Separate units of Ozark National Forest are in the northeastern corner and in the southwest. • Named for Richard Searcy (? -1832), jurist • First established 1835; name changed to Marion in 1836, then in 1838 a new Searcy County was formed from Marion • Cattle, hogs; timber.

SEBASTIAN *Fort Smith and Greenwood* • 115,071 (the fourth most populated county in AR) • 536 • Western AR, bounded on the west by the OK state line and on the north by the Arkansas River, with the source of Petit Jean River in the south. The Ouachita Mountains are also in the south (comprising part of Ouachita National Forest). Fort Chaffee Maneuver Training Center crosses the northern part of the county from Fort Smith east into Franklin County. Lock and Dam No. 13 on the Arkansas River is east of Fort Smith. • Named for William K. Sebastian (?–1865), jurist and U.S. senator from AR • 1851 from Crawford • Fort Smith was one of the first U.S. military posts in the Louisiana Territory. Serving as a base of operations for enforcing Indian policy and keeping the peace from 1817 to 1896, it was presided over in its unruly later years by "Hanging" Judge Isaac C. Parker (his restored courtroom part of Fort Smith National Historic Site). • Explorer and frontiersman Benjamin-Louis-Eulalie de Bonneville died here. • Coal and gas; timber; dairying, cattle, hogs, fruit, poultry; manufacture of furniture, automobiles, glass, food products, paper and plastic products, metal fabrication • Fort Smith has more than 900 acres of parks. "Miss Laura's," a restored Victorian House in Fort Smith, is the only former bordello listed on the National Register of Historic Places.

SEVIER (one of three counties so named) *De Queen* • 15,757 • 564 • Southwestern AR, bounded on the west by the OK state line, on the south by the Little River, and on the east by the Saline River (with Dierks Lake reservoir in the northeast corner); drained by the Cossatot River (designated as a National Scenic and Recreational River). DeQueen Lake reservoir is in the northwest; part of Millwood Lake reservoir (the Little and Saline rivers) is in the southeastern corner. Cossatot National Wildlife Refuge is located between the Little and Cossatot rivers in the south. • Named for Ambrose H. Sevier (1801–48), territorial legislator and delegate to U.S. Congress, U.S. senator from AR, and minister to Mexico • 1828 (prior to statehood) from Hempstead • Cattle, hogs, poultry; timber; manufacturing.

SHARP *Ash Flat* • 17,119 • 604 • Northern AR, bounded on the north by the MO state line; drained by the Strawberry and Spring rivers. Rock Creek Natural Area is here. • Named for Ephraim Sharp, AR state legislator • 1868 from Izard • Hay, chickens, cattle, hogs, timber; fishing.

STONE (one of three counties so named) *Mountain View* • 11,499 • 607 • North-central AR, bounded on the northeast by the White River; drained by the Middle Fork of the Little Red River. The county is located in the Ozark region and draws tourists for Blanchard Springs Caverns, the Ozark Folk Center, and Ozark National Forest, part of which is in the north. • Named for the natural stone formations, rocky hills and mountains in the area • 1873 from Izard and Independence • Cattle, poultry, hay; pine, hardwood timber; some manufacturing; tourism.

UNION (eighteen counties so named) *El Dorado* • 45,629 • 1,039 (the largest county in AR) • Southern AR, bounded on the south by the LA state line, and on the northeast and east by the Ouachita River. Felsenthal Lock and Dam, which impounds Lake Jack Lee on the eastern border, and H.K. Thatcher Lock and Dam are both located on the Ouachita River. Parts of the Felsenthal National Wildlife Refuge are here. The Southern Arkansas Arboretum is in El Dorado. • The county was given its name for the union of states • 1829 (prior to statehood) from Hempstead and Clark • Union is major oil and gas center with natural gas drilling, refining, and manufacture of petroleum products; also cattle, hogs, chickens, vegetables • Conservation methods pioneered in Schuler oil field have been adopted by the petroleum industry at large. The Arkansas Museum of Natural Resources in Smackover offers tours of actual oil fields to tell the story of the 1920's oil boom in South AR. The Rialto, located in El Dorado, is the only working art deco theatre left in AR.

VAN BUREN *Clinton* • 16,192 • 712 • North-central AR; drained by Archeys Fork of the Little Red River. Part of Ozark National Forest is here, as is part of Greers Ferry Lake reservoir. • One of four counties named for President Martin Van Buren • 1833 (prior to statehood) from Independence • Cattle, hogs, poultry; timber.

WASHINGTON *Fayetteville* • 157,715 (40% increase since 1990; the third fastest growing and second most populated county in AR) • 950 (the fourth largest county in AR) • Northwestern AR, bounded on the west by the OK state line; drained by the Illinois and White rivers. The county is located in the Ozark region. Increasingly urbanized in the north-center, it enjoys seasonal population swells, with significant retiree immigration. Located here are Devils Den State Park, parts of Ozark National Forest and part of Beaver Lake reservoir (White River). • One of thirty-one counties named for President George Washington • 1828 (prior to statehood) from the eastern portion of former Lovely County • The county suffered greatly during the Civil War. It was the scene of the December 7, 1862 Battle of Prairie Grove (commemorated by a state park). Following the Battle of Fayetteville (April 18, 1863), the city remained under Federal occupation until the end of the war. • Architect Edward Durell Stone • Cattle, hogs, chickens, turkeys, dairying, strawberries, grapes, apples, peaches; timber; coal, manufacture of clothing, farm implements, golf clubs, fishing rods; poultry processing canning, lumber production • Fayetteville, home of the University of AR, acquired an early reputation as an education center: Sophia Sawyer's Fayetteville Female Seminary was established in 1839. Arkansas College, established in 1852 and destroyed during the Civil War, was the state's first degree-granting college.

WHITE (one of five counties so named) *Searcy* • 67,165 • 1,034 (the second largest county in AR) • Central AR; bounded on the east by the White River and on the south in part by Cypress Bayou; drained by the Bayou Des Arc (forming part of the southern boundary) and Departee Creek; in-

tersected by the Little Red River. Bald Knob National Wildlife Refuge is in the east. • Named for either Hugh L. White (1773–1840), TN legislator, U.S. senator, and candidate for U.S. president in 1836; or for the White River • 1835 (prior to statehood) from Pulaski, Jackson and Independence • The explosion of a Titan II missile at a U.S. Air Force base here on August 9, 1965 resulted in the loss of 53 lives. • The county leads AR in strawberry production; other farm products: cotton, potatoes, vegetables, poultry, eggs, pecans, rice, wheat, soybeans, cattle, hogs; timber; mineral springs; light manufacturing; education (Harding U.).

WOODRUFF *Augusta* • 8,741 • 587 • East-central AR, bounded on the west by the White River; drained by the Cache River, Cache Bayou and Bayou DeView. Two units of Cache River National Wildlife Refuge are here. • Named for William E. Woodruff (1795–1885), publisher who established the *Arkansas Gazette*, the state's first newspaper • 1862 from White • Cotton, rice, wheat, soybeans, sorghum; diversified manufacturing; commercial fishing; mussel-shell gathering; timber.

YELL *Danville and Dardanelle* • 21,139 • 928 (the fifth largest county in AR) • West-central AR, bounded on the northeast by the Arkansas River; drained by the Fourche La Fave and Petit Jean rivers. Much of the county lies in Ouachita and Ozark national forests. Dutch Creek Mountain Scenic Area is on the western border. Mount Nebo State Park is also in the county, as are Nimrod Lake and part of Blue Mountain Lake reservoirs. • Named for Archibald Yell (1797–1847), U.S. representative from AR and governor of the state • 1840 from Pope • Cattle, hogs, chickens, wheat, soybeans; timber; sand and gravel.

CALIFORNIA

Eureka (I Have Found It)

Most of California's fifty-eight counties have a five-member board of supervisors and a number of elected officials, including assessor, auditor, clerk, coroner, district attorney, sheriff, superintendent of schools, and treasurer. County home rule is provided for by the California constitution.

ALAMEDA *Oakland* • 1,443,741 (the twenty-first most populated county in the U.S.) • 738 • Western CA, bounded on the west by San Francisco Bay, on the south in part by Coyote Creek; drained by Alameda Creek. Coastal ranges cross the county to the San Joaquin Valley in the northeast corner. The county includes Livermore Valley and part of the Diablo Range in the southeast. Hetch Hetchy Aqueduct runs east-west through the county and carries water from the Sierra Nevada to San Francisco. The county has several reservoirs, including San Antonio, part of Calaveras, Upper San Leandro,

and Del Valle. Anthony Chabot and Coyote Hills regional parks are here. Alameda County has other regional preserves, wilderness areas and parks. Part of Don Edwards San Francisco Bay National Wildlife Refuge is in the extreme south. • Named for Alameda Creek • 1853 from Contra Costa and Santa Clara • Oakland was chosen as the terminus of the first transcontinental railroad, completed in 1869. After the 1906 earthquake in San Francisco, the city received a large influx of refugees. Its growth was stimulated by military and naval installations built here during World War II. Major damage was done to the county on October 17, 1989 by an earthquake, which measured 7.1 on the Richter scale and collapsed a mile-long section of Interstate 880 highway. • Writer Jack London; aviator and army general James H. Doolittle; tennis players Don Budge and Helen Wills; geologist Richard Joel Russell; work efficiency expert Lilian Evelyn Gilbreth; baseball player and manager Billy Martin; actor Tom Hanks; composer and instrument builder Harry Partch. Evangelist Aimee Semple McPherson, astronomer Robert Grant Aitken, physicists Luis W. Alvarez and Arthur Holly Compton, educator and mathematician Florian Cajori, scientist Frederick G. Cottrell, physical chemist William F. Giauque, anthropologist Edward W. Gifford, zoologists Richard B. Goldschmidt and Charles A. Kofoid died here. • Cattle, nursery products, carnations, roses (especially white) and rose seedlings, grapes, honey, oats; gypsum, limestone, sand and gravel, clay quarrying, magnesite mining, stone quarrying; manufacture of industrial glass fabrics, cheese and other food products, school buses, transportation equipment, electronic equipment, metal products, plastics, building materials, industrial chemicals; shipping (Oakland is the fourth busiest port in the U.S.); research (especially high tech, nuclear physics, and nuclear weapons); education (U. of CA, Berkeley; Merritt College; Cal State U., Hayward; Holy Names College, Mills College; others) • The corporate headquarters of six Fortune 1000 companies are located here. Mission San Jose de Guadalupe in Fremont is the mother house of the Dominican Sisters. Oakland is home to the Athletics and Raiders (Network Associates Coliseum) and the Golden State Warriors (the Arena in Oakland).

ALPINE *Markleeville* • 1,208 (the least populated county in CA) • 739 • Eastern CA, bounded on the northeast by the NV state line; drained by the North Fork of the Mokelumne River, the Middle and Clark forks of the Stanislaus River, and the East and West forks of the Carson River, all of which have their sources here. The county is located along the crest of the Sierra Nevada Mountains south of Lake Tahoe and mostly is occupied by national forests: El Dorado in the north, Humboldt-Toiyabe east of the Sierra Divide, and Stanislaus west of the Divide. The Pacific Crest Trail and the Divide of the Sierra Nevada runs north-south through the center of county. The Clark Fork of the Stanislaus forms the southern boundary of the county. Grover Hot Springs State Park and Kirkwood Ski Resort are also here. • Named for the mountainous terrain of the Sierra Nevada • 1864 from Calaveras, Amador, El Dorado, and Mono • The county had a silver boom from the 1850s to the 1870s; ruins of silver towns remain. The Western side of the famous Comstock Lode (Virginia City, Yerington NV) is here. • Some hay, some beef-cattle and sheep grazing; some gold mining; hunting, fishing.

AMADOR *Jackson* • 35,100 • 593 • Central and eastern CA, bounded on the south in part by the Mokelumne River and its north fork, and on the north in part by the Cosumnes River and its south fork. The county extends from the Sacramento Valley in the west to the Sierra Nevada in the east, where Mokelumne Peak rises to 9,332 feet. Part of El Dorado National Forest is in east. Pardee and Camanche reservoirs (both on Mokelumne River) are on southern boundary in the southwest. • Named for J.M. Amador (1794-1883), miner, and early landowner • 1854 from Calaveras • The 1849 gold rush here, centered around Jackson, was made famous by the tales of Mark Twain and Bret Harte. Many old gold camps survive. • Astronomer Robert G. Aitken • Barley, corn, oats, grapes, walnuts, cattle; timber; gold mining; clay, sand and gravel quarrying; recreational tourism.

BUTTE (one of three counties so named) *Oroville* • 203,171 • 1,639 • North-central CA, bounded on the west in part by the Sacramento River and Butte Creek, and on the south in part by South Honcut Creek. Flatlands of the Sacramento Valley in the west rise to approximately 6,600 ft. in the Sierra Nevada Mountains in the east. The county contains parts of Lassen (in the northeast) and Plumas (in the east) national forests. Sacramento River National Wildlife Refuge is in the west. Lake Oroville reservoir and State Recreation Area (Feather River) are in east-center. Thermalito Afterbays Reservoir, used for irrigation, is west of Oroville in south-center. • Named for the Sutter Buttes of the Sacramento Valley • 1850 (original county) • Chico experienced significant industrial expansion after WW II. • Pioneer and politician John Bidwell (state historic park) • Rice, nuts (especially almonds), kiwi fruit, olives, prunes, peaches, barley, corn, oats, wheat, beans, cattle; extensive logging and lumber production; gold, silver, platinum; food processing; manufacture of matches, conveyor systems, toothpaste tubes; education (CA State U.–Chico).

CALAVERAS *San Andreas* • 40,554 • 1,020 • Central CA, in the Sierra Nevada Mountains, bounded in the north by the Mokelumne River and its North Fork, and on the south by the Stanislaus River and its North Fork; drained by the Calaveras River and its North Fork, and by the South Fork of the Mokelumne River. Stanislaus National Forest and part of Calaveras Big Trees State Park (redwoods) are located on the southeastern boundary. Angels Camp, the scene of Mark Twain's famous "The Jumping Frog of Calaveras County" and other old 1849 California Gold Rush towns survive. Camanche Reservoir (Mokelumne River) is on the north boundary, in the northwest. New Melones and Tulloch reservoirs (Stanislaus River) are on the southeast boundary. The dams throughout the county store water for power, water supply and irrigation. • Named for the Calaveras River • 1850 (original county) • Gold mining; timber; cement production; cattle, walnuts, olives, honey, oats, grapes; tourism (winter sports area; camping, hunting, fishing, spelunking in its many caverns).

COLUSA *Colusa* • 18,804 • 1,151 • North-central CA, bounded on the east by the Sacramento and Butte rivers. The county rises from lowlands of the Sacramento and Colusa rivers to Coast Ranges in the west. The Tehama Colusa (irrigation) Canal passes north-south through the center of the

---

county. East Park Reservoir (Stony River) is in the northwest; Colusa-Sacramento River State Recreation Area is in the northeast, north of Colusa. The county includes part of Mendocino National Forest. National wildlife refuges in the county include part of Sacramento, and all of Delevan and Colusa. • Named for the Colus Indians • 1850 (original county) • Rice, beans, wheat, oats, barley, corn, sugar beets, almonds, walnuts, tomatoes, cattle; sand and gravel; hunting (waterfowl, pheasant, deer).

CONTRA COSTA *Martinez* • 948,816 • 720 • Western CA, bounded on the west by San Francisco Bay and San Pablo Strait, on the northwest by San Pablo Bay, on the north by Carquinez Strait, Suisun Bay, San Joaquin/Sacramento estuary, and the San Joaquin River, and on the east by the Old San Joaquin River (old channel). The county is highly urbanized in the north, west, and center; these population centers continue to grow. The northeast comprises part of the fertile delta of the San Joaquin River. The county contains a number of parks; Mount Diablo is prominent in the center. The Mokelumne Aqueduct crosses east-west. Concord Naval Weapons Detachments are in the north. • The name of the county comes from the Spanish for "opposite coast," designating the northeastern shore of San Francisco Bay • 1850 (original county) • Professional baseball player Joe DiMaggio; naturalist John Muir; zoologist Clarence E. McClung; jazz pianist and composer Dave Brubeck. Historian Hubert H. Bancroft and educator and chemist Joel H. Hildebrand died here. Dramatist Eugene O'Neill wrote several of his best known plays near Danville. • Asparagus, tomatoes, apples, walnuts, wheat, oats, barley, corn, nursery stock; shipbuilding; food processing; manufacture of steel products, bathroom fixtures, aircraft and aerospace components, electronics, petroleum products, petrochemicals, chemicals, tiles; quarrying of stone, clay, sand and gravel, pumice; natural gas wells; education (St. Mary's College of CA; J.F.K. University) • Richmond is one of the busiest ports on the Pacific coast. The region around Antioch is called the "Everglades of the West," for its hundreds of crisscrossing waterways protected by levees.

DEL NORTE *Crescent City* • 27,507 • 1,008 • Extreme northwestern CA, bounded on the north by the OR state line, on the west by the Pacific Ocean; drained by the Smith and Klamath rivers. The county is predominantly mountainous except for its narrow coastal strip. Part of Yurok Indian Reservation is located in the south. Redwood trees are found in Jedediah Smith Redwoods and Del Norte Coast Redwoods state parks. A northern unit of Redwood National Park is here, along the coast, as are Pelican State Beach and Castle Rock National Wildlife Refuge • From Spanish "north" for the county's location in the state • 1858 from Klamath County • Lumbering and sawmilling; dairying, cattle, grapes, apples, asparagus, tomatoes, walnuts, nursery stock; silver and gold mining, sand and gravel quarrying; ocean fisheries and game fishing, hunting; processing industries.

EL DORADO *Placerville* • 156,299 • 1,711 • East-central CA, bounded on the west in part by the American River and its reservoir Folsom Lake, on the north in part by the North Fork of the American and the Rubicon rivers, and on the south by the Consumnes River and its South Fork; drained by the American, Rubicon and Consumnes rivers. The county rises from the Sierra Nevada foothills in the west to the crest of the range and includes Free and Pyramid peaks. Lake Tahoe lies on the northeast boundary between CA and NV. The county includes parts of Eldorado National Forest. • The name El Dorado comes from the Spanish for "the golden one," referring to gold found in the area in 1848 • Original county; organized 1850 (prior to statehood) • Coloma was the site of the gold discovery in 1848 that touched off the legendary California gold rush. It was at Sutter's Mill that John A. Sutter's boss carpenter, James W. Marshall, found gold on January 24, 1848 (state historical park). This and other old mining towns of the Mother Lode survive. • Tourism: winter sports, hunting, fishing, camping, hiking; lumber; limestone, gold; grapes, apples, walnuts, cattle, lambs, poultry.

FRESNO *Fresno* • 799,407 • 5,963 (the forty-first largest county in the U.S.) • Central CA, bounded in large part on the north by the San Joaquin River; drained by the Kings and Fresno rivers. The county stretches across San Joaquin Valley from the Diablo Range in the west to the crest of the Sierra Nevada in the east; there are peaks here over 14,000 ft. high. The California Aqueduct crosses the county in the southwest-center. There are several reservoirs in the county, including Pine Flat Lake, Courtright and Millerton Lake (with state recreation area attached) on the Madera county line. A large part of Kings Canyon National Park and parts of Sierra National Forest (its headquarters in the city of Fresno) and Sequoia National Forest are in the east. The north unit of Giant Sequoia National Monument is also in the county. • The name of the county comes from the Spanish "ash (tree)" for the abundant ash trees found here. • 1856 from Mariposa and Merced • The city of Fresno was built by the Central Pacific Railroad. In 1872, a line was extended into the San Joaquin Valley by its founder Leland Stanford, who felt the area had farming potential. • Physicist William W. Hansen; film director Sam Peckinpah; writer William Saroyan. World War II flying ace Pappy Boyington died here. • The county, one of the most agriculturally productive in the U.S., grows virtually the entire U.S. raisin crop. Farmers here raise over 200 other crops, most important among them table grapes, cotton, figs (the largest orchards in the U.S. are here), nectarines, oranges, almonds, lettuce, garlic, tomatoes, sugar beets, rice, corn, beans, barley, oats and wheat. Also here, dairying, cattle, wineries; manufacture of electric wiring, automobile heaters, blue jeans, wood products, concrete pipe, chemicals, ceramics, farm machinery, vending machines; sand and gravel, stone quarrying, oil and gas; pine, fir, cedar; food processing, packing and shipping; tourism; education (Fresno Pacific U.; CA State U. Fresno).

GLENN *Willows* • 26,453 • 1,315 • North-central CA,

bounded in part on the east by Butte Creek; watered by the Sacramento River (forming part of its eastern boundary). The eastern part of the county is in the Sacramento Valley, rising in the west to Coast Ranges. The county includes part of Mendocino National Forest, part of Sacramento National Wildlife Refuge, Stony Gorge Reservoir, and Black Butte Reservoir (on the northern boundary). • Named for Dr. Hugh J. Glenn (1824-82), the most important wheat grower in CA and a prominent politician during the latter half of the 1800s • 1891 from Colusa • Cattle, sheep, dairying, sugar beets, rice, corn, beans, barley, olives, almonds, walnuts, pistachios, prunes, honey, citrus; timber; waterfowl, pheasant and deer hunting.

HUMBOLDT (one of three counties so named) *Eureka* • 126,518 • 3,572 • Northwestern CA, bounded on the west by the Pacific Coast; drained by the Klamath, Trinity, Mad, Eel, and Mattole rivers. Cape Mendocino is the westernmost point in the state. The county lies mainly in the Coast Ranges. Part of the Klamath Mountains are here, as are the King Mountain Range and Rainbow Ridge. The county includes part of Six Rivers National Forest (its headquarters in Eureka), part of Hoopa Valley and Yurok Indian reservations, Humbolt Bay National Wildlife Refuge, part of Redwood National Park, several state parks (including the large Humboldt Redwoods State Park) and state recreation areas. Kings Range National Conservation Area is in the southwest. • Named for Humboldt Bay • 1853 from Trinity; in 1874 it annexed part of Klamath • Fort Humboldt (now a state historic monument) was the scene of several Indian uprisings from 1853 to 1865. • Timber (redwood, Douglas fir, cedar, spruce); dairying, cattle, lambs, sheep (Merino wool); recreation tourism; salmon, crabs; sand and gravel, clay, silver mining • The world's tallest tree (364 feet high) is near Dyerville.

IMPERIAL *El Centro* • 142,361 • 4,175 • Extreme southeastern CA, bounded on the south by the Mexican state of Baja California and on the east by the Colorado River (forming the AZ state line). The county lies in the Colorado Desert; the Superstition Mountains and Chocolate Mountains enclose the canal irrigated agriculturally productive Imperial Valley. The New and Alamo rivers carry wastewater to the Salton Sea in the northwest. The Sonny Bono Salton Sea National Wildlife Refuge is situated on its southern shore. Part of the Chocolate Mountains Gunnery Range is in the north. Imperial Sand Dunes Recreation Area is in the south. Fort Yuma Indian Reservation is situated in the extreme southeast; part of Torres-Martinez Indian Reservation is in the northwest. Part of Anza Borrego Desert State Park is also in the county. The Cibola and Imperial national wildlife refuges are found along its eastern border. • Named for the Imperial Valley, itself named for the Imperial Land Company that was organized to colonize the southern CA Desert • 1907 from San Diego • Asparagus, broccoli, cauliflower, carrots, onions, tomatoes, melons, other fruits, dates, corn, sugar beets, wheat, cotton, alfalfa, hay, cattle, sheep; gypsum, sand and gravel • El Centro is the largest settlement in the U.S. below sea level (fifty-

two feet). The National Parachute Test Range is located in El Centro.

INYO *Independence* • 17,945 • 10,203 (the second largest county in CA and the ninth largest county in the U.S.) • Eastern CA, bounded on the east by the NV state line, and on the west by the crest of the Sierra Nevada, which contain ten peaks over 14,000 feet, including Mount Whitney on the border with Tulare County. Standing at 14,494 feet, it is the highest peak in the U.S. outside Alaska. To the east is Badwater Basin in Death Valley National Park (which occupies most of the eastern half of the county). At 282 feet below sea level, the basin is the lowest point in the U.S. (The county earns the distinction of having both the highest and lowest elevations in the contiguous forty-eight states.) Death Valley is the hottest and driest place in the U.S.; the highest shade temperature ever recorded here was 134 degrees F. at Furnace Creek Ranch. Between the Sierra Nevada and the Panamint Range are arid basins such as Owens Valley, and the Inyo Mountains and other ranges. The Owens River supplies water to the Los Angeles Aqueduct. The Amargosa River and Furnace Creek vanish in Death Valley. The Lone Pine Indian Reservation is in Owens Valley. Ancient Bristlecone Pine Forest in Inyo National Forest contains representatives of the oldest living organism on earth. The China Lake Naval Air Weapons Station is in the southwest. • Named for the Inyo Mountains • 1866 from Tulare • Manzanar (national historic site) was the first of the permanent Japanese American internment camps to open, receiving its first detainees on March 21, 1942. • Anthropologist Leslie A. White died here. • The county is the leading producer in the state of lead, tungsten, and talc. Also mined here are molybdenum, zinc, silver, borax, potash, salt, and soda. Stock raising, dairying; tourist and recreational activities, especially in Death Valley National Park. • Death Valley Scotty and Albert Mussey Johnson built their Castle in the Desert here in the late 1920s; it is a major county tourist draw.

KERN *Bakersfield* • 661,645 • 8,141 (the third largest county in CA and the nineteenth largest county in the U.S.) • South-central CA, walled in by the Tehachapi Mountains in the south, the southern part of the Sierra Nevada in the east and Coast Ranges in the west; drained by the Kern River. Part of the Mojave Desert extends into the county from the west. The Los Angeles Aqueduct crosses the county north-south in the east. The California Aqueduct crosses northwest-southeast in the west. The county contains part of Sequoia National Forest and part of Los Padres National Forest. Edwards Air Force Base is in the extreme southeast. Also found here are the Kern National Wildlife Refuge and Tule State Elk Reserve. Part of China Lake Naval Air Weapons Station is in the extreme northeast. • Named for the Kern River, itself named by John C. Frémont for Edward M. Kern, topographer and artist who almost drowned in the river. • 1866 from Los Angeles and Tulare • The county was benefited around the turn of the 20th century through investment by San Francisco capitalists who helped to develop an extensive irrigation system to distribute the waters of the Kern River and make the area agriculturally productive. A strong petroleum industry, centered in Bakersfield, grew from the discovery of the Kern River oil fields in 1899. Bakersfield was ravaged by a fire in 1889 and a widespread earthquake in 1952. • Baritone Lawrence Tibbett • Cotton, potatoes, hay, grains, nuts, table grapes and vineyards (the county produces one quarter of all the wine produced in CA), citrus fruits, apples, plums carrots, tomatoes, peppers, cattle, dairying; limestone, gypsum quarrying, clay mining, borax, tungsten, silver, gold mining, oil and natural gas. (Kern is the state's leading petroleum-producing county); manufacture of steel products, textiles, bedding materials, electronic parts; education (CA State U., Bakersfield); tourism.

KINGS (one of two counties so named; the other in NY) *Hanford* • 129,461 • 1,391 • South-central CA; drained by the Kings and Tule rivers. The county lies on irrigated farmland of the San Joaquin Valley. Tulare Lake irrigation reservoir is the center of the county. Kettleman Hills (rich in oil and natural gas) are in the southwest. Part of Lemoore Naval Air Station is in the northwest. Part of the Diabolo Range is in the far southwest. • Named for the Kings River • 1893 from Tulare • Cotton, oats, wheat, barley, fruits, vegetables, dairying, turkeys; farm product processing, oil refining; gypsum quarrying.

LAKE (one of twelve counties so named) *Lakeport* • 58,309 • 1,258 • Northwestern CA, in the Coast Ranges; drained by the Eel River and Cache Creek. The county lies in a scenic recreational region, dominated in the center by Clear Lake. Part of Mendocino National Forest, including Lake Pillsbury Recreation Area, is in the north. South of the lake are Clear Lake State Park, Boggs Mountain Demon State Forest, and Anderson State Historic Park. Part of Cache Creek Cooperative Management Area is in the east. Several small Indian reservations are located in the county. Indian Valley Reservoir is in the east. • Named for Clear Lake • 1861 from Napa • Oats, pears, grapes, walnuts, cattle; timber; resort (hot springs) tourism, camping, hunting, fishing; mineral-water bottling; quick-silver, sand and gravel.

LASSEN *Susanville* • 33,828 • 4,557 • Northeastern CA, bounded on the east by the NV state line; drained by the Pit and Susan rivers. The county lies on a high volcanic plateau extending east from the Cascade Range. The Sierra Nevada follows the southwest and southern borders of the county. Part of Lassen Volcanic National Park is in the west. Also here are a large part of Lassen National Forest (its headquarters in Susanville) and parts of Plumas and Modoc national forests. Eagle Lake is in the center of the county. The Sierra Army Depot is in the southeast. • Named for Mount Lassen, itself named for Peter Lassen, a Danish-born pioneer in northeastern California • 1864 from Plumas and Shasta • After gold was struck in 1853, Susanville became a bustling mining town. In 1856, early settler Isaac Roop established a short-lived "republic" called Nataqua and made Susanville its capital. Residents put up armed resistance to California jurisdiction (the

Sagebrush War) until the county was formed in 1864. • Motion picture art director Cedric Gibbons died here. • Pine, fir, and cedar logging, lumber milling; cattle, irrigated farming producing potatoes, rice, wheat, barley, oats, garlic, strawberries; fishing, hunting, camping, winter sports.

LOS ANGELES *Los Angeles* • 9,519,338 (the most populated county in the U.S.) • 4,061 • Southern CA, bounded on the west by the Pacific Ocean. The county, formerly comprising some of the nation's most valuable farmland, has been largely replaced by heavy urbanization in the Los Angeles basin. In the northeast the San Gabriel Mountains rise to peaks of over 10,000 feet. The coast is indented by San Pedro and Santa Monica bays. The county includes Santa Catalina Island across the San Pedro Channel, and San Clemente Island. The intermittent Los Angeles and San Gabriel rivers (both large culverts) and their tributaries flow through the county. The California and Los Angeles aqueducts bring in greatly needed water. Part of the Santa Monica Mountains and its national recreation area are in the west; parts of Angeles National Forest are in the San Gabriel Mountains in the center. Part of the Mojave Desert is in the northeast; a portion of Edwards Air Force Base is also here. Part of Antelope Valley is in the northwest. State beaches dot the coast. Saddleback Butte and Placerita Canyon state parks are also in the county. Los Angeles is the most populated city located within a single county (3,694,820), and one of the largest in the U.S. in area. Eighty-four other cities make up the county. • Named for the Los Angeles River • Original county; organized 1850 (prior to statehood) • Franciscan priests built Mission San Gabriel, just east of the future city of Los Angeles in 1771. Pioneers from Guaymas, Mexico founded the Pueblo of Los Angeles in 1781. The area was an early ranching center. With the completion of the Panama Canal and the artificial harbor at San Pedro in 1914, the city of Los Angeles became a major seaport. Since the 1910s the county's film industry has attracted world attention, the word Hollywood becoming synonymous with manufactured glitz and glamour. Rioting in the Los Angeles neighborhood of Watts in 1965 left thirty-four dead and about $40 million in property damage. In 1970, brush fires that spread from the San Fernando Valley to Malibu killed eleven people and destroyed 400 homes. The next year an earthquake centered in San Fernando caused sixty-five deaths and extensive property damage. A 1987 earthquake in the county caused significant damage as well. An acquittal of white police officers in Los Angeles charged with beating black motorist Rodney King in March, 1991 ignited rioting, looting, and arson in the South-Central section of the city, resulting in fifty-one deaths, and over $1 billion in property damage. • A sampling of the many famous individuals who resided and/or died here: jazz musician Miles Davis; biologist Max Delbrück; showman Walt Disney; novelist Theodore Dreiser; frontiersman Wyatt Earp; singer Ella Fitzgerald; actors W.C. Fields, Henry Fonda, Clark Gable, Lucille Ball, Humphrey Bogart and Gary Cooper; short story writer and novelist F. Scott Fitzgerald;

presidential contender and diplomat Adlai E. Stevenson; engineer and architect R. Buckminster Fuller; composer George Gershwin; broadcast pioneer Lee De Forest; operetta composer Rudolf Friml; inventor and manufacturer King Camp Gillette; writer Zane Grey; playwright William Inge; novelist and playwright Christopher Isherwood; sculptor and designer Isamu Noguchi; general George S. Patton; astronaut Sally Ride; dancer Fred Astaire; boxer Max Baer; comedians Jack Benny and George Burns; baseball player Roy Campanella; army officer Adna R. Chaffee; singer Nat King Cole; composer and pianist Sergei Rachmaninoff. • Los Angeles is the industrial, financial, and trade center of the western U.S., the largest manufacturing center in the U.S., and a major television and film production center. Among its many manufactures are aircraft, aerospace equipment, clothing, furniture, rubber, tires, automobiles, food products, electronic products, computer equipment and software, missiles. Oil and natural gas; oil refining (one of the nation's top centers). Farm products include cattle, poultry, honey, strawberries, almonds, peaches, onions, barley, ornaments and bedding plants, dairy products. Also, printing and publishing; music recording; commercial fishing and canning; research; education (numerous institutions of higher learning, including UCLA, USC, Loyola Marymount U., CA State U.; Whittier College; Mount St. Mary's College, Occidental College, Pepperdine U., Woodbury U.,CA State Polytechnic U.); tourism. The Port of Los Angeles handles a greater annual value of cargo than any other port in the U.S., most of the trade between the U.S. and Japan flowing through the port. • The county is corporate headquarters to twenty-two Fortune 1000 companies. It has one of the world's most extensive freeway systems, with over 650 miles of expressways. Los Angeles's celebrated Hollywood Bowl seats more than 20,000 people. Some of the world's greatest paintings are housed at the Henry E. Huntington Library and Art Gallery in San Marino. The first orange grove in the county was planted in Glendora in 1866. Lawndale, long associated with the mortuary business, was the first city to utilize synthetic grass material in the landscaping of its public rights-of-way. Automobile crash test dummies are made in Sierra Madre. Formerly a major production and shipping center for citrus fruits, Covina was said to have shipped a million oranges a day in the 1930s. Douglas Fairbanks and Mary Pickford, who built Pickfair in 1919, were the vanguard of hundreds of film and television stars and executives who built lavish homes in Beverly Hills. Glendale's Forest Lawn Memorial Park is known for its elaborate statuary, including reproductions of famous shrines and works of art. The historic British transatlantic ocean liner *Queen Mary* serves as museum and hotel in the Long Beach harbor. Pasadena is know for its Tournament of Roses parade, held each New Year's Day since 1890. Los Angeles is home to the Dodgers (Dodger Stadium), Clippers, Lakers, and Kings (Staples Center).

MADERA *Madera* • 123,109 (40% increase since 1990; the third fast growing county in CA) • 2,136 • Central CA, bounded on the southwest, south, and southeast by the San Joaquin River, and on the northwest in part by the Chowchilla River; watered by the Fresno River and Madera Canal. The county stretches from the San Joaquin Valley in the west, northeast to the crest of the Sierra Nevada. It includes part of Yosemite National Park, part of Sierra National Forest and Devil Postpile National Monument. The Pacific Coast Trail crosses near its the northeastern border. Also here are part of Millerton Lake State Recreation Area and Wassama Roundhouse State Historic Park. • The name of the county is Spanish for "lumber" because the town around which it developed was a lumbering center. • 1893 from Fresno • Cotton, oats, wheat, barley, beans, pistachios, almonds, apples, figs, oranges, raisins, vegetables, honey, dairying, cattle, turkeys, poultry; pine; mining of pumice, gold, copper, sand and gravel, granite quarries; manufacturing; tourism.

MARIN *San Rafael* • 247,289 • 520 • Western CA. The wooded, hilly Marin Peninsula includes many suburbs of San Francisco. It is linked to the city by the Golden Gate Bridge. The county lies between San Pablo and San Francisco bays, and the Pacific Ocean. The Pacific coast here is indented by Bodega, Tomales, Drakes, and Bolinas bays. The county includes Mount Tamalpais, Angel Island, Tomales Bay, China Camp, and Samuel P. Taylor state parks. Also here are Muir Woods National Monument (with its virgin stand of coastal redwoods), Point Reyes National Seashore, Olompali State Historic Park, and part of Golden Gate National Recreation Area. The state prison at San Quentin is also located here. • Named for the local bay, islands, and peninsula by this name • 1850 • Mission San Rafael Arcangel was founded on December 14, 1817 as a health retreat for priests and locals. • Novelist and short story writer Kay Boyle, criminal writer Caryl Chessman, dancer Harold Christensen, and scholar and senator S.I. Hayakawa all died here. • Dairying, poultry, cattle, sheep; oats, nuts, fruits; oysters, clams, mussels; nurseries; stone, sand, gravel, quarrying, mercury; manufacture of electronics, lumber and wood products, chemicals; printing and publishing; food processing; education (Dominican U. of San Rafael) • San Rafael's civic center was designed by Frank Lloyd Wright.

MARIPOSA *Mariposa* • 17,130 • 1,451 • Central CA, on the western slope of the Sierra Nevada, the southern end of gold country, bounded on the south in part by the Chowchilla River; drained by the Merced River (forming McClure Reservoir). The county has peaks over 10,000 feet in the northeast. Part of Yosemite National Park, with some of the nation's most photographic scenery and its tallest waterfalls, is also in the northeast. The county includes parts of Sierra and Stanislaus national forests. The Merced and Mariposa groves of giant sequoias are here. • Named for the Mariposa Creek, Spanish for "butterfly" • Original county; organized 1850 (prior to statehood) • Ruins of old gold camps at Mariposa, Hornitos, and Coulterville are in the county. (The CA Mining and Mineral Museum is located in Mariposa.) • Cattle, sheep, hogs, poultry; sand and gravel pits, silver.

MENDOCINO *Ukiah* • 86,265 • 3,509 • Northwestern CA, bounded on the west by the Pacific Ocean; traversed by several of the Coast Ranges, with summits over 6,000 ft. in the east; drained by the Eel, Russian, Big, Novo, and Navarro rivers. The county includes part of Mendocino National Forest in the east, as well as a number of state parks, state beaches, state reserves, and state recreation areas. There are large stands of redwood trees near the coast. Jackson Demonstration State Forest is west-center. • Named for Cape Mendocino, north of the county. • Original county; organized 1850 (prior to statehood) • The great racehorse Seabiscuit • Timber and sawmilling; wineries, breweries, cattle, sheep, poultry, fruit (including apples, pears, and grapes), hops, beans, dairying; urchins, fish; manufacture of cylinders; hot springs resorts, trout and steelhead fishing, deer hunting; education (Mendocino College).

MERCED *Merced* • 210,554 • 1,929 • Central CA, extending across the San Joaquin Valley from the Diablo Range (west and southwest) to the foothills of the Sierra Nevada (east and northeast). Agriculture in the county is irrigated by the Merced, San Joaquin, and Chowchilla rivers. The county is crossed in the southwest (southeast to northwest) by the Delta Mendota Canal and the California Aqueduct. The county includes San Luis and Merced national wildlife refuges, McConnell State Recreation Area, Great Valley Grasslands and Pacheco state parks and San Luis Reserve State Recreation Area on the San Luis Reservoir. • Named for the Merced River • 1855 from Mariposa • Grapes, alfalfa, grain, sweet potatoes, tomatoes, corn, cantaloupes, wheat, barley, oats, rice, beans, sugar beets, nuts, dairying, cattle, turkeys and other poultry; sand and gravel; processing of farm products; lumber milling; manufacture of cement, carpets and draperies, recreational vehicles; metal fabrication; publishing.

MODOC *Alturas* • 9,449 • 3,944 • Extreme northeastern CA, bounded on the north by the OR state line, on the east by the NV state line; drained by Pit River. The county lies on a high semiarid volcanic plateau and has an extensive lava bed. It rises to Eagle Peak (9,892 feet) in the Warner Mountains in the east. Clear Lake Reservoir is in the northwest, encircled by Clear Lake National Wildlife Refuge. Part of Goose Lake is also in the county. A large percentage of the county is covered by Modoc National Forest. Part of Tule Lake and a part of Tule Lake National Wildlife Refuge are in the northwest. Surprise Valley in the east contains intermittently dry lakes. Fort Bidwell and XI Indian reservations are also found in the county. Modoc National Wildlife Refuge is here as well. • Named for the Modoc Indian tribe • 1874 from Siskiyou • Cattle, sheep, timber, potatoes, onions, horseradishes, wheat, barley, oats, sugar beets; pumice, sand and gravel; hunting and fishing.

MONO *Bridgeport* • 12,853 • 3,044 • Eastern CA, bounded on the east by the NV state line; drained by the Owens, East Walker, and West Walker rivers. The crest of the Sierra Nevada Range (with peaks over 13,000 ft.) is in the west and is crossed by Tioga Pass (the eastern entrance to Yosemite National Park). The Sweetwater Mountains are in the northeast, the White Mountains in the southeast. A large part of the county lies within Humboldt-Toiyabe and Inyo national forests. Also in the county are Bodie State Historical Park, part of John Muir Trail (on the western boundary), Mono Basin National Forest Scenic Area, saline Mono Lake, Mammoth Lakes, Lake Crowley, and Mammoth Lakes ski area. • Named for the Mono Indians • 1861 from Calaveras and Fresno • Recreational tourism; cattle, sheep; mining of pumice, gold, lead, silver, andalusite; pine.

MONTEREY *Salinas* • 401,762 • 3,322 • Western CA, bounded on the west by the Pacific Ocean and Monterey Bay, on the north by the Pajaro River valley. The Salinas River valley flows through the center of the county, flanked on the east by the Gabilan and Diablo ranges, and on the west by the Santa Lucia Range. The Monterey Peninsula is a major resort area. Scenic Highway 1 extends south along the coast from Monterey and includes Big Sur, several state parks and Point Lobos State Reserve; Los Padres National Forest is just east. Part of Camp Roberts is in the south, as is all of Fort Hunter Liggett Military Reservation. A small part of Pinnacles National Monument is on the northeast boundary. Lake San Antonio is in the south. Several state beaches are located along Monterey Bay. Three Franciscan missions are found in the county. • Named for Monterey Bay • Original county; organized 1850 (prior to statehood) • From the 1770s to the 1840s Monterey was the capital of vast Alta California under both Spain and Mexico. The state constitutional convention met in the city in 1849, paving the way for statehood in 1850. An early whaling center, Monterey was considered the sardine capital of the world in the 1940s, its industry centered at Cannery Row. Carmel-by-the-Sea was founded by artists in 1904 and remains a major art center. • Novelist John Steinbeck (who featured the county prominently in his work); actor, director, and mayor Clint Eastwood. Photographers Ansel Adams and Wynn Bullock, social organizer Saul Alinsky, naturalist and author Roy Chapman Andrews, actor Jean Arthur, humorist Josh Billings, advertising executive Fairfax M. Cone, businessman and banker Charles Crocker, aviator and army general James Doolittle, science fiction author Robert A. Heinlein, political philosopher Lincoln Steffens, first woman member of the House of Representatives Jeannette Rankin all died here. • Grain, tomatoes, asparagus, artichokes, celery, lettuce, peppers, sugar beets, olives, dairying; food processing; asbestos mining, sand and gravel; tourism; education (CA State U., Monterey Bay) • Each summer Salinas holds the California Rodeo. Point Pinos Light Station is the oldest operating lighthouse on the West Coast. The arrival of large numbers of migrating monarch butterflies to Pacific Grove each October is celebrated by the Butterfly Festival. The Monterey Bay National Marine Sanctuary is the nation's largest marine sanctuary. The renowned Monterey Jazz Festival is the oldest of its kind in the world.

NAPA *Napa* • 124,279 • 754 • Western CA. Though San Pablo Bay is south, boundaries of neighboring counties Sonoma and Solano have been drawn so that Napa County does not access the bay. Napa Valley extends southeast from the base of Mount St. Helena. The county lies in a mountainous area, in Coast Ranges. Napa County contains a petrified redwood forest and hot springs resorts. Robert Louis Stevenson State Park, Las Posadas State Forest, part of Bothe-Napa Valley State Park, and Bale Grist Mill (built in 1846) are here. • The derivation of the county name is uncertain; it is of Indian origin, from a now extinct tribe. • Original county; organized 1850 (prior to statehood) • Winemaking has been a principal industry here since the 1850s; more than fifty wineries are located in the county. Also, table grapes, walnuts, nursery products, dairying, cattle; fruit processing; manufacture of steel pipe, sheepskin coats, electrical power switching units; mining and quarrying of mercury, pumice, sand and gravel; fruit shipping.

NEVADA (one of two counties so named; the other in AR) *Nevada City* • 92,033 • 958 • Eastern CA, bounded on the east by the NV state line, on the south in part by the Bear River, and on the northwest by the Middle Yuba and Yuba rivers; drained by the South Yuba River, its Middle and South forks converging at Englebright Reservoir to form the Yuba River. The county extends eastward across the foothills to the crest of the Sierra Nevada, and is crossed here by Donner Pass. It has many lakes and lies in a popular recreational region. Most of the eastern two-thirds is in Tahoe National Forest. Malakoff Diggins and Empire Mine state historic parks are here. • Named for Nevada City, CA • 1851 from Yuba • Situated at the northern end of gold country, it was a leading county in gold production, with its peak years from the 1850s to 1950s. • Idealist philosopher and teacher Josiah Royce • Apples, nursery stock, cattle; timber; gold, silver, sand and gravel.

ORANGE (One of eight counties so named) *Santa Ana* • 2,846,289 (the second most populated county in CA and the fifth most populated county in the U.S.) • 789 • Southern CA; drained by the Santa Ana River. The county rises to the Santa Ana Mountains along its eastern border. The San Gabriel River forms part of its western boundary. Orange is part of the extensive Los Angeles metropolitan area and includes a number of resorts and large scale tourist attractions, anchored by Disneyland in Anaheim. State beaches are found along the coast. There are wilderness parks in the east. Part of Cleveland National Forest blankets the Santa Ana Mountains. Seal Beach Naval Weapons Station and Los Alamitos Joint Forces Training Center are in the southwest. • Named for local orange groves • 1889 from Los Angeles • Anaheim was founded by German immigrants in 1857 as a cooperative agricultural community. The county played a major role in the state's oil boom in the early 1900s. It experienced rapid urbanization after World War II. In 1995, it declared bankruptcy as a result of imprudent investments. • President Richard M. Nixon. Philosopher W.T. Stace; Cambodian politician and soldier

Lon Nol died here. C.C. Chapman made innovative improvements in citrus production in Fullerton in the early 1900s. • Beans, celery, avocados, artichokes, peppers, tomatoes, strawberries, oranges, eggs, cut flowers, livestock; extensive petroleum and natural gas fields (the county is among the foremost oil producers in the state); oil refining; packing, canning and food processing; manufacture of metal products, concrete blocks, plastic and rubber products, furniture, chemicals, carpets, jewelry, quartz crystals, aerospace components, boats and sports equipment, oil drilling supplies; electronic and computer industries; education (CA State U., Fullerton; Southern CA College; U. of CA, Irvine; Saddleback College; Chapman U.); tourism • The flourishing artists' colony of Laguna Beach is home to the Festival of Arts and Pageant of the Masters. San Clemente is distinguished by its many homes with red tile roofs. The harbor at Newport Beach contains one of the largest fleets of private recreational boats in the U.S. The architecturally significant mission at San Juan Capistrano, founded on November 1, 1776, and largely destroyed in an 1812 earthquake, is known for its nesting swallows, which arrive from their winter homes in the south around March 19 (St. Joseph's Day) and depart around October 23 (St. John's [death] Day). Anaheim hosts nearly one million convention delegates at its convention center each year, the largest center on the West Coast. Garden Grove's Crystal Cathedral televises its Sunday services worldwide from its all-glass structure. The city's annual strawberry festival attracts nearly one half million visitors each year. "Surf City USA," Huntington Beach hosts more than a dozen surfing contests each year, including the U.S. Open of Surfing, and is the site of the International Surfing Museum. Anaheim is home to the Angels (Edison International Field) and Mighty Ducks (Arrowhead Pond).

PLACER *Auburn* • 248,399 (44% increase since 1990; the second fastest growing county in CA) • 1,404 • Central and eastern CA, bounded on the east in part by the NV state line; drained by the Bear River (forming part of the county's northern border), the Rubicon River and the Middle Fork of the American River. The county extends east from the Sacramento Valley, across the foothills and crest of the Sierra Nevada to Lake Tahoe (Tahoe State Recreation Area here). Donner Pass lies along its northern border. Parts of Tahoe National Forest are in the eastern half of the county. A small part of El Dorado National Forest is found along the southern border. The county has ghost towns from its gold rush days. Its southwestern corner is urbanized as part of the Sacramento metropolitan area. Folsom Lake reservoir and State Recreation Area (American River) is on the southeastern boundary. • Named for the surface gold deposits in the area • 1851 from Yuba and Sutter • Auburn was founded in 1848 by prospectors who discovered gold here on their way to the famous gold strike at Sutter's Mill. (Many buildings from the early 1850s survive in the city's "Old Town" section. • Recreational tourism (many ski resorts near Lake Tahoe); nursery products, apiary products, rice, walnuts, fruit (especially plums &, kiwis), wheat, oats, corn, cattle, sheep, turkeys; mining and quarrying of clay, gold, sand and gravel; pine, fir, and cedar lumbering.

PLUMAS *Quincy* • 20,824 • 2,254 • Northeastern CA, in the Sierra Nevada; drained by the North, Middle, and South forks of the Feather River. All of the county except the extreme southeast, north, and southwest corners lies in a national forest; these include parts of Plumas and Lassen. Also here are part of Lassen Volcanic National Park, Lake Almanor, Lake Davis, and Plumas-Eureka State Park. Pacific Crest National Scenic Trail crosses the county in the west. • Named for the Feather River • 1854 from Butte • Tennis player Alice Marble • Recreational tourism, including hunting, fishing, winter sports, hot springs; pine, cedar; livestock, alfalfa, hay; Christmas trees; gold, copper, silver mining, sand and gravel.

RIVERSIDE *Riverside* • 1,545,387 (the sixteenth most populated county in the U.S.) • 7,207 (the fourth largest county in CA and the twenty-sixth largest county in the U.S.) • Southern CA, bounded on the east by the Colorado River (forming the AZ state line) and on the west by the Santa Ana Mountains. The center of the county is crossed northwest-southeast by the San Jacinto and San Bernardino ranges, and the Little San Bernardino Mountains. Part of the Colorado Desert is here, with the Coachella Valley in the center and the northern part of Salton Sea in the south. Other ranges in the county include the Chocolate, McCoy, and Chuckwalla Mountains. Most of Joshua Tree National Park is here, as are San Bernardino National Forest, Santa Rosa and San Jacinto Mountains National Monument, Coachella Valley Preserve, and Mount San Jacinto State Park. Among the Indian reservations here are the Cahuilla and parts of the Torres-Martinez. Part of Cleveland National Forest is in the far west. • Named for the city of Riverside • 1893 from San Bernardino and San Diego • Palm Springs developed as a fashionable, internationally known resort in the 1930s, a backyard playground for Hollywood glitterati. • Numerous entertainers reside or have resided here. One of the county's most illustrious residents was Bob Hope. (The Bob Hope Golf Classic is a popular Palm Springs event.) Physician and psychoanalyst Franz Alexander; film directors Busby Berkeley, Frank Capra, and John Ford; pilot Jacqueline Cochran; author and lawyer Erle Stanley Gardner; aircraft designer Donald Douglas; tennis player Alice Marble; singer and actor Mary Martin all died here. • Cotton, peppers, nursery stock, avocados, citrus fruits (Riverside has been a top orange producer since the late 1800s; its Orange Blossom Festival and the California Citrus State Historic Park are reminders), grapes, dates, melons, eggs, poultry, wheat, alfalfa, barley, oats, corn, beans; limestone, gypsum, clay, sand and gravel, iron, salt deposits; large farm produce packing and processing industries; manufacture of glass, ceramics, orchard equipment, lemon byproducts, cottonseed oil; education (Mount San Jacinto College; U. of CA, Riverside and others); resort tourism • The Palm Springs Aerial

Tramway, carrying passengers over a 13,200-foot-long cableway to the top of Mount San Jacinto, is the longest of its kind in the U.S. The Fabulous Palm Springs Follies is a popular annual event. Free-for-all auto races were held in Corona from 1913 to 1916. Indio, located in a large date-growing area, hosts the national date festival each February. Some fifty golf courses lie within a twenty-mile radius of Palm Springs.

SACRAMENTO *Sacramento* • 1,223,499 • 966 • Central CA, in the Central Valley, bounded on the west by the Sacramento River, on the south by the San Joaquin and Consumnes rivers and Dry Creek; drained by the Consumnes and American rivers (the latter forming Folson Lake reservoir). The county is urbanized around Sacramento. It includes Stone Lakes National Wildlife Refuge and Cosumnes River Preserve. • Named for the Sacramento River • Original county; organized 1850 (prior to statehood) • Sacramento, near the site of the colony of New Helvetia established by Captain John Sutter in 1849, prospered as gateway to Gold Rush country. After being established the capital of the state in 1854, the city suffered devastating floods and fires. It was the western terminus of the Pony Express and the terminus of the first California railroad (the Sacramento Valley Railroad to Folsom). • Actor Mary Anderson; designer Ray Eames; governor and senator Hiram Johnson; U.S. Supreme Court justice Anthony Kennedy; writer Joan Didion • Dairying, cattle, turkeys, nursery stock, corn, rye, wheat, barley, oats, rice, tomatoes, pears, grapes, sugar beets, beans; processing, packing and shipping center; manufacture of computer and aerospace components, boxes, fertilizer; food processing; printing; natural gas (a leading CA county); gold dredging, sand and gravel, silver mining; government operations; education (CA State U., Sacramento) • The *Union*, CA's oldest newspaper, began publishing in Sacramento in 1851. Sacramento is home to the Sacramento Kings professional basketball team (ARCO Arena).

SAN BENITO *Hollister* • 53,234 (45% increase since 1990; the fastest growing county in CA) • 1,389 • Western CA, bounded in part on the south by Lewis Creek and the Pajaro River. The San Benito River flows through the San Benito Valley between the Gabilan Range in the west and the Diablo Range in the east. The upper part of the Santa Clara Valley is in the north. The county contains part of Pinnacles National Monument. San Juan Bautista State Historical Park and Hollister Hills State Recreation Area are also here. • Named for the San Juan Creek, originally called San Benito • 1874 from Monterey • Lettuce, peppers, onions, grapes, eggs, poultry, wheat, barley, oats; granite, sand, gravel, mercury, limestone.

SAN BERNARDINO *San Bernardino* • 1,709,434 (the fourth most populated county in CA and the thirteenth most populated county in the U.S.) • 20,053 (the largest county in the U.S.) • Southern CA; bounded on the east by the NV and AZ state lines, the latter formed by the Colorado River. The southwest corner (San Bernardino Valley) lying south and west of the San Gabriel Mountains and San Bernardino Mountains (with peaks over 11,000 feet) comprises part of the expanding Los Angeles metropolitan area and is the county's population center. The Mojave Desert dominates the rest of the county. Part of San Bernardino National Forest (its headquarters in the city of San Bernardino) is in the southwest; part of Joshua Tree National Monument is in the south; and part of Death Valley National Monument is in the north. The county has several state parks and recreation areas. Several Indian reservations lie entirely or partially within the county. Mojave National Preserve is in the northeast. The county is home to the Twentynine Palms Marine Corps Air Ground Command Center, Fort Irwin National Training Center, parts of China Lake Naval Air Weapons Station, and Goldstone Deep Space Communications Complex. Part of Edwards Air Force Base is in the west. • Named for the San Bernardino Mountains • 1853 from Los Angeles • The city of San Bernardino was laid out by Mormons in 1852. • Film costume designer Edith Head. Baseball pitcher Fat Freddie Fitzsimmons died here. • Manufacture of aircraft and aircraft parts, plastics, printing machinery, prefabricated structural metal, electronic equipment, baked goods, industrial glass, apparel, filter aids; sand and gravel, potash, borax, iron, gold, talc, bentonite, clay, lead, zinc, agate, jasper mining, limestone, salt; printing and publishing; dairying, cattle, thoroughbred horses, eggs, chickens, alfalfa, strawberries, citrus fruits (the National Orange Show has been held in San Bernardino city since 1915), vegetables, nursery products, roses, barley; vineyards (including the world's largest); education (Chaffey College; U. of Redlands; Crafton Hills College; CA State U., San Bernardino; Loma Linda U.); tourism • The A.K. Smiley Public Library in Redlands has the largest collection of Lincoln memorabilia west of the Mississippi River. Needles, with high temperatures often exceeding 100 degrees F., is often described as the hottest city in the nation. The Ontario Motor Speedway is the scene of the annual California "500" auto race. Victorville and its back country have been used as backdrops for many Western films.

SAN DIEGO *San Diego* • 2,813,833 (the third most populated county in CA and the sixth most populated county in the U.S.) • 4,200 • Southern CA, bounded on the west by the Pacific Ocean, on the south by the Mexican state of Baja California; drained by the following intermittent rivers: the Santa Margarita, San Luis Rey, Sweetwater, Otay, Tijuana, and San Diego, and by Cottonwood Creek. Rolling coastal plain characterizes the west, Coast Ranges in the center, and the Colorado Desert in the east. The Mount Palomar astronomical observatory is located at Palomar Mountain State Park. There are several state beaches along the Pacific Coast. Camp Pendleton Marine Corps Base is in the northwest. The county includes part of the largest state park in CA, Anza Borrego Desert State Park. A number of Indian reservations are found here, including Los Coyotes in the north. Cuyamaca Rancho State Park is in the center of the county. • Named for San Diego Bay • Original county; organized 1850 (prior to statehood) • The Cabrillo National Monument, located at Point

Loma, honors the Portuguese explorer who sailed into San Diego Bay in 1542. Called the "Birthplace of California," the area that was to become San Diego County saw the construction of CA's first military fort and mission here in 1769; San Diego de Alcalá was the first of CA's twenty-one Franciscan missions. In 1846 California forces under General Andrés Pico fought U.S. Army troops under Brig. General Stephen W. Kearny in the Battle of San Pasqual here. In 1915, San Diego hosted the Panama-California Exposition. During World War II, San Diego's airplane plants attracted thousands of workers from throughout the U.S. • Tennis player Maureen Connolly; actor Gregory Peck; baseball player Ted Williams. Detective fiction writer Raymond Chandler, composer Paul Creston, operatic soprano Amelita Galli-Curci; writer and illustrator of children's books Theodor (Dr. Seuss) Geisel, architect Irving Gill, cartoonist Harold Gray, physicist Maria Goeppert Mayer, British geophysicist Stanley Runcorn, and composer and instrument builder Harry Partch died here. • Dairying, eggs, cattle, carnations, roses, avocados (the county is one of the top producers in the world), cucumbers, tomatoes, oranges, lemons, strawberries, grain; manufacture of aircraft and aerospace products, missiles, electronic and oceanographic equipment, precision dental instruments, athletic equipment, clothing, ink, processed foods, educational toys, kitchen cabinets, scientific instruments; shipbuilding; ocean fisheries; tourism (sport fishing, coast and mountain resorts, hot springs); education (U. of CA, San Diego; U.S. International U.; San Diego State U.; Point Loma Nazarene U.; Scripps Institution of Oceanography). San Diego is located in a naturally deep harbor and has become one of the chief naval centers in the U.S. with roughly one quarter of its workers employed by the U.S. government or working in military-related industries. San Diego Naval Base provides headquarters for several U.S. Pacific Fleet commands. • Five Fortune 1000 companies have their corporate headquarters in the county. The San Diego Zoo has over 3,400 animals, one of the largest collections in the world. Gray whales migrate along the county's coast on their way to Baja each winter. The Reuben H. Fleet Space Theater in San Diego is one of the largest planetariums in the world. Chula Vista is home to the ARCO Olympic Training Center, the nation's first year-round, warm weather Olympic training facility. San Diego is home to the Padres and Chargers (Qualcomm Stadium).

SAN FRANCISCO *San Francisco* • 776,733 • 47 (the smallest county in CA and one of the fifty smallest counties in the U.S.) • Western CA, at the northern end of the San Francisco-Santa Cruz Peninsula, bounded on the west by the Pacific Ocean, on the north by Golden Gate Strait, and on the east by San Francisco Bay. The county includes Alcatraz (the federal prison which operated here from 1934 to 1963 held some of the most dangerous criminals in the U.S.), Treasure, and Yerba Buena islands in San Francisco Bay, and the Farallon Islands (national wildlife refuge here) to the west in the Pacific. The county is coterminous with the city of San Francisco, but the two are politically separate. It includes part of Golden Gate National Recreation Area, Fort Point National Site, and Lake Merced reservoir (in the southwest.) Golden Gate Park, covering 1,017 acres, is one of the nation's largest city parks. The main span of the Golden Gate Bridge, which links the county to Marin County, places the bridge among the world's longest (4,200 feet). • Named for the city of San Francisco • 1850 (original county) • The area was settled in 1776 by Spanish soldiers and priests as presidio and mission named in honor of Saint Francis of Assisi. A port developed in the northeastern corner of the peninsula alongside the town of Yerba Buena, which, when captured by Commander John B. Montgomery in the Mexican War, was renamed San Francisco. During the Gold Rush of 1849, San Francisco, a supply center for the miners, found its harbors clogged with hundreds of ships. Loans from San Francisco banks played a key role in the early development of the mining industry in the Western U.S. In 1873, the essential cable car was invented here by Andrew S. Hallidie. The severe April 18, 1906 earthquake and the fires it propagated left 3,000 dead and the area in ruins. During World War II, the county was one of the world's largest shipbuilding centers. It was here that fifty nations came together in 1945 to form the United Nations. Another strong earthquake struck the city on October 17, 1989. • Born and/or resided here: writers Mark Twain, Ambrose Bierce, Bret Harte, Frank Norris, Jack London, the "Beat" poets, Robert Frost; baseball player Joe DiMaggio; photographer Ansel Adams; dancer Isadora Duncan; actor Clint Eastwood; U.S. Supreme Court justice Stephen Breyer; boxing champion James J. Corbett.; U.S. defense secretary Robert McNamara; television executive Barry Diller; physicist Luis W. Alvarez; political philosopher Lincoln Steffens. Died here: photographer Dorothea Lange, business executive Stephen D. Bechtel, propagandist George Creel, anthropologist William R. Bascom, President Warren G. Harding. • Fish, nursery products; banking and finance (The Bank of America, headquartered here, was one of the largest commercial banks in the world. San Francisco has been nicknamed the "Wall Street of the West."); education (U. of San Francisco; San Francisco State U. and others); tourism; diversified manufactures, including apparel, food products, electronic equipment, metal products; publishing and printing; high tech industry. • The corporate headquarters of fourteen Fortune 1000 companies are in the county. It has one of the largest Asian-American populations in the mainland U.S. Built on and around more than forty hills, some rising as much as 376 feet, San Francisco has some of the steepest streets in the world. San Francisco's ballet company, founded in 1933, is one of the nation's oldest. San Francisco is home to the Giants (Pacific Bell Stadium) and 49'ers (3Com Park).

SAN JOAQUIN *Stockton* • 563,598 • 1,399 • Central CA, bounded on the north by Dry Creek and the San Joaquin River and on the south in part by the Stanislaus River; drained by the San Joaquin, Mokelumne, Columnes, and Calaveras

rivers. The San Joaquin Valley here touches Coast Ranges in the southwest and the foothills of the Sierra Nevada in the east, with partly reclaimed marshy delta of the San Joaquin River in the west. The Mokelumne Aqueduct passes east-west through the center of the county, the Delta Mendota Canal crosses north-south. Caswell Memorial State Park is in the south. • Named for the San Joaquin River • Original county; organized 1850 (prior to statehood) • Stockton was an important supply station during the 1849 gold rush. • Cattle, dairying, apples, pumpkins, cherries, almonds, walnuts, grapes, cauliflower, onions, cucumbers, tomatoes, asparagus, celery, nursery products, wheat, barley, oats, corn, sugar beets, beans; wineries, canning, beet-sugar refineries; manufacture of fabricated metal products, iron castings, rubber products, cake mixes and other food products, laminated glass, wood products, recycled paper products, asbestos, cement pipe; shipbuilding; sand and gravel, clay, stone, limestone, natural gas; education (U. of the Pacific; Humphreys College). • Stockton is CA's major inland port.

SAN LUIS OBISPO *San Luis Obispo* • 246,681 • 3,304 • Southwestern CA, bounded on the west by the Pacific Ocean and on the south by the Cayama River (forming Twitchell Reservoir) and Santa Maria River; drained by the Salinas River. The Santa Lucia Range runs along the coast. Two of CA's twenty-one Franciscan missions, San Miguel Arcangel and Mision San Luis Obispo de Tolosa, are in the county. Carrizo Plain National Monument is on the Carrizo Plain in the southeast. (Dry Soda Lake is here.) Los Padres National Forest covers mountains in the La Panza Range. Also in the county are Morro Bay, San Simeon, and Montaña de Oro state parks, and several state beaches. Lake Nacimiento reservoir and part of Camp Roberts Military Reservation are in the north. The Hearst-San Simeon State Historical Monument features William Randolph Hearst's Spanish castle-styled home and retreat La Casa Grande. • Named for Mision San Luis Obispo de Tolosa • Film director Don Siegel died here. • Original county; organized 1850 (prior to statehood) • Peas, celery, beans, cauliflower, peppers, avocados, strawberries, flowers, nursery products, grapes, wheat, barley, oats, cattle, wineries; oil and natural gas, clay, sand and gravel, chromite, mercury mining; oil refining; resort tourism, mineral springs; manufacture of metal furniture, electronic products; education (CA Poly State U. San Luis Obispo).

SAN MATEO *Redwood City* • 707,161 • 449 • Western CA, on the San Francisco-San Mateo peninsula, bounded on the west by the Pacific Ocean, on the east by San Francisco Bay, and on the southeast by San Francisquito Creek. The San Mateo and Dumbarton bridges connect the county to Alameda County across the bay. The county is residential and industrial in the north (south of San Francisco). The Santa Cruz Mountains divide the suburbs, which line the bay, from the sparsely populated Pacific coast, dotted by state beaches. The San Francisco International Airport is found here. Part of Golden Gate National Recreation Area is in the north. Upper and Lower Crystal Springs reservoirs, and San Andreas Reservoir are located along the San Andreas Fault. San Mateo County has several state and county parks, including part of Big Basin Redwoods State Park on the southern border. • Named for San Mateo Creek, originally called Arroyo de San Matheo • 1856 from San Francisco • San Mateo was established by men who turned their gold rush fortunes into large estates. The first airplane flight on the Pacific coast took off from Tanforan Race Track in San Bruno in 1910. A year later Eugene Ely took off from Tanforan and made the first plane landing on a naval vessel. Belmont was center for sanitariums in the early part of the 1900s. • Painter Sam Francis. Dancer and choreographer Lew Christensen, billiards player Welker Cochran, banker A.P. Giannini, and historian Allan Nevins died here. • Timber, Christmas trees; ornamentals, flowers (especially chrysanthemums) artichokes, beans, Brussels sprouts, oats, barley; manufacture of cement (from oyster shells), lithographic products, wire products, electronics, computer software, rubber goods, chemicals, paper products, furniture, air conditioning units, gunsights, electrical equipment, paints and enamels, aluminum alloy forgings, building materials, textiles, aircraft parts; salt evaporating; magnesium extraction from sea water; quarrying of stone, sand, gravel, salt; meatpacking; publishing; research (the Stanford Research Institute is located in Menlo Park), education (Menlo College; College of Notre Dame and others).

SANTA BARBARA *Santa Barbara* • 399,347 • 2,737 • Southwestern CA, bounded on the north by the Santa Maria and Cuyama rivers (the latter forming Twitchell Reservoir) and on the west by the Pacific Ocean; drained by the intermittent Sisquoc and Santa Ynez rivers. The county includes Channel Islands National Park on the Channel Islands. Point Conception and Point Arguello are west and south of Vanderburg Air Force Base. The county rises from coastal plain to the Santa Madre and San Rafael Mountains in the east. Part of Los Padres National Forest (its headquarters in the city of Santa Barbara) is in the east. La Purisma (one of the most completely restored CA missions), Santa Barbara, and Santa Ines missions are here. There are also state beaches, state parks and state historical parks in the county. • Named for the Santa Barbara Channel and Mission Santa Barbara, Virgen y Martir • Original county; organized 1850 (prior to statehood) • Graphic artist and painter Herbert Bayer, actors Dame Judith Anderson, Ronald Coleman, Marie Dressler, and Georgiana Barrymore, soprano Lotte Lehmann, manufacturer C.W. Post, and essayist/poet Kenneth Rexroth all died here. • Cauliflower, broccoli, celery, squash, carrots, peas, cabbages, spinach, tomatoes, lettuce, avocados, strawberries, lemons, grapes, flowers and flower seeds (Lompoc has an annual festival celebrating the importance of the industry to the area), cattle, wheat, barley, oats, beans; manufacture of sound recordings, tire molds, cable, marine hardware, aerospace components; food processing and sugar refining; tourism; education (Westmont College; U. of CA, Santa Barbara); Santa Barbara is a leading county

in CA in diatomite mining; also produced here are asphalt, clay, and petroleum. • The Santa Barbara Mission (established in 1786) is the western headquarters of the Franciscan Order, and has been in continuous use since its founding. After the 1925 earthquake, many buildings in Santa Barbara were restored to Spanish colonial style; a law was subsequently passed preserving the city's special adobe character.

SANTA CLARA *San Jose* • 1,682,585 (the fifth most populated county in CA and the fourteenth most populated county in the U.S.) • 1,291 • Western CA, bounded in the northwest by San Francisquito Creek; drained by Coyote, Los Gatos, and Guadalupe creeks. The county includes the northern part of the Santa Clara Valley, extending southeast from San Francisco Bay between the Diablo Range and the Santa Cruz Mountains. Henry W. Coe State Park is in the county. Moffett Federal Air Field is north of Sunnyvale. • Named for Mision de Santa Clara de Asis • Original county; organized 1850 (prior to statehood) • San Jose was founded in 1777 as a Spanish military-supply base. It supplied wheat, vegetables, and cattle to the military garrisons at Monterey and San Francisco during the Spanish colonial and Mexican periods. After occupation of CA by the U.S. in 1846, San Jose briefly served as the state's first capital. It was here that the first state legislative assembly convened in December, 1849. In 1850, San Jose became the first chartered city in CA. It was a major trade depot for the gold fields during the California Gold Rush. In the early 1900s, Mountain View was the center of a large religious book publishing industry. Like most of the cities in the county, San Jose was an early dried fruit processing center (as well as manufacturer of orchard supplies and agricultural equipment). It experienced rapid growth during and after World War II through the shift to the manufacturing of durable goods. With the rise of computer-manufacturing and software production in the area ("Silicon Valley"), its growth exploded, more than tripling from 1960 to 1980, and it continued to grow until the tech bust of the late 1990s and early 2000s. • Banker A.P. Giannini; figure skater Peggy Fleming. Botanist Douglas H. Campbell, zoologist Charles Manning Child, physician and pathologist George Frederick Dick, physicist William W. Hansen, ichthyologist David S. Jordan, railroad builder Leland Stanford, engineer and teacher William B. Shockley, and experimental poet Kenneth Patchen died here. • Grapes, peppers, lettuce, tomatoes, oriental vegetables, onions, garlic (Gilroy is the "garlic capital of the world"), beans, nursery products, mushrooms, flowers, strawberries, cherries, dried fruits (especially prunes) dairying, cattle, eggs, poultry, wheat, barley, oats, corn; manufacture of magnesium products, machinery, canning and packing equipment, food products (also packing, canning), electrical equipment, chemicals, paper, fiber glass, electronics, computer circuits, high tech components, cement, guided missiles; printing and publishing; clay, sand and gravel, quicksilver; research (high tech and electronics, and aeronautics; the Ames Research Center of NASA is near Mountain View); education (San Jose State U.;

Stanford U.; Santa Clara U., the oldest institution of higher learning in the state) • The county is corporate headquarters for eighteen Fortune 1000 companies. Sunnyvale was settled in 1849 by the family of Martin Murphy, Jr. who built his house in pieces in Boston, transported it by ship around Cape Horn and assembled it here. Founded in 1892, the Leland Stanford Museum at Stanford University is one of the oldest museums west of the Mississippi River. The Hoover Institution of War, Revolution, and Peace is recognized for its documents on world conflict. The Stanford Linear Accelerator Center includes a linear electron accelerator two miles long. Palo Alto was named for a 1,200-year-old giant redwood that stands in the city. San Jose is home to the San Jose Sharks professional hockey team (Compaq Center).

SANTA CRUZ (one of two counties so named, the other in AZ) *Santa Cruz* • 255,602 • 445 • Western CA, at the base of the San Francisco-Mateo peninsula, in the Santa Cruz Mountains, bounded on the southwest by the Pacific Ocean and on the south by Monterey Bay and the Pajaro River; drained by the San Lorenzo River and Soquel Creek. There are several state beaches along the coast. Forest of Nisene Marks State Park is in the north. The Santa Cruz Mountains are home to giant redwood forests, especially in Henry Cowell Redwoods and Big Basin Redwoods state parks. • Named for Mision la Exaltacion de la Santa Cruz • Original county; organized 1850 (prior to statehood) • The redwood lumber business was a prosperous mainstay here as early as 1840. Whaling ships often stopped in Santa Cruz for fresh food. The center of Santa Cruz's downtown business area was destroyed by the earthquake that rocked the San Francisco Bay area on October 17, 1989. • Mathematician and educator Eric Temple Bell • Berries, artichokes, cauliflower, lettuce, flowers, apples, mushrooms, nursery products, celery, Brussels sprouts; farm products packaging and processing (the county is one of the leading frozen food processors in the U.S.); manufacture of furniture, electronics equipment, lumber; fisheries; cement, clay, sand, granite, gravel, limestone quarrying; resort tourism; education (U. of CA, Santa Cruz) • The Santa Cruz Beach Boardwalk is the last remaining seaside amusement park in the state.

SHASTA *Redding* • 163,256 • 3,785 • Northern CA, bounded on the south in part by the Cottonwood River and its Middle Fork, and Battle Creek; drained by the Sacramento, Pit, and McCloud rivers. The county is largely mountainous, with the Cascade Range rising in the east. The part of Lassen Volcanic National Park that lies within the county comprises the area that was affected by intermittent eruptions from 1914 to 1921, and includes Lassen Peak, a still active volcano. Part of Shasta National Forest (its headquarters in Redding) is in the north; part of Lassen National Forest is in the southeast; and part of Trinity National Forest is in the southwest corner. Castle Crags State Park is on the northern border. Ahjumawi Lava Springs and McArthur-Burney Falls Memorial state parks are also in the county. Parts of Whiskeytown-Shasta-Trinity National

Recreation Area are also here. Shasta Lake is a popular recreation destination. • Named for Mount Shasta, itself named in 1827 by Peter Skene Ogden probably for a local Indian tribe • Original county; organized 1850 (prior to statehood) • Timber; cattle, honey and other apiary products, walnuts, olives, strawberries, wheat, barley, oats; sand and gravel; processing of farm products; tourism (hunting, fishing, camping); education (Simpson College).

SIERRA (one of two counties so named, the other in NM) *Downieville* • 3,555 • 953 • Northeastern CA, in the Sierra Nevada, bounded on the east by the NV state line; drained by the Yuba River and its tributaries. The county is crossed by Yuba Pass and Pacific Crest National Scenic Trail through the center. Much of the county is occupied by parts of Tahoe National Forest. Plumas National Forest overlaps its northern boundary. Gold Lake and other (fishing) lakes are in the north. • Named for the Sierra Nevada Mountains • 1852 from Yuba • Gold, lead, silver, sand and gravel; pine, fir, cedar; cattle, sheep, hay, alfalfa, field crops; tourism.

SISKIYOU *Yreka* • 44,301 • 6,287 (the fifth largest county in CA and the thirty-fifth largest county in the U.S.) • Northern CA, bounded on the north by the OR state line; drained by the Klamath River and its tributaries. The Klamath Mountains are in the west. In the east-center is part of the Cascade Range with peaks rising to 14,000 feet; its glacier-fed springs are sources of the Shasta, Sacramento, and McCloud rivers. Lava Beds National Monument is in the northeast. The county also contains part of Shasta National Forest, part of Klamath National Forest, part of Modoc National Forest, part of Castle Crags State Park, and Tule Lake and Lower Klamath Lake national wildlife refuges. The Pacific Crest National Scenic Trail threads through the mountains in the west. • Named for the Siskiyou Mountains • 1852 from Klamath and Shasta; in 1874 the county annexed part of Klamath • Novelist and screenwriter Anita Loos • Wheat, barley, oats, potatoes, onions, sugar beets, cattle, lambs; sand and gravel.

SOLANO *Fairfield* • 394,542 • 829 • Central and western CA, bounded on the far southwest by San Pablo Bay, on the south by Carquinez Strait, and Suisun and Grizzly bays, on the southeast by the Sacramento River, and on the north by Putah Creek. The county is largely level, with marshland in the south, north of Grizzly Bay. Delta lands near the Sacramento River are protected by levees. Travis Air Force Base and part of Concord Naval Weapons Detachment are here. A strip of the San Pablo Bay National Wildlife Refuge is in the county. Benicia State Recreation Area is in the south. • Named for Soscol and Suisun Indian chief, baptised Chief Francisco Solano • Original county; organized 1850 (prior to statehood) • The county was home to two state capitals: Vallejo served in this capacity in 1852 and 1853; Benicia was capital in 1853 and 1854 (historic park). • Extensive fruit orchards, including apricots and pears; also safflower, beans, sugar beets, tomatoes, sunflowers, nursery products, almonds, prunes, grapes, cattle, lambs, wheat, barley, oats, corn; clay, natural gas; shipbuilding (the Mare Island Naval Shipyard in Vallejo is the oldest and largest naval shipyard on the West Coast.); manufacture of explosives, textiles; flour milling, meat packing; waterfowl hunting; education (CA Military Academy).

SONOMA *Santa Rosa* • 458,614 • 1,576 • Western CA, bounded on the west by the Pacific Ocean, on the south in part by San Pablo Bay and the Petaluma River; drained by the Russian River and coastal streams. The county lies in Coast Ranges, with Mount St. Helena on the eastern border. Sonoma includes Kruse Rhododendron and Armstrong Redwoods state reserves (the latter, a stand of old growth redwoods, including Colonel Armstrong and Parson Jones, two trees that tower over 310 feet); Salt Point, Sugarloaf Ridge, and Annadel state parks; Fort Ross, Sonoma, and Jack London state historic parks; Sonoma Coast State Beach; and Austin Creek State Recreation Area. • Named for the town of Sonoma and Sonoma Mission • Original county; organized 1850 (prior to statehood) • Established in 1823, Mission San Francisco Solano was the last and most northerly of the twenty-one Franciscan California missions. A small band of American settlers invaded the area and captured General Mariano Vallejo and his Mexican garrison on June 14, 1846. The settlers raised an improvised Bear Flag of California and declared a republic, which lasted until July 9. Hungarian count Agoston Haraszthy laid the basis for the state's wine industry by planting thousands of cuttings from European grape vines here in the 1850s. • Cartoonist Robert Ripley; tennis player Hazel Wightman; film critic Pauline Kael. World War II commanding general Henry H. Arnold died here. Horticulturist Luther Burbank developed more than 800 new varieties of plants in Santa Rosa. • Large wine industry (some of the state's finest wines are produced here); sheep, turkeys, chickens, dairying, nursery products, vegetables, apples, grapes, wheat, oats, corn; urchins, fish; stone quarries; some timber; resort tourism (hot springs, geyser fields, petrified forest attracting visitors); processing industries, fish packing; manufacture of machinery, clothing, shoes, optical coating • Jack London wrote of the Sonoma Valley in his *The Valley of the Moon.*

STANISLAUS *Modesto* • 446,997 • 1,494 • Central CA, in the San Joaquin Valley, bounded on the west by Coast Ranges, on the north in part by the Stanislaus River; watered by the San Joaquin, Tuolumne, and Stanislaus rivers. The county is crossed east-to-west by the Modesto Main Canal and Hetch Hetchy Aqueduct, north-to-south by the Delta Mendota Canal, among others. Irrigation water in the county is supplied by Modesto, Turlock, and Don Pedro reservoirs. The county is experiencing rapid urbanization around Modesto and Turlock. Turlock Lake and George J. Hatfield state recreation areas are in the county. • Named for the Stanislaus River, itself an Anglicization of Estanislao, the Spanish name given to a local Indian leader • 1854 from Tuolumne • Swimmer Mark Spitz; film producer and director George Lucas • Catfish, cattle, chickens, turkey, eggs, dairying, almonds, walnuts,

peaches, grapes, berries, melons, tomatoes, beans, broccoli, cauliflower, onions, peas, peppers, spinach, pumpkins, wheat, barley, oats, alfalfa, rice; wineries; manufacture of chemicals, tin cans, fabricated metals, wood and paper products; food processing, including fruit and vegetable canning and dehydrating; gypsum and clay; education (CA State U., Stanislaus).

SUTTER *Yuba City* • 78,930 • 603 • North-central CA, in the Sacramento Valley, bounded on the west by the Sacramento and Butte rivers, on the east in part by the Feather and Bear rivers; drained by the Feather River. Sutter Buttes (with its natural gas wells) are in the north. Sutter National Wildlife Refuge is in the center of the county. • Named for John A. Sutter (1803-1880) on whose property gold was discovered in 1848, setting off the California Gold Rush • Original county; organized 1850 (prior to statehood) • Nursery products, alfalfa, safflower, beans, wheat, barley, oats, corn, rice, sugar beets, tomatoes, prunes, peaches, melons; processing of farm products; steel fabrication; waterfowl hunting, fishing.

TEHAMA *Red Bluff* • 56,039 • 2,951 • Northern CA, across the northern part of the Central Valley, bounded on the north in part by the Battle River; drained by the Sacramento River and the South Fork of the Cottonwood River. Extensions of the Klamath Mountains and the Coast Ranges are in the west; the Sierra Nevada are in the east. A small part of Lassen Volcanic National Park is in the extreme northeast, as are parts of Lassen, Mendocino, and Trinity national forests. Black Butte Lake reservoir is on the southern boundary. The county also contains Woodson Bridge State Recreation Area and William B. Ide State Historical Park. • Named for the town of the same name • 1856 from Butte, Colusa, and Shasta • Choral and orchestral conductor Robert Shaw • Red Bluff is home to the Elberta peach. Also, cattle, honey, alfalfa, wheat, barley, oats, rice, corn, beans, almonds, walnuts, olives; lumbering of pine, fir, and cedar; wood industries; sand and gravel; processing of olives and olive oil, fruit dehydrating • Red Bluff's annual Roundup is a well known rodeo.

TRINITY (one of two counties so named, the other in TX) *Weaverville* • 13,022 • 3,179 • Northern CA; drained by the Trinity (designated a National Wild, Scenic, and Recreational River), Eel, and Mad rivers. The county lies mostly within the Klamath Mountains, with Coast Ranges in the southwest. Pacific Crest Scenic Trail follows its northeast boundary. The Trinity Unit of Whiskeytown-Shasta-Trinity National Recreation Area, Clair Eagle Lake reservoir (Trinity River), part of Six Rivers National Forest, part of Mendocino National Forest, parts of Trinity National Forest, part of Shasta National Forest, and Weaverville Joss House State Historical Park are all in the county. • Named for the Trinity River • Original county; organized 1850 (prior to statehood) • Gold mining, sand and gravel; hay, nursery products; timber; tourism.

TULARE *Visalia* • 368,021 • 4,824 • Central CA, extending east from the San Joaquin Valley to the crest of the Sierra

Nevada; drained by the Kaweah, St. Johns, Tule and Kern rivers. Mt. Whitney, at 14,495 feet, the highest point in the contiguous U.S., is on its boundary with Inyo County. Pacific Crest Scenic Trail runs north-south near the eastern boundary. Sequoia National Park is in the county, as are part of Kings Canyon National Park, Inyo and Sequoia national forests, Tule River Indian Reservation, Pixley National Wildlife Refuge, and Col. Allensworth State Historical Park. • Named for the San Joaquin Valley, which was originally a reedy marshland, "tullin" meaning cattails or rushes in Aztec. • 1852 from Mariposa • The city of Tulare was the division headquarters of the Southern Pacific Railroad from 1872 to 1891. It was destroyed by fire and rebuilt three times, in 1875, 1883, and 1886. Visalia, founded in 1852, was a center of pro-Confederate sympathy during the Civil War. It later opposed the Southern Pacific Railroad. • Sugar beets, beans, wheat, oats, corn, citrus fruit, nuts, olives, berries, grapes, apples, nursery products, cotton, turkeys, cattle, hogs; fir; sand and gravel; tungsten, clay deposits, marble and granite quarries; farm-produce packing, processing and shipping; lumber milling. • The General Sherman Tree in Sequoia National Park is the world's largest living thing. Estimated to be about 2,500 years old, it rises to a height of 275 feet; its trunk measures 37 feet wide.

TUOLUMNE *Sonora* • 54,501 • 2,235 • Central and eastern CA, in the Sierra Nevada, bounded on the northwest by the Stanislaus River and its North Fork; drained by the Middle and South forks of the Stanislaus River and by the Tuolumne River. The county is crossed by Sonora Pass. The northern half of Yosemite National Park is in the east. A large part of Stanislaus National Forest is in the center of the county. Also in the county are part of Calaveras Big Trees State Park; Columbia and Railtown 1897 historic parks; and Cherry Lake, Don Pedro, and Hetch Hetchy reservoirs. Hetch Hetchy Aqueduct, running across the south, delivers water to the San Francisco Bay Area. • Named for either the Tuolumne River or the Tuolumne Indians • Original county; organized 1850 (prior to statehood) • The western portion of the county was a part of the 1849 California Gold Rush region and included gold camps Sonora, Jamestown and Columbia. • Hay, apples, cattle, fruit, hay, poultry; pine, fir, cedar; gold, marble, limestone, sand and gravel; tourism.

VENTURA *Ventura* • 753,197 • 1,845 • Southern CA, bounded on the south by the Pacific Ocean; drained by the Ventura and Santa Clara rivers. The county includes Santa Barbara Island in the Channel Islands (part of Channel Islands National Park here), Mount Pinos and Pine Mountain, part of Los Padres National Forest, several state beaches, Point Mugu State Park, and part of Santa Monica Mountains National Recreation Area. Hopper Mountain National Wildlife Refuge is in the east. The Naval Construction Battalion Center and Seabee Museum are in Port Hueneme. Point Mugu Naval Air Station is in the southeast. • Named for the city and Mission Spanish San Buenaventura • 1872 from Santa Barbara

• San Buenaventura was the ninth and last mission founded by Juníperio Serra (1782). • Cartoonist Sergio Aragonés; philosopher J. Krishnamurti; crime novelist Erle Stanley Gardner (who set many of his Perry Mason stories in Ventura). Wild animal trainer Clyde Beatty died here. • Avocados, broccoli, beans, cabbage, celery, lettuce, spinach, strawberries, citrus fruits, walnuts, barley, flowers, nursery products, bee products, dairying; oil and natural-gas, refineries, stone quarrying; agricultural processing, packing and shipping; manufacture of electronics, precision instruments, plastics, paper containers, drinking cups; aerospace industries; education (CA Lutheran U.; Moorpark College); tourism • The Ronald Reagan Presidential Library is in Simi Valley. The California Oil Museum in Santa Paula depicts the history of the state's industry. Ojai, a community of artists and craftsmen, has had a history of attracting followers of New Age philosophies and the occult.

YOLO *Woodland* • 168,660 • 1,013 • Central CA, in the Sacramento Valley, bounded on the east by the Sacramento River and on the south in part by Putah Creek; drained by Cache and Putah creeks. The Sacramento metropolitan area extends into the eastern part of the county. Berryessa Peak is on the western boundary. The Sacramento Deep Water Canal runs north-south, joining the Sacramento River at West Sacramento. Part of Cache Creek Cooperative Management Area is in the extreme northwest. • Named for the Yolo Indians. The name that was officially adopted when the county was organized was Yola, but over time it evolved to Yolo. • Original county; organized 1850 (prior to statehood) • Geneticist and evolutionist Theodosius Dobzhansky died here. • Sugar beets, tomatoes, asparagus, barley, wheat, rice, fruits, olives, beans, nuts, sheep, cattle, dairying; sand and gravel, mercury, natural gas; food processing, including olive oil and beet sugar production, fruit canning and dehydrating; manufacture of steel products, plastics, mobile homes, farm machinery; education (U. of CA, Davis) • The California Regional Primate Research Center (for research on non-human primates) was founded in Davis in 1962. Woodland has a number of well-preserved Victorian buildings. The Woodland Opera House is maintained within a state historic park.

YUBA *Marysville* • 60,219 • 631 • North-central CA, extending northeast from the Feather River (forming the county's western boundary) through the Sacramento Valley to the lower western slopes of the Sierra Nevada; drained by the Yuba River (forming part of the eastern boundary) and Bear River (forming the southern boundary). The county includes parts of Plumas and Tahoe national forests, and Beale Air Force Base. • Named for the Yuba River • Original county; organized 1850 (prior to statehood) • Maryville grew as a miner's supply depot and collection point during the 1849 California gold rush. • Peaches, grapes, prunes, kiwi fruit, olives, nuts, rice, wheat, oats, corn, dairying, cattle; pine, fir, cedar; platinum, silver, sand and gravel; gold dredging; hunting and fishing.

COLORADO

Nothing Without Providence

Sixty-three of Colorado's sixty-four counties are governed by either a three or five person commission. The city and county of Denver operate as a single government.

ADAMS (one of twelve counties so named) *Brighton* • 363,857 (the fifth most populated county in CO) (note: this figure has not been adjusted to compensate for the removal of the fraction that includes the population of Broomfield, which became its own county in December, 2001) • 1,177 • North-central CO; drained by Badger, Bijou and Boxelder creeks. The Denver metropolitan area extends into the county in the west. Barr Lake State Park and Rocky Mountain Arsenal National Wildlife Area are found in the county. • Named for Alva Adams (1850-1922), statesman and governor • 1902 from Arapahoe County; annexed part of Denver County in 1909 • Sugar beets (growing, processing, shipping), cattle, horses, wheat, hay, sunflowers, oats, barley, corn, dry beans; manufacture of telephone switching equipment, electromechanical products • Brighton holds the largest county fair in CO. At the turn of the 20th century, the Presbyterian Church built Westminster College using the services of renowned architect Stanford White. (Only the law school still operates, and is now located in Denver.) A fundamentalist church group, the Pillar of Fire, bought the property in 1920 and has since maintained Belleview College there.

ALAMOSA *Alamosa* • 14,966 • 723 • Southern CO, bounded on the east by the crest of the Sangre de Cristo Mountains; watered by the Rio Grande. San Luis Valley extends north-south between the Sangre de Cristo and San Juan Mountains. Part of San Isabel National Forest is here and includes Zapata Blanca Sand Castle B.L.M. Recreation Area. The county also includes part of Great Sand Dunes National Park, which contains some of the largest and highest dunes in the U.S. San Luis Lakes State Park, Alamosa National Wildlife Reserve, and part of Monte Vista National Wildlife Reserve are also located in the county. • Named for Alamosa Creek and the town of Alamosa, which means "shaded with cottonwood trees" • 1913 from Costilla • Cattle, sheep, wheat, hay, oats, barley, vegetables, potatoes (especially, Red McClures); education (Adams State College).

ARAPAHOE *Littleton* • 487,967 (the fourth most populous county in CO) • 803 • North-central CO; drained by the South Platte River. The western part of the county is highly urbanized, the east rural and sparsely populated. Cherry Creek Lake Reservoir and State Park are here, as is the Plains Conservation Center. Buckley Air National Guard Base is at Aurora. Two exclaves of the county (one including the city of Glendale) are totally encompassed by the county and city of Denver. • Named for the Arapaho Indians • Original county; organized 1861 (prior to statehood) • Aurora, founded in 1891, flourished during the silver boom as a mining center. In 1893, a silver panic closed the mines. During World War I, Aurora was chosen as the site for an Army Recuperation Camp that later became Fitzsimmons Army Medical Center. Littleton was the scene of a shooting spree on April 20, 1999 at Columbine High School that took the lives over fourteen students (including the two assailants) and one teacher. • Dairy products, wheat, sunflowers, nursery co-ops, cattle; recreational enterprises; light manufacturing, including fishing tackle and sporting goods, electronic equipment, luggage, precision metal products; research and development in computer, chemical, and aerospace industries.

ARCHULETA *Pagosa Springs* • 9,898 • 1,350 • Southwestern CO, bounded on the south by the NM state line and on the east by the San Juan Mountains (the Continental Divide closely following the boundary); drained by the Piedra and Navajo rivers. A large part of the county is in the San Juan National Forest, especially in the north; a small part of Rio Grande National Forest is in the southeastern corner. Chimney Rock Archeological Area (Anasazi Ruins), Navajo State Park, and part of Navajo Reservoir are also here. Part of Southern Ute Indian Reservation is in the southwest. • Named for either Antonio Archuleta (1855–?), member of the first CO state legislature, or for his father Jose M. Archuleta, head of a prominent local family • 1885 from Conejos • Sheep, cattle; resorts (mineral hot springs); manufacture of aircraft equipment; publishing.

BACA *Springfield* • 4,517 • 2,556 • Extreme southeastern CO, bounded on the south by the OK and NM state lines, and on the east by the KS state line; drained by tributaries of the Cimarron River, the North Fork of the Cimarron River, Bear Creek, Two Buttes Creek and Sand Arroyo. Two Buttes Reservoir (State Fishing Area) is located here, as is a part of Comanche National Grassland. Picture Canyon in the Grasslands contains prehistoric petroglyphs. • Named for an early pioneer family from Trinidad, CO • 1889 from Las Animas County • Wagon tracks and other landmarks can be found along the Cimarron Route of the Santa Fe Trail, which crossed the county. • Grain, livestock.

BENT *Las Animas* • 5,998 • 1,514 • Southeastern CO; drained by the Purgatoire and Arkansas rivers which form John Martin Reservoir. Fort Lynn National Cemetery is also here. • Named for either Bent's Fort or for the Bent brothers who built it, including William Bent (1809-69), an early settler, fur trader, and Indian agent. • Organized 1870, from Greenwood County (prior to statehood), which was organized in 1874 and abolished in 1878 • Scout and Indian agent Kit Carson died here (museum) • Cattle, wheat, hay, sorghum, barley, corn, irrigated vegetables • The county's courthouse, built in 1888, is the oldest still active in the state.

BOULDER *Boulder* • 291,288 (note: this figure has not been adjusted to compensate for the removal of the fraction that includes the population of Broomfield, which became its own county in December, 2001) • 732 • North-central CO, bounded on the west by the Continental Divide; drained by Boulder and St. Vrain creeks. Part of Rocky Mountain National Park is in the northwest; Front Range is in the west. Part of Roosevelt National Forest, Eldorado Canyon State Park, and Eldorado Mountain ski area are located in the county. • Named for Boulder City and Boulder Creek, themselves named for the large rock formations in the area • Original county; organized 1861 (prior to statehood) • Biochemist Edward L. Tatum. Physicists Sydney Chapman, Edward U. Condon, George E. Uhlenbeck, and George Gamow died here. • Cattle, fruit, vegetables, wheat, hay, beans, barley, corn, sugar beets, poultry, dairying; mining of coal, gold; manufacture of business machines, oil and air filters, chemicals, electronic equipment, camp trailers; beet-sugar refining, food processing and canning; education (U. of CO); scientific and environmental research (located in the county are a key section of the National Bureau of Standards, the U.S. branch of the World Data Center for Solar-Terrestrial Physics, and the National Center for Atmospheric Research.) • Boulder gets part of its water from the Arapahoe Glacier, sitting high on the Continental Divide. The city owns 6,000 acres of mountain parklands.

BROOMFIELD *Broomfield* • 42,684 • 34 (the smallest county in CO; only four U.S. counties are smaller) North-central CO. The county and the city of Broomfield are coterminous. • Named for the city of Broomfield • 2001 (the newest county in the U.S.) from Adams, Boulder, Jefferson and Weld • The city of Broomfield experienced rapid population growth in the 1970s–1990s. • Manufacture of spring-energized seals, space-vehicle equipment, fabricated metal products, epitaxial wafers, flame-retardant clothing, motor vehicles, furniture, medical supplies and equipment; machinery, networking products, electronic equipment, consumer goods, acoustical products, riboflavin; printing.

CHAFFEE *Salida* • 16,242 • 1,013 • Central CO, bounded on the west by the Continental Divide; drained by the Arkansas River, its valley running north-south through the center of the county. Parts of San Isabel National Forest are here, as is part of the Sawatch Range. Monarch ski area and Arkansas Headwaters Recreation Area are also found in the county. • Named for Jerome B. Chaffee (1825-86), CO territorial legislator and U.S. senator • Organized as Lake, 1861 (prior to statehood); name changed, 1879 • Anthropologist Leslie A. White • Cattle, some wheat and vegetables • The county has more peaks

over 14,000 ft. in elevation (fifteen) than any other county in the U.S. Chaffee boasts the largest historic district in the state of CO.

CHEYENNE *Cheyenne Wells* • 2,231 • 1,781 • Eastern CO, bounded on the east by the KS state line; drained by Big Sandy Creek. The source of the Smoky Hill River is in the center of the county. • One of three counties named for the Cheyenne Indians • 1889 from Bent and Elbert • Wheat, sunflowers, sorghum, corn, cattle; oil production.

CLEAR CREEK *Georgetown* • 9,322 • 395 • North-central CO, bounded on the west by the Continental Divide; drained by Clear Creek. The county includes parts of Pike and Arapaho national forests. Part of Mount Evans Wilderness Area is in the southeast. • Named for the stream in the county • Original county; organized 1861 (prior to statehood). It was originally called Vasquez. • Georgetown was established in 1864 following the discovery of the rich Belmont Lode nearby. Silver mining infused the town with money; the Hotel de Paris, built in 1875 by the eccentric Frenchman Louis de Puy, was once one of the most elegant hotels west of the Mississippi River. • Gold, silver, lead, copper, zinc; tourism (a winter and summer recreational area, skiing, ghost towns) • The Mount Evans Byway to the summit of Mount Evans (14,264 ft.) is the highest road in the U.S.

CONEJOS *Conejos* • 8,400 • 1,287 • Southern CO, bounded on the east by the Rio Grande and on the south by the NM state line; drained by the Conejos River (forming Platoro Reservoir in the northwest) and La Jara Creek (forming La Jara Reservoir). The Continental Divide closely follows the northwestern boundary. San Luis Valley extends north to south. The county also includes part of the San Juan Mountains and the Rio Grande National Forest. Part of Rio Grande B.L.M. Recreation Area is on the eastern boundary. • Named for the Conejos River and the town of Conejos • Original county; organized as Guadalupe in 1861 (prior to statehood); its name changed the same year. • Boxer Jack Dempsey (museum) • Sheep, cattle, wheat, hay, oats, barley, potatoes, vegetables • Conejos (founded 1854) is one of the oldest towns in CO and the terminus of the Cumbres and Toltec Scenic Railway.

COSTILLA *San Luis* • 3,663 • 1,227 • Southern CO, bounded on the south by the NM state line and on the west by the Rio Grande; drained by Trinchera Creek (which forms Mountain Home and Smith reservoirs in the north). Part of San Luis Valley is in the west. Part of Culebra Range forms the eastern boundary. Part of the Rio Grande B.L.M. Recreation Area is also here. • Named for the Costilla River and the town of Costilla. Originally in CO, the town is now in Taos County, NM, the boundaries between CO and NM having been changed by the U.S. Supreme Court in 1925. • Original county; organized 1861 (prior to statehood) • Established by ME land grant settlers, San Luis is the oldest settlement in the state • Cattle, sheep, wheat, hay, oats, barley, potatoes, vegetables.

CROWLEY *Ordway* • 5,518 • 789 • Southeast-central CO, bounded partly on the south by the Arkansas River; drained by Horse and Pond creeks. Lake Meredith is in the south. • Named for John H. Crowley (1849–?), fruit grower and state senator from Otero County when Crowley was formed • 1911 from Otero • Cattle, wheat, sorghum, vegetables, melons • The many lakes and irrigated cropland of the county attract Canadian and snow geese during the fall, and bald eagles and sandhill cranes during winter months. The National Sugar Company of Baltimore, MD opened a sugar mill here in 1900, resulting in the formation of Sugar City.

CUSTER *Westcliffe* • 3,503 • 739 • South-central CO, bounded on the west by the crest of the Sangre de Cristo Mountains, with two peaks here rising over 14,000 feet; drained by Grape Creek (forming De Weese Reservoir). The Wet Mountains cross along the eastern boundary. Parts of San Isabel National Forest are also here. • One of six counties named for General George Armstrong Custer • 1877 from Fremont • Silver Cliff was a booming silver camp in 1881. • Sheep, cattle, dairying; silver and lead mining; tourism.

DELTA (one of three counties so named) *Delta* • 27,834 • 1,142 • Western CO; drained by the Gunnison River. Grand and Buck mesas extend along the northwest and northeast boundaries; the West Elk Mountains cross in the southeast. Parts of Grand Mesa and Gunnison national forests are here. The county includes Crawford and Sweitzer state parks and part of Gunnison Gorge National Conservation Area. • Named for the city, itself named for its location on the delta of the Uncompahgre River. • 1883 from Gunnison • Coal-mining; cattle, sheep, wheat, hay, beans, oats, corn, fruit, vegetables • The Ute Council Tree is located here; a historic cottonwood, it marked the site of peace-pipe diplomacy from 1857 to 1882 between white settlers and Chief Ouray and his wife Chipeta (said to have been the only Indian woman ever permitted to sit in council meetings). Fort Uncompahgre Living History Museum is in Delta.

DENVER *Denver* • 554,636 (the most populated county in CO) • 153 (one of the fifty smallest counties in the U.S.) • North-central CO. The city and county are coterminous. Denver is the fulcrum of a large metropolitan area, which envelopes the communities of six counties. The Denver International Airport is captured from Adams County by gerrymandering. • Named for General James W. Denver (1817-92), CA legislator, Commissioner of Indian Affairs, and governor of KS Territory • Organized 1901 from Adams. • Denver was founded in 1858 when prospectors discovered gold at nearby Cherry Creek and established the community as a supply point for their mining settlements. Denver served as capital of the territory of CO from 1867 to 1876. When the territory was admitted to the union in 1876 it became the state capital. • Actor Douglas Fairbanks; engineer Herbert T. Herr; dramatist Mary Chase, soldier Homer Lea; actor and director Antoinette Perry; orchestra conductor Paul Whiteman. Mountain man Jim Beckwourth, publisher Frederick G. Bonfils, "Buffalo Bill" Cody, and governor and founder of Northwestern University John Evans all died here. • Denver is the chief distribution center for the Rocky Mountain region and the national or regional headquarters of more federal agencies than any other U.S. city outside of Washington, D.C. Also, food processing; diversified manufacturing, including defense, high technology, and transportation equipment. The Denver Stockyards constitute one the nation's major livestock centers. • The headquarters of eight Fortune 1000 companies are located in the county. The Denver Art Museum owns one of the world's finest collections of Native American art. Established in 1891, the Elitch Summer Theatre is the nation's oldest theatre with a permanent group of performers. Denver also owns its own ski resort, Winter Park, located in the Rocky Mountains. The Denver mint makes millions of coins each year. Denver is home to the Nuggets and Avalanche (Pepsi Center), Rockies (Coors Field), and Broncos (Invesco Field at Mile High).

DOLORES *Dove Creek* • 1,844 • 1,067 • Southwestern CO, bounded on the west by the UT state line; drained by the Dolores River (its source in the eastern part of the county) and Disappointment Creek. The San Miguel Range is in the northeast; Taylor Mesa is located in the southeast. The county contains part of San Juan and part of Uncompahgre national forests. The Delores River B.L.M. Recreation is attached to the river. A small part of Canyons of the Ancients National Monument is also here. • Named for the Dolores ("sorrows") River, which was named by the Dominguez-Escalante expedition after the loss of one of its members here. • 1881 from Ouray • The county contains the ancient remains of dwellings and artifacts of the Anasazi Indians. The last Indian battle in CO took place in 1885 at the Beaver Creek Massacre site located in the west. • Zinc mining; cattle, wheat, hay, beans, sheep.

DOUGLAS *Castle Rock* • 175,766 (191% increase since 1990; the fastest growing county in CO) • 840 • Central CO, bounded on the west by the South Platte River (which forms Chatfield and Cheesman Lake reservoirs); drained by Plum and Cherry creeks. The western part of the county extends into the Front Range of the Rocky Mountains, the remainder is on the western edge of the Great Plains. The Denver metropolitan area is urbanizing the county in the northwest. The county contains Castlewood Canyon, and part of Chatfield and Roxborough state parks. Part of Pike National Forest is also here. • One of twelve counties named for Stephen Arnold Douglas • Original county; organized 1861 (prior to statehood) • Wheat, oats, fruit, vegetables, cattle, dairying; timber; manufacture of magnetic pulleys, asphalt.

EAGLE *Eagle* •41,659 • 1,688 • West-central CO; bounded partly on the southeast by the Continental Divide; drained by the Colorado, Eagle and Fryingpan rivers (the Fryingpan forming the Ruedi Reservoir on the southern boundary). The Upper Colorado River B.L.M. Recreation Area extends along the Colorado River. The county includes parts of White River National Forest. Sylvan Lake State Park is also here. Ranges of the Rocky Mountains are in the south and east, and include numerous ski areas. • Named for the Eagle River • 1883 from Summit • Vail is a young town; it was founded by developers in 1962 as a skiing resort in the style of a quiet Alpine village (and is now the largest ski resort in North America). • Sheep; silver, lead, copper, zinc, gypsum; timber; tourism (other skiing resorts at Avon and Beaver Creek) • Vail was host to the World Alpine Ski Championships in 1989.

ELBERT (one of two counties so named, the other in GA) *Kiowa* • 19,872 (106 % increase since 1990; the second fastest growing county in CO) • 1,851 • East-central CO; drained by Big Sandy, Beaver, Boxelder, and East and West Bijon creeks. • Named for Samuel H. Elbert (1833-1899), CO territorial governor and chief justice of the CO Supreme Court • 1874 from Douglas and Greenwood prior to statehood; the latter was abolished after being divided between Bent and Elbert • Cattle, wheat, hay, oats, sunflowers.

EL PASO (one of two counties so named, the other in TX) *Colorado Springs* • 516,929 (the third most populated county in CO) • 2,126 • East-central CO; drained by Fountain and Big Sandy creeks. The county includes part of Pike National Forest in the west, Aiken Canyon Preserve, Cave of the Winds, the red sandstone monoliths of the Garden of the Gods, and Seven Falls. Pikes Peak (14,110 feet) may be accessed by the Barr National Recreation Trail and the Pikes Peak Cog Railway. The U.S. Air Force Academy is here, as are part of Fort Carson Military Reservation and Schriever Air Force Base. The county is urbanized around Colorado Springs in west-center. • El Paso is Spanish for "the pass" (through the mountains), referring to Ute Pass, west of Colorado Springs • Original county; organized 1861 (prior to statehood) • Colorado City (between Colorado Springs and Manitou Springs) was the capital of Colorado Territory in 1862. A single legislative session was held here. • Novelist Anne Parrish; sociologist Talcott Parsons; actor Lon Chaney; photographer Laura Gilpin. Electronics engineer Seymour R. Cray and poet/playwright William Vaughn Moody died here. • Cattle, wheat, oats, sorghum; coal mining; manufacture of electronic components; printing; tourism; education (CO School for the Deaf and Blind; U. of CO–Colorado Springs; The CO College; Nazarene Bible College). Strong contributors to the county's economy are the U.S. Air Force Academy at Colorado Springs, Fort Carson Military Reservation, and Paterson Air Force Base, headquarters for the U.S. Space Command and the North American Aerospace Defense Command (NORAD), its command and control facilities housed in the excavated interior of Cheyenne Mountain. (Since 1966, it has been the nation's primary base for aerospace defense and for the tracking of orbiting objects.) • The World Figure Skating Museum and Hall of Fame is in Colorado Springs.

FREMONT *Canon City* • 46,145 • 1,533 • South-central CO, bounded on the southwest by the crest of the Sangre de Cristo Range; drained by the Arkansas River (Arkansas Headwaters Recreation Area here). Royal Gorge, in the center of the county, is spanned by a bridge 1,053 feet above the river. Part of Fort Carson Military Reservation is on the eastern boundary. The county contains parts of San Isabel National Forest, Pike National Forest and the Wet mountains. • Named for John Charles Frémont (1813-90), soldier and explorer who led five expeditions to the West, U.S. senator from CA and governor of the AZ Territory • Original county; organized 1861 (prior to statehood) • Poet Joaquin Miller • Sheep, cattle, vegetables; foundries, canneries; tourism; manufacture of firebrick concrete, hand tools, conveyors, model rockets, ore concentrates. CO State Penitentiary is here. • Fossils of prehistoric dinosaurs were discovered at Oil Creek in 1878. Buckskin Joe is a reconstructed mining town at the entrance to Royal Gorge. The Colorado Territory Prison Museum is here.

GARFIELD *Glenwood Springs* • 43,791 • 2,947 • Western CO, on the Roan Plateau, bounded on the west by the UT state line; drained by the Colorado River. The U.S. Naval Oil-Shale Reserve is near the town of Grand Valley. Part of Grand Mesa National Forest is in the south; parts of White River National Forest (its headquarters in Glenwood Springs) are in the northeast and southeast, and include Glenwood Canyon and Deep Creek B.L.M. Recreation Area; part of Routt National Forest is in the northeast corner. Rifle Gap, Rifle Falls, and Harvey Gap state parks are in the county. A dam near Glenwood diverts water from the Colorado through a 2.7 mile tunnel, supplying power, via the Shoshone Hydroelectric plant, to Denver. • One of six counties named for President James A. Garfield • 1883 from Summit • With the arrival of the Colorado Midland Railway in 1885, Glenwood Springs became a major health spa and year-round resort. • Astronaut James B. Irwin. Gunman Doc Holliday died here. • Cattle, sheep, hay, oats, timber; tourism.

GILPIN *Central City* • 4,757 • 150 (one of the fifty smallest counties in the U.S.) • North-central CO, bounded on the northwest by the Continental Divide. Parts of Roosevelt National Forest and Front Range are here. • Named for Col. William Gilpin (1815-94), first territorial governor of CO • Original county; organized 1861 (prior to statehood) • Central City was the center of a gold stampede in 1859. During its boom days in the 1860s the city was known as the "richest square mile on earth," its population burgeoning to 15,000 and rivaling Denver as CO's leading city. With the drop in gold production, it was nearly a ghost town by the 1930s. • Tourism (gambling); mining of gold, silver, lead, copper, zinc, uranium; cattle • Central City is known for the drama and opera festival held in its restored Opera House (1878) each summer. Glory Hole, a huge mining pit 900 feet long and 300 feet deep, is in Quartz Hill.

GRAND *Hot Sulphur Springs* • 12,442 • 1,847 • North-central CO, bounded on the north, east and southeast by the Continental Divide, on the east by Front Range; drained by the Colorado River (here forming Grand Lake, Lake Granby, and Shadow Mountain Lake reservoirs). Arapaho National Recreation Area and part of Rocky Mountain National Park are in the county. Parts of Arapaho and Routt national forests are also found here. Silver Creek and Winter Park ski areas are in the east. • Named for Grand Lake and the Grand River (which was later renamed the Colorado) • 1874 (prior to statehood) from Summit • Sheep-grazing, some farming; timber, sawmills; tourism (mineral springs, winter ski resorts).

GUNNISON *Gunnison* • 13,956 • 3,239 (the fourth largest county in CO) • West-central CO, bounded on the east by the Continental Divide, which extends along the crest of the Sawatch Range; drained by the Gunnison River (forming Blue Mesa Reservoir, part of Curecanti National Recreation Area). The county contains numerous ranges of the Rocky Mountains and part of Gunnison National Forest (its headquarters in Gunnison) as well as a part of Uncompahgre National Forest, including Powderhorn B.L.M. Recreation Area. Crested Butte ski area is also here. • Named for John W. Gunnison (1812-53), killed by Indians in UT while surveying for a proposed railroad • 1877 from Lake • Gunnison was established as a silver-mining town in 1879. • Sheep, cattle; mining of coal, gold and silver; light manufacturing; education (Western State College of CO); resort tourism.

HINSDALE *Lake City* • 790 • 1,118 • Southwestern CO; drained by the Lake Fork of the Gunnison and Cebolla Creek, Los Pinos and Piedra rivers (both branches of the San Juan), and headwaters of the Rio Grande. The Continental Divide crosses the county twice and forms part of its northeastern border. Most of the county lies within national forests; parts of Uncompahgre, Gunnison, Rio Grande, and San Juan national forests are here. Parts of Powderhorn and Alpine Triangle B.L.M. recreation areas are also in the county. • Named for George A. Hinsdale (1826-74), a former lieutenant governor of CO Territory • 1874 from Conejos and Summit (prior to statehood) • Sheep; timber; tourism.

HUERFANO *Walsenburg* • 7,862 • 1,591 • Southern CO, bounded on the west by the crest of the Sangre de Cristo Mountains; drained by the Cucharas River (forming Cucharas Reservoir) and the Huerfano River. Part of San Isabel National Forest is in the county, as well as part of Great Sand Dunes National Preserve, Lathrop State Park, and Cuchara Mountain ski area. The twin Spanish Peaks on the border with Las Animas County are remnants of ancient volcanoes. • Named for the Huerfano River • Original county; organized 1861 (prior to statehood) • Coal-mining; livestock grazing; flour milling, sawmills, meat packing; manufacture of transportation equipment, sporting goods; tourism (hunting and fishing) • Walsenburg is home to the Barbed Wire Museum. The Spanish El Fandango is a popular annual festival in Walsenburg.

JACKSON (one of twenty-four counties so named) *Walden* • 1,577 • 1,613 • Northern CO, bounded on the south and west by the Continental Divide, on the north by the WY state line, and on the east by the Medicine Bow Mountains; drained by the headwaters of the North Platte River. Most of Colorado State Forest, part of Routt National Forest, a small part of the Arapaho National Forest, and part of Park Range are in the county. Summits in the county rise to 12,950 feet. Thousands of Canada geese nest in the Arapaho National Wildlife Refuge each spring. North Sand Hills B.L.M. Recreation Area is also here. • One of twenty-two counties named directly or indirectly for President Andrew Jackson • 1909 from Larimer • Over the years, silver, gold, copper, and fluorspar have been mined in the county. • Jim Bridger, Old Bill Williams, and Kit Carson all hunted and trapped here. • Livestock; lumber. • In 1995 the CO Senate designated Walden the Moose Viewing Capital of the state.

JEFFERSON *Golden* • 527,056 (the second most populated county in CO) (note: this figure has not been adjusted to compensate for the removal of the fraction that includes the population of Broomfield, which became its own county in December, 2001) • 768 • Central CO, bounded on the southeast by the South Platte River (forming Chatfield and Cheesman Lake reservoirs); drained by Clear Creek. Jefferson is a constituent county of the Denver metropolitan area. All but the northeast part of the county is in the Front Range of the Rocky Mountains and its foothills. It includes parts of Pike National Forest, part of Chatfield State Park, and part of Golden Gate Canyon State Park. • One of twenty-six counties named directly or indirectly for President Thomas Jefferson • Original county; organized 1861 (prior to statehood) • Golden served as the capital of CO Territory from 1862 to 1867. • Plant physiologist Dennis Hoagland. "Buffalo Bill" Cody's Gravesite and Museum is located outside of Golden. • Sugar beets, wheat, beans, livestock; fur farms; clay, gold, coal mining; manufacture of porcelain, firebrick; beer brewing; education (CO School of Mines) • The National Earthquake Information Center is in Golden. Red Rocks Park and Amphitheatre, overlooking a 200-mile panorama, hosts a number of special events each year. Dinosaur Ridge contains more than 100 dinosaur tracks. The White Ash Mine Museum commemorates the collapse of the White Ash Coal Mine here. The Colorado Railroad Museum is in Golden.

KIOWA (one of three counties so named) *Eads* • 1,622 • 1,771 • Eastern CO, bounded on the east by the KS state line; watered by Big Sandy and Adobe creeks and reservoirs. Adobe Creek Reservoir is on the southern boundary in the southwest. Neeso Pah and Nee Noshe reservoirs are in the south-center. • 200 Cheyenne and Arapaho Indians were killed by U.S. troops under the command of Col. John Chivington in November, 1864, in what became known as the Sand Creek Massacre (national historic site). • Named for the Indian tribe • 1889 from Bent • Cattle, wheat, sunflowers, sorghum, poultry.

KIT CARSON *Burlington* • 8,011 • 2,161 • Eastern CO, bounded on the east by the KS state line; drained by the South Fork of the Republican River and the North Fork of the Smoky Hill River, and by Spring, Sand, Landsman, and Little Beaver creeks. Flagler Reservoir and Flagler State Wildlife Area are in the west. • Named for Christopher (Kit) Carson (1809-68), frontiersman, guide, and Indian agent • 1889 from Elbert • Cattle, wheat, hay, sunflowers, beans, sorghum, oats, corn; printing and publishing.

LAKE (one of twelve counties so named) *Leadville* • 7,812 • 377 • Central CO, bounded on the northwest by the Continental Divide; drained by headwaters of the Arkansas River. A large part of the county is in San Isabel National Forest. The Sawatch Mountains extend north to south and include Mount Elbert, at 14,433 feet, the highest point in CO and in the U.S. Rocky Mountains. Turquois Lake reservoir is also in the county. • Named for Twin Lakes in the southern part of the county. • Original county; organized 1861 (prior to statehood). Originally Carbonate County; named changed 1879 • Climax became one of the state's most prosperous mining towns after the value of local molybdenum deposits (discovered here in 1903) was established and world demand for the metal escalated. The Bartlett Mountain mine is the largest molybdenum source in the world. Leadville enjoyed a lead and silver boom beginning in 1877. Within one year its population of 15,000 made it CO's second-largest city. • Mining magnate Horace A. W. Tabor and his impoverished wife "Baby Doe" Tabor • The county is situated in the center of one of the nation's most celebrated mining districts: gold, silver, lead, copper, zinc, molybdenum. Also, dairying, livestock; tourism • Leadville's mining boom years are recalled by the National Mining Hall of Fame and Museum, Horace Tabor's Matchless Mine, and the Tabor Opera House.

LA PLATA *Durango* • 43,941 • 1,692 • Southwestern CO, bounded on the southwest by the NM state line and on the northwest by the La Plata Mountains; drained by the Animas and Florida rivers (the latter forming Lemon Reservoir). The county includes part of San Juan National Forest (its headquarters in Durango) in the north. Part of Southern Ute Indian Reservation is here, as are Purgatory and Hesperus ski areas. • Named for La Plata River and La Plata Mountains • 1874 from Conejos and Lake (prior to statehood) • Astronaut Stuart Roosa • Cattle, sheep; gold, silver, lead, uranium, vanadium, and coal mines; timber; light manufacturing; education (Fort Lewis College) • Established in 1822, the Durango-Silverton narrow-gauge railway, also in San Juan County, is a popular sight-seeing vehicle.

LARIMER *Fort Collins* • 251,494 • 2,601 • Northern CO, bounded on the north by the WY state line and on the southwest by the Continental Divide; drained by the Cache la Poudre River (designated here a National Wild and Recreational River) and Laramie River. Its substantial irrigation system includes the Laramie-Poudre (or Greeley-Poudre) Tunnel, which connects the two rivers. The county contains part of Rocky Mountain National Park and Front Range. Part of Roosevelt National Forest (its headquarters in Fort Collins) is here, as are Picnic Rock, Lory and Boyd Lake state parks. A small part of Colorado State Forest is on the western boundary. The county's population center is in the east. • Named for General William Larimer (1809-75), a founder of Denver and

prominent early settler • Original county; organized 1861 (prior to statehood) • U.S. Supreme Court justice Byron R. White • Limestone; timber; cattle, sheep, fruit (especially cherries), vegetables, alfalfa, wheat, hay, beans, barley, corn, sugar beets; sugar refining, canning, meat packing; manufacture of electronic components, furniture, prefabricated and mobile homes, combustion engines, arc welders and rods, cement, toys, motion picture film, dental hygiene appliances, miscellaneous plastics; education (CO State U.) • Trail Ridge Road, extending from Estes Park across the Continental Divide and then south to Grand Lake, is the highest continuous highway in the U.S.

LAS ANIMAS *Trinidad* • 15,207• 4,772 (the largest county in CO) • Southeastern CO, bounded on the south by the NM state line; drained by the Purgatoire and Apishapa rivers. Part of Culebra Range and part of San Isabel National Forest are in the west. Trinidad Lake State Park and part of Comanche National Grassland are also located in the county. Fort Carson Military Reservation is in the north. • From part of the original name of the Purgatoire River, El Rio de las Animas Perdidas en Purgatorio, Spanish for "river of souls lost in Purgatory" • 1866 from Huerfano (prior to statehood) • A monument erected by the United Mine Workers near Ludlow honors the strikers who lost their lives in the "Ludlow Massacre" during the Great Colorado Coalfield Wars of 1913-14. 11,000 miners went on strike against the Rockefeller-owned Colorado Fuel and Iron Corporation, resulting in Rockefeller-bankrolled National Guard atrocities perpetrated against both miners and their families, and subsequent outcry by union supporters and progressives throughout the U.S. • Coal-mining; cattle, horses, wheat, hay, sorghum; dairying, meat packing, wood processing; manufacture of bricks, structural clay products, plastics.

LINCOLN (one of twenty-four counties so named) *Hugo* • 6,087 • 2,586 • East-central CO; drained by Big Sandy, Horse, Rush, and Hell creeks. The source of the South and North forks of the Arikaree River and the South Fork of the Republican River are in the north. • One of eighteen counties named for President Abraham Lincoln • 1889 from Bent and Elbert • Wheat, sunflowers, cattle; manufacture of concrete.

LOGAN (one of ten counties so named) *Sterling* • 20,504 • 1,839 • Northeastern CO, bounded on the north by the NE state line; drained by the South Platte River. North Sterling Reservoir (state park on its northern shore) and part of Julesburg Reservoir are here. • One of five counties named for General John Alexander Logan (1826-86), major general in the Union Army, U.S. senator from IL, and originator of Memorial Day • 1887 from Weld • Sugar beets, beans, wheat, hay, sunflowers, corn, cattle; dairying; oil and natural gas; sugar refining, meat processing; manufacture of steel tanks, cinder blocks, concrete; railroad shops • The Overland Trail Museum displays artifacts from pioneer days.

MESA *Grand Junction* • 116,255 • 3,328 • Western CO,

bounded on the west by the UT state line; drained by the Delores, Colorado and Gunnison rivers. The northern section of the county is part of an extensively irrigated farming area. The county includes a large part of Grand Mesa National Forest. Also here are parts of White River and Uncompahgre national forests, and a small part of Manti-La Sal National Forest. Highline and Vega state parks, and two units of Colorado River State Park (Island Acres and Corn Lake) are in the county. Powderhorn ski area is here, as are numerous reservoirs and B.L.M. recreation areas. The county's most popular attraction, Colorado National Monument, is known for its towering monoliths, steep-walled canyons and colorful sandstone formations. Petrified logs and dinosaur fossils are also found in the park. • Spanish for the local tablelands, but particularly for Grand Mesa • 1883 from Gunnison • Peaches (large orchards here), grapes, beans, sugar beets, tomatoes, cantaloupes, cucumbers, wheat, hay, oats, alfalfa, barley, corn, potatoes, cattle, sheep; marble quarrying, oil and natural gas; processing of uranium and vanadium; manufacture of electronics products; tourism; education (Mesa State College) • The Museum of Western CO is in Grand Junction.

MINERAL (one of four counties so named) *Creede* • 831 • 876 • Southwestern CO, bounded in part on the north by the Continental Divide, which also crosses along the crest of the San Juan Mountains in the south; drained by the headwaters of the Rio Grande. The county includes ranges of the Rocky Mountains. Most of the northern three-fourths of the county is in Rio Grande National Forest, with the remainder in the San Juan National Forest. Wheeler Geological Area (a former national monument) is also here. Wolf Creek ski area is in the southeast. • Named for the rich mineral resources in the area • 1893 from Saguache and Rio Grande counties • A silver boom town founded in 1890, Creede had a population of 8,000 by 1893. • Silver, lead; timber; tourism and recreation.

MOFFAT *Craig* • 13,184 • 4,742 (second largest county in CO) • Extreme northwestern CO, bounded on the west by the Utah state line, on the north by the WY state line, and partly on the east by Elkhead Creek; drained by the Yampa, Little Snake and Green rivers. The Danforth Hills cross the southern boundary. Part of Dinosaur National Monument, and small sections of Routt and White River national forests are here. Browns Park National Wildlife Refuge and Little Yampa Canyon B.L.M. Recreation Area are also located in the county. • Named for David H. Moffat (1839-1910), mine owner and president of the Rio Grande Railroad • 1911 from Routt • Cattle, wheat, oats, barley; logging, sawmilling; gas and oil wells.

MONTEZUMA *Cortez* • 23,830 • 2,037 • Extreme southwestern CO, bounded on the south by the NM state line, on the west by the UT state line, and on the east by La Plata Mountains; drained by the Dolores River. The southwestern corner forms part of Four Corners Monument (the only point common to four states). The county is crossed by the Dolores River, which forms McPhee Reservoir in the north. It includes part of Canyons of the Ancients and Yucca House national monuments, part of Ute Mountain Indian Reservation, part of San Juan National Forest, Mancos State Park, and units of Hovenweep National Monument, which contain pre-Columbian towers, pueblos, and cliff dwellings. The pre-Columbian cliff dwellings and other works of early man in Mesa Verde National Park in the east are probably the best preserved examples of such ruins in the U.S. • Named for Montezuma II (1466-1520), Aztec Indian emperor of Mexico who was conquered by Hernando Cortés • 1889 from La Plata • Sheep, wheat, hay, beans, oats, barley, cattle, peaches; aspens; manufacture of concrete; meat and flour processing; Indian pottery making.

MONTROSE *Montrose* • 33,432 • 2,241 • Western CO; bounded on the west by the UT state line; drained by the Dolores, San Miguel, Gunnison, and Uncompahgre rivers. The county includes parts of Uncompahgre, Gunnison, and Manti-La Sal national forests, and Black Canyon of the Gunnison National Park (one of the last national parks to be established). Also here are the Delores River B.L.M. Recreation Area and Gunnison Gorge National Conservation Area. The Uncompahgre Plateau bisects the county northwest-southeast. • Named for the city, itself named for *A Legend of Montrose* (1819) by Sir Walter Scott, admired by one of its founders • 1883 from Gunnison • Fruit, beans, hay, livestock; mining of uranium, radium, coal, silver, copper; wood-processing • The seven-mile-long Gunnison Tunnel, acclaimed as a National Historic Civil Engineering Landmark, was an early Bureau of Reclamation project designed to bring water to the Uncompahgre Valley (1910).

MORGAN (one of eleven counties so named) *Fort Morgan* • 27,171 • 1,285 • Northeastern CO; drained by the South Platte River. Part of Empire Reservoir is on the western boundary, with Bijou Reservoir also in the west. Jackson Lake Reservoir and Jackson Lake State Park are also here. • Named for Fort Morgan, which was named for Christopher A. Morgan (? - 1866), colonel in the Union Army and inspector general • 1889 from Weld • Cattle, wheat, hay, sunflowers, brans, barley, corn, sugar beets, potatoes, alfalfa; oil; manufacture of hand tools, irrigation pipes, concrete products.

OTERO (one of two counties so named, the other in NM) *La Junta* • 20,311 • 1,263 • Southeastern CO; drained by the Purgatoire, Apishapa, and Arkansas rivers (the last forming part of the northern boundary), as well as Horse and Timpas creeks. A large part of Comanche National Grassland is here, as is Bent's Old Fort National Historic Site. • Named for Miguel A. Otero (1829-1882), delegate to the U.S. Congress from NM Territory and founder of La Junta, CO • 1889 from Bent • Bent's Fort, constructed in 1833, was the first permanent American settlement in CO. It was a principal rendezvous for white settlers on the Santa Fe Trail. La Junta was located at the convergence of the Santa Fe and Navajo trails. • Cattle, poultry, sugar beets, wheat, hay, beans, corn, melons, vegetables, cantaloupes. • The Koshare Indian Museum and Kiva are in La Junta.

OURAY *Ouray* • 3,742 • 540 • Southwestern CO; drained by the Uncompahgre River. The county includes parts of Uncompahgre National Forest, including Ouray Hot Springs and Box Canyon Falls, and a small part of San Juan Forest. Ranges of the Rocky Mountains are here, as is Ridgway State Park. • Named for Ouray (1833?–1880), chief of the Uncompahgre Utes • Organized as Uncompahgre County 1877 from San Juan; name changed 1883 • Gold, silver, lead, copper; grain, potatoes, livestock; printing and publishing; mineral hot springs.

PARK (one of three counties so named) *Fairplay* • 14,523 (102% increase since 1990; the third fastest growing county in CO) • 2,201 • Central CO, bounded on the northwest by the Continental Divide; drained by the headwaters of the South Platte River (with its source in the north). The county includes part of Park Range in the west. Part of Pike National Forest is here, as are part of Arapaho National Forest, Antero Reservoir, Spinney Mountain Reservoir and State Park, Eleven-Mile Canyon Reservoir, and Eleven-Mile State Park. • Named for the large mountain valley known as "South Park" • Original county; organized 1861 (prior to statehood) • Gold, silver, lead; cattle, sheep • Fairplay has twenty log homes that survive from the 1880s.

PHILLIPS (one of four counties so named) *Holyoke* • 4,480 • 688 • Northeastern CO, bounded on the east by the NE state line; drained by the North Fork of Frenchman Creek. • Named for Rufus O. Phillips (1859–?), an official in the Lincoln Land Company, which organized many of the towns in eastern CO • 1889 from Logan • Cattle, poultry, wheat, hay, sorghum, beans, sunflowers, oats, corn, sugar beets; light manufacturing.

PITKIN *Aspen* • 14,872 • 970 • West-central CO, bounded on the east by the Continental Divide, in the Sawatch Range; drained by the Roaring Fork of the Colorado River. White River National Forest covers much of the county and includes part of Thompson Creek B.L.M. Recreation Area. The county contains some of highest peaks of the Rocky Mountains, and has numerous ski areas in the vicinity of Aspen. • Named for Frederick W. Pitkin (1837-86), governor of CO • 1881 from Gunnison • Founded around 1878, Aspen was a silver-mining boomtown of 15,000 by 1887. It declined rapidly with the collapse in silver prices in the early 1890s. Its revival began in the late 1930s, spearheaded by the efforts of Walter Paepcke to turn it into a recreational and cultural center. • Editor Harold Ross • Sheep; mining of silver and lead; resort tourism • Major summer attractions in the county are the Aspen Music Festival and the Aspen Institute for Humanistic Studies. The Smuggler Mine once produced a nugget weighing over 2,000 pounds and constituting 93% silver.

PROWERS *Lamar* • 14,483 • 1,640 • Southeastern CO, bounded on the east by the KS state line; drained by the Arkansas River and Two Butte and Big Sandy creeks. • Named for John W. Prowers (1838-84), successful cattleman of the Arkansas Valley and member of the CO state legislature • 1889 from Bent • Clay; wheat, hay, sorghum, barley, corn, cattle; food processing; manufacture of transit buses, forage tubs, clay products, alfalfa products.

PUEBLO *Pueblo* • 141,472 • 2,389 • South-central CO; drained by the Arkansas and St. Charles rivers. The county includes part of San Isabel National Forest (its headquarters in Pueblo), part of Fort Carson Military Reservation, and Pueblo Reservoir, encompassed by Lake Pueblo State Park. Pueblo Chemical Depot and the Federal Railroad Administration's Transportation Technology Center are in the northeast. • Named for the city, from the Spanish, "town" • 1861 (prior to statehood) • Colorado City was the capital of the CO Territory in 1862. A disastrous flood of the Arkansas River in 1921 spurred the development of an expansive flood-control system upstream from Pueblo. • Electrical engineer and entrepreneur David Packard • Cattle, wheat, hay, beans, sorghum, corn; food processing, meat packing; manufacture of steel and steel products, machinery, transportation equipment, building products, fabricated plastic products, fuel oil, beverages, consumer goods, skiwear; printing and publishing; education (U. of Southern CO) • The annual Colorado State Fair and Industrial Exposition is held in Pueblo. The Weisbrod Aircraft Museum and B-24 Museum are located at Pueblo Memorial Airport.

RIO BLANCO *Meeker* • 5,986 • 3,221 (the fifth largest county in CO) • Northwestern CO, bounded on the west by the UT state line; drained by the White River (the White River Museum is in Meeker) and Piceance Creek. The county lies on East Tavaputs and Roan plateaus in the south, rising to the Cathedral Bluffs and Danforth Hills in the north. Parts of the White River and Routt national forests are here, as is the Canyon Pintado National Historic District. • Spanish name for the White River • 1889 from Garfield • Meeker Monument marks the spot where Ute Indians killed a small group of whites in 1879, including Nathan Meeker, Indian agent and co-founder of the city of Greeley. The county enjoyed an oil boom in the 1940s from the productive Rangely oil field. • The state's richest coal and oil fields are here. Also, natural gas; cattle, sheep, hay.

RIO GRANDE *Del Norte* • 12,413 • 912 • Southern CO; drained by the Rio Grande. The source of the San Juan River and part of San Juan National Forest are in the southwest corner. The Continental Divide passes through the county's southwest corner following the crest of the San Juan Mountains. Part of Rio Grande National Forest (its headquarters in Monte Vista) dominates two-thirds of the county. Monte Vista National Wildlife Refuge is also here. • Named for the Rio Grande • 1874 from Conejos • Potatoes, wheat, hay, oats, barley, sheep, cattle; mining of gold and silver; light manufacturing, including starches; tourism (dude ranches).

ROUTT *Steamboat Springs* • 19,690 • 2,362 • Northwestern CO, bounded on the north by the WY state line and on the northeast and east by the Continental Divide, extending along Park Range; drained by the Yampa River and Elkhead Creek. The county includes parts of Routt and White River national forests and Steamboat Lake, Pearl Lake, and Stagecoach state parks. Several ski resorts are near Steamboat Springs. • Named for John L. Routt (1826-1907), last territorial governor and first CO state governor • 1877 from Grand • Cattle, sheep, wheat, hay, barley; hot mineral springs, resort tourism, skiing; diversified light manufacturing; publishing and printing; coal.

SAGUACHE *Saguache* • 5,917 • 3,168 • South-central CO, bounded on the east by the crest of the Sangre de Cristo Mountains; drained by Saguache Creek. The Continental Divide crosses the county and forms part of its southwest border. Located in a predominantly irrigated agricultural area, the county includes the northern part of the San Luis Valley in the east. It includes ranges of the Rocky Mountains and parts of Rio Grande National Forest. Gunnison National Forest is also here and includes La Ventana Natural Arch. The dunes of Great Sand Dunes National Park, among the largest and highest in the U.S., have been formed by wind blowing through the passes of the Sangre de Cristo Mountains for thousands of years. • Named for Saguache Creek and other local geographical features with this name • 1866 from Costilla (prior to statehood) • Sheep, cattle, wheat, hay, oats, barley, potatoes, vegetables; mining of gold, silver, copper.

SAN JUAN (one of four counties so named) *Silverton* • 558 (the least populated county in CO; only seven U.S. counties have fewer people) • 387 • Southwestern CO; drained by the Animas River; crossed in the east by the Continental Divide. The source of the Rio Grande is east of the Divide, the source of Uncompahgre River in the north. The San Juan Mountains dominate the county, its many slopes sheltered by the San Juan National Forest, and part of the Rio Grande and Uncompahgre national forests. • Named for the San Juan River, San Juan Mountains, and the region • 1876 from La Plata • Lead, silver, gold, copper, zinc mining; tourism; publishing and printing. • The Durango-Silverton narrow gauge railway (also in La Plata County) was established in 1888 and is now a popular sight-seeing vehicle.

SAN MIGUEL *Telluride* • 6,594 •1,287 • Southwestern CO, bounded on the west by the UT state line; drained by the Dolores and San Miguel rivers (both attached to B.L.M. recreation areas). The county includes part of the San Miguel Mountains. Sections of Uncompahgre National Forest are also found here. Bridal Veil Falls is near Telluride ski area. • Named for the San Miguel River and San Miguel Mountains, themselves named for St. Michael (the Archangel). It is one of two counties (the other in NM) named directly or indirectly for St. Michael. • Organized 1861; named changed from Ouray when Uncompahgre became Ouray in 1883 • Gold, silver, lead, uranium; sheep, dairying, cattle, wheat; tourism; printing and publishing.

SEDGWICK *Julesburg* • 2,747 • 548 • Extreme northeastern CO, bounded on the northeast by the NE state line; watered by the South Platte River. Julesburg Reservoir is on the western boundary of the county. • Named for Fort Sedgwick, itself named for Major General John Sedgwick (1813-64), Indian fighter and Union officer in the Civil War. (It is one of two counties, the other in KS, named directly or indirectly for Major Sedgwick) • 1889 from Logan • Sugar beets, cattle, poultry, wheat, sunflowers, beans, oats, corn • The only Colorado pony express "home" station was located in Julesburg. The remains of the elaborate "Italian caves," dug by eccentric Uberto Gibello, beginning in 1887, are located south of Julesburg.

SUMMIT (one of three counties so named) *Breckenridge* • 23,548 • 608 • Central CO, bounded on the south and east by the Continental Divide; drained by the Blue River, which forms Dillon Reservoir at the center. The county includes Green Mountain Reservoir. Most of the county is in the Arapaho National Forest. • Named Summit for its mountainous terrain • Original county; organized 1861 (prior to statehood) • The county was formerly a mining and sheep-grazing region. The site of the town of Frisco was a Ute Indian camp for 7,000 years. • Zinc, gold, silver mining; livestock; manufacture of concrete; gravel processing; recreational tourism (several ski resorts are located here.)

TELLER *Cripple Creek* • 20,555 • 557 • Central CO; drained by High and Cripple creeks. The county includes part of Front Range and Pike National Forest in the north and east. Florissant Fossil Beds National Monument, with its unusual display of petrified sequoia stumps, and Mueller State Park are here. The Cripple Creek and Victor Narrow Gauge Railroad is located in the southwest. • Named for Henry M. Teller (1830-1914), one of CO's first two U.S. senators and U.S. secretary of the interior • 1889 from El Paso and Fremont • In 1891, gold was discovered in Poverty Gulch by Robert Womack (who died impoverished) and in Victor by Winfield S. Stratton (who left a fortune of $20 million). Cripple Creek suffered a devastating fire in 1894. Labor disputes in 1903-04 resulted in much violence and loss of life. Reaching a population of 50,000 by 1901, Cripple Creek had only 1,000 residents by 1960. • Mining of gold and silver; ranching and livestock-grazing • The Lowell Thomas Museum, which chronicles the life and career of the famous journalist, is located in Victor.

WASHINGTON *Akron* • 4,926 • 2,521 • Northeastern CO; drained by the South Platte and Arikaree rivers and by Gordon and Beaver creeks. Prewitt Reservoir, on a tributary of the South Platte River, is also here. • One of thirty-one counties named for President George Washington • 1887 from Weld • Summit Springs Battlefield was the scene of the July 1869 defeat by U.S. Cavalry of Cheyenne and Sioux under the command of Chief Tall Bull. • The county leads CO in the production of hard red winter wheat. Also, hay, sunflowers, beans, oats, corn, sugar beets, cattle.

WELD *Greeley* • 180,936 • 3,987 (the third largest county in

CO) (note: this figure has not been adjusted to compensate for the removal of the fraction that includes the population of Broomfield, which became its own county in December, 2001) • Northern CO, bounded on the north by the WY and NE state lines; watered by the South Platte, Cache la Poudre, and Big and Little Thompson rivers. Two units of Pawnee National Grassland are in the north. The county also contains Milton, Empire, and Riverside reservoirs. Barbour Ponds State Park and the Colorado National Speedway are in the southwest. Most of the county's population is centered in the west and southwest, peripheral to the Fort Collins and Denver metropolitan areas. • Named for Lewis L. Weld (1833-65), first Secretary of the CO Territory and major of the 41st Colored Infantry • Original county; organized 1861 (prior to statehood) • Greeley was founded in 1870 by Nathan Cook Meeker, head of the Union Colony Company, which was a cooperative venture organized by the eponymous Horace Greeley, editor of the *New York Tribune*. • It is the state's richest agricultural county: sugar beets (principal crop) wheat, hay, corn, sunflowers, beans, sorghum, oats, barley, fruit, vegeta-

bles, cattle, poultry, eggs; also oil and gas; processing of beet sugar, flour, and other agricultural products, canning and bottling; education (U. of Northern CO).

YUMA *Wray* • 9,841 • 2,366 • Northeastern CO, bounded on the east by the KS and NE state lines; drained by the Arikaree River, and the North and South forks of the Republican River (the latter forming Bonny Reservoir in the southeast). Bonny State Park is here, as is Beecher Island Battleground site. The island, lost in a flood in 1935, is commemorated with a monument placed near the Arikaree River. • Named for the town of Yuma, itself named for the Yuma Indian tribe. It is one of two counties (the other in AZ) named directly or indirectly for the tribe. • 1889 from Washington County • The county is one of the largest corn producers in the world. Also, cattle, dairying, wheat, hay, sunflowers, beans, sorghum, oats. • The largest cattle feedlot in the United States is located here. The majority of the state's endangered prairie chickens live on private grasslands within the county.

CONNECTICUT

He Who Transplanted Still Sustains

County government in the state no longer exists. All of Connecticut's eight counties remain as geographical units within the state but carry no additional function.

FAIRFIELD (one of three counties so named) • no county seat • 882,567 (the most populated county in CT) • 626 • Southwestern CT, bounded on the south by the Long Island Sound, on the west by the NY state line, and on the east by the Housatonic River; drained by the Housatonic, Norwalk, Aspetuck, Saugatuck, and Pequonnock rivers. Many of its residential communities lie within commuting distance of New York City. There are resorts on the shore and at Lake Candlewood, the largest man-made lake in the state. The county has several state parks. Paugussett and Pootatuck state forests are in the north. • Named for the city of Fairfield; the name is descriptive of the area • Original county; 1666 • The Great Swamp Fight in Westport in July, 1637, ended the Pequot Indian War. Norwalk was a major oyster center in its early years. Greenwich was invaded and plundered by British light cavalry under Governor William Tryon during the American Revolution. On April 27, 1777, 2,000 British soldiers under the command of Tryon set fire to Danbury. Militia and neighborhood farmers led by General Benedict Arnold attempted to halt their retreat at the Battle of Ridgefield. Tryon's men

burned Fairfield and Norwalk in 1779. Jasper McLevy served as socialist mayor of Bridgeport for twenty-four years beginning in 1933. • Composer Charles Ives; senator Joseph Lieberman; showman P.T. Barnum (who was mayor of Bridgeport); his star performer Charles S. Stratton ("Tom Thumb"). Singer and actor Ezio Pinza, painter and sculptor Frederic Remington, blind and deaf author and educator Helen Keller, pioneer in aircraft design Igor Sikorsky, and writer Mark Twain died here. • Manufacture of electrical and electronic equipment, firearms, hats, machinery, metal products, apparel, textiles, drugs, chemicals, rubber, paper, golf clubs, wood and glass products, aircraft, tools, surgical supplies; dairying; research; education (Western CT State U.; Sacred Heart U.; U. of Bridgeport; other colleges. Several private preparatory schools are located in the county, including Whitby School, headquarters of the Montessori Society in America, in Greenwich.) • The county has one of the largest concentrations of corporate headquarters in the U.S. Twenty-three Fortune 1000 companies are located here. One of the first artists' colonies in the U.S. was founded near New Canaan in the early 1900s. Danbury was known as the "hat city of the world" for its manufacture of men's hats until early in the 20th century.

HARTFORD • no county seat • 857,183 (the second most populated county in CT) • 735 • Central and northern CT, bounded on the north by the MA state line; divided by the Connecticut River; drained by the Farmington, Quinnipiac, Pequabuck, Hockanum, and Scantic rivers. The county includes several state parks and forests, including Tunxis State Forest in the extreme northwest. • Named for Hertford, England. The spelling reflects English pronunciation • Original county; organized 1666 • Wethersfield is the site of the first permanent English settlement in CT (1634). Hartford was home to the first constitution of the Connecticut Colony, the Fundamental Orders (1639), sometimes called the first written constitution. Simsbury was burned during King Philip's War (1675–76). Hartford was joint capital with New Haven from 1701 until 1875, when it became the state's only capital. The first copper coins in the American colonies were minted in Simsbury in 1737. The first American tinware was made in Enfield in 1740. It was also in Enfield that Jonathan Edwards preached his famous sermon, "Sinners in the Hands of an Angry God" in 1741. The first powder mill in America was built on the Hockanum River in 1775. Bristol was a Tory stronghold during the Revolutionary War. Wethersfield was the site of the Yorktown Conference held in May, 1781 between General George Washington and French general Count de Rochambeau. At the Hartford Convention, which took place here from December 15, 1814 to January 5, 1815, New Englanders gathered to express opposition to the War of 1812. Samuel Colt invented the first successful repeating pistol in Hartford in 1836. • Lexicographer Noah Webster; actor Katharine Hepburn; landscape architect Frederick Law Olmsted; author Mark Twain; firearms manufacturer Eliphalet Remington; author Harriet Beecher Stowe; financial and industrial organizer J. P. Morgan. Poet Padraic Colum died here. • Manufacture of airplanes, machinery, hardware (New Britain is known as the "Hardware City"), tools, woven felt, building materials, paper, clothing, food products, rubber products, leather products, furniture, fabricated metal products, textiles, soap, plastics, gauges, greeting cards, wood and paper products, consumer goods, electronic and electrical goods, industrial machinery, computer components, aircraft engines, chemicals; insurance; government offices; printing; tobacco, dairy products, poultry, vegetables, fruit, corn, potatoes, nursery products, seeds; education (U. of Hartford; St. Joseph College; Trinity College; U. of CT at Hartford) • The corporate headquarters for eight Fortune 1000 companies are located in the county. Established in 1764, the *Hartford Courant* is the oldest continuously published newspaper in the U.S. Amelia Simmons' *American Cookery*, the first cookbook written by an American, was published in Hartford in 1796. Bristol's New England Carousel Museum has over 300 antique carousel figures. The city's American Clock and Watch Museum is the preeminent institution in the U.S. devoted entirely to American horologic history. The American School for the Deaf, founded by Thomas Gallaudet in 1817 in West Hartford is the oldest institution of its kind in the U.S. The rose gardens in West Hartford's Elizabeth Park attract thousands of visitors a year. The Wadsworth Atheneum in Hartford was one of the first public art museums in the U.S.

LITCHFIELD • no county seat • 182,193 (the fifth most populated county in CT) • 920 (the largest county in CT) • Northwestern CT, bounded on the west by the NY state line, and on the north by the MA state line; drained by the Housatonic, Naugatuck, Shepaug, Pomperang and Still rivers. The county contains many small state parks and forests, along with mountain resorts. Mount Frissell, at 2,380 feet, is the highest point in CT. Part of Lake Candlewood and Barkhamsted Reservoir are here, as are other lakes and reservoirs, including Waramaug, Wononskopomuc, Highland, and Bantam. The Appalachian Trail traverses the county in the west. • Named for the town of Litchfield, in honor of Lichfield in England • 1751 from Hartford and Fairfield • The first law school in the U.S. was established in Litchfield in 1774; Aaron Burr and John C. Calhoun were students here. Litchfield was a supply point and rest stop for American troops on their way to Boston during the American Revolution. During the war, Torrington's entire male population over the age of twenty enlisted in the Continental Army. Clocks have been made in Thomaston since 1812, when Seth Thomas established his business here. • Revolutionary leader Ethan Allen; author Harriet Beecher Stowe; Congregational minister Henry Ward Beecher; Declaration of Independence signer Oliver Wolcott; abolitionist John Brown; politician Orville Hitchcock Platt; consumer advocate Ralph Nader; lawyer and educator Charles G. Finney. Educator Helen Parkhurst, cartoonist Al Frueh, and World War II guerilla Marine officer Evans Carlson died here. • Manufacture of metal products, electrical equipment, clocks and watches, machine tools, hosiery, pines, fish line, appliances, machinery, glass and plastic products, textiles, apparel, machinery, furniture, mattresses, brass goods; also dairy products, vegetables, fruit, tobacco, poultry; resort tourism; education.

MIDDLESEX • no county seat • 155,071 (8% increase since 1990; the fastest growing county in CT) • 369 (the smallest county in CT) • Southern CT, bounded on the south by the Long Island Sound; divided and drained by the Connecticut River (which also forms part of the county's eastern boundary in the south); also drained by the Hammonasset and Salmon rivers. The county includes Lake Pocotopaug and several state parks and forests, including Cockaponset State Forest. It is the former site of Haddam Neck nuclear power plant, which was built in the 1960s on the banks of the Connecticut River and closed in 1996 for safety reasons. • One of four counties named for Middlesex County in England • 1785 (prior to statehood) from Hartford, New London and New Haven • Middletown was an early seaport and shipbuilding center, a base of the triangular trade in rum, slaves and molasses, and later a center for China clipper trade. The first official pistol maker for the U.S. government, Simeon North, began operating a factory here in 1799. • Supreme Court Justice Stephen J. Field • Tobacco, potatoes, produce, fruit, dairy products, poultry; manufacture of tools, hardware, electrical equipment, boats, textiles, metal products, consumer goods, piano parts, paper and fiber products, clothing, transportation equipment, agricultural machinery, chemicals, asbestos, cigars, aircraft engines; fishing; sandstone and feldspar quarries; insurance, banking: education (Wesleyan U.) • Middletown is home to the Submarine Library and Museum. The Museum of Fife and Drum is at Ivoryton.

NEW HAVEN • no county seat • 824,008 (the third most populated county in CT) • 606 • Southern CT, bounded on the south by the Long Island Sound and on the east by the Housatonic River; also drained by the Naugatuck, Quinnipiac, and Hammonasset rivers. Several state parks and state forests are found here, including units of Naugatuck State Forest. Lake Gaillard is in the southeast. • Named for New Haven colony and the city of New Haven • Original county; organized 1666 • New Haven and Hartford were joint capitals of CT from 1701 until 1875, when Hartford became the only capital. British troops under General William Tryon sacked the town of West Haven on July 5, 1779. Thousands of acres of undersea oysters were once harvested near Milford. In the first half of the 1800s, Cheshire was a copper- and barite-mining center. In 1802, David Humphreys brought the first merino sheep from Spain to Seymour and opened a woolen mill here. In 1839, Charles Goodyear discovered the vulcanization of rubber in Naugatuck. The first telephone exchange in the world opened in New Haven in January, 1878. The first mohair plush made in the U.S. was produced in Seymour by John Tingue in 1880. Simon Lake invented his even-keel submarine torpedo boat in Milford in 1894. • President George W. Bush; television producer Norman Lear; civil rights leader Adam Clayton Powell, Jr.; clock manufacturer Seth Thomas; inventors Eli Whitney (who helped develop mass production in Hamden in the early 1800s) and Samuel F. B. Morse; Declaration of Independence drafting committee member Roger Sherman; pediatrician Benjamin Spock. Novelist and playwright Thornton Wilder died here. • Manufacture of metal products, hardware, firearms, rubber goods, silverware (Meriden is one of the world's largest manufacturers), electrical and communications equipment, nuclear instrumentation, tools, dies, molds and patterns, bathroom accessories, jewelry, plastics, candy, appliances, brass (Waterbury was once the nation's largest producer of brass products), copper sheets, wire cables, bricks, textiles, aircraft engine parts; oil refining; fruit, vegetables, dairy products, poultry, seed growing; fisheries; tourism at shore resorts; education (Yale U., the third oldest institution of higher learning in the U.S.; Southern CT State U.; Albertus Magnus College; Quinnipiac U.; U. of New Haven; Teikyo Post U.) • The Branford Trolley Museum in East Haven exhibits electric street and in-

terurban railway cars. Guilford is the site of the Henry Whitfield House, the oldest stone house in the U.S. New Haven was once called "Elm City" for its many elm-lined streets. The city has one of the oldest symphony orchestras in the country. The Yale University Art Gallery is the oldest university art museum in the nation. Its Beinecke Rare Book and Manuscript Library is one of the largest buildings in the world devoted to rare books and manuscripts. The football tackling dummy was invented on the Yale campus in 1889 by Amos Alonzo Stagg, a Yale football player and future coach. Cheshire is home to the Barker Character, Comic and Cartoon Museum.

NEW LONDON • no county seat • 259,088 (the fourth most populated county in CT) • 666 • Southeastern CT, bounded on the south by the Long Island Sound, on the east by the RI state line, and on the west in part by the Connecticut River; drained by the Shetucket, Thames, Mystic, Quinebaug, and Niantic rivers. Parts of Pachaug State Forest are in the east; parts of Nehantic State Forest are in the west. Several state parks are found here. Pachaug Pond is in the northeast. • Named for the city of New London, in honor of London, England • Original county; organized 1666 • CT's first printing press was established in New London in 1709 by Thomas Short. Norwich was a major shipbuilding and shipping center from 1750 to 1800. On September 6, 1781, Fort Griswold was attacked by a British force led by turncoat Benedict Arnold; when fighting ended the garrison was massacred. New London was a whaling center from 1784 to 1909. Some of America's fastest clipper ships were built in Mystic; from its shipyards the first regular iron-clad vessel, the *Galena* was launched in 1861. • Revolutionary War traitor Benedict Arnold; diplomat Silas Dean; educator Daniel C. Gilman; sea captain and explorer Nathaniel B. Palmer; CT governor Jonathan Trumbull; novelist E. Annie Proulx. Economist Richard T. Ely and actor James O'Neill died here. • New London is the site of the U.S. Coast Guard Academy. The U.S. Submarine Officers School is here. The construction of submarines is a major industry in the county. (The *Nautilus*, the first nuclear-powered submarine, was launched from New London in 1954, the U.S.S. *Ohio*, the first "Ohio" class sub, in 1981.) Diversified manufactures include textiles, metal products, chemicals, antibiotics, clothing, consumer goods, silverware, boats, leather products, electronic equipment; also dairying, poultry, fruit, vegetables; tourism, gambling resorts; education (CT College) • The Yale-Harvard crew races are held each June on the Thames River at New London. The Mystic Marine Life Aquarium features more than 2,000 aquatic specimens. The Eugene O'Neill Memorial Theater Center in Waterford is the site of the prestigious National Playwrights' Conference. Lyme gave its name to Lyme disease, a tick-borne viral condition that was first identified and described in the area of the town.

TOLLAND • no county seat • 136,364 • 410 • Northeastern CT, bounded on the north by the MA state line; drained by the Willimantic, Hockanum, Scungamaug, Fenton, and Hop rivers. The county has several state parks, lake resorts and state forests, including parts of Nipmuck and Shenipsit state forests in the north. • Named for the town of Tolland, itself named for the town of Tolland in Somersetshire, England • 1785 (prior to statehood) from Windham • Patriot Nathan Hale (homestead preserved here); publisher and editor Jared Sparks • Manufacture of textiles, lumber, thread, wood products, buttons, paper goods, sutures, boats, snowmobile trailers, baseballs, fishline, paint; machine parts; fabric dyeing and finishing; also dairy products, poultry, vegetables, potatoes (a major crop), tobacco, fruit; education (U. of CT) • The county is home to a number of eclectic museums, including the New England States Civilian Conservation Corps Museum, the Special Joys Doll and Toy Museum and the Connecticut State Museum of Natural History.

WINDHAM (one of two counties so named, the other in VT) • no county seat • 109,091 (the least populated county in CT)

• 513 • Northeastern CT; bounded on the north by the MA state line and on the east by the RI state line; drained by the Quinebaug, Natchaug, Shetucket, Little, and Mossup rivers. The county has several state parks and forests, with resorts on small lakes. Natchaug State Forest is prominent in the center. • Named for the town of Windham, itself probably named for Wymondham, Norfolk, England • 1726 from Hartford and New London • Physicist Harold D. Arnold; journalist Charles H. Dow; Congregational minister Manasseh Cutler; linguist and anthropologist Kenneth L. Pike; jeweler Charles Lewis Tiffany • Dairying, vegetables, poultry; manufacture of machinery, cutlery, metal products, clothing, paper and rubber goods, shoes, chemicals, furniture, optical goods and wood products; education (Eastern CT State U.). Willimantic was long known as the Thread City; cotton was spun here beginning in 1822. • The New England Center for Contemporary Art is in Brooklyn. An interesting relic of the Revolutionary War in Windham is the "Bacchus of Windham," a wooden statue carved by British sailors held prisoner here in 1776.

DELAWARE

Liberty and Independence

Each of Delaware's three counties is slightly different from the others in government organization. New Castle is led by a six-member council headed by an elected president. Sussex's council has five members, with one councilman serving as president. Kent County is governed by a seven member county commission called the levy court. All members of the counties' governing bodies serve four-year terms. Other elected county officials in the state include the comptroller, sheriff, and recorder of deeds. Delaware's counties are divided into hundreds. It is unique among the states in this respect.

KENT (one of five counties so named) *Dover* • 126,697 (the least populated county in DE) • 590 • Central DE, bounded on the north in part by the Smyrna River, on the west by the MD state line, on the south by part of the Misspillion River, on the east by the Delaware River and Delaware Bay (both comprising the NJ state line); drained by the Leipsic, Choptank, Murderkill, and St. Jones rivers, and Marshyhope Creek. The county is level coastal plain, with some marshland. Bombay Hook National Wildlife Refuge, W.S. Taber State Forest, Murderkill River Nature Preserve, and Killens Pond State Park are here. Dover Air Force Base is the principal air cargo terminal supplying U.S. forces around the world. • One of two counties (the other in RI) named for Kent County in England • Organized as Saint Jones in 1680 from Horre Kill District, which was organized in 1664; name changed in 1682 • Dover became the capital of the state in 1777. • Astronomer Annie Jump Cannon; Declaration of Independence signer Caesar Rodney; jurist and publicist John Bassett Moore • Corn, vegetables, wheat, fruit, poultry, dairying; fishing, oysters; fruit

and vegetable canning; processing of dairy products; manufacture of gelatin food products (one of the largest single-plant users of sugar in the world is in Dover), synthetic polymers, adhesives, elastomers, latex, chemical coatings, resins, specialty chemicals; government offices; education (DE State U.; Wesley College) • Dover contains a number of notable examples of Georgian colonial architecture.

NEW CASTLE *Wilmington* • 500,265 (the most populated county in DE) • 426 (the smallest county in DE) • Northern DE, bounded on the north by the PA state line, on the west by the MD state line, on the south in part by the Smyrna River, on the east by the Delaware River (forming the NJ state line); drained by the Christina River, and Brandywine, Red Clay and White Clay creeks. The county is crossed east-west at its center by the Chesapeake and Delaware Canal, part of the Intracoastal Waterway. It is highly urbanized in the north, especially around Wilmington, and constitutes an extension of the Philadelphia metropolitan area from the northeast. Several state parks are located here. Two small sections of DE, including Finn's point are on the NJ side of the Delaware River. The county's northern boundary with PA is formed by the arc of a perfect circle (making New Castle the only county in the nation with part of its border formed in this manner); the circle is centered at the dome of the Court House in New Castle. • Named for either the town of New Castle or for the Duke of Newcastle, William Cavendish (1592–1676); originally named New Amstel • Original county; 1673 • Fort Christina, the first settlement in the Wilmington area, was established by Swedish colonists in 1638. The settlement was seized by the Dutch in 1655 and by the English in 1664. A convention in New Castle on September 21, 1776, proclaimed the state of Delaware. The city served briefly as capital. On September 3, 1777, Cooch's Bridge on Christina Creek was the scene of the only Revolutionary War battle fought in the state. • Colonial preacher Samuel Davies; economist Pierre-Samuel Du Pont; munitions producer Pierre Samuel du Pont; inventor Oliver Evans; microbiologist Daniel Nathans; illustrator Howard Pyle; author and editor Henry S. Canby; novelist John P. Marquand; jurist George Ross; physician and manufacturer Edward R. Squibb. Statesman John Dickinson and newspaper publisher Hezekiah Niles died here. • Dairy products, poultry, livestock, corn, wheat; shipping; education (U. of DE; Goldey-Beacom College; Wilmington College) manufacture of chemicals (Wilmington, home to several leading chemical firms, including the DuPont Company — the birthplace of nylon in the 1930s — is sometimes called the "Chemical Capital of the World"), frozen desserts, machinery, steel products, rayon, aircraft, vulcanized fiber, concrete products, processed foods, dyed fabrics, military equipment; automobile assembly; research • One of the best collections of Early American furniture is displayed at the Henry Francis du Pont Winterthur Museum. The courthouse in New Castle, seat of PA's "Lower Counties" until 1776, is one of the oldest buildings in the U.S. Christmas seals were introduced in the U.S. in 1907 in Wilmington. The headquarters of four Fortune 1000 counties are located in the county.

SUSSEX *Georgetown* • 156,638 (40% increase since 1990; the fast growing county in DE) • 938 (the largest county in DE) • Southern DE, bounded on the south and west by the MD state line, on the north, in part, by the Mispillion River, on the northeast by Delaware Bay (forming the NJ state line) and on the east by the Atlantic Ocean; drained by the Broadkill, Indian, Pocomoke and Nanticoke rivers. The county includes Barnes Woods Nature Preserve; Trap Pond, Cape Henlopen, Delaware Seashore, and Fenwick Island state parks; Prime Hook National Wildlife Refuge; Cypress Swamp; and Ellendale and Redden state forests. • One of three counties named for Sussex County in England • Organized as Deale County in 1680 from Horre Kill District, which was organized in 1664; name changed in 1682 • Founded in 1631, Lewes was the first white settlement along the Delaware River. The town's seafaring tradition goes back more than 300 years. During the War of 1812, it was bombarded by the British, and is the site of numerous shipwrecks. • Fruit, grain, livestock, dairying; fish processing, canning (especially clams); manufacture of clothing; tourism, sport fishing • The Zwaanendael House, a replica of part of the town hall of Hoorn, the Netherlands, was built by the state in Lewes in 1931 to commemorate settlement of the area by the Dutch in 1631. Rehoboth Beach was the site of the first beauty contest in the U.S. (1880); Thomas Edison was one of the three judges who decided the winner of the title "Miss United States."

FLORIDA

In God We Trust

Most of Florida's sixty-seven counties are governed by a board of five commissioners and divided into five districts, with a commissioner coming from each district. Other elected officials in the county include the circuit court clerk, supervisor of elections, property appraiser, tax collector, and sheriff. County officers serve four-year terms.

ALACHUA *Gainesville* • 217,955 • 874 • North-central FL, bounded on the north by the Sante Fe River. The county has many lakes, including Orange, Newnans and Sante Fe. Paynes Prairie State Preserve and San Felasco Hammock State Preserve are here. • Named for an early Indian settlement called Alachua. • 1824 from Duval and Saint Johns • Gainesville sits on part of a grant of 289,000 acres made in 1817 to Don Fernando de la Mata Arredondo by the King of Spain. • Author Marjorie Kinnan Rawlings (state historic site) • Hay, soybeans, corn, vegetables, peanuts, cotton, tobacco, citrus fruit, nuts (pecan, tung), livestock; lumber and naval stores; limestone, phosphate and flint; education; light industry, including production of tung oil • A large cultural complex is affiliated with the University of FL, comprising the Florida Museum of Natural History, the Samuel P. Harn Museum of Art, and the University Gallery.

BAKER (one of three counties so named) *Macclenny* • 22,259 • 585 • Northeastern FL, bounded on the north by the GA state line and on the northeast by St. Mary's River (forming the GA state line). Parts of Okefenokee National Wildlife Refuge and Osceola National Forest are in the west. • Named for James M. Baker (1822–92), FL Confederate legislator and jurist • 1861 from New River • The only significant Civil War battle fought in FL took place on February 20, 1864 at Olustee and resulted in a Confederate victory (state historic site). • Corn, vegetables, peanuts, cotton; lumber, naval stores.

BAY (one of two counties so named, the other in MI) *Panama City* • 148,217 • 764 • Northwestern FL, in the panhandle, bounded on the south by the Gulf of Mexico. The county includes Pine Log State Forest and St. Andrews State Recreation Area. Panama City's deepwater, landlocked harbor is on the Atlantic Intracoastal Waterway, which crosses from West Bay to East Bay. • Named for St. Andrews Bay • 1913 from Calhoun and Washington • During the Revolutionary War, the area that would become Bay County was settled by British Loyalists who engaged in lumbering and naval store industries, and established indigo plantations. Saltworks, serving the Confederacy, were destroyed by Union sea-raids in 1863. Panama City became a shipbuilding and industrial center during World War II. • Commercial and sport fishing; cattle, some cotton, peanuts and sugarcane; manufacture of chemicals, forestry and paper products, steam generators, pipe, clothing; tourism (including sailing) • The Naval Surface Warfare Center (diving school) and Tyndall Air Force Base are in the county.

BRADFORD (one of two counties so named, the other in PA) *Starke* • 26,088 • 293 • Northeastern FL, bounded on the south by the Santa Fe River. • Named for Captain Richard Bradford, first Florida officer killed in the Civil War • Organized as New River County 1858; name changed 1861 • Corn, strawberries, vegetables, tobacco, pecans, livestock; forestry.

BREVARD *Titusville* • 476,230 • 1,018 • Eastern FL, bounded on the east by the Atlantic Ocean. Barrier beaches border a lowland region enclosing Indian River and Banana River lagoons, and Merritt Island. (Merritt Island National Wildlife Refuge is here.) The western part of the county is marshy peat; several lakes are formed by the St. Johns River, which drains it. The southern portion of Canaveral National Seashore extends into the county. The Atlantic Intracoastal Waterway passes through the Indian River. Patrick Air Force Base is in the south, Cape Canaveral Air Station east-central. The county is undergoing rapid urbanization. • Named for Theodore W. Brevard (1804–77), FL state comptroller • Organized as Saint Lucie 1844 from Mosquito; name changed 1855 • Astronauts Roger B. Chaffee and Virgil Grissom died here (Cape Kennedy) • Citrus fruits (the county is famous for its Indian River citrus crops), vegetables; tourism, including boating, sailing; commercial and sport fishing; aerospace industries including the U.S. space program (Kennedy Space Center); education (FL Institute of Technology, FL Air Acad-

emy). As the "Technology Capital of the Southeast," Melbourne manufactures high-level mathematics systems, aviation products, computer software, electronic power supplies, and optical devices. • The Melbourne bone beds, an area of deposits along the east coast, contain important Pleistocene fossils.

BROWARD *Fort Lauderdale* • 1,623,018 (the second most populated county in FL and fifteenth most populated county in the U.S.) • 1,205 • Southeastern FL, bounded on the east by the Atlantic Ocean. The county is one of FL's most urbanized, experiencing much of its growth in the last thirty years. Beach resorts line the coast. Inland is the peat-underlaid Everglades, which are crossed by drainage canals between Lake Okeechobee and the coast. Miccosukee Indian Reservation is in the extreme west. • Named for Napoleon Bonaparte Broward (1857–1910), FL governor who played a leading role in draining the Everglades • 1915 from Dade and Palm Beach • Tennis player Chris Evert • Extensive winter vegetable market; business and retail centers; large planned retirement communities; light manufacturing; major tourism; education (FL Atlantic U.; FL Metro U.; Fort Lauderdale College; Nova U.) • Fort Lauderdale's Port Everglades is the deepest harbor on the Atlantic coast south of Norfolk VA. A port of entry, it ranks with Jacksonville and Tampa in volume of cargo handled, especially tanker-borne fuel. Fort Lauderdale continues to be a major spring break destination for thousands of vacationing college students. The International Swimming Hall of Fame is in the city. Sunrise is home to the Florida Panthers professional hockey team (Office Depot Center).

CALHOUN *Blountstown* • 13,017 • 567 • Northwestern FL, in the panhandle, bounded on the east by the Apalachicola River; drained by the Chipola River. The county includes the northern end of Dead Lake reservoir. • One of eleven counties named for John C. Calhoun (1782–1850), U.S. statesman and champion of Southern causes • 1838 (prior to statehood) from Jackson • Corn, peanuts, sugarcane, vegetables, hogs, cattle; lumber, naval stores; clay pits.

CHARLOTTE (one of two counties so named, the other in VA) *Punta Gorda* • 141,627 • 694 • Southwestern FL, bounded on the west by the Gulf of Mexico (Charlotte Harbor). The county is sparsely populated inland; most of its residents live on Charlotte Harbor or on the Gulf. Don Pedro Island State Recreation Area and Island Bay National Wildlife Refuge are here. • Named for Charlotte Harbor, itself named for Queen Charlotte, wife of King George III. • 1921 from DeSoto • The county is a major retirement center; also cattle, vegetables; fishing; tourism.

CITRUS *Inverness* • 118,085 • 584 • West-central FL, bounded on the west by the Gulf of Mexico and on the north and east by the Withlacoochee River. The county contains Tsala Apopka Lake, and the Homosassa Islands off its swampy coast. Withlacoochee State Forest is in the south. Crystal River and part of Chassahowitzka national wildlife refuges are also here. Fort Cooper State Park is in the east. • Named for the major agricultural crop of the area • 1887 from Hernando • Located near Crystal River, Crystal River State Archeological Site was active from 200 BC–1400 AD, making it one of the longest continually occupied sites in Florida. • Corn, peanuts, citrus fruits, cattle, hogs; fishing; lumbering; quarrying of phosphate, limestone and clay • The geographical center of Florida is in this county. The Ted Williams Museum and Hitters Hall of Fame honors Williams along with the best of baseball's best batters.

CLAY (one of eighteen counties so named) *Green Cove Springs* • 140,814 • 601 • Northeastern FL, bounded on the east by the St. Johns River. Jennings State Forest and Mike Roess Gold Head Branch State Park are here, as is Camp Blanding Training Site. The county has many small lakes in the southwest. • One of fifteen counties named for Henry Clay (1777–1852), U.S. senator from KY, known as the "Great Pacificator" for his advocacy of compromise to avert national crises • 1858 from Duval • Investment banker Charles E. Merrill • Livestock, dairying, corn, vegetables, peanuts; lumbering; clay pits.

COLLIER *Naples* • 251,377 (65% increase since 1990; the third fastest growing county in FL) • 2,025 (the largest county in FL) • Southwestern FL, bounded on the west by the Gulf of Mexico. The Everglades and Big Cypress Swamp (Big Cypress National Preserve) are prominent in the east. Okaloacoochee Slough State Forest is in the north. The county's population is centered around Naples on the coast. It is ancestral home to the Seminoles who have reservations here. Ten Thousand Islands dot the southwest coast. • Named for Barron G. Collier (1873–1939), advertising tycoon and a promoter active in the development of southern FL • 1923 from Lee and Monroe • Truck farming; fishing; lumbering; oil wells; tourism; education (International College) • The Corkscrew Swamp Sanctuary has the largest nesting colony of wood storks in North America. Sunniland was the site of the first oil wells in FL. Excavations in the 1970s revealed a civilization, characterized by enormous shell mounds possibly dating from 3500 B.C., and perhaps ancestral to the Calusa Indians.

COLUMBIA (one of eight counties so named) *Lake City* • 56,513 • 797 • Northern FL, bounded on the north by the GA state line, on the northwest by the Suwannee River, and on the south by the Santa Fe River. Parts of Osceola National Forest and Big Shoals State Forest are here. O'Leno and Ichetucknee Springs state parks and River Rise State Preserve are in the south. • The county's name is a feminine form of Columbus, a poetic and honorific reference to Christopher Columbus and America • 1832 (prior to statehood) from Alachua • Lake City occupies the site of a Seminole village once ruled by a chief called Halpatter-Tustennuggee (meaning "alligator warrior"). The tribe left under the terms of an 1824 treaty. Lake City was called Alligator until 1859. • Corn, peanuts, cotton, tobacco, livestock; lumber and forestry products, naval stores; phosphate deposits; some manufacturing, including aircraft repair; tourism.

DE SOTO *Arcadia* • 32,209 • 637 • Central FL; drained by the Peace River and Horse Creek. • One of four counties named for Hernando De Soto (1500–1542), Spanish explorer of the southern U.S • 1887 from Manatee • Citrus fruits, vegetables, corn, cattle, poultry.

DIXIE *Cross City* • 13,827 • 704 • Northern FL, bounded on the south and west by the Gulf of Mexico and on the east by the Suwannee River. The county includes part of Lower Suwannee National Wildlife Refuge. • Dixie is a nickname for the south • 1921 from Lafayette • Lumbering; cattle, corn, peanuts; fishing.

DUVAL *Jacksonville* • 778,879 • 774 • Northeastern FL, bounded on the east by the Atlantic Ocean and on the north in part by the Nassau River and Thomas Creek; drained by the St. Johns River. The county is swampy in the northeast. The Timucuan Ecological and Historic Preserve north of Jacksonville includes cultural sites of the prehistoric Timucuan Indians and others associated with the Spanish American War of 1898. Jacksonville and Mayport naval stations are located in the county. Cary State Forest is on the northwest border. • Named for William P. DuVal (1784–1854), first governor of the FL Territory • 1822 from Saint Johns (prior to statehood). • The French and Spanish began two centuries of national rivalry in North America at the site of Fort Caroline (national memorial). The French Huguenot colony here (1564–65) represented the second attempt by the French to settle within the area. Jacksonville was occupied intermittently by Union troops during the Civil War. It endured a crippling yellow-fever epidemic in 1888 and widespread destruction by fire in 1901. • Writer and film producer Merian C. Cooper; poets James Weldon Johnson and George Hill Dillon; physicist John A. Wheeler • Dairying, poultry, corn, vegetables; naval stores, lumber; fishing; manufacture of pulp and paper products, furniture, machinery, cigars, drugs, fertilizers, transportation equipment; beach tourism; Jacksonville Naval Air Station and other naval installations; education (Jacksonville U.; Edward Waters College; U. of North FL). Jacksonville is a wholesale distribution center for the southeastern U.S., and FL's foremost transportation and commercial center. • When Jacksonville consolidated with most of the county in 1968, it became one of the nation's largest cities in area (851 sq. miles, including inland water). The city is home to the Jaguars (Alltel Stadium).

ESCAMBIA (one of two counties so named, the other in AL) *Pensacola* • 294,410 • 662 • Extreme northwestern FL, in the panhandle, bounded on the west by the Perdido River (forming the AL state Line), on the north by the AL state line, on the east by the Escambia River and Escambia Bay, and on the south by the Gulf of Mexico. Part of Gulf Islands National Seashore is located on the barrier islands, including Perdido Key and Big Lagoon state recreation areas. • Named for the river which forms its eastern border • Original county; organized 1822 (prior to statehood). Escambia was one of the first two counties established in FL; the other, Saint Johns • The Spanish Fort San Carlos (built 1698) was destroyed in French-

Spanish colonial fighting in 1719–20. During the American Revolution the British-dominated area was a haven for Tories, but in 1781 it was repossessed by a Spanish force from New Orleans. General Andrew Jackson captured Pensacola in 1818. It was ceded to the U.S. in 1821 and acquired a federal navy yard. Despite the occupation by Federals of Fort Pickens offshore, the city was seized by Confederates at the outbreak of the Civil War, but was evacuated in 1862. Established in 1914 in Pensacola, the U.S. Navy Aeronautic Station was the first training center for Navy pilots. (Today, all U.S. Navy pilots begin their training at the facility, which is now known as the Pensacola Naval Air Station.) • Pilot Jacqueline Cochran; Air Force officer Daniel (Chappie) James, Jr.; Creek Indian chief Alexander McGillivray • Corn, peanuts, cotton, vegetables, dairying; lumber, naval stores; commercial fishing; shipyards; diversified manufacturing, including chemicals • Pensacola celebrates the Fiesta of Five Flags, which reflects the city's colorful, multi-national history.

FLAGLER *Bunnell* • 49,832 (74% increase since 1990; the fastest growing county in FL) • 485 • Northeastern FL, bounded on the east by the Atlantic Ocean and on the west in part by Crescent Lake. The county includes Washington Oaks State Gardens and Gamble Rogers Memorial State Recreation Area. Its rapid growth since 1980 has made it the center of the "Palm Coast" coastal strip between Daytona Beach and St. Augustine. • Named for Henry M. Flagler (1830–1913), FL railroad tycoon and a leader in developing Florida's east coast as a resort area • 1917 from St. Johns and Volusia • Corn, vegetables, citrus fruit, livestock; lumber, naval stores.

FRANKLIN (one of twenty-five counties so named) *Apalachicola* • 11,057 • 544 • Northern FL, in the panhandle, bounded on the south by the Gulf of Mexico, on the west by the Apalachicola River, and on the east by the Ochlockonee River. St. Vincent, St. George, and Dog islands are separated from the mainland by Apalachicola Bay and St. George Sound. Much of the county is covered by Tate's Hell State Forest. St. Vincent National Wildlife Refuge and St. George Island State Park are also here. • One of twenty-three counties named for Benjamin Franklin • 1832 from Jackson (prior to statehood) • Apalachicola was an important shipping port from 1830 until implementation of the U.S. Civil War blockade. • Apalachicola physician John W. Gorrie is known as the father of refrigeration for his invention of a refrigerant apparatus in the 1840s to cool the rooms of his yellow-fever patients. • Commercial fishing (oysters, shrimp), fish canning; lumber and naval stores; cattle • A notable Apalachicola landmark is the Ionic-columned Old Trinity Church (1839), which was shipped in wooden sections from NY. The state's oldest maritime festival, the Florida Seafood Festival, is hosted by Apalachicola each November. St. George Island stages the largest regional chili cook-off in the U. S. in March. Carrabelle is the site of the world's smallest police station, a tiny phone booth in the city's business district.

GADSDEN *Quincy* • 45,087 • 516 • Northern FL, in the panhandle, bounded on the north by the GA state line, on the south and east by the Ochlockonee River and Lake Talquin reservoir, and on the northwest by the Apalachicola River. The county includes Lake Talquin State Forest and part of Torreya State Park. • Named for James Gadsden (1788–1858), U.S. commissioner for the removal of the FL Seminole Indians to reservations and negotiator of the Gadsden Purchase • 1823 (prior to statehood) from Jackson • Truck farming, corn, peanuts, tobacco, vegetables, dairy products, poultry, hogs; manufacture of food products, including soft drinks, cigars, cellulose, building materials; lumber; large deposits of fuller's earth, also clay, sand and gravel • The county is the site of the Florida State Hospital for the mentally ill, the largest such facility in the state, with about 6,000 patients.

GILCHRIST *Trenton* • 14,437 • 349 • North-central FL, bounded on the north by the Santa Fe River and on the west by the Suwannee River. • Named for Captain Albert W. Gilchrist (1858–1926), Spanish American War officer, FL legislator, and governor • 1925 from Alachua • Corn, vegetables, peanuts, cattle; lumbering • The county was originally to be named Melon; the name was changed to honor Gilchrist who was dying at the time of its establishment.

GLADES *Moore Haven* • 10,576 • 774 • Central FL, bounded on the east by Lake Okeechobee, the largest lake in FL; crossed by the Caloosahatchee River. The county includes Brighton Indian Reservation. • Glades is a shortened form of "Everglades" • 1921 from De Soto • Cattle, some farming and fishing.

GULF *Port Saint Joe* • 13,332 • 555 • Northern FL, in the panhandle, bounded on the south by the Gulf of Mexico and on the east by the Apalachicola River. The county is comprised of swampy lowlands, bordered by long sandpits which enclose St. Joseph Bay. It contains Lake Wimico and part of Dead Lake (state recreation area to the west). St. Joseph Peninsula State Park is located on a peninsula separated from the mainland by St. Joseph Bay. St. Joseph Aquatic Preserve is in St. Joseph Bay. Gulf is one of only a few counties in the U.S. divided by a time zone boundary, with Central in the north and Eastern in the south. • Named for the Gulf of Mexico • 1925 from Calhoun • Constitution Convention State Monument and Museum commemorates territorial FL's first State Constitutional Convention, held here in 1838. The Confederate Salt Works, located on the Cape, was the site of a major salt processing facility, later destroyed by Union troops. • Pulp harvesting, fishing.

HAMILTON (one of ten counties so named) *Jasper* • 13,327 • 515 • Northern FL, bounded on the north by the GA state line, on the south and east by the Suwannee River, and on the west by the Withlacoochee River; drained by the Alapaha River. The county includes Suwannee River State Park. • One of eight counties named for Alexander Hamilton • 1827 from Duval (prior to statehood) • Before settlement in 1826, White Springs was held sacred by local Indians who came here to recuperate after battle. The area was known as "Rebel's Refuge" during the Civil War after many plantation owners moved here to remove themselves from Union invasion routes. White Springs was promoted for the medicinal properties of its spring waters in the early 20th century. • Corn, peanuts, cotton, tobacco, vegetables, hogs, cattle; lumbering; phosphate mining • White Springs is the headquarters of the Suwannee River Water Management District. The Stephen Foster State Folk Culture Center holds the Florida Folk Festival each May. A 200-foot tower at the Foster Memorial houses a 97-bell carillon that plays the composer's works each day.

HARDEE *Wauchula* • 26,938 • 637 • Central FL; drained by the Peace River and Horse Creek. The county includes Paynes Creek State Historic Site. • Named for Cary A. Hardee (1876–1957), governor of FL • 1921 from DeSoto • Citrus fruits, strawberries, cattle, poultry.

HENDRY *La Belle* • 36,210 • 1,153 • South-central FL, touching Lake Okeechobee in the northeast; crossed in the northwest corner by the Caloosahatchee River. The county is located in the Everglades. Seminole Big Cypress Indian Reservation is in the southeast, and includes Ah-Tah-Thi-Ki Museum. • Named for Captain Francis A. Hendry (1833–1917), the "Cattle King of South Florida" • 1923 from Calhoun • Sugar cane, cattle.

HERNANDO *Brooksville* • 130,802 • 478 • West-central FL, bounded on the northeast by the Withlacoochee River and on the west by the Gulf of Mexico. Part of Withlacoochee State Forest, including McKethan Lake Recreation Area, is also here. A portion of the Chassahowitzka National Wildlife Refuge is in the northwest • One of four counties named for Hernando De Soto (1500–1542), Spanish explorer of southern U.S. • 1843 (prior to statehood). The name was changed to Benton in 1844 and back to Hernando in 1850. • Poultry, cattle, hogs, corn, citrus fruit, peanuts; sawmilling; limestone quarrying.

HIGHLANDS *Sebring* • 87,366 • 1,028 • Central FL, bounded on the east by the Kissimmee River; drained by Fisheating Creek. It has many lakes, including Istokpoga. Highlands Hammock State Park is in the west. The southeastern corner lies in the Everglades. The southern half of Avon Park Air Force Range is here. • Named for its perceived rolling terrain • 1921 from DeSoto • Librarian Melvil Dewey died here. • Citrus fruit, cattle, vegetables, poultry; pottery manufacturing • The annual International Grand Prix Sports Car Race takes place every March in Sebring.

HILLSBOROUGH *Tampa* • 998,948 (the fourth most populated county in FL) • 1,051 • West-central FL; bounded on the south and southwest by Tampa Bay, constituting part of the Gulf of Mexico; drained by the Hillsborough River (Hillsborough River State Park) and Alafia River. The county has many small lakes, especially in the northwest. It is becoming increasingly urbanized as part of the metropolitan Tampa area. MacDill Air Force base is south of the city. • Named for Hillsborough Bay, itself named for Wills Hill, Earl of Hillsborough (1718–93); one of two counties, the other in NH, named

directly or indirectly for the earl. • 1834 (prior to statehood) from Alachua and Monroe • Explorers Juan Ponce de León, Pánfilo de Narváez and Hernando de Soto all visited the site of Tampa in the 1520s and 1530s. The military post of Fort Brooke was established here in 1824 to oversee the removal of the Seminole Indians. The city was captured by the Union Navy during the Civil War. Cigar manufacturing was introduced to Tampa in 1886 by Vincente M. Ybor; cigars are still made in Tampa's Latin quarter, Ybor City. Tampa was the chief port of embarkation for troops bound for Cuba during the Spanish-American War in 1898. Theodore Roosevelt made the Tampa Hotel his headquarters. • English novelist and travel writer Alice Waugh died here. • Citrus fruit, tomatoes, strawberries, peanuts, corn, dairying, poultry; fishing, especially shrimping; food and tobacco processing. Tampa is one of the most industrialized cities in the state. Its manufactures include fabricated steel, electronic equipment, cigars, beer, paint, fertilizer, wood products; phosphate (Tampa is a leading phosphate-shipping port), sand, shells; education (U. of Southern FL; U. of Tampa; FL Metro U.–Tampa College, Brandon). • The city's Gasparilla festival each February includes a pirate invasion of the old port city. • Tampa is home to the Buccaneers (Raymond James Stadium). The Tampa Bay Lightning play at the Ice Palace.

HOLMES (one of three counties so named) *Bonifay* • 18,564 • 482 • Northwestern FL, in the panhandle, bounded on the north by the AL state line and on the east by Holmes Creek; drained by the Choctawhatchee River • Named for Holmes Creek • 1848 from Walton and Calhoun • Corn, peanuts, cotton, vegetables, livestock; lumber, naval stores • The Ponce de Leon Springs State Recreation Area contains a large spring that is often referred to by locals as the "The Fountain of Youth."

INDIAN RIVER *Vero Beach* • 112,947 • 503 • Eastern FL, bounded on the east by the Atlantic Ocean. Its barrier beach encloses Indian River lagoon. The interior of the county is marshy peat surrounding Blue Cypress Lake. The county is part of the Indian River citrus growing district. When established by President Theodore Roosevelt in 1903, Pelican Island National Wildlife Refuge became the first federal wildlife refuge in the U.S. • Named for the Indian River • 1925 from Saint Lucie • Industrial designer Donald Deskey died here. • Citrus fruits, especially oranges; other farm produce, sugarcane, cattle; tourism; light industry • Vero Beach is the site of the Los Angeles Dodgers' training base.

JACKSON (one of twenty-four counties so named) *Marianna* • 46,755 • 916 • Northwestern FL, in the panhandle, bounded on the north by the AL state line, on the northwest by Holmes Creek, and on the east by the Chattahoochee River, forming the GA state line; drained by the Chipola River. The county includes Florida Caverns State Park and Three Rivers State Recreation Area on the western shore of Lake Seminole reservoir. • One of twenty-two counties named directly or indirectly for President Andrew Jackson • 1822 (prior to statehood) from Escambia. In 1834 it annexed Fayette County, which was organized in 1832. • Black American journalist T. Thomas Fortune • Peanuts, corn, cotton, vegetables, hogs; food product manufacturing; limestone quarrying.

JEFFERSON *Monticello* • 12,902 • 598 • Northern FL, in the panhandle, bounded on the north by the GA state line, on the south by the Gulf of Mexico, and on the east in part by the Aucilla River. The county contains part of St. Marks National Wildlife Refuge along the coast. Lake Miccosukee is in the northwest. • One of twenty-six counties named directly or indirectly for President Thomas Jefferson • 1827 (prior to statehood) from Leon • Corn, peanuts, cotton, vegetables, tung nuts, hogs, cattle; lumber; naval stores.

LAFAYETTE (one of six counties so named) *Mayo* • 7,022 • (The county is virtually tied with Liberty for FL county with the least number of people [Liberty: 7,021; Lafayette: 7,022].) • 543 • North-central FL, bounded on the east and northeast by the Suwannee River. • One of seventeen counties named for the Marquis de Lafayette (1757–1834), French statesman and soldier who fought with Americans during the Revolutionary War • 1856 from Madison • Corn, peanuts, tobacco, cattle; lumbering; limestone, phosphate deposits.

LAKE (one of twelve counties so named) *Tavares* • 210,528 • 953 • Central FL, bounded on the northeast by the St. Johns River. The county is characterized by rolling terrain with more than 500 lakes of 10 acres or more spread throughout. Ocala National Forest extends into the northeastern corner. • Named for its many lakes • 1887 from Orange and Sumter • Stock car racer Glenn "Fireball" Roberts • Citrus fruits, vegetables, grapes, watermelons, corn, peanuts, cotton, poultry; canneries and packing houses; manufacture of house trailers, furniture, wooden and cardboard boxes, frozen fruit juices.

LEE (one of twelve counties so named) *Fort Myers* • 440,888 • 804 • Southwestern FL, bounded on the west by the Gulf of Mexico; drained by the Caloosahatchee River. The county, located in a lowland area and swampy in the southeast, is bordered by a chain of barrier islands sheltering several lagoons and Pine Island. It is rapidly urbanizing. Caloosahatchee, Pine Island, and J.N. "Ding" Darling national wildlife refuges, and Lower Key State Recreational Area are here. Mound Key State Archeological Site is located on a barrier island. • One of eight counties named for Robert E. Lee • 1887 from Monroe • The side-by-side winter estates of Henry Ford and Thomas Edison are located in Fort Myers. • Gladioli, chrysanthemums, citrus fruits, vegetables, cattle; commercial fishing, including shrimping; resort tourism (water sports, fishing); retirement centers; education (FL Gulf Coast U.) • The Bailey-Matthews Shell Museum, located on Sanibel Island, is the only museum of its kind in the U.S. Fort Myers is called the "City of Palms" for the many royal palms that line its streets. The city holds a seven-day Pageant of Light each February in honor of Thomas Edison's seasonal residency here. Fort Myers is also the western terminus of the cross-state Okeechobee Waterway, which links the Atlantic Ocean and the Gulf of Mexico.

LEON (one of two counties so named, the other in TX) • *Tallahassee* (also state capital) • 239,452 • 667 • Northern FL, in the panhandle, bounded on the north by the GA state line and on the northwest by the Ochlockonee River (here forming Lake Talquin). Part of Apalachicola National Forest is here, and includes Rocky Bluff Scenic Area and Leon Sinks Geological Area. Maclay State Gardens and Lake Jackson Mounds Archeological Site are also here. • Named for Juan Ponce de Leon (1460–1521), Spanish colonial governor and explorer of Florida while in search of the "fountain of youth." • 1824 (prior to statehood) from Gadsden • Several Francisco missions were established in the area, with their headquarters at Fort San Luis (1633). The fort was destroyed by Governor James Moore of SC during Queen Anne's War (1702–13) to punish the Spanish who had been fomenting Indian attacks against English settlers. Tallahassee was selected as capital of FL Territory in 1824 because of its central location between previous joint capitals St. Augustine and Pensacola. Although the county was the scene of a Civil War engagement on March 6, 1865 at Natural Bridge (state historic site), Tallahassee was the only Confederate capital east of the Mississippi River not captured by Union forces. The FL Supreme Court in Tallahassee was a major player in the 2000 Presidential Election saga. • Prince Achille Murat, nephew of Napoleon I and his wife Catherine Willis, great-grandniece of George Washington. Sociologist William F. Ogburn died here. • Corn, peanuts, cotton, vegetables, cattle, hogs, poultry, dairy products; forestry, lumbering; some manufacturing; education (FL A and M Univ.; FL State U.).

LEVY *Bronson* • 34,450 • 1,118 • Northern FL, bounded on the southwest by the Gulf of Mexico, on the west by the Suwannee River, and on the south by the Withlacoochee River. The county includes part of Lower Suwanee National Wildlife Refuge, as well as Cedar Keys National Wildlife Refuge. Part of Goethe State Forest is in the southeast. Waccasassa Bay State Preserve and Cedar Key Scrub State Reserve are also here. • Named for David Levy (Yulee) (1810–86), West Indian-born, one of the first two U.S. senators from FL • 1845 from Alachua and Marion • Hogs, cattle, corn, vegetables, peanuts; lumbering; fishing; some quarrying of limestone and dolomite.

LIBERTY (one of four counties so named) *Bristol* • 7,021 (virtually tied with Lafayette County [pop. 7,022] as the least populated county in FL) • 836 • Northern FL, in the panhandle, bounded on the east by the Ochlockonee River and on the west by the Apalachicola River; drained by the New River. The southern half of the county is included in Apalachicola National Forest. Torreya State Park is in the north. • The county was given this name to honor the objective of the nation's founding fathers. • 1855 from Franklin and Gadsden • Lumber; livestock, corn, peanuts.

MADISON *Madison* • 18,733 • 692 • Northern FL, bounded on the west by the Aucilla River, on the northeast by the Withlacoochee River, and on the southeast by the

Suwannee River. The county includes part of Twin Rivers State Forest. • One of twenty counties named directly or indirectly for President James Madison • 1827 (prior to statehood) from Jefferson • Army officer Colin P. Kelly • Corn, peanuts, cotton, tobacco, hogs, poultry; lumber, naval stores.

MANATEE *Bradenton* • 264,002 • 741 • West-central FL, bounded on the west by the Gulf of Mexico and Tampa Bay; drained by the Manatee and Myakka rivers. Lakes are scattered throughout the county. Lake Manatee State Recreation Area is in the center. The county contains part of Sarasota Bay and small offshore islands, including Ann Maria Key. Passage Key National Wildlife Refuge is here. Part of Myakka River State Park is in the south. • Named for the manatee, or sea cow • 1855 from Hillsborough • The (Hernando) De Soto National Memorial west of Bradenton marks the spot of the explorer's probable landing in FL in 1539. • Confederate vice president, secretary of war, and secretary of state Judah P. Benjamin (his Gamble Mansion is FL's chief Confederate shrine.) • Citrus fruits, dairying, poultry; some fishing and lumbering; light industries, including boat building.

MARION *Ocala* • 258,916 • 1,579 (the fifth largest county in FL) • North-central FL, bounded on the northeast by the Oklawaha River and on the southwest by the Withlacoochee River. The county includes lakes Weir and Kerr. Part of Ocala National Forest is in the east. The city of Ocala is a regional headquarters of the U.S. and FL forest services. Silver River and Rainbow Springs state parks are here. • One of seventeen counties named for Gen. Francis Marion (c. 1732–1795), SC soldier and legislator, known as "The Swamp Fox" for his tactics during the Revolutionary War • 1844 (prior to statehood) from Alachua • Outlaw gang matriarch Ma Barker died here. • Citrus fruits, vegetables, corn, cotton, tobacco, tung nuts, peanuts, poultry, cattle, hogs, thoroughbred horses; lumber, naval stores; quarrying of limestone and phosphate; dairy products; manufacture of mobile homes, boxes, crates, hampers; tourism • Rainbow Springs and Silver Springs offer glass-bottom boat excursions. Silver Springs, a collection of more than 100 springs, discharges about 530,000,000 gallons of water a day, and contains more than 480 tons of minerals.

MARTIN (one of six counties so named) *Stuart* • 126,731 • 556 • Southeastern FL, bounded on the west by Lake Okeechobee and on the east by the Atlantic Ocean. The county is partly sheltered on the east by Jupiter Island (barrier beach). It is located in a lowland area, with swamps and many small lakes in the west. The county is crossed by St. Lucie Canal. • Named for John W. Martin (1884–1958), governor of FL • 1925 from Palm Beach • Physicist Arthur J. Dempster died here. • Produce, citrus fruits, cattle; fishing • The Maritime and Yachting Museum is located in Stuart. The Hobe Sound National Wildlife Refuge and Nature Center is a popular nesting site for sea turtles. The Barley Barber Swamp, a 400-acre freshwater cypress swamp preserve is located in Indiantown.

MIAMI-DADE *Miami* • 2,253,362 (the most populated county in FL and the eighth most populated county in the U.S.) • 1,946 (the third largest county in FL) • Southeastern FL, bounded by the FL Keys, enclosing Biscayne Bay on the east and part of Florida Bay, on the south. The coastal fringe is heavily urbanized as part of the Miami metropolitan area, and serves as southern anchor to the string of resort and retirement communities that populate the "Gold" coastline. The interior lies in the Everglades and includes part of Everglades National Park, the largest remaining subtropic wilderness in the coterminous U.S. Homestead Air Force Reserve Base is in the south. • The name Miami comes from the city of Miami, itself named for the Miami River. The county is one of three named in part or in full for Major Francis L. Dade (?–1835), U.S. army officer killed in the Seminole War. The name was changed from Dade to Miami-Dade in 1997. • 1836 (prior to statehood) from Monroe • Coconut Grove, South Florida's first settlement, was founded in the 1880s by New England intellectuals and Blacks from the Bahamas. Miami was founded in 1896, the same year that railroad builder Henry M. Flagler extended his Florida East Coast Railroad into the area. A real estate boom in the 1920s was dampened by destructive hurricanes in 1926 and 1928. When Fidel Castro became dictator of Cuba in 1959, hundreds of thousands of Cubans fled to Miami. In the late 1970s the city received a heavy infusion of Haitian refugees along with immigrants from other Central and South American countries. A race riot in 1980 left seventeen dead and over $100 million in damage. In August, 1992, Hurricane Andrew, the most expensive natural disaster to hit the U.S., devastated the community of Homestead. Financial woes plagued Miami in the 1990s. • Attorney general Janet Reno; baseball pitcher Steve Carlton; actor Sidney Poitier. Chicago mayor Anton J. Cermak was assassinated here in an attempt on the life of President-Elect Franklin D. Roosevelt. Industrialist Harvey S. Firestone, civil rights leader Adam Clayton Powell, Jr., Confederate military leader John Brown Gordon, Jewish scholar Meyer Waxman, Yiddish writer Isaac Bashevis Singer, crime syndicate head Meyer Lansky, pianist Harold Bauer, and presidential candidate Thomas E. Dewey all died here. • Truck vegetables, citrus fruit; manufacture of food and wood products, construction materials, textiles, aircraft, solid-propellant rocket fuels, pharmaceuticals, furniture, metal goods, clothing, transportation equipment; commercial fishing; tourism; education (FL International U.; Barry U.; U. of Miami; FL Mem. College; St. Thomas U.) The Latin American corporate headquarters of a number of major oil and manufacturing companies are in the county. • In 1925, William Randolph Hearst purchased a 12th century Spanish Monastery of St. Bernard de Clairvaux, and had it reassembled in Miami. The National Hurricane Center of the National Weather Service is in Sweetwater. Miami Beach, designated an Art Deco National Historic District, has the world's largest concentration of art deco-styled buildings. Aircraft designer Glenn Curtiss founded Opa-locka in 1926 with hopes that it would resemble a town in the *Arabian Nights*, and some of it does. Coral Gables is known for its unique "villages" in various international styles. Hialeah RaceTrack (which opened in 1925) became known for its flamingos and elaborate landscaping. On August 8, 1933, the First Federal Savings and Loan Association of Miami became the first such association in the U.S. Miami is home to the Florida Marlins and Dolphins (Pro Player Stadium) and Heat (American Airlines Arena).

MONROE *Key West* • 79,589 • 997 • Southwestern FL, at the tip of the peninsula. The county consists of part of the Everglades area and includes Cape Sable, Whitewater Bay, part of Everglades National Park, part of Big Cypress National Preserve, and all of the Florida Keys enclosing Florida Bay. • One of seventeen counties named for President James Monroe • 1823 (prior to statehood) from Saint Johns • In 1822, Key West was occupied by U.S. forces under Matthew C. Perry. A naval depot was established by David Porter to combat pirates. Much of Key West was destroyed by fire in 1886. The ambitious Florida East Coast Railroad uniting the keys, begun in 1912 by Henry M. Flagler, resulted in great loss of life among its construction force, and was ultimately destroyed by the 1935 Hurricane. • Novelist Ernest Hemingway; President Harry S. Truman (retreat); Cuban poet Cintio Vitier. Novelist and journalist John Hershey died here. • Fishing; dairying, poultry, limes; significant tourism • An inmate of Fort Jefferson, which occupies most of Garden Key in Dry Tortugas National Park, was Dr. Samuel Mudd, implicated in the Lincoln assassination plot. Connected by forty-two bridges, the Overseas Highway, running from the mainland to Key West, is the longest overwater road in the world. The John Pennekamp Coral Reef State Park, the first underseas park in the U.S., contains the largest living coral formations in North America. The National Key Deer Refuge on Big Pine Key is sanctuary for the tiny key deer. More than 600 varieties of fish swim in the waters of the keys.

NASSAU (one of two counties so named, the other in NY) *Fernandina Beach* • 57,663 • 652 • Extreme northeastern FL, bounded on the east by the Atlantic Ocean, on the north and west by St. Mary's River (forming the GA state line), and on the south by the Nassau River. The county is in a lowland area with Amelia barrier island in the east, and includes Amelia Island State Recreation Area. Fort Clinch State Park is on the coast. Part of Cary State Forest is also here. • Named for the Nassau River, which forms part of the boundary between Nassau and Duval counties • 1824 (prior to statehood) from Duval • Fernandina Beach is located on a site occupied by the Timucuan Indians until the French, and later, the Spanish, around 1680, built a fort and mission here. Control shifted to the British in 1673 and a large number of Tories settled here during the American Revolution. With the return of Spanish control, the settlement became a haven for slave traders, pirates, and smugglers; it became a free port in 1808, was held by Scottish military adventurer St. Gregor MacGregor, then claimed for Mexico by pirate Luis Aury. The U.S. took formal possession after 1821. Seized by Confederates in 1861, Fort Clinch

(State Park) was a staging area for blockade running until its capture by a Union naval force in 1862. • Poultry, dairying, corn; naval stores, lumber, pulp and paper milling; fishing (crab and shrimp); production of fish oil, fertilizer, and livestock feed • Fernandina Beach is FL's northern entry point to the Atlantic Intracoastal Waterway.

OKALOOSA *Crestview* • 170,498 • 936 • Northwestern FL, in the panhandle, bounded on the north by the AL state line and on the southwest by the Gulf of Mexico; drained by the Blackwater, Yellow and Shoal rivers. It includes part of Blackwater River State Forest; covering 183,153 acres, it is the largest state forest in FL. The southern half of the county lies within the boundaries of Eglin Air Force Base, one of the largest air force installations in the world, encompassing over 724 square miles. Fred Gannon Rocky Bayou and Henderson Beach state recreation areas are also here. • Okaloosa is possibly the Choctaw name for the Blackwater River • 1915 from Santa Rosa and Walton • Corn, peanuts, cotton, hogs, cattle, poultry; commercial and sport fishing, tourism; manufacture of electronic equipment, lumber, concrete, brick • The Old Spanish Trail Festival, held in the spring, commemorates the 16th century trade route between El Paso, TX and Jacksonville, FL.

OKEECHOBEE *Okeechobee* • 35,910 • 774 • Central FL, bounded on the west by the Kissimmee River and on the south by Lake Okeechobee. • Named for Lake Okeechobee • 1917 from Osceola and Palm Beach • Cattle, poultry, vegetables.

ORANGE (one of eight counties so named) *Orlando* • 896,344 • 907 • Central FL, bounded on the east by the St. Johns River. The county is heavily urbanized as a result of recent expansion of the Orlando metropolitan area. It contains many lakes, most notably Lake Apopka on the northwest border. • Named for the orange groves in the area • Organized as Mosquito County, 1824 (prior to statehood) from Indian lands; name changed 1845 • Settlement in the area began around 1844 with the establishment of Fort Gatlin, an army post. With the development of the Cape Canaveral Aerospace complex sixty miles east, and the establishment of Walt Disney World southwest of the city, Orlando experienced a major boost to its economy and accelerated population growth. • Folklorist and writer Zora Neale Hurston. Methodist evangelist John R. Mott and novelist Winston Churchill died here. • Substantial citrus fruit-growing, winter vegetables, small scale farming, dairying, poultry; manufacture of aerospace and high-tech electronics, food products; education (Rollins College; U. of Central FL). The county is a national recreation destination with a wide variety of attractions, the Disney complex alone covering some 28,000 acres. There are many government installations in the county. • The loose-skinned mandarin type Temple orange was first cultivated in Winter Park. Orlando is home to the Orlando Magic professional basketball team (American Airlines Arena).

OSCEOLA *Kissimmee* • 172,493 • 1,322 • Central FL,

bounded on the southwest by the Kissimmee River (here forming Lake Kissimmee). The county contains numerous lakes, especially in the northwest, including Tohopekaliga and East Tohopekaliga. It is sparsely settled except for its northeastern corner, constituting part of the Orlando metropolitan area. • One of three counties named for Osceola (?–1838), the Seminole leader • 1887 from Brevard and Orange • Citrus fruit, vegetables, cattle; lumber; tourism (The city of Kissimmee is a gateway to Walt Disney World and other local attractions, many in Orange County to the north.) • The Silver Spurs Rodeo is held in Kissimmee every February and July. The Monument of the States, a pyramidal structure built in stones from each of the 50 states is a popular Kissimmee attraction. Many of the large galleried frame houses built by wealthy cattlemen in the early 20th century are preserved in the city.

PALM BEACH *West Palm Beach* • 1,131,184 (the third most populated county in FL) • 1,974 (the second largest county in FL) • Southeastern FL, bounded on the east by the Atlantic Ocean. The county is heavily urbanized for ten miles inland from the coast, and constitutes the fastest growing part of the southeastern FL (Gold Coast) megalopolis. Lake Okeechobee to the northwest is linked by several drainage canals to the Atlantic Ocean. Arthur R. Marshall Loxahatchee National Wildlife Refuge is southeast. • Named for the town of Palm Beach • 1909 from Dade • Palm Beach earned its name from an 1878 shipwrecked cargo of coconuts that washed up on its beach and took root. Riviera was settled in the 1920s by descendants of fishermen who had left the Bahamas during World War I and relocated on Singer's Island, opposite the site. Boca Raton was incorporated in 1925 after the architect Addison Mizner promoted a luxury resort centering on the extravagant Cloister Inn. A devastating hurricane hit the county in 1928 causing widespread damage and killing hundreds, especially in Belle Glade. Most of the beach resort communities in the county benefited economically from the extension of Henry Flagler's Florida East Coast Railroad. • Industrialist Meyer Guggenheim, WW I Canadian flying ace William A. Bishop, financier and developer Henry M. Flagler, theatrical manager Edward F. Albee, and journalist Kent Cooper all died in the county. • Winter vegetables, flowers, sugarcane, cattle, dairying, poultry; resort tourism; manufacture of food and wood products, fertilizers, cattle feed, crates, wooden boxes; commercial and sports fishing; electronics and engineering industries; education (FL Atlantic U.; Lynn U.) • Lake Worth's municipally owned pier, with a length of 1,000 feet, is the longest on FL's east coast.

PASCO *Dade City* • 344,765 • 745 • West-central FL, bounded on the west by the Gulf of Mexico. The county has experienced substantial urbanization as Tampa has expanded from the south. It has many small lakes. • Named for Samuel Pasco (1834–1917), English-born FL legislator and U.S. senator • 1887 from Hernando • Citrus fruits, poultry, cattle; education (Trinity College of FL; St. Leo U.).

PINELLAS *Clearwater* • 921,482 (the fifth most populated

county in FL) • 280 • West-central FL. The county is largely a peninsula (the Pinellas peninsula) between the Gulf of Mexico to the west and Tampa Bay to the east; it is bordered on the west by a chain of barrier islands. It includes Honeymoon Island State Recreation Area, Caladesi Island State Park, Brooker Creek Preserve, and Pinellas National Wildlife Refuge. Lake Tarpon is in the north. The county is largely urbanized. • Named for Pinellas Peninsula and Point Pinellas, which were derived from Spanish punta pinal, "point of pines" • 1911 from Hillsborough • The natural sponge industry in Tarpon Springs, established in 1890, became one of the world's largest; at its peak it comprised more than 200 boats. In the late 1940s St. Petersburg became one of the first FL cities to encourage tourists to spend their retirement years there. • Author and reformer George W. Cable, poet and novelist Jack Kerouac, art critic Sadakichi Hartmann, and baseball umpire and football player Cal Hubbard all died here. • Canning, packing, shipping of citrus fruits; fish canning; wood processing, remnant sponge-fishing; tourism. Manufacture of sail boats and yachts, electronics; education (Eckerd College). • Formerly, the county manufactured nuclear weapons parts. St. Petersburg is home to the Tampa Bay Devil Rays (Tropicana Field).

POLK (one of twelve counties so named) *Bartow* • 483,924 • 1,874 (the fourth largest county in FL) • Central FL, bounded on the east by the Kissimmee River and partly on the north by the Withlacoochee River; drained by the Peace River. The county is located in a hilly lake region; lakes include Hancock, Hamilton, Hatchineha, Weohyakapka and Crooked. There are swamps in the north. The northern half of Avon Park Air Force Range is in the south. The county also includes General James A. Van Fleet State Trail, A.D. Broussard Catfish Creek State Preserve, and Lake Wales Ridge State Forest. Lake Kissimmee State Park is on the eastern border. • One of eleven counties named for President James Knox Polk • 1861 from Brevard and Hillsborough • Editor Edward Bok and football player Red Grange died here. • The county is located in a major citrus-fruit growing and phosphate-mining center; also truck farming, vegetables, strawberries, corn, cattle, poultry; education (Webber College; FL Southern College, with a large group of buildings designed by Frank Lloyd Wright); tourism • Mountain Lake Sanctuary, on the slopes of Iron Mountain (at 324 feet, the highest point in peninsular FL) is known for its bird life, as well as for the (Edward) Bok Singing Tower with its carillon of fifty-seven bells. The Bone Valley Phosphate Museum near Bartow traces the history of the phosphate industry. Winter Haven attracts visitors to its Slocum Water Gardens, Cypress Gardens, and Florida Citrus Showcase.

PUTNAM (one of nine counties so named) *Palatka* • 70,423 • 722 • Northeastern FL; drained by the St. Johns River. The county is in a lake and swamp area, which includes part of Lake George and part of Crescent Lake. Etoniah Creek State Forest and Ravine State Gardens are also here. • Named for either General Benjamin A. Putnam (1801–69), officer in the Seminole Indian War and surveyor-general of FL; or for Israel Putnam (1718–1790), major-general in the Continental Army • 1849 from Alachua, Duval, Marion, Mosquito (now Orange) and Saint Johns • Army officer Joseph (Uncle Joe) W. Stilwell; trade unionist and civil-rights leader A. Philip Randolph • Corn, vegetables, peanuts, citrus fruit, poultry, livestock; lumber, naval stores; fishing; kaolin, peat, sand; resort tourism.

SAINT JOHNS *Saint Augustine* • 123,135 • 609 • Northeastern FL, bounded on the west by the St. Johns River and on the east by the Atlantic Ocean. The county lies in a partly swampy lowland area. Anastasia State Recreation Area is on Anastasia Island (a barrier beach). Faver-Dykes State Park is on the southern border. • Named for the St. Johns River • Original county; organized 1822 (prior to statehood). It was one of the first two counties established in FL (the other, Escambia). • St. Augustine is the oldest continuously settled city in the U.S. Ponce de León landed here in 1513 in search of the legendary Fountain of Youth and claimed the area for Spain. Admiral Pedro Menéndez de Avilés founded the city in 1565. Throughout the 256 years that followed except for the years 1763 to 1783 in which FL belonged to England, St. Augustine was the northernmost outpost of the Spanish colonial empire. The imposing Castillo de San Marcos, constructed in 1672, is the oldest standing fort in the U.S. (now a national monument). In 1821, St. Augustine became part of the U.S. The city was plundered by the English sea raider Sir Francis Drake. It was a refuge for Tories during the American Revolution. During the Indian wars it served as a prison for captured Seminole Indians, including Osceola. During the last three years of the Civil War it was occupied by Union troops. • Army officer Edmund Kirby-Smith. Artist Randolph Caldecott and author Marjorie Kinnan Rawlings died here. • Corn, potatoes, vegetables, poultry, dairy products; commercial fishing; naval stores, lumber; railroad shops; education (Flagler College); tourism • San Augustín Antiguo in St. Augustine is a re-creation of the old Spanish city. • Fort Matanzas (National Monument) was built by the Spanish in 1740–42 to warn St. Augustine of the approach from the south of the British and other enemies.

SAINT LUCIE *Fort Pierce* • 192,695 • 572 • Eastern FL, bounded on the east by the Atlantic Ocean. The county is largely swampy with most of its population concentrated along the coast. A barrier beach encloses Indian River lagoon. Saint Lucie has experienced recent urban growth as part of Florida's "Treasure Coast." The federally maintained Port of Fort Pierce is on the Atlantic Intracoastal Waterway. • Named for an old Spanish Fort Santa Lucia, itself named for Saint Lucy, early Christian martyr • The state's first county by this name was organized in 1844 (prior to statehood) from Mosquito; name changed to Brevard, 1855. The present-day Saint Lucie County was organized from Brevard, 1905. • Fort Pierce was built 1838–42 during the Seminole War. Permanent white settle-

ment began in the 1860s. • Folklorist and writer Zora Neale Hurston died here. • Citrus, tomatoes, cattle, poultry; commercial fishing, including shrimping; boating, tourism • The Manatee Observatory and Education Center, dedicated to preserving the endangered species, offers viewing of manatees in their natural habitat during the winter months. During June and July, sea turtles can be found nesting along the beaches of the county. Since 1959, salvaging operations offshore have yielded large quantities of gold and silver coins, bullion, artifacts, and relics from a sunken Spanish "Silver Fleet," lost in a 1715 hurricane.

SANTA ROSA *Milton* • 117,743 • 1,017 • Northwestern FL, in the panhandle, bounded on the north by the GA state line, on the south by the Gulf of Mexico, and on the west by the Escambia River; drained by the Blackwater and Yellow rivers. The county includes part of Pensacola Bay and Santa Rosa Sound, as well as part of Gulf Islands National Seashore. A large portion of Blackwater River State Forest is in the northeast. At 183,153 acres, it is the largest state forest in FL. Eglin Air Force Base, one of the largest air force installations in the world, is prominent in the southeast, south of the Yellow River. • Named for Santa Rosa Island, which lies off its southern coast, itself named for Santa Rose of Viterbo, a Christian saint • 1842 (prior to statehood) from Escambia • Corn, peanuts, cotton, vegetables, livestock; lumber, naval stores. • The world's longest fishing pier is in Gulf Breeze.

SARASOTA *Sarasota* • 325,957 • 572 • West-central FL, bounded on the west by the Gulf of Mexico; drained by the Myakka River. The county lies in a lowland area with its coastal section bordered by barrier beaches and Sarasota Bay. It is heavily urbanized in the west. Part of the Myakka River State Park is in the east. Oscar Scherer State Park is also here. • The derivation of the county's name is uncertain. • 1921 from Manatee • Sarasota was popularized as a resort by Chicago socialite and cattle rancher Bertha Palmer. In 1927, John Ringling selected the city as winter headquarters for the Ringling Brothers and Barnum and Bailey Circus. It moved to Venice in 1960. • Circus clown Emmett Kelly died here. • Vegetables, citrus, cattle; fishing; quarrying of coquina, dolomite, limestone; boat building; electronics research; tourism • Sarasota is known for the Ringling museums, including a large gallery of Baroque art, highlighted by a collection of the work of Peter Paul Rubens. The Asolo Theater, built in 1790, was brought from Venice, Italy, and assembled in Sarasota by the State of FL. The Circus Hall of Fame and Museum of the Circus are also here.

SEMINOLE *Sanford* • 365,196 • 308 • Eastern FL, bounded on the north and east by the St. Johns River (here forming lakes Monroe and Harney). Lake Jessup and many smaller lakes are found here. There has been major suburban growth in the south due to an expansion of the Orlando metropolitan area. • One of three counties named for the Seminole Indians • 1913 from Orange • Celery, citrus fruit (growing, packing, shipping), corn, poultry, livestock; some wood- and food-processing; manufacture of boats, mobile homes, clothing, commercial telephone equipment and capacitors; electronic systems research and development

SUMTER *Bushnell* • 53,345 (70% increase since 1990; the second fastest growing county in FL) • 546 • Central FL, bounded partly on the west and south by the Withlacoochee River. The county contains many scattered lakes, including Lake Panasoffkee. Several sections of Withlacoochee State Forest are also here. • One of four counties named for Gen. Thomas Sumter (1734–1832), American Revolutionary officer, U.S. representative from GA and U.S. senator • 1853 from Marion and Orange • The Dade Massacre, which occurred here in 1835 (Dade Battlefield Historical Site) started the Second Seminole Indian War. • Citrus fruit, corn, cattle, poultry; lumber, naval stores • An annual reenactment of the daily life of an American or Allied soldier during World War II is held at Bushnell's Dade Battlefield Park.

SUWANNEE *Live Oak* • 34,844 • 688 • North-central FL, bounded on the north and southwest by the Suwannee River and on the south by the Santa Fe River. Suwanee River State Park and Peacock Springs State Recreation Area are here. • Named for the Suwannee River • 1858 from Columbus • Corn, peanuts, cotton, tobacco, vegetables, hogs, cattle; some lumbering.

TAYLOR (one of seven counties so named) *Perry* • 19,256 • 1,042 • North-central FL, bounded on the southwest by the Gulf of Mexico and on the west by the Aucilla River. The county includes Forest Capital State Museum. Econfina River State Park is in the west. • One of four counties named for President Zachary Taylor • 1856 from Madison • Lumber, naval stores; cattle, corn, peanuts; fishing; limestone.

UNION (one of eighteen counties so named) *Lake Butler* • 13,442 • 240 (the smallest county in FL) • North-central FL, bounded on the south by the Santa Fe River. • The county was given the name Union as an expression of unity between political parties in the division of Bradford County, from which it was formed • 1921 • Fort Call, near Dukes settlement, and Fort Clinch, on the northern banks of Lake Butler, were erected to protect settlers during the seven-year Seminole War. • Farming, corn, vegetables, peanuts, cattle; lumber, naval stores.

VOLUSIA *De Land* • 443,343 • 1,103 • Eastern FL, bounded on the west and part of the south by the St. Johns River and on the east by the Atlantic Ocean. The county is comprised of lowlands, rising to hills in the west, and includes many lakes and swamps, with lagoons in the east, Halifax and Hillsborough rivers and Mosquito Lagoon. Part of Ocala National Forest is in the west. • Named for the former settlement of Volusia Landing on the St. Johns River • 1854 from Saint Lucie • Ormond Beach was developed about 1875 as a health center for the employees of a lock company in New Britain CT. Its hotel was bought and enlarged by resort promoter Henry M. Flagler, spurring development of the area as a general resort destination. The hard, white sand Ormond-Daytona beach has been used for automobile speed trials since 1903 when Henry Ford, Ransom E. Olds, and Louis Chevrolet began testing their new models here. Sir Malcolm Campbell drove his "Bluebird" over the course at 276.82 m.p.h. in 1935. • Industrialist and philanthropist John D. Rockefeller died here (at his winter home, "The Casements"). Race car driver Dale Earnhardt also died in the county. • Citrus fruit, vegetables, dairy products, poultry; lumber, naval stores; fishing; tourism; education (Bethune-Cookman College) • The endangered manatees make their winter home in Blue Spring in Orange City. The county is home to the largest population of bald eagles in the contiguous forty-eight states. Turtle Mound, a forty-foot shell midden in Canaveral National Seashore, is one of the largest of its kind in the U.S. The Jackie Robinson Memorial Stadium in downtown Daytona commemorates the site of the first integrated professional sporting event, a baseball spring training game. Daytona is home to both the Daytona 500 auto race and the Firecracker Stock Car 400. The Antique Car Festival is held in Ormond Beach every Thanksgiving weekend.

WAKULLA *Crawfordville* • 22,863 • 607 • Northern FL, in the panhandle, bounded on the south by Apalachee Bay (of the Gulf of Mexico) and on the west by the Ochlockonee River; drained by the St. Marks and Wakulla rivers. The county lies in a lowland area with its western interior in the Apalachicola National Forest. St. Marks National Wildlife Refuge, San Marcos de Apalache State Historic Site, and Ochlockonee River State Park are also here. • Named for either Wakulla Springs or the Wakulla River • 1843 (prior to statehood) from Leon • Cattle, hogs, corn, peanuts, vegetables; forestry, lumber naval stores; fishing • Wakulla Springs State Park features a natural underground spring which flows at the rate of more than 600,000 gallons per minute.

WALTON (one of two counties so named, the other in GA) *De Funiak Springs* • 40,601 • 1,058 • Northwestern FL, in the panhandle, bounded on the east in part by the Choctawhatchee River, on the north by the AL state line, and on the south by the Gulf of Mexico; drained by the Shoal River. Its rolling terrain rises to 345 feet (the highest point in the state). The county's peninsula is separated from the mainland by Choctawhatchee Bay, and includes Point Washington State Forest, and Henderson Beach and Grayton Beach state recreation areas. The eastern portion of Eglin Air Force Base is also here. • Named for Col. George Walton, secretary for territorial Florida • 1824 (prior to statehood) from Jackson • Aviator Jacqueline Cochran • Corn, peanuts, poultry, cattle, hogs.

WASHINGTON *Chipley* • 20,973 • 580 • Northwestern FL, in the panhandle, bounded on the west by the Choctawhatchee River; drained by Holmes Creek (forming part of its northern boundary). The county includes Falling Waters State Recreation Area. • One of thirty-one counties named for President George Washington • 1825 (prior to statehood) from Jackson and Walton • Corn, peanuts, cotton, vegetables, livestock; lumber milling, naval stores.

GEORGIA

Wisdom, Justice, and Moderation

One hundred forty-nine of Georgia's 159 counties are governed by a board of commissioners consisting of from three to eleven members. The other ten are governed by one commissioner. Muscogee County has a joint council-manager government with the city of Columbus. The same form of shared government is in effect in Clarke County (Athens) and Richmond County (Augusta).

APPLING *Baxley* • 17,419 • 509 • Southeastern GA, bounded on the northeast by the Altamaha River and on the southwest by Big Satilla Creek. • Named for Daniel Appling (1787–1818), hero in the War of 1812 • 1818 (prior to statehood) from Creek cession • Author Carolyn Miller • Tobacco, corn, peanuts, soybeans, cotton, cattle, hogs, poultry; timber • Appling County was once known as "the turpentine capital of the world."

ATKINSON *Pearson* • 7,609 • 338 • Southern GA, bounded on the west by the Alapaha River; drained by the Satilla River (forming part of the northern and eastern boundary). • Named for William Y. Atkinson (1854–99), governor of GA • 1917 from Coffee and Clinch • Cotton, corn, peanuts, tobacco, cattle, hogs, poultry, nursery products; timber • Throughout the 1960s and 1970s, Pearson was known as the "Chess Capital" of the state. The town hosted four consecutive championships, Pearson residents making up a quarter of the membership of the GA Chess Association.

BACON *Alma* • 10,103 • 285 • Southeastern GA, bounded on the northeast by Big Satilla Creek; drained by Little Hurricane and Hurricane creeks. • Named for Captain Augustus O. Bacon (1839–1914), Confederate army officer and U.S. senator from GA • 1914 from Appling, Pierce and Ware • Timber; soybeans, tobacco, cotton, corn, peanuts, blueberries. (A festival every June celebrates the importance of the large blueberry industry here.) • The name of the county seat is an acronym composed of the first letter in each of GA's four state capitals: Augusta, Louisville, Milledgeville, and Atlanta.

BAKER (one of three counties so named) *Newton* • 4,074 • 343 • Southwestern GA, bounded on the southeast by the Flint River; drained by Ichawaynochaway and Chickasawhatchee creeks. • Named for Col. John Baker (?–1792), Army officer and GA legislator • 1825 from Early • Indian villages were first recorded in the area that would later comprise the county in 1540 by Hernando de Soto. The last battle of the Creek Indian War of 1836 was fought at Chickasawhatchee Swamp near Red Bluff. • Corn, peanuts, sugarcane, cotton, canola, pecans, cattle, hogs, poultry; timber • The Ichauway Plantation houses the Joseph W. Jones Ecological Research Center, one of the largest outdoor research centers in the world, which studies over thirty-two species of endangered plants and animals.

BALDWIN *Milledgeville* • 44,700 • 258 • Central GA; drained by the Oconee River (forming part of the county's southeastern boundary). Lake Sinclair reservoir forms part of the northern boundary. The county is located in the Piedmont region • One of two counties (the other in AL) named for Abraham Baldwin (1754–1807), member of the Continental Congress, and U.S. senator from GA • 1803 from Creek Indian lands and Hancock, Washington, and Wilkinson • Milledgeville served as the capital of GA from 1807 to 1867, the only city in the U.S. designed specifically as a state capital. According to the National Trust for Historic Preservation, Milledgeville is the only surviving example of a complete "Federal Period" city. • Long-term congressman Carl Vinson; writer Flannery O'Connor, comedian Oliver Hardy • Corn, pecans, fruit, cattle, poultry; timber; education (GA College and State U.); light manufactures including clay products, textiles.

BANKS *Homer* • 14,422 • 234 • Northeastern GA; drained by the headstreams of the Broad River. The county is located in the Piedmont area of the state. The Chattahoochee National Forest is on its northern boundary. • Named for Richard Banks (1784–1858), a noted local surgeon • 1858 from Franklin and Habersham • Baseball player Ty Cobb • Hay, sweet potatoes, fruit, poultry, cattle; timber • The county is the home of the World's Largest Easter Egg Hunt hosted by Garrison Farms. For over 110 years, the Sunday School Celebration, honoring the county's churches, has been held each July.

BARROW *Winder* • 46,144 • 162 • North-central GA, bounded on the south and southwest by the Apalachee River. The county is located in the Piedmont agricultural area. Fort Yargo State Park is here. • Named for David. C. Barrow (1852–1929), professor and chancellor of the University of Georgia • 1914 from Jackson, Walton and Gwinnett • Fort Yargo State Park includes old Fort Yargo, a log fort constructed in 1792 for protection from the Creek and Cherokee Indians. • Cotton, corn, hay, sweet potatoes, fruit; textile manufacturing.

BARTOW *Cartersville* • 76,019 • 459 • Northwestern GA; drained by the Etowah River, forming Allatoona Lake reservoir in the east. Barnesley Gardens, Etowah Indian Mounds State Historic Site and Red Top Mountain State Park are also here. • Named for Confederate general Francis S. Bartow (1816–1861), first officer of such rank to be killed in action during the Civil War. The county was originally named for

Lewis Cass but his abolitionist views eventually prompted the pro-slavery citizenry to advocate a name change. • Organized in 1832 from Indian lands; name changed 1861 • First female U.S. senator Rebecca Latimer Felton; philosopher and humorist Bill Arp; and author Corra Harris. • Barite, bauxite, slate, potash, manganese, iron ore, and limestone mining; manufacture of rugs, textiles, tire cord fabric, plastics and lumber products; hay, sweet potatoes, fruit, cattle, hogs, poultry • Cassville, the county seat in 1833, was the site of GA's first post office. Cartersville was the site of the world's first outdoor Coca-Cola wall advertisement (1894). GA's oldest covered bridge (Euharlee/Lowery Bridge, 1886) is here.

BEN HILL *Fitzgerald* • 17,484 • 252 • South-central GA, bounded on the northeast by the Ocmulgee River and on the west by the Alapaha River. • Named for Benjamin H. Hill (1823–82), GA legislator and U.S. senator • 1906 from Irwin and Wilcox • Cotton, corn, tobacco, peanuts, cattle, hogs; meat packing; timber; manufacture of textiles and steel products • Fitzgerald was founded by former Union soldiers on a 50,000 acre tract owned by the American Soldier's Colony Company. The town was laid out symmetrically with street names honoring leaders of both armies. To this day the town holds separate Memorial Day commemorations, one for the Union and one for the Confederacy. The Blue and Gray Museum is also here.

BERRIEN *Nashville* • 16,235 • 452 • Southern GA; drained by the Alapaha River (forming the southeastern boundary) and the Withlacoochee River (forming part of the western boundary). • One of two counties (the other in MI) named for John M. Berrien (1781–1856), U.S. senator from GA and U.S. attorney general • 1856 from Lowndes, Coffee, and Irwin • Berrien County had one of the state's earliest post roads, the Coffee Road, opened in 1823 to channel settlers' crops to FL. • The county has been called "the Bell Pepper Capital of the World." Also, cotton, corn, tobacco, peanuts, cattle, hogs; fish farming; forestry.

BIBB *Macon* • 153,887 • 250 • Central GA; drained by the Ocmulgee River (forming part of the southern and northeastern boundary) and intersected by the Fall Line. Ocmulgee National Monument contains massive temple mounds of a Mississippian Indian ceremonial complex that thrived between A.D. 900 and 1100. • One of two counties (the other in AL) named for William W. Bibb (1781–1820), US senator from GA and first governor of AL • 1822 from Jones, Monroe, Twiggs, and Houston • Macon's city hall served as the temporary state capitol from November, 1864 to March, 1865. Macon was a Confederate gold depository and supply depot until General Howell Cobb surrendered it to Union general James H. Wilson on April 20, 1865. • Poet Sidney Lanier • Textiles, brick, tile, wood products; hogs, poultry, cattle, dairying; clay mining (one of the world's largest deposits of kaolin is here); food processing and distribution; education (Mercer U.; Macon State College.) • Wesleyan College, founded in 1836 as the GA Female College, was the first col-

lege in the world chartered to grant degrees to women. The GA State Fair is held each October in Macon.

BLECKLEY *Cochran* • 11,666 • 217 • Central GA, bounded on the northwest by the Ocmulgee River; drained by the Little Ocmulgee River and Gum Swamp. • Named for Logan E. Bleckley (1827–1907), Confederate soldier and chief justice of the GA Supreme Court • 1912 from Pulaski • Corn, peanuts, cotton, wheat, fruit, cattle, hogs • Cochran is home to Middle Georgia College, recognized as the oldest two-year college in America.

BRANTLEY *Nahunta* • 14,629 • 444 • Southeastern GA, bounded on the north and northwest by the Satilla River and by Big Satilla Creek. Part of Dixon Memorial State Forest is here, as is a small portion of Okefenokee National Wildlife Refuge. • Named for either William G. Brantley (1860–1934), state senator; or for Benjamin D. Brantley (1832–91), state representative • 1920 from Charlton, Pierce and Wayne • Fort McIntosh was built in the early years of the American Revolution to protect the extensive herds of cattle in the area. It was placed under siege by Tories in 1777 and eventually surrendered. Fort Mudge was built at about the same time, and was immortalized by Walt Kelly in his "Pogo" comic strip. • Tobacco, cattle, hogs; timber; manufacture of lumber and millwork products.

BROOKS (one of two counties so named, the other in TX) *Quitman* • 16,450 • 494 • Southern GA, bounded on the south by the FL state line, on the east by the Little and Withlacoochee rivers. • Named for Preston S. Brooks (1819–1857), SC Congressman infamous for caning Senator Charles Sumner • 1858 from Lowndes and Thomas • Tobacco, cotton, corn, peanuts, cattle, hogs; apparel and other textile products • The county's courthouse, constructed in 1864, was paid for in Confederate money, a currency that soon thereafter became worthless.

BRYAN (one of two counties so named, the other in OK) *Pembroke* • 23,417 • 442 • Southeastern GA, bounded on the southeast by the Atlantic Ocean and on the northeast by the Ogeechee River; drained by the Canoochee River. The county includes Ossabaw Island Heritage Preserve. The Intracoastal Waterway extends from St. Catherines Sound to Ossabaw Sound. The county is divided north-south by Fort Stewart, a large U.S. Army training facility. • Named for Jonathan Bryan (1708–88), a founder of the Georgia Colony at Savannah, jurist and GA legislator • 1793 from Chatham • Henry Ford made one of his homes here (Richmond Hill Plantation) and provided health care and educational opportunities for many county residents. • Peanuts, tobacco, cattle; forestry; fishing • Bryan is a county of forts, including Fort Argyle, established by General Oglethorpe on the Ogeechee River to protect Savannah from Florida's Spaniards, and Fort McAllister (state historic park), which has the best preserved earthwork fabrications of the Confederate Period.

BULLOCH *Statesboro* (the only city in the U.S. by this name)

• 55,983 • 682 • Eastern GA, bounded on the northeast by the Ogeechee River and on the west, in part, by Lotts Creek. • Named for Archibald Bulloch (?–1777), "president and commander in chief of GA" after the departure of the British royal governor • 1796 from Bryan and Screven • Tobacco, cotton (also ginning and warehouses), corn, peanuts (cultivation and processing), cattle, hogs; forestry products; hunting; education (GA Southern U.) • The town of Hopeulikit was named for a famous dance hall of the big band swing era. The county abounds in festivals including the Brooklet Peanut Festival, Portal's Cat Face Turpentine Festival, and the Bulloch County Azalea Festival. Georgia Southern University provides a sanctuary for bald eagles and other native birds of prey.

BURKE (one of three counties so named) *Waynesboro* • 22,243 • 830 (the second largest county in GA) • Eastern GA, bounded on the northeast by the Savannah River (forming the SC state line), and on the south in part by the Ogeechee River; drained by Brier Creek. Named for Edmund Burke (1729–97), British statesman, orator, and defender of the American colonies • Original county; 1777 (prior to statehood) from Saint George Parish • Burke is the "County of Governors." Lyman Hall had a plantation here; the county has connections through birth, residence, or marriage to nine other GA governors. • Cotton, corn, soybeans, oats, peanuts, wheat, cattle, hogs; timber • Waynesboro is known as the "Bird Dog Capital of the World." The GA Field Trials is one of the nation's oldest hunting dog competitions. The Redbreast Festival celebrates the Ogeechee River's unique variety of redbreasted bream.

BUTTS *Jackson* • 19,522 • 187 • Central GA, bounded on the northeast by the South River and on the east by the Ocmulgee River, here forming Jackson Lake, one of the first reservoirs in GA. The county lies in the Piedmont. Indian Springs State Park is here. • Named for Captain Samuel Butts (1777–1814), captain in the War of 1812; killed in combat with Indians • 1825 from Henry and Monroe • Indian Springs is reputed to be the oldest state park in the U.S. It was the site of the treaty that ceded the Creek Indian lands to the state of GA in 1825. • Publisher Robert Grier (*Grier's Almanac*) • Cattle, hogs.

CALHOUN *Morgan* • 6,320 • 280 • Southwestern GA, bounded on the east by Chickasawhatchee Creek, and on the extreme southwest by Spring Creek; intersected by Ichawaynochaway Creek • One of eleven counties named for John Caldwell Calhoun (1782–1850), U.S. statesman and champion of Southern causes • 1854 from Early and Baker • Fifty percent of the county's land has been designated prime farmland by the U.S. Dept. of Agriculture. Crops include cotton, corn, truck crops, peanuts, and pecans. Also produced here are cattle, hogs, poultry and timber.

CAMDEN (one of four counties so named) *Woodbine* • 43,664 • 630 • Extreme southeastern GA, bounded on the south by the St. Marys River (forming the FL state line), on the east by the Atlantic Ocean, and on the north by the Little Satilla River; intersected by the Satilla River (forming part of the western boundary). The Intracoastal Waterway crosses from the southeast to St. Andrew Sound. The county includes Cumberland Island National Seashore and Crooked River State Park. • Named for Charles Pratt, 1st Earl of Camden (1714–94), English statesman who supported the American colonies before the Revolutionary War • Original county; organized 1777 (prior to statehood) from Saint Mary and Saint Thomas parishes • American Revolution officer "Light Horse" Harry Lee is buried on Cumberland Island. The county is also the site of the ruins of Dungeness, the mansion of the family of Andrew Carnegie. • Lumbering; fishing; farming, cattle • Kings Bay Naval Submarine Base, home of the Trident Nuclear Submarine, is here.

CANDLER *Metter* • 9,577 • 247 • East-central GA, bounded on the northeast by Lotts Creek; drained by the Canoochee River. The county includes the Charles C. Harrold Nature Preserve, home of the rare gopher tortoise, and part of George L. Smith State Park. • Named for Col. Allen D. Candler (1834–1910), GA legislator and governor • 1914 from Bulloch, Emanuel, and Tattnall • Cotton, corn, tobacco, soybeans, pecans, peanuts, cattle, hogs; timber • Metter's whimsical slogan is "Everything's better in Metter." The town is home to Michael Guido and the Guido Evangelical Association, familiar to many for its "seeds from the sower" radio programs.

CARROLL (one of thirteen counties so named) *Carrollton* • 87,268 • 499 • Western GA, bounded on the west by the AL state line and on the southeast by the Chattahoochee River; drained by the Little Tallapoosa River. J. Tanner State Park is here. • One of twelve counties named for Charles Carroll (1737–1832), a signer of the Declaration of Independence, and U.S. senator from MD • Original county; established 1825 from Indian lands • Actress Susan Haywood • Poultry and textiles are most important; also cattle, hogs; lumbering; manufacture of shoes, fertilizers, aluminum and copper cable and wire; food processing; education (State U. of West GA) • The 480-acre McIntosh Reserve recreation site was once the plantation of Creek Indian Chief William McIntosh, who was murdered in 1825 by a group of Upper Creek Indians angry over his transfer of Creek lands to white settlers.

CATOOSA *Ringgold* • 53,282 • 162 • Northwestern GA, bounded on the north by the TN state line. The county includes part of Chattahoochee National Forest • Named for Catoosa Springs • 1853 from Walker and Whitfield • A major Confederate victory and one of the bloodiest battles of the Civil War took place at Chickamauga Creek on September 19–20, 1863; it is remembered at Chickamauga and Chattanooga National Military Park, part of which lies in the county. It was the first national military park established in the U.S. Sherman began his march through GA from Ringgold Depot. • Cotton, potatoes, corn, fruit, cattle, poultry, muscadine wines; timber; textile manufacturing.

CHARLTON *Folkston* • 10,282 • 781 (the fifth largest county in GA) • Southeastern GA, bounded on the south and southeast by the FL state line (formed here by St. Marys River) and on the northeast by the Satilla River; drained by the Suwanee River. The western part of the county is dominated by the Okefenokee National Wildlife Refuge, one of the oldest and best preserved freshwater areas in America, home to Native Americans for as long as 4,500 years, and later occupied by escaped slaves. The cypress-forested swamps are teeming with wildlife. Stephen C. Foster State Park is here. • Named for either Thomas U. P. Charlton (1779–1835), GA legislator and GA attorney general; or for Robert M. Charlton (1807–54), GA legislator, jurist and U.S. senator • 1854 from Camden • Sugarcane, tobacco, cattle; lumber, logging (pine), sawmilling, wood products. • The county comprises one of the richest titanium reserves in the world. Folkston, for years the self-proclaimed "Marriage Capital of the World," tempted many nearby Floridians to cross the state line for "express nuptials." The three-day Fall Pow Wow in October, is sponsored by the Cherokee of GA Tribal Council.

CHATHAM *Savannah* • 232,048 • 438 • Eastern GA, bounded on the east by the Atlantic Ocean, on the northeast by the Savannah River (forming the SC state line), and on the south by the Ogeechee River. The county includes Tybee and Skidaway (state park) islands. Fort Pulaski National Monument is on Tybee Island; bombardment here in 1862 first demonstrated the ineffectiveness of old-style masonry fortifications. National wildlife refuges here include Tybee, Wassaw, and part of Savannah. • One of two counties (the other in NC) named for William Pitt (the Elder, 1708–78), 1st earl of Chatham, known as "the Great Commoner," for his support of the American colonies prior to the Revolutionary War. • Original county; organized 1777 (prior to statehood) from Saint Phillips and Christ Church parishes • The county includes the site on which General James Oglethorpe landed in 1733 to establish the Georgia Colony. Savannah was the colonial government seat and capital of the state until 1786. Methodist founders John and Charles Wesley came in 1736 to preach to the colonists and the Indians. George Whitefield came in 1738 to found Bethesda, the first orphanage in America. British troops captured Savannah in December, 1778 and remained here until colonial forces drove them out in 1782. The *Savannah*, the first steamboat to cross the Atlantic, left the city for Liverpool in 1819. Savannah, the objective of Gen. William Tecumseh Sherman's march to the sea, was captured on Dec. 21, 1864. It recovered fairly rapidly despite a yellow-fever epidemic in 1876. • Writer Conrad Aiken; explorer John C. Frémont; religious leader Father Divine; Confederate General William J. Hardee; writer Flannery O'Connor; Supreme Court justice Clarence Thomas; songwriter Johnny Mercer; first Postmaster of the U.S. Joseph Habersham • Dairy farming; fishing; shipbuilding; manufacture of paper, food products, chemicals, transportation equipment; shipping; army installations; education (Savannah State U., Armstrong-Atlantic

State U.) • Savannah includes a major National Historic Landmark district incorporating 1,100 architecturally significant buildings, including one of the nation's largest collections of Victorian dwellings. The city hosts the second largest St. Patrick's Day parade and celebration in the U.S. Juliette Gordon Low founded the Girl Scouts of the U.S.A. in Savannah on March 12, 1912.

CHATTAHOOCHEE *Cusseta* • 14,882 • 249 • Western GA, bounded on the west by the Chattahoochee River (here forming the AL state line) and on the northwest by Upatoi Creek. Most of the county is occupied by part of Fort Benning Military Reservation. • Named for the Chattahoochee River • 1854 from Muscogee and Marion • Political strategist James Carville; U.S. senator Phil Graham. • Poultry. • Fort Benning, the world's largest infantry camp, is also the county's largest employer. Often called the "West Point of the South," it is the home of a Regional Civilian Personnel Center, serving 40,000 civilian employees of the Department of the Army in the Southeast. The National Infantry Museum is in the county.

CHATTOOGA *Summerville* • 25,470 • 313 • Northwestern GA, bounded on the west by the AL state line. The county is crossed by the Appalachian Mountains and includes part of Chattahoochee National Forest (Armuchee Ranger District) in the east. James H. "Sloppy" Floyd State Park is also here. • Named for the Chattooga River, which runs diagonally through the county • 1838 from Floyd and Walker • Cherokee leader Sequoyah, credited with developing the Cherokee written alphabet. • Cotton, corn, hay, sweet potatoes, fruit, cattle, hogs, poultry; textile manufacturing; sawmilling.

CHEROKEE *Canton* • 141,903 • 424 • Northwestern GA; drained by the Etowah River (which forms Allatoona Lake reservoir here). The county is part of the Atlanta metropolitan area. • One of eight counties named for the Cherokee Indians • Original county; established 1830 from Cherokee lands • Secretary of State Dean Rusk, golfer Bobby Jones • Manufacture of textiles; poultry, eggs, cattle, hogs; education (Reinhardt College) • Harness racing pioneer A.L. Coggins's Crescent Farm produced the world-class race horse, Abbedale.

CLARKE (one of five counties so named) *Athens* • 101,489 • 121 (the smallest county in GA and one of the fifty smallest counties in the U.S.) • North-central GA, in the Piedmont, bounded on the southwest in part by McNutt Creek; drained by the Oconee River • Named for General Elijah Clarke (1733–99), an officer in the Revolutionary War • 1801 from Jackson and Greene • Athens is home to the oldest state-chartered university in the U.S., the University of Georgia. The world's only double-barreled cannon was built here. • Blood researcher Dr. William Lorenzo Moss; journalist Henry W. Grady, Secretary of State Dean Rusk • Cattle, hogs, poultry (raising and processing), dairying; manufacture of textiles, cotton garments, cord, tire fabric, cottonseed products, fertilizer, wood products, electrical transformers, clocks, milk cartons; education • Athens was home to a tree that "owned it-self" when its owner university professor William Jackson, willed the oak on his property the eight feet of land around its trunk. After it blew down in 1942, the Junior Ladies' Garden Club planted a new one from one of the tree's acorns. The Georgia Museum of Art has a permanent collection of over 7,000 works of art.

CLAY (one of eighteen counties so named) *Fort Gaines* • 3,357 • 195 • Southwestern GA, bounded on the west by the Chattahoochee River (forming the AL state line and Walter F. George Reservoir). The Walter F. George Lock and Dam includes the second highest lock east of the Mississippi. George T. Bagby State Park is also here. • One of fifteen counties named for Henry Clay (1777–1852), U.S. senator from KY, known as the "Great Pacificator" for his advocacy of compromise to avert national crises • 1854 from Early and Randolph • Senator and NATO ambassador Walter F. George • Cotton, corn, truck farming, peanuts, cattle, hogs.

CLAYTON (one of two counties so named, the other in IA) *Jonesboro* • 236,517 (the fifth most populated county in GA) • 143 (one of the fifty smallest counties in the U.S.) • Central GA; drained by the Flint River (forming part of the western boundary). It is a rapidly growing Atlanta suburban county and site of Atlanta Hartsfield International Airport, one of the world's largest. • Named for Augustin S. Clayton (1783–1839), GA jurist and U.S. representative • 1858 from Fayette and Henry • There was bitter fighting in Forest Park during the Civil War. The Battle of Jonesboro marked the end of the Atlanta Campaign; when Union troops seized control of the railroad there, all supplies to Atlanta were cut off. • Virologist Thomas M. Rivers • Atlanta Army Depot (supply and maintenance installation); education (Clayton College and State U.) • The Atlanta State Farmer's Market is the largest open-air farmer's market in the U.S. Mary Blalock, president of the Bank of Jonesboro, was the first woman bank president in the U.S. Margaret Mitchell drew inspiration for *Gone with the Wind* from the story of her great-grandfather Philip Fitzgerald, a county resident. The Clayton County Water Authority maintains one of the most successful and innovative wastewater treatment systems in the world. Its land application system is studied by treatment industry personnel from around the world.

CLINCH *Homerville* • 6,878 • 809 (the fourth largest county in GA) • Southern GA, bounded on the south by the FL state line; drained by the Suwannee River, its eastern edge lying within Okefenokee National Wildlife Refuge. • Named for Brig. Gen. Duncan L. Clinch (1787–1849), Army officer and U.S. representative from GA • 1850 from Ware and Lowndes • Timber, forest products; blueberries, honey, cattle, hogs, tobacco, sweet potatoes, alligator farming; diversified manufacturing, including metal fabrication.

COBB *Marietta* • 607,751 (the third most populated county in GA) • 340 • Northwest-central GA, bounded on the south-east by the Chattahoochee River. The county includes part of Allatoona Lake reservoir in the northwest. It contains large suburbs of Atlanta. Kennesaw Mountain National Battlefield Park and Marietta National Military Cemetery (with over 17,000 soldier interments) are here. Cobb County has an extensive system of parks and recreation centers, including several units of Chattahoochee River National Recreation Area. Dobbins Air Reserve Base is here. • Named for Thomas W. Cobb (1784–1830), U.S. senator from GA and judge of the GA superior court • 1832 from Cherokee • Two engagements took place at Kennesaw Mountain between Union and Confederate forces during the Atlanta Campaign in June and July, 1864. • Army officer Lucius D. Clay; secretary of the treasury William G. McAdoo • Aircraft manufacturing; education (Kennesaw State U.; Southern Polytechnic State U.); recreational activities • B-29 bombers were made here during WW II.

COFFEE (one of three counties so named) *Douglas* • 37,413 • 599 • South-central GA, bounded on the north by the Ocmulgee River; drained by the Satilla River and Suwanee Creek. The county is in the Wiregrass region of the state. General Coffee State Park here contains a pioneer village. • Named for General John Coffee (1782–1836), an officer in the Indian wars, U.S. representative from GA and cousin to John Coffee of TN • 1854 from Clinch, Irwin, Telfair and Ware • Tobacco (one of the state's most important markets), cotton, corn, peanuts, cattle, hogs, poultry, dairying; marble; timber; manufacture of mobile homes, clothing • South Georgia College, in Douglas, is the state's oldest state-supported junior college. Broxton Rocks represent the largest outcrop of ancient sandstone anywhere on the coastal plain of the Southeastern U.S. Each November the county hosts Mule Day, a festival of all things mule-related.

COLQUITT *Moultrie* • 42,053 • 552 • Southern GA, bounded on the east by the Little River; drained by the Ochlockonee and Withlacoochee rivers and Warrior Creek. Reed Bingham State Park is here. • Named for Walter T. Colquitt (1799–1855), jurist, Methodist minister, and U.S. senator • 1856 from Thomas and Lowndes • A leading producer of cotton and tobacco; also corn, soybeans, wheat, melons, peanuts, cattle, hogs, poultry; timber; hunting (bobtail quail, wild turkey, deer, dove) • The annual Sunbelt Agricultural Exposition in Moultrie draws thousands of visitors from around the country. Moultrie, home to a world class diving well, hosts international diving tournaments and served as a training site for the 1996 Olympic Games.

COLUMBIA (one of eight counties so named) *Appling* • 9,288 • 290 • Eastern GA, bounded on the east by the Savannah River (forming the SC state line) and on the north by the Little River; intersected by the Fall Line. Clarks Hill Lake is part of J. Strom Thurmond Lake, the largest man-made lake east of the Mississippi River. It was created in 1946 when the Army Corps of Engineers built the Clarks Hill Dam on the Savannah River. Mistletoe State Park and a small portion of Fort Gordon Military Reservation are here. • The name of the county is a poetic and honorific reference to Christopher Columbus • 1790 from Richmond • Comedian Oliver Hardy • Cotton, corn, potatoes, cattle; timber.

COOK (one of three counties so named) *Adel* • 15,771 • 229 • Southern GA, bounded on the west by the Little River and on the southeast by the Withlacoochee River. Part of Reed Bingham State Park is here. • Named for General Philip Cook (1817–94), Confederate officer and U.S. representative from GA • 1918 from Berrien • Tobacco, watermelons, cotton, corn, peanuts, fruit, cattle, hogs; pine timber; some manufacturing • One of the first roads cut through the Wiregrass Territory ran through the county at Cecil; built by Gen. John Coffee, it was a main thoroughfare for early settlers traveling to Tallahasseee and the Gulf Coast. The county has several oddly named festivals, including the Brushy Creek Muzzleloaders Spring Shoot and Rendezvous, the Annual Turnip Trot, and the Lean-Ox Festival.

COWETA *Newnan* • 89,215 • 443 • Western GA, bounded on the northwest by the Chattahoochee River. • Named for the Coweta or Lower Creek Indians • 1825 from Indian lands • Author Erskine Caldwell; columnist Lewis Grizzard • Textile manufacturing; stone quarries; sawmills; melons, pecans, peaches, cattle, hogs and poultry • The county holds the Homemade Ice Cream Festival and Powers Crossroads Country Fair and Arts Festival each year.

CRAWFORD (one of eleven counties so named) *Knoxville* • 12,495 • 325 • Central GA, bounded on the southwest by the Flint River, on the northeast by Echeconnee Creek; intersected by the Fall Line. • One of six counties named directly or indirectly for William H. Crawford (1772–1834), GA statesman • 1822 from Houston • Peaches, cotton, corn, vegetables, pecans, wheat, cattle, poultry • On the courthouse square in Knoxville is a monument to Joanna Toutman who designed and sewed the Lone Star Flag adopted by the State of Texas. It was presented to a group of GA volunteers who were on their way to assist in the Texas fight for independence in 1835.

CRISP *Cordele* • 21,996 • 274 • South-central GA, bounded on the west by the Flint River (which forms Lake Blackshear reservoir here). Georgia Veterans State Park is on the banks of Lake Blackshear. • Named for Charles F. Crisp (1845–96), Confederate army officer and Speaker of the U.S. House of Representatives (county native) • 1905 from Dooly • In 1930, Crisp became the first county in the U.S. to own and operate its own electrical power plant, with Lake Blackshear providing its power source. • Cotton, corn, peanuts, pecans, soybeans, wheat, cattle, hogs, poultry; lumber; processing of agricultural and forest products, manufacture of textiles, machinery, air conditioners, fertilizer, soft drinks • Cordele claims the title "Watermelon Capital of the World," and celebrates the harvest with its Watermelon Days Festival each July.

DADE • *Trenton* • 15,154 • 174 • Extreme northwestern GA, bounded on the north by the TN state line and on the west

by the AL state line; drained by Lookout Creek; crossed by the Lookout and Sand mountains. Most of the county lies in the valley between the two. Cloudland Canyon State Park is here. • One of three counties named in part or in full for Major Francis L. Dade (?–1835), U.S. army officer killed in the Seminole War • 1837 from Walker • Pro-south and vehemently secessionist, the county strongly supported the sentiments of its state assemblyman Colonel R. H. Tatum when he stated just prior to the outbreak of the Civil War that if GA didn't withdraw from the Union, Dade County would. It is believed that at one meeting called to address the secessionist issue, a "Declaration of Independence" was presented and passed, declaring the county a "Free State." Dade County did not officially acknowledge its return to the Union fold until July 4, 1945. • Coal; timber; fruit, vegetables, corn, grain, cotton, cattle, poultry • The county seat of Trenton received its name in honor of industrial engineers from Trenton, New Jersey who came to the area in search of coal and iron.

DAWSON (one of four counties so named) • *Dawsonville* • 15,999 • 211 • Northern GA, in the Blue Ridge (north) and Piedmont (south) regions; drained by the Etowah and Chestatee rivers. An arm of Lake Sidney Lanier reservoir forms the eastern boundary. Chattahoochee National Forest is in the north. Amicalola Falls State Park surrounds 729-foot high Amicalola Falls, the highest waterfall east of the Rocky Mountains. • Named for William C. Dawson (1798–1856), jurist and U.S. senator from GA • 1857 from Gilmer and Lumpkin • Race car driver Bill Elliot • Corn, hay, sweet potatoes, cattle, hogs, poultry; timber; manufacture of apparel and textiles.

DECATUR *Bainbridge* • 28,240 • 597 • Southwestern GA, bounded on the south by the FL state line; intersected by the Flint River. Jim Woodruff Dam, in the extreme southwest, forms Lake Seminole reservoir. The county is underlaid by a broken limestone aquifer creating many caves. • One of five counties named for Stephen Decatur (1779–1820), naval hero in the War of 1812 and in actions against the Barbary pirates near Tripoli • 1823 from Early • The area that would become the county of Decatur was the site of several battles between Indians and early settlers. In the early 1700s, both the Spanish and English fought the Creeks. In 1818, Gen. Andrew Jackson led troops from TN, KY, and GA to victory over the Seminoles here. • A leading county in the production of fuller's earth. Also corn, cotton, tobacco, wheat, sugarcane, peanuts, pecans, cattle, hogs, poultry; timber • The Town of Climax hosts "Swine Time," a pork festival each November. Lake Seminole is considered one of the nation's best lakes for large mouth bass fishing.

DE KALB *Decatur* • 665,865 (the second most populated county in GA) • 268 • Central GA. It is the largest suburban county in the metropolitan Atlanta area. The Center for Disease Control and Prevention is located here. The world's largest bas-relief sculpture, depicting Jefferson Davis, Robert E. Lee and "Stonewall" Jackson, was carved on Stone Mountain employing a design by Gutzon Borglum. The mountain constitutes the world's largest exposed mass of granite. • One of six counties named for Johann, Baron de Kalb (1721–80), German-born French soldier who fought with the Americans during the Revolutionary War • 1822 from Fayette, Henry, Gwinnett, and Newton • De Kalb pioneered the urban county concept in which the county provides most services to its residents. • First female U.S. senator Rebecca Ann Felton • The county is an important corporate, warehousing, retail and distribution center. Diversified manufactures include electrical equipment, farm machinery, lumber, abrasives, medical supplies; education (Emory U.; Oglethorpe U.; Agnes Scott College, and others). • One of the largest jails in the U.S. (with over 3,000 beds) is in the county.

DODGE (one of four counties so named) *Eastman* • 19,171 • 500 • Central GA, bounded on the southwest by the Ocmulgee River; drained by the Little Ocmulgee River. • Named for William E. Dodge (1805–83), U.S. representative from NY and owner of a vast estate in GA, who urged moderation in Reconstruction measures • 1870 from Montgomery, Pulaski, and Telfair • Cotton, corn, peanuts, soybeans, tobacco, wheat, cattle, hogs; lumber; textile manufacturing • Eastman, the home of the original Stuckey's candy plant, is referred to as the "Candy Capital of Georgia." What began as one roadside candy stand has grown to over 400 highway marts nationwide.

DOOLY *Vienna* • 11,525 • 393 • Central GA, bounded on the west by the Flint River. • Named for Captain John Dooly (1740–80), American Revolutionary War officer in GA who was killed by British sympathizers • Original county; organized 1821 from Indian lands • Politicians Walter F. George and George Busbee; presidential press secretary Jody Powell • Cotton, corn, soybeans, wheat, peanuts, pecans, cattle, hogs, poultry; timber; hunting.

DOUGHERTY *Albany* • 96,065 • 330 • Southwestern GA, bounded on the west by Chickasawhatchee Creek; intersected by the Flint River (forming part of its northern boundary). Radium Springs, the largest springs in GA, is in the county. Traces of radium isotopes found here suggested the name. The United States Marine Corps Logistics Base is also here. • Named for Charles Dougherty (?–1853), leader of the Whig party in GA and western circuit judge • 1853 from Baker • Trumpeter and band leader Harry James; composer Wallingford Riegger; golfer Nancy Lopez; singer Ray Charles; first African-American to win an Olympic gold medal Alice Coachman • Pecans (a top producer in the U.S.), corn, soybeans, Spanish peanuts, cotton, wheat, cattle, dairying; limestone quarries; timber; manufacture of aircraft and farm implements; education (Albany State U.) • Albany's St. Teresa's Catholic Church, built in 1859, is the oldest Catholic Church in continuous use in GA.

DOUGLAS *Douglasville* • 92,174 • 199 • Western GA, bounded on the southeast by the Chattahoochee River. The county includes suburbs of Atlanta. • One of twelve counties named for Stephen A. Douglas (1813–61), U.S. orator and statesman • 1870 from Carroll and Campbell • Cattle, poultry • The ruins of the New Manchester Manufacturing Company's cotton factory on the banks of Sweetwater Creek testify to the destructive force of General Sherman's March to the Sea. Lithia Springs was a nationally prestigious hotel until fire destroyed it in 1911.

EARLY *Blakely* • 12,354 • 511 • Southwestern GA, bounded on the west by the Chattahoochee River, forming the AL state line; drained by Spring Creek. Kolomoki Mounds State Park contains a mound, believed to have been a temple base, that is possibly the largest in the U.S. • Named for Peter Early (1773–1817), U.S. representative from GA, jurist and governor • Original county; organized 1818 from Creek Indian lands • Cotton, corn, peanuts (raised and processed), pecans, soybeans, sorghum, wheat, cattle, hogs; lumber • The importance of peanuts to this top-producing county is emphasized by a statue of a peanut erected on the square in Blakely. Also standing outside the county courthouse is the only known extant Confederate flagpole, erected in 1861.

ECHOLS *Statenville* • 3,754 • 404 • Southern GA, bounded on the south by the FL state line; drained by the Alapaha and Suwannee rivers. • Named for General Robert M. Echols (?–1847), a GA officer killed during the Mexican War, and GA state legislator • 1858 from Clinch and Lowndes • Corn, cotton, tobacco, cattle; lumber • Echols County is the only county in GA with no incorporated municipalities in the traditional sense. Statenville, its county seat, is unincorporated except for the boundaries of its courthouse.

EFFINGHAM (one of two counties so named, the other in IL) *Springfield* • 37,535 • 479 • Eastern GA, bounded on the east by the Savannah River (forming the SC state line) and on the west by the Ogeechee River. The county includes part of Savannah National Wildlife Refuge in the southeast. • One of two counties (the other in IL) named for Thomas Howard, 3rd Earl of Effingham (1746–91), a pro-colonist English army officer • Original county; organized 1777 (prior to statehood) from Saint Mathew and Saint Phillips parishes • The county lies in one of the oldest settled areas in the U.S. The Lutheran Salzburg community, established in 1734 at Ebenezer, was the second settlement in GA. • Corn, soybeans, peanuts, fruit, tobacco, wheat, cotton, cattle, hogs; timber • Sandhill Park hosts an annual model plane fly-in.

ELBERT (one of two counties so named, the other in CO) *Elberton* • 20,511 • 369 • Northeastern GA, bounded on the east by the Savannah River (here forming the SC state line and Russell Lake reservoir) and on the southwest by the Broad River. Richard B. Russell and Bobby Brown state parks are here. • Named for General Samuel Elbert (?–1788), Revolutionary War officer and GA governor • 1790 from Wilkes • Revolutionary War heroes Nancy Morgan Hart and Stephen Heard; political leader William H. Crawford; U.S. Supreme Court Justice Joseph R. Lamar • Elberton is known as the

"Granite Capital of the World." The county's more than forty quarries produce more granite monuments than any other area in the world. Also, cotton, fruit, soybeans, wheat, cattle, poultry.

EMANUEL *Swainsboro* • 21,837 • 686 • Eastern GA, bounded on the north by the Ogeechee River; drained by the Ohoopee River (forming part of the southwestern and southeastern boundary) and the Canoochee River. George L. Smith State Park is here. • Named for David Emanuel (?–1808), GA legislator and governor • 1812 from Montgomery and Bulloch • Cotton, corn, tobacco, wheat, soybeans, peanuts, hogs, cattle, timber; education (East GA College) • The county has the unfortunate distinction of having had its courthouse destroyed by fire five times: in 1841, 1855, 1857, 1919 and 1938.

EVANS *Claxton* •10,495 • 185 • Eastern GA, bounded on the northeast by the Canoochee River. Fort Stewart in the southeast is used as a flight-training center. • Named for General Clement A. Evans (1833–1911), GA officer during the Civil War, jurist and Methodist minister • 1914 from Bulloch and Tattnall • Cotton, corn, soybeans, wheat, tobacco, peanuts, cattle, hogs, poultry; timber. Claxton claims to be the "Fruitcake Capital of the World," producing over 5.5 million pounds of fruitcake a year. • The Evans County Wildlife Club hosts a Rattlesnake Roundup each March. Old Sunbury Road, laid through the county in the 1790s, is considered one of the longest vehicular thoroughfares of the post-revolutionary period.

FANNIN *Blue Ridge* • 19,798 • 386 • Northern GA, on the TN and NC state lines; drained by the Toccoa River (which forms Blue Ridge Lake here). The county is situated in the Blue Ridge and partly in the Chattahoochee National Forest. The Cohutta Wilderness Area, which extends into the county from TN, is the largest national wilderness area east of the Mississippi River. • One of two counties (the other in TX) named for James W. Fannin (1804–1836), GA soldier executed in the Texas War of Independence • 1854 from Gilmer and Union • Some members of the Cherokee Nation found shelter in the mountains of Fannin County while the rest of their tribe was forcibly moved west in 1838. • Apparel, textiles, wood products, dairy products; cattle, poultry, hogs, fruit, corn, hay, potatoes. Copper mines in adjacent Polk County, TN are a major employer of Fannin residents. • The terminus of the Appalachian Trail is in the Ed Jenkins National Recreation Area on Springer Mountain along the border with Gilmer County.

FAYETTE (one of eleven counties so named) *Fayetteville* • 91,263 • 197 • West-central GA, in the Piedmont, bounded on the east in part by the Flint River. • One of seventeen counties named for the Marquis de Lafayette (1757–1834), French statesman and soldier who fought with the Americans during the Revolutionary War • Original county; organized 1821 from Indian lands (Creek Indian Territory) • Pecans, peaches, dairying, cattle • The county courthouse in Fayette, built in 1825,

is the oldest in the state. It also boasts the "world's largest courthouse bench," situated alongside the building's entrance. Every Halloween, local children fill the courthouse square with elaborately decorated jack-o-lanterns.

FLOYD (one of six counties so named) *Rome* • 90,565 • 513 • Northwestern GA, bounded on the west by the AL state line; drained by the Coosa, Etowah and Oostanaula rivers. The county includes part of Chattahoochee National Forest in the north. Part of Weiss Lake reservoir is on the western boundary. • Named for General John Floyd (1769–1839), officer in the War of 1812 and U.S. representative • 1832 from Cherokee • Union General Sherman all but destroyed Rome during his "March to the Sea." The city suffered a disastrous flood in 1886. • Blues vocalist Ma Rainey died here. • Cotton, corn, wheat, soybeans, cattle, hogs, poultry; stone quarrying; manufacture of carpets, electrical equipment, foundry products, furniture, frozen foods, lumber, paper; education (Shorter College; Berry College, which, at 26,000 acres, claims to have the largest college campus in the world.) • The discovery of bauxite (aluminum ore) was made here in 1887. The World's Largest Bed race is held in Rome. Capitoline Wolf is a 1,500-pound sculpture given to the city of Rome by Italian dictator Benito Mussolini in 1929. The world's largest natural springs swimming pool is in Cave Spring. A notable county landmark is the 104-foot clock tower, built atop one of Rome's hills.

FORSYTH (one of two counties so named, the other in NC) *Cumming* • 98,407 (123% increase since 1990; the fastest growing county in GA) • 226 • Northern GA, bounded on the east by the Chattahoochee River (here forming Lake Sidney Lanier reservoir). The county lies in the Piedmont Region. • Named for John Forsyth (1780–1841), U.S. secretary of state and minister to Spain when FL was ceded to the U.S. • 1832 from Cherokee • Signers of the Treaty of New Echota (which established the terms for the removal of the Cherokee Indians) William Rogers, Johnson Rogers, and George Welch • Manufacture of fabricated metal products, food products, apparel; printing and publishing • Several Indian archaeological sites are located in the county.

FRANKLIN (one of twenty-five counties so named) *Carnesville* • 20,285 • 263 • Northeastern GA, bounded on the northeast by the Tugaloo River (here forming the SC state line and part of Lake Hartwell reservoir) and on the south in part by the Hudson River; drained by forks of the Broad River. The county is located in the Piedmont agricultural region of the state. It also includes Victoria-Bryant and Tugaloo state parks. • One of twenty-three counties named for Benjamin Franklin • Original county; organized 1784 (prior to statehood) from Cherokee lands • Baseball player Ty Cobb • The county leads the state in poultry production. Also, cotton, corn, hay, soybeans, wheat, cattle, hogs; textiles; lumber; education (Emmanuel College) • Lavonia is the smallest city in the U.S. with an original Carnegie Library Building.

FULTON (one of eight counties so named) *Atlanta* • 816,006 (the most populated county in GA) • 529 • Northwestern GA, bounded on the northwest by the Chattahoochee River. The county includes a major part of the Atlanta metropolitan area. The northern and southern sections are rapidly urbanizing. Units of Chattahoochee River Recreation Area are here. • One of seven counties named for Robert Fulton (1765–1815), builder of the Clermont, the first commercially successful steamboat. Some contend the county was named for Hamilton Fulton, chief engineer of the state of GA. • 1853 from De Kalb; in 1932 the county annexed Campbell (organized 1828 from Carroll, Coweta, De Kalb, Fayette, and Cherokee) and Milton (organized 1857 from Cobb, Cherokee and Forsyth) • Railroads have played a large role in the development of Atlanta (first called Terminus). By 1860, several railroads had converged on the city. East Point was an important defense post for the Confederacy during the Civil War; forts and ammunition depots were here. A supply depot and an industrial center for the Confederacy, Atlanta was the prime military objective of General William Tecumseh Sherman whose Union troops entered the city on September 1, 1864 and converted it into a military camp. Sherman burned the city before continuing his march to the sea. A center of federal government activities for the south during Reconstruction and early advocate of reconciliation with the North, the city became state capital in 1868. It was at the Cotton States and International Exposition in 1895 that Booker T. Washington made his famous declaration, urging blacks to seek economic security before political and social equality with whites. (Piedmont Park, designed by noted architect Frederick Law Olmsted, served as the grounds for the exposition.) A fire in 1917 destroyed about 2,000 buildings in the city. Atlanta hosted the Summer Olympic Games in 1996. • Historian Daniel Boorstin; golfers Bobby Jones and Louise Suggs; civil rights leaders Martin Luther King, Jr. (national historic site) and Vernon E. Jordan; author Margaret Mitchell. Journalist and orator Henry W. Grady, author Joel Chandler Harris, civil rights leader Ralph David Abernathy, and poet and novelist James Dickey died here. • Atlanta is the principal trade and transportation center of the southeastern U.S. Manufacture of automobiles, glass products, airplane parts, textiles, electronic and electrical equipment, processed foods, chemicals, pulp and paper products; commercial fertilizers; printing and publishing; banking and insurance; government operations (both state and federal); education (Morehouse College; American Intercontinental U.; Atlanta Christian College; GA Institute of Technology; Morris Brown College; Clark Atlanta U.; GA State U.; Spelman College; others) • The corporate headquarters for nineteen Fortune 1000 companies are located here. Atlanta is the site of the King Center for Nonviolent Social Change and the Jimmy Carter Presidential Center. Hartsfield-Atlanta International Airport, located partially in the county, is one of the nation's busiest. Atlanta's High Museum of Art is known for its Renaissance paintings. Atlanta is home to the Atlanta Thrashers (CNN Center), Falcons (Georgia Dome), Hawks (Phillips Arena), and Braves (Turner Field).

GILMER (one of two counties so named, the other in WV) *Ellijay* • 23,456 • 427 • Northern GA, in the Blue Ridge; drained by the Ellijay and Coosawattee rivers. Nearly half the county is in Chattahoochee National Forest. • Named for George R. Gilmer (1790–1859), U.S. representative from GA and governor • 1832 from Cherokee • The county is GA's "Apple Capital" (with a festival each October). Also, corn, cattle, hogs; timber; textiles; tourism.

GLASCOCK *Gibson* • 2,556 • 144 (one of the fifty smallest counties in the U.S.) • Eastern GA, bounded on the west by the Ogeechee River. • Named for General Thomas Glascock (1790–1841), GA army officer during the War of 1812 and the Seminole War, and U.S. representative from GA • 1857 from Warren • Cotton, corn, soybeans, wheat, cattle, hogs; timber; kaolin mining and processing.

GLYNN *Brunswick* • 67,568 • 422 • Southeastern GA, bounded on the east by the Atlantic Ocean, on the northeast by the Altamaha River, and on the southwest by the Little Satilla River. The county includes St. Simons, Little St. Simons, and Jekyll islands. The Intracoastal Waterway crosses from St. Andrew Sound to Altamaha Sound. Fort Frederica National Monument, including the Bloody Marsh Battlefield Site on St. Simons, preserves the ruins of a fort built by General James E. Oglethorpe between 1736 and 1748, the southernmost British outpost in America. Hofwyl-Broadfield Plantation State Historic Site is also here. • Named for John Glynn (1722–79), a pro-colonist member of the British Parliament • Original county; organized 1777 (prior to statehood) from St. David and St. Patrick parishes • Professional football player Jim Brown; tobacco magnate R.J. Reynolds; architect William Portman • Shrimp, conch, crabs; forestry; cattle, dairying; manufacture of seafood products, naval stores, pulp boxes, paperboard, chemicals, paints, varnishes, clothing, industrial boilers, concrete and gypsum products; tourism. The Federal Law Enforcement Training Center is located here • The area was made famous by Sidney Lanier's poem "Marshes of Glynn." Glynn Academy, established in Brunswick in 1778, is the oldest school in the state. Jekyll Island Park is a major golf and convention center.

GORDON *Calhoun* • 44,104 • 356 • Northwestern GA; drained by the Oostanaula, Conasauga, and Coosawattee rivers, the last forming part of the northern boundary. The county includes part of Chattahoochee National Forest. • Named for William W. Gordon (1796–1842), a prominent GA railroad official • 1850 from Bartow (then called Cass) and Floyd • The written Cherokee language, developed by Sequoyah, and the newspaper, the *Cherokee Phoenix*, were born in New Echota, site of the last capital (1825–1838) of the Cherokee Nation (state historic site). Calhoun was virtually wiped out by Sherman's Union troops on their "March to the Sea." • Singer Roland Hayes • Cotton, corn, soybeans, wheat, cattle, dairying, hogs, poultry; manufacture of bricks and textiles.

GRADY (one of two counties so named, the other in OK) *Cairo* • 23,659 • 458 • Southwestern GA, bounded on the south by the FL state line; drained by the Ochlockonee River. • Named for Henry W. Grady (1850–89), editor, and part-owner of the *Atlanta Constitution* • 1905 from Decatur and Thomas • Hernando De Soto is believed to have come through what is now Grady County during his trek across the southeast in 1540. • Baseball player Jackie Robinson • Tobacco, corn, peanuts, pecans, tung nuts, cotton, soybeans, wheat, cattle, hogs, poultry; lumber and naval stores; some manufacturing • Calvary's Mule Day Parade attracts 30,000 to 40,000 spectators each November.

GREENE (one of fourteen counties so named) *Greensboro* • 14,406 • 388 • Northeast-central GA, bounded on the west by the Apalachee River (here forming part of Oconee Lake reservoir); drained by the Oconee and Ogeechee rivers. The county is located in the Piedmont region of the state. • One of sixteen counties named for General Nathanael Greene (1742–86), hero of the Revolutionary War, quartermaster general and commander of the Army of the South • 1786 (prior to statehood) from Washington, Oglethorpe and Wilkes • Blues singer and harmonica player Sonny Terry • Cotton, corn, grain, fruit, cattle, poultry; textile manufacturing; timber • Greenesborough (later Greensboro) is reputed to be the first town in the U.S. to be burned and its inhabitants killed by Indians (in 1787). By special arrangement with the county, the top floor of the Greene County courthouse (1848–49) was constructed as a Masonic Lodge.

GWINNETT *Lawrenceville* • 588,448 (the fourth most populated county in GA) • 433 • North-central GA, bounded on the northwest by the Chattahoochee River; drained by the Apalachee and Yellow rivers. Part of the Atlanta metropolitan area, it is one of the fastest growing counties in the U.S. A small part of Lake Sidney Lanier reservoir is on the northern border. • Named for Button Gwinnett (?–1777), a signer of the Declaration of Independence and acting president of GA • Original county; organized 1818 from Indian lands • High-tech manufacturing, business and industrial parks • The graves of seven soldiers killed in a battle with Indians in 1830 lie beneath the county's courthouse grounds. Gwinnett boasts the largest retail mall in the state. Stone Mountain, standing on the border with De Kalb County, is the world's largest exposed mass of granite.

HABERSHAM *Clarkesville* • 35,902 • 278 • Northeastern GA, in the Blue Ridge and Piedmont area, bounded on the east by the Tugaloo River (here forming the SC state line) and on the west by the Chattahoochee River. Part of Chattahoochee National Forest is in the north. Part of Tallulah Gorge, considered to be the Grand Canyon of the South, is located in the county. • Named for Col. Joseph Habersham (1751–1815), member of the Continental Congress and U.S. postmaster general • 1818 from Cherokee lands • Confederate presidential contender Robert Toombs • Timber; textile manufacturing; cotton, hay, sweet potatoes, peaches, poultry, cat-

tle, hogs, apples (A large apple monument, weighing 5,200 pounds, was erected in 1925 as a symbol of the area's productive orchards. Cornelia hosts the Big Red Apple Festival each October.); education (Piedmont College) • The Eastern Continental Divide runs through downtown Cornelia on South Main Street; water falling on the north side of the street runs into the Chattahoochee River and the Gulf of Mexico, while water draining to the south of the street ends up in the Savannah River and the Atlantic Ocean.

HALL (one of three counties so named) *Gainesville* • 139,277 • 394 • Northeastern GA; drained by the Chattahoochee and Oconee rivers. Lake Sidney Lanier reservoir dominates the southwest and forms part of the boundary. The county is located in the Piedmont region of the state. • Named for Lyman Hall (1724–90), a signer of the Declaration of Independence, and GA governor • Original county; organized 1818 from Cherokee lands • Gainesville was heavily damaged and many lives were lost in a tornado that struck the city in 1936. • Confederate general James Longstreet • Gainesville stakes its claim as the "Poultry Capital of the World." Also soybeans, hay, sweet potatoes, cattle, eggs; granite and marble; manufacture of textiles and furniture; education (Brenau U.). • With the construction of its municipal power plant in 1899, Gainesville became the first southern city to have electric streetlights. The city serves as headquarters for both the Oconee and Chattahoochee national forests.

HANCOCK *Sparta* • 10,076 • 473 • East-central GA, bounded on the east by the Ogeechee River, on the west by the Oconee River; intersected by the Fall Line. Lake Sinclair is formed by the impoundment of the Oconee River by Sinclair Dam • One of ten counties named for John Hancock • 1793 from Greene and Washington • Millmore Gristmill was the site of the historic 1786 peace treaty between GA and the Creek Indian Nation. • Civil rights leader Charles L. Harper • Cotton, corn, forage, pecans, cattle; lumber and wood products • Four GA governors have come from this sparsely populated county.

HARALSON *Buchanan* • 25,690 • 282 • Northwestern GA, bounded on the west by the AL state line; drained by the Tallapoosa River • Named for Gen. Hugh A. Haralson (1805–54), U.S. representative from GA • 1856 from Carroll and Polk • Corn, cattle, hogs, poultry; textile manufacturing, sawmilling • Tallapoosa is known for its beautiful Dogwood trees. The annual Dogwood Festival is held each April. The first free school in GA was established in Tallapoosa in 1889.

HARRIS (one of two counties so named, the other in TX) *Hamilton* • 23,695 • 464 • Western GA, bounded on the west by the Chattahoochee River (forming the AL state line). Franklin D. Roosevelt State Park is here. Reservoirs on the Chattahoochee are created by Langdale, Riverview, Bartletts Ferry, and Goat Rock dams. • Named for Charles Harris (1772–1827), mayor of Savannah • 1827 from Muscogee and Troup • Cattle, hogs, cotton, wheat, vegetables, fruit;

sawmilling • Callaway Gardens, a 12,000-acre resort, comprises one of the largest botanical gardens in the world.

HART (one of two counties so named, the other in KY) *Hartwell* • 22,997 • 232 • Northeastern GA, bounded on the north and east by the Savannah and Tugaloo rivers (forming the SC state line and Hartwell Lake reservoir). The reservoir is one of the three most visited Corps of Engineers lakes in the U.S. The county also includes Hart State Park. • Named for Nancy Morgan Hart, spy, sharpshooter, and heroine of the American Revolution. • 1853 from Elbert and Franklin • Cotton, wheat, soybeans, corn, hay, sweet potatoes, cattle, hogs, poultry • The Cherokee Indian "Center of the World" was the site of council meetings and trade with white settlers. The *Hartwell Sun* is over 120 years old.

HEARD *Franklin* • 11,012 • 296 • Western GA, in the Piedmont, bounded on the west by the AL state line; bisected by the Chattahoochee River, and part of West Point Lake reservoir. • Named for Stephen Heard (1740–?), chief executive officer and de facto governor of GA • 1830 from Carroll, Coweta and Troup • Hay, vegetables, fruit, cattle, poultry; gravel; apparel, textiles • The Labor Day Powers Crossroads Festival held on the border between Coweta and Heard counties has been rated as one of the ten best arts and crafts festivals in the U.S. The county has old gristmills and cotton gins scattered throughout.

HENRY (one of ten counties so named) *McDonough* • 119,341 (103% increase since 1990; the second fastest growing county in GA) • 323 • Central GA, bounded on the northeast in part by the South River. The county is rapidly urbanizing from the expanding Atlanta metropolitan area. It is bisected by I-75, which has become an important force in its economic growth. The Panola Mountain State Conservation Park, located on the county's border with Rockdale County, surrounds Panola Mountain, a million-year-old granite monadnock • One of ten counties (including Patrick County, VA) named for patriot Patrick Henry • 1821 from Indian lands • Martin Luther King, Sr.; civil rights leader James Weldon Johnson • The Atlanta Motor Speedway, in Hampton, stages two major NASCAR events.

HOUSTON (one of five counties so named) *Perry* • 110,765 • 377 • Central GA, bounded on the east by the Ocmulgee River. • Named for John Houstoun (1744–96), American Revolutionary patriot and GA governor, with spelling changed by clerical error • Original county; organized 1821 from Indian lands • Senator Sam Nunn • Cotton, corn, melons, soybeans, wheat, peanuts, pecans, peaches, cattle, hogs, poultry; timber • The Museum of Aviation in Warner Robins is considered one of the best air museums in the U.S. The Georgia National Fair is held each year in Perry. Robins Air Force Base, GA's largest single employer, was once the home of the "Flying Tigers," and is now headquarters for the Air Force Reserve.

IRWIN *Ocilla* • 9,931 • 357 • South-central GA; drained by the Alapaha (forming part of the southwest and northwest

boundaries) and Satilla rivers. • Named for General Jared Irwin (?–1818), twice governor of GA. Irwin was admired for his opposition to the Yazoo Law of 1795, by which the state of GA sold a vast tract of land at one and a half cents per acre to four companies, including one owned by Senator James Gunn. Irwin rescinded the law in 1796 during his term as governor. • Original county; organized 1818 from Indian lands • Union soldiers captured Confederate president Jefferson Davis at Irwinville. (The event is memorialized at Jefferson Davis State Historic Site and Museum.) • Wheat, cotton, corn, tobacco, peanuts, peaches, cattle, hogs, poultry; timber.

JACKSON (one of twenty-four counties so named) *Jefferson* • 41,589 • 342 • Northeastern GA; drained by the Oconee River • Named for General James Jackson (1757–1806), an officer in the American Revolution, GA governor and U.S. senator • 1796 from Franklin • Hay, sweet potatoes, apples, peaches, cattle, hogs, poultry; textile manufacturing • Crawford W. Long reputedly discovered ether as an anesthetic while studying in Jefferson. The city's top track facilities draw state high school track and field championships.

JASPER *Monticello* • 11,426 • 370 • Central GA, bounded on the west by the Ocmulgee River (which forms Jackson Lake reservoir here) and on the northwest by the Alcovy River; drained by the Little River. Oconee National Forest and Piedmont National Wildlife Refuge are in the south. • One of eight counties named for Sergeant William Jasper (1750–79), Revolutionary War hero. (GA is one of five states in which Jasper and Newton counties have been placed adjacent to one another to honor the allied efforts of sergeants William Jasper and John Newton to rescue captive colonial soldiers near Savannah.) • Organized as Randolph, 1807 from Baldwin; name changed 1812 • Cattle, poultry; timber; feldspar mining.

JEFF DAVIS (One of two counties so named, the other in TX) *Hazlehurst* • 12,684 • 333 • Southeast-central GA, bounded on the northwest by the Ocmulgee River and on the north by the Altamaha River, the largest free-flowing waterway in GA; drained by Big Satilla and Hurricane creeks. • One of four counties named for Jefferson Davis (1808–89), president of the Confederate States of America • 1905 from Appling and Coffee • Cotton, soybeans, tobacco, corn, sugarcane, peanuts, pecans, cattle, hogs, poultry; textile manufacturing.

JEFFERSON *Louisville* • 17,266 • 528 • Eastern GA, bounded on the northeast by Brier Creek; drained by the Ogeechee River (which forms part of the county's western boundary). • One of twenty-six counties named directly or indirectly for President Thomas Jefferson • 1796 from Burke and Warren • Louisville was GA's third state capital, serving from 1796 to 1806. The Jefferson County Courthouse, built in 1904, stands on the site of GA's first permanent capitol, constructed in 1795. Louisville was the scene of the burning of the infamous Yazoo Act, in which GA sold 35 million acres to four companies, including one owned by GA senator and Jefferson County native son, James Gunn, for one and a half per acre. Louisville was also the site of the Constitutional Convention of 1798 in which the state's pre-Civil War constitution was adopted. • Politician Howell Cobb; Republic of Texas president Mirabeau B. Lamar • Cotton, corn, peanuts; sawmilling; manufacture of trusses, textiles, apparel, consumer goods; printing and publishing.

JENKINS *Millen* • 8,575 • 350 • Eastern GA; intersected by the Ogeechee River. Magnolia Springs State Park is in the county. • Named for Charles J. Jenkins (1805–83), GA legislator, jurist, and governor • 1905 from Bulloch, Burke, Screven and Emanuel • Cotton, corn, soybeans, peanuts, tobacco, wheat, cattle, hogs; lumber and wood products • Millen was originally called Seventy-Nine or Old 79 because of its distance from Savannah. Within the county is the site of Fort Lawton; at forty-two acres, it was the largest stockade built by the Confederacy to receive prisoners-of-war. One of the oldest structures in GA is the Millen Big Buckhead Church, constructed in 1830.

JOHNSON (one of twelve counties so named) *Wrightsville* • 8,560 • 304 • Central GA, bounded on the west by the Oconee River; drained by the Ohoopee and Little Ohoopee rivers. • Named for Herschel V. Johnson (1812–80), middle circuit court judge, GA governor, and vice-presidential candidate • 1858 from Emanuel, Laurens, and Washington counties • Professional football player Herschel Walker • Cotton, corn, potatoes, soybeans, peanuts, fruit; manufacture of apparel, textiles, lumber and millwork; wholesale trade

JONES (one of six counties so named) *Gray* • 23,639 • 394 • Central GA, bounded on the southwest by the Ocmulgee River; intersected by the Fall Line. Part of Oconee National Forest is in the north. Jarrell Plantation State Historic Site lies within Piedmont National Wildlife Refuge. • Named for James Jones (?—1801), GA legislator and U.S. representative from GA. • 1807 from Baldwin • Peaches, soybeans, pimientos, cattle, poultry, hogs; sawmilling. • The first iron foundry in GA was established by Samuel Griswold here in 1820; it was destroyed by Union forces because it provided ordnance to the Confederate army. The architecture of old Clinton, built in 1809, shows a New England influence; many of the early settlers to the town were from that region.

LAMAR (one of four counties so named) *Barnesville* • 15,912 • 185 • West-central GA; drained by Potato Creek. • One of three counties named for Lucius Q. C. Lamar (1825–93), U.S. statesman and U.S. Supreme Court justice • 1920 from Monroe and Pike • Cotton, corn, soybeans, wheat, cattle, hogs, poultry; lumber and wood products • Barnesville, once home to four buggy companies, was designated the "Buggy Capital of the World." Barnesville Buggy Days festival is one of GA's largest community festivals, attracting over 50,000 people.

LANIER *Lakeland* • 7,241 • 187 • Southern GA; intersected by the Alapaha River (forming the northwest and southwest boundaries). Part of Moody Air Force Base is in the west. Banks Lake National Wildlife Refuge is here. • Named for Sidney C. Lanier (1842–81), important post-Civil War southern poet • 1920 from Berrien, Lowndes and Clinch • Corn, tobacco, peanuts, soybeans, cotton, fruit, cattle, hogs; forestry products.

LAURENS (one of two counties so named, the other in SC) *Dublin* • 44,874 • 812 (the third largest county in GA) • Central GA; intersected by the Oconee River (forming part of the southeastern boundary) • Named for John Laurens (1753–82), lieutenant colonel in the American Revolution • 1807 from Wilkinson • The Ocute Indian Mounds at Blackshear's Ferry date back to 1000 B.C. • Tobacco, wheat, cotton, corn, peanuts, cattle, hogs; timber • Dublin's two-week-long St. Patrick's Festival includes the world's biggest Irish stew.

LEE (one of twelve counties so named) *Leesburg* • 24,757 • 356 • Southwest-central GA, bounded on the east by the Flint River; drained by Kinchafoonee Creek (forming part of the western boundary) and Muckalee Creek. Part of Lake Blackshear reservoir is on the extreme northeast. Chewhaw Indian Monument is also here. • Named for Richard Henry Lee (1732–94), signer of the Declaration of Independence and U.S. senator • Original county; organized 1826 from Indian lands • Peanuts, soybeans, cotton, wheat, corn, cattle, hogs; timber; hunting, fishing • In June, Lee County hosts the Southern Heritage Festival. The county was once the site of Kennard's Settlement and Cowpens, a major Creek Indian center named for Jack and William Kennard, two Lower Creek chiefs who were friendly to white settlers.

LIBERTY (one of four counties so named) *Hinesville* • 61,610 • 519 • Southeastern GA, bounded on the southeast by the Atlantic Ocean, on the northeast by the Canoochee River. The Intracoastal Waterway crosses from Sapelo Sound to St. Catherines Sound. The county includes St. Catherines Island and Fort Morris State Historic Site. Fort Stewart Military Reservation is here. • Named for the fervent patriotism of the citizens of Midway during the Revolutionary War • Original county; organized 1777 (prior to statehood) from Saint Andrew, Saint James, Saint Johns and Tatnall parishes • GA governor and signer of the Declaration of Independence Lyman Hall; naturalist and scholar Louis LeConte (His home is now the site of the LeConte Botanical Gardens.) • Corn, sugarcane, rice, tobacco, cattle, hogs, poultry; logging and wood products; fishing.

LINCOLN (one of twenty-four counties so named) *Lincolnton* • 8,348 • 211 • Northeastern GA, bounded on the northeast by the Savannah River (forming the SC state line and J. Strom Thurmond Reservoir) and on the south by the Little River (forming Clark Hills Lake reservoir). • One of four counties named for General Benjamin Lincoln (1733–1810), Revolutionary War officer and U.S. secretary of war • 1796 from Wilkes • Revolutionary War hero Elijah Clarke and his wife are buried in Elijah Clark State Park. • Cotton, corn, hay, fruits, cattle, hogs, poultry; manufacture of apparel, textiles; sawmilling • The Lewis Family Homecoming and Bluegrass Festival is a nationally recognized bluegrass festival. Over

160 buildings in the county are listed in the National Register of Historic Places.

LONG *Ludowici* • 10,304 • 401 • Southeastern GA, bounded on the southwest by the Altamaha River. Part of Fort Stewart Military Reservation is in the north. • Named for Crawford W. Long (1815–78), prominent GA surgeon, first in history to administer sulphuric ether as an anesthetic • 1920 from Liberty • Old Barrington Road, originally an Indian trail, became an important trade route between the Carolinas and Florida in the early 1700s, and was of critical importance for Continental Army troop movements. • Corn, soybeans, tobacco, hogs, cattle; forestry.

LOWNDES *Valdosta* • 92,115 • 504 • Southern GA, bounded on the south by the FL state line, on the east in part by the Alapaha River, and on the west in part by the Little River; drained by the Withlacoochee River (which forms part of its western boundary). Moody Air Force Base is in the northeast. • One of three counties named for William J. Lowndes (1782–1822), SC legislator and U.S. representative from SC • 1825 from Irwin • Gunslinger Doc Holliday • Tobacco, watermelons, cotton, soybeans, peanuts, corn, wheat, vegetables, cattle, hogs; lumber and naval stores, especially turpentine; manufacture of casual and western wear, cotton and nylon fabrics, aluminum trim for automobiles, polyethylene bags; education (Valdosta State U.) • Valdosta was once the smallest American town with a streetcar system.

LUMPKIN *Dahlonega* • 21,016 • 284 • Northern GA; drained by the Chestatee and Etowah rivers. The county is in the Blue Ridge. The Appalachian Trail closely follows the northern boundary. The county's northern half is occupied by Chattahoochee National Forest and includes DeSoto Falls Scenic Area. • Named for Wilson Lumpkin (1783–1870), U.S. senator and GA governor who worked to remove Cherokees from GA. • 1832 from Cherokee, Hall and Habersham • Gold was discovered near Dahlonega in 1838. A U.S. mint operated in the city from 1837 until 1861 when GA seceded from the Union • Corn, hay, potatoes, broiler poultry, cattle, hogs; timber; education (North GA College and State U.) • Constructed in 1838, the Lumpkin County Courthouse is the oldest public building in north GA. The Dahlonega Gold Museum (and state historic site) is the state's second most visited museum.

MACON *Oglethorpe* • 14,074 • 403 • Central GA; drained by the Flint River • One of six counties named for Nathaniel Macon (1758–1837), U.S. representative and senator • 1837 from Houston and Marion • More than a quarter of the 45,000 Union soldiers held in Andersonville Civil War prison camp at the southwest tip of the county died from disease caused by overcrowding and poor water (Andersonville National Historic site and National Prisoner of War Museum; also in Sumter County). • Sam H. Rumph developed the Elberta Peach here; this variety is responsible for establishing GA as the peach state. • Cotton, corn, soybeans, wheat, peanuts; timber • There is a large Mennonite colony near Montezuma.

MADISON *Danielsville* • 25,730 • 284 • Northeastern GA, bounded on the north and southeast by the Broad River; drained by the Broad River • One of twenty counties named directly or indirectly for President James Madison • 1811 from Clarke, Elbert, Franklin, Jackson and Oglethorpe • Physician Crawford W. Long • Manufacture of apparel, textiles, wood products; printing and publishing; cotton, wheat, soybeans, sweet potatoes, hay, cattle, poultry, eggs, hogs • Madison and Oglethorpe counties share Watson Mill Bridge State Park, the site of the longest covered bridge in GA (with a span of 229 feet).

MARION *Buena Vista* • 7,144 • 367 • Western GA, bounded on the north in part by Upatoi Creek; drained by the Kinchafoonee River • One of seventeen counties named for General Francis Marion (?–1795), SC soldier and legislator, known as "The Swamp Fox" • 1827 from Lee and Muscogee • Baseball player Josh Gibson • Soybeans, wheat, corn, peanuts, cattle, poultry, hogs; timber • Buena Vista is becoming a miniature version of Branson, MO, with music museums and performing venues.

MCDUFFIE *Thomson* • 21,231 • 260 • Eastern GA, bounded on the north by the Little River (forming Clarks Hill Lake reservoir in the northeast) and on the south by Brier Creek; intersected by the Fall Line. Part of Fort Gordon Military Reservation is here. • Named for George McDuffie (1790–1851), SC governor and U.S. senator • 1870 from Columbia and Warren • Gold was discovered near Thomson in 1823, and before it was mined out, produced about $80,000 in bullion. • "Father of Rural Free Delivery" Thomas Edward Watson • Cotton, vegetables, fruit, cattle; timber • The "no kill" Belle Meade Fox Hunt draws participants from all over the U.S. and Europe.

MCINTOSH (one of three counties so named) *Darien* • 10,847 • 433 • Southeastern GA, bounded on the southeast by the Atlantic Ocean and on the southwest by the Altamaha River. The Intracoastal Waterway crosses from Altamaha Sound to Sapelo Sound. The county contains Harris Neck, Blackbeard Island, and Wolf Island national wildlife refuges, and Sapelo Island National Estuarine Research Reserve. Lewis Island Natural Area and Fort King George State Historic Site are also here. • Named for either all or one of the McIntosh family of early settlers; or for William McIntosh (?–1825), Creek Indian leader who became a brigadier general in the U.S. Army • 1793 from Liberty • Fort King George was the first English fort in GA. The county enjoyed an economic boom after the War of 1812 due to the demand for lumber harvested from surrounding forest lands. During the Civil War, the Rev. Mansfield French who was known as the "White Jesus," formed an "army" of black crusaders who burned the city of Darien on July 11, 1863. • Fishing; sawmilling; seafood canning. (Darien is the source of 90% of the caviar sold in GA.)

MERIWETHER *Greenville* • 22,534 • 503 • Western GA,

bounded on the east by the Flint River. The county lies in the Piedmont. • Named for General David Meriwether (1755–1822), officer in the Revolutionary War, representative from GA, and commissioner to the Creek Indians • 1827 from Troup • Large peach production here; also pecans, melons, peppers, cattle, hogs; lumber; manufacture of apparel, textiles, wood products; printing and publishing • The therapeutic waters of Warm Springs were promoted by President Franklin D. Roosevelt, through the Warm Springs Foundation, which he organized in 1927. The town was the site of FDR's "Little White House" (state historic site) where he died on April 12, 1945.

MILLER (one of three counties so named) *Colquitt* • 6,383 • 283 • Southwestern GA; drained by Spring Creek. • Named for Andrew J. Miller (1806–56), GA legislator • 1856 from Baker and Early • Corn, peanuts, sugarcane, cotton, oats, cattle, hogs • Colquitt is the "Mayhaw Capital of the World." A festival celebrating the importance of this small, red berry to the area draws almost 20,000 visitors a year.

MITCHELL (one of five counties so named) *Camilla* • 23,932 • 512 • Southwestern GA, bounded on the west by the Flint River. • Named for General Henry Mitchell (1760–1837), Revolutionary War hero and president of the GA Senate. • 1857 from Baker • Corn, pecans, soybeans, peanuts, cotton, tobacco, cattle, hogs, poultry; sawmilling; manufacturing.

MONROE *Forsyth* • 21,757 • 396 • Central GA, bounded on the east by the Ocmulgee River drained by the Towaliga and Tobesofkee rivers. High Falls State Park is in the north. • One of seventeen counties named for President James Monroe • Original county; organized in 1821 from Indian lands • Corn, wheat, vegetables, pecans, fruit, cattle, poultry; timber; textile manufacturing • Culloden is the site of the oldest Methodist church in GA. Juliette's Whistle Stop Café still serves fried green tomatoes.

MONTGOMERY (One of eighteen counties so named) *Mount Vernon* • 8,270 • 245 • East-central GA, bounded on the west by the Oconee River, which joins the Ocmulgee to form the Altamaha along the southern border. • One of sixteen counties named directly or indirectly for General Richard Montgomery (1738–75), American Revolutionary War officer who captured Montreal, Canada • 1793 from Washington County • Manufacture of apparel, textiles, beer, distilled beverages; cotton, corn, tobacco, peanuts, cattle, hogs; timber; education (Brewton-Parker College).

MORGAN (One of eleven counties so named) *Madison* • 15,457 • 350 • North-central GA, bounded on the northeast by the Apalachee River (forming part of Oconee Lake in the southeast); drained by the Little River. Hard Labor Creek State Park is the largest park in GA. • One of nine counties named for General Daniel Morgan (1736–1802), an officer in the Revolutionary War and U.S. representative from VA • Organized as Cotaco in 1807 from Baldwin; named changed 1821 • During the Civil War the town of Madison was spared

destruction by Sherman's army because it was the home of pro-Union senator Joshua Hill. • Inventor Lancelot Johnson • Cotton, corn, wheat, peaches, cattle, hogs, poultry; lumbering • The Madison Collegiate Institute (later GA Female College) and the Methodist Female College, both founded in Madison (neither extant), were among the first women's colleges in the U.S.

MURRAY *Chatsworth* • 36,506 • 344 • Northwestern GA, bounded on the north by the TN state line, on the west by the Conasauga River, and on the south in part by the Coosawattee River. The Appalachian Mountains cross the county, which includes part of Chattahoochee National Forest in the east. The county also includes Fort Mountain State Park, which contains possibly the oldest fortifications in North America, believed to have been built in 1530 to defend against De Soto's men. Chief Vann House State Historic Site is also here. • Named for Thomas W. Murray (1790–1832), GA legislator • 1832 from Cherokee • Corn, hay, soybeans, fruit, cattle, hogs, poultry; textile manufacturing; sawmilling; talc mining.

MUSCOGEE *Columbus* • 186,291 • 216 • Western GA, bounded on the west by the Chattahoochee River (forming the AL state line and Lake Oliver reservoir) and on the southeast by Upatoi Creek; intersected by the Fall Line. Fort Benning Military Reservation, partly located here, is one of the largest infantry bases in the world. • Named for the Muskogee Indians' Creek members • 1826 from Creek lands • Columbus was an arsenal and arms manufacturer for the Confederate army during the Civil War. Union forces under General James H. Wilson, unaware of Lee's surrender to Grant one week earlier, captured the city on April 16, 1865. One million officers and troops were trained at Fort Benning during WW II. • Blues vocalist Ma Rainey; industrialist Robert W. Woodruff; Coca-Cola inventor Dr. John Pemberton; novelist and short story writer Carson McCullers • Dairying, cattle, vegetables; manufacture of machinery, fabricated iron and steel, concrete pipe, storage batteries, upholstery fabric, clothing, hosiery, processed foods, packed meats, soft drinks, lumber products, fertilizer; education (Columbus State U.) • Columbus's Confederate Naval Museum displays the salvaged hulk of the gunboat *Muscogee*, which was built here and sunk by the Union army in the Chattahoochee River in 1865.

NEWTON (one of six counties so named) *Covington* • 62,001 • 276 • North-central GA, bounded on the southwest by the Smith River; drained by the Alcovy and Yellow Rivers. Two arms of Jackson Lake reservoir form the southern tip of the county. • One of five counties named for Sergeant John Newton (?–1780), Revolutionary War hero. (GA is one of five states in which Jasper and Newton counties have been placed adjacent to one another to honor the allied efforts of sergeants William Jasper and John Newton to rescue captive colonial soldiers near Savannah.) • 1821 from Henry, Walton and Jasper • Gold mining was important in the county in the late 1800s. • Fruit, cattle, poultry; textile manufacturing.

OCONEE (one of two counties so named, other in SC) *Watkinsville* • 26,225 • 186 • Northeastern GA, bounded on the southeast by the Oconee River, on the southwest by the Apalachee River, and on the north and northeast by McNutt Creek. • Named for the Oconee River • 1875 from Clarke • Pacifist congresswoman Jeanette Rankin had a summer home here. • Furniture, fixtures, wholesale goods; cotton, soybeans, fruit, cattle, hogs • Several Indian mounds have been discovered at Keowee Town, which was an important Cherokee settlement.

OGLETHORPE *Lexington* • 12,635 • 441 • Northeastern GA, bounded on the northeast by the Broad River and on the southwest by the Oconee River. The county is located in the Piedmont. Watson Mill Bridge State Park (partly in Madison) is the site of the largest bridge in GA. A small part of Oconee National Forest is in the southwest. • Named for Gen. James E. Oglethorpe (1696–1785), founder of GA who proposed that GA be settled by former prisoners • 1793 from Wilkes • Wheat, fruit, cattle, hogs, poultry; timber.

PAULDING *Dallas* • 81,678 (96% increase since 1990; the third fastest growing county in GA) • 313 • Northwestern GA. The county, lying in the Piedmont, is part of the expanding Atlanta metropolitan area. • One of two counties (the other in OH) named for John Paulding (?–1818), one of the captors of John Andre, British spy, during the American Revolution • 1832 from Cherokee • Prior to heading to Kennesaw in 1864, Sherman's forces clashed with Confederate troops at Pickett's Mill (state historic site). • Fruit, cattle, poultry; timber.

PEACH *Fort Valley* • 23,668 • 151 (one of the fifty smallest counties in the U.S.) • Central GA, bounded on the west by the Flint River. • Named for its location in the most productive peach-growing region in the state • 1924 from Houston and Macon (the last county created in GA) • Manufacture of apparel, textiles and chemicals; peaches (more than ninety percent of the state's peaches are shipped from this county), cotton, corn, soybeans, wheat, peanuts, pecans, cattle; timber; education (Fort Valley State U.) • The Blue Bird Corporation in Fort Valley is the largest school bus manufacturer in the world. The USDA Research Station in Byron has created more than thirty-seven varieties of peaches. Massee Lane Gardens is headquarters for the American Camellia Society.

PICKENS *Jasper* • 22,983 • 232 • Northern GA. Mount Oglethorpe is located on the northeastern boundary. • One of three counties named for General Andrew Pickens (1739–1817), officer in the American Revolutionary War and U.S. representative from SC • 1853 from Cherokee and Gilmer • Corn, cotton, hay, fruit, cattle, poultry; sawmilling; tourism; marble quarrying. One of the largest marble veins in the world runs at least four miles within the county. Over sixty percent of the monuments in Washington D.C. are made from marble quarried here. • The county school system pioneered the first Head Start Program in the U.S.

PIERCE (One of five counties so named) *Blackshear* • 15,636 • 343 • Southeastern GA, bounded on the south by the Satilla River and on the northeast by Big Satilla Creek; drained by Hurricane Creek. • One of four counties named for President Franklin Pierce • 1857 from Appling and Ware • During the last months of the Civil War the county held 5,000 Union prisoners who had been transferred here from other camps so that Union General Sherman would not be able to free them on his march south. • Manufacture of apparel and textiles; tobacco, cotton, soybeans, corn, cattle, hogs, poultry, eggs.

PIKE *Zebulon* • 13,688 • 218 • West-central GA, bounded on the west by the Flint River. The county lies in the Piedmont. • One of ten counties named for Gen. Zebulon M. Pike (1779–1813), U.S. army officer and discoverer of Pikes Peak in CO • 1822 from Monroe • Cotton, peaches, corn, soybeans, wheat, cattle, poultry; food products; sawmilling.

POLK (one of twelve counties so named) *Cedartown* • 38,127 • 311 • Northwestern GA, bounded on the west by the AL state line. • One of eleven counties named for President James Knox Polk • 1851 from Paulding and Floyd • Cedartown was built on the site of a Cherokee Indian meeting ground. • Public relations pioneer Ivy Ledbetter Lee • Cotton, corn, hay, sweet potatoes, fruit, cattle, poultry; cedar, pine, poplar, oak logging; manufacture of tire-cord fabric, cotton yarn, woolen cloth, shirts, cheese, vitamins, chemicals, paper products, furniture, disc plows and harrows, butane gas cylinders, prefabricated homes; iron mining; limestone • Cedartown's Big Spring is the largest natural limestone spring in the South.

PULASKI *Hawkinsville* • 9,588 • 247 • South-central GA; intersected by the Ocmulgee River (forming part of the southern boundary) • One of seven counties named for Count Casimir Pulaski (1748–79), Polish soldier who fought for America during the Revolutionary War • 1808 from Laurens • Pulaski was once the site of the capital of the Creek Indian Confederacy. • Peanuts, corn, wheat, fruit, cattle, hogs; apparel and textile manufacture • Hawkinsville is home to one of the last harness racing training facilities in the U.S. The town's long horse racing past is celebrated by the Hawkinsville Harness Festival every spring.

PUTNAM (one of nine counties so named) *Eatonton* • 18,812 • 345 • Central GA, bounded on the east by the Oconee River (forming Oconee Lake reservoir in the northeast and Lake Sinclair reservoir in the southeast); drained by the Little River. Part of Oconee National Forest is in the west. The Rock Eagle Effigy, near Eatonton, is a ten-foot high mound of quartz shaped like a large prone bird, and believed by archaeologists to have been used by ancient Indians for religious ceremonies. • One of eight counties definitively named for General Israel Putnam (1718–90), Revolutionary War officer and American commander at the Battle of Bunker Hill • 1807 from Baldwin • Authors Alice Walker and Joel Chandler Harris. (Eatonton is home of the Uncle Remus Museum, as well as a Br'er Rabbit Statue standing on the courthouse square.) • Industrial machinery, wood product manufacturing; peaches, cattle. Dairying is important.

QUITMAN *Georgetown* • 2,598 • 152 (one of the fifty smallest counties in the U.S.) • Southwestern GA, bounded on the west by the Chattahoochee River (here forming the AL state line and part of Walter F. George Reservoir). A portion of Eufala National Wildlife Refuge is in the northwest. • One of two counties (the other in MS) named for John A. Quitman (1798–1858), governor of MS and U.S. representative • 1858 from Randolph and Stewart • Cotton, corn, peanuts, pecans, cattle; sawmilling • The world's first long distance phone call was reputedly made from Georgetown.

RABUN *Clayton* • 15,050 • 371 • Extreme northeastern GA, bounded on the north by the NC state line and on the east by the Chattooga River (a National Wild, Scenic, and Recreational River, which forms the SC state line); drained by the Tallulah River (dammed, it forms lakes Burton and Rabun) and the Little Tennessee River. The county is located in Chattahoochee National Forest and the Blue Ridge. The waterfall at Tallulah Gorge State Park is the highest in the state. The county also includes Black Rock Mountain and Moccasin Creek state parks. • Named for William Rabun (1771–1819), GA legislator and governor • 1819 from Cherokee land • Parts of the county were once ruled by Chief Attakullakulla, "Little Carpenter," who mediated early conflicts between the Cherokee Indians and white settlers. • Hay, potatoes, fruits, cattle, poultry; timber; tourism • Persistent trillium, a federally protected flower, grows only in the Tallulah Gorge area. According to Indian legend, Rabun Bald Mountain is inhabited by fire-breathing demon people. Campers often report hearing strange sounds throughout the night.

RANDOLPH (one of eight counties so named) *Cuthbert* • 7,791 • 429 • Southwestern GA, bounded on the southeast by Ichawaynochaway Creek. • One of four counties named for John Randolph (1773–1833), VA statesman and U.S. minister to Russia • 1828 from Lee. An earlier Randolph County was renamed Jasper in 1812. • Jazz orchestra pioneer Fletcher Henderson • Wheat, sorghum, soybeans, cotton, corn, peanuts, fruits, cattle, hogs; timber. One of the first pecan trees brought to GA from TX was planted in Cuthbert. The tree became known as the "mother of the GA pecan industry." • Andrew College was the second school in the nation to confer degrees on women.

RICHMOND (one of four counties so named) *Augusta* • 199,775 • 324 • Eastern GA, bounded on the southwest by Brier Creek and on the northeast by the Savannah River (forming the SC state line). The county contains most of Fort Gordon Military Reservation. • One of two counties (the other in NC) named for Charles Lennox (1735–1806), Third Duke of Richmond who favored the American colonies and wanted troops withdrawn in 1778 • Original county; organized 1777 (prior to statehood) from Saint Paul Parish • Hernando de Soto explored the area in 1540. In 1735, a fortified fur-trading post was established on the site of Augusta by GA founder James Oglethorpe. The city changed hands several times during the violent years of the Revolutionary War. During the war it served briefly on two occasions as the temporary capital of GA. It was the capital again from 1786 to 1795. The GA state convention, which ratified the U.S. Constitution, was held here on January 2, 1788. The largest gunpowder factory in the Confederacy was located in Augusta during the Civil War, its 176-foot chimney still standing. Augusta was an early southern milling town and center for cotton trading. Augusta and Richmond County were consolidated in 1995. • Singer James Brown; operatic singer Jessye Norman; painter Jasper Johns; educator John Hope • Cotton, wheat, soybeans, peanuts, fruit, corn; clay mining; timber; manufacture of textiles, firebrick and related products; education (Augusta State U.; Medical College of GA) • Augusta is the home of the Augusta National Golf Club, which hosts the annual Masters Tournament. The Morris Museum of Art reputedly has the largest collection of Southern U.S. art in the world.

ROCKDALE *Conyers* • 70,111 • 131 (one of the fifty smallest counties in the U.S.) • North-central GA; drained by the Yellow and South rivers. Formerly agricultural, the county is becoming more urbanized as part of the expanding Atlanta metropolitan area. The Panola Mountain State Conservation Park, the state's first conservation park, contains a 100-acre granite monadnock often compared to Stone Mountain. • Named for the Rockdale Church, which was itself named for the underlying bed of granite in this part of the state • 1870 from Henry and Newton • Vegetables, fruits, cattle; textile manufacturing • The county was the site of the Georgia International Horse Park equestrian competition during the 1996 summer Olympic Games.

SCHLEY *Ellaville* • 3,766 • 168 • West-central GA; drained by the Muckalee River and Buck Creek. • Named for William Schley (1786–1858), U.S. representative from GA and governor of the state • 1857 from Marion and Sumter • Cotton, corn, peanuts, wheat, pecans, peaches, poultry (broilers), hogs, cattle; manufacture of portable classrooms and offices • The City of Ellaville's water system is one of only two in the state that use duckweed as a natural water filter instead of chemicals.

SCREVEN *Sylvania* • 15,374 • 648 • Eastern GA, bounded on the east by the Savannah River (forming the SC state line) and on the southwest by the Ogeechee River; drained by Brier Creek. • Named for General James Screven (?–1778), an officer in the Revolutionary War • 1793 from Burke and Effingham • The founding of Sylvania is said to have been the result of a curse. An itinerant minister attacked by rowdies in 1821 in the county seat of Jacksonborough prayed for the town to be destroyed. Within thirty years, thanks to mysterious fires and floods, the town had disappeared. By 1847, a new town, Sylvania, had grown up south of the site and became the county seat. • Cotton, corn, soybeans, tobacco, potatoes, peanuts, cattle, hogs; timber.

SEMINOLE *Donalsonville* • 9,369 • 238 • Extreme southwestern GA, bounded on the west by the Chattahoochee River (forming the AL and FL state lines), on the southwest and southeast by arms of Lake Seminole reservoir, and on the east in part by Spring Creek. The creation of the lake behind the Jim Woodruff Lock and Dam inundated many acres of the county. Seminole State Park is also here. • One of three counties named for the Seminole Indians • 1920 from Decatur and Early • Apparel, textiles, industrial machining; cotton, corn, vegetables, soybeans, wheat, almonds, peanuts, cattle, hogs; sawmilling • Notches still visible on some of the county's trees marked the Three-Notch Road built here in 1814.

SPALDING *Griffin* • 58,417 • 198 • West-central GA, bounded on the west in part by the Flint River. The county, located in the Piedmont, is part of the growing Atlanta metropolitan area. • Named for Thomas Spalding (1774–1851), early GA cotton planter, GA legislator and U.S. representative • 1851 from Henry, Pike and Fayette • Gunman Doc Holliday; Olympic runner Wyomia Tyus • Cotton, corn, peppers, wheat, soybeans, fruit, cattle, hogs, poultry; timber; manufacture of cotton textiles, towels, corduroy, velveteen, hosiery, underwear, utility truck bodies; canning of fruits and vegetables.

STEPHENS (one of three counties so named) *Toccoa* • 25,435 • 179 • Northeastern GA, bounded on the east by the Tugaloo River (forming the SC state line and Hartwell Lake reservoir); drained by head streams of the Broad River. Part of Chattahoochee National Forest is in the county. Traveler's Rest State Historic Site is also here. Toccoa Falls, located on the campus of the college named for them, plunges 186 feet. • One of two counties (the other in TX) named for Alexander Hamilton Stephens (1812–83), GA statesman and vice president of the Confederacy • 1905 from Franklin and Habersham • In November, 1977, the Kelley Barnes earthen dam on Toccoa Creek burst following torrential rains, and flooded the campus of Toccoa Falls College, leaving thirty-nine people dead. • Cotton, corn, hay, sweet potatoes, cattle; stone quarrying; manufacture of textiles, furniture, metal products, heavy machinery, caskets.

STEWART (one of two counties so named, the other in TN) *Lumpkin* • 5,252 • 459 • Southwestern GA, bounded on the west by the Chattahoochee River (forming the AL state line). Part of Walter F. George Reservoir and Eufala National Wildlife Refuge are in the southwest. Providence Canyon State Conservation Park contains canyons (including "Grandfather Canyon 300 feet wide and 150 feet deep) and gullies caused by erosion from poor farming practices previously in use in the area. The park also has the largest natural collection of the rare "Plumleaf Azalea" in the world. Florence Marina State Park is also here. • Named for General Daniel Stewart (1759–1829), an officer in the American Revolution and the War of 1812 • 1830 from Randolph • Architect John Root • Manufacture of mobile homes and electronic equipment; cotton, corn, peanuts, fruit, cattle, poultry, hogs; sawmilling • The pseudo-

town of Westville is made up of more than twenty-five historic homes, shops, and public buildings gathered here from other counties. Located in Lumpkin is the Singer Company, the oldest hardware store in the state.

SUMTER *Americus* • 33,200 • 485 • Southwest-central GA, bounded on the east by the Flint River (forming Lake Blackshear reservoir in the southeast) and on the southwest by Kinchafoonee Creek; drained by Muckalee Creek. • One of four counties named for Thomas Sumter (1734–1832), American Revolutionary officer, U.S. representative from SC and U.S. senator • 1831 from Lee • President Jimmy and Rosalynn Carter (national historic site) • Cotton, corn, soybeans, peanuts, wheat, oats, cattle, hogs, poultry; manufacture of mobile homes, terry cloth garments, electrical fixtures, caskets; education (GA Southwestern State U.) • Charles A. Lindbergh made his first solo flight at Souther Field near Americus. The city is the headquarters of Habitat for Humanity, International, a non-profit organization dedicated to eliminating substandard housing around the world. Part of Andersonville National Historic Site is in the north (shared with Macon County).

TALBOT *Talbotton* • 6,498 • 393 • Western GA, bounded on the northeast by the Flint River and on the south in part by Upatoi Creek; intersected by the Fall Line. • Named for Matthew Talbot (?–1827), GA legislator and interim governor • 1827 from Muscogee • The first session of the GA Supreme Court was held in Talbotton on January 26, 1846. The state's first fifteen attorneys were sworn in and qualified to practice law in the state here. • Lazarus Straus, an immigrant from Bavaria established a business here in the 1850s that was the forerunner of Macy's department store. • Peaches, cattle; sawmilling; sand.

TALIAFERRO *Crawfordville* • 2,077 (the least populated county in GA) • 195 • Northeastern GA, in the Piedmont, bounded on the northeast in part by the Little River; drained by the Little and Ogeechee rivers. • Named for Captain Benjamin Taliaferro (1750–1821), officer in the Continental Army and U.S. representative from GA • 1825 from Greene, Hancock, Oglethorpe, Warren and Wilkes • Confederate vice president Alexander H. Stephens (state historic park and memorial); poet Roselle M. Montgomery (who often wrote about Crawfordville) • Cotton, corn, grain, fruit, cattle, hogs; sawmilling • Among the county's festivals is the Twelve Oaks Barbecue and Ball, featuring two days of Confederate reenactments.

TATTNALL *Reidsville* • 22,305 • 484 • East-central GA, bounded on the southwest by the Altamaha River; drained by the Ohoopee River. Gordonia Alatamaha State Park is named for a rare tree, the "Lost Camilla," found only in GA. The county also includes Big Hammock Natural Area and part of Fort Stewart Miltary Reservation. • Named for General Josiah Tattnall (1764–1803), an officer in the American Revolution, U.S. senator from GA and governor or the state • 1801 from

Montgomery • Vidalia onions (annual festival in Glennville), corn, soybeans, wheat, cotton, tobacco, peanuts, cattle, hogs, poultry; sawmilling • The Georgia State Penitentiary is the state's oldest (1936).

TAYLOR (one of seven counties so named) *Butler* • 8,815 • 377 • West-central GA, bounded on the north and east by the Flint River; intersected by the Fall Line. • One of four counties named for President Zachary Taylor • 1852 from Macon, Marion, and Talbot • Sociologist William F. Ogburn • Cotton, corn, peanuts, soybeans, wheat, cattle, poultry; sawmilling.

TELFAIR *McRae* • 11,794 • 441 • South-central GA, bounded on the south by the Ocmulgee River and on the northeast by the Little Ocmulgee River. The county includes part of Little Ocmulgee State Park. • Named for Edward Telfair (?–1807), signer of the Articles of Confederation and governor of GA • 1807 from Wilkinson • The county was primarily settled by Scottish Presbyterians from the Carolinas • Father and son GA governors Eugene and Herman Talmadge • Wheat, oats, cotton, corn, peanuts, tobacco, pecans, cattle, hogs; timber • Replicas of the Statue of Liberty and the Liberty Bell are at "Liberty Square." Lumber City has fifty artesian wells.

TERRELL (one of two counties so named, the other in TX) *Dawson* • 10,970 • 335 • Southwestern GA, bounded on the northeast by Kinchafoonee Creek and on the southwest by Ichawaynochaway Creek; drained by Chickasawhatchee Creek. • Named for Dr. William Terrell (1778–1855), U.S. representative and benefactor of the University of Georgia. • 1856 from Lee and Randolph • A Creek uprising, the Battle of Echouanotchaway Swamp was fought here in 1836. Shortly after Atlanta's capture in the Civil War, Governor Joseph E. Brown arranged for a camp at Dawson to shelter refugees. This "Exile Camp" was later used to house a detachment of fifty Union soldiers assigned to keep order in the area. • Cotton, corn, peanuts, wheat, soybeans, cattle, hogs.

THOMAS (one of three counties so named) *Thomasville* • 42,737 • 548 • Southern GA, bounded on the south by the FL state line; drained by the Ochlockonee and Aucilla rivers. The county includes Lapham–Patterson House State Historic Site. Limestone sinks are common here. • Named for General Jett Thomas (1776–1817), officer of the GA militia; supervisor of the construction of the state capitol at Milledgeville and the first university building at Franklin College (now the University of Georgia) • 1825 from Decatur and Irwin • Thomasville was a popular winter resort for wealthy northern families in the late 1890s and early 1900s. • Cotton, tobacco, corn, soybeans, wheat, peanuts, cattle, hogs; timber; manufacture of clothing, mobile homes, baked goods; meat and poultry packing; quail hunting • Thomasville's annual rose festival is a popular event. The Glen Arven golf course is the fifth oldest in continuous operation in the U.S.

TIFT *Tifton* • 38,407 • 265 • Southern GA, bounded on the northeast in part by the Alapaha River; intersected by the Little River • Named for Captain Nelson Tift (1810–1891), GA legislator, officer in the Confederate Navy, U.S. representative, and founder and editor of the *Albany Patriot*. • 1905 from Berrien, Irwin and Worth • Peanuts, corn, wheat, soybeans, cotton, tobacco, cattle, hogs, nurseries; manufacture of fertilizers, textiles, shoes, aluminum extrusions, concrete products, mobile homes • Tifton is the site of the rural development center of the University of Georgia, and an agricultural research station. Tift County is home to possibly the largest Southern magnolia in the world. The Magnolia Tree Foundation preserves and protects it for future generations.

TOOMBS *Lyons* • 26,067 • 367 • East-central GA, bounded on the south by the Altamaha River and on the northeast by the Ohoopee River. • Named for General Robert A. Toombs (1810–85), U.S. senator, secretary of state for the Confederacy, and officer in the Confederate Army • 1905 from Emanuel, Montgomery and Tattnall • Diversified manufacturing; wheat, soybeans, cotton, corn, peanuts, tobacco, cattle, hogs. The county is famous for its sweet Vidalia onions, the state vegetable of GA. The Vidalia Onion Festival is held here every spring. • The county's Ladson Genealogical Library is one of the largest such libraries in the southeastern U.S.

TOWNS *Hiawassee* • 9,319 • 167 • Northeastern GA, bounded on the north by the NC state line; drained by the Hiawassee River, forming Chatuge Lake in the north. The county is located in Chattahoochee National Forest and the Blue Ridge and includes High Shoals Scenic Area. The Appalachian Trail crosses the county in the east. • Named for George W. B. Towns (1801–54), U.S. representative from GA and governor of the state • 1856 from Rabun and Union • During the 1800s and the early part of the 1900s the county's highlands were a summer escape from the heat and disease prevalent in the larger population areas of the region. • Textiles, apparel; corn, hay, potatoes, fruit, cattle, hogs, lumber; tourism; education (Young Harris College).

TREUTLEN *Soperton* • 6,854 • 201 • East-central GA, bounded on the southwest by the Oconee River and on the northeast by the Ohoopee River. The county is located in a coastal plain agricultural area. • Named for John A. Treutlen (1726–82), first governor of GA • 1917 from Emanuel and Montgomery • Tobacco, corn, peanuts, nuts, potatoes; trout fishing; mineral springs, tourism; manufacture of pine by-products • Soperton earned the nickname "Million Pines City" after James Fowler planted over seven million pine seedlings on 10,000 acres in the county. The Million Pines Arts and Crafts Festival is held here each November. On March 31, 1933, the *Soperton News* became the first newspaper in the U.S. to print on pine-pulp paper.

TROUP *La Grange* • 58,779 • 414 • Western GA, bounded on the west by the Chattahoochee River (forming the AL state line and West Point Lake reservoir, which dominates the western section of the county) • Named for George M. Troup (1780–1856), U.S. senator from GA and governor • 1826 from

Indian lands • Fort Tyler, the last fort of the Confederacy, fell on April 16, 1865 to 3,000 of "Wilson's Raiders" following a defense of fewer than 300 Confederates, their number including boys, militia, and convalescents of Reid Hospital. • Fruits, cattle; timber; manufacture of textiles (dating back to 1866), plastics, fertilizer, boats, beverages, sports equipment; education (La Grange College) • La Grange has the distinction of being the home base of the "Nancy Harts," the only female militia unit organized during the Civil War.

TURNER (one of two counties so named, the other in SD) *Ashburn* • 9,504 • 286 • South-central GA, bounded on the northeast by the Alapaha River; drained by the Little River. • Named for Capt. Henry G. Turner (1839–1904), officer in the Confederate Army, U.S. representative from GA and associate justice of the GA Supreme Court • 1905 from Dooly, Irwin, Wilcox and Worth • Following the boll weevil assault in the 1920s, Turner became the first GA county to institute "cow-hog-hen" programs to diversify its farming output. • Peanuts, cotton, corn, tobacco, soybeans, wheat, cattle, hogs.

TWIGGS *Jeffersonville* • 10,590 • 360 • Central GA, bounded on the west by the Ocmulgee River. • Named for Major General John Twiggs (1750–1816), an officer in the American Revolution and Indian commissioner • 1809 from Wilkinson • Cotton, corn, peanuts, cattle, hogs; timber; kaolin (There are thirty-six mines and nearly 3,800 acres in the county used for kaolin and sand production) • The county is located in the geographical center of the state.

UNION (one of eighteen counties so named) *Blairsville* • 17,289 • 323 • Northern GA, bounded on the north by the NC state line; drained by the Nottely River (its dam and reservoir in the north). The Appalachian Trail closely follows the southeastern border. The county is located in the Blue Ridge; at 4,784 feet, Brasstown Bald is the highest point in the state. Chattahoochee National Forest covers the entire county. Also here are Cooper Creek Scenic Area and Vogel State Park. • Named for the union of the states • 1832 from Cherokee • Corn, cattle, hogs, stone quarrying.

UPSON *Thomaston* • 27,597 • 325 • West-central GA, bounded on the west and south by the Flint River; intersected by Potato Creek. Sprewell Bluff State Park is in the west. • Named for Stephen Upson (?–1824), attorney, trustee of the University of Georgia, and state legislator • 1824 from Crawford and Pike • Confederate military leader and politician John Brown Gordon • Largely peaches; also cotton, cattle, hogs, poultry, dairying; timber; manufacture of lumber, tire cord, linens.

WALKER (one of three counties so named) *La Fayette* • 61,053 • 447 • Northwestern GA, bounded on the southwest by the AL state line and on the north by the TN state line. The Appalachian Mountains cross the county. It includes parts of Chickamauga and Chattanooga National Military Park (where, in September, 1863, Confederate troops won the first great Civil War battle fought in the state) and Chattahoochee

National Forest. Zahnd Natural Area is in the southwest. • Named for Freeman Walker (1780–1827), GA legislator, U.S. senator, mayor of Augusta • 1833 from Murray • Cherokee chief John Ross • Corn, soybeans, wheat, cattle, hogs; limestone; tourism • Lookout Mountain, at 2,392 feet, is the highest point in northwest GA, and home of the well-advertised Rock City Gardens, which opened in 1932. The mountain is also the site of the first miniature golf park. John B. Gordon Hall is the oldest standing brick school building in the state (1836).

WALTON (one of two counties so named, the other in FL) *Monroe* • 60,687 • 329 • North-central GA, bounded on the northeast by the Apalachee River; drained by the Alcovy River. The county is found in the Piedmont. Located between Atlanta and Athens, it is becoming more suburban. • Named for George Walton (?–1804), a signer of the Declaration of Independence, GA governor and U.S. senator • Original county; organized 1818 from Cherokee lands • Jacks Creek, near Monroe, was the site of a massacre by whites of a large encampment of Creek Indians in 1787. • Walton is the county of GA governors; seven made their home here. • Soybeans, peaches, cattle, poultry; manufacturing • Monroe holds a popular Crepe Myrtle Festival each September.

WARE *Waycross* • 35,483 • 902 (the largest county in GA) • Southeastern GA, bounded on the south by the FL state line; drained by the Satilla River (forming part of the eastern boundary). Okefenokee Swamp (National Wildlife Refuge) occupies the southern part of the county. Laura S. Walker State Park, near Waycross, is one of the few state parks in GA named for a woman. Part of Dixon Memorial State Forest is also here. • Named for Nicholas Ware (?–1824), GA legislator, mayor of Augusta and U.S. senator from GA • 1824 from Appling • Okefenokee Swamp served as a refuge for Indians and escaped slaves. • Tobacco, corn, wheat, honey, pecans, cotton, soybeans, cattle, hogs, poultry; timber, naval stores, forest products; manufacture of footwear, cigars, crates, boxes, mobile homes, concrete bricks and blocks, missile parts • Waycross is often referred to as the largest city in the largest county in the largest state east of the Mississippi River.

WARREN *Warrenton* • 6,336 • 286 • Eastern GA, bounded on the west by the Ogeechee River, on the southeast by Brier Creek, and on the north by the Little River; intersected by the Fall Line. • One of fourteen counties named for Gen. Joseph Warren (1741–75), Revolutionary War patriot and member of the Committee of Safety who dispatched Paul Revere on his famous ride • 1793 from Hancock, Wilkes, Richmond and Columbus • Manufacture of apparel, textiles, wood products; cotton, cattle, hogs; timber; granite and stone quarrying; hunting.

WASHINGTON *Sandersville* • 21,176 • 680 • East-central GA, bounded on the northeast by the Ogeechee River and on the southwest by the Oconee River. The county is intersected by Williamson Swamp. Hamburg State Park is in the north.

• The first of thirty-one counties named for George Washington, it was created in 1784 prior to statehood and before Washington became president. • The county was settled by Revolutionary War veterans, who were given land grants for their service. • Cotton, corn, wheat, oats, peanuts, cattle, hogs; kaolin-clay mining. The county is called the "Kaolin Capital of the World" and holds a Kaolin Festival each year. • Local resident Willy Lee Duckworth improvised the familiar "Sound Off" during a WW II training march; it became the anthem of all the troops who followed.

WAYNE (one of sixteen counties so named) *Jesup* • 26,565 • 645 • Southeastern GA, bounded on the northeast by the Altamaha River and on the southwest by Big Satilla Creek. The county is a railroad hub for southeastern GA. • One of fifteen counties named for Revolutionary War general and statesman "Mad" Anthony Wayne (1745–96) • Original county; organized 1803 from Indian lands • Tobacco, honey, peanuts, soybeans, cotton, corn, cattle, hogs; timber; textile manufacturing • Often called the "town that trains made," Jesup collected passenger fares that averaged $1,000 per day in 1890. Its rail yard could hold 500 cars.

WEBSTER *Preston* • 2,390 • 210 • Western GA; intersected by Kinchafoonee Creek. • One of eight counties named for statesman Daniel Webster • 1853, as Kinchafoonee, from Stewart (named changed to Webster County in 1856 following citizen petition, when outsiders made fun of the name) • The first Confederate flag to fly in GA was raised on the Webster County Courthouse lawn in 1861. • Politician and statesman Walter F. George • Corn, cotton, wheat, peanuts, cattle, hogs; sawmilling.

WHEELER (one of four counties so named) *Alamo* • 6,179 • 298 • Southeast-central GA, bounded on the north and east by the Oconee River, on the south by the Ocmulgee River, and on the southwest by the Little Ocmulgee River. Part of Little Ocmulgree State Park is in the west. • Named for Joseph Wheeler (1836–1906), Confederate general, author, and U.S. representative from AL • 1912 from Montgomery • Corn, wheat, soybeans, cotton, tobacco, peanuts, cattle, hogs.

WHITE (one of five counties so named) *Cleveland* • 19,944 • 242 • Northeastern GA; drained by the Chattahoochee River. The Appalachian Trail closely follows the northwestern boundary. Chattahoochee National Forest is in the north, and includes Raven Cliffs and Anna Ruby Falls scenic areas. Uncoi State Park is also here. • The derivation of this county's name has never been firmly established. It was possibly named for David T. White (1812–71), GA legislator; or for Col. John White, a hero of the Revolutionary War • 1857 from Habersham • Gold was found here in the late 1820s on land belonging to the Cherokees. After local miners and settlers pressured the U.S. government to remove the Indians, the land was profitably mined until the 1930s, with as many as nine mines in operation here. • Corn, poultry, cattle, hogs; timber; tourism; education (Truett Mcconnell College) • Helen, built to look like an alpine village, holds one of the largest Oktoberfests in the U.S.

WHITFIELD *Dalton* • 83,525 • 290 • Northwestern GA, bounded on the north by the TN state line and on the east by the Conasauga River. The Appalachian Mountains cross the county. Part of Chattahoochee National Forest is here. • Named for the Reverend George Whitefield (1714–70), prominent Church of England clergyman who established Bethesda, one of the first orphanages in the U.S. The spelling was changed by clerical error. • 1851 from Murray • Dalton, founded in 1837, developed as a shipping point for copper mined nearby. During the Civil War, it was the headquarters for Confederate General Joseph Johnston. • Political journalist Duff Green died here. • Corn, cattle, hogs, broiler poultry; timber; marble; education (Dalton State College); manufacture of tufted textiles (Dalton produces much of the national output), yarn, thread, chairs, machinery. Dalton is known for its candlewick bedspreads, produced here since 1895.

WILCOX (one of two counties so named, the other in AL) *Abbeville* • 8,577 • 380 • South-central GA, bounded on the east by the Ocmulgee River; drained by the Alapaha River. • Named for either Captain John Wilcox, early settler and Indian fighter, or for his son Major General Mark Wilcox (?–1850), officer in the GA militia and GA legislature. • 1857 from Dooly, Irwin and Pulaski • The county is a leading grower of canteloupes, and the second largest producer of watermelons in the state. Also, cotton, corn, peanuts; lumber • Wild boar hunts are conducted along the banks of the Ocmulgee River. Abbeville holds a Wild Hog Festival each May.

WILKES (one of two counties so named, the other in NC) *Washington* • 10,687 • 471 • Eastern GA, located in the Piedmont, bounded in part on the south by the Little River (forming Clarks Hill Lake reservoir in the southeast) and on the north by the Broad River • Named for John Wilkes (1727–1797), writer and British member of Parliament who supported the colonists before the Revolutionary War • 1777 from original territory • The Battle of Kettle Creek, fought near Washington, disrupted British plans to recapture GA in 1779. The world's first cotton gin was developed by Eli Whitney on a plantation here in 1794. The county was also the site of the first cotton mill in the south. Jefferson Davis formally dissolved the Confederacy in Washington on May 5, 1865. • Vice president of the Confederacy Alexander H. Stephens; secretary of state for the Confederacy Robert A. Toombs (state historic site); U.S. Supreme Court justice John A. Campbell • Hay, sweet potatoes, peaches, cattle, hogs, poultry; timber; lumber and textile manufacturing • Laid out in 1780, Washington was one of the first communities in the U.S. to be named in honor of George Washington. Washington has more antebellum homes than any other city its size in the state.

WILKINSON *Irwinton* •10,220 • 447 • Central GA, bounded on the northeast by the Oconee River. Baldwin State Forest is in the north. • One of two counties (the other in MS) named for James Wilkinson (1757–1825), officer under Washington, and first governor of the Louisiana Territory • Original county; organized 1803 from Creek cession. • Cotton, peanuts; kaolin clay mining; timber • Wilkinson County has lost its courthouses to fire in 1829, 1854, 1864, and 1924.

WORTH *Sylvester* • 21,967 • 570 • South-central GA, bounded in part on the west by the Flint River; drained by the Ochlockonee River and Warrior Creek. Lake Blackshear reservoir is in the northwest corner. • One of three counties named for William J. Worth (1794–1849), officer in the War of 1812 and hero of the Mexican War, and commandant of West Point • 1853 from Dooly and Irwin • Peanuts, cotton, tobacco, corn, wheat, soybeans, cattle, hogs, poultry; timber; manufacture of wood products, apparel, textiles • Sylvester is home to Peter Pan peanut butter. The Georgia Peanut Festival is held here.

HAWAII

The Life of the Land Is Perpetuated in Righteousness

Hawaii has no self-governing incorporated municipalities. All of the state's populated places are administered as part of the county in which they are located. Each county is governed by an elected mayor and county council, except for Kalawao, which is administered by the state department of health.

HAWAII *Hilo* • 148,677 • 4,028 (the largest county in HI) • The county is coextensive with the island of Hawaii, the largest in the state. It also includes several islets along the northeast coast. Hawaii was formed by five volcanoes. Kilauea is the focal point of Hawaii Volcanoes National Park. Still active, its lava flows continue to increase the size of the county through accretion. Scientists of the U.S. Geological Survey study volcanic activity at the Hawaiian Volcanic Observatory on the rim of Kilauea. Mauna Loa erupts less frequently. At 13,796 feet, Mauna Kea is the highest point in the state. The county has a number of forest reserves, beach parks, and state recreation areas. Puuhonua o Honaunau National Historic Park on the western Kona coast preserves the sacred sanctuary offered here to the vanquished and conscientious objectors of early Hawaii. Akaka Falls State Park is in the east. • Named for the island of Hawaii • 1905 • British navigator and explorer James Cook arrived here in November, 1778 and traded with the Hawaiians who considered him a great chief with divine powers. He was killed on February 14, 1779 in a quarrel between his men and the islanders over a stolen boat. Chief Kamehameha gained control of the island in a bloody ten-year war that began in 1782. He captured and united the other main islands of the chain (except for Kauai and Niihau) in 1795, with the aid of firearms obtained from white traders. Hilo was established in 1824 as a missionary center on the island. It became a thriving whaling port. A devastating tsunami struck the city in 1946. • Sugarcane (a large producer in the state), fruit, flowers (especially orchids and anthuriums), cattle (large ranches), macadamia nuts, coffee; commercial fishing; education (U. of HI at Hilo); tourism • Ka Lae (South Point) is the southernmost point in the U.S. Naalehu is the southernmost town.

HONOLULU *Honolulu* • 876,156 (the most populated county in HI) • 600 • Central Hawaii between Kauai and Molokai. The county includes all of the island of Oahu as well as a string of unpopulated islands west of Kaula and Niihau (except for Midway, which is administered by the U.S. Navy). The county has several naval reservations. Hickam Air Force Base and the Hawaii Marine Corps Base are also here. Forest reserves are spread throughout the island of Oahu, which is ringed by beach parks. Diamond Head State Monument and Waikiki Beach are major tourist draws. Oahu consists of a rolling, fertile valley flanked by two verdant mountain ranges, the Koolau in the east and the Waianae in the west. Pearl Harbor is one of the largest natural harbors in the Pacific Ocean (and headquarters for the U.S. Pacific fleet). Because Hawaii has no self-governing, incorporated cities or towns, Honolulu is officially known as the City and County of Honolulu. • Named for the city of Honolulu • 1905 • Nuuanu Pali, the cliff at the upper end of Nuuanu Valley, was the scene of King Kamehameha I's routing of island defenders (some driven over the cliff) when he conquered Oahu in 1795. Honolulu flourished first as a center for the sandalwood trade and later as whaling base. Pearl Harbor has been an American naval base since 1887 when King Kalakaua granted the U.S. exclusive rights in exchange for trading privileges. The December 7, 1941 surprise attack by Japanese warplanes on the harbor plunged the U.S. into World War II. Honolulu was made capital of Hawaii in 1845, remaining so when the islands became a territory of the U.S. in 1900, and continuing as capital when statehood was achieved in 1959. • Hawaiian Queen Liliuokalani; archaeologist and politician Hiram Bingham; corporate executive Steve Case; Hawaiian leader Lorrin A. Thurston; singer and actor Bette Midler. Anthropologist Sir Peter Buck, author Joseph Campbell, baseball rules codifier

Alexander J. Cartwright, muralist Jean Charlot, Hawaiian president Sanford B. Dole, Philippine president Ferdinand E. Marcos, missionary Gerrit P. Judd, trombonist and composer Kid Ory, first president of the Republic of Korea Syngman Rhea all died here. • Dairying, eggs, pineapples; commercial fishing; food processing; printing; petroleum processing; manufacture of clothing, chemicals, cement, furniture, glass products, plastics; government operations; military operations, service industries, education (U. of HI; Chaminade U. of Honolulu; HI Pacific U.; Brigham Young U.–Hawaii Campus); tourism • Eight of every ten Hawaiians make their "hale" in the county. The Polynesian Cultural Center has several villages representing various South Pacific cultures.

KALAWAO • 147 (the least populated county in HI; only Loving County, TX has fewer people) • 13 (the smallest county in the U.S) • North-central Molokai Island, on Kalaupapa Peninsula. Kalaupapa National Historic Park is here. • The county was named for a land division on Molokai Island. In Polynesian it means "mountainous area." • 1905 • Kalawao occupies land that was formerly part of the colony for victims of leprosy (Hansen's disease) shepherded by Belgian priest, Father Joseph Damien de Veuster from 1873 until his death in 1885. The colony came to an end in 1969. Kalawao exists as a county in name only. It is administered by the state department of health. • It has the largest percentage of Asians in the nation (66%) Some of its present residents are leprosy patients whose disease has been controlled and contagion eliminated by modern drugs.

KAUAI *Lihue* • 58,463 • 622 • The western Hawaiian islands of Kauai, Niihau, Kaula, and Lehua. Waimea Canyon's colorful walls resemble those of the rock formations of the Grand Canyon. The steep Na Pali cliffs (state park) in the northwest make it impossible to build a road circumscribing the island. The county is separated from neighboring Honolulu County (Oahu Island) by the Kauai Channel. It has a number of forest reserves and national wildlife reserves. Polihale State Park is in the west; Wailua River State Park is in the east. Called the "Garden Isle" for its verdant slopes, Kauai is geologically the oldest of the major Hawaiian islands. • Named for the island of Kauai, from the Polynesian word for "drying place." • 1905 • The first Polynesians to reach the Hawaiian islands are said to have arrived on Kauai 1,000 years ago, settling at the mouth of the Wailua River. It was at Waimea on January 20, 1778 that English navigator-explorer Captain James Cook, made his first landing on the Hawaiian (Sandwich) Islands. In 1810, the islands of Kauai and Niihau became the last to accept the rule of King Kamehameha I. Russians made an ill-

fated attempt to seize the island in 1815. Hawaii's first permanent sugar cane plantation began operating on Kauai in 1835 at Koloa; it was owned by the American firm, Ladd and Company. Damage to the Hawaiian Islands by Hurricane Iniki in 1992 was most heavily sustained on the island of Kauai, with property damage estimated at $1 billion. Niihau was purchased from King Kamehameha V in 1864 by Mrs. Elizabeth Sinclair for $10,000. (Her descendants, the Robinson family, run a cattle ranch that covers nearly the entire island. It is one of the few places in which residents still speak the Hawaiian language.) • Cattle, hogs, sugarcane, tropical fruits; diversified manufacturing, especially of tourist-oriented goods; commercial fishing; resort tourism • Kauai is the wettest county in the U.S. An average of 460 inches of rain fall on Mount Waialeale each year, making it the wettest place on earth. (Deep canyons have been carved into the island by the dozens of streams flowing from this spot.)

MAUI *Wailuku* • 128,094 (28% increase since 1990; the fastest growing county in HI) • 1,159 • Comprised of the Hawaiian islands of Maui, Lanai, Kahoolawe, and most of Molokai. Haleakala National Park is on eastern Maui Island; it contains the largest dormant volcano crater in the world (20 miles around and 2,000 feet deep). Waianapanapa and Makena state parks, Kealia Pond National Wildlife Refuge, and Halekii-Pihana Heiau State Monument are on Maui; Palaau State Park is on Molokai. Kahoolawe is owned by the U.S. military. The cluster of islands that make up the county are separated from the island and county of Hawaii to the southeast by Alenuihaha Channel and from Honolulu County and the island of Oahu by the Kaiwi Channel. The two volcanic mountains that form the island of Maui are cut by scenic canyons; between them lies a broad, low isthmus of sugar cane plantations. • Named for the island of Maui, itself named for a Polynesian god • 1905 • In 1790, the Battle of Kepaniwai added Maui to the kingdom of Kamehameha the Great. Lahaina was made the capital of the Hawaiian kingdom in 1810 by King Kamehameha I, but in 1845 the capital was transferred to Honolulu. From 1845 to 1865 the city was the whaling capital of the mid-Pacific. • Union military commander Samuel Chapman Armstrong. Aviator Charles A. Lindbergh died here. • Cattle, hogs, sugarcane, pineapples (highest yield in the U.S.), tropical fruits; sugarcane refining, pineapple canning; tourism; commercial fishing; manufacture of textiles, woodworking products, shoes, hula supplies • Ninety-eight percent of the island of Lanai is owned by Castle and Cooke, Inc., the maker of Dole pineapple products.

IDAHO

It Is Perpetual

Each of the state's forty-four counties is governed by three commissioners, two elected to two-year terms, the third elected to a four-year term. Other county officials, all elected to four-year terms, include the sheriff, assessor, coroner, prosecuting attorney, treasurer (who also serves as tax collector), and clerk of the district court (who is also auditor and recorder).

ADA *Boise* • 300,904 (the most populated county in ID) • 1,055 • Southwestern ID, bounded on the southwest by the Snake River; drained by the Boise River. Bogus Basin ski area is on its northern boundary. Eagle Island and Lucky Peak state parks are here, as is Snake River Birds of Prey National Conservation Area, which covers the southern half of the county. The World Center for Birds of Prey and Kuna Cave are also here. Part of Boise National Forest (its headquarters in Boise) is on the northern boundary. • Named for Ada C. Riggs (1863–?), the first white child born in Boise City • 1864 (prior to statehood) from Boise County • Boise, established in 1863, was located at the crossroads of the Oregon Trail and the routes to Boise River basin, site of an 1860s gold rush. The city has served as the capital of ID since 1864. Hundreds of Basques from northern Spain moved to the county in the late 1800s. (Today Boise is the chief center of the U.S. Basque community.) It grew rapidly in the early 20th century due to the growth of the commercial lumber industry in the area and agricultural expansion facilitated by the Boise Irrigation Project in 1902. The county was also the site of one of the world's largest construction companies. In the Ada County courthouse in 1907 Clarence Darrow won an acquittal for union leader William D. Haywood, charged with directing the murder of former ID governor Frank Steuenberg. • Dairying, hay, alfalfa, wheat, barley, oats, corn, sugar beets, fruit, vegetables, cattle, sheep; manufacture of lumber products, electronics, mobile homes, metal products, paints; government operations; education (Boise State U.; Boise Bible College) • The headquarters of four Fortune 1000 companies are located in Boise.

ADAMS (one of twelve counties so named) *Council* • 3,476 • 1,365 • Western ID, bounded on the west by the Snake River (forming the OR state line); watered by headstreams of the Weiser and Little Salmon rivers. This mountainous county includes the West Mountains in the south and Brundage Mountain and Little Ski Hill ski areas in the northeast. Parts of Payette and Boise national forests and Lost Valley State Forest are here. Part of Hells Canyon National Recreation Area lies along the western border and includes Hells Canyon Seven Devils Scenic Area. • One of eight counties named for President John Adams • 1911 from Washington County • Council was once the site of Native American peace talks, tribal games and trading. • Physicist James Rainwater • Cattle, apples, plums, alfalfa, oats, barley.

BANNOCK *Pocatello* • 75,565 • 1,113 • Southeastern ID, bounded on the northwest corner by part of American Falls Reservoir (Snake River); drained by the Portneuf River. The Snake River Plain is in the north, with the Bannock Range along the western border. The county is urbanized in the northwest around Pocatello. Parts of Caribou National Forest (its headquarters in Pocatello) are here. Part of Fort Hall Indian Reservation is in the north. • Named for the Bannock Indians, a branch of the Shoshone • 1893 from Bingham • Settled in 1882, Pocatello was a stopover point on the Oregon Trail. It was later an important railroad depot on the Union Pacific line between Omaha, NE and Portland, OR. • Wheat, alfalfa, barley, sheep, cattle, dairying; manufacture of electronic components, steel, cement, mining machinery, cheese products, phosphorus, phosphate fertilizer; potato and meat processing; manganese deposits. • Idaho State University is located here. Its Minidome is the first indoor football stadium ever built on a university campus.

BEAR LAKE *Paris* • 6,411 • 971 • Extreme southeastern ID, bounded on the east by the WY state line and on the south by the UT state line. Wasatch-Cache National Forest is in the west and includes Minnetonka Cave. Part of Caribou National Forest is in the northeast. Bear Lake State Park and Bear Lake National Wildlife Refuge are at the northern end of the lake. • Named for Bear Lake, half of which lies in ID (Franklin County) • 1875 from Oneida • Sculptor Gutzon Borglum • Hay, alfalfa, oats, barley, wheat, sheep, cattle, turkeys, dairying.

BENEWAH *St. Maries* • 9,171 • 776 • Northern ID, bounded on the west by the WA state line; drained by the St. Joe and St. Maries rivers. (At more than 2,100 feet above sea level, the St. Joe River is the world's highest commercially navigable river.) The Palouse region is in the west. Heyburn State Park is in the north at the southern tip of Coeur d'Alene Lake. A portion of St. Joe National Forest is in the south, and includes part of Mary M. McCroskey State Park. Coeur d'Alene Indian Reservation is in the western half of the county. • Named for Benewah, a chief of the Coeur d'Alene Indian tribe • 1915 from Kootenai • Lumber; lentils, wheat, oats, barley, cattle • Annually, on Labor Day weekend, St. Maries holds Paul Bunyan Days festivities, which include lumber jack competitions.

BINGHAM *Blackfoot* • 41,735 • 2,095 • Southeastern ID; drained by the Snake and Blackfoot rivers and American Falls

Reservoir. Part of the Snake River Plain lies in the west, and includes extensive lava beds. Hell's Half Acre Lava Flow is located north of Blackfoot. Part of Fort Hall Indian Reservation is in the south. Part of Idaho National Engineering and Environmental Laboratory (U.S. Department of Energy) is in the northwest. • Named for Henry H. Bingham (1841–1912), U.S. representative from PA and a former Union officer • 1885 (prior to statehood) from Oneida • The county was created by anti-Mormons to add one new county to the state without a Mormon majority. • Blackfoot evolved from Fort Hall trading post built by the Hudson's Bay Company in 1834. • Potatoes, sugar beets, barley, wheat, oats, alfalfa, sheep, cattle, dairying.

BLAINE *Hailey* • 18,991 • 2,645 • South-central ID, bounded on the south by the Snake River (here forming Lake Walcott reservoir; drained by the Big Wood River. The county is one of the most irregularly-shaped in the country. Part of Minidoka National Wildlife Refuge, Sawtooth National Forest and part of Sawtooth National Recreation Area are located here. Part of Craters of the Moon National Monument is here, as well. The Pioneer and Sawtooth mountains are in the north, with peaks rising to over 10,000 feet. (The Sun Valley ski area here is a major winter resort destination.) The Snake River Plain is in the south. Magic Reservoir is on the southwestern boundary. • One of four counties named for James G. Blaine (1830–93), Speaker of the House from ME, U.S. senator, and candidate for President • Organized 1895 from Alturas County, which was itself organized in 1864 and abolished in 1895, and from Logan County, which was organized in 1889 and abolished in 1895 • Sun Valley Lodge was built by the Union Pacific Railroad in 1936 and is one of the nation's oldest ski resorts. • Poet Ezra Pound. Novelist and short story writer Ernest Hemingway died here. • Sheep, cattle, potatoes, sugar beets, alfalfa, hay, wheat, barley, oats; silver, lead, gold, zinc, copper; tourism.

BOISE *Idaho City* • 6,670 (90% increase since 1990; the fastest growing county in ID) • 1,902 • Western ID, bounded on the south by the Boise River (here forming Arrow Rock Reservoir and part of Lucky Peak Lake) and by the Middle Fork of the Boise River, and on the southeast by the North Fork of the Boise River. The county is located in a mountainous area cut by canyons of the Payette River and its Middle and South forks. Boise National Forest and Packer John State Forest are here, as is part of Sawtooth Wilderness Area in the Sawtooth Range. • Named for the Boise River • Original county; organized 1864 • Following the discovery of gold here in 1862, Idaho City became one of the most populated cities in the Northwest, burgeoning at one point to 40,000 residents. It served as territorial capital for a short time. With the decline in placer mining, the population had dropped to 1,000 by 1869, and by the early 1900s the town had become a fire- and decay-ravaged quasi-ghost town. It is now a revived tourist center. • Gold, silver, lead; cattle; lumber; tourism.

BONNER *Sandpoint* • 36,835 • 1,738 • Northern ID, in the panhandle, bounded on the east by the MT state line, and on the west by the WA state line; drained by the Priest and Pend Oreille rivers and Clark Fork. The northwest extension of the county comes to within ten miles of the Canadian border. Priest Lake (known for its giant trout, the Mackinaw and Dolly Varden), Priest Lake State Park and State Forest, and Upper Priest Lake Scenic Area are here. Along the shores of the lake is part of the Roosevelt Grove of Ancient Cedars; some of these 800-year-old trees stand more than 150 feet high. The county also includes Round Lake State Park, part of Kaniksu National Forest, part of Kootenai National Forest, part of Lake Pend Oreille, Albeni Falls Dam (on the Pend Oreille River), Cabinet Gorge Dam on Clark Fork, and Schweitzer Mountain ski area. • Named for Edwin L. Bonner, an early settler of northern ID who operated a ferry on the Kootenai River in 1864 • 1907 from Kootenai • Silver, lead, copper; lumber; cattle, alfalfa, hay, oats, grains • The Pacific Northwest Sled Dog Championship Races are held each February at Priest River Airport.

BONNEVILLE *Idaho Falls* • 82,522 (the fourth most populated county in ID) • 1,868 • Southeastern ID, bounded on the east by the WY state line; drained by the Snake River and Willow Creek. The Caribou Mountains and part of the Snake River Range cross in the east. Snake River Valley extends through the northwest. Part of Caribou National Forest is in the east. Part of Grays Lake and Grays Lake National Wildlife Refuge are also here. Palisades Reservoir is on the eastern boundary. • Named for Benjamin Louis Eulalie de Bonneville (1793–1878), French-born officer in the Mexican-American War and ID explorer who was immortalized in *The Adventures of Captain Bonneville* by Washington Irving • 1911 from Bingham • Wheat, barley, oats, rye, hay, alfalfa, potatoes, sugar beets, sheep, cattle, dairying; beet sugar processing; manufacture of potato food products, concrete and stone products, specialized farm implements, steel products, camper-trailers; atomic energy research • The Idaho Falls Mormon Temple, constructed in 1944, is a riverbank landmark.

BOUNDARY *Bonners Ferry* • 9,871 • 1,269 • Northern ID, in the panhandle, bounded on the west by the WA state line, on the north by the Canadian province of British Columbia, and on the east by the MT state line; drained by the Kootenai, Moyie, Pack, and Upper Priest rivers. Kaniksu National Forest and Priest Lake State Forest extend throughout most of the county. Part of Kootenai National Forest, Kootenai National Wildlife Refuge, and Kootenai Indian Reservation are here. Smith and Moyie falls are also here. • The county was probably given this name because of its boundary with Canada • 1915 from Kootenai and Bonner • Cattle, alfalfa, hay, hops, oats, barley, wheat; timber; silver, lead, thorium.

BUTTE (one of three counties so named) *Arco* • 2,899 • 2,233 • Southeast-central ID; watered by the Big Lost and Little Lost rivers. Parts of the Lost River and Lemhi ranges cross in the north, while the Snake River Plain and extensive lava beds cover the southern half of the county. The county includes part of Craters of the Moon National Monument, part of Salmon-Challis National Forest, and part of Targhee National Forest. A large part of Idaho National Engineering and Environmental Laboratory is in the eastern part of the county. • Named for either Big Southern Butte in the southeast or for Three Buttes (of which Big Southern Butte is a constituent). Big Southern Butte was a conspicuous landmark for pioneers moving through the area. • 1917 from Bingham, Blaine, and Jefferson • Sheep, cattle, alfalfa, hay, oats, barley, some wheat; silver, lead, manganese • The King Mountain Hang-gliding Championship near Arco takes place each June.

CAMAS *Fairfield* • 991 (the least populated county in ID) • 1,075 • South-central Idaho, bounded on the southeast in part by the Big Woods River (here forming Magic Reservoir); drained by Camas Creek. The county is the source of the South Fork of the Boise River in the north. Part of the Sawtooth Mountain Range is in the north and is covered by Sawtooth National Forest. Soldier Mountain ski area is also here. • Named for Big Camas Prairie • 1917 from Blaine • Cattle, alfalfa, hay, barley; timber; deposits of lead, silver, zinc, gold, copper.

CANYON *Caldwell* • 131,441 (the second most populated county in ID) • 590 • Southwestern ID, bounded on the southwest by the Snake River and on the west by the OR state line; drained by the Boise River. Deer Flat National Wildlife Refuge encompasses Lake Lowell reservoir in the south. • Named for either for the canyon of the Boise River near Caldwell, or for the Snake River canyon • 1891 from Ada • Dairying (creameries), sheep, cattle, alfalfa, hay, oats, barley, wheat, corn, sugar beets, potatoes, vegetables, tree fruits; meat and fruit packing; manufacture of mobile homes; dehydrating plants; education (Albertson College of ID; Northwest Nazarene U.).

CARIBOU *Soda Springs* • 7,304 • 1,766 • Southeastern ID, bounded on the east by the WY state line; crossed by the Blackfoot River, forming Blackfoot Reservoir in the northwest. The Webster Range extends across the northeast. Parts of Caribou National Forest are in the east and northwest, and a small part of Wasatch-Cache National Forest is in the south. Part of Fort Hall Indian Reservation and part of Grays Lake National Wildlife Refuge are also in the county. Formation Springs and Cave Preserve issue spring water determined to be 13,000 years old. • Named for either the Caribou Mountains or for Caribou Mountain within the range. • 1919 from Bannock and Oneida • Wagon ruts left by pioneers traveling along the Oregon Trail can be seen at Oregon Trail Park near Soda Springs. • Wheat, barley, alfalfa, cattle, sheep, hogs, dairying; phosphate mining; chemical manufacturing • Naturally occurring carbonated springs can be found in and around Soda Springs. The town lies at the center of the world's largest phosphate fields. Capped and controlled by a timer to erupt every hour, the geyser at Geyser Park in Soda Springs, is the only captive geyser in the world.

CASSIA *Burley* • 21,416 • 2,566 • Southern ID, bounded on the south by the UT and NV state lines, and on the north by the Snake River; drained by the Raft River and Goose Creek. Parts of Sawtooth National Forest are scattered throughout. Pomerelle ski area is here, as well. • Named for Cassia Creek • 1879 (prior to statehood) from Oneida • Potatoes, sugar beets, dry beans, wheat, barley, oats, corn, alfalfa, hay, cattle, dairying.

CLARK (one of twelve counties so named) *Dubois* • 1,022 • 1,765 • Eastern ID, bounded on the north by the Continental Divide (here forming the MT state line); drained by Camas, Medicine Lodge, and Birch creeks, all of which flow into the Snake River Aquifer south of the county. The U.S. Sheep Experimental Station is here. Part of Targhee National Forest is in the county. Clark also includes Lidy Hot Springs and Sheridan Reservoir. • Named for Sam K. Clark, pioneer cattleman and first state senator from the county • 1919 from Fremont • Sheep, horses, cattle, potatoes, wheat, alfalfa, hay; lumber; gold, iron and silver mining • Opal was first discovered in the area in 1948 by local deer hunters; visitors may dig for the gem stones in Spencer. The rare star opal comes from this county, which has one of the largest opal deposits in the U.S.

CLEARWATER *Orofino* • 8,930 • 2,461 • Northern ID, bounded on the east by the Bitterroot Range and the MT state line and on the southwest in part by Lolo Creek; crossed by the North Fork of the Clearwater River; drained by the Clearwater River. Clearwater National Forest and the Clearwater Mountains extend over half the county. Elk Creek Falls Recreation Area, and Lolo and Orofino state forests are also here. Dworshak Dam, Reservoir, Fish Hatchery, and State Park are in the county, as is Bald Mountain ski area. Part of Nez Perce Indian Reservation is in the southwest. • Named for the Clearwater River • 1911 from Nez Perce • Gold was first discovered in ID by prospector E. D. Pierce on Orofino Creek in 1860 (Pierce Historic Site) • Timber; cattle, alfalfa, barley, wheat; silver, lead • Dworshak Dam is the largest straight-axis dam in North America, and standing at a height of 717 feet, is the third highest dam in the country.

CUSTER *Challis* • 4,342 • 4,925 (the third largest county in ID) • Central ID, bounded in part on the northeast by Big Creek, on the northwest in part by the Middle Fork of the Salmon River, and on the north in part by Cames Creek; drained by the Big Lost River and crossed by the Salmon River. Borah Peak, at 12,662 feet, the highest point in Idaho, is in the Lost River Range. The Boulder and Pioneer mountains are also here, their crests forming part of the southwestern boundary. The county also includes parts of Salmon-Challis and Sawtooth national forests, part of Sawtooth National Recreation Area, Land of the Yankee Fork Historic Area, and Mackay Reservoir Wildlife Viewing Area. Several ghost towns are also here. • Named for the General Custer mine, itself named for General George Armstrong Custer (1839–76), U.S. officer and Indian fighter (one of six counties named directly or indirectly for General Custer) • 1881 (prior to statehood) from Alturas and Lemhi • Cattle, alfalfa, hay, barley, oats; mining of gold, molybdenum, silver, lead, copper; recreational tourism • The rugged mining roads of the White Knob Mountains are used today for the Annual White Knob Challenge, the longest-running mountain bike race in the Northwest.

ELMORE (one of two counties so named, the other in AL) *Mountain Home* • 29,130 • 3,078 • Southwestern ID, bounded on the north by the Boise River and its Middle and North forks (forming Arrowrock and Lucky Peak Lake reservoirs) and on the south by the Snake River, which drains the southeast corner of the county and forms Strike Reservoir. Mountain Home Air Force Base and part of Snake River Birds of Prey National Conservation Area are in the southwest corner. The county also includes Three Islands Crossing State Park, and parts of Sawtooth and Boise national forests (including part of the Sawtooth Wilderness Area). • Named for the Ida Elmore Quartz Mine, one of the largest gold- and silver-producing mines of the 1860s • 1889 (prior to statehood) from Alturas • Sheep, cattle, potatoes, vegetables, sugar beets, alfalfa, hay, wheat; gold deposits.

FRANKLIN (one of twenty-five counties so named) *Preston* • 11,329 • 665 • Southeastern ID, bounded on the south by the UT state line; drained by the Bear River. Weston Canyon is here, as are Caribou National Forest in the west and Wasatch-Cache National Forest in the east. • Named for the first permanent white settlement in ID, itself named for Franklin Dewey Richards (1821–99), a Mormon apostle, politician and judge • 1913 from Oneida • Dairying is strong here. Also sugar beets, sweet corn, wheat, alfalfa, barley, cattle, sheep, horses, poultry.

FREMONT *Saint Anthony* • 11,819 • 1,867 • Eastern ID, bounded on the northeast and northwest by the Continental Divide (here forming the MT state line) and on the east by the WY state line; drained by Henrys Fork and the Teton River (forming part of the southern boundary). Part of Targhee National Forest is in the north and the northeast, and includes a thin strip of Yellowstone National Park, Island Park Reservoir with Harriman State Park, and Henrys Lake reservoir and State Park. Also here are Upper and Lower Mesa Falls and St. Anthony Sand Dunes. • One of four counties named for John C. Frémont (1813–90), soldier and explorer who led five expeditions to the West and was governor of the AZ Territory • 1893 from Bingham • On June 5, 1976, the Teton Dam on the Teton River collapsed killing eleven people downstream. • Wheat, barley, hay, sugar beets, potatoes, cattle, sheep; lumber • Island Park claims the nation's longest main street, which runs thirty-three miles through the village, actually a long stretch of resorts that became incorporated into one town.

GEM *Emmett* • 15,181 • 563 • Western ID; drained by the Payette River and Squaw Creek. The county is located in the Snake River Plain. Part of Boise National Forest and Black Canyon Recreation Area are here. • The name of the county comes from "Gem State," the state's nickname. • 1915 from Boise and Canyon • Hay, alfalfa, oats, corn, barley, wheat, sugar beets, vegetables, potatoes, apples, pears, peaches, plums, cherries, nectarines, dairying.

GOODING *Gooding* • 14,155 • 731 • Southern ID, in the Snake River Plain with extensive lava beds, bounded on the south and southwest by the Snake River. The county includes Malad Gorge, Box Canyon, and Niagara Springs state parks. Thousand Springs is in the south near the Snake River. Here water from the Big and Little Lost rivers emerge from the Snake River Plain Aquifer in a series of waterfalls in a deep canyon. • Named for Frank R. Gooding (1859–1929), governor of Idaho and U.S. senator • 1913 from Lincoln • Potatoes, dry beans, sugar beets, alfalfa, corn, wheat, watermelons, cranberries, sheep, cattle, dairying. • When the Idaho Irrigation Company opened 70,000 acres along the Big Wood River near Gooding to the public, handbills were distributed that read, "Come to Gooding, and you'll come for good."

IDAHO *Grangeville* • 15,511 • 8,485 (the largest county in ID and the eighteenth largest county in the U.S.) • Central ID, bounded on the east by the Bitterroot Range and the MT state line, and on the west by Hells Canyon of the Snake River (here forming the OR state line); drained by the South and Middle forks of the Clearwater River, and the Salmon, Lochsa, and Selway rivers (the last three designated National Scenic rivers). A large part of Nez Perce National Forest permeates the county except in the northwest. The Clearwater Mountains and part of Clearwater National Forest are also here. Several units of the Nez Perce National Historic Park are here, including White Bird Battlefield, East Kamiah Site, and Clearwater Battlefield. The Bitterroot National Forest is in the east. Snowhaven and Cottonwood Butte ski areas are here, as is part of Nez Perce Indian Reservation. • Named for the steamer Idaho, launched June 9, 1860 on the Columbia River to serve miners in the gold rush • Original county; organized 1864 (prior to statehood). Originally established in 1861 as the third county of WA Territory, now in ID. • The Nez Perce Indians, resisting forced removal to the Lapwai Reservation, defeated U.S. troops in a battle at White Bird Canyon on June 17, 1877. The Indians were later forced to surrender upon retreat. • Wheat, barley, alfalfa, hay, sheep, cattle; copper, gold, silver, lead.

JEFFERSON *Rigby* • 19,155 • 1,095 • Eastern ID; drained by the Snake River, forming part of the southeastern boundary. The county is in the Snake River Plain and includes numerous lava beds. Part of Idaho National Engineering and Environmental Laboratory (U.S. Department of Energy) is on the western boundary. The county also includes Jefferson and Mud Lake reservoirs, and Camas National Wildlife Refuge. • One of twenty-six counties named directly or indirectly for Thomas Jefferson • 1913 from Fremont • Clover, legumes, sugar beets, potatoes, alfalfa, orchards, wheat, barley, oats, sheep, cattle, poultry.

JEROME *Jerome* • 18,342 • 600 • Southern ID, bounded on the south by the Snake River. The county lies in the Snake

River Plain and contains extensive lava beds. Shoshone Falls is in the west; Wilson Lake reservoir is in the east. Minidoka Internment National Monument is also here. • Probably named for Jerome Kuhn, son of W.S. Kuhn, president of Twin Falls North Side Irrigation Project • 1919 from Gooding and Lincoln • Sheep, cattle, dairying, corn, barley, wheat, alfalfa, hay, potatoes, apples, sugar beets • Over eighty percent of the commercial trout served in U.S. restaurants comes from this county.

KOOTENAI *Coeur d'Alene* • 108,685 (56% increase since 1990; the third fastest growing county and the third most populated county in ID) • 1,245 • Northern ID, in the panhandle, bounded on the west by the WA state line; watered by Coeur d'Alene Lake and the Spokane and Coeur d'Alene rivers. The county is growing more urbanized in the corridor between Coeur d'Alene and Spokane, WA, fifteen miles west of the state line. Old Mission State Park is in the southeast. The county includes part of the Coeur d'Alene Mountains in Coeur d'Alene National Forest in the east. The forest's headquarters is located in the city of Coeur d'Alene. Part of Coeur d'Alene Indian Reservation is in the south. Farragut State Park is at the southern end of Lake Pend Oreille. • Named for the Kutenai Indian tribe • Original county; organized 1864 (prior to statehood) • Coeur d'Alene was founded in 1878 as a military outpost. The town's economy was energized by the discovery of silver and lead in the area in 1882. It was the scene of widespread industrial strife between mine owners and unionized workers in the 1890s and early 1900s. • World War II flying acre Pappy Boyington • Lumbering; wheat, oats, alfalfa, cattle, dairying, fruits, vegetables; manufacture of furniture, wood products, dairy foods; tourism.

LATAH *Moscow* • 34,935 • 1,077 • Northern ID, in the Palouse region, bounded on the west by the WA state line; drained by the Palouse and Potlatch rivers. The county includes part of St. Joe National Forest. • Named for Latah Creek • 1888 (prior to statehood) from Kootenai • Lumber; sheep, cattle, alfalfa, wheat, oats, barley, peas, lentils; clay. The city of Moscow is a research and education center. On the campus of the University of Idaho is the state Bureau of Mines and Geology. The university maintains agricultural and other research stations in the area.

LEMHI *Salmon* • 7,806 • 4,564 (the fourth largest county in ID) • Eastern ID, bounded on the east by Bitterroot Range and Beaverhead Mountain (the Continental Divide forming the MT state line) and on the southwest by the Pahsimeroi River, and Big and Carnes creeks; drained by the Salmon River and its tributaries. The Salmon River and Yellowjacket Mountains are here, as is the Lemhi Range. Parts of Salmon-Challis National Forest are found throughout the county. Also here are a small part of Targhee National Forest and part of Frank Church River of No Return Wilderness Area. • Named for Fort Lemhi, a Mormon mission on the Salmon River • 1869 (prior to statehood) from Idaho County • Here, in the fall of 1805, the Lewis and Clark Exhibition was forced to abandon

its quest to pursue the Salmon River as a navigable route to the Pacific Ocean. The Viola Mine, located in what is now the ghost down of Nichola, was once one of the richest lead mines in the world. In 1855, Mormon missionaries from Salt Lake City established a missionary colony called Fort Lemhi here. • Lewis and Clark's Indian guide Sacajawea was probably born here. • Sheep, cattle, alfalfa, oats; lead, silver, copper, manganese and uranium deposits; recreational tourism, including white water rafting • The county touts itself as the "Whitewater Capital of the World." It has one of the largest elk herds in the west. It is also home to at least a dozen ghost towns. Two annual events, the Great Salmon Valley Balloon Fest and the Idaho Cowboy Poetry Gathering take place in the county.

LEWIS (one of seven counties so named) *Nezperce* • 3,747 • 479 • Western ID, bounded on the east by the Clearwater River and on the south in part by the Salmon River and Lawyer's Creek. The county includes part of Nez Perce Indian Reservation, which covers all but its southern end. Winchester Lake State Park is on the western boundary. • One of five counties named for Meriwether Lewis (1774–1809), co-leader of the Lewis and Clark expedition • 1911 from Nez Perce • Cattle, alfalfa, barley, wheat, beans; lumber.

LINCOLN (one of twenty-four counties so named) *Shoshone* • 4,044 • 1,206 • Southern ID, in the Snake River Plain; watered by the Big Wood and Little Wood rivers. Shoshone Ice Caves and Mammoth Cave are in the northwest. A small portion of Craters of the Moon National Monument is also here. • One of eighteen counties named for President Abraham Lincoln • 1895 from Blaine • Cattle, alfalfa, oats, barley, corn, sugar beets, potatoes, dry beans • Many of the buildings of Fairfield are constructed with the lava rock found in the area. The fourteen lava tubes that make up the T-Maze caves are considered by geologists to be the best examples of their kind in the state. The Big Wood River is known as the "upside down river"; in one stretch it is about 100 feet deep and four feet wide, while another section is about 100 feet wide and four feet deep.

MADISON *Rexburg* • 27,467 • 472 • Eastern ID, in the Snake River Plain, bounded on the southwest by the Snake River and on the north in part by the Teton River. The Teton River joins Henrys Fork River in the north, which in turn joins the Snake River in the southwest. Part of Caribou National Forest and the Snake River Range are in the southeast. Kelly Canyon ski area is also here. • One of twenty counties named directly or indirectly for President James Madison • 1913 from Fremont • Potatoes, sugar beets, wheat, barley, alfalfa, sheep, cattle, dairying. • The Teton Flood Museum in Rexburg memorializes the June 5, 1976 Teton Dam collapse and subsequent flood, which killed eleven people.

MINIDOKA *Rupert* • 20,174 • 760 • Southern ID, on the Snake River Plain, bounded on the south and southeast by the Snake River. Lake Walcott on the Snake River is formed by Minidoka Dam (on the southeastern boundary of the county).

Part of Minidoka National Wildlife Refuge and Lake Walcott State Park are in the southeastern corner. Part of Craters of the Moon National Monument is also here. • Named for either the town of Minidoka or for the Minidoka Reclamation Project • 1913 from Lincoln • Potatoes, sugar beets, dry beans, alfalfa, sheep, dairying, oats, barley, wheat.

NEZ PERCE *Lewiston* • 37,410 • 849 • Western ID, bounded on the west by the Snake River (designated here a National Wild and Scenic River, and forming the WA and OR state lines) and on the far south by the Salmon River; drained by the Clearwater River. Part of Nez Perce National Historic Indian Reservation, its headquarters at Lapwai, is in the east, covering about half of the county; it includes Nez Perce Historic Park. Hells Gate State Park and part of Winchester Lake State Park are also here. • Named for the Indian tribe • Original county; organized 1864 (prior to statehood). It was previously established by WA Territory in 1861. • Lewiston is the state's oldest community. It was incorporated on the site of an 1805 and 1806 Lewis and Clark expedition encampment, and served as ID Territory's first capital from 1863 to 1865. • Lumber; diversified agriculture; light manufacturing; tourism; education (Lewis-Clark State College). The Port of Lewiston is the terminus of river barge traffic from Astoria-Portland, OR, and serves barge traffic from four states.

ONEIDA (one of three counties so named) *Malad City* • 4,125 • 1,200 • Southeastern ID, bounded on the south by the UT state line; crossed by the Little Malad River and its tributaries. The county is crossed by the Sublette Range and Bannock Range (the latter forming part of the northeastern border). Part of Caribou National Forest, part of Sawtooth National Forest, and Curlew National Grassland are in the county. • Named for either Lake Oneida, New York, former home of early settlers, or for the city of Oneida, New York • Original county; organized 1864 (prior to statehood) • Cattle, wheat, alfalfa, barley.

OWYHEE *Murphy* • 10,644 • 7,678 (the second largest county in ID and the twenty-fifth largest county in the U.S.) • Southwestern ID, on the Snake River Plain and Columbia Plateau, bounded on the west by the OR state line, on the south by the NV state line, and on the northeast by the Snake River; drained by the Bruneau River and forks of the Owyhee and Snake rivers. Part of Duck Valley Indian Reservation is on the NV state line. Bruneau Dunes State Park and part of Snake River Birds of Prey National Conservation Area are here. • Named for the Owyhee River, itself named for a corrupt spelling of Hawaii, in honor of three Hawaiians who were hired to trade with the Indians and disappeared • Original county; organized 1863 (prior to statehood) • The county was the site of bitter competition to control the rich silver lodes in the War Eagle and Florida mountains. A 500-pound silver crystal from the Poorman Mine won a gold medal at the Paris Exposition in 1867. Silver City was one of the few silver boomtowns to survive the collapse of silver prices due to the advanced technology of its mines, extensive British investments

and productive railroad infrastructure. Eventually, mining activity declined and the city's residents moved elsewhere. • Sheep, cattle, dairying, hay, alfalfa, sugar beets, potatoes, beans, oats, barley, wheat; gold, silver and zinc mining.

PAYETTE *Payette* • 20,578 • 408 (the smallest county in ID) • Western ID, bounded on the west by the Snake River (here forming the OR state line); drained by the Payette River. • Named for the river • 1917 from Canyon • Dairying, hay, alfalfa, sugar beets, vegetables, potatoes, apples, peaches, plums, sheep, cattle.

POWER *American Falls* • 7,538 • 1,406 • Southeastern ID; drained by the Snake River and Bannock Creek, and lying partly in the Snake River Plain. The Sublette and Bannock ranges are here. American Falls Dam at American Falls Reservoir is located near the northern border. Part of Fort Hall Indian Reservation is here, as are Massacre Rocks State Park, part of Sawtooth National Forest, part of Minidoka National Wildlife Refuge and part of Craters of the Moon National Monument, including Crystal Ice Cave. • Named for the output of the Idaho Power Company • 1913 from Bingham, Cassia, Oneida, and Blaine • Cattle, sheep, dairying, alfalfa, wheat, rye, potatoes, barley • The construction of American Falls Dam destroyed the falls for which it was named, an early scenic tourist attraction.

SHOSHONE *Wallace* • 13,771 • 2,634 • Northern ID, bounded on the east by the Bitterroot Range, forming the MT state line; crossed by the Coeur d'Alene and St. Joe rivers (the latter designated a National Wild and Recreation River). At more than 2,100 feet above sea level, the St. Joe River is the world's highest commercially navigable river. The Coeur d'Alene mining district is in the Coeur d'Alene Mountains. Also in the county are parts of the Coeur d'Alene and St. Joe national forests, and part of Floodwood State Forest. Silver Mountain and Lookout Pass ski areas, and Hobo Cedar Grove Botanical Area are also here. • Named for the Shoshone Indian tribe • The first organized unit of government in ID; created in 1858 as part of WA Territory, effective in 1861; reorganized 1864 (prior to statehood) • Kellogg developed as a mining and smelting center for lead, zinc and silver. In 1972, the Sunshine Mine was the scene of a disastrous fire that left ninety-one miners dead. • Some agriculture, cattle; wood working; smelting; mining of silver, zinc and lead. Bunker Hill and Sullivan mines together form one of the world's largest lead mines. The Sunshine Mine is one of the largest single-lode producers of silver in the U.S.

TETON (one of three counties so named) *Driggs* • 5,999 (74% increase since 1990; the second fastest growing county in ID) • 450 • Eastern ID, bounded on the east by the WY state line and on the north by Bitch Creek and the Teton River. The foothills of the Teton Range are on the eastern boundary. The county also contains parts of Targhee and Caribou national forests. • Named for the Teton Mountains • 1915 from Madison • Dairying, potatoes, dry beans, alfalfa, barley, cattle.

TWIN FALLS *Twin Falls* • 64,284 (the fifth most populated county in ID) • 1,925 • Southern ID, bounded on the south by the NV state line and on the north by the Snake River. The county includes part of Snake River Plain in the north; it is mountainous in the south. Salmon Falls Creek and Cedar Creek reservoirs are in the southwest. Also located here are Hagerman Fossil Beds National Monument, Balanced Rock, Magic Mountain ski area, Magic Hot Springs, and part of Sawtooth National Forest. • Named for the falls on the Snake River • 1907 from Cassia • Potatoes, dry beans, sugar beets, onions, apples, peaches, cherries, cattle; commercial fish hatchery • The hydroelectric dam built by the Idaho Power Company partially blocks the twin falls, transforming them into a single cascade.

VALLEY (one of three counties so named) *Cascade* • 7,651 • 3,678 (the fifth largest county in ID) • Central ID, bounded on the east in part by the Middle Fork of the Salmon River (designated here a National Wild and Recreational River); drained by the North and Middle forks of the Payette River.

The Salmon River Mountains cross in the northeast. Most of the county is covered by national forests, including Payette and Boise. Part of Frank Church River of No Return Wilderness Area is here, as are Ponderosa and Cascade state parks. The county has several small lakes and reservoirs in its western half. • Named for Long Valley • 1917 • Cattle, oats; lumbering; mercury, gold, silver, and lead mining.

WASHINGTON *Weiser* • 9,977 • 1,456 • Western ID, bounded on the west by the Snake River (here forming the OR state line); crossed by the Weiser River. The county includes part of Payette National Forest and Hornet Creek State Forest. Brownlee Dam and Reservoir, Steck Park, and Weiser Sand Dunes are also here. • One of thirty-one counties named for President Washington • 1879 (prior to statehood) from Boise • Weiser suffered a disastrous fire in 1890 and was rebuilt. • Cattle, sheep, dairying, potatoes, sugar beets, hay, alfalfa, wheat, apples, plums; iron and mercury deposits, mining of silver, lead, copper; manufacture of metal products, beverages; flour mills.

ILLINOIS

State Sovereignty — National Union

Most of the state's 102 counties are divided into townships. With the exception of Cook County, each is governed by a board of supervisors. Cook County is governed by a board of commissioners. Counties without townships are also governed by boards of commissioners.

ADAMS (one of twelve counties so named) *Quincy* • 68,277 • 857 • Western IL, bounded on the west by the Mississippi River (forming the MO state line); drained by Bear and McKee creeks. Part of Siloam Springs State Park is in the southeast. Mark Twain National Wildlife Refuge and Burton Cave Nature Preserve are also here. • One of two counties (the other in IN) named for President John Quincy Adams • 1825 from Pike; Highland was organized from Adams and Marquette in 1847 and eliminated in 1848; Marquette was organized in 1843 from Adams and eliminated in 1847 • In Quincy sixty-five community leaders chartered the Adams County Antislavery Society, the first in IL. During the winter of 1838–39 Mormons found refuge here before heading north to Nauvoo. Quincy's Washington Park was the site of the sixth debate between Lincoln and Douglas, on Oct. 13, 1858. Because of its strategic location on the Mississippi River, the city was once the second largest in the state. • Biblical scholar Edgar J. Goodspeed; historian Allan Nevins; engineer William B. Stout • Hogs, cattle, corn, wheat, soybeans, barley, sorghum, dairying; manufacture of metal wheels, air compressors, agricultural equipment, truck and tractor bodies; limestone quarries; education (Quincy U.).

ALEXANDER (one of two counties so named, the other in NC) *Cairo* • 9,590 • 236 • Extreme southern IL, bounded on the west and south by the Mississippi River (forming the MO state line), on the southeast by the Ohio River (forming the KY state line), and on the east in part by the Cache River. The county includes part of Shawnee National Forest, part of Cypress Creek National Wildlife Refuge, and Horseshoe Lake Conservation Area. • Named for William M. Alexander, an early settler and IL legislator • 1819 from Johnson • A busy cotton port, Cairo was also a concentration point for the Union army during the western campaigns of the Civil War. General Ulysses Grant established his headquarters here in 1861; his troops were quartered just south of the city at Fort Defiance (state park). The city was protected by its levees from destruction during the 1937 flood when the Ohio River rose to record heights. Cairo suffered racial strife during the turbulent late 1960s and early 1970s. • Livestock, corn, cotton, fruit; manufacture of lumber products, plastics, fiber-glass boats, workmen's apparel, pipe fittings, polyurethane foam, soybean products • Charles Dickens expressed his unhappiness with Cairo during a visit in 1842 by making it a prototype for the nightmare city of Eden in his 1843 novel *Martin Chuzzlewit*.

BOND *Greenville* • 17,633 • 380 • Southwestern IL; drained by the Kaskaskia River and Shoal Creek. Part of Coffeen Lake State Fish and Wildlife Area is on the northern border. • Named for Shadrach Bond (1773–1832), IL legislator and first governor • 1817 (prior to statehood) from Madison • Corn, wheat, dairy, livestock; bituminous mines, natural gas mines; manufacture of clothing and rubber products; education (Greenville College).

BOONE (one of eight counties so named) *Belvidere* • 41,786 • 281 • Northern IL, bounded on the north by the WI state line; drained by the Kishwaukee River • One of seven counties named for Daniel Boone • 1837 from Winnebago • Baseball player Fred Schulte. Potowatomi Indian chief Big Thunder is buried here. • Livestock, corn, oats, vegetables, dairying; manufacture of machine parts, paper, metal products, motor vehicles, casket trimmings, commercial scales • The Pettit Memorial Chapel in Belvidere Cemetery was designed by Frank Lloyd Wright in 1907.

BROWN (one of nine counties so named) *Mount Sterling* • 6,950 • 306 • Western IL, bounded on the southeast by the Illinois River and on the northeast by La Moine River; drained by McKee Creek. Part of Siloam Springs State Park is here. • One of four counties named for General Jacob J. Brown (1775–1828), an officer in the War of 1812 and commander of the U.S. Army • 1839 from Schuyler • Cattle, hogs, corn, sorghum, soybeans; bituminous coal.

BUREAU *Princeton* • 35,503 • 869 • Northern IL, bounded on the southeast by the Illinois River; drained by the Green and Spoon rivers, and Big Bureau Creek; crossed by the old Illinois and Mississippi Canal. The county includes Lake Depue, a bayou of the Illinois River, and Hennepin Canal Parkway State Park. Several state fish and wildlife areas are also here. • Named for Bureau Creek • 1837 from Putnam • Anthropologist William R. Bascom; journalist and humorist Don Marquis • Corn, soybeans, cattle, hogs, dairying; sand and gravel pits; industrial machinery, hardware, jewelry, environmental controls • The Elijah P. Lovejoy home in Princeton was one of several local underground railroad "stations."

CALHOUN *Hardin* • 5,084 • 254 • Western IL, bounded on the south and west by the Mississippi River (forming the MO state line) and on the east by the Illinois River, which join at the county's southeastern tip. The county is a hilly peninsula with portions of the Mark Twain National Wildlife Refuge on both rivers. The Center for American Archeology and Calhoun County Conservation Area are also here. • One of eleven counties named for John C. Calhoun (1782–1850), U.S. statesman and champion of Southern causes • 1825 from Pike • Large apple-growing region, also hogs, vinegar.

CARROLL (one of thirteen counties so named) *Mount Carroll* • 16,674 • 444 • Northwestern IL, bounded on the west by the Mississippi River (forming the IA state line); drained by the Plum River and Elkhorn Creek. The Upper Mississippi River National Wildlife and Fish Refuge extends along the river. The county includes Mississippi Palisades State Park and Ayers Sand Prairie Nature Preserve. • One of twelve counties named for Charles Carroll (1737–1832), a signer of the Declaration of Independence, U.S. senator from MD and founder of the Baltimore and Ohio Railroad • 1839 from Jo Daviess • Livestock, corn, hay, wheat, oats, produce, dairying; manufacture of refrigeration equipment.

CASS (one of nine counties so named) *Virginia* • 13,695 • 376 • West-central IL, bounded on the north by the Sangamon River and on the west by the Illinois River. The county includes Sanganois and Jim Edgar Panther Creek state fish and wildlife areas, and Shick Shack Sand Pond Nature Preserve. • One of eight counties named for General Lewis Cass (1782–1866), military and civil governor of MI Territory, U.S. secretary of war and U.S. secretary of state • 1837 from Morgan • Corn, soybeans, sorghum, sweet potatoes, cattle, hogs; manufacture of gloves; shipping.

CHAMPAIGN (one of two counties so named, the other in OH) *Urbana* • 179,669 • 997 (the fifth largest county in IL) • Eastern IL; drained by the Sangamon, Kaskaskia, and Embarras rivers and by forks of the Vermilion River. The county also includes the commercial and industrial center of Champaign-Urbana. • Named for the county in OH. In lieu of his $900 fee, surveyor John W. Vance asked for the privilege of naming the county; he selected the county where his first wife was buried. • 1833 from Vermilion • Built in 1917 and closed in 1993, Chanute Air Force Base was one of the oldest and largest technical-training centers of the U.S. Air Force. • Biochemist Robert W. Holley; Olympian Bonnie Blair; film critic Roger Ebert; authors Mark and Carl Van Doren; musicians Julius and Sol Cohen; physicist John Bardeen; economist James Tobin. Chemist Roger Adams died here. • Corn, wheat, soybeans, alfalfa, livestock, dairying; manufacture of machinery, electronic components, metal castings, refrigeration and air-conditioning equipment, apparel, consumer goods, concrete, edible oils and other processed foods, computer software and book publishing, athletic equipment. The presence of the University of Illinois makes the county an important education center. • The University's experimental agricultural fields have been in continuous cultivation since 1867. The school's assembly hall has one of the world's largest edge-supported domes. A plaque at the Urbana Courthouse marks the site where, in 1854, Lincoln delivered his third speech against slavery.

CHRISTIAN (one of three counties so named) *Taylorville* • 35,372 • 709 • Central IL, bounded on the north by the Sangamon River; drained by the South Fork of the Sangamon River. Sangchris Lake State Park is in the northwest. Lake Taylorville is also here. • Named for the county in KY, itself named for Col. William Christian (?–1786), army officer, Indian fighter, and legislator • Organized as Dane, 1839 from Sangamon; name changed 1840 • Physicist E. M. Purcell • Corn, wheat, soybeans, sorghum; bituminous-coal mining, oil; light manufacturing, including paper; commercial rose growing • Abraham Lincoln practiced law in the county courthouse.

CLARK (one of twelve counties so named) *Marshall* • 17,008 • 502 • Eastern IL, bounded on the east by the IN state line, and on the southeast by the Wabash River; drained by the North Fork of the Embarras River. Lincoln Trail State Park is here. • One of six counties named for General George Rogers Clark (1752–1818), officer in the Revolutionary War and frontiersman in the Northwest Territory • 1819 from Crawford • Author James Jones (who wrote *From Here to Eternity* in Marshall) • Corn, wheat, soybeans, cattle, hogs; paper products, machinery, electronic equipment • The Archer House in Marshall, the oldest hostelry in IL in continuous operation, hosted Presidents Lincoln and Cleveland. Marshall was located on the Cumberland Trail.

CLAY (one of eighteen counties so named) *Louisville* • 14,560 • 469 • South-central IL, bounded on the east, in part, and drained by the Little Wabash River • One of fifteen counties named for Henry Clay (1777–1852), U.S. senator from KY and statesman • 1824 from Lawrence, Wayne and Fayette • Wheat, soybeans, sorghum, cattle; oil, natural-gas wells; manufacture of apparel, lighting equipment, auto parts, paints, plastic bottles.

CLINTON (one of nine counties so named) *Carlyle* • 35,535 • 474 • Southern IL, bounded on the south in part by the Kaskaskia River. Part of Carlyle Lake reservoir is in the northeast. South Shore and Eldon Hazlet state parks are on the lake. Centralia Correctional Center is in the southeast. • One of eight counties named for De Witt Clinton (1769–1828), governor of NY and supporter of the Erie Canal (including De Witt County in IL) • 1824 from Washington, Bond and Fayette • Corn, wheat, sorghum; metal, wood and plastics manufacturing, food products; bituminous-coal mines.

COLES *Charleston* • 53,196 • 508 • East-central IL; drained by the Kaskaskia, Embarras and Little Wabash rivers. The county includes Fox Ridge State Park and Lincoln Log Cabin State Historic Site. • Named for Edward Coles (1786–1868), humanitarian and IL governor • 1830 from Clark and Edgar • Charleston was the scene of the fourth Lincoln-Douglas debate in September, 1858. • Geologist Thomas C. Chamberlin; cinematographer Gregg Toland • Corn, wheat, soybeans, livestock; manufacture of photo lamps, shoes, brooms, business forms, ceramics for the steel industry; railroad shops; lumber mills; education (Eastern IL U.) • Abraham Lincoln's father and stepmother are buried in Shiloh Cemetery.

COOK (one of three counties so named) *Chicago* • 5,376,741 (the most populated county in IL and second most populated county in the U.S.) • 946 • Northeastern IL, bounded on the east by Lake Michigan and the IN state line, and traversed by the Chicago and Des Plaines rivers, and other links in the Chicago Sanitary and Ship Canal System. The county is dominated by Chicago, its vast metropolitan area extending well beyond Cook County. It contains Midway Airport and shares O'Hare International Airport with DuPage County. • Named for Daniel P. Cook (1794–1827), first attorney general of IL and U.S. representative • 1831 from Putnam • After the Great Fire of 1871 destroyed much of Chicago, architects such as Louis Sullivan and Daniel Burnham designed innovative skyscrapers in a style that came to be known as the Chicago School. The world's first metal-frame skyscraper, the ten story Home Insurance Building, was designed by William Le Baron Jenney and completed in 1885. The city hosted world's fairs in 1893 and 1933. In 1900, engineers reversed the flow of the Chicago River to prevent its polluted waters from reaching the city's water supply in Lake Michigan. Until the 1950s, Chicago was the world's leading meat packing center, rhapsodized by Carl Sandburg as "Hog Butcher for the World." Jane Adams and Ellen Starr founded Hull House in 1889 to help immigrant workers. In 1942, the University of Chicago set off the first nuclear chain reaction, leading to the development of the atomic bomb. South Holland was the first northern community against which federal action was brought under the 1964 Civil Rights Act to force desegregation of public schools. • Novelists Ernest Hemingway, Frank Norris, Raymond Chandler, James Gould Cozzens; market research engineer A.C. Nielsen; industrialist George M. Pullman; U.S. attorney general John Ashcroft; publisher Hugh Hefner; U.S. defense secretary Donald Rumsfeld; U.S. Supreme Court justice John P. Stevens; Archbishop Edward Egan; mayor Richard M. Daley; first ladies Betty Ford and Hillary Clinton; ventriloquist Edgar Bergen; baseball executive Charles Comiskey; film producer Walt Disney; jurist Arthur Joseph Goldberg; clarinetist Benny Goodman; playwright Lorraine Hansberry; musician Gene Krupa; poet Archibald MacLeish; TV and radio executive William Paley; newspaper columnist Drew Pearson, author William Shirer; actress Gloria Swanson; Vice President Charles G. Dawes. Died here: political leader Stephen A. Douglas; lawman Eliot Ness; bank robber John Dillinger • Diversified industries in Chicago and neighboring Cook County municipalities place Cook among the top manufacturing and transportation centers in the U.S. Remnant agriculture (corn and soybeans) is in the extreme northwest and southwest corners of the county. The county is a major education center, especially in Evanston. (Institutions of higher learning located here include Northeastern IL U.; De Paul U.; Loyola U. Chicago; Northwestern U.; IL Institute of Technology; U. of Chicago; Concordia U.; Chicago State U.; and U. of IL at Chicago.) • Over forty Fortune 1000 counties have headquarters in the county. At 110 stories high, the Sears Tower in Chicago is the tallest building in the U.S. Lincolnwood's name honors Abraham Lincoln and has inspired the planting of 10,000 trees that distinguish the village. Previously Al Capone's duchy, Cicero contains one of the greatest industrial concentrations in the world, with more than 150 factories within an area of 1.75 square miles. Almost half of Forest Park is occupied by cemeteries. Evanston is the national headquarters for the National Merit Scholarship Corporation, Rotary International, and the National Women's Christian Temperance Union. Oak Park has twenty-four buildings designed by architect Frank Lloyd Wright, who once lived and kept his studio there. The Baha'i House of Worship in Wilmette is the center of the Baha'i faith in North America. Chicago is home to the Bears (Soldier Field), Blackhawks and Bulls (United Center), Cubs (Wrigley Field), and White Sox (Comiskey Park).

CRAWFORD (one of eleven counties so named) *Robinson* • 20,452 • 444 • Southeastern IL, bounded on the east by the Wabash River (forming the IN state line); drained by the North Fork of the Embarras River. The county contains the Crawford County Sate Fish and Wildlife Area and part of Chauncy Marsh Nature Preserve. • One of six counties named directly or indirectly for William Harris Crawford (1772–1834), U.S. senator from GA, U.S. secretary of war, and U.S. secretary of the treasury • 1816 (prior to statehood) from Edwards • Wabash River ports here were important trade centers in the 19th century. • Novelist James Jones • Livestock, wheat, soybeans, hay; oil drilling, refining; manufacture of pottery, food, rubber and metal products • Palestine, settled in the late 17th century, is the oldest established town in IL. Hutsonville's thriving button factory used mussel shells from the Wabash River; a large pearl found in one of its mussels is now part of the Crown Jewels of England. The Heath English Toffee bar originated in Robinson.

CUMBERLAND (one of eight counties so named) *Toledo* • 11,253 • 346 • Southeast-central IL; drained by the Embarras River. • Named for the Cumberland Road, the first national thoroughfare, which ran through the county. • 1843 from Coles • Livestock, hay, soybeans, corn, dairying, wheat; light manufacturing.

DE KALB *Sycamore* • 88,969 • 634 • Northern IL; drained by branches of the Kishwaukee River. Shabbona Lake State Park is in the south. • One of six counties named for Johann, Baron de Kalb (1721–80), German-born French soldier who fought with the Americans during the Revolutionary War • 1837 from Kane • The barbed wire industry began in De Kalb in 1875 when Joseph F. Glidden invented a practical machine for its manufacture. • Sheep, hogs, hybrid seed corn, soybeans, poultry, truck gardening; manufacture of electrical, electronic, and precision equipment, plastic products, asphalt; education (Northern IL U.) • The American Farm Bureau Federation was founded in De Kalb in 1912.

DE WITT (one of two counties so named, the other in TX) *Clinton* • 16,798 • 398 • Central IL; drained by Salt and Kickapoo creeks. Clinton Lake reservoir is here, as are Clinton Lake State Recreation Area and Weldon Springs State Park • One of eight counties named for De Witt Clinton (1769–1828), governor of NY and supporter of the Erie Canal (one of two counties named for Governor Clinton in IL, the other being Clinton) • 1839 from McLean and Macon • Grain, corn, soybeans, livestock; manufacture of fabricated metal products; printing and publishing.

DOUGLAS *Tuscola* • 19,922 • 417 • East-central IL; drained by the Embarras and Kaskaskia rivers. Rockome Gardens is in the southwest. • One of twelve counties named for Stephen A. Douglas (1813–61), U.S. orator and statesman • 1859 from Coles • Cartoonist John B. Gruelle • Corn, wheat, soybeans, broomcorn, livestock, poultry; dairy and other food products; manufacture of brooms, road machinery, oil tanks, burial vaults, caskets, office equipment, wood products.

DU PAGE *Wheaton* • 904,161 (the second most populated county in IL) • 334 • Northeastern IL, bounded on the southeast by Des Plaines River; drained by the DuPage River. The county lies in the Chicago metropolitan area and is predominantly urban and suburban. Argonne National Lab and Fermi National Accelerator Lab are here. • Named for the DuPage River • 1839 from Cook • Jurist and steel corporation organizer Elbert H. Gary; astronomer Grote Reber; publisher Robert R. McCormick. Socialist Eugene Debs died here. • Diversified manufacturing; railroad shops; limestone quarries; nurseries; education (a number of colleges and universities) • Several Fortune 1000 companies have their headquarters in the county. Lilacia Park in Lombard, the former estate of Col. William Plum, offers viewing of more than 300 varieties of lilacs, which Plum collected from around the world. Wheaton and Carol Stream have been called the "Protestant Vatican of the Midwest" for their denominational and interdenominational institutions and activities, including the headquarters of the Theosophical Society of America, and the National Association of Evangelicals. *Christianity Today* is published in Wheaton.

EDGAR *Paris* • 19,704 • 624 • Eastern IL, bounded on the east by the IN state line; drained by small tributaries of the Wabash River. • Named for John Edgar (?–1832), pioneer merchant and politician • 1823 from Clark • Corn, soybeans, sorghum, cattle, hogs; food processing; farm machinery.

EDWARDS (one of three counties so named) *Albion* • 6,971 • 222 • Southeastern IL, bounded on the east by Bonpas Creek; drained by the Little Wabash River. The southeastern corner touches the Wabash River. • Named for Ninian Edwards (1775–1833), first governor of IL Territory and one of IL's first two senators • 1814 (prior to statehood) from Madison and Gallatin • Editor Benjamin O. Flower • Cattle, wheat, sorghum, oil; fisheries; manufacture of auto parts.

EFFINGHAM (one of two counties so named, the other in GA) *Effingham* • 34,264 • 479 • Southeast-central IL; drained by the Little Wabash River. The county includes Rock Cave Nature Preserve. • Named for either Thomas Howard (1746–91), 3rd Earl of Effingham, who supported the Americans during the Revolutionary War, or for Edward Effingham, surveyor who laid out the county • 1831 from Fayette and Crawford • The town of Effingham grew with the extension of the Cumberland (National) Road into the area in 1831. • Corn, wheat, sorghum, soybeans, hogs, cattle, dairying; manufacture of dairy and other food products, wood products, leather gloves, mittens, home appliances, air conditioners, fertilizers, housing components; oil; printing.

FAYETTE (one of eleven counties so named) *Vandalia* • 21,802 • 716 • South-central IL; drained by the Kaskaskia River. Ramsey Lake State Park and Dean Hills Nature Preserve are here. Carlyle Lake State Fish and Wildlife Area is on the northern end of Carlyle Lake reservoir. Vandalia is the site of Vandalia State House Historic Site and Vandalia Correction Center. • One of seventeen counties named for the Marquis de Lafayette (1757–1834), French statesman and soldier who fought with the Americans during the Revolutionary War • 1821 from Bond, Jefferson, Wayne and Clark • The Cumberland (National) Road ended at Vandalia, the second of three IL state capitals (1820–1839). Abraham Lincoln and political rival Stephen A. Douglas served in the legislature here; in the Supreme Court Lincoln received his license to practice law. • Businessman Haroldson L. Hunt • Corn, wheat, soybeans, sorghum, cattle, dairy products; oil and natural gas wells; manufacture of rubber and plastic products • Vandalia owns one of two extant Lincoln life masks.

FORD (one of two counties so named, the other in KS) *Paxton* • 14,241 • 486 • East-central IL; drained by the Mackinaw River and the Middle Fork of the Vermilion River (designated here a National Scenic River) • Named for Thomas Ford (1800–1850), IL Supreme Court justice and governor of IL • 1859 from Vermilion. Ford was the last of IL's 102 counties to organize. • Corn, soybeans, wheat, livestock; manufacture of machinery, brooms and brushes.

FRANKLIN (one of twenty-five counties so named) *Benton* • 39,018 • 412 • Southern IL, bounded on the northwest by the Little Muddy River; drained by the Big Muddy River. The southern half of Rend Lake (the second largest manmade lake in IL) is in the north. • One of twenty-three counties named for Benjamin Franklin • 1818 (prior to statehood) from White and Gallatin • Labor leader John L. Lewis lived for a time in Benton and worked in nearby coal fields • Bituminous coal; poultry; corn, wheat, fruit; manufacture of textiles and boats • Wayne Fitzgerrell State Park hosts annual field dog trials.

FULTON (one of eight counties so named) *Lewistown* • 38,250 • 866 • West-central IL, bounded on the southeast by the Illinois River; drained by Spoon River. The county includes a group of bayou lakes along the Illinois. Emiquon National Wildlife Refuge, Anderson Lake Conservation Area, and Rice Lake State Fish and Wildlife Area are here. Many square miles of the county have been scarred by coal strip mining. • One of seven counties named for Robert Fulton (1765–1815), builder of the *Clermont*, the first commercially successful steamboat • 1823 from Pike • Canton was severely damaged by a tornado in 1835. • Inventors and manufacturers Charles E. and J. Frank Duryea • Cattle, corn, wheat, soybeans, sorghum, dairy products; bituminous-coal mining, clay deposits; manufacture of textiles, furniture, metals, kitchen cabinets, overalls, agricultural implements (Canton was the

site of one of the world's largest tillage-implement factories, the P. and O. Plow Works, absorbed by International Harvester Company in 1919). • Spoon River was made famous by poet Edgar Lee Masters' 1915 *Spoon River Anthology.*

GALLATIN (one of three counties so named) *Shawneetown* • 6,445 • 324 • Southeastern IL, bounded on the northeast by the Wabash River (forming the IN state line) and on the southeast by the Ohio River (forming the KY state line); drained by the Saline River and its north and south forks. The southern part of the county is in Shawnee National Forest. • One of two counties (the other in KY) named for Albert Gallatin (1761–1849), U.S. secretary of the treasury, and minister to France and Great Britain • 1812 (prior to statehood) from Randolph • Shawneetown State Historic Site marks the site of Old Shawneetown, once a major river port. The John Marshall home, built here in 1818, served as the first bank in Illinois Territory and gained notoriety in 1830 for refusing a loan application from a Chicago investment group, noting that "Chicago would not amount to anything." The oldest post office in continuous operation in IL and the state's second newspaper, the *Illinois Immigrant* began here in 1818. Floods repeatedly devastated the county; after the flood of 1937, the state moved the buildings of Shawneetown four miles to the west. • Union army officer James Harrison Wilson • Corn, soybeans; bituminous-coal mining, oil, natural gas • A plaque in New Haven marks the site where, around 1800, the brother of Daniel Boone established a mill. The Salt Festival in Equality recalls the contributions of the oldest salt works west of the Alleghenies.

GREENE (one of fourteen counties so named) *Carrollton* • 14,761 • 543 • Western IL, bounded on the west by the Illinois River; drained by Macoupin Creek (forming part of the southern boundary) and Apple Creek. • One of sixteen counties named for General Nathanael Greene (1742–86), hero of the Revolutionary War • 1821 from Madison • Politician Henry T. Rainey • Cattle, hogs, corn, wheat, soybeans, sorghum, oats, fruit, dairy products; potter's clay; manufacture of paper products.

GRUNDY *Morris* • 37,535 • 420 • Northeastern IL; drained by the Illinois, Des Plaines, and Kankakee rivers. The county includes Gebhard Woods State Park and Goose Lake Prairie State Nature Area. The Illinois and Michigan Canal, completed in 1848, bisects the county. • One of four counties named for Felix Grundy (1777–1840), chief justice of the KY Supreme Court, U.S. senator from TN, and U.S. attorney general • 1841 from La Salle • Corn, soybeans, dairying; clay, limestone; manufacture of paper products, aluminum products, rubber and plastic products, chemicals, and allied products • Morris hosts a dulcimer festival each July.

HAMILTON (one of ten counties so named) *McLeansboro* • 8,621 • 435 • Southeastern IL; drained by the North Fork of the Saline River. Hamilton County Conservation Area is in the east and Ten Mile Creek State Fish and Wildlife Area is in the west. • One of eight counties named for Alexander Hamilton (1757–1804), first U.S. secretary of the treasury • 1821 from White • Livestock, fruit, wheat, corn, redtop seed.

HANCOCK *Carthage* • 20,121 • 795 • Western IL, bounded on the west by the Mississippi River (forming the IA and MO state lines); drained by La Moine River and Bear Creek. The county includes Nauvoo State Park. • One of ten counties named for John Hancock (1737–93), noted signer of the Declaration of Independence; governor of MA and statesman • 1825 from Pike and unorganized territory • The Mormons, having settled in Nauvoo in 1839, were forced to abandon the city in 1846 after Joseph and Hyram Smith, awaiting trail for treason, were murdered by a mob in Carthage on June 27, 1844. After establishing a settlement in Fannin County, TX, Etienne Cabot, a French Icarian, relocated his communist community to the abandoned Nauvoo in 1849. • Poet Ina Donna Coolbrith • Wine (extensive orchards), blue-cheese, corn, wheat, apples, soybeans, fruit, cattle, hogs, dairying; limestone quarries, sand pits; milling of whole wheat flour; tourism • Before the Mormons left Nauvoo, it was the most populated city in IL.

HARDIN (one of six counties so named) *Elizabethtown* • 4,800 • 178 • Southeastern IL, bounded on the south and east by the Ohio River (forming the KY state line) and on the northeast by the Saline River; drained by Big Creek. About ninety percent of the county lies in Shawnee National Forest. Part of Cave-in-Rock State Park (a pirate den in the 1790s and later a hideout for outlaws) is here. • Named for the county in KY, former home of many settlers • 1839 from Pope • The Illinois Iron Furnace was the first charcoal-fired iron furnace in IL and the principal source of iron during the Civil War. • Wheat, corn, sorghum, livestock; timber; manufacture of fluorspar products from imported fluorspar. (The last IL fluorspar mine closed in 1996.)

HENDERSON (one of five counties so named) *Oquawka* • 8,213 • 379 • Western IL, bounded on the west by the Mississippi River (forming the IA state line); drained by Henderson Creek. Big River State Forest, Delabar State Park, and Henderson County Conservation Area are here, with beaches and campsites along the Mississippi. • Named for either the county in KY, former home of many settlers, or Henderson Creek • 1841 from Warren • Cattle, hogs, poultry, corn, soybeans; limestone.

HENRY (one of ten counties so named) *Cambridge* • 51,020 • 823 • Northwestern IL, bounded on the northwest by the Rock River; drained by the Green and Edwards rivers. The Old Illinois and Mississippi Canal crosses the county. Johnson-Sauk Trail State Park is in the east. • One of ten counties (including Patrick County in VA) named for Patrick Henry (1736–99), patriot, governor of VA, and statesman • 1825 from Fulton • Bishop Hill began as a communistic settlement established in 1846 by Erik Jansson and other Swedish Pietist immigrants. (Designated a state historic site in 1946, the vil-

lage has several restored buildings constructed by member carpenters and craftsmen.) • Cartoonist Rollin Kirby • Corn, soybeans, vegetables, cattle, hogs, dairy products; food products, metal industries; manufacture of heating equipment, farm implements, work clothes; coal mining.

IROQUOIS *Watseka* • 31,334 • 1,116 (the third largest county in IL) • Eastern IL, bounded on the east by the IN state line; drained by the Iroquois River and Sugar Creek. Hooper Branch Savanna Nature Preserve and Iroquois County State Wildlife Area are here. • Named for the Iroquois River, itself named for the Indian tribe • 1833 from Vermilion • Architect Henry Bacon; peace officer Bat Masterson • Corn, sorghum, soybeans, cattle, hogs, dairying; manufacture of food products, wood products, industrial machinery, condensers, transformers, electric parts, business forms.

JACKSON (one of twenty-four counties so named) *Murphysboro* • 59,612 • 588 • Southern IL, bounded on the southwest by the Mississippi River (forming the MO state line); drained by the Big Muddy and Little Muddy rivers and Beaucoup Creek. The county includes part of Shawnee National Forest, including Pomona Natural Bridge and Little Grand Canyon. Part of Crab Orchard and Mark Twain national wildlife refuges are here, as are Lake Murphysboro and Grant City state parks. Lake Kincaid and Cedar Lake reservoirs are also here. • One of twenty-two counties named directly or indirectly for President Andrew Jackson • 1816 (prior to statehood) from Randolph and Johnson • Sociologist Willard W. Waller • Wheat, sorghum, fruit, truck vegetables, cattle, dairying; manufacture of wood products, paper products, fabricated metal products, gloves, dresses, concrete, tape; bituminous-coal mining; railroad shops; education (Southern IL U. Carbondale) • General John A. Logan, county native and commander of the Grand Army of the Republic, issued the order of Carbondale (1868) designating May 30 as Memorial (Decoration) Day.

JASPER *Newton* • 10,117 • 494 • Southeast-central IL; drained by the Embarras River and its North Fork. Newton Lake is in the southwest with Newton Lake State Fish and Wildlife Area on its western shore. Sam Parr State Fish and Wildlife Area is also here. • One of eight counties named for Sergeant William Jasper (?–1779), Revolutionary War hero. • 1831 from Crawford and Clay • Soybeans, corn, sorghum, wheat, cattle, hogs, dairy products; oil; manufacture of auto parts.

JEFFERSON *Mount Vernon* • 40,045 • 571 • Southern IL; drained by the Big Muddy River. The northern half of Rend Lake (the second largest manmade lake in IL) is in the south. The lake is noted for its Canadian goose population. Over 1,500 blue herons nest at the Rend Lake State Fish and Wildlife Area. • One of twenty-six counties named directly or indirectly for President Thomas Jefferson • 1819 from Edwards and White counties • The southern division of the IL Supreme Court was located in Mount Vernon from 1856 to 1896; Abraham Lincoln argued and won a tax case here in 1859. • Cattle, sorghum, wheat; manufacture of railroad cars, rubber products, machinery, electronic equipment; bituminous-coal mining, oil.

JERSEY *Jerseyville* • 21,668 • 369 • Western IL, bounded on the south in part by the Mississippi River (forming the MO state line) and on the west by the Illinois River; drained by Macoupin Creek (forming part of the northern boundary). The county includes the Mississippi River State Fish and Wildlife Area, Pere Marquette State Park, and the Great River Road bicycle trail. Its limestone cliffs are noted for bald-eagle nesting. • Named for the town of Jerseyville, many of whose residents came from New Jersey • 1839 from Greene • Soybeans, sorghum, apples, corn, wheat, cattle, hogs, dairying; resort tourism; education (Principia College).

JO DAVIESS *Galena* • 22,289 • 601 • Extreme northwestern IL, bounded on the north by the WI state line, and on the west by the Mississippi River (here forming the IA state line); drained by the Apple, Plum and Galena rivers. Charles Mound, near the WI border, is the highest point in IL (1,235 feet). The county contains Apple River Canyon State Park, a portion of the Upper Mississippi River National Wildlife and Fish Refuge and several nature preserves. The Savannah Army Depot is in the southwest on the Mississippi River. • One of four counties named for Col. Joseph H. Daveiss (1774–1811), VA soldier and attorney who unsuccessfully attempted to indict Aaron Burr for treason. The name was misspelled in the act creating the county and allowed to stand. • 1827 from Mercer, Henry and Putnam • Lead sulfide deposits were mined in the area beginning in the early 1700s, and led to the name Galena for the town established here in 1826. In the late 1840s and 1850s, Galena was IL's wealthiest city. Much of its original architecture survives. • President Ulysses S. Grant (state historic site) • Tourism, cattle, hogs, sheep, oats, alfalfa, dairying; lead and zinc mines; dairy products, metal products, fertilizer, iron.

JOHNSON (one of twelve counties so named) *Vienna* • 12,878 • 345 • Southern IL; drained by the Cache River (forming part of the southern boundary). The county includes part of Shawnee National Forest in the north. Ferne Clyffe State Park is in the northwest; Cache River and Little Black Slough state nature areas are here, as is Cave Creek Glade Nature Preserve. • One of five counties named for Col. Richard M. Johnson (1780–1850), officer in War of 1812, U.S. senator from KY and U.S. vice president • 1812 (prior to statehood) from Randolph • Fruit, sorghum, wheat, cattle, dairy products; lumbering; wood products.

KANE (one of two counties so named, the other in UT) *Geneva* • 404,119 (the fifth most populated county in IL) • 520 • Northeastern IL; drained by the Fox River and Mill Creek The county has industrial centers along the Fox River. Its eastern margin has experienced urban growth as part of the Chicago metropolitan area. • Named for Elish K. Kane (1794–1835), IL legislator, jurist and U.S. senator • 1836 •

Literary historian Vernon L. Parrington; Speaker of the House Dennis Hastert; journalist Bob Woodward; biologist Edmund B. Wilson • Diversifed manufacturing; limestone quarries; education (several schools, including Aurora U.) • Elgin was once known the world over for its watches. Built in 1881, Aurora's street lighting system, with powerful arc lamps placed on tops of buildings and 150-foot towers, is said to have been the world's first complete lighting system. Aurora's Blackberry Historical Farm Village, features a large carriage collection. The Aurora Historical Museum displays mastodon bones found here.

KANKAKEE *Kankakee* • 103,833 • 677 • Northeastern IL, bounded on the east by the IN state line; drained by the Kankakee and Iroquois rivers. Kankakee River State Park is in the northwest. Gooseberry Island, Iroquois Woods, and Hooper Branch Savanna Nature preserves are here. • Named for the Kankakee River • 1853 from Iroquois and Will • Originally a campsite for French fur trappers, the area became popular with French immigrants through the mid-1880s. • Cartoonist Harold Gray • Corn, soybeans, livestock, dairying; manufacture of industrial machinery, wood products, food products, paper products, chemicals, plastic products, tile, industrial machinery, metal products, furniture, stoves, paint, farm implements, pharmaceuticals; corn- and soybean-processing plants; limestone deposits; education (Olivet Nazarene College). The Kankakee State Hospital for the mentally ill was established in 1877.

KENDALL (one of two counties so named, the other in TX) *Yorkville* • 54,544 (39% increase since 1990; the third fastest growing county in IL) • 321 • Northeastern IL; drained by the Fox River. The county lies in a rich farming area, with the beginnings of urbanization in the extreme northeast corner (Chicago metropolitan area). Silver Springs State Park is in the central west. • Named for Amos Kendall (1789–1869), U.S. postmaster general and journalist • 1841 from La Salle and Kane • Corn, soybeans, wheat; dairy products; manufacture of fabricated metal products, electronic equipment.

KNOX *Galesburg* • 55,836 • 716 • Northwestern IL; drained by Spoon River, and Pope and Henderson creeks. The county contains Snakeden Hollow State Fish and Wildlife Area.• One of nine counties named for General Henry Knox (1750–1806), Revolutionary War officer and first U.S. secretary of war • 1825 from Fulton • Galesburg was founded in 1837 by a group of pioneers from the east who set out to establish a college here. The fruit of their efforts, Knox College, witnessed one of the historical Lincoln-Douglas debates at its Old Main building in 1858. • Collegiate football player Willie Heston; poet and historian Carl Sandburg (state historic site); geographer and explorer Ellsworth Huntington; pharmacist and businessman Charles R. Walgreen • Corn, wheat, soybeans, livestock, dairy products; clay, gravel; manufacture of mowers, marine parts and accessories, garage doors, farm gates and fencing, malleable iron castings, hydraulic rubber hose.

LAKE (one of twelve counties so named) *Waukegan* • 644,356 (the third most populated county in IL) • 448 • Extreme northeastern IL, bounded on the east by Lake Michigan and on the north by the WI state line; drained by the Fox and Des Plaines rivers. The county lies in a rapidly growing urban area which includes many northern suburbs of Chicago. It has two ski resorts, Illinois Beach State Park and Chain O' Lakes State Park offering fishing and duck hunting. There is a major military presence in the county with the Great Lakes Naval Training Station and Philip Sheridan Arms Reserve Center located here. • Named for either Lake Michigan or for the several small lakes within the county. • 1839 from McHenry • A strike at a manufacturing plant in North Chicago in 1937 led to a major U.S. Supreme Court ruling in 1939 (National Labor Relations Board v. Fansteel Metallurgical Company) declaring sit-down strikes illegal. • Science fiction author Ray Bradbury; football player and coach Otto Graham; photographer Edward Weston; politician Adlai E. Stevenson II; comedian Jack Benny. Advertising executive Leo Burnett died here. • Sand, gravel, stone deposits; dairying; diversified manufacturing; education (several colleges, including Lake Forest) • Highland Park is the site of one of the nation's most prominent music festivals and the summer home of the Chicago Symphony Orchestra. The county is headquarters to eight Fortune 1000 companies. Zion was established in 1901 by John Alexander Dowie as the headquarters of his Christian Catholic Church; until 1935 it was, in effect, a theocracy, with the church controlling all business activities in the town.

LA SALLE *Ottawa* • 111,509 • 1,135 (the second largest county in IL) • Northern IL; drained by the Illinois, Fox, Vermilion, and Little Vermilion rivers. The county includes part of the Illinois and Michigan Canal Parkway. It also includes Starved Rock, Buffalo Rock, Illini and Matthiessen state parks. Wild Bill Hickok State Memorial is here. • One of three counties named for Robert Cavelier (1643–87), Sieur de La Salle, French adventurer and explorer who claimed the land west of the Mississippi River for France • 1831 from Putnam and Vermilion • In 1682, La Salle established a fort in the area that would later bear his name. Lincoln participated in the first in a series of seven senatorial debates with Stephen Douglas in Ottawa. • Astronomer James Keeler; writer Clarence E. Mulford • Corn, soybeans, wheat, cattle, hogs, dairy products; clay, coal, silica sand, gravel; manufacture of glass and plastic materials; chemical, zinc, and metal works.

LAWRENCE (one of eleven counties so named) *Lawrenceville* • 15,452 • 372 • Southeastern IL, bounded on the east by the Wabash River (forming the IN state line); drained by the Embarras river. The county includes Red Hills State Park. • One of nine counties named for Captain James Lawrence (1781–1813), U.S. naval officer in the war with Barbary pirates near Tripoli and commander of the U.S.S. Chesapeake in the War of 1812 • 1821 from Crawford and Edwards • Oil and natural gas wells; oil refineries and other manufacturing; livestock, soybeans, corn, wheat.

LEE (one of twelve counties so named) *Dixon* • 36,062 • 725 • Northern IL; drained by the Rock, Green, and Kyte rivers, and Big Bureau Creek. Green River State Wildlife Area and part of Foley-Sand Prairie Nature Preserve are here. • Named for either Henry "Lighthorse Harry" Lee (1756–1818), governor of the state of VA, or for Richard Henry Lee (1732–1794), VA statesman, a signer of the Declaration of Independence, and U.S. senator from VA • 1839 from Ogle • Fort Dixon was built by General Henry Atkins as a base for his campaign in 1832 against Chief Black Hawk. It was here in its Blockhouse that Abraham Lincoln, Jefferson Davis, and Zachary Taylor met as comrades-in-arms. • President Ronald Reagan • Corn, soybeans, cattle, poultry, dairying; manufacture of food products, cement products, metal products, industrial machinery, auto parts; sand and gravel pits • The John Deere Historic Site, south of Grand Detour, marks the spot where Deere built the first successful self-scouring steel plow in 1837. The Nachusa Grasslands, a privately-held nature preserve owned by the Nature Conservancy, represents a rare remnant of native Illinois prairie. The Franklin Creek State Nature Area, north of Franklin Grove, contains the oldest bedrock outcropping in the state.

LIVINGSTON (one of six counties so named) *Pontiac* • 39,678 • 1,044 (the fourth largest county in IL) • East-central IL; drained by the Vermilion River. The Sunbury Railroad Prairie Nature Preserve is in the central north. • One of three counties definitively named for Edward Livingston (1764–1836), senator from LA and U.S. secretary of state • 1837 from La Salle and McLean • Physician Francis E. Townsend • Corn, wheat, soybeans, livestock, dairying; limestone, clay; manufacture of furniture, industrial storage equipment, lawn mowers, gloves, shoe heels; commercial printing; Pontiac Correctional Center • Pontiac is an integral part of the Route 66 tour.

LOGAN (one of ten counties so named) *Lincoln* • 31,183 • 618 • Central IL; drained by Salt, Kickapoo and Sugar creeks. Edward R. Madigan State Park, and Postville Courthouse and Mount Pulaski Courthouse state historic sites are here. • Named for Dr. John Logan (1788–1852), IL legislator, and father of John A. Logan, U.S. general • 1839 from Sangamon • Abraham Lincoln helped to plan the town of Lincoln and practiced law here from 1847 to 1859. The town was the first in the nation to be named for Lincoln prior to his becoming president. • Corn, wheat, soybeans, cattle, hogs; manufacture of glass containers, plate glass, store fixtures, corrugated boxes, electrical equipment, cosmetics; sand and gravel; education (Lincoln Christian College) • Mount Pulaski was the landing site for Walter Brookins' plane after his record-breaking race with a steam train. The Illinois State Geological Survey designated Chestnut as the geographical center of the state.

MACON *Decatur* • 114,706 • 581 • Central IL; drained by the Sangamon River, dammed to form Lake Decatur (a recreational area). The county contains Spitler Woods State Nature Area and Lincoln Trail Homestead State Memorial. • One of six counties named for Nathaniel Macon (1757–1837), U.S. representative and senator • 1829 from Shelby • In 1830, Abraham Lincoln's family built its first IL home in what is now Lincoln Trail Homestead Park. Lincoln was a lawyer in the county from 1847 to 1857. At the State Republican Convention held in the county in 1860, Lincoln received his first endorsement for the presidency of the U.S. • Chemist Karl A. Folkers; historian Stephen E. Ambrose • Soybeans, corn, livestock; bituminous-coal mining; manufacture of iron, steel and brass products, automobile products, tires, electronic components, earth-moving equipment, glass, chemicals, food products, nonedible derivatives of corn and soybeans, clothing, plastic products, kites, tractors, gas and watermain equipment • Founded in 1857, Decatur's municipal band is the oldest in the U.S. The 1st post of the Grand Army of the Republic was organized in Decatur in 1866.

MACOUPIN *Carlinville* • 49,019 • 864 • West-central IL; drained by Macoupin, Cahokia, and Otter creeks. Beaver Dam State Park and Denby Prairie Nature Preserve are here. • Named for Macoupin Creek • 1829 from Madison and Greene • The first Civil War regiment in IL was organized in Carlinville; four U.S. Civil War generals lived in the town. Attended by fraud and scandal, Carlinville's imposing "million dollar" limestone county courthouse was completed in 1870. Virden was the scene of a coal-mine-related riot on Oct. 12, 1898 in which ten people were killed and the city fell under several days of martial law. The incident was seen by the union movement as a milestone in efforts to win workers the eight-hour day. • Novelist and essayist Mary Austin; Texas cattleman Charles Goodnight; sociologist Edward A. Ross. Missionary to the Cherokees Gideon Blackburn died here • Corn, wheat, soybeans, sorghum, cattle, hogs, poultry, dairy products; bituminous-coal mining; clay pits; manufacture of transportation equipment, food products, wood products, dresses, small boats, steel pipe fittings, agricultural implements, cotton gloves • Blackburn College became known internationally in 1912 for its self-help plan and student management policies.

MADISON *Edwardsville* • 258,941 • 725 • Southwestern IL, bounded on the west by the Mississippi River (forming the MO state line); drained by Cahokia and Silver creeks. Horseshoe Lake State Park, with its large oxbow lake, is here. As part of the St. Louis metropolitan area, the county is fairly urbanized. • One of twenty counties named directly or indirectly for President James Madison • 1812 (prior to statehood) from Saint Clair • It was from the mouth of the Wood River here that Lewis and Clark embarked on their trip to the Pacific Northwest on May 14, 1804 (state memorial). Elijah P. Lovejoy, killed in 1837 while defending his Alton printing press from a pro-slavery mob, became a symbol for the abolitionist cause. The final Lincoln-Douglas senatorial debate was held in Alton on Oct. 15, 1858. • Musician Miles Davis; assassin James Earl Ray • Wheat, soybeans, sorghum, cattle, poultry, dairying; oil and oil refining, manufacture of steel products, corn products, glass, paper, plastic ammunition, hardware, machinery;

education (Southern IL U. at Edwardsville) • Edwardsville is the birthplace of seven IL governors. Highland is one of the oldest and largest Swiss communities in the U.S. In Alton a life-sized bronze sculpture was created in memory of Robert Wadlow, reputedly the tallest man in the world. Leclair Village was an experimental community founded by industrialist N.O. Nelson on the principles of profit-sharing and Britain's cooperative movement. The Collinsville water tower, constructed in 1949, is the world's tallest replica of a catsup bottle.

MARION *Salem* • 41,691 • 572 • South-central IL; drained by Skillet Fork and the East Fork of the Kaskaskia River. Stephen A. Forbes State Park is here. Miller Shrub Swamp Nature Preserve is on Skillet Fork in the extreme southeast. • One of seventeen counties named for Francis Marion (?–1795), SC soldier and legislator, known as "The Swamp Fox" for his tactics during the Revolutionary War • 1823 from Fayette and Jefferson • Two of the participants in the Scopes "monkey" trial were born in Salem, the Populist politician (and prosecutor) William Jennings Bryan and John Thomas Scopes, the teacher-defendant • Large-scale oil production; also wheat, soybeans, corn, sorghum, cattle, poultry, dairying; manufacture of metal products, plastic products, machinery, transportation equipment, fiber glass products, stoves and furnaces, food products, clothing; railroad shops.

MARSHALL (one of twelve counties so named) *Lacon* • 13,180 • 386 • North-central IL; drained by the Illinois River (here forming Goose Lake) and Sandy Creek. The county includes Marshall State Fish and Wildlife Area. • One of eight counties named for John Marshall (1755–1835), fourth Chief Justice of the U.S. • 1839 from Putnam • Corn, wheat, soybeans, fruit, livestock; manufacture of food products, books, chemicals, clothing.

MASON (one of six counties so named) *Havana* • 16,038 • 539 • Central IL, bounded on the west by the Illinois River and on the south by the Sangamon River and Salt Creek. Several slough lakes, including Lake Chautauqua and Crane Lake, are located along the Illinois. The county includes part of Chautauqua National Wildlife Refuge, Sand Ridge State Forest, and Long Branch Sand Prairie, Mantanzas Prairie, and Revis Hill Prairie nature preserves. • Named for the county in KY, former home of many of the settlers • 1841 from Tazewell • Corn, wheat, soybeans, vegetables, melons; diversified manufacturing; river and railroad shipping.

MASSAC *Metropolis* • 15,161 • 239 • Extreme southern IL, bounded on the south by the Ohio River (forming the KY state line), on the northwest by the Cache River. The county includes part of Shawnee National Forest along its northeast border. Fort Massac State Park (IL's first state park) and Mermet Lake Conservation Area are also here. Lock and Dam No. 52 is near Brookport. • Named for Fort Massac, an old French fort within the county • 1843 from Pope and Johnson • Wheat, sorghum, corn, soybeans, cattle; manufacture of clothing, chemicals, cement • Metropolis was declared the official hometown of Superman by IL House Resolution No. 572, dated June 9, 1972. Vice President Aaron Burr and General James Wilkinson allegedly drew up plans to conquer Mexico and the American southwest at Fort Massac during the summer of 1805.

MCDONOUGH *Macomb* • 32,913 • 589 • Western IL; drained by La Moine River and its East Fork. The county includes Argyle Lake State Park. • Named for Captain Thomas Macdonough (1783–1825), naval officer in the war against Barbary pirates near Tripoli and in the War of 1812. Coincidentally, the Macdonough family name was previously spelled "McDonough." • 1826 from Schuyler • Cartoonist and illustrator Peter Newell • Livestock, corn, sorghum, soybeans, hay, dairying; bituminous-coal mining, clay pits; manufacture of pottery, porcelain products, roller bearings; education (Western IL U.).

MCHENRY (one of two counties so named, the other in ND) *Woodstock* • 260,077 (42% increase since 1990; the fastest growing county in IL) • 604 • Northeastern IL, bounded on the north by the WI state line; drained by the Fox and Kishwaukee rivers. Urban growth from Chicago has extended into the county. There are several fishing lakes. The Illinois Railway Museum is east of Marengo. • Named for Major William McHenry (?–1835), officer in the War of 1812 and the Black Hawk War, and IL legislator • 1836 from Cook • Cartoonist Chester Gould. Gunman and bank robber Baby Face Nelson died here. • Dairying, livestock, corn, hay; manufacture of typewriters, beds, metal products.

MCLEAN (one of three counties so named) *Bloomington* • 150,433 • 1,184 (the largest county in IL) • Central IL; drained by the Sangamon and Mackinaw rivers, and Kickapoo, Salt, Money and Sugar creeks. The county includes Lake Bloomington, Evergreen Lake and Moraine View State Park. Funks Grove Nature Preserve is in the southwest. • Named for John McLean (1791–1830), first U.S. representative from IL and U.S. senator • 1830 from Tazewell • At Old Majors Hall in Bloomington, on May 29, 1856, Lincoln delivered his "lost speech," an anti-slavery oration so passionate that reporters reputedly were unable to take notes. The Pullman, the first successful railroad sleeping car, was built by George M. Pullman in Bloomington in 1858. • Playwright Rachel Crothers; physicist Clinton J. Davisson; printer and typographer Frederic W. Goudy; publisher and author Elbert Hubbard; army officer and businessman James G. Harbord; poet Richard Hovey; politician James R. Mann; historian and educator James H. Robinson; cartoonist Sidney Smith; journalist Melville E. Stone; U.S. vice president Adlai E. Stevenson and his grandson, statesman Adlai E. Stevenson. Supreme Court justice David Davis died here • Corn, wheat, soybeans, livestock, dairying; canning; gravel and sand pits; manufacture of builders' supplies, electronic tubes, heating and ventilating equipment, cotton pulp for paper, agricultural equipment,

vacuum cleaners; insurance; education (IL State U.; IL Wesleyan U.) • The baseball used in the first World Series game is on display at the Old Courthouse Museum in Bloomington. Normal was one of four IL towns chartered with a special legislative prohibition against the sale of alcohol. An annual spring event in Bloomington is the production of the American Passion Play.

MENARD (one of two counties so named, the other in TX) *Petersburg* • 12,486 • 314 • Central IL; drained by the Sangamon River and Salt Creek (both forming the northern boundary of the county). The county includes Lincoln's New Salem State Historic Site, a reconstruction of the town in which Lincoln worked as grocery clerk, surveyor and postmaster from 1831 to 1837. • Named for Lt. Col. Pierre Menard (1766–1844), jurist, first presiding officer of IL territorial legislature, and the state's first lieutenant governor • 1839 from Sangamon • Poet Edgar Lee Masters; Lincoln's beloved Ann Rutledge • Corn, wheat, soybeans; manufacture of electrical components, concrete products.

MERCER (one of eight counties so named) *Aledo* • 16,957 • 561 • Northwestern IL, bounded on the west by the Mississippi River (forming the IA state line); drained by the Edwards River and Pope Creek. Two portions of Mark Twain National Wildlife Refuge are in the west. • One of six counties definitively named for Gen. Hugh Mercer (?–1777), Revolutionary War officer and physician • 1825 from Pike • Cattle, hogs, corn, soybeans, hay, dairy products; some manufacturing.

MONROE *Waterloo* • 27,619 • 388 • Southwestern IL, bounded on the west by the Mississippi River (forming the MO state line) and on the east by the Kaskaskia River. The northern part of the county is urbanized as part of the St. Louis metropolitan area. Also here are Fults Hill Prairie Nature Preserve and Illinois Caverns State Nature Area. • One of seventeen counties named for President James Monroe • 1816 • A large portion of the western part of the county was damaged by floods in 1993; Valmeyer relocated to a bluff 400 feet above its original site as a result of this. • Wheat, hay, barley, sorghum, poultry, dairy products; limestone quarries; spelunking.

MONTGOMERY (one of eighteen counties so named) *Hillsboro* • 30,652 • 704 • South-central IL; drained by Shoal and Macoupin creeks. The county has several recreational reservoirs, including Lake Lou Yeager, Lake Glenn Shoals, and Coffeen Lake. Coffeen Lake State Fish and Wildlife Area is located on the southern border. • One of sixteen counties named directly or indirectly for Gen. Richard Montgomery (1738–75), American Revolutionary War officer who captured Montreal, Canada • 1821 from Bond and Madison • Physicist Samuel W. Stratton • Corn, wheat, sorghum, soybeans, cattle, dairy products; manufacture of food products, paper boxes, glass jars, metal products, industrial machinery, transportation equipment.

MORGAN (one of eleven counties so named) *Jacksonville* • 36,616 • 569 • West-central IL, bounded on the west by the Illinois River; drained by Apple, Sandy, Mauvaise Terre, and Indian creeks. The county includes part of Lake Meredosia, attached on the west to Meredosia National Wildlife Refuge. Meredosia Hill Prairie Nature Preserve is also here. • One of nine counties named for Gen. Daniel Morgan (1736–1802), an officer in the Revolutionary War and U.S. representative from VA • 1823 from Sangamon • Political leaders Stephen A. Douglas and William Jennings Bryan; dentist Greene V. Black; classicist Edward Capps; geneticist Alfred H. Sturtevant • Corn, wheat, sorghum, soybeans, cattle, hogs, dairying; food processing; manufacture of paper products, chemicals, ferris wheels, polyethylene film; bookbinding; coal; education (MacMurray College; Illinois College — the first in the state to graduate a college class) • Jackson is home to several state institutions that care for the blind, deaf and mentally disabled.

MOULTRIE *Sullivan* • 14,287 • 336 • Central IL; drained by the Kaskaskia River. Two units of Shelbyville State Fish and Wildlife Area border the northeast shore of Lake Shelbyville reservoir in the south. • Named for General William Moultrie (1730–1805), an officer in the Revolutionary War and governor of SC • 1843 from Macon and Shelby • Corn, wheat, soybeans, livestock; manufacture of candy, wood products, farm machinery.

OGLE *Oregon* • 51,032 • 759 • Northern IL; drained by the Rock, Leaf, and Kyte rivers. The county includes White Pines Forest, Lowden and Castle Rock state parks, and Lowden-Miller State Forest. • Named for Lieutenant Joseph Ogle (1741–1821), first Methodist layman in IL and captain of the territorial militia.• 1836 from Jo Daviess • Sportsman and businessman Albert G. Spalding; writer Harry L. Wilson; industrialist John Deere • Cattle, hogs, dairy products, corn, soybeans, hay; food processing plants, manufacture of pianos, printing plates, road-building equipment, paper products; textile finishing, die-casting • Eagle's Nest Camp was a retreat used by Lorado Taft and other artists from 1898 to 1942; Taft's "Soldiers Monument" is in Oregon's courthouse square.

PEORIA *Peoria* • 183,433 • 620 • Central IL, bounded on the east and south by the Illinois River, Lake Peoria, and Upper Lake Peoria; drained by Spoon River and Kickapoo Creek. • Named for the Peoria tribe of the Illinois Nation • 1825 from Fulton • Peoria is one of IL's oldest settled locations. The area was occupied by the French under La Salle as early as 1680. Between 1825 and 1831, Chicago was attached to Peoria County and its county affairs administered in Peoria. Jubilee College State Historic Site marks the location of one of the first colleges in the state, established around 1840. Here, on October 16, 1854, Abraham Lincoln denounced slavery in a rebuttal to a speech by Stephen A. Douglas. • Feminist Betty Friedan; sculptor Lorado Taft. Clergyman and bishop Philander Chase died here. • Corn, soybeans, cattle, vegetables, dairy products; bituminous-coal mines, sand and gravel deposits; manufacture of tractors, earth-moving equipment,

trailers, steel, wire, paper products, chemicals; food processing and packing, distilling, brewing; education (Bradley U.) The U.S. Department of Agriculture's Northern Region Research Laboratory is here.

PERRY *Pinckneyville* • 23,094 • 441 • Southern IL, bounded on the east in part by the Little Muddy River; drained by Beaucoup and Galum creeks. The county includes Pyramid State Park and Du Quoin State Fairgrounds. • One of ten counties named for Oliver Hazard Perry (1785–1819), U.S. naval officer during the War of 1812 • 1827 from Randolph and Jackson • Plant geneticist and botanist Edward M. East • Corn, wheat, dairy products, livestock, poultry; bituminous-coal mining; manufacture of textiles, metal products, consumer goods, electronic equipment.

PIATT *Monticello* • 16,365 • 440 • Central IL; drained by the Sangamon River. Bryant Cottage State Historic Site is south of Monticello. • Possibly named for James A. Piatt, Sr. (1789–1838), an early settler • 1841 from De Witt and Macon • Corn, soybeans, livestock; some manufacturing; grain and mill products.

PIKE *Pittsfield* • 17,384 • 830 • Western IL; bounded on the west and southwest by the Mississippi River (forming the MO state line) and on the east by the Illinois River; drained by Bay and McCraney creeks. The county includes Mark Twain National Wildlife Refuge on the Mississippi River and Ray Norbut State Fish and Wildlife Area on the Illinois River. Grubb Hollow Prairie Nature Preserve is also here. • One of ten counties named for Zebulon Montgomery Pike (1779–1813), U.S. army officer and discoverer of Pikes Peak in CO. • 1821 from Madison, Bond and Clark • Novelist and radical journalist Floyd Dell • Corn, wheat, hay, sorghum, apples, cattle, hogs; dairy products, flour and cheese manufacturing.

POPE (one of three counties so named) *Golconda* • 4,413 (the least populated county in IL) • 371 • Southeastern IL, bounded on the southeast by the Ohio River (forming the KY state line); drained by Bay and Lusk creeks, small tributaries of the Ohio River. All but the southern tip and southwestern corner of the county are in Shawnee National Forest. The county also contains Dixon Springs State Park. • Named for Nathaniel Pope (1784–1850), first secretary of IL Territory and U.S. district judge for IL • 1816 (prior to statehood) from Johnson and Gallatin • During the years 1838 and 1839, close to 13,000 Cherokee crossed the Ohio River at Golconda on their "Trail of Tears" to Oklahoma. • Grain, cattle; timber; wood products; fluorspar mining • The Smithland Lock, the world's largest twin navigational locks system, is located on the Ohio River. The *Herald-Enterprise*, established in Golconda in 1858, is one of the oldest newspapers in the state. Petroglyphs and evidence of a Late Woodland Indian Village site is located at Millstone Bluff. Lusk Creek Canyon contains many plants found only in this area, left behind during the retreat of the last ice age.

PULASKI *Mound City* • 7,348 • 201 • Extreme southern IL, bounded on the southeast by the Ohio River; Cypress Creek National Wildlife Refuge is located along the Cache River, which forms part of the county's western boundary. Mound City National Cemetery is north of Mound City. • One of seven counties named for Count Casimir Pulaski (1748–79), Polish soldier who fought for America during the Revolutionary War • 1843 from Johnston • Grain, fruit, dairy products.

PUTNAM (one of nine counties so named) *Hennepin* • 6,086 • 160 (the smallest county in IL) • North-central IL, bounded on the north and west by the bend of the Illinois River. The county includes Senachwine and Sawmill lakes (bayous of the Illinois River), Donnelley State Wildlife Area, and George S. Park Memorial Woods Nature Preserve. • One of eight counties definitively named for General Israel Putnam (1718–90), Revolutionary War officer and American commander at Battle of Bunker Hill • 1825 from Fulton • Zoologist Charles A. Kofoid • Corn, soybeans, wheat, livestock, poultry, dairy products; manufacture of chemicals, steel products.

RANDOLPH (one of eight counties so named) *Chester* • 33,893 • 578 • Southwestern IL, bounded on the southwest by the Mississippi River (forming the MO state line); drained by the Kaskaskia River. Several state fish and wildlife areas are located here. The county also includes Fort Kaskaskia and Fort de Chartres state historic sites. Kaskaskia Island and village, the first state capital of IL, is located on the MO side of the Mississippi River, separated from the IL mainland by a flood. • One of two counties (the other in WV), named for Edmund Jennings Randolph (1753–1813), governor of VA, first U.S. attorney general and U.S. secretary of state • 1795 (prior to statehood) from Saint Clair • The French Jesuit mission, founded in 1703 at "Old" Kaskaskia, was a center for French colonization of IL Territory. In 1733, Fort Kaskaskia was built as an outpost against English penetration of the region. When turnover to the British seemed imminent in 1763, the villagers destroyed the fort. The region was captured by George Rogers Clark for the U.S. in 1778. Kaskaskia was the capital of IL Territory from 1809 to 1818, and IL's state capital from 1818 to 1820. The village was gradually inundated when the Mississippi changed its course, and had disappeared altogether by the 1890s. • Cartoonist Elzie Segar; fur trader and pioneer Pierre Menard (state historic site) • Wheat, corn, soybeans, sorghum, cattle, poultry, dairy products; manufacture of textiles, hosiery, leather goods, aluminum products, flour mills, grain elevators, industrial machinery; bituminous-coal mining, stone quarries; state institutions; tourism • On Kaskaskia Island visitors can view the Liberty Bell of the West which predates the Philadelphia Liberty Bell by seven years (state memorial). The Popeye (the Sailor) Museum in Chester is a popular tourist attraction. The village of Ruma is the home of the Convent of the Adorers of the Blood of Christ; buried in its cemetery are five nuns martyred in Liberia in 1992. Prairie du Rocher was founded in 1722, making it the oldest town in IL.

RICHLAND (one of seven counties so named) *Olney* • 16,149 • 360 • Southeastern IL, bounded partly on the southwest by the Little Wabash River; drained by the Fox River and by Bonpas Creek. East Fork Lake is north of Olney. • Named for the county in OH • 1841 from Clay and Lawrence • Corn, soybeans, wheat, apples, cattle, poultry, dairying; oil and natural gas deposits; food processing, manufacture of toys, transportation equipment • The town of Olney is home to the protected, rare white squirrel.

ROCK ISLAND *Rock Island* • 149,374 • 427 • Northwestern IL, bounded on the north and west by the Mississippi River (forming the IA state line) and on the east in part by the Rock River; drained by the Rock River. Part of the Upper Mississippi River Wildlife and Fish Refuge is here. Three of the Quad cities are in the county: Moline, East Moline and Rock Island (Davenport is in IA). • Named for an island in the Mississippi River • 1831 from Jo Daviess • Campbell's Island State Memorial marks the site of an 1814 battle during the War of 1812 between troops led by Lieutenant John Campbell and Indians under Chief Black Hawk. John Deere invented an improved steel plow in his workshop in Moline in 1847; by 1890, "Plow City" had become a center of plow production. • Political scientist Gabriel A. Almond; inventor and industrialist Vincent Bendix; Indian Chief Keokuk; editor Henry Cantwell Wallace • Cattle, hogs, poultry, corn, soybeans, dairy products; manufacture of farm implements, aluminum products, machinery, wood products, clothing, elevators, escalators, foundry equipment; education (Augustina College). • Rock Island, a 1,000-acre limestone formation in the Mississippi River, has been the site of one of the largest manufacturing arsenals in the world since the Civil War. It also served as a prisoner-of-war camp, where many Confederates died and were buried in its Confederate cemetery. A national cemetery is also on the island. Black Hawk State Park, at Rock Island City's southern edge, was once the site of the Sauk and Fox Indian capitals.

SAINT CLAIR (one of four counties so named) *Belleville* • 256,082 • 664 • Southwestern IL, bounded on the northwest by the Mississippi River (forming the MO state line) and on the southwest in part by the Kaskaskia River; drained by Silver Creek. The county is highly industrialized around East St. Louis. • One of three counties named for General Arthur St. Clair (1736–1818), an officer in the Revolutionary War, and governor of the Northwest Territory • 1790 (prior to statehood) from the Northwest Territory; it was the first county in IL • Cahokia, originating as a French mission in 1699, was the first permanent white settlement in IL. It passed to the British in 1765 and to the U.S. in 1778. East St. Louis was the scene of a race riot in July, 1917 that left forty blacks and eight whites dead, and 6,000 homeless. The violence was touched off by the employment of black workers in a factory holding government contracts. • Social worker Mary Ellen Richmond; tennis player Jimmy Connors. Ottawa Indian Chief Pontiac died here. • River shipping; bituminous coal, clay, limestone;

timber; wheat, barley, soybeans, sorghum, apples, dairy products, hogs, poultry; oil refining; diversified manufacturing, including chemicals, steel products, glass, building materials; Scott Air Force Base • Cahokia Mounds World Heritage Site (a large part located in the county) commemorates a vast native American Indian city, believed to have been the largest prehistoric settlement in what is now the U.S. It contains a large circular calendar similar to Stonehenge. The National Shrine of Our Lady of the Snows is the largest outdoor shrine in the U.S. and draws more than one million pilgrims a year. The Gateway Geyser in East Saint Louis is the world's tallest fountain. The Cahokia Courthouse on the outskirts of East St. Louis is believed to be the oldest courthouse west of the Allegheny Mountains (state historic site).

SALINE (one of five counties so named) *Harrisburg* • 26,733 • 383 • Southeastern IL; drained by the North and South forks of the Saline River. The county contains part of Shawnee National Forest in the south and Saline County Conservation Area in the southeast. • Possibly named for the Saline River • 1847 from Gallatin • Grain, fruit, cattle; bituminous coal fields, oil; manufacture of textiles and hats.

SANGAMON *Springfield* • 188,951 • 868 • Central IL; drained by the Sangamon River (forming the southeastern boundary) and its South Fork, and by Spring, Bush, and Sugar creeks. The county includes artificial Lake Springfield. • Named for the Sangamon River • 1821 from Bond and Madison • In 1837, the capital of IL was transferred to Springfield from Vandalia, largely due to the efforts of Abraham Lincoln and eight other members of the IL legislature (known as the "Long Nine" because they were all over six feet tall). It was here in the Old State Capitol that Lincoln practiced before the state Supreme Court, delivered his "House Divided" address, and maintained an office as president-elect. • Astronomer Seth B. Nicholson; manufacturer C.W. Post; merchant and philanthropist Julius Rosenwald; cattleman Joseph G. McCoy; poet Vachel Lindsay; lawyer Robert Todd Lincoln; The house where Abraham and Mary Todd Lincoln lived for seventeen years before moving to the White House is now the Lincoln Home National Historic Site; Lincoln's Tomb and Monument is located in Springfield's Oak Ridge Cemetery. • Corn, sorghum, wheat, soybeans, cattle, hogs, poultry, dairying; bituminous-coal mining, oil, sand and gravel deposits; diversified manufacturing, including industrial tractors, garage equipment, brick and concrete products, paints; also insurance; government operations; tourism; education (U. of IL at Springfield) • Thomas Rees Memorial Carillon in Springfield, is the fourth largest in the world. Springfield is the site of the annual IL State Fair. Camp Butler National Cemetery was established on the site of a Civil War prison camp.

SCHUYLER *Rushville* • 7,189 • 437 • Western IL, bounded on the southeast by the Illinois River; drained by La Moine River (forming the southwestern boundary). Weinberg-King State Park is in the northwest. • One of three counties named for General Philip John Schuyler (1733–1804), an officer in the

Revolutionary War, member of the Continental Congress, and one of NY's first two U.S. senators • 1825 from Pike and Fulton • Economist Wesley C. Mitchell; newspaper publisher Edward W. Scripps • Livestock, dairy, meat products, corn, soybeans, wheat, fruit.

SCOTT (One of eleven counties so named) *Winchester* • 5,537 • 251 • West-central IL, bounded on the west by the Illinois River; drained by Sandy and Mauvaise Terre creeks. • Named for the county in KY • 1839 from Morgan • Dentist Greene Vardiman Black • Corn, wheat, soybeans, livestock.

SHELBY *Shelbyville* • 22,893 • 759 • Central IL; drained by the Kaskaskia and Little Wabash rivers. The county includes Lake Shelbyville reservoir, with Eagle Creek and Wolf Creek state parks on opposite sides of the lake. Hidden Springs State Forest is also here. • One of nine counties named directly or indirectly for General Isaac Shelby (1750–1826), officer in the Revolutionary War and KY's first governor • 1827 from Fayette • Wheat, corn, hay, soybeans sorghum, dairy products, hogs, cattle; manufacture of construction machinery, paper products.

STARK (one of three counties so named) *Toulon* • 6,332 • 288 • North-central IL; drained by Spoon River and Indian Creek. The county includes Rock Island Trail State Park and part of Rock Island Trail Prairie Nature Preserve along the south-central boundary. • One of two counties (the other in OH) named for General John Stark (1728–1822), officer in the French and Indian War and the Revolutionary War • 1839 from Knox and Putnam • Corn; bituminous coal; manufacturing.

STEPHENSON *Freeport* • 48,979 • 564 • Northern IL, bounded on the north by the WI state line; drained by the Pecatonica River, and Yellow and Richland creeks. Lake Le-Aqua-Na State Park is in the northwest. • Named for Benjamin Stephenson (?–1822), adjutant general of IL Territory • 1837 from Winnebago and Jo Daviess • Lincoln and Douglas met in Freeport on August 27, 1858 for the second of their debates, in which Douglas stated in his "Freeport Doctrine" that a territory had the right to exclude slavery in spite of contrary Supreme Court decisions. "Lincoln, the Debater," a statue by Leonard Crunelle in Taylor Park, commemorates the event. • Political scientist and philosopher Arthur F. Bentley; newspaper columnist Louella Parsons • Livestock, corn, wheat, oats, nursery products; manufacture of textiles, hardware, medicines, batteries, precision switches, paper matrices, paper box cartons and bags, steel tanks, shop machinery, tires, toys, plastic products, stock feeds, fertilizers; metal plating; insurance.

TAZEWELL (one of two counties so named, the other in VA) *Pekin* • 128,485 • 649 • Central IL, bounded on the northwest by the Illinois River; drained by the Mackinaw River. The county is part of the Peoria metropolitan area. It includes Banner Marsh and Mackinaw River state fish and wildlife areas. • Named for Littleton Waller Tazewell (1774–1860), VA legislator, U.S. senator and governor of VA • 1827 from Fayette • Fort Creve Coeur was the first French fort in IL. • Political leader Everett Dirksen; businessman and government official David E. Lilienthal • Corn, hay, soybeans, barley, cattle, hogs, poultry, dairying; sand and gravel deposits, coal; manufacture of tractors, machinery, food products, alcohol, liquor, steel tanks, barrels, burial vaults, copper, brass, iron and aluminum castings; education (IL Central College).

UNION (one of eighteen counties so named) *Jonesboro* • 18,293 • 416 • Southern IL, bounded on the west by the Mississippi River (forming the MO state line) and on the extreme northwest corner by the Big Muddy River; drained by the Cache River. The county includes part of Shawnee National Forest. Trail of Tears State Forest, part of Giant City State Park, Union County Conservation Area, and Berryville Shale Glade Nature Preserve are in the county. • Named for the temporary union of the Baptists and Dunkards in 1816 or 1817. (In 1850, County Commissioners adopted a seal that depicted two preachers standing and shaking hands.) • 1818 (prior to statehood) from Johnson • Grain, fruit, vegetables, sorghum, cattle, dairy products; manufacturing; limestone, granite, marble quarries.

VERMILION (one of three counties named either Vermilion or Vermillion) *Danville* • 83,919 • 899 • Eastern IL, bounded on the east by the IN state line; drained by the Vermilion River and its Middle Fork, and the Little Vermilion River. Kickapoo State Park is here. • Named for the Vermilion River • 1826 from Edgar • Danville, founded in 1827, had a profitable salt works before turning to coal and brick production. • Editor and scholar Samuel Putnam; chemist Charles S. Palmer. Political leader Joe Cannon died here. • Corn, soybeans, dairy products, cattle, poultry; bituminous-coal mining; manufacture of automotive parts, food products, lift trucks, ballasts, hair accessories.

WABASH *Mount Carmel* • 12,937 • 223 • Southeastern IL, bounded on the southeast by the Wabash River (forming the IN state line) and on the west by Bonpas Creek; Beall Woods State Park is in the southeast. • One of two counties (the other in IN) named for the Wabash River • 1824 from Edwards • Ornithologist Robert Ridgway • Corn, soybeans; some manufacturing; petroleum, natural gas, coal.

WARREN *Monmouth* • 18,735 • 543 • Western IL; drained by Henderson and Swan creeks. Massagauga Prairie Nature Preserve is here. • One of fourteen counties named for General Joseph Warren (1741–75), Revolutionary War patriot and member of the Committee of Safety who dispatched Paul Revere on his famous ride • 1825 from Pike • Billiards player Ralph Greenleaf; lawman Wyatt Earp • Corn, soybeans, poultry, cattle, hogs; manufacture of machinery, pottery, sheet metal products, furnaces, processed meats and pet foods, other light manufacturing; education (Monmouth College).

WASHINGTON *Nashville* • 15,148 • 563 • Southern IL, bounded on the north by the Kaskaskia River; drained by the Little Muddy River and Beaucoup Creek. Washington County Conservation Area is in the south. • One of thirty-one counties named for President George Washington • 1818 (prior to statehood) from Saint Clair • U.S. Supreme Court justice Harry Blackmun • Wheat, soybeans, corn, sorghum, hogs, poultry, dairy products; processing of flour; manufacture of machinery, bituminous-coal mining, oil • Nashville lays claim to one of the smallest country chapels in the world.

WAYNE (one of sixteen counties so named) *Fairfield* • 17,151 • 714 • Southeastern IL; drained by the Little Wabash River and Skillet Fork. Sam Dale Lake Conservation Area is here. • One of fifteen counties named for General Anthony Wayne (1745–96), PA soldier and statesman, nicknamed "Mad Anthony" for his daring during the Revolutionary War • 1819 from Edwards • Senator William E. Borah; physician Benjamin F. Stephenson • Livestock, cattle, sorghum, wheat, hay, soybeans, corn, dairying; oil wells; manufacture of auto parts.

WHITE (one of five counties so named) *Carmi* • 15,371 • 495 • Southeastern IL, bounded on the east by the Wabash River (forming the IN state line); drained by the Little Wabash River. • Possibly named for Leonard White, a delegate to the IL Constitutional Convention and state legislator • 1815 (prior to statehood) from Gallatin • Wheat, corn, soybeans, sorghum, cattle, poultry; manufacture of clothing, wood products, dairy products, soft drinks; food processing; coal, oil, and natural-gas wells.

WHITESIDE *Morrison* • 60,653 • 685 • Northwestern IL, bounded on the northwest by the Mississippi River (forming the MO state line); drained by the Rock River, and Rock and Elkhorn creeks. The Upper Mississippi River National Wildlife and Fish Refuge extends along the river. Prophetstown and Morrison-Rockwood state parks are here, as are Big Bend State Fish and Wildlife Area and Thomson-Fulton Sand Prairie Nature Preserve. • Named for General Samuel Whiteside, officer in the War of 1812 and the Black Hawk War, and IL legislator • 1836 from Jo Daviess and Henry • President Ronald W. Reagan • Cattle, hogs, poultry, corn, soybeans, hay; limestone quarries; processing of farm and dairy products, manufacture of steel and steel products, builders' hardware, nuts and bolts, mobile homes, barber supplies.

WILL *Joliet* • 502,266 (41% increase since 1990; the second fastest growing county and fourth most populated county in IL) • 837 • Northeastern IL, bounded on the east by the IN state line; drained by Des Plaines, Du Page, and Kankakee rivers. The Chicago metropolitan area extends into the county in the northeast. Midewin National Tallgrass Prairie is in the Southwest. • Named for Dr. Conrad Will (?–1835), physician and IL legislator • 1836 from Cook and Iroquois • The site that would become Joliet was visited by missionary Jacques Marquette and French explorer Louis Jolliet in 1673. • Singer Nora Bayes; dancer and choreographer Katherine Dunham; journalist Robert Novak; naturalist and photographer Edwin W. Teale; labor leader John Mitchell; Canadian railroad executive Sir William Cornelius Van Horne; sociologist Lester Frank

Ward. Reformer John Peter Altgeld died here. • Corn, soybeans, poultry, dairy products; coal, limestone (Joliet was once called "stone city," its limestone used in public projects throughout the Midwest.); manufacture of construction materials and equipment, machinery, earth-moving and road equipment, wire, chemicals, paper, oil refinery projects, meat processing; printing and publishing; penal and criminal justice offices and institutions; education (Governors State U.; Lewis U.).

WILLIAMSON (one of three counties so named) *Marion* • 61,296 • 423 • Southern IL; drained by the Big Muddy River, the South Fork of the Saline River and Crab Orchard Creek dammed to form Crab Orchard Lake. The reservoir is surrounded by Crab Orchard National Wildlife Refuge. Shawnee National Forest is in the southeast and includes Lake Egypt reservoir. • Named for Williamson County, TN, former home of many early settlers • 1839 from Franklin • Settled in 1818, Herrin was a coal-mining center until after World War II. It was the scene of the 1922 Herrin Massacre, a tragedy arising from a labor dispute in which nonunion laborers were fired upon by striking coal miners, leaving twenty dead and many wounded. A grand jury returned 214 indictments for murder and other offenses; there were no convictions. • Bituminous-coal mining; corn, wheat, fruit, livestock, dairy products; manufacture of textiles, household appliances, neon signs, staple machines, upholstery, dresses • One of the few remaining outdoor drive-in theatres, the Egyptian, is reputed to have the world's largest outdoor movie screen (twelve stories high by ninety-five feet wide).

WINNEBAGO (one of three counties so named) *Rockford* • 278,418 • 514 • Northern IL, bounded on north by the WI state line; drained by the Rock, Pecatonica, and Kishwaukee rivers. Rock Cut State Park and Rockton Bog Nature Preserve are here. Several forest preserves are located around Rockford. • Named for the Winnebago Indian tribe • 1836 from Jo Daviess • Camp Grant served as a reception and medical center during both world wars. • Balloonist Ben Abruzzo; Egyptologist James H. Breasted; entomologist Leland O. Howard; social welfare worker Julia Clifford Lathrop; explorer and naturalist Martin E. Johnson • Dairying, corn, oats, soybeans, cattle, hogs, sheep; manufacture of machine tools, fasteners, hardware, furniture, seeds, farm implements. (Rockford's farm-machinery industry began in the early 1850s with the development by local inventor John Manny of the reaper and mower combination.) Also, education (Rockford College). • The Time Museum in Rockford's Clock Tower Inn houses a noted collection of antique timepieces.

WOODFORD (one of two counties so named, the other in KY) *Eureka* • 35,469 • 528 • Central IL, bounded on the west by Lake Peoria, a widening of the Illinois River; drained by the Mackinaw River and Panther Creek. Woodford State Fish and Wildlife Area is located on Lake Peoria. The county includes a slice of the Peoria metropolitan area. Metamora Courthouse State Historic Site is also here. • Named for Woodford County, KY, former home of many settlers • 1841 from Tazewell and McLean • Bishop Fulton John Sheen • Corn, oats, soybeans, cattle, hogs, poultry, dairying; manufacture of tile, concrete blocks, dairy and food products, feed.

INDIANA

The Crossroads of America

All of Indiana's ninety-two counties except one are governed by boards of county commissioners. Each is composed of three members, elected to four-year terms. Marion County and Indianapolis, employing a metropolitan government plan, are together governed by a mayor and twenty-nine member council, all elected to four year terms.

ADAMS (one of twelve counties so named) *Decatur* • 33,625 • 339 • Eastern IN, bounded on the east by the OH state line; drained by the Wabash and St. Mary's rivers. Limberlost State Historic Site is on the southern boundary. • One of two counties (the other in IL) named for President John Quincy Adams • Organized 1836 from Warren • Industrial designer Walter D. Teague; sculptor David Smith; scholar John Livingston Lowes • Cattle, hogs, poultry, soybeans, oats, wheat, dairying; timber; diversified manufacturing, including the processing of dairy products and other foods.

ALLEN (one of five counties so named) *Fort Wayne* • 331,849 (the third most populated county in IN) • 657 (the largest county in IN) • Northeastern IN, bounded on the east by the OH state line; drained by the Maumee, St. Joseph, and St. Mary's rivers • One of two counties (the other in KY) named for Col. John Allen (?–1813), KY legislator and army officer • 1823 from Indian lands • The city of Fort Wayne began as a French trading post (and later fort) on the site of the Kekionga, the chief town of the Miami Indians in the late 17th century. It took its name from the log stockade constructed by General Anthony Wayne in 1794 after the Battle of Fallen Timbers in what is now Toledo, OH. • Physician and pathologist George Frederick Dick; Indian leader Little Turtle; editor and critic George Jean Nathan; journalist William R. Nelson; sculptor Frederick W. Sievers; Greek scholar Edith Hamilton; actress Carole Lombard. Johnny (Appleseed) Chapman is buried here • Wheat, oats, corn, soybeans, hogs, dairying; limestone; manufacture of machinery, automotive and electrical equipment and parts, diamond-set cutting tools; education (Concordia Theological Seminary; IN U.–Purdue U. Fort Wayne; U. of St. Francis; Taylor U.–Fort Wayne Campus) • Blanche Stuart Scott made the first professional flight by a woman on October 23, 1910 in Fort Wayne. The Allen County Public Library system has one of the largest genealogical research centers in the U.S. The Lincoln Museum and Library has the largest private collection of Lincoln memorabilia and artifacts in the world. Jenny Electric provided lighting for the world's first night baseball game, which was held in Fort Wayne in 1883. On May 4, 1871, Fort Wayne hosted the first professional league baseball game; the Fort Wayne Kekiongas defeated the Cleveland Forest Citys, 2–0. Baking powder, jukeboxes, and hand-held calculators were all invented in Fort Wayne.

BARTHOLOMEW *Columbus* • 71,435 • 407 • South-central IN; drained by the East Fork of the White River and its tributaries. Grouse Ridge State Fishing Area is in the southwest. • Named for General Joseph Bartholomew (1766–1840), officer wounded at the Battle of Tippecanoe and IN legislator • 1821 from Indian lands • Journalist Kent Cooper • Wheat, vegetables, soybeans, corn, tomatoes, hogs, cattle; timber; manufacture of automobile parts, diesel engines, appliances, cement products, furniture, textiles • Partly as a result of the philanthropy of the Cummins Engine Foundation, which pays the fees of architects who design public buildings, Columbus has more buildings by distinguished architects than any other U.S. city of its size. Among the architects whose work is represented here are Cesar Pelli, Robert Venturi and John Rausch, Harry Weese, Eliel and Eero Saarinen, Robert Trent Jones, I.M. Pei, James Stewart Polshek, and Eliot Noyes.

BENTON (one of nine counties so named) *Fowler* • 9,421 • 406 • Western IN, bounded on the west by the IL state line; drained by Sugar and Big Pine creeks • One of seven counties named for Thomas Hart Benton (1782–1858), U.S. journalist and statesman • 1840 from Indian lands • Corn, wheat, oats, rye, hay, soybeans, hogs, poultry; limestone.

BLACKFORD *Hartford City* • 14,048 • 165 • Eastern IN; drained by the Salamonie River and Lick Creek • Named for Isaac N. Blackford (1786–1859), IN legislator, justice of the IN Supreme Court, and legal writer • 1838 from Jay • Livestock, corn, soybeans, oats; gas and oil wells, stone quarries; some manufacturing.

BOONE (one of eight counties so named) *Lebanon* • 46,107 • 423 • Central IN; drained by Sugar, Big Raccoon, and Big Walnut creeks, and the Eel River. Boone's Pond State Fishing Area is in the southeast. The county is part of the Indianapolis metropolitan area. • One of seven counties named for

Daniel Boone • 1830 from Indian lands • Diversified manufacturing; corn, soybeans, vegetables, hogs, cattle, dairying • The county courthouse features what may be the largest solid limestone pillars in the world.

BROWN (one of nine counties so named) *Nashville* • 14,957 • 312 • South-central IN; drained by Beanblossom Creek and by Salt Creek and its north fork. The county lies in a heavily forested area with Hoosier National Forest in the extreme south and Yellowwood State Forest in the west. Part of Morgan-Monroe State Forest is in the northwest corner. Brown County State Park is in the southwest. • One of four counties named for General Jacob J. Brown (1775–1828), an officer in the War of 1812 and commander of the U.S. Army • 1836 from Monroe, Jackson, and Bartholomew • Fruit, vegetables, hogs, livestock; timber.

CARROLL (one of thirteen counties so named) *Delphi* • 20,165 • 372 • Central IN, bounded on the northwest by the Tippecanoe River (here forming Lake Freeman reservoir); drained by Wildcat and Deer Creeks, and intersected by the Wabash River. • One of twelve counties named for Charles Carroll (1737–1832), a signer of the Declaration of Independence, U.S. senator from MD (1789–92), and founder of the Baltimore and Ohio Railroad • 1828 from Indian lands • Delphi was an important port of call on the Wabash and Erie Canal in the early 19th century. • Dairying, rye, oats, corn, soybeans, hogs; furniture manufacture; crushed limestone; meat and poultry packing; timber, lumber milling and other manufacturing.

CASS (one of nine counties so named) *Logansport* • 40,930 • 413 • North-central IN; drained by the Eel River and Deer Creek; intersected by the Wabash River. • One of eight counties named for General Lewis Cass (1782–1866), governor of MI Territory, U.S. secretary of war, and U.S. secretary of state • 1828 from Indian lands • Logansport was founded in 1828; for many years it was the seat of the U.S. agency for the Potawatomi and Miami Indians. • Naval officer Charles V. Gridley • Hogs, poultry, corn, fruit, produce, nurseries, shipping of farm products; timber; manufacture of storage batteries, thermal and electromagnetic control devices, precision mechanical springs, automotive and industrial suspension blocks, foundation garments, meat processing.

CLARK (one of twelve counties so named) *Jeffersonville* • 96,472 • 375 • Southeastern IN, bounded on the southeast by the Ohio River (here forming the KY state line); drained by Silver Creek and other small tributaries of the Ohio River. The county is part of the Louisville, KY metropolitan area. Part of Clark State Forest is in the northwest, and includes Deam Lake State Recreation Area. Charlestown State Park is located in the east. • One of six counties named for General George Rogers Clark (1752–1818), officer in the Revolutionary War and frontiersman in the Northwest Territory • 1801 (prior to statehood) from Knox • Clarksville was founded in 1784 by frontiersman George Rogers Clark. Jeffersonville was laid out in 1802 on a plan suggested by Thomas Jefferson for whom it was named. The city was a successful steamboat construction center in the 19th century; among the many paddlewheelers it turned out were the *Natchez* and the *J.M. White*. The largest steamboat ever made, the 382-foot *Mississippi Queen* was built here, and commissioned in 1976 for luxury cruises. In 1937, Jeffersonville was inundated by flood. • Soybeans, corn, tobacco, grains, strawberries, hogs, cattle, dairying; manufacture of ordnance, sporting goods (including Louisville Slugger baseball bats), chemicals, soaps, aluminum products, foundries; limestone quarries • The Howard National Steamboat Museum in Jeffersonville houses a rich collection of steamboat memorabilia. The forty-foot diameter of the Colgate clock in Jeffersonville makes it one of the largest in the world.

CLAY (one of eighteen counties so named) *Brazil* • 26,556 • 358 • Western IN; drained by the Eel River and Birch Creek. • One of fifteen counties named for Henry Clay (1777–1852), U.S. senator from KY, named the "Great Pacificator" for his advocacy of compromise to avert national crises • 1825 from Indian lands • Labor leader James Hoffa • Livestock, grain; bituminous-coal mining, clay pits, some manufacturing.

CLINTON (one of nine counties so named) *Frankfort* • 33,866 • 405 • Central IN; drained by Sugar Creek and forks of Wildcat Creek. Eunice H. Bryan Nature Preserve is in the northwest. • One of eight counties named for De Witt Clinton (1769–1828), governor of NY and supporter of the Erie Canal • 1830 from Indian lands • Seven railroad lines once converged at Frankfort's roundhouse, which still exists in its original form. • Astronomer Vesto Slipher; children's author (Dick and Jane) Zerna Sharp • Soybeans, apples, corn, wheat, oats, cattle, hogs, sheep, dairying; manufacture of plumbing fixtures, electronic equipment, porcelain products, aluminum windows, travel trailers; farm products processing; oil refining • The famous racehorse "Dan Patch" made his home in Frankfort.

CRAWFORD (one of eleven counties so named) *English* • 10,743 • 306 • Southern IN, bounded on the south by the OH River (here forming the KY state line), and on the east in part by the Blue River; drained by the Little Blue River. Hoosier National Forest occupies the western three-fourths of the county. Harrison-Crawford State Forest and Wyandotte Caves are here. The county also contains Marengo Cave, part of Newton-Stewart State Recreation Area and part of Patoka Lake reservoir (Patoka River). • Named for either William Crawford (1732–1782), colonel in the American Revolutionary War; or for William Harris Crawford (1772–1834), senator from GA, U.S. secretary of war and U.S. secretary of the treasury • 1818 from Harrison • Electrical engineer Frederick E. Terman • Dairy products, cattle, poultry, tobacco; manufacture of lime, wood products; timber; limestone quarries.

DAVIESS *Washington* • 29,820 • 431 • Southwestern IN, bounded on the south by the East Fork of the White River and

on the west by the White River. Glendale State Fish and Game Preserve (including East Fork State Fish Hatchery) is in the southeast. West Boggs Reservoir is also in the county. • One of four counties named for Col. Joseph H. Daveiss (1774–1811), VA soldier and attorney who unsuccessfully attempted to indict Aaron Burr for treason. The name was misspelled in the act creating the county and allowed to stand. • 1816 from Indian lands • Corn, soybeans, watermelon, fruit, cattle, turkeys, nurseries; bituminous-coal, gas and oil wells; manufacturing.

DEARBORN *Lawrenceburg* • 46,109 • 305 • Southeastern IN, bounded on the east by the OH state line, on the southeast by the Ohio River (forming the KY state line), and on the south by Laughery Creek; drained by the Whitewater River. The county has experienced some urban growth around Lawrenceburg due to its proximity to Cincinnati, Ohio. Perfect North Slope ski area is north of Greendale. • Named for General Henry Dearborn (1751–1829), an officer in the Revolutionary War, U.S. secretary of war and minister to Portugal • 1803 (prior to statehood) • Construction engineer and business executive Stephen D. Bechtel; engineer James B. Eads; broadcaster Elmer Davis; senator John Spooner • Cattle, tobacco; food manufacturing, wood products, liquor.

DECATUR *Greensburg* • 24,555 • 373 • Southeast-central IN; drained by the Flatrock River, and Clifty and Sand creeks. • One of five counties named for Stephen Decatur (1779–1820), U.S. naval officer during the War of 1812 and in actions against the Barbary pirates near Tripoli • 1821 from Indian lands • Corn, soybeans, hogs, cattle; limestone; manufacturing.

DE KALB *Auburn* • 40,285 • 363 • Northeastern IN, bounded on the east by the OH state line; drained by Cedar and Fish creeks, and the St. Joseph River. The county is part of northeastern IN's (glacial) Lake Region. • One of six counties named for Johann, Baron de Kalb (1721–80), German-born French soldier who fought for the Americans during the Revolutionary War • 1835 from Allen • The Auburn-Cord-Duesenberg Museum and the National Automotive and Truck Museum recall Auburn's importance as a pioneer in the early development of the automobile industry. It was the home of the Auburn Automobile Company (1902–1933). • Critic and humorist Will Cuppy • Cattle, sheep, poultry, soybeans, corn, wheat, oats, dairying; manufacture of automotive parts, rubber products, foundry and metal products, stokers, oil burners, calendars, greeting cards.

DELAWARE (One of six counties so named) *Muncie* • 118,769 • 393 • Eastern IN; drained by the Mississinewa River, the West Fork of the White River, and Muncie and Buck creeks. Prairie Creek Reservoir is here. • Named for the Delaware Indians • 1827 from Indian lands • Muncie was famously described in Robert and Helen Lynd's sociological studies *Middletown* (1929) and *Middletown in Transition* (1937) as the average American town. • About four-fifths of the county is under cultivation: corn, wheat, oats, hogs, soybeans, tomatoes; also dairying; shipping, diversified manufacturing, including automobile and marine transmissions, steel forgings, storage batteries, dies and metal stampings, wire products, power transformers; petroleum; education (Ball State U.) • Muncie remains the corporate headquarters for the Ball corporation, which produces glass jars and fittings for home canning. Members of the Ball family have been city benefactors for many years. The National Model Aviation Museum is also in Muncie.

DUBOIS *Jasper* • 39,674 • 430 • Southwestern IN, bounded on the north in part by the East Fork of the White River; drained by the Patoka River (Patoka Dam and Lake are in the northeast) and Huntley Creek. Lick Fork State Recreation Area is near Patoka Dam. Part of Hoosier National Forest and Ferdinand State Forest are in the county. • Named for Toussaint Dubois (?–1816), a French immigrant who fought with the Americans as "commandant of spies" at the Battle of Tippecanoe • 1817 from Orange and Perry • Corn, soybeans, cattle, poultry, hogs; bituminous coal, clay pits; timber; stone quarries; diversified manufacturing.

ELKHART *Goshen* • 182,791 (the fifth most populated county in IN) • 464 • Northern IN, bounded on the north by the MI state line; drained by the Elkhart and St. Joseph rivers • Possibly named for the Elkhart River • 1830 from Indian lands • Film director Howard Hawks • Dairying, hogs, cattle, poultry, soybeans, corn, wheat, oats, potatoes, hay, mint, onions, fruit. The county is one of the leading manufacturing centers in IN, producing electrical controls, electronic components, steel products, rubber products, furniture, recreational vehicles, pharmaceuticals, automotive products, plastic extrusions, fire fighting equipment, metal window casings. Also, timber; education (Goshen College). • Charles G. Conn began making brass cornets in Elkhart city in 1875; his company, now one of the world's largest manufacturers of musical instruments, and others, make Elkhart the band instrument center of the U.S. Elkhart has been a major railroad center for years; at the city's western edge is the Robert R. Young classification yard of the Penn Central System. There are large concentrations of Mennonites and Amish in the county.

FAYETTE (one of eleven counties so named) *Connersville* • 25,588 • 215 • Eastern IN; drained by the West Fork of the Whitewater River. Shrader-Weaver Nature Preserve is in the northwest. • One of seventeen counties (Lafayette and Fayette) named for the Marquis de Lafayette (1757–1834), French statesman and soldier who fought with the Americans during the Revolutionary War • 1818 from Wayne • Connersville was an early shipping point on the Whitewater Canal, and once the place of manufacture for Auburn, Cord, and Duesenberg cars. • Corn, soybeans, wheat, cattle, hogs; manufacture of automobile parts, machine tools, dies, castings, household appliances, blowers, air conditioners, caskets, building supplies • Connersville organized the first high school band in the U.S. The nation's first industrial park was constructed in the city.

The annual Armed Forces Parade in Connersville is reputed to be the largest parade honoring the military in the U.S.

FLOYD (one of six counties so named) *New Albany* • 70,823 • 148 (one of the fifty smallest counties in the U.S.) • Southern IN, bounded on the south by the Ohio River (here forming the KY state line); drained by small tributaries. This hilly county is part of the Louisville metropolitan area (also called Falls City Area). • Named for either John Floyd (?–1783), surveyor, Indian fighter, and American Revolutionary War figure; or for Davis Floyd (1772–?), auditor and treasurer of IN Territory and judge • 1819 from Harrison and Clark • New Albany was the largest city in IN during the 1840s and early 1850s and an important steamboat-building center; the riverboats *Robert E. Lee* and *Eclipse* were built here. The first public school in IN was established in New Albany in 1853. President Abraham Lincoln established a National Cemetery here in 1862. • U.S. Supreme Court justice Sherman Minton; sociologist Robert S. Lynd; educator Felix E. Schelling; poet-dramatist William Vaughn Moody • Corn, strawberries, tobacco, cattle, poultry, dairying; timber; sand and gravel; manufacture of plywood, veneer, prefabricated houses, furniture, electronic equipment, machinery, clothing; education (IN U. Southeast) • New Albany High School was the first in the U.S. to run and operate its own FM radio station. The New Albany Glass Works was the first company in the U.S. to produce plate glass windows.

FOUNTAIN *Covington* • 17,954 • 396 • Western IN, bounded on the north and west by the Wabash River; drained by Coal Creek. Portland Arch Nature Preserve is in the northwest. Part of Shades State Park is in the southeast corner. • Named for Major James Fountain (originally Fontaine) (?–1790), KY army officer killed near Fort Wayne in the Battle of Maumee • 1825 from Montgomery • Bituminous-coal mining, sand and gravel, clay pits; dairying, wheat, corn, rye, soybeans, fruit, tomatoes, cattle, hogs, sheep, poultry; manufacture of steel casings, bricks, cement, vaults, clothing, electronic equipment; canning.

FRANKLIN (one of twenty-five counties so named) *Brookville* • 22,151 • 386 • Southeastern IN, bounded on the east by the OH state line; drained by the Whitewater River and its East Fork (here forming Brookville Lake reservoir). The county includes Mounds State Recreation Area, and Whitewater Canal State Historic Site. • One of twenty-three counties named for Benjamin Franklin • 1810 (prior to statehood) from Wayne and Ripley • Soldier and writer Lew Wallace • Corn, wheat, dairying, cattle, hogs; some manufacturing.

FULTON (one of eight counties so named) *Rochester* • 20,511 • 369 • Northern IN; drained by the Tippecanoe River. The county includes Lake Manitou and Menominee State Fishing Area. • One of seven counties named for Robert Fulton (1765–1815), builder of the *Clermont*, the first commercial steamboat • 1835 from Indian lands • Sculptor John Chamberlain • Vegetables, corn, soybeans, cattle, poultry, hogs, dairy products; manufacturing; timber; resort tourism • The county is known for its unusual round barns.

GIBSON (one of two counties so named, the other in TN) *Princeton* • 32,500 • 489 • Southwestern IN, bounded on the west by the Wabash River (here forming the IL state line) and on the north by the White River; drained by the Patoka River and Pigeon Creek. Hemmer Woods Nature Preserve is in the southeast. Part of Patoka River National Wildlife Refuge is also here. • Named for General John Gibson (1740–1822), an officer in the Revolutionary War, jurist and secretary of IN Territory • 1813 (prior to statehood) from Knox • Baseball player Gil Hodges • Corn, wheat, barley, hogs, poultry, truck, melons; manufacture of concrete products, food products; natural-gas and oil wells; timber; education (Oakland City U.).

GRANT (one of fifteen counties so named) *Marion* • 73,403 • 414 • Central IN; drained by the Mississinewa River. Marion is the site of a National Cemetery. • Named for Samuel and Moses Grant, killed in 1789 in Indian battles • 1831 from Delaware County • U.S. troops fought Miami and Delaware Indians in the Battle of the Mississinewa here in 1812. Discovery of natural gas here in 1887 resulted in rapid industrialization and population growth. • Microbiologist Thomas Francis, Jr.; actor James Dean (memorial); U.S. Supreme Court justice Willis Van Devanter • Hogs, poultry, corn, vegetables, wheat, tomatoes, popcorn, soybeans, oats, fruit, dairy products; manufacture of automotive parts, radio and television parts, plastics, wire, glass, foundry products; natural-gas and oil wells; education (Taylor U.; IN Wesleyan U.).

GREENE *Bloomfield* • 33,157 • 542 (the fourth largest county in IN) • Southwestern IN; drained by the White and Eel rivers. Part of Shakamak State Park is here. Greene-Sullivan State Forest is on the western boundary. A small portion of Naval Surface Warfare Center (Crane Division) is also here. • One of sixteen counties named for General Nathanael Greene (1742–86), hero of the Revolutionary War • 1821 from Knox • Wheat, corn, soybeans, hogs, cattle; bituminous-coal mines; timber; diversified manufacturing.

HAMILTON (one of ten counties so named) *Noblesville* • 182,740 (68% increase since 1990; the fastest growing county in IN) • 398 • Central IN; drained by the West Fork of the White River, and by Cicero (forming Morse Reservoir), Prairie and Buck creeks. Part of the Indianapolis metropolitan area extends into the county from the south. Geist Reservoir is on Fall Creek in the southeast. • One of eight counties named for Alexander Hamilton (?–1804), U.S. statesman and first secretary of the treasury • 1823 from Hancock and Marion • The Quaker community of Westfield was a well-known stop on the Underground Railroad. For the first time in U.S. history, white settlers were held accountable for killing Indians in the Fall Creek Massacre of 1874. • Lawyer and peace advocate Salmon O. Levinson; writer Rex T. Stout • Soybeans, corn, wheat, dairy products, cattle, hogs; diversified manufacturing, pro-

cessing of farm products • Conner Prairie, located in Fishers, has been ranked as one of the nation's top living history museums. In 1826, thousands of squirrels inexplicably migrated from the west side of the county eastward, destroying everything in their path.

HANCOCK *Greenfield* • 55,391 •306 • Central IN; drained by Sugar and Brandywine creeks, and the Big Blue River. Part of the county lies in the Indianapolis metropolitan area. • One of ten counties named for John Hancock (1737–93), noted signer of the Declaration of Independence and governor of MA • 1827 from Madison • Poet James Whitcomb Riley (home and museum) • Vegetables, corn, wheat, hogs, cattle, dairying; manufacture of prefabricated steel buildings, screw machine products, rayon underwear, biological and pharmaceutical research.

HARRISON (one of eight counties so named) *Corydon* • 34,325 • 485 • Southern IN, bounded on the southeast, south, and southwest by the Ohio River (here forming the KY state line) and on the west by the Blue River; drained by Indian and Buck creeks. Part of Harrison Crawford State Forest is in the west, and includes Wyandotte Woods State Recreation Area. Battle of Corydon Memorial Park is also here. • One of four counties named for President William Henry Harrison • 1808 (prior to statehood) from the Northwest Territory • Corydon was settled in about 1805 on land that was originally owned by then territorial governor William Henry Harrison, who named the town for a shepherd in a popular song of the day, "Pastoral Elegy." It served as the capital of Indiana Territory from 1813 to 1816, then as state capital until 1825. (The first statehouse is preserved as the Corydon Capitol State Historic Site.) The first constitution for IN was drafted in Corydon in June, 1816. • Daniel Boone's brother Squire Boone is buried at Squire Boone Caverns, which he discovered while hiding from Indians. • Soybeans, burley tobacco, corn, wheat, beef and dairy cattle, poultry, eggs; natural gas, limestone; lumber milling, manufacture of furniture, glass, dairy products; stone quarries; timber • IN's oldest county fair is held in Corydon each summer.

HENDRICKS *Danville* • 104,093 (38% increase since 1990; the second fastest growing county in IN) • 408 • Central IN; drained by Big Walnut, Mill, and White Lick creeks. The county is part of the Indianapolis metropolitan area. • Named for William Hendricks (1782–1850), IN's first Congressman, senator from IN, and governor • 1823 from Indian lands • Zoologist William T. Hornaday • Corn, fruit, hogs, cattle, sheep; flour milling; processing of dairy products; lumber.

HENRY (one of ten counties so named) *New Castle* • 48,508 • 393 • Eastern IN; drained by the Big Blue River, Flatrock River, and Fall Creek. The county also includes Summit Lake State Park. • One of ten counties named for Patrick Henry (1736–99), patriot, governor of VA, and statesman • 1821 from Delaware County • In the early 1900s New Castle's economy was substantially enhanced by automobile and piano manufacturing, and large-scale commercial rose growing. • Historian Charles A. Beard; aviation pioneer Wilbur Wright (state memorial) • Corn, soybeans, hogs, poultry; manufacture of transportation equipment, steel products • The Indiana Basketball Hall of Fame is in New Castle.

HOWARD (one of seven counties so named) *Kokomo* • 84,964 • 293 • Central IN; drained by Wildcat Creek • One of two counties (the other in IA) named for Tilghman A. Howard (1797–1844), TN legislator and charge d'affaires to the Republic of Texas • Organized as Richardville in 1844 from Indian lands; named changed 1846 • Kokomo's industrial development began in 1886 with the discovery of natural gas nearby. In 1893 the first practical gasoline-driven American automobile was invented in Kokomo by Elwood Haynes. A monument east of the city marks the place where one of the first clutch-driven automobiles with electric ignition was successfully road-tested on July 4, 1894. Through his metallurgical experiments here Haynes also paved the way for the manufacture of stainless steel, and a durable cobalt-chromium-tungsten alloy called Stellite. Kokomo was an important manufacturing center during World War II. • Jockey Tod Sloan • Corn, soybeans, wheat, hogs, cattle, poultry; manufacture of electrical machinery, automobile parts and supplies, aluminum castings, radios, steel, wire, plumbing supplies; education (IN U. Kokomo) • The county is the home of the Elwood Haynes and Greentown Glass museums.

HUNTINGTON (one of two counties so named, the other in PA) *Huntington* • 38,075 • 383 • Northeast-central IN; drained by the Wabash, Salamonie, and Little Wabash rivers. The county includes part of Salamonie Lake reservoir and Huntington Reservoir. Kil-So-Quah, Little Turtle, and Mount Etna state recreation areas are also here. • Named for Samuel Huntington (1731–96), a signer of the Declaration of Independence; president of the Continental Congress, chief justice of the CT Superior Court, and governor of CT • 1832 from Grant • Inventor and businessman Edwin A. Link • Corn, soybeans, tomatoes, poultry, hogs, cattle, dairy products; manufacture of electronics parts, canning equipment, brake linings, rubber goods; limestone quarrying; timber; education (Huntington College).

JACKSON (one of twenty-four counties so named) *Brownstown* • 41,335 • 509 • Southern IN, bounded on the south by the Muscatatuck River and on the extreme northeast by Sand Creek; drained by the East Fork of the White River and tributaries of the Muscatatuck. The county includes Hoosier National Forest, part of Muscatatuck National Wildlife Refuge (on the eastern border), Starve Hollow State Recreational Area, Hemlock Bluff Nature Preserve, and part of Jackson-Washington State Forest. • One of twenty-two counties named directly or indirectly for President Andrew Jackson • 1815 (prior to statehood) from Washington County • Corn, wheat, vegetables, cattle, hogs, truck vegetables, poultry; timber; manufacture of wood products, heavy machinery, shoes, textiles, paper and packaging materials.

JASPER *Rensselaer* • 30,043 • 560 (the third largest county in IN) • Northwestern IN, bounded on the north by the Kankakee River; drained by the Iroquois River. Part of Jasper-Pulaski State Fish and Wildlife Area is on the northeast border. • One of eight counties named for Sgt. William Jasper (?–1779), Revolutionary War soldier. (IN is one of five states in which Jasper and Newton counties have been placed adjacent to one another to honor the allied efforts of sergeants William Jasper and John Newton to rescue captive colonial soldiers near Savannah.) • 1835 from Indian lands • Football player Tom Harmon; politician Charles A. Halleck; writer Eleanor Atkinson • Corn, soybeans, cattle, hogs, dairying; education (St. Joseph's College).

JAY *Portland* • 21,806 • 384 • Eastern IN, bounded on the east by the OH state line; drained by the Salamonie River • Named for John Jay (1745–1829), first Chief Justice of the U.S. and governor of NY • 1835 from Randolph • Inventor and automobile pioneer Elwood Haynes; dancer and choreographer Twyla Tharp • Corn, oats, vegetables, soybeans, hogs, cattle, poultry; diversified manufacturing; timber, lumber milling; natural-gas and oil wells • Dunkirk, known as the "Glass Capital of Indiana," has two glass factories and a museum dedicated to glass. Portland hosts the world's largest antique tractor and engine show every August.

JEFFERSON *Madison* • 31,705 • 361 • Southeastern IN, bounded in part on the south by the Ohio River (here forming the KY state line); drained by Big Creek, Clifty Creek, and Indian-Kentuck Creek. The county includes Clifty Falls State Park and part of Hardy Lake State Recreation Area. Lanier Mansion State Historic Site is in Madison. • One of twenty-six counties named directly or indirectly for President Thomas Jefferson • 1810 (prior to statehood) from Indian lands • Settled about 1808, Madison flourished as a river port until it was eclipsed by the development of Louisville and Cincinnati. It was briefly the largest town in the state. • Novelist David Graham Phillips • Madison's large tobacco warehouses hold auctions for buyers from all over the U.S. Crops grown in the county include corn, cattle, poultry, and hogs. It manufactures road machinery, small motors, electric organs, chemicals, shoes, clothing, furniture and boats. Also timber; education (Hanover College) • The county has a number of antebellum homes, many finely preserved. Madison holds a July regatta and Governor's Cup Race for hydroplanes.

JENNINGS *Vernon* • 27,554 • 377 • Southeastern IN; drained by the Muscatatuck River (forming part of the southern boundary) and by Vernon Fork, and Graham and Sand creeks. The county includes Brush Creek State Fish and Wildlife Area, Selmier State Forest, Crosley State Fish and Wildlife Area, and part of Muscatatuck National Wildlife Refuge. • Named for Jonathan Jennings (1787–1834), U.S. representative from IN and first IN governor • 1816 from Indian lands • Corn, wheat, tobacco, cattle, hogs; manufacturing; timber; limestone quarries • Jessamyn West, the author of *The Friendly Persuasion*, was born near North Vernon and set her novel there.

JOHNSON (one of twelve counties so named) *Franklin* • 115,209 (31% increase in 1990; the third fastest growing county in IN) • 320 • Central IN; drained by the White River and tributaries of the East Fork of the White River. The county is urbanized in the north as an extension of the Indianapolis metropolitan area. Atterbury State Fish and Wildlife Area is here. • Named for John Johnson (?–1817), a judge of the first IN Supreme Court • 1822 • On January 1, 1900, the Indianapolis-Greenwood Electric Railway Company dispatched its first interurban car, which operated until 1941. Camp Atterbury, established in 1942, served as a POW camp for German and Italian prisoners and was home to the Wakeman Army Hospital, the largest in the U.S. during World War II. Italian prisoners built the "Chapel in the Meadow" at Camp Atterbury, now restored and open to the public. • Psychologist Lewis M. Terman; painter William Merritt Chase • Wheat, corn, soybeans, tomatoes, dairying, hogs, cattle, poultry; manufacture of textiles, appliances, automobile parts, tools and dies, lumber, canned goods, flour; education (Franklin College).

KNOX *Vincennes* • 39,256 • 516 • Southwestern IN, bounded on the west by the Wabash River (here forming the IL state line) and on the east and south by the White River; drained by Maria and Pond creeks, and the Deschee River. The county contains the Indiana Territory Memorial and George Rogers Clark National Historical Park (containing one of the largest monuments outside of Washington, D.C.). It also includes Cypress Pond, an oxbow lake of the Wabash River. The pond marks the northern-most point in the U.S. in which the bald cypress grows naturally. • One of nine counties named for General Henry Knox (1750–1806), Revolutionary War officer and first U.S. secretary of war • 1790 (prior to statehood) from the Northwest Territory (IN's first county) • The state's oldest city, Vincennes, was settled in 1702 by French traders. Fort Sackville, erected here in 1732, was ceded to the British in 1763. The fort was taken by American forces under George Rogers Clark in 1779. Vincennes was the capital of IN Territory from 1800 to 1813. The territory's first newspaper, the *Indiana Gazette*, was published here by Elihu Stout in 1804. Governor (later President) William Henry Harrison negotiated several treaties with the Indians here, launching the campaign that led to the Battle of Tippecanoe in November, 1811. • Army officer and politician Henry Dodge; pantomimist and comedian Red Skelton • Fruits, including watermelons, vegetables, grain; oil, natural gas, bituminous coal, sand and gravel; manufacture of batteries, paper products, glass; auto seat assembling; fruit-packing plants, creameries; nurseries.

KOSCIUSKO *Warsaw* • 74,057 • 538 (the fifth largest county in IN) • Northern IN, in the center of the glacial lake region (including lakes Wawasee and Winona); drained by the Tippecanoe and Eel rivers, and Turkey Creek. Wawasee State Fishing Area and Tri-County State Fish and Wildlife Area are here. • Named for Thaddeus Kosciusko (1746–1817), Polish soldier who fought with the Americans during the Revolu-

tionary War • 1835 • Journalist and poet John J. Piatt • Poultry, hogs, cattle, dairy products, corn, soybeans, vegetables; timber; manufacturing; education (Grace College).

LAGRANGE *Lagrange* • 34,909 • 380 • Northeastern IN, bounded on the north by the MI state line; drained by the Pigeon and Elkhart rivers. Pigeon River State Fish and Wildlife Area is here. Olin Lake Nature Preserve is in the south. There are about twenty-seven small glacially formed lakes in the county, most concentrated in its southeastern quarter. • Named for the country home near Paris of the Marquis de Lafayette • 1832 from unorganized territory in Elkhart County • Dairying, soybeans, oats, wheat, corn, grain, cattle, sheep, hogs, poultry hatcheries; processing of dairy products.

LAKE (one of twelve counties so named) *Crown Point* • 484,564 (the second most populated county in IN) • 497 • Extreme northwestern IN, bounded on the north by Lake Michigan, on the west by the IL state line, and on the south by the Kankakee River; traversed by the Grand Calumet and Little Calumet rivers. The county lies in the heavily industrialized Calumet region, and is part of the Chicago metropolitan area. It has harbors at Gary and East Chicago (Indiana Harbor). Part of Indiana Dunes National Seashore and Calumet Prairie State Nature Preserve are also here. La Salle State Fish and Wildlife Area is in the southwestern corner. • Named for its location on the southern shore of Lake Michigan • 1836 from Porter and Newton • In 1868, George H. Hammond established a meat-packing plant in the town named for him. Here he devised a method of refrigerating and shipping dressed beef to markets in the east. The industry moved to Chicago following a disastrous fire in 1901. Established in 1887, East Chicago experienced increased industrial development with the construction of Indiana Harbor, connected to the Grand Calumet River by a thirty-mile canal. Whiting is the birthplace of the Standard Oil Company of Indiana; when constructed in 1889, it was the "world's largest complete oil refinery." Gary was laid out by the U.S. Steel Corp as an adjunct to its large manufacturing complex here. It became a leader in the progressive education movement in the early 20th century when William A. Wirt established the "platoon school," designed to attract underprivileged children. • Astronaut Frank Borman; economist Paul Samuelson; Singer Michael Jackson and family • It is one of the world's most important steel-manufacturing centers; also foundries, oil refineries, diversified manufacturing, including agricultural implements, industrial tanks and valves, chemicals, candy, books, soap, margarine, corn products, railroad equipment. The county also grows vegetables, poultry, soybeans, corn. Dairying is important. Its institutions of high learning include Purdue University Calumet and Indiana University N.W.

LA PORTE *La Porte* • 110,106 • 598 (the second largest county in IN) • Northwestern IN, bounded on the northwest by Lake Michigan, on the north by the MI state line, and on the south in part by the Kankakee River. Kingsbury State Fish and Wildlife Area is here, as is part of Kankakee State Fish and

Wildlife Area. The county contains natural, glacially formed lakes. • The name is French for "the door," referring to a natural opening through the forest that served as a gateway to the north. • 1832 from Indian lands • Michigan City was the site of a meeting in 1674 between Father Marquette and the Potawatomi Indians. The city was laid out in 1830 as the terminus of the Michigan Road from the Ohio River. It was an early producer of Pullman cars. • Resort tourism; diversified manufacturing, including steel, farm equipment, precision castings, air compressors, adhesive tapes, food products, clothing, furniture, plastic and rubber products; fruit, wine, corn, soybeans, hogs, cattle; lake shipping; fisheries; timber; education (Purdue U. North Central); tourism. The Indiana State Prison is in Michigan City. • International Friendship Gardens east of Michigan City has flowers and plants representative of a number of countries.

LAWRENCE (one of eleven counties so named) *Bedford* • 45,922 • 449 • Southern IN; drained by Salt Creek and the East Fork of the White River (forming part of the southeastern border). The county includes Williams Dam State Fishing Area, Spring Mill State Park, and two sections of Hoosier National Forest (its headquarters in Bedford). Salt Creek State Recreation Area is on the northern boundary. • One of nine counties named for Captain James Lawrence (1781–1813), U.S. naval officer in the war with Barbary pirates near Tripoli and commander of the U.S.S. Chesapeake in the War of 1812. • 1818 from Orange • Astronauts Virgil Grissom, Ken Bowersox, and Charles Walker; outlaw Sam Bass • Large limestone quarries (Bedford, the "Limestone Capital of the World," provided stone for the Empire State Building and the Pentagon); fruit, cattle, grain, corn, soybeans; manufacture of textiles, electronic and transportation equipment, aluminum, cranes, saws, refrigerators, furniture, clothing • Oolitic has, inexplicably, a limestone statue of Sunday comic strip character Joe Palooka.

MADISON *Anderson* • 133,358 • 452 • Central IN; drained by the West Fork of the White River, and by Fall and Buck creeks. The Indiana Reformatory is in the south at Pendleton. Mounds State Park, containing the largest human-made prehistoric earthwork discovered in the state, is also here. • One of twenty counties named directly or indirectly for President James Madison • 1823 from Fayette • Presidential candidate Wendell Willkie • Hogs, cattle, corn, wheat, tomatoes, soybeans, vegetables, poultry; manufacture of automotive ignition and lighting equipment, automotive regulators and pumps, fire trucks, mobile homes, furniture, glassware, recreation equipment, wall and floor tile, packaging material, corrugated paper boxes, mattresses; processing of farm and dairy products; limestone quarrying (rock wood, a limestone product and insulation material, is Alexandria's chief product); education (Anderson U.) • Anderson is the national headquarters for the Church of God.

MARION *Indianapolis* • 860,454 (the most populated county in IN) • 396 • Central IN; drained by the White River and Eagle, Fall, and Buck creeks. The county, largely urbanized, is dominated by the city of Indianapolis, a major commercial, political and manufacturing center. (In 1970, Indianapolis consolidated with the county, except for the municipalities of Lawrence, Speedway, Southport, and Beech Grove). Indianapolis International Airport is in the southwest. Fort Harrison State Park is in the northeast. Called the "Crossroads of America," Indianapolis serves as the junction of several highways and railway routes. Part of Geist Reservoir is in the northeast; Eagle Creek Reservoir is in the northwest. • One of seventeen counties named for Gen. Francis Marion (?–1795), SC soldier and legislator, known as "The Swamp Fox" for his tactics during the Revolutionary War • 1821 from Ohio County • Indianapolis has been state capital since 1825. Commissioners who chose the site in 1820 thought the nearby White River navigable. It was not, this fact making Indianapolis one of the largest U.S. cities not situated on a navigable waterway. The National Road reached the city in 1830. With the location of Western Electric Company in Indianapolis in 1950, the city earned the distinction of making more telephones than any other city in the world. • President Benjamin Harrison; poet James Whitcomb Riley; physicist Philip W. Anderson; golfer Chick Evans; bank robber John Dillinger; architect and designer Michael Graves; jazz composer and trombonist J.J. Johnson; U.S. vice president Dan Quayle; archaeologist George A. Reisner; novelist and dramatist Booth Tarkington; poet Sarah T. Bolton; editor Margaret Caroline Anderson; journalist Janet Flanner; theatre owner Sidney Grauman; novelist Kurt Vonnegut, Jr.; Sir Edwin Major; architect Nathaniel Alexander Owings; army officer Walter B. Smith; television personality David Letterman. Politician and historian Albert Beveridge, and U.S. vice presidents Charles W. Fairbanks and Thomas A. Hendricks died here. • Dairy, cattle, hogs, corn, other vegetables; food processing; manufacture of electrical equipment, electronic products, computer software, automotive transmissions, locomotive parts, aircraft engines, truck bodies, chemicals, pharmaceuticals, steel casings, machine-tool parts, clothing; railroad shops; government operations; insurance; printing and publishing; education (Marian College; Butler U.; Martin U.) • The corporate headquarters of eight Fortune 1000 companies are located in the county. Built in 1909, the Indianapolis 500 Speedway auto racetrack at Speedway is the world's oldest continually operated racetrack. 300,000 spectators show up for the famed Memorial Day weekend event. The national headquarters for the American Legion is in Indianapolis. The payroll for the entire U.S. Army is prepared at Fort Benjamin Harrison. A national center for amateur sports, Indianapolis is headquarters of several governing organizations, including the Amateur Athletic Union. The Raggedy Ann doll was created by Marcella Gruelle in Indianapolis in 1914. Indianapolis is home to the Colts (RCA Dome) and Pacers (Conseco Fieldhouse).

MARSHALL (one of twelve counties so named) *Plymouth* •

45,128 • 444 • Northern IN; drained by the Yellow and Tippecanoe rivers. The county has several glacially formed lakes in the southwest; the largest is Lake Maxinkuckee. Chief Menominee Monument is in Twin Lakes. • One of eight counties named for John Marshall (1755–1835), fourth Chief Justice of the U.S. • 1835 from Indian lands • Plymouth was founded in 1834 near the site of the area's last Potawatomi Indian village; in 1838 more than 800 members of the tribe were dispossessed and moved to a reservation in KS, many dying of malaria along the way. • The county is noted for raising mint and vegetables. Also grain, soybeans, oats, fruit, dairy products, cattle, poultry, hogs; processing of spearmint and peppermint oil; manufacture of light machinery, batteries, chemical fertilizers; resorts.

MARTIN (one of six counties so named) *Shoals* • 10,369 • 336 • Southwestern IN; drained by the Lost River and the East Fork of the White River (forming the southwestern boundary). Hoosier National Forest is in its southeast quarter. It also includes Martin State Forest and the Naval Surface Warfare Center's Crane Division (with Greenwood Lake reservoir within). • The derivation of the county's name has never been firmly established; it could have been named for one of several men named Martin. • 1820 from Indian lands • Corn, hay, cattle, hogs; gypsum, limestone; timber; manufacturing.

MIAMI (one of four counties, including Miami-Dade FL, so named) *Peru* • 36,082 • 376 • North-central IN; intersected by the Wabash, Mississinewa, and Eel rivers, and by Deer Creek. Grissom Air Reserve Base (and Air Museum) is in the southwest. Part of Mississinewa Lake reservoir and Miami State Recreation Area are in the southeast. • Named for the Miami Indians • 1832 from Cass • Composer and lyricist Cole Porter • Grain, fruit, livestock, poultry, dairy products; manufacture of electrical and heating equipment, plastics, paper, wood, and fabricated metal products. • The Circus City Festival Museum is a reminder of Peru's early fame as the nation's primary circus winter quarters.

MONROE *Bloomington* • 120,563 • 394 • South-central IN; drained by the White River, and Salt, Beanblossom and Clear creeks. Hoosier National Forest is in the southeast corner. Several state recreation areas are found on the banks of Monroe Reservoir. Part of Morgan-Monroe State Forest is in the northeast, north of Lake Lemon reservoir. The scenic southern hills of the county are pocked by sinkholes of karst topography. • One of seventeen counties named for President James Monroe • 1818 from Orange • Zoologist and ecologist Warder C. Allee; songwriter Hoagy Carmichael • Corn, cattle, dairying; timber; manufacture of television equipment, other electronic and electrical products, refrigerators; education (IN U. Bloomington); clay, limestone (Bloomington has been a center of quarrying and processing for many years.)

MONTGOMERY (one of eighteen counties so named) *Crawfordsville* • 37,629 • 505 • West-central IN; drained by Sugar and Big Raccoon creeks. Shades State Park is in the southwest.

• One of sixteen counties named directly or indirectly for General Richard Montgomery (1738–75), American Revolutionary War officer who captured Montreal, Canada • 1823 from Indian lands • Author and general Lew Wallace; statesman Henry S. Lane; poet and novelist Maurcie Thompson. Educator Caleb Mills died here. • Soybeans, corn, wheat, cattle, hogs, sheep, poultry, dairy products; clay pits; timber; printing and bookbinding; manufacturing and commerce; education (Wabash College).

MORGAN (one of eleven counties so named) *Martinsville* • 66,689 • 406 • Central IN, bounded on the northwest by Mill Creek; drained by the White River, White Lick Creek and Indian Creek. Part of Morgan-Monroe State Forest is on the southern boundary. • One of nine counties named for General Daniel Morgan (1736–1802), an officer in the Revolutionary War and U.S. representative from VA • 1821 from Indian lands • Hogs, wheat, corn, fruit, poultry; manufacturing; clay deposits; timber; artesian springs.

NEWTON (one of six counties so named) *Kentland* • 14,566 • 402 • Northwestern IN, bounded on the west by the IL state line, on the north by the Kankakee River; also drained by the Iroquois River. The county includes Willow Slough and part of La Salle state fish and wildlife areas. • One of five counties named for Sgt. John Newton (?–1780), Revolutionary War hero. (IN is one of five states in which Jasper and Newton counties have been placed adjacent to one another to honor the allied efforts of sergeants William Jasper and John Newton to rescue captive colonial soldiers near Savannah.) • 1858 from Jasper • Playwright George Ade • Corn, rye, oats, soybeans, cattle, hogs; some manufacturing; shipping of seed and grain; limestone quarrying • This was the last county organized in IN.

NOBLE (one of three counties so named) *Albion* • 46,275 • 411 • Northeastern IN; drained by the Elkhart River. The county includes Chain O' Lakes State Park and part of Tri-County State Fish and Wildlife Area. There are about twenty small glacially formed lakes scattered throughout the county. The largest is Sylvan Lake. • Named for either James Noble (1785–1831), U.S. senator from IN, or for Noah Noble (1794–1844), governor of IN • 1835 from Elkhart • Author Gene Stratton-Porter (state historic site) • Hogs, cattle, poultry, fruit, corn, soybeans, dairying; dairy and farm-products processing; gravel pits.

OHIO (one of three counties so named) *Rising Sun* • 5,623 (the least populated county in IN) • 87 (the smallest county in IN and one of the fifty smallest counties in the U.S.) • Southeastern IN, bounded on the east by the Ohio River (here forming the KY state line), and on the northwest by Laughery Creek. • Named for the Ohio River • 1844 from Dearborn • Hogs, cattle, tobacco; some manufacturing.

ORANGE (one of eight counties so named) *Paoli* • 19,306 • 400 • Southern IN; drained by the Lost and Patoka rivers, and Lick Creek. Lost River runs east to west below the surface through limestone karst topography in the northern part of the county. The county includes Springs Valley State Fish and Wildlife Area, Tillery Hill and Jackson state recreation areas, and Patoka Lake reservoir. Hoosier National Forest occupies over half of the county (in the west and south), and includes Pioneer Mothers Memorial Forest. • Named for Orange County, NC, former home of many early settlers • 1815 (prior to statehood) from Crawford and Washington • Since 1840, French Lick, site of sulphur springs, has been a popular health resort. IN political leader Tom Taggart developed hotels here. • Political scientist and philosopher Arthur F. Bentley died here. • Corn, fruit, cattle, hogs, poultry, dairying; stone quarrying; resort tourism (mineral springs, notably French Lick); some manufacturing. • West Baden Springs Hotel is a former grand resort hotel of note.

OWEN *Spencer* • 21,786 • 385 • Southwest-central IN; drained by the White River (forming part of the eastern boundary) and Mill Creek. McCormick's Creek State Park is in the east; Cataract Falls, Owen-Putnam State Forest, and part of Lieber State Recreation Area on Cagles Mill Lake reservoir are in the north. • One of two counties (the other in KY) named for Col. Abraham Owen (1769–1811), killed in the Battle of Tippecanoe • 1818 from Indian lands • Poet and playwright William Vaughn Moody • Soybeans, corn, wheat, fruits, hogs, cattle, dairying; manufacturing; lumber milling; limestone quarrying; timber.

PARKE *Rockville* • 17,241 • 445 • Western IN, bounded on the west by the Wabash River; drained by Sugar and Big Raccoon creeks. Turkey Run State Park is here, as are parts of Shades State Park, Raccoon Lake State Recreation Area and Cecil M. Harden Lake reservoir. Mansfield Roller Mill State Historic Site is also here. • Named for Benjamin Parke (1777–1835), attorney general of IN Territory and judge of the U.S. District Court of IN • 1821 from Indian lands • Psychologist Gordon W. Allport; lawyer and horticulturist James H. Logan; baseball player "Three Finger" Mordecai Brown • Bituminous-coal mining, clay and gravel pits; manufacturing; corn, wheat, rye, hogs, cattle, sheep; timber; mineral springs, tourism; maple syrup • The county has thirty-one covered bridges. An annual Covered Bridge Festival is held in October.

PERRY *Cannelton* • 18,899 • 381 • Southern IN, bounded on the south and partly on the east by the Ohio River (here forming the KY state line); drained by the Anderson River (forming part of the western boundary). The eastern three-fourths of the county is dominated by Hoosier National Forest, and includes Buzzard Roost Overlook. • One of ten counties named for Oliver Hazard Perry (1785–1819), U.S. naval officer during the War of 1812 • 1814 (prior to statehood) from Harrison and Warrick • Psychiatrist Charles F. Menninger • Corn, soybeans, dairy products, poultry, cattle, hogs; manufacturing; timber; sandstone quarries.

PIKE *Petersburg* • 12,837 • 336 • Southwestern IN, bounded on the north by the White River and its East Fork; drained by the Patoka River, with Patoka River National Wildlife Refuge situated along its banks. Pike State Forest is also found in the county. • One of ten counties named for Zebulon Montgomery Pike (1779–1813), U.S. army officer and discoverer of Pikes Peak in CO • 1816 from Indian lands • Diplomat John W. Foster • Bituminous-coal mines, oil wells, clay pits; timber; grain, livestock; manufacturing.

PORTER *Valparaiso* • 146,798 • 418 • Northwestern IN, bounded on the north by Lake Michigan and on the south by the Kankakee River; drained by the Little Calumet and Grand Calumet rivers. Indiana Dunes National Lakeshore (with dunes rising 180 feet) and Indian Dunes State Park are along Lake Michigan. • Named for Commodore David Porter (1780–1843), naval hero in the War of 1812 and commander-in-chief of the Mexican navy • 1835 from Indian lands • Valparaiso was originally a point on the old Sauk Trail, a thoroughfare for Sauk Indians traveling to Detroit to collect payment from the British for services contracted in the War of 1812. The state's economy was boosted in 1970 by the opening of the Port of Indiana in Burns Harbor to serve oceangoing ships sailing through the St. Lawrence Seaway. • Corn, fruit, grain, hogs, cattle, poultry, dairying, popcorn; manufacture of magnets, steel products, die castings, dresses, automobile accessories, food-processing machinery, electrical specialties; resort tourism; education (Valparaiso U.).

POSEY *Mount Vernon* • 27,061 • 409 • Extreme southwestern IN, bounded on the west by the Wabash River (forming the IL state line) and on the south by the Ohio River (forming the KY state line). The county includes Harmonie State Park and Twin Swamps Nature Preserve. • Named for General Thomas Posey (1750–1818), officer in the American Revolution, U.S. senator from LA, and IN territorial governor • 1814 (prior to statehood) from Knox • The settlement of Harmonie was founded in 1814–15 by George Rapp, a German Pietist preacher. Unrest brought on by hostile neighbors resulted in its sale, in 1825, to Robert Owen, a British reformer who founded the cooperative community of New Harmony (state historic site). Despite its economic failure, the scientists and educators it attracted stayed on to develop one of the most notable pre-Civil War cultural centers in the U.S. The nation's first geologist, David Dale Owen, built a laboratory here that later became the headquarters of the U.S. Geological Survey. The Workingmen's Institute, established in 1894, was one of the nation's first free public libraries. • The ashes of theologian Paul Tillich are interred in Tillich Park in New Harmony. • Corn, wheat, melons, hogs, poultry; manufacture of food products, petroleum fields.

PULASKI *Winamac* • 13,755 • 434 • Northwestern IN; drained by the Tippecanoe River. Tippecanoe River State Park, Winamac State Fish and Wildlife Area, part of Jasper-Pulaski State Fish and Wildlife Area, and Berns-Meyer Nature Preserve are all in the county. • One of seven counties named for Count Casimir Pulaski (1748–79), Polish soldier who fought for America during the Revolutionary War • 1835 from Cass • Corn, soybeans, oats, rye, dairy products, poultry, hogs, cattle; manufacturing.

PUTNAM (one of nine counties so named) *Greencastle* • 36,019 • 480 • West-central IN, bounded on the southeast by Mill Creek; drained by Big Walnut, Deer, Raccoon, and Mill creeks. Lieber State Recreation Area and Cagles Mill Lake reservoir are on the southern boundary. Oscar and Ruth Hall Woods Nature Preserve is also in the county. • One of eight counties definitively named for General Israel Putnam (1718–90), Revolutionary War officer and American commander at the Battle of Bunker Hill • 1821 from Indian lands • Corn, soybeans, wheat, hogs, sheep, cattle; manufacture of zinc products, business machines, capacitors; timber; limestone quarries, crushed stone; education (DePauw U.).

RANDOLPH (one of eight counties so named) *Winchester* • 27,401 • 453 • Eastern IN, bounded on the east by the OH state line; drained by the Mississinewa, Whitewater, and White rivers. • Named for either Thomas Randolph (?–1811), attorney-general of IN Territory killed at the Battle of Tippecanoe, or for Randolph County, NC, former home of many early settlers • 1818 from Wayne • Mass murderer and cult leader Jim Jones; film director Robert Wise • Corn, oats, wheat, soybeans, cattle, hogs, poultry, dairy products; manufacture of glass products and glass-making molds; stone quarrying.

RIPLEY *Versailles* • 26,523 • 446 • Southeastern IN; drained by Laughery and Graham creeks. Versailles State Park is here. • One of two counties (the other in MO) named for General Eleazar W. Ripley (1782–1839), officer in the War of 1812, MA legislator, and U.S. representative from LA • 1816 from Indian lands • Wheat, corn, tobacco, cattle, hogs, dairying; limestone quarries; timber; manufacturing, farm products processing.

RUSH (one of two counties so named, the other in KS) *Rushville* • 18,261 • 408 • East-central IN; drained by the Big Blue and Flatrock rivers, and Clifty Creek • Named for Benjamin Rush (1745–1813), surgeon general in the Continental Army and a signer of the Declaration of Independence • 1821 from Franklin • Boxer Norman Selby • Wheat, soybeans, corn, livestock, poultry, dairying; stone quarrying; manufacturing.

SAINT JOSEPH (one of two counties so named, the other in MI) *South Bend* • 265,559 (the fourth most populated county in IN) • 457 • Northern IN, bounded on the north by the MI state line; drained by the St. Joseph, Yellow, and Kankakee rivers. Potato Creek State Park is here, as is Twin Branch State Fish Hatchery. • Named for the St. Joseph River • 1830 from Indian lands • Robert Cavelier, Sieur de La Salle, the French explorer, visited the site of South Bend in 1679; under Council Oak Tree (still standing) he parleyed with chiefs of the Miami and Illinois Indian confederation. Former industries in South Bend were the Studebacker Brothers Manufacturing Company and the Singer Sewing Machine Company cabinet

works. Several thousand Belgian World War I refugees formed a strong Flemish-speaking community in Mishawaka. • Baseball pitcher Fat Freddie Fitzsimmons; essayist and poet Kenneth Rexroth; chemist Harold C. Urey; writers Ruth McKenney and Rose A. Thorpe; jurist Sherman Minton; biologist Maclyn McCarty. Mythic football player at University of Notre Dame George Gipp died here. • Dairy products, corn, grain, fruit, mint, livestock; diversified manufacturing, including rubber, plastic, and food products, power-transmission units, electrical and heavy machinery, structural steel, foundry equipment, missiles; resort tourism; education (U. of Notre Dame; St. Mary's College; Bethel College) • Hesburgh Memorial Library on the campus of the University of Notre Dame is one of the world's largest college libraries.

SCOTT (one of eleven counties so named) *Scottsburg* • 22,960 • 190 • Southeastern IN, bounded on the north by the Muscatatuck River; drained by its tributaries. The county contains Hardy Lake State Recreation Area, part of Clark State Forest, and Pigeon Roost State Historic Site. • One of two counties (the other in KY) named for Gen. Charles Scott (1739–1813), officer in the Revolutionary War and governor of KY • 1820 from Clark and Jackson • Grain, livestock, poultry; timber; manufacturing.

SHELBY *Shelbyville* • 43,445 • 413 • Central IN; drained by the Big Blue, Little Blue, and Flatrock rivers, and by Sugar Creek. The county is part of the Indianapolis metropolitan area. • One of nine counties named directly or indirectly for General Isaac Shelby (1750–1826), officer in the Revolutionary War and first governor of KY • 1821 from Indian lands • Indiana's first railroad was in Shelbyville. Completed in 1834, it was horse-drawn upon wooden tracks. • Dairying, corn, hay, wheat, soybeans, hogs, cattle; manufacture of electrical and heating equipment, fiber glass, paper-plastics, furniture, radio and television parts, airplane and rocket parts.

SPENCER *Rockport* • 20,391 • 399 • Southwestern IN, bounded on the south by the Ohio River (forming the KY state line); drained by the Anderson River (forming part of the county's eastern boundary) and Little Pigeon Creek. Lincoln State Park and Lincoln Boyhood National Memorial, the farm where Abraham Lincoln spent his boyhood years, is in the northern part of the county. Col. William Jones State Historic Site is also here. • One of two counties (the other in KY) named for Captain Spear Spencer (? –1811), a KY officer killed at the Battle of Tippecanoe • 1818 from Warrick. In the 1950s there was an organized effort to change the county's name from Spencer to Lincoln to coincide with the sesquicentennial of Abraham Lincoln's birth. With the failure of the movement, IN still has no county named for its regional hero. • President Abraham Lincoln's mother Nancy Hanks is buried here. • Soybeans, corn, wheat, tobacco, hay, peas, dairying, hogs, cattle; manufacture of brick, tile, concrete blocks, flour; education (St. Meinrad College) • The town of Santa Claus remails more than one million pieces of Christmas mail each year with the Santa Claus postmark.

STARKE *Knox* • 23,556 • 309 • Northwestern IN, bounded on the northwest by the Kankakee River; drained by the Yellow River and other tributaries of the Kankakee. The county includes Bass Lake State Beach and Fish Hatchery. Part of Kankakee State Fish and Wildlife Area is on the northwestern border. • One of three counties named for General John Stark (1728–1822), an officer in the French and Indian Wars and hero in the American Revolution. (No reason exists for why the spelling was altered.) • 1835 from Marshall • Mint, onions, corn, soybeans, cattle, hogs, poultry; some manufacturing.

STEUBEN *Angola* • 33,214 • 309 • Extreme northeastern IN, bounded on the north by the MI state line, and on the east by the OH state line; drained by the Pigeon River. The county has fifteen small lakes, glacial in origin, the largest being Lake James in Pokagon State Park. Part of Pigeon River State Fish and Wildlife Area is here. • One of two counties (the other in NY) named for Friedrich Wilhelm, Baron von Steuben (1730–94), Prussian soldier named inspector general of the U.S. Continental Army • 1835 from Indian lands • Army officer Lewis B. Hershey • Wheat, hay, corn, hogs, sheep, cattle, poultry, dairying; education (Tri-State U.).

SULLIVAN (one of six counties so named) *Sullivan* • 21,751 • 447 • Southwestern IN, bounded on the west by the Wabash River (here forming the IL state line); drained by Busseron, Turman, and Maria creeks. Part of Greene-Sullivan State Forest is here, as is part of Shakamak State Park. • Possibly for Daniel Sullivan (?–1790), early settler and Indian fighter • 1816 from Knox • Lawyer and politician Will Hays • Corn, wheat, soybeans, fruit, melons, livestock; bituminous-coal mines, sand and gravel, oil and natural-gas wells; timber; manufacturing.

SWITZERLAND *Vevay* • 9,065 • 221 • Southeastern IN, bounded on the east and south by the Ohio River (here forming the KY state line). The county is heavily forested. • Named by Swiss settlers for the European country • 1814 (prior to statehood) from Indian lands • Librarian John Shaw Billings; clergyman Edward Eggleston • Hay, tobacco, cattle; manufacturing.

TIPPECANOE *Lafayette* • 148,955 • 500 •West-central IN; intersected by the Wabash and Tippecanoe rivers, and Wildcat Creek. Tippecanoe Battlefield State Memorial is in the north. Prophetstown State Park and Celery Bog Nature Area are also in the county. • Named for the Tippecanoe River and/or Tippecanoe Battleground • 1826 from Montgomery • Fort Ouiatanon, established here in 1719, was the first white settlement in what would become IN; a trading and military post, it was controlled at different times by the French, British, and Indians of the area. In the Battle of Tippecanoe on November 7, 1811, Governor William Henry Harrison and his small army defeated an Indian confederacy led by Prophet, brother of Tecumseh. (Tippecanoe County Historical Museum displays many artifacts from the battle.) • Organist and composer Clarence Dickinson; athlete Ray Ewry; novelist George B. McCutcheon; printer and book designer Bruce Rogers; Cable TV executive and journalist Brian Lamb; playwright George Ade. Botanist J.C. Arthur and collegiate basketball coach Piggy Lambert died here. • Wheat (busy grain market), corn, soybeans, hogs, cattle; sand and gravel; diversified manufacturing, including aluminum, electrical and rubber products, prefabricated houses, pharmaceuticals; education (Purdue U.).

TIPTON (one of two counties so named, the other in TN) *Tipton* • 16,577 • 260 • Central IN; drained by Cicero Creek, Turkey Creek and the South Fork of Wildcat Creek. Tipton is the flattest county in IN. • Named for John Tipton (1786–1839), captain in the Battle of Tippecanoe, IN legislator and U.S. senator from IN • 1844 from Hamilton • Corn, soybeans, wheat, hogs, cattle; some manufacturing.

UNION (one of eighteen counties so named) *Liberty* • 7,349 • 162 • Eastern IN, bounded on the east by the OH state line; drained by the East Fork of the Whitewater River. The northern half of Brookville Reservoir is in the southwest, with Quakertown State Recreation Area on the western shore and Whitewater Memorial State Park on the eastern shore. • Named Union in support of the federal union of the states • 1821 from Wayne • Union general Ambrose E. Burnside; poet Joaquin Miller • Soybeans, hay, corn, cattle, hogs, dairying; some manufacturing.

VANDERBURGH *Evansville* • 171,922 • 235 • Southwestern IN, bounded on the south by the Ohio River (here forming the KY state line); drained by Pigeon Creek. Angel Mounds Historic Site Memorial, a large prehistoric Indian archaeological site, is in the southeast. • Named for Captain Henry Vanderburgh (1760–1812), officer in the Revolutionary War and judge of the first court in IN Territory • 1818 from Indian lands • The Wabash and Erie Canal was completed in 1853, linking Evansville and the Ohio River to Lake Erie. Evansville experienced substantial growth in its early years as the metropolitan center of southwestern IN and adjacent areas of KY and IL. • Politician Edwin Denby; writer Annie Johnston • Extensive manufactures, including pharmaceuticals, agricultural implements, refrigeration and air conditioning equipment, aluminum, plastic and rubber products; shipping operations; wheat, soybeans, corn; bituminous-coal mining; education (U. of Evansville; U. of Southern IN).

VERMILLION (one of three counties named either Vermillion or Vermilion) *Newport* • 16,788 • 257 • Western IN, bounded on the west by the IL state line and on the east by the Wabash River; drained by the Vermilion River. Ernie Pyle State Historic Site is at Dana. Newport Chemical Depot is southwest of Newport. • Named for the Vermilion River, which runs across the northern part of the county. No explanation exists for the difference in spelling between county and river. • 1824 from Parke • Bituminous coal; soybeans, corn, cattle; timber; some manufacturing.

VIGO *Terre Haute* • 105,848 • 403 • Western IN, bounded on the west by the IL state line; intersected by the Wabash

River (forming part of the western border); drained by Lost, Otter, and Prairie creeks. • Named for Joseph Maria Francesco Vigo (1747–1836), private in the Spanish army, fur trader, and spy for George Rogers Clark • 1818 from Indian lands • Fort Harrison, established in 1811 by territorial governor William Henry Harrison, was later defended by Captain Zachary Taylor against Indian attack. Laid out in 1816, Terre Haute became an important community on the Cumberland (National) Road (1835), the Wabash and Erie Canal (1849), and the Richmond Railroad (1852). The city was the scene of militant union activity • Socialist leader Eugene Debs; novelist Theodore Dreiser. Domestic terrorist Timothy McVeigh was executed here. • The county is a commercial and banking center. Also, corn, soybeans, wheat, hogs, cattle; timber; bituminous-coal mining; manufacture of fabricated metals, industrial and agricultural chemicals, medicines, packaging materials, processed foods, paint products; education (St. Mary-of-the-Wood College; IN state U.) • In 1930, Ellen Church Marshall of Terre Haute became the world's first airline flight attendant. On August 8, 1911, the Johnson Brothers of Terre Haute made the first monoplane flight in U.S. history. Terre Haute is the setting for Indiana's state song, "On the Banks of the Wabash," written by resident Paul Dresser. The Coca Cola bottle was designed in Terre Haute by employees of the Root Glass Company.

WABASH *Wabash* • 34,960 • 413 • Northeast-central IN; drained by the Wabash, Eel, Salamonie and Mississinewa rivers. Laketon Bog National Preserve is in the north; several state recreation areas are located in the south around Mississinewa and Salamonie lakes (reservoirs). Salomonie River State Forest is also here. • One of two counties (the other in IL) named for the Wabash River • 1832 from Huntington • Wabash was settled on land ceded to the U.S. by the Potawatomi Indian chief Pierish in the Treaty of Paradise Springs in 1826. In 1880, it became one of the world's first electrically lighted cities. • Journalist and author Ed Howe; Vice President Thomas R. Marshall; author Gene Porter • Cattle, hogs, dairying, soybeans, wheat, corn; manufacture of rubber and paper products; education (Manchester College).

WARREN *Williamsport* • 8,419 • 365 • Western IN, bounded on the west by the IL state line, on the southeast by the Wabash River. • One of fourteen counties named for Dr. Joseph Warren (1741–75), Revolutionary War general and member of the Committee of Safety who dispatched Paul Revere on his famous ride • 1827 from Indian lands • Historical markers dot the trail left by William Henry Harrison and his troops as they made their way to the Battle of Tippecanoe. • Wheat, corn, oats, soybeans, hogs, cattle; manufacturing • Rural Warren County calls itself "the only county in Indiana with no traffic signal." The Williamsport Falls are the state's highest free falling waterfall, with a drop of close to 100 feet.

WARRICK *Boonville* • 52,383 • 384 • Southwestern IN, bounded on the south by the Ohio River (forming the KY state line here); drained by Pigeon and Little Pigeon creeks. •

Named for Capt. Jacob Warrick (?–1811), early settler and officer who died at the Battle of Tippecanoe • 1813 (prior to statehood) from Indian lands • One of IN's leading coal producing counties (bituminous); corn, hay, soybeans, cattle; diversified manufacturing.

WASHINGTON *Salem* • 27,223 • 514 • Southern IN, bounded on the north by the Muscatatuck River and the East Fork of the White River; drained by the Blue and Lost rivers, and Twin Creek. A unit of Jackson-Washington State Forest is in the north. Part of Clark National Forest in the extreme east. Karst topography marks the southwest. • One of thirty-one counties named for President Washington • 1813 (prior to statehood) from Indian lands • Banker and industrialist Washington C. De Pauw; diplomat John Hay; army officer Thomas J. Rodman • Corn, hay, cattle, dairying; limestone quarrying; timber; manufacturing.

WAYNE (one of sixteen counties so named) *Richmond* • 71,097 • 404 • Eastern IN, bounded on the east by the OH state line; drained by the East and West forks of the Whitewater River. The highest point in the state (1,257 feet) is in the northeast. • One of fifteen counties named for "Mad" Anthony Wayne (1745–96), Revolutionary War general from PA and statesman • 1810 (prior to statehood) from Indian lands • Settled in 1806 by Quakers from NC, Richmond continues to be a center of Quaker influence and organizations, including the general offices for Friends United Meeting. • Philologist George O. Curme; ethnologist James Mooney; anthropologist Clark Wissler; abolitionist Levi Coffin (state historic site) • Corn, wheat, soybeans, cattle, hogs, poultry, dairy products, flower growing; manufacture of transportation equipment, machinery, fabricated metals, truck and bus bodies, automotive parts, multispindle drilling machines, appliances, home insulation; timber; education (Earlham College; IN U. East) • Richmond's large greenhouse rose-growing industry is reflected in its annual rose festival. (Two million roses are shipped each year from the county to all parts of the U.S.) The Indiana Football Hall of Fame is here.

WELLS (one of two counties so named, the other in ND) *Bluffton* • 27,600 • 370 • Eastern IN; drained by the Wabash and Salamonie rivers. Ouabache State Park was established in 1933 as part of the Civilian Conservation Corps program. • Named for Captain William Wells (?–1812), a white man adopted by Miami Indian Chief Little Turtle who served with the Indians; he later returned to white civilization and served as Indian agent • 1835 from Indian lands • Gene Stratton Porter set her novel *A Girl of the Limberlost* in the county's peat bogs, which have since been drained. • Livestock, dairy products, soybeans, wheat, corn; farm-products processing; limestone quarrying • Once considered the piano capital of the world, more pianos were built and shipped from Bluffton than from any other place in the U.S. Edward Bruce Williamson from Bluffton and Paul Howard Cook from Poneto formed Longfield Iris Farm, and along with their families, introduced award-winning iris hybrids.

WHITE (one of five counties so named) *Monticello* • 25,267 • 505 • Northwest-central IN, bounded on the east in part by the Tippecanoe River (here forming Lake Freeman reservoir); drained by the Tippecanoe River, Big Monon Creek and Little Monon Creek. Lakes Shafer and Freeman are resort and recreational areas. • Named for Col. Isaac White (?–1811), killed at the Battle of Tippecanoe • 1834 from Carroll • Corn, oats, rye, cattle, hogs; diversified manufacturing; quarries; tourism.

WHITLEY *Columbia City* • 30,707 • 336 • North-eastern IN; drained by the Eel River. The county includes Crooked Lake Nature Preserve in the north. • One of two counties (the other in KY) named for Col. William Whitley (1749–1813), soldier in the War of 1812 who enlisted at the age of sixty-three • 1835 from Huntington • Cowboy and writer Andy Adams; clergyman and novelist Lloyd C. Douglas • Poultry, corn, wheat, soybeans, dairy products; some manufacturing.

IOWA

Our Liberties We Prize and Our Rights We Will Maintain

A board of supervisors governs each of the state's ninety-nine counties. In most counties, the board is composed of three members. Other elected officials include the county attorney, sheriff, auditor, clerk of the court, treasurer, and recorder.

ADAIR (one of four counties so named) *Greenfield* • 8,243 • 569 • Southwestern IA; drained by the Middle, North, and Thompson rivers, and by the Middle and East branches of the Nodaway River. • Named for John Adair (1757–1840), U.S. senator from KY and governor of KY • 1851 from Cass • The county was the site of the first train robbery in the west (Jesse James in 1873). • Vice President Henry A. Wallace • Corn, soybeans, cattle, hogs, poultry; manufacturing; bituminous-coal deposits • Wagon wheel ruts are still visible along the Mormon Trail, which cut through the county in 1846. A forestry area at the Wallace Research Satellite Farm, planted by the Civilian Conservation Corps, contains several rare native tree species.

ADAMS (one of twelve counties so named) *Corning* • 4,482 (the least populated county in IA) • 424 • Southwestern IA; drained by the Middle and East branches of the Nodaway River, the Little Platte River and One Hundred and Two River. Lake Icaria reservoir is north of Corning. • One of eight counties named for President John Adams • 1851 from Taylor • Television personality Johnny Carson • Corn, hogs, cattle, poultry; bituminous-coal deposits; clay, sand and gravel pits, limestone quarries.

ALLAMAKEE *Waukon* • 14,675 • 640 • Extreme northeastern IA, bounded on the north by the MN state line, and on the east by the Mississippi River (forming the WI state line); drained by the Upper Iowa River. The county is mostly rolling prairie and includes the hilly, forested "Little Switzerland" district. Lock and Dam No. 9 on the Mississippi River lies above Harpers Ferry. The Upper Mississippi River National Wildlife and Fish Refuge extends along the river. The Yellow River State Forest is in the southeast. Fish Farm Mounds State Preserve is in the northwest. Effigy Mounds National Monument contains examples of prehistoric American Indian mounds, some in the shapes of birds and bears. • Possibly named for an Indian trader named "Allan Makee" • 1847 from Clayton •

There was extensive local flooding here in 1993. • Religious leader John R. Mott; biochemist Edwin G. Krebs • Extensive dairying, hogs, poultry, cattle, corn; limestone quarries, lead, zinc and iron deposits; some manufacturing. • The county contains one of the few log barns still in existence (ca. 1860) near New Albin.

APPANOOSE *Centerville* • 13,721 • 496 • Southern IA, bounded on the south by the MO state line; drained by the Chariton River. Part of Stephens State Forest is located in the northeast. Sharon Bluffs State Park is southeast of Centerville. Rathbun Dam and Lake, with Honey Creek State Park on its northern shore, are in the northwest. • Named for a respected chief of the Sac and Fox tribes, prominent in IA in the 1830s and 1840s • 1843 (prior to statehood) from Davis • Sheep, hogs, cattle, poultry, corn, soybeans, hay; shale, limestone quarrying, gypsum and bituminous-coal mining; manufacture of camp trailers, farm equipment, electrical appliances, food wrappings, fertilizer, beverages, boxes, clay concrete, metal, shale and wood products; processing of grain, meal and milk products; printing • Centerville's annual fall festival, Pancake Day, draws as many as 50,000 visitors.

AUDUBON *Audubon* • 6,830 • 443 • West-central IA; drained by the East Nishnabotna River. • Named for John James Audubon (1785–1851), naturalist painter and ornithologist • 1851 from Cass and Black Hawk • Cattle, hogs, poultry, corn, hay, oats.

BENTON (one of nine counties so named) *Vinton* • 25,308 • 716 • East-central IA; drained by the Cedar River and Wolf Creek. • One of seven counties named for Thomas Hart Benton (1782–1858), U.S. journalist and statesman • 1837 (prior to statehood) from Indian lands • The county suffered extensive flooding of its rivers in 1993. • Hogs, cattle, poultry (raising, packing), corn, oats; limestone quarries; manufacture of screw machines, farm implements; vegetable canning. • The state school for the blind is in Vinton; graduates may matriculate at any college in IA.

BLACK HAWK *Waterloo* • 128,012 (the fourth most populated county in IA) • 567 • East-central IA; drained by the Cedar River. George Wyth Memorial State Park is located in Waterloo and Cedar Falls. • Named for Black Hawk (1767–1838), famous Indian warrior and chief of the Sac and Fox tribes • 1843 (prior to statehood) from Delaware County • There was extensive flooding here in 1993. • Historian Carl Becker; the Sullivan brothers (five brothers all killed in action during World War II on the same day: Nov. 13, 1942); writer Bess G. Aldrich • Hogs, cattle, poultry, corn, oats, soybeans; meat packing; manufacture of rotary pumps, tractors, farm equipment, golf-course equipment, humidifiers, air-conditioners, heating grills and registers, tools and dies; education (U. of N. IA) • Waterloo has the distinction of being the only city west of the Mississippi awarded two Carnegie libraries. It hosts the National Dairy Cattle Congress each September.

BOONE (one of eight counties so named) *Boone* • 26,224 • 571 • Central IA; drained by the Des Moines River and Beaver Creek. Seven Oaks ski area is southwest of Boone. Holst State Forest is in the north. Ledges State Park and Iowa Arboretum are in the south. • Named for Captain Nathan Boone (1780–?), son of Daniel, officer in the U.S. Dragoons and early explorer of IA • 1846 from Polk • There was widespread flooding here in 1993. • First Lady Mamie Eisenhower • Hogs, cattle, poultry, corn, oats, soybeans; bituminous-coal deposits; light manufacturing; railroad industry • There are a number of summer camps for youth organizations in the county. The Kate Shelley High Bridge (crossing the Des Moines River) is one of the highest (185 feet above the river) and longest (2,685 feet) railroad bridges in the US.

BREMER *Waverly* • 23,325 • 438 • Northeastern IA; drained by the Cedar, Wapsipinicon, and Shell Rock rivers. • Named for Frederika Bremer (1801–65), Swedish novelist, traveler, and early feminist • 1851 from Winnebago Indian Reserve • There was general flooding here in 1993. • Hogs, cattle, poultry, corn, oats, dairying; limestone quarries, sand and gravel pits; manufacture of excavating equipment, food processing (especially condensed milk); education (Wartburg College).

BUCHANAN *Independence* • 21,093 • 571 • Eastern IA; drained by the Wapsipinicon River and Buffalo Creek. • One of three counties named for President James Buchanan • 1837 (prior to statehood), from Delaware County • The county experienced widespread flooding in 1993. • Mathematician Leonard E. Dickson • Cattle, hogs, poultry, corn, oats; sand and gravel pits; some limestone quarries.

BUENA VISTA *Storm Lake* • 20,411 • 575 • Northwestern IA; drained by the Little Sioux River and by headstreams of the North Raccoon, Boyer and Maple rivers. This prairie-dominated county includes reclaimed swampland and has a system of drainage ditches. Wanata State Park is in the northwest corner. Storm Lake in the south has several local parks along its shores. • Named for the Battle of Buena Vista • 1851 from Sac and Clay • Hogs, cattle, poultry, corn, oats, soybeans; sand and gravel pits; education (Buena Vista U.).

BUTLER (one of eight counties so named) *Allison* • 15,305 • 580 • North-central IA; drained by the Shell Rock River and the West Fork of the Cedar River. Henry Woods State Park is in the east. • One of three counties named for Major William O. Butler (1791–1880), officer in the War of 1812 and Mexican War, and U.S. representative from KY • 1851 from Buchanan and Black Hawk • The county experienced widespread flooding in 1993. • Cattle, hogs, poultry, corn, oats, soybeans; limestone quarries, sand and gravel pits.

CALHOUN *Rockwell City* • 11,115 • 570 • Central IA; drained by the North Raccoon River. Twin Lakes State Park is in the north. • One of eleven counties named for John C. Calhoun (1782–1850), U.S. statesman and proponent of southern causes • Established as Fox 1851 from Greene; name changed 1853. Iowa legislators agreed to the name on the condition that its neighboring county would be named for Calhoun's political foe Daniel Webster. • Corn, oats, soybeans, hogs, cattle, poultry; bituminous-coal deposits, sand and gravel pits • At twenty-three miles wide, the largest intact on-land meteorite crater in the U.S. is located near Manson.

CARROLL (one of thirteen counties so named) *Carroll* • 21,421 • 569 • West-central IA; drained by the South, North, and Middle Raccoon rivers, and by the East and West Nishnabotna rivers. Swan Lake State Park is in the center of the county. • One of twelve counties named for Charles Carroll (1737–1832), a signer of the Declaration of Independence and U.S. senator from MD • 1851 from Guthrie • There was widespread flooding here in 1993. • Merle Hay, the first Iowan and one of the first U.S. soldiers killed in World War I, is buried at the Merle Hay Memorial Cemetery near Glidden. • Cattle, hogs, poultry, corn, oats; insurance; meat processing, manufacture of oven timers, windows, soft drinks, farm equipment, fertilizer, feed, seed, refrigeration equipment; bituminous-coal deposits • The Missouri-Mississippi Drainage Divide, directing water east of the divide to the Mississippi River, and west, to the Missouri River, is designated by a marker near Arcadia.

CASS (one of nine counties so named) *Atlantic* • 14,684 • 564 • Southwestern IA; drained by the East Nishnabotna and West Nodaway rivers. Anita Lake and Cold Springs state parks are both here. • One of eight counties named for Lewis Cass (1782–1866), OH legislator, governor of Michigan Territory, U.S. secretary of war, and U.S. secretary of state • 1851 from Pottawattamie • The winter headquarters for travelers along the Mormon Trail was located near Lewis. Other historic trails and routes passed through the county: the Oregon Trail, the Handcart Trails of 1856–57, the 49er's Gold Rush Trail and White Pole Road. • Cattle, hogs, poultry, corn; coal deposits, some manufacturing • Hitchcock House, built in Lewis in 1856, is a restored "station" on the Underground Railroad.

CEDAR (one of three counties so named) *Tipton* • 18,187 •

580 • Eastern IA; drained by the Cedar River. • Named for the Cedar (or Red Cedar) River • 1837 (prior to statehood) from Wisconsin Territory • President Herbert Hoover (gravesite, presidential library and museum at the Herbert Hoover National Historic Site in West Branch) • Hogs, cattle, corn, oats, soybeans; limestone quarries.

CERRO GORDO *Mason City* • 46,447 • 568 • Northern IA; drained by the Shell Rock River and Lime Creek. Clear Lake reservoir is in the west, Clear Lake State Park on its southern shore and McIntosh Woods State Park on its northern shore. • Named for the battle of Cerro Gordo, an important American victory in the Mexican War. • 1851 from Floyd • Cattle, hogs, poultry, corn, oats, soybeans; limestone quarries, sand and gravel pits; manufacture of cement, bricks and drain tile, steel door frames, electronic equipment, grain drying equipment, meat products, baked goods; resort tourism • With winds averaging seventeen miles per hour, Clear Lake was selected as the site for the Cerro Gordo Wind Farm Project. The Surf Ballroom in Clear Lake was the site of Buddy Holly's last concert in 1959. A memorial in the county marks the site where Buddy Holly, Ritchie Valens and The Big Bopper were killed in a plane crash. Mason City was the inspiration for the "River City" of favorite son Meredith Willson's hit musical *The Music Man*. The city is still known for its interest in band music and barbershop quartet harmonies; the North Iowa Band Festival is an annual event.

CHEROKEE *Cherokee* • 13,035 • 577 • Northwestern IA; drained by the Little Sioux River and its West Fork, and the Maple River. The county includes Steele Prairie State Preserve. • One of eight counties named for the Indian tribe • 1851 from Crawford • When the railroad from Fort Dodge to Sioux City failed to cross the Little Sioux River where anticipated in 1870, the townspeople of Cherokee dragged houses, shops, and the county courthouse a mile and a half to the new depot. • Cherokee is one of the state's largest hogs- and cattle-raising counties. Also, sheep, poultry, corn, oats, soybeans; manufacture of farm implements; meat packing • Pilot Rock, an errant twenty-foot high boulder left behind by the retreating ice of the last continental glacier, served as a guidepost for Indians and settlers. Spring Lake was formed when, in 1855, the Illinois Central Railroad excavated a hill near Cherokee for its gravel, and the resulting pit filled up with natural spring water.

CHICKASAW *New Hampton* • 13,095 • 505 • Northeastern IA; drained by the Cedar, Wapsipinicon, and Little Cedar rivers. • One of two counties (the other in MS) named for the Indian tribe • 1851 from Fayette • Dairying, hogs, cattle, corn, soybeans; limestone quarries, sand and gravel pits • The Little Brown Church in the Vale, located in Nashua, was the inspiration for the hymn of the same name.

CLARKE (one of five counties so named) *Osceola* • 9,133 • 431 • Southern IA; drained by the Chariton and South rivers and White Breast Creek. A unit of Stephens State Forest is here. • Named for James Clarke (1812–50), newspaper publisher and

last governor of IA Territory • 1846 from Lucas • The first white settlers in the county were Mormons traveling from Nauvoo, IL to Salt Lake City, UT along the Mormon Trail. (Murray Trail Days, held in June, commemorates the town's location on the Mormon Trail.) • Hogs, cattle, poultry, corn; bituminous-coal deposits.

CLAY (one of eighteen counties so named) *Spencer* • 17,372 • 569 • Northwestern IA; drained by the Little Sioux and Ocheyedan rivers. The northeastern part of the county is in the Iowa lakes district (with glacial origins); these include Elk, Round, and Trumbull lakes, Dan Green Slough, and part of Lost Island Lake. • Named for Lt. Col. Henry Clay, Jr. (?–1847), son of the statesman; killed at the Battle of Buena Vista during the Mexican War • 1851 from Indian lands • Hogs, cattle, sheep, poultry, corn, oats, soybeans; some manufacturing • The Clay County Fair has one of the largest displays of agricultural machinery in the U.S.

CLAYTON (one of two counties so named, the other in GA) *Elkader* • 18,678 • 779 (the fifth largest county in IA) • Northeastern IA, bounded on the east by the Mississippi River (here forming the WI state line); drained by the Turkey and Volga rivers. The north is in the "Little Switzerland" district of the state. Mississippi River Lock and Dam No. 10 is at Guttenberg. Turkey River Mounds and Bixley preserves and Pikes Peak State Park are here. White Pine Hollow State Forest and Preserve is on the southern border. Upper Mississippi National Wildlife Refuge extends along the eastern boundary. • Named for John M. Clayton (1796–1856), U.S. senator from DE and U.S. secretary of state • 1837 (prior to statehood) from Dubuque • Cattle, hogs, poultry, corn, hay; limestone quarries, sand and gravel pits; lead and zinc • The Osborne Conservation Center features one of IA's largest wildlife exhibits and includes over fifty species of native animals. The Froelich Monument near Monona marks the site where the Froelich tractor was invented.

CLINTON (one of nine counties so named) *Clinton* • 50,149 • 695 • Eastern IA, bounded on the east by the Mississippi River (forming the IL state line) and on the south by the Wapsipinicon River. Lock and Dam No. 13 is north of Clinton. The Upper Mississippi River National Wildlife and Fish Refuge extends along the eastern border. • One of eight counties named for De Witt Clinton (1769–1828), governor of NY and supporter of the Erie Canal • 1837 (prior to statehood) from Dubuque • Singer and actress Lillian Russell • Hogs, cattle, corn, oats; limestone quarries; manufacturing.

CRAWFORD (one of eleven counties so named) *Denison* • 16,942 • 714 • Western IA; drained by the Boyer, Soldier, and West Nishnabotna rivers. • One of six counties named directly or indirectly for William Harris Crawford (1772–1834), U.S. senator from GA, U.S. secretary of war, and U.S. secretary of the treasury • 1851 from Shelby • Attorney Jim Garrison • Hogs, poultry, sheep, corn, oats, barley; bituminous-coal deposits.

DALLAS (one of five counties so named) *Adel* • 40,750 (37% increase since 1990; the fastest growing county in IA) • 586 • Central IA; drained by the Raccoon River system and by Beaver Creek. Part of Saylorville Lake reservoir is in the northeast. • One of three counties named for George Mifflin Dallas (1792–1864), U.S. minister to Great Britain and U.S. vice president • 1846 from Polk • Cattle, poultry, corn, oats, soybeans; coal mines • The rail bed for the defunct Chicago, Milwaukee and St. Paul line now serves as the route for the thirty-four mile Raccoon River Valley Bike Trail from Waukee to Yale in Guthrie County.

DAVIS (one of two counties so named, the other in UT) *Bloomfield* • 8,541 • 503 • Southeastern IA, bounded on the south by the MO state line; drained by the Des Moines, Fox, North Fabius, and North and South Wyaconda rivers. The county includes Lake Wapello State Park and part of Stephens State Forest. • Named for Garret Davis (1801–72), U.S. senator and representative from KY • 1843 (prior to statehood) from Van Buren • Sheep, hogs, cattle, poultry, corn, soybeans, hay; bituminous-coal deposits • Between 1846 and 1860 more than 80,000 Mormons on their western trek to Utah passed through the county; some of the ruts left by their wagons are still visible along the trail. There is a large Amish community in the county. Mars Hill Church, built in 1857, is the oldest log church still in use in the nation.

DECATUR *Leon* • 8,689 • 532 • Southern IA, bounded on the south by the MO state line; drained by the Thompson and Weldon rivers. Nine Eagles State Park is here. • One of five counties named for Stephen Decatur (1779–1820), U.S. naval officer during the War of 1812 • 1846 from Appanoose • Cattle, poultry, corn, alfalfa; bituminous-coal deposits; education (Graceland U.).

DELAWARE (one of six counties so named) *Manchester* • 18,404 • 578 • Eastern IA; drained by the Maquoketa River. Backbone State Park (IA's first state park) is here. • Named for the state, as a tribute to John Middleton Clayton, U.S. senator from DE • 1837 (prior to statehood) from Dubuque • Hogs, cattle, poultry, corn, oats; limestone quarries • In Greeley stands a life-size replica of a Clydesdale horse, a tribute to the Brady brothers, two local hitch drivers.

DES MOINES *Burlington* • 42,351 • 416 • Southeastern IA, bounded on the east by the Mississippi River (forming the IL state line) and on the south by the Skunk River. Lock and Dam No. 18 is located northwest of Burlington. Malchow Mounds State Preserve and the Iowa Army Ammunition Plant are also here. • Named for the Des Moines River, which runs through the southeastern part of the state • 1834 (prior to statehood) from Wisconsin Territory • For many years Burlington was the only adequate steamboat landing on the western bank of the Mississippi River for a stretch of eighty miles. It served briefly (1837) as the Wisconsin territorial capital and then as the Iowa territorial capital from 1838 to 1841. There was extensive flooding here in 1993 along the Missis-

sippi and its tributaries. • Chemist and inventor of nylon Wallace H. Carothers; forester Aldo Leopold; engineer Robert N. Noyce • Hogs, cattle, corn, soybeans; gypsum and limestone quarries; grain shipping; manufacture of electrical and electronic equipment, boilers, steam turbines, furniture, office equipment, tractors and farm equipment, explosives, chemicals • The American Music Festival in Burlington attracts jazz musicians from all over the U.S.

DICKINSON (one of three counties so named) *Spirit Lake* • 16,424 • 381 (the smallest county in IA) • Northwestern IA, bounded on the north by the MN state line; drained by the Little Sioux River. The county is situated in a glacial lake region with many state parks and preserves, including Mini-Waken, Pikes Point, Gull Point and Trappers Bay state parks, and Cayler Prairie (a 4½ mile swath of untouched prairie) State Preserve. • One of two counties (the other in KS) named for Daniel S. Dickinson (1800–66), U.S. senator from NY • 1851 from Kossuth • In 1857, many settlers were killed here by the Sioux during the Spirit Lake Massacre. • Cattle, hogs, poultry, corn, oats, hay; lumbering, sand and gravel; tourism.

DUBUQUE *Dubuque* • 89,143 • 608 • Eastern IA, bounded on the east by the Mississippi river (forming the WI and IL state lines here); drained by the North Fork of the Maquoketa River. Lock and Dam No. 11 is at Dubuque city. The Upper Mississippi River National Wildlife and Fish Refuge extends along the entire eastern border. Mines of Spain State Recreation Area, Crystal Lake Cave, and Sundown Mountain ski area are also here. • Named for Julien Dubuque (1762–1810), first permanent white settler in Iowa • 1834 (prior to statehood) from Wisconsin Territory. Present boundaries were established in 1837. • Dubuque is IA's oldest city; early settlers arrived in the late 1700s to mine lead and trade with the Mesquakie Indians. The city's Old Shot Tower utilized locally mined lead for bullets during the Civil War. • Novelist and playwright Richard Bissell; geologist and anthropologist William John McGee; Speaker of the House of Representatives David Henderson. Senator William B. Allison died here. • Hogs, cattle, corn, oats; lead and zinc deposits; limestone quarrying; meat packing; manufacture of wood products and machinery; education (Loras and Clarke colleges) • The "Field of Dreams" — a baseball diamond carved from a cornfield depicted in the film of the same name — is in the west. Dyersville has a museum containing thousands of farm toys and truck replicas. The town is known as the "Farm Toy Capital of the World." The Basilica of St. Francis Xavier in Dyersville is the only basilica in the U.S. found in a rural community. Fenelon Street Elevator, the Midwest's shortest and steepest railroad to the top of the bluffs of the Mississippi River, is in Dubuque.

EMMET *Estherville* • 11,027 • 396 • Northern IA, bounded on the north by the MN state line; drained by the Des Moines River and its East Fork. The county is in the Iowa lakes region and contains Swan, Ingham, High, Twelve Mile, and Okamandpedan lakes. The county includes Fort Defiance and Okamandpedan state parks, and Riverside Hills ski area. •

One of two counties (the other in MI) named for Robert Emmet (1778–1803), celebrated Irish patriot executed by the English for revolutionary acts • 1851 from Kossuth and Dickinson • Cattle, hogs, poultry, corn, oats, soybeans; sand and gravel pits • On May 10, 1879, one of North America's largest meteorites, weighing a total of 744 pounds, burst into three separate pieces before crashing throughout the county; the three large fragments are displayed in museums in Vienna, London and at the University of Minnesota in Minneapolis. O.C. Bates, editor of Estherville's *Northern Vindicator,* is credited with using the word "blizzard" with its present definition for the first time in print on April 23, 1870.

FAYETTE (one of eleven counties so named) *West Union* • 22,008 • 731 • Northeastern IA; drained by the Volga, Maquoketa, and Turkey rivers, and by Buffalo Creek. Echo Valley State Park is here, as are Brush Creek Canyon State Preserve and Volga River State Recreation Area. Montauk Historic Site is near Clermont. • One of seventeen counties named for the Marquis de Lafayette (1757–1834), French statesman and soldier who fought with the Americans during the Revolutionary War • 1837 (prior to statehood) from Clayton • Hogs, cattle, poultry, corn, oats, dairying; limestone quarries, sand and gravel pits; some manufacturing; education (Upper IA U.).

FLOYD (one of six counties so named) *Charles City* • 16,900 • 501 • Northern IA; drained by the Shell Rock, Cedar and Little Cedar rivers. • Possibly for Sergeant Charles Floyd (?–1804), a member of the Lewis and Clark expedition • 1851 from Chickasaw • During World War II, the U.S. government subsidized the farming of hemp, primarily grown in the Rockford area, for the war effort. There was widespread flooding in the county in 1993 • Suffragist Carrie Chapman Catt; automotive manufacturers Frederick and August Duesenberg (who ran a bicycle shop in Rockford) • Hogs, cattle, poultry, corn, soybeans, oats, plant nurseries; limestone quarries, some clay and gravel pits; manufacture of tractors, pharmaceuticals, wood products • Charles City is the birthplace of the farm tractor, and home to the Hart-Parr Co., the first tractor factory in the world. In 1901, Charles Hart and Charles Parr produced one of the first gasoline traction engines for agricultural and industrial use. A rare "creeping juniper," thought to have been deposited from the glaciers during the Ice Age, can be found only in Floyd County and one area in PA.

FRANKLIN (one of twenty-five counties so named) *Hampton* • 10,704 • 582 • North-central IA; drained by the West Branch of the Iowa River and the West Fork of the Cedar River. Beeds Lake State Park is here. • One of twenty-three counties named for Benjamin Franklin • 1851 from Chickasaw • Naval officer William D. Leahy • Cattle, hogs, poultry, corn, oats, soybeans; limestone quarries.

FREMONT *Sidney* • 8,010 • 511 • Extreme southwestern IA, bounded on the south by the MO state line and on the west by the Missouri River (forming the NE state line); drained by the Nishnabotna River and its East and West forks, and Walnut Creek. The county includes Waubonsie State Park. • One of four counties named for John C. Frémont (1813–90), soldier and explorer who led five expeditions to the West, U.S. senator from CA, and governor of the AZ Territory • 1847 from Pottawattamie • The county annexed part of Otoe County, NE in 1943. • Cattle, hogs, poultry, corn; bituminous-coal deposits; some manufacturing.

GREENE *Jefferson* • 10,366 • 568 • Central IA; drained by the Raccoon River. Spring Lake State Park is here. The Mahany Memorial Carillon Tower is in Jefferson. • One of sixteen counties named for General Nathanael Greene (1742–86), hero of the Revolutionary War, quartermaster general, and commander of the Army of the South • 1851 from Dallas • Pollster George H. Gallup • Bituminous-coal deposits, sand and gravel pits; hogs, cattle, poultry, corn, soybeans.

GRUNDY *Grundy Center* • 12,369 • 503 • Central IA; drained by Blackhawk and Wolf creeks. • One of four counties named for Felix Grundy (1777–1840) chief justice of the KY Supreme Court, U.S. senator from TN and U.S. attorney general • 1851 from Black Hawk • Hogs, cattle, corn, soybeans, oats • "Grundy Soil," a very rich and black soil, was named for Grundy County, known for its fertile farmland. Grundy Center, world headquarters for the Two Cylinder Club, hosts its annual Two Cylinder Expo featuring exhibits of restored, vintage John Deere products.

GUTHRIE *Guthrie Center* • 11,353 • 591 • West-central IA; drained by the Middle Raccoon (here forming Panorama Lake reservoir) and South Raccoon rivers and by the Middle River and Brushy Creek. Springbrook State Recreation Area is here. Sheeder Prairie State Preserve, one of the few untouched tracts of prairie left in IA, is also in the county. • Named for Captain Edwin Guthrie (1806–1847), army officer from IA killed during the Mexican War • 1851 from Jackson • Hogs, cattle, poultry, corn, oats; sand and gravel pits.

HAMILTON (one of ten counties so named) *Webster City* • 16,438 • 577 • Central IA; drained by the Boone River and the South Fork of the Skunk River. Little Wall Lake is in the south. • Named for William Hamilton, president of the IA senate at the time the county was established • 1856 from Webster • Writer MacKinlay Kantor • Hogs, poultry, cattle, corn, soybeans, oats; bituminous-coal deposits; manufacture of washing machines, frozen foods, farm equipment, metal castings, electric scoreboards, aluminum boats.

HANCOCK *Garner* • 12,100 • 571 • Northern IA; drained by branches of the Iowa River, and Boone and Winnebago rivers. The county contains small glacial lakes. Pilot Knob Lake and State Park are on the northeastern boundary. • One of ten counties named for John Hancock (1737–93), noted signer of the Declaration of Independence, governor of MA, and statesman • 1851 from Wright • Cattle, hogs, poultry, corn, oats; sand and gravel pits.

HARDIN (One of six counties so named) *Eldora* • 18,812 • 569 • Central IA; drained by the Iowa River. Pine State Park is here. • Named for Col. John J. Hardin (1810–47), officer in the Black Hawk and Mexican wars, and U.S. representative from IL • 1851 from Black Hawk • Hogs, cattle, poultry, corn, oats, soybeans; limestone quarries, sand, clay, and gravel pits.

HARRISON (one of eight counties so named) *Logan* • 15,666 • 697 • Western IA, bounded on the west by the Missouri River (forming the NE state line); drained by the Boyer, Soldier, and Little Sioux rivers, and Willow and Pigeon creeks. Part of Wilson Island State Park and De Soto Bend National Wildlife Refuge and Visitor's Center are in the southwest. • One of four counties named for President William Henry Harrison • 1851 from Pottawattamie • Cattle, hogs, corn, barley, oats • The county's most prominent geological feature, the Loess Hills, formed by wind-blown dust after the Ice Age, are unique in the western hemisphere. The Loess Hills Scenic Byway here was named one of the ten most outstanding scenic byways in the U.S. Mormons established settlements in the area in the 1850s. The Bertrand Museum displays artifacts recovered from the *Bertrand*, a sternwheeler which sank in the Missouri River in 1865.

HENRY (one of ten counties so named) *Mount Pleasant* • 20,336 • 434 • Southeastern IA; drained by the Skunk River and Cedar Creek. Oakland Mills and Geode state parks are in the county. (The latter is known for its quartzite geodes.) • One of three counties named for Col. Henry Dodge (1782–1867), officer in the War of 1812, governor of WI Territory and U.S. senator from WI • 1836 (prior to statehood) from Wisconsin Territory • Physicist James Alfred Van Allen • Sheep, cattle, corn, soybeans; limestone quarries; livestock shipping; manufacture of bus bodies; education (IA Wesleyan College) • Salem, founded in 1835, was the first Quaker settlement west of the Mississippi.

HOWARD (one of seven counties so named) *Cresco* • 9,932 • 473 • Northeastern IA, bounded on the north by the MN state line; drained by the Upper Iowa, Wapsipinicon, and Turkey rivers. Hayden Prairie State Preserve contains a 200-acre tract of virgin prairie. • One of two counties (the other in IN) named for Tilghman A. Howard (1797–1844), TN legislator, U.S. representative from IN, and TX patriot • 1851 from Chickasaw and Floyd • Agricultural scientist Norman E. Borlaug • Hogs, cattle, poultry, corn, oats, dairying; limestone quarries, sand and gravel pits.

HUMBOLDT *Dakota City* • 10,381 • 434 • North-central IA; drained by the Des Moines River and its East Fork. Silver Creek ski area is in the county. • One of three counties named for Alexander von Humboldt (1769–1859), German explorer and naturalist • Created in 1851 from Webster, never organized, re-established in 1857 • Professional free-style wrestler Frank Gotch • Hogs, cattle, corn, oats, soybeans; bituminous-coal deposits; limestone quarries.

IDA *Ida Grove* • 7,837 • 432 • Western IA; drained by the Maple and Soldier rivers • Named for Mount Ida on the Isle of Crete • 1851 from Cherokee • Cattle, hogs, poultry, corn, oats, soybeans; sand and gravel pits, bituminous-coal deposits.

IOWA (one of two counties so named, the other in WI) *Marengo* • 15,671 • 586 • East-central IA; drained by the Iowa and English rivers. In the northeast are seven villages of the Amana colonies. • Named for the Iowa River • 1843 (prior to statehood) from Washington County • Spiritual leader of the county's Amana Colony Barbara Heinemann died here. • Cattle, hogs, sheep, poultry, corn, oats; manufacturing • The small community of Koszta is known for its interest in the Belgian sport of "rolle bolle."

JACKSON (one of twenty-four counties so named) *Maquoketa* • 20,296 • 636 • Eastern IA, bounded on the east by the Mississippi River (forming the IL state line); drained by the Maquoketa River and its North Fork. Lock and Dam No. 12 on the Mississippi River is near Bellevue. Maquoketa Caves and Bellevue state parks are in the county. Part of the Upper Mississippi River National Wildlife and Fish Refuge extends along the entire eastern border. • One of twenty-two counties named directly or indirectly for President Andrew Jackson • 1837 (prior to statehood) from Wisconsin Territory • Hogs, cattle, poultry, corn, oats, soybeans; limestone quarries • St. Donatus, a picturesque Luxembourger village, was settled by Luxembourg immigrants. The oldest Way of the Cross in the U.S., established in 1865, is located here. Several historic barns, including unusual hexagonal and polygonal structures, are located throughout the county. The Young Museum in Bellevue displays one of the world's best collections of Parian ware.

JASPER *Newton* • 37,213 • 730 • Central IA; drained by the North and South Skunk rivers. Rock Creek Lake and State Park are here, as is Neal Smith National Wildlife Refuge. • One of eight counties named for Sgt. William Jasper (?–1779), Revolutionary War hero. • 1846 from Mahaska County • Writer Emerson Hough • Hogs, cattle, poultry, corn, oats; bituminous-coal deposits; manufacture of washing machines, farm and road-building machinery, dairy foods (especially blue cheese) • The washing machine industry began in 1898 in Newton with the manufacture of ratchet-slat washers. It was also in Newton that Frederick L. Maytag invented a "hand power" washing machine in 1907 and a motor-driven one in 1911, both revolutionizing the industry.

JEFFERSON *Fairfield* •16,181 • 435 • Southeastern IA; drained by the Skunk River and Cedar Creek • One of twenty-six counties named directly or indirectly for President Thomas Jefferson • 1839 (prior to statehood) from Indian lands • Hogs, cattle, poultry, corn, soybeans, hay; coal mines, limestone quarries; manufacture of dairy products, feed, washing machines, farm equipment, textiles, gray and malleable iron castings; education (Maharishi U. of Management).

JOHNSON (one of twelve counties so named) *Iowa City* • 111,006 (the fifth most populated county in IA) • 614 • Eastern IA; drained by the Iowa River. This prairieland county includes Lake Macbride State Park in the north. Coralville Reservoir (on the Iowa River) is north of Iowa City. • One of five counties named for Col. Richard Mentor Johnson (1780–1850), officer in the War of 1812, U.S. senator from KY and U.S. vice president • 1837 (prior to statehood) from Des Moines County • Iowa City was the capital of IA Territory from 1841 to 1846, and capital of the state from 1846 to 1857. Thousands of Mormons used the Coralville area as a departure point on their journey west in the 1850s. In the summer of 1856, in particular, 1,300 Mormons bound for Utah built handcarts here for their goods before leaving the county on foot. • Astronomer Allan Rex Sandage. Artist Grant Wood died here. • Corn, soybeans, hogs, cattle, poultry; limestone quarrying; small, light manufacturing, including adhesive paper, toothbrushes, toiletries; education (U. of IA; its presence in Iowa City has influenced the growth of the city as a cultural center.) • Iowa City claims to have elected the world's first woman mayor, Emma Harvat, in 1922. The city is the headquarters of the state historical society and the state geological survey. Also here are a Veterans Administration hospital, a psychopathic hospital, a hospital for handicapped children, and the state bacteriological laboratory.

JONES (one of six counties so named) *Anamosa* • 20,221 • 575 • Eastern IA; drained by the Wapsipinicon River, and the North and South Forks of the Maquoketa River. Wapsipinicon State Park is in the west. Searryl's Cave State Preserve is also here. • Named for George W. Jones (1804–96), surveyor of public lands for WI and IA territories and one of IA's first two U.S. senators • 1837 (prior to statehood) from Wisconsin Territory • The county lay at the heart of the "Black Hawk Purchase." Following the Black Hawk War, a treaty was made in 1832 with the Sac and Fox Indians, opening land west of the Mississippi for settlement. • Painter Grant Wood (Memorial Park and Art Festival in June) • Cattle, hogs, poultry, corn, oats; limestone quarries, sand and gravel pits • Anamosa is the self-proclaimed "Pumpkin Capital of Iowa" with a pumpkinfest each October.

KEOKUK *Sigourney* • 11,400 • 579 • Southeastern IA; drained by the Skunk River, the North and South Skunk rivers, and the English River. • Named for Keokuk (1780–1848), appointed chief of the Sauk tribe by General Winfield Scott • 1843. A different Keokuk County was created in 1837 and abolished in 1840. • Widespread river flooding occurred here in 1993. • Hogs, cattle, sheep, poultry, corn, oats; limestone quarries, clay pits.

KOSSUTH *Algona* • 17,163 • 973 (the largest county in IA) • Northern IA, bounded on the north by the MN state line; drained by the East Fork of the Des Moines River, the Blue Earth River, and Union Slough. The county lies in part of the Iowa lakes district; it is characterized by rolling prairie. Ambrose A. Call State Park and Union Slough National Wildlife Refuge are here. • Named for Lajos Kossuth (1802–94), foremost Hungarian resistance leader against Austrian domination • 1851 from Webster • The county experienced widespread flooding in 1993. • Cattle, hogs, poultry, corn, oats, soybeans; sand and gravel.

LEE (one of twelve counties so named) *Fort Madison and Keokuk* • 38,052 • 517 • Extreme southeastern IA, bounded on the northeast by the Skunk River, on the east by the Mississippi River (forming the IL state line), and on the south by the Des Moines River (forming the MO state line). Lock and Dam No. 19 is at Keokuk. Part of Shimek State Forest is in the west. • Named for either Albert M. Lea (1808–?), a surveyor of the Des Moines River who mapped the Iowa District; or for William E. Lee, an official of the New York Land Company, which had extensive landholdings in the area • 1836 (prior to statehood) from Des Moines County • Fort Madison was founded as a military post in 1808. After repeated attacks by Indians led by Chief Black Hawk, it was burned in 1813. A permanent settlement was established here in 1838, making Fort Madison one of IA's oldest cities. • Columnist Elsa Maxwell • Hogs, cattle, poultry, sheep, corn, oats, soybeans; limestone quarries, coal deposits; food processing and packaging; manufacture of rubber products, steel casings, fabricated metal products, paper, waxed paper products, paints, industrial brushes, corrugated board and containers, truck and trailer vans, pens. The IA state penitentiary (established in 1839) is in the county. • The *George M. Verity*, a stern-wheeler, has been turned into a popular riverboat museum at Keokuk. The only national cemetery in IA is located in the county.

LINN *Cedar Rapids* • 191,701 (the second most populated county in IA) • 717 • Eastern IA; drained by the Cedar and Wapsipinicon rivers, and Buffalo Creek. The county includes Palisades-Kepler State Park, built by the Civilian Conservation Corps in the 1930s with many original stone buildings still standing. Pleasant Creek State Recreation Area is on the western border. • One of four counties named for Lewis F. Linn (1795–1843), U.S. senator from MO • 1837 (prior to statehood) from Wisconsin Territory • Novelist and critic Carl Van Vechten. Aerodynamicist Alexander M. Lippisch died here. • Hogs, cattle, poultry, corn, oats; limestone quarries, sand and gravel pits; agriculture-related industry, including cereal production, meat packaging, stock feed production, manufacture of milk-processing machinery, farm implements; education (Coe College; Mount Mercy College) • Cornell College in Mount Vernon was the first institution of higher education in IA to admit women and the only college in the U.S. to have its entire campus listed in the National Register of Historic Places. The large Quaker Oats plant in Cedar Rapids is a riverside landmark. Cedar Rapids' Masonic Library and Grand Lodge Office Building houses one of the world's largest collections of Masonic material.

LOUISA (one of two counties so named, the other in VA) *Wapello* • 12,183 • 402 • Southeastern IA, bounded on the east by the Mississippi River (forming the IL state line). The eastern section of the county between the Iowa and Mississippi rivers is artificially drained. Mark Twain National Wildlife Refuge is here, as is Toolesboro Indian Mounds. Lock and

Dam No. 17 is above Toolesburg. • Named for Louisa Massey, pioneer heroine who shot and wounded her brother's murderer • 1836 (prior to statehood) from Des Moines County • Cattle, hogs, poultry, corn, oats, wheat, soybeans; gypsum and limestone quarries.

LUCAS *Chariton* • 9,422 • 431 • Southern IA; drained by the Chariton River and White Breast Creek. Red Haw State Park is in the southeast. Two units of Stephens State Forest are located here. • One of two counties (the other in OH) named for Robert Lucas (1781–1853), governor of OH and first territorial governor of IA • 1846 from Monroe • Hogs, cattle, poultry, corn, hay; bituminous-coal deposits.

LYON (one of five counties so named) *Rock Rapids* • 11,763 • 588 • Extreme northwestern IA, bounded on the north by the MN and SD state lines, and on the west by the Big Sioux River (forming the SD state line); drained by the Rock and Little Rock rivers. Gitchee Manitou State Preserve is in the northwest. • One of four counties named for General Nathaniel Lyon (1818–61), Union commander in the Civil War, killed in the Battle of Wilson's Creek • Established as Buncombe County, 1851 from Woodbury; name changed 1862. • Sheep, hogs, cattle, poultry, corn, oats.

MADISON *Winterset* • 14,019 • 561 • South-central IA; drained by the North and Middle rivers. Pammel State Park and Badger Creek State Recreation Area are here. • One of twenty counties named directly or indirectly for President James Madison • 1846 • Actor John Wayne (birthplace site). Winterset's George Washington Carver Memorial Park honors the scientist who resided here for two years. • Hogs, cattle, corn, soybeans; bituminous-coal deposits, clay, limestone • The county, popularized in Robert James Wallers' novel *The Bridges of Madison County*, is home to the Madison County Covered Bridge Festival, which celebrates the six historic covered bridges located here. The last remaining Woman's Relief Corps Hall in Iowa is located in Macksburg. The red Delicious apple was developed on an orchard near East Peru in the 1880s.

MAHASKA *Oskaloosa* • 22,335 • 571 • South-central IA; drained by the Des Moines, North and South Skunk rivers. The county includes Lake Keomah State Park. • Named for Mahaska (1784–1834), a chief of the Iowa tribe • 1843 (prior to statehood) from Indian lands • Hogs, cattle, sheep, poultry, corn, oats, hay; bituminous-coal deposits, limestone quarries; education (William Penn U.) • The county seat Oskaloosa was named for one of Chief Mahaska's wives. • The Nelson Pioneer Farm and Museum is north of Oskaloosa.

MARION *Knoxville* • 32,052 • 554 • South-central IA; drained by the South Skunk and Des Moines rivers, and by White Breast Creek. It includes Sunset ski area and Lake Red Rock reservoir (Des Moines River), with Elk Rock State Park encompassing the reservoir. • One of seventeen counties named for General Francis Marion (?–1795), SC soldier and legislator, known as "The Swamp Fox" for his tactics during the Revolutionary War • 1845 (prior to statehood) from Washington County • There was widespread flooding along its rivers in 1993. • Hogs, cattle, poultry, sheep, corn; bituminous-coal mines, some limestone quarries; education (Central College) • Dixie Cornell Gebhart of Knoxville designed the Iowa State Flag. The Sprint Car National Championship Races are held every August in Knoxville on one of the fastest half mile dirt tracks in the U.S. The National Sprint Car Hall of Fame and Museum is also here.

MARSHALL (one of twelve counties so named) *Marshalltown* • 39,311 • 572 • Central IA; drained by the Iowa and North Skunk rivers. • One of eight counties named for John Marshall (1755–1835), Chief Justice of the U.S. • 1846 from Jasper • Professional baseball player Adrian "Cap" Anson • Cattle, hogs, poultry, corn, oats; bituminous-coal deposits, limestone quarries; manufacture of control valves, heating and air conditioning equipment, die castings, lawn mowers, farm equipment. • Marshalltown is the site of the Wolfe Eye Clinic, renowned for corrective eye treatment.

MILLS (one of two counties so named, the other in TX) *Glenwood* • 14,547 • 437 • Southwestern IA, bounded on the west by the Missouri River (forming the NE state line); drained by the West Nishnabotna River, and by Keg and Silver creeks. Part of the Loess Hills Scenic Byway runs through the county. • Named for Major Frederick D. Mills (?–1847), IA officer killed in the Battle of Churubusco during the Mexican War • 1851 from Pottawattamie • Mormons established several temporary settlements in the county on their journey from Nauvoo, IL to Utah. John Brown, the abolitionist, often delivered runaway slaves to Hoyt House, near present-day Hastings. • Hogs, cattle, poultry, corn, oats; bituminous-coal deposits.

MITCHELL (one of five counties so named) *Osage* • 10,874 • 469 • Northern IA, bounded on the north by the MN state line; drained by the Wapsipinicon, Cedar, and Little Cedar rivers. • Named by Irish settlers for John Mitchell (1815–75), Irish journalist and patriot who was imprisoned for helping to lead a revolt against Britain and who escaped to the U.S. in 1853 • 1851 from Chickasaw • Dairying, cattle, hogs, corn, hay; limestone quarries, sand, clay and gravel pits.

MONONA *Onawa* • 10,020 • 693 • Western IA, bounded on the west by the Missouri River (forming the NE state line); drained by the Little Sioux, Maple, and Soldier rivers. Blue Lake, an oxbow lake of the Missouri River, is in the west. Lewis and Clark State Park is on the northern end of Blue Lake near the Missouri River. Preparation Canyon State Park and Loess Hills State Forest are in the south. • The county's name is an Indian word meaning "unknown" • 1851 from Harrison • The county lost territory to Burt County, NE in 1943. • Corn, hogs, cattle, poultry; bituminous-coal deposits, sand and gravel pits. • The Loess Hills Visitor Center in the heart of the Loess Hills (formed by windblown dust after the Ice Age) is located in Moorhead.

MONROE *Albia* • 8,016 • 433 • Southern IA. A unit of Stephens State Forest is in the northwest. • One of seventeen counties named for President James Monroe • Established as Kishkekosh in 1843 (prior to statehood) from Wapello; name changed 1846 • Writer James F. Stevens • Hogs, cattle, poultry, sheep, corn, oats, hay; coal-mining.

MONTGOMERY (one of eighteen counties so named) *Red Oak* • 11,771 • 424 • Southwestern IA; drained by the East Nishnabotna and West Nodaway rivers, and by Tarkio and Walnut creeks. Viking Lake State Park is in the southeast. • One of sixteen counties named directly or indirectly for General Richard Montgomery (1738–75), American Revolutionary War officer who captured Montreal, Canada • 1851 from Polk • Hogs, cattle, corn, wheat, oats; bituminous-coal deposits • The Thomas D. Murphy Company, one of the largest manufacturers of art calendars in the U.S., was located in Red Oak. Stanton, the "Swedish Capital of Iowa," features the world's largest coffee pot (a water tower in this shape). In 1946, a Saturday Evening Post article ranked casualties sustained by citizens of Red Oak during World War II among the highest (per capita) in the U.S.

MUSCATINE *Muscatine* • 41,722 • 439 • Southeastern IA, bounded on the southeast by the Mississippi River (forming the IL state line); drained by the Cedar River. Wildcat Den State Park and Fairport State Recreation Area are here. Lock and Dam No. 16 is at Muscatine. • Named for Muscatine Island, Iowa • 1836 (prior to statehood) from Des Moines County • Muscatine, formerly called the "Pearl Button Capital of the World," was the largest freshwater pearl button manufacturing center anywhere, its buttons fashioned from Mississippi River mussel shells. • Humorist Ellis Parker Butler • Sheep, hogs, cattle, poultry, corn, melons, vegetables, soybeans; limestone, sand and gravel pits, bituminous-coal deposits; manufacture of buttons, food products, industrial alcohol, fertilizers, plastics, metal products. • Muscatine Island is noted for its experimental farm, operated by Iowa State University.

O'BRIEN *Primghar* • 15,102 • 573 • Northwestern IA; drained by the Little Sioux and Floyd rivers. The county includes Mill Creek State Park. • Named for William S. O'Brien (1803–64), leader of the Irish rebellion of 1848 • 1851 from Cherokee • Attorney Joseph N. Welch • Cattle, sheep, poultry, corn, oats, barley.

OSCEOLA *Sibley* • 7,003 • 399 • Northwestern IA, bounded on the north by the MN state line; drained by the Ocheyedan River and Otter Creek. The county includes the highest spot in the state six miles northeast of Sibley (1,670 feet). Iowa and Rush lakes are in the northeast. • One of three counties named for Osceola (?–1838), Seminole leader during the early years of the Second Seminole War • 1851 from Woodbury • Hogs, cattle, poultry, corn, oats, soybeans.

PAGE (one of two counties so named; the other in VA) *Clarinda* • 16,976 • 535 • Southwestern IA, bounded on the south by the MO state line; drained by the East and West Nodaway, and East Nishnabotna rivers and by West Tarkio and Tarkio creeks. • Named for Captain John Page (?–1846), killed at the Battle of Palo Alto during the Mexican War • 1847 from Pottawattamie • Composer and trombonist Glenn Miller • Corn, hogs, cattle, poultry; bituminous-coal deposits.

PALO ALTO *Emmetsburg* • 10,147 • 564 • Northern IA; drained by the Des Moines and Lizard rivers. Virgin, Silver, and Rush lakes are near the western boundary. Five Island Lake is northeast of Emmetsburg. Lost Island Prairie Wetland Nature Center is on the northern end of Lost Island Lake. • Named for the battle of Palo Alto in 1846 • 1851 from Kossuth • Cattle, hogs, poultry, corn, oats, soybeans; sand and gravel pits.

PLYMOUTH (one of two counties so named, the other in MA) *Le Mars* • 24,849 • 864 (the fourth largest county in IA) • Northwestern IA, bounded on the west by the Big Sioux River, forming the SD state line; drained by the Floyd River and the West Fork of the Little Sioux River. A portion of the Loess Hills Scenic Byway runs through the county. • Named for New England's Plymouth colony • 1851 from Woodbury • In the 1880s, the sons of English aristocrats were sent to the Le Mars area to learn farming and to keep out of trouble. In 1933, Judge Charles Bradley was kidnapped and almost lynched by farmers angry over foreclosures. • Anthropologist Clyde Kluckhorn • Area, cattle, hogs, poultry, sheep, corn, oats, barley; sand and gravel.

POCAHONTAS *Pocahontas* • 8,662 • 578 • North-central IA; drained by the Lizard River and Cedar Creek. Kalsow Prairie State Preserve, comprising one of the few remaining tracts of virgin land in the state, is in the southeast. • One of two counties (the other in WV) named for the daughter (?–1617) of chief Powhatan who prevented the execution of Captain John Smith. • 1851 from Humboldt and Greene • The Battle of Pilot Creek, a skirmish pitting the Sioux against the Winnebagos in 1859, was the last Indian battle in IA. • Cattle, hogs, poultry, corn, oats, soybeans; coal deposits • A twenty-five-foot statue of Pocahontas, erected in 1956, towers over its namesake town.

POLK (one of twelve counties so named) *Des Moines* • 374,601 (the most populated county in IA) • 569 • Central IA; drained by the Des Moines River (forming part of the southeastern boundary), Raccoon and Skunk rivers, and by Beaver Creek. Saylorville Lake Reservoir and Dam, and Big Creek and Walnut Woods state parks are here. • One of eleven counties named for President James K. Polk • 1846 from Indian lands • Established first as Fort Des Moines in 1843 to protect the rights of the Sauk and Fox Indians, the city developed as a military training center, especially during the two world wars. The Women's Army Corps (WAC) was founded here in 1942. Des Moines has been the capital of IA since 1857. The city expanded rapidly from 1910 to 1920 because of the development of local coal deposits. • Public relations consultant Carl Byoir; zoologist Libbie Henrietta Hyman; communications engineer John Robinson Pierce • Hogs, cattle, poultry, corn, soybeans, oats; manufacture of machinery, food products, fabricated metal goods, glass products, tires, farm implements; insurance; printing and publishing (especially farm journals); bituminous-coal mining; government operations; education (Drake U.; Grand View College) • The Iowa State Fair Grounds is in Des Moines. Living History Farms in Urbandale traces the history of agriculture through several working farms from different periods.

POTTAWATTAMIE *Council Bluffs* • 87,704 • 954 (the second largest county in IA) • Southwestern IA, bounded on the west by the Missouri River, forming the NE state line; drained by the East and West Nishnabotna rivers, and by Silver and Walnut creeks. The western part of the county constitutes part of the Omaha, NE metropolitan area. The county contains Lake Manawa and part of Wilson Island state parks. • One of three counties named for the Potawatomi Indian tribe • 1848 from Indian lands • The Lewis and Clark expedition passed through the area in 1804. The explorers held a powwow with the Indians at a place called Council Hill or Council Bluff. (A monument commemorates the meeting.) The original site of Council Bluffs was settled by Mormons in 1846. The city was designated by Abraham Lincoln as the eastern terminus of the Union Pacific Railroad following a visit here in 1859. (A granite monument marks the spot where the declaration was made.) Major flooding of the county's rivers occurred in 1993. • Inventor and broadcasting pioneer Lee De Forest; educator Nathan Pusey; silent screen actor Harry Langdon. Civil engineer Grenville M. Dodge, Potawatomi Indian chief Sauganash, and reformer Amelia Bloomer died here. • Oats, corn, cattle, hogs; bituminous-coal deposits; manufacture of cast-iron pipe, furniture, playground equipment. • Part of the county (containing the town of Carter Lake) is actually located on the NE side of the Missouri River, having been cut off from the rest of IA by a change in the course of the Missouri River. The Pottawattamie County Jail, which operated from 1885 until 1969, incorporated unique pie-shaped cells that rotated around a central core to align with a single door on each floor.

POWESHIEK *Montezuma* • 18,815 • 585 • Central IA; drained by the English and North Skunk rivers. Fun Valley ski area is here. • Named for the Fox Indian chief (1797–?) • 1843 (prior to statehood) from Keokuk, Iowa, Johnson, and Mahaska • Hogs, cattle, poultry, corn, oats, hay; bituminous-coal deposits; manufacture of gloves and shoes; education (Grinnell College). • It was Horace Greeley's famous advice to Josiah Bushnell Grinnell, "Go West, young man, go West and grow up with the country!" that propelled the Congregationalist minister in 1854 to move to the county and establish the town of Grinnell here.

RINGGOLD *Mount Ayr* • 5,469 • 538 • Southern IA, bounded on the south by the MO state line; drained by the West Fork of Big Creek, by the Platte River, and the Grand River and its Middle and East forks. • Named for Major

Samuel Ringgold (1800–1846), officer in the Seminole War and the Mexican War • 1847 from Taylor • Hogs, cattle, poultry, corn, oats; bituminous-coal deposits; fish hatchery.

SAC *Sac City* • 11,529 • 576 • Western IA; drained by the North Raccoon and Boyer rivers. Black Hawk Lake State Park is here. • Named for the Sauk Indians • 1851 from Greene • Cattle, hogs, corn, oats; gravel pits, coal deposits.

SCOTT (one of eleven counties so named) *Davenport* • 158,668 • 458 • Eastern IA, bounded on the east and south by the Mississippi River (forming the IL state line) and on the north in part by the Wapsipinicon River. Buffalo Bill Cody Homestead is here. Lock and Dam No. 15 is at Davenport; Lock and Dam No. 14 is below Le Claire. Davenport is the largest of the Quad-Cities and the only one in IA. Cameron Woods State Preserve and part of the Upper Mississippi River National Wildlife and Fish Refuge are here. • One of five counties named for General Winfield Scott (1786–1866), officer in the War of 1812 and the Mexican-American War • 1837 (prior to statehood) from Wisconsin Territory • Settled in 1808, the area was the scene of several battles with Indians. A treaty signed with Chief Black Hawk in 1832 opened the county for settlement. The first railroad bridge across the Mississippi was opened in 1856. The county experienced severe flood damage along its rivers in 1993. • Jazz cornetist Bix Beiderbecke; novelist and poet George C. Cook; buffalo hunter and showman "Buffalo Bill Cody" (museum); dramatist and novelist Susan Glaspell; biologist Robert A. Harper; scholar Paul Shorey. Film actor Cary Grant died here. • Hogs, cattle, poultry, corn, oats; manufacture of clothing, airplane parts and accessories, tractor parts, wheels, iron and steel, industrial timers, cement, wood products, flour and meat products; coal deposits, limestone quarries; education (Marycrest International U.; Palmer College of Chiropractic [the first college of its kind]; St. Ambrose U.) One of the world's largest aluminum rolling mills is here. • The Davenport Municipal Art Gallery has a notable collection of paintings by Iowan Grant Wood.

SHELBY *Harlan* • 13,173 • 591 • Western IA; drained by the West Nishnabotna River and by Pigeon, Silver, and Mosquito creeks. Prairie Rose State Park is in the south • One of nine counties named directly or indirectly for General Isaac Shelby (1750–1826), officer in the Revolutionary War and first governor of Kentucky • 1851 from Cass • Cattle, hogs, poultry, corn, alfalfa; bituminous-coal deposits • The only authentic Danish windmill outside of Denmark is located in Elk Horn.

SIOUX (one of three counties so named) *Orange City* • 31,589 • 768 • Northwestern IA, bounded on the west by the Big Sioux River (forming the SD state line); drained by the Rock River, the Floyd River, and its west branch. Oak Grove State Park is in the west. • One of five counties named for the Sioux Indians, also known as the Dakota • 1851 from Plymouth • Television evangelist Robert Schuller • Hogs, cattle, poultry, corn, oats, hay; education (Dordt College; Northwestern College).

STORY *Nevada* • 79,981 • 573 • Central IA; drained by the South Skunk River and Indian Creek. • Named for Joseph Story (1779–1845), representative from MA and U.S. Supreme Court justice • 1846 from Jasper, Polk, and Boone • Evangelist Billy Sunday • Hogs, cattle, poultry, corn, oats, soybeans; manufacturing; limestone quarries, sand and gravel pits, bituminous-coal deposits; education (IA State U. of Science and Technology — its College of Veterinary Medicine [1879] the oldest in the U.S.). Ames is the headquarters of the IA State Highway Commission, the National Animal Disease Center, the Ames Laboratory, and other federal and state institutions. • Story City's Story Theatre is the oldest continuously operating theatre in the state (established in 1913). Cambridge was home in 1855 to the largest group of Norwegians to come to IA, all members of the Norwegian Lutheran Church.

TAMA *Toledo* • 18,103 • 721 • Central IA; drained by the Iowa River and Wolf Creek. The county has several parks, including Union Grove State Park and Casey's Paha State Preserve. Sac and Fox/Meskwaki Indian Reservation is here. • Named for the chief of the Fox Indians • 1843 (prior to statehood) from Boone and Benton • Hogs, cattle, poultry, corn, oats, soybeans.

TAYLOR (one of seven counties so named) *Bedford* • 6,958 • 534 • Southwestern IA, bounded on the south by the MO state line; drained by the One Hundred and Two, Platte, and East Nodaway rivers. Lake of Three Fires State Park is in the county. • One of four counties named for President Zachary Taylor • 1847 from Page • Corn, hogs, hay, cattle, poultry.

UNION (One of eighteen counties so named) *Creston* • 12,309 • 424 • Southern IA; drained by the Platte and Thompson rivers. Summit Lake and Twelve Mile Lake reservoirs, and Green Valley State Park are in the county. • Probably named for the preservation of America's union of states • 1851 from Clarke • Hogs, cattle, poultry, corn, oats; bituminous-coal deposits.

VAN BUREN *Keosauqua* • 7,809 • 485 • Southeastern IA, bounded on the south by the MO state line; drained by the Des Moines River (forming part of the southeastern boundary) and Fox River. Lacey-Keosauqua State Park is here, as are units of Shimek State Forest. • One of four counties named for President Martin Van Buren • 1836 (prior to statehood) from Des Moines County • Hogs, cattle, sheep, poultry, corn, soybeans, hay; bituminous-coal mines, limestone quarries.

WAPELLO *Ottumwa* • 36,051 • 432 • Southeastern IA; drained by the Des Moines River and Cedar Creek. • Named for Wapello (1787–1842), a Fox Indian chief who figured prominently in the signing of several treaties; his gravesite is at Agency. • 1843 (prior to statehood) from Indian lands • Following a disastrous flood in 1947, Ottumwa regained its position as a commercial and manufacturing center through a locally financed program of self-help called "Operation Bootstrap." • Hogs, sheep, cattle, poultry, corn, soybeans, wheat; bituminous-coal mines; meat packing; manufacture of farm

equipment, automotive products, electronic components, materials-handling equipment • The Air Power Museum, southwest of Ottumwa, displays more than twenty antique airplanes, artifacts from the early days of aviation, and several hundred model airplanes. The "American Gothic" house in the southeast.

WARREN *Indianola* • 40,671 • 572 • South-central IA, bounded on the northeast by the Des Moines River; drained by the North, South and Middle rivers. Lake Ahquabi State Park is here. • One of fourteen counties named for Dr. Joseph Warren (1741–75), Revolutionary War patriot and member of the Committee of Safety who sent Paul Revere on his famous ride. • 1846 from Polk • Cattle, hogs, poultry, corn, oats; bituminous-coal deposits; feed milling; manufacture of pickup campers; education (Simpson College) • Indianola is the site of the National Balloon Museum and the National Hot Air Balloon Championship, held each August.

WASHINGTON *Washington* • 20,670 • 569 • Southeastern IA, bounded on the northeast by the Iowa River; drained by the Skunk and English rivers. Lake Darling State Park is here. • One of thirty-one counties named for President George Washington • Created in 1837 from Wisconsin Territory as Slaughter. Name changed in 1839. • Hogs, cattle, poultry, corn, oats • Riverside is the future birthplace of Star Trek's James T. Kirk.

WAYNE (one of sixteen counties so named) *Corydon* • 6,730 • 526 • Southern IA, bounded on the south by the MO state line; drained by a branch of the Chariton River. Bobwhite State Park is here. • One of fifteen counties named for Gen. "Mad Anthony" Wayne (1745–96), Revolutionary War soldier from PA and statesman • 1846 from Appanoose • Hogs, sheep, cattle, poultry, corn, soybeans, oats; bituminous-coal deposits.

WEBSTER *Fort Dodge* • 40,235 •715 • Central IA; drained by the Des Moines and Lizard rivers. Dolliver Memorial State Park, Brushy Creek State Recreation Area, and Woodman Hollow State Preserve are all in the southeast. • One of eight counties named for Daniel Webster (1782–1852), U.S. statesman and orator from MA. Iowa legislators chose this name to counter the naming of a neighboring county for John C. Calhoun, Webster's political foe. • 1853 from Yell and Risley counties, both of which were organized in 1851 and abolished in 1853. • The county experienced widespread flooding in 1993. • Cattle, hogs, poultry, corn, soybeans, hay; meat packing; gypsum bed (one of the world's largest), coal deposits, clay, sand and gravel; manufacture of farm machinery, chemical fertilizer, feeds, soybean products, brick and tile • Gypsum quarried near Fort Dodge was used to carve the infamous Cardiff Giant in 1869. The petrified man hoax fooled thousands of visitors to Cardiff, New York. Fort Dodge Historical Museum, Fort Museum and Frontier Village all have pioneer exhibits.

WINNEBAGO (one of three counties so named) *Forest City* • 11,723 • 400 • Northern IA, bounded on the north by the

MN state line; drained by the Winnebago River. Lake Harmon is in the north; Rice Lake and Rice Lake State Park are on the eastern boundary. Pilot Knob State Park is on the southern boundary. • Named for the Winnebago Indians • 1847 from Kossuth • Writer Wallace Stegner • Hogs, poultry, corn, oats; sand and gravel pits.

WINNESHIEK *Decorah* • 21,310 • 690 • Northeastern IA, bounded on the north by the MN state line; drained by the Upper Iowa and Turkey rivers. Fort Atkinson and Malanaphy Springs State preserves and Nor-Ski Runs ski area are located here. • Named for the Winnebago chief (1812–?) who participated in the Black Hawk War. • 1847 from Indian lands • Mathematician Oswald Veblen • Hogs, cattle, poultry, corn, oats, hay, dairying; limestone quarrying; education (Luther College) • The World's Smallest Church is at Festina. The county has an eclectic mix of museums, including the Norwegian-American, Bily Clock, and Laura Ingalls Wilder museums.

WOODBURY *Sioux City* • 103,877 • 873 (the third largest county in IA) • Western IA, bounded on the west by the Big Sioux River (which forms the SD state line) and the Missouri River (which forms the NE state line); drained by the Little Sioux River and its West Fork. The county contains Stone State Park. • Named for Levi Woodbury (1789–1851), governor of NH, U.S. secretary of the navy, U.S. secretary of the treasury and U.S. Supreme Court justice • Created as Wahkaw in 1851 from Indian lands; named changed 1853. • The site of Sioux City was visited in 1804 by the Lewis and Clark expedition. Sergeant Charles Floyd, the trip's only fatality, was buried here, the spot commemorated by the nation's first historic landmark. The area was settled by Theophile Bruguier, a French-Canadian trader, who arrived in 1849 with his Sioux Indian wives and their father Chief War Eagle (his gravesite here). With the arrival of the railroad and growth of its local meat packing industry in the 1870s, Sioux City grew rapidly and by 1920 had reached a population of more than 70,000. The city was a supply center and departure point for miners in the Black Hills of SD and for settlers bound for the Northwest in the mid 19th century. • Statistician and educator W. Edwards Deming; New Deal administrator Harry Hopkins; advice columnists Ann Landers and Abigail Van Buren • Hogs, cattle, corn, oats, barley; meat packing, food processing; manufacture of fabricated metals, machinery; education (Briar Cliff College; Morningside College).

WORTH *Northwood* • 7,909 • 400 • Northern IA, bounded on the north by the MN state line; drained by the Shell Rock River. Silver Lake is in the northwest, and Rice Lake and Rice Lake State Park are on the western border. • One of three counties named for General William J. Worth (1794–1849), officer in the War of 1812, Seminole War, and Mexican War • 1851 from Mitchell • Hogs, cattle, poultry, corn, oats, soybeans, dairying.

WRIGHT (one of three counties so named) *Clarion* • 14,334 • 581 • North-central IA; drained by the West Branch of the Iowa and Boone rivers. The county contains Morse, Cornelia, Elm, and Wall lakes. • Named for Joseph A. Wright (1810–67), IN governor; and for Silas Wright (1795–1847), U.S. senator from NY and governor of NY • 1851 from Webster • There was widespread flooding here in 1993. • Livestock, corn, oats, soybeans, grain; bituminous-coal, sand and gravel pits.

KANSAS

To the Stars Through Difficulties

Each of Kansas' 105 counties is governed by a board of commissioners consisting of three or five members. Each commissioner is elected from a separate district and serves a four-year term. Other county officials include the county clerk, register of deeds, sheriff, county attorney, and treasurer. The four most populous counties have an election commissioner, as well.

ALLEN (one of five counties so named) *Iola* • 14,385 • 503 • Southeastern KS; drained by the Neosho River. • Named for William Allen (1803–79), U.S. senator from OH and governor of OH • Original county; organized 1855 (prior to statehood) • Professional baseball player Walter Johnson; Major Brig. General Frederick Fuson • Cattle, hogs, wheat, soybeans, sorghum, dairying, honey; manufacture of rubber and plastic products, cement, clothing, building materials, consumer goods, motor-vehicle parts; oil and gas fields • Iola has a Buster Keaton celebration each year. It is reputed to have the largest town square in the country.

ANDERSON (one of five counties so named) *Garnett* • 8,110 • 583 • Eastern KS; watered by Cedar Creek. The county contains Prairie Spirit Rail Trail. • Named for Joseph C. Anderson, a member of the first KS territorial legislature • Original county; organized 1855 (prior to statehood) • Poet and novelist Edward Lee Masters; publisher and politician Arthur

Capper • Cattle, grain, dairying, corn, soybeans, oats, wheat, sorghum; manufacture of clothing, fabricated metal, food processing; oil wells • Harry Houdini's escape from the Garnett town jail in 1897 helped to launch his career as an escape-artist.

ATCHISON *Atchison* • 16,774 • 432 • Northeastern KS, bounded on the east by the Missouri River (forming the MO state line); drained by the Delaware River. The county includes Atchison State Fishing Lake and the International Forest of Friendship. • Named for the town of Atchison, which was itself named for David Rice Atchison (1807–86), statesman and U.S. senator from MO (one of two counties, the other in MO, named directly or indirectly for Atchison) • Original county; organized 1855 (prior to statehood) • During the fight between free-soil and slavery parties for political control of "bleeding" KS, Atchison was headquarters for the pro-slavery group. The *Squatter Sovereign*, an anti-abolitionist journal, was published here. With the granting of a charter in 1859 for the Atchison and Topeka Railroad, Atchison became an important railroad town. • Aviator Amelia Earhart (museum) • Hogs, cattle, poultry, corn, wheat, oats, alfalfa, fruit, sorghum, soybeans, hay; oil; manufacture of industrial alcohol, textiles, flour and feed; education (Benedictine College).

BARBER *Medicine Lodge* • 5,307 • 1,134 • Southern KS, bounded on the south by the OK state line; drained by the Medicine Lodge River and the Salt Fork of the Arkansas River. Barber State Fishing Lake is in the northeast. The county lies in the Red Hills region of the state. Gypsum Hills is a scenic area of canyons, towering mesas, and buttes. • The county was given this name as a memorial to Thomas W. Barber (?–1855), a Free State martyr, murdered near Lawrence, KS • Organized as Barbour 1867 from Harper; spelling changed 1883 • Plains Indians peacefully shared a "lodge" on the site that was to become Medicine Lodge. Here in 1867 the Five Tribes met with U.S. commissioners, and a treaty was negotiated that fixed the boundary between KS and Indian Territory. Temperance activist Carry Nation lived in Medicine Lodge (memorial), and attacked her first saloon here with an umbrella. • Cattle, wheat, sorghum; gas, gypsum mines.

BARTON (one of two counties so named, the other in MO) *Great Bend* • 28,205 • 894 • Central KS; drained by the Arkansas River and Cow Creek. Pawnee Rock State Historic Site is in the southwest corner. • Named for Clara Barton (1821–1912), Civil War nurse and founder of the American Red Cross (the only KS county named for a woman) • 1867 from Ellsworth • The county lies in the alleged vicinity of the mythical city of Quivira sought by Francisco Coronado in the 16th century. It was visited by explorer Zebulon Pike and was a stopping point on the Santa Fe Trail. The Great Bend Army Airfield was a B-29 bomber training base during World War II. • Wheat, alfalfa, corn, cattle, poultry; food processing; extensive oil and natural-gas production • The Cheyenne Bottoms Preserve contains what is considered to be the largest

marsh in the interior of the U.S. and has been designated "Wetland of International Importance."

BOURBON (one of two counties so named, the other in KY) *Fort Scott* • 15,379 • 637 • Southeastern KS, bounded on the east by the MO state line; watered by the Marmaton and Little Osage rivers. Bourbon State Fishing Lake is here, as are Fort Scott National Historic Site and National Cemetery. • Named for Bourbon County, KY, former home of Samuel A. Williams, a member of the first Kansas legislature. • Original county; organized in 1855 (prior to statehood) • Fort Scott was established in 1842 as a base for the U.S. Army's peacekeeping efforts along the "permanent Indian frontier." In 1862, Congress established National Cemetery No. 1 in Fort Scott for those killed in the vicious struggle between pro- and anti-slavery groups in the late 1850s, and in the Civil War. • Photographer and filmmaker Gordon Parks • Cattle, hogs, corn, oats, wheat, soybeans, hay; manufacture of fabricated aluminum products, monuments, concrete, waterproofing material, clothing; meat packing; printing; gas, coal, limestone • In 1891, Fort Scott's public library was organized by poet and lawyer Eugene Fitch Ware who wrote under the name "Ironquill." The term "jay-hawker" was allegedly first used at the Free State Hotel in Fort Scott, when Pat Devlin referred to his harassment of pro-slavery farmers as "jayhawking."

BROWN (one of nine counties so named) *Hiawatha* • 10,724 • 571 • Northeastern KS, bounded on the north by the NE state line; watered by headstreams of the Delaware River. The county is situated in the Loess Hills region of the state. Kickapoo, Iowa, Sac and Fox Indian reservations are here. The county also includes Brown State Fishing Lake. • Probably for Orville H. Browne, a member of the 1855 KS territorial legislature. • Original county; organized as Browne in 1855 (prior to statehood). The "e" was left off the county seal by accident, and allowed to stand. • Wheat, sorghum, corn, soybeans, hay, cattle, hogs.

BUTLER (one of eight counties so named) *El Dorado* • 59,482 • 1,428 (the largest county in KS) • Southeastern KS, in the Flint Hills region; drained by the Walnut River. Butler State Fishing Lake is in the southeast. El Dorado Reservoir (with El Dorado State Park on its shore) is also here. • Named for Andrew P. Butler (1796–1857), jurist, and U.S. senator from SC • Original county; organized 1855 (prior to statehood) • There was a devastating tornado in Andover in 1991. • Newspaper editor William Allen White (who had his first job at a newspaper in El Dorado); Painter and sculptor Frederic Remington (who owned a sheep ranch near Whitewater). • Cattle, hogs, poultry, sorghum, soybeans, alfalfa, hay; manufacture of plastics, small arms, insulated doors and windows; oil and oil refineries. • The Great Osage Indian trail cuts across the county east-west. Near Potwin a sink hole appeared in 1937, growing to dimensions of 200 feet wide, 250 feet long, and 50 feet deep. The Old Frisco water tower is the last remaining wooden railroad water tower in KS.

CHASE (one of two counties so named, the other in NE) *Cottonwood Falls* • 3,030 • 776 • East-central KS; drained by the Cottonwood River. The county is located in the Flint Hills region of the state. Tallgrass Prairie National Preserve is north of centrally located Chase State Fishing Lake. • Named for Salmon P. Chase (1808–73), U.S. senator from OH, governor of OH, and Chief Justice of the U.S. • 1859 (prior to statehood) from Butler • Cottonwood Falls served as a shipping point for Texas cattle. • College football coach Knute Rockne died here. • Cattle, wheat, soybeans, hay, hogs, poultry.

CHAUTAUQUA (one of two counties so named, the other in NY) *Sedan* • 4,359 • 642 • Southeastern KS, bounded on the south by OK; drained by the Caney River. The county lies in the Osage Questas region of the state. • Named for Chautauqua County, NY, home of a member of the KS legislature • 1875 (prior to statehood) from Howard, which was organized in 1855, and abolished at the time of its division into Chautauqua and Elk counties • Circus clown Emmett Kelly • Cattle, hay, oats, wheat; oil and gas fields.

CHEROKEE *Columbus* • 22,605 • 587 • Extreme southeastern KS, bounded on the south by the OK state line and on the east by the MO state line; drained by the Spring and Neosho rivers, and Lightning Creek. The county lies in the Cherokee Lowlands region of the state. • One of eight counties named for the Indian tribe • 1855 as McGee County; the name was changed at some point in the 1860s. • In the late 1860s Baxter Springs was a major shipping point for longhorn cattle driven over trails from Texas. • Cattle, hogs, wheat, soybeans, apples, sorghum; textiles; mining of coal, lead, zinc; manufacture of mining supplies • Victims of the raid on the town of Baxter Springs by Confederate guerrillas under William Quantrill in 1863 are buried in Baxter Springs National Cemetery.

CHEYENNE *Saint Francis* • 3,165 • 1,020 • Extreme northwestern KS, bounded on the north by the NE state line and on the west by the CO state line; drained by the South Fork of the Republican River. Arikaree Breaks are in the northwest. St. Francis Sandpits State Fishing Lake is also here. • One of three counties named for the Cheyenne Indians • 1873 from Kirwin Land District • Barley, wheat, sheep, cattle, hogs • After his famous transatlantic flight, Charles Lindbergh flew over Bird City in the "Spirit of St. Louis" and dropped a note to his former aeronautics teacher Banty Rogers, who lived here.

CLARK (one of twelve counties so named) *Ashland* • 2,390 • 975 • Southern KS, bounded on the south by the OK state line; drained by the Cimarron River and Bluff Creek. The county is located in the Red Hills region. Big Basin Prairie Preserve is in the west. Clark State Fishing Lake is also here. • Named for Captain Charles F. Clarke (?–1862), Union officer in the Civil War. (The "e" was subsequently dropped.) • 1867; abolished in 1883; recreated in 1885 • Grain, wheat, sorghum, alfalfa, cattle.

CLAY (one of eighteen counties so named) *Clay Center* • 8,822 • 644 • Northern KS; drained by the Republican River. Part of Milford Lake reservoir is on the eastern border. • One of fifteen counties named for Henry Clay (1777–1852), U.S. senator from Kentucky, known as the "Great Pacificator" for his advocacy of compromise to avert national crises • Original county; organized 1857 (prior to statehood) • Wheat, sorghum, cattle, hogs, sheep, poultry, corn, soybeans.

CLOUD *Concordia* • 10,268 • 716 • Northern KS; drained by the Republican and Solomon rivers. • Named for William F. Cloud (1825–1905), who fought in the Mexican War, and for the Union Army in the Civil War. • Organized as Shirley County 1860 (prior to statehood) from unorganized territory; name changed 1867 • Wheat, cattle, hogs, sheep, sorghum, soybeans, alfalfa, hay, corn.

COFFEY *Burlington* • 8,865 • 630 • Eastern KS; drained by the Neosho River. John Redmond Reservoir, surrounded by Flint Hills National Wildlife Refuge, is in the northwestern quarter of the county. Wolf Creek Reservoir is also here. • Named for Col. Asbury M. Coffey (1804–1879), member of the first KS territorial legislature and later a Confederate officer • 1855 (prior to statehood) from Kiowa • Cattle, poultry, corn, wheat, sorghum, soybeans, hay, grain; manufacture of puppets and plush products.

COMANCHE *Coldwater* • 1,967 • 788 • Southern KS, bounded on the south by the OK state line; drained by the Salt Fork of the Arkansas River, the Cimarron River, and Mule and Bluff creeks. The county lies in the Red Hills region. • One of three counties named for the Comanche Indians • 1867 from Kiowa • Cattle, wheat, barley, alfalfa.

COWLEY *Winfield* • 36,291 • 1,126 • Southern KS, bounded on the south by the OK state line; drained in the west by the Arkansas and Walnut rivers. The county lies in the Flint Hills region. Cowley State Fishing Lake is in the south. • Named for Lieutenant Matthew Cowley (?–1864), a Union officer • Created in 1855 as Hunter; the name was changed after the Civil War • The county was the staging area for the 1893 settlement of the Cherokee Strip in Indian Territory (museum). A helium plant opened in Dexter in 1927. • Extensive oil and natural gas fields; cattle, hogs, sheep, wheat, sorghum, alfalfa, apples, hay; manufacture of plastic products, tile, gas burners, water cans, oil-field equipment, steel products; railroad repair shops; oil refining; flour milling, meat packing, food processing; education (Southwestern College) • Winfield places special emphasis on music in its schools.

CRAWFORD (one of eleven counties so named) *Girard* • 38,242 • 593 • Southeastern KS, bounded on the east by the MO state line. The county is located in the Osage Questas region of the state. Crawford State Park is in the north. • Named for Col. Samuel J. Crawford (1835–1913), Union army officer and governor of KS • 1867 from Bourbon and Cherokee • Wheat, cattle, sorghum, soybeans, corn, hay; manufacture of motor vehicles and equipment, coal-mining equipment, clay tile and pipe, plastic pipe, wallboard, polyethylene bags, ammonium nitrate; extensive coal deposits; education (Pittsburg State U.).

DECATUR *Oberlin* • 3,472 • 894 • Northwestern KS, bounded on the north by the NE state line; watered by Sappa, Prairie Dog, and Beaver creeks, and the North Fork of the Solomon River. • One of five counties named for Stephen F. Decatur (1779–1820), U.S. naval officer during the War of 1812 and in actions against the Barbary pirates near Tripoli • 1873 from Norton • The county was the scene of the last Indian raid on KS soil in 1878. • Wheat, sorghum, corn, alfalfa, cattle, hogs • Hardy young Russian thistle plants in the county were blown into Oberlin by strong winds in 1909 and buried houses under piles as high as twenty feet.

DICKINSON (one of three counties so named) *Abilene* • 19,344 • 848 • Central KS; drained by the Smoky Hill River. The county is situated in the Flint Hills region. An arm of Milford Lake Reservoir is in the northeast corner. • One of two counties named for Daniel S. Dickinson (1800–66), U.S. senator from NY • Original county; organized 1855 (prior to statehood) • The northern terminus of the Texas cattle drives, Abilene enjoyed its biggest year in 1871 when more than 5,000 cowboys driving 700,000 head over the Chisholm Trail arrived at the town's yards. Famed gunman Wild Bill Hickok served as Abilene's second marshal. • President Dwight D. Eisenhower (buried at Eisenhower Center) • Soybeans, alfalfa, sorghum, rye, wheat, cattle, sheep, poultry; light manufacturing, including machinery • For her axe-demolition of a local saloon, Carry Nation was pelted with eggs and run out of Enterprise by the women of the town who found her actions unladylike. Abilene claims the first use of the lunch wagon; when local restaurants were unable to serve the large number of cowboys who had descended upon the town, the cattle outfits' chuck wagons rolled into town.

DONIPHAN *Troy* • 8,249 • 392 • Extreme northeastern KS, bounded on the east and north by the Missouri River, forming the MO state line. The northeastern corner touches the NE border. The county lies in the Loess Hills region. The Native American Heritage Museum State Historic Site is east of Highland. • Named for Alexander W. Doniphan (1808–87), MO legislator and officer in the Mexican War • Original county; organized 1855 (prior to statehood) • Poultry, cattle, hogs, corn, wheat, strawberries, hay, dairying, apples (Troy has an Apple Blossom Festival each August.) • At one time Elwood was the largest city in Kansas Territory, but flooding from the Missouri river discouraged further growth.

DOUGLAS *Lawrence* • 99,962 (22.2% increase since 1990; the third fastest growing and fifth most populated county in KS) • 457 • Eastern KS, bounded on the north and drained by the Kansas (Kaw) River and by the Wakarusa River, which forms Clinton Lake. Clinton State Park is on its northern shore. The county also contains Douglas State Fishing Lake. • One of twelve counties named for Stephen A. Douglas

(1813–61), U.S. orator and statesman • Original county; organized 1855 (prior to statehood) • Lawrence, famed as the stronghold of the free-state, abolitionist movement in the KS-MO area before and during the Civil War, was founded by the New England Emigrant Aid Society, which encouraged abolitionists from the east to settle in KS. It was sacked in 1856 by pro-slavery militia. In 1863, 150 of its citizens were massacred by Confederate guerrillas under William C. Quantrill and the town razed. • Basketball inventor James A. Naismith died here. • Cattle, corn, sorghum, soybeans; limestone quarries; manufacturing; major education center (U. of KS; Baker U.; Haskell Indian Nations University — one of the oldest and largest Indian schools in the U.S.).

EDWARDS (one of three counties so named) *Kinsley* • 3,449 • 622 • South-central KS; drained by the Arkansas River and Rattlesnake Creek. • Probably named for William C. Edwards (1846–?), early KS lumberman • 1874 from Kiowa • Wheat, cattle, hogs, corn, soybeans, alfalfa; manufacture of power cylinders, concrete.

ELK (one of two counties so named, the other in PA) *Howard* • 3,261 • 648 • Southeastern KS; drained by Elk, Caney and Fall rivers. The county lies partly in the Flint Hills region. • Named for the Elk River • 1875 from Howard, which was organized in 1855 (named Godfrey and changed to Seward in 1867) and abolished at the time of its division into Chautauqua. • Cattle, oats, wheat, hay, corn; oil and natural-gas fields.

ELLIS (one of three counties so named) *Hays* • 27,507 • 900 • Central KS; drained by the Saline and Smoky Hill rivers, and Big Creek. The county lies in the Smoky Hills region of the state. Fort Hays State Historic Site is here. • Named for George Ellis (?–1854), KS infantryman killed during the Civil War • 1867 from unorganized territory • Automobile manufacture Walter P. Chrysler (home and museum); Wild Bill Hickok was elected sheriff of Ellis County in 1869. • Wheat, cattle, hogs; oil, natural gas; manufacture of granite products; education (Fort Hays State U.) • The Cathedral of the Plains (1909–1911) is in Victoria.

ELLSWORTH *Ellsworth* • 6,525 • 716 • Central KS; drained by the Smoky Hill River. The county lies in the Smoky Hills region of the state. Kanopolis Lake reservoir and Kanopolis State Park are here. Mushroom Rock State Park is also in the county. • Named for Fort Ellsworth, KS, itself named for Lieutenant Allen Ellsworth who supervised its construction. • 1867 from Saline • Cattle, sheep, hogs, winter wheat, sorghum, hay; manufacture of feed, industrial valves; oil and gas • Kanopolis was founded in 1886 by promoters who printed advertisements predicting a city of 150,000 by 1900. In 2000, the population was 543.

FINNEY *Garden City* • 40,523 (22.5% increase since 1990; the second fastest growing county in KS) • 1,300 (the second largest county in KS) • Southwestern KS; drained by the Arkansas and Pawnee rivers. Concannon and Finney state fishing lakes are here. • Named for David W. Finney (1839–?) lieutenant governor of KS and KS legislator • Organized as Sequoyah in 1873 from Arapahoe and Foote; name changed to Finney in 1883 • Wheat, sorghum, soybeans, alfalfa (also meal mills), sugar beets, cattle; meat packing, dairy food processing, machine shops, manufacture of masonry products, plastics, farm machinery, irrigation pipe; oil and natural gas. • The Lee Richardson Zoo in Garden City is the largest zoological park in Kansas. The Finney Game Refuge protects a large buffalo herd.

FORD (one of two counties so named, the other in IL) *Dodge City* • 32,458 • 1,099 • Southern KS; drained by the Arkansas River and Saw Log Creek. The county includes Hain and Ford state fishing lakes. • Named for James H. Ford (?–1867), Indian fighter and first commander of Fort Dodge • 1867 from unorganized territory • The county was the scene of large buffalo slaughters prior to the introduction of a thriving cattle industry here. As a primary shipping point for longhorn herds driven from Texas, Dodge City saw years in which as many as eight million head passed through. Lawlessness and gunfights necessitated a succession of marshals and sheriffs, including Bat Masterson and Wyatt Earp, and the establishment of Boot Hill Cemetery. Fort Dodge was built in 1864 to protect travelers and wagon trains on the Santa Fe Trail. • Wheat, sorghum, corn, soybeans, alfalfa, sugar beets, cattle; food processing, meat packing; manufacture of feed mixers, cattle-handling equipment, crop sprayers, tillage tools, bale movers, athletic equipment, mobile homes • Kingsdown received its name in 1887 when a group of card players in the unnamed shack town decided to name it for the next card drawn from the deck.

FRANKLIN (one of twenty-five counties so named) *Ottawa* • 24,784 • 574 • Eastern KS; drained by the Marais des Cygnes River. • One of twenty-three counties named for Benjamin Franklin • Original county, organized 1855 (prior to statehood) • Cattle, hogs, poultry, sorghum, soybeans, wheat, hay, apples, corn; manufacture of textiles, plastic and metal products, navigation equipment; oil and gas fields; education (Ottawa University).

GEARY *Junction City* • 27,947 • 384 • East-central KS; drained by the Smoky Hill and Republican rivers, which join at Junction City to form the Kansas River. Geary State Fishing Lake is in the southwest. • Named for John W. Geary (1819–73), territorial governor of KS and governor of PA • Organized as Davis 1855 from Riley; named changed 1889 • A military post was established at Fort Riley in 1853; it later became headquarters for Lt. Col. George A. Custer and his Seventh Cavalry. The fort was also the site of the first territorial capitol of KS (state historic site). • Livestock, grain, dairying; manufacture of electronic equipment; railroad shops, feed mills; limestone quarrying.

GOVE *Gove* • 3,068 • 1,071 • West-central KS; drained by the Smoky Hill River and Big Creek. The county lies in the Smoky

Hills region. Monument Rocks National Landmark and Chalk Pyramids are in the southwest. Castle Rock is in the southeast. • Named for Captain Grenville L.Gove (?–1864), Union army officer from KS • 1868 from Rooks • Wheat, sorghum, cattle; farm machinery • Grinnell claims provenance of the term "jerky" for dried meat, the arid air here allowing the meat to be "jerked" off the bone in layers that could be dried and preserved indefinitely.

GRAHAM (one of three counties so named) *Hill City* • 2,946 • 898 • Northern KS; drained by the South Fork of the Solomon River and Bow Creek. • Named for Captain John L. Graham (?–1863), a KS infantry officer killed at Chickamauga • 1867 from Rooks • Wheat, sorghum, cattle

GRANT (one of fifteen counties so named) *Ulysses* • 7,909 • 575 • Southwestern KS; drained by the Cimarron River and its North Fork. Wagon Bed Springs is in the south. • One of twelve counties named for President Ulysses S. Grant • 1873 from Finney and Kearny • Wheat, corn, sorghum, alfalfa, cattle; small natural-gas fields; manufacture of chemicals, concrete, machinery; petroleum refining.

GRAY (one of two counties so named, the other in TX) *Cimarron* • 5,904 • 869 • Southwestern KS; drained by the Arkansas River and Crooked Creek. • Named for Alfred Gray (1830–1880), KS legislator, and the first secretary of the KS Board of Agriculture • 1887 from Finney and Ford • Wheat, sorghum, corn, soybeans, alfalfa, cattle.

GREELEY *Tribune* • 1,534 (the least populated county in KS) • 778 • Western KS, bounded on the west by the CO state line; drained by White Woman Creek. The county is located in the Smoky Hill River valley. It is one of only four counties in KS that lie within the Mountain time zone. • One of two counties (the other in NE) named for Horace Greeley (1811–72), editor of the New York Tribune and champion of westward expansion • 1873 • Cattle, wheat, corn, sorghum.

GREENWOOD (one of two counties so named, the other in SC) *Eureka* • 7,673 • 1,140 (the fifth largest county in KS) • Southeastern KS, in the Flint Hills; drained by the Fall and Verdigris rivers. Fall River Lake reservoir and State Park are in the southeast. Part of Toronto Lake reservoir and Toronto State Park are on the eastern boundary. • Named for Alfred B. Greenwood (1811–89), U.S. representative from AR • Original county; organized 1855 (prior to statehood) • Cattle, hay, wheat, soybeans; extensive oil and natural gas production.

HAMILTON (one of ten counties so named) *Syracuse* • 2,670 • 997 • Southwestern KS, bounded on the west by the CO state line; drained by the Arkansas River. The county includes Hamilton State Fishing Lake. It is one of only four counties in the state that lie within the Mountain time zone. • One of eight counties named for Alexander Hamilton (?–1804), first U.S. secretary of the treasury • 1873 from unorganized territory • Wheat, sorghum, cattle.

HARPER (one of two counties so named, the other in OK)

Anthony • 6,536 • 801 • Southern KS, bounded on the south by the OK state line; drained by the Chikaskia River and Bluff Creek. The county is in the Red Hills region of the state. • Named for Sergeant Marion Harper (?–1863), soldier in the Kansas cavalry killed in the Civil War • 1867 from Kingman • Wheat, barley, oats, sheep, cattle; food processing; manufacturing.

HARVEY *Newton* • 32,869 • 539 • South-central KS; drained by the Little Arkansas River and Walnut Creek. The county contains Dyck Arboretum of the Plains. • Named for Captain James M. Harvey (1833–94), U.S. senator from KS and governor of the state • 1872 from McPherson, Butler and Sedgwick • Mennonite farmers from Russia settled in the county in the 1870s and began raising Turkey Red Hard winter wheat with such success that the variety became the state's principal agricultural product. Newton was a railhead for the Chisholm Trail cattle drives from 1871 to 1873. • Anthropologist and archaeologist Emil W. Haury; basketball coach Adolph Rupp • Wheat, corn, oats, barley, soybeans, apples, cattle, poultry; millwork, manufacture of industrial machinery, mobile homes, farm equipment; railroad shops; food processing • Bethel College, founded in 1887, is the oldest Mennonite college in the U.S.

HASKELL (one of three counties so named) *Sublette* • 4,307 • 577 • Southwestern KS; drained by the Cimarron River. The county contains sand dunes in the extreme north. • Named for Dudley C. Haskell (1842–83), KS legislator and U.S. representative from KS • 1887 from Finney • Wheat, corn, alfalfa, sorghum, cattle; small natural-gas fields.

HODGEMAN *Jetmore* • 2,085 • 860 • Central KS, watered by the Pawnee River and Buckner Creek. • Named for Captain Amos Hodgman (?–1863), officer in the KS Cavalry who died in the Civil War. (The "e" was mistakenly inserted when the county was named.) • 1873 from Indian lands • Wheat, sorghum, cattle.

JACKSON (one of twenty-four counties so named) *Holton* • 12,657 • 657 • Northeastern KS; watered by the Delaware River. The county is dominated by Prairie Band Potawatomi Indian Reservation. Nebo State Fishing Lake is also here. • One of twenty-two counties named directly or indirectly for President Andrew Jackson • Organized as Calhoun 1855 (prior to statehood); name changed 1859 • Holton was settled by Free State men from Milwaukee and was a station on the Underground Railroad in the 1850s and 1860s. • Wheat, sorghum, soybeans, cattle, hogs; manufacture of rotary mowers; feed, sausage and prepared meat.

JEFFERSON *Oskaloosa* • 18,426 • 536 • Northeastern KS, bounded on the south in part by the Kansas River. Its many hills are crossed by the Delaware River, here forming Perry Lake reservoir. Perry State Park is at the dam. • One of twenty-six counties named directly or indirectly for President Thomas Jefferson • Original county; organized 1855 (prior to statehood) • Corn, hogs, cattle, sorghum, hay, wheat, dairying;

limestone mining • Local legend has it that Buffalo Bill Cody was once tied to an oak tree here by pro-slavery men and horsewhipped for making Free State speeches.

JEWELL *Mankato* • 3,791 • 909 • Northern KS, bounded on the north by the NE state line; drained by the Republican River and White Rock Creek. The county contains Jewell State Fishing Lake and Lovewell State Park. • Named for Lt. Col. Lewis R. Jewell (1822–1862), officer in the Kansas cavalry killed during the Civil War • 1867 from Mitchell • Wheat, corn, sorghum, alfalfa, hogs, sheep, cattle.

JOHNSON (one of twelve counties so named) *Olathe* • 451,086 (27% increase since 1990; the fastest growing and second most populated county in KS) • 477 • Eastern KS, bounded on the north by the Kansas River and on the east by the MO state line. Most of the northeastern section of the county is urbanized as an extension of the Kansas City metropolitan area. • Named for the Reverend Thomas Johnson (1802–65), missionary to the Shawnee Indians, murdered for his pro-Union views • Original county; organized 1855 (prior to statehood) • The Shawnee Indians made their headquarters in Shawnee in 1828, when it was known as Gum Springs. Shawnee served as temporary capital of KS Territory in 1854–55. • Greeting card magnate Joyce C. Hall • Wheat, soybeans, hay, cattle, dairying; manufacture of paper products, chemicals, glass and plastics products, electronic equipment; sand and gravel, scattered oil and gas fields • Overland Park was the site of the first aviation school in the western U.S. • The first newspaper in KS, the *Shawnee Sun* was founded in Shawnee in 1835 and printed in the Shawnee language at the Baptist Mission.

KEARNY *Lakin* • 4,531 • 870 • Southwestern KS; drained by the Arkansas River. Lake Mckinney reservoir is here. • Named for General Philip Kearny (?–1862), hero of the Mexican War and Civil War • Established in 1873 as Kearney from Finney. Name changed from Kearney to Kearny in 1889. • Wheat, cattle, sorghum, sugar beets, alfalfa .

KINGMAN *Kingman* • 8,673 • 864 • Southern KS, watered by the Chikaskia River and the South Fork of the Ninnescah River. Kingman State Fishing Lake, part of Cheney Reservoir and Dam, and Cheney State Park are all in the county. • Named for Samuel A. Kingman (1818–1904), Chief Justice of the KS Supreme Court • 1872 from unorganized territory • Wheat, sheep, cattle, hogs, rye, sorghum, strawberries; meat packing; manufacture of metal stampings, auto accessories.

KIOWA *Greensburg* • 3,278 • 722 • Southern KS, watered by Rattlesnake and Mule creeks, and Medicine Lodge River. The rolling plains of the county are located in the Red Hills region. Kiowa State Fishing Lake is here. • One of three counties named for the Kiowa Indians • 1867 from Comanche and Edwards; abolished in 1875, and recreated in 1886 • Wheat, cattle, sorghum, corn, hay, soybeans; education (Barclay College) • A well dug in Greensburg in 1885 is reputedly the deepest hand-dug well in the world (109 feet deep).

LABETTE *Oswego* • 22,835 • 649 • Southeastern KS, bounded on the south by the OK state line; drained by the Neosho River. Big Hill Lake reservoir is here. • Named for the creek, which runs through the county • 1867 from Neosho • Aircraft manufacturer T. Claude Ryan • Cattle, hogs, strawberries, wheat, sorghum, soybeans, hay, dairying; oil and gas fields, coal deposits; manufacture of pottery, construction machinery, cultured marble products, truck and bus bodies, ammunition, fabricated wire products, paper products, concrete, plastics, appliances, apparel.

LANE (one of two counties so named, the other in OR) *Dighton* • 2,155 • 717 • West-central KS; drained by the North and South forks of Walnut Creek. The county is located in the Smoky Hills region of the state. • Named for Col. James H. Lane (1814–66), officer in the Mexican War, U.S. representative from IN and one of the first two U.S. senators from KS • 1873 from Finney • Wheat, sorghum, cattle.

LEAVENWORTH *Leavenworth* • 68,691 • 463 • Northeastern KS, bounded on the east by the Missouri River (forming the MO state line) and on the south by the Kansas River. Leavenworth State Fishing Lake is here. • Named for Fort Leavenworth, itself named for General Henry Leavenworth (1783–1834), who established it. • 1855 (prior to statehood) • The federal government established an army post here in 1827 to protect travelers on the Santa Fe Trail. Leavenworth City was founded in 1854 by pro-slavery settlers from MO. It was the first incorporated community in the KS Territory. On December 3, 1859, Abraham Lincoln gave a major speech here attacking Stephen A. Douglas's state sovereignty doctrines. • Frontiersman Wild Bill Hickok; scout and showman Buffalo Bill Cody. Restauranteur Fred Harvey, gangster Bugs Moran, and temperance advocate Carry Nation all died here. • Wheat, sorghum, soybeans, hay, vegetables, apples, cattle, hogs, poultry, dairying; oil; flour milling; manufacture of steel, woodworking products, batteries, agricultural equipment, paper products, including greeting cards, furniture, industrial machinery; federal penitentiary, veterans hospital, state prison; education (Saint Mary College). As the only commercial shipyard on the Missouri River, towboats and barges are built and repaired here. Fort Leavenworth includes the U.S. Army Command and General Staff College.

LINCOLN (one of twenty-four counties so named) *Lincoln* • 3,578 • 719 • Central KS; drained by the Saline River and Salt Creek. The county is in the Smoky Hills region. • One of eighteen counties named for President Abraham Lincoln • 1867 from Ellsworth • Cattle, sheep, wheat, sorghum, alfalfa, hay • When Lincoln won the election for county seat from its rival Abram, it placed most of the town's buildings on wheels and moved them across the prairie to Lincoln.

LINN *Mound City* • 9,570 • 599 • Eastern KS, in the state's Prairie region, bounded on the east by the MO state line; drained by the Marais des Cygnes River. Marais des Cygnes National Wildlife Refuge is on the eastern border. • One of

four counties named for Lewis F. Linn (1795–1843), governor of MO and U.S. senator from MO • Original county; organized 1855 (prior to statehood) • Immortalized by John Greenleaf Whittier in his poem, "Le Marais du Cygne," the Marais des Cygnes Massacre (state historic site) was the scene of the bloodiest single incident in the KS/MO border struggles of 1854–1861; on May 19, 1858, thirty pro-slavery Missourians seized eleven KS Free-staters, killing five and wounding five. The only decisive Civil War battle fought on Kansas soil, the Battle of Round Mound in 1864, was won by Union General Pleasanton for whom the town here was named (Mine Creek Battlefield State Historic Site). • Cattle, hogs, wheat, fruit, sorghum, soybeans, hay.

LOGAN (one of ten counties so named) *Oakley* • 3,046 • 1,073 • Western KS; drained by the Smoky Hill River. Logan State Fishing Lake is here. • One of five counties named for General John A. Logan (1826–86), officer in the Mexican War and Civil War, U.S. senator from IL and governor of KS • Organized as Saint John 1881 from Wallace; name changed 1887 • Wheat, sorghum, livestock, dairying • Oakley's placement in the extreme northeastern corner of the county makes it unusual among county seat locations.

LYON (one of five counties so named) *Emporia* • 35,935 • 851 • East-central KS; drained by the Neosho and Cottonwood rivers. The county is located in the Flint Hills region of the state and includes part of Flint Hills National Wildlife Refuge. Also here is Lyon State Fishing Lake. • One of four counties named for General Nathaniel Lyon (1818–61), Union commander in the Civil War, killed at Wilson's Creek • Established as Breckinridge 1857 (prior to statehood) from Madison (which was abolished at the time it was divided between Leon and Greenwood); name changed 1862. • Established in 1857, Emporia prohibited the use and sale of liquor by town charter, making it the first "dry town" in the Midwest. Droughts plagued the county until 1938 when the Kahola Valley was dammed. • Journalist and publisher of the *Emporia Gazette*, William Allen White, whose editorials commanded worldwide attention • Poultry, cattle, hogs, corn, wheat, sorghum, hay, dairying; education (Emporia State U.).

MARION *Marion* 13,361 • 943 • East-central KS; drained by the Cottonwood River (forming Marion Lake reservoir). • Named for Marion County, Ohio, itself named for General Francis Marion (?–1795), SC soldier and legislator, known as "the Swamp Fox" for his tactics during the Revolutionary War (one of seventeen counties named directly or indirectly for General Marion) • 1855 (prior to statehood) from Chase; it disappeared in 1857; in 1860 the present Marion County was established. • Wheat, corn, sorghum, apples, cattle, poultry; manufacture of industrial machinery, transportation equipment, feeds, food processing, including dairy products; bookbinding; marble and granite; education (Tabor College) • The Mennonite Heritage Museum is in Goessel.

MARSHALL (one of twelve counties so named) *Marysville* •

10,965 • 903 • Northeastern KS, bounded on the north by the NE state line; drained by the Big Blue, Black Vermillion, and Little Blue rivers. • Named for Francis J. Marshall (1816–1895), local businessman and member of the first KS territorial legislature. (The county seat was named for his wife.) • Original county; organized 1855 (prior to statehood) • A spur of the Oregon Trail crossed the county via a ferry crossing at Marysville on the Big Blue River. The county was also on the Pony Express route (museum). • Transportation equipment, gypsum products; wheat, sorghum, strawberries, soybeans, hogs, cattle, dairying; poultry packing; honey; meat processing; manufacture of machinery, paper products • In 1899, the city government of Beattie was composed entirely of women.

MCPHERSON *McPherson* • 29,554 • 900 • Central KS; drained by the Smoky Hill River. McPherson State Fishing Lake and Maxwell Game Preserve are here. • One of three counties named for General James B. McPherson (1828–64), commander of the Union Army of the Tennessee during the Civil War who was killed in the Battle of Atlanta • 1867 from unorganized territory • Wheat, soybeans, alfalfa, hay, poultry, cattle, hogs, sheep; flour milling; manufacture of chemicals, petroleum products, mineral wool, plastic pipe, mobile homes, aluminum products; oil and gas fields • Bethany College in Lindsborg has been presenting Handel's "Messiah" every year since 1822. McPherson College's museum displays the world's first synthetic diamond.

MEADE (one of three counties so named) *Meade* • 4,631 • 978 • Southwestern KS, bounded on the south by the OK state line; drained by Crooked Creek and the Cimarron River. Meade State Park is here. • Named for General George G. Meade (1815–72), commander of the Union army that defeated General Robert E. Lee at Gettysburg • Created 1873 from unorganized territory and abolished 1883; re-created 1885 • Wheat, corn, sorghum, cattle; volcanic ash deposits • The Dalton Gang hideout was near Meade. An abundant supply of water from artesian wells make the county an oasis of green on the brown prairie.

MIAMI *Paola* • 28,351 • 577 • Eastern KS, bounded on the east by the MO state line; drained by the Marais des Cygnes River and Pottawatomie Creek. The county includes Miami and Louisburg-Middlecreek state fishing lakes. Hillsdale Lake reservoir is also in the county, with Hillsdale State Park on its southern shore. • One of three counties named for the Miami Indians • Organized as Lykins 1855 (prior to statehood); named changed 1861 • Osawatomie was settled in 1854 with support from the New England Emigrant Aid Company, and was the headquarters of John Brown's militant Free State activities in the Territory (state historic site). The town was ransacked and burned on Aug. 30, 1856 by Missourians in retaliation for Brown's slaying of five pro-slavery settlers at Pottawatomie Creek. • Corn, oats, soybeans, sorghum, hogs, cattle; manufacture of metal products, navigation equipment; railroad shops; oil and gas fields.

MITCHELL (one of five counties so named) *Beloit* • 6,932 • 700 • Northern KS; drained by the Solomon River and Salt Creek. The county lies in the Smoky Hills region in the state. Waconda Lake reservoir and Glen Elder State Park (at the dam) are in the west. • Named for Captain William D. Mitchell (?–1865), Union officer killed at the Battle of Monroe's Cross Roads, NC • 1867 from Kirwin Land District • Cattle, hogs, wheat, rye, soybeans; manufacture of farm machinery; flour milling • E. H. Cawker won the privilege of naming Cawker City after himself in a poker game. Cawker City is also home to the world's largest ball of twine, weighing 17,320 pounds.

MONTGOMERY (one of eighteen counties so named) *Independence* • 36,252 • 645 • Southeastern KS, bounded on the south by the OK state line; drained by the Verdigris and Elk rivers. Elk City Lake reservoir is in the west, with Elk City State Park on its eastern shore. Montgomery State Fishing Lake is also here. • One of sixteen counties named directly or indirectly for General Richard Montgomery (1738–75), officer in the American Revolution • 1867 from Labette • Politician Alf Landon; dramatist William Inge. Four of the five outlaws in the Dalton gang were killed following a bank robbery in Coffeyville in October, 1892. (Dalton Defenders Museum) • Livestock, grain, dairying, wheat, sorghum, soybeans, hay, strawberries; oil and gas fields; petroleum refining; manufacture of plastics products, industrial machinery, oil equipment, aircraft parts, house trailers, furniture, clothing, paint pigments, evaporated milk, cement, boats, electronic equipment.

MORRIS (one of three counties so named) *Council Grove* • 6,104 • 697 • East-central KS; located in the Flint Hills region; watered by the Neosho River, (forming Council Grove Lake reservoir is in the east). Kaw Mission State Historic Site is also here. • Named for Thomas Morris (1776 -1844), opponent of slavery and U.S. senator from OH • Organized as Wise 1855 (prior to statehood) from Madison; name changed 1859 • With the conclusion of a treaty in 1825 between the U.S. government and the Kansas and Osage Indians to permit the surveying of the Santa Fe Trail, Council Grove was established as the last supply point before Santa Fe. • Hogs, cattle, poultry, wheat, barley, hay, soybeans; industrial machinery • Frontier landmarks in the county include the Madonna of the Trail Monument honoring pioneer women, the Pioneer Jail (the only one on the Santa Fe Trail), and Custer's Elm which supposedly sheltered Lt. Col. George A. Custer's troops in 1867 during an expedition against the Indians.

MORTON *Elkhart* • 3,496 • 730 • Extreme southwestern KS, bounded on the west by the CO state line, and on the south by the OK state line; drained by forks of the Cimarron River. Cimarron National Grassland covers most of the county. • One of two counties (the other in ND) named for Oliver H. P. T. Morton (1823–77), jurist, governor of IN, and U.S. senator from IN. • 1886 from Stanton • Wheat, grain sorghum, cattle, livestock; gas field.

NEMAHA *Seneca* • 10,717 • 719 • Northeastern KS, bounded on the north by the NE state line; drained by the South Fork of the Big Nemaha River. • Named for the Nemaha River • Original county; organized 1855 (prior to statehood) • Cattle, hogs, poultry, corn, oats, soybeans, wheat; food products; manufacture of machinery, rubber products, control systems, fabricated metal products, furniture, wood products.

NEOSHO *Erie* • 16,997 • 572 • Southeastern KS; drained by the Neosho River. Neosho State Fishing Lake is here. • Named for the Neosho River • Organized as Dorn 1855 (prior to statehood) from Labette; name changed 1861 • Sorghum, wheat, soybeans, hay, hogs, cattle, poultry, dairying; manufacture of textiles, plastic products, transportation equipment, cement, drilling equipment, work clothes, chemicals; oil (also refining), gas, coal • The artifacts in Chanute's Safari Museum highlight the careers of African explorers Martin and Osa Johnson. (Osa was born in Chanute.)

NESS *Ness City* • 3,454 • 1,075 • West-central KS; drained by Walnut Creek and its North and South forks, which converge in the center of the county, and by the Pawnee River. Goodman State Fishing Lake is here. • Named for Noah V. Ness (?–1864), a corporal in the Kansas cavalry killed in the Civil War • 1867 • Wheat, sorghum, cattle; oil and gas extraction.

NORTON *Norton* • 5,953 • 878 • Northern KS, bounded on the north by the NE state line; watered by Beaver and Prairie Dog creeks, and the North Fork of the Solomon River. Prairie Dog State Park and Keith Sebelius Lake reservoir are here. • Named for Captain Orloff Norton (1837–1864), Kansas army officer presumed killed at Cane Hill by Confederate guerrillas. • Established as Oro 1859 (prior to statehood) from unorganized territory; named changed to Norton in 1867; changed to Billings 1873; changed back to Norton 1874. • Wheat, barley, oats, corn, sorghum, cattle, hogs, dairying; manufacture of furniture, fabricated metal products.

OSAGE (one of three counties so named) *Lyndon* • 16,712 • 704 • Eastern KS; drained by the Marais des Cygnes River and Dragoon Creek. Osage State Fishing Lake is here, as are Pomona Lake reservoir and Pomona State Park. Eisenhower State Park is on the shore of Melvern Lake reservoir. • Named for the Marais des Cygnes River, originally named the Osage. • Original county, organized as Weller 1855 (prior to statehood); name changed 1859 • Pharmacologist and physiologist Earl W. Sutherland, Jr. • Hogs, cattle, soybeans, wheat, apples, sorghum, hay; manufacture of paper and metal products, prefabricated wooden buildings.

OSBORNE *Osborne* • 4,452 • 893 • North-central KS, in the Smoky Hills region; drained by the North and South forks of the Solomon River. The northern arm of Waconda Lake reservoir is in the northeast. • Named for Vincent B. Osborne (1839–1879), sergeant with the Second Kansas Volunteer cavalry, and KS legislator • 1867 from Mitchell • Cattle, hogs,

wheat, rye, barley, sorghum; manufacture of farm equipment; food processing • The Geodetic Center of the U.S. is in the southeast (at Meades Ranch).

OTTAWA *Minneapolis* • 6,163 • 721 • North-central KS; drained by the Solomon River and Salt Creek. Ottawa State Fishing Lake is near the center. Rock sandstone formations (Rock City) are in the west-center. • One of four counties named for the Ottawa Indians • 1860 (prior to statehood) from Saline • Wheat, sorghum, alfalfa, cattle; grain storage; manufacture of motor homes • Delphos was the home of Grace Bedell Billings, who as a young girl wrote to Abraham Lincoln suggesting that he would look better with whiskers.

PAWNEE (one of three counties so named) *Larned* • 7,233 • 754 • Central KS; drained by the Arkansas and Pawnee rivers. Fort Larned National Historic Site is centrally located. • Named for the Pawnee River, itself named for the Pawnee Indians • 1867 from Rush and Stafford • Astronomer Clyde Tombaugh • Wheat, sorghum, sugar beets, alfalfa, cattle • The Santa Fe Trail Center near Larned commemorates the historical importance of the trail in KS.

PHILLIPS (one of four counties so named) *Phillipsburg* • 6,001 • 886 • Northern KS, bounded on the north by the NE state line; drained by the North Fork of the Solomon River which forms Kirwin Reservoir in the southeast. Kirwin National Wildlife Refuge surrounds the reservoir. Old Fort Bissell is near Phillipsburg. • Named for William A. Phillips (?–1856), a free-state man murdered at Leavenworth by proslavery bushwhackers • 1867 from Kirwin Land District • Corn, wheat, sorghum, beans, sunflowers, oats, corn, sugar beets.

POTTAWATOMIE (one of two counties so named, the other in OK) *Westmoreland* • 18,209 • 844 • Northeastern KS, bounded on the south by the Kansas River and on the west by the Big Blue River (forming Tuttle Creek reservoir); drained by Vermillion Creek. The county includes Pottawatomie State Fishing lakes No. 1 and 2, and part of Tuttle Creek State Park. • One of three counties named for the Potawatomi Indian tribe (including Pottawattomie in IA) • 1857 (prior to statehood) from Indian lands • Automobile manufacturer Walter P. Chrysler; prizefighter Jess Willard • Cattle, hogs, poultry, corn, apples, wheat, hay; manufacture of machinery.

PRATT *Pratt* • 9,647 • 735 • Southern KS; drained by Sand Creek, the South Fork of the Ninnescah River and the Chikaskia River. The county includes the Kansas Wildlife and Parks Museum. • Named for Lieutenant Caleb S. Pratt (?–1861), Union officer killed in the Battle of Wilson's Creek • 1867. The county was fraudulently organized with no bona fide settlers at the time. Official recognition was given in 1879. • Wheat, sorghum, cattle, sheep; small gas and oil fields.

RAWLINS *Atwood* • 2,966 • 1,070 • Northwestern KS, bounded on the north by the NE state line; watered by headstreams of Sappa, Beaver, and Little Beaver creeks. • Named for General John A. Rawlins (1831–69), aide-de-camp to General Grant, officer in the Civil War and U.S. secretary of war under Grant • 1873 from Kirwin Land District • Barley, wheat, corn, sorghum, cattle.

RENO *Hutchinson* • 64,790 • 1,255 (the third largest county in KS) • South-central KS; drained by the Arkansas River and the North Fork of the Ninnescah River (forming Cheney Reservoir in the southeast). Part of Quivira National Wildlife Refuge is in the northwest corner, a salt marsh area. Sand Hills and Cheney state parks are also here. • Named for General Jesse L. Reno (1823–62), officer in the Mexican War and the Civil War • 1867 from Sedgwick • Geneticist and agronomist Donald F. Jones • Wheat; food processing; manufacture of metal and paper products, chemicals, industrial machinery, transportation equipment; salt mining and processing • The KS State Fair and national junior college basketball tournament are held each year in Hutchinson. The city has twenty-one parks.

REPUBLIC *Belleville* • 5,835 • 717 • Northern KS, bounded on the north by the NE state line; drained by the Republican River. Pawnee Indian Village State Historic Site is across the Republican River from the village of Rossville. • Named for the Republican River • 1860 (prior to statehood) from Washington and Cloud counties • Corn, wheat, strawberries, sorghum, alfalfa, hogs, cattle, sheep; manufacture of plastic products.

RICE (one of two counties so named, the other in MN) *Lyons* • 10,761 • 727 • Central KS; drained by the Little Arkansas and Arkansas rivers and Cow Creek. The county is in a rolling plain region. Part of Quivira National Wildlife Refuge and its salt marshes are in the southwest corner. Coronado-Quivira Museum (archaeological site) is at county center. • Named for General Samuel A. Rice (1828–64), attorney general for IA and Union officer in the Civil War • 1867 from Reno County • Wheat, alfalfa, sorghum, cattle, hogs; oil and gas fields; education (Sterling College) • County fathers wanted their seat in the exact center of the county, and so this is where Lyons was laid out in 1876.

RILEY *Manhattan* • 62,843 • 610 • Northeastern KS, bounded on the east by the Big Blue River (here forming Tuttle Creek Lake reservoir); drained by the Kansas River. The county includes Tuttle Creek State Park on the western shore of the reservoir. Fort Riley Military Reservation is here. • Named for Fort Riley, itself named for General Bennet Riley (1787–1853), professional soldier and military governor of CA • 1855 (prior to statehood) from Wabaunsee • Wheat, rye, corn, hay, apples, strawberries, cattle, sheep, hogs, poultry; manufacture of farm machinery; poultry packing; bottling; machine-shop services; education (KS State U.; Manhattan Christian College).

ROOKS *Stockton* • 5,685 • 888 • North-central KS; drained by the South Fork of the Solomon River and Bow Creek. Webster Reservoir (in Webster State Park) and Rooks State Fishing Lake are centrally located. Nicodemus National Historic Site is in the west. The county is in the Smoky Hills region of the state. • Named for John C. Rooks (1835–1862), private who died at the Battle of Prairie Grove, AR. Rooks is the only county named for a Civil War private. • 1867 from Kirwin Land District • Rye, cattle; manufacture of mobile homes; oil fields.

RUSH (one of two counties so named, the other in IN) *La Crosse* • 3,551 • 718 • Central KS; watered by Walnut Creek • Named for Alexander Rush (?–1864), captain of the Second Kansas Colored Volunteer infantry, killed at Jenkins Ferry, AR • 1867 from unorganized territory • Wheat, cattle, poultry • The Barbed Wire Museum in La Crosse defines an important historical component of the cattle ranching industry in Kansas.

RUSSELL (one of four counties so named) *Russell* • 7,370 • 885 • Central KS; drained by the Saline and Smoky Hills rivers. The county is located in the Smoky Hills region of the state. Wilson State Park is on the shore of Wilson Lake reservoir. • Named for Captain Avra P. Russell (1833–1862), Union army officer who died of wounds received at Prairie Grove • 1867 from Ellsworth • Senator Robert Dole • Cattle, wheat, hay; transportation equipment; oil fields.

SALINE (one of five counties so named) *Salina* • 53,597 • 720 • Central KS; intersected by the Smoky Hill, Saline, and Solomon rivers. The county is partially located in the Smoky Hills region (museum) of the state. Coronado Heights, a campsite of early Spanish explorers is here. Saline State Fishing Lake is also in the county. • Named for the Saline River • 1860 (prior to statehood) • Saline was rebuilt after being largely destroyed by floods in 1903. • Winter wheat, alfalfa, sorghum, cattle, hogs, poultry packing; grain storage operations, flour mills, food processing; manufacture of aircraft, electronic and transportation equipment; education (KS Wesleyan U.) • The Union Pacific Railroad sponsored the planting of maple trees in Brookville's city park, making the town an oasis on the treeless prairie. The hills around the town were used as a hideout by Jesse James and his gang of outlaws.

SCOTT (one of eleven counties so named) *Scott City* • 5,120 • 718 • Western KS; drained by Ladder and White Woman creeks, the latter flowing into White Woman Basin Lake near the center of the county. El Cuartelejo Pueblo Ruins and Lake Scott State Park are in the county. • One of five counties named for General Winfield Scott (1786–1866), officer in the War of 1812 and the Mexican War; general in chief of the U.S. Army and commander of the Union armies at the beginning of the Civil War • 1873 from Finney • Wheat, cattle, hogs, sorghum, corn.

SEDGWICK *Wichita* • 452,869 (the most populated county in KS) • 1,000 • Southern KS; drained by the Arkansas and Little Arkansas rivers. The eastern part of the county is in the Flint Hills region of the state. • One of two counties (the other in CO) named directly or indirectly for General John Sedgwick (1813–1864), Indian fighter and Union officer in the Civil

War • 1867 from Butler • A trading post was established at the site of Wichita, an Indian village, in 1864. The tracks set down by the heavily laden wagons of James R. Mead and Cherokee Jesse Chisholm between the post and points south became the famous Chisholm Trail. In its early years, Wichita was a stopover on cattle drives to Abilene and other points as the railroad moved west. • Communist party leader Earl Browder; television journalist Jim Lehrer; photojournalist W. Eugene Smith; jazz bandleader Stan Kenton. • Wheat, sorghum, hay, soybeans, cattle, hogs, sheep, poultry, strawberries, peaches; manufacture of furniture, plastic products, fabricated metal products, chemicals, machinery, aircraft; food processing and storage; scattered oil and gas fields; education (Friends U.; Newman U.) McConnell Air Force Base is a large employer. • The Wichita Mid-Continent Airport was the headquarters of the International Flying Farmers. The restored Cowtown is a replica of Wichita in the 1870s.

SEWARD *Liberal* • 22,510 • 640 • Southwestern KS, bounded on the south by the OK state line; drained by the Cimarron River. • One of two counties (the other in NE) named for William H. Seward (1801–1872), U.S. secretary of state, noted for negotiating the purchase of Alaska • Organized as Godfrey from Indian lands; name changed to Seward 1861; changed to Howard 1867. In 1873 the name Seward was given to a new county organized in the present location. • Wheat, sorghum, corn, cattle; meat packing; aircraft manufacturing; oil and natural gas.

SHAWNEE *Topeka* • 169,871 (the third most populated county in KS) • 550 • Northeastern KS; drained by the Kansas River (forming part of the eastern and western boundaries), Soldier Creek, and the Wakarusa River. Shawnee State Fishing Lake is here. • Named for the Shawnee Indian tribe • Original county; organized 1855 (prior to statehood) • The present site of Topeka was chosen in 1854 by antislavery settlers from Lawrence, led by Charles Robinson, a resident agent of the New England Emigrant Aid Company. It was the scene of several conflicts between Free Soil groups and pro-slavery advocates. Topeka was the temporary capital of KS Territory in 1856. It was made permanent capital of the state of KS in 1861. The city was headquarters for the building of the Atchison, Topeka and Santa Fe Railway system. The Supreme Court's 1954 ruling in Brown v. Board of Education of Topeka made racial segregation in public schools unconstitutional. The suit was brought by Oliver Brown in 1951 against the board for not allowing his daughter to attend an all-white school near her home (national historic site). • Poet Gwendolyn Brooks; journalist and newspaper editor Frank I. Cobb; psychiatrists Karl Augustus, William C., and Charles F. Menninger (Menninger Clinic) • Cattle, corn, wheat, soybeans, hay, strawberries, general agriculture; food processing, publishing and printing; state government offices; insurance; education (Washburn U.) • The statehouse in Topeka was modeled after the U.S. Capitol.

SHERIDAN *Hoxie* • 2,813 • 896 • Northwestern KS; drained by the Saline River, the North and South forks of the Solomon River, and Bow Creek. Cottonwood Ranch State Historic Site is east of Sheridan State Fishing Lake. • One of five counties named directly or indirectly for General Philip H. Sheridan (1831–1888), Union officer during the Civil War and commander in chief of the U.S. army • 1873 from unorganized territory • Wheat, barley, corn, cattle, sheep, hogs.

SHERMAN (one of four counties so named) *Goodland* • 6,760 • 1,056 • Northwestern KS, bounded on the west by the CO state line; watered by the North Fork of the Smoky Hill River and by Beaver and Sappa creeks. Sherman State Fishing Lake is in the south. The county lies within the Mountain time zone. • One of three counties named for General William Tecumseh Sherman (1820–1891), officer during the Civil War and general-in-chief of the U.S. army • 1873 from Kirwin Land District • Wheat, corn, cattle.

SMITH (one of four counties so named) *Smith Center* • 4,536 • 895 • Northern KS, bounded on the north by the NE state line; drained by the North Fork of the Solomon River. • Named for Major James Nelson Smith (1837–1864), Union officer killed at the Battle of Little Blue, MO • 1867 from unorganized territory • Silent film comedian Fatty Arbuckle. Brewster Higley wrote the lyrics of "Home on the Range" in his homestead cabin here in 1873. • Corn, hay, wheat, cattle, hogs, sorghum, alfalfa • The traditional geographical center of the contiguous United States is in the county, eleven miles east-northeast of Smith Center.

STAFFORD (one of two counties so named, the other in VA) *Saint John* • 4,789 • 792 • Central KS; watered by Rattlesnake Creek and the North Fork of the Ninnescah River. Part of Quivira National Wildlife Refuge is in the county. • Named for Captain Lewis Stafford (?–1863), Union army officer killed at Young's Point, LA • 1867 from unorganized territory • Cattle, wheat, sorghum, soybeans, alfalfa.

STANTON *Johnson* • 2,406 • 680 • Southwestern KS, bounded on the west by the CO state line; drained by Bear and Sandy Arroyo creeks. • One of two counties (the other in NE) named for Edwin M. Stanton (1814–1869), U.S. attorney general, and U.S. secretary of war. • Created 1873, later abolished and made part of Hamilton. In 1887 Stanton was reorganized from Hamilton. • Wheat, sorghum, soybeans, alfalfa, cattle.

STEVENS (one of three counties so named) *Hugoton* • 5,463 • 728 • Southwestern KS, bounded on the south by the OK state line; crossed in the northwest by the Cimarron River. • Named for Thaddeus Stevens (1792–1868), U.S. representative from PA and leader of the Radical Republicans • 1873 from Indian lands • Cattle, wheat, sorghum, corn, alfalfa.

SUMNER (one of two counties so named, the other in TN) *Wellington* • 25,946 • 1,182 (the fourth largest county in KS) • Southern KS, bounded on the south by the OK state line; drained by the Chikaskia, Ninnescah, and Arkansas rivers. •

Named for Charles Sumner (1811–74), a founder of the Free-Soil Party and U.S. senator from MA • 1867 from Cowley • Wellington was a favorite camping ground for travelers on the old Chisholm Trail (museum). • Sumner is the largest wheat-producing county in KS. Also corn, sorghum, flour milling, dairy and beef cattle, hogs; manufacture of industrial machinery, aircraft components, furniture; oil. (There are over 100 producing wells in the Wellington Oil Field.) • Women's Christian Temperance Union officer Susanna Salter became the first woman mayor in the U.S. in 1887 after her name was put on the ballot by anti-Prohibitionists as a joke.

THOMAS (one of three counties so named) *Colby* • 8,180 • 1,075 • Northwestern KS; drained by the Saline River and headstreams of the Solomon River and Sappa Creek. • Named for General George H. Thomas (1816–70), Union officer in the Civil War • 1873 from Kirwin Land District; reorganized 1895 with territory annexed from Logan • Wheat, barley, sorghum, cattle, sheep, hogs.

TREGO *Wakeeney* • 3,319 • 888 • Central KS; drained by the Saline and Smoky Hill rivers. The county is located in the Smoky Hills region of the state. Cedar Bluff Reservoir and State Park are in the south. • Named for Captain Edgar P. Trego (?–1863), Union army officer killed at Chickamauga, TN • 1867 • Wheat, sorghum, corn, cattle.

WABAUNSEE *Alma* • 6,885 • 797 • East-central KS, bounded on the north by the Kansas River; drained by Mill and Dragoon creeks. • Named for Waubansee, a Potawatomi chief • Organized as Richardson County 1855 (prior to statehood); name changed 1859. • Poultry, cattle, hogs, wheat, sorghum, hay, soybeans; meat processing. • The Beecher Bible and Rifle Colony was located on the Kansas River; supported by abolitionist minister Henry Ward Beecher who raised money to purchase twenty-five rifles, colonizers settled here from Connecticut, referring to their community as the "New Haven of the West."

WALLACE *Sharon Springs* • 1,749 • 914 • Western KS, bounded on the west by the CO state line; drained by the North and South Forks of the Smoky Hill River and Ladder Creek. The county is characterized by gently sloping to rolling plains with the highest point in Kansas, Mount Sunflower, in the west on the CO state line (4,039 feet). It is one of only four counties in KS that lie within the Mountain time zone. • Named for General William H. L. Wallace (1821–1862), Union officer in the Civil War who died of wounds received at Shiloh, TN • 1868 from Indian lands • Cattle, sheep, barley, wheat, sorghum, corn.

WASHINGTON *Washington* • 6,483 • 899 • Northern KS, bounded on the north by the NE state line; drained by the Little Blue River and branches of the Republican River. Washington State Fishing Lake is here. The Hollenberg Pony Express Station State Historic Site is on the eastern boundary of the county. • One of thirty-one counties named for George Washington • Original county; organized 1857 (prior to statehood) • Corn, hogs, cattle, poultry, wheat, sorghum, soybeans, alfalfa, dairying.

WICHITA *Leoti* • 2,531 • 719 • Western KS; drained by White Woman and Ladder creeks. • One of two counties (the other in TX) named for the Wichita Indians • 1873 from Indian lands • Wheat sorghum, corn, cattle.

WILSON (one of four counties so named) *Fredonia* • 10,332 • 574 • Southeastern KS; drained by the Verdigris and Fall rivers. The county contains Wilson State Fishing Lake in the northeast. • Named for Hiero T. Wilson (1806–?), member of the first legislature of KS Territory, settler, and merchant • Original county; organized 1855 (prior to statehood) • Cattle, hogs, wheat, sorghum, soybeans, hay, strawberries; some manufacturing.

WOODSON *Yates Center* • 3,788 • 501 • Southeastern KS; crossed by the Neosho and Verdigris rivers. Toronto Lake reservoir and Toronto State Park are in the southwestern corner. Woodson State Fishing Lake is also in the southwest. • Named for Daniel Woodson (1824–1894), secretary of KS Territory • Original county; organized 1855 (prior to statehood) • Silent film comedian Buster Keaton • Cattle, hogs, corn, wheat, soybeans, hay; textiles; some oil production.

WYANDOTTE *Kansas City* • 157,882 (the fourth most populated county in KS) • 151 (the smallest county in KS and one of the fifty smallest counties in the U.S.) • Northeastern KS, bounded in part on the north by the Missouri River (here forming the MO state line) and on the east by the MO state line; drained by the Kansas River, which forms part of its southern border. About eighty percent of the county lies within the Kansas City limits. Grinter Place State Historic Site and Historic Huron Indian Cemetery are also here. • One of two counties (the other, Wyandot, in OH) named for the Wyandot Indians • Original county; organized 1859 (prior to statehood) • Rapid development of Kansas City began after the passage of the 1854 Kansas-Nebraska Act when rival settlements of pro-slavery and Abolitionist supporters rushed into the area. The county was the site of the writing of the Kansas constitution, under which the territory entered the U.S. in 1861. In 1863, it became the eastern terminus of the first transcontinental railroad, the Union Pacific, Eastern Division (later the Kansas Pacific). With the arrival of vast herds of Texas cattle to the railheads here, the county became a major site for marketing, reshipment, stockyards and meatpacking plants, an industry that remains strong today. Serious damage was caused by floods in 1903, 1951, and 1977. • Sand and gravel; diversified manufacturing, including chemicals, paper goods, automobiles, railroad cars, petroleum and soap products, fabricated steel, dairy products; some agriculture, including vegetables, peaches, strawberries.

KENTUCKY

United We Stand, Divided We Fall

One hundred nineteen of the state's 120 counties are managed by fiscal courts, each presided over by a county judge executive. The exception is Fayette, whose top official is the mayor.

ADAIR (one of four counties so named) *Columbia* • 17,244 • 407 • Southern KY; drained by the Green River and Russell Creek. Part of Green River Lake reservoir is in the northeast. • Named for John Adair (1757–1840), governor of KY and senator from the state • 1802 from Green • The Battle of Gradyville was fought here in 1861. In 1863, John Hunt Morgan fought Union soldiers at Tebb's Bend on his way to IN and OH. • Hay, alfalfa, wheat, corn, hogs, cattle, poultry, dairying, burley tobacco; timber; some manufacturing; education (Lindsey Wilson College).

ALLEN (one of five counties so named) *Scottsville* • 17,800 • 346 • Southern KY, bounded on the south by the TN state line and on the northeast by the Barren River (which forms Barren River Lake reservoir); drained by Bays Fork and Trammel Fork rivers. • One of two counties (the other in IN) named for Lt. Col. John Allen (?–1813), KY legislator and officer in the War of 1812 who died at the Battle of River Raisin • 1815 from Warren and Barren • Cattle, poultry, dairying, hay, alfalfa, soybeans, wheat, corn, burley tobacco; oil wells, hardwood timber; some manufacturing • The county was noted for names carved on trees by early settlers, including that of Daniel Boone in 1778 near Barren Lake.

ANDERSON (one of five counties so named) *Lawrenceburg* • 19,111 • 203 • Central KY, bounded on the east by the Kentucky River and on the southwest by Beech Fork; drained by the Salt River. The county lies in the Bluegrass region of the state. Beaver Lake and (part of) Taylorsville Lake reservoirs are here. • Named for Richard C. Anderson, Jr. (1788–1826), U.S. representative from KY and U.S. minister to Colombia • 1827 from Franklin, Mercer, and Washington • Speaker of the House Champ Clark • Burley tobacco, poultry, hogs, horses, cattle, hay, alfalfa, corn; manufacturing; stone quarrying.

BALLARD *Wickliffe* • 8,286 • 251 • Western KY, bounded on the southwest by the Mississippi River (forming the MO state line), on the west, northwest and north by the Ohio River (forming the IL state line), and on the south in part by Mayfield Creek. Wyckliffe Mounds are in the west. The county contains many small lakes. Ballard County and Peal wildlife management areas are also here. Lock and Dam No. 53 is in the north on the Ohio River. • Named for Major Bland W. Ballard (1761–1853), professional Indian fighter and scout, army officer, and KY legislator • 1842 from McCracken and Hickman • Dark tobacco, burley tobacco, sorghum, hay, alfalfa, soybeans, wheat, corn, hogs, cattle, poultry, dairying; timber; clay pits.

BARREN *Glasgow* • 38,033 • 491 • Southern KY, bounded on the southwest by the Barren River; drained by Beaver and Skaggs creeks. A small part of Mammoth Cave National Park is in the northwest corner. Other limestone caves, including Diamond Caverns, Crystal Onyx Cave, and Jesse James and Hundred Domes Caves, are in the northwest. Barren River Lake reservoir and State Resort Park lie on the county's southwest border. • Named for the Kentucky barrens, a prairie grassland • 1798 from Warren and Green • Political writer Arthur B. Krock • Hogs, cattle, poultry, burley tobacco, hay, alfalfa, soybeans, wheat, corn; oil and gas wells; hardwood timber; stone quarries; some manufacturing.

BATH (one of two counties so named, the other in VA) *Owingsville* • 11,085 • 279 • Northeastern KY, bounded on the northeast by the Licking River (forming Cave Run Lake reservoir) and on the west by Hinkston Creek; drained by Slate Creek. The county is in the state's Bluegrass region. It includes part of Daniel Boone National Forest. • Named for the once-famous mineral baths here. (During the 19th century, the county's mineral springs made it a popular resort destination.) • 1811 from Montgomery • Confederate general John B. Hood • Burley tobacco, corn, soybeans, hay, alfalfa, cattle, poultry, dairying; timber.

BELL (one of two counties so named, the other in TX) *Pineville* • 30,060 • 361 • Southeastern KY, bounded on the south by the TN state line and on the southeast by the VA state line; drained by the Cumberland River and its tributaries. The Cumberland Mountains cross along the southeast border. The county includes Pine Mountain State Resort Park, parts of Daniel Boone National Forest, and part of Cumberland Gap National Historical Park. Kentucky Ridge State Forest is also here. • Named for Joshua F. Bell (1811–1870), KY legislator and U.S. representative from KY • Organized as Josh Bell County in 1867 from Knox and Harlan counties; name shortened 1872 or 1873 • Despite the fact that Middlesboro was located on the old Wilderness Road through a natural pass in the mountains, the site was not settled until 1889. The city was developed by English investors who hoped to make it an iron and steel center; their company went bankrupt when the financing bank in London failed in 1893. Eventually Middlesboro recovered and became an important coal center. • Bituminous-coal mining, limestone quarries, iron deposits; dairying, cattle, burley tobacco, fruit; manufacture of plastic pipe, elastic webbing, mobile homes; tanning, food processing; education (Clear Creek Baptist Bible College).

BOONE (one of eight counties so named) *Burlington* • 85,991 (49% increase in 1990; the second fastest growing county in KY) • 246 • Northern KY, bounded on the north and west by the Ohio River, which forms the OH state line on the north and the IN state line on the west; drained by Gunpowder Creek. The northeast part of the county lies within the urbanized Cincinnati metropolitan area. The Cincinnati-Northern Kentucky International Airport is here. Bullock Pen Lake reservoir (on Ten Mile Creek) is in the south. • One of seven counties named for Daniel Boone • 1798 from Campbell • Burley tobacco, corn, soybeans, alfalfa, hay, cattle, poultry, dairying; diversified manufacturing • Big Bone Lick State Park contains fossil remains of mastodons and other extinct animals who apparently gathered here to lick the earth near the salt spring.

BOURBON (one of two counties so named, the other in KS) *Paris* • 19,360 • 291 • North-central KY, bounded on the east in part by Hinkston Creek and on the north in part by Silas Creek; drained by the South Fork of the Licking River and Houston, Stoner and Hinkston creeks. The county lies in the Bluegrass region of the state. • Named for the French royal dynasty who contributed funds to the American colonies during the Revolutionary War • 1786 from Fayette • Politician Thomas Corwin. U.S. Supreme Court justice Robert Trimble died here. • Burley tobacco, grass seed, soybeans, wheat, corn, hay, alfalfa, hogs, cattle, horses, poultry, dairying; limestone quarries; manufacture of textiles, auto parts, mining machinery • The first patent for the automatic traffic signal was granted to Garrett A. Morgan of Paris in 1877. Bourbon whiskey, which was named after the county, was first distilled in Paris in 1790. The name was later applied to any corn whiskey made from this distillery's formula. Duncan Tavern Historic Shrine (1788) in Paris was once a rendezvous point for frontiersmen such as Daniel Boone. In 1804, Barton W. Stone started a religious movement in Paris called the New Lights, which merged with the "Campbellites" in 1832 to become the Disciples of Christ or Christian Church.

BOYD (one of two counties so named, the other in NE) *Catlettsburg* • 49,752 • 160 • Northeastern KY, bounded on the northeast by the Ohio River (forming the Ohio state line), and on the east by the Big Sandy River (forming the WV state line); drained by the East Fork of the Little Sandy River. The county comprises part of the Huntington, WV metropolitan area. • Named for Linn Boyd (1800–1859), U.S. representative from KY and speaker of the House • 1860 from Carter, Lawrence and Greenup • Ashland was settled in 1815; its proximity to coal and timber regions, as well as to iron-ore deposits (no longer mined) aided its growth as KY's major iron and steel center, and the chief city of northeastern KY. The continuous sheet mill process of manufacture was developed here. • Bituminous-coal mines, oil and gas wells, clay pits, limestone and sandstone quarries, iron deposits; lumber; hay, alfalfa, cattle; diversified manufacturing • Ashland's Central Park is known for its old-forest trees and prehistoric Indian mounds.

BOYLE *Danville* • 27,697 • 182 • Central KY, bounded on the east by the Dix River (forming Herrington Lake reservoir); drained by the Salt, Beech Fork, and North Rolling Fork rivers. The county lies partly in the Bluegrass region. • Named for John Boyle (1774- ?), U.S. representative from KY and jurist • 1842 from Lincoln and Mercer (having the same county seat as the now-abolished Kentucky County, which was organized in 1776 from Fincastle County, VA) • Danville was settled in 1775. As the capital of the Kentucky District of VA, it became a political center. Between 1784 and 1791 nine conventions were held here to consider the creation of the state of KY. The first state constitution was drafted in Danville in 1792 (state historic site). Perryville (Battlefield State Historic Site) was the scene of KY's bloodiest Civil War battle on Oct. 8, 1862. The defeat of Confederate forces here marked the end of the Confederate attempt to take KY. • Abolitionist James G. Birney; U.S. Supreme Court justice John Marshall Harlan • Burley tobacco, hemp, hay, alfalfa, soybeans, wheat, corn, berries, hogs, cattle, horses, poultry, dairying; stone quarries; light manufacturing; education (KY School for the Deaf; Centre College) • The first post office west of the Alleghenies was established in 1792 in Danville. The first college west of the Alleghenies, Transylvania Seminary, was chartered in 1780 in Danville. The first successful operation for the removal of an ovarian tumor was performed by Doctor Ephraim McDowell in 1809 in Danville.

BRACKEN *Brooksville* • 8,279 • 203 • Northern KY, bounded on the north by the Ohio River, which forms the OH state line, and on the south in part by the North Fork of the Licking River. The county lies in the northern part of the Bluegrass region. Captain A. Meldahl Lock and Dam is on the Ohio River here. • Named either directly for William Bracken, an early settler; or for Big Bracken Creek and Little Bracken Creek, which were named for him • 1796 from Campbell and Mason • Burley tobacco, corn, hay, alfalfa, cattle, poultry, dairying; some shipping and manufacturing.

BREATHITT *Jackson* • 16,100 • 495 • East-central KY, in the Cumberland Mountains; drained by the North and Middle forks of the Kentucky River, Troublesome Creek, and several other creeks. • Named for John Breathitt (1786–1834), KY legislator and governor of KY • 1839 from Estill, Clay, and Perry • The county has been nicknamed "Bloody Breathitt" because of the feuds among family clans that took place here. • Cattle, honey, apples, sweet and Irish potatoes, burley tobacco, hay; bituminous-coal mining; timber; education (KY Mountain Bible College).

BRECKINRIDGE *Hardinsburg* • 18,648 • 572 • Northwestern KY, bounded on the northwest by the Ohio River, which forms the IN state line, and on the south by the Rough River, which forms Rough River Lake reservoir; drained by the South Fork of Panther Creek and Sinking Creek. Rough River Dam State Resort Park is here, as well as Yellowbank Wildlife Management Area. • Named for John Breckinridge (1760–1806), Speaker of the KY House, U.S. senator from KY, and U.S. attorney general • 1799 from Hardin • U.S. Supreme Court justice Wiley B. Rutledge • Burley tobacco, corn, soybeans, wheat, hay, alfalfa, cattle; timber; limestone quarries; some manufacturing.

BULLITT *Shepherdsville* • 61,236 • 299 • Northern KY, bounded on the northwest by the Ohio River, on the west by the Salt River, and on the southwest by Rolling Fork; drained by Floyds Fork and the Salt River. Part of Fort Knox Military Reservation is in the west; part of Bernheim Forest Arboretum and Nature Center (the official state arboretum) is also here. The Louisville metropolitan area is beginning to encroach into the northern part of the county. • Named for Alexander S. Bullitt (?–1816), first president of the KY senate and the state's first lieutenant-governor • 1796 from Jefferson and Nelson • Bullitt's Lick, near Shepherdsville, was the site of the first commercial industry in KY: salt production. • Cattle, poultry, burley tobacco, hay, alfalfa, soybeans, corn, dairying; manufacturing • A whiskey distillery at Clement has been in operation since 1795.

BUTLER (one of eight counties so named) *Morgantown* • 13,010 • 428 • West-central KY, bounded on the southwest by the Mud River; drained by the Green River (forming part of the southeast and northwest borders) and the Barren River • One of three counties named for Maj. Gen. Richard Butler (?–1791), officer and Indian commissioner after the American Revolution • 1810 from Logan and Ohio • Burley tobacco, dark tobacco, hay, soybeans, wheat, corn, hogs, cattle, catfish; coal mines, stone quarries; timber.

CALDWELL (one of five counties so named) *Princeton* • 13,060 • 347 • Western KY, bounded on the northeast by the Tradewater River. The county includes part of Pennyrile Forest State Resort Park and Lake Beshear reservoir on its eastern boundary. • Named for General John W. Caldwell (1757–1804), soldier, member of the KY conventions, and KY legislator • 1809 from Livingston • Caldwell County was the scene of the "Black Patch War" (1906–08) in which local night-riding farmers sought to end price controls set by the Tobacco trust by successfully destroying their factories. • Tobacco, hay, alfalfa, soybeans, wheat, corn, hogs, cattle, poultry, dairying; coal; timber; limestone quarries • The annual Black Patch Festival in Princeton celebrates the tobacco farming industry of the area.

CALLOWAY *Murray* • 34,177 • 386 • Western KY, bounded on the south by the TN state line and on the east by the Tennessee River (forming Kentucky Lake reservoir); drained by the East and West forks of the Clark River and by Mayfield Creek. Part of Kenlake State Resort Park is here. • Named for Col. Richard Callaway (?–1780), one of the founders, with Daniel Boone, of Boonesborough. The difference in the spelling was due to a clerical error. • 1821 from Hickman • Teacher and critic Cleanth Brooks • Tobacco, hay, alfalfa, soybeans, wheat, corn, hogs, cattle, poultry, dairying; manufacturing; education (Murray State U.) • The first radio transmission was pub-

licly demonstrated by Nathan Stubblefield in 1892 in Murray. The National Scouting Museum is in Murray.

CAMPBELL (one of five counties so named) *Alexandria* • 88,616 • 152 (one of the fifty smallest counties in the U.S.) • Northern KY, bounded on the north and east by the Ohio River (forming the OH state line) and on the west by the Licking River. The county is located in the northern part of the Bluegrass region. Urbanization has taken place in the north, part of the Cincinnati, Ohio metropolitan area. • Named for John Campbell (?–1799), fur trader and large KY landowner • 1794 from Scott, Harrison and Mason • Newport was the scene of a seven-year strike by steelworkers (1921–28). • Legislator and government official John G. Carlisle; jurist Horace H. Lurton • Manufacture of steel, transportation equipment, printing presses, chemicals, beverages, wood products, clothing, recreational equipment, cement blocks; printing; agricultural products including vegetables, tobacco, fruit, hay, alfalfa, soybeans, corn, cattle; education (Northern KY U.).

CARLISLE *Bardwell* • 5,351 • 192 • Western KY, bounded on the west by the Mississippi River (forming the MO state line) and on the north in part by Mayfield Creek; drained by the West Fork of Mayfield Creek. • Named for John G. Carlisle (1835–1910), Speaker of the House of Representatives, U.S. senator from KY and U.S. secretary of the treasury • 1886 from Ballard • Dark and burley tobacco, corn, hay, alfalfa, soybeans, wheat, sorghum, hogs, cattle, poultry, dairying; timber.

CARROLL (one of thirteen counties so named) *Carrollton* • 10,155 • 130 (one of the fifty smallest counties in the U.S.) • Northern KY, bounded on the north by the Ohio River (forming the IN state line) and on the southeast by Eagle Creek; drained by the Kentucky and Little Kentucky rivers. The county lies in the outer Bluegrass region. General Butler State Resort Park is here. • One of twelve counties named for Charles Carroll (1737–1832), signer of the Declaration of Independence, U.S. senator from MD, and founder of the B and O Railroad • 1838 from Gallatin • Burley tobacco, hay, alfalfa, soybeans, corn, hogs, cattle, horses; sand and gravel pits; some manufacturing.

CARTER (one of five counties so named) *Grayson* • 26,889 • 411 • Northeastern KY; drained by the Little Sandy River (forming Grayson Lake reservoir and part of the southern boundary) and Tygarts Creek. Tygarts State Forest, Carter Caves State Resort Park, and Grayson Lake State Park are here. The county contains several caves and natural bridges. • Named for William G. Carter (?–1850), KY state senator who donated the land on which the county courthouse was built. • 1838 from Greenup and Lawrence • Burley tobacco, corn, hay, alfalfa, cattle; clay, sand, gravel, limestone, iron, asphalt; timber; manufacturing; education (KY Christian College).

CASEY *Liberty* • 15,447 • 446 • Central KY, bounded on the east corner by Fishing Creek; drained by the Green River, the Big South Fork of Rolling Fork, and Casey Creek. • Named for Col. William Casey (1754–1816), Revolutionary War veteran, pioneer settler, and KY legislator • 1806 from Lincoln • Corn, hay, alfalfa, burley tobacco, soybeans, hogs, cattle, poultry, dairying; timber; limestone quarries; manufacturing • The nation's largest Buckeye tree (144 feet tall) is located here.

CHRISTIAN (one of three counties so named) *Hopkinsville* • 72,265 • 721 (the second largest county in KY) • Southwestern KY, bounded on the south by the TN state line and on the northeast by the Pond River; drained by the Tradewater River, the Little River and its North and South Forks, the West Fork of the Pond River, and the West Fork of the Red River. The county contains part of Pennyrile Forest State Resort Park and part of Fort Campbell Military Reservation. • Named for Col. William Christian (?–1786), army officer in the French and Indian War and Revolutionary War, VA legislator, and brother-in-law of Patrick Henry. (Counties in IL and MO are named for this county.) • 1796 from Logan • Jefferson Davis (state shrine in Fairview marked by a 351-foot high obelisk); U.S. vice president Adlai E. Stevenson • Dark and burley tobacco, corn, wheat, soybeans, hay, alfalfa, cattle, poultry, dairying; coal mines, gas wells; hardwood timber; light manufacturing • Cherokee chiefs Fly Smith and White Path who died along the Trail of Tears were buried in Hopkinsville. The Trail of Tears Commemorative Park is here.

CLARK (one of twelve counties so named) *Winchester* • 33,144 • 254 • Central KY, bounded on the south by the Kentucky River; drained by Stoner Creek. The county lies in the Bluegrass region. Fort Boonesborough State Park and Boone Station State Historic Site are here. • One of six counties named for George Rogers Clark (1752–1818), general in the American Revolution and frontiersman in the Northwest Territory • 1792 from Bourbon and Fayette • Fort Boonesboro was built here in 1775 by Daniel Boone and a company of NC men under Col. Richard Henderson who had just opened Boone's Trace through the Cumberland Gap. The group claimed all the land between the Kentucky and Cumberland rivers and called it Transylvania. The first legislative assembly west of the Appalachians was held here in May, 1775: the Transylvania Convention. The marriage here between Richard's younger brother Samuel and Betsy Calloway was the first in KY. Fort Boonesboro was abandoned in 1778. • Journalist Helen Thomas • Burley tobacco, hay, alfalfa, soybeans, wheat, corn, hogs, cattle, sheep, horses, turkeys, dairying; limestone quarries; manufacture of clothing, lumber, bricks, beverages, tubing, bedsprings, projection lamps • The oldest trail in the U.S., the Warrior's Path, passes through Winchester. Henry Clay made his first and last speeches in the Clark County Court House.

CLAY (one of eighteen counties so named) *Manchester* • 24,556 • 471 • Southeastern KY, in the Cumberland foothills, bounded on the east in part by the Red Bird River; drained by the South Fork of the Kentucky River and its headstreams, including Goose, Collins Fork, and Sexton creeks. All of the county is in Daniel Boone National Forest. • Named for General Green Clay (1757–1826), wealthy KY landowner, VA and KY legislator, and officer in the War of 1812 • 1806 from Madi-

son, Knox and Floyd • Burley tobacco, corn, hay, hogs, cattle; bituminous-coal mines; hardwood timber.

CLINTON (one of nine counties so named) *Albany* • 9,634 • 197 • Southern KY, bounded on the south by the TN state line and on the northwest corner by the Cumberland River (an arm of Lake Cumberland is in the north); drained by several creeks. The county includes part of Dale Hollow Lake reservoir and State Resort Park. It lies in the Cumberland foothills. • Probably named for De Witt Clinton (1769–1828), governor of NY, and supporter of the Erie Canal • 1836 from Wayne and Cumberland • Burley tobacco, hay, alfalfa, soybeans, corn, hogs, cattle, poultry, dairying; coal mines; stone quarrying; timber.

CRITTENDEN (one of two counties so named, the other in AR) *Marion* • 9,384 • 362 • Western KY, bounded on the northwest by the Ohio River (forming the IL state line), on the northeast by the Tradewater River and on the southwest corner by the Cumberland River; drained by Crooked Creek. • Named for John J. Crittenden (?–1863), U.S. senator from KY, U.S. attorney general and governor of KY • 1842 from Livingston • Hogs, cattle, poultry, burley tobacco, hay, alfalfa, soybeans, wheat, corn; limestone quarries.

CUMBERLAND (one of eight counties so named) *Burkesville* • 7,147 • 306 • Southern KY, bounded on the south by the TN state line; drained by the Cumberland River (which forms part of the county's southwest and northeast boundary) and Marrowbone Creek. The county lies in the Cumberland foothills. Part of Dale Hollow Lake reservoir (and State Resort Park) is in the southeastern corner. • Named for the Cumberland River • 1798 from Green • In 1829, the world's first free-flowing oil well was drilled near Burkesville; the oil was never collected and flowed unused into the Cumberland River. • Hay, alfalfa, soybeans, corn, cattle, poultry, dairying.

DAVIESS *Owensboro* • 91,545 • 462 • Northwestern KY, bounded on the north by the Ohio River (forming the IN state line), on the west by the Green River, and on the northeast by Blackford Creek; drained by Panther Creek, and its North and South forks. Ben Hawes State Park is in the county. • One of four counties named for Col. Joseph H. Daveiss (1774–1811), VA soldier and attorney who attempted without success to indict Aaron Burr for treason. The state legislature later passed an act correcting the name of the county, but the erroneous name continued in use. • 1815 from Ohio • During the Civil War, Owensboro was the site of the Federal Camp Silas B. Miller. The town repelled a Confederate assault in 1862, but in August, 1864, it was attacked by guerillas and partially burned. • Daviess is a leading KY county in tobacco production (both burley and dark), also corn, wheat, sorghum, hay, alfalfa, soybeans, cattle, hogs, poultry, dairying; oil and gas wells, coal mines; manufacture of bourbon whiskey, electronic components, electric motors, plastics, aluminum, furniture, iron and steel products, chemicals, cigars; meat packing; canning; education (KY Wesleyan

College; Brescia U.) • The nation's largest sassafras tree (seventy-six feet tall) is located in Owensboro. The city holds a Festival of the Arts every September, and the Owensboro Hydroplane Regatta in June.

EDMONSON *Brownsville* • 11,644 • 303 • Central KY; drained by the Green and Nolin rivers, and Bear Creek. The county includes most of Mammoth Cave National Park, the longest recorded cave system in the world, with nearly 330 miles explored and mapped. There are also other limestone caves in the county. Nolin River Lake State Park and part of Nolin River Reservoir are in the northeast. • Named for Captain John M. Edmonson (?–1813), an American officer in the War of 1812, killed at the Battle of River Raisin • 1825 from Hart, Warren and Grayson • Burley tobacco, hay, alfalfa, soybeans, wheat, corn, hogs, cattle, poultry, dairying; resort tourism.

ELLIOTT *Sandy Hook* • 6,748 • 234 • Northeastern KY; drained by the Little Sandy River (forming Grayson Lake reservoir in the northeast) and several creeks. • Probably named for John M. Elliott (1820–79), KY legislator, U.S. representative from KY, and jurist • 1869 from Lawrence, Morgan, and Carter • Burley tobacco, hay, alfalfa, cattle; coal mines.

ESTILL *Irvine* • 15,307 • 254 • East-central KY, bounded on the northwest and drained by the Kentucky River; bounded on the north by the Red River. The county is also drained by Station Camp and Red Lick creeks. Daniel Boone National Forest is in the east and south. • Named for Capt. James Estill (1750–82), Indian fighter, soldier and early pioneer who established Fort Estill in 1781 • 1808 from Madison and Clark • Burley tobacco, hay, alfalfa, soybeans, corn, hogs, cattle.

FAYETTE (one of eleven counties so named) *Lexington* • 260,512 (the second most populated county in KY) • 284 • Central KY, bounded on the southeast by the Kentucky River; drained by Elkhorn Creek and its north branch. The county lies in the heart of the Bluegrass region. It is coterminous with the city limits of Lexington. • One of seventeen counties named for the Marquis de Lafayette (1757–1834), French statesman and soldier who fought with the Americans during the Revolutionary War • 1780 (prior to statehood) from Kentucky County • The site of Lexington was so named in 1775 by a group of settlers who were camped there when news of the Battle of Lexington was received. In 1817, Lexington, now called the "Athens of the West," for its emphasis on education and culture, presented the first Beethoven symphony heard in the U.S. In 1974, the county and its seat were combined and given an "urban-county government." • Politician Francis P. Blair, Jr.; Supreme Court justice Louis Brandeis; Vice President John C. Breckinridge; welfare worker Sophonisba Preston Breckinridge; zoologist and geneticist Thomas H. Morgan; statesman Henry Clay (Ashland); Confederate cavalry leader John Hunt Morgan; First Lady Mary Todd Lincoln. Sportsman Edward R. Bradley, folksinger John Jacob Niles, and basketball coach Adolph Rupp died here. • Thoroughbred and saddle horses, tobacco, hay, alfalfa, soybeans, wheat, corn, hogs, cattle, spring lambs, bluegrass seed; limestone quarries; diversified manufacturing, including bourbon whiskey, paper products, electronic equipment; education (U of KY; Transylvania U.— the oldest college west of the Alleghenies) • The world's largest burley tobacco producer and market is in Lexington. The American Thoroughbred Breeders Association has its headquarters in Lexington. The county also contains the "International Museum of the Horse," the world's largest museum dedicated to all breeds of the horse (Lexington), as well as the only park of its kind in the world dedicated to the horse, The Kentucky Horse Park. The first newspaper west of the Alleghenies, the *Kentucky Gazette* (1787), was published in Lexington.

FLEMING *Flemingsburg* • 13,792 • 351 • Northeastern KY, bounded on the southwest by the Licking River and on the northeast by its North Fork; drained by Fleming Creek. The county lies in the northern part of the Bluegrass region. Three of KY's thirteen covered bridges are found in the county. • Named for Col. John Fleming (1735–?), surveyor who constructed Fleming Station • 1798 from Mason • Burley tobacco, corn, hay, alfalfa, soybeans, wheat, hogs, cattle, poultry, dairying • After his soda factory in Elizaville failed, Dwight Baldwin relocated to Cincinnati and started the Baldwin Piano Company. A monument in Elizaville Cemetery honors Pfc. Franklin Sousley, one of the Marines who raised the flag at Iwo Jima. James Andrews, resident of Flemingsburg, and his Andrews Raiders, stole a locomotive from the Confederacy and led soldiers on a chase into northern Georgia.

FLOYD (one of six counties so named) *Prestonburg* • 42,441 • 394 • Eastern KY, in the Cumberland Mountains; drained by Levisa Fork and Beaver Creek. Dewey Lake reservoir is on John's Creek. The county also contains Jenny Wiley State Resort Park. • Named for John Floyd (?–1783), KY surveyor and Indian fighter who destroyed British vessels in the Revolutionary War • 1799 from Fleming, Mason and Montgomery • Bituminous-coal mining, oil and gas wells, hay, corn, livestock.

FRANKLIN (one of twenty-five counties so named) *Frankfort* • 47,687 • 210 • North-central KY; drained by the Kentucky River, and by Elkhorn Creek and its North Branch. The county is located in the Bluegrass region. KY National Fish Hatchery is in the north, on Elkhorn Creek. • One of twenty-three counties named for Benjamin Franklin • 1794 from Woodford, Mercer, and Shelby • Frankfort was founded in 1786 by the notorious Gen. James Wilkinson. It became the state capital in 1793. Twice during its early history, the statehouse was burned; both times Louisville and Lexington sought to supplant the city as state capital and failed. The city was occupied briefly in 1862 by Confederate General Braxton Bragg. Governor William Goebel was assassinated in Frankfort on Feb. 3, 1900. The city suffered widespread damage in a 1937 flood. • Politician Albert Fall; political journalist Duff

Green. Statesman John J. Crittenden and U.S. Supreme Court justice Thomas Todd died here. KY's first settlers, Daniel Boone and his wife Rebecca, are buried in Frankfort Cemetery. • Burley tobacco, hay, alfalfa, corn, cattle, Thoroughbred horses; stone quarries (especially "Kentucky marble," used in construction), lead and zinc deposits; manufacture of air brakes, bolts, nuts, hardware, automotive trim, baby furniture and accessories, thermometers, shoes, undergarments, candy; government operations; education (KY State U.) • Bibb lettuce was developed by John Bibb in the 1850s in Frankfort. A three-block section of Frankfort known as the "Corner of Celebrities" contains the homes of KY generals, judges, and statesmen. In 1910, the first Boy Scout troop in the U.S. was chartered in Frankfort (as "Troop No. 1") by permission of Lord Baden-Powell, the organization's British founder.

FULTON (one of eight counties so named) *Hickman* • 7,752 • 209 • Extreme southwestern KY, bounded on the west by the Mississippi River (forming the MO state line) and on the south by the TN state line; drained by Obion Creek and Bayou de Chien. Madrid Bend is totally detached from the remainder of the state by the Mississippi River. Part of Reelfoot National Wildlife Refuge is in the county. • One of seven counties named for Robert Fulton (1765–1815), builder of the *Clermont*, the first commercially successful steamboat • 1845 from Hickman • Cotton, corn, hay, alfalfa, soybeans, wheat, walnuts, dark tobacco, hogs; timber.

GALLATIN (one of three counties so named) *Warsaw* • 7,870 (46% increase since 1990; the third fastest growing county in KY) • 99 (technically the smallest county in KY, although Robertson, at 100 square miles, is only slightly larger; ranks as one of the fifty smallest counties in the U.S.) • Northern KY, bounded on the north by the Ohio River (forming the IN state line) and on the south by Eagle Creek. The county is in the northern part of the Bluegrass region. Markland Locks and Dam on the Ohio River is in the northwest. • One of two counties (the other in IL) named for Albert Gallatin (1761–1849), Swiss-born U.S. statesman and diplomat, and U.S. secretary of the treasury • 1798 from Franklin and Shelby • Burley tobacco, corn, hay, alfalfa, soybeans, cattle, poultry, horses, dairying; some manufacturing.

GARRARD *Lancaster* • 14,792 • 231 • Central KY, bounded on the north by the Kentucky River, on the west by the Dix River (which forms Herrington Lake reservoir in the northwest), and on the northeast by Paint Lick Creek (its source in the southeast). The county lies in the Bluegrass region. • Named for James Garrard (1749–1822), second governor of KY • 1796 from Madison, Lincoln and Mercer • Temperance advocate Carry Nation • Burley tobacco, corn, hay, alfalfa, hogs, cattle, poultry, dairying • The Thomas Kennedy Plantation, no longer in existence, is believed to have been the setting for Harriet Beecher Stowe's *Uncle Tom's Cabin*.

GRANT (one of fifteen counties so named) *Williamstown* • 22,384 • 260 • Northern KY; drained by Ten Mile and Fort Lick creeks and the South Fork of Grassy Creek. The county lies in the Bluegrass region. Williamstown Lake reservoir is also in the county. • Named for one or more brothers of a local family named Grant • 1820 from Pendleton • Burley tobacco, corn, hay, alfalfa, cattle, hogs, poultry, dairying.

GRAVES *Mayfield* • 37,028 • 556 • Southwestern KY, bounded on the south by the TN state line; drained by the West Fork of the Clarks River, Mayfield Creek, its West Fork, Obion Creek, and Bayou de Chien. • Named for Col. Benjamin F. Graves (1771–1813), an officer during the War of 1812 killed at the Battle of River Raisin • 1823 from Hickman • The Confederate base of Camp Beauregard and the city of Mayfield were both captured in 1862 by Federal forces. • Vice President Alben Barkley • Dark and burley tobacco, sorghum, hay, alfalfa, soybeans, wheat, corn, hogs, cattle, poultry, dairying; ball clay (for ceramics and china); timber; some manufacturing; education (Mid Continent College).

GRAYSON (one of three counties so named) *Leitchfield* • 24,053 • 504 • West-central KY, bounded on the north by the Rough River (forming Rough River Lake reservoir), and on the southeast by the Nolin River (forming Nolin River Lake reservoir); drained by Bear and Caney creeks. • One of two counties (the other in VA) named for William Grayson (?–1790), aide-de-camp to General George Washington and one of VA's first two U.S. senators • 1810 from Hardin and Ohio County • Burley tobacco, hay, alfalfa, soybeans, wheat, corn, hogs, cattle, poultry, dairying, honey; asphalt, bituminous-coal mines, stone quarries.

GREEN (one of two counties so named) *Greensburg* • 11,518 • 289 • Central KY; drained by the Green and Little Barren rivers, and Russell and Big Pitman creeks. • One of sixteen counties (two Greens and fourteen Greenes) named for Gen. Nathanael Greene (1742–86), Revolutionary War officer and quartermaster general • 1792 from Lincoln and Nelson • Burley tobacco, hay, alfalfa, soybeans, corn, hogs, cattle, poultry, dairying; cedar; manufacturing.

GREENUP *Greenup* • 36,891 • 346 • Northeastern KY, bounded on the north and east by the Ohio River (forming the OH state line); drained by the Little Sandy River and Tygarts Creek. The eastern part of the county is urbanized as part of the Huntington, WV — Ashland, KY metropolitan area. Greenbo Lake State Resort Park is here. Greenup Locks and Dams are on the Ohio River in the east. • Named for Col. Christopher Greenup (?–1818), officer in the Revolutionary War, one of KY's first two representatives in the U.S. House, and governor of the state • 1803 from Mason • Corn, burley tobacco, apples, hay, alfalfa, soybeans, cattle; iron deposits; some manufacturing.

HANCOCK *Hawesville* • 8,392 • 189 • Northwestern KY, bounded on the north and northeast by the Ohio River (forming the IN state line); drained by Blackford Creek, forming part of the western border. Cannelton Lock and Dam is on the Ohio River in the northeast. • One of ten counties named for

John Hancock (1737–93), noted signer of the Declaration of Independence, governor of MA and statesman • 1829 from Breckinridge, Ohio, and Daviess • Burley tobacco, corn, hay, alfalfa, soybeans, wheat, cattle, hogs.

HARDIN (one of six counties so named) *Elizabethtown* • 94,174 (the fourth most populated county in KY) • 628 (the fourth largest county in KY) • North-central KY, bounded on the extreme north by the IN state line (formed by the Ohio River) and on the northeast by the Salt River and Rolling Fork; drained by the Rough and Nolin rivers. Part of Vernon-Douglas State Nature Preserve is here. • One of two counties (the other in OH) named for Gen. John Hardin (1753–92), Revolutionary War officer and Indian fighter with George Rogers Clark in the trans-Ohio campaigns • 1792 from Nelson • During the Civil War, Elizabethtown was bombarded by Confederate forces under General John Morgan. • Burley tobacco, corn, wheat, hay, alfalfa, soybeans, hogs, cattle, poultry, dairying; limestone quarries, sand pits, asphalt deposits; manufacture of magnets, electronic timing devices, concrete blocks, ice cream, soft drinks and cheese • The U.S. gold depository, the largest in the world, is at the Fort Knox Military Reservation in the north, its $6 billion in gold bullion representing nearly all of the gold owned by the U.S. government. The Coca-Cola Memorabilia Museum in Elizabethtown is the largest private collection of its kind in the world.

HARLAN (one of two counties so named, the other in NE) *Harlan* • 33,202 • 467 • Southeastern KY, bounded on the south and east by the VA state line; drained by the Cumberland River and its numerous forks. The county lies in the Cumberland Mountains and includes Black Mountain, which, at 4,139 feet, is the highest point in KY. Kentenia State Forest is here, as well as part of Daniel Boone National Forest, and a small part of Cumberland Gap National Historical Park. Part of Kingdom Come State Park is also in the county. • Named for Major Silas Harlan (?–1782), an officer in the Revolutionary War and Indian fighter under George Rogers Clark • 1819 from Floyd and Knox • Labor conflicts between coal operators and miners here (which gave the county the nickname "Bloody Harlan)" have been bitter and recurrent. Following twenty turbulent years, the mines were unionized in 1941. • Harlan is one of the leading coal-producing counties in KY; also, burley tobacco, livestock; hardwood timber.

HARRISON (one of eight counties so named) *Cynthiana* • 17,983 • 310 • Northern KY, bounded on the northeast by the Licking River and on the south by Silas Creek; drained by the South Fork of the Licking River and several creeks. • Named for Col. Benjamin Harrison (?–1808), officer in the Revolutionary War and KY legislator • 1793 from Bourbon and Scott • Burley tobacco, hay, alfalfa, soybeans, wheat, corn, hogs, cattle, poultry, dairying; timber; limestone quarries; some manufacturing. • The Appalachian Cultural and Fine Arts Center is in Cumberland.

HART (one of two counties so named, the other in GA) *Mun-*

fordville • 17,445 • 416 • Central KY, bounded on the northeast by the Nolin River (forming part of Nolin River Lake reservoir); drained by the Green River. The county contains part of Mammoth Cave National Park, along with many other limestone caves, including Kentucky, Mammoth, Onyx, and Hidden River. The American Cave Museum is in Horse Cave. • Named for Captain Nathaniel G.S. Hart (?–1813), officer in the War of 1812 killed at the Battle of River Raisin • 1819 from Hardin and Barren • Confederate general Simon B. Buckner; WW II army general Simon B. Buckner, Jr. • Burley tobacco, corn, wheat, soybeans.

HENDERSON (one of five counties so named) *Henderson* • 44,829 • 440 • Northwestern KY, bounded on the north by the Ohio River (forming the IN state line), on the southwest by Highland Creek, and on the east and southeast by the Green River, which also drains it. The county includes Diamond Island in the Ohio River. John James Audubon State Park and Sauerheber Wildlife Management Area are here. Newburgh Lock and Dam is on the Ohio River. A portion of the county lies on the Indiana side of the Ohio River four miles south of Evansville, IN, having been isolated by a change in the river's course. • Named for Richard Henderson (1735–85), who backed Daniel Boone's explorations and founded the Transylvania Company. • 1798 from Christian • American Revolution heroine Nancy Hart (buried here). It was here in Henderson that failed general store owner John James Audubon was inspired by a chance visit to his store by ornithologist Alexander Wilson to begin his own career as artist-ornithologist. (The city's Audubon Memorial Museum contains many of his original paintings.) • Dark and burley tobacco, corn, wheat, soybeans, alfalfa, hay, hogs, cattle; bituminous-coal mines, oil wells, clay, sand and gravel; manufacture of clothing, furniture, chemicals, plastics • Mother's Day was first observed by Henderson school teacher Mary S. Wilson in 1887. • James C. Ellis Park and Audubon Raceway offer summer Thoroughbred and harness racing.

HENRY (one of ten counties so named) *New Castle* • 15,060 • 289 • Northern KY, bounded on the east by the Kentucky River; drained by the Little Kentucky River. • One of ten counties (including Patrick County, VA) named for Patrick Henry (1736–99), patriot, governor of VA, and statesman • 1798 from Shelby • The county once had productive zinc and lead mines in the south. • Burley tobacco, corn, hay, alfalfa, soybeans, wheat, cattle, hogs, horses, poultry, dairying; timber; metal industries, manufacture of electronics.

HICKMAN (one of two counties so named, the other in TN) *Clinton* • 5,262 • 244 • Western KY, bounded on the west by the Mississippi River (forming the MO state line) and on the southeast corner by the TN state line; drained by Obion Creek and Bayou de Chien. The county includes Columbus-Belmont State Park. Wolf Island on the MO side of the Mississippi River is in the county. • Named for Captain Paschal Hickman (?–1813), army officer in the War of 1812 who was killed in the Battle of River Raisin • 1821 from Caldwell and

Livingston • The county comprised the entire KY portion of the Jackson Purchase, bought from the Chickasaw Indians in 1818. • Dark and burley tobacco, soybeans, wheat, corn, hay, hogs, cattle, poultry, dairying; manufacturing.

HOPKINS (one of two counties so named, the other in TX) *Madisonville* • 46,519 • 551 • Western KY, bounded on the east by the Pond River, on the west by the Tradewater River. • Named for Gen. Samuel Hopkins (1753–1819), KY legislator, and U.S. representative from KY • 1806 from Henderson • Burley and dark tobacco, hay, alfalfa, soybeans, wheat, corn, hogs, cattle; bituminous-coal mines, oil wells; hardwood timber; some manufacturing.

JACKSON (one of twenty-four counties so named) *McKee* • 13,495 • 346 • Central KY, in the Cumberland foothills, bounded on the southwest by the South Fork of the Rockcastle River; drained by the Middle Fork of the Rockcastle River, and by Station Camp Creek. A large part of the county is in Daniel Boone National Forest. • One of twenty-two counties named for President Andrew Jackson • 1858 from Madison, Owsley, Estill, Laurel, Clay and Rockcastle • Burley tobacco, hay, alfalfa, corn, cattle, poultry, dairying; timber; limestone.

JEFFERSON *Louisville* • 693,604 (the most populated county in KY) • 385 • Northern KY, bounded on the west and north by the Ohio River (forming the IN state line); drained by Floyds Fork. Dominated by Louisville, the state's largest city and a major transportation, commercial and manufacturing center, the county is largely urbanized, with small pockets dedicated to agriculture in the south and east. It contains numerous city and county parks and E.P. "Tom" Sawyer State Park. • One of twenty-six counties named for President Thomas Jefferson • 1780 (prior to statehood) from Kentucky County • Louisville was established in 1778 by a group of pioneers led by George Rogers Clark. During the Civil War, it was a supply depot for northern troops. The flood of 1937 caused the city over $52 million in damage. • Frontier military leader George Rogers Clark; actress Irene Dunne; pathologist and bacteriologist Simon Flexner; educator Abraham Flexner; Roman Catholic leader Benedict J. Flaget; educator Patty Smith Hill; sociologist Charles S. Johnson; folksinger John Jacob Niles; philanthropist and social leader Bertha Palmer; Union general John Pope; heavyweight boxing champion Marvin Hart; writer Sue Grafton. Confederate terrorist William C. Quantrill died here. • Diversified manufacturing, including gin and whiskey, chemicals, electric appliances, paint, plumbing fixtures, sporting goods; meat packing; lumber milling; printing (the American Printing House for the Blind is the world's largest publisher of braille products); tobacco processing; quarrying of limestone, clay, sand and gravel; education (U. of Louisville—the first municipal college in the U.S., established in 1798; other institutions) • Louisville contains the world's largest museum dedicated to the Thoroughbred horse, the Kentucky Derby Museum. It is the site of the oldest continuously contested horse race in America, the Kentucky Derby, which has been held at Churchill

Downs since 1875. The county contends that the first cheeseburger was served here in 1934 at Kaelin's, a Louisville restaurant. The first public display of electricity by Thomas Edison occurred at the Southern Exposition in Louisville in 1883. Louisville is the national headquarters for the Presbyterian Church of the U.S.

JESSAMINE *Nicholasville* • 39,041 • 173 • Central KY, bounded on the southwest, south and southeast by the Kentucky River; drained by Hickman Creek. The county lies in the Bluegrass region of the state. The Palisades of the Kentucky River (gorge) and Daniel Boone's Cave are here. The Jim Beam Nature Preserve protects the largest concentration of rare plant species within the Bluegrass region. • Probably named for the jessamine flower (a type of jasmine) that grows along the banks of Jessamine Creek • 1798 from Fayette • Burley tobacco, corn, hay, alfalfa, soybeans, cattle, horses, poultry, dairying. • The first cantilevered bridge, High Bridge (once the highest railroad bridge over a navigable stream), was built over the Kentucky River near Wilmore in 1877. Camp Nelson, the nation's third largest recruitment and training center for Black troops during the Civil War, also served as a refugee camp for escaped slaves. Asbury College's Bethel Academy in Wilmore is the oldest Methodist academy west of the Alleghenies and the second Methodist school in the U.S. The Valley View Ferry, the oldest continuous business in KY, is presently the only ferry still operating on the Kentucky River.

JOHNSON (one of twelve counties so named) *Paintsville* • 23,445 • 262 • Eastern KY; drained by Levisa Fork. Part of Paintsville Lake reservoir is here, with Paintsville Lake State Park located on its eastern shore. • One of five counties named for Richard Mentor Johnson (1780–1850), U.S. senator from KY and vice president • 1843 from Lawrence, Floyd, and Morgan • Burley tobacco, hay, some cattle, hogs; coal mines, oil wells.

KENTON *Independence* • 151,464 (the third most populated county in KY) • 163 • Northern KY, bounded on the north by the Ohio River (forming the OH state line) and on the east by the Licking River. The county is located in the northern part of the Bluegrass region. It is urbanized in the north as part of the Cincinnati metropolitan area, and rural and agricultural in the south. • Named for Simon Kenton (1755–1836), KY scout and Indian fighter • 1840 from Campbell • Painter and sculptor Frank Duveneck; Boy Scouts of America founder Dan Carter Beard; drama teacher Frederick H. Koch • Cattle, poultry, corn, burley tobacco, hay, alfalfa, dairying; education (Thomas More College); manufacture of machine tools, freight cars, prison equipment, electrical equipment, paper bags, processed fruits, stained glass. • The world's largest stained glass window (67 feet high) graces the Cathedral Basilica of the Assumption in Covington, a replica of Notre Dame in Paris. • Situated at the confluence of the Licking and Ohio rivers, Covington is linked to Cincinnati by three bridges, one of them a suspension bridge designed by John A. Roebling and opened in 1866.

KNOTT *Hindman* • 17,649 • 352 • Eastern KY; drained by Carr Fork of the Kentucky River, and Troublesome and Buckhorn creeks. The county lies in the Cumberland foothills. Carr Fork Lake State Park (and reservoir) is in the south. • Named for J. Proctor Knott (1830–1911), MO legislator, U.S. representative from KY and governor of the state • 1884 from Floyd, Letcher, Perry and Breathitt • Bituminous-coal mining; livestock, some tobacco; education (Alice Lloyd College).

KNOX *Barbourville* • 31,795 • 388 • Southeastern KY, in the Cumberland Mountains; drained by the Cumberland River. The Dr. Thomas Walker State Historic Site has a replica of the first house (cabin) in KY, built in 1750 by Walker, discoverer of the Cumberland Gap. • One of nine counties named for Gen. Henry Knox (1750–1806), Revolutionary War officer and first U.S. secretary of war • 1799 from Lincoln • Bituminous-coal mining, oil wells; corn, hay, burley tobacco, vegetables, sorghum, cattle; timber; light industry; education (Union College) • Barbourville is a gateway to Daniel Boone National Forest.

LARUE *Hodgenville* • 13,373 • 263 • Central KY, bounded on the east and northeast by Rolling Fork; drained by the Nolin River. • Named for John LaRue (1746–1792), large KY landowner • 1843 from Hardin • President Abraham Lincoln was born here (national historic site). Knob Creek Farm where Lincoln's family moved when he was two is seven miles northeast of the birthplace. The Lincoln Museum is at Hodgenville. • Burley tobacco, corn, hay, alfalfa, soybeans, wheat, hogs, cattle, poultry, dairying; limestone quarries, natural-gas wells; timber.

LAUREL *London* • 52,715 • 436 • Southeastern KY, bounded on the west by the Rockcastle River, on the northeast by the South Fork of the Rockcastle River and on the south by the Laurel River (forming Laurel River Lake reservoir); drained by several creeks. The county lies in the foothills of the Cumberland Mountains. It includes Levi Jackson Wilderness Road State Park and part of Daniel Boone National Forest in the western half. • Named for either the Laurel River or for the laurel shrubs that grow along its banks • 1825 from Rockcastle, Knox, Clay and Whitley • Cattle, hogs, poultry, dairying, burley tobacco, corn, hay, alfalfa; coal mines; timber.

LAWRENCE (one of eleven counties so named) *Louisa* • 15,569 • 419 • Northeastern KY, bounded on the east by the Big Sandy River and Tug Fork of the Big Sandy River (both forming the WV state line); drained by Levisa Fork, the Big Sandy River, and Blaine Creek (forming Yatesville Lake reservoir; Yatesville Lake State Park is on its northern shore). • One of nine counties named for Capt. James Lawrence (1781–1813), U.S. Navy commander in the War of 1812 • 1821 from Floyd and Greenup • Chief Justice of the U.S. Fred M. Vinson • Corn, burley tobacco, hay, alfalfa, cattle; oil and gas wells, coal mines, fireclay and sand pits; timber.

LEE (one of twelve counties so named) *Beattyville* • 7,916 • 210 • East-central KY, in the Cumberland Mountains; drained by the Kentucky River, and its North, Middle, and South forks. The county includes part of Daniel Boone National Forest in the western half. • One of eight counties named for Robert E. Lee (1807–70), American general and commander-in-chief of the Confederate forces during the Civil War • 1870 from Owsley, Breathitt, Estill and Wolfe • Livestock, burley tobacco, hay; coal, oil, limestone; hardwood timber.

LESLIE *Hyden* • 12,401 • 404 • Southeastern KY, in the Cumberland Mountains, bounded on the west by the Red Bird River; drained by the Middle Fork of the Kentucky River (forming Buckhorn Lake reservoir on the northern boundary). The county lies in Daniel Boone National Forest. • Named for Preston H. Leslie (1819–1907), KY legislator, governor of KY, and territorial governor of MT • 1878 from Clay, Harlan and Perry • Livestock, burley tobacco; timber; bituminous-coal mines.

LETCHER *Whitesburg* • 25,277 •339 • Southeastern KY, in the Cumberland Mountains, bounded on the east and southeast by the VA state line; drained by the North Fork of the Kentucky River and Poor Fork of the Cumberland River, and Rockhouse Creek. The county includes part of Pine Mountain and part of Jefferson National Forest, both on the southeast boundary. Part of Kingdom Come State Park, Lilley Cornett Woods, and Big Branch State Nature Preserve are also here, as is Pine Mountain Wildlife Management Area. • Named for Robert P. Letcher (1788–1861), U.S. representative from KY, governor of KY, and U.S. minister to Mexico • 1842 from Harlan and Perry • Pilot Francis Gary Powers • Bituminous coal, clay, sand and gravel pits; stone quarries; timber; livestock, burley tobacco.

LEWIS (one of seven counties so named) *Vanceburg* • 14,092 • 485 • Northeastern KY, bounded on the north by the Ohio River (forming the OH state line) and on the southwest by the North Fork of the Licking River; drained by Grassy Fork and Kinniconick Creek. Ohio River Islands National Wildlife Refuge is here. • One of five counties named for Meriwether Lewis (1774–1809), co-leader of the Lewis and Clark Expedition • 1806 from Mason • Burley tobacco, hay, alfalfa, soybeans, wheat, corn, cattle, poultry, dairying; some manufacturing.

LINCOLN (one of twenty-four counties named Lincoln) *Stanford* • 23,361 • 337 • Central KY; drained by the Dix and Green rivers, and Fishing and Buck creeks. The county lies partly in the outer Bluegrass region. Isaac Shelby Cemetery and William Whitley House state historic sites are here. • One of four counties directly named for Gen. Benjamin Lincoln (1733–1810), Revolutionary War officer, and U.S. secretary of war • 1780 (prior to statehood) from Kentucky County • It is one of the three original counties of the Kentucky district of Virginia. • Burley tobacco, hay, alfalfa, soybeans, wheat, corn, hogs, cattle, poultry, dairying; timber.

LIVINGSTON (one of six counties so named) *Smithland* • 9,804 • 316 • Western KY, bounded on the west and north by the Ohio River (forming the IL state line) and on the south by the Tennessee River (joining the Ohio River at the southwestern tip of the county); crossed by the Cumberland River (forming part of the southeastern boundary). Kentucky Dam and part of Kentucky Lake reservoir are on the southern boundary (Tennessee River). Barkley Dam and part of Lake Barkley reservoir are on the southeastern boundary. Smithland Lock and Dam is on the Ohio River here. • One of two counties (the other in NY) definitively named for Robert R. Livingston (1746–1813), NY patriot, statesman, and a drafter of the Declaration of Independence • 1798 from Christian • Tobacco, corn, wheat, soybeans, hay, alfalfa, hogs, cattle, poultry, dairying; catfish; limestone quarries.

LOGAN (one of ten counties so named) *Russellville* • 26,573 • 556 • Southern KY, bounded on the south by the TN state line; drained by the Mud, Red, and Gasper rivers, and by Whippoorwill, Wolf Lick, and Elk Lick creeks. Part of Lake Malone reservoir is in the northwest corner. Lake Herndon reservoir is in the center of the county. • One of two counties (the other in OH) named for Benjamin Logan (?–1802), early settler, KY legislator, and general in the KY militia • 1792 from Lincoln • In 1805, Shakers from New York purchased 3,000 acres of land near South Union; Shakertown was a settlement for over 100 years. • Texas Revolution hero Jim Bowie • Dark and burley tobacco, corn, wheat, barley, soybeans, alfalfa, hay, cattle, hogs, poultry, dairying; timber; bituminous-coal and asphalt mines; limestone quarries; manufacturing • The famous Jackson-Dickinson duel was fought at "Popular Bottom" in Adairville in 1806.

LYON (one of five counties so named) *Eddyville* • 8,080 • 216 • Western KY, bounded on the southwest by the Tennessee River (Kentucky Lake reservoir) and on the northwest by the Cumberland River. The county includes part of Kentucky Woodlands Nature Center and the northern quarter of Land Between the Lakes Recreation Area. Barkley Dam on the Cumberland River on the western boundary forms Lake Barkley reservoir, which crosses the county. Two units of West Kentucky Farm Center are in the north. Mineral Mound State Park is also in the county. • Named for either Chittenden Lyon (?–1842), U.S. representative from KY; or for Matthew Lyon (?–1822), U.S. representative from VT and KY, and U.S. factor to the Cherokee Indians • 1854 from Caldwell • Burley and dark tobacco, corn, wheat, soybeans, hay, alfalfa, hogs, cattle; catfish; limestone quarries; hardwood timber. • The first air-boiling process for manufacturing steel (now called the Bessemer Process) was developed by William Kelly in 1851 near Eddyville.

MADISON *Richmond* • 70,872 • 441 • Central KY, bounded on the northwest, north and northeast by the Kentucky River and on the west in part by Paint Lick creek; drained by Silver, Muddy, and Red Lick creeks. The county lies in the Bluegrass region of the state. A small part of Daniel Boone National Forest is here. Blue Grass Army Depot is in the east. • One of twenty counties named for President James Madison • 1785

(prior to statehood) from Lincoln • KY's first Confederate victory took place in Richmond on Aug. 29–31, 1862, when Gen. Kirby-Smith's troops defeated Union forces under Gen. William Nelson, capturing the city and pushing the Union troops into northern retreat. The courthouse was used as a hospital during the war. • Abolitionist Cassius M. Clay (White Hall Historic Site); U.S. Supreme Court justice Samuel Freeman Miller • Burley tobacco, corn, hay, alfalfa, poultry, cattle, horses, dairying; bituminous-coal mines; clay pits; light manufacturing; education (Eastern KY U.; Berea College) • The oldest continuously operating pottery west of the Alleghenies, Bybee, near Richmond, was established in 1845.

MAGOFFIN *Salyersville* • 13,332 • 309 • Eastern KY, in the Cumberland Mountains; drained by the Licking River and several creeks. • Named for Beriah Magoffin (1815–85), KY legislator and governor • 1860 from Floyd, Johnson and Morgan • Publisher Larry Flynt • Burley tobacco, corn, hay, cattle; bituminous-coal mines; oil wells; timber.

MARION *Lebanon* • 18,212 • 347 • Central KY; drained by Rolling Fork and Beech Fork. The county lies partly in the Bluegrass region. • One of seventeen counties named for Gen. Francis Marion (?–1795), SC soldier and legislator, known as "The Swamp Fox" for his tactics during the Revolutionary War • 1834 from Washington County • Burley tobacco, corn, alfalfa, soybeans, wheat, hogs, cattle, poultry, dairying; timber; stone quarries; manufacturing.

MARSHALL (one of twelve counties so named) *Benton* • 30,125 • 305 • Western KY, bounded on the north and east by the Tennessee River, forming Kentucky Lake reservoir on the east (Kentucky Dam); drained by the East and West forks of the Clarks River. Kentucky Dam Village State Park is here. • One of eight counties named for John Marshall (1755–1835), fourth Chief Justice of the U.S. • 1842 from Calloway • Corn, dark and burley tobacco, alfalfa, hay, soybeans, wheat, corn, hogs, cattle; timber; clay pits; manufacturing.

MARTIN (one of six counties so named) *Inez* • 12,578 • 231 • Eastern KY, in the Cumberland Mountains, bounded on the east by the Tug Fork of the Big Sandy River (forming the WV state line); drained by several creeks. • Named for John P. Martin (1811–62), KY legislator and U.S. representative from KY • 1870 from Johnson, Pike, Floyd and Lawrence • Livestock, tobacco; bituminous-coal mines.

MASON (one of six counties so named) *Maysville* • 16,800 • 241 • Northeastern KY, bounded on the north by the Ohio River (forming the OH state line); drained by the North Fork of the Licking River. The county lies in the northern part of the Bluegrass region. • One of two counties (the other in WV) named for George Mason (1725–92), patriot and author of the VA Declaration of Rights • 1788 (prior to statehood) from Bourbon • Maysville was established as Limestone in 1787 at the site of a tavern operated (1786–89) by Daniel Boone and his wife, Rebecca. By 1792 it had become a landing point for pioneers. • Justice of the peace and saloon keeper Roy Bean;

Supreme Court justice Stanley Reed; singer Rosemary Clooney; President Ulysses S. Grant (attended school here). The childhood home of Confederate Gen. Albert Johnston, located in Washington, was later owned by Union Gen. William "Bull" Nelson. • Maysville is considered the second largest burley tobacco market in the world. Also, corn, wheat, soybeans, hay, alfalfa, cattle, poultry, dairying; limestone; some manufacturing • The National Underground Railroad Museum in Maysville preserves artifacts that chronicle the history of the Underground Railroad. Several stations were located throughout the county.

MCCRACKEN *Paducah* • 65,514 • 251 • Western KY, bounded on the north by the Ohio River (forming the IL state line) and on the northeast by the Tennessee River (entering the Ohio River); drained by the Clarks River and its East and West forks, and by Mayfield Creek. Metropolis Lake State Nature Preserve is in the north. Lock and Dam No. 52 is on the Ohio River at Paducah. • Named for Captain Virgil McCracken (?–1813), KY legislator, killed during the War of 1812 at the Battle of River Raisin • 1824 from Hickman • The site that would become Paducah was part of a grant to soldier and frontiersman George Rogers Clark. It was inherited by his brother, the explorer William Clark, who laid out the town in 1827. Because of its strategic river facilities, Paducah was occupied by Grant's forces during the Civil War and was raided by Confederate General Nathan Bedford Forrest. Due to its location in one of the world's greatest power-generating regions, the county's growth has been greatly enhanced by TVA and Atomic Energy Commission (now U.S. Department of Energy) projects. • Journalist and humorist Irvin S. Cobb; Vice President Alben W. Barkley • Dark and burley tobacco, corn, strawberries, sorghum, hay, soybeans, wheat, hogs, cattle, poultry, dairying; clay, sand and gravel, coal; timber; manufacture of aluminum, zinc castings, wire, beverages, clothing; uranium separation.

MCCREARY *Whitley City* • 17,080 • 428 • Southern KY, in the Cumberland Mountains, bounded on the south by the TN state line, on the north and northeast by the Cumberland River, and on the west by part of the Little South Fork River; drained by the South Fork of the Cumberland River. Daniel Boone National Forest covers the entire county. It includes part of Big South Fork National River and Recreation Area. • Named for Lt. Col. James B. McCreary (1838–1918), Confederate army officer, governor of KY, and U.S. senator from KY • 1912 from Pulaski, Wayne, and Whitley • Bituminous-coal mining; timber, some lumber milling; oil wells; burley tobacco, hay, cattle • The only "moonbow" in the Western Hemisphere (a rainbow-like spectrum produced from a combination of moonlight and mist) occurs at Cumberland Falls.

MCLEAN (one of three counties so named) *Calhoun* • 9,938 • 254 • Western KY, bounded on the west by the Green and Pond rivers; drained by the Green River (forming part of the southwestern boundary) and Cypress Creek. • Named for Captain Alney McLean (1779–1841), U.S. representative from

KY and jurist • 1854 from Daviess, Ohio and Muhlenberg counties • In 1861, Lt. Col. Nathan Bedford Forrest and his troops battled Union forces near Sacramento (an event reenacted each May). • Soybeans, corn, wheat, dark and burley tobacco, tomatoes, hay, alfalfa, hogs, cattle, timber; bituminous-coal mines; some manufacturing.

MEADE (one of three counties so named) *Brandenburg* • 26,349 • 308 • Northern KY, bounded on the north and northwest by the Ohio River (forming the IN state line); drained in the east by Otter Creek. Part of Fort Knox Military Reservation is here. Otter Creek Park is also in the county. • Named for Captain James Meade (?–1813), an officer in the War of 1812 killed in the Battle of River Raisin • 1823 from Breckinridge and Hardin • Burley tobacco, hay, alfalfa, soybeans, wheat, hogs, cattle; timber; limestone.

MENIFEE *Frenchburg* • 6,556 • 204 • East-central KY, bounded on the northeast by the Licking River (forming Cave Run Lake reservoir) and on the south by the Red River (designated a Wild and Recreational River); drained by several creeks. Most of the county, except for its east and west ends, lies in Daniel Boone National Forest. Part of Red River Geological Area, including Red River Gorge, is in the south. • Named for Richard H. Menefee (1809–41), U.S. representative from KY. The spelling discrepancy is attributed to spelling error. • 1869 from Montgomery, Bath, Wolfe, and Morgan • Burley tobacco, hay, cattle; oil and gas wells; timber, some sawmills.

MERCER (one of eight counties so named) *Harrodsburg* • 20,817 • 251 • Central KY, bounded on the northeast by the Kentucky River and on the southeast by the Dix River, Dix Dam forming Herrington Lake; drained by the Salt and Chaplin rivers. The county lies in the Bluegrass region of the state. It includes Old Fort Harrod State Park. • One of six counties definitively named for Gen. Hugh Mercer (?–1777), physician and Revolutionary War officer who died at the Battle of Princeton • 1785 (prior to statehood) from Lincoln • KY's first permanent settlement, and the first west of the Alleghenies, Harrodsburg, established in 1774, was also the site of KY's first court of law, school and religious service. • Burley tobacco, soybeans, wheat, corn, hay, alfalfa, hogs, cattle, poultry, dairying; calcite mines, limestone quarries; manufacturing • Shaker Village at Pleasant Hill is the largest restored Shaker settlement in the United States. • High Bridge, which spans the Kentucky River connecting Mercer and Jessamine counties, was the highest railroad trestle in the world when constructed in 1877.

METCALFE *Edmonton* • 10,037 • 291 • Southern KY; drained by the Little Barren River, and Beaver and Marrowbone creeks. • Named for Capt. Thomas Metcalfe (1780–1855), KY legislator, U. S representative from KY and governor of the state • 1860 from Adair, Monroe, Cumberland, Barren and Green • Corn, wheat, burley tobacco, soybeans, hay, alfalfa, cattle, poultry, dairying; timber.

MONROE *Tomkinsville* • 11,756 • 331 • Southern KY,

bounded on the south by the TN state line; drained by the Cumberland River (forming part of the eastern boundary), Barren River, and Skaggs Creek. The county includes Old Mulkey Meetinghouse State Historic Site. • One of seventeen counties named for President James Monroe • 1820 from Barren and Cumberland • Corn, wheat, hay, alfalfa, burley tobacco, soybeans, cattle, poultry, dairying; timber; limestone quarries.

MONTGOMERY (one of eighteen counties so named) *Mount Sterling* • 22,554 • 199 • East-central KY; drained by Hinkston (forming part of the northeast boundary) and Slate creeks. The county lies in the northeast part of the Bluegrass region of the state. • One of sixteen counties named for Gen. Richard Montgomery (1738–75), American Revolutionary War officer who captured Montreal, Canada • 1796 (prior to statehood) from Clark • On March 22, 1782, Captain Estill and his troops were defeated here at the Battle of Little Mountain. • Burley tobacco, corn, soybeans, hay, alfalfa, cattle, poultry, dairying; manufacturing.

MORGAN (one of eleven counties so named) *West Liberty* • 13,948 • 381 • Eastern KY; drained by the Licking River (the upper reach of Cave Run Lake reservoir is in the northwest) and several creeks. The county is in the Cumberland foothills. It includes part of Daniel Boone National Forest and part of Paintsville Lake reservoir. • One of nine counties named for Gen. Daniel Morgan (1736–1802), officer in the Revolutionary War • 1822 from Floyd and Bath • Corn, burley tobacco, sorghum, hay, alfalfa, cattle; bituminous-coal mines • The nation's largest Kentucky Coffee Tree (78 feet tall) is located here.

MUHLENBERG *Greenville* • 31,839 • 475 • Western KY, bounded on the northeast by the Green River, on the east by the Mud River, and on the west by the Pond River; drained by Pond, Cypress, and Rocky creeks. Lake Malone reservoir (Rocky Creek) and State Park are on the southern boundary. • Named for Gen. John P. G. Muhlenberg (1746–1807), an officer in the Revolutionary War, Vice President of PA, and representative from PA in both houses of Congress • 1798 from Christian and Logan • Bituminous-coal mining; soybeans, burley and dark tobacco, wheat, hay, alfalfa, corn, hogs, cattle; timber; limestone; manufacturing.

NELSON (one of three counties so named) *Bardstown* • 37,477 • 423 • Central KY, bounded on the southwest by Rolling Fork and on the southeast by the Chaplin River. Nelson is a Bluegrass county. Part of Taylorsville Lake reservoir is in the northeast corner. "Federal Hill," a Georgian house now enshrined in My Old Kentucky Home State Park, is reputedly where Stephen Foster wrote the song for which the park was named. Part of Bernheim Forest Nature Center is also in the county. • One of two counties (the other in VA) named for Thomas Nelson (1738–89), a signer of the Declaration of Independence and governor of VA • 1784 (prior to statehood) from Jefferson • Established by act of the Virginia Legislature

in 1788, Bardstown is the second-oldest city in KY. It was occupied in September, 1862 by Confederate Forces under General Braxton Bragg. • The county is famous for its whiskey distilling (the Museum of Whiskey History is here); also burley tobacco, soybeans, wheat, corn, hay, alfalfa, hogs, cattle, poultry, dairying; hardwood timber; some manufacturing • The oldest continuously operated tavern west of the Alleghenies, the Old Talbott Tavern, founded in 1779, is located in Bardstown. The first patent for a steamboat was given to John Fitch of Bardstown in 1791. St. Joseph's Cathedral, built in Bardstown in 1819, is the oldest Roman Catholic cathedral west of the Alleghenies. Its paintings are believed to have belonged to King Louis Philippe of France.

NICHOLAS (one of two counties so named, the other in WV) *Carlisle* • 6,813 • 197 • Northern KY, bounded on the northeast by the Licking River and on the southwest by Hinkston Creek. The county lies in the Bluegrass region of the state. • Named for Col. George Nicholas (?–1799), officer in the Revolutionary War and first attorney general of KY • 1799 from Bourbon and Mason • In the Battle of Blue Licks, which took place here in 1782 along the Licking River (and partly in Robertson County on the other side of the river), Shawnee Indians and British troops routed a KY militia. Daniel Boone was a participant in this, the last Revolutionary War battle fought in KY; Boone's son Israel was among the many casualties (Blue Licks Battlefield State Park). • Burley tobacco, hay, alfalfa, corn, cattle, poultry, dairying.

OHIO (one of three counties so named) *Hartford* • 22,916 • 594 (the fifth largest county in KY) • Western KY, bounded on the southwest and southeast (in part) by the Green River; drained by the Rough River, Caney Creek, and the South Fork of Panther Creek. • Named for the Ohio River, which formed its northern border when the county was created • 1798 from Hardin • Burley and dark tobacco, hay, alfalfa, soybeans, wheat, corn, hogs, cattle; bituminous-coal mines; limestone quarries; timber.

OLDHAM (one of two counties so named, the other in TX) *La Grange* • 46,178 • 189 • Northern KY, bounded on the west and northwest by the Ohio River (forming the IN state line); drained by Floyds Fork and Harrods Creek. The county is located in the northern part of the Bluegrass region. It is urbanized in the southwest, constituting an extension of the Louisville metropolitan area. • Named for Col. William Oldham (1753–1791), officer in the American Revolution • 1823 from Jefferson, Shelby, and Henry • Silent film director D.W. Griffith; Masonic leader Rob Morris • Burley tobacco, corn, wheat, hay, alfalfa, soybeans, hogs, cattle, poultry, dairying; limestone.

OWEN *Owenton* • 10,547 • 352 • Northern KY, bounded on the southwest by the Kentucky River and on the northwest (and drained) by Eagle Creek. The county lies in the Bluegrass region. Elmer Davis Lake and Elk Lake reservoirs are in the center of the county. • One of two counties (the other in IN) named for Abraham Owen (1769–1811), KY legislator, aide-de-camp to Gen. William Henry Harrison, killed at the Battle of Tippecanoe • 1819 from Scott, Gallatin, and Franklin • Burley tobacco, corn, hay, alfalfa, cattle, poultry, dairying; lead and zinc mines, limestone quarries.

OWSLEY *Booneville* • 4,858 • 198 • East-central KY, in the Cumberland Mountains; drained by the South Fork of the Kentucky River, and several creeks. Parts of Daniel Boone National Forest are in the northwest and southeast. • Named for William Owsley (1782–1862), jurist and governor of KY • 1843 from Clay, Estill and Breathitt • Livestock, burley tobacco, hay; bituminous-coal mines; timber.

PENDLETON *Falmouth* • 14,390 • 280 • Northern KY, bounded in the northeast by the Ohio River (forming the OH state line); drained by the Licking River and its South Fork, and the South Fork of Grassy Creek. The county is located in the northern part of the Bluegrass region. Kincaid Lake State Park is here. • One of two counties (the other in WV) named for Edmund Pendleton (1721–1803), member of the Continental Congress and presiding judge of the VA court of appeals • 1787 from Campbell and Bracken • Molecular biologist Phillip Sharp • Burley tobacco, hay, corn, alfalfa, soybeans, cattle, sheep, poultry, dairying; some manufacturing.

PERRY *Hazard* • 29,390 • 342 • Southeastern KY, in the Cumberlands; drained by the North Fork, Middle and Carr forks of the Kentucky River, and Troublesome Creek. Buckhorn Lake Reservoir and State Resort Park (on the Middle Fork of the Kentucky River) is in the northwest. • One of ten counties named for Oliver Hazard Perry (1785–1819), U.S. naval officer during the War of 1812 • 1820 from Clay and Floyd • Bituminous-coal mining, oil and gas wells; timber; burley tobacco, livestock; manufacturing.

PIKE *Pikeville* • 68,736 • 788 (the largest county in KY) • Eastern KY, in the Cumberland Mountains, bounded on the northeast by Tug Fork (forming the WV state line) and on the southeast by the VA state line; drained by the Levisa and Russell Fork rivers. The county includes Breaks of Big Sandy River (in Breaks Interstate Park) and part of Jefferson National Forest. Fishtrap Lake reservoir is also here. • One of ten counties named for Gen. Zebulon Montgomery Pike (1779–1813), U.S. army officer and discoverer of Pikes Peak in CO • 1821 from Floyd • Pike is one of the leading counties in KY in bituminous-coal production; livestock, hay; timber; some manufacturing; education (Pikeville College). The county was made famous by the mountain-family feud between the local McCoy family and the Hatfields of Logan County, WV.

POWELL (one of two counties so named, the other in MT) *Stanton* • 13,237 • 180 • East-central KY; drained by the Red River (designated a National Wild and Recreational River) and several creeks. It includes Pilot Knob State Nature Park and part of Natural Bridge State Park. Red River Gorge in Red River National Geological Area is in the northeast corner. Part of Daniel Boone National Forest is in its eastern half. • Named

for Lazarus W. Powell (1812–1867), governor of KY and U.S. senator from KY • 1852 from Montgomery, Clark and Estill • Corn, hay, burley tobacco, cattle; bituminous-coal mines, limestone quarries; timber; manufacturing.

PULASKI *Somerset* • 56,217 • 662 (the third largest county in KY) • Southern KY, bounded on the east by the Rockcastle River; drained by the Cumberland River (forming Lake Cumberland reservoir), and by Fishing, Pitman, and Buck creeks. The county lies partly in the Cumberland foothills. It includes Mill Springs National Cemetery, part of Daniel Boone National Forest in the east and southeast, and General Burnside State Park. • One of seven counties named for Count Casimir Pulaski (1748–79), Polish soldier who fought for America during the Revolutionary War • 1798 from Lincoln and Green • Confederate General Felix Zollicoffer was killed here on Jan. 19, 1862 at the Battle of Mill Springs. Zollicoffer Memorial Park is accompanied by a national cemetery ten miles west of Somerset. • Burley tobacco, corn, hay, alfalfa, soybeans, wheat, cattle, hogs; stone quarries; timber; manufacture of auto parts, glass, clothing, plumbing fixtures, lumber, furniture, feed products.

ROBERTSON (one of three counties so named) *Mount Olivet* • 2,266 (the least populated county in KY) • 100 (only one square mile larger than KY's smallest county Gallatin and one of the fifty smallest counties in the U.S.) • Northern KY, bounded on the west and southwest by the Licking River, on the north by the North Fork of the Licking River; drained by Johnson Creek. The county is situated in the Bluegrass region. • Named for George Robertson (1790–1874), U.S. representative from KY and chief justice of KY Court of Appeals • 1867 from Nicholas, Harrison, Bracken and Mason • In the Battle of Blue Licks, which took place in 1782 along the Licking River (and partly in Nicholas County on the other side of the river), Shawnee Indians and British troops routed a KY militia. Daniel Boone was a participant in this, the last Revolutionary War battle fought in KY; Boone's son Israel was among the many casualties (Blue Licks Battlefield State Park). • Cattle, poultry, burley tobacco, corn, hay, alfalfa.

ROCKCASTLE *Mount Vernon* • 16,582 • 318 • Central KY, bounded on the southeast by the Rockcastle River; drained by the Dix River and Roundstone Creek. The county includes part of Daniel Boone National Forest in the east, including Great Saltpeter Cave. • Named for the Rockcastle River • 1810 from Lincoln, Pulaski, Madison, and Knox • Burley tobacco, hay, alfalfa, corn, cattle, hogs, poultry, dairying; bituminous-coal mines, limestone and sandstone quarries, oil wells; timber.

ROWAN (one of two counties so named, the other in NC) *Morehead* • 22,094 • 281 • Northeastern KY, bounded on the southwest by the Licking River, forming Cave Run Lake reservoir. Daniel Boone National Forest covers most of the county. • Named for John Rowan (1773–1843), senator and representative from KY • 1856 from Fleming and Morgan • Clay mining, sandstone quarries; timber; burley tobacco, hay, alfalfa, soybeans, corn, cattle; manufacturing; education (Morehead State U.).

RUSSELL (one of four counties so named) *Jamestown* • 16,315 • 254 • Southern KY; drained by the Cumberland River and Russell Creek. The county lies in the Cumberland foothills. Lake Cumberland reservoir is on the Cumberland River, and dominates the southeastern part of the county. Lake Cumberland State Resort Park is here. Natural Bridge is in the west. • One of two counties (the other in VA) named for William Russell (1758–1825), VA soldier and statesman who served in the legislatures of VA and KY • 1825 from Wayne, Adair, and Cumberland • Corn, burley tobacco, hay, alfalfa, soybeans, wheat, hogs, cattle, poultry, dairying; manufacturing.

SCOTT (one of eleven counties so named) *Georgetown* • 33,061 • 285 • Northern KY, bounded on the southwest by Elkhorn Creek; drained by Eagle and North Elkhorn creeks. The county lies in the Bluegrass region. • One of two counties (the other in IN) named for Gen. Charles Scott (1739–1813), career soldier and governor of KY • 1792 from Woodford • Burley tobacco, corn, hay, alfalfa, hogs, cattle; limestone quarries; manufacturing; education (Midway College; Georgetown College) • In 1789, Rev. Elijah Craig reputedly invented bourbon whiskey in Georgetown. Located in Georgetown, KY's largest spring, Royal Spring, gushes twenty-seven million gallons of water a day.

SHELBY *Shelbyville* • 33,337 • 384 • Northern KY; drained by Beech, Plum, Clear, and Guist creeks. The county is located in the Bluegrass region. Guist Creek Lake reservoir is here. • One of nine counties named for Gen. Isaac Shelby (1750–1826), officer in the Revolutionary War and first governor of KY • 1792 from Jefferson • Daniel Boone's frontiersman father Richard built a fort about two miles from present-day Shelbyville, but had to abandon it in 1781 after an Indian attack. • Novelist and short-story writer Alice Rice • Burley tobacco, corn, wheat, soybeans, alfalfa, hay, hogs, cattle, poultry, dairying; some manufacturing, including fertilizers, utensils, metal products; flour and feed mills; printing.

SIMPSON (one of two counties so named, the other in MS) *Franklin* • 16,405 • 236 • Southern KY, bounded on the south by the TN state line; drained by the West Fork of Drakes Creek. • Named for Captain John Simpson (?–1813), KY legislator, killed at the Battle of River Raisin during the War of 1812 • 1819 from Logan, Warren, and Allen • Dark and burley tobacco, strawberries, barley, wheat, corn, soybeans, hay, alfalfa, hogs, cattle, poultry, dairying; timber; limestone quarries; manufacturing • The jag or nick in the KY-TN line on the county's southern border is attributed to the "hospitality" of landowner Sanford Duncan who reputedly plied surveyors with wine and cider to keep his holdings in KY.

SPENCER *Taylorsville* • 11,766 (73% increase since 1990; the fastest growing county in KY) • 186 • North-central KY; drained by the Salt River (forming Taylorsville Lake reservoir

in the east) and several creeks. The county lies in the Bluegrass region. Taylorsville Lake State Park is here. • One of two counties (the other in KY) named for Captain Spear Spencer (?–1811), KY officer killed at the Battle of Tippecanoe • 1824 from Nelson, Shelby, and Bullitt • Hay, alfalfa, soybeans, wheat, corn, burley tobacco, hogs, cattle, poultry, dairying; manufacturing.

TAYLOR (one of seven counties so named) *Campbellsville* • 22,927 • 270 • Central KY; drained by the Green River (forming Green River Lake reservoir in the south), Big Pitman and Robinson creeks. Green River Lake State Park is here. • One of four counties named for President Zachary Taylor • 1848 from Green • Burley tobacco, corn, oats, hay, wheat, alfalfa, soybeans, hogs, poultry, cattle, dairying; timber; limestone quarries; manufacture of wood products, furniture, ready-mixed concrete, men's clothing, dairy products, livestock feeds; education (Campbellsville U.).

TODD (one of three counties so named) *Elkton* • 11,971 • 376 • Southern KY, bounded on the south by the TN state line; drained by the Pond River, and the Elk and West forks of the Red River. An arm of Lake Malone reservoir is also in the county. • Named for John Todd (1750–1782), VA legislator killed in the American Revolution in the Battle of Blue Licks • 1819 from Logan and Christian • Lawyer and statesman Benjamin H. Bristow; President of the Confederate States of America Jefferson Davis (State Historic Site); architect Paul Rudolph; author Robert Penn Warren; United Daughters of the Confederacy founder Caroline Meriwether Goodlett; U.S. Supreme Court justice James McReynolds • Dark tobacco, hay, alfalfa, soybeans, wheat, barley, corn, fruits, hogs, cattle, poultry, dairying; timber; stone quarries.

TRIGG *Cadiz* • 12,597 • 443 • Southwestern KY, bounded on the south by the TN state line and on the west by the Tennessee River (forming Kentucky Lake Reservoir); drained by the Cumberland River (Lake Barkley reservoir), and the Little River and its Muddy Fork. The middle third of the Land Between the Lakes Recreational Area (TVA) is here. Lake Barkley State Resort Park is also in the county. Part of Fort Campbell Military Reservation is in the southeast. Lake Barkley State Resort Park is west-center. • Named for Col. Stephen Trigg (1742–1782), an officer killed in action against Indians at Blue Licks • 1820 from Christian and Caldwell • Tobacco, wheat, corn, hay, alfalfa, soybeans, hogs, cattle; limestone quarries; timber.

TRIMBLE *Bedford* • 8,125 • 149 (one of the fifty smallest counties in the U.S.) • Northern KY, bounded on the north and west by the Ohio River (forming the IN state line); drained by the Little Kentucky River. The county is located in the northern part of the Bluegrass region. • Named for Robert Trimble (?–1828), associate justice of the U.S. Supreme Court • 1837 from Gallatin, Oldham, and Henry • Burley tobacco, hay, alfalfa, soybeans, wheat, corn, cattle, poultry, dairying; timber; stone quarries, sand and gravel.

UNION (one of eighteen counties so named) *Morganfield* • 15,637 • 345 • Western KY, bounded on the west by the IL state line (formed by the Ohio River), on the north by the IN state line (also formed by the Ohio River), and on the south by the Tradewater River. Uniontown Lock and Dam is on the Ohio River, two miles east of the confluence of the Wabash River. Higginson-Henry Wildlife Management Area is here. • Possibly named for the united desire to create this new county • 1811 from Henderson • Corn, wheat, hay, alfalfa, soybeans, hogs, cattle; bituminous coal, sand and gravel; manufacturing.

WARREN *Bowling Green* • 92,522 (the fifth most populated county in KY) • 545 • Southern KY, bounded on the north by the Green River; drained by the Barren River, Gasper Creek, Drakes Creek, and its Trammel and West forks. • One of fourteen counties named for Gen. Joseph Warren (1741–75), Revolutionary War patriot and member of the Committee of Safety • 1796 from Logan • Bowling Green was founded in 1780 by settlers from VA. It was named for the green on which lawyers and court officials played bowls during recess periods. The city was designated the Confederate capital of KY in 1861. It was occupied by Confederate troops under General Simon B. Buckner until Union forces commanded by Ulysses S. Grant and Don Carlos Buell forced their retreat in 1862. • Food critic and writer Duncan Hines • Burley tobacco, corn, strawberries, hay, alfalfa, soybeans, wheat, poultry, hogs, cattle, dairying; limestone quarries, oil and gas wells; diversified manufacturing; education (Western KY U.) • The only Chevrolet Corvette manufacturing plant in the world is in Bowling Green, which is also home to the National Corvette Museum.

WASHINGTON *Springfield* • 10,916 • 301 • Central KY, in the Bluegrass region, bounded on the northwest by Beech Fork and the Chaplin River (both of which cross the county) and on the southwest by Hardins Creek. The county includes Lincoln Homestead State Park. • One of thirty-one counties named for President George Washington • 1792 from Nelson • This was the first county formed after KY became a state. • Burley tobacco, hay, alfalfa, soybeans, sorghum, wheat, corn, poultry, hogs, cattle, dairying; some timber.

WAYNE (one of sixteen counties so named) *Monticello* • 19,923 • 459 • Southern KY, in the Cumberland foothills, bounded on the south by the TN state line and on the east in part by the South and Little South forks of the Cumberland; crossed by the Cumberland River (forming Lake Cumberland reservoir, including two large arms; also forming part of the northern and northwestern county border); drained by Beaver Creek. The county includes a small part of Daniel Boone National Forest in the southeastern corner. • One of fifteen counties named for Gen. Anthony Wayne (1745–96), PA soldier and statesman, nicknamed "Mad Anthony" for his daring during the Revolutionary War • 1800 from Pulaski and Cumberland • Burley tobacco, hay, alfalfa, soybeans, wheat, corn, hogs, cattle, poultry, dairying, bituminous-coal mines, oil wells, rock quarries; timber.

WEBSTER *Dixon* • 14,120 • 335 • Western KY, bounded on the northeast by the Green River and on the southwest by the Tradewater River. • One of eight counties named for Daniel Webster (1782–1852), U.S. statesman and orator from MA • 1860 from Hopkins, Union and Henderson • Burley and dark tobacco, sorghum, alfalfa, soybeans, wheat, corn, hogs, cattle; bituminous-coal mines, gas wells; timber; some manufacturing.

WHITLEY *Williamsburg* • 35,865 • 440 • Southeastern KY, bounded on the south by the TN state line, on the north by the Laurel River (forming Laurel River Lake reservoir), and on the northwest by the Cumberland River, which crosses east to west. The county is located on the Cumberland Plateau. Part of Daniel Boone National Forest is here. Part of Cumberland Falls State Resort Park is also in the county. • One of two counties (the other in IN) named for William Whitley (1749–1813), the soldier believed by some to have killed Shawnee Chief Tecumseh • 1818 from Knox • Burley tobacco, hay, corn, cattle; bituminous-coal mining, gas wells; hardwood timber; education (Cumberland College).

WOLFE *Campton* • 7,065 • 223 • East-central KY; drained by the Red River. The county is located in the Cumberland Mountains and includes parts of Natural Bridge State Resort Park, Daniel Boone National Forest, and Red River National Geological Area. • Named for Nathaniel Wolfe (1810–65), KY legislator • 1860 from Breathitt, Morgan, Powell and Owsley • Burley tobacco, hay, corn, cattle.

WOODFORD (one of two counties so named) *Versailles* • 23,208 • 191 • Central KY, bounded on the south, southwest, and west by the Kentucky River, and on the north and northeast by Elkhorn Creek. • Named for William Woodford (?–1780), French and Indian War and Revolutionary War general • 1788 (prior to statehood) from Fayette (the last county formed while KY was still a part of VA) • Statesman John J. Crittenden • Burley tobacco, hay, alfalfa, soybeans, dairying, poultry, wheat, corn, cattle, horses; manufacture of whiskey, clothing, boats, brooms; flour and feed mills.

LOUISIANA

Union, Justice, and Confidence

Louisiana is unique among the states in calling its counties parishes. Originally the word referred to the administrative units of the Roman Catholic Church during the years in which the area was under Spanish rule. The state constitution of 1845 directed the state to drop its county organization and turn over to parishes the counties' governmental functions. Most of Louisiana's sixty-four parishes have a central government body called the police jury, similar in structure and function to the county board of commissioners. The sheriff is the chief enforcement officer and tax collector in the parish.

ACADIA *Crowley* • 58,861 • 655 • Southern LA, bounded on the west by Bayou Nezpique and the Mermentau River, on the south by Bayou Queue de Tortue; drained by Bayou des Cannes. • Named for the original county of Acadia in Orleans Territory, itself named for French Acadie, an area in northeastern Canada and ME, former home of present-day Cajuns, descendents of French settlers displaced by English troops • 1886 from Saint Landry Parish • The parish produces one fourth of the nation's rice. Also corn, wheat, soybeans, vegetables, sweet potatoes, cattle, horses, poultry; aquaculture; oil and natural gas; cotton ginning; manufacture of textiles, pipe fittings, sporting goods, burlap bags, concrete blocks, machine-shop products, fertilizer, clothing; lumber • Called the "Rice Capital of America," Crowley hosts the International Rice Festival each October. A rice-growing experiment station here is both state and federally administered.

ALLEN (one of five counties/parishes so named) *Oberlin* • 25,440 • 765 • Southwest-central LA, bounded on the southeast by Bayou Nezpique; drained by the Calcasieu River, and Bundick and Whiskey Chitto creeks. Coushatta Indian Reservation is in the southeast. • Named for Henry W. Allen (1820–66), Confederate general and governor of LA • 1912 from Calcasieu Parish • Lumber milling, logging; manufacture of clothing, wood products, plastic resins; rice, corn, sweet potatoes, peaches, vegetables, soybeans, pecans, livestock, dairying; crawfish.

ASCENSION *Donaldsonville* • 76,627 (31.6% since 1990; the second fastest growing parish in LA) • 292 • Southeastern LA, bounded on the northeast by the Amite, Petite Amite, and Blind rivers, on the north by Bayou Manchac; intersected by the Mississippi River. • Named for the old Catholic District of Ascension • 1807 (prior to statehood) from Acadia Parish • The parish was settled by Acadians between 1764 and 1772. Donaldsonville served as capital of the state in 1830 and 1831. • Strawberries, home gardening, nursery crops, sugarcane, pecans, peppers, cattle, horses, hogs, ostriches; crawfish, alligators; petrochemicals; natural gas wells; logging; some manufacturing • The county is known for its antebellum homes.

ASSUMPTION *Napoleonville* • 23,388 • 339 • Southeastern LA, bounded on the west in part by the Belle River; intersected by the navigable Bayou Lafourche. The parish includes Lake Verret in the west. • Named for the Roman Catholic Church of the Assumption at Plattenville, LA, the oldest church in the state. • 1807 (prior to statehood) from Lafourche • Sugar cane, rice, corn, home gardens, cattle, horses; crawfish, crabs; sugar milling.

AVOYELLES *Marksville* • 41,481 • 833 • East-central LA, bounded in part on the north and east by the Red River, and on the east by the Atchafalaya River. It is the northernmost of the Acadian parishes of southern LA. There are several lakes in the northeast. The parish includes Marksville State Historic Site, Tunica-Biloxi Indian Reservation, and part of Grand Cote and Lake Ophelia national wildlife refuges. The Eola oil and natural gas field is here. • Named for the Avoyel Indians who built temple mounds at the site of Marksville • Original parish; organized 1807 (prior to statehood) • Writer Ruth Stuart • Cotton, berries, corn, sorghum, hay, soybeans, sugar cane, sweet potatoes, vegetables, cattle, hogs, horses, honey; crawfish; manufacture of food products and clothing; logging; gambling. • Marksville hosts the "Egg Knocking Festival" every Easter Sunday morning. On October 23, 1947, thousands of fish rained from the sky upon the town.

BEAUREGARD *De Ridder* • 32,986 • 1,160 • Western LA, bounded on the west by the Sabine River, here forming the TX state line; drained by Bear Head, Bundick, and Whiskey Chitto creeks. The parish includes Bundicks Fish and Game Preserve at Bundick Lake reservoir. • Named for Pierre G. T. Beauregard (1818–93), superintendent at West Point who resigned to join the Confederate army and directed the bombardment of Fort Sumter and the battles of Bull Run and Shiloh • 1912 from Calcasieu • Blueberries, feed grains, hay, nursery crops, rice, soybeans, squash, watermelons, cattle, exotic fowl; dairying; manufacture of clothing, chemicals, plastics, resins; logging, paper mills; sand and gravel.

BIENVILLE *Arcadia* • 15,752 • 811 • Northwestern LA, bounded partly on the west by Lake Bistineau and Black Lake Bayou; drained by several tributaries of the Red River. At 535 feet, Driskill Mountain, in the northeast, is the highest point in the state. Kepler Creek Lake and Mill Creek reservoirs are also found in the parish. • Named for Jean Baptiste Le Moyne,

Sieur de Bienville (1680- ?), founder of New Orleans and governor of the French colony of LA • 1848 from Claiborne • Cotton, berries, peaches, hay, sweet potatoes, squash, watermelons, horses, cattle, poultry, dairying; logging • Bank robbers Bonnie Parker and Clyde Barrow were gunned down near Gibsland.

BOSSIER *Benton* • 98,310 • 838 • Northwestern LA, bounded on the north by the AR state line, on the west by the Red River, on the southeast by Loggy Bayou and Lake Bistineau, on the northeast by Bodcau Bayou; drained by the Bodcau and Red Chute bayous. Barksdale Air Force Base is the headquarters of the Strategic Air Command's Second Air Force. The parish also includes Cypress Bayou and Black Bayou reservoirs. • Named for Pierre E. J. B. Bossier (1797–1844), LA legislator and U.S. representative from LA • 1843 from Claiborne • The Confederates erected Fort Smith in Bossier City for the defense of sister city Shreveport. • The parish lies in one of the greatest oil- and gas-producing areas of the U.S. Oil refineries also operate here. Cotton, corn, sorghum, blueberries, pecans, soybeans, home garden fruits and vegetables, wheat, cattle, horses, rabbits, honey; manufacture of chemicals, playground equipment, lumber, wood and paper products, mattresses, fertilizer, cottonseed oil, candy, clothing; gambling.

CADDO (one of two counties/parishes so named, the other in OK) *Shreveport* • 252,161 (the fourth most populated parish in LA) • 882 • Extreme northwestern LA, bounded on the west by the TX state line, on the north by the AR state line, on the east by the Red River, and on the south by Bayou Pierre. The parish includes Cross Lake reservoir and part of Caddo Lake reservoir on the TX boundary. Black Bayou Lake reservoir and Wallace Lake reservoir (on the southern boundary) are also here. • Named for the Caddo Indian tribe • 1838 from Natchitoches • Shreveport, the last stronghold of the Confederacy, became the capital of Confederate LA in 1863. The discovery of oil at Caddo Lake was an economic boon to the parish (museum). • Football player Terry Bradshaw; attorney Johnnie L. Cochran, Jr.; pianist Van Cliburn • Shreveport is a commercial and industrial center for a three-state region (known as the Ark-La-Tex), with large oil production, natural gas wells, oil and gas refineries, pipelines. (Several of the nation's largest natural gas companies have their headquarters here.) The parish is situated in one of the state's leading cotton regions. Also, berries, peaches, corn, sorghum, hay, home gardens, nursery crops, vegetables, rice, cattle, horses, hogs, poultry, exotic fowl, dairying; timber, logging; manufacture of chemicals, paper, glass products, metal products, industrial machinery, motor vehicles, food products, apparel; milling of cotton and cottonseed; shipping; printing; education (Centenary College of LA; LA State U. in Shreveport) • The LA State Fair is held in Shreveport each autumn. Holiday in Dixie is a popular spring festival.

CALCASIEU *Lake Charles* • 183,577 • 1,071 • Southwestern LA, bounded on the west by the Sabine River, here forming the TX state line, on the far east by Bayou Lacassine; drained by the Houston and Calcasieu rivers. The parish includes Sam Houston Jones State Park, Nibletts Bluff Park, and part of Calcasieu Lake in the south. The Intracoastal Waterway parallels the southern border. • Possibly named for the Calcasieu River • 1840 from Saint Landry • Surgeon Michael E. De Bakey • The parish lies in one of the principal rice-growing regions of the U.S. Also, sorghum, home gardens, soybeans, honey, cattle, horses, sheep, hogs; crawfish, crabs; sulphur mines, oil and natural gas, coal; logging; fur-trapping; diversified manufacturing, including the processing of farm, lumber and petrochemical products; sport fishing, boating; education (McNeese State U.) • Lake Charles, on the Calcasieu River, is the fourth-largest inland port in the nation and the largest rice-exporting port in the U.S. In 1895, the Frasch process for mining sulfur was first employed in the vicinity of Sulphur to extract the large deposits in the area.

CALDWELL (one of five county/parishes so named) *Columbia* • 10,560 • 529 • Northeast-central LA, bounded on the east by the Boeuf River; intersected by the Ouachita River, Bayou Lafourche, and Castor Creek. • Named for either Matthew Caldwell, a pioneer from NC; or for the Caldwell family, local residents • 1838 from Catahoula and Ouachita • Cotton, hay, soybeans, cattle, horses; aquaculture; logging; oil and natural gas.

CAMERON *Cameron* • 9,991 • 1,313 (the third largest parish in LA) • Extreme southwestern LA, in a marshy coastal area, bounded on the west by Sabine Lake and the Sabine River, and on the south by the Gulf of Mexico. Navigable waterways within the parish include the Calcasieu, Mermentau, and Sabine rivers, and the Intracoastal Waterway. Calcasieu and Grand lakes are also here. Sabine National Wildlife Refuge, which extends from Sabine Lake to Calcasieu Lake, is the largest waterfowl refuge on the Gulf Coast. The parish also contains Cameron Prairie and Lacassine national wildlife refuges, and part of Rockefeller National Wildlife Refuge, known internationally for its alligator research center. • Named for Simon Cameron (1799–1889), U.S. senator from PA and U.S. secretary of war • 1870 from Calcasieu and Vermilion • The parish held a prisoner of war camp during World War II. • Crawfish, oysters, shrimp, crabs, finfish, alligators; nutria trapping; hay, rice, soybeans, cattle, horses; oil and natural gas. • Large concentrations of Indian archeological finds have been unearthed along the shores of Grand Lake. A shrine, at the Catholic church, "Our Lady Star of the Sea," was presented by Italy as a memorial to those who lost their lives in 1957 during Hurricane Audrey.

CATAHOULA *Harrisonburg* • 10,920 • 704 • Eastern LA, bounded on the east by the Black and Tensas rivers, on the south by the Red River, and Big Saline Bayou, and on the north by the Boeuf River and Deer Creek; intersected by the Ouachita and Little rivers, and Bushley Creek. Larto Lake is in the south. • Possibly named for Catahoula Lake, which lay within the parish until La Salle was carved from it • 1808 (prior to statehood) from Rapides • Cotton, corn, soybeans, sorghum, hay, sweet potatoes, peas, cattle, horses; turtles, catfish; sand and gravel pits; logging.

CLAIBORNE *Homer* • 16,851 • 755 • Northern LA, bounded on the north by the AR state line, and on the southwest by Black Lake Bayou; drained by Bayou D'Arbonne (forming Lake Claiborne reservoir in the center of the parish), its Middle Fork, and Corney Bayou (forming Corney Lake reservoir in the northeast corner). Lake Claiborne State Park is here, as are units of Kisatchie National Forest. • One of three counties/parishes named for William C. C. Claiborne (1775–1817), governor of the Mississippi Territory of the Orleans Territory, and LA's first governor • 1828 from Natchitoches • Oil wells, natural gas; logging; hay, watermelons, nursery crops, grains.

CONCORDIA *Vidalia* • 20,247 • 696 • East-central LA, bounded on the east by the Mississippi River (forming the MS state line) on the west by the Black and Tensas rivers, on the south and southwest by the Red River (its outflow channel to the Mississippi River passing through the southern part); drained by Bayou Cocodrie. The parish has several lakes, including Cocodrie, Concordia, and St. John. Two units of Bayou Cocodrie National Wildlife Refuge are here. • Named for a Spanish military post located near present-day Natchez, MS. • Original parish; organized 1807 (prior to statehood) • Politician John R. Lynch • Oil, natural gas; lumber; sweet potatoes, vegetables, wheat, cattle, horses, exotic fowl; fishing.

DE SOTO *Mansfield* • 25,494 • 877 • Northwestern LA, bounded on the west by the TX state line, on the southwest by the Sabine River (here forming Toledo Bend Reservoir and the TX state line), and on the north and east by Bayou Pierre. The parish includes Clear Lake, Smithport Lake, and Wallace Lake reservoirs. Mansfield State Historic Site is also here. • One of four counties/parishes named for Hernando de Soto (1500–42), Spanish explorer of southern U.S. • 1843 from Natchitoches • Cotton, blueberries, hay, poultry, cattle, dairying; oil and natural gas; logging; manufacture of wood and paper products.

EAST BATON ROUGE *Baton Rouge* • 412,852 (the third most populated parish in LA) • 456 • Southeast-central LA, bounded on the east by the Amite River, on the south in part by Bayou Manchac, and on the west by the Mississippi River; drained by Comite River. Port Hudson State Commemorative Area is here. • The name is French for "red stick," the pole separating the hunting grounds of two Indian tribes • 1810 (prior to statehood) from Spanish West Florida • Since the French built and garrisoned a fort on the site of Baton Rouge in 1719, the citizens of the area have lived under seven flags: France, Great Britain, Spain, the Republic of West Florida, the U.S., the Republic of LA, and the Confederate States of America. Baton Rouge replaced New Orleans as state capital in 1849. After Union forces invaded LA in 1862, the capital was moved to Opelousas. That year the city was captured by a Union

squadron under Capt. David G. Farragut. The city remained under federal control until 1877. It became the capital again in 1882. The parish's growth as an industrial center began with the building of the Standard Oil Company's giant refinery in 1909. By WW II, Baton Rouge had become an important center for petrochemical production. From 1940 to 1950 its population trebled. • Professional basketball player Bob Pettit. Governor Huey Long was assassinated in the state capitol. • Manufacture of petrochemicals, fabricated metals, food products, lumber and wood products, printed materials, synthetic rubber; shipping; oil and gas fields, sand and gravel; timber; home gardens, peas, sugar cane, vegetables, cattle, horses, poultry, goats, exotic fowl, dairying; alligators; education (LA State U. and A and M College; Southern U. and A. and M College; Our Lady of the Lake College); state government offices • The skyscraping state capitol built by Governor Huey Long in 1931–32 is one of the most architecturally significant buildings in the state. It is constructed of marble and other stone brought from around the world. Its grounds include a sunken garden containing the governor's grave.

EAST CARROLL *Lake Providence* • 9,421 • 421 • Extreme northeastern LA, bounded on the east by the Mississippi River (forming the MS state line), on the west by Bayou Macon, and on the north by the AR state line. The source of the Tensas River and Lake Providence are here. • The parish was originally named for Charles Carroll (1737–1832), signer of the Declaration of Independence and U.S. senator from MD • 1877 from the division of Carroll, which had been formed in 1832, into east and west parishes • Cotton, corn, sorghum, home gardens, rice, soybeans, wheat, pecans, cattle • Poverty Point archeological site dates to between 700 and 1700 BC. The parish contains remnants of the failed "Grant's Canal," one of a series of canals dug by Union troops to allow Federal gunboats to by-pass Vicksburg's fortifications.

EAST FELICIANA *Clinton* • 21,360 • 453 • Southeastern LA, bounded on the east by the Amite River, on the west by Thompson Creek, and on the north by the MS state line; drained by the Comite River. Centenary State Historic Site is here. • Named for Spain's Distrito de Feliciana in West Florida • 1824 from Feliciana (when the parish was divided into East and West Feliciana parishes), the original parish formed in 1810 • East Feliciana was one of the Florida parishes of Southeastern Louisiana. • Blueberries, peaches, corn, hay, sweet potatoes, cattle, horses, hogs, dairying; wineries; sod production; logging • Clinton Confederate Cemetery is located at the parish seat.

EVANGELINE *Ville Platte* • 35,434 • 664 • South-central LA, bounded in part on the north by Cocodrie Lake reservoir, on the southwest in part by Bayou Nezpique, and on the south in part by Bayou des Cannes. The parish includes Chicot State Park and Louisiana State Arboretum. • Named for the heroine of Henry Wadsworth Longfellow's poem of the same name. • 1910 from Saint Landry • Rice, cotton, corn, hay, sugar cane, sweet potatoes, home gardens, cattle, dairying; fishing, crawfish, alligators; logging, manufacture of apparel, oil and gas field machinery, carbon black; sand and gravel.

FRANKLIN (one of twenty-five counties/parishes so named) *Winnsboro* • 21,263 • 623 • Northeastern LA, bounded on the east by the Tensas River and Bayou Macon, on the west by the Boeuf River and Big Creek, and on the south in part by Deer Creek. The parish contains Turkey Creek Lake reservoir. • One of twenty-three counties/parishes named for Benjamin Franklin • 1843 from Catahoula, Ouachita, and Madison • Cotton, corn, sorghum, hay, rice, soybeans, wheat, sweet potatoes, cattle, hogs; catfish; logging, manufacture of food products, apparel, boats; oil and gas. • The Franklin Parish Catfish Festival, held each April, is the largest one-day festival in the state. The Louisiana University Sweet Potato Experiment Station is located near Winnsboro.

GRANT (one of fifteen counties/parishes so named) *Colfax* • 18,698 • 645 • Central LA, bounded in the east by the Little River, on the west and southwest by the Red River. Within the parish are Lake Iatt and Lake Nantachie reservoirs, and part of Camp Beauregard. A large part of a unit of Kisatchie National Forest dominates the eastern half of the parish. • One of twelve counties/parishes named for President Ulysses S. Grant • 1869 from Rapides and Winn • Cotton, corn, soybeans, sweet potatoes, vegetables, watermelons, home gardens, cattle, horses; some manufacturing; logging, timber.

IBERIA *New Iberia* • 73,266 • 575 • Southern LA, on the Gulf of Mexico, bounded on the southwest by Vermilion Bay, and on the east by the Belle River, forming Lake Fausse Pointe reservoir; intersected by Bayou Teche, Big Bayou Pigeon, and Atchafalaya Main Channel. The parish is crossed by the Intracoastal Waterway. Part of Cypremort Point State Park is in the parish. Beyond Vermilion Bay to the south lies Marsh Island and the Shell Keys (National Wildlife Refuge). Rip Van Winkle Gardens are on Jefferson Island, and Jungle Gardens are located on Avery Island. • Named for the city of New Iberia, LA • 1868 from Saint Martin and Saint Mary • The parish was first settled in the 18th century by the French, Spanish and Acadians. New Iberia was occupied by Union forces in 1863 because of its proximity to important salt mines. • Oil and gas, salt and sulphur mining; fisheries (crawfish, catfish, shrimp, crabs, finfish); sugar cane (the Louisiana Sugar Cane Festival is held here each September), soybeans, rice, vegetables, nursery crops, home gardens, peppers, cattle, dairying; manufacture of pepper products, apparel, metal products, industrial machinery; shipbuilding; hunting and fur trapping. • The moss-draped oak trees of New Iberia shade many beautiful antebellum buildings. Tabasco sauce originated on Avery Island.

IBERVILLE *Plaquemine* • 33,320 • 619 • Southeast-central LA, bounded on the west by the Atchafalaya River; intersected by the Mississippi River; drained by the Grand River; intersected by Bayou Maringouin and Bayou des Glaises. The southern half of the parish lies in the Atchafalaya Basin. Part of Atchafalaya National Wildlife Refuge is in the northwest corner. Locks in the parish connect the Mississippi River to the Plaquemine branch of the Port Allen-Morgan City canal (state historic site). • Named for Pierre le Moyne, Sieur d'Iberville (1661–1706), French-Canadian naval officer who explored the Mississippi River delta, founded French colonies at present-day Biloxi and Mobile, and served as the first governor of French-controlled LA • 1807 (prior to statehood) • The parish was occupied by Union troops during the Civil War. • Corn, hay, soybeans, nursery crops, sugar cane, home gardens, cattle, horses, exotic fowl; crawfish, catfish, alligators; logging; manufacture of chemicals, plastics, lumber, metal products, industrial machinery; oil and gas • Nottoway Plantation, located here, is the largest plantation home in the south. Madonna Chapel, reputed to be the smallest chapel in the world, is located in Point Pleasant. Saint Gabriel Catholic Church is believed to be the oldest Catholic church in the state. The Gillis Long Hansen's Disease Center, the only long-term treatment facility for Hansen's Disease (leprosy), is located in the east.

JACKSON (one of twenty-four counties/parishes so named) *Jonesboro* • 15,397 • 570 • North-central LA, bounded on the southwest by the Dugclemona River; drained by Castor Creek. Caney Creek Lake State Park and reservoir are in the parish. • One of twenty-two counties named directly or indirectly for President Andrew Jackson • 1845 from Claiborne, Ouachita, and Union • The "Singing Governor" Jimmie Davis • Hay, vegetables, cattle, poultry; logging, timber, manufacture of paper products.

JEFFERSON *Gretna* • 455,466 (the second most populated parish in LA) • 306 • Southeastern LA, in the delta of the Mississippi River, which intersects the parish in the north, bounded on the south by the Gulf of Mexico, on the north by Lake Pontchartrain, and on the west by Cataouatche, Salvador, and Little lakes. The parish constitutes part of the New Orleans metropolitan area. The New Orleans International Airport is at Kenner. The parish is traversed by the Intracoastal Waterway. It also includes Grand Isle and Bayou Segnette state parks and Jean Lafitte National Historical Park and Preserve (Barataria Preserve). The Lake Pontchartrain Causeway which connects the parish to St. Tammany Parish twenty-nine miles to the north is the world's longest bridge. • One of twenty-six counties/parishes named directly or indirectly for President Thomas Jefferson • 1825 from Orleans • Gretna was once the main shipping point for nearby plantations. It has since developed into a residential suburb of New Orleans. • Diversified industries, including mahogany processing, manufacture of soft drinks, glass, barrels, safety matches; home gardens, nursery crops, horses; oysters, shrimp, crabs, finfish, alligators; exotic fowl; oil and natural gas; warehouses; railroad facilities.

JEFFERSON DAVIS (one of two counties/parishes so named) *Jennings* • 31,435 • 652 • Southwestern LA, bounded on the east by Bayou Nezpique, on the southeast by Lake Arthur, and on the west by Bayou Lacassine; drained by the Calcasieu River and Bayou Serpent. • One of four counties/parishes named for Jefferson Davis (1808–89), president of the Confederate States of America • 1912 from Calcasieu • Oil, natural gas, sorghum, cotton, rice, soybeans, sweet potatoes, cattle, sod production; exotic fowl; crawfish, catfish; manufacture of apparel; logging; shipbuilding.

LAFAYETTE (one of six counties/parishes so named) *Lafayette* • 190,503 • 270 • Southern LA, bounded on the north by Bayou Carencro and on the south in part by Bayou Queue de Tortue; drained by the Vermilion River (forming part of the southern boundary). Jean Lafitte National Historical Park (Acadian Cultural Center) is here. • One of seventeen counties/parishes named for the Marquis de Lafayette (1757–1834), French statesman and soldier who fought with the Americans during the Revolutionary War • 1823 from Attakapas and Saint Martin • Lafayette was settled in the late 18th century by exiled Acadians from Nova Scotia. In the mid 20th century the city became a major supply center of the growing oil and gas industry of southern LA. • Home gardens, corn, sorghum, hay, nursery crops, rice, sugar cane, cotton, sweet potatoes, cucumbers, other vegetables, honey, cattle, horses, exotic fowl, dairying; crawfish; lumber; oil and natural gas; diversified manufacturing; education (U. of LA at Lafayette) • Lafayette, though now a cosmopolitan community, maintains many of its older Cajun customs, including the celebration of Mardis Gras each year. The Live Oak Society in Lafayette works to preserve the city's noted oaks.

LAFOURCHE *Thibodaux* • 89,974 • 1,085 • Southeastern LA, bounded on the south by the Gulf of Mexico, on the southwest by Bayou Pointe Aux Chenes, on the east in part by Barataria Bay, on the north by Bayou Des Allemands and Lac Des Allemands, and on the northeast by Lake Salvador; intersected by Bayou Lafourche; crossed by the Intracoastal Waterway. • Named for Bayou Lafourche • 1807 (prior to statehood) • Thibodaux was founded as a river depot about 1750 and settled by French, Spanish, Acadians, and Des Allemands (Germans enticed over by John Law's Mississippi Venture). • Confederate general Braxton Bragg; soldier Jim Bowie • Home gardens, truck farming, sugar cane, cotton, vegetables, cattle, horses, quail, pheasants; crawfish, alligators, shrimp, crabs, finfish; natural gas, oil; logging; manufacture of paper products, industrial machinery; shipbuilding; food processing; education (Nicholls St. U.). • The Wetlands Acadian Cultural Center in Jean Lafitte National Historical Park features exhibits and demonstrations on Cajun life along Bayou Lafourche. St. John's Episcopal Church was established in 1841 in Thibobaux by Leonidas Polk, the "Fighting Bishop" of the Confederacy. The parish has several preserved antebellum plantation homes, including those of LA's acting governor Henry Schuyler Thibodaux and Chief Justice Edward Douglass White (historic site).

LA SALLE *Jena* • 14,282 • 624 • Central LA, bounded on the west by the Little River, Castor Creek, and Big Saline Bayou. The parish includes Catahoula Lake in the center, with Cata-

houla National Wildlife Refuge on its eastern shore. Saline Lake is on the parish's southern border. The Catahoula Lake Diversion Canal crosses in the south. • One of three counties/parishes named for Rene Robert Cavelier (1643–87), Sieur de La Salle, French adventurer and explorer who claimed the land west of the Mississippi River for France • 1908 from Catahoula • Oil, natural gas; cotton, sugar cane, home gardens, soybeans, hay, cattle, hogs; logging, timber, lumber milling.

LINCOLN (one of twenty-four counties/parishes so named) *Ruston* • 42,509 • 471 • Northern LA; drained by the Middle Fork of Bayou D'Arbonne. • One of eighteen counties/parishes named for President Abraham Lincoln • 1873 from Bienville, Jackson and Union • Peaches (Ruston holds the Louisiana Peach Festival each year), blueberries, home gardens, cotton, corn, hay, cattle, poultry; processing of milk products, cottonseed oil; lumber; manufacture of wood products, glass containers, metal products, lighting fixtures; oil and natural gas; education (Grambling State U.; LA Tech U.).

LIVINGSTON (one of six counties/parishes so named) *Livingston* • 91,814 (30% increase since 1990; the third fastest growing parish in LA) • 648 • Southeastern LA, bounded on the west by the Amite River, on the south by the Petite Amite and Blind rivers, partly on the east by the Natalbany River, and on the southeast by Lake Maurepas; drained by the Tickfaw River. Tickfaw State Park is located here. • Named for either Edward Livingston (1764–1836), U.S. representative and senator from LA, and secretary of state; or for his brother Robert R. Livingston (1746–1813), NY patriot, statesman, and a drafter of the Declaration of Independence • 1832 from Saint Helena • The parish was part of the former British Colony of West Florida. • Home gardens, nursery crops, cucumbers, peppers, cattle, horses, poultry, exotic fowl, hogs, dairying; alligators; logging; hunting and fishing.

MADISON *Tallulah* • 13,728 • 624 • Northeastern LA, bounded on the west by Bayou Macon, on the east by the Mississippi River (forming the MS state line); intersected by the Tensas River. The parish includes many Native American mounds. Part of Tensas River National Wildlife Refuge is here. • One of twenty counties/parishes named directly or indirectly for President James Madison • 1838 from Concordia Parish. • Cotton, corn, sorghum, rice, soybeans, wheat, cattle, hogs, home gardens; crawfish; fishing and waterfowl hunting on oxbow lakes formed by the Mississippi River.

MOREHOUSE *Bastrop* • 31,021 • 794 • Northeastern LA, bounded on the east by the Boeuf River, on the west by the Ouachita River, and on the north by the AR state line; intersected by Bayou Bartholomew and Bayou Bonne Idee. It contains Chemin-a-Haut State Park, Handy Brake National Wildlife Refuge, and a small part of Upper Ouachita National Wildlife Refuge. • Named for Abraham Morhouse (?–1813), early settler and colonizer of LA. The discrepancy in spelling is due to error at time of establishment. • 1844 from Ouachita Territory • With the discovery of natural gas in 1916, Bastrop experienced an industrial boom. • Professional baseball catcher Bill Dickey • Cotton, corn, wheat, sorghum, home gardens, rice, soybeans, sweet potatoes, vegetables, cattle, horses; catfish; processing of agricultural products; timber; manufacture of paper products, apparel, wood products, carbon black, chemicals • Bastrop is the site of the North Louisiana Cotton Festival and Fair each year.

NATCHITOCHES *Natchitoches* • 39,080 • 1,256 (the fourth largest parish in LA, although only one square mile larger than Terrebonne) • Northwest-central LA, bounded on the east by the Saline (here a national scenic river) and Red rivers, and on the northwest in part by Black Lake Bayou and Bayou Pierre; intersected by the Red River and Cane River. The parish is bisected by Black Lake. It also includes Rebel, Los Adaes, and Fort St. Jean Baptiste state historic sites, and a large section of Kisatchie National Forest. Cane River Creole National Historic Park is also here. • Named for the Natchitoches Indian tribe • 1807 (prior to statehood) • Natchitoches, the oldest settlement in the Louisiana Purchase (founded in 1714), came under U.S. control in 1803. • Cotton, corn, sorghum, hay, rice, soybeans, pecans, cattle, poultry; catfish, crawfish, alligators; timber; manufacture of plywood, paper products, brick and tile, farm products; oil and natural gas; U.S. fish hatchery; education (Northwestern State U. of LA). • Natchitoches has over fifty buildings, many from the French colonial era, designated as National Historic landmarks. The Magnolia Plantation is one of only two National Bicentennial farms west of the Mississippi. The first cotton in the state was planted at Oakland Plantation. Several historic highways, including the Natchez Trace from the east and El Camino Real from Mexico, converged in Natchitoches.

ORLEANS (one of three counties/parishes so named) *New Orleans* • 484,674 (the most populated parish in LA) • 181 (the smallest parish in LA) • Southeastern LA; coextensive with the city of New Orleans, bounded on the north by Lake Pontchartrain, in part on the east, south, and southeast by the Mississippi River. Bayou Sauvage National Wildlife Refuge and Fort Pike State Historic Site are in the northeast. The Intracoastal Waterway crosses the eastern two-thirds of the parish to join the Mississippi River. • Named for either the city in France or for Philippe II, Duke of Orleans • 1807 (prior to statehood) • New Orleans is the South's oldest major city. It was founded by Jean Baptiste le Moyne, Sieur de Bienville in 1718. It was made the capital of the French colony of Louisiana (covering the central third of present day U.S.) in 1722, turned over to the Spanish in 1762, returned to France, and sold to the U.S. as part of the Louisiana Purchase in 1803. Britain's unsuccessful attempt to capture the city during the War of 1812 culminated in Andrew Jackson's victory at the Battle of New Orleans on January 8, 1815. After the war, New Orleans thrived as a cotton port and slave-trading center. The city served as capital of LA from 1812 to 1830, 1831 to 1849, and 1862 to 1882. Repeated yellow fever epidemics took their toll on the city; about 7,700 residents died in 1832. An even worse epidemic struck in 1853, killing more than 11,000 and ranking as the nation's worst. (A third, in 1878, killed more than 3,800.) New Orleans was forced to surrender to Union Captain David Farragut on May 1, 1862. Union troops remained in the city until 1877. A voting dispute in 1866 resulted in a race riot that left fifty dead. New Orleans helped give birth to jazz in the early 1900s. A world's fair was held here in 1984. • Jazz trumpeter Louis Armstrong; song writer Fats Domino; Confederate general P.G.T. Beauregard; jazz forefather Buddy Bolden; pianist and composer Louis Moreau Gottschalk; playwright Lillian Hellman; gospel singer Mahalia Jackson; accused assassin Lee Harvey Oswald; civil rights leader Andrew Young; author and reformer George W. Cable; writer Truman Capote; singer Harry Connick, Jr.; musicians Branford and Wynton Marsalis. Pathologist and bateriologist Aristedes Agramonte y Simoni, novelist and short story writer Roark Bradford, Flying Tigers creator Claire L. Chennault, Guatemalan dictator Jorge Ubico, architect and civil engineer Benjamin Latrobe, and Confederate general John B. Hood died here. • New Orleans is one of the South's major centers of business, industry, and transportation. Its port ranks among the world's busiest, handling more trade with Latin America than any other U.S. port. Shipping; shipbuilding; manufacture of aerospace components (the Saturn 5 rocket that launched the Apollo 11 astronauts to the moon in 1969 was made here), food products, petrochemicals, petroleum products, primary metals; home gardens; oysters, shrimp, crabs, finfish; education (Tulane U.; Loyola U.; New Orleans Baptist Theological Seminary; Southern U. at New Orleans; U. of New Orleans; Dillard U.; others); tourism • Because much of the parish lies below sea level and lacks natural drainage, Orleans relies on levees and one of the world's greatest systems of drainage pumps. A Spanish architectural style dominates New Orleans's French Quarter due to fires that swept through the area in 1788 and 1794; at the time of rebuilding, Spain ruled LA. New Orleans's Mardi Gras festival climaxes the city's carnival season and is widely attended. The St. Louis Cathedral (originally built as a small parish church in 1716) is the oldest cathedral in continuous use in the U.S. The Louisiana Superdome, home of the New Orleans Saints, is the world's largest steel-constructed room unobstructed by posts. The stadium holds the world record for the largest attendance at an indoor event: 87,500 for a Rolling Stones concert in 1981. The longest boxing match in history took place on April 6–7, 1893 in New Orleans; Andy Bowen and Jack Burke fought through 110 rounds to a draw. New Orleans is home to the Hornets (New Orleans Arena).

OUACHITA (one of two counties/parishes so named, the other in AR) *Monroe* • 147,250 • 611 • Northeast-central LA, bounded on the east by Bayou Lafourche; intersected by the Ouachita River and Bayou D'Arbonne. Part of D'Arbonne National Wildlife Refuge is here. • Named for the Ouachita Indians • 1807 (prior to statehood) • The parish comprises an area explored by Hernando de Soto in 1541. Monroe was founded in 1785 by French pioneers from southern LA under

Jean-Baptiste Filhiol. It was first established as a trading post (Ft. Miro) on a land grant from King Charles X of Spain. • Professional basketball player Bill Russell • Cotton, rice, soybeans, blueberries, peaches, sorghum, corn, home gardens, nursery crops, vegetables, cattle, dairying; horses, exotic fowl; alligators, natural-gas fields (the parish sits above one of the largest fields in the U.S.), gas pipelines; logging; manufacture of food products, apparel, paper products, plastic products, furniture, agricultural chemicals, electronic equipment, industrial machinery, metal products, carbon black; education (U. of LA at Monroe). • The Northeastern Louisiana Delta African American Heritage Museum is in Monroe.

PLAQUEMINES *Pointe a la Hache* • 26,757 • 845 • Extreme southeastern LA, occupying all of the central part of the delta of the Mississippi River below New Orleans, with part of the New Orleans metropolitan area in the north. Barataria Bay and the Gulf of Mexico are on the west and south, Breton Sound and the Gulf on the east. The parish is mostly swamp in the south. A peninsula, ten to fifteen miles wide, is in the southeast. The leveed Mississipi River flows through the parish, radiating into three passes as it enters the Gulf, each bounded by narrow strips of land on both sides. The parish's land mass is shrinking due to compaction, subsidence, and dredging. Lakes and bayous abound. Plaquemines Parish includes the Breton Islands in Breton Sound, an extension of the Chandeleur Islands, part of Breton National Wildlife Refuge, and Delta National Wildlife Refuge, containing one of the country's largest colonies of snowy egrets. • Its name is a French rendering of an Indian word meaning persimmon • 1807 (prior to statehood) from Orleans Parish • Oysters, shrimp, crabs, finfish, alligators; natural gas, oil; manufacture of chemicals, electronic equipment; boat building; petroleum refining; food processing; hunting, fishing, fur trapping (nutria).

POINTE COUPEE *New Roads* • 22,763 • 557 • Southeastern LA, bounded on the east by the Mississippi River, on the north in part by Old River (a former channel of the Red River), and on the west by the Atchafalaya River; drained by Bayou Maringouin and Bayou Des Glaises. Parlange Plantation is located near False River, a long owbow lake. • The name comes from the French for "cut-off point," referring to a place where the Mississippi River shortened itself to produce a new channel • 1807 (prior to statehood) • Cotton, corn, pecans, rice, soybeans, sugar cane, vegetables, wheat, cattle, hogs, horses; crawfish; logging; manufacture of wood products, lumber.

RAPIDES *Alexandria* • 126,337 • 1,323 (the second largest parish in LA) • Central LA, bounded on the north in part by the Red River, and on the northeast by Big Saline Bayou and Little River; drained by the Calcasieu and Red rivers. The parish includes sections of Kisatchie National Forest (its headquarters in Alexandria). Castor Creek Scenic Area is here. Part of Camp Beauregard is on the parish's northeast border. Part of Grand Cote National Wildlife Refuge is also found in the parish, as is Alexander State Forest, including Indian Creek Recreation Area. Cocodrie Lake is on the southern boundary.

Kincaid Reservoir, Cotile Lake, and Lake Rodemacher are also in the parish. • Rapides is French for the former "rapids" on the Red River • 1807 (prior to statehood) • In May, 1863, and again in March, 1864, Alexandria was occupied by Union forces under Admiral David Porter and General Nathaniel P. Banks. Situated on the Red River where rapids once obstructed navigation, the city was partially dismantled to dam the river so gunboats could be floated over the rough water. Later the Federals set fire to the city, and all civic records were lost. Alexandria was rebuilt after the war. The rapids were permanently eliminated, the name of the parish kept as historic reminder. • Writer Arna Bontemps • Cotton, corn, sorghum, hay, rice, sugar cane, sweet potatoes, soybeans, vegetables, home gardens, nursery crops; cattle, horses, poultry, exotic fowl, dairying; catfish, crawfish; logging; oil refining; diversified manufacturing, including brick, tile roofing, road machinery, turpentine, tar, valves, pipe fittings, concrete products, food, wood, metal, paper, and paper products; chemicals; education (LA State U. at Alexandria; LA College) The Louisiana Seminary of Learning was formed in Alexandria in 1860. It later became Louisiana State University in Baton Rouge. • Alexandria National Cemetery is located in the parish.

RED RIVER *Coushatta* • 9,622 • 389 • Northwestern LA, bounded on the west by Bayou Pierre, and on the east by Black Lake Bayou, forming Black Lake in the extreme southeast; intersected by the Red River. • One of two counties/parishes (the other in TX) named for the Red River • 1871 from Caddo, Bossier, Bienville, Natchitoches, and De Soto • Cotton, peaches, berries, corn, wheat, hay, soybeans, vegetables, watermelons, cattle, horses, exotic fowl; oil and natural gas; logging, lumber milling.

RICHLAND (one of seven counties/parishes so named) *Rayville* • 20,981 • 559 • Northeastern LA, bounded on the west by Bayou Lafourche, on the far east by Bayou Macon, and on the southeast by Big Creek; intersected by Bayou Bonne Idee and the Boeuf river. • The parish's name is descriptive of its fertile soil. • 1852 from Ouachita, Carroll, Franklin, and Morehouse • Cotton, corn, sorghum, hay, rice, soybeans, wheat, vegetables, cattle; logging; cotton processing; aluminum rolling and drawing; boat building; manufacture of apparel, industrial machinery; hunting and fishing.

SABINE (one of two counties/parishes so named, the other in TX) *Many* • 23,459 • 865 • Western LA, bounded on the west by the Sabine River, here forming Toledo Bend Reservoir (the largest manmade body of water in the South) and the TX state line; drained by tributaries of the Sabine, including Bayou Toro (which forms part of the southeastern boundary). North Toledo Bend State Park is in the west. The parish also contains Fort Jesup State Historic Site. • Named for the Sabine River • 1843 from Natchitoches Parish • Home gardens, vegetables, cattle, poultry, exotic fowl, dairying; natural gas, oil fields; timber.

SAINT BERNARD *Chalmette* • 67,229 • 465 • Southeastern

LA, its mainland portion bounded on the north by Lake Borgne, on the east by Chandeleur Sound, on the south by Breton Sound, on the southwest by Bayou Terre Boeufs, and on the west by the Mississippi River. The parish includes the Chandeleur Islands in the Gulf of Mexico. St. Bernard State Park, Jean Lafitte National Historical Park (Chalmette Battlefield), and part of Breton National Wildlife Refuge are also here. • Named for the old Catholic District called Saint Bernard Parish • 1807 (prior to statehood) from Orleans • Among the parish's earliest settlers were Islenos from the Canary Islands. • Diversified industries, including sugar refineries, oil refineries, stockyards, manufacturing; oil and natural gas extraction; home gardens, nursery crops, vegetables, tomatoes, exotic fowl; oysters; hunting and fishing.

SAINT CHARLES (one of two counties/parishes so named, the other in MO) *Hahnville* • 48,072 • 284 • Southeastern LA, bounded on the north by Lake Pontchartrain, on the southeast by Salvador and Catouatche lakes, and on the southwest by Bayou and Lac Des Allemands; intersected by the Mississippi River. Bonnet Carre Spillway here carries floodwaters from the Mississippi River to Lake Pontchartrain. Timken and Salvador wildlife management areas are also in the parish. • Named for an old Catholic district by this name • 1807 (prior to statehood) from German Coast Parish • Early settlers included many Germans from AR; for a time the area was called "the German Coast." • Nursery crops, sugar cane, vegetables, cattle, horses, exotic fowl; alligators, catfish, crabs; oil and natural gas production and refining; manufacturing.

SAINT HELENA *Greensburg* • 10,525 • 408 • Southeastern LA, bounded on the west by the Amite River and on the north by the MS state line; intersected by the Tickfaw River. • Named for the Spanish district in West Florida, Distrito de Santa Helena • 1810 (prior to statehood) from Feliciana • The parish was one of the West Florida parishes. • Vegetables, hay, cattle, poultry, dairying; logging.

SAINT JAMES *Convent* • 21,216 • 246 • Southeast-central LA; divided by the Mississippi River; drained by the Blind River. Sunshine Bridge is the only bridge that crosses the Mississippi River between Baton Rouge and New Orleans. • Named for the old Catholic district by this name • Original parish; organized 1807 (prior to statehood) • Named for James the Apostle, disciple of Jesus Christ • Saint James Parish is the only place in the world that grows perique tobacco. Other products include chemicals; sugar cane, vegetables, cattle, horses; crawfish • Among the historic plantations located here are Oak Alley and Laura. The Laura Plantation contains the largest collection of family plantation artifacts in the state. In its slave quarters were first recorded the west-African folktales known in English as "Br'er Rabbit."

SAINT JOHN THE BAPTIST *Edgard* • 43,044 • 219 • Southeastern LA, bounded on the north by Lake Maurepas and Pass Manchac, on the east by Lake Pontchartrain, and on the south and east in part by Lake Des Allemands (home to one of the country's largest colonies of little blue herons); divided by the Mississippi river. • Named for the old Catholic district with this name • 1807 (prior to statehood) from German Coast Parish • Trombonist and composer Kid Ory • Soybeans, sugar cane, vegetables, cattle; catfish, crawfish, alligators; manufacture of food products, chemicals, plastic products, steel products; oil (retrieval and refining) and natural gas.

SAINT LANDRY *Opelousas* • 87,700 • 929 • South-central LA, bounded on the east by the Atchafalaya River, on the extreme west by Bayou des Cannes; drained by Bayou Teche and other bayous. Jean Lafitte National Historical Park (Prairie Acadian Cultural Center) is here. • Named for the old Catholic district with this name • 1807 (prior to statehood) from Opelousas • Opelousas was founded in 1720 as a French garrison and trading post. It became a sanctuary for Acadians who had been exiled from Nova Scotia. The State Supreme Court was located here until 1819. In 1862, it became the temporary Confederate capital of LA. • Sweet potatoes, cotton, peaches, corn, sorghum, hay, rice, sugar cane, vegetables, wheat, cattle, horses, sheep, hogs, dairying; crawfish, catfish; manufacture of fertilizers, drugs, processed foods; logging; natural gas, petroleum. • Most of the residents of the parish are descendants of its Acadian immigrant settlers. French is widely spoken. Opelousas, holds a yam festival, the "Yambilee," each October. The Jim Bowie Museum in Opelousas exhibits Bowie mementos and French and Indian items. The parish is known for its antebellum houses in the Greek Revival architectural style.

SAINT MARTIN *Saint Martinville* • 48,583 • 740 • Southern LA, bounded on the extreme southeast corner by Lake Palourde; traversed by the Atchafalaya and Grand rivers and Bayou Teche. The parish is unusual among counties and parishes in the U.S. in its partition into detached sections, separated not by water but by land (Iberia Parish). Much of the parish lies in the Atchafalaya Basin, especially in the east and south. Longfellow-Evangeline State Historic Site contains the grave and statue of Emmeline Labiche in the yard of the St. Martin de Tours Catholic Church; Labiche was the alleged inspiration for the heroine of Longfellow's poem "Evangeline." • Named for the old Catholic District called St. Martin Parish • 1811 from Attakapas • Saint Martinville was settled about 1760. In 1765, a colony of Acadians arrived, having been expelled from Nova Scotia by the British. St. Martin's Church, completed in 1838, replaced an earlier structure that had been the mother church of the Acadians. The arrival in St. Martinville of many Royalist refugees from the French Revolution earned the town the nickname, "Le Petit Paris." The community thrived as a river resort for New Orleans society until a string of disasters struck the parish: yellow fever, a destructive fire, and hurricane. A reduction in steamboat travel also contributed to its economic decline. • Rice, soybeans, sugar cane, sweet potatoes, cotton, cabbage, peppers, cattle, horses, hogs, exotic fowl; crawfish, catfish, alligators; logging; manufacture of food products, apparel; chemicals, natural gas, oil; fur trapping; tourism.

SAINT MARY *Franklin* • 53,500 • 613 • Southern LA, bounded on the west and south by West Cote Blanche, East Cote Blanche, and Atchafalaya bays, and on the northeast by Grand Lake (a widening of the Atchafalaya River); crossed by the Intracoastal Waterway and drained by the Atchafalaya River. The parish is indented by Wax and Sweet Bay lakes. Also in the parish are Jean Lafitte National Historical Park (Chitimacha Cultural Center), Chitimacha Indian Reservation, and part of Cypremont Point State Park • Named for the old Catholic District called St. Mary Parish • 1811 (prior to statehood) from Attakapas • Soybeans, sugar cane, rice, cattle, hogs; salt mines, natural gas, oil; fisheries, crawfish, oysters, crabs, shrimp (Morgan City is the base of a large shrimp fleet), alligators; seafood canning, sugar refining; manufacture of carbon black, structural metal, ships, chemicals, machinery; sport fishing, hunting of small game and ducks. • The Wedell Williams Memorial Aviation Museum is here.

SAINT TAMMANY *Covington* • 191,268 (32.4% increase since 1990; the fast growing and the fifth most populated parish in LA) • 854 • Southeastern LA, bounded on the south by Lake Pontchartrain, on the extreme southeast by Lake Borgne, on the east by the Pearl River (here forming the MS state line); drained by Bogue Chitto, Bogue Falaya and the Tchefuncte River. The parish is located in the piney woods section of LA, often called the Ozone Belt. Lake Ramsay and Pearl River wildlife management areas, and Fairview Riverside and Fontainebleau state parks are in the parish. Also here are Big Branch Marsh and part of Bogue Chitto national wildlife refuges. The Lake Pontchartrain Causeway, which connects the parish to Jefferson Parish twenty-nine miles to the south, is the world's longest bridge. • Named for Tamenend, Delaware Indian chief popular with the American colonists in the late 1600s • 1810 (prior to statehood) from Feliciana • The parish was formerly part of the British Colony of West Florida. • Novelist Walker Percy • Blueberries, hay, sorghum, vegetables, cattle, horses, exotic animals, dairying; catfish, shrimp, crabs, alligators; manufacture of food products, apparel, concrete, machinery; shipbuilding.

TANGIPAHOA *Amite* • 100,588 • 790 • Southeastern LA, bounded on the east in part by the Tchefuncte River, on the south by Lake Maurepas, Pass Manchac, and Lake Pontchartrain, on the north by the MS state line, and on the west in part by the Natalbany River; drained by the Tangipahoa River. Joyce Wildlife Management Area is in the parish, as are Zemurray Gardens and Global Wildlife Center. • Named for the Tangipahoa Indian tribe • 1869 from Livingston, Saint Tammany, Saint Helen, and Washington parishes • The parish was one of the Florida parishes of southeastern LA's former British Colony of West Florida. • It is a large strawberry producer. Also, peppers, home gardens, nursery crops, sweet potatoes, vegetables, cattle, poultry, horses, rabbits, dairying; catfish,

shrimp, alligators; manufacture of bricks, clothing; logging; clay; resort tourism, hunting, fishing; education (Southeastern LA U.).

TENSAS *Saint Joseph* • 6,618 (the least populated parish in LA) • 603 • Eastern LA, bounded on the east and southeast by the Mississippi River (forming the MS state line), on the west by the Tensas River, which also drains the parish. Part of Tensas River National Wildlife Refuge is in the parish. Winter Quarters State Historic Site and Lake Bruin State Park are also here. • Named for the Taensa Indian tribe • 1843 from Concordia Parish • Cotton, corn, sorghum, peanuts, rice, soybeans, wheat, cattle, hogs; logging; manufacture of apparel; fish hatchery, fishing.

TERREBONNE *Houma* • 104,503 • 1,255 (the fifth largest parish in LA, although Natchitoches is only one square mile larger) • Southeastern LA, bounded on the south by the Gulf of Mexico, on the east in part by Bayou Pointe Aux Chenes, and on the west by the Atchafalaya River; drained by Grand Caillou, Du Large, Terrebonne, and Black bayous; intersected by Bayou Terrebonne and many smaller bayous. The swamps of the coast are indented by Atchafalaya, Caillou, and Terrebonne bays. The parish is crossed by the Intracoastal Waterway. The Houma Navigation Canal connects the waterway and Houma with the Gulf. Mandalay National Wildlife Refuge is also here. • Several possibilities exist for the derivation of the name Terrebonne, including, simply, the French translation of "good land." • 1822 from Lafourche Parish • Canning and shipping of seafood; oil and natural gas; pipeline servicing; iron and steel fabrication; manufacture of machinery; shipbuilding; sugar milling; sugar cane, vegetables, cattle; crawfish, oysters, shrimp, crabs, finfish, alligators; fur trapping, hunting and fishing. • The parish has a number of antebellum homes of note, including the Southdown Plantation (c.1850).

UNION (one of eighteen counties/parishes so named) *Farmerville* • 22,803 • 878 • Northern LA, bounded on the north by the AR state line, on the east by the Ouachita River; drained by Bayou de Loutre, Corney Bayou and Bayou D'Arbonne. Bayou D'Arbonne Lake reservoir and Lake D'Arbonne State Park are here, as are Upper Ouachita National Wildlife Refuge and part of D'Arbonne National Wildlife Refuge. • Possibly named for the union of the United States • 1839 from Ouachita Parish • Natural gas; home gardens, vegetables, watermelons, cattle, horses, poultry, hogs, dairying; fishing; logging, wood products; chemicals.

VERMILION (one of three counties/parishes named Vermilion or Vermillion) *Abbeville* • 53,807 • 1,174 • Southern LA, bounded on the south by the Gulf of Mexico, on the north in part by Bayou Queue de Tortue, on the northwest by Lake Arthur, and on the southeast by Vermilion Bay; drained by the Vermilion River. The parish is crossed by the Intracoastal Waterway. The Southwest Pass separates the southeastern corner from Marsh Island (in Iberia Parish). A large part of the parish is composed of marshland. It includes White Lake (home to one of the nation's largest colonies of common egrets) and part of Rockefeller National Wildlife Refuge. • Named for the Vermilion River and Vermilion Bay • 1844 from Lafayette Parish • Abbeville, founded by a Capuchin missionary in 1843, was settled by Acadians and Mediterranean immigrants. It was originally modeled after a French village. • Home gardens, nursery crops, rice, sugar cane, soybeans, vegetables, cattle, horses, dairying, hogs, exotic fowl; crawfish, shrimp, crabs, alligators; logging; rice milling, cotton ginning; manufacture of apparel; oil and natural gas. • Abbeville holds a French-Acadian dairy festival each year.

VERNON (one of three counties/parishes so named) *Leesville* • 52,531 • 1,329 (the largest parish in LA) • Western LA, bounded on the west by the Sabine River (here forming the TX state line) and Bayou Toro; drained by the Calcasieu River and Bayou Anacoco (forming part of the parish's southern boundary). Vernon Parish includes part of Kisatchie National Forest (including Longleaf Scenic Area and Fullerton Mill Site), Fort Polk Military Reservation, and Anacoco Lake and Vernon Lake reservoirs. • There are several possibilities for the derivation of its name. The most outrageous: for a local mule. • 1871 from Natchitoches, Rapides, and Sabine • Activist Ward Connerly • Home gardens, sweet potatoes, watermelons, cattle, poultry, hogs, dairying; logging, lumber; manufacture of apparel; sand and gravel.

WASHINGTON *Franklinton* • 43,926 • 670 • Southeastern LA, bounded on the north and east by the MS state line (formed by the Pearl River), and on the west in part by the Tchefuncte River; drained by Bogue Chitto. • One of thirty-one counties named for President George Washington • 1819 from Saint Tammany Parish • Washington was one of the Florida parishes of Southeastern LA, a former British Colony of Western Florida. Bogalusa was founded in 1906 by the Great Southern Lumber Company. • Logging of yellow pine, lumber milling and products. (Through reforestation programs the parish has remained a major logging center since the early 1900s.) Also, hay, home gardens, nursery crops, sweet potatoes, vegetables, watermelons, cattle, exotic fowl, dairying; tung oil; light manufacturing; oil and natural gas. The LA State U. Forestry School, and state and federal agricultural experiment stations are here.

WEBSTER *Minden* • 41,831 • 596 • Northwestern LA, bounded on the north by the AR state line, on the east in part by Black Lake Bayou, and on the west in part by Bodcau Bayou; drained by Bayou Dorcheat. The parish includes part of Kisatchie National Forest and Lake Bistineau State Park. • One of eight counties/parishes named for Daniel Webster (1782–1852), U.S. statesman and orator from MA. • 1871 from Bossier, Claiborne, and Bienville • Cotton, hay, sweet potatoes, vegetables, watermelons, cattle, horses, poultry, dairying;

oil and natural gas and refineries, sand and gravel; logging, lumber and paper milling.

WEST BATON ROUGE *Port Allen* • 21,601 • 191 • Southeast-central LA, bounded on the east by the Mississippi River. The parish has many Indian mounds. • Baton Rouge is French for "red stick," the pole that separated the hunting grounds of two local Indian tribes • 1807 from Baton Rouge (when the parish was divided into East and West Baton Rouge parishes) • Corn, hay, soybeans, sugar cane, cattle, horses, exotic fowl; crawfish; logging; manufacture of food products, chemicals, petroleum and coal products, metal products; lumber; clay deposits.

WEST CARROLL *Oak Grove* • 12,314 • 359 • Northeastern LA, bounded on the east by Bayou Macon, on the west by the Boeuf River, and on the north by the AR state line. Located here is Poverty Point National Monument and State Historic Site, one of the largest and most intricate geometrical earthworks in North America. • The parish was originally named for Charles Carroll (1737–1832), signer of the Declaration of Independence and U.S. senator from MD • 1877 from Carroll (when the parish was divided into East and West Carroll parishes), the original parish formed in 1832 • Cotton, peaches, corn, sorghum, wheat, rice, soybeans, sweet potatoes, vegetables, cattle, hogs, dairying; manufacture of leather gloves, mittens, prefabricated metal buildings; logging; oil and natural-gas wells.

WEST FELICIANA *Saint Francisville* • 15,111 • 406 • Southeast-central LA, bounded on the west by the Mississippi River, on the northwest in part by Old River Lake and the Red River, on the north by the MS state line, and on the east by Thompson Creek. The state penitentiary is in the northwest. Lake Rosemound is in the parish. Locust Grove and Audubon state historic sites are also found here. • Named for Spain's Distrito de Feliciana in West Florida • 1824 from Feliciana (when the parish was divided into East and West Feliciana parishes), the original parish formed in 1810 • The parish was one of the Florida Parishes of Southeastern LA, a former British Colony of West Florida. • Cotton, corn, soybeans, sweet potatoes, cattle, dairying; logging; sand and gravel; paper mills. • The Annual Audubon Pilgrimage is held here.

WINN *Winnfield* • 16,894 • 951 • North-central LA, bounded on the west by Saline Lake and the Saline River (here a national scenic river), and on the southeast by Castor Creek; intersected by the Dugdemona River. Part of Kistachie National Forest is here and includes Dogwood Trail in the west. • Probably named for Walter O. Winn, state legislator and founder of the forerunner of Louisiana State University • 1852 from Natchitoches, Catahoula and Rapides • Politician Huey P. Long. • Blueberries, hay, vegetables, cattle, poultry; logging, lumber, millwork; gypsum quarrying.

MAINE

I Direct

Maine's sixteen counties serve as court and jail districts. Each elects three commissioners.

ANDROSCOGGIN *Auburn* • 103,793 (the fifth most populated county in ME) • 470 • Southwestern ME. The Androscoggin and Little Androscoggin rivers flow through the county. Several lakes are recreational centers. Range Ponds State Park is here. Lost Valley ski area is a resort destination. • Named for either the Arosaguntacook Indians or for the Androscoggin River • 1854 from Cumberland, Oxford, and Kennebec • Poet Louise Bogan; Union officer Oliver O. Howard; critic Oscar Cargill; politicians Nelson Dingley and Israel Washburn; painter Marsden Hartley; geologist George P. Merrill; businessman James S. Sanborn; educator Chauncey Tinker • Manufacture of textiles, footwear and shoe accessories, glass fabrics, bakery products, livestock and poultry feeds, concrete and brick, electrical equipment, fabricated metals; dairying, eggs, apples, vegetables; education (Bates College); tourism • Two hydroelectric dams provide waterpower to the twin cities of Lewiston and Auburn. One of the first electronically automated poultry hatcheries is in Lewiston.

AROOSTOOK *Houlton* • 73,938 • 6,672 (the largest county in ME, the thirtieth largest county in the U.S., and the largest county east of the Mississippi River) • Northern ME, bounded on the north and east by the Canadian province of New Brunswick and on the north and northwest by the Canadian province of Quebec; drained by the Allagash, Aroostook, Fish, Little Madawaska, Machias, Mattawamkeag, Meduxnekeag and St. John rivers (the last forming most of the northern boundary). The county has large tracts of lake-dotted wilderness, and includes the Allagash Wilderness Waterway. There are several areas of public reserved land here. Aroostook State Park is also here. • Named for the Aroostook River • 1839 from Washington and Penobscot • Houlton played an active role in the bloodless Aroostook (Maine-New Brunswick border) War of 1839; it was the headquarters for the Maine militia. Federal troops were also stationed here. A transatlantic radiotelephone receiving station operated in Houlton from 1927 to the late 1950s. In August, 1978, Presque Isle served as lift-off point for the "Double Eagle II," the first balloon to cross the Atlantic Ocean from the U.S. to France; it was manned by Max Anderson, Ben Abruzzo and Larry Newman. • Educator Ashley H. Thorndike • Aroostook is a leading potato-growing county. Also, poultry, dairying, grain; manganese; manufacture of wood and paper products, burlap bags, farm machinery, food products, fertilizers; hunting, fishing and canoeing; education (U. of ME at Presque Isle; U. of ME at Fort Kent) • The Webb Museum of Vintage Fashion is in Island Falls. Fort Kent is the terminus of Highway No. 1 from Key West, FL.

CUMBERLAND (one of eight counties so named) *Portland* • 265,612 (the most populated county in ME) • 836 • Southwestern ME, bounded on the southeast by Casco Bay (Atlantic Ocean), on the southwest in part by the Saco River, and on the northeast in part by the Androscoggin River; drained by the Fore, Presumpscot, Nonesuch, Royal, and Stroudwater rivers. There are resort areas at Casco Bay, Sebago and Long lakes. The county has several state parks. • One of four counties named for William Augustus, Duke of Cumberland (1721–65), British general and second son of King George II • 1760 (prior to statehood) • The village that would later become Portland was raided by Indians in 1676 and by the French and Indians in 1690. In 1775, the settlement (then known as Falmouth) was bombarded and burned by the British. Portland served as state capital from 1820 to 1832. Naval shipbuilding was important to the county during the two world wars. • Astronomer William C. Bond; antislavery leader John A. Andrew; politician and temperance advocate Neal Dow; poet Robert P. T. Coffin; film director John Ford; Nazi radio propagandist Mildred Gillars; electrical engineer Greenleaf Whittier Pickard; composer Walter Piston; Speaker of the House Thomas B. Reed; poet Henry Wadsworth Longfellow; politician Rufus King; editor and writer Nathaniel Parker Willis; religious leader Ellen Gould White; publisher George Palmer Putnam; naval officer Edward Preble; organist John Knowles Paine; entomologist Alpheus S. Packard; writer John Neal; zoologist Edward S. Morse; clergyman Joseph H. Ingraham; physicist Edwin Herbert Hall; publisher Cyrus Curtis; painter Samuel Colman; novelist Stephen King. Harriet Beecher Stowe wrote *Uncle Tom's Cabin* in 1852 while her husband taught at Bowdoin College, whose students included Franklin Pierce, Longfellow and Hawthorne. The rocky coast of Prouts Neck inspired many of the paintings of resident Winslow Homer. • Manufacture of paper and wood products, apparel, furniture, textiles, shoes; dairying, chemicals, metal goods, machinery, crushed-stone products, jewelry; tourism; publishing; commercial fishing; education (Bowdoin College; U. of New England — Westbrook College; U. of Southern ME; St. Joseph's College) • Portland is closer to Europe than any other major port in the U.S. • The city is a major petroleum port and the eastern terminus of the Portland-Montreal oil pipeline. Portland Head Lighthouse, erected in 1791 on orders from George Washington, is one of the oldest lighthouses in the U.S. The Camp Fire Girls originated in Sebago Lake in 1910.

FRANKLIN (one of twenty-five counties so named) *Farmington* • 29,467 • 1,698 • Western ME, bounded on the north by the Canadian province of Quebec. The county lies in a recreational and lumbering region and includes Rangeley Lake and Mount Blue state parks. The Androscoggin is its chief river. Located in the White and Appalachian mountains, the county is crossed by the Appalachian Trail. Numerous ski areas are also here. • One of twenty-three counties named for Benjamin Franklin • 1838 from Cumberland • Soprano Lillian Nordica; poet Elizabeth Anne Allen; teacher and writer Jacob Abbott • Lumbering; manufacture of paper, pulp, and wood products, bricks, shoes, plastic products; wood turning; canning; fruit, (especially blueberries), vegetables, dairying; hunting, fishing, tourism; education (U. of ME at Farmington) • Earmuffs were invented by Chester Greenwood in Farmington about 1873. Each year on the first Saturday in December, townspeople and their pets celebrate this fact by wearing them en masse. County lakes are known for their many loons.

HANCOCK *Ellsworth* • 51,791 • 1,589 • Southern and southeastern ME, bounded on the west by the Penobscot River and Penobscot Bay; drained by the West Branch of the Union River. Mount Desert Island includes units of Acadia National Park (its headquarters in Bar Harbor, one of the most famous resorts in the U.S.). The county is characterized by bays, islands and inland lakes (resorts). Lamoine State Park is south of Ellsworth. • One of ten counties named for John Hancock (1737–93), president of the Continental Congress, noted signer of the Declaration of Independence, and governor of MA • 1789 (prior to statehood) from Lincoln • A trading post was established by the Plymouth Colony in Castine in 1626. Fort George was built here by the British in 1770. Most of Bar Harbor was destroyed by fire in 1947. • U.S. vice president Nelson A. Rockefeller; writer Mary Ellen Chase; physician Henry G. Davis; publisher Edwin Ginn. Orchestra conductor Pierre Monteux died here. • Dairying; granite quarrying; hunting and fishing; manufacture of machinery, wood and paper products, woolen goods; shipbuilding; education (The Maine Maritime Academy; College of the Atlantic).

KENNEBEC *Augusta* • 117,114 (the fourth most populated county in ME) • 867 • Southern ME. The county receives water power from the Sebasticook and Kennebec rivers (the latter forming part of the northern boundary). It has many resorts, especially in the Belgrade and China lakes regions. Great Pond is the largest of its many lakes. • Named for the Kennebec River • 1799 (prior to statehood) from Lincoln • Fort Halifax, constructed by the British in 1754, commanded a strategic Indian route during the French and Indian War. Augusta became the capital of the state in 1832. One of the first workable steam automobiles in the U.S. was built in Gardiner in 1858. • Political leader George Mitchell; writer Holman Francis Day; jurist Melville Weston Fuller; teacher and writer Jacob Abbott; psychologist Henry H. Goddard; abolitionist Elijah P. Lovejoy; anthropologist John R. Swanton; poet Edwin Arlington Robinson (Gardiner is considered to be the "Tilbury Town" of his poems). Laura E. Richards wrote many of her novels, including *Captain January,* in Gardiner. • Man-

ufacture of apparel, textiles, food products, shoes, paper, wood and pulp products; dairying and shipping of farm and orchard produce; education (Colby College; U. of ME at Augusta); government offices; tourism • Built in 1754, Old Fort Western, located in Augusta, is New England's oldest surviving wooden fort. The Samantha Smith Memorial, which honors the memory of the young girl who wrote a letter to Soviet Premier Yuri Andropov and was then invited to tour the Soviet Union, is located at the Maine State Capitol Complex. The State House in Augusta (1829–32) was designed by architect Charles Bulfinch. A 2,100 feet bridge of cantilever deck truss design (1850) spans the Kennebec, which divides the city.

KNOX *Rockland* • 39,618 • 366 • Southern ME, bounded on the southeast by Penobscot Bay (Atlantic Ocean); drained by the St. George River. Birch Point Beach State Park and part of Camden Hills State Park are here. • One of nine counties named for General Henry Knox (1750–1806), first U.S. secretary of war • 1860 from Lincoln and Waldo • Actress Maxine Elliott; poet Edna Saint Vincent Millay; composer Walter Piston • Resort tourism; commercial fishing (major landing and distribution point for lobsters); shipbuilding; poultry, apples; manufacture of boats, leather, yarns, textiles, millwork, cement; limestone quarrying • The Maine Seafood Festival is held each August in Rockland. The city's William A. Farnsworth Library and Art Museum houses a notable collection of paintings by the Wyeths.

LINCOLN (one of twenty-four counties so named) *Wiscasset* • 33,616 • 456 • Southern ME. Resorts are spread out along its coast and islands, Sheepscot and Eastern rivers, Damariscotta and Medomak inlets. Damariscotta Lake State Park is here. Colonial Pemaquid (Fort William Henry) State Historic Site is also found in the county. • Named for the town of Lincoln, England, chosen to honor Thomas Pownall (1722–1805), royal governor of Massachusetts Bay Colony who was born there. • 1760 (prior to statehood) from York • Religious leader Augusta Emma Stetson • Fishing; resort tourism; some mixed agriculture; boat building; manufacture of canvas goods, boats, food products; canning and shipping of seafood • Boothbay Harbor is crowded with old schooners during its annual Windjammer Days festivities.

OXFORD *South Paris* • 54,755 • 2,078 • Western ME, bounded on the east by the NH state line and on the north by the Canadian province of Quebec; drained by the Androscoggin River. Part of White Mountain National Forest is in the west. There are winter sports at Newry and Locke Mills, summer resorts in Rangeley Lakes region. The county is crossed by the Appalachian Trail, located in the White Mountains. • Named for the town of Oxford, MA • 1805 (prior to statehood) from York and Cumberland • Humorist Charles F. Brown; clergyman Cyrus Hamlin; sociologist Albion W. Small; satirist Seba Smith; zoologist Charles O. Whitman • Manufacture of shoes, paper, wood products, lumber mills; dairying; tourism • Oxford is a "Scandinavian county," with towns named Norway, Sweden and Denmark. The Bryant Pond Telephone Museum is here.

PENOBSCOT *Bangor* • 144,919 (the third most populated county in ME) • 3,396 (the fourth largest county in ME) • Central ME; drained by the Penobscot and Seboeis rivers. The county has numerous lakes. Sunkhaze Meadows National Wildlife Refuge is in the southeast. • Named for the Penobscot River • 1816 (prior to statehood) from Hancock • The first white visitor to the county was French explorer Samuel de Champlain, who sailed up the Penobscot in 1604. British occupied the town of Bangor during the War of 1812. In the 19th century, the city was one of the leading lumber ports in the world. Shipbuilding has also made a strong contribution to the local economy over the years. • Reformer Dorothea Dix; botanist Merritt L. Fernald; novelist Blanche Willis Howard. Joshua Chamberlain, born in Brewer, accepted Confederate General Robert E. Lee's surrender at Appomattox. • Lumbering; manufacture of pulp, paper, wood products, canoes, bricks, fabricated steel, awnings, textiles, concrete products, sweaters, women's shoes, electronic equipment; hunting, fishing and other outdoor recreation; education (U. of ME; Husson College) • Bangor's public library, with more than 400,000 volumes, is one of the largest in New England.

PISCATAQUIS *Dover-Foxcroft* • 17,235 (the least populated county in ME) • 3,966 (the second largest county in ME) • North-central ME; drained by the Piscataquis and Pleasant rivers and the West Branch of the Penobscot. The county has hundreds of lakes, including the largest in the state, Moosehead; its western shore forms part of the county's western boundary. Piscataquis also boasts the highest mountain in ME, Katahdin (5,267 feet), located in 200,000-acre Baxter State Park. The mountain serves as the northern terminus of the Appalachian Trail. The county also includes several sections of public reserved land, Peaks Kenny State Park and Katahdin Iron Works State Historic Site. • Named for the Piscataquis River • 1838 from Penobscot and Somerset • During the Civil War, soldiers from Piscataquis played a key role for the Union in the Battle of Gettysburg. • British inventor Sir Hiram Maxim • Manufacture of wood products, lumbering; resort tourism, hunting, fishing, canoeing • Piscataquis is mentioned in the work of Henry David Thoreau and John Steinbeck.

SAGADAHOC *Bath* • 35,214 • 254 (the smallest county in ME) • Southwestern ME, bounded on the southwest by Casco Bay and on the south by the Gulf of Maine (Atlantic Ocean). The Androscoggin River joins the Kennebec River at Merrymeeting Bay. Pond Island National Wildlife Refuge, and Reid and Popham Beach state parks are on the coast. • Named for the lower portion of the Kennebec River • 1854 from Lincoln • The first English colony in New England was founded at Fort St. George (now Popham Beach) in 1607. The *Virginia*, thought to be the first vessel built in America (in 1607), came from Popham. Bath's shipbuilding (recalled in its Maine Maritime Museum) dates from 1762, when Captain William

Swanton launched the *Earl of Bute*. The Bath Iron Works has been building ships since 1889, production spiking during the world wars. Among the better-known yachts and sailboats built in Bath were J.P. Morgan's *Corsair*. • Sculptor William Zorach; geographer Henry Gannett; promoter Charles W. Morse • Manufacture of wood products and building supplies, windlasses, deck machinery, nautical lights, bottles, shirts; canning; fishing, duck hunting, tourism; dairying.

SOMERSET (one of four counties so named) *Skowhegan* • 50,888 • 3,927 (the third largest county in ME) • Central and western ME, bounded on the west by the Canadian province of Quebec; drained by the Kennebec and Moose rivers. Moosehead Lake (forming part of the eastern boundary) and Jackman-Moose River regions are known for hunting, canoeing and fishing. (The county has many lakes, especially in the north.) Lumber camps are in the northwest in the Appalachian Mountains. • Named for Somersetshire in England • 1809 (prior to statehood) from Kennebec • Colonel Benedict Arnold's Continental troops camped on Skowhegan Island on their expedition against the British in Quebec in the autumn of 1775. • Work efficiency expert Frank B. Gilbreth; senator Margaret Chase Smith • Manufacture of shoes, paper, pulp and wood products; farming, dairying; lumber; fishing and hunting • The Skowhegan State Fair, held since 1818, is the oldest state fair in the U.S. The Skowhegan Indian has cast his shadow over the town since 1969 when he was erected to honor the state's Native Americans in conjunction with Maine's sesquicentennial celebration. At sixty-two feet high, he is regarded as "the world's tallest Indian."

WALDO *Belfast* • 36,280 • 730 • Southern ME, bounded on the southeast by Penobscot Bay; drained by the Sebasticook, Sheepscot, and Penobscot rivers (the last forming the eastern boundary). The county contains several state parks, including part of Camden Hills situated on the bay. Fort Knox State Historic Site is in the east. • Named for General Samuel Waldo (1695–1759), an officer in the French and Indian Wars, and promoter of settlement in the area that became Maine • 1827 from Hancock • Mental healer Phineas P. Quimby died here. • Apples, potatoes, poultry, garden vegetables, dairying; fishing (sardines, lobsters); manufacture of ski apparel, shoes; tourism; education (Unity College) • An early seaport and port of entry, Belfast retains significant architecture from the sailing era. • Searsport was once home to eleven shipyards, and had more shipmasters than any other town in the U.S. Between 1810 and 1890 more than 200 vessels anchored here.

WASHINGTON *Machias* • 33,941 • 2,569 (the fifth largest county in ME) • Eastern ME, bounded on the east by the Canadian province of New Brunswick, on the south by the Atlantic Ocean, and on the southeast by Grand Manan Channel; drained by the St. Croix River (forming the New Brunswick border), Machias, East Machias, and Dennys rivers. Indian Township Indian Reservation is here, as are national wildlife refuges (including units of Moosehorn), public reserved land areas and state parks, including Quoddy Head, the easternmost in the U.S. • One of thirty-one counties named for President Washington • 1789 (prior to statehood) from Lincoln • The French attempted to settle on Saint Croix Island in 1604 (international historic site), a first step toward the founding of New France. Machias sheltered Atlantic pirates and was later a center of Revolutionary War activity. Probably the first naval engagement of the Revolutionary War took place off Machiasport when the British schooner *Margaretta* was captured in June, 1775. Eastport was captured by the British in the War of 1812 and not returned to the U.S. until 1818. The Passamaquoddy Tidal Power Project, initiated by the federal government in the 1930s to harness the high tides of the bay for hydroelectric power was never completed. • Theatre manager Edward F. Albee; ethnologist Otis T. Mason. President Franklin D. Roosevelt had his summer home at Campobello Island (now an international park). • The county is the world's largest producer of blueberries; also lumbering; manufacture of pulp, paper, and wood products; resort tourism, hunting; poultry, dairying; recreational and commercial fishing; sardine and herring packing, other fish-related industries; education (U. of ME at Machias); granite quarrying • The most powerful radio station in the world, the Navy's Very Low Frequency radio station, is located in Cutler. The "Old Sow Whirlpool," one of the world's largest and most dangerous, is located between Eastport and Deer Island, New Brunswick. The tremendous tides at Mahar's Point in West Pembroke create the "Reversing Salt Water Falls." A granite stone in Perry marks the halfway point between the Equator and the North Pole. Eastport and Lubec share the distinction of being the easternmost community in the U.S.

YORK (one of five counties so named) *Alfred* • 186,742 (13.5% increase since 1990; the fastest growing and the second most populated county in ME) • 991 • Southwestern ME, bounded on the west and southwest by the NH state line and on the southeast by the Gulf of Maine (Atlantic Ocean); drained by the Saco River (forming part of the northeastern boundary), the Pascataqua, Salmon Falls (both rivers forming part of the southwestern boundary), and the Mousam and Ossippee rivers. Ferry Beach and Fort Foster state parks and Rachel Carson National Wildlife Refuge are also here. • Named for either the town of York, ME or for Yorkshire, England • Original county (formerly Yorkshire County, MA), organized 1652 (prior to statehood) • Kittery, the oldest town in the state, was settled in 1624. In 1641, York became the first English city on the American continent when Sir Fernando Gorges endowed it with a city charter under the name Gorgeana. A shipbuilding center since Revolutionary War times, Kittery saw the launch in 1777 of John Paul Jones' *Ranger*, the first ship to fly the American flag. The Portsmouth Naval Shipyard, though attached economically to Portsmouth, NH, is actually in York County. It was here that 1905 treaty negotiations ended the Russo-Japanese War and earned President Theodore Roosevelt his Nobel Prize. Since 1900 it has been a center for the building and repair of submarines. • Writers Sarah Orne Jewett, Carlos Heard Baker, and Kenneth Lewis Roberts; native American baronet Sir William Pepperrell; pioneer and newspaperman Samuel Brannan; lawyer and financier Hugh McCulloch; politician Edith Rogers; Revolutionary War leader William Whipple. U.S. Supreme Court justices Nathan Clifford and Wiley B. Rutledge died here. Walker's Point at Kennebunkport is the vacation retreat of President Bush père and President Bush fils. • Manufacture of textiles, wood products, shoes, machinery, plastics, electrical products, apparel, aircraft and aircraft components, automotive parts, medical gases, acrylic plastic sheets; market gardening; dairying; lumbering; commercial fishing and lobstering; summer tourism; education (U. of New England) • Old Orchard Beach features one of the longest stretches of hard-packed sand on the Atlantic Coast. York's jail, now the Old Gaol Museum, is the oldest English public building in North America still standing and open to the public. Kennebunkport, long a literary and art colony, is also home to the Seashore Trolley Museum, which displays more than 100 antique streetcars.

MARYLAND

Manly Deeds, Womanly Words

About half of Maryland's twenty-three counties are governed by elected boards of county commissioners, which serve both executive and legislative functions. Its members are elected to four-year terms. The remaining counties are administered by either county councils or county executives, or by a combination of the two, all members serving four-year terms. Other county officials include the circuit court clerk, state's attorney, sheriff, register of wills, and financial director or treasurer. Baltimore is an independent city, unaffiliated with any county in the state.

ALLEGANY (one of two counties so named, the other in NY; one of five counties named Allegany with variant spellings) *Cumberland* • 74,930 • 425 • Western MD, bounded on the north by the PA State Line (Mason-Dixon Line), on the south by the Potomac River and its North Branch (forming the WV state line); drained by Evitts, Wills, and other creeks. An Appalachian ridge and valley county, Cumberland includes the Alleghenies, Green Ridge State Forest, and Dans Mountain and Rocky Gap state parks. The Cumberland Narrows is a natural gateway through the Appalachians to the Ohio Valley. • Named for the Allegheny Mountains • 1789 from Washington County • The national road, the first highway built with Federal funds, cut through the gorge of the Narrows at Cumberland. The city of Cumberland lies at the end of the Chesapeake and Ohio Canal. George Washington and General Edward Braddock made their headquarters at Fort Cumberland during the French and Indian Wars of the 1750s. On February 21, 1865, two sleeping Union generals, Benjamin Kelley and George Crook, were surprised and captured at Union-occupied Cumberland by McNeill's Rangers. • Journalist and author Fitz-James O'Brien • Apples, peaches, maple syrup, dairying; bituminous- and lignite-coal mining, clay pits; timber; manufacture of glass, clay and stone products, food products, apparel, paper products, transportation equipment, sheet metal, missile components, synthetic fibers; hunting and fishing; railroad shops.

ANNE ARUNDEL *Annapolis* • 489,656 (the fourth most populated county in MD) • 416 • Central MD, bounded on the east by the Chesapeake Bay, on the north and northeast by the Patapsco River, and on the west by the Patuxent River. The county has a number of resorts, recreational parks and beaches. The U.S. Naval Research Development Center is also here. The northern part of the county constitutes part of the large Baltimore metropolitan area; Baltimore Washington International Airport is here. Fort George G. Meade Military Reservation is also in the county. Sandy Point State Park is on the shore of Chesapeake Bay. • Named for Anne Arundell Calvert (1615–1649), wife of Cecilius Calvert, Lord Baltimore; one of twelve MD counties named for the Calverts, their friends, and relations • Original county; organized 1650 • In 1694, Annapolis was made provincial capital. It remained capital after Maryland became a state. The city had its own "tea party" on October 18, 1774, forcing the owner of the ship *Peggy Stewart* to burn his cargo of taxed tea. While Congress was in session in Annapolis (from November 26, 1783 to June 3, 1794), George Washington resigned as commander in chief of the Continental Army (December 23, 1783). Congress ratified the Treaty of Paris here, ending the Revolutionary War. The 1786 Annapolis Convention addressed changes to the Articles of Confederation; it paved the path to the meeting in Philadelphia the next year that drew up the Constitution of the U.S. Many soldiers wounded during the Civil War were hospitalized here. • Diplomat and statesman William Pinkney; Declaration of Independence signer Charles Carroll; politicians Daniel Dulany and Reverdy Johnson; merchant and philanthropist John Hopkins. Novelist James M. Cain died here. Naval hero John Paul Jones is buried in the crypt of the chapel of the U.S. Naval Academy. • Vegetables, fruit,

tobacco, poultry, livestock, dairy products; fish, oyster, crabs; manufacture of search and navigational equipment and boatworks; resort tourism; education (Saint John's College; U.S. Naval Academy); government offices • Annapolis's State House (1772–80) is the oldest state capitol still in legislative use. Annapolis has more than sixty pre-Revolutionary houses, including those belonging to three signers of the Declaration of Independence: William Paca, Samuel Chase, and Charles Carroll.

BALTIMORE *Towson* • 754,292 (the third most populated county in MD) • 599 (the third largest county in MD) • Northern MD, bounded on the north by the PA state line, on the southeast by the Gunpowder River and Chesapeake Bay, and on the southwest by the Patapsco River; drained by Gunpowder Falls (stream). The county is largely suburban around the independent city of Baltimore, which it almost completely surrounds. Estates (including Hampton National Historic Site) are in a district known for horse racing, fox hunting, and jousting. Patapsco State Park, units of Gunpowder Falls State Park and Lake Roland are in the county. Prettyboy Reservoir is in the north. • Named for the barony of Baltimore in Ireland, source of the hereditary title Lord Baltimore of the Calvert family, proprietors of the colony of MD • Original county; its legal origin is not known, but it was in existence by 1659 • Baltimore was split into the discrete constituents of county and city in 1851. Worldwide publicity came to the Catonsville Nine, a group of citizens who burned the records of the local draft board in protest against the War in Vietnam in 1968. • Biochemist Christian Andinsen died here. • Manufacture of steel, ships, aircraft, communications equipment, electric tools, scientific instruments; fruit, dairying; education (Towson U.; Goucher College; U. of MD, Baltimore County; Villa Julie College) • Ballestone Museum (c. 1780) at the Rocky Point Golf Course was built by George Washington's grandfather. The Maryland State Fairgrounds is here.

CALVERT *Prince Frederick* • 74,563 (45% increase since 1990; the fastest growing county in MD) • 215 (the smallest county in MD) • Southern MD, a narrow tidewater peninsula, bounded on the east by the Chesapeake Bay, on the south and west by the Patuxent River; drained by many small creeks. Calvert Cliffs State Park is here. • Given the family name of the Lords Baltimore, proprietors of MD. It is one of twelve MD counties named for the Calverts, their friends and relations • Original county; organized as Charles in 1650; name changed to Calvert in 1654 and later that year changed to Patuxent; name changed again in 1658 • Revolutionary War leader Thomas Johnson; soldier and adventurer James Wilkinson; Chief Justice of the U.S. Roger Brooke Taney • Tobacco, grain, truck crops, livestock; fisheries, oysters, crabs, fish; timber; some boat building; resort area fishing, hunting and water sports.

CAROLINE (one of two counties named Caroline, the other in VA) • *Denton* • 29,772 • 320 • Eastern MD, on the Eastern Shore, bounded on the east by the DE state line, on the west by the Choptank River and Tuckahoe Creek. Tuckahoe State Park is on the western boundary; Martinak State Park is also in the county. • Named for Caroline Calvert Eden, wife of Robert Eden, colonial governor of MD at the time the county was created; one of twelve MD counties named for the Calverts, their friends and relations • 1774 (prior to statehood) from Dorchester and Queen Anne's counties • Tomatoes, fruit, dairy products, corn, soybeans, barley, poultry, livestock; hardwoods, evergreens; vegetable canneries, poultry-dressing plants; manufacture of paper products.

CARROLL (one of thirteen counties so named) *Westminster* • 150,897 • 449 • Northern MD, bounded on the northwest by the Monocacy River and on the north by the PA state line; drained by branches of the Patapsco River. • One of twelve counties named for Charles Carroll (1737–1832), signer of the Declaration of Independence, U.S. senator from MD and founder of the Baltimore and Ohio Railroad • 1836 from Baltimore and Frederick counties • Composer of the "Star Spangled Banner" Francis Scott Key; diplomat R. Sargent Shriver, Jr. • Dairying, stock, poultry, corn, wheat, potatoes, vegetables, apples; stone quarries; manufacture of electronic equipment; lumbering; education (Western MD College) • Just northwest of Westminster is Whittaker Chambers's farm; here Chambers buried the "Pumpkin papers," evidence in the trial of Alger Hiss.

CECIL *Elkton* • 85,951 • 348 • Extreme northeastern MD, at the head of Chesapeake Bay and at the base of the Eastern Shore, bounded on the south by the Sassafras River, on the east by the DE state line, on the north by the PA state line, and on the west by the Susquehanna River; drained by the Elk, Northeast, and Bohemia rivers, and Octoraro Creek. The county includes Elk Neck State Park and State Forest. • Named for Cecilius Calvert, 2nd Lord Baltimore (1605–75), founder and first proprietor of the colony of MD, though he never visited it; one of twelve MD counties named for the Calverts, their friends and relations • 1674 from Baltimore and Kent counties • The area that became Cecil county was explored by Captain John Smith in 1608. A boundary dispute in the northern part of the county between Lord Baltimore and William Penn was resolved by the drawing of the Mason-Dixon line in 1765. Prior to their attack on Philadelphia in 1777, British troops under General Sir William Howe landed on Elk Neck promontory. During the War of 1812, Elkton was attacked by a British naval squadron, which was repulsed. • Businessman and philanthropist Robert S. Brookings; U.S. Supreme Court justice David Davis • Livestock raising, dairying, wheat, corn, vegetables, fruit; granite quarries, sand and gravel pits; manufacture of transportation equipment, medical instruments, rubber goods, explosives, propellants, plastics, clothing; commercial fisheries; boatbuilding • Until a 1938 law mandated a 48-hour waiting period, Elkton earned a reputation as the "Gretna Green of the East" for facilitating "quickie" marriages. It is still a destination for eloping couples.

CHARLES *La Plata* • 120,546 • 461 • Southern MD, bounded on the east by the Potomac River and partly on the southeast by the Wicomico River. Doncaster Demonstration Forest is in the west. Smallwood State Park is also in the county. • Named for Charles Calvert, 3rd Baron Baltimore (1637–1715), second proprietor of the colony of MD and colonial governor of MD; one of twelve counties named for the Calverts, their friends and relations • Original county; organized 1658 • John Wilkes Booth's leg was set by Dr. Samuel Mudd here following Booth's assassination of President Abraham Lincoln. • American Revolutionary leader John Hanson; explorer Matthew Henson; Confederate naval officer Raphael Semmes • Lumbering; commercial fishing and oystering; tobacco (Auctions are conducted every spring in La Plata, Hughesville, and Waldorf.) • The county comprises the oldest active Jesuit parish in the U.S.

DORCHESTER (one of two counties so named, the other in SC) *Cambridge* • 30,674 • 558 (the fourth largest county in MD) • Eastern Shore of MD, bounded on the east by the DE state line. Chesapeake Bay islands that make up part of the county include Barren, Hooper, and Bloodsworth (Bloodsworth Island U.S. Naval Reservation here). The county's shores are indented by many inlets. Large flocks of Canada geese rest and feed in Blackwater National Wildlife Refuge. • Possibly named for Richard Sackville II, 5th Earl of Dorset (1622–77), friend of the Calvert family; one of twelve MD counties named for the Calverts, their friends and relations. • Original county, whose legal origin is unknown, but it was in existence by 1669 • Abolitionist Harriet Tubman • Fruit (especially canteloupes), vegetables (especially tomatoes), barley, soybeans, corn, wheat, dairying, poultry; seafood (fish, crabs, oysters); canning of vegetables and seafood, packing houses; lumbering; flour milling; muskrat trapping; sport fishing, duck hunting, yachting; light manufacturing.

FREDERICK (one of two counties so named, the other in VA) *Frederick* • 195,277 • 663 (the largest county in MD) • Northern MD, bounded on the north by the PA state line, on the southwest by the Potomac River, forming the VA state line, and on the northeast by the Monocacy River; also drained by Catoctin Creek. The county's extreme western section is in the Blue Ridge (locally called the South and Catoctin mountains) and Middletown Valley. It includes Sugar Loaf Mountain, part of Gathland and part of Washington Monument state parks, Cunningham Falls State Park, and Catoctin Mountain Park, the abandoned Chesapeake and Ohio Canal, and Gambrill State Park. • Probably named for Frederick Calvert, 6th Baron of Baltimore (1731–71), fifth and last proprietor of the colony of MD; one of twelve MD counties named for the Calverts, their friends and relations. • 1748 from Baltimore and Prince George's counties • The British Stamp Act received its first repudiation from judges in the Frederick County Court House in November, 1765. The town of Frederick also supplied 1,700 men to join George Washington at Valley Forge. Frederick's residents were spared an attack on their city when local banks paid Confederate General Jubal A. Early $200,000 in July, 1864. At Monocacy (national battlefield), Early defeated Union forces commanded by Brig. Gen. Lew Wallace. Tradition has it that Confederate General Stonewall Jackson spared the life of 95-year-old Barbara Fritchie (immortalized in John Greenleaf Whittier's poem) when she defiantly displayed the U.S. flag at her home in Frederick. • "The Star Spangled Banner" author Francis Scott Key; U.S. Chief Justice Roger Brooke Taney. U.S. Supreme Court justice Thomas Johnson died here. • Wheat, corn, hay, dairy products, fruit, poultry, livestock; manufacture of electronics, eyeglass frames, clothing, lime-cement products, brushes; canning; black-bass and trout fishing, resorts; education (Hood College) • The Maryland School for the Deaf is in Frederick.The 200-acre presidential retreat, Camp David, is in Catoctin Mountain Park. The first American chapter of the Sisters of Charity was founded in Emmitsburg in 1806 by St. Elizabeth Ann Seton (the first native-born American to be canonized by the Roman Catholic Church). The first national Catholic shrine in the U.S. is nearby.

GARRETT *Oakland* • 29,846 • 648 (the second largest county in MD) • Extreme western MD, bounded on the southeast by the North Branch of the Potomac River (here forming the WV state line), on the west by the WV state line, on the north by the PA state line; drained by the Youghiogheny, Casselman, Savage, and Stoney rivers. Backbone Mountain, at 3,360 feet, the highest point in MD, is in the county. Muddy Creek, at 64 feet, the state's highest waterfall, is also here. The county also includes several state parks and state forests, including units of Savage River State Forest. Deep Creek Lake is also here. • Named for John W. Garrett (1820–84), president of the Baltimore and Ohio Railroad • 1872 from Allegany (the last county to be formed in MD) • Bituminous-coal mining, fireclay; lumbering; dairy products, grain, livestock; maple sugar and syrup; hunting and fishing.

HARFORD *Bel Air* • 218,590 • 441 • Northeastern MD, bounded on the north by the PA state line, on the northeast by the Susquehanna River, on the southeast and south by Chesapeake Bay. The Coastal plain (on the county's southern fringe) is dominated by the Aberdeen Proving Ground (a major research and testing installation of the U.S. Materiel Command). The county includes many large estates. Susquehanna, units of Gunpowder Falls, and Rocks state parks are here, as well. • Named for Henry Harford (1758–1834), illegitimate son of Frederick Calvert 6th Lord of Baltimore, and the last proprietor of the colony of MD; one of twelve MD counties named for the Calverts, their friends and relations. • 1773 (prior to statehood) from Baltimore County • Cokesbury College, the first Methodist college in the Western Hemisphere, was here from 1785 to 1795. • Actor Edwin Booth. Physiologist Haldan K. Hartline died here. • Dairy products, vegetables, fruit, grain, poultry; stone quarries; commercial fisheries, shore resorts; vegetable canneries; clothing.

HOWARD (one of seven counties so named) *Ellicott City* • 247,842 (32% increase since 1990; the third fastest growing and fifth most populated county in MD) • 252 • Central MD, bounded on the northeast by the Patapsco River (Patapsco Valley State Park) and on the west and southwest by the Patuxent River. (Patuxent River State Park). (Howard is the only MD county that doesn't border either the Chesapeake Bay or the boundary of another state. • Named for John E. Howard (1752–1827), governor of MD and U.S. senator from the state • Organized as Howard District in 1838 from Anne Arundel; formed as a county in 1851 • The first section of the Baltimore and Ohio Railroad, which began operation on May 24, 1830, ran from Baltimore to Ellicott City. • Dairying, poultry, vegetables, apples, some grain; manufacture of furniture, chemicals, fabricated metals, electronics. • The Merriweather Post Pavillion in Columbia is the summer home of the Baltimore Symphony.

KENT (one of five counties so named) *Chestertown* • 19,197 (the least populated county in MD) • 280 • Eastern MD, peninsula on the Eastern Shore, bounded on the east by the DE state line and on the west by Chesapeake Bay. • Named for Kent Island, MD • Original county; organized 1642 • Before being carved into other counties, Kent took in all of the Eastern Shore. • Vegetables, fruit, corn, wheat, livestock, dairy products; oysters; summer resorts, fishing, hunting; education (chartered here in 1783, Washington College was named for George Washington with his permission.)

MONTGOMERY (one of eighteen counties so named) *Rockville* • 873,341 (the most populated county in MD) • 495 (the fifth largest county in MD) • Central MD, bounded on the northeast by the Patuxent River, on the south by the District of Columbia, on the west and southwest by the Potomac River (forming the VA state line); drained by Rock Creek. The county contains a number of residential suburbs, with some remnant agriculture in the northwest. Montgomery operates 168 parks, covering a total area of 19,000 acres. • One of sixteen counties named directly or indirectly for General Richard Montgomery (1738–75), an officer in the Revolutionary War • 1776 (prior to statehood) from Frederick • The county ceded sixty square miles to the Federal government in 1790 to form the District of Columbia. Silver Spring was the closest point to the center of Washington that was reached by forces under Confederate General Jubal Early in July, 1864. • Priest and ethnologist John M. Cooper; American Red Cross founder Clara Barton. Novelist and radical journalist Floyd Dell, first U.S. secretary of defense James V. Forrestal, secretary of state Cordell Hull, U.S. Supreme Court justice Thurgood Marshall, and politician Hiram Johnson died here. Novelist F. Scott Fitzgerald and his wife Zelda are buried in St. Mary's Cemetery in Rockville. • Dairying, truck farming, apples, wheat, hay, cattle, poultry; manufacture of scientific instruments, wood products; research and technology. Government installations, including offices of the Department of Health and Human Services, the FDA, and the National Institutes of Health, as well as the Naval Medical Center and the National Library of Medicine employ thousands. • Eight Fortune 1000 corporations have their headquarters in the county. When founded in 1945, the Takoma Park Campus of Montgomery College was the first junior college in the U.S. Josiah Henson, the inspiration for Harriet Beecher Stowe's novel *Uncle Tom's Cabin* was a slave in the county. The headquarters of the Seventh-day Adventists is in Silver Spring.

PRINCE GEORGE'S *Upper Marlboro* • 801,515 (the second most populated county in MD) • 487 • Central MD, bounded on the west by the Potomac River (forming the VA state line and D.C. boundary) and on the east and northeast by the Patuxent River; drained by the Anacostia River. The county is suburban outside of Washington D.C. It includes some of the National Capital parks in the west, part of Cedarville State Forest, the National Agricultural Research Center, and part of Patuxent Wildlife Research Center. The U.S. Bureau of the Census, Navy Hydrographic Office, and Andrews Air Force Base are in the county. The NASA Goddard Space Flight Center is also here, as are Merkle Wildlife Sanctuary and Cedarville State Forest. • Named for Prince George of Denmark (1653–1708), husband of Queen Anne of England • 1695 from Charles and Calvert • Bladensburg was the scene of a battle on August 24, 1814 in which a poorly prepared army of American defenders under the command of Brig. General William H. Winder failed to halt the advance of British regulars on Washington, D.C. (which they burned). Greenbelt was built in 1935–38 to house middle-income families, employing a garden city plan by the Federal Resettlement Administration. Presidential candidate George C. Wallace was seriously wounded in an assassination attempt in Laurel on May 15, 1972. • First U.S. Roman Catholic bishop John Carroll. Novelist James M. Cain, astrophysicist C.G. Abbot, urban designer Pierre-Charles L'Enfant, and American Revolution leader John Hanson died here. • Tobacco, truck, dairy products, corn, wheat; manufacture of machine tools, transportation equipment, chemicals; banking; education (U. of MD; Howard U. Beltsville Campus) • The Army Aviation School at College Park airfield opened in 1909 with Wilbur Wright as an instructor. The Washington D.C. International Horse Race is run each November at Laurel Race Course. Landover is home to the Washington Redskins (FedEx Field).

QUEEN ANNE'S *Centreville* • 40,563 • 372 • Eastern MD, on the Eastern Shore, bounded on the east by the DE state line, on the west by Chesapeake Bay. Eastern Bay and a narrow channel lie between Chesapeake Bay shore and Kent Island. Wye Island National Recreation Area is in the south. • Named for Anne (1665–1714), queen of Great Britain and Ireland • 1706 from Talbot • Kent Island was the site of the first permanent English settlement in MD. It was founded in 1631 by William Claiborne, who claimed it for VA. • Painter Charles Willson Peale. Financier John Jakob Raskob died here. • Vegetables, fruit, wheat, corn, dairying, poultry; fishing, oystering, canneries; tourism; education (Chesapeake College)

• The county's courthouse is one of only two built in the 18th century (1706) still standing in the state.

SAINT MARY'S *Leonardtown* • 86,211 • 361 • Southern MD, a tidewater peninsula, bounded on the northeast by the Patuxent River, on the east by Chesapeake Bay, and on the south by the Potomac (which forms the VA state line here). Patuxent River Naval Air Station is here. The county also includes Point Lookout, St. Clement's Island, Greenwell, and St. Mary's River state parks. • Named for Mary, the mother of Jesus Christ. The ships Ark and Dover, carrying colonists, landed on St. Clement's Island on March 25, 1624, the Feast of the Annunciation of Mary. • The first original county, organized 1637 • Saint Mary's City was the first settlement in the colony of MD. The town was the colonial capital from 1634 to 1694. • Detective fiction writer Dashiell Hammett • Chiefly tobacco; some lumbering and commercial fishing; resort tourism; education (St. Mary's College of MD) • Much of the county is still held under patents of the Lords Baltimore.

SOMERSET (one of four counties so named) *Princess Anne* • 24,747 • 327 • Southeastern MD, on the Eastern Shore, bounded on the southeast by the Pocomoke River, on the south by the Pocomoke Sound (here forming the VA state line), and on the west by the Tangier Sound of Chesapeake Bay. The county lies in a partly marshy tidewater area, its shores indented by Wicomico, Manokin, and Big Annemessex river estuaries. In the bay are South Marsh and Smith islands (the latter partially occupied by Glenn Martin National Wildlife Refuge). Jane Island State Park is north of Crisfield. • Named for Mary Arundell Somerset, sister-in-law of Cecilius Calvert, 2nd Lord Baltimore; one of twelve MD counties named for the Calverts, their friends and relations • Original county; organized 1666 • Supreme Court justice Samuel Chase • White potatoes, vegetables, poultry, dairy products; timber; seafood fishing and canning; lumber mills; fishing equipment, apparel; education (U. of MD Eastern Shore).

TALBOT *Easton* • 33,812 • 269 • Eastern MD, on the Eastern Shore, bounded on the west by the Chesapeake Bay. The county is in a tidewater agricultural area. Wye Oak State Park is here, as are several Chesapeake Bay islands. • Probably named for Grace Calvert Talbot (1614–1672), sister of Cecilius Calvert, first proprietor of the colony of MD; one of twelve counties named for the Calverts, their friends and relations • In existence by 1662; organized from Kent • Naval officer Franklin Buchanan; statesman John Dickinson • Large seafood industry (fish, oysters, crabs); yachting, hunting, fishing; vegetables, grain, dairy products, poultry, cattle; canneries.

WASHINGTON *Hagerstown* • 131,923 • 458 • Western MD, bounded on the north by the PA state line, and on the south and southwest by the Potomac River; drained by Antietam, Conococheague, Beaver, and several other creeks. Cumberland (Hagerstown) Valley is bordered on the east by the Blue Ridge (South Mountain and Elk Ridge), and on the west by the Bear

Pond Mountains and Sideling Hill. South Mountain State Park is on the eastern border. The county also contains Fort Frederick, Greenbrier, and Washington Monument state parks. Part of Gathland State Park is in the southeast. • The first of thirty-one counties named for President George Washington • 1776 from Frederick • The county was settled by Swiss, French, English, and Scottish colonists. General Robert E. Lee's first invasion of the North was halted on the battlefield of Antietam (Sharpsburg) on September 17, 1862 (national battlefield). The battle represented the bloodiest single day's fighting in the entire Civil War with over 10,000 men on both sides either killed or wounded; yet the outcome was essentially a draw. • Lutheran theologian and educator S.S. Schmucker • Wheat, corn, peaches, apples, berries, poultry, dairying; ornamental fish, aquatic fish; limestone quarrying, sand pits; manufacture of aircraft, furniture, pipe organs, textiles; railroad shops; canneries, grain mills; hunting and fishing.

WICOMICO *Salisbury* • 84,644 • 377 • Southeastern MD, bounded on the north by the DE state line, on the east in part by the Pocomoke River, and on the west by the Nanticoke River. Wicomico Demonstration Forest is in the east. • Named for the Wicomico River • 1867 from Somerset and Worcester • Clergyman and prohibitionist James Cannon • The county is in one of the largest chicken-raising areas in the U.S. Also, strawberries, vegetables, sweet potatoes, dairy products; vegetable and fruit processing; manufacture of cabinets, wood products, clothing, printing computer forms, plastics, service-station pumps, hoists; commercial fishing, muskrat trapping; duck hunting; education (Salisbury State U.) • The first stone marker of the Mason and Dixon Line was laid seven miles northwest of Salisbury in 1763. Salisbury is the site of the annual National Indoor Tennis Tournament.

WORCESTER (one of two counties so named, the other in MA) *Snow Hill* • 46,543 (33% increase since 1990; the second fastest growing county in MD) • 473 • Eastern Shore of MD (Delmarva Peninsula), bounded on the south by the VA state line, on the north by the DE state line, on the southwest in part by the Pocomoke River (which traverses the county), and on the east in part by the Atlantic Ocean (the only MD county that borders the ocean). Off its Atlantic shore is a north-south chain of bays forming inland waterways between the mainland and barrier islands which comprise Assateague Island National Seashore, with its wild ponies. The great cypress swamps of Pocomoke River State Forest lie along the Pocomoke River, as does Pocomoke River State Park. • Probably named for Edward Somerset, Earl of Worcester (1601–67), son-in-law of George Calvert; one of twelve MD counties named for the Calverts, their friends and relations • 1742 from Somerset • U.S. vice president Spiro Agnew; naval commander Stephen Decatur • Potatoes, fruit, dairy products, poultry; sport and commercial fishing; manufacture of clothing; lumbering; vegetable canning; resort tourism (Ocean City's population swells to 150,000 in the summer; it has been a resort city since the 1870s.)

MASSACHUSETTS

By the Sword We Seek Peace, but Peace Only Under Liberty

Since 1997, the governments of six Massachusetts counties have been abolished. The state government has absorbed many of these functions. All the remaining eight except for Nantucket and Suffolk elect commissioners and treasurers. Massachusetts' counties are divided into districts, with each county having one or more district courts.

BARNSTABLE *Barnstable* • 222,230 • 396 • Southeastern MA, coextensive with Cape Cod. The county is a major summer resort destination; Cape Cod National Seashore occupies much of the northeast spit. Camp Edwards Military Reservation is in the west. • Named for the town of Barnstable, MA • 1685 from Old Plymouth Colony • In Providencetown Harbor on November 21, 1620, the Pilgrims made their first temporary landing in America and signed their compact for self-government. Here, Peregrine White, the first European child born in New England, entered this world on board the Mayflower. During the 18th century, Barnstable was a thriving port, trading in molasses and rum. Falmouth was bombarded by the British during the American Revolution, and again during the War of 1812. In the 19th century, the county was a major shipbuilding, shipping, and whaling center. Clipper ships were built in Shiverick Shipyard (East Dennis). Provincetown attracted a large number of Portuguese fishermen in the 1800s. Charles Hawthorne founded the Cape Cod School of Art in Provincetown in 1901. The playwriting career of Eugene O'Neill was launched by the Provincetown Players in 1916 with the production of his first play *Bound East for Cardiff*. • "America the Beautiful" author Katherine Lee Bates; Revolutionary War statesman James Otis, Jr.; jurist Lemuel Shaw. U.S. Chief Justice Charles Evans Hughes, U.S. army officer Lucius D. Clay, dramatist and novelist Susan Glaspell, psychoanalyst Erik H. Erikson, painter Robert

Motherwell, biochemist Albert Szent Györgyi, and poet and novelist John Peale Bishop died here. President John F. Kennedy had a summer home in Hyannis Port. • Cranberries, asparagus; fishing, oystering; tourism; manufacture of plastic and concrete products, machinery, navigation equipment • The Sandwich Glass Museum features exhibits of the rare pressed glassware that was made in Sandwich from 1825 to 1888, the special formula for which has been lost. Located at Woods Hole are the Marine Biological Laboratory, the National Marine Fisheries Service Aquarium, and Woods Hole Oceanographic Institute. Barnstable is the site of the Sturgis Library; built in 1645, it is one of the oldest library buildings in the U.S.

BERKSHIRE *Pittsfield* • 134,953 • 931 (the second largest county in MA) • Western MA, bounded on the north by the VT state line, on the west by the NY state line, and on the south by the CT state line. The county comprises most of the Berkshire Hills, a popular summer and winter resort area, and includes some manufacturing towns. Standing at a height of 3,491 feet, Mount Greylock is the highest point in MA. Rivers that flow through the county include the Housatonic, Hoosic, and Farmington. The Appalachian Trail traverses it north-south. The county has numerous state forests, state parks, and state reserves. • Named for Berkshire County in England • 1761 from Hampshire • Pioneer suffragist Susan B. Anthony; sociologist and black leader W.E.B. Du Bois; scholar and editor Bliss Perry; financier Cyrus W. Field. Industrialist and philanthropist Andrew Carnegie, physician and physiologist André Cournand, sculptor Daniel Chester French, and theologian Reinhold Niebuhr died here. Herman Melville completed *Moby Dick* in Pittsfield. • Manufacture of textiles, paper, plastic, and metal products, industrial machinery, leather products, ordnance supplies, search and navigation equipment, electronic capacitors, wire, photographic products; livestock, hay, fruit, nursery products, dairying; insurance; education (MA College of Liberal Arts. Prominent graduates of Williams College include President James A. Garfield and William Cullen Bryant, who is said to have written "Thanatopsis" while a student here.) • The Berkshire Music Festival is held each year at Tanglewood, summer home of the Boston Symphony Orchestra. A 19th century writers colony drew such authors here as Fanny Kemble, Catharine Sedwick, Henry Ward Beecher, and Edith Wharton. Nathaniel Hawthorne wrote *Tanglewood Tales* here.

BRISTOL (one of two counties so named, the other in RI) *Taunton, Fall River and New Bedford* • 534,678 • Southeastern MA, bounded on the south by Buzzards Bay in the Atlantic Ocean; intersected by the Taunton River. Freetown–Fall River State Forest is northeast of Fall River. The county has several state parks and state reserves scattered throughout. • Named for the town of Bristol, RI • 1685 from Old Plymouth County • Dartmouth was nearly destroyed by Indians during King Philip's War (1675–76). A taxpayer revolt in Taunton in 1684 was an early colonial incarnation of the Revolutionary

creed, "No taxation without representation." Norton was a center of witchcraft hysteria in the early 1700s. New Bedford, a privateering base during the Revolutionary War, was burned by the British in September, 1778. Later the foremost whaling port on the Atlantic coast, it was, by 1857, the world's richest city per capita. New Bedford's Seaman's Bethel (1832) was featured in Herman Melville's *Moby Dick*. Fall River, once a leading cotton-textile center, was the scene of numerous labor strikes; its mill workers made a large contribution to the American labor-union movement. • Suspected murderer Lizzie Borden; financier Hetty Green; painter Albert Pinkham Ryder; Britannia-ware inventor Isaac Babbitt. Fairhaven was the home port of Captain Joshua Slocum, who, in 1895–96, became the first man to circumnavigate the globe alone. • Manufacture of pottery, paper products, shellac and varnish, silverware, electronic components, textiles, clothing, rubber and latex products, textile machinery, luggage, jewelry (the leading industry of Attleboro), scientific instruments, fabricated metal products, chemicals, plastics, electrical equipment, bleach, optical goods, leather; hay, livestock, poultry, fruit, vegetables; resorts; education (Wheaton College; Stonehill College; U. of MA Dartmouth) • The Florence Pilkington Manchester Collection in the Fall River Public Library contains 3,000 mineral specimens. Battleship Cove at Fall River harbors famous vessels of the U.S. Navy, among them the USS *Massachusetts*.

DUKES *Edgartown* • 14,987 (30% increase since 1990; the second fastest growing county in MA) • 104 (one of the fifty smallest counties in the U.S.) • Southeastern MA. The county comprises the island of Martha's Vineyard and the Elizabeth Islands. Manuel F. Correllus State Forest is in the center of Martha's Vineyard. • Named for King James II (1633-1701), Duke of York and Albany, who was administrator of the colonies at the time of naming • Organized 1695 from Martha's Vineyard • English explorer Bartholomew Gosnold established the first settlement in New England on Cuttyhunk Island in 1602; it survived only a few weeks. Edgartown was one of the first whaling ports in New England. It was the site of the world's largest sperm-oil candle factory during the whaling era. • Preacher Jonathan Mayhew. Actress Katharine Cornell, photojournalist Alfred Eisenstaedt, and playwright Lillian Hellman died here. • Significant summer tourism; fishing • One of the best-known weekly newspapers in the U.S. is the *Vineyard Gazette*, founded and published in Edgartown. • Edgartown has preserved a number of architecturally notable houses built by successful whalers and merchants.

ESSEX *Salem, Lawrence and Newburyport* • 723,419 (the third most populated county in MA) • 498 • Northeastern MA, bounded on the east by the Atlantic Ocean and on the north by the NH state line; intersected by the Merrimack and Ipswich rivers. The county contains both industrial centers and resorts. It has several state parks and forests; Willowdale State Forest is in the center. Parker River National Wildlife Refuge is on Plum Island. • One of five counties named for Essex County in England • Original county; organized 1643 • Lynn was a world center of shoe manufacturing from the 1600s through the early 20th century. The first Congregational Church of America was organized in Salem in 1629; Rhode Island colony founder Roger Williams served as an early pastor. Saugus was the site of the first successful integrated ironworks in North America (1646-1668). The first examinations of suspected witches in the region took place in Danvers, originally called Salem Village, in 1692. A year later, Amesbury also became seized by witchcraft-related hysteria. The schooner *Hannah*, the first ship of the American navy, sailed from Beverly on its first cruise on September 5, 1775. During the War of 1812, the waters near Marblehead were the scene of an engagement between the American *Chesapeake* and the British *Shannon*. Several renowned clipper ships were built in Newburyport. The first meeting of Christian Scientists (led by Mary Baker Eddy) was held in Lynn in 1875. Lawrence was the scene of a famous strike of textile workers in 1912 pitting out-of-town militia against members of the Industrial Workers of the World. Four blocks of downtown Lynn were destroyed by fire on November 28, 1981. • Poets Anne Bradstreet, Dr. Oliver Wendell Holmes, and John Greenleaf Whittier; chemist Elias J. Corey; financier and philanthropist George Peabody; diplomat Caleb Cushing; civil engineer Grenville M. Dodge; abolitionist William Lloyd Garrison; U.S. Supreme Court justices William Moody and Oliver Wendell Holmes; Revolutionary War general Israel Putnam; politician Henry Cabot Lodge, Jr.; President William Howard Taft. Political activist James Otis, astronomer Maria Mitchell, and Congregational minister Manasseh Cutler died here. • Nursery products, fruits, livestock; diversified manufactures, including shoes, textiles, metal products, electrical and electronic components, flatware, shoes, chemicals, plastic and metal products, machinery, leather; tourism; education (Endicott College; Salem State College; Merrimack College; Bradford College) • The first successful U.S. turbojet engine was designed and built in Lynn in 1941. Abbot Hall in Marblehead contains the original of Archibald Willard's painting *The Spirit of '76*. Built before 1636, the Balch House in Beverly is thought to be the oldest house in the U.S. In 1810, America's first Sunday School was organized in Beverly. Gloucester's maritime heritage has inspired many books, including Kipling's *Captains Courageous*. Fisherman's Memorial, a bronze statue facing the city's harbor, honors the estimated 10,000 fishermen who have died at sea. *The House of the Seven Gables* by Nathaniel Hawthorne was set in Salem and immortalizes the house built here by Captain John Turner in 1668. Samuel F. Smith wrote the words for "America" in Andover in 1832.

FRANKLIN (one of twenty-five counties so named) *Greenfield* • 71,535 • 702 (the fourth largest county in MA) • Northwestern MA, bounded on the north by the VT and NH state lines and in part on the southeast by Quabbin Reservoir; bisected by the Connecticut River; drained by the Deerfield and Millers rivers. The county is predominantly rural. Small state

forests are sprinkled throughout. • One of twenty-three counties named for Benjamin Franklin • 1811 from Hampshire • The Connecticut Valley here was one of the first inland regions of the colonies to be settled. During King Philip's War, colonials were massacred at "Bloody Brook" (now South Deerfield) in 1675 and at Turners Falls in 1676. On February 29, 1704, the village of Deerfield was burned by French soldiers and Indians; forty-nine villagers were killed, and more than 100 taken captive to Canada. (An account of the incident, *The Redeemed Captive Returning to Zion*, written the Rev. John Williams, the village minister, is considered one of the best narratives of early colonial life in the region.) Northfield native and evangelist Dwight Lyman Moody founded the Student Volunteer Movement here in 1886. The now decommissioned Yankee-Rowe nuclear power plant twenty-one miles northeast of Pittsfield was the oldest nuclear power plant in the U.S. • Film director Cecil B. DeMille; architect Benjamin Asher; department store owner Marshall Field; journalist and reformer George Ripley; historian and educator Herbert B. Adams; painter George Fuller; educator Mary Lyon. Poet and critic Horace Gregory and theologian Helmut R. Niebuhr died here. • Dairying, poultry, onions, fruit (especially apples), tobacco, cattle, nursery products; food processing; manufacture of wood and paper products, plastics, hand tools, hardware, industrial machinery, silverware, electronic components. One of the first cutlery factories in the U.S. was established in Greenfield in the early 1800s. • Deerfield has a number of colonial structures and is home to several private schools, most notably Deerfield Academy, founded in 1797.

HAMPDEN *Springfield* • 456,228 • 618 • Southwestern MA, bounded on the south by the CT state line; bisected by the Connecticut River. The Connecticut Valley lowland is formed in the middle of the county. State parks and state forests are spread throughout. • Named for John Hampden (1594-1643), English parliamentarian who joined forces with Oliver Cromwell to oust King Charles I • 1812 from Hampshire • A cliff along the Chicopee River at Ludlow was the scene of a plunge to the death of a band of Indians led by Roaring Thunder, fleeing pursuers in King Philip's War (1675–76). Springfield was the site of Shays' Rebellion in 1786, an uprising of indebted and overtaxed farmers. The first friction matches were made in Chicopee in 1834. The massive doors to the east and west wings of the U.S. Capitol were cast at the Ames Company's bronze statuary factory, established in Chicopee in 1853. The city also produced three-quarters of the bicycles manufactured in the U.S. in the 1890s. James Naismith originated the game of basketball in Springfield in 1891. (The Naismith Memorial National Basketball Hall of Fame is here.) Volleyball was invented by William G. Morgan at the YMCA in Holyoke in 1895. (The Volleyball Hall of Fame is here.) • British spy Edward Bancroft; publisher and inventor Albert E. Beach; writer and children's book illustrator Theodor "Dr. Seuss" Geisel; writer Edward Bellamy; geologist Ferdinand V. Hayden; Helen Keller's teacher Anne Sullivan Macy.

Firearms engineer John C. Garand and architect Asher Benjamin died here. • Manufacture of paper and paper products (especially fine quality stationery), food, rubber and plastic products, metal products, industrial machinery and equipment, consumer goods, textiles; printing and publishing; vegetables, fruits, livestock, dairying, nursery products; education (Elms College; Springfield College; American International College; Western New England College) • From 1794 to 1968 the Springfield Armory was the center for the manufacture of small military arms in the U.S (including Springfield and Garand rifles). A large weapons museum is housed at the national historic site established here. Eastern States Exposition Park in West Springfield is the site of one of the largest industrial-agricultural fairs in the eastern U.S. Westfield was once the source of nearly all the whips made in the U.S.

HAMPSHIRE (one of two counties so named, the other in WV) *Northampton* • 152,251 • 529 • West-central MA, bounded in part on the east by Quabbin Reservoir; drained by the Westfield River and other small streams; bisected by the Connecticut River. The county is in a forested and agricultural area, bisected by the Connecticut Valley lowland. The Berkshire Mountains touch the western section of the county. • Named for the county in England, home of many early Puritan settlers in Massachusetts Bay Colony • 1662 from Middlesex • During the 1800s, Northampton was a major silk manufacturing center. Calvin Coolidge was mayor of the city in 1910 and 1911. • Poets Emily Dickinson, Robert Frost, William Cullen Bryant, and Eugene Field; author Helen Hunt Jackson; theologian Timothy Dwight; lexicographer Noah Webster; clergyman and university president Jonathan Dickinson; Union general Joseph Hooker. Historian and educator Herbert B. Adams, journalist Ray Stannard Baker, children's author Howard R. Garis, and botanist and geneticist Albert F. Blakeslee died here. The English regicides Edward Whalley and William Goffe lived secretly (and died) in Hadley. • Tobacco, hay, vegetables, fruit, poultry, livestock, dairying; manufacture of textiles, paper, plastic and metal products, machinery, photographic equipment, consumer goods, stainless steel cutlery, hosiery, brushes, silverware, optical and precision instruments, electronic equipment; education (Amherst College; University of MA; Smith College; Mount Holyoke College — one of the first institutions of higher learning for American women).

MIDDLESEX *Cambridge* • 1,465,396 (the third most populated county in MA and the nineteenth most populated county in the U.S.) • 823 (the third largest county in MA) • Northeastern MA, bounded on the north by the NH state line; drained by the Charles, Concord, Sudbury and Assabet rivers, and intersected by the Merrimack and Nashua rivers. • One of four counties named for the ancient county in England, from which a large number of early Puritan settlers came • Original county; organized 1643 • Stephen Day set up the first printing press in the colonies at Cambridge in 1639. General synods of the New England churches met in Cambridge

in 1637 and 1647 to settle disputed points of doctrine. The Battle of Lexington, regarded as the first military engagement of the American Revolution, was fought here on April 19, 1775. At Concord that same day was fired "the shot heard round the world." George Washington assumed leadership of the Continental forces at what is now Cambridge Common on July 3, 1775. During the Revolution, the MA Provisional Assembly and General Court met at Watertown (which is also known as the "cradle of the town meeting"). Lowell, called the "City of Spindles," was one of the nation's major textile centers in the 1800s. Charles Goodyear discovered the process of vulcanizing rubber in Woburn in 1839. That same year the first public teacher's training school in the U.S. was established in Lexington. The first training school in the U.S. for nurses (outside of hospital wards) was started in Waltham in 1885. • Poet Henry Wadsworth Longfellow; authors Louisa May Alcott, Nathaniel Hawthorne, and Margaret Sidney; actors Bette Davis and Edwin Booth; Christian Science founder Mary Baker Eddy; poet-diplomat James Russell Lowell; U.S. Supreme Court justice David Souter; attorney F. Lee Bailey; patriot Roger Sherman; orator Edward Everett; publisher Edwin Ginn; identically named father and son horticulturist and engineer Loammi Baldwin; scientist Benjamin "Count Rumford" Thompson; poet and novelist Jack Kerouac. Astronomer William C. Bond, electrical engineer and photographer Harold E. Edgerton, and educator John D. Pierce died here. Woburn's old burial ground contains the graves of the ancestors of four U.S. presidents (Cleveland, B. Harrison, Pierce and Garfield) • The county has a number of industrial towns, which produce a wide variety of products, including shoes, textiles, machinery, and other metal products, electronic and computer components, watches, food and wood products, rubber goods. It is a major research and education center (Boston College; MA Institute of Technology; Radcliffe College; Lesley College; U. of Lowell; Tufts U.; Brandeis U. and others. Harvard University, founded in 1636, is the oldest institution of higher education in the U.S. It has the world's largest university library system.) • Wayside Inn, which opened in 1686 in Sudbury, was the setting for Longfellow's *Tales of a Wayside Inn.* Lowell was America's first planned industrial city. The headquarters of the Smithsonian Astrophysical Observatory is in Cambridge. The Concord grape was perfected by Ephraim Bull around 1850 in Concord. Eight Fortune 1000 companies are headquartered in the county.

NANTUCKET *Nantucket* • 9,520 (Despite a 58% increase in population since 1990, the county remains the least populated in MA.)• 48 (the smallest county in MA and one of the fifty smallest counties in the U.S.) • Southeastern MA, south of Cape Cod and across Muskeget Channel from Martha's Vineyard to the west. It comprises the island of Nantucket and small adjacent islands. • Named for Nantucket Island, MA • Original county; organized 1695 • First visited by English navigator Bartholomew Gosnold in 1602 and purchased by Thomas Mayhew from the Plymouth Colony in 1641, Nantucket was administered as part of NY until cession to MA in 1692. It was settled by Quakers in 1659 and later functioned as a major whaling port (with more than 125 whaling ships ported here during peak years in the 1770s). It later became a resort and artists' colony. • Astronomer Maria Mitchell; reformer Lucretia Mott • Tourism, fishing • The first U.S. lightship station (established in 1856) is located here. Sankaty Head Lighthouse, established on the East Coast bluff in 1850, is a tourist attraction.

NORFOLK *Dedham* • 650,308 (the fifth most populated county in MA) • 400 • Eastern MA, south of Boston, bounded on the southwest by the RI state line; drained by the Charles and Neponset rivers. An exclave of the county is to the northeast, sandwiched between Middlesex and Suffolk counties; another is to the east, encompassed by Plymouth County and Massachusetts Bay. Norfolk is heavily suburbanized in the northeast, with some farmland in the southwest. F. Gilbert Hills and Franklin state forests are in the southwest. Borderland State Park is on the border of Bristol County. • Named for the county in England, home of many Puritan settlers • 1793 from Suffolk • The Suffolk Resolves, which protested the Intolerable Acts of Britain against the colonies, were initially drafted in Stoughton, discussed in Dedham, and adopted in Milton on September 9, 1774. The highly publicized and politically charged Sacco and Vanzetti murder trial took place in the Norfolk County courthouse in Dedham in 1921. • The county is the birthplace of four U.S. presidents: John Adams, John Quincy Adams, John F. Kennedy, and George H.W. Bush; famous residents also include first lady Abigail Adams; diplomat Charles Francis Adams; writers and historians Henry and Brook Adams; poet Amy Lowell; patriot John Hancock; general Sylvanus Thayer (birthplace); educator Horace Mann; short story writer Mary E. Wilkins Freeman; senators Robert F. and Edward M. Kennedy; colonial soldier Deborah Sampson; explorer and author Jonathan Carver; presidential contender Michael Dukakis; engineer and architect R. Buckminster Fuller; landscape architect Frederick Law Olmsted; television journalist Mike Wallace. Canton was the site of Paul Revere's brass and bell foundry. (During the War of 1812 Revere ran a powder mill here.) • Manufacture of furniture, apparel, textiles, metal, paper and wood products, soap, building materials, industrial resins, chemicals, machinery, rubber products, electrical, electronic and medical equipment, surgical dressings, floor coverings, sporting goods; printing and publishing; lobstering; education (Pine Manor College; Babson College, with one of the largest outdoor globes in the world; Wellesley College; Curry College); tourism • The corporate headquarters for four Fortune 1000 companies are located in the county. The Fairbanks house in Dedham, part of which was built in 1636, is believed to be the oldest frame house existing in the U.S. The first free public school in America to be supported by a general tax was opened in Dedham in 1644. Brookline is the largest place in the state still operating under town government, using the limited town meeting.

The first U.S. lifeboat station was constructed on Pleasant Beach in 1807. Foxboro is home to the New England Patriots (CMGI Stadium).

PLYMOUTH (one of two counties so named, the other in IA) *Plymouth* • 472,822 • 661 (the fifth largest county in MA) • Southeastern MA, bounded on the east by Massachusetts Bay and Cape Cod Bay. Miles Standish State Forest is in the southeast; Wompatuck and Ames-Nowell state parks are in the north. • Named for Plymouth, Devonshire, England (from which the Mayflower sailed for America) and/or for Plymouth Colony • 1685 from Old Plymouth Colony • Plymouth was the first settled town in MA (by the Pilgrims in 1620). Related historical sites include Plymouth Rock (where the Pilgrims, according to tradition, landed on December 26), Mayflower II, and Plymouth Plantation. Duxbury was founded by Myles Standish, William Brewster, John Alden and other Pilgrims in 1624. Plymouth Colony was absorbed into Massachusetts Bay Colony in 1691. The first cannons made in the U.S. were cast at the Abington foundry, where Paul Revere learned to cast bells. Abington, a major station on the Underground Railroad, was a center of abolitionist activity from 1846 to 1865. Brockton began manufacturing shoes in the mid-18th century, and was one of the nation's chief shoemakers until the 20th century. Abington, also a shoe center, is reputed to have produced half of all the boots worn by the Union army in the Civil War. • Geologist and paleontologist James Hall; poet and playwright Samuel Woodworth; abolitionist Samuel May; author Louisa May Alcott; poet and editor Richard Henry Stoddard; Continental army officer Benjamin Lincoln • Cranberries (the Cranberry World Visitor Center is here), vegetables, poultry; manufacture of nails, cordage, machine tools; printing; resort tourism in its shore communities; education (Bridgewater State College. Derby Academy, founded in 1784 as Derby School, is the oldest private coeducational school in the U.S.). • Brockton, one of the first cities in the U.S. to adopt electric street lighting, was also one of the first to pioneer in the operation of electric-powered streetcars. Its municipal system of inland sewage disposal, implemented in 1893, was widely copied. Hingham's Old Ship Church (1681) is considered the oldest house of worship in continuous use in the U.S.

SUFFOLK *Boston* • 689,807 (the fourth most populated county in MA) • 59 (one of the fifty smallest counties in the U.S.) • Eastern MA, on Massachusetts Bay and Boston Bay. • One of two counties (the other in NY) named for Suffolk County in England • Original county, organized 1643 • Founded by Puritans in 1630, Boston had become, by the mid-1700s, a leading commercial, fishing, and shipbuilding center of the American colonies. The city has been the only capital of both the colony and state of MA, and played a key role in winning independence for the United States from England, earning itself the nickname "Cradle of Liberty." One of the earliest events that led to the Revolutionary War was the Boston Massacre, a street clash with British soldiers that took place on March 5, 1770, and resulted in five deaths. The

Boston Tea Party occurred here on December 16, 1773. Charlestown, now a part of Boston, was the scene of the Battle of Bunker Hill (actually Breed's Hill) on June 17, 1775. In March, 1776, colonials forced the evacuation of British troops by occupying Dorchester Heights, overlooking Boston Harbor. More than 500,000 Irish immigrants fled to Boston to escape starvation during the potato famine of the 1840s. Alexander Graham Bell invented the telephone in Boston; it was patented on March 7, 1876. The Boston Marathon, the world's oldest annual foot race, was first held here in 1897. The Boston Pilgrims beat the Pittsburgh Pirates in the first World Series, which was played in Boston from October 1 to October 13, 1903. A police strike in Boston in 1919 was put down by Governor Calvin Coolidge, his firm stand against police unionizers ultimately earning him a spot on the Republican national ticket of 1920. In 1974 and 1975 Boston suffered the throes of school integration-related conflicts. • Renaissance man Benjamin Franklin; U.S. Supreme Court justice Oliver Wendell Holmes, Jr.; Congregational minister Cotton Mather; poet Edgar Allen Poe; patriot and folk hero Paul Revere; television journalist Barbara Walters. Dramatist Eugene O'Neill and Polar explorer Richard E. Byrd died here. Patriots Samuel Adams and John Hancock are buried at the Old Granary Burying Ground. A literary center in the 1800s, Boston was home to authors Ralph Waldo Emerson, Louisa May Alcott, Nathaniel Hawthorne, and Henry Wadsworth Longfellow • Diversified manufacturing, including textiles, shoes, paint, furniture, air conditioners, electrical controls, heating equipment; insurance, government offices; education (in 1635, the first public school in the Western Hemisphere was built in Boston, which eventually became one of the leading learning centers in the U.S. with over 20 colleges and universities, including Northeastern U., the New England Conservatory of Music, U. of MA Boston, Harvard Medical School, and Simmons College); tourism • Nine Fortune 1000 companies have their corporate headquarters in the county. The Freedom Trail, a one-and-a-half-mile marked path which winds from downtown to the North End, includes such historic locations as Faneuil Hall, the Boston Massacre site, Paul Revere's house, and the Old North Church. The forty-five-acre Boston Common, established in 1634, is the nation's oldest public park. The first chocolate mill in the U.S. was built in Dorchester, now part of Boston, in 1765. Dorchester also originated the town meeting form of local government. The U.S.S. *Constitution*, also known as "Old Ironsides" of the War of 1812, is docked at the Charlestown Navy Yard. Boston's *Publick Occurrences Both Forreign and Domestick*, published in 1690, was the first newspaper in the American colonies. With an estimated cost of $15 billion, Boston's "Big Dig" is the largest urban construction project in the U.S. and the final piece of the U.S. highway interstate system. Boston is home to the Red Sox (Fenway Park), Celtics and Bruins (Fleet Center).

WORCESTER (one of two counties so named, the other in MD) *Worcester and Fitchburg* • 750,963 (the second most populated county in MA) • 1,513 (the largest county in MA) • Central MA, bounded on the north by the NH state line, on the south by the CT and RI state lines, on the east in part by Quabbin Reservoir; drained by the Blackstone, Nashua, Assabet, Millers, and Ware rivers. Wachusett Mountain and part of Wachusett Reservoir are here. The county also includes numerous state parks, state forests and resort lakes. • Named for Worcester, England • 1731 from Middlesex and Suffolk • Worcester was an early textile center; the first corduroy cloth in the U.S. was made here. The city was the site of the National Woman's Rights Convention on October 23 and 24, 1850, the first national gathering of women in favor of female suffrage. Leominster incurred great damage from a fire on July 10, 1873, and from a hurricane on September 21, 1938. • Red Cross founder Clara Barton; missionary John Eliot; clockmaker Simon Willard; Revolutionary War leader Artemas War; orchardist Johnny Appleseed; first Christian Native American Jack Straw; inventor Eli Whitney; colonial minister and diarist Ebeneza Parkman; historian George Bancroft; horticulturist Luther Burbank; composer Earle Brown; inventor and manufacturer Irving W. Colburn; architect Wallace K. Harrison; poet and literary theorist Charles Olson; feminist Lucy Stone. Journalist and social reformer Jacob Riis died here. Rocketry pioneer and native son Robert H. Goddard fired the first liquid-fuel rocket in Auburn in 1926. • Dairying, vegetables, poultry; manufacture of carpets, looms, wire products, metal products, furniture, optical goods, glass, precision instruments; tools, cutlery, plastics, abrasives, leather, machinery, chemicals, apparel, strollers, woolen yarns and worsteds, paper and leather goods, toys (Winchendon is popularly known as Toy Town); education (Atlantic Union College; Fitchburg State College; Nichols College; Anna Maria College; Assumption College; Clark U.; College of the Holy Cross; Becker College; UMass Mem. Health Care; Worcester Polytechnic Institute) • Old Sturbridge is a full-scale replica of a 19th century New England Village. Worcester's John Woodman Armory Museum exhibits its notable collection of medieval armor. Lake Chaubunagungamaug's full name is Chargoggagoggmauchauggagoggchaubunagungamaugg, which, in Nipmuc, means, "You fish your side of the lake; I fish my side; nobody fish in the middle." The annual Worcester Music Festival is the oldest such festival in the U.S.; it began in 1858.

MICHIGAN

If You Seek a Pleasant Peninsula, Look About You

The county board of commissioners serves as the legislative body for each of Michigan's eighty-three counties, and is made up of representatives from each part of the county. Other county officers are the county clerk, county treasurer, prosecuting attorney, sheriff, and register of deeds. The county is Michigan's chief unit of local government.

ALCONA • *Harrisville* • 1,719 • 674 • Northeastern MI, bounded on the east by Lake Huron; drained by the Au Sable (a National Scenic River), Pine and Little Wolf Creek rivers. The county includes part of Huron National Forest in its southwestern third. A separate small unit is in the northeast. Hubbard Lake is in the north. Alacona Dam Pond is in the county, along with several other small lakes. Also here are Negwegon and Harrisville state parks (both on Lake Huron). • Alcona is a contrived or pseudo-Indian name coined by Henry R. Schoolcraft • Established as Negwegon 1840 from Alpena; name changed 1843 • Cattle, sheep, poultry; fisheries; nurseries.

ALGER *Munising* • 9,862 • 918 • Northern Upper Peninsula MI, bounded on the north by Lake Superior; drained by the Whitefish, Indian, and Sturgeon rivers (all three designated as National Scenic and Recreational rivers). The county contains Grand Island National Recreation Area. Wagner Falls and Laughing Whitefish Falls scenic sites and part of Hiawatha National Forest are also here. Pictured Rocks National Lakeshore was the first national lakeshore. • Named for General Russell A. Alger (1836–1907), governor of MI, U.S. secretary of war and U.S. senator from MI • 1885 from Schoolcraft • Dairying, cattle, sheep; some manufacturing, lumbering, paper mills, commercial fishing; resort tourism.

ALLEGAN *Allegan* • 105,665 • 828 • Southwestern MI, bounded on the west by Lake Michigan; drained by the Kalamazoo and two Black rivers. The county contains Kal-Haven Trail and Saugatuck Dunes state parks. Part of Yankee Springs State Recreation Area is on its eastern boundary. There are numerous lakes throughout the county. Bittersweet ski area is in the south. • Named for the Alleghany Indians • 1831 (prior to statehood) from Kalamazoo • Apples, peaches, cherries, grapes, dairying, onions, cucumbers, potatoes, soybeans, corn, grain, forage crops, hay, cattle, hogs, poultry; diversified manufacturing; fisheries; resort tourism.

ALPENA *Alpena* • 31,314 • 574 • Northeastern MI, bounded on the east by Lake Huron; drained by the Thunder Bay River and its affluents. The county includes part of Long Lake, part of Fletcher Pond reservoir, Thunder Bay Underwater Preserve, with its high density of shipwrecks, and Michigan Islands National Wildlife Refuge. Parts of Mackinaw State Forest are found throughout. • Alpena is a contrived or pseudo-Indian name coined by Henry R. Schoolcraft • Established as Anamickee County in 1840 from Presque Isle; named changed 1843

• During the last half of the 19th century, Alpena was a major sawmilling center. • Dairying, cattle, beans, grain, raspberries; manufacture of hardboard, paper, cement, concrete blocks, hydraulic cylinders; printing and publishing; limestone quarries, iron; timber; resort tourism (hunting and fishing) • Alpena holds a popular annual winter carnival.

ANTRIM *Bellaire* • 23,110 • 477 • Northwestern MI, bounded on the west by Grand Traverse Bay; drained by the Jordan River. The western part of the county is dominated by Torch Lake, which roughly parallels Grand Traverse Bay. The county contains Intermediate and Bellaire lakes. Elk Lake forms part of the southwestern boundary. It has numerous smaller lakes, mostly in the west. Shanty Creek ski area is in the south. Part of Mackinaw State Forest is here. • Named for the county in Ireland • Established as Meegisee 1840 from Mackinac; name changed 1843 • Cattle, sheep, poultry, dairy products, cherries, apples, forage crops, grain; food processing, manufacture of industrial machinery; resort tourism.

ARENAC *Standish* • 17,269 • 367 • Eastern MI, bounded on the southeast by Saginaw Bay; drained by the Rifle and Au Gres rivers. Portions of the Au Sable State Forest are scattered throughout the county. Isabella Indian Reservation is on the southern boundary. • Arenac is a contrived or pseudo-Indian word coined by Henry R. Schoolcraft • 1831 (prior to statehood) • Dairying, cattle, poultry, potatoes, corn, sugar beets, wheat, oats, soybeans, grain, beans, cucumbers; manufacture of metal products, industrial machinery; commercial fishing; resorts.

BARAGA *L'Anse* • 8,746 • 904 • Northwestern Upper Peninsula, MI, bounded in part on the north by Keweenaw and Huron bays; drained by the Sturgeon River (a National Wild and Scenic River) and Silver River. The county includes L'Anse Indian Reservation, and Craig Lake and Baraga state parks. Parts of Ottawa National Forest and Copper Country state forests are found here. Mount Arvon, at 1,979 feet, and Mount Curwood, at 1,978 feet, in the Huron Mountains, are the highest points in the state. • Named for the Reverend Irenaeus Frederich Baraga (1797–1868), Slovenian-born Roman Catholic missionary to the Ojibways who became a bishop in 1853 • 1875 from Houghton • The region was settled by Finnish immigrants. • Dairying, cattle, forage crops, lumbering; manufacture of industrial machinery, mineral wool; resorts.

BARRY *Hastings* • 56,755 • 556 • Southwestern MI; drained by the Thornapple River. The county includes many small lakes, including Gun Lake in the west (Yankee Springs State Recreation Area is here). • Named for William T. Barry (1784–1835), KY legislator, U.S. senator from KY and U.S. postmaster general • 1829 (prior to statehood) from Eaton • Cattle, hogs, sheep, poultry, dairy products, oats, wheat, soybeans, beans, corn; manufacture of electronic equipment, industrial machinery, rubber and plastic products.

BAY (one of two counties so named, the other in FL) *Bay City* • 110,157 • 444 • Eastern MI, bounded on the east and northeast by Saginaw Bay; drained by the Saginaw and Kawkawlin rivers. The county contains Bay City State Recreation Area. • Named Bay for its location at the head of Saginaw Bay • 1857 from Saginaw and Midland • Bay City, settled in the 1830s, was an early lumber boom town. By 1872, there were thirty-six saw mills operating on the banks of the Saginaw River. After the depletion of the local pine forests, the city turned to soft-coal mining, commercial fishing and beet-sugar manufacturing. • Animal psychologist Theodore Christian Schneirla; singer Madonna • Sugar beets, beans, soybeans, potatoes, melons, cucumbers, dairy products, cattle, hogs, poultry; diversified manufacturing, including power shovels, cement, auto and aircraft equipment, petrochemicals; shipbuilding; ocean shipping; resort and recreational tourism.

BENZIE *Beulah* • 15,998 • 321 (the smallest county in MI) • Northwestern MI, bounded on the west by Lake Michigan; drained by the Betsie and Platte rivers. The county includes the large Crystal and Platte lakes in the west, along with other smaller lakes. Part of Sleeping Bear Dunes National Lakeshore is in the northwest. Pere Marquette State Forest covers much of the county. • Possibly given the name Benzie as a variation on the name of the village of Benzonia. Another possibility is that the county name is a conflation of Benzonia and the Betsie River. • 1863 from Manistee and Grand Traverse • Journalist and historian Bruce Catton died here. • Apples, cherries, grapes, plums, forage crops; resort tourism • Benzonia was established about 1858 by a group of Protestants looking to found a Christian colony with an institution of higher learner similar to those in Oberlin, OH and Olivet, MI. Grand Traverse College was chartered in 1863, and operated until 1918.

BERRIEN *Saint Joseph* • 162,453 • 571 • Extreme southwestern MI, bounded on the south by the IN state line and on the west by Lake Michigan; drained by the St. Joseph, Paw Paw, and Galien rivers. Paw Paw Lake is in the north. Warren Dunes and Grand Mere state parks lie along Lake Michigan. Warren Woods Natural Area is also here. • One of two counties (the other in GA) named for Col. John M. Berrien (1781–1856), U.S. senator from GA and U.S. attorney general • 1829 (prior to statehood) from Indian lands • The explorer La Salle established Fort Miami at the site of St. Joseph in 1679 to use as a base (historic site). The House of David, a religious sect, established a colony in Benton Harbor in 1903. • Criminal Caryl Chessman; writer Ring Lardner; mail order innovator Montgomery Ward • Fruit growing is important to the

county's economy. Also, corn, soybeans, hogs, cattle, dairying, vineyards; manufacture of machinery, castings, rubber goods, hosiery, paper boxes, auto parts, microphones; commercial fishing; resort tourism; education (Andrews U.) • Niles is called the "four flags city" because it is the only city in the state to have been under the control of France, Britain, Spain, and the U.S.

BRANCH *Coldwater* • 45,787 • 507 • Southern MI, bounded on the south by the IN state line; drained by the St. Joseph and Coldwater rivers. The county contains many small (resort) lakes, especially on the Coldwater River, and includes Coldwater Lake State Park. • Named for John Branch (1782–1863), NC governor, U.S. secretary of the navy, and governor of FL territory • 1829 (prior to statehood) from St. Joseph • Forage crops, wheat, corn, soybeans, tomatoes, apples, cherries, grapes, cattle, hogs, sheep, poultry; dairy products; manufacturing; marl and clay deposits.

CALHOUN *Marshall* • 137,985 • 709 • Southern MI; drained by the Kalamazoo and St. Joseph rivers, and Battle Creek. The county includes Whitehouse Nature Center and part of Fort Custer Training Center. Huron Potawatomi Indian Reservation is in the southwest corner. • One of eleven counties named for John C. Calhoun (1782–1850), U.S. statesman and proponent of Southern causes • 1829 (prior to statehood) from Indian lands • Battle Creek, settled in 1831, was an early flour and woolen mill center, and the site of a Seventh-day Adventist colony, which, in 1866, founded the Western Health Reform Institute (renamed Battle Creek Sanitarium in 1876, and Battle Creek Health Center in 1959). The sanitarium, under the direction of John Harvey Kellogg, gained national attention for its experimentation with health foods, and the eventual manufacture of ready-to-eat cereals, now the city's main industry. The W.K. Kellogg Foundation to improve the well being of children, was established here in 1930. • Civil rights pioneer Sojourner Truth • Cattle, hogs, sheep, poultry, oats, wheat, soybeans, hay, onions, corn, apples, dairy products; manufacture of auto parts, trucks, farm equipment, paper products. • Each June, Battle Creek's Cereal City Festival sets the "world's longest breakfast table."

CASS (one of nine counties so named) *Cassopolis* • 51,104 • 492 • Southwestern MI, bounded on the south by the IN state line; drained by the St. Joseph and Dowagiac rivers. The county is urbanized in the southwest corner as part of the South Bend/ Niles MI metropolitan area. Swiss Valley ski area is in the east. • One of eight counties named for General Lewis Cass (1782–1866), OH legislator, governor of MI Territory, U.S. secretary of war, and U.S. secretary of state • 1829 (prior to statehood) from Indian lands • Vegetables, peppermint, apples, cherries, grapes, hogs, cattle, sheep, dairy products; manufacture of wood and plastic products, transportation equipment.

CHARLEVOIX *Charlevoix* • 26,090 • 417 • Northwestern MI, bounded on the northwest by Lake Michigan; drained by the Boyne and Jordan rivers. The county includes the Beaver Islands group. Fisherman's Island and Young state parks are located near Lake Charlevoix. Sections of Mackinaw State Forest are also here. • Named for Pierre F. X. de Charlevoix (1682–1761), French Jesuit explorer and writer who traveled from the Great Lakes down the Illinois and Mississippi rivers to New Orleans • Established as Reshkauko County 1840; named changed 1843. • Beaver Island was the site of a Mormon colony from 1847 to 1856 founded by James Jesse Strang, and a source of antagonism to neighboring non-Mormons. Strang was crowned king in 1850, his reign ending in assassination by rebellious followers. • Dairying, cattle, poultry, potatoes, cherries, apples, seed; iron foundries, plastic products; flour and lumber mills; fisheries; resorts, hunting and fishing.

CHEBOYGAN *Cheboygan* • 26,448 • 716 • Northern MI, bounded on the north by the Straits of Mackinac; drained by the Black and Sturgeon rivers. The county includes Mullet, Black, Douglas, and Burt lakes, and sections of Mackinaw State Forest. Cheboygan, Aloha, and Burt Lake state parks and Old Mill State Historic Park are also here. The University of Michigan Biological station is on Douglas Lake. • Named for the Cheboygan River • 1840 from Antrim • Settlement of the site of Mackinaw City began in 1673 with a French trading post, which in 1715 developed as Fort Michilimackinac. After being taken over by the British, the fort was destroyed in 1763 and its garrison massacred by a band of Chippewa-Sauk Indians under Chief Minavavana. A village was laid out in 1857, its name shortened from Michilimackinac to Mackinaw in 1894. • Cattle, dairy products, potatoes, forage crops; manufacturing; limestone quarrying, sawmilling, metal industries; tourism. • Cheboygan is the site of the Northern Michigan State Fair and the Cheboygan 250, a popular snowmobile race.

CHIPPEWA (one of three counties so named) *Sault Sainte Marie* • 38,543 • 1,561 (the second largest county in MI) • Eastern Upper Peninsula of MI, bounded on the east by the St. Mary's River, on the north by Whitefish Bay, and on the south in part by Lake Huron; drained by the Tahquamenon River (a National Wild and Recreational River). The county includes Sugar, Neebish and Drummond islands. Bay Mills Indian Reservation, Western Unit, is on Lake Superior; its Eastern Unit is on Sugar Island. Parts of Tahquamenon Falls and Brimley state parks are here. Hiawatha National Forest dominates the western half of the county. Also here are Harbor Island National Wildlife Refuge and a national fish hatchery. Sault Sainte Marie is a hub of the St. Lawrence Seaway. (Its first set of locks to bypass the St. Marys River went into operation in 1855.) St. Mary's Falls Canal (including four parallel locks, popularly called Soo Locks) is operated by the U.S. Army Corps of Engineers. It raises or lowers vessels the twenty-one feet between lakes Superior and Huron in six to fifteen minutes. • Named for the Chippewa Indians • 1826 (prior to statehood) from Mackinac • Sault Sainte Marie is the oldest

permanent settlement in MI; in 1668 the Jesuits established a mission here under Father Jacques Marquette • Indian agent Henry Rowe Schoolcraft lived in Sault Ste. Marie; his writings inspired Longfellow to compose "The Song of Hiawatha." • Potatoes, forage crops, oats, cattle, sheep, poultry, dairying; lumber and veneer; tourism; education (Lake Superior State U.) • The Great Lakes Shipwreck Museum is at Whitefish Point, near Whitefish Point Natural Wildlife Refuge and Bird Observatory. The John Johnson Home (1796) is one of the oldest houses in MI.

CLARE *Harrison* • 31,252 • 567 • Central MI; drained by the Muskegon, Tobacco, and Cedar rivers. There are many lakes in the county, especially in the southwest. Wilson State Park and Snowsnake Mountain ski area are here. Au Sable State Forest covers the upper third of the county. • Named for the county in Ireland • Established as Kaykakee 1840 from Isabella; name changed 1843 • Cattle, hogs, sheep, forage crops, dairy products, wheat, oats, soybeans, potatoes, corn, beans; some manufacturing.

CLINTON (one of nine counties so named) *Saint Johns* • 64,753 • 571 • South-central MI; drained by the Maple, Looking Glass, and Grand rivers, and by Stony Creek. Part of the city of Lansing extends into the county in the south. Sleepy Hollow State Park is in the east. • One of eight counties named for De Witt Clinton (1769–1828), governor of NY and supporter of the Erie Canal • 1831 (prior to statehood) from Shiawassee • Advertising executive Leo Burnett; American Idealist philosopher Ralph T. Flewelling • Soybeans, corn, wheat, oats, vegetables, sugar beets, peppermint, beans, apples, cattle, hogs, sheep, poultry, dairying; manufacturing.

CRAWFORD (one of eleven counties so named) *Grayling* • 14,273 • *558* • North-central MI; drained by the North, Middle, and South branches of the Au Sable River (one of the most highly touted trout streams in the Midwest), and by the Manistee River. The county includes part of Huron National Forest in the southeast quarter of the county, two state forests, part of Camp Grayling Army and Air National Guard Training Center, Hanson Hills and Skyline ski areas, and Hartwick Pines State Park. • One of three counties named for Col. William Crawford (1732–82), VA officer in the Revolutionary War, Indian fighter, and surveyor • 1840 as Shawono; name changed 1843 • Potatoes, oats; lumber mills; industrial machinery; tourism (boating, fishing, skiing) • Grayling holds a winter sports festival in February, the World Championship Au Sable Canoe Marathon in July, and the Au Sable River Longboat Regatta in August.

DELTA (one of three counties so named) *Escanaba* • 38,520 • 1,170 (the fifth largest county in MI) • Southern Upper Peninsula, MI, bounded on the south by Lake Michigan and arms (Big Bay De Noc, Little Bay De Noc) of Green Bay; drained by the Ford, Escanaba, and Whitefish (its east and west branches both National Scenic and Recreational) rivers. Part of Hiawatha National Forest (its headquarters in Escanaba) occupies the eastern two-thirds of the county. The county includes Gladstone ski area. Fayette State Historic Park is on Garden Peninsula. Lake Superior State Forest and sections of Escanaba River State Forest are also in the county. • Named for the Greek letter, which the shape of the county resembles • 1843 from Schoolcraft • Lumber operations in the county began in the 1830s. Escanaba developed rapidly after the Chicago and North Western Railway Company built the first iron-ore dock, the only one on Lake Michigan, and the city became an important component of the Chicago steel industry. • Lumbering; dairying, beans, barley, oats, potatoes, cattle, hogs, poultry; shipping of iron ore, coal, lumber, and other freight; manufacture of paper, veneers, foundry products, flooring, furniture, chemicals, concrete blocks, beverages; commercial fishing; resort tourism • Escanaba holds the Upper Peninsula State Fair each August.

DICKINSON (one of three counties so named) *Iron Mountain* • 27,472 • 766 • Southwestern Upper Peninsula, MI, bounded on the southwest by the WI state line; drained by the Menominee, Ford and Escanaba rivers. Copper Country State Forest occupies much of the county. Pine Mountain and Norway Mountain ski areas are here. Guided tours are given of the underground shafts of the Iron Mountain Iron Mine, which ceased operation in 1945. The county is only one of four in MI that lie within the Central time zone. • Named for Donald M. Dickinson (1846–1917), leader of MI's Democratic political machine and U.S. postmaster-general • 1891 from Marquette • Explorer and filmmaker Robert Flaherty • Dairying, cattle, apples, potatoes, hay; manufacture of heavy mining and marine equipment, tools, castings, chemicals, furniture; some lumbering; resorts (hunting, fishing, winter sports) • Iron Mountain is the site of the Pine Mountain Ski Slide, one of the highest artificial ski jumps in the world.

EATON *Charlotte* • 103,655 • 577 • South-central MI; drained by the Grand and Thornapple rivers, and by Battle Creek. The northeastern corner of the county is urbanized as part of the Lansing metropolitan area. • Named for John H. Eaton (1790–1856), U.S. senator from TN, U.S. secretary of war, governor of FL Territory, and Andrew Jackson's biographer • 1829 • Wheat, corn, beans, soybeans, vegetables, fruit, cattle, hogs, poultry, dairying, stockbreeding; manufacture of glass, lumber, road machinery, silos, aluminum appliances, iron products, furniture; food processing; mineral springs; education (Olivet College; Great Lakes Christian College).

EMMET *Petoskey* • 31,437 • 468 • Northern MI, bounded on the west by Little Traverse Bay and Lake Michigan, and on the north by the Straits of Mackinac; drained by the Maple River. The county includes Wycamp, Pickerel, Crooked, and Paradise lakes. Walloon Lake is in the southwest. The county also includes Wilderness and Petoskey state parks, and Mackinaw State Forest. • One of two counties (the other in IA) named for Robert W. Emmet (1778–1803), Irish rebel executed by the British • Established as Tonedagana in 1840 from Mackinac; name changed 1843 • Journalist and historian Bruce Catton.

Inventor Ephraim Shay died here. • Dairy products, potatoes, cattle, poultry; manufacturing; sawmills; fisheries; resort tourism (hiking, fishing, camping, winter sports) • Colonial Fort Michilimackinac includes a maritime museum, the old Mackinac Point Lighthouse and the reconstructed 18th century wooden sloop *Welcome*. The beaches and gravel pits of the county offer colorful and unusually fossilized stones. One found here, the Petoskey Stone, was adopted as the official state stone in 1965.

GENESEE (one of two counties so named, the other in NY) *Flint* • 436,141 (the fifth most populated county in MI) • 640 • Southeast-central MI; drained by the Flint and Shiawassee rivers • Named for Genesee County, New York, former home of many early settlers • 1835 (prior to statehood) from Oakland • Settled in the 1830s, Flint progressed as a fur-trading, lumbering and agricultural center. By 1900, the city was producing more than 100,000 horse-drawn vehicles a year. The body, spring, and wheel companies of the carriage industry became suppliers for the Buick Motor Company, organized by W. C. Durant in 1903. In 1908, Flint's major manufacturing resources were consolidated into the General Motors Company. By the 1950s, General Motors had become the largest single manufacturing complex in the U.S., and Flint second only to Detroit in the manufacture of automobiles, and auto parts and supplies in the nation. Closures and relocation in the industry left the city with a shrinking economy and population by the mid-1990s. • Dairying, cattle, poultry, apples, strawberries, corn, wheat, oats, soybeans, cucumbers, forage crops, beans; diversified manufacturing; summer resorts; education (U. of MI–Flint; Kettering U.; Davenport U.; Baker College of Flint) • The Mott Foundation was founded in Flint in 1926.

GLADWIN *Gladwin* • 26,023 • 507 • Central MI; drained by the Tittabawassee and Tobacco rivers. The county has several small lakes and reservoirs (called "ponds" in MI); the largest is Wixom Lake reservoir on the southern border. Au Sable State Forest covers the eastern third of the county. • Named for General Henry Gladwin (1729–91), British soldier during the French and Indian War and defender of Detroit against Chief Pontiac • 1831 (prior to statehood) from unorganized territory • Cattle, hogs, sheep, poultry, grain, seed, sugar beets, corn, wheat, oats; dairy products; manufacture of industrial machinery.

GOGEBIC *Bessemer* • 17,370 • 1,102 • Western Upper Peninsula, MI, bounded on the northwest by Lake Superior and on the southwest by the WI state line; drained by the Montreal, Presque Isle, and Ontonagon rivers. Much of the county is in Ottawa National Forest (its headquarters in Ironwood). Lake Gogebic is on the northern boundary. The Gogebic Range crosses the northern part of the county and includes several ski areas. The county contains many small lakes, national scenic and recreational rivers, and waterfalls. Lake Gogebic State Park and Lac Vieux Desert Indian Reservation are also here. It is one of only four counties in MI that lie within the

Central time zone. • Named for Lake Gogebic and the Gogebic Iron district • 1887 from Ontonagon • Ironwood, situated near the Penokee-Gogebic Range of iron deposits, became a major shipping point for iron ore after 1884. The county's prosperous deep-shaft-iron-mining industry ceased operations in 1967 and many miners went to work in the Ontonagon County copper mines. • Lumbering, cattle, dairying; manufacture of clothing, sports equipment; food processing; retail center; resort tourism • Ironwood's most noted landmark is a fifty-two-foot statute of Hiawatha.

GRAND TRAVERSE *Traverse City* • 77,654 • 465 • Northwestern MI, bounded on the north in part by the east and west arms of Grand Traverse Bay; drained by the Boardman and Betsie rivers. Traverse City and Interlochen state parks are here. Old Mission Peninsula is in the extreme north. Its tip (marked by a lighthouse) is exactly midway between the equator and the North Pole. This forested county contains Green, Duck, and Skegemog lakes. • Named for Grand Traverse Bay • Organized as Omeena, 1840; name changed 1851; boundaries corrected 1853 • Collegiate football player Willie Heston and golfer Walter Hagen died here. • Traverse City is one of the nation's chief marketing centers for cherries (and the site of the National Cherry Festival). Also, apples, plums, grapes, potatoes, cattle, hogs, poultry; manufacturing; fisheries; resorts. • Traverse City is home to the Interlochen Center for the Arts (at Interlochen State Park); its Arts Academy hosts a nationally recognized camp each summer.

GRATIOT *Ithaca* • 42,285 • 570 • Central MI; drained by the Maple, Pine, and Bad rivers. • Named for either Fort Gratiot or for its builder, General Charles Gratiot (1786–1855), chief engineer of the U.S. Army. • 1831 from Saginaw • Poultry, cattle, hogs, sugar beets, wheat, soybeans, grain, beans, corn, dairy products; light manufacturing, food processing; petroleum refineries; mineral springs; education (Alma College).

HILLSDALE *Hillsdale* • 46,527 • 599 • Southern MI, bounded on the south by the OH state line and on the southwest by the IN state line; drained by headstreams of the Kalamazoo River and by the St. Joseph River. The county has many small lakes. • The name of the county is descriptive of its topography of hills and dales • 1829 (prior to statehood) from Lenawee • Forage crops, corn, wheat, oats, apples, soybeans, cattle, hogs, sheep, dairy products; manufacture of consumer goods, plastic products, bakery products, playground equipment, transportation equipment; machining; education (Hillsdale College).

HOUGHTON *Houghton* • 36,016 • 1,012 • Northwestern Upper Peninsula MI, bounded in part on the southeast by Keweenaw Bay in Lake Superior and on the northwest by Lake Superior; drained by the Ontonagon and Sturgeon rivers (the former a National Wild, Scenic, and Recreational River, the latter a National Wild and Scenic River); divided by Portage Lake and traversed by Copper Range. The county includes the southern part of the Keweenaw Peninsula, extending into Lake Superior. F. J. McLain and Twin Lakes state parks are here. Mount Ripley ski area is also in the county. The southern third lies in Ottawa National Forest. • Named for Douglass Houghton (1809–45), MI's first state geologist who conducted studies of the upper and lower peninsulas of MI • 1845 from Marquette, Schoolcraft, and Ontonagon • The county was settled by Finn immigrants • Notre Dame football player George Gipp • Manufacture of hardwood flooring, explosives, handles; cattle, poultry, forage crops, oats, dairy products (especially cheese); lumbering; copper mining; commercial fishing; resort tourism; education (MI Technological U.; Finlandia U.) • Houghton is the mainland headquarters for Isle Royale National Park in Lake Superior.

HURON (one of two counties so named, the other in OH) *Bad Axe* • 36,079 • 837 • Eastern MI, at the tip of the "thumb" of southern Lake Huron, bounded on the east and north by Lake Huron, on the west by Saginaw Bay (and containing numerous islands off Saginaw Bay shores); drained by headwaters of the Cass River and by the Pigeon and Willow rivers. Albert E. Sleeper and Port Crescent state parks are in the north. • Named for either the Huron Indians or for Lake Huron • 1840 from Sanilac and Tuscola • Supreme Court justice Frank Murphy • Poultry, cattle, hogs, dairying, beans, sugar beets, corn, wheat; manufacture of plastic and metal products, industrial machinery; some resorts.

INGHAM *Mason* • 279,320 • 559 • South-central MI; drained by the Grand and Red Cedar rivers, and Sycamore Creek. The county is urban and suburban in its northwest corner. • Named for Samuel D. Ingham (1779–1860), U.S. representative from PA and U.S. secretary of the treasury • 1829 (prior to statehood) from unorganized territory • Lansing has been the capital of MI since 1847. The city became an industrial center with the establishment of the Reo Motor Car Company by Ransom Eli Olds (and is now an automotive production center) • Journalist Ray Stannard Baker; biologist A.D. Hershey; basketball player Magic Johnson. Canadian poet and anthologist A. J. M. Smith died here. • Apples, wheat, soybeans, corn, hay, beans, onion, cucumbers, carrots, hogs, cattle, poultry, dairy products; diversified manufacturing; oil and gas extraction; education (Founded as Michigan Agricultural College in 1855, Michigan State University is the world's oldest agricultural college and the nation's oldest land-grant college.)

IONIA *Ionia* • 61,518 • 573 • South-central MI; drained by the Flat, Looking Glass and Maple rivers; intersected by the Grand River. Ionia Recreation Area is centrally located. • Named for the ancient province in Greece • 1831 (prior to statehood) from unorganized territory • Poultry, cattle, hogs, forage crops, wheat, oats, barley, corn, green beans, peas, strawberries, apples, peaches; diversified manufacturing; lake resort tourism.

IOSCO *Tawas City* • 27,339 • 549 • Northeastern MI,

bounded on the east by Lake Huron; drained by the Au Sable and Au Gres rivers. Huron National Forest and Au Sable State Forest are in the northern half of the county. Tawas Point State Park is in the east. The county also includes Tawas and Van Ettan lakes. • Named for a fictional American Indian hero invented by Henry R. Schoolcraft • Established as Kanotin County 1840 from unorganized territory; name changed 1843. • Cattle, hogs, corn, wheat, oats, barley, dairying; manufacture of metal forgings, industrial machinery, gypsum products; resorts.

IRON (one of four counties so named) *Crystal Falls* • 13,138 • 1,167 • Southwestern Upper Peninsula, MI, bounded on the south by the WI state line; drained by the Brule (forming part of the southern boundary), Michigamme, Paint (a National Recreational River), and Iron rivers. The county has many small lakes and streams. Part of Ottawa National Forest is here, as is Bewabic State Park, and Brule Mountain ski area. The county also includes part of the Menominee Iron Range. The University of Michigan's forestry school's summer camp is here. Iron is one of only four counties in MI that lie within the Central time zone. • Named for the iron mines in the area • 1885 from Marquette and Menominee • Lumbering; cattle, sheep, potatoes, oats, forage crops; dairying; manufacturing; resort tourism • Although the iron ore industry has been inactive here since 1979, some mines are open for tours.

ISABELLA *Mount Pleasant* • 63,351 • 574 • Central MI; drained by the Chippewa and Pine rivers. Isabella Indian Reservation dominates the county. • Named for Isabella (1451–1504), queen of Spain who financed Christopher Columbus's expeditions • 1831 (prior to statehood) from unorganized territory • After the discovery of crude oil here in 1928, the county became a center for oil production in the state. • Cattle, hogs, poultry, sheep, dairying, sugar beets, beans, wheat, oats, soybeans, hay, asparagus; oil production and related industries and products; manufacture of automobile parts, stock and dog feeds, food-service equipment; education (Central MI U.).

JACKSON (one of twenty-four counties so named) *Jackson* • 158,422 • 707 • Southern MI; drained by the Grand and Raisin rivers, and headstreams of the Kalamazoo River. The county contains many small lakes in its eastern half. • One of twenty-two counties named directly or indirectly for President Andrew Jackson • 1829 (prior to statehood) from Washtenaw • A state political convention held in Jackson on July 6, 1854, was one of the first to use the name "Republican Party" for its coalition of antislavery advocates. Jackson was an early leader in the production of automobiles. • U.S. Supreme Court justice Potter Stewart. Geologist Grove K. Gilbert died here. • Forage crops, corn, hay, apples, soybeans, wheat, oats, cattle, hogs, sheep, dairy products; manufacture of auto parts, tires, steel, air-conditioning equipment, aircraft parts, surgical appliances, plastic products, forgings and stampings, machine tools; education (Spring Arbor College) • The Michigan Space and Science Center in Jackson is housed in a geodesic dome.

The illuminated Cascade Falls, a series of man-made waterfalls, attracts summer visitors to Jackson.

KALAMAZOO *Kalamazoo* • 238,603 • 562 • Southwestern MI; drained by the Kalamazoo River and Portage Creek. The county has numerous small lakes in the southwest. Gull Lake is in the northeast. • Named for the Kalamazoo River • 1829 (prior to statehood) from Saint Joseph • Incorporated as a village in 1843, Kalamazoo enjoyed its claim to being the most populous village in the U.S. Celery was introduced into the county in 1856 by Dutch farmers, becoming the county's chief crop and earning Kalamazoo the nickname "Celery Capital of the U.S." • Novelist and short story writer Edna Ferber; surgeon and pioneer in cardiac transplantation Norman E. Shumway. Operatic tenor Richard Tucker died here. • Cattle, hogs, poultry, dairy products, celery, apples, grapes, cherries, strawberries, corn, wheat, oats, soybeans; manufacture of paper and paper products, chemicals, automobile parts, aircraft and missile components, machine tools, metal products, air-conditioning and transportation equipment, clothing, musical instruments, food stuffs, pharmaceuticals; wholesaling; education (Western MI U.; Kalamazoo College; Davenport U.).

KALKASKA *Kalkaska* • 16,571 • 561 • Northwest-central MI; drained by the Boardman River and the North Branch of the Manistee. Pere Marquette State Forest covers over half of the county. Part of Camp Grayling Army and Air National Guard Training Center is here, as is part of Lake Skegemog (southern extension of Elk Lake). • The county's name comes from an Indian word of uncertain origin and meaning • Established as Wabassee 1840 from Crawford; name changed in 1843 to Kalcasca and to its present spelling in 1871. • Potatoes, corn, wheat, cattle, hogs; logging, wood products; resort tourism.

KENT (one of five counties so named) *Grand Rapids* • 574,335 (the fourth most populated county in MI) • 856 • Southwestern MI; intersected by the Grand River; drained by the Flat and Thornapple rivers. The county has numerous lakes in the northeast, as well as the state fish hatchery. Pando and Cannonsburg ski areas are in the center. Grand Rapids and its suburbs make the southwest quarter highly urbanized. • Named for James Kent (1763–1847), chief justice of the NY Supreme Court • 1831 (prior to statehood) from unorganized territory • Located on the southern edge of MI's great pine forest, Grand Rapids had become a major lumber center by the 1860s. Many Dutch and Polish crafts workers settled here during the mid-1800s and helped to develop its furniture-manufacturing industry. Although much of the industry has been relocated to the South since the early 1900s, Grand Rapids' present output still justifies its nickname, "Furniture City." Melville R. Bissell invented the first practical carpet sweeper in Grand Rapids in 1876. • Astronaut Roger B. Chaffee; actress and singer Judy Garland; historian and philosopher John H. Randall; composer and organist Leo Sowerby; presidential press secretary James Brady. The Gerald R. Ford Museum commemorates the life and political career of Grand Rapid's presidential native son. • Apples, peaches, wheat, oats, barley, soybeans, cucumbers, onions, corn, potatoes, beans cattle, hogs, sheep, dairying; manufacture of refrigerators, automobile bodies, metals, aircraft equipment, electronics, cleaning and home care goods; publishing and printing; gypsum quarries, gravel pits; education (Aquinas College; Grand Bible College; Cornerstone U.) • Downtown Grand Rapids features a forty-three foot high steel sculpture by artist Alexander Calder, and hosts the annual Calder Arts Festival every spring.

KEWEENAW *Eagle River* • 2,301 (The county, though the least populated in the state, grew by 35% in 1990) • 541 • Northwestern Upper Peninsula, MI. It lies on the northern end of the Keweenaw Peninsula in Lake Superior. Manitou Island is off the eastern end of the peninsula. Isle Royal National Park is to the northwest. Located in a resort area, two-thirds of the county's residences are seasonal. Keweenaw is traversed by the Copper Range. Fort Wilkins State Historic Park is east of Copper Harbor. The county lies in one of the heaviest snowfall areas in the U.S. • Named for the Keweenaw Peninsula • 1861 from Houghton • Copper mining; tourism.

LAKE (one of twelve counties so named) *Baldwin* • 11,333 (32% increase since 1990; the third fastest growing county in MI) • 568 • West-central MI; drained by the Little Manistee River and the Little Branch of the Pere Marquette River. The Pine River, which cuts through the northeast, is designated as a National Scenic River. Together, Manistee National Forest and Pere Marquette State Forest cover over seventy-five percent of the county. • The county was given its name because of the numerous lakes here. • Established as Aishcum 1840; named changed 1843 • Cattle, dairy products, forage crops; lumbering; resort tourism.

LAPEER *Lapeer* • 87,904 • 654 • Eastern MI; drained by the Flint (Holloway Reservoir on the western boundary) and Belle rivers, and by Mill Creek. Metamora-Hadley Recreation Area is in the southwest and Seven Ponds Nature Center is in the southeast. The county has many lakes, especially in the west. • Lapeer is the French name for the Flint River • 1822 (prior to statehood) from Oakland and St. Clair • Cattle, hogs, sheep, poultry, dairying, apples, corn, wheat, oats, soybeans, barley, potatoes, carrots, sugar beets, beans, celery, onions; manufacture of motor vehicle parts, fabricated metal products, machining, plumbing equipment, plastic products.

LEELANAU *Leland* • 21,119 • 349 • Northwestern MI, a peninsula (Leelanau Peninsula) bounded on the west by Lake Michigan and on the east by Grand Traverse Bay and its western arm. Grand Traverse Lighthouse and Leelanau State Park are at the tip of the peninsula. The county also includes Sleeping Bear Dunes National Seashore (its headquarters in Empire) on the shore of Lake Michigan, North and South Manitou Islands, and Glen Lake and Lake Leelanau. The Homestead and Sugar Loaf ski areas are also in the county. • Named for a fictional American Indian maiden attributed to Henry R. Schoolcraft • 1840 • Cherries, apples, plums, strawberries, grapes, corn, wheat, cattle, hogs, poultry; fisheries; resorts.

LENAWEE *Adrian* • 98,890 • 751 • Southeastern MI, bounded on the south by the OH state line; drained by the River Raisin and its branches. The county includes Walter J. Hayes State Park, Lake Hudson Recreation Area, and Devils Lake. • Lenawee is an Indian word meaning "people" • 1822 (prior to statehood) from Indian lands • Theatrical designer Norman Bel Geddes; anthropologist Elman R. Service • Soybeans, wheat, oats, sugar beets, corn, beans, cattle, hogs, sheep, dairy products; manufacture of auto parts, aluminum, paper and wood products, aircraft parts, silicones and other chemicals, garden and farm gates; sand and gravel; chrysanthemums; lake resorts; education (Adrian College; Siena Heights U.).

LIVINGSTON (one of six counties so named) *Howell* • 156,951 (36% increase since 1990; the fastest growing county in MI) • 568 • Southeastern MI; drained by the Red Cedar and Huron rivers. The county has numerous small lakes in the southeast and extreme northeast and is a resort destination. Island Lake and Brighton recreation areas are here, as is Mount Brighton ski area. • One of three counties definitively named for Edward Livingston (1764–1836), U.S. representative from NY, U.S. representative and senator from LA; and U.S. secretary of state • 1833 (prior to statehood) from Shiawassee • Cattle, hogs, sheep, poultry, corn, wheat, oats, soybeans, apples, dairy products; manufacturing.

LUCE *Newberry* • 7,024 • 903 • Northeastern Upper Peninsula, MI, bounded on the north by Lake Superior; drained by the Tahquamenon and Two Hearted rivers. The county includes part of Manistique Lake and North Manistique Lake, and is largely covered by a portion of Lake Superior Forest. Part of Tahquamenon Falls State Park (the Upper Falls) and Muskallonge Lake State Park are also in the county. • Named for Cyrus G. Luce (1824–1905), governor of MI and early conservationist • 1887 from Chippewa • Forage crops, potatoes, hay, oats, livestock; lumbering; manufacturing.

MACKINAC *Saint Ignace* • 11,943 • 1,022 • Southeastern Upper Peninsula, MI, bounded on the south by lakes Michigan and Huron, and by their connection, the Straits of Mackinac; drained by the Carp (a National Wild, Scenic, and Recreational River) and Pine rivers. The county lies in the historic Mackinac region and includes Mackinac and Bois Blanc islands. Among its lakes are Brevoort, Milakokia, Millecoquins, South Manistique, and Manistique (part). The county also includes part of Hiawatha National Forest, and parts of Lake Superior State Forest, Straits and Mackinac Island state parks. • Mackinac is an Indian word meaning "turtle" • Original county; established as Michilimackinac 1818 (prior to statehood); name changed 1843 • One of MI's oldest cities, Saint Ignace, was founded in 1671 when Jacques Marquette established a mission here. Marquette is buried here. Mackinac Island has a rich history. It was an ancient Indian burial ground ("Michilimackinac"). The French explored it in the 1600s, and the British established a fort here in 1780. It was headquarters for John Jacob Astor's American Fur Company, and was occupied by the British during the War of 1812.

• Supreme Court justice William R. Day died in the county • Forage crops, oats, cattle, truck and fruit farming, dairying; resort tourism; fisheries • Mackinac Island maintains old world charm through the banning of cars, and the use of bicycles and horse and buggy for transport. U.S. army surgeon William Beaumont studied human digestion at Old Fort Mackinac through the open stomach of Alexis St. Martin, a wounded French-Canadian trapper.

MACOMB *Mount Clemens* • 788,149 (the third most populated county in MI) • 480 • Southeastern MI, just north of Detroit, bounded on the southeast by Lake St. Clair and Anchor Bay; drained by the Clinton River and its affluents. The county is highly urbanized in the south, and mostly residential and commercial in the west. It contains Selfridge Air National Guard Base. W.C. Wetzel State Park is also here. • Named for Alexander Macomb (1782–1841), officer in the War of 1812 and commanding general of the U.S. Army • Original county; established 1818 (prior to statehood) • Corn, wheat, oats, soybeans, apples, peaches, dairying, truck farming, poultry; manufacture of metal and paper products, transportation equipment, steel fabrications, mechanical hoists, vinyl-coated fabrics • Mount Clemens is noted for its pottery, and is one of the largest producers of roses under glass in the U.S. Young Thomas Edison first learned telegraphy at Grand Trunk Station in Mount Clemens. The General Motors Technical Center and the Detroit Arsenal (U.S. Army Tank Automotive Command) are in Warren.

MANISTEE *Manistee* • 24,527 • 544 • Northwestern MI, bounded on the west by Lake Michigan; drained by the Manistee River (designated a National Scenic River), the Little Manistee River, and Bear Creek. The county includes part of Manistee National Forest in the south and southeast. Little River Indian Reservation is located near Orchard Beach State Park. Manistee and Bear lakes are also in the county, as are Tippy Dam Pond and part of Hodenpyl Dam Pond. • Named for the Manistee River • 1840 • Manistee was one of the state's liveliest lumber camps in the mid-19th century, but was largely destroyed by fire in 1871. It later developed as a health resort, and was a leading producer of salt. • Fruit, hogs, poultry, potatoes, forage crops; manufacture of paper products, chemicals, mineral products; salt mines; fisheries; resorts (hunting and fishing).

MARQUETTE *Marquette* • 64,634 • 1,821 (the largest county in MI) • Northwestern Upper Peninsula, bounded on the north in part by Lake Superior; drained by the Yellow Dog (here a National Wild River) and Michigamme rivers, and by several branches of the Escanaba River. The county includes the Marquette Iron Range. (The Michigan Iron Industry Museum is in Negaunee.) Van Riper State Park and several ski areas are here. Sections of Escanaba River State Forest are scattered throughout. • One of two counties (the other in WI) named for Jacques Marquette (1637–75), French Jesuit missionary and explorer with Louis Joliet • 1843 from Schoolcraft • Marquette was largely destroyed by fire in 1868, but quickly rebuilt. • Nuclear chemist Glenn T. Seaborg; archaeologist Alfred V. Kidder • Cattle, forage crops, potatoes; iron ore mining, marble quarrying; lumbering; manufacture of mining machinery, explosives, iron-ore pellets, cement blocks, flooring, garments; recreational tourism (fishing, hunting and camping); education (Northern MI U.) • Ishpeming was one of the first ski centers in the U.S. and is the site of the U.S. Ski Hall of Fame and Ski Museum. At Mud Lake, Lewis H. Morgan collected data for his book, *The American Beaver and Its Works* (1868). Marquette is a Roman Catholic diocesan seat (St. Peter's Cathedral 1933).

MASON (one of six counties so named) *Ludington* • 28,274 • 495 • Western MI, bounded on the west by Lake Michigan; drained by the Pere Marquette (a National Scenic River), Big Sable and Little Manistee rivers. Parts of Manistee National Forest are located in the east and north. Several resorts are here. Ludington State Park, with large sand dunes, is in the west on Big Sable Point. • Named for Stevens T. Mason (1811–43), acting governor of MI Territory and first governor of the state of MI • Organized as Notipekago in 1840 from Ionia; name changed 1843 • French Jesuit missionary/explorer Jacques Marquette died here in 1675. (A large lighted cross on the shore of Lake Michigan marks the spot.) • Cattle, apples, cherries, peaches, green beans, dairy products; manufacture of wood and metal products, watchcases, game boards; automotive and railway equipment, chemicals; resort tourism.

MECOSTA *Big Rapids* • 40,553 • 556 • Central MI; drained by the Muskegon, Little Muskegon, Chippewa, and Pine rivers. A small portion of Manistee National Forest is on the western border, as is White Pine Trail State Park. • Named for the Potawatomi chief • 1840 from Newaygo and Osceola • Cattle, hogs, sheep, potatoes, apples, corn, dairy products; manufacturing; resorts; fish hatchery; education (Ferris State U.).

MENOMINEE (one of two counties so named, the other in WI) *Menominee* • 25,326 • 1,044 • Southern Upper Peninsula, MI, bounded on the southeast by Green Bay and on the southwest by the Menominee River (forming the WI state line); drained by the Big Cedar, and Little Cedar rivers. Hannahville Indian Community is here, as is J.W. Wells State Park. A small part of Escanaba River State Forest is also here. The county is one of only four in MI that lie within the Central time zone. • Named for the Menominee River • Established as Bleecker 1861 from Marquette; name changed 1863 • Fur trading here led to lumbering in the 1830s, ending a century later. • Cattle, poultry, forage crops, corn, oats, dairy products (cheese important); manufacture of paper products, furniture, electrical equipment, helicopters; resort tourism (hunting and fishing); lumbering.

MIDLAND (one of two counties so named, the other in TX) *Midland* • 82,874 • 521 • Central MI; drained by the Tittabawassee (Sanford Lake reservoir in the north), Pine and Chippewa rivers. Parts of Au Sable State Forest are in the county. • Named for its location in the geographic center of the state • 1831 (prior to statehood) from Saginaw • Cattle, hogs, corn, wheat, oats, soybeans, beans, sugar beets; oil wells, salt deposits, coal mines; chemical and metallurgical manufacturing; education (Saginaw Valley College; Northwood U.) • Midland's chemical industry, established in the 1880s on the basis of local brine deposits, expanded with the growth of Dow Chemical Company, which now maintains the nation's largest single chemical complex, producing over 500 different products. Dow Corning is the leading manufacturer of silicones in the U.S.

MISSAUKEE *Lake City* • 14,478 • 567 • North-central MI; drained by the Muskegon River and its affluents. Numerous lakes are clustered west of Lake City, the largest being Lake Missaukee. Pere Marquette State Forest and Missaukee Mountain ski area are here. • Named for the Ottawa chief • 1840 from unorganized territory • Cattle, hogs, corn, oats, forage crops, dairy products; manufacturing; resorts.

MONROE *Monroe* • 145,945 • 551 • Extreme southeastern MI, bounded on the south by the OH state line, on the east by Lake Erie, and on the northeast by the Huron River; drained by the River Raisin. Sterling State Park is located near the city of Monroe, the state's only port on Lake Erie. • One of seventeen counties named for President James Monroe. Monroe was the first American president to travel as far west as MI (August, 1817). • Original county; established 1817 (prior to statehood) • Monroe was the scene of the Raisin River Massacre (January 23, 1813) of General James Winchester's troops by Indian allies of England. The county was a prominent player in the Toledo War, a boundary dispute between Michigan and Ohio (1835). • Lt. Col. George A. Custer once lived in Monroe. • Cattle, hogs, sheep, poultry, dairying, corn, wheat, soybeans, sugar beets, apples, nurseries; manufacturing; limestone quarrying; shipping and diversified manufactures, including paper products and automobile parts.

MONTCALM *Stanton* • 61,266 • 708 • Central MI; drained by the Flat and Pine rivers. A small part of Manistee National Forest is in the northwest corner. • Named for Louis Joseph de Montcalm (1712–59), commander of French troops against the British in Canada • 1831 (prior to statehood) from Isabella • Potatoes, apples, corn, wheat, beans, cattle, hogs, sheep, dairy products; manufacturing; lake resorts.

MONTMORENCY *Atlanta* • 10,315 • 548 • Northern MI; drained by the Thunder Bay and Black rivers. Small lakes are shaded by Mackinaw State Forest, which covers half of the county. Clear Lake State Park is here. Part of Fletcher Pond is on the county's eastern boundary. • Probably named for one of many members of the French House of Montmorency. • Established as Cheonoquet 1840 from Alpena; name changed 1843 • Dairying, corn, cattle; industrial machinery.

MUSKEGON *Muskegon* • 170,200 • 509 • Southwestern MI, bounded on the west by Lake Michigan; drained by the Muskegon and White rivers, and by Crockery Creek. P.J.

Hoffmaster, Muskegon, and Duck Lake state parks are here. Part of Manistee National Forest is in the north. • Named for the Muskegon River • 1859 from Newaygo • Muskegon, early a major sawmill center and shipping point for lumber to Chicago, was destroyed by fire in 1890. • Radio and television executive Frank Stanton • Cattle, hogs, apples, cherries, vegetables, corn, wheat, oats, grain, dairy products; diversified manufactures including tool and dies, machinery, chemicals, food products, furniture; fisheries; resort tourism • Muskegon is the largest port on Lake Michigan's eastern shore and has extensive international trade. The Seaway Festival, honoring the port activities, is held here every summer.

NEWAYGO *White Cloud* • 47,874 • 842 • Western MI; drained by the Muskegon, White, and Big and Little south branches of the Pere Marquette. The county includes Newaygo State Park. The Loda Lake Wildflower Sanctuary is centrally located. Manistee National Forest covers the northeast two-thirds of the county except for the extreme northeastern corner. • Possibly named for the Ojibway Indian chief, signer of the Saginaw Treaty of 1819 • 1840 from unorganized territory • Cattle, hogs, poultry, dairying, onions, carrots, asparagus, apples, cherries, peaches, grains; some manufacturing; resort tourism.

OAKLAND *Pontiac* • 1,194,156 (the second most populated county in MI) • 873 • Southeastern MI, drained by the Shiawassee, Huron, and Clinton rivers, and by the River Rouge. The county, comprising part of the Detroit metropolitan area, is highly urbanized in the south. It contains many small resort lakes, especially in the west, and has a number of state parks and state recreational areas, as well as four ski areas. • Named for the many oak trees in the area at the time the county was formed • Original county; established 1819 (prior to statehood) • Bandleader and jazz drummer Elvin Jones; physician-assisted-suicide activist Jack Kevorkian. Architect Eliel Saarinen died here. • Apples, vegetables, wheat, oats, corn, cattle, hogs, sheep, poultry, dairy products, nurseries; diversified manufacturing including machine tools, steel products, electronics, tractors, golf carts. Pontiac is a major automobile manufacturing center • The county has ten Fortune 1000 companies headquartered within its borders. The Detroit Lions football team plays in Pontiac. The Detroit Zoological Park is in Royal Oak. The Cranbrook Foundation's 300-acre estate devoted to art, science and religion in Bloomfield Hills, contains four buildings designed by Eliel Saarinen. Oakland University in Rochester holds the summer Meadow Brook Music Festival. Controversial "radio priest" Charles E. Coughlin was pastor of Royal Oak's Shrine of the Little Flower. Auburn Hills is home to the Detroit Pistons (Palace at Auburn Hills).

OCEANA *Hart* • 26,873 • 540 • Western MI, bounded on the west by Lake Michigan; drained by the White and Pentwater rivers. The county includes Charles Mears, Hart-Montague Trail, and Silver Lake state parks. Over half of the county is blanketed by Manistee National Forest. Several lakes are located in the east and northwest. • Possibly named for its location on the shore of large Lake Michigan • 1831 (prior to statehood) from Newaygo • Apples, cherries, peaches, vegetables, cattle, hogs, poultry, dairying; some manufacturing; fisheries; resort tourism.

OGEMAW *West Branch* • 21,645 • 564 • Northeast-central MI; drained by the Au Gres and Rifle rivers. Part of Huron National Forest and Au Sable State Forest are here. The county contains Rifle River Recreation Area and many small lakes. • Named for Ogemakegato (1794–1840), chief of the Saginaw band of Indians • 1840 • Cattle, hogs, corn, wheat, oats, barley, dairy products.

ONTONAGON *Ontonagon* • 7,818 • 1,312 (the third largest county in MI) • Northwestern Upper Peninsula, MI, bounded on the north by Lake Superior; drained by the Ontonagon River (designated a National Wild, Scenic, and Recreational River), and by the Iron and Fire Steel rivers. Part of the Porcupine Mountains are here, including Porcupine Mountains Wilderness State Park. Part of Ottawa National Forest is in the southern half of the county and part of Gogebic Lake is on its southern boundary. Ontonagon Indian Reservation is also in the county. • Named for the Ontonagon River • 1843 from Michilimackinac and Chippewa • Lumber; cattle, oats, hay, dairy products; fishing, resorts; some manufacturing.

OSCEOLA *Reed City* • 23,197 • 566 • Central MI; intersected by the Muskegon River; drained by the Pine River. Part of Manistee National Forest is in the county. • One of three counties named for the Seminole chief (?–1838), who led the second Seminole War against the U.S. • Established as Unwattin 1840; name changed 1843 • Forage crops, cattle, hogs, poultry, wheat, oats, corn, dairy products; manufacturing; resorts.

OSCODA *Mio* • 9,418 • 565 • North-central MI; intersected by the Au Sable River (designated a National Scenic River); drained by the South Branch of the Thunder Bay River. The county includes parts of Huron National Forest, Mackinaw State Forest, Kirtlands Warbler National Wildlife Refuge, and several small lakes. Mio Mountain ski area is here. • Oscoda is a contrived or pseudo-Indian name coined by Henry R. Schoolcraft • 1840 from unorganized territory • Grain, cattle, sheep, dairy products, poultry; manufacture of wood products and metal products; resort tourism.

OTSEGO *Gaylord* • 23,301 • 515 • Northern MI; drained by the Sturgeon and Black rivers, and by the North Branch of the Au Sable River. The county lies in a year-round resort area. It includes many small lakes and sections of Mackinaw State Forest. Otsego Lake State Park is here, as are Treetops Sylvan and Hidden Valley ski areas. A small part of Camp Grayling Army and Air National Guard Training Center is in the south. • Probably named for Otsego, NY, home of some early settlers • Established as Okkuddo 1840; name changed 1843 • Cattle, hogs, potatoes, wheat, oats, dairy products; manufacture of wood products, electronic equipment.

OTTAWA *Grand Haven* • 238,314 • 566 • Southwestern MI, bounded on the west by Lake Michigan; drained by the Grand River. Spring Lake, a large backwater lake of Lake Michigan, receives the Grand River in the northwestern corner. The county includes Mulligan's Hollow ski area, and Grand Haven and Holland state parks. • One of four counties named for the Ottawa Indians • 1831 (prior to statehood) • Artist and filmmaker Winsor McCay • Hogs, cattle, sheep, poultry, apples, cherries, onions, asparagus, grain, dairy products; large variety of manufactures, including printing presses, pianos, refrigerators, plumbing fixtures, boilers, marine engines, leather and gloves, plastics, electronic devices, radar antennas; fisheries; resort tourism; education (Grand Valley State U.) • A popular attraction in Grand Haven is a large electronically controlled musical fountain. Holland, founded in 1847 by a secessionist church group from the Netherlands, maintains elements of Dutch culture; wooden shoes are still sold here, as are thousands of tulip bulbs. The annual Tulip Time Festival is held in May. Hope College and Western Theological Seminary here are both affiliated with the Reformed Church of America.

PRESQUE ISLE *Rogers City* • 14,411 • 660 • Northeastern MI, bounded on the northeast by Lake Huron; drained by the Black, Rainy, and Ocqueoc rivers, and by the North Branch of the Thunder Bay River. Grand Lake and part of Long Lake are on the eastern end of the county. Part of Black Lake is on the western end. Onaway State Park is in the northwest, on Black Lake. P.H. Hoeft and Thompson's Harbor state parks are on Lake Huron. Parts of Mackinaw State Forest are also here. • The county was named for the Presque Isle peninsula • 1840 from unorganized territory • Dairying, cattle, hogs, poultry, oats, beans; manufacturing; limestone quarries; fisheries; resorts.

ROSCOMMON *Roscommon* • 25,469 • 521 • North-central MI; drained by the Muskegon River and branches of the Tittabawassee and Au Sable rivers. The county includes Houghton and Higgins lakes, and Lake St. Helen. South Higgins Lake and North Higgins Lake state parks are here. Au Sable State Forest and Huron National Forest cover much of the county. • Named for the county in Ireland • Established as Mikenauk 1840; name change 1843 • Manufacture of automotive stampings; dairy products, livestock; resorts.

SAGINAW *Saginaw* • 210,039 • 809 • East-central MI; drained by the Saginaw River and its affluents, by the Cass, Flint, Shiawassee, Bad and Tittabawassee rivers, and by Mistaguay Creek. Apple Mountain ski area is here, as are Shiawassee National Wildlife Refuge and Crow Island State Game Area. • Named for the Saginaw River • 1822 (prior to statehood) from unorganized territory • On September 24, 1819, a treaty was signed in Saginaw between MI Territory's governor Lewis Cass and the Chippewa Indians, which ceded large tracts of land to the U.S. Saginaw was one of the leading lumbering centers in the nation in the latter half of the 19th century. • Singer and songwriter Stevie Wonder • Sugar beets (cultivation and refining), soybeans, beans, wheat, oats, potatoes, cucumbers, corn, cattle, hogs, poultry, dairy products; coal, oil and salt deposits; manufacture of automobile parts, fabricated metals, machinery, food products; tourism (especially focused on the German town of Frankenmuth); education (Saginaw Valley State U.).

SAINT CLAIR (one of four counties so named) *Port Huron* • 164,235 • 724 • Eastern MI, bounded on the east by Lake Huron and the St. Clair River (the latter forming the border with Ontario) and on the south by Lake St. Clair; drained by the Belle and Black rivers, and by Mill Creek. Lakeport State Park is in the northeast on Lake Huron. Lake Algonac State Park is in the south. • Named for the township by this name in MI territory • Original county; established 1820 (prior to statehood) • Thomas Edison lived in the county in his youth. • Cattle, hogs, poultry, corn, wheat, oats, sugar beets, soybeans, dairy products; manufacture of cement, machinery, tool and auto parts, brass; salt mines; fisheries • Fort Gratiot Lighthouse, built in 1829, is the oldest on the Great Lakes. Originally a lumber and shipbuilding center, Port Huron is now a railway and St. Lawrence Seaway terminal, possessing one of the few natural deepwater ports on the Great Lakes.

SAINT JOSEPH (one of two counties so named, the other in IN) *Centreville* • 62,422 • 504 • Southwestern MI, bounded on the south by the IN state line; drained by the St. Joseph River and its affluents. Small (resort) lakes are distributed throughout the county, especially on the St. Joseph River. • Named for the St. Joseph River • 1829 (prior to statehood) from Indian lands • Cattle, hogs, sheep, poultry, wheat, soybeans, corn, dairy products; manufacturing.

SANILAC *Sandusky* • 44,547 • 964 • Eastern MI, bounded on the east by Lake Huron; drained by the Black and Cass rivers. Sanilac Petroglyphs is in the northwest, on Lake Huron. • Named for the Wyandot chief who is the main character in Henry Whiting's poem "Sannilac." • 1822 (prior to statehood) • Beans, sugar beets, apples, cattle, hogs, poultry, corn, wheat, oats, barley, dairy products; manufacturing; fisheries; resorts.

SCHOOLCRAFT *Manistique* • 8,903 • 1,178 (the fourth largest county in MI) • Southern Upper Peninsula MI, bounded on the south by Lake Michigan; drained by the Indian River (designated a National Scenic and Recreational River) and by the Manistique River and its affluents. Palms Book and Indian Lake state parks are on Indian Lake. Seney National Wildlife Refuge is also in the county, as is part of Hiawatha National Forest. McDonald and Gulliver lakes are in the southeast; numerous small lakes are in the west and far north. • Named for Henry R. Schoolcraft (1793–1864), explorer, MI legislator, author, and superintendent of Indian Affairs for MI. Schoolcraft coined the largest number of artificial county names of anyone in U.S. history. • 1843 from Michilimackinac and Chippewa • Cattle, forage crops; manufacturing; lumbering; resorts; fish hatchery.

SHIAWASSEE *Corunna* • 71,687 • 539 • South-central MI; drained by the Shiawassee, Maple, and Looking Glass rivers. • Named for the Shiawassee River • Presidential candidate Thomas E. Dewey; novelist James O. Curwood (The Curwood Castle is located in Owosso) • Beans, corn, potatoes, cattle, hogs, sheep, poultry, dairy products; manufacturing.

TUSCOLA *Caro* • 58,266 • 813 • Eastern MI, bounded on the northwest by Saginaw Bay; drained by the Cass River and its affluents. • Tuscola is a contrived or pseudo-Indian name coined by Henry R. Schoolcraft • 1840 from Sanilac • Sugar beets, beans, corn, wheat, oats, soybeans, barley, potatoes, fruit, livestock, poultry, dairy products; fisheries.

VAN BUREN *Paw Paw* • 76,263 • 611 • Southwestern MI, bounded on the west by Lake Michigan; drained by the Paw Paw and Black rivers. Van Buren Trail and Van Buren state parks are here, as is Timber Ridge ski area. There are small lakes throughout the county. • One of four counties named for President Martin Van Buren • 1829 (prior to statehood) from unorganized territory • Apples, cherries, peaches, plums, strawberries, grapes, carrots, green beans, asparagus, livestock, poultry, dairy products; wineries, vineyards; manufacturing; resort tourism; fisheries, nurseries. • Lake Michigan Maritime Museum is in South Haven.

WASHTENAW *Ann Arbor* • 322,895 • 710 • Southeastern MI; drained by the Huron and Raisin rivers. The county has several (resort) lakes. It is growing more urbanized as the Detroit metropolitan area extends westward. Pinckney Recreation Area is in the north. • Washtenaw is the Indian name for the Grand River • 1822 (prior to statehood) • The plant at Willow Run in Ypsilanti, was the production center for B-24 bombers during World War II. • Physicist Samuel C.C. Ting • Cattle, sheep, hogs, poultry, wheat, oats, corn, soybeans, apples, dairy products; diversified manufactures, including automobiles (Willow Run auto plants); research; education (U. of MI, Eastern MI U.; Cleary College; Concordia College) • The Gerald R. Ford Library is in Ann Arbor, as is the National Center for the Study of Frank Lloyd Wright. The University of Michigan Library is considered one of the best in the nation. The university also has the largest pre-law and pre-med programs in the country.

WAYNE (one of sixteen counties so named) Detroit • 2,061,162 (the most populated county in MI and the eleventh most populated county in the U.S.) • 614 • Southeastern MI, bounded on the east by the Detroit River (forming the border with the Canadian province of Ontario) and Lake St. Clair, touching Lake Erie in the extreme southeast; drained by the Huron River, River Rouge and its branches. The county is highly urbanized and industrialized with the city of Detroit occupying most of its northeastern quarter. The Detroit Metro Wayne County Airport is in Romulus. • One of fifteen counties named for General Anthony Wayne (1745–96), PA soldier and statesman, nicknamed "Mad Anthony" for his daring during the Revolutionary War • Original county; 1815 (prior to statehood) • Detroit is the oldest city in the Midwest, founded in 1701 by Antoine de la Mothe Cadillac for Louis XIV of France. At Council Point (now Lincoln Park) on April 27, 1763, Ottawa Indian chief Pontiac made plans to capture Detroit from the British, thus launching Pontiac's War. The British refused to surrender Fort Lernoult, located in present day Detroit, until 1796, thirteen years after the end of the Revolutionary War. Trenton was the scene of several decisive skirmishes and encounters between British and American troops during the War of 1812, including the Battle of Monguagon. Detroit served as MI's first capital from 1837 to 1847. From 1872 until 1920 Wyandotte was a major ship-building center for the Great Lakes. A blast furnace constructed here in 1864 produced the first commercial Bessemer steel in the U.S. The county became the center of the U.S. automobile industry in the early 1900s. Henry Ford opened his first Model T automobile plant in Highland Park in 1910, introducing the assembly-line method of automobile production here. Called "center line safety stripes," the first traffic lines to mark traffic lanes were painted near Trenton in 1911. The first all-metal multi-engine commercial airliner in the U.S. was built at Ford Airport in Dearborn (1924–1933). The first contract airmail service on domestic routes was inaugurated here as well. A strike against General Motors in 1937 by the United Automobile Workers greatly strengthened the labor movement in the U.S. Detroit was the scene of two of America's worst race riots: in June, 1943, 34 people were killed and over 1,000 injured; in July, 1967, more than 40 died and 2,000 were injured. • Industrialists Henry Ford and Henry Ford II; aviator Charles A. Lindbergh; Union leader James P. Hoffa; boxers Sugar Ray Robinson and Joe Louis; director Francis Ford Coppola. Engineer and manufacturer Henry M. Leland died here. • Diversified manufacturing, including motor vehicles (General Motors, Ford, others), auto parts (number one county in the U.S.), dental supplies and equipment, industrial ovens,

marine engines, cement, chemicals, steel, plastics, boats, glass, machinery, industrial diamonds, food products; sand and gravel; remnant agriculture: soybeans, corn, hogs, poultry; fishing; salt mining; lake- and ocean-shipping facilities; education (U. of Detroit; Marygrove College; Wayne State U.; Madonna U.; U. of MI Dearborn) • The corporate headquarters of eleven Fortune 1000 companies are located in the county. One of the largest salt mines in the nation, covering nearly two square miles, lies under Detroit. The Motown Historical Museum chronicles the popularity of Barry Gordy's "Motown Sound." Greenfield Village in Dearborn is a collection of about 100 historic buildings, gathered by Henry Ford from around the country (including Edison's laboratory and the courthouse where Lincoln first practiced law.) The Henry Ford Museum is also here. Detroit has the country's largest population of Bulgarians, Chaldeans, Belgians, and Arabs. The city is home to the Detroit Redwings (Joe Louis Arena), the Tigers (Comerica Park), and the Lions (Ford Field).

WEXFORD *Cadillac* • 30,484 • 566 • Northwestern MI; intersected by the Manistee River (forming Hodenpyl Dam Pond on its western boundary). Part of Manistee National Forest is located in the southwestern third of the county. (Cadillac is headquarters for both Manistee and Huron national forests.) A state fish hatchery is at Harrietta. The county also contains Caberfae Peaks ski area. Lakes Mitchell and Cadillac are here, as are William Mitchell and White Pine Trail state parks. • Named for the county in Ireland • Established as Kautawaubet County in 1840 from unorganized territory; name changed 1843. • Cadillac was settled by lumbermen in the 1860s. • Cattle, mixed grains, green beans, dairy products; manufacture of castings, rubber and plastic goods, boats, lumber, women's clothing; tourism (summer and winter resorts); education (Baker College of Cadillac).

MINNESOTA

The Star of the North

Each of Minnesota's eighty-seven counties is governed by a board of commissioners, usually consisting of five members, each of whom is elected to a four-year term. Other county officials in the state include the attorney, auditor, coroner, treasurer, and sheriff.

AITKIN *Aitkin* • 15,301 • 1,819 • East-central MN; drained by the Mississippi, Willow, Rice, and Sandy rivers. Savanna State Forest in the northeast includes Savanna Portage State Park and Big Sandy Lake, with Sandy Lake Indian Reservation along its shore. Part of Hill, Solana, and Weatherwood state forests are here, as is part of Mille Lacs Lake in the south-

west. Rice Lake National Wildlife Refuge is found in the county. Part of the Cuyuna Iron Range is in the west. The fertile soil of this county is attributed to a prehistoric lake, which covered a large area and left bogs and swamps behind when it disappeared. • Named for William A. Aitkin (1785–1851), a local fur trader • 1857 as Aiken (prior to statehood) from Cass and Itasca; the spelling was corrected in 1872 • Hay, wild rice, turkeys, dairy products, fruit; deposits of marl and peat; shipping; timber.

ANOKA *Anoka* • 298,084 (the fourth most populated county in MN) • 424 • Eastern MN, bounded on the southwest by the Mississippi River; drained by the Rum River. The county has become urbanized in the south from an expansion of the Minneapolis-St. Paul metropolitan area. Part of the Carlos-Avery Wildlife Area is in the county. Anoka has many lakes, especially in the center. • Named for the town of the same name • 1857 (prior to statehood) from Hennepin; annexed Manomin County in 1869 • Author and broadcaster Garrison Keillor (whose many talents include being able to quickly recite the names of all of Minnesota's counties in alphabetical order) • Cattle, alfalfa, rye, dairying, poultry; deposits of marl and peat; manufacture of refrigerators and heating equipment.

BECKER *Detroit Lakes* • 30,000 • 1,310 • Western MN; watered by numerous lakes, the Buffalo River and the South Branch of the Wild Rice River. Part of White Earth Indian Reservation is in the north. Hamden Slough and Tamarac national wildlife refuges are here. Two Inlets and Smoky Hills state forests are in the east; part of White Earth State Forest is in the northeast. The county also includes a small part of Itasca State Park. • Named for George L. Becker (1829–1904), who was elected U.S. representative from MN, but not allowed to serve due to a change in Congressional seat allotment; naming the county after him was a consolation. He was later a railroad executive. • 1858 from Indian lands • Oats, barley, wheat, hay, alfalfa, soybeans, sunflowers, sugar beets, wild rice, beans, hogs, cattle, sheep, poultry, dairying; timber.

BELTRAMI *Bemidji* • 39,650 • 2,505 (the fourth largest county in MN) • Northwestern MN; drained by the headwaters of the Mississippi River in the south (with its source to the southwest in Clearwater County). The county includes a large part of Red Lake Indian Reservation; part of Leech Lake Indian Reservation is in the southeast. The center of the county is dominated by Upper and Lower Red Lakes. Also here are parts of Beltrami Island, Red Lake, Mississippi Headwaters, Buena Vista, and Blackduck state forests, and part of Chippewa National Forest. Lake Bemidji State Park is in the south. • Named for Giacomo C. Beltrami (1779–1855), an Italian who searched for the source of the Mississippi River • 1866 from unorganized territory • Bemidji was originally a major logging and sawmilling center. (An eighteen-foot statue of mythical lumberman Paul Bunyan and his blue ox Babe stands on the shore of Lake Bemidji.) • Oats, barley, wheat, wild rice, hay, alfalfa, sunflowers, sheep, cattle, poultry, dairying; freshwater fishing; tourism; manufacture of woolens, plywood, hardwood, cement; education (Bemidji State U.).

BENTON (one of nine counties so named) *Foley* • 34,226 • 408 • Central MN, bounded on the west by the Mississippi River. Little Rock Lake is in the west, near the Mississippi. The southern part of the county comprises part of the St. Cloud metropolitan area. • One of seven counties named for Thomas Hart Benton (1782–1858), U.S. journalist and statesman • Original county; established Oct. 27, 1849 (prior to statehood) • Sauk Rapids, an early sawmill town, suffered a devastating cyclone in 1886, but emerged to become a flour milling center. • Dairying, livestock, poultry, grain, soybeans; deposits of marl in the northwest; manufacture of surgical appliances and supplies.

BIG STONE *Ortonville* • 5,820 • 497 • Western MN, bounded on the west and southwest by Big Stone Lake (forming the SD state line) and on the south by the Minnesota River (which flows out of Big Stone Lake). Artichoke Lake is in the east; Marsh Lake (formed by the Minnesota River) is in the southeast. Big Stone Lake State Park and part of Big Stone Lake National Wildlife Refuge are in the southwest. • Named for Big Stone Lake • 1862 from Pierce County (which was abolished the same year). Laid out in 1873, Ortonville flourished as a western outpost. • Alfalfa, wheat, corn, oats, barley, soybeans, hogs.

BLUE EARTH *Mankato* • 55,941 • 752 • Southern MN, bounded on the north in part by the Minnesota River; drained by the Blue Earth, Watonwan, Maple, Big Cobb, and Le Sueur rivers. Minneopa State Park is in the north, as is Sakatah Singing Hills State Trail. Several small natural lakes, including Madison and Eagle, are in the county, especially in the northeast corner. • Named for the Blue Earth River • 1853 (prior to statehood) from unorganized territory • French explorer Pierre Le Sueur built a fort near Mankato and sent large quantities of the blue-green earth back to France, mistakenly believing it was filled with copper ore. Thirty-eight Sioux were hanged in Mankato at Camp Lincoln (now Sibley park) in 1862 following the failure of an Indian uprising at New Ulm. • Author and literary biographer W. Jackson Bate. U.S. Vice President Schuyler Colfax died here. • Corn, oats, soybeans, alfalfa, peas, hogs, cattle, sheep; processing of farm products; limestone quarrying; manufacture of farm equipment, cans, generators, fishing reels, boats, paper products, plastics; education (MN State U., Mankato) tourism (ski resort at Mount Kato).

BROWN (one of nine counties so named) *New Ulm* • 26,911 • 611 • Southern MN, bounded on the northeast by the Minnesota River; drained by the Cottonwood and Little Cottonwood rivers. Lake Hanska reservoir is in the south; Flandrau State Park is in the northeast at New Ulm. • Named for Joseph R. Brown (1805–70), MN and WI territorial legislator who helped to draft MN's state constitution • 1855 (prior to statehood) from Nicollet • New Ulm was almost destroyed in the

Sioux Uprising of 1862. The related battles are commemorated by the Defenders' Monument next to the courthouse square. • Corn, oats, hay, alfalfa, soybeans, peas, hogs, sheep, cattle, poultry, dairying; quartzite, silica • German influence is strong in the city of New Ulm, founded in 1854 by German immigrants and named for Ulm in Württemberg. Overlooking the city on a bluff is a 102-foot high bronze statue honoring German tribal leader Hermann (Arminius) who defeated the Romans at the Teutoburg Forest in 9 AD. Dr. Martin Luther College dates from 1884.

CARLTON *Carlton* • 31,671 • 860 • Eastern MN, bounded on the east in part by the WI state line; drained by the St. Louis River, Kettle, Moose, and Nemadji rivers. The county includes parts of Fond du Lac Indian Reservation and Fond du Lac State Forest, both in the north. Part of Nemadji State Forest is in the southeast corner. Jay Cooke and Moose Lake state parks are also here. • Named for Reuben B. Carlton (1812–1863), farmer and blacksmith for the Ojibway Indians who served in MN's first state senate • 1857 (prior to statehood) from Pine • When the building of the Northern Pacific Railway was begun, Carlton was distinguished by having the first spike driven here. • Dairying, poultry, alfalfa, hay, oats.

CARVER *Chaska* • 70,205 (47% increase since 1990; the third fastest growing county in MN) • 357 • South-central MN, bounded on the southeast by the Minnesota River; drained by the South Crow River. The county lies within a predominately agricultural area with a fringe of the Minneapolis/St. Paul metropolitan area in the northeast. It contains numerous small natural lakes, especially in the northeast, including Lake Waconia and the southern extremity of Lake Minnetonka. Part of the Minnesota Valley National Wildlife Refuge extends along the Minnesota River. • Named for Captain Jonathan Carver (1710–1780), an officer in the French and Indian War, explorer, and author • 1855 (prior to statehood) from Hennepin • Dairying, sugar beets, cattle, poultry, hogs, wheat, corn, soybeans, oats, hay, alfalfa, manufacture of plastic products, surgical and medical instruments, sporting and athletic goods.

CASS (one of nine counties so named) *Walker* • 27,150 • 2,018 • North-central MN, bounded on the south by the Crow Wing River, and on the north by the Mississippi River (forming Lake Winnibigoshish reservoir here). Leech Lake and Leech Lake Indian Reservation, and Chippewa National Forest dominate the northern half of the county. Several state forests are scattered throughout. Pine Point Nature Area and Schoolcraft State Park are also here. Part of Gull Lake reservoir (with Ski Gull ski area on its northern shore) is in the extreme southeast. • One of eight counties named for General Lewis Cass (1782–1866), governor of MI Territory, U.S. secretary of war, and U.S. secretary of state • Original county;

established 1851 (prior to statehood) • Dairying, cattle, sheep, poultry, wild rice, hay, alfalfa, oats; timber.

CHIPPEWA (one of three counties so named) *Montevideo* • 13,088 • 583 • Southwestern MN, bounded on the southwest by the Minnesota River (forming Lac qui Parle here); drained by the Chippewa River. Part of Lac qui Parle State Park and Lac qui Parle Mission are in the northwest. • One of two counties (the other in WI) named for the Chippewa River • 1862 from Pierce County, which was abolished that same year • Wheat, corn, oats, soybeans, sugar beets, alfalfa, hogs, sheep.

CHISAGO *Center City* • 41,101 • 418 • Eastern MN, bounded on the east by the St. Croix River (forming the WI state line); drained by the Sunrise River; watered by several small lakes including Rush Lake. Part of Carlos-Avery Wildlife Area is here, as well as part of St. Croix National Scenic Riverway. Wild River and Interstate state parks are located on the eastern boundary. • Named for Chisago Lake, largest in the county • 1851 (prior to statehood) from Washington County • Cattle, poultry, hay, corn, oats, rye, alfalfa, dairying.

CLAY (one of eighteen counties so named) *Moorhead* • 51,229 • 1,045 • Western MN, bounded on the west by the Red River of the North (forming the ND state line); drained by the Buffalo River and the South Branch of the Wild Rice River. Buffalo River State Park is here. The western part of the county comprises part of the Fargo-Moorhead metropolitan area. • One of fifteen counties named for Henry Clay (1777–1852), statesman and U.S. senator from KY • Established as Breckinridge in 1858; name changed in 1862 • Alfalfa, hay, oats, barley, soybeans, beans, sunflowers, wild rice, sugar beets (cultivation and refining), potatoes (cultivation and processing), hogs, cattle, poultry, dairying; manufacture of farm equipment and fiberglass boats; education (MN State U., Moorhead; Concordia College).

CLEARWATER (one of two counties so named, the other in ID) *Bagley* • 8,423 • 995 • Northwestern MN, bounded on the northeast by Lower Red Lake reservoir; drained by the Clearwater, Red Lake, Wild Rice, and Mississippi rivers. The county includes part of Red Lake and White Earth Indian reservations. Itasca State Park is in the southeast corner and includes Lake Itasca, source of the Mississippi River. Parts of White Earth and Mississippi Headwaters state forests are in the south. • Named for the Clearwater River and Lake • 1902 from Beltrami • Oats, wheat, barley, hay, alfalfa, potatoes, sunflowers, sheep, cattle, poultry, dairying; timber.

COOK (one of three counties so named) *Grand Marais* • 5,168 • 1,451 • Extreme northeastern MN, bounded on the southeast by Lake Superior and on the north by the Canadian province of Ontario (separated by a chain of lakes). The county is watered by many lakes. It is occupied by Superior National

Forest and several state forests. It includes part of Boundary Waters Canoe Area Wilderness. Grand Portage Indian Reservation and Grand Portage National Monument are in the extreme east. Cook has several state parks and state waysides along the shoreline of Lake Superior. Eagle Mountain, at 2,301 feet, is the highest point in the state. • Named for Major Michael Cook (1828–64), an officer in the Civil War and MN legislator • 1874 from Lake • Fisheries; timber; resort tourism.

COTTONWOOD *Windom* • 12,167 • 640 • Southwestern MN; watered by the Des Moines and Watonwan rivers. Talcot Lake Wildlife Area is in the southwest and Jeffers Petroglyphs is in the northeast. • Named for the Cottonwood River • 1857 (prior to statehood) from Brown • Soybeans, alfalfa, hogs, cattle, sheep.

CROW WING *Brainerd* • 55,099 • 997 • Central MN; drained by the Mississippi River and watered by numerous lakes. Crow Wing State Park is in the county. Crow Wing, Emily, and part of Land O'Lakes state forests are here. Among the county's large lakes is Mille Lacs on the eastern boundary. Part of Cuyuna Iron Range is in the east. • Named for the Crow Wing river, which forms the southwestern border of the county • 1857 (prior to statehood) from Cass and Aitkin • The county was formerly in a productive lumbering region. (Its importance to the area is recalled in Lumbertown, a replica of a Minnesota camp in the 1870s, and a lumber carnival held at the Paul Bunyan Amusement Center.) • Baseball player Charles Albert Bender • Cattle, poultry, hay, alfalfa, oats, wild rice; iron mining; railroad shops; manufacture of high-grade paper, sportswear, dairy products; resort tourism • The county is strongly identified with legendary lumberjack Paul Bunyan and boasts a twenty-six-foot-high replica of him, immortalized in the film *Fargo*.

DAKOTA *Hastings* • 355,904 (the third most populated county in MN) • 570 • Southeastern MN, bounded on northeast and north (in part) by the Mississippi River, and on the northwest by the Minnesota River; drained by the Vermillion and Cannon rivers (the latter forming part of the southern boundary). The northern part of the county is adjacent to St. Paul (to the north) and Minneapolis (to the northwest) and is highly urbanized. Part of Richard J. Dorer Memorial Hardwood State Forest is in the southeast. Parts of Fort Snelling State Park and Minnesota Valley National Wildlife Refuge are in the northwest. • One of five counties named for the Dakota Indians, also known as the Sioux. • Original county; established 1849 (prior to statehood); originally spelled Dakotah • Two waterfalls on the Vermillion River were the site of MN's first milling industries. • Cattle, hogs, sheep (South Saint Paul is one of the largest livestock markets in the world and terminal point for producers in several states.), hay, alfalfa, oats, corn, soybeans, peas, poultry, dairying; sand and gravel; food processing and diversified manufactures, includ-

ing office equipment, brick, tile, machinery, toys, sporting goods, boating equipment, brick, tile • South Saint Paul is the site of the extensive St. Paul Union Stockyards (est. 1886) and the Farmers Union Central Exchange, a large farm-supply cooperative.

DODGE (one of four counties so named) *Mantorville* • 17,731 • 440 • Southeastern MN; drained by the South and Middle Forks of the Zumbro River. Part of Rice Lake State Park is on the western boundary. • Named for either General Henry Dodge (1782–1867), officer in the War of 1812, governor of WI territory, and U.S. senator from WI; or for both Henry and August C. Dodge (1812–1883), one of IA's first two U.S. senators • 1855 (prior to statehood) from Olmstead • Soybeans, corn, oats, peas, sheep, hogs, cattle, poultry; dairying; manufacturing.

DOUGLAS *Alexandria* • 32,821 • 634 • Western MN; watered by the Long Prairie, Chippewa, and Little Chippewa rivers. Lake Carlos State Park is here. The county has numerous natural lakes, including Lake Miltona and Lake Christina. • One of twelve counties named for Stephen A. Douglas (1813–61), U.S. orator and statesman • 1858 from Todd • The possibility of early Norse exploration of the area is promoted by a twenty-eight-foot-high statue of a Viking in Alexandria and the controversial Kensington Stone, containing runic inscriptions reputed to describe a 1362 visit by Norsemen. • Wheat, corn, oats, barley, alfalfa, hay, sheep, hogs, cattle, poultry, dairying; resort tourism; light industry.

FARIBAULT *Blue Earth* • 16,181 • 714 • Southern MN, bounded on the south by the IA state line; drained by the Blue Earth River, and its East and West forks. Rice and Minnesota lakes are in the north, Walnut Lake and Wildlife Area in east-center. • Named for Jean B. Faribault (1774–1860), a French-Canadian fur trader in the Northwest Territory who established a trading post in present day Carver County • 1855 (prior to statehood) from Blue Earth • Industrial designer Donald Deskey • Corn, oats, soybeans, alfalfa, peas, hogs, cattle, sheep, poultry; food processing • One of Blue Earth's earliest industries, ice cream, brought the town the claim of inventing the ice cream sandwich. Blue Earth is home to the Jolly Green Giant.

FILLMORE (one of two counties so named, the other in NE) *Preston* • 21,122 • 861 • Southeastern MN, bounded on the south by the IA state line; watered by the Root River, and by its South, Middle and North branches. Part of Richard J. Dorer Memorial Hardwood State Forest is here. Harmony-Preston Valley and Root River state trails are also here. The county includes Forestville/Mystery Cave State Park southwest of Preston. • One of three counties named for President Millard Fillmore • Original county; established 1853 (prior to statehood) • Merchant Richard Sears • Poultry, cattle, sheep, hogs, corn, soybeans, oats, alfalfa, hay, dairying; limestone.

FREEBORN *Albert Lea* • 32,584 • 708 • Southern MN, bounded on the south by the IA state line. Several natural lakes are found in the county. Albert Lea Lake is in the center, with Myre Big Island State Park on its shore. Freeborn Lake is also in the county. • Named for William Freeborn (1816–?), pioneer and MN territorial legislator • 1855 (prior to statehood) from Blue Earth and Rice • Albert Lea became the county seat as the result of a race won by a local horse (Old Tom) over one backed by neighboring town Itasca (Itasca Fly). The town of Itasca no longer exists. • Cattle, sheep, hogs, dairying, hay, alfalfa, oats, corn, soybeans, peas, potatoes; diversified industries, including large meat-packing plants.

GOODHUE *Red Wing* • 44,127 • 759 • Southeastern MN, bounded on the northeast by the Mississippi River, forming the WI state line; drained by the Cannon River. Prairie Island Indian Community is here, as is part of Richard J. Dorer Memorial Hardwood State Forest. The county also includes Frontenac State Park and several ski areas. • Named for James M. Goodhue (1810–52), lawyer and editor of the first newspaper in MN Territory • 1853 (prior to statehood) from Wabasha • Ethnologist Frances Densmore • Hay, corn, oats, barley, alfalfa, soybeans, peas, sheep, hogs, cattle, poultry, dairying • Pine Island, settled by the Swiss, was previously known as the Cheese Center of Minnesota, and once entered a 6,000 pound cheese in the state fair at St. Paul.

GRANT (one of fifteen counties so named) *Elbow Lake* • 6,289 • 546 • Western MN; drained by the Mustinka, Chippewa, and Pomme de Terre rivers. The county includes numerous small lakes, notably Pomme de Terre and Pelican. Tipsinah Mounds Park is also here. • One of twelve counties named for President Ulysses S. Grant • 1868 from Stearns • Alfalfa, wheat, corn, oats, barley, soybeans, sugar beets, beans, sunflowers, hogs, sheep, poultry, dairying.

HENNEPIN *Minneapolis* • 1,116,200 (the most populated county in MN) • 557 • Eastern MN, bounded on the northeast and southeast by the Mississippi River, on the northwest by the Crow River, and on the south by the Minnesota River. Minnesota Valley National Wildlife Refuge is on the southern border. Fort Snelling National Cemetery and State Park is in the southeast. Minnehaha Falls, on the Mississippi River, was immortalized by poet Henry Wadsworth Longfellow in his poem "The Song of Hiawatha." Lake Minnetonka is in the southwest. There are numerous other lakes throughout the county, with twenty-two found within the city limits of Minneapolis, nicknamed the "City of Lakes." Minneapolis-St. Paul International Airport is in the southeast. • Named for Louis Hennepin (1640–1705), Franciscan missionary and explorer (with La Salle) who named the Falls of St. Anthony in the Mississippi River at present-day Minneapolis • Original county; established 1852 (prior to statehood) • Eighteen of the structures that are part of historic Fort Snelling, MN's first settlement, have been restored or reconstructed. From 1882 to 1930, Minneapolis led the world in flour production. The city led the world in lumber production from 1899 to 1905. • Oil billionaire J. Paul Getty; newspaper columnist Westbrook Pegler; cartoonist Charles Schulz; wrestler and governor Jesse Ventura; novelist and short-story writer Anne Tyler; NATO commander Lauris Norstad; singer Prince. Flour miller Charles A. Pillsbury died here. • Corn, soybeans, oats, alfalfa, cattle, sheep, poultry, dairying, nursery stock, truck farming; manufacture of controls for guided missiles, X-ray equipment, floor scrubbers and sanders, flour and baked goods, peanut butter, window and door frame units, canvas products, computers, air conditioners, microwave ovens, construction equipment, farm machinery, munitions, plastic and rubber parts, precision machined parts, cast aluminum cookware; service industries; education (U. of MN; Crown College; North Central U.) • The county serves as corporate headquarters for over twenty Fortune 1000 companies. The home thermostat was invented and first manufactured here in 1885, by Alfred M. Butz. The Mall of America in Bloomington is one of the largest indoor shopping malls in the U.S. Minneapolis has one of the largest Native American populations of any city in the U.S. The Guthrie Theater in Minneapolis is home to one of the best-known theater groups in the country. The Walker Art Center owns one of the country's finest collections of modern art. Minneapolis is home to the Minnesota Timberwolves (Target Center), Twins and Vikings (HHH Metrodome).

HOUSTON (one of five counties so named) *Caledonia* • 19,718 • 558 • Extreme southeastern MN, bounded on the east by the Mississippi River (forming the WI state line) and on the south by the IA state line; drained by the Root River. Beaver Creek Valley State Park is here. Part of Richard J. Dorer Memorial Hardwood State Forest is also in the county. It includes parts of Upper Mississippi River National Wildlife and Fish Refuge, as well. • One of three counties named for Samuel Houston (1793–1863), governor of TN, president of the Republic of Texas, U.S. senator from TX, and TX governor • 1854 (prior to statehood) from Fillmore • Corn, oats, soybeans, hay, alfalfa, hogs, cattle, poultry, dairying; timber; sand and gravel, limestone • MN's abundance of dandelions is blamed on Caledonia resident Jacob Webster who sent for dandelion seed from New England, not realizing how well the plant would take to MN soil.

HUBBARD *Park Rapids* • 18,376 • 923 • Northwest-central MN; drained by the Mississippi River. The county has numerous small natural lakes. Parts of Paul Bunyan State Forest are here. The county includes Badoura State Forest and part of Lake Itasca State Park. Also here are Heartland and Paul Bunyan state trails. • Named for General Lucius F. Hubbard

(1836–1913), Union officer in the Civil War and the Spanish-American War, MN legislator and governor of the state • 1883 from Cass • Alfalfa, oats, barley, rye, potatoes, beans; timber; peat deposits.

ISANTI *Cambridge* • 31,287 • 439 • Eastern MN; drained by the Rum River. The county has numerous small lakes. • Named for the Santee Indians, a tribe of the Dakotas who inhabited the area • 1857 (prior to statehood) from Anoka • Corn, soybeans, oats, rye, alfalfa, hogs, sheep, poultry, dairying.

ITASCA *Grand Rapids* • 43,992 • 2,665 (the third largest county in MN) • Northern MN; drained by the Mississippi River (forming part of its southwestern boundary, including Lake Winnibigoshish reservoir). The county contains part of Leech Lake Indian Reservation, a section of Bois Forte Indian Reservation, part of Chippewa National Forest, and several state parks and state forests, including George Washington State Forest in the northeast. It has many lakes, including Bowstring and Pokegama. • Named for Itasca Lake, its name coined by explorer and ethnologist Henry R. Schoolcraft, who believed it to be the true source of the Mississippi River. The lake is now in Clearwater County. • Original county; established 1849 (prior to statehood) • Hay, alfalfa, cattle, some dairying; timber; peat deposits, iron mining.

JACKSON (one of twenty-four counties so named) *Jackson* • 11,268 • 702 • Southwestern MN, bounded on the south by the IA state line; watered by the Des Moines River and headwaters of the Little Sioux River. The county includes part of Coteau des Prairies, Kilen Woods State Park, and Heron and South Heron lakes. There are numerous small lakes here, primarily near the southern boundary. • Probably named for Henry Jackson (1811–57), an early merchant in St. Paul, first postmaster and territorial legislator • 1857 (prior to statehood) from unorganized lands • Corn, oats, soybeans, alfalfa, sheep, hogs, cattle.

KANABEC *Mora* • 14,996 • 525 • Eastern MN; drained by the Snake, Knife, Ann, and Groundhouse rivers. Parts of Rum River State Forest, Mille Lacs Wildlife Area, and Snake River State Forest are located here. • Kanabec was named for the Snake River; it is the Ojibway word for "snake." • 1858 from Pine • Alfalfa, hay, oats, barley, potatoes, hogs, cattle, sheep, poultry, dairying.

KANDIYOHI *Willmar* • 41,203 • 796 • Central MN; watered by several natural lakes, notably Green Lake and Big Kandiyohi Lake; drained by the Crow River. Sibley State Park and Glacier Lakes State Trail are here. • Named for the many Kandiyohi lakes • 1858 from Meeker; annexed Monongalia in 1870 • Oats, wheat, corn, alfalfa, hay, soybeans, sugar beets, beans, peas, hogs, sheep, cattle, poultry, dairying; manufacture of children's furniture; foundries, machine shops, printing. • A two-day "Kaffee Fest" takes place in Willmar every year in June.

KITTSON *Hallock* • 5,285 • 1,097 • Extreme northwestern MN, bounded on the west by the Red River (forming the ND state line) and on the north by the Canadian province of Manitoba; drained by Two Rivers and its North, Middle and South branches. Lake Bronson State Park is on Lake Bronson reservoir. Twin Lakes Wildlife Area is also in the county. • Named for Norman W. Kittson (1814–88), fur trader, territorial legislator and mayor of St. Paul • Established as Pembina, 1862 from unorganized lands; name changed 1878 • Wheat, alfalfa, hay, flax, oats, barley, sugar beets, beans, sunflowers, sheep.

KOOCHICHING *International Falls* • 14,355 • 3,102 (the second largest county in MN) • Northern MN, bounded on the north by the Rainy River, and on the northeast by Rainy Lake, both marking the border with Ontario; drained by the Big Fork and Little Fork rivers. The county includes parts of Bois Forte and Red Lake Indian reservations. Koochiching and Pine Island state forests cover seventy-five percent of the county. It also includes Franz Jevne State Park, Smokey Bear State Forest, and part of Voyageurs National Park. • Koochiching is an Indian word for the falls of the Rainy River at International Falls • 1906 from Itasca • Alfalfa, clover, potatoes, vegetables, cattle, some dairying; timber; resort tourism; lumber and paper milling • In the winter, the county often records the daily lowest temperature among the forty-eight contiguous states.

LAC QUI PARLE *Madison* • 8,067 • 765 • Southwestern MN, bounded on the west by the SD state line and on the north and northeast by the Minnesota River (bordered by Lac qui Parle Wildlife Area); drained by the Lac qui Parle River and its West Fork, and by the Yellow Bank River. Lac qui Parle State Park, part of Big Stone National Wildlife Refuge, and Camp Release State Historical Wayside Park are found along the Minnesota River. • The name of the county is French for "talking lake," possibly for the echoes reflected from the surrounding cliffs • Organized 1862 north of the Minnesota River, disestablished in 1868, then recreated 1871 south of the river • Corn, oats, wheat, soybeans, hay, alfalfa, hogs, cattle, sheep • Madison is the Lutefisk capital of the world.

LAKE (one of twelve counties so named) *Two Harbors* • 11,058 • 2,099 (the fifth largest county in MN) • Northeastern MN, bounded on the southeast by Lake Superior and on the north by a chain of lakes along the border of the Canadian province of Ontario. The southern half of the county is drained by small streams, which feed into Lake Superior; the northern half is drained by many lakes linked by rivers. Part of Superior National Forest (including part of Boundary Waters Canoe Area Wilderness in the northern two-thirds of the county) is part of a recreational region known as "Arrowhead Country." There are several state parks on or near the shore of Lake Superior. Insula Lake and Finland state forests are found here. • Named for Lake Superior • 1856 (prior to statehood); name changed from Doty • Timber, some dairying; tourism.

LAKE OF THE WOODS *Baudette* • 4,522 • 1,297 • Northwestern MN, bounded on the northeast by the Rainy River, and on the north and northwest by Lake of the Woods, both forming the border with the Canadian province of Ontario. An exclave of the county (occupied by a unit of the Red Lake Indian Reservation) is found on the western shore of Lake of the Woods in Ontario. Part of Beltrami Island State Forest covers close to half of the county. Other units of the Red Lake Indian Reservation are in the south and west. Zippel Bay State Park is on the south shore of Lake of the Woods. • Named for the Lake of the Woods in Canada • 1922, from Beltrami; the last county formed in MN • Oats, wheat, barley, alfalfa, potatoes, flax, sunflowers; timber.

LE SUEUR *Le Center* • 25,426 • 449 • Southern MN, bounded on the west by the Minnesota River. Part of Sakatah Lake State Park is in the southeast corner. The county contains numerous small lakes, especially in the south and east. • Named for Pierre Charles Le Sueur (1657–1704), French-Canadian fur trader and explorer of the upper Mississippi River and its tributaries • 1853 (prior to statehood) from unorganized lands • Physician William James Mayo • Soybeans, alfalfa, peas, sheep, hogs, cattle, poultry, dairying; silica, sand, marble, limestone.

LINCOLN (one of twenty-four counties so named) *Ivanhoe* • 6,429 • 537 • Southwestern MN, bounded on the west by the SD state line; drained by the Lac qui Parle and Yellow Medicine rivers, and Flandreau Creek. The county includes part of Coteau des Prairie. There are several lakes spread throughout, including Lake Benton in the south and Lake Hendricks on the western boundary. Hole-in-the-Mountain ski area is also here. • One of eighteen counties named for President Abraham Lincoln • 1873 • Oats, wheat, soybeans, hay, alfalfa, sheep, hogs, cattle, poultry, dairying.

LYON (one of five counties so named) *Marshall* • 25,425 • 714 • Southwestern MN; drained by the Yellow Medicine, Cottonwood, and Redwood rivers. Camden State Park is in the southwest. • One of four counties named for General Nathaniel Lyon (1818–61), officer in the Seminole War, Mexican War and Civil War • 1868 from Yellow Medicine • Corn, oats, wheat, hay, alfalfa, soybeans, hogs, sheep, cattle, poultry, dairying, honey; education (Southwest State U.).

MAHNOMEN *Mahnomen* • 5,190 • 556 • Northwestern MN; drained by the Wild Rice and White Earth rivers. The entire county lies within White Earth Indian Reservation. Parts of White Earth State Forest are here. • Mahnomen is an Ojibway word for the wild rice that grows in the area. • 1906 from Norman • Wheat, hay, alfalfa, oats, barley, sunflowers, wild rice.

MARSHALL (one of twelve counties so named) *Warren* • 10,155 • 1,772 • Northwestern MN, bounded on the west by the Red River of the North (forming the ND state line); drained by the Snake, Thief, Tamarac, and Middle rivers. The county includes Agassiz National Wildlife Refuge (surrounding Mud Lake reservoir), and Old Mill State Park. • Named for General William R. Marshall (1825–96), Union officer in the Civil War and governor of MN • 1879 from Kittson • Wheat, oats, flax, hay, alfalfa, sugar beets, beans, sunflowers, potatoes.

MARTIN (one of six counties so named) *Fairmont* • 21,802 • 709 • Southern MN, bounded on the south by the IA state line; watered by numerous lakes, and Elm Creek. • Named for either Morgan L. Martin (1805–87), U.S. representative from WI Territory who introduced the bill for the organization of the Territory of MN; or for Henry Martin (1829–1908), CT speculator with large holdings in the area • 1857 (prior to statehood) from Faribault • Vice President Walter Mondale • Corn, oats, soybeans, alfalfa, hogs, sheep, cattle.

MCLEOD *Glencoe* • 34,898 • 492 • South-central MN; watered by the South Fork of the Crow River and Buffalo Creek. The county has many small lakes. • Named for Martin McLeod (1813–60), fur trader, and a president of the MN territorial legislature. • 1856 (prior to statehood) from Carver • Corn, oats, wheat, hay, alfalfa, soybeans, peas, hogs, cattle, poultry, dairying.

MEEKER *Litchfield* • 22,644 • 609 • South-central MN; drained by the North and South forks of the Crow River. There are numerous small lakes in the county. Washington Lake is in the southeast. Lake Koronis is on the northern boundary. • Named for Bradley B. Meeker (1813–73), associate justice of the MN Territory Supreme Court • 1856 (prior to statehood) from Wright • Corn, oats, barley, wheat, hay, alfalfa, soybeans, beans, peas, sheep, hogs, cattle, poultry dairying.

MILLE LACS *Milaca* • 22,330 • 574 • East-central MN; drained by the Rum River. The southern half of Mille Lacs Lake is in the north, with Mille Lacs National Wildlife Refuge and Father Hennepin and Mille Lacs Kathio state parks on its southern shore. Mille Lacs Indian Reservation is in the northwest corner of the county. It also includes parts of Rum River State Forest. • Named for Mille Lacs Lake • 1857 (prior to statehood) from Kanabec • Alfalfa, hay, corn, oats, barley, rye, hogs, cattle, poultry, dairying; timber; peat; sand and gravel.

MORRISON *Little Falls* • 31,712 • 1,125 • Central MN, bounded on the northwest by the Crow Wing River; bisected by the Mississippi River. There are numerous small lakes in the northwest, including Lake Alexander. The county also contains Camp Ripley Military Reservation. Crane Meadow National Wildlife Refuge is near Little Falls. • Named for the Morrison brothers: William (1785–1866), fur trader and explorer; and Allen (1803–77), fur trader and representative in the first territorial legislature • 1856 (prior to statehood) from Benton and Stearns • Aviator Charles A. Lindbergh (house state park) • Alfalfa, hay, potatoes, corn, oats, barley, rye, sunflowers, beans, sheep, hogs, cattle, poultry, dairying; timber; deposits of marl and peat.

MOWER *Austin* • 38,603 • 712 • Southeastern MN, bounded on the south by the IA state line; drained by the Cedar River and headwaters of the Root and Little Cedar rivers. Lake Louise State Park is here. • Named for John E. Mower (1815–79), MN territorial and state legislator • 1855 (prior to statehood) from Fillmore • Poet Richard Eberhart • Meat processing important; also hay, soybeans, corn, oats, peas, alfalfa, sheep, hogs, cattle, poultry, dairying; limestone; manufacture of metal containers, paper boxes • Austin is the home of the Hormel Institute, a unit of the graduate school of the University of Minnesota, where research is conducted on fats and oils, and their connection to heart disease. The county has several agricultural shows each year.

MURRAY (one of three counties so named) *Slayton* • 9,165 • 704 • Southwestern MN; drained by the Des Moines river, which forms Lake Shetek in the north, with Shetek State Park on its southeastern shore. The county has several lakes. • Named for William P. Murray (1825–1910), MN legislator • 1857 from Lyon • Corn, oats, alfalfa, soybeans, hogs, sheep, cattle, poultry, dairying • The End-O-Line Railroad Park and Museum, first developed as a local 4-H project, features an authentically restored depot and other historic buildings.

NICOLLET *Saint Peter* • 29,771 • 452 • Southern MN, bounded on the southwest and east by the Minnesota River. Swan and Middle lakes are near the center of the county. Part of Fort Ridgely State Memorial Park is in the extreme northwest. • Named for Joseph N. Nicollet (1786–1843), French explorer of the upper Midwest • 1853 (prior to statehood) from unorganized lands • Corn, oats, alfalfa, hay, soybeans, peas, hogs, sheep, cattle, poultry, dairying • A proposal to move MN's capital from Saint Paul to Saint Peter when the territory entered the union in 1858 failed, leaving the town of Saint Peter with the prematurely erected "Old State Capitol Building."

NOBLES *Worthington* • 20,832 • 715 • Southwestern MN, bounded on the south by the IA state line; drained by the West Branch of the Little Rock River. The county includes part of Coteau des Prairies. There are several small natural glacially formed lakes including Ocheda, Okabena, and West and East Graham. • Named for William H. Nobles (1816–76), explorer who discovered Nobles Pass through the Rocky Mountains • 1857 (prior to statehood) from Jackson • Corn, oats, soybeans, alfalfa, hogs, sheep, cattle, poultry, dairying.

NORMAN *Ada* • 7,442 • 876 • Northwestern MN, bounded on the west by the Red River of the North (forming the ND state line); drained by the Wild Rice River. • Possibly named for the many Norwegians living in the area • 1881 from Polk • Wheat, oats, barley, sugar beets, beans, sunflowers, soybeans, potatoes, alfalfa, hay.

OLMSTED *Rochester* • 124,277 • 653 • Southeastern MN; drained by the Root River and the South and Middle forks of the Zumbro River. Part of Whitewater State Park is in the northeast corner; part of Richard J. Dorer Memorial Hardwood State Forest is in the south. Douglas State Trail is also here. • Probably named for David Olmsted (1822–61), president of the upper house of MN's first territorial legislature and first mayor of St. Paul • 1855 (prior to statehood) from unorganized lands • Mail order merchant R.W. Sears; chemical manufacturer Herbert H. Dow. Baseball team owner Walter O'Malley died here. • Corn, oats, soybeans, peas, hay, alfalfa, sheep, hogs, cattle, poultry, dairying; manufacture of computers, tractor cabs, medical instruments, electronic, business and recording equipment; food processing. Rochester, home of the Mayo Clinic, established by William W. and his two sons William and Charles in 1889, is a major medical center.

OTTER TAIL *Fergus Falls* • 57,159 • 1,980 • Western MN; drained by the Pelican, Pomme de Terre, and Otter Tail rivers. Numerous lakes are here, chief among them Lake Lida, Dead Lake, and Otter Tail Lake. The county includes Inspiration Peak State Wayside, and Maplewood and Glendalough state parks. • Named for Otter Tail lake and river • 1858 from Pembina and Cass • Alfalfa, hay, wheat, corn, oats, barley, soybeans, sugar beets, beans, sunflowers, hogs, sheep, cattle, poultry, dairying; flour mills, cooperative creamery, meat packing; garment manufacturing • Fergus Falls is the council headquarters of the Church of the Lutheran Brethren and the site of a Lutheran seminary.

PENNINGTON (one of two counties so named, the other in SD) *Thief River Falls* • 13,584 • 617 • Northwestern MN; drained by the Red Lake and Thief rivers. • Named for Edmund Pennington (1848–1926), president of the Saint Paul and Sault Sainte Marie Railroad • 1910 from Red Lake • Wheat, hay, alfalfa, oats, barley, sunflowers, dairying, poultry, sheep.

PINE *Pine City* • 26,530 • 1,411 • Eastern MN, bounded on the east by the WI state line and on the southeast by the St. Croix River (forming the WI state line); drained by the Kettle River. Part of St. Croix National Scenic Riverway follows the St. Croix River in the southeast. The county has several small natural lakes. It also includes Hinckley Fire Monument and Historic Site, and Banning and St. Croix state parks. The county is shaded by several state forests. Willard Munger State Trail is in the west. • Possibly named for the pine forests that were extensive here when the county was created • 1856 (prior to statehood) from unorganized lands; annexed Buchanan County in 1861 • Alfalfa, hay, oats, cattle, sheep, dairying, poultry; timber; sandstone quarries.

PIPESTONE *Pipestone* • 9,895 • 466 • Southwestern MN, bounded on the west by the SD state line; drained by the Rock River. Split Rock Creek State Park is here. The county includes part of Coteau des Prairies. • Named for the red stone (catlinite) quarried by local Indians • Established mistakenly as Rock in 1857 (prior to statehood) from Murray; name changed 1862 • Hogs, sheep, cattle, poultry, dairying, corn, oats • Pipestone's concrete water tower, built in 1920, is one of only two such towers in the U.S. designed by L. P. Wolff still standing. Pipestone, reddish-colored stone used by Plains Indians in the area to make ceremonial peace pipes, is called catlinite in honor of the artist George Catlin, among the first white men to visit the quarries. The stone in Pipestone National Monument is reserved for Indians who quarry it under special permits issued by the National Park Service. Longfellow popularized the quarries in "The Song of Hiawatha."

POLK (one of twelve counties so named) *Crookston* • 31,369 • 1,970 • Northwestern MN, bounded on the west by the Red River of the North (forming the ND state line); drained by the Poplar, Sand Hill and Red Lake rivers. Rydell National Wildlife Refuge is centrally located. • One of eleven counties named for President James K. Polk • 1858 from Indian lands • East Grand Forks was devastated by floodwaters from the Red River in the spring of 1997, forcing massive evacuation of residents. • Wheat, hay, alfalfa, oats, barley, sugar beets, soybeans, beans, sunflowers, potatoes, cattle, poultry, sheep, hogs, dairying; manufacture of fertilizer, sashes and doors; education (U. of MN-Crookston).

POPE (one of three counties so named) *Glenwood* • 11,236 • 670 • Western MN; drained by the Chippewa, Little Chippewa, and East Chippewa rivers; watered by several small lakes, with larger Lake Minnewaska in the center of the county. Glacial Lakes State Park is also in the county. • Named for General John Pope (1822–1892), explorer and career army officer in the Mexican War and the Civil War • 1862 from Pierce County, which was abolished the same year • Wheat, corn, oats, barley, alfalfa, hay, soybeans, beans, honey, sheep, hogs, cattle, poultry, dairying.

RAMSEY *Saint Paul* • 511,035 (the second most populated county in MN) • 156 (the smallest county in MN) • Eastern MN; crossed in the south by the Mississippi River which forms part of its southern and western boundaries. The county is urbanized as part of the Minneapolis–St. Paul metropolitan area. It has numerous small lakes, especially in the north. White Bear Lake is on the eastern boundary. Bald Eagle Lake is on the northern boundary. • One of two counties (the other in

ND) named for Alexander Ramsey (1815–1903), first MN territorial governor, state governor, U.S. senator, and U.S. secretary of war • Original county; established 1849 (prior to statehood) • Originally named Pig's Eye for the French Canadian trader who founded the settlement in 1840, St. Paul has been the capital of MN since 1849, serving as center of government for both the territory and state. • Novelist and short story writers F. Scott Fitzgerald and Kay Boyle; Chief Justice of the U.S. Warren E. Burger; biochemist Melvin Calvin; sculptor Paul Manship; author and feminist Kate Millett; railroad builder and financier James J. Hill; publisher De Witt Wallace • Manufacture of electronics, machinery, automobiles, cosmetics, fabricated metals, wood products, plastics, transportation equipment, sailboats; printing; government operations; truck farming; education (Metro State U.; Bethel College; Hamline U.; U. of St. Thomas; Concordia U.; Macalester College; College of St. Catherine) • Seven Fortune 1000 companies have their corporate headquarters in the county. Cellophane transparent tape was invented and patented by Richard Gurley Drew in St. Paul. The Minnesota Manufacturing and Mining Co. began producing the tape in 1930. Built in 1915, the Cathedral of St. Paul was modeled after St. Peter's in Rome. Ice-fishing contests are held at White Bear Lake as part of the St. Paul Winter Carnival. The *St. Paul Pioneer Press* is the oldest newspaper in the state. St. Paul has the nation's longest skyway system of pedestrian bridges linking its many downtown buildings. The Minnesota State Fair takes place each year at the State Fairgrounds here. St. Paul is home to the Minnesota Wild (Xcel Energy Center).

RED LAKE *Red Lake Falls* • 4,299 • 432 • Northwestern MN; drained by the Red Lake, Poplar, and Clearwater rivers. Old Crossing Treaty State Historic Wayside Park is on the Red Lake River in the west. • Named for the Red Lake River • 1896 from Polk • Wheat, hay, alfalfa, oats, barley, sugar beets, sunflowers, potatoes, cattle.

REDWOOD *Redwood Falls* • 16,815 • 880 • Southwestern MN, bounded on the northeast by the Minnesota River; drained by the Redwood and Cottonwood rivers. Lower Sioux Indian Reservation is located along the Minnesota River. • Named for the Redwood River • 1862 from Brown • Corn, oats, wheat, soybeans, alfalfa, sugar beets, peas, sheep, hogs, cattle, poultry, dairying • The Laura Ingalls Wilder Museum is located in Walnut Grove.

RENVILLE (one of two counties so named, the other in ND) • *Olivia* • 17,154 • 983 • Southern MN, bounded on the southwest by the Minnesota River. The county includes part of Fort Ridgely State Memorial Park, Birch Coulee Battlefield, and Joseph R. Brown State Historical Wayside Park, all located along the Minnesota River. • Named for Joseph Renville (?–1846), captain in the British Army during the War of 1812, assistant to missionaries to the Sioux, and participant in the translation of the Bible into Sioux. • 1855 (prior to statehood) from unorganized lands • Oats, corn, wheat, hay, alfalfa, soybeans, beans, sugar beets, peas, hogs, cattle, poultry, sheep, dairying; sand and gravel.

RICE (one of two counties so named, the other in KS) *Faribault* • 56,665 • 498 • Southeastern MN; drained by the Cannon and Straight rivers. Nerstrand Big Woods and part of Sakatah Lake state parks are here. • Named for Henry M. Rice (1816–94), MN territorial delegate to Congress and one of MN's first two U.S. senators • 1853 (prior to statehood) from Nobles • Alfalfa, hay, soybeans, corn, oats, sheep, cattle, hogs, poultry (especially frozen turkeys), dairying, garden nurseries, peonies, chrysanthemums, blue cheese (cured in caves along the Straight River); manufacture of heating and air-conditioning equipment, automatic ice-cube makers, plastics, precision office machines, computer parts, amusement park equipment. Several state schools are in Faribault, including those serving the blind, deaf, and mentally and physically challenged. Institutions of higher education include Carlton College and St. Olaf College.

ROCK (one of three counties so named) *Luverne* • 9,721 • 483 • Extreme southwestern MN, bounded on the west by the SD state line and on the south by the IA state line; drained by the Rock River. Blue Mounds State Park is here. • Named for the outcrop of quartzite called "the Mound" near Luverne. • In 1857, the southwestern-most county of the state was named Pipestone and the county adjacent to the north was named Rock. When legislators discovered in 1862 that the mound for which Rock had been named was actually in Pipestone, the names of the two counties were switched. In 1866, when legislators attempted another name change, from Rock to Lincoln, frustrated residents ignored the act. • Corn, oats, hay, alfalfa, soybeans, hogs, cattle, sheep, poultry, dairying.

ROSEAU *Roseau* • 16,338 • 1,663 • Northwestern MN, bounded on the northeast by Muskeg Bay of Lake of the Woods and on the north by the Canadian province of Manitoba; drained by the Roseau River and its North and South forks. The county includes Hayes Lake State Park, part of Beltrami Island and Lost River state forests, and Roseau River Wildlife Area. • Named for Roseau lake and river • 1894 from Kittson • Wheat, hay, flax, barley, oats, alfalfa, sunflowers, cattle, sheep, poultry, dairying; timber; peat deposits.

SAINT LOUIS (one of two counties so named, the other in MO) *Duluth* • 200,528 • 6,226 (the largest county in MN and the thirty-sixth largest county in the U.S.) • Northeastern MN, bounded on the north by the Canadian province of Ontario (the border formed largely by the international lakes Rainy, Namakan, Loon, Lac La Croix, and Crooked), and on the southeast by Lake Superior; drained by the St. Louis, Little Fork, Whiteface, Vermilion, and numerous other rivers. The county has many lakes and reservoirs, especially in the north, including Pelican, Kabetogama, Vermilion, Trout, and Burntside. Much of the northern half of the county is covered by forest; parts of Superior National Forest (its headquarters in Duluth), and Kabetogama, Lake Jeanette, Burntside, Bear Island, and Sturgeon River state forests are here. Cloquet Valley, Whiteface River, and part of Savanna and Fond Du Lac state forests are in the south. Part of Fond du Lac and Bois Forte Indian reservations extend into the county. Most of Voyageurs National Park is in the northwest corner. Bear Head Lake and McCarthy Beach state parks are also in the county. Duluth was built on a steep slope that rises about 800 feet above the shore of Lake Superior. • Named for the St. Louis River • Established 1855 (prior to statehood) as Superior County from Lake County (then called Doty). Name changed the same year. • The area was originally occupied by Ojibway Indians. It was visited in the 1600s by French voyageurs. The fur-trading post of Fond du Lac (in what is now western Duluth) was controlled by the Hudson's Bay Company in 1692, by the North West Company in 1793, and by the American Fur Company (run by John Jacob Astor) from 1817 until 1854. • Singer and composer Bob Dylan; labor union official Ralph Helstein; professional baseball player Roger Maris • There are productive mines in the Vermilion Iron Range in the northeast and the Mesabi Iron Range extending east to west through the central part of the state. Eveleth's taconite mines produce much of the nation's ore. Also, potatoes, hay, oats, dairying, poultry; timber; food processing; manufacture of underwear; machine shops; paper mills; printing and publishing; tourism (fishing, hunting, skiiing); education (College of St. Scholastica; U. of MN—Duluth) • Duluth, MN—Superior, WI is the busiest freshwater port in North America, and the farthest inland ocean port in the U.S. The combined harbor is the western terminus of the St. Lawrence Seaway. It ranks second only to New York City among U.S. ports in tonnage handled. The U.S. Hockey Hall of Fame is in Eveleth. Nearby, the Leonidas Mine is, at a depth of 650 feet, one of the world's deepest underground iron mines. The world's largest open-pit iron mine, the now exhausted Hull-Rust-Mahoning Mine, at Hibbing, is 535 feet deep, nearly five miles across, and up to one mile wide. The original Northland-Greyhound bus line was established near Hibbing in 1925 as a commuter service between old and new Hibbing. The Minnesota Museum of Mining is a few miles north.

SCOTT (one of eleven counties so named) *Shakopee* • 89,498 (54.7% increase since 1990; the fastest growing county in MN) • 357 • Southeast-central MN, bounded on the north and west by the Minnesota River. The county lies on the southwest fringe of the Minneapolis-St. Paul metropolitan area. Minnesota Valley State Recreation Area and Trail are here, as is Shakopee Mdewakanton Sioux Indian Community. The county also includes Minnesota Valley National Wildlife Refuge, which extends along the river There are several small lakes in the county. • One of five counties named for Gen. Winfield Scott (1786–1866), officer in the War of 1812 and the Mexican War; general-in-chief of the U.S. Army and commander of the Union armies at the beginning of the Civil War • 1853 (prior to statehood) from Dakota • Hay, corn, soybeans, oats, alfalfa, hogs, cattle, poultry, dairying; limestone, sand and gravel.

SHERBURNE *Elk River* • 64,417 (53.6% increase since 1990; the second fastest growing county in MN) • 437 • Central MN, bounded on the west and south by the Mississippi River; drained by the Elk River. Sherburne National Wildlife Refuge and Sand Dunes State Forest are in the county. • Named for Moses Sherburne (1808–68), associate justice of the MN Territory Supreme Court and active in the formation of the state • 1856 (prior to statehood) from Anoka • Corn, oats, rye, alfalfa, potatoes, soybeans, hogs; sand and gravel.

SIBLEY *Gaylord* • 15,356 • 589 • Southern MN, bounded on the east by the Minnesota River; drained by the Rush River and High Island Creek. There are several small lakes in the county, especially in the north-center and northeast. Rush River State Wayside is also here. • Named for Henry H. Sibley (1811–1891), first governor of MN • 1853 (prior to statehood) from unorganized lands • Corn, oats, wheat, soybeans, hay, alfalfa, sugar beets, peas, sheep, hogs, cattle, poultry, dairying.

STEARNS *Saint Cloud* • 133,166 • 1,345 • Central MN, bounded on the east by the Missisippi River and on the southeast by the Clearwater River; watered by the Sauk River. The county has numerous small lakes, especially in the south. Part of Birch Lakes State Forest is in the county. Powder Ridge ski area is also here. • Named for Charles T. Stearns (1807–98), territorial legislator and hotelier • 1855 (prior to statehood) from unorganized lands • Before the first railroad reached St. Cloud in 1866, it was a terminus of the Hudson's Bay Company; furs were brought down from the Red River valley in wooden oxcarts. During the Sioux uprising of 1862, the settlement was a refuge for frightened settlers. • Novelist Sinclair Lewis's boyhood home, Sauk Centre, was the model for the town of Gopher Prairie in his 1920 novel *Main Street*, as well as the setting for other Lewis novels. • Corn, oats, barley, wheat, rye, alfalfa, hay, soybeans, beans, sheep, hogs, cattle, poultry, mink, dairying; colored granite; railroad shops; manufacture of refrigerating equipment, paper and paper products, iron and brass products, optical goods; education (St. Cloud State U.; St. John's U.).

STEELE *Owatonna* • 33,680 • 430 • Southeastern MN; drained by the Straight River. Rice Lake State Park is on the eastern border. • Named for Franklin Steele (1813–80), lumberman, landowner, and member of the first board of regents of the University of Minnesota • 1855 (prior to statehood) from unorganized territory • Corn, oats, alfalfa, hay, soybeans, peas, hogs, sheep, cattle, poultry, dairying (cooperative creameries with high butter production); manufacture of jewelry, tools, farm equipment. • Owatonna was the site of MN's only state orphanage (1886–1945), as well as the state's first known health spa, now in Mineral Springs Park. Architect Louis Sullivan designed Owatonna's National Farmers' Bank Building in 1908.

STEVENS (one of three counties so named) *Morris* • 10,053 • 562 • Western MN; drained by the Pomme de Terre and Chippewa rivers. Several small lakes are scattered throughout the county. • One of two counties (the other in WA) named for Gen. Isaac I. Stevens (1818–62), an officer in the Mexican War and the Civil War, and first governor of WA Territory. The MN legislature had intended to honor Stevens with a county in 1855; through a clerical error the name of the first county was accidentally changed to Stearns and left to stand. This county represented legislative amends. • 1862 from Pierce, which was abolished the same year • Wheat, corn, oats, barley, soybeans, alfalfa, beans, sunflowers, hogs, sheep, cattle; education (U. of MN — Morris).

SWIFT *Benson* • 11,956 • 744 • Western MN, bounded in the southwest corner by the Minnesota River (its dam forming Marsh Lake reservoir); drained by the Pomme de Terre and Chippewa rivers. The county lies partially in the Lac qui Parle Wildlife Area. Monson Lake State Park is here. Swift has small natural lakes in the far west and northeast. • Named for Henry A. Swift (1823–69), president of the MN senate and governor of the state • 1870 from Chippewa • Wheat, corn, oats, alfalfa, hay, soybeans, sugar beets, beans, sheep, hogs, cattle, poultry, dairying.

TODD (one of three counties so named) *Long Prairie* • 24,426 • 942 • Central MN, bounded on the northeast by the Crow Wing River; watered by the Long Prairie River. The county has numerous small lakes, including Sauk and Big Birch, in the south and east. Part of Lake Osakis is on the western border. • One of two counties (the other in SD) named for John B. S. Todd (1814–72), army officer in the Seminole Wars, the Mexican War, and the Civil War; delegate to Congress for Dakota, and Dakota Territory legislator • 1855 (prior to statehood) from Stearns • Brans, potatoes, hay, alfalfa, oats, barley, hogs, cattle, poultry, dairying; deposits of marl and peat.

TRAVERSE *Wheaton* • 4,134 (the least populated county in MN) • 574 • Western MN, bounded on the west by the Bois de Sioux River (forming the SD and ND state lines and Lake

Traverse and Mud Lake reservoirs); watered by the Mustinka River and its West Branch. • Named for Lake Traverse • 1862 from Wilkin (then called Toombs) • Alfalfa, wheat, corn, oats, barley, soybeans, sugar beets, beans, sunflowers, hogs, sheep.

WABASHA *Wabasha* • 21,610 • 525 • Southeastern MN, bounded on the east by the Mississippi River (forming the WI state line); drained by the Zumbro River. Lock and Dam No. 4 is on the Mississippi River, below Lake Pepin. The Upper Mississippi River National Wildlife and Fish Refuge extends along the river. The county includes Carley State Park, and part of Whitewater Wildlife Area. Part of Richard J. Dorer Memorial Hardwood State Forest is in the south. • Named for the town of Wabasha • Original county; established 1849 (prior to statehood); originally spelled Wabashaw • Hay, alfalfa, corn, oats, barley, soybeans, peas, apples, sheep, hogs, cattle, poultry, dairying.

WADENA *Wadena* • 13,713 • 535 • Central MN; drained by the Leaf, Redeye, and Crow Wing rivers (the last forming part of the southeastern boundary). The county has several small lakes, especially in the north, and includes Lyons and Huntersville state forests. • Named for the Wadena trading post • 1858 from Cass and Todd • Hay, alfalfa, oats, barley, rye, beans, sheep, cattle, poultry, dairying; peat deposits.

WASECA *Waseca* • 19,526 • 423 • Southern MN; drained by the Le Sueur and Little Cobb rivers. Lake Elysian is in the northwest. • Waseca is a Dakota word meaning "fertile" • 1857 (prior to statehood) from Steele • Soybeans, alfalfa, corn, oats, sheep, hogs, cattle, poultry, dairying.

WASHINGTON *Stillwater* • 201,130 (the fifth most populated county in MN) • 392 • Eastern MN, bounded on the south by the Mississippi River (Lock and Dam No. 2 forming Spring Lake) and on the east by the St. Croix River (which forms Lake St. Croix and the WI state line). A fossilized face of sandstone is exposed alongside the St. Croix National Scenic Riverway. The county also includes Afton and William O'Brien state parks, as well as numerous small glacial lakes. • One of thirty-one counties named for President George Washington • Original county; established 1849 (prior to statehood) • Stillwater was the site of an August 26, 1848 convention that undertook the organization of MN Territory. It was also the first town site in the state. The Minnesota State Prison was established in Stillwater in 1851. The county was a large lumbering center in the mid-19th century. • Hay, corn, soybeans, oats, alfalfa, cattle, sheep; food processing; manufacture of reflector products, precision parts for aircraft, metal products, shoes, ventilating fans, boats, electronic goods.

WATONWAN *Saint James* • 11,876 • 435 • Southern MN; drained by the Watonwan River and its South Fork. • Named for the Watonwan Township, Blue Earth County, MN • 1860 from Brown • Soybeans, alfalfa, corn, oats, hogs, cattle, sheep, poultry.

WILKIN *Breckenridge* • 7,138 • 751 • Western MN, bounded on the west by the Bois de Sioux and Red River of the North (both forming the ND state line); drained by the Otter Tail and Rabbit rivers. Rothsay Wildlife Area is in the northeast. • Named for Col. Alexander Wilkin (1820–64), an officer in the Union army killed at the Battle of Tupelo. • 1858 from Cass; name changed from Toombs County to Andy Johnson County in 1863, and Andy Johnson to its present name in 1868 • The county was originally named for Robert Toombs, U.S. senator from GA who angered local residents by becoming the Confederate secretary of state. The name was changed to honor the seventeeth U.S. president, Andrew Johnson, who then angered some residents by his subsequent political stands. • Wheat, alfalfa, soybeans, corn, oats, barley, sugar beets, beans, sunflowers, hogs.

WINONA *Winona* • 49,985 • 626 • Southeastern MN, bounded on the east and northeast by the Mississippi river, forming the WI state line. Upper Mississippi River National Wildlife and Fish Refuge extends along the river in the northeast. Parts of Richard J. Dorer Memorial Hardwood State Forest are found throughout the county, which also includes John A. Latsch and Great River Bluffs state parks, parts of Whitewater State Park, and Whitewater Wildlife Area. Locks and dams Nos. 5, 5A, 6 and 7 are on the Mississippi River. • Named for the town that became the county seat • 1854 (prior to statehood) from unorganized lands • Hay, soybeans, corn, oats, barley, alfalfa, sheep, hogs, cattle, poultry, dairying; food processing; brick manufacturing; limestone quarrying; education (Winona State U.; St. Mary's U.) • Downtown Winona displays a life-size statue of the legendary Indian maiden by this name, popularized by several 19th century writers.

WRIGHT (one of three counties so named) *Buffalo* • 89,986 • 661 • South-central MN, bounded on the north by the Mississippi River, and on the northwest by the Clearwater River (forming Clearwater Lake reservoir); drained by the Crow River (forming the county's southeast border) and its north fork. Numerous small natural lakes are scattered throughout the county, including Pelican Lake. Lake Maria State Park is also here. • Named for Silas Wright (1795–1847), NY governor and friend of a member of the county organization committee • 1855 (prior to statehood) • Alfalfa, hay, corn, oats, barley, soybeans, sheep, hogs, cattle, poultry, dairying.

YELLOW MEDICINE *Granite Falls* • 11,080 • 758 • Southwestern MN, bounded on the west by the SD state line and on the northeast by the Minnesota River; drained by the Lac qui Parle and Yellow Medicine rivers. Upper

Sioux Agency State Park, and Upper Sioux Indian Reservation are located along the Minnesota River. • Named for the Yellow Medicine River • 1871 from Redwood • Corn, oats, wheat, soybeans, alfalfa, sugar beets, hogs, cattle, sheep; granite.

MISSISSIPPI

By Valor and Arms

Each of Mississippi's eighty-two counties is made up of five districts. An elected member from each district serves on the board of supervisors for each county. The county is the chief unit of local government in the state.

ADAMS (one of twelve counties so named) *Natchez* • 34,340 • 460 • Southwestern MS, bounded on the west by the Mississippi River (forming the LA state line), and on the south by the Homochitto River; drained by St. Catherine Creek. The county includes part of Homochitto National Forest and St. Catherine Creek National Wildlife Refuge. Natchez State Park is in the northeast. Natchez Trace National Parkway from Nashville terminates in Natchez; the city includes Natchez National Historical Park and Natchez National Cemetery. • One of eight counties named for President John Adams • 1799 (prior to statehood) from Natchez District • Five flags have flown over the city of Natchez. Passing from France to England in 1763, it was a haven for Loyalists during the American Revolution. It was captured by a Spanish expedition under Bernardo de Gálvez in 1779, and remained under Spanish dominion until 1798 when the U.S. took possession. The steamboat era, beginning in 1811, made Natchez a wealthy city, and one of the world's most successful cotton ports. It served as capital of MS Territory from 1798 to 1802 and of the state of MS from 1817 to 1821. Jefferson Davis attended historic Jefferson College in Washington; it was also here that Aaron Burr was given a preliminary trial for treason in 1807 and the state's first constitution convention was held on March 1, 1817. Natchez was occupied by the Union army in July 1863. • Novelist and short story writer Richard Wright • Cotton, corn, soybeans; timber; oil and natural gas, clay, limestone; manufacture of rubber, wood, and paper products, and textiles • Natchez retains its Old South ambience, especially through annual "pilgrimage" tours of many of its antebellum homes.

ALCORN *Corinth* • 34,558 • 400 (the smallest county in MS) • Northeastern MS, bounded on the north by the TN state line; drained by the Hatchie and Tuscumbia rivers • Named for James L. Alcorn (1816–94), governor of MS and U.S. senator from the state • 1870 from Tippah, Tishomingo, and Wilkinson • An early strategic railroad center, Corinth was the scene of a Civil War battle (October 3–4, 1862) in which General W.S. Rosecrans' Union troops repulsed E. Van Dorn's Confederates. (Approximately 6,000 Union soldiers are buried in the Corinth National Cemetery.) One of the fiercest and bloodiest battles in the war, it marked the beginning of the end of the War in the West. Corinth was a marriage capital from the 1930s through the 1950s. From the 1940s to the 1960s, the city was a hide-away for several Chicago mob affiliates, a group from AL called the "State line Mob." • Pole-vaulter Earle Meadows • Corn, cotton, dairying, soybeans, cattle, hogs; lumbering; light manufactures, including electrical motors, plastics, chemicals, textiles; farm-products processing.

AMITE *Liberty* • 13,599 • 730 • Southwestern MS, bounded on the south by the LA state line and on the northwest by the Homochitto River; drained by the East and West forks of the Amite River (which join just south of the state line). The county includes part of Homochitto National Forest in the northwest and Percy Quin State Park. • Named for the Amite River • 1809 (prior to statehood) from Wilkinson • Cotton, corn, cattle, catfish, dairying; timber; light manufacturing.

ATTALA *Kosciusko* • 19,661 • 735 • Central MS, bounded on the west by the Big Black River; intersected by the Yockanookany River and Lobutcha Creek. Natchez Trace National Parkway crosses the county north-south. • Named for Atala, the fictional American Indian heroine from the pen of Francois Rene, Vicomte de Chateaubriand. (The difference in spelling is due to clerical error.) • 1833 from Choctaw cession • Television personality Oprah Winfrey • Corn, cotton, hay, soybeans, cattle; timber; light manufacturing, including paper products and textiles.

BENTON (one of nine counties so named) *Ashland* • 8,026 • 407 • Northern MS, bounded on the north by the TN state line; drained by the Wolf River and Tippah Creek. Holly Springs National Forest covers about two-thirds of the county. • Named for Samuel Benton (1820–1864), MS state legislator and Confederate officer killed in the Battle of Atlanta • 1870 from Marshall and Tippah • Cotton, corn, hay, sweet potatoes, soybeans, cattle; timber; manufacture of bulletin boards, auto parts, furniture and wood products.

BOLIVAR *Cleveland and Rosedale* • 40,633 • 876 (the second largest county in MS) • Western MS, bounded on the west by the Mississippi River (forming the AR state line); drained by the Big Sunflower River. Great River Road State Park is in the west. Bolivar County State Fishing Lake is in the center of the county. Lakes Beulah and Whittington, oxbow lakes of the Mississippi River form part of the state line. Dahomey National Wildlife Refuge is in the county. • Named for Simon Bolivar (1783–1830), Venezuelan leader of the South American revolt against Spanish rule; known as "the liberator" and "George Washington of South America." • 1836 from Choctaw cession • Soybeans, cotton, corn, wheat, sorghum, rice, alfalfa, cattle; timber; manufacture of ceramic tile, pharmaceuticals, automobile trim, and tool and die products; education (Delta State U.).

CALHOUN *Pittsboro* • 15,069 • 587 • North-central MS; drained by the Skuna and Yalobusha rivers. • One of eleven counties named for John C. Calhoun (1782–1850), U.S. statesman and champion of Southern causes • 1852 from Chickasaw, Lafayette, and Yalobusha • Cotton, corn, sorghum, soybeans, cattle; timber; bauxite, lignite, clay deposits; manufacture of apparel, wood products, leather, furniture, machinery, concrete.

CARROLL (one of thirteen counties so named) *Carrollton and Vaiden* • 10,769 • 628 • Central MS; drained by the Big Black and Yalobusha rivers. • One of twelve counties named for Charles Carroll (1737–1832), signer of the Declaration of Independence, U.S. senator from MD, and founder of the B and O Railroad • 1833 from Choctaw cession • Soybeans, cotton, corn, wheat, other grains, cattle; timber.

CHICKASAW *Houston and Okolona* • 19,440 • 502 • Northeast-central MS; drained by the Yalobusha River and Chookatonchee Creek. The Natchez Trace National Parkway passes north-south through the center of the county. Part of Tombigbee National Forest is in the north, and includes Owl Creek Indian Mounds. • One of two counties (the other in IA) named for the Chickasaw Indians • 1836 from Chickasaw cession of 1832 • Cotton, corn, soybeans, wheat, cattle, dairying; timber; clay deposits; manufacture of furniture, fiber optics, apparel, cotton batting, paper products, carpet padding, lumber.

CHOCTAW *Ackerman* • 9,758 • 419 • Central MS, bounded on the north in part by the Big Black River; drained by the Noxubee and Yockanookany rivers (the source of both here). Natchez Trace National Parkway crosses the county. Part of Tombigbee National Forest is in the southeast. • One of three counties named for the Choctaw Indians • 1833 from the Chickasaw cession of 1832 • Cotton, corn, lespedeza, sweet potatoes, cattle; timber; manufacture of shirts and sportswear, wood chips, industrial flanges, lumber.

CLAIBORNE *Port Gibson* • 11,831 • 487 • Southwestern MS, bounded largely on the west by the Mississippi River (forming the LA state line) and on the north by the Big Black River; drained by Bayou Pierre. The state line extends west of the Mississippi River to Yocatan Lake, an oxbow lake and former river channel. Grand Gulf Military Park on the Mississippi

River occupies the townsite of the former Grand Gulf where the Confederate forts of Cobun and Wade once stood; it was the scene of several Civil War engagements. • One of three counties named for William C. C. Claiborne (1775–1817), governor of MS Territory and the first governor of LA • 1802 (prior to statehood) from Jefferson • The presence of many antebellum buildings in Port Gibson is owed to Gen. Ulysses S. Grant's remark that the town was "too beautiful to burn," this delivered on his march to Vicksburg after victory at the Battle of Port Gibson on May 1, 1863 at nearby Magnolia Church. • Cotton, corn, soybeans, cattle; timber; manufacture of cable assemblies, paper products, plastic products, lumber, cottonseed oil; education (Alcorn U.) • Twenty-two Gothic columns are all that remain of Windsor, considered to be MS's most extravagant Greek Revival mansion, completed in 1860, and burned down in 1890.

CLARKE (one of five counties so named) *Quitman* • 17,955 • 691 • Eastern MS, bounded on the east by the AL state line; drained by the Chickasawhay River (formed in the northwest by the joining of Chunky and Okatibbee creeks), and also drained by Buckatunna Creek. Clarkco State Park is in the north-center. • Named for Joshua G. Clarke (?–1828), first chancellor of the MS Supreme Court of Chancery • 1833 (prior to statehood) from Choctaw cession • Cotton, corn, cattle, timber; manufacture of lumber and wood products, automotive parts, feeds, textiles, PVC pipe, apparel.

CLAY (one of eighteen counties so named) *West Point* • 21,979 • 409 • Eastern MS, bounded on the east by the Tombigbee River (Tennessee-Tombigbee Waterway; Columbus Lake reservoir in the southeast corner); drained by Line Creek (forming part of the southern boundary) and Chookantonchee Creek. • One of fifteen counties named for Henry Clay (1777–1852), U.S. senator from KY, known as the "Great Pacificator" for his advocacy of compromise to avert national crises • Established as Colfax County 1871 from Chickasaw, Oktibbeha, and Lowndes; name changed 1876 • Cotton, soybeans, corn, wheat, hay, hogs, poultry, cattle, dairying; catfish; timber; manufacture of textiles, metal and rubber products, consumer goods, furniture, lumber and wood products, chemicals, machining; printing and publishing; meat packing • The Prairie Arts Festival is held here each year in late summer.

COAHOMA *Clarksdale* • 30,622 • 554 • Northwestern MS, bounded on the northwest and west by the Mississippi River (forming the AR state line); drained by the Big Sunflower River. Moon Lake, an oxbow lake in the northwest near the Mississippi River and source of the Big Sunflower River, is a prehistoric channel of the Mississippi River. De Soto Lake is in the southwest; also an oxbow lake, it forms part of the AR-MS state line. • Possibly named for Sweet Coahoma, daughter of a Choctaw Chief named Sheriff • 1836 from Chickasaw cession • Sunflower Landing, fourteen miles west of Clarksdale, is presumed to be the spot where Hernando de Soto first viewed the Mississippi River in 1541 • Soybeans, corn, rice, sorghum, wheat, cattle; cotton seed, dairy and bakery products; timber; manufacture of farm machinery, conveyor systems, engine heaters, inner tubes, furniture • The Delta Blues Museum is in Clarksdale.

COPIAH *Hazlehurst* • 28,757 • 777 • Southwestern MS, bounded on the east by the Pearl River; drained by the Homochitto River and Bayou Pierre. Part of Homochitto National Forest is in its southwest corner. • Copiah is an Indian word meaning "screaming panther." • 1823 from Hinds • Blues composer and guitarist Robert Johnson • Cotton, corn, soybeans, tomatoes, cattle, poultry, dairying; timber; sand and gravel; manufacture of furniture, concrete, fabricated metal products, lumber, plastics, processing of poultry and meat.

COVINGTON *Collins* • 19,407 • 414 • South-central MS; drained by the Leaf River and by Oakohay, Okatoma and Bowie creeks. Bowie Creek forms part of the southwestern boundary. Mike Conner State Fishing Lake is in the southwest. • One of two counties (the other in AL) named for Leonard W. Covington (1773–1813), general in the War of 1812, killed in the Battle of Chrysler's Farm • 1819 from Lawrence and Wayne • Cotton, soybeans, dairying, corn, cattle, poultry; timber; manufacture of apparel, wood products, transportation equipment.

DESOTO *Hernando* • 107,199 (57% increase since 1990; the fastest growing and fifth most populated county in MS) • 478 • Extreme northwestern MS, bounded on the west in part by the Mississippi River (forming the AR state line), and on the north by the TN state line; drained by the Coldwater River which forms part of its southern boundary and Arkabutla Lake reservoir also on its southern boundary. The northern edge of the county is suburbanized as part of the Memphis, TN metropolitan area. • One of four counties named for Hernando De Soto (c.1500–42), Spanish explorer of southern U.S. (The Hernando de Soto Memorial Trail traces his route through the county.) • 1836 from Indian lands • Cotton, corn, sorghum, wheat, soybeans, cattle, dairying; manufacture of aluminum and paper products, electrical goods, wood products, processed beef products, sheet metal products, food seasonings, textiles, machinery, furniture, motor vehicles, aircraft; crushed stone; printing and publishing.

FORREST *Hattiesburg* • 72,604 • 467 • Southeastern MS; drained by the Leaf River, and Black and Bowie creeks. (Black Creek is designated a National Scenic River.) Most of the southern half of the county is in De Soto National Forest. Paul B. Johnson State Park and part of Camp Shelby Training Site (National Guard) base are in the center. • Named for General Nathan Bedford Forrest (1821–77), Confederate officer, and organizer and grand wizard of the Ku Klux Klan. • 1906 from Perry • Cotton, corn, poultry; timber; sand and gravel; oil and natural gas; manufacture of lumber products, explosives, chemicals, sheet metal, concrete pipes, paint, clothing; education (U. of Southern MS, William Carey College). • At a site a few miles south of Hattiesburg, the last world heavyweight bare-knuckle boxing championship took place

on July 8, 1889; John L. Sullivan defeated Jake Kilrain in seventy-five rounds.

FRANKLIN (one of twenty-five counties so named) *Meadville* • 8,448 • 565 • Southwestern MS; drained by the Homochitto River, which forms part of the southern boundary in the southwest. A large part of the county is in Homochitto National Forest in the west, south and east-center. • One of twenty-three counties named for Benjamin Franklin • 1809 (prior to statehood) from Adams • Cotton, corn; pine and hardwood timber; oil field; manufacture of apparel.

GEORGE *Lucedale* • 19,144 • 478 • Southeastern MS, bounded on the east by the AL state line; drained by the Pascagoula (formed by the joining of the Leaf and Chickasawhay rivers in the northwest) and Escatawpa rivers, and Black and Red creeks. Part of De Soto National Forest is in the northwest. • Named for General James Z. George (1826–97), Confederate army officer, U.S. senator from MS, and Chief Justice of the MS Supreme Court • 1810 (prior to statehood) from Greene and Jackson • Corn and other vegetables, cotton; timber; manufacture of storage tanks, jewelry, concrete, wood products, knitting kits • Palestine Gardens is a 20-acre scale model of the Holy Land.

GREENE *Leakesville* • 13,299 • 713 • Southeastern MS, bounded on the east by the AL state line; drained by the Leaf and Chickasawhay rivers. Parts of De Soto National Forest are in the north and southwest corner of the county. • One of sixteen counties named for General Nathanael Greene (1742–86), hero of the Revolutionary War, quartermaster general and commander of the Army of the South • 1811 (prior to statehood) from Amite, Franklin, and Wayne • Cotton, corn, cattle, poultry; timber; manufacture of lumber, wood products.

GRENADA *Grenada* • 23,263 • 422 • North-central MS; drained by the Yalobusha and Skuna rivers (together forming Grenada Lake reservoir). Camp McCain National Guard base is in the southeast. Hugh White State Park and part of Tallahatchie National Wildlife Refuge are here. • Named for the city of Grenada, MS • 1870 from Carroll and Tallahatchie • Grenada's cotton economy was virtually destroyed during the Civil War. Confederate General Pemberton headquartered here while resisting General Grant's troops at Vicksburg in 1862. • Senator Trent Lott • Soybeans, cotton, corn, cattle, dairying; timber; light manufacturing. • The union of two rival towns Pittsburg and Tullahoma to form the city of Grenada in 1836 was symbolized by an actual wedding ceremony in which the bride came from Tullahoma and the groom from Pittsburg.

HANCOCK *Bay Saint Louis* • 42,967 (35% increase since 1990; the third fastest growing county in MS) • 477 • Southeastern MS, bounded on the west by the Pearl River (forming the LA state line) and on the south and southeast by the Mississippi Sound (Gulf of Mexico); drained by the Jourdan and Wolf rivers. Buccaneer State Park is on the coast in the southeast. Stennis Space Center (NASA's MS Test Facility) is in the west. • One of ten counties named for John Hancock (1737–93), noted signer of the Declaration of Independence, governor of MA and statesman • 1812 (prior to statehood) from Mobile District • Bay Saint Louis was the scene of an 1814 British naval victory known as the Battle of Pass Christian, the last engagement to take place in continental U.S. waters against a foreign foe. • Corn, cotton, pecans; timber; seafood; manufacture of electrical appliances, steel and aluminum products, plastics, leather goods; tourism.

HARRISON (one of eight counties so named) *Gulfport and Biloxi* • 189,601 (the second most populated county in MS) • 581 • Southeastern MS, bounded on the south by the Mississippi Sound (Gulf of Mexico); drained by the Biloxi, Wolf, and Tchoutacabouffa rivers, and Bernard Bayou. The county includes part of De Soto National Forest in the northeast. Part of Gulf Islands National Seashore is here. • One of four counties named for President William Henry Harrison • 1841 from Hancock and Jackson • The county has been under the flags of France, Spain, Great Britain, the West Florida Republic, the Confederacy, and the U.S. Fort Louis, the site of present-day Biloxi, was established in 1719 and served as the territorial capital from 1720 to 1722. Fort Massachusetts on Ship Island was used as a detention center for Confederate prisoners during the Civil War. Pass Christian was, early on, a popular resort for plantation owners, with railroads later bringing in hundreds of winter visitors from the North, including presidents T. Roosevelt, Wilson, and Truman. The county was in the path of devastation wreaked by hurricane Camille on August. 17, 1969. • Jefferson Davis (his last 12 years spent at his "Beauvoir"); Astronaut Fred Wallace Haise • Corn, pecans, citrus, cattle; timber; extensive seafood industries; tourism and gambling; boat building • Annual festivals include the blessing of the shrimp fleet and the Biloxi Mardi Gras. Biloxi is the site of a 700-acre U.S. Veterans Administration center, which includes a national soldiers' home. The first yacht club on the Gulf coast was organized at Pass Christian in 1849. Gulfport's terminal is the leading U.S. port for importation of bananas. The world's largest fishing rodeo is held in Gulfport every July 4 weekend.

HINDS *Jackson and Raymond* • 250,800 (the most populated county in MS) • 869 (the third largest county in MS) • Western MS, bounded on the east by the Pearl River, and on the northwest and on the west in part by the Big Black River. The county is urbanizing in the east around Jackson, the state's largest city. LeFleur's Bluff State Park is in the east in Jackson. Dockery State Fishing Lake is also in the east. Natchez Trace (National) Parkway crosses the county and includes an incomplete section. • Named for General Thomas Hinds (1780–1840), officer during the War of 1812, U.S. representative from MS, and member of the three member commission set up to select the site of the capital of MS. • 1821 from Choctaw cession • Selected as the site for the state capital, Jackson was laid out in April, 1822 using Thomas Jefferson's checkerboard plan, designating alternate squares as parks. The

state legislature first met here on Dec. 23, 1822. During the Vicksburg campaigns the city was occupied four times by Federal forces, and its burning in July, 1863 by General Sherman's troops earned it the unfortunate nickname of "Chimneyville." The Governor's Mansion served as headquarters for generals Grant and Sherman. After the Civil War, Jackson was troubled by a corrupt city government run by carpetbaggers, and its recovery proceeded slowly until the arrival of new railroads in the 1880s. The world's first heart transplant into a human being was performed in Jackson in 1964; Dr. James D. Hardy replaced a human heart with the heart of a chimpanzee at the University of Mississippi Medical Center. • Writers Eudora Welty and Richard Ford • Cotton, corn, soybeans, vegetables, potatoes, cattle, poultry; timber; natural gas, paper and pulp manufacturing, other manufactures; education (Millsaps College, Belhaven College, MS College, Jackson State U., U. of MS Medical Center, MS Universities Center) • Jackson is the site of the MS Arts Festival, State Fair, State Horse Show, and the quadrennial USA International Ballet Competition.

HOLMES (one of three counties so named) *Lexington* • 21,609 • 756 • Central MS, bounded on the east by the Big Black River and on the northwest and southwest in part by the Yazoo River; drained by Tchula Lake Creek which forms part of the western boundary. Bee Lake oxbow lake of the Yazoo River is in the southwest corner. Also found in the county are Morgan Brake and Hillside national wildlife refuges. Holmes County State Park is in the east. • Named for David Holmes (1770–1832), governor of MS Territory, MS's first and fifth state governor, and U.S. senator from the state • 1833 from Yazoo • Cotton, corn, soybeans, sorghum, cattle; timber; clay deposits, sand and gravel; manufacture of textiles, apparel.

HUMPHREYS (one of two counties so named, the other in TN) *Belzoni* • 11,206 • 418 • Western MS, bounded on the west in part by the Big Sunflower River and on the east in part by Tchula Lake Creek. The county is drained by the Yazoo River (which forms part of the county's boundary in the northeast and southeast) and its tributaries. • Named for Benjamin G. Humphreys (1808–82), general in the Confederate army. He was elected governor of MS but was physically ejected by Reconstruction armed forces. • 1918 from Holmes, Washington, Yazoo, and Sunflower • Catfish raising and processing (Belzoni is the self-proclaimed "Catfish Capital of the World.") Also, cotton, corn, rice, soybeans, wheat, cattle; timber; manufacture of consumer goods, apparel.

ISSAQUENA *Mayersville* • 2,274 (the least populated county in MS) • 413 • Western MS, bounded largely on the west by the Mississippi River, forming the LA state line. The state boundary follows the old channel of the Mississippi River, and includes Albemarle Lake and other oxbow lakes on either side of the river. The northwestern corner of the county touches the southwestern corner of AR. The Yazoo River forms part of the county's southern and eastern boundaries. The county includes part of Delta National Forest in the southeast. • Its name comes from the Choctaw translation of Deer Creek

• 1844 from Washington • Cotton, corn, oats, sorghum, soybeans, wheat, cattle; timber.

ITAWAMBA *Fulton* • 22,770 • 532 • Northeastern MS, bounded on the east by the AL state line; drained by the East Fork of the Tombigbee River. Natchez Trace (National) Parkway passes through the county's northwest corner. • Itawamba was an honorary Chickasaw name given to Levi Colbert (?–1834), unofficial chairman of the Chickasaw Council • 1836 from Indian lands • Dance-band leader Jimmie Lunceford • Cotton, corn, soybeans, poultry, cattle; timber; manufacture of furniture, wood products, lumber, leather boots, copper tubing; beef and pork processing; printing and publishing.

JACKSON (one of twenty-four counties so named) *Pascagoula* • 131,420 (the third most populated county in MS) • 727 • Extreme southeastern MS, bounded on the east by the AL state line and on the south by the Mississippi Sound in the Gulf of Mexico; drained by the Pascagoula and Escatawpa rivers. The county includes part of De Soto National Forest in the northwest. Grand Bay and Mississipi Sandhill Crane national wildlife refuges are here. Shepard State Park is in the south and J. L. Scott Marine Education Center is in the southwest. The visitors center for Gulf Islands National Seashore is on the mainland in the southwestern part of the county. • One of twenty-two counties named directly or indirectly for President Andrew Jackson • 1812 (prior to statehood) from Mobile District • Ocean Springs developed around the site of Old Biloxi, where Pierre Le Moyne d'Iberville established Fort Maurepas in 1699, the first permanent European settlement in the lower Mississippi River valley and the first capital (1699–1702) of the Louisiana Territory. Pascagoula was a thriving lumber-shipping port in the 19th century. • Cotton, corn, pecans; honey; timber; saltwater fish, shrimp, crabs; catfish farming; manufacture of paper products, synthetic rubber, chemicals, textiles, fish meal, ships and barges • The large Ruskin Oak on the Many Oaks Estate at Ocean Springs was named after John Ruskin, the English writer and artist who is said to have visited the spot in 1885. The Pascagoula River is called the "Singing River" by locals because of strange humming sounds that emanate from the area.

JASPER *Bay Springs and Paulding* • 18,149 • 676 • East-central MS; drained by Tallahala and other creeks. The county includes part of Bienville National Forest in the northwest. Claude Bennett State Fishing Lake is in the northeast. • One of eight counties named for Sergeant William Jasper (?–1779), American Revolutionary War hero. (MS is one of five states in which Jasper and Newton counties have been placed adjacent to one another to honor the allied efforts of sergeants William Jasper and John Newton to rescue captive colonial soldiers near Savannah.) • 1833 from Indian lands • Corn, cotton, poultry, cattle, dairying; timber; oil fields; manufacture of auto engine parts, lumber, apparel, household appliances; meat processing; printing and publishing.

JEFFERSON *Fayette* • 9,740 • 519 • Southwestern MS, bounded largely on the west by the Mississippi River, including Rodney Lake on the northwest, an oxbow lake and former channel of the Mississippi River (forming the LA state line). The county includes part of Homochitto National Forest in the east and southeast. Natchez Trace (National) Parkway passes north-south through the county. • One of twenty-six counties named directly or indirectly for Thomas Jefferson • 1799 (prior to statehood) from Pickering • Cotton, corn, soybeans, cattle; timber; manufacture of wood products; education (Alcorn State U.) • Jefferson County has the highest percentage of African Americans in the nation (86%). Springfield Plantation (c.1788) was the site of Andrew Jackson's marriage to Rachel Robards in 1791.

JEFFERSON DAVIS (one of two counties so named) *Prentiss* • 13,962 • 408 • South-central MS; drained by Bowie Creek (which forms part of its eastern boundary) and Black Creek. Jeff Davis State Fishing Lake is here. • One of four counties named for Jefferson Davis (1808–89), president of the Confederate State of America • 1906 from Covington and Lawrence • Cotton, corn, poultry, cattle, hogs and pork processing; timber.

JONES (one of six counties so named) *Ellisville and Laurel* • 64,958 • 694 • Southeastern MS; drained by the Leaf River and Tallahala Creek. The county includes part of De Soto National Forest in the southeast. Boque Homa State Fishing Lake is in the northeast. • Named for John Paul Jones (1747–92), commander of the "Bon Homme Richard" in its victory over the British ship *Serapis* during the American Revolution. • 1826 from Covington and Wayne • By 1920 Laurel was the world's largest shipping center for yellow-pine lumber. With the depletion of area forests, the city, facing economic collapse, was saved by William Mason who developed a type of hardboard (Masonite) made from sawmill waste here. • Long jumper Ralph Boston; lyric soprano Leontyne Price; novelist James Street, who, in his *Tap Roots* (1942), popularized the legend that Jones County had seceded from the Confederacy during the Civil War. • Cotton, corn, sweet potatoes, honey, poultry, cattle, dairying; timber; oil and natural gas; manufacture of fiberboard, wood products, apparel; education (Southeastern Baptist College) • The Lauren Rogers Library and Museum of Art is noted for its collection of North American Indian baskets.

KEMPER *De Kalb* • 10,453 • 766 • Eastern MS, bounded on the east by the AL state line; drained by Sucarnoochee and Okatibbee creeks. Kemper County State Fishing Lake is in the county. • Named for the Kemper brothers, Reuben, Nathan, and Samuel, agitators along the Spanish-controlled FL border. Some sources say the county was only named for Reuben. • 1833 from Indian lands • Cotton, corn, cattle; catfish; timber; manufacture of construction materials, transportation equipment, food, apparel.

LAFAYETTE (one of six counties so named) *Oxford* • 38,744 • 631 • Northern MS, bounded on the north in part by the

Tallahatchie River; also drained by the Yocona River. Part of Sardis Lake reservoir (Tallahatchie River) is in the northwest. Part of Holly Springs Forest is in the northeast. • One of seventeen counties named for the Marquis de Lafayette (1757–1834), French statesman and soldier who fought with Americans during the Revolutionary War • 1836 from Chickasaw cession of 1832 • Oxford was given its academic name by founding fathers who desired a university here. The University of Mississippi opened in 1848. It served as a hospital when the city was occupied by Federal troops during the Civil War. In the fall of 1962 it was the scene of rioting over the enrollment of black student James Meredith to the previously white-only university. • Novelist William Faulkner drew heavily from Lafayette County for his fictional Yoknapatawpha County. • Cotton, corn, soybeans, cattle, poultry, dairying, truck farming; pine, hardwood timber; manufacture of electric motors and appliances.

LAMAR (one of four counties so named) *Purvis* • 39,070 • 497 • Southeastern MS; drained by the Wolf River (its source in the southwest) and by Black and Red creeks. The Hattiesburg metropolitan area extends into the northeast corner of the state. • One of three counties named for Lucius Q. C. Lamar (1825–93), U.S. statesman and U.S. Supreme Court justice. • 1904 from Marion and Pearl River • Cotton, corn, pecans, poultry, cattle; pine timber; oil and natural gas; manufacture of wood pallets, apparel, lumber.

LAUDERDALE *Meridian* • 78,161 • 704 • Eastern MS, bounded on the east by the AL state line; drained by Chunky, Okatibbee, and Buckatunna creeks. Meridian Naval Air Station (a training base for jet pilots) is here, as are Sam Dale Historic Site, Okatibbee Lake reservoir and Tom Bailey State Fishing Lake. • One of three counties named for Col. James Lauderdale (?–1814), officer killed at the Battle of New Orleans during the War of 1812 • 1833 from Choctaw cession • During the Civil War, Meridian served as a Confederate military camp. It was the state capital for one month in 1863; General Sherman's Union forces captured the city on Feb. 16, 1864. His troops systematically destroyed the arsenals, storehouses, and the railroads near the city, rendering it useless as a rail center for the remainder of the war. • Meridian native Jimmie Rodgers, the "Singing Brakeman," is honored by a museum and a country music festival every May. • Cotton, corn, sweet potatoes, cattle, hogs; timber; manufacture of textiles, wood and clay products, chemicals, machinery, foodstuffs, structural steel, automobile parts, weighing scales, aircraft assemblies, roofing supplies, insulation board, sound equipment • An early railroad junction site, Meridian was given this name by a settler who thought the word meant "junction."

LAWRENCE (one of eleven counties so named) *Monticello* • 13,258 • 431 • South-central MS; drained by the Pearl River. Mary Crawford State Fishing Lake is here. • One of nine counties named for Captain James Lawrence (1781–1813), U.S. Navy commander in the War of 1812 •1814 (prior to statehood) from Marion • Cabinet secretary Roderick R. Paige •

Cotton, corn, poultry, cattle, hogs; timber; manufacture of linerboard, sportswear, industrial screens, lumber.

LEAKE *Carthage* • 20,940 • 583 • Central MS; drained by the Pearl and Yockanookany rivers and Lobutcha Creek. The county includes two small Native American reservations in the center and southeast. Natchez Trace (National) Parkway passes through the northwest. Part of Golden Memorial State Park is also here. • Named for Walter Leake (1762–1825), judge of the MS Territory, one of the first two U.S. senators from MS, and governor of the state • 1833 from Choctaw cession • Cotton, poultry, cattle, dairying; timber.

LEE (one of twelve counties so named) *Tupelo* • 75,755 • 450 • Northeastern MS; drained by Chiwapa and Oldtown creeks. Tombigbee State Park and Lamar Bruce State Fishing Lake are also located in the county. The Natchez Trace (National) Parkway passes southwest-northeast through it. (Tupelo is the headquarters and focal point for the parkway.) • One of eight counties named for Robert E. Lee (1807–70), American general and commander in chief of the Confederate forces during the Civil War • 1866 from Itawamba and Pontotoc • On June 10, 1864, Federal forces were defeated by Lt. Gen. Nathan Bedford Forrest at Brice Cross Roads. On July 13–14 at Tupelo, Forrest's cavalry fought a Union force of 14,000 sent to keep Forrest from cutting the railroad supplying Major General William T. Sherman's march to the sea. The Union Army fought off the Confederates but were forced to retreat due to diminished supplies. (Both battles are commemorated at national battlefields in the county.) In April, 1936, Tupelo was struck by a tornado, which killed 201 and injured 1,000. • Elvis Presley • Cotton, corn, soybeans, wheat, honey, poultry, cattle, dairying; timber; manufacture of textiles, electronic equipment, furniture.

LEFLORE *Greenwood* • 37,947 • 592 • West-central MS. The Tallahatchie and Yalobusha rivers join in the east-center to form the Yazoo River (and part of its southern boundary). The county includes Matthews Brake National Wildlife Refuge and Florewood River Plantation State Park. • One of two counties (the other in OK) named for Greenwood Leflore (1800–65), large landowner in MS and Texas, and chief of the Western District of the Choctaw Indian nation. • 1871 from Carroll and Sunflower • Blues composer and guitarist Robert Johnson; guitarist B.B. King; politician Marion Barry • Long-staple cotton, rice, sorghum, wheat, soybeans, cattle; catfish; food processing, manufacture of cottonseed products, farm implements, electronic testing apparatus, indexing equipment, fishing tackle, picture frames, metal lockers, pianos, seat belts, pharmaceuticals, trailers, heavy machinery, bridge materials; education (MS Valley State U.).

LINCOLN (one of twenty-four counties so named) *Brookhaven* • 33,166 • 586 • Southwestern MS; drained by the Bogue Chitto River and the East Fork of the Amite River. A small section of Homochitto National Forest is here. Lake Lincoln State Park is in the northeast corner. • One of eighteen counties named for

Abraham Lincoln • 1870 from Amite, Pike, Lawrence and Franklin • Cotton, corn, cattle, poultry, dairying; timber; manufacture of thermometers, lawn mowers, wire cloth, pressed brick, tile, lumber products, animal feeds, apparel.

LOWNDES *Columbus* • 61,586 • 502 • Eastern MS, bounded on the east by the AL state line and on the north in part by the Buttahatchee River; drained by the Tombigbee River (which forms Columbus Lake reservoir on the northwestern boundary) and Luxapallila Creek. Lake Lowndes State Park is here. Columbus Air Force Base is in the north. • One of three counties named for William J. Lowndes (1782–1822), U.S. Representative from SC • 1830 from Monroe • Confederates kept a large arsenal in Columbus during the Civil War. The town also served as temporary state capital when Jackson fell in 1863. Confederate Decoration Day, a forerunner of Memorial Day, originated at Friendship Cemetery in Columbus on April 25, 1866. • Boxer Henry Armstrong; pro football player Walter Payton; playwright Tennessee Williams • Cotton, corn, hay, soybeans, wheat, cattle; timber; manufacture of chemicals, lumber, apparel, rubber, marble, bricks, soft drinks. • Founded in Columbus in 1821, Franklin Academy was the first public school in MS. Mississippi State University for Women, founded in Columbus in 1884 as Columbus Industrial Institute and College, was the first state-supported women's college in the U.S. Columbus is the headquarters for the Tennessee-Tombigbee Waterway Development Authority (1958).

MADISON *Canton* • 74,674 (39% increase since 1990; the second fastest growing county in MS) • 719 • Central MS, bounded on the southeast by the Pearl River (here forming Ross Barnett Reservoir) and on the northwest by the Big Black River. The southern part of the county is urbanized as part of the Jackson metropolitan area. Mississippi Petrified Forest is in the county. Natchez Trace (National) Parkway passes through the southeast. • One of twenty counties named directly or indirectly for President James Madison • 1828 from Yazoo • Cotton, corn, hay, vegetables, potatoes, pecans, poultry, cattle, dairying; timber; manufacture of lumber, furniture and furniture parts, fertilizers, pesticides, textiles, canvas tents, gun covers, liquid carbon dioxide, computer keyboards, printing, concrete, plastic products • The county has many antebellum homes.

MARION *Columbia* • 25,595 • 542 • Southern MS, bounded in part in the south by the LA state line; drained by the Pearl River. Columbia State Fishing Lake is in the east. • One of seventeen counties named for "The Swamp Fox," Francis Marion (?–1795), Revolutionary War general and legislator • 1811 (prior to statehood) from Amite, Wayne, and Franklin • The Pearl River Convention of 1816, which petitioned for MS's admission to the Union, took place in a pioneer home south of Columbia. The town served as the capital of MS for three months in 1821. • Cotton, corn, cattle, dairying; timber; manufacture of clothing, hosiery, canned goods, naval stores, concrete, asphalt, paper products, furniture.

MARSHALL (one of twelve counties so named) *Holly Springs* • 34,993 • 706 • Northern MS, bounded on the north by the TN state line, and on the south in part by the Tallahatchie River; drained by the Coldwater River. The county includes part of Holly Springs National Forest and Wall Doxey State Park. • One of eight counties named for John Marshall (1755–1835), fourth Chief Justice of the U.S. • 1836 from Indian lands • More than 60 skirmishes were fought around Holly Springs, including an 1862 raid by Confederate General E. Van Dorn that delayed Grant's drive to Vicksburg, and destroyed a Union supply depot. In 1878, a yellow-fever epidemic killed more than 300 residents of the town. • Journalist Ida Bell Wells-Barnett • Cotton, corn, hay, soybeans, wheat, cattle, dairying; processing of farm products; manufacture of clay products, wall paneling, industrial machinery, kitchen appliances, bricks, metal stampings; steel and alloy fabrication; printing and publishing; education (Rust College) • The Kate Freeman Clark Art Gallery in Holly Springs has a collection of more than 1,000 paintings by the artist, who was a native. The county is also known for its many fine antebellum homes.

MONROE *Aberdeen* • 38,014 • 764 • Eastern MS, bounded on the east by the AL state line; drained by the Buttahatchee River (forming part of the southern boundary) and the East Fork of the Tombigbee River, which forms Aberdeen Lake reservoir in the center. Monroe State Fishing Lake is located on the reservoir. The Tennessee-Tombigbee Waterway runs parallel to the river. • One of seventeen counties named for President James Monroe • 1821 from Chickasaw cession of 1821 • Clergyman Robert Paine; columnist William E. Evans. Hiram R. Revels, the first African American elected to the U.S. Senate, died here. • Cotton, corn, soybeans, wheat, cattle, dairying; timber; manufacture of apparel, furniture, building materials, transportation equipment, metal and plastic products, furniture; printing; chemical processing; metal fabrication; gas wells • The Amory Regional Museum is in the county.

MONTGOMERY (One of eighteen counties so named) *Winona* • 12,189 • 407 • Central MS; drained by the Big Black River (forming part of the eastern boundary) • One of sixteen counties named directly or indirectly for General Richard Montgomery (1738–75), American Revolutionary War officer who captured Montreal, Canada • 1871 from Carroll and Choctaw • Cotton, corn, soybeans, cattle; timber; manufacture of apparel, lumber products, motor vehicle parts, furniture, plastics, steel fabrication.

NESHOBA *Philadelphia* • 28,684 • 570 • East-central MS; drained by the Pearl River. The county includes Mississippi Choctaw Indian Reservation. Part of Nanih Waiya Historic Site is here, as is Neshoba State Fishing Lake. The source of Chunky Creek is in the east. • The county's name is a Choctaw word meaning "wolf." • 1833 from Choctaw cession • Philadelphia was settled on an old Indian site following the Treaty of Dancing Rabbit Creek. The headquarters of the Choctaw Indian Agency was established here in 1918 and a majority of MS's Choctaw live in the vicinity. Notoriety came to the county in 1964 with the murder and burial of three civil-rights workers here during a voter-registration drive. • Cotton, corn, poultry, cattle, dairying; timber; light manufactures including textiles, electrical motors, lumber products, electronic equipment, concrete; printing and publishing. • The Choctaw Indian Fair is held in Philadelphia.

NEWTON (one of six counties so named) *Decatur* • 21,838 • 578 • East-central MS; drained by Chunky and Potterchitto creeks. Part of Bienville National Forest is here. • Probably for Sgt. John Newton (?–1780), Revolutionary War hero (MS is one of five states in which Jasper and Newton counties have been placed adjacent to one another to honor the allied efforts of sergeants William Jasper and John Newton to rescue captive colonial soldiers near Savannah.) • 1836 from Neshoba • Cotton, corn, poultry, cattle, dairying; timber; manufacture of electronic products, fabricated metal products, furniture, cheese, feeds, plastic products, transportation equipment, apparel, wood products.

NOXUBEE *Macon* • 12,548 • 695 • Eastern MS, bounded on the east by the AL state line; drained by the Noxubee River. Part of Aliceville Lake reservoir is on its eastern boundary; part of Noxubee National Wildlife Refuge is in the northwest corner. • Named for the Noxubee River • 1833 from Choctaw cession of 1830 • Cotton, corn, wheat, soybeans, cattle, dairying; timber; manufacture of bricks, apparel, vinyl products, feeds, transportation equipment, lumber.

OKTIBBEHA *Starkville* • 42,902 • 458 • Eastern MS; drained by the Noxubee and Oktibbeha rivers. The county includes Oktibbeha County State Fishing Lake and part of Noxubee National Wildlife Refuge. A small part of Tombigbee National Forest is in the southwest. • Named for one of two waterways with this name • 1833 from Choctaw cession of 1830 • Baseball player Cool Papa Bell • Cotton, corn, hay, soybeans, honey, cattle, dairying; timber; manufacture of textiles, clocks, parking meters, furniture; education (MS State U.) • Starkville is the site of a federal agricultural research station and a state agricultural center.

PANOLA (one of two counties so named, the other in TX) *Batesville and Sardis* • 34,274 • 684 • Northwestern MS; drained by the Tallahatchie and Yocona rivers. Part of Enid Lake reservoir on the Yocona River is in the southeast. The county also contains John W. Kyle State Park at the dam of Sardis Lake reservoir on the Tallahatchie River. • Its name comes from the Choctaw word meaning "cotton." • 1836 from Indian lands • Cotton, corn, poultry, hay, sorghum, soybeans, wheat, cattle, hogs; timber; clay and gravel deposits; manufacture of building materials, plastic, wood, and felt products, hospital furniture, concrete, sports equipment.

PEARL RIVER *Poplarville* • 48,621 • 812 (the fourth largest county in the state) • Southern MS, bounded on the west by the Pearl River (forming the LA state line); also drained by

Hobolochitto and Catahoula creeks and by the Wolf River. Part of De Soto National Forest and Bogue Chitto Wildlife Refuge are here. • Named for the river • 1890 from Hancock and Marion • Politician Theodore Bilbo • Cotton, corn, tung nuts, pecans, blueberries, blackberries, cattle, dairying; timber; sand and gravel.

PERRY *New Augusta* • 12,138 • 647 • Southeastern MS; drained by the Leaf River, and Thompson, Tallahala, and Black creeks (the last, a National Scenic River). Part of De Soto National Forest covers the southern half of the county. Perry State Fishing Lake and Camp Shelby Training Site are centrally located. • One of ten counties named for Oliver Hazard Perry (1785–1819), U.S. naval officer during the War of 1812 • 1820 from Greene • Cotton, corn, poultry; timber; manufacture of plywood, telephone poles, pulpwood processing.

PIKE *Magnolia* • 38,940 • 409 • Southwestern MS, bounded on the south by the LA state line; drained by the Bogue Chitto and Tangipahoa rivers. A portion of Percy Quin State Park is here. • One of ten counties named for Zebulon Montgomery Pike (1779–1813), U.S. army officer and discoverer of Pikes Peak in CO • 1815 (prior to statehood) from Marion • Military historian Jacob Dolson Cox died in Magnolia. • Cotton, corn, soybeans, cattle, dairying; timber; manufacture of wire products, printing and publishing, textile products, concrete, lumber, poultry processing.

PONTOTOC (one of two counties so named, the other in OK) *Pontotoc* • 26,726 • 497 • Northern MS; drained by the Skuna and Yocona rivers, and Chiwapa Creek. A small part of Tombigbee National Forest is here, as is a small part of Holly Springs National Forest. Trace State Park is also in the county. Natchez Trace (National) Parkway crosses its southeastern corner. • Named for the town of Pontotoc, MS, from the Chickasaw term probably meaning "cattails growing on the prairie" • 1836 from Chickasaw cession • Cotton, corn, soybeans, wheat, cattle, dairying; timber; clay and bauxite deposits; manufacture of textiles, furniture, consumer goods, transportation equipment, fabricated metal products, medical equipment, apparel; pork processing.

PRENTISS *Booneville* • 25,556 • 415 • Northeastern MS; drained by the East Fork of the Tombigbee and Tuscumbia rivers. Natchez Trace (National) Parkway passes through its southeast corner. Part of Bay Springs Reservoir is on the Tennessee-Tombigbee Waterway. Pharr Mounds is in the southeastern corner. • Named for Sergeant Smith Prentiss (1808–50), MS legislator and U.S. representative from the state • 1870 from Tishomingo • Booneville was the scene of a Union victory won by General P.H. Sheridan in 1862. • Cotton, corn, soybeans, wheat, hay, cattle, dairying; timber and lumber processing; clay deposits; manufacture of furniture, paper and vinyl products, cheese, machinery, apparel, office supplies, fabricated metal products; meat processing.

QUITMAN *Marks* • 10,117 • 405 • Northwestern MS; drained by the Coldwater and Tallahatchie rivers. A small portion of the Tallahatchie National Wildlife Refuge is in the southeast. • One of two counties (the other in GA) named for John A. Quitman (1798–1858), governor of MS and U.S. representative from the state • 1877 from Panola and Coahoma • Cattle, cotton, corn, rice, sorghum, soybeans (grown and processed), wheat; timber; manufacture of apparel, electrical equipment.

RANKIN *Brandon* • 115,327 (the fourth most populated county in MS) • 775 • Central MS, bounded on the west, northwest, and north by the Pearl River (forming Ross Barnett Reservoir). The county is urbanized in the west and center, as part of the Jackson metropolitan area. • Named for Christopher Rankin (1788–1826), U.S. representative from MS • 1828 from Hinds • Cotton, corn, potatoes, sweet potatoes, other vegetables, poultry, cattle; timber; natural gas; manufacture of fabricated metal and plastic products, carbon dioxide, hydrogen sulfide, wood products, transportation equipment, paper products, furniture, steel products; machining; education (Wesley College).

SCOTT (one of eleven counties so named) *Forest* • 28,423 • 609 • Central MS, bounded on the northwest by the Pearl River; drained by the Strong and Leaf rivers, and Pelahatchie Creek. Roosevelt State Park and part of Golden Memorial State Park are here. Part of Bienville National Forest covers much of the county in the south, center, and northwest, and includes Bienville Pines Scenic Area. • Named for Abram M. Scott (?–1833), governor of MS • 1833 from Choctaw cession of 1830 • Cotton, corn, soybeans, poultry (grown and processed), cattle; timber and lumber processing; manufacture of electronics, bakery goods.

SHARKEY *Rolling Fork* • 6,580 • 428 • Western MS, bounded on the southeast by the Yazoo River and on the west in part by Indian Bayou; drained by the Big Sunflower (forming part of the eastern boundary) and Little Sunflower rivers, and Deer Creek. Much of the southeastern part of the county is in Delta National Forest. • Named for William L. Sharkey (1797–1873), MS legislator, circuit court judge and provisional governor • 1876 from Warren, Washington, and Issaquena • Blues guitarist and singer Muddy Waters • Cotton, corn, oats, rice, soybeans, sorghum, wheat, timber; light manufacturing.

SIMPSON *Mendenhall* • 27,639 • 589 • South-central MS, bounded on the west by the Pearl River; drained by the Strong River and Okatoma Creek. Simpson County Legion State Fishing Lake is here. • Named for Josiah Simpson (?–1817), a judge in Mississippi Territory • 1824 from Copiah • Cotton, corn, poultry, cattle; timber and lumber processing; manufacture of apparel, wood products, building materials; millwork, steel fabrication.

SMITH (one of four counties so named) *Raleigh* • 16,182 • 636 • South-central MS; drained by the Leaf and Strong rivers, and Oakohay Creek. The county includes part of Bienville National Forest. Ross Barnett State Fishing Lake is also here. •

Named for David Smith (1753–1835), major in the KY militia and father-in-law of Governor Hiram G. Runnels • 1833 from Indian lands • Corn, cotton, poultry, cattle, hogs; timber and lumber processing (including plywood and particleboard); bentonite mining; manufacture of automotive and industrial engine starters, apparel; sausage processing.

STONE (one of three counties so named) *Wiggins* • 13,622 • 445 • Southeastern MS; drained by the Biloxi River, and Red and Black creeks. Part of De Soto National Forest is in the county. Flint Creek reservoir is also here. • Named for John M. Stone (1830–1900), president pro tem of the MS state senate, who was elevated to governor when the black Reconstruction lieutenant governor Alexander K. Davis, following the resignation of Governor Adelbert Ames, was preemptively impeached • 1916 from Harrison • Cotton, corn, honey, tung and pecan groves; poultry; timber; manufacture of metal products, lumber products.

SUNFLOWER *Indianola* • 34,369 • 694 • Western MS; drained by the Big Sunflower and Quiver rivers. • Named for the Sunflower River • 1844 from Bolivar • Cotton, corn, oats, rice, soybeans, wheat, pecans, hay, alfalfa, cattle; timber; catfish; meat and pecan processing, paper products.

TALLAHATCHIE *Charleston and Sumner* • 14,903 • 644 • Northwest-central MS; drained by the Tallahatchie River (forming part of the southern boundary). Parts of Tallahatchie National Wildlife Refuge are here. • Named for the Tallahatchie River • 1833 from Indian lands • Cotton, corn, soybeans, rice, sorghum, wheat, cattle; timber and lumber milling; manufacture of paper products, apparel, furniture, textiles; clay, fuller's earth pits.

TATE *Senatobia* • 25,370 • 404 • Northwestern MS, bounded on the west and northwest by the Coldwater River, (forming Arkabutla Lake reservoir). • Named for either Thomas Simpson Tate, MS legislator active in the creation of the county, or for his family • 1873 from DeSoto, Marshall, and Tunica • Senatobia was burned by Union troops in the Civil War. • Actor James Earl Jones; historian and editor Dumas Malone • Cotton, corn, wheat, soybeans, hay, cattle, dairying; timber; manufacture of aluminum products, chemicals, furniture, apparel, concrete; printing.

TIPPAH *Ripley* • 20,826 • 458 • Northern MS, bounded on the north by the TN state line; drained by the Hatchie River and Tippah Creek. Part of Holly Springs National Forest is in the northwest. Tippah County State Fishing Lake is in the center of the county. • Named for either the wife of Chickasaw Chief Pontotoc, or for Tippah Creek which was named for her • 1836 from Chickasaw cession • Cotton, corn, soybeans, cattle, dairying; pine timber; manufacture of furniture, shoe soles and heels, boat oars, upholstery material, oil absorbents, apparel; education (Blue Mountain College).

TISHOMINGO *Iuka* • 19,163 • 424 • Extreme northeastern MS, bounded on the east by the AL state line, on the north by the TN state line, and on the northeast by Pickwick Lake reservoir and its Bear River arm (forming the AL state line); drained by tributaries of the Tennessee and Tombigbee rivers. Woodhall Mountain, at 806 feet, is the highest point in the state. The county includes Tishomingo and J. P. Coleman state parks. Natchez Trace (National) Parkway and the Tennessee-Tombigbee Waterway both pass through the county. Bay Springs Lake reservoir is in the south. • Named for Tishomingo, the last full-blooded chief of the Chickasaw Indians • 1836 from Chickasaw cession, divided in 1870 into Alcorn, Prentiss, and Tishomingo counties • Iuka was the scene of a Civil War battle in 1862. • Soybeans, wheat, corn, sweet potatoes, hogs; timber; manufacture of wood products; clay (extraction and products), sandstone, limestone, phosphorus, and bauxite deposits.

TUNICA *Tunica* • 9,227 • 455 • Northwestern MS, bounded largely on the northwest and west by the Mississippi River (forming the AR state line) and on the east in part by the Coldwater River. Tunica Lake is a twelve-mile-long oxbow lake of the Misssssippi on the western boundary of the county. • Named for the Tunica Indians • 1836 by the Treaty of Pontotoc from Chickasaw cession of 1832 • The introduction of gambling to the county in the early 1990s erased Tunica's unheralded claim to being one of the nation's poorest counties. • Gambling and related tourism; cotton, corn, sorghum, soybeans, wheat, rice, cattle; timber; catfish (raised and processed); manufacture of chemicals, bedding.

UNION (one of eighteen counties so named) *New Albany* • 25,362 • 415 • Northern MS; drained by the Tallahatchie and Hatchie rivers, and Oldtown Creek. The county includes part of Holly Springs National Forest. • Probably named for the re-uniting of the states after the Civil War • 1870 from Pontotoc and Tippah • Novelist William Faulkner • Cotton, corn, soybeans, cattle, dairying; timber; manufacture of machinery, marble tops, asphalt and foam products, apparel, furniture, concrete; printing and publishing.

WALTHALL *Tylertown* • 15,156 • 404 • Southern MS, bounded on the south by the LA state line; drained by the Bogue Chitto River and McGee Creek. • Named for General Edward C. Walthall (1831–98), Confederate army officer and U.S. senator from MS • 1910 from Marion and Pike • Cotton, corn, cattle, dairying; timber and lumber processing; manufacture of apparel, saw blades and sawmill equipment; meat processing.

WARREN *Vicksburg* • 49,644 • 587 • Western MS, bounded on the southeast by the Big Black River and on the west largely by the Mississippi River (forming the LA state line). A large section of the county lies west of the Mississippi River due to isolation by a new river channel. • One of fourteen counties named for Gen. Joseph Warren (1741–75), Revolutionary War patriot who died at the Battle of Bunker Hill • 1809 (prior to statehood) from Natchez District • Vicksburg was besieged for forty-seven days during General Ulysses S. Grant's campaign

for control of the Mississippi River in the Civil War, finally surrendering on July 4, 1863. (Vicksburg National Military Park includes Vicksburg National Cemetery, with 18,244 interments.) • Cotton, corn, soybeans, cattle; timber; manufacture of lumber, wood and paper products, chemicals, light fixtures, prefabricated housing, petroleum products, fabricated metal products, boats; tourism. • Coca-Cola was first bottled in 1894 in Vicksburg.

WASHINGTON *Greenville* • 62,977 • 724 • Western MS, bounded on the west largely by the Mississippi River (forming the AR state line), on the east in part by the Big Sunflower River; intersected by Deer Creek and several bayous. The southwestern corner of the county touches the northeastern corner of LA. Lake Lee and Lake Ferguson, both oxbow lakes, form part of the AR-MS state line. Lake Washington, an oxbow lake of the Mississippi River is also here, as are Yazoo National Wildlife Refuge, Leroy Percy State Park, and Winterville Mounds Historic Site. • One of thirty-one counties named for President George Washington • 1827 from Warren and Yazoo • Historian Shelby Foote; lawyer and poet Walter Percy • Cotton, alfalfa, corn, wheat, vegetables, soybeans, rice, sorghum, cattle, dairying, poultry; timber; catfish; cottonseed oil; manufacture of insulating board, automobile parts, saws, screws.

WAYNE (one of sixteen counties so named) *Waynesboro* • 21,216 • 810 (the fifth largest county in MS) • Southeastern MS, bounded on the east by the AL state line; drained by the Chickasawhay River, and Buckatunna and Thompsons creeks. The county includes part of De Soto National Forest. Lakeland Park State Fishing Lake is here. • One of fifteen counties named for General Anthony Wayne (1745–96), PA soldier and statesman, nicknamed "Mad Anthony" for his daring during the Revolutionary War • 1809 (prior to statehood) from Washington • Cotton, corn, poultry, cattle; timber and lumber processing; printing and publishing; manufacture of industrial chemicals, electric blankets, poultry feed.

WEBSTER *Walthall* • 10,294 • 423 • Central MS; drained by the Big Black River (forming most of the southern border). Natchez Trace (National) Parkway passes north/south through the eastern end of the county. • One of eight counties named for Daniel Webster (1782–1852), U.S. statesman and orator from MA • Organized as Sumner 1874 from Montgomery; name changed 1882 • Cotton, corn, soybeans, cattle; timber and lumber processing; manufacture of transportation equipment, apparel, furniture, plastic products.

WILKINSON *Woodville* • 10,312 • 677 • Extreme southwestern MS, bounded on the south by the LA state line, on the west largely by the Mississippi River, here forming the LA state line, and on the north by the Homochitto River; drained by the Buffalo River. The county includes part of Homochitto National Forest. Old River Lake, an oxbow lake of the Mississippi River, is on the northwest border. Clark Creek State

Park is also in the county. • One of two counties (the other in GA) named for James Wilkinson (1757–1825), negotiator of the Louisiana Purchase, and first governor of Louisiana Territory who conspired to form a second nation allied with Spain • 1802 (prior to statehood) from Adams • Composer and conductor William G. Still; jazz saxophonist Lester Young • Cotton, corn, cattle, dairying; timber; manufacture of hardwood chips, children's clothing.

WINSTON (one of two counties so named, the other in AL) *Louisville* • 20,160 • 607 • East-central MS; drained by the Noxubee River and Lobutcha Creek, source of the Pearl River. Part of Nanih Waiya Historic Site is on the southern boundary. The county includes Legion State Park, part of Tombigbee National Forest, and part of Noxubee National Wildlife Refuge in the north. • Named for Louis Winston, judge of the Second Circuit Court • 1833 from Indian lands • Cotton, corn, poultry, cattle, dairying; timber; manufacture of apparel, furniture, bricks, lumber, consumer goods, motor vehicle parts, construction equipment.

YALOBUSHA *Coffeeville and Water Valley* • 13,051 • 467 • North-central MS; drained by the Yocona River (forming Enid Lake reservoir) and the Skuna River (forming the northern arm of Grenada Lake reservoir). The county includes sections of Holly Springs National Forest. George Payne Cossar State Park is also here. • Named for the Yalobusha River, which flowed here before the county was reduced in size. • 1833 from Choctaw cession in 1830 • Cotton, corn, watermelons, soybeans, hogs, cattle, poultry (raised and processed); timber; manufacture of textiles, tool and die, fuel injection systems.

YAZOO *Yazoo City* • 28,149 • 920 (the largest county in MS) • West-central MS, bounded on the east and southeast by the Big Black River and on the west in part by the Big Sunflower River; intersected by the Yazoo River and its tributaries. Panther Swamp National Wildlife Refuge is in the east. • Named for either the Yazoo River or for the Yazoo Indians • 1823 from Hinds • During the Civil War, Yazoo City was the site of a Confederate naval yard and twice burned. Its riverfront was the scene of several Civil War battles. In 1904 it was nearly destroyed by fire and later rebuilt. • Cotton, corn, hay, wheat, sorghum, soybeans, cattle; timber; catfish; oil (retrieval and refining); manufacture of nitrogen, chemicals, fertilizer, machinery, textiles, apparel. • The Casey Jones Museum is here.

MISSOURI

The Welfare of the People Should Be the Supreme Law

County commissioners serve as the chief administrators in the state's 114 counties. Other county officials include the sheriff, recorder of deeds, prosecuting attorney, collector of revenue, assessor, treasurer, public administrator, surveyor, and coroner. St. Louis is an independent city, unaffiliated with any county in the state.

ADAIR (one of four counties so named) *Kirksville* • 24,977 • 568 • Northern MO; drained by the Chariton River and the North Fork of the Salt River. Thousand Hills State Park and Union Ridge Conservation Area are here. • Named for Adair County, KY, itself named for KY governor John Adair (1757–1840) • 1841 from Macon • The Battle of Kirksville, part of the Western Campaign to secure the Mississippi River for the Union, took place here in 1862. Dr. Andrew Taylor developed Osteopathic Medicine in Kirksville in the 1890s (Kirksville College of Osteopathic Medicine). The county is a former coal-mining center. • Actor Geraldine Page • Corn, soybeans, grain, hogs, sheep, cattle, mules, poultry; limestone; manufacture of electrical items, clothing; education (Truman State U.).

ANDREW *Savannah* • 16,492 • 435 • Northwestern MO, bounded on the west by the Nodaway River and on the southwest by the Missouri River (forming the KS state line); drained by the One Hundred and Two and Platte rivers. The south is becoming urbanized through its proximity to St. Joseph. • Named for Andrew J. Davis, a prominent St. Louis attorney • 1841 from Platte Purchase • Corn, wheat, cattle, hogs; some manufacturing.

ATCHISON *Rock Port* • 6,430 • 545 • Extreme northwestern MO, bounded on the west by the Missouri River, forming the NE state line, and on the north by the IA state line; drained by the Tarkio River. • One of two counties (the other in KS) named directly or indirectly for David Rice Atchison (1807–86), MO statesman and U.S. senator • 1843 from Holt • Severe flooding occurred along all its rivers in 1993. • Corn, wheat, hogs, cattle.

AUDRAIN *Mexico* • 25,853 • 693 • North-central MO; drained by the West Fork of the Cuivre River. There is a large Amish area in the west. • Probably named for James H. Audrain (1782–1831), MO legislator • 1836 from Pike, Callaway, and Ralls • Corn, wheat, soybeans, oats, cattle, hogs, saddle horses (the American Saddle Horse Museum is here), sheep; diversified manufactures; fire-clay deposits, coal; lumber.

BARRY *Cassville* • 34,010 • 779 • Southwestern MO, bounded on the south by the AR state line; drained by the White River (here forming part of Table Rock Lake reservoir). The county is located in the Ozarks with part of Mark Twain National Forest in the southeast corner. Roaring River State Park is also in the county. • Named for either John Barry (?–1803), American Revolution naval hero, or for William T. Barry (1784–1835), KY legislator, U.S. senator and U.S. postmaster general • 1835 from Greene • Cassville served as the Capital of Confederate MO for one week (October 31 to November 7, 1861), after the state assembly was forced out of Neosho. • Apples, grapes, peaches, cattle, turkeys, broiler chickens, dairying, goats; hardwood timber; sport fishing, tourism; manufacturing.

BARTON (one of two counties so named, the other in KS) *Lamar* • 12,541 • 594 • Southwestern MO, bounded on the west by the KS state line; drained by a branch of the Spring River and by affluents of the Osage River. Prairie State Park and Shawnee Trail Conservation Area are here. • Named for David Barton (1783–1837), one of the first two senators from MO. • 1855 from Jasper • President Harry S. Truman (birthplace state historic site) • Wheat, corn, hay, oats, soybeans, livestock; coal deposits; manufacturing.

BATES *Butler* • 16,653 •849 • Western MO, bounded on the west by the KS state line, on the north in part by the South Grand River, and on the south in part by the Osage River; drained by the Marais des Cygnes and South Grand rivers. Settle's Ford Conservation Area is here. • Named for one of two brothers: Edward Bates (1793–1869), U.S. attorney general, or Frederick Bates (1777–1825), early governor of MO • 1841 from Cooper County • Science fiction author Robert A. Heinlein. General Joseph Shelby, reputedly the only ranking Confederate who never surrendered to the Union, lived on a farm near Adrian while serving as a U.S. marshal. • Corn, wheat, sorghum, popcorn, pecans, cattle, coal, oil. • Butler was called "Electric City." It has the oldest continuously operated municipal power system in the U.S., and was the second city west of the Mississippi River to have electricity.

BENTON (one of nine counties so named) *Warsaw* • 17,180 • 706 • Central MO; drained by the Osage, South Grand, and Pomme de Terre rivers, all three forming Harry S. Truman Lake reservoir (Harry S. Truman State Park is here) and Lake of the Ozarks. The county lies in the Ozark Region. • One of seven counties named for Thomas Hart Benton (1782–1858), U.S. journalist and statesman, and ardent advocate of free land for settlers • 1835 from Cooper • The Battle of Cole Camp took place here on June 19, 1861; a mass grave at Union Church cemetery in Crockerville attests to the routing of Federal troops by Confederate forces. • Corn, cattle, poultry; lake fishing; resort and recreational tourism; lumber; hydroelectricity.

BOLLINGER *Marble Hill* • 12,029 • 621 • Southeastern MO; crossed by the Castor and Whitewater rivers. Part of Mark

Twain National Forest is in the northwest. • Named for George F. Bollinger (?–1842), colonizer and state legislator • 1851 from Cape Girardeau, Madison, Stoddard, and Wayne • Corn, soybeans, wheat, livestock; timber.

BOONE (one of eight counties so named) *Columbia* •135,454 • 685 • Central MO, bounded on the southwest by the Missouri River and on the east in part by the Cedar River. The county includes Rock Bridge Memorial State Park, Jewell Cemetery State Historic Site, Finger Lakes State Park (a reclaimed strip mine), and parts of Mark Twain National Forest. • One of seven counties named for Daniel Boone • 1820 (prior to statehood) from Howard • In 1839, residents of Columbia pledged $117,900 for the location in their city of a state university (now the University of Missouri), the first west of the Mississippi River. The world's first school of journalism opened here in 1908. On September 27, 1864, bushwhacker Bill Anderson ransacked Centralia and robbed the North Missouri Railroad after it arrived in town, killing over twenty unarmed Federal soldiers in the process. • Corn, wheat, soybeans, hay, pumpkins, cattle, sheep; lumber; limestone; insurance; light manufacturing; a major education center. (Established in 1833, Stephens College [originally the Columbia Female Academy] is the oldest women's college west of the Mississippi. Columbia College is also here.) • Thomas Jefferson's original tombstone is located on the Francis Quadrangle of the University of Missouri. The original tombstones of Daniel and Rebecca Boone are part of the historical collections of Stephens College.

BUCHANAN *St. Joseph* • 85,998 • 410 • Northwestern MO, bounded on the west by the Missouri River (here forming the KS state line); drained by the Little Platte. Lewis and Clark State Park is in the southwest. Kneib Memorial Conservation Area is also in the county. • One of three counties named for President James Buchanan • 1838 from Platte • St. Joseph was departure point and supply depot for parties bound for Oregon Territory and the gold fields of CA. The Pony Express operated between St. Joseph and Sacramento, CA in 1860 and 1861 (Pony Express Stables Museum). During the Civil War, the city was a center for guerrilla operations and was frequented by Confederate terrorist W. C. Quantrill. • Saxophonist Coleman Hawkins; television journalist Walter Cronkite; governor and director of U.S. mint Nellie Tayloe Ross; outlaw Jesse James; journalist and poet Eugene Field (his "Lovers' Lane, Saint Jo" was a remembrance of the St. Joseph street where he courted his wife); politician Thomas J. Pendergast • Cattle, hogs, corn, wheat, hay, apples, tobacco; limestone; meat packing, dairy product processing; manufacture of concrete, structural steel, wire rope, auto cables, fire fighting equipment, boats, chemicals, paper products, machinery, clothing; education (MO Western State College). St. Joseph is a trading point for fifteen counties in MO, IA, NE, and KS.

BUTLER (one of eight counties so named) *Poplar Bluff* • 40,867 • 698 • Southeastern MO, bounded on the east by the

St. Francis River and on the south by the AR state line; drained by the Black River. The Ozark Mountains are in the northwest. Coon Island Conservation Area is also here. The county includes parts of Mark Twain National Forest and a small part of Lake Wappapello reservoir. • One of three counties named for Major William O. Butler (1791–1880), officer in the War of 1812 and Mexican-American War, and U.S. representative from KY • 1849 from Wayne • Cotton, corn, soybeans, rice, apples, livestock; lumber; manufacturing.

CALDWELL (one of five counties so named) *Kingston* • 8,969 • 429 • Northwestern MO; drained by Shoal Creek • Named for either Matthew Caldwell (?–1842), signer of the TX Declaration of Independence, or for General John W. Caldwell (1757–1804), KY Indian fighter and legislator • 1836 from Ray • Merchant J.C. Penney (museum) • Corn, wheat, oats, soybeans, cattle, hogs; some manufacturing.

CALLAWAY *Fulton* • 40,766 • 839 • Central MO, bounded on the south by the Missouri River and on the west by the Cedar River. The county includes Katy Trail State Park and part of Mark Twain National Forest. There has been some urban growth from Jefferson City in the south. • Named for Captain James Callaway (1783–1815), grandson of Daniel Boone, killed in a battle with Indians • 1820 (prior to statehood) from Howard, Boone, and Montgomery • During the Civil War, the county seceded from the U.S. and by treaty with the state militia formed the "Kingdom of Callaway." Serious flooding in 1993 damaged part of the county. • Corn, wheat, oats, soybeans, hay, cattle, hogs, saddle horses; fire clay, coal, limestone; manufacture of firebrick from local clay deposits, farm machinery, electrical equipment, shoes; education (William Woods U.; state hospital and school for the deaf) • On March 5, 1946, Sir Winston Churchill delivered his famous "Iron Curtain" speech at Westminster College. To commemorate the event, the Winston Churchill Memorial and Library was created on the campus in 1965. It is a brick-by-brick reconstruction of the Church of St. Mary the Virgin, Aldermanbury, London, designed by Sir Christopher Wren in 1677 and largely destroyed by bombing in World War II.

CAMDEN (one of four counties so named) *Camdenton* • 37,051 • 655 • Central MO, crossed by Lake of the Ozarks (forming part of the northern boundary); drained by the Niangua River. The county is in the Ozarks, and includes Lake of the Ozarks State Park and Ha Ha Tonka State Park (which features an outstanding example of a karst site, formed by the collapse of a major cave system). The county is underlaid by many caves and springs. There has been a large increase in seasonal and permanent residents on the lake over the last thirty years. • Named for Camden County, NC, itself named for Charles Pratt (1714–94), first Earl of Camden, English statesman who supported the American colonies before the Revolutionary War • Organized 1841 as Kinderhook from Pulaski, Morgan and Benton counties; name changed 1843 • Corn, wheat, dairying, turkeys, cattle; oak, cedar, pine; manufacturing; resort and recreational tourism.

CAPE GIRARDEAU *Jackson* • 68,693 • 579 • Southeastern MO, bounded on the east by the Mississippi River (here forming the IL state line), crossed by the Whitewater River, with drainage channels in the south. The county contains Trail of Tears State Park. Bollinger Mill State Historic Site is also here. • Named for the Spanish District of Cape Girardeau, itself named for Jean Girardot, a French naval officer stationed at Kaskaskia, IL and later a trading-post operator • Original county; organized 1812 (prior to statehood) • Cape Girardeau city was a bustling port until occupation by Union troops during the Civil War. • Radio talk show host Rush Limbaugh • Corn, soybeans, hay, peaches, cattle; lumber; dairy products; meat packing; manufacture of cement, paper products, electrical appliances, clothing, shoes; education (Southeast MO State U.).

CARROLL (one of thirteen counties so named) *Carrollton* • 10,285 • 695 • Northwest-central MO, bounded on the south by the Missouri River, on the east by the Grand River. Bunch Hollow Conservation Area is in the north. • One of twelve counties named for Charles Carroll (1737–1832), U.S. senator from MD and founder of the Baltimore and Ohio Railroad. (Originally intended to be named Wakenda for the county's large east-west creek; the name was changed when news was received of the November 1832 death of Marylander Charles Carroll, the last surviving signer of the Declaration of Independence) • 1833 from Ray • Wheat, corn, soybeans, pecans, hogs, cattle; manufacturing.

CARTER (one of five counties so named) *Van Buren* • 5,941 • 508 • Southern MO; drained by the Current River. The county includes part of Mark Twain National Forest and Big Spring, a former state park. Peck Ranch Conservation Area is also here. Ozark National Scenic Riverways follows the Current River from north to south through the center of the county. More than two-thirds of the county is occupied by national forest, national park or state forest. • Named for Zimri A. Carter (1794–1870), the county's first settler and later its richest resident • 1859 from Ripley, Reynolds, Shannon, and Oregon • Livestock; lumber, timber; tourism.

CASS (one of nine counties so named) *Harrisonville* • 82,092 • 699 • Western MO; drained by the South Grand River (forming part of the southern boundary). The Kansas City metropolitan area extends into the northern part of the county. • One of eight counties named for Gen. Lewis Cass (1782–1866), U.S. secretary of war, U.S. secretary of state and 1848 Democratic presidential candidate • Organized as Van Buren County 1835 from Jackson. Name changed in 1849 • The Dalton Brothers outlaw gang • Corn, wheat, sorghum, sweet corn, cattle, horses, poultry; oil and gas wells, limestone.

CEDAR (one of three counties so named) *Stockton* • 13,733 • 476 • Western MO, in the Ozark region; drained by the Sac River (forming Stockton Lake reservoir in the southeast). Stockton State Park is on the peninsula at the center of the lake. • Named for Cedar Creek, which flows through it • 1845 from Dade and Saint Clair • Corn, wheat, hay, soybeans, cattle; hardwood timber.

CHARITON *Keytesville* • 8,438 • 756 • North-central MO, bounded on the south by the Missouri River and on the west by the Grand River; drained by the Chariton River and Mussel Fork. The county includes Swan Lake National Wildlife Refuge. • Named for either the Chariton River or the town of Chariton • 1820 (prior to statehood) from Howard • Army officer Maxwell Davenport Taylor • Corn, wheat, soybeans, hogs, cattle, sheep; bituminous coal; some manufacturing • The General Sterling Price Museum is located in Keytesville.

CHRISTIAN (one of three counties so named) *Ozark* • 54,285 (66% increase since 1990; the fastest growing county in MO) • 563 • Southwestern MO, in the Ozark Mountains; drained by the James River. Part of Mark Twain National Forest is in the southeast quarter. There is urban growth from Springfield to the north. • Named for Christian County in KY, itself named for Col. William Christian (?–1786), army officer, Indian fighter, and legislator • 1859 from Taney, Greene, and Webster • Health spas thrived near the Reno and Eau de Vie springs during the 1880s. • Playwright Lanford Wilson; MO's Poet Laureate George Nicholas Rees; Vaudeville family of performers, the Weavers • Corn, wheat, hay, berries, apples, peaches, dairying, cattle, horses; timber; manufacturing.

CLARK (one of twelve counties so named) *Kahoka* • 7,416 • 507 • Extreme northeastern MO, bounded on the southeast by the Mississippi River (forming the IL state line), and on the northwest by the Des Moines River (forming the IA state line); drained by the Fox and Wyaconda rivers. Fox Valley Lake Conservation Area and Battle of Athens State Historic Park are here. • One of three counties named for William Clark (1770–1838), explorer and co-leader of the Lewis and Clark Expedition (The county is adjacent to Lewis County.) • 1836 from Lewis • Flooding in 1993 heavily damaged the eastern part of the county. • Sociologist Neil Joseph Smelser • Soybeans, corn, sheep, cattle, hogs.

CLAY (one of eighteen counties so named) *Liberty* • 184,006 • 396 • Western MO, bounded on the south by the Missouri River. The county is highly urbanized in the south as part of the Kansas City metropolitan area, and rural in the north. Part of Smithville Lake reservoir and Watkins Mill State Park (the only 19th century textile factory in the U.S. with original machinery) are here. • One of fifteen counties named for Henry Clay (1777–1852), U.S. senator from KY, known as the "Great Pacificator" for his advocacy of compromise to avert national crises • 1822 from Ray • Outlaws Jesse and Frank James (farm and museum) • Corn, oats, wheat, soybeans, pumpkins, tobacco, cattle; coal deposits, limestone; light manufactures, including plastics; education (William Jewell College). The county has a large underground mine storage space used for wholesaling and frozen food containment. • Joseph Smith,

first prophet and president of the Mormon Church, was incarcerated in the historic Liberty jail. The Hall of Waters, built in Excelsior Springs in 1937, originally featured the world's largest mineral baths. Visitors today may drink at the world's largest water bar and sample from among a variety of healthful waters, including the only natural supply of iron manganese mineral water in the U.S.

CLINTON (one of nine counties so named) *Plattsburg* • 18,979 • 419 • Northwestern MO; drained by the Little Platte River and Shoal Creek. Part of Smithville Lake (reservoir) and Wallace State Park are here. • One of eight counties named for De Witt Clinton (1769–1828), governor of NY and supporter of the Erie Canal • 1833 from Clay and Ray • Corn, wheat, soybeans, cattle, sheep, hogs; natural gas.

COLE *Jefferson City* • 71,397 • 392 • Central MO, bounded on the north by the Missouri River, and on the east by the Osage River. The northern part of the county is urbanized. • Named for Captain Stephen Cole (?–1822), an Indian fighter • 1820 (prior to statehood) from Cooper • Located near the geographical center of the state, Jefferson City was laid out by Daniel M. Boone, son of the KY frontiersman on land donated under an act of the U.S. Congress that specified it be within forty miles of the mouth of the Osage river. The city became the state capital in 1826. The present capitol (1911–18) contains murals by Thomas Hart Benton. • Wheat, hay, corn, dairying, poultry, livestock, limestone quarrying; manufacturing • Lincoln University, now racially integrated, was founded in Jefferson City in 1866 by Black Union Army veterans.

COOPER *Boonville* • 16,670 • 565 • Central MO, bounded on the north by the Missouri River; drained by the Lamine and Blackwater rivers • Named for either Sarshall Cooper, an early settler; or for Benjamin Cooper, early settler and legislator • 1818 (prior to statehood) from Howard • Settled in 1810, Boonville was an important depot for pioneers traveling to the Southwest via the Santa Fe Trail. On June 17, 1861, Union troops defeated state forces here in the first Civil War battle west of the Mississippi. • MO congressman and fur trader William Henry Ashley • Wheat, corn, soybeans, peaches, dairying, cattle, turkeys; limestone; manufacture of electrical appliances, fiber-glass boats, fiber board, wood products, women's shoes • Kemper Military School, the oldest military academy west of the Mississippi (1844), is still operating in Boonville. • The first herd of purebred shorthorn cattle was raised in Ravenswood. The largest corn cob pipe factory in the U.S. was located here. The Ouija Board, crockpot, and self-closing barn door latch were all invented here. Thespian Hall (1855–57), the oldest theater building west of the Alleghenies, hosts the Big Muddy Folk Festival and the Missouri River Festival. It was a supply depot, barracks, and hospital during the Civil War.

CRAWFORD (one of eleven counties so named) *Steelville* • 22,804 • 743 • East-central MO; drained by the Meramec River. The county is located in the Ozark Mountains. Mark

Twain National Forest is here, as are Onondaga Cave State Park and Huzzah Conservation Area. • One of six counties named directly or indirectly for William Harris Crawford (1772–1834), U.S. senator from GA, U.S. secretary of war, and U.S. secretary of treasury • 1829 from Gasconade • Wheat, corn, hay, grapes, cattle; oak; fire clay; manufacturing; wineries; tourism (canoeing, fishing) • The population center of the U.S. in 1990 was 9.7 miles southeast of Steelville.

DADE *Greenfield* • 7,923 • 490 • Southwestern MO; drained by the Sac River (here forming part of Stockton Lake reservoir in the northeast). The county lies in the Ozarks. • One of three counties named in part or in full for Francis L. Dade (?–1835), U.S. army officer killed in the Second Seminole War • 1841 from Polk and Barry • Greenfield was often raided by Confederate soldiers because of the location of the Union garrisons here. • Wheat, hay, corn, sorghum, fruit, soybeans, dairying, livestock; coal, limestone; manufacturing.

DALLAS (one of five counties so named) *Buffalo* • 15,661 • 542 • Southwest-central MO; drained by the Niangua and Little Niangua rivers. The county is located in the Ozarks. Bennett Spring State Park and Lead Mine Conservation Area are here. • One of three counties named for George Mifflin Dallas (1792–1864), senator from PA, U.S. vice president, and U.S. minister to Russia and Great Britain • Organized as Niangua in 1841 from Polk; name changed in 1844 • Cattle, poultry; timber; manufacturing.

DAVIESS *Gallatin* • 8,016 • 567 • Northwestern MO; drained by the Grand River. There is an Amish community near Jamesport. • One of four counties named for Col. Joseph H. Daveiss (1774–1811), VA soldier and attorney who unsuccessfully attempted to indict Aaron Burr for treason. The name was misspelled in the act creating the county and allowed to stand. • 1836 from Ray • The James gang robbed the Daviess County Savings Association in 1869; one of their last robberies occurred in nearby Winston. Frank James was acquitted by a jury of southern sympathizers in Gallatin of an 1881 train robbery and murder in Winston. • Corn, wheat, hay, soybeans, cattle, sheep, hogs, dairying. The rotary jail in Gallatin, from a design patented by W.H. Brown of Indianapolis in 1881, is one of only three still standing.

DE KALB *Maysville* • 11,597 • 424 • Northwestern MO; drained by branches of the Grand and Platte rivers. Pony Express Lake is in the south. • One of six counties named for Johann, Baron de Kalb (1721–1780), German-born French soldier who fought with the Americans during the Revolutionary War • 1845 from Clinton • Corn, wheat, soybeans, cattle.

DENT *Salem* • 14,927 • 754 • Southeast-central MO; drained by the Meramec and Current rivers. Indian Trail Conservation Area, Montauk State Park, and part of Mark Twain National Forest are all here. • Named for Lewis Dent, early settler and MO legislator • 1851 from Shannon and Crawford • Except for a brief period in 1864 when raiders burned the courthouse and jail, Salem was occupied by the Union army during the Civil War, Federal forces having repulsed the Confederates in a battle fought here on December 3, 1861. Iron mines were developed here in the 1870s. • Corn, wheat, hay, cattle; oak, pine; manufacture of charcoal briquets, shoes, clothing; mining of lead, zinc, copper; tourism, canoeing.

DOUGLAS *Ava* • 13,084 • 815 • Southern MO; drained by the North Fork of the White River and Bryant Creek. The county lies in the Ozark Mountains, with parts of Mark Twain National Forest in the east and in the southwest corner. Honey Branch Cave is also here. • One of twelve counties named for Stephen A. Douglas (1813–61), U.S. orator and statesman • 1857 from Ozark • Corn, hay, apples, dairying, beef cattle, poultry; oak; tourism; manufacturing. • Assumption Abbey, a Cistercian (Trappist) monastery, was founded here in 1950.

DUNKLIN *Kennett* • 33,155 • 546 • In the boot heel of extreme southeastern MO, bounded on the west by the St. Francis River (here forming the AR state line) and on the south by the AR state line. The county is traversed by drainage channels. • Named for Daniel Dunklin (1790–1844), governor of MO • 1845 from Stoddard • The county's land surface was altered by the New Madrid earthquakes of 1811–12. • Cotton, rice, corn, wheat, melons, fruit, popcorn, soybeans, poultry; manufacturing. • After learning that the proposed 1818 AR Territory line would place his property in AR, John H. Walker lobbied to set MO Territory's southeastern line at the 36th parallel, resulting in MO's distinctive boot heel.

FRANKLIN (One of twenty-five counties so named) *Union* • 93,807 • 922 (the fourth largest county in MO) • East-central MO, bounded on the north by the Missouri River; drained by the Meramec and Bourbeuse rivers. Part of the St. Louis metropolitan area is in the eastern half of the county. Meramec Caverns is here, as are Meramec and Robertsville state parks. • One of twenty-three counties named for Benjamin Franklin • 1818 (prior to statehood) from Saint Louis County • The county experienced major German settlement from the 1830s to the 1860s. • Wheat, corn, soybeans, hay, vegetables, dairying, cattle, hogs, horses, mules; lumber; fire clay, limestone; manufacturing. Washington is the world's largest producer of corncob pipes. The Old Springs Cemetery in Gerald features late 19th century and early 20th century folk art embellishments on its markers.

GASCONADE *Hermann* • 15,342 • 519 • East-central MO, bounded on the north by the Missouri River; drained by the Gasconade and Bourbeuse rivers. The county is located in the Ozark Mountain region. Canaan Conservation Area is here. Deutschheim State Historic Site (interpreting 19th century German culture through architecture and exhibits) is located at Hermann. • Named for the Gasconade River • 1820 (prior to statehood) from Franklin • Corn, wheat, grapes (wineries), dairying, cattle, poultry; timber; fire clay; tourism; manufacture of grain products, lumber products, shoes • Hermann holds annual Oktoberfest and Maifest celebrations that attract thousands of tourists.

GENTRY *Albany* • 6,861 • 492 • Northwestern MO; drained by the Grand River • Name for Richard Gentry (1788–1837), officer in the Black Hawk War who died fighting the Seminoles in Florida • 1841 from Clinton • Corn, soybeans, cattle, hogs, poultry; light manufacturing.

GREENE *Springfield* • 240,391 (the fourth most populated county in MO) • 675 • Southwestern MO; drained by the James, Sac, Little Sac, and Pomme de Terre rivers. The county is a tourist center in the southwest Ozarks. Fantastic Caverns and Crystal Cave are north of Springfield; Wilson's Creek National Battlefield is in the south. • One of sixteen counties named for Nathanael Greene (1742–86), general in the Revolutionary War • 1833 from Wayne and Crawford • At Wilson's Creek on August 10, 1861, the first major Civil War engagement west of the Mississippi took place; several months after nominal success by the Confederate army, Federal forces in MO regrouped and took Springfield, the turnover setting events in motion to keep the state in the union. • Outlaw matriarch Ma Barker; zoologist Carl Richard Moore; "Wild Bill" Hickok (who was acquitted in Springfield of the murder of Dave Tutt); pioneer Nathan Boone (state historic site). The "Bird Man of Alcatraz" Robert Stroud died here. • Wheat, soybeans, vegetables, peaches, apples, strawberries, grapes, tomatoes, dairying, cattle, poultry; limestone; manufacture of steel products, televisions, paper containers, refrigeration motors, V-belts; major educational center (Southwest Missouri State U.; Central Bible College; Baptist Bible College; Drury U.; Evangel U.) • The International Headquarters of the Assemblies of God Church is in Springfield.

GRUNDY *Trenton* • 10,432 • 436 • Northern MO; drained by the Thompson and Weldon rivers. Crowder State Park is in the west. • One of four counties named for Felix Grundy (1777–1840), chief justice of KY Supreme Court, U.S. senator from TN, and U.S. attorney general • 1841 from Livingston and Ray • Corn, wheat, cattle; some manufacturing; education (North Central MO College).

HARRISON (one of eight counties so named) *Bethany* • 8,850 • 725 • Northwestern MO, bounded on the north by the IA state line; drained by the Thompson and Grand rivers. The county includes Grand Trace Conservation Area. • Named for Albert G. Harrison (?–1839), U.S. representative from MO • 1845 from Daviess and Ray • Corn, wheat, hay, sheep, cattle; limestone; light manufacturing.

HENRY (one of ten counties so named) *Clinton* • 21,997 • 702 • West-central MO; drained by the South Grand River. South Grand and Tebo Arms of Harry S. Truman Reservoir enter the county from the east. Montrose Conservation Area is in the southwest. • One of ten counties named for Patrick Henry • Organized as Rives 1834 from Lafayette; named changed 1841 • Corn, wheat, soybeans, sorghum, cattle; strip coal mines; some manufacturing; fishing, boating. • Lawrence Brown of Clinton invented Chinkerchek (Chinese checkers) from Chinese chess, and ran a thriving factory here during the 1930s.

HICKORY *Hermitage* • 8,940 • 399 • Central MO; drained by the Pomme de Terre and Little Niangua rivers. Pomme de Terre State Park, Pomme de Terre Lake reservoir, and an arm of Harry S. Truman Reservoir are in the county. • One of twenty-two counties named for President Andrew Jackson; "Old Hickory" was his nickname. • 1845 from Benton and Polk • Corn, wheat, soybeans, hay, dairying, cattle. • One of the best mastodon skeletons ever assembled was first discovered near Hermitage in the mid-1880s (and is now owned by the British Museum).

HOLT (one of two counties so named, the other in NE) *Oregon* • 5,351 • 462 • Northwestern MO, bounded on the west by the Missouri River (here forming the NE state line), on the south and southwest by the Missouri River (here forming the KS state line), and on the east by the Nodaway River; drained by the Tarkio River. Squaw Creek National Wildlife Refuge and Big Lake State Park are here. River Breaks Conservation Area is in the south. • Named for David R. Holt (1803–40), MO legislator • Organized as Nodaway 1841 from Platte Purchase; name changed three weeks later • Corn, wheat, apples, cattle, hogs.

HOWARD (one of seven counties so named) *Fayette* • 10,212 • 466 • Central MO, bounded on the west and south by the Missouri River. • Named for General Benjamin Howard (1760–1814), governor of LA Territory and & MO Territory • 1816 (prior to statehood) from St. Louis and St. Charles counties • Howard is known as the "Mother of Missouri counties" for its large original size and for the fact that so many counties have been formed from it. It was the original eastern terminus of the Santa Fe Trail in the 1820s. • Two of Daniel Boone's sons operated a salt manufacturing business here between 1806 and 1811 (Boone's Lick State Historic Site) • Corn, wheat, apples, soybeans, cattle, hogs, poultry; manufacturing; education (Central Methodist College). • The Great Red Spot of Jupiter was first observed at the Morrison Observatory at Prichett College in 1878.

HOWELL *West Plains* • 37,238 • 928 (the third largest county in MO) • Southern MO, in the Ozarks, bounded on the south by the AR state line; drained by the Eleven Point River (designated here a National Scenic River). Mark Twain National Forest is in the northwest. White Ranch Conservation Area is also here. • Named for either an early settler whose name was James or Josiah Howell, or for Howell Valley • 1857 from Oregon County • Cattle, goats, horses, corn, hay; oak, cedar, pine; stone quarries; manufacture of charcoal, pallets, staves, furniture, electronic equipment, shoes, truck bodies; tourism, canoeing.

IRON (One of four counties so named) *Ironton* • 10,697 • 551 • Southeast-central MO, in the Ozarks. The county rests in the St. Francois Mountains and includes Taum Sauk, at 1,772 feet, the highest mountain in the state. Units of Mark Twain National Forest are in the southeast and west. The county also includes Elephant Rocks State Park. Mina Sauk Falls, the highest waterfall in MO, with a drop of 132 feet, is located near Arcadia. • Named for the area's rich iron deposits • 1857 from Madison, Saint Francois, Wayne, Washington, and Reynolds • Cattle, hogs, mixed farming; manganese, lead, iron, granite, zinc; oak, pine; recreational resorts • While stationed in Ironton, Ulysses Grant received papers designating him as Brigadier General of the Union Army. Every three years in September, the Battle of Pilot Knob is reenacted by Civil War buffs at Fort Davidson State Historic Site. The first excursion train with a mystery theme ran from Arcadia to St. Louis on May 21, 1932.

JACKSON (One of twenty-four counties so named) *Independence* • 654,880 (the second most populated county in MO) • *605* • Western MO, bounded on the north by the Missouri River, the Kansas River entering the Missouri in the northwest corner of the county, and on the west by the KS state line. The oldest and most densely populated part of Kansas City is in the county. Also here are Army Corps of Engineers reservoirs Lake Jacomo, Longview Lake, and Blue Springs Lake. Lake Jacomo Park, and James A. Reed Memorial and Burr Oak Woods wildlife areas are here, as well. • One of twenty-two counties named directly or indirectly for Andrew Jackson • 1826 from Lafayette • Employees of the American Fur Company were the first permanent white settlers at the site of what is now Kansas City. They established a trading post here in 1821. The county was designated as the original Garden of Eden by Mormon prophet Joseph Smith. Independence was the western terminus of transportation on the Missouri River and the starting point for pioneers following the California, Oregon, and Santa Fe trails. Confederates occupied Independence on two occasions at the height of guerrilla activity during the Civil War, each time for only a day. The county's economy, seriously damaged during the war, began to rebound in 1869 when the first railroad bridge over the Missouri River was constructed. Kansas City was a center of the defense industry during World War II. In 1981, the walkway above the Hyatt Regency Hotel lobby collapsed, killing 114. • Actors Jean Harlow, Wallace Beery, and Ginger Rogers; painter Thomas Hart Benton; film director Robert Altman; pianist and composer Louis Horst; artist Robert Morris; pianist Bennie Moten; editor and publisher William Rockhill Nelson; baseball player Satchel Paige; saxophonist Charlie Parker; politician Thomas Pendergast; poet James Tate; composer and music critic Virgil Thomson; U.S. president Harry S. Truman (Library and Museum and national historic site in Independence); blues singer Big Joe Turner; business executive Robert E. Wood; gambler and fight promoter Tex Rickard; dancer Ted Shawn; journalist and author Edgar Snow. Painter George Caleb Bingham and jazz pianist and composer Fats Waller died here. • Wheat, corn, soybeans, dairy products; grain and livestock industries (Kansas City ranks as the largest winter wheat market in the U.S.); manufacture of chemicals, automobiles, clothing, electric equipment, soap, jet fuel, steel products, munitions, farm and industrial machinery, crushed stone, food products (especially ice cream); printing and publishing; wholesale-retail trade, oil refining; education (U. of MO — Kansas City; Avila College; others). Only Buffalo produces more wheat flour than Kansas City. • Independence is the world headquarters of the Reorganized Church of Jesus Christ of Latter Day Saints. Kansas City is second only to Minneapolis-St. Paul, MN, in the capacity of its grain elevators. The Kansas City Livestock Exchange is one of the largest in the nation. Swope Park in Kansas is one of the largest city parks in the U.S. Kansas City is home to the Chiefs (Arrowhead Stadium) and Royals (Kauffman Stadium).

JASPER *Carthage* • 104,686 • 640 • Southwestern MO, bounded on the west by the KS state line; drained by the Spring River. The county has numerous abandoned surface and underground mines. • One of eight counties named for Sgt. William Jasper (?–1779), Revolutionary War soldier. (MO is one of five states in which Jasper and Newton counties have been placed adjacent to one another to honor the allied efforts of sergeants William Jasper and John Newton to rescue captive colonial soldiers near Savannah.) • 1841 from Barry • Carthage was the scene of border warfare between pro- and anti-slavery forces in MO (state historic site); it was destroyed by Confederate guerrillas in 1863 and rebuilt in 1866. The Battle of Carthage, fought on July 5, 1861, was one of the earliest skirmishes of the Civil War. • Baseball player Carl Hubbell; poet Langston Hughes; outlaw Belle Starr • Small grains, soybeans, fruit, poultry, cattle, dairying; manufacture of leather goods, clothing, shoes, spring wire products, typesetting equipment, furniture, insulation materials, explosives, hydraulic pumps, aircraft and missile parts, batteries, chemicals; zinc and lead smelting (mining of the ores was earlier a major industry); limestone (gray marble) quarries; oak; education (MO Southern State College; Ozark Christian College) • The Joplin reading plan, an innovative program for the teaching of reading, won national recognition for the Joplin school system where it was first implemented in 1953.

JEFFERSON *Hillsboro* • 198,099 (the fifth most populated county in MO) • 657 • Eastern MO, bounded on the east by the Mississippi River (forming the IL state line) and on the northeast and northwest by the Meramec River; drained by the Big River. The county is urbanized in the north and east as part of the St. Louis metropolitan area. Mastodon and Sandy Creek Covered Bridge state historic sites are located here. • One of twenty-six counties named directly or indirectly for President Thomas Jefferson • 1818 (prior to statehood) from Saint Genevieve and Saint Louis counties • Basketball player and politician Bill Bradley • Corn, hay, livestock; sand, barite mines; manufacturing. The largest lead smelter in the U.S. (225,000 tons of lead refined annually) operates near Herculaneum.

JOHNSON (one of twelve counties so named) *Warrensburg* • 48,258 • 831 • West-central MO; drained by the Blackwater River. Knob Noster State Park and Whiteman Air Force Base are here. • One of five counties named for Col. Richard Mentor Johnson (1780–1850), officer in the War of 1812, U.S. senator from KY, and U.S. vice president • 1834 from Lafayette • Due to divided loyalties, troops of both the Union and the Confederacy occupied the town of Warrensburg during the Civil War. The county's original courthouse was the scene of future U.S. senator George Vest's classic oration, "Tribute to the Dog," a reaction to an 1870 trial over the killing of a dog by a local farmer. • Automobile manufacturer Erret Lobban Cord • Corn, wheat, sorghum, soybeans, hay, grapes, cattle, horses, coal mines (formerly), sandstone quarries, clay pits; manufacture of clothing, shoes, textiles, lawn mowers, electronic products, chemicals, metal castings; education (Central MO State U.).

KNOX *Edina* • 4,361 • 506 • Northeastern MO; drained by the North Fork of the Salt River, and the Middle and South Fabius rivers • One of nine counties named for General Henry Knox (1750–1806), Revolutionary War officer and first U.S. secretary of war • 1845 from Scotland County • Corn, wheat, hay, soybeans, hogs; lumber; limestone quarrying.

LACLEDE *Lebanon* • 32,513 • 766 • South-central MO, in the Ozarks; drained by the Gasconade River and Osage Fork. Part of Mark Twain National Forest is in the east. Part of Bennett Spring State Park is on the western border. • Named for Pierre Laclede Liguest (?–1778), founder of St. Louis • 1849 from Pulaski, Wright and Camden • Because of its strategic location on the military road between Springfield and St. Louis, the town of Lebanon was occupied alternately by Federal and Confederate forces. • Cattle, wheat, corn, fruit, hay; timber; manufacture of aluminum boats. clothing, barrels; tourism • Harold Bell Wright set his novel *The Calling of Dan Matthews* (1909) at the Lebanon Christian Church, where he earlier served as pastor.

LAFAYETTE (one of six counties so named) *Lexington* • 32,960 • 629 • West-central MO, bounded on the north by the Missouri River. Confederate Memorial State Historic Site is here. • One of seventeen (Fayette and Lafayette) counties named for the Marquis de Lafayette (1757–1834), French statesman and soldier who fought with the Americans during the Revolutionary War • Organized as Lillard 1820 (prior to statehood) from Cooper; name changed 1825 • The nation's first Masonic college operated in Lexington from 1846 to 1859. At the beginning of the Civil War, Lexington commanded the river approach to Fort Leavenworth, KS, and was the most important river town between St. Louis and St. Joseph. At the bloody Battle of Lexington on September 18 and 19, 1861, Union troops under Col. James A. Mulligan were defeated by Confederate forces under Major General Sterling Price (state historic site). • Propagandist George Creel • Higginsville is the "Seed Corn Capital of the U.S." Also, wheat, soybeans, apples, peaches, sorghum, cattle, hogs; limestone rock quarries, coal mines; manufacture of cables, dies, wood products, shirts; tourism.

LAWRENCE (one of eleven counties so named) *Mount Vernon* • 35,204 • 613 • Southwestern MO, in the Ozarks;

drained by the Spring River • One of nine counties named for Captain James Lawrence (1781–1813), U.S. naval officer in the war with Barbary pirates near Tripoli and the War of 1812 • 1845 from Dade and Barry • Wheat, hay, oats, barley, corn, apples, peaches, vegetables, turkeys, cattle, dairying; processing of dairy and grain products.

LEWIS (one of seven counties so named) *Monticello* • 10,494 • 505 • Northeastern MO, bounded on the east by the Mississippi River (forming the IL state line); drained by the Wyaconda River, and North and Middle Fabius rivers. Deer Ridge Conservation Area and Wakonda State Park are here. • One of five counties named for Meriwether Lewis (1774–1809), co-leader of the Lewis and Clark Expedition. (The county is adjacent to Clark County.) • 1833 from Marion • Corn, wheat, soybeans, hogs, cattle; lumber; manufacturing; education (Established in 1853, Culver-Stockton College is the oldest college west of the Mississippi specifically chartered as coeducational.) • The Standard Machine Company in Canton is the world's only manufacturer of flatbed wooden pickle separating machines, and still produces around thirty-five each year.

LINCOLN (one of twenty-four counties so named) *Troy* • 38,944 • 631 • Eastern MO, bounded on the east by the Mississippi river (forming the IL state line); drained by the Cuivre River. Cuivre River State Park is here. • Named for Lincoln counties in KY and NC, themselves named for General Benjamin Lincoln (1733–1810), Revolutionary War officer and U.S. secretary of war • 1818 (prior to statehood) from St. Charles • Publisher Frederick Gilmer Bonfils • Soybeans, corn, apples, cattle, hogs; limestone; manufacturing.

LINN *Linneus* • 13,754 • 620 • North-central MO; drained by Locust Creek. The county includes Pershing State Park and Locust Creek Covered Bridge State Historic Site. • One of four counties named for Lewis F. Linn (1795–1843), U.S. senator from MO • 1837 from Chariton • Walt Disney; General John J. Pershing (state historic site) • Corn, wheat, hay, soybeans, sheep, cattle, hogs; coal; manufacture of pharmaceuticals, uniforms, shoes.

LIVINGSTON (one of six counties so named) *Chillicothe* • 14,558 • 535 • North-central MO; drained by the Grand River. The Grand River Museum is in Chillicothe. The county includes Poosey Conservation Area. • One of three counties definitively named for Edward Livingston (1764–1836), U.S. representative from NY, senator from LA, and U.S. secretary of state • 1837 from Carroll • Corn, wheat, soybeans, cattle; manufacture of filters for farm and road machinery, gloves, mobile homes • A stone column in Chillicothe marks the site where, in 1859, east and west tracks were joined, thus completing the first railroad across MO. Earl and Foreman Sloan first compounded Sloan's Liniment (purported to bring "muscular relief to man and beast") while they operated a livery stable in Chillicothe in the 1870s.

MACON *Macon* • 15,762 • 804 • North-central MO; drained by the Chariton River and the Middle Fork of the Salt River. Long Branch Lake and State Park, and Thomas Hill Reservoir are here. • One of six counties named for Nathaniel Macon (1758–1837), Revolutionary War soldier, NC legislator, representative and senator from NC • 1837 from Randolph and Chariton • The county is in a former coal-mining area. • Corn, wheat, soybeans, hay, cattle, sheep, hogs; manufacturing.

MADISON *Fredericktown* • 11,800 • 497 • Southeastern MO; drained by the St. Francis and Castor rivers. The county lies partly in the St. Francois Mountains. Part of Mark Twain National Forest extends across the county from east to west. • One of twenty counties named directly or indirectly for President James Madison • 1818 (prior to statehood) from Saint Genevieve and Cape Girardeau counties • Recreational tourism (St. Francis River); wheat, corn, hay, livestock; tungsten, manganese, lead, zinc, iron, cobalt, copper, antimony, nickel, granite; manufacturing.

MARIES *Vienna* • 8,903 • 528 • Central MO, in the Ozark Mountains; drained by the Gasconade River (forming part of the southern boundary). Spring Creek Gap Conservation Area is here. • Named for the Maries River and Little Maries River, which flow through the county • 1855 from Osage and Pulaski • Wheat, corn, cattle; timber; charcoal.

MARION *Palmyra* • 28,289 • 438 • Northeastern MO, bounded on the east by the Mississippi River (forming the IL state line); drained by the North and South Fabius rivers. • One of seventeen counties named for the "Swamp Fox," SC Revolutionary War general Francis Marion (?–1795) • 1822 from Ralls • Aided by steamboats and the arrival of the Hannibal and St. Joseph Railroad, Hannibal was a prosperous trading center. MO's first city-owned power and light company was built here in 1886 and MO's first tax-supported library was constructed here in 1889. • Parvenu Molly Brown; electrical engineer and industrialist William P. Lear; Mark Twain, who drew heavily from his boyhood in Hannibal for *Tom Sawyer* and *Huckleberry Finn.* (Reputedly the first statue in the U.S. to commemorate a literary character, the "Tom and Huck," was erected in Hannibal in 1926. The Tom Sawyer Days festival is an annual event in the town.) • Corn, wheat, soybeans, dairying, hogs, cattle; diversified manufacturing; limestone; education (Hannibal–La Grange College).

MCDONALD *Pineville* • 21,681 • 540 • Extreme southwestern MO, in the Ozarks, bounded on the west by the OK state line and on the south by the AR state line; drained by the Elk River. Huckleberry Ridge Conservation Area and Bluff Dwellers Cave are here. • Named for Sergeant Alexander McDonald, a soldier in the American Revolution • 1849 • Berries, grapes, tomatoes, vegetables, grain, dairying, turkeys, a major chicken broiler producer; lumber; tourism.

MERCER (one of eight counties so named) *Princeton* • 3,757 • 454 • Northern MO, bounded on the north by the IA state line; drained by the Weldon River. Lake Paho is in the county.

• The derivation of this county's name has never been firmly established. It was most likely named for Gen. Hugh Mercer (?–1777), Revolutionary War officer, and if so, is one of seven counties named for the general. • 1845 from Grundy and Livingston • Soybeans, corn, hogs, cattle; manufacturing.

MILLER (one of three counties so named) *Tuscumbia* • 23,564 • 592 • Central MO, in the Ozark region; drained by the Osage River. Bagnell Dam on the Osage River forms Lake of the Ozarks in the southwest, a major recreation area. Lake of the Ozarks State Park is the largest state park in MO. • Named for Col. John Miller (1781–1846), officer in the War of 1812, governor of MO and U.S. representative • 1837 from Cole and Pulaski • Corn, wheat, cattle, poultry; timber; hydroelectricity; manufacturing.

MISSISSIPPI (one of two counties so named, the other in AR) *Charleston* • 13,427 • 413 • Southeastern MO, bounded on the north and east by the Mississippi River (forming the IL and KY state lines). Big Oak Tree State Park and Towosahgy State Historical Site are here. • Named for its location on the Mississippi River • 1845 from Scott • The Battle of Belton, fought on November 7, 1861, was reputedly Ulysses S. Grant's first battle. • Corn, cotton, soybeans, wheat, potatoes, popcorn, melons, livestock; cotton processing; lumber; manufacture of shoes • Several Indian mounds are located in the county.

MONITEAU *California* • 14,827 • 417 • Central MO, bounded on the northeast by the Missouri River • Named for Moniteau Creek, its western portion flowing through the county • 1845 from Cole and Morgan; annexed a small part of Morgan in 1881 • Wheat, corn, soybeans, cattle, poultry; limestone; manufacturing.

MONROE *Paris* • 9,311 • 646 • Northeastern MO; drained by the Middle and North Forks of the Salt River (the latter forming Mark Twain Lake reservoir in the east). Mark Twain State Park and Birthplace is in Florida. Union Covered Bridge State Historic Site is also here. • One of seventeen counties named for President James Monroe • 1831 from Ralls • Cattle, sheep, saddle horses; lumber; manufacturing.

MONTGOMERY (One of eighteen counties so named) *Montgomery City* • 12,136 • 539 • East-central MO, bounded on the south by the Missouri River; drained by the Cuivre River. Graham Cave State Park is here. • One of sixteen counties named directly or indirectly for General Richard Montgomery (1738–75), American Revolutionary War officer who captured Montreal, Canada • 1818 (prior to statehood) from St. Charles • Danville was burned in 1864 by the infamous bushwhacker Bill Anderson. Flooding destroyed Rhineland and McKittrick in 1993. • Corn, wheat, soybeans, cattle, sheep, hogs; manufacturing; limestone, fire-clay pits. • The formula for 7-Up was invented by Charles Leeper Griggs at Price's Branch.

MORGAN (one of eleven counties so named) *Versailles* •

19,309 • 597 • Central MO, on the Ozarks; drained by the Osage River (here forming Lake of the Ozarks reservoir along the southern boundary). Much development has occurred along the reservoir. • One of nine counties named for General Daniel Morgan (1736–1802), an officer in the Revolutionary War and U.S. representative from VA • 1833 from Cooper • Zebulon Pike and his 1806 expedition followed the Osage River as it snaked through present day Morgan County. The Butterfield Overland Mail, which ran from 1858 to 1861, had relay stations at Syracuse and Florence. • Wheat, corn, cattle, poultry; manufacturing; timber; tourism • Versailles has a large Amish community.

NEW MADRID *New Madrid* • 19,760 • 678 • Southeastern MO, bounded on the east by the Mississippi River (here forming the KY and TN state lines); crossed by the Little River and drainage channels. Hunter-Dawson State Historic Site is in New Madrid. • Named for the New Madrid Spanish district • Original county; organized 1812 (prior to statehood) • The county was settled about 1788 by French Creoles and Americans. • The worst earthquakes in U.S. history occurred here in 1811 and 1812. Floods and shifts in the course of the Mississippi River caused several removals of New Madrid city to different sites, and transformed the county's land surface and drainage patterns. Union General John Pope gained control over New Madrid and a portion of the river in 1862 during the Battle of Island #10. • Cotton, rice, soybeans, corn, grain sorghum, wheat, melons, livestock; some lumbering; aluminum processing; manufacture of shoes, clothing, canvas products, toys, locks, milk cartons, telecommunications shelters, electrical conductors.

NEWTON (one of six counties so named) *Neosho* • 52,636 • 626 • Southwestern MO, in the Ozarks, bounded on the west by the KS and OK state lines. The county includes part of the city of Joplin in the northwest. It has nine flowing springs, the largest of which is in Big Spring State Park within the city limits of Neosho. • One of five counties named for Sgt. John Newton (?–1780), Revolutionary War hero. (MO is one of five states in which Jasper and Newton counties have been placed adjacent to one another to honor the allied efforts of sergeants William Jasper and John Newton to rescue captive colonial soldiers near Savannah.) • 1838 from Barry • The Civil War Secession Legislature met at the courthouse in Neosho in October, 1861. During the war, the county was the scene of many battles and skirmishes. Newtonia saw fighting on April 30, 1861 and October 28, 1864. • Black agronomist George Washington Carver (national monument); painter Thomas Hart Benton • Vegetables, berries, hay, apples, corn, wheat, dairying, cattle, horses, poultry; oak; light manufacturing, including clothing, wire products, furniture; rocket-engine testing; lead and zinc mining • Camp Crowder, the largest U. S. Army Signal Corps Camp in the world when built in 1941, is located in Neosho. Herman Jaeger, a Swiss immigrant to the county, was awarded the French Legion of Honor in 1889 after he sent

seventeen boxcars of local grape cuttings to replace the blighted vines in France. Neosho has one of the oldest U.S. Fish and Wildlife Service hatcheries, established in 1887.

NODAWAY *Maryville* • 21,912 • 877 (the fifth largest county in MO) • Northwestern MO; drained by the Nodaway (forming part of the southwestern boundary), Little Platte and One Hundred and Two rivers. • Named for the Nodaway River • 1845 from Andrew • Opera conductor and impresario Sarah Caldwell; public speaking pioneer Dale Carnegie • Corn, wheat, oats, soybeans, cattle, hogs; manufacturing; education (Northwest MO State U.).

OREGON *Alton* • 10,344 • 791 • Southern MO, in the Ozarks, bounded on the south by the AR state line; drained by the Eleven Point (designated as a National Scenic River) and Spring rivers. Grand Gulf State Park and part of Mark Twain National Forest are here. Several natural springs are located near Alton, an area that is reputed to have MO's largest daily volume of flowing spring water. • Named for Oregon Territory • 1845 from Ripley • Hay, cattle, hogs, dairying; oak, hickory, walnut; manufacturing.

OSAGE (one of three counties so named) *Linn* • 13,062 • 606 • Central MO, in the Ozark region, bounded on the north by the Missouri River and on the west by the Osage River; drained by the Gasconade and Maries rivers. The county is known for its picturesque villages. • Named for the Osage River • 1841 from Gasconade • The county was settled by German immigrants beginning in the 1830s. • Corn, wheat, vegetables, hay, cattle, poultry, dairying; wineries; fire-clay pits.

OZARK *Gainesville* • 9,542 • 747 • Southern MO, bounded on the south by the AR state line; drained by the North Fork of the White River. Caney Mountain Conservation Area and parts of Mark Twain National Forest are here. Arms of Bull Shoals Lake reservoir are in the southwest. • Named for the Ozark Mountains • 1841 from Taney; name changed 1843 to Decatur; name changed back to Ozark in 1845 • Hay, cattle; cedar, oak, pine; recreational tourism.

PEMISCOT *Caruthersville* • 20,047 • 493 • In the boot heel of extreme southeastern MO, bounded on the east by the Mississippi River (here forming the TN state line) and on the south by the AR state line. • Its name comes from the county's principal bayou • 1851 from New Madrid • The county's land surface and drainage were modified by the New Madrid earthquakes of 1811–12. • Cotton, rice, corn, soybeans; manufacturing. • After learning that the proposed 1818 AR Territory line would place his property in AR, John H. Walker lobbied to set MO Territory's southeastern line at the 36th parallel, resulting in MO's distinctive boot heel.

PERRY *Perryville* • 18,132 • 475 • Eastern MO, bounded on the east by the Mississippi River (forming the IL state line). • One of ten counties named for Oliver H. Perry (1785–1819), U.S. naval officer who won the Battle of Lake Erie in the War of 1812 • 1820 (prior to statehood) from St. Genevieve • Corn, wheat, soybeans, hogs, cattle; lumber; manufacturing • The county is noted for its German heritage, especially through the location of the Lutheran-Missouri Synod here. The Log Cabin College, built in 1839 and now located in Altenburg, was the first Lutheran seminary west of the Mississippi; it later became Concordia Seminary and was transferred to St. Louis in 1849. The world's largest pipeline suspension bridge (2,150 feet) crosses the Mississippi River near Wittenberg, delivering natural gas from the TX coast to the Chicago market.

PETTIS *Sedalia* • 39,403 • 685 • Central MO; drained by the Lamine River. Bothwell Lodge State Historic Site is here, as is Katy Trail State Park. • Named for Spencer Pettis (1802–31), U.S. senator and representative from MO • 1833 from Saline and Cooper • Sedalia was a Federal military post during the Civil War and was raided by Confederate general Sterling Price. Union generals Nathaniel Lyon and John C. Frémont outfitted their troops here. With the arrival of the Missouri-Kansas-Texas Railroad, the town became the site of large railroad shops. Sedalia claims to be the birthplace of the ragtime craze, based upon the fact that Scott Joplin wrote and played "Maple Leaf Rag" (and other rags) at the town's Maple Leaf Saloon. • Corn, wheat, hay, dairying, eggs, poultry, cattle, horses, mules; manufacture of glass, textiles, prefabricated houses, truck bodies, disinfectants, dog food, chemicals, shoes, clothing, tools, home appliances; photo processing; steel fabrication; limestone quarries • Sedalia is the site of the Missouri State Fair.

PHELPS (one of two counties so named, the other in NE) *Rolla* • 39,825 • 673 • Central MO, in the Ozarks; drained by the Meramec and Gasconade rivers (the latter forming part of the northwest boundary). Part of Mark Twain National Forest is in the southwest. The county also contains Onyx Mountain Caverns. • Named for John S. Phelps (1814–86), MO legislator, U.S. representative and governor • 1857 from Crawford • Rolla, the end of the line of railroad transportation to the south and the west in 1860, served as a staging area for Union troops before they transferred to the battles of Wilson Creek in Missouri, and Pea Ridge and Prairie Grove in Arkansas. • Wineries; grapes, fruit, corn, hay, livestock; timber; fire-clay pits; manufacturing; education (U. of MO-Rolla — containing an experimental mine, mineral museum, and a partial replica of Stonehenge) • Based upon data from the 2000 census, the center of population for the U.S. is 2.8 miles east of Edgar Springs.

PIKE *Bowling Green* • 18,351 • 673 • Eastern MO, bounded on the east by the Mississippi River (forming the IL state line); crossed by the Salt River. Ted Shanks and Dupont Reservoir conservation areas are here. • One of ten counties named for Zebulon M. Pike (1779–1813), U.S. army officer and discoverer of Pikes Peak, CO • 1818 (prior to statehood) from St. Charles • Wheat, corn, soybeans, apples, cattle, hogs; limestone; manufacturing • There is an Amish community near Curryville.

PLATTE (one of three counties so named) *Platte City* • 73,781 • 420 • Western MO, bounded on the south and west by the Missouri River (forming the KS state line); drained by the Platte River. The county is partly urbanized as part of the Kansas City metropolitan area. Weston Bend State Park is here, as is Kansas City International Airport. Snow Creek ski area is also here. • Named for the Platte Purchase (of lands from the Indians) • 1838 from Platte Purchase • Wheat, corn, tobacco (the only market west of the Mississippi River); alcohol distilling; education (Park U.) • Lewis and Clark State Park honors the expedition that journeyed through the county.

POLK (one of twelve counties so named) *Bolivar* • 26,992 • 637 • Southwest-central MO, in the Ozarks; drained by the Pomme de Terre River and Little Sac River. Pomme de Terre Lake reservoir is on the northern border and Little Sac arm of Stockton Lake reservoir is in the southwest. Snow Bluff ski area is here. • One of eleven counties named for President James Knox Polk • 1835 from Greene and Laclede • Corn, wheat, sorghum, hay, cattle, horses, poultry; timber; manufacturing; education (Southwest Baptist U.) • A plaque in Brighton marks the site of a Butterfield stagecoach way station and the first telegraph office in southwest MO. A statue of Simon Bolivar was presented to its namesake city by Venezuela president Romulo Gollegos and dedicated by President Harry S. Truman in 1948.

PULASKI *Waynesville* • 41,165 • 547 • Central MO, in the Ozark Mountains; drained by the Gasconade and Big Piney rivers. Part of Mark Twain National Forest occupies the southern half of the county. Fort Leonard Wood Military Reservation, a basic training facility and airport, is in the south. • One of seven counties named for Count Casimir Pulaski (1748–79), Polish soldier who fought for America during the Revolutionary War • 1833 from Crawford • Corn, wheat, fruit, livestock; manufacturing.

PUTNAM (one of nine counties so named) *Unionville* • 5,223 • 518 • Northern MO, bounded on the east by the Chariton River and on the north by the IA state line; drained by Locust Creek. Lake Thunderhead is here. Rebel's Cove Conservation Area is in the northwest. • One of eight counties definitively named for General Israel Putnam (1718–90), Revolutionary War officer and American commander at the Battle of Bunker Hill • Established 1843 from Adair, Sullivan, and Linn; annexed Dodge in 1853 • Corn, wheat, soybeans, sheep, cattle; manufacturing.

RALLS *New London* • 9,626 • 471 • Northeastern MO, bounded on the northeast by the Mississippi River (forming the IL state line); drained by the Salt River. Lock and Dam No. 21 is on the Mississippi River in the north. Clarence Cannon Dam and part of Mark Twain Lake reservoir are here. • Named for Daniel Ralls (?–1820), a MO legislator • 1820 (prior to statehood) from Pike • Soybeans, corn, wheat, cattle, hogs.

RANDOLPH (one of eight counties so named) *Huntsville* • 24,663 • 482 • North-central MO; drained by tributaries of the Chariton and Salt rivers. Thomas Hill Dam and Reservoir are in the northwest. • One of four counties named for John Randolph (1773–1833), VA statesman and U.S. minister to Russia • 1829 from Chariton and Ralls • Army general Omar Bradley; leftist writer Jack Conroy • Corn, wheat, oats, soybeans, cattle; manufacturing; bituminous coal, limestone quarries; education (Central Christian College) • MO's only life-size statue of Abraham Lincoln is located in the Oakland Cemetery in Moberly.

RAY *Richmond* • 23,354 • 569 • West-central MO, bounded on the south by the Missouri River; drained by the Crooked River. • Named for John Ray (?–1820), a MO legislator when the county was named • 1820 (prior to statehood) from Howard • Ray was formerly a coal mining county. • Confederate guerrilla Capt. William "Bloody Bill" Anderson was killed in Orrick by Federal forces in 1864. • Corn, wheat, soybeans, vegetable farming, hogs, cattle; manufacture of plastics • Richmond, the self-proclaimed "Morel Mushroom Capital of the World," hosts the Mushroom Festival every spring. Two witnesses to Joseph Smith's revelations are buried in local cemeteries.

REYNOLDS *Centerville* • 6,689 • 811 • Southeastern MO, in the Ozarks; drained by the Black River (forming Clearwater Lake reservoir on the southeast border). Part of Mark Twain National Forest is in the northwest. Deer Run Conservation Area and Johnson Shut-ins State Park are here. • Named for Thomas Reynolds (1796–1844), IL legislator, MO legislator, and governor of MO • 1845 from Shannon • Livestock, hay; pine, oak; granite, lead; wood products.

RIPLEY *Doniphan* • 13,509 • 629 • Southern MO, in the Ozarks; drained by the Current and Little Black rivers. The Current River Heritage Museum is in Doniphan. Part of Mark Twain National Forest is in the northwest quarter of the county. • One of two counties (the other in IN) named for General Eleazar W. Ripley (1782–1839), officer in the War of 1812, MA legislator, and U.S. representative from LA • 1833 from Wayne • Recreational tourism; hay, livestock; timber; rock quarries; wood-product industries.

SAINT CHARLES (one of two counties so named, the other in LA) *Saint Charles* • 283,883 (the third most populated county in MO) • 561 • Eastern MO, bounded on the east and north by the Mississippi River (forming the IL state line) and on the south by the Missouri River, which enters the Mississippi here. The county is located in the extensive St. Louis metropolitan area. Flooding often occurs on the low-lying alluvial peninsula between the Missouri and Mississippi rivers. • Named for the Saint Charles Spanish district • Original county; organized 1812 (prior to statehood) • Saint Charles city was settled in 1769 by French pioneers. It was from Saint Charles (then called San Carlos) that Lewis and Clark began their westward expedition in May, 1804. The city served as MO's first capital from 1821 to 1826 (state historic site). The eastern part of the county experienced extensive flood damage in 1993. • Frontiersman Daniel Boone (his last home here),

Chicago founder Jean Baptiste Point du Sable, and Saint Rose Philippine Duchesne all died here. • Corn, soybeans, wheat, oats, hay; manufacture of automobiles, dresses, beer, dairy products, aluminum products, electronic equipment; education (Lindenwood U. [est. 1827] was the first college west of the Mississippi to offer degrees to women).

SAINT CLAIR (one of four counties so named) *Osceola* • 9,652 • 677 • Western MO; drained by the Osage and Sac rivers. Part of Schell-Osage Conservation Area is here. The Taberville Prairie here is, at 1,360 acres, the state's largest prairie natural area, and has one of the state's largest populations of prairie chickens. The Osage arm of Harry S. Truman Reservoir extends southwest to Roscoe. • One of three counties named for General Arthur St. Clair (1736–1818), officer in the Revolutionary War and governor of the Northwest Territory • 1841 from Rives • Mining engineer and metallurgist Daniel C. Jackling • Corn, sorghum, hay, pecans, cattle, poultry; coal, sand and gravel.

SAINT FRANCOIS *Farmington* • 55,641 • 449 • Eastern MO, located partly in the St. Francois Mountains; drained by the Big River and St. Francis River. Semi-urban, the county has large residential developments. Missouri Mines State Historic Site, and St. Francois and St. Joe state parks are here. Part of Mark Twain National Forest is in the extreme east. • Named for the St. Francis River • 1821 from Saint Genevieve, Jefferson, and Washington • Formerly located in a region of great mining importance, the county saw extensive lead mining from the early 1800s until the 1960s. Center of the "Lead Belt," it was once the nation's leading lead producer. • Corn, wheat, hay, livestock; timber. • Rain and underground springs have created more than seventeen miles of navigable waterways in the abandoned Bonne Terre Mine (called the largest man-made cavern in the world.) The Bonne Terre City Hall is reportedly a replica of William Shakespeare's home.

SAINT LOUIS (one of two counties so named, the other in MN) *Clayton* • 1,016,315 (the most populated county in MO) • 508 • Eastern MO, bounded on the east by the Mississippi River (forming the IL state line), on the northwest by the Missouri River, and on the southeast and southwest by the Meramec River. • Named for the St. Louis Spanish district • Original county; organized 1812 • Settled by the French about 1785, Florissant was a center for early Jesuit missionaries. The city of St. Louis separated from St. Louis County in 1876 and became independent. A building boom in the 1960s in Clayton created a second downtown for the St. Louis metropolitan area. In 1982, the Missouri Department of Health and Centers for Disease Control evacuated the dioxin-contaminated Times Beach; the town was razed in 1991. • Jazz clarinetist Pee Wee Russell • Corn, wheat, hay, horticulture, dairying; limestone, shale, clay; lumber products; diversified manufacturing; education (Washington U.; St. Louis Christian College; MO Baptist College; Maryville U. of St. Louis; University of MO–St. Louis; Fontbonne College; Webster U.

Concordia Seminary is the world's largest Lutheran Seminary.) • Lambert-St. Louis International Airport is here. Museums in the county include the AKC Museum of the Dog and St. Louis Aviation Museum. The Washington University Art Galley, established in 1881, was reputedly the first fine arts museum west of the Mississippi. The first parachute jump from an airplane was made on March 1, 1912, 1,500 feet over Jefferson Barracks (historic park) by Captain Albert Berry. St. Stanislaus Seminary is reportedly the world's oldest Jesuit novitiate still in existence. The Black Madonna Shrine and Grottoes in Eureka, a massive folk art project, took Franciscan brother Bronislaus Luszca twenty-two years to complete.

SAINTE GENEVIEVE *Sainte Genevieve* • 17,842 • 502 • Eastern MO, bounded on the northeast by the Mississippi River (forming the IL state line). Part of Mark Twain National Forest is here, as is Hawn State Park. • Named for the Sainte Genevieve Spanish district • Original county; organized 1812 (prior to statehood) • Sainte Genevieve, the first permanent white settlement in MO, was founded in 1735 by French Canadians. (Its French origin is celebrated in Jour de Fête à Ste. Genevieve each August.) • Grapes, corn, wheat, hay, cattle, dairying; wineries; limestone for hydrated lime and pulverized carbonate, limestone for marble; manufacture of wooden sashes, doors, clothing • Sainte Genevieve's museum contains a display of birds mounted by John James Audubon, who lived briefly in the city.

SALINE (one of five counties so named) *Marshall* • 23,756 • 756 • Central MO, bounded on the north and east by the Missouri River; drained by the Blackwater River. Arrow Rock State Historical Site is here. Van Meter State Park is also in the county. • Named for the many local salt springs • 1820 (prior to statehood) from Cooper • Corn, wheat, soybeans, sorghum, cattle, hogs, dairy products; manufacturing; education (MO Valley College).

SCHUYLER *Lancaster* • 4,170 • 308 • Northern MO, bounded on the north by the IA state line and on the west by the Chariton River; drained by the Middle and South Fabius rivers. • One of three counties named for Gen. Philip J. Schuyler (1733–1804), an officer in the Revolutionary War and one of NY's first two senators • 1845 from Adair • Corn, wheat, soybeans, sheep, hogs, cattle, poultry.

SCOTLAND (one of two counties so named, the other in NC) *Memphis* • 4,983 • 438 • Northeastern MO, bounded on the north by the IA state line; drained by the North and Middle Fabius rivers, and North and South Wyaconda rivers. Indian Hills Conservation Area is in the south. • Named for the country, former home of early settlers • 1841 from Clark, Lewis and Shelby • Corn, soybeans, cattle, sheep, hogs; manufacturing.

SCOTT (one of eleven counties so named) *Benton* • 40,422 • 421 • Southeastern MO, bounded on the east by the Mississippi River and on the west by the Little River • Named for John Scott (?–1861), first U.S. representative from MO • 1821 from New Madrid • Corn, cotton, wheat, soybeans, melons, pumpkins, hay, lumber; manufacture of shoes, canvas products, toys, locks and milk cartons.

SHANNON (one of two counties so named, the other in SD) *Eminence* • 8,324 • 1,004 (the second largest county in MO) • Southern MO, in the Ozark Mountains; drained by the Current River. Parts of Mark Twain National Forest are in the southeast and northeast corners. Ozark National Scenic Riverways (National Park) follows the Current and Jacks Fork rivers. The county includes Sunklands, Angeline, and Birch Creek conservation areas. Round Spring Cave is also here. • Named for George F. "Peg-leg" Shannon (1787–1836), a member of the Lewis and Clark expedition, and U.S. attorney for MO • 1841 from Ripley • Cattle, hay; lumber; manufacturing; recreational tourism.

SHELBY *Shelbyville* • 6,799 • 501 • Northeastern MO; drained by the North Fork of the Salt and North rivers • One of nine counties named directly or indirectly for General Isaac Shelby (1750–1826), first governor of KY • 1835 from Marion • Prussian immigrant William Keil established a utopian society in Bethel in 1844. A German Mennonite community settled in Cherry Box in the late 1850s. • Corn, wheat, hay, soybeans, cattle, hogs, dairying; limestone; lumber.

STODDARD *Bloomfield* • 29,705 • 827 • Southeastern MO, bounded on the west by the St. Francis River and on the east, in part, by the Little River; drained by lower Castor River and drainage channels of the Little River. Mingo National Wildlife Refuge is on the northwest border. Crowley's Ridge runs from the southwest to the northeast through the center of the county. • Named for Captain Amos Stoddard (1762–1813), major participant in the transfer of Louisiana Territory to the U.S. • 1835 from Cape Girardeau • Rice, corn, soybeans, wheat, cotton (grown and processed); lumber; manufacturing. • The official newspaper of the Overseas Department of Defense, *The Stars and Stripes*, was first printed in Bloomfield in 1861; one of the three existing original issues is displayed at the county museum.

STONE (one of three counties so named) *Galena* • 28,658 (50% increase since 1990; the third fastest growing county in MO) • 463 • Southwestern MO, in the Ozark Mountains; drained by the White and James rivers, here forming Table Rock Lake reservoir, which dominates the southern part of the county. Mark Twain National Forest is also in the south. Part of Table Rock State Park is on the southeastern boundary. The derivation of the county's name is uncertain. • 1851 from Taney • Vegetables (especially corn), fruit, hay, cattle; manufacturing; recreation and tourism • Silver Dollar City, a replica of an 1870 Ozark mining town is nine miles west of Branson. Galena's Y Bridge, built in 1928, is one of the few of its type constructed in the U.S.

SULLIVAN (one of six counties so named) *Milan* • 7,219 • 651 • Northern MO; drained by Mussel Fork and Locust Creek • Probably named for Sullivan County, TN, which was itself named for General John Sullivan (1740–95), Revolutionary War officer, member of the Continental Congress, chief executive and governor of NH • 1845 from Linn • Corn, soybeans, hay, sheep, cattle, hogs; agricultural processing.

TANEY *Forsyth* • 39,703 (55% increase since 1990; the second fastest growing county in MO) • 632 • Southwestern MO, in the Ozarks; drained by the White River and the Arkansas River. Bull Shoals, Lake Taneycomo, and Table Rock Lake reservoir are on the White River. Part of Lake Table Rock State Park and part of Mark Twain National Park are here. Branson has gained national recognition as a major resort, recreation, and entertainment center, with emphasis on country music halls. • Named for Roger Brooke Taney (1777–1864), Chief Justice of the U.S., who wrote the decision in the Dred Scott Case • 1837 from Greene • Cedar, pine, oak; tourism and retirement communities • The community of Branson formed the setting for the novel *The Shepherd of the Hills* written in 1907 by Harold Bell. College of the Ozarks is tuition-free; students pay their way by working in a number of college-affiliated industries.

TEXAS (one of two counties so named, the other in OK) *Houston* • 23,003 • 1,179 (the largest county in MO) • South-central MO, in the Ozarks; drained by the Big Piney and Jacks Fork rivers. Part of Mark Twain National Forest is here. • Named for the Republic of Texas • Organized as Ashley County 1843 from Shannon and Wright; name changed 1845 • Clown Emmett Kelly • Cattle, corn, wheat, hay; pine, oak, cedar; manufacturing; recreational tourism.

VERNON (one of three counties so named) *Nevada* • 20,454 • 834 • Western MO, bounded on the north in part by the Osage River; drained by the Little Osage and Marmaton rivers. Part of Schell-Osage Conservation Area is in the northeast corner. Osage Village State Historic Site is also here. • Named for Col. Miles Vernon (1786–1866), veteran of the Battle of New Orleans and MO legislator • 1855 from Bates • In 1863, Nevada, known as the "Bushwhacker Capital," was burned by Federal troops after giving residents ten minutes to pack and leave. Camp Clark was used as a World War II prisoner of war camp. • Film director John Huston • Corn, wheat, soybeans, sorghum, hay, pecans, cattle, poultry; strip coal mines, oil wells; manufacturing. • The Bushwhacker Museum in Vernon recalls the town's Confederate sympathies during the Civil War.

WARREN *Warrenton* • 24,525 • 432 • East-central MO, bounded on the south by the Missouri River. Reifsnider State Forest and Daniel Boone Conservation Area are here. The Daniel and Rebecca Boone Grave and Monument is east of Marthasville. • One of fourteen counties named for General Joseph Warren (1741–75), Revolutionary War patriot and member of the Committee of Safety who dispatched Paul Re-

vere on his famous ride • 1833 from Montgomery • The county was heavily damaged in the floods of 1993. • Theologians Helmut and Reinhold Niebuhr; geographer Carl O. Sauer • Wheat, corn, soybeans, apples, grapes, livestock; manufacturing.

WASHINGTON *Potosi* • 23,344 • 760 • East-central MO, in the Ozarks; drained by the Big River. Pea Ridge Iron Mine is in the northwest corner. Much of the county has been scarified by mining activity. Washington State Park and part of Meramec State Park are here. Part of Mark Twain National Forest is in the county as well. • One of thirty-one counties named for President George Washington • 1813 (prior to statehood) from Ste. Genevieve • The county, lying in one the largest lead districts in the world, has been heavily mined since the 18th century. • Corn, hay, livestock; barite, iron, manufacturing; penal employment (Missouri State Correctional Center at Potosi).

WAYNE (one of sixteen counties so named) *Greenville* • 13,259 • 761 • Southeastern MO; drained by the St. Francis (here forming Wappapello Lake reservoir) and Black rivers. The county is located in the Ozarks, with parts of Mark Twain National Forest in the south. The county also contains Mingo National Wildlife Refuge, Sam A. Baker State Park, and Coldwater Conservation Area. • One of fifteen counties named for "Mad" Anthony Wayne (1745–96), Revolutionary War general and statesman • 1818 (prior to statehood) from Cape Girardeau and Lawrence • Corn, hay, livestock; oak, pine, hickory; manufacturing; outdoor recreation.

WEBSTER *Marshfield* • 31,045 • 593 • South-central MO; drained by the James and Niangua rivers and Osage Fork. There is an Amish community near Seymour. • One of eight counties named for Daniel Webster (1782–1852), U.S. statesman and orator from MA • 1855 from Greene • Astronomer Edwin P. Hubble • Corn, wheat, fruit, tomatoes, apples, cattle; oak; manufacturing.

WORTH *Grant City* • 2,382 (the least populated county in MO) • 267 (the smallest county in MO) • Northwestern MO, bounded on the north by the IA state line; drained by the Grand River • One of three counties named for General William J. Worth (1794–1849), officer in the War of 1812, Seminole War, and the Mexican War • 1861 from Gentry • Bandleader Glenn Miller learned how to play the trombone in Grant City. • Wheat, corn, cattle; some manufacturing.

WRIGHT (one of three counties so named) *Hartville* • 17,955 • 682 • South-central MO; drained by the Gasconade River. The county is in the Ozarks, with Mark Twain National Forest in the northeast corner. • Named for Silas Wright (1795–1847), NY governor, U.S. representative, and senator from NY • 1841 from Pulaski • Peaches, apples, hay, cattle, dairying, lumber. • The Laura Ingalls Wilder Historic Home and Museum is located near Mansfield.

MONTANA

Gold and Silver

Of Montana's fifty-six counties, fifty-three elect three county commissioners to govern the county, each serving a six-year term. Two of the remaining counties are administered by elected chief executives. A manager, appointed by commissioners, administers the remaining county.

BEAVERHEAD *Dillon* • 9,202 • 5,543 (the largest county in MT and forty-sixth largest county in the U.S.) • Southwestern MT, bounded on the west and south by the ID state line and the Continental Divide, and on the north by the Continental Divide in the Anaconda Range; crossed by the Big Hole (forming part of the northern boundary), Beaverhead, and Red Rock rivers. The Beaverhead Mountains extend along the western border of the county; the Centennial Mountains are found along the southern boundary. Upper and Lower Red Rock lakes are formed by the Red Rock River. Red Rock Lake National Wildlife Refuge is a trumpeter swan nesting area. The county includes Maverick Mountain ski area, Beaverhead Rock and Clark's Lookout state parks, and scattered sections of Beaverhead-Deerlodge National Forest. Sacagawea Historic Area, Lewis and Clark Memorial and Clark Canyon Reservoir Recreation Area are also here. • Named for the Beaverhead River • Original county; organized 1865 (prior to statehood); annexed part of Madison County in 1911 • The ghost town of Bannack (state park), the site of Montana's first major gold strike (1862), was MT's first territorial capital (1864–65). One of the Nez Perce Indians' most dramatic struggles against U.S. Army troops' efforts to confine them to reservations occurred at Big Hole in 1877 (Big Hole National Battlefield–Nez Perce National Historic Park) • Talc mining; sheep, cattle, alfalfa, hay, barley, seed potatoes; education (Western MT College of the U. of MT — MT's first normal school); skiing and dude ranch tourism.

BIG HORN (one of two counties so named, the other in WY) *Hardin* • 12,671 • 4,995 (the fifth largest county in MT) • Southern MT, bounded on the south by the WY state line and on the southwest by the Bighorn River; drained by the Bighorn and Little Bighorn rivers, and by Lodge Grass and Hanging Woman creeks. Part of Crow and Northern Cheyenne Indian reservations are here. The county also includes the Pryor, Bighorn, and Rosebud Mountains. Bighorn Lake Reservoir, formed by the Bighorn River, is in Bighorn Canyon National Recreation Area (and includes Yellowtail Dam). Rosebud Battlefield, Chief Plenty Coups, and Tongue River Reservoir state parks are also here. • Named for its bighorn sheep. • 1913 from Rosebud and Yellowstone • The Battle of Little Big Horn between twelve companies of the 7th U.S. Cavalry and the Sioux and Northern Cheyenne Indians was fought here on June 25–26, 1876 (commemorated at Little Bighorn Battlefield National Monument). Lt. Col. George A. Custer and his entire unit were killed. The battle is said to have included probably the largest gathering of Indian warriors in Western history. • Wheat, barley, oats, hay, beans, sugar beets, cattle.

BLAINE *Chinook* • 7,009 • 4,226 • Northern MT, bounded on the north by the Canadian province of Saskatchewan and on the south by the Missouri River (designated a National Wild and Recreational River); drained by the Milk River, and Peoples, Cow, and Lodge creeks. Part of Upper Missouri River Breaks National Monument is in the south. Fort Belknap Indian Reservation and Black Coulee National Wildlife Refuge are also here. • One of four counties named for James G. Blaine (1830–93), U.S. representative and senator from ME and U.S. secretary of state • 1912 from Chouteau • Chief Joseph and the Nez Perce surrendered to the U.S. Army at Bear Paw Battlefield in 1877 (Nez Perce National Historic Park) • Wheat, barley, oats, hay, beans, cattle, sheep, hogs; oil, and natural gas.

BROADWATER *Townsend* • 4,385 (32% increase since 1990; the third fastest growing county in MT) • 1,191 • West-central MT, bounded in part on the southeast and drained by the Missouri River, which forms Canyon Ferry Lake reservoir in the north. The Big Belt Mountains extend along the northeast border. Sections of Helena National Forest cover much of the county. Missouri Headwaters State Park is also here. • Named for Col. Charles A. Broadwater (1840–92), president of the Montana Central Railroad, and commercial developer • 1895 from Jefferson and Meagher • Wheat, barley, hay, hogs, sheep; gold.

CARBON (one of four counties so named) *Red Lodge* • 9,552 • 2,048 • Southern MT, bounded on the south by the WY state line and on the southeast by the Bighorn River; drained by Clark's Fork of the Yellowstone River (designated a National Wild River). The Beartooth Range extends along the western border and the Pryor Mountains cross in the east. Cooney Reservoir and State Park are here, as are numerous small glacially-formed lakes. The county also includes sections of Custer National Forest and part of Gallatin National Forest. Part of Big Horn Canyon National Recreation Area and Big Ice Cave are in the east. • Named for the abundant coal deposits in the county • 1895 from Park and Yellowstone • Cattle, sheep, barley, oats, hay, corn, sugar beets, beans; coal, natural gas.

CARTER (one of five counties so named) *Ekalaka* • 1,360 • 3,340 • Extreme southeastern MT, bounded on the east by the SD state line and on the south by the WY state line; drained by the Little Missouri River and Boxelder Creek. Chalk Buttes cross in the center of the county. The source of O'Fallon Creek is in the northwest. Two sections of Custer National Forest are also here. Capitol Rock, a deposit of volcanic ash eroded into the shape of our nation's capitol, is located near the eastern border. • Named for Thomas H. Carter (1854–1911), U.S. senator and first U.S. representative from MT • 1917 from Fallon • Teepee rings are still visible at Medicine Rocks State Park, the historical staging area for the Sioux and Cheyenne prior to the Battle of the Little Bighorn. • Wheat, oats, hay, cattle, sheep.

CASCADE *Great Falls* • 80,357 (the third most populated county in MT) • 2,698 • West-central MT; drained by the Missouri, Sun, and Smith rivers. Part of Lewis and Clark National Forest is here (its headquarters in Great Falls), as is part of the Little Belt Mountains. Ulm Pishkun State Park is one of the world's largest prehistoric bison kill sites. Sluice Boxes State Park and Benton Lake National Wildlife Refuge are also in the county. (Benton Lake is one of the most productive waterfowl nesting sites in the U.S. About 10,000 shore birds and 25,000 waterfowl are raised here annually.) Malmstrom Air Force Base, east of Great Falls, is the site of an ICBM installation. Each day, about 390 million gallons of water gush from the ground at Giant Springs Heritage State Park, site of one of the world's largest freshwater springs. • Named for the falls in the Missouri River, which runs through the northern part of the county, named Great Falls by explorers Lewis and Clark in 1805. • 1887 (prior to statehood) from Chouteau and Meagher • Wheat (flour processing), barley oats, hay, some corn, potatoes, cattle, sheep, hogs, dairying; timber; publishing and printing; meatpacking; processing of copper, zinc, aluminum; education (U. of Great Falls; Montana School for the Deaf and Blind) • Great Falls is the site of the annual MT state fair and rodeo. The city also contains the original art studio and museum of Western painter and sculptor Charles M. Russell, and displays the largest collection of his work in the world. The Roe River, near Great Falls, is reputedly the world's shortest river. Lewis and Clark National Historic Trail Interpretive Center is in Great Falls.

CHOUTEAU *Fort Benton* • 5,970 • 3,973 • North-central MT, bounded by Arrow Creek in the southwest; drained by the Missouri (designated a National Wild and Recreational River), Teton, and Marias rivers. There are several lakes in the southern center of the county. Part of Rocky Boy's Indian Reservation is in the northeast; part of Lewis and Clark National Forest is in the south; a small part of Benton Lake National Wildlife Refuge is in the southwest. Upper Missouri River Breaks National Monument begins at Fort Benton in the center of the county, and follows the Missouri River east into Blaine and Fergus counties. Coal Banks and Judith Landing BLM recreation sites are also here. • Named for one or more members of the Chouteau family, including Auguste and Pierre, both fur traders • Original county; organized 1865 (prior to statehood) • Fort Benton (national historical monument), established as an American Fur Company outpost in 1846 and serving as head of steamboat river navigation on the Missouri River, became a boom town supply point for gold prospectors and cattlemen on their way west. The ruins of the old fort are currently under archeological study. • Irish Revolutionary leader and MT Territory acting governor Thomas F. Meagher died here. • Wheat, barley, oats, hay, cattle, hogs, sheep • The House of 1000 Dolls in Loma displays dolls and toys from 1830 to the present. Ferry crossings on the Missouri River near Carter and Virgelle link back road routes throughout the county. The Museum of the Upper Missouri is in Fort Benton.

CUSTER *Miles City* • 11,696 • 3,783 • Southeastern MT; drained by the Yellowstone and Powder rivers, and by Pumpkin, Tongue, and Mizpah creeks. Fort Keogh Agricultural Experiment Station is here, as is Pirogue Island State Park. • One of six counties named for Gen. George Armstrong Custer (1839–76), U.S. army officer defeated at the Battle of Little Bighorn • Original county; organized as Big Horn County 1865 (prior to statehood); name changed 1877 • Wheat, oats, hay, corn, sugar beets, horses, cattle, sheep (wool); saddles • Roundups and rodeos are annual events in the cowboy town of Miles City. The Range Riders Museum is nearby.

DANIELS *Scobey* • 2,017 • 1,426 • Northeastern MT, bounded on the north by the Canadian province of Saskatchewan; drained by the East and West forks of the Poplar River. The southern fifth of the county comprises part of Fort Peck Indian Reservation. • Named for Mansfield A. Daniels (1858–1919), an early rancher and storekeeper • 1920 from Sheridan and Valley • Wheat, barley, oats, hay, cattle.

DAWSON (one of four counties so named) *Glendive* • 9,059 • 2,373 • Eastern MT; drained by the Yellowstone River. Makoshika ("hell cooled over") State Park contains badlands rock formations. Dinosaur fossils are found throughout the county. • Named for Major Andrew Dawson (1817–1871), commander of Fort Benton for the American Fur Company • Original county; organized 1869 (prior to statehood) • Wheat, barley, oats, hay, corn, beans, sugar beets, potatoes, cattle, sheep, hogs, chickens, geese, ducks, turkeys; education (Dawson College). Glendive became headquarters of the Montana-Dakota Utilities Company following the discovery of oil, gas, and coal in the county, and is now supply center for the Williston Basin oil fields. • The rare paddle fish are found in the Yellowstone River here.

DEER LODGE *Anaconda* • 9,417 • 737 • Southwestern MT, bounded on the southwest by Pintlar Creek and on the south by Big Hole River; also drained by the Clark Fork River and Dutchman Creek. The Continental Divide crosses the county east-west, and forms parts of its eastern and western boundaries. Lost Creek State Park is here, as are Mount Haggin

Recreational Area, Georgetown Lake (on the western boundary), and part of Beaverhead-Deerlodge National Forest. The Flint Creek and Anaconda ranges are also in the county. • Named for the town of Deer Lodge, Idaho Territory, now in Powell County • Original county; organized 1865 (prior to statehood) • The county is indelibly associated with copper magnate Marcus Daly who turned his Anaconda plant into the world's largest nonferrous and reduction works, its 585-foot smokestack a structural exclamation point to his success, which also included one of the most ornate hotels in the nation and a newspaper, the *Anaconda Standard,* printed in an ultra-modern plant. Daly lost his political fight with Helena in 1891 to make Anaconda the state capital. Copper smelting and the manufacture of phosphate products remained the county's economic mainstay until 1980 when Atlantic Richfield, owner at the time, permanently closed the smelter. In 1977, the governments of Anaconda and Deer Lodge County were consolidated to form the city of Anaconda-Deer Lodge County. • Cattle, hay; mining.

FALLON *Baker* • 2,837 • 1,620 • Eastern MT, bounded on the east by the ND and SD state lines; drained by O'Fallon and Little Beaver creeks. • Named for Benjamin O'Fallon (1793–1842), army officer, Indian agent, and nephew of the explorer William Clark • 1913 from Custer. • Oil and gas; wheat, barley, oats, corn, hay, beans, sugar beets, hogs, cattle, sheep • The Fallon County Museum in Baker displays the preserved carcass of the world's largest steer (5'11" tall and 3,980 lbs.).

FERGUS *Lewistown* • 11,893 • 4,339 • Central MT, bounded on the north by the Missouri River (designated a Wild and Recreational River) and on the northwest by Arrow Creek; drained by the Judith River and numerous creeks. A section of Lewis and Clark National Forest is located in the Big Snowy Mountains in the south. Part of Charles M. Russell National Wildlife Refuge, including Kipp BLM Recreation Area, and part of Upper Missouri River Breaks National Monument extend along the northern border. The Judith Mountains cross in the center. • Named for James Fergus (1813–1902), cattleman, miner, MT territorial legislator, and one of several who originated the idea of establishing Yellowstone National Park • 1885 (prior to statehood) from Meagher • Chief Joseph and the Nez Perce traveled through the county on their flight toward Canada. • Grain, wheat, barley, oats, hay, cattle, sheep, hogs • Its county seat, Lewistown, sits in the exact center of the state. The MT Cowboy Poetry Gathering is held every August in Lewistown.

FLATHEAD *Kalispell* • 74,471 (the fourth most populated county in MT) • 5,099 (the third largest county in MT) • Northwestern MT, bounded on the north by the Canadian province of British Columbia and on the east by the Continental Divide (running southeast-northwest through the center of Glacier National Park); drained by the Flathead River and its North, Middle, and South forks; also by the Stillwater, Whitefish, and Little Bitterroot rivers. Several mountain ranges cross the county. The Middle Fork of the Flathead River (a National Wild and Scenic River) is in the east along the border of Glacier National Park. Sections of Flathead National Forest are in the southeast, south and north. Part of Flathead Lake is on the southern boundary. The county also contains Lone Pine and Whitefish Lake state parks, Hungry Horse Reservoir on the South Fork of the Flathead River, Coal Creek State Forest, part of Stillwater State Forest, and several ski areas. A small part of Flathead Indian Reservation is in the south. • Named for the Salish or Flathead Indians • 1893 from Missoula County; annexed part of Deer Lodge County before 1900 • Cherries, wheat, barley, rape seeds, hay, potatoes, peas, lentils, mint, Christmas trees, cattle, horses, hogs, llamas; mining; manufacture of forest products, furniture, pre-fabricated log houses; tourism.

GALLATIN (one of three counties so named) *Bozeman* • 67,831 (34% increase since 1990; the second fastest growing and fifth most populated county in MT) • 2,617 • Southwestern MT, bounded on the south by the Continental Divide (forming the ID state line), on the southeast by the WY state line, and on the northwest by the Jefferson and Missouri rivers; drained by the Gallatin and Madison rivers, and Sixteenmile Creek. The Missouri River is formed in the northwest, near Three Forks, by the junction of the Gallatin River and the Jefferson and Madison rivers. The southern half of the county is covered by part of Gallatin National Forest (its headquarters at Bozeman), with another section in the north. Part of Gallatin Range crosses in the east. Part of Yellowstone National Park is in the southeast, the town of West Yellowstone a western gateway to the park. Madison Buffalo Jump State Park, Gallatin Petrified Forest, and Hebgen Lake reservoir are also here. • Named for the Gallatin River, itself named by Lewis and Clark in 1805 for Albert Gallatin, U.S. secretary of the treasury at the time • Original county; organized 1865 (prior to statehood) • Cattle, sheep, hogs, llamas, potatoes, hay, wheat, barley, oats; timber and lumber industries; gold, talc, phosphate; manufacturing; tourism; education (MT State U. –Bozeman).

GARFIELD *Jordan* • 1,279 • 4,668 • East-central MT, bounded on the north by the Missouri River (Fort Peck Lake reservoir) and on the west by the Musselshell River; drained by Big Dry, Little Dry, and Sand creeks. The reservoir is encompassed by Charles M. Russell National Wildlife Refuge, which includes Hell Creek State Park and Hell Creek Fossil Area. • One of six counties named for President James Abram Garfield • 1919 from Valley and McCone • Wheat, barley, oats, hay, sheep, cattle, hogs.

GLACIER *Cut Bank* • 13,247 • 2,995 • Northern MT, bounded on the north by the Canadian province of Alberta; drained by the St. Mary River and the North and South Forks of the Milk River, Two Medicine Canal, and Cut Bank Creek (the latter two waterways joining on the southeastern corner of the county to form the Marias River). Blackfeet Indian

Reservation covers all but the east and west margins of the county. Part of Glacier National Park is in the west; the Continental Divide forms the western boundary of the county and runs through the center of the park. Part of Lewis and Clark Forest is in the southwest corner. • Named for Glacier National Park • 1919 from Flathead and Teton • Grain, wheat, barley, oats, hay, hogs; petroleum, natural gas. • The Museum of the Plains Indian is in Browning.

GOLDEN VALLEY (one of two counties so named, the other in ND) *Ryegate* • 1,042 • 1,175 • Central MT; drained by the Musselshell River, and by Currant and Fish creeks. Part of Lewis and Clark National Forest and the Big Snowy Mountains are in the northwest. • The county was given this name, indicative of its rich soil and abundant streams, to attract settlers • 1920 from Musselshell and Sweet Grass • Wheat, rye, hay, sheep, cattle, hogs, poultry.

GRANITE *Philipsburg* • 2,830 • 1728 • Western MT, bounded on the southeast by the Continental Divide in the Anaconda Range, and in part by Georgetown Lake; drained by the Clark Fork River, and by Flint and Rock creeks. The Sapphire Mountains extend along the western border, and the Garnet Mountains cross on the extreme northeast. Parts of Beaverhead-Deerlodge and Lolo national forests are here. Flint Creek Range is in the east. Beavertail Hill State Park is also located in the county. • Named for the Granite Mountain Silver Mine, itself named for the granite rock within the mine • 1893 from Deer Lodge • In the 1880s Granite Mountain Silver Mine produced between $20 and $25 million worth of silver and gold. Today, the mine is inactive and the town of Granite, a ghost town. • Silver, sapphires, hay, cattle; ski and other tourist resorts.

HILL *Havre* • 16,673 • 2,896 • Northern MT, bounded on the north by the Canadian provinces of Alberta and Saskatchewan; drained by the Milk River (forming Fresno Reservoir), and by Lodge, Big Sandy, and Sage creeks. Part of Rocky Boy's Indian Reservation is in the south. Beaver Creek Park is the largest county park in the U.S., encompassing 10,000 acres. Creedman Coulee and Lake Thibadeau national wildlife refuges are in the northeast. • Named for James J. Hill (1838–1916), president of the Great Northern Railroad • 1912 from Chouteau • Cattle, sheep, hogs, wheat, barley, oats, hay; education (MT State U. – Northern) • Ft. Assinniboine, established in 1879 and the 1890s home to the Black 10th Cavalry Regiment, is one of the oldest forts in existence, and the largest in Montana. A re-creation of one of the first "underground malls" is located in Havre beneath the historic Pepin-Broadwater block.

JEFFERSON (one of twenty-six counties so named) *Boulder* • 10,049 • 1,657 • Southwest-central MT, bounded on the south by the Jefferson River and on the west by the Continental Divide; drained by the Boulder River. Lewis and Clark Caverns and Elkhorn state parks, part of Beaverhead-Deerlodge National Forest, and part of Helena National Forest are here.

• Named for the Jefferson River itself named by Lewis and Clark for President Thomas Jefferson (one of twenty-two counties named directly or indirectly for President Jefferson) • Original county; organized 1865 (prior to statehood) • Cattle, sheep, hogs, hay, wheat, oats; gold, silver, lead, zinc.

JUDITH BASIN *Stanford* • 2,329 • 1,870 • Central MT; drained by the Judith River, and Arrow and Wolf creeks. Part of Lewis and Clark National Forest is here. The Little Belt and Highwood mountains and Ackley Lake State Park are also in the county. • Named for the basin of the Judith River by Lieutenant William Clark for his sweetheart (and later wife) "Judy" Hancock • 1920 from Fergus and Cascade • Wheat, barley, hay, cattle, sheep, poultry; sapphires, silver and other metals • The settings for many of Charles Russell paintings can be found throughout the county, and especially along Highway 87, designated by the MT Legislature as "Charles M. Russell Trail."

LAKE (one of twelve counties so named) *Polson* • 26,507 • 1,494 • Northwestern MT; drained by the Flathead River (which forms part of the western boundary) and the Swan River. Five of six units of Flathead Lake State Park are in the north, along the shore of Flathead Lake. Lake Mary Ronan State Park is in northwest. Flathead Indian Reservation comprises most of the county and includes Nine Pipe and Pablo national wildlife refuges, St. Ignatius Mission, and part of the National Bison Range. Swan River State Forest is in the northeast. (Swan River National Wildlife Refuge is here.) The Mission Range of the Rocky Mountains extends along the southeastern border. • Named for Flathead Lake • 1923 from Flathead and Missoula • Wheat, barley, corn, oats, potatoes, rape seed, hay, cattle, sheep, hogs, horses, llamas, cherries, dairying.

LEWIS AND CLARK *Helena* • 55,716 • 3,461 • West-central MT, bounded on the north by the Sun River, forming Gibson Reservoir; drained by the Missouri, Dearborn (forming part of the northeast boundary), and Blackfoot rivers. The Continental Divide crosses the county and forms part of its northwest and southwest boundaries. Part of Lewis and Clark national Forest is in the northwest, while sections of Helena National Forest and Lincoln State Forest are scattered throughout the south. Hauser Lake and Spring Meadow Lake state parks are here, as are Missouri River Recreational Road, Holter Lake and Canyon Ferry B.L.M. recreational areas. • Named for Meriwether Lewis (1774–1809) and William Clark (1770–1838), explorers and leaders of the expedition (1804–06) to explore the American northwest. (There are five other counties named for Meriwether Lewis, and three other counties named for William Clark.) • Original county; organized as Edgerton County 1865 (prior to statehood); name changed 1867 • Gold and silver were discovered in the county in 1864. By 1868, $16 million worth of gold had been uncovered in Helena. Last Chance Gulch, site of the original gold discovery in Helena, is now the city's main street. Helena has been the capital of MT since 1875. • Film actors Gary Cooper and Myrna Loy • Wheat, barley, oats, hay, cattle, sheep; sand and gravel; gold mining; smelters, quartz crushing, and zinc reduction works; manufacture of concrete, ceramics, paints, bakery products, sheet metal, chemicals, prefabricated houses; government operations; education (Carroll College).

LIBERTY (one of four counties so named) *Chester* • 2,158 • 1,430 • Northern MT, bounded on the north by the Canadian province of Alberta; drained by the Marias River. The source of Sage Creek is in the northeast. Tiber Dam forms Lake Elwell reservoir in the west. • Its name was possibly inspired by U.S. victory in WW I • 1920 from Chouteau and Hill • Wheat, barley, oats, hogs; light manufacturing.

LINCOLN (one of twenty-four counties so named) *Libby* • 18,837 • 3,613 • Extreme northwestern MT, bounded on the north by the Canadian province of British Columbia, and on the west by the ID state line; drained by the Kootenai River (Lake Koocanusa formed by Libby Dam), and the Fisher and Yaak rivers. The Whitefish Range extends along the northeast border, and the Cabinet Mountains cross the southwest. The Purcell and Salish mountains are also here. Kootenai National Forest blankets most of the county, with a small section of Stillwater State Forest in the northeast and part of Kaniksu State Forest in the southwest. Ross Creek Cedars, Northwest Park, and Ten Lakes scenic areas are in the county. • One of eighteen counties named for President Abraham Lincoln • 1909 from Flathead • Cattle, sheep; lead, silver, gold.

MADISON *Virginia City* • 6,815 • 2,643 • Southwestern MT, bounded on the southeast corner by the ID state line, formed by the Continental Divide; drained by the Madison, Ruby, Beaverhead, and Jefferson rivers. Part of Beaverhead Rock State Park is here, as are Ennis Lake reservoir, part of Earthquake Lake (formed in 1959), parts of Beaverhead-Deerlodge National Forest, and part of Gallatin National Forest. The county also includes the Tobacco Root Mountains, the Gravelly Mountains, and part of the Madison and Ruby ranges. • Named for the Madison River, itself named by Lewis and Clark for James Madison, then secretary of state (one of twenty counties named directly or indirectly for President Madison) • Original county; organized 1865 (prior to statehood) • Virginia City was established in 1863 when one of the richest deposits of gold ever found in the U.S. was discovered in nearby Alder Gulch. It served as the territorial capital from 1865 to 1875. The infamous Plummer gang of outlaws was exterminated by vigilantes who organized in Virginia City in the 1860s. Nearly $300 million in gold was mined in the area during the boom. • Cattle, sheep, horses, hay, wheat, barley, potatoes; talc, marble, gold, silver, lead, lignite; tourism • The *Post*, first issued in Virginia City on August 27, 1864, was MT's first newspaper. Nevada City is a popular reconstructed gold camp in the county.

MCCONE *Circle* • 1,977 • 3,587 • Northeastern MT, bounded on the north by the Missouri River; drained by the Redwater River. Part of the Dry Arm (Big Dry Creek) of Fort Peck Lake reservoir is in the west and is surrounded by Charles M. Russell National Wildlife Refuge. • Named for George

McCone (1854–?), a MT state legislator active in establishing the county • 1919 from Dawson and Richland • Wheat, barley, hay, sheep, cattle; oil.

MEAGHER *White Sulphur Springs* • 1,932 • 2,392 • Central MT, bounded on the west by the Big Belt Mountains; drained by the Smith River, Sixteenmile Creek, and the South and North forks of Musselshell River. Smith River State Park, part of the Little Belt Mountains, parts of Lewis and Clark and Helena national forests, and a small part of Gallatin National Forest are all in the county. • Named for Thomas F. Meagher (1823–67), Irish revolutionary tried for sedition, Union army leader of the "Irish Brigade" in the Civil War and acting governor of MT Territory • Original county; organized 1867 (prior to statehood) from Chouteau and Gallatin counties; annexed part of Fergus in 1911 • Barley, wheat, hay, cattle, sheep, hogs.

MINERAL (one of four counties so named) *Superior* • 3,884 • 1,220 • Western MT, bounded on the west by the ID state line; drained by the St. Regis River. The Bitterroot Range crosses along the southwest border; the Coeur D'Alene Mountains are in the north. Lolo National Forest covers all of the county except for margins of the Clark Fork. • Named Mineral for its many mines • 1914 from Missoula • Some sheep, cattle, hay; lumbering; mining. • The Gideons began their practice of placing Bibles in hotel rooms in October, 1908, courtesy of the Superior Hotel.

MISSOULA *Missoula* • 95,802 (the second most populated county in MT) • 2,598 • Western MT, bounded on the southwest by the ID state line; drained by the Clark Fork, Bitterroot, Swan, Clearwater, and Blackfoot rivers. The Rocky Mountains cross in the northeast. The county has numerous recreational areas, including Frenchtown Pond, Council Grove, Placid Lake, and Salmon Lake state parks. Part of Flathead National Forest and Mission Mountains Wilderness Area are in the north, as is part of Flathead Indian Reservation. A small part of Bitterroot National Forest is on the county's southern boundary. Parts of Lolo National Forest are also found throughout the county. • Missoula is a Salish Indian word, its meaning unknown • Original county; organized 1865 (prior to statehood) • First woman member of the U.S. Congress Jeannette Rankin • Wheat, barley, hay, cattle, dairying, poultry; timber; mining; manufacture of lumber, wood products, packed meats, chemicals, concrete, dental equipment; education (U. of MT-Missoula).

MUSSELSHELL *Roundup* • 4,497 • 1,867 • Central MT; drained by the Musselshell River, and by Currant, Pole, Willow, and North Willow creeks. The Bull Mountains extend along the southern border. Lake Mason National Wildlife Refuge is in the northwest. • Named for the Musselshell River, which forms part of the county's eastern border, itself named for the mussel shells found on its banks by Lewis and Clark • 1911 from Fergus, Yellowstone, and Meagher • Wheat, oats, hay, some corn, dairying, cattle, sheep, hogs; oil, gas and coal.

PARK (one of three counties so named) *Livingston* • 15,694 • 2791 • Southern MT, bounded on the south by the WY state line; drained by the Yellowstone and Shields rivers. The county contains part of Yellowstone National Park, Paradise Valley (of the Yellowstone River), Cottonwood Reservoir, and several units of Gallatin National Forest. Granite Peak, at 12,799 feet, the highest point in the state, is in the extreme southeast. Part of the Crazy Mountains are in the northeast. The Absaroka Range crosses in the southwest. • Named for Yellowstone National Park • 1887 from Gallatin (prior to statehood) • Wheat, barley, oats, hay, vegetables, cattle, sheep, hogs, horses, dairying; lumber; marble, coal; tourism (especially dude ranches) • Livingston is the site of the National Fresh Water Trout Derby. Grasshopper Glacier was named for the thousands of grasshoppers that became embedded in the ice long ago.

PETROLEUM *Winnett* • 493 (the least populated county in MT; only five U.S. counties have fewer people) • 1,654 • Central MT, bounded on the north by the Missouri River (Fort Peck Lake) and on the east by the Musselshell River; drained by Box Elder, Yellow Water, and Flatwillow creeks. Part of Charles M. Russell National Wildlife Refuge extends along the northern border. UL Bend National Wildlife Refuge encompasses Fort Peck Lake and the Musselshell River in the northeast. Two units of War Horse National Wildlife Refuge are located near several reservoirs, including Yellow Water, War Horse Lake, and Wild Horse Lake. • Named for the petroleum production in the Cat Creek fields • 1925 from Fergus • Mosby Dome was the site of MT's first commercially successful oil strike in 1920. At its peak, 150 oil wells were in operation at Cat Creek. • Wheat, barley, hay, cattle, sheep; petroleum, natural gas.

PHILLIPS (one of four counties so named) *Malta* • 4,601 • 5,140 (the second largest county in MT) • Northern MT, bounded on the north by the Canadian province of Saskatchewan and on the south by the Missouri River (its upper reach at Fort Peck Lake reservoir); drained by the Milk River, and Whitewater, Frenchman, and Beaver creeks. Hewitt Lake and Bowdoin reservoirs and national wildlife refuges are here, as are parts of Charles M. Russell and UL Bend national wildlife refuges, which extend along the southern border. A portion of Fort Belknap Indian Reservation is in the west. • Named for Benjamin D. Phillips (1857–?), a local sheep rancher and MT state legislator • 1915 from Blaine and Valley • Wheat, barley, oats, hay, cattle, sheep, hogs; natural gas.

PONDERA *Conrad* • 6,424 • 1,625 • Northern MT, bounded in part on the north by the Marias River and in the extreme west by the Continental Divide; drained by Lake Frances, Dupuyer and Birch creeks, and Two Medicine Canal. Part of Blackfeet Indian Reservation and part of Lewis and Clark National Forest are here. • Possibly named for either the Pondera River or the Pend d' Oreille Indians • 1919 from Teton and Chouteau • Wheat, barley, oats, hay, cattle, hogs, sheep; coal, oil • The Great North Trail passes through the western edge of the county. An interpretive marker, located west of Valier,

commemorates Lewis and Clark's confrontation with the Blackfeet Indians.

POWDER RIVER *Broadus* • 1,858 • 3,297 • Southeastern MT, bounded on the south by the WY state line; drained by the Powder and Little Powder rivers, and Pumpkin and Mizpah creeks. A large portion of Custer National Forest is in the west. • Named for the river. Its name comes from either the fine black sand resembling gunpowder that is found along its banks, or from an incident in which a group of soldiers was attacked by Indians, and one yelled "hide the powder." • 1919 from Custer • Wheat, oats, hay, cattle, sheep; oil and natural gas, coal.

POWELL *Deer Lodge* • 7,180 • 2,326 • West-central MT; drained by the Blackfoot, Little Blackfoot, and Clark Fork rivers, and by the South Fork of the Flathead River (designated a National Wild and Recreational River). The Continental Divide forms the county's southeastern border and its extreme northeastern corner. It includes part of the Flint Creek and Garnet ranges, and parts of Beaverhead-Deerlodge, Helena, and Lolo national forests. Part of Lincoln State Forest is in the northeast. • Named for John Wesley Powell (1834–1902), geologist and explorer of the Grand Canyon, director of the U.S. Geological Survey, and first head of the U.S. Bureau of Reclamation • 1901 from Deer Lodge • Potatoes, hay, cattle, sheep; lumber; phosphate, lignite. • A living museum of the western cattle industry of the 1860s to 1930s, the Grant-Kohrs Ranch National Historic Site, was once the home of one of the largest and best known range ranches of its day.

PRAIRIE (one of two counties so named, the other in AR) *Terry* • 1,199 • 1,737 • Eastern MT; drained by the Yellowstone and Powder rivers, and O'Fallan, Cabin, and Timber creeks. • The county's name is descriptive of most of the eastern half of the state. • 1915 from Custer, Dawson and Fallon • Wheat, barley, oats, corn, hay, sugar beets, beans, sheep, hogs, poultry; gravel, some oil.

RAVALLI *Hamilton* • 36,070 (44% increase since 1990; the fastest growing county in MT) • 2,394 • Western MT, bounded on the west and south by the ID state line; drained by the Bitterroot River. The Continental Divide in the Anaconda Range forms the southeastern county line. The Bitterroot Range extends along the western border, and the Sapphire Mountains cross in the northeast. Bitterroot National Forest covers much of the county. Painted Rocks and Fort Owen (site of St. Mary's Mission) state parks, Lee Metcalf National Wildlife Refuge, and Sula State Forest are also here. Lost Trail Powder Mountain ski area is in the southeast. • Named for Father Antonio Ravalli (1811–84), Jesuit missionary to the Kalispel, Coeur d'Alene, and Salish Indians • 1893 from Missoula • Wheat, barley, oats, potatoes, mint, apples, hay, cattle, sheep, hogs, llamas; forest industries; mining.

RICHLAND (one of seven counties so named) *Sidney* • 9,667 • 2,084 • Northeastern MT, bounded on the east by the ND state line and on the north by the Missouri River; drained by the Yellowstone River. • The county was named Richland in a promotional attempt to attract visitors and/or new residents. • 1914 from Dawson. Its present boundaries were established in 1919. • Wheat, barley, oats, corn, beans, sugar beets, hay, cattle, sheep, hogs; oil, coal, limestone. • The MonDak Heritage Center is located in Sidney.

ROOSEVELT *Wolf Point* • 10,620 • 2,356 • Northeastern MT, bounded on the east by the ND state line and on the south by the Missouri River; drained by the West Fork of the Poplar River and Big Muddy Creek. The county includes part of Medicine Lake National Wildlife Refuge (Homestead Lake unit), and part of Fort Union Trading Post National Historic Site (on the ND boundary). Fort Peck Indian Reservation covers all of the county west of the Big Muddy River. • One of two counties (the other in NM) named for President Theodore Roosevelt • 1919 from Sheridan • Manufacture of textiles, fabricated metal products; wheat, barley, oats, corn, beans, sugar beets, hay, cattle, hogs, sheep. • The Tribal Culture Center and Museum is located in Poplar.

ROSEBUD *Forsyth* • 9,383 • 5,012 (the fourth largest county in MT) • East-central MT, bounded on the extreme west by the Musselshell River; drained by the Yellowstone River, and by Big Porcupine, Tongue, Rosebud, and Sandy creeks. The county includes part of Custer National Forest and part of Northern Cheyenne Indian Reservation. • Named for Rosebud Creek • 1901 from Custer • Wheat, barley, oats, hay, corn, beans, sugar beets, cattle, sheep; timber; oil, open-pit coal mining, bentonite,

SANDERS *Thompson Falls* • 10,227 • 2,762 • Northwestern MT, bounded on the west by the ID state line and on the east in part by the Flathead River; also drained by the Clark Fork of the Flathead River and the Thompson River. Clark Fork forms Cabinet Gorge and Noxon Rapids reservoirs. The Cabinet Mountains of the Bitterroot Range are on the northeastern border, and the Coeur D'Alene Mountains cross along the southwest boundary. Kaniksu National Forest and Thompson River State Forest cover two-thirds of the county, with the eastern third occupied by Flathead Indian Reservation. Thompson Falls and Logan state parks are also here. • Named for Wilbur F. Sanders (1834–1905), pioneer, mine operator, and one of MT's first two U.S. senators • 1907 from Missoula • The Oregon Steam Navigation Company of Portland ran a line of steamboats on the Clark Fork River between Thompson Falls and Lake Pend Oreille from 1865 to 1869. • Cattle, sheep, hay, barley; timber; antimony • The National Bison Range is the protected habitat of one of the last remaining herds of free-range bison.

SHERIDAN *Plentywood* • 4,105 • 1,677 • Extreme northeastern MT, bounded on the north by the Canadian province of Saskatchewan and on the east by the ND state line; drained by Big Muddy and Lake creeks. Part of Fort Peck Indian Reservation is here. Numerous lakes are here, including Medicine Lake, which is encompassed by Medicine Lake National Wildlife Refuge, and Homestead Lake on the southern bound-

ary. • One of five counties named directly or indirectly for Gen. Philip H. Sheridan (1831–88), Union officer during the Civil War and commander in chief of the U.S. army • 1913 from Valley • Wheat, barley, oats, hay, sugar beets, cattle, hogs, sheep; oil, coal.

SILVER BOW *Butte (officially Butte-Silver Bow)* • 34,606 • 718 (the smallest county in MT) • Southwestern MT, bounded on the southwest by the Big Hole River; drained by Silver Bow Creek. The county is crossed by the Continental Divide, which also forms most of its eastern boundary. Parts of Beaverhead-Deerlodge National Forest are distributed throughout the county. The city of Butte is coterminous with the county, except for Walkerville. • Named for Silver Bow Creek • 1881 from Deer Lodge • Placer gold was discovered here in 1864. Silver was first successfully treated in the county in 1875. By 1900 the area around Butte was yielding half the nation's output of copper. The city of Butte-Silver Bow was created in 1977 with the merging of the county and the city of Butte. • Copper, zinc, lead, gold, silver, manganese, phosphorus; dairying, cattle, hay; light industry; education (MT Tech of the U. of MT); tourism.

STILLWATER *Columbus* • 8,195 • 1,795 • Southern MT; drained by the Yellowstone and Stillwater rivers. Big Lake (intermittent) is in the north. Hailstone and Halfbreed Lake national wildlife refuges are in the county, as is part of Custer National Forest. The Beartooth Range extends along the southeast border. • Named for the Stillwater River • 1913 from Carbon, Sweet Grass, and Yellowstone • Sugar beets, beans, wheat, barley, hay, cattle, sheep, hogs; coal.

SWEET GRASS *Big Timber* • 3,609 • 1,855 • Southern MT; drained by the Yellowstone and Boulder rivers and Sweet Grass Creek. The Absaroka Range crosses in the southwest; the Crazy Mountains are on the northwest border. The county includes parts of Gallatin National Forest, a small part of Lewis and Clark National Forest, Greycliff Prairie Dog Town State Park, part of Custer National Forest, and part of Natural Bridge State Park. • There are several possibilities for the derivation of the county's name, including Sweet Grass Creek, Sweet Grass Hills, and the abundant fragrant grass of the genus Glyceria, at the suggestion of Mrs. Paul Van Cleve • 1895 from Meagher, Park and Yellowstone • Wheat, barley, hay, cattle, sheep, hogs.

TETON (one of two counties so named, the other in WY) *Choteau* • 6,445 • 2,273 • North-central MT, bounded in part on the south by the Sun River and on the west by the North Fork of the Sun River and the Continental Divide; drained by the Teton River. Part of Lewis and Clark National Forest is here. The county also includes Pine Butte Swamp Reserve, Freezeout Lake, Bynum and Pishkun reservoirs. • Named for the Teton River and Teton Peak in the Teton Mountains • 1893 from Chouteau • Wheat, barley, oats, alfalfa, hay, cattle, sheep, hogs • In 1977, fossilized dinosaur eggs were discovered at Egg Mountain, site of an ongoing archeological dig.

TOOLE *Shelby* • 5,267 • 1,911 • Northern MT, bounded on the north by the Canadian province of Alberta; drained by the Marias River (which forms part of its southwestern boundary) and Willow Creek. Lake Elwell reservoir is here. • Named for Joseph K. Toole (1851–1929), first governor of the state of MT • 1914 from Hill and Teton • The Dempsey-Gibbons heavy-weight championship was held in Shelby in 1923. Related memorabilia is displayed at the Marias Museum of History and Art. • Wheat, barley, hay, cattle, sheep, hogs; petroleum, natural gas.

TREASURE *Hysham* • 861 • 979 • South-central MT, bounded on the west in part by the Bighorn River; drained by the Yellowstone River. • Named for the nickname of Montana, the "Treasure State." • 1919 from Rosebud • Wheat, barley, corn, sugar beets, beans, hay, cattle, sheep.

VALLEY (one of three counties so named) *Glasgow* • 7,675 • 4,921 • Northeastern MT, bounded on the north by the Canadian province of Saskatchewan and on the south by the Missouri River, forming Fort Peck Lake reservoir; drained by the Milk River and the West Fork of the Poplar River, and by Porcupine, Willow, and Rock creeks. Glasgow Air Force Base is now a site for aircraft testing. Part of Charles M. Russell National Wildlife Refuge extends along the southern border. Fort Peck Indian Reservation is in the east. • Named for the several valleys in the county • 1893 from Dawson • Wheat, barley, oats, hay, cattle, sheep, hogs; bentonite.

WHEATLAND *Harlowton* • 2,259 • 1,423 • Central MT, bounded in part on the north by the Little Belt Mountains; drained by the Musselshell River. Martinsdale Reservoir is on the western border. Parts of Lewis and Clark National Forest are in the southwest corner and in the northwest. • Named for the major crop of the county • 1917 from Meagher and Sweet Grass • Wheat, barley, oats, hay, cattle, hogs, sheep • The longest stretch of electric railway in North America is located near Harlowton.

WIBAUX *Wibaux* • 1,068 • 889 • Eastern MT, bounded on the east by the ND state line; drained by Beaver Creek. The Yellowstone River is on the northwest border. Lamesteer National Wildlife Refuge is here. • Named for Pierre Wibaux (1858–?), a Huguenot immigrant who owned one of the largest herds of cattle in MT • 1914 from Dawson, Fallan, and Richland • Wheat, barley, hay, cattle, sheep, oil.

YELLOWSTONE *Billings* • 129,352 (the most populated county in MT) • 2,635 • Southern MT, bounded in part on the northeast by the Bighorn River; drained by the Yellowstone River and Pryor Creek. Part of Crow Indian Reservation, and Lake Elmo and Pictograph Cave (containing prehistoric artifacts) state parks are here. 200-foot high Pompey's Pillar (National Monument) was a famous landmark for migrating pioneers; it was first seen by explorer William Clark in 1806. Billings is the metropolis of the "Midland Empire," a rangeland and irrigated agricultural river valley. • Named for the Yellowstone River • 1883 • Hay, wheat, barley, oats, corn, beans, sugar beets, cattle, sheep (wool); sulfur, limestone, clay, coal; manufacturing; education (MT State U.–Billings; Rocky Mountain College); tourism.

NEBRASKA

Equality Before the Law

About two thirds of Nebraska's ninety-three counties have the commissioner-precinct form of government. The rest have the supervisor-township form. Commissioner-precinct counties are governed by a board of commissioners of three or five members. Supervisor-township counties are governed by a seven-member board of supervisors. Other county officials include the county clerk, treasurer, attorney, and sheriff. The consolidation of administrative offices in two or more counties is permitted by the state constitution.

ADAMS (one of twelve counties so named) *Hastings* • 31,151 • 563 • Southern NE; drained by the Little Blue River and the West Fork of the Big Blue River. Crystal Lake and DLD state recreation areas are in the county. • One of eight counties named for President John Adams • 1867 from Clay • Wheat, corn, sorghum, cattle, dairying, hogs, poultry; food processing; grain processing and storage facilities; government beef-research station; manufacture of cooling and heating machinery, farm and irrigation equipment, farm tools, sheet metal, millwork products; education (Hastings College). A U.S. naval munitions depot is here. • The House of Yesterday contains historical, geological and biological collections, as well as the J.M. McDonald Planetarium.

ANTELOPE *Neligh* • 7,452 • 857 • Northeastern NE; drained by the Elkhorn River. Ashfall State Historic Park is on the northern boundary. • The county was named for a specific antelope shot here by NE legislator Leander Gerrard while on the trail of Indians • 1871 from Pierce • Elgin is known as the "Vetch capital." Also, rye, corn, soybeans, wild hay, alfalfa, cattle, dairying, hogs • The Neligh Mill (state historic site), constructed in 1873–74 on the Elkhorn River, is one of the oldest and best examples of a water-powered mill in the U.S. The county is the western terminus of the Cowboy Trail, NE's first state recreational trail.

ARTHUR *Arthur* • 444 (the least populated county in NE; only four U.S. counties have fewer people) • 715 • West-central NE; watered by several small lakes. The Sand Hills cover much of the county. • Named for President Chester A. Arthur • County approved 1887 from unattached lands; formed 1913 • Cattle • The Haybale Church, built in 1927 in Arthur, is believed to be the only baled straw church in the world. Fence posts along Highway 61 outside of the town of Arthur are capped with old boots, a tradition long respected by locals.

BANNER *Harrisburg* • 819 • 746 • Western NE, bounded on the west by the WY state line; drained by Rocky Hollow and Pumpkin creeks. Wildcat Hills State Recreation Area is on the northern boundary. • The name of the county was inspired by a boast by its citizens that it would be the "banner county" of the state • 1888 from Cheyenne • Cattle, hogs, wheat, potatoes, sunflower seeds.

BLAINE *Brewster* • 583 (only eight U.S. counties have fewer people) • 711 • Central NE; drained by the North Loup, Middle Loup, and Dismal rivers. Part of the manmade ponderosa- and red cedar-rich Nebraska National Forest is here. • One of four counties named for James G. Blaine (1830–93), U.S. representative from ME, U.S. senator, and U.S. secretary of state • 1885 from Custer • Cattle, hogs, grain.

BOONE (one of eight counties so named) *Albion* • 6,259 • 687 • East-central NE; drained by the Cedar River and Beaver Creek. • One of seven counties named for Daniel Boone • 1871 from Platte • Cattle, hogs, corn, alfalfa, sorghum, dairying.

BOX BUTTE *Alliance* • 12,158 • 1,075 • Northwestern NE; drained by the Niobrara River. Several small natural lakes are here, including Kilpatrick Lake. • Named for a rectangular-shaped butte near Alliance • 1886 from Dawes • Railroad shops; cattle, hogs, poultry products, wheat, beans, alfalfa, corn, sugar beets, potatoes (including seed potatoes). Alliance has a federal seed-potato testing ground. • Intrigued by England's mystical Stonehenge, a farmer from Alliance created Carhenge. At a 1991 festival, over 750 people used methods employed by the ancients to raise the "Heel Stone," a 1962 Cadillac. Some locals contend that the county was named for a message box placed on a hill, which served as an information center for early settlers.

BOYD (one of two counties so named, the other in KY) *Butte* • 2,438 • 540 • Northern NE, bounded on the north by the SD state line, on the south by the Niobrara River (designated a National Scenic and Recreational River), and on the northeast by the Missouri River (designated here a National Recreational River); drained by the Keya Paha River and Ponca Creek. • Named for James E. Boyd (1834–1906), governor of NE • 1891 from Holt • Cattle, hogs, dairying, corn, sorghum, alfalfa.

BROWN (one of nine counties so named) *Ainsworth* • 3,525 • 1,221 • Northern NE, bounded on the north by the Niobrara River (designated here a National Scenic and Recreational River); drained in the south by the Calamus River. The county contains several small natural lakes, Niobrara Valley Preserve, and Long Pike, Long Lake, and Keller Park state recreation areas. • Possibly named for five members of the NE state legislature named Brown at the time the county was formed. • 1883 from unorganized territory • Cattle, hogs, dairying, corn • Ainsworth, designated by the NE Legislature as the "Country Music Capital of Nebraska," hosts the annual National Country Music Festival in August. The city periodically hosts the World Horseshoe Tournament. Bison herds roam north of Johnstown on land owned by the Nature Conservancy.

BUFFALO (one of three counties so named) *Kearney* • 42,259 (the fifth most populated county in NE) • 968 • South-central NE, bounded on the south by the Platte River; drained by the South Loup and Wood rivers. Ravenna Lake, Windmill, and Union Pacific state recreation areas are here. • Named for the large bison herds that once roamed NE • Original county; organized 1855 (prior to statehood); not officially recognized until 1870 • Dairying, cattle, hogs, potatoes, wheat, sugar beets, soybeans, corn, sorghum, alfalfa; manufacture of oil filters, automotive valves, pipeline valves, grain-drying equipment, irrigation pipes, rubber pharmaceutical products, truck generators; education (the U. of NE at Kearney) • Gibbon was once a soldiers' colony; free home sites and reduced railroad fare were offered to Union veterans recruited from the east who began to arrive in 1871. Elm Creek was almost a "doom" town; in its first 25 years following settlement in 1873, it experienced several blizzards and a major fire. 18,000 Austrian and Ponderosa pines and red cedars were planted along a four-and-one-half-mile stretch of Route 2 in 1961 as a "Living Snow Fence" (located partly in Hall County). The Nebraska Wild Horse and Burro Facility is located here.

BURT *Tekamah* • 7,791 • 493 • Eastern NE, bounded on the east by the Missouri River (forming the IA state line); drained by Logan Creek. A small part of Omaha Indian Reservation is in the extreme north. Pelican Point and Summit Lake state recreation areas are in the county. • Named for Francis Burt (1807–54), SC legislator and first governor of NE Territory (who served for only two days) • Original county; organized 1854 (prior to statehood) • Decatur, the second oldest community in the state, is best known for the Dry Land Bridge, a historic bridge built to cross the Missouri River that was left dry-docked when the river shifted its channel in 1950. In 1954 the U.S. Corps of Engineers rerouted the river back to its original channel. • Corn, sorghum, cattle, hogs, dairying • On the face of Golden Springs' sandstone cliff, five miles south of Decatur, are names carved by pioneers who stopped here on their way west. The Troll Stroll in Oakland is a nature walk through a forest inhabited by two dozen handmade "trolls" designed by local students.

BUTLER (one of eight counties so named) *David City* • 8,767 • 584 • Eastern NE, bounded on the north by the Platte River; drained in the southwest by the Big Blue River. • One of three counties named for General William O. Butler (1791–1880), U.S. representative from KY and officer in the Mexican War. • 1856 from unorganized territory • Executive Joyce C. Hall • Cattle, hogs, poultry, corn, soybeans, sorghum, alfalfa, dairy products.

CASS (one of nine counties so named) *Plattsmouth* • 24,334 • 559 • Southeastern NE, bounded on the east by the Missouri River (forming the IA state line), and on the north by the Platte River. Louisville State Recreation Area, and Mahoney and Platte River state parks are here. • One of eight counties named for Gen. Lewis Cass (1782–1866), military and civil governor of MI Territory, U.S. secretary of war, and U.S. secretary of state • Original county; organized 1854 (prior to statehood) • Cattle, dairying, hogs, corn, sorghum, alfalfa; manufacture of freight cars. • Each September Plattsmouth holds the King Korn Karnival, a harvest fair.

CEDAR (one of three counties so named) *Hartington* • 9,615 • 740 • Northeastern NE, bounded on the north by the SD state line, formed by the Missouri River (designated here a National Recreational River); drained by Logan Creek. • Named for the abundant cedar trees in the county • 1857 • On August 5, 1944, two bombers collided near Laurel. The B-17 Memorial Site here recalls the tragedy. • Cattle, dairying, hogs, corn, barley, alfalfa.

CHASE (one of two counties so named, the other in KS) *Imperial* • 4,068 • 895 • Southwestern NE, bounded on the west by the CO state line; drained by Frenchman and Stinking Water creeks. Enders Reservoir and Champion Lake state recreation areas and Champion Mill State Historical Park (containing the last functional water-powered mill in NE) are located in the county. • Named for Champion S. Chase (1820–1898), mayor of Omaha, NE and first attorney general of NE • 1873 from Keith • Cattle, hogs, corn, wheat, popcorn, beans, potatoes.

CHERRY *Valentine* • 6,148 • 5,961 (the largest county in NE and the forty-second largest county in the U.S.) • Northern NE, bounded on the north by the SD state line; drained by the Niobrara, Snake, North Loup and Middle Loup rivers. Merritt Reservoir and Cottonwood Lake state recreation areas are here. The county also includes Bowring Ranch State Historical Park, Smith Falls State Park, Fort Niobrara and Valentine national wildlife refuges, Samuel R. McKelvie National Forest, and numerous small natural lakes. The Sand Hills cover much of the county. (Sandhills Museum is located in Valentine.) Part of the county lies in the Central time zone and part in the Mountain time zone. • Named for Lieutenant Samuel A. Cherry (1850 -1881), an army officer stationed at Fort Niobrara • 1883 from unorganized territory • Cattle, hogs, dairying, alfalfa, wild hay.

CHEYENNE *Sidney* • 9,830 • 1,196 • Western NE, bounded on the south by the CO state line; drained by Lodgepole and Rush creeks. • One of three counties named for the Cheyenne Indians who once lived in the area • 1867 from Lincoln • Most of the western trails, including the Emigrant Trail, Mormon Trail, Oregon Trail, Overland Trail, Sidney-Deadwood Trail, and the Pony Express Trail passed through the county. Fort Sidney (museum) was established in 1867 to protect the Union Pacific Transcontinental Railroad workers. The town of Sidney was ruled by lawlessness in the 1870s; among its many visitors were "Doc" Middleton, Sam Bass, Butch Cassidy, Calamity Jane, and Wild Bill Hickok. During WW II, Sidney was the site of the Sioux Ordnance Depot, an installation of hundreds of above-ground ammunition storage bunkers, most still standing, and now providing farm storage for local farmers. • Cattle, hogs, wheat, sunflower seeds, sugar beets; oil and gas.

CLAY (one of eighteen counties so named) *Clay Center* • 7,039 • 573 • Southern NE; drained by the Little Blue River and Big Sandy Creek. The U.S. Meat Animal Research Center is west of Clay Center. The Oregon Trail crossed the county's southwest corner. • One of fifteen counties named for Henry Clay (1777–1852), U.S. senator from KY, known as the "Great Pacificator" for his advocacy of compromise to avert national crises • Original county; organized 1855 (prior to statehood) • Cattle, hogs, corn, wheat, sorghum, alfalfa, dairy products • The arrival of over one million snow geese and other wild fowl to this region each year is celebrated in the Spring Wing Ding in Clay Center.

COLFAX *Schuyler* • 10,441 • 413 • Eastern NE, bounded on the south by the Platte River; drained by Shell and Maple creeks. • One of two counties (the other in NM) named for Schuyler Colfax (1823–85), U.S. vice president under Ulysses S. Grant • 1869 from Platte • Cattle, hogs, poultry, corn, soybeans, alfalfa, dairying.

CUMING *West Point* • 10,203 • 572 • Northeastern NE; drained by the Elkhorn River. Part of Omaha Indian Reservation is in the northeast corner. • Named for Thomas B. Cuming (1828–1858), first secretary of NE territory and acting governor of NE Territory • 1855 from Burt • Poet Laureate of Nebraska John G. Neihardt (state historic site) • Cattle, dairying, hogs, corn, alfalfa.

CUSTER *Broken Bow* • 11,793 • 2,576 (the second largest county in NE) • Central NE; drained by the Middle Loup and South Loup rivers and Clear Creek. Arnold and Victoria Springs state recreation areas are here. • One of six counties named for Gen. George Armstrong Custer (1839–76), U.S. army officer and Indian fighter • Organized 1877 from unorganized territory • Cattle, dairying, hogs, corn, wheat, sorghum, alfalfa; manufacture of blood collecting tubes • The county is home to the Nebraska One Box Pheasant Hunt, attended by a variety of celebrities, corporate executives and government officials each year since 1961.

DAKOTA (one of two counties so named) *Dakota City* • 20,253 (21% increase since 1990; the second fastest growing county in NE) • 264 • Northeastern NE, bounded on the east and northeast by the Missouri River, forming the IA and SD state lines. The eastern part of the county is in the Sioux City/South Sioux City metropolitan area. • One of five counties named for the Dakota Indians, also known as the Sioux • Original county; organized 1855 • Manufacture of food, leather, fabricated metal products, machinery; corn, cattle, hogs.

DAWES *Chadron* • 9,060 • 1,396 • Northwestern NE, bounded on the north by the SD state line; drained by the White and Niobrara rivers. Part of Oglala National Grasslands is here, as is the Pine Ridge unit of Nebraska National Forest which crosses the county from east-center to the southwest. Chadron State Park (NE's oldest state park), Pine Ridge National Recreation Area, and Box Butte Reservoir State Recreation Area are also here. • Named for James W. Dawes (1844–1918), governor of NE • 1885 from Sioux • For over 70 years Fort Robinson (state park) was the most important military outpost in the region. It was the site of the Cheyenne Outbreak and home to the Red Cloud Agency. Crazy Horse surrendered to the U.S. army here on May 6, 1877 and was killed by a soldier as he was being put into a jail cell. • Cattle, wheat, alfalfa, hogs, dairying, poultry, beans, potatoes; education (Chadron State College) • The Museum of Fur Trade traces the history of fur trapping and trade, and includes a reconstructed 1837 trading post. Chadron was the starting point of the June, 1893 Cowboy Horse Race to Chicago, almost 1000 miles away. The winner, John Berry, completed the race in thirteen days, sixteen hours, and won $1000.

DAWSON (one of four counties so named) *Lexington* • 24,365 (22% increase since 1990; the fastest growing county in NE) • 1,013 • South-central NE; drained by the Platte and Wood rivers, and Buffalo Creek. Gallagher Canyon and Johnson Lake state recreation areas are here. • Named for Jacob Dawson, first postmaster of Lancaster (now Lincoln) • 1860 from Buffalo • In 1864, the Plum Creek Massacre occurred in the bluffs near Lexington, forcing settlers to flee to the safety of Fort Kearney. • Corn, alfalfa, wheat, soybeans, hogs, dairy and poultry products. • An historic Pony Express Station is located near Gothenburg.

DEUEL (one of two counties so named, the other in SD) *Chappell* • 2,098 • 440 • Western NE, bounded on the south by the CO state line; drained by Lodgepole Creek and the South Platte River. The Old Oregon Trail passes through the county. • Named for Henry (or Harry) P. Deuel (1836–1914), an early settler of Omaha and later a local railroad official • 1889 from Cheyenne • Visible wagon ruts attest to the countless wagons that passed through what is now Deuel County on their journey west along the Oregon Trail. The Pony Express also galloped through here. The Waterman Sod House was one of the last of the famous sod houses built by pioneers on the prairie. Deuel County was the site of the first Union Pacific train robbery. It also contains the crash site of a B-24 bomber which exploded over the county on June 7, 1944; a marker here honors the many bomber crew members who sacrificed their lives during WWII. • Cattle, hogs, wheat, sorghum, sunflower seeds.

DIXON *Ponca* • 6,339 • 476 • Northeastern NE, bounded on north by the SD state line, formed by the Missouri River (designated here a National Recreational River); watered by Logan Creek. Ponca State Park and Tarbox Hollow Living Prairie are here, as is a small part of Winnebago Indian Reservation (in the extreme southeastern corner). • Named for an early settler of the area • Original county; organized Dec. 1856 (prior to statehood) from Dakota • Cattle, hogs, corn, soybeans, alfalfa, oats, poultry; food processing, dairy products • The Ionia "Volcano" site frightened early settlers to the area; until washed away by the Missouri River in 1878, iron pyrite beds here produced dense, seemingly inexplicable smoke and fire.

DODGE (one of four counties so named) *Fremont* • 36,160 • 535 • Eastern NE, bounded on the south by the Platte River; drained by the Elkhorn River and Logan Creek. Dead Timber and Fremont Lakes state recreation areas are here. • Named for Augustus C. Dodge (1812–83), one of IA's first two U.S. senators and minister to Spain • Original county, organized 1854 (prior to statehood) • Electrical engineer and photographer Harold E. Edgerton • Cattle, hogs, corn, soybeans, sorghum, alfalfa, fruits, dairying, poultry; manufacture of flour, feeds, cement and tile products, machine parts, refrigeration equipment; education (Midland Lutheran College).

DOUGLAS *Omaha* • 463,585 (the most populated county in NE) • 331 • Eastern NE, bounded on the west by the Platte River and on the east by the Missouri River, forming the IA state line; drained by the Elkhorn River. The county lies in an industrial region, highly urbanized in and around Omaha, primarily rural in the southeast. Two Rivers State Recreation Area is here, as are Glen Cunningham Lake and Standing Bear Lake, both local recreation areas. • One of twelve counties named for Stephen A. Douglas (1813–61), U.S. orator and statesman • Original county; organized 1854 (prior to statehood) • Explorers Lewis and Clark passed through what is now the county of Douglas on their journey in 1804. Omaha served as the winter headquarters for over 4,000 Mormons on their trek from IL to UT. It was also an outfitting point for wagon trains headed for the newly discovered Colorado gold fields in the late 1850s. Omaha was the capital of NE Territory from 1855 to 1867. The "Trans-Mississippi and International Exposition," held in Omaha in 1898, saw attendance of over two million. Boys Town, a municipality administered by homeless boys and girls, was established here in 1919 by Father Flanagan. • Dancer Fred Astaire; professional boxer Max Baer; actor Marlon Brando; President Gerald R. Ford; baseball player Bob Gibson; economist Lawrence Klein; investor Warren Buffett; black militant leader Malcolm X. Irish nationalist John O'Neill died here. • Omaha is one of the world's leading food-processing centers, with meat packing its major industry and frozen food production important. It is also one of the largest insurance centers in the U.S. Also, cattle, dairying, hogs, corn; manufacture of machinery, telephone and electrical equipment; printing and publishing; education (U. of NE at Omaha; U. of NE Medical Center; Creighton U.; College of St. Mary; Grace U.) • The headquarters of six Fortune 1000 companies are located in Omaha. Omaha's Rosenblatt Stadium has hosted baseball's College World Series since 1950. Omaha is the headquarters of the Union Pacific Railroad, which began building west from the city in 1865 as part of the first U.S. transcontinental line.

DUNDY *Benkelman* • 2,292 • 920 • Southwestern NE, bounded on the south by the KS state line and on the west by the CO state line; drained by the Republican River and its North Fork. The county has fish hatcheries, one of them at Rock Creek State Recreation Area, which contains tiger muskies, crossbred from northern pike and muskellunge. • Named for Elmer S. Dundy (1830–96), U.S. circuit judge for the district of NE • 1873 from unorganized territory • Massive cattle herds were driven from TX to Dundy County, and then moved up to Ogallala. By 1883, the Texas Trail Canyon was serving as a major stopping point for cattle branding and disease inspection. In 1886, the last year of the trail drives, 150,000 head of cattle moved through the county. • Cattle, hogs, corn, wheat, beans, sorghum.

FILLMORE *Geneva* • 6,634 • 577 • Southeastern NE; drained by Turkey Creek and the Big Blue River. Some of the county's wet areas are preserved as wildlife refuges. • One of three counties named for President Millard Fillmore • 1856 from unorganized territory • Welfare leader Kate Barnard • Corn, soybeans, sorghum, cattle, hogs, dairy and poultry products.

FRANKLIN (one of twenty-five counties so named) *Franklin* • 3,574 • 575 • Southern NE, bounded on the south by the KS state line; drained by the Republican River. • One of twenty-three counties named for Benjamin Franklin • 1867 from Kearney • Corn, wheat, soybeans, sorghum, livestock, dairy products.

FRONTIER *Stockville* • 3,099 • 975 • Southern NE; drained by Medicine, Deer, and Red Willow creeks. Part of Red Willow State Recreation Area (Hugh Butler Lake) and Medicine Creek State Recreation Area (Harry Strunk Lake) are in the south. • Named for its location on the NE frontier at the time of its creation • 1872 from unorganized territory • Corn, wheat, sorghum, livestock.

FURNAS *Beaver City* • 5,324 • 718 • Southern NE, bounded on the south by the KS state line; drained by the Republican River, and Beaver and Sappa creeks. • Named for Col. Robert W. Furnas (1824–1905), a Union Army officer and governor

of NE • 1873 from unorganized territory • George Norris began his long political career here, serving as prosecuting attorney of the county in 1892. • Cattle, hogs, dairying, corn, wheat, sorghum, alfalfa.

GAGE *Beatrice* • 22,993 • 855 • Southeastern NE, bounded on the south by the KS state line; drained by the Big Blue River and the North Fork of the Big Nemaha River. Homestead National Monument, comprising the Dan Freeman farm, represents the first claim entered under the Homestead Act of 1862. Rockford State Recreation Area is also in the county. • Named for William D. Gage (1803–85) Methodist minister and chaplain of the first legislative assembly of NE Territory • Original county; organized 1855 • Cattle, hogs, corn, wheat, soybeans, sorghum, alfalfa, dairy and poultry products.

GARDEN *Oshkosh* • 2,292 • 1,705 • Western NE; drained by the North Platte River and Blue Creek. The Oregon Trail followed the southern banks of the North Platte River. Ash Hollow State Historical Park (with Oregon Trail wagon ruts and gravesites) is here, as is Crescent Lake National Wildlife Refuge. The county is located in the Sand Hills, and has numerous small natural lakes teeming with abundant animal life. • Named by John T. and William R. Twiford, area developers who thought it would become the "garden spot of the west." • 1909 from Deuel • In the Battle of Ash Hollow at Blue Water Creek (1855) General Harney's forces killed a number of Brule Sioux in retaliation for the Grattan Massacre of 1854. • Cattle, hogs, corn, wheat, alfalfa, sugar beets.

GARFIELD *Burwell* • 1,902 • 570 • Central NE; drained by the North Loup, Calamus, and Cedar rivers. Calamus Reservoir State Recreation Area is in the west. • One of six counties named for President James A. Garfield • 1884 from Wheeler • Fort Hartsuff, a U.S. Army Infantry Post, was established here in 1874 to provide protection for the settlers from Sioux attack. • Corn, wild hay, cattle, hogs.

GOSPER *Elwood* • 2,143 • 458 • Southern NE, bounded on the northeast corner by the Platte River; drained by Muddy Creek. Elwood and Johnson Lake reservoirs are in the north, the latter on the Tri-County Supply Canal. • Named for John J. Gosper (?–1913), NE secretary of state and acting governor of AZ Territory • 1873 from unorganized territory • Corn, wheat, sorghum, cattle, hogs.

GRANT (One of fifteen counties so named) *Hyannis* • 747 • 776 • West-central NE. The Sand Hills cover much of the county. • One of twelve counties named for President Ulysses S. Grant • 1887 from unorganized territory • Cattle.

GREELEY *Greeley* • 2,714 • 570 • East-central NE; drained by the Cedar and North Loup rivers. Happy Jack Chalk Mine and Peak is in the southwest corner. • One of two counties (the other in KS) named for Horace Greeley (1811–72), editor who championed westward expansion • 1871 from Boone • Cattle, hogs, dairying, soybeans, corn, alfalfa, dairy products.

HALL (one of three counties so named) *Grand Island* • 53,534 (the fourth most populated county in NE) • 546 • South-central NE; drained by the Platte, Wood, and South Loup rivers. War Axe, Cheyenne, and Mormon Island state recreation areas are here, as is Crane Meadows Nature Center. • Named for Augustus Hall (1814–61), U.S. representative from IA and chief justice of NE Territory • Original county; organized 1858 (prior to statehood) • Grand Island sits on the site of old Fort Independence, built by William Stolley (Stolley State Park). The city was struck by a devastating series of seven tornadoes on June 3, 1980, which destroyed hundreds of buildings and left several dead. • Actor Henry Fonda; Puppeteer Bil Baird • Corn, soybeans, wheat, hay, sorghum, vegetables, cattle, hogs, dairying, poultry; meat packing, dairy processing, flour milling; manufacture of farm and irrigation equipment, stock foods, pumps, concrete walls, munitions, house trailers, plastic tile, beverages • 18,000 Austrian and Ponderosa pines and red cedars were planted along a four-and-one-half-mile stretch of Route 2 in 1961 as a " Living Snow Fence" (located partly in Buffalo). The Stuhr Museum of the Prairie Pioneer in Grand Island was designed by Edward Durell Stone.

HAMILTON (one of ten counties so named) *Aurora* • 9,403 • 544 • Southeast-central NE, bounded on the north and northwest by the Platte River; drained by the Big Blue River and its West Fork. • One of eight counties named for Alexander Hamilton (?–1804), first U.S. secretary of treasury • 1867 from York • Cattle, hogs, dairying, corn, soybeans, sorghum.

HARLAN (one of two counties so named, the other in KY) *Alma* • 3,786 • 553 • Southern NE, bounded on the south by the KS state line; drained by the Republican River, here impounded by the Harlan County Dam. • Named for either Thomas Harlan, a pioneer; or for James Harlan (1820–99), U.S. senator from IA and U.S. secretary of the interior. • 1871 from Lincoln • Cattle, hogs, corn, wheat, sorghum, dairy and poultry products.

HAYES *Hayes Center* • 1,068 • 713 • Southern NE; drained by Frenchman, Red Willow, and Stinking Water creeks. • Named for President Rutherford B. Hayes • 1877 from unorganized territory • The county was the scene of an 1872 visit by Russian Grand Duke Alexis (son of Russian Czar Alexander II) who, led by Gen. Custer and Buffalo Bill Cody, participated in the slaughter of fifty-six buffalo. • Cattle, hogs, corn, wheat, beans.

HITCHCOCK *Trenton* • 3,111 • 710 • Southern NE, bounded on the south by the KS state line; drained by the Republican River, and Driftwood and Stinking Water creeks. Swanson Reservoir and State Recreation Area is here. Massacre Monument is also in the county. • Named for Phineas W. Hitchcock (1831–81), U.S. senator from NE • 1873 from unorganized territory • The August 5, 1873 Massacre Canyon Battle (Massacre Canyon Monument), the last battle fought between the Pawnee and Sioux nations, resulted in a routing of the Pawnees and death to a number of the tribe's warriors, women and children. • Corn, wheat, sorghum, sunflower seeds, cattle, hogs; petroleum.

HOLT (one of two counties so named, the other in MO) *O'Neill* • 11,551 • 2,413 (the fifth largest county in NE) • Northern NE, bounded on the north by the Niobrara River (designated a National Scenic and Recreational River); drained by the Elkhorn River. Atkinson Lake State Recreation Area is here. • Named for Joseph Holt (1807–94), U.S. postmaster general, secretary of war, and judge advocate general for the U.S. army who prosecuted those accused of assassinating President Lincoln • Organized as West in 1860; name changed in 1862 • Cattle, hogs, corn, alfalfa, wild hay, soybeans, dairy, poultry.

HOOKER *Mullen* • 783 • 721 • Central NE; drained by the Middle Loup and Dismal rivers. The Sand Hills cover much of the county. • Named for Joseph Hooker (1814–79), Union general during the Civil War • 1889 from unorganized territory • Cattle, hogs.

HOWARD (one of seven counties so named) *Saint Paul* • 6,567 • 570 • East-central NE; drained by the North Loup and Middle Loup rivers. The two rivers merge northwest of the south canal to become Loup Reservoir. North Loup State Recreation Area is also here. • Named for Gen. Oliver O. Howard (1830–1909), Union officer in the Civil War, and one of the founders and president of Howard University • 1871 from Hall • Professional baseball player Grover Cleveland Alexander • Cattle, hogs, corn, alfalfa, soybeans, dairy and poultry products • Dannebrog is the Danish capital of NE. The state's Baseball Hall of Fame is located in St. Paul.

JEFFERSON *Fairbury* • 8,333 • 573 • Southeastern NE, bounded on the south by the KS state line; drained by the Little Blue River. The old Oregon Trail crosses the county from southeast to northwest, passing through the historic Rock Creek Station (state historic park) southeast of Fairbury. Alexandria State Recreation Area is in the northwest. • One of twenty-six counties named directly or indirectly for President Thomas Jefferson • In 1856, Jones and Jefferson counties were created. Over the years that followed the counties evolved and county lines shifted, ultimately resulting in adjacent counties Jefferson (east) and Thayer (west). • Cattle, hogs, corn, wheat, soybeans, sorghum, alfalfa, dairying; clay quarrying.

JOHNSON (one of twelve counties so named) *Tecumseh* • 4,488 • 376 • Southeastern NE; drained by branches of the North Fork of the Big Nemaha River. • One of five counties named for Col. Richard Mentor Johnson (1780–1850), officer in the War of 1812, U.S. senator from KY, and U.S. vice president • 1855 (prior to statehood) • Cattle, hogs, poultry, corn, sorghum, soybeans, wheat, dairying, poultry products, feed.

KEARNEY *Minden* • 6,882 • 516 • Southern NE, bounded on the north by the Platte River. Pioneer Village is in Minden. • Named for Fort Kearny, itself named for Stephen W. Kearny (1794–1848), officer in the War of 1812 and the Mexican War. The "e" in the last syllable was added from established use of the name spelled this way elsewhere. • Original county; organized 1860 (prior to statehood) • Fort Kearney, established in 1848, served as a government outpost to protect pioneers on the Oregon Trail (Fort Kearney State Historical Park). • Cattle, hogs, corn, soybeans, wheat, sorghum, alfalfa, sunflower seeds, dairy products • Axtell, often called the town of windmills, was settled by the Swedish. The county is the center of a refueling area for half a million sandhill cranes. The excitement of the crane season is enhanced by Kearney's Wildlife Celebration.

KEITH *Ogallala* • 8,875 • 1,061 • Southwest-central NE; drained by the North Platte and South Platte rivers. Lake C. W. McConaughy reservoir (Kingsley Dam) is on the North Platte and is bordered by Lake McConaughy State Recreation Area. Lake Ogallala State Recreation Area is also in the county. • Named for Morell C. Keith (1824–1899), famous ranchman and the grandfather of NE governor Keith Neville • 1873 from Lincoln • Ogallala was a major shipping point for beef. • Cattle, hogs, wheat, corn, alfalfa, beans, sunflower seeds.

KEYA PAHA *Springview* • 983 • 773 • Northern NE, bounded on the north by the SD state line and on the south by the Niobrara River (designated here a National Scenic and Recreational River); drained by the Keya Paha River. • Named for the Keya Paha River • 1884 from Brown • Cattle, dairying, hogs, corn, alfalfa, wild hay.

KIMBALL *Kimball* • 4,089 • 952 • Western NE, bounded on the south by the CO state line and on the west by the WY state line; drained by Lodgepole Creek. The highest point in the state (5,424 feet, unnamed) is in the southwest corner of the county. The county includes the Oliver Reservoir State Recreation Area. • Named for the town of Kimball, NE • 1888 from Cheyenne • Kimball began as a water station for the Union Pacific Railroad in 1867. • Cattle, hogs, wheat, potatoes, sunflower seeds • A Titan missile is on display in Kimball's city park.

KNOX *Center* • 9,374 • 1,108 • Northeastern NE, bounded on the north by the SD state line, formed by the Missouri River (designated here a National Recreational River and dammed in the northeast corner of the county to form Lewis and Clark Lake); drained by the Niobrara River. Niobrara State Park is here, as is Lewis and Clark State Recreation Area, and Santee Indian Reservation. • One of nine counties named for Gen. Henry Knox (1750–1806), Revolutionary War officer and first U.S. secretary of war • Original county; organized as L'Eau Qui Court in 1857 (prior to statehood); name changed to Emmett in 1867; then to its present name in 1873 • Explorers Lewis and Clark met with the Yankton Sioux at Calumet Bluff in August, 1804. • Cattle, hogs, corn, wild hay, alfalfa, soybeans, dairying • Verdigre holds a Czech festival every June.

LANCASTER (one of four counties so named) *Lincoln* • 250,291 (the second most populated county in NE) • 839 • Southeastern NE; drained by the Salt Creek. The county has seven state recreational areas. • Named for Lancaster County, PA, former home of many settlers • Original county, organized

in 1855 (prior to statehood) • Lincoln has served as the capital of NE since 1867. Its capitol, constructed between 1922 and 1932, has been declared one of the modern architectural wonders of the world by the American Institute of Architects. • Anthropologist Loren Eiseley; psychologist Edwin Ray Guthrie; botanist Roscoe Pound; senator Bob Kerry; U.S. vice president Richard Cheney • Corn, wheat, sorghum, soybeans, cattle, hogs, dairying; manufacture of computer software, grain products, electrical circuits, laboratory equipment, recreational vehicles, rubber belting; state government operations; education (U. of NE–Lincoln; NE Wesleyan U.; Union College) • One of the top five paleontological museums in the U.S. is at the University of Nebraska–Lincoln. Charles Lindbergh took lessons at the Lincoln Flying School. The city of Lincoln was so named to annoy residents of the area who held Confederate sympathies. The National Museum of Roller Skating is in Lincoln. Post Number Three in Lincoln is the world's largest American legion post. The 911 system of emergency communications was developed and first used here. Authorized off-premise banking was first developed in Lincoln.

LINCOLN (one of twenty-four counties so named) *North Platte* • 34,632 • 2,564 (the third largest county in NE) • Central NE. The Platte River is formed by the juncture of the South Platte and North Platte rivers here. Ft. McPherson National Cemetery is in the county, as are Maloney Reservoir and Sutherland Reservoir state recreation areas. The old Oregon Trail follows the southern bank of the Platte/South Platte River. • One of eighteen counties named for President Abraham Lincoln • Organized as Shorter in 1860 (prior to statehood) from unorganized territory; name changed 1866 • William F. "Buffalo Bill" Cody (who organized his famous Wild West Show at his ranch here, now a state recreation area and historic park). • Cattle, hogs, dairying, corn, wheat, alfalfa, sugar beets, rye, soybeans, wild hay, sunflowers • The Buffalo Bill Rodeo is held annually in North Platte, which claims to have held the earliest rodeo in the U.S. on July 4, 1882. Bailey Yard at North Platte (Union Pacific Railroad) is the nation's largest railroad classification yard. The largest mammoth fossil ever found, measuring 13 feet 4½ inches tall, was unearthed in 1922 near Wellfleet.

LOGAN (one of ten counties so named) *Stapleton* • 774 • 571 • Central NE; drained by the South Loup River. The Sand Hills cover much of the county. • One of five counties named for General John A. Logan (1826–86), officer in the Mexican War and Union Army during the Civil War, who came up with the idea for Memorial Day • 1885 from Custer • Cattle, hogs, corn.

LOUP *Taylor* • 712 (only nine U.S. counties have fewer people) • 570 • Central NE; drained by the Calamus and North Loup rivers. A large portion of Calamus Reservoir is on its eastern border. • Named for the North Loup River • Organized as Taylor County 1855 from unorganized territory (prior to statehood); name changed 1883 • A number of Indian skirmishes took place in the county, including the Spring Creek Incident of 1870, the Battle of Sioux Creek in 1873, and the Battle of the Blowout in 1876. • NE's first Black cowboy Amos Harris. Cattle and horse rustlers "Doc" Middleton and "Kid" Wade frequented the county in its early days. • Cattle, hogs, corn.

MADISON *Madison* • 35,226 • 573 • Northeast-central NE; drained by the Elkhorn River. • Named for the city of Madison, WI, former home of early German settlers • 1867 from Platte • Norfolk was settled in 1866 by German farmers from WI. • Entertainer Johnny Carson; inventor Orville Carlisle • Cattle, hogs, dairying, poultry, corn, soybeans; manufacture of medical equipment, electronic resistors and circuits; education (NE Christian College) • The county is the eastern terminus of the nation's longest rail to trail conversion, the Cowboy Trail, NE's first state recreation trail. Norfolk is home to "the cave that children built," the Verges cave, dug in 1910 under supervision of a former miner. Subsequently enlarged and appropriately equipped, the cave was put to use as shelter and public gathering place.

MCPHERSON *Tryon* • 533 (only six U.S. counties have fewer people) • 859 • West-central NE; drained by Birdwood Creek. Much of the county is in the Sand Hills. Several small lakes, including Diamond, Bar, and Whitewater, are located here. • One of three counties named for Gen. James Birdseye McPherson (1828–64), commander of the Union army in Tennessee during the Civil War • 1887 from Lincoln and Keith • Cattle, hogs, corn.

MERRICK *Central City* • 8,204 • 485 • East-central NE, bounded on the south by the Platte River. Hord Lake State Recreation Area is in the county. • Named for Elvira Merrick De Puy, wife of Rep. Henry W. De Puy, who introduced the bill for the county's establishment • Original county; organized 1858 (prior to statehood) • Central City is an historic crossroad community where the Oregon, California and Mormon trails met near the Platte River. Also here is the junction with the historic Lincoln Highway (U.S. 30) and the Union Pacific Railroad. • Novelist Wright Morris • Manufacture of mobile homes, chemicals, and fertilizer; cattle, hogs, dairying, corn.

MORRILL *Bridgeport* • 5,440 • 1,424 • Western NE; drained by the North Platte River and its branches. Several small natural lakes are in the northeast corner. The spire of Chimney Rock in Chimney Rock National Historic Site was mentioned more often in the diaries of pioneers moving along the Mormon and Oregon trails than any other feature; hundreds climbed up the cone to carve their names there. Other unusual geological features of note here are Courthouse Rock and Jail Rock. Bridgeport State Recreation Area is in the center of the county. • Named for Charles Henry Morrill (1843–1928), bank president and president of the Board of Regents for the University of NE. • 1908 from Cheyenne • Several trails crossed the county. Ruts of the Oregon Trail may still be seen

indenting the prairie sod in places. The Mud Springs Pony Express Station was the scene of an attack by a local band of Indians in 1865, in which nineteen men forestalled defeat long enough to be rescued by cavalry troops from Fort Laramie and Fort Mitchell in true Western melodrama fashion. • Sugar beets, beans, cattle, hogs, corn, wheat.

NANCE *Fullerton* • 4,038 • 441 • East-central NE; drained by the Loup and Cedar rivers. • Named for Albinus Nance (1848–1911), governor of NE • 1879 from Merrick, encompassing the entire former Pawnee Reservation • Cattle, hogs, dairying, corn, soybeans, sorghum.

NEMAHA *Auburn* • 7,576 • 409 • Southeastern NE, bounded on the east by the Missouri River (forming the MO state line); drained by the Little Nemaha River and Muddy Creek. Brownville State Recreation Area is here. • Named for the Nemaha River • Original county; organized 1855 (prior to statehood) • Soybeans, wheat, corn, sorghum, cattle, hogs, dairy and poultry products; education (Peru State College).

NUCKOLLS *Nelson* • 5,057 • 575 • Southern NE, bounded on the south by the KS state line; drained by the Republican and Little Blue rivers. The old Oregon Trail is in the northeast. • Named for either Stephen F. Nuckolls (1825–79), pioneer, NE territorial legislator, and delegate to Congress from WY Territory; or for both Stephen and his brother Lafayette, a NE territorial legislator • 1871 from unorganized territory; a county originally named Nuckolls is now Thayer County • Buried in Superior's Evergreen Cemetery is NE's only member of the British nobility, Lady Evelyn Vesty, who was also the highest paid woman executive in the world in the 1910s and 1920s. • Cattle, dairying, hogs, corn, wheat, sorghum.

OTOE *Nebraska City* • 15,396 • 616 • Southeastern NE, bounded on the east by the Missouri River, forming the IA and MO state lines; drained by the Little Nemaha River. Riverview Marina State Recreation Area is in the east. • Named for the Oto Indians • Organized as Pierce in 1854; name changed in 1855 • Nebraska City grew as an unloading point on the Missouri River for westbound freight. • Cattle, hogs, apples, corn, wheat, soybeans, sorghum; manufacture of gas meters; education (NE School for the Visually Handicapped) • The National Arbor Day Foundation is headquartered near the home of founder Sterling Morton in Arbor Lodge State Historical Park in Nebraska City. Located in the county was John Brown's Cave, a station on the Underground Railroad; as well as headquarters for the Pony Express and the Overland Trail passing point.

PAWNEE (one of three counties so named) *Pawnee City* • 3,087 • 432 • Southeastern NE, bounded on the south by the KS state line; drained by branches of the North and South forks of the Big Nemaha River and Turkey Creek. Burchard Lake is here. • One of two counties (the other in OK) named for the Pawnee Indians • Original county; organized 1855 (prior to statehood) • Silent screen actor Harold Lloyd • Cattle, hogs, sorghum, corn, soybeans, dairying; limestone • One of the largest barbed wire collections in the U.S. is displayed at the Historical Society Museum in Pawnee City.

PERKINS (one of two counties so named, the other in SD) *Grant* • 3,200 • 883 • Southwest-central NE, bounded on the west by the CO state line; drained by Red Willow and Stinking Water creeks. • Named for Charles E. Perkins (1840–1907), president of the Chicago, Burlington and Quincy Railroad • 1887 from Keith • Wheat, corn, beans, cattle, hogs, dairying.

PHELPS (one of two counties so named, the other in MO) *Holdrege* • 9,747 • 540 • Southern NE, bounded on the north by the Platte River. The Oregon Trail follows the south bank of the river. Sandy Channel State Recreation Area is in the county. • Named for Captain William Phelps (1808–?), an early settler and former steamboat captain • 1873 from unorganized territory • Camp Atlanta, a WW II prisoner of war camp, was located southwest of Holdrege. In 1934, a large stratosphere balloon, sponsored by the National Geographic Society for high altitude exploration, crashed to the ground near Loomis. • Cattle, hogs, corn, dairy products; manufacturing • Migrating bald eagles can be seen in the northwest from November through March.

PIERCE (one of five counties so named) *Pierce* • 7,857 • 574 • Northeastern NE; drained by branches of the Elkhorn River. Willow Creek State Recreation Area is in the county. • One of four counties named for President Franklin Pierce • 1856 from Madison • Cattle, hogs, dairying, corn, alfalfa, dairy products.

PLATTE (one of three counties so named) *Columbus* • 31,662 • 678 • East-central NE, bounded on the south by the Platte River; drained by the Loup River and Shell Creek. • Named for the Platte River • Original county; organized as Loup County 1856 (prior to statehood); name changed 1859 • Columbus was founded in 1856 at the North Fork Ferry of the Oregon Trail by settlers from Columbus, OH. After the arrival of the Union Pacific Railroad in 1860, the town became an outfitting post for wagon trains, and center for cattle feeding. • Corn, alfalfa, soybeans, wheat, cattle, hogs, dairying; manufacture of farm machinery, electronic equipment; surgical equipment. Several public power agencies have their headquarters in Columbus. • The city has one of the state's largest business districts in continuous use. Columbus Days include a re-enactment of the coronation of King Ferdinand and Queen Isabella.

POLK (one of twelve counties so named) *Osceola* • 5,639 • 439 • East-central NE, bounded on the north by the Platte River; drained by the Big Blue River • One of eleven counties named for President James Knox Polk • 1856 (prior to statehood) from Butler • Cattle, hogs, corn, sorghum, dairying.

RED WILLOW *McCook* • 11,448 • 717 • Southern NE, bounded on the south by the KS state line; drained by Beaver, Red Willow, Driftwood, and Medicine creeks, and by the Re-publican River. Part of Red Willow Reservoir State Recreation Area is located on the northwest boundary. • Named for Red Willow Creek • 1873 from unorganized territory • Senator George Norris (state historic site) • Dairying, corn, wheat, sorghum, cattle, hogs; petroleum. • The Museum of the High Plains is located in McCook.

RICHARDSON *Falls City* • 9,531 • 553 • Extreme southeastern NE, bounded on the east by the Missouri River (forming the MO state line) and on the south by the KS state line; drained by the Nemaha River and its North and South forks. Indian Cave State Park and Verdon Lake State Recreation Area are in the county. Also found here are Sac and Fox Indian Reservation and Iowa Indian Reservation. • Named for Major William A. Richardson (1811–75), officer in the Mexican War, U.S. senator from IL and governor of NE Territory • Original county; organized 1854 (prior to statehood) • Manufacture of agricultural equipment, food products, feed; corn, soybeans, wheat, sorghum, cattle, hogs, dairying.

ROCK (one of three counties so named) *Bassett* • 1,756 • 1,009 • Northern NE, bounded on the north by the Niobrara River (designated here a National Scenic and Recreational River); drained by the Elkhorn River. Several small natural lakes are found in the county. • Named for Rock Creek • 1888 from Brown • Cattle, hogs, corn, dairying.

SALINE (one of five counties so named) *Wilber* • 13,843 • 575 • Southeastern NE; drained by the Big Blue River and its West Fork. Part of Blue River State Recreation Area is on the northern border. • The county was named Saline in the unfounded belief that salt deposits were located here • 1855 from Gage and Lancaster • Manufacture of flour, tools, animal feed; cattle, hogs, corn, wheat, soybeans, dairying; education (Doane College) • Wilber claims the title "Czech Capital of Nebraska and the USA," and hosts an annual festival celebrating the Czech heritage of the area. The county was the setting for Willa Cather's *My Antonia*.

SARPY *Papillion* • 122,595 (19% increase since 1990; the third fastest growing and third most populated county in NE) • 241 (the smallest county in NE) • Eastern NE, bounded on the east by the Missouri River (forming the IA state line) and on the west and south by the Platte River. The county is becoming more urbanized as part of the Omaha metropolitan area. Schramm Park State Recreation Area is in the extreme southwest. • Named for Col. Peter A. Sarpy (1805–65), an early settler, fur trader and quartermaster for the NE volunteer regiment • 1857 from Douglas • Bellevue, established in the early 1800s as a fur trading post and later serving as an important missionary center and Indian agency, is NE's oldest continuous settlement. The town was the capital of NE Territory in 1864. The state's first newspaper, the *Nebraska Palladium*, was published here in 1854. The county lost territory in 1943 to Pottawattamie County in IA. • Military services; manufacture of textiles, concrete products, food processing, feed and fertilizer, computer cable; printing; cattle, hogs, corn, fruit, dairying; education (Bellevue U.) • The Offutt Air Force Base is headquarters of the U.S. Strategic Air Command. The Strategic Air Command Museum here displays many of the Air Force's most famous aircraft.

SAUNDERS *Wahoo* • 19,830 • 754 • Eastern NE, bounded on the east and north by the Platte River. The county includes Todd Valley (former valley of the Platte River). Pioneer and Memphis state recreation areas are located here. • Named for Alvin Saunders (1817–99), governor of NE Territory and U.S. senator from NE • Organized as Calhoun County 1856 (prior to statehood); name changed 1862 • Geneticist George Wills Beadle; composer Howard Hanson; film producer Darryl F. Zanuck • Feed, food processing and other industries; cattle, hogs, corn, soybeans, sorghum, alfalfa, vegetables, dairying; limestone.

SCOTTS BLUFF *Gering* • 36,951 • 739 • Western NE, bounded on the west by the WY state line; drained by the North Platte River. Scotts Bluff National Monument in the center of the county includes Scotts Bluff, a massive promontory and landmark along the Oregon Trail (which crosses the county along the south bank of the Platte River). Wildcat Hills State Recreation Area is on the county's southern boundary. Also found in the county are Lake Minatare State Recreation Area and two units of the North Platte National Wildlife Refuge. • Named for the prominent bluff on the North Platte River • 1888 from Cheyenne • Cattle, hogs, corn, alfalfa, beans, potatoes, dairying; oil; manufacture of food products and machinery • The nationally recognized Riverside Zoo is active in many endangered species programs. Lake Minatare Lighthouse is one of only seven inland lighthouses in the U.S.

SEWARD *Seward* • 16,496 • 575 • Southeastern NE; drained by the Big Blue River and its branches. Blue Valley State Recreation Area is here. • One of two counties (the other in KS) named for William H. Seward (1801–72), U.S. secretary of state who negotiated the purchase of Alaska • Organized as Greene County 1855 (prior to statehood) from Lancaster County; name changed in 1862 • A tornado in 1913 leveled a large part of the town of Seward, killing a number of its residents. • Corn, wheat, soybeans, sorghum, dairy products; limestone; manufacture of crossarms, wood products, transportation equipment; education (Concordia U.) • Seward is recognized as NE's Fourth of July city, its festivities attracting 40,000 people a year. Seward was also named the Small Town Fourth of July City for the U.S. Bicentennial in 1976. The world's largest time capsule, buried here in 1975, is scheduled to be opened on July 4, 2025.

SHERIDAN *Rushville* • 6,198 • 2,441 (the fourth largest county in NE) • Northwestern NE, bounded on the north by the SD state line; drained by the Niobrara and Snake rivers. The county lies in the heart of the Sand Hills, which comprise the world's largest area of grass-stabilized sand dunes. Numerous small natural lakes are scattered throughout. The county also includes Walgren Lake State Recreation Area. •

One of five counties named directly or indirectly for Gen. Philip Henry Sheridan (1831–88), Union officer during the Civil War and commander in chief of the U.S. army • 1885 from Sioux • Crazy Horse began his final journey to Fort Robinson from the Spotted Tail Agency here. During WW I, water from the alkali lakes of the Sand Hills was used to produce potash fertilizer to aid in the war effort. The towns that grew up around the production plants have since died. • Biographer Mari Susette Sandoz • Corn, wheat, alfalfa, cattle, hogs, dairying.

SHERMAN (one of four counties so named) *Loup City* • 3,318 • 566 • Central NE; drained by the Middle Loup River and Clear Creek. The county contains the Sherman Reservoir and State Recreation Area, and Bowman Lake State Recreational Area. • One of three counties named for Gen. William Tecumseh Sherman (1820–91), Union officer in the Civil War • 1871 from Buffalo • Corn, alfalfa, cattle, hogs, dairying • Litchfield is 1,733 miles from the east coast and 1,733 miles from the west coast.

SIOUX (one of three counties so named) *Harrison* • 1,475 • 2,067 • Extreme northwestern NE, bounded on the north by the SD state line and on the west by the WY state line; drained by branches of the White and Niobrara rivers. It also includes part of Fort Robinson State Park (on the eastern boundary) and part of Oglala National Grassland, including Toadstool Geologic Park, Warbonnet Monument, and Hudson–Meng Bison Bonebed. The second richest fossil bed in the U.S. is found in Agate Fossil Beds National Monument in the center of the county. • One of five counties named for the Sioux Indians, also known as the Dakota. • 1877 from unorganized territory • Cattle, hogs, corn, alfalfa, beans, sugar beets • Sioux Sundries in Harrison sells what is reputed to be America's largest hamburger.

STANTON *Stanton* • 6,455 • 430 • Northeastern NE; drained by the Elkhorn River. • One of two counties (the other in KS) named for Edwin M. Stanton (1814–69), U.S. secretary of war under presidents Lincoln and Johnson • Organized as Izard in 1855; name changed in 1862 • Cattle, hogs, corn, alfalfa, soybeans, dairying.

THAYER *Hebron* • 6,055 • 575 • Southeastern NE, bounded on the south by the KS state line; drained by the Little Blue River and Big Sandy Creek. The old Oregon Trail bisects the county from east to west on the northern side of the Little Blue River. • Named for Gen. John M. Thayer (1820–1906), a Union officer in the Civil War, U.S. senator from NE and governor of NE • Organized as Jefferson County in 1856; boundaries and names adjusted over succeeding years. • Pollster Elmo Roper • Corn, wheat, soybeans, alfalfa, cattle, hogs, dairying; manufacture of farm machinery, irrigation systems, brooms and mops.

THOMAS (one of three counties so named) *Thedford* • 729 • 713 • Central NE; drained by the Middle Loup and Dismal rivers. Much of the county is located in the Sand Hills. Part of the Halsey Unit of the Nebraska National Forest is in the east. The forest encompasses 90,000 acres of rolling sandhills prairie interspersed with the largest "man-made" forest in the U.S., containing 22,000 acres of Ponderosa pine, Eastern red cedar and Jack pine. • One of two counties (the other in KS) named for General George Henry Thomas (1816–70), career army officer, including commander of the Army of the Cumberland • 1887 from Blaine • Cattle, hogs, grain.

THURSTON (one of two counties so named, the other in WA) *Pender* • 7,171 • 394 • Northeastern NE, bounded on the east by the Missouri River, forming the IA state line; drained by Logan Creek. The county is divided between the Winnebago Indian Reservation in the north and the Omaha Indian Reservation in the south. • Named for John M. Thurston (1847–1916), U.S. senator from NE who was active in establishing the county. • Organized as Blackbird County in 1855; name changed in 1889 • Omaha Chief Blackbird; first Native American woman physician Dr. Susan LaFlesche Picotte • Cattle, hogs, corn, dairying; some manufacturing • Each summer ceremonial dances and pow wows are organized here by the Winnebago, Santee Sioux, and Omaha Indians. Robbers Cave in a sandstone bluff on the Missouri River was reputedly the headquarters of the notorious James Brothers.

VALLEY (one of three counties so named) *Ord* • 4,647 • 568 • Central NE; drained by the North Loup and Middle Loup rivers. Fort Hartsuff State Historical Park is here. • Named for the North Loup River and Middle Loup River valleys in the county. • 1871 from unorganized territory • Cattle, hogs, corn, dairy products.

WASHINGTON *Blair* • 18,780 • 391 • Eastern NE, bounded on the east by the Missouri River, forming the IA state line. The De Soto Bend National Wildlife Area in the former river bend of the Missouri (on the IA side on land belonging to NE) is stopover point for half a million snow geese on their fall migration. Boyer Chute National Wildlife Refuge is also found in the county. • One of thirty-one counties named for President George Washington • Original county; organized 1854 (prior to statehood) • Manual Lisa established a post for the St. Louis Missouri Fur Company in 1812 near the site of Lewis and Clark's council with local Indian tribes. The largest mil-

itary post west of the Missouri, Fort Atkinson (state historic site) was established in 1820, and by 1827 had 1,000 soldiers stationed within. Originally scheduled to be one of a string of posts across the plains, Atkinson remained the only fort on the Missouri River, due to budget considerations. • Cattle, dairying, hogs, corn, alfalfa; limestone; manufacture of metal products; education (Dana College).

WAYNE (one of sixteen counties so named) *Wayne* • 9,851 • 443 • Northeastern NE; drained by Logan Creek. • One of fifteen counties named for "Mad Anthony" Wayne (1745–96), Revolutionary general and statesman • 1871 from Thurston • Cattle, hogs, poultry, corn, alfalfa, dairy and poultry products; manufacture of modular homes, refrigerated semi-truck trailers, fabricated metal, pillows, mattresses, kiosks and signs, feed; printing; education (Wayne State College).

WEBSTER *Red Cloud* • 4,061 • 575 • Southern NE, bounded on the south by the KS state line; drained by the Republican and Little Blue rivers. • One of eight counties named for Daniel Webster (1782–1852), U.S. statesman and orator from MA • 1867 (prior to statehood) from unorganized territory • Author Willa Cather used Red Cloud as the setting for many of her novels including *O Pioneers!* (1913), *My Antonia* (1918), and *A Lost Lady* (1923) (state historic site). • Cattle, dairying, hogs, corn, wheat, soybeans, sorghum, alfalfa; cheese- and meat-processing plants; limestone.

WHEELER (one of four counties so named) *Bartlett* • 886 • 575 • Northeast-central NE; drained by the Cedar River and Beaver Creek. Pibel Lake State Recreation Area is in the south. • Named for Daniel H. Wheeler (1834–1912), county clerk of Cass County and mayor of Plattsmouth • 1877 from Boone • Cattle, hogs, dairying, corn.

YORK (one of five counties so named) *York* • 14,598 • 576 • Southeastern NE; drained by the Big Blue River and its West Fork. • Named for one or more of the following: York, England; York County, PA (former home of early settlers); England's Royal House of York; or King James II. • Original county; boundaries defined 1855 (prior to statehood) • Dairy and poultry products; cattle, hogs, corn, soybeans, sorghum; manufacture of farm implements, mobile homes, aircraft parts; education (York College); tourism.

NEVADA

All for Our Country

Thirteen of Nevada's sixteen counties are governed by three-member boards of county commissioners. Clark County is served by a seven-member board. Voters in Lyon and Washoe counties elect five-member boards. All commissioners serve four-year terms. Other elected county officials are the assessor, auditor and recorder, district attorney, clerk, public administrator, and sheriff. Carson City is an independent city, which functions as a county.

CHURCHILL *Fallon* • 23,982 • 4,929 • West-central NV; watered in the west by the Caron River and diversions from the Truckee River, forming Lahontan Reservoir on the western border. Carson Sink is in the north and includes Fallon National Wildlife Refuge. Clan Alpine Mountains and the Stillwater Range are here. The county also contains part of Lahontan State Recreation Area and several units of Fallon Naval Air Station. Part of Walker River Indian Reservation is in the southwest. Fallon Paiute Shoshone Indian Reservation is also here. • Named for Fort Churchill • Original county; organized 1861 (prior to statehood) • Alfalfa, cantaloupes, hay, vegetables; diatomite, salt, sand and gravel, lime, gypsum, silica sand. • The county courthouse, built in 1903, is the only wood frame government building still in use within the state of Nevada. The county's Newlands Project is the first federally sponsored reclamation project in the U.S. Stillwater National Wildlife Refuge includes the largest marsh in NV. It is the only county in the U.S. that owns its own telephone company. Churchill is the home of "Singing" Sand Mountain, one of only three singing sand dunes in North America. The county contains remnants of the forty-mile desert portion of the Emigrant Trail, Simpson Route, Pony Express Trail (including several stations), Transcontinental Telegraph, and the Lincoln Highway.

CLARK (one of twelve counties so named) *Las Vegas* • 1,375,765 (85% increase since 1990; the fastest growing and most populated county in NV, and twenty-fifth most populated county in the U.S.) • 7,911 (the twenty-second largest county in the U.S.) • Southeastern NV, bounded on the east by the AZ state line, formed, in part, by the Colorado River, and on the southwest by the CA state line; drained by the Virgin River. Red Rock Canyon National Conservation Area, which includes Spring Mountain Ranch State Park, is west of Las Vegas. Desert National Wildlife Range is in the northwest, as is part of Nellis Air Force Range Complex. Sections of Nellis Air Force Base are northeast of Las Vegas. Moapa River Indian Reservation and Valley of Fire State Park are in the north. Also here is Lake Mead National Recreation Area. The lake, one of the world's largest artificially formed bodies of water, was created by Hoover Dam, one of the highest concrete dams in the world. The Spring Mountains are in the west, the McCullough Range and Eldorado Mountains, in the south. • Named for William A. Clark (1839–1925), Railroad executive

and U.S. senator from MT • 1909 from Lincoln • With the legalization of gambling in the state in 1931, small casinos began to appear in Las Vegas; its first large gambling casino opened in 1946. By the mid-1950s, gambling here had made the city one of the leading tourist destinations in the U.S. A fire in 1980 destroyed the MGM Grand Hotel and left eighty-five dead. Henderson sprung up during WW II, when large industrial plants were built here to process magnesium for military purposes. • Tennis player Jack Kramer. Boxer Sonny Liston died here. • Magnesium deposits, sand and gravel, lime, gypsum, silicon sand; manufacture of sponge titanium, titanium ingots, chlorine, caustic hydrogen, heavy chemicals, lime products, insecticides, ammonium perchlorate; dairying, cattle, vegetables; tourism (gambling and entertainment); education (U. of NV Las Vegas) • The corporate headquarters of six Fortune 1000 companies are located here. Boulder City, built in 1931 to house workers employed by area construction projects, including Hoover Dam, is headquarters for the U.S. Water and Power Resources Service, and for the Lake Mead National Recreation Area. Each December, Las Vegas hosts the National Finals Rodeo competition.

DOUGLAS *Minden* • 41,259 • 710 • Western NV, bounded on the west and southwest by the CA state line (formed in part in the west by Lake Tahoe); watered by the Carson River (east and west forks) and West Walker River. The county lies in the foothills of the Sierra Nevada. Washoe Indian Reservation is here. • One of twelve counties named for Stephen A. Douglas (1813–61), U.S. orator and statesman • Original county; organized 1861 (prior to statehood) • Genoa was the first settlement in NV. Guided by Kit Carson, Captain John C. Frémont and his expedition arrived in the area in 1844. • Ferris Wheel inventor George Ferris; pony express rider Bob Haslett • Poultry, cattle, sheep, sand, gravel; gambling, entertainment, tourism.

ELKO *Elko* • 45,291 (the third most populated county in NV • 17,182 (the second largest county in NV and the fourth largest county in the U.S.) • Northeastern NV, bounded on the north by the ID state line, and on the east by the UT state line. The county is in a mountainous and plateau region, crossed by the Humboldt River. Part of Duck Valley Indian Reservation is here, as is South Fork Indian Reservation. Sections of Humboldt-Toiyabe National Forest (its headquarters in Elko) are here. Part of Ruby Lake National Wildlife Refuge

NEVADA (Esmeralda)   250

is in the south. The county has several recreation areas. • Named for the town of Elko, NV • 1869 from Lander • Elko served as a way station for wagon trains heading westward. • Singer Bing Crosby (who owned a cattle ranch near Elko) • Gold, silver, copper, sand and gravel; freight handling; cattle, sheep • The county has a large Basque-American population.

ESMERALDA *Goldfield* • 971 (the least populated county in NV) • 3,589 • Southern NV, bounded on the southwest by the CA state line. The Silver Peak Range and White Mountains are in the west. The county also includes Columbus Salt Marsh. A small part of Inyo National Forest is in the west, including Boundary Peak on the CA border; at 13,140 feet, it is the highest point in the state. A small part of Death Valley National Monument is in the far south. • Named for the Esmeralda mining district • Original county; organized 1861 (prior to statehood) • Established in 1860, the Esmeralda mines produced $29 million worth of ore during their first decade of operation. In 1861, the state of CA claimed the Esmeralda mining district and made the mining town of Aurora the county seat of Mono; the disputed area was subsequently awarded to NV. Goldfield was the site of a gold rush that began in 1902; the mining boom that followed lasted until 1918. At its peak in 1910, the ore produced here was valued at more than $11,000,000. The area endured a bitter labor struggle between miners and operators in 1907 and 1908, resulting in the stationing of Federal troops here. • Lithium, gold, silver, diatomite, clay.

EUREKA *Eureka* • 1,651 • 4,176 • North-central NV; crossed in the north by the Humboldt River. The chief ranges are the Diamond Mountains (forming the east-central boundary) and the Cortez Mountains (south of the Humboldt River). Part of Antelope Valley is in the south. The county contains part of Humbolt-Toiyabe National Forest, Geyser basin, parts of the Tuscarora Mountains, and Emigrant Pass. • Named for the town of Eureka, NV, itself named for the mining district • 1873 from Lander • Gold, silver; cattle.

HUMBOLDT *Winnemucca* • 16,106 • 9,648 (the fourth largest county in NV and the thirteenth largest county in the U.S.) • Northwestern NV, bounded on the north by the OR state line; watered by the Quinn, Little Humboldt, and Humboldt rivers. The Santa Rosa Range in the northeast lies chiefly within Humboldt-Toiyabe National Forest. The county also includes Summit Lake and Fort McDermitt Indian reservations. Also here are part of the Sheldon National Wildlife Refuge, Lahontan Cutthroat Trout Natural Area, and part of Black Rock Desert-High Rock Canyon Emigrant Trails National Conservation Area. • Named for either the Humboldt or the Little Humboldt River • Original county; organized 1861 (prior to statehood) • Cattle, sheep, hay, potatoes; silver, copper, gold, sand and gravel, clay.

LANDER *Battle Mountain* • 5,794 • 5,494 (the forty-eighth largest county in the U.S.) • North-central NV; drained by the Humboldt and Reese rivers. Parts of Humboldt-Toiyabe Na-

tional Forest are here, as are the Shoshone, Toiyabe, and Toquima mountain ranges. The geographic center of the state is in the county's southeast corner. • Named for General Frederick W. Lander (1821–62), Union army officer, railroad surveyor, and transcontinental explorer • Organized 1862 (prior to statehood). Originally Lander encompassed a third of the state and was called "Great East" and later "mother of counties." • Gold, silver, lead, copper mining; cattle, sheep.

LINCOLN (one of twenty-four counties so named) *Pioche* • 4,165 • 10,635 (the third largest county in NV and the seventh largest county in the U.S.) • Southeastern NV, bounded on the east by the AZ and UT state lines; watered by Meadow Valley Wash. The county includes part of Desert National Wildlife Range, part of Nellis Air Force Range Complex, and Pahranagat National Wildlife Refuge. Also here are Beaver Dam, Kershaw-Ryan, Spring Valley, Echo Canyon, and Cathedral Gorge state parks, Leviathan Cave Geologic Area, and a small part of Humboldt National Forest. Part of Egan Range is in the north. • One of eighteen counties named for Abraham Lincoln • 1866 • Perlite, sand, gravel mining; ranching.

LYON (one of five counties so named) *Yerington* • 34,501 (72% increase since 1990; the third most populated county in NV) • 1,994 • Western NV; drained by the Carson River, forming Lahontan Reservoir (supplying water for irrigation). The East and West Walker rivers form the Walker River above Yerington in the center of the county. Part of Toiyabe National Forest is in the Sierra Nevada in the south. Part of Walker River Indian Reservation, Campbell Ranch Indian Reservation, Fort Churchill State Historical Park, part of Lahontan State Recreation Area, and Dayton State Park are all located here. • Named for either General Nathaniel Lyon (1818–61), an officer in the Seminole War, Mexican War, and Civil War; or for Captain Robert Lyon, a hero of the Indian Wars • Original county; organized 1861 (prior to statehood) • Cattle, sheep, poultry, dairying, hay, vegetables: cement, sand and gravel, gypsum, copper, gold, silver, diatomite.

MINERAL (one of four counties so named) *Hawthorne* • 5,071 • 3,757 • Western NV, bounded on the southwest by the CA state line. Walker Lake (with Walker Lake B.L.M. State Recreational Area on its western shore) and Wassuk Range are in the west. Hawthorne Army Depot is near the county seat. Part of Walker River Indian Reservation is here, as are the Excelsior Mountains, Gillis Range, and part of Humbolt-Toiyabe and Inyo national forests. • Named for the variety of minerals in the county • 1911 from Esmeralda • Gold, silver, scheelite (calcium tungstate), sand and gravel; cattle; recreation.

NYE *Tonopah* • 32,485 (83% increase since 1990; the second fastest growing county in NV) • 18,147 (the largest county in NV and third largest county in the U.S.) • Southern and central NV, bounded on the south by the CA state line; drained by the Amargosa, Reese, and White rivers. There are large sections of Humboldt-Toiyabe National Forest in the north.

Amargosa Desert, and part of Death Valley National Park (mostly in CA) are in the south, as is Pahute Mesa, which includes a large part of Nellis Air Force Range Complex. The county also includes Ash Meadows National Wildlife Refuge, including Devils Hole, Lunar Crater Volcanic Field National Natural Landmark, Belmont Courthouse State Historic Site, and Berlin Ichthyosaur State Park. Yomba and Duckwater Indian reservations are also here. • Named for James Warren Nye (1814–76), the only governor of NV Territory and one of NV's first two U.S. senators • 1864 from Esmeralda • Mining of silver, gold, clay, magnesium, sand and gravel; cattle, sheep. Angry at the Reagan administration for storing nuclear waste at Yucca Mountain, the Nevada legislature, in 1987, created Bullfrong County, population 0, for the purpose of punitively taxing the federal government. The court abolished the "county" two years later.

PERSHING *Lovelock* • 6,693 • 6,009 (the fortieth largest county in the U.S.) • Northwest-central NV; crossed by the Humboldt River. The county includes Rye Patch Reservoir State Recreation Area. Chief ranges here are the Tobin, Humboldt, Seven Troughs, and Trinity. Part of Black Rock Desert, which includes part of Black Rock Desert–High Rock Canyon Emigrant Trails National Conservation Area, is in the extreme northwest. • Named for General John J. "Black Jack" Pershing (1860–1948), commander in chief of the American Expeditionary Force during World War I, and U.S. army chief of staff • 1919 from Humboldt • Mining of mercury, tungsten, gold, silver, copper, diatomite; barley, cattle, sheep, dairying.

STOREY *Virginia City* • 3,399 • 263 (the smallest county in NV) • Western NV, bounded on the north by the Truckee River. • Named for Edward F. Storey (1828–60), army officer killed by Paiute Indians • Original county; organized 1861 (prior to statehood) • In 1859, the Comstock Lode, one of the richest deposits of gold and silver, was discovered on Mount Davidson above present-day Virginia City. When the Nevada Territory was created in 1861, Virginia City had more than three quarters of the new territory's population. Its population reached 30,000 before the city was destroyed by fire in 1875. • Diatomite, gold, silver mining; cattle, poultry, dairying, hay; tourism • The county courthouse is noteworthy for having one of the only unblindfolded Statues of Justice. Established in 1961, the Virginia City Landmark District is one of the largest in the nation, and includes most of Storey County and part of neighboring Lyon County. A reporter on the *Territorial Enterprise* in Virginia City first tried out a new pen name here: "Mark Twain."

WASHOE *Reno* • 339,486 (the second most populated county in NV) • 6,342 (the thirty-fourth largest county in the U.S.) • Northwestern NV, bounded on the west by the CA state line, on the north by the OR state line, and on the south, in part, by the Truckee River. Pyramid Lake, encompassed by Pyramid Indian Lake Reservation, includes Anaho Island National Wildlife Refuge. The northeastern part of Lake Tahoe is in the southwest corner. The county also contains Smoke Creek Desert and the Granite Range. Part of Sheldon National Wildlife Refuge and Black Rock Desert–High Rock Canyon Emigrant Trails National Conservation Area are in the northeast. Part of Humboldt-Toiyabe National Forest (its headquarters in Reno), and part of Lake Tahoe Nevada State Park are in the southwest corner. • Named for the Washo Indians • Original county; organized 1861 (prior to statehood); in 1883 it annexed Roop County, also an original county • Part of the Pyramid Lake Indian War took place here. Seventy-six whites are believed to have died in one encounter a few miles northwest of the lake in May, 1860. In a second encounter in early June at the big bend in the Truckee River, the Indians were outnumbered and routed by the army. Thanks to liberal state laws, Reno became a busy marriage and divorce center by the early 1900s. First Negro heavyweight champion Jack Johnson defeated Jim Jeffries in the "Fight of the Century" staged in Reno in 1910. • Automobile manufacturer Erret L. Cord, physicist Samuel A. Goutsmit, and electrical engineer and industrialist William P. Lear died here. • Cattle, hay, potatoes, onions; sand, gravel, gold, silver, gypsum; manufacturing; gambling, strong tourist trade; education (U. of NV, Reno). Due to NV's Free Port Law, under which merchandise moving in interstate commerce may be stored and assembled in transit tax-free, Reno has become an important warehousing and distribution center. • Pyramid Lake, located on the Paiute Indian Reservation, is the only habitat of the endangered Cui-ui fish. The National Championship Air Races, hosted by Reno, is the world's largest running air race and show. The Reno Rodeo is the third largest rodeo in the U.S. The National Judicial College, part of the University of Nevada, is the only training facility in the U.S. for trial court judges, administrative law judges, and court personnel.

WHITE PINE *Ely* • 9,181 • 8,877 (the fifth largest county in NV and the seventeenth largest county in the U.S.) • Eastern NV, bounded on the east by the UT state line. Snake and Schell ranges are in the east. Egan Range is in the center of the county; the White Pine Mountains are in the southwest. (The bristlecone pine trees found here are the slowest growing and longest lived organisms on earth, with some over 3,000 years old.) Portions of Humboldt-Toiyabe National Forest are distributed throughout the county. Great Basin National Park, with its remnant ice field on Wheeler Peak, and Lehman Caves are here. The county also includes part of Ruby Lake National Wildlife Refuge, part of Goshute Indian Reservation, Cave Lake State Park, and Ward Charcoal Ovens State Historical Park, with preserved stone beehive ovens used to produce charcoal for smelting in the 1870s. • Named for the White Pine mining district, itself named for the White Pine Mountains • 1869 from Lander • Ely was established in 1868 as a gold-mining camp. It expanded after 1907 with extensive copper mining. • First Lady Pat Nixon • Gold and silver mining, sand and gravel; cattle, sheep; tourism (ghost towns, recreational facilities) • The Nevada Northern Railway Museum in Ely attracts visitors to the area.

NEW HAMPSHIRE

Live Free or Die

County officials in each of New Hampshire's ten counties are the county commissioners, sheriff, attorney, treasurer, register of probate, and register of deeds. All are elected to two-year terms.

BELKNAP *Laconia* • 56,325 • 401 • Central NH, bounded on the northeast by Lake Winnipesaukee, on the extreme north by Squam Lake, and on the west by the Pemigewasset River; drained by the Winnipesaukee, Merrymeeting, and Suncook rivers. The county also includes Winnisquam Lake, Crystal Lake, and Upper and Lower Suncook Lakes, Ellacoya State Park and Gunstock ski area. • Named for Jeremy Belknap (1744–98), clergyman and NH's first historian • 1840 from Strafford • The nation's first cotton mill was built in Laconia in 1811. NH's first radio station began broadcasting from the city in 1922. • Resort tourism; nursery crops, apples, corn, berries, cattle, poultry, dairying; sugar maples; manufacture of boats, skis, textiles, textile machinery, metal and leather products; resort tourism • Laconia holds snowmobile championships in the winter and boating regattas in the summer. Lake Winnipesaukee was the backdrop for comic shenanigans in the film *What About Bob?*

CARROLL (one of thirteen counties so named) *Ossipee* • 43,666 (23% increase since 1990; the fastest growing county in NH) • 934 (virtually tied with Merrimack as the third largest county in NH) • Eastern NH, bounded on the east by the ME state line, on the southwest by Lake Winnipesaukee, and on the west by Squam Lake; drained by the Saco, Swift, Ellis, Pine, Cold, and Ossipee rivers. Wentworth State Park is on the northern shore of Lake Wentworth. Crawford Notch State Park is in the extreme northwest. The county also contains Hemenway and Pine River state forests, part of White Mountain National Forest, General John Wentworth State Historic Site, and White Lake and Echo Lake state parks. Several ski areas are located here, as are Heath Pond Bog and Madison Boulder natural areas. • One of twelve counties named for Charles Carroll (1737–1832), signer of the Declaration of Independence, U.S. senator from Maryland, and founder of the Baltimore and Ohio Railroad • 1840 from Strafford, Coos, and Grafton • Ski instructor Hannes Schneider died here. • Vegetables, nursery crops, corn, apples, cattle, hogs, poultry, dairying; granite quarrying; some manufacturing; winter and summer resort tourism.

CHESHIRE *Keene* • 73,825 • 707 • Southwestern NH, bounded on the west by the Connecticut River (forming the VT state line) and on the south by the MA state line; drained by the Ashuelot River and headwaters of the Contoocook River. The county contains numerous lakes and ponds, including Spofford Lake and part of Highland Lake. Part of Honey Brook State Park is on the northern boundary. The county also contains Pisgah, Rhododendron and Monadnock state parks, as well as Chesterfield Gorge, Wantastiquet Mountain and Bear's Den natural areas. • Named for Cheshire County in England • Original county; organized 1769 • Journalist Charles A. Dana; educator John Davis Pierce; governor general of the Philippines Leonard Wood; U.S. Supreme Court justice Harlan Fiske Stone • Mica and feldspar mining and processing, granite quarrying; timber; apples, vegetables, corn, nursery crops, hay, cattle, sheep, poultry, dairying; manufacture of small engineering products, optical instruments, furniture, textiles, shoes; resort tourism; education (Keene State College).

COOS (one of two counties so named, the other in OR) *Lancaster* • 33,111 • 1,801 (the largest county in NH) • Northern NH, bounded on the west (and drained) by the Connecticut River (forming the VT state line), on the northwest and north by Quebec, and on the east by the ME state line; drained by the Androscoggin and Upper Ammonoosuc rivers. The Presidential Range of the White Mountains and sections of White Mountain National Forest are here. The county has several state parks including Mount Washington, its feature peak, at 6,288 feet, the highest in the state. Wayside parks and forests are also found here; prominent is Nash Stream Forest in the center. • Coos is an Indian word meaning either "pine trees" or "crooked," the latter referring to the Connecticut River. • 1803 from Grafton • Potatoes, nursery crops, vegetables, hay, apples, cattle, poultry, dairying; timber; manufacture of paper and wood pulp; ski resorts • Berlin has one of the highest steel ski towers in the U.S.; the Berlin Nansen Ski Jump stands at 181.5 feet. Residents of Dixville Notch gather at 12:01 A.M. each election day to cast the first votes in the nation.

GRAFTON *Woodsville* • 81,743 • 1,714 (the second largest county in NH) • Central and western NH, bounded on the west and north by the Connecticut River; drained by the Ammonoosuc, Pemigewasset, Gale, Mascoma and Baker rivers. A large part of the White Mountains and White Mountain National Forest are here. State parks include Bedell Bridge, Cardigan, Wellington, and Franconia Notch (where the Old Man of the Mountain rock formation collapsed in 2003). Province Road State Forest, Sculptured Rocks and Plummer Ledge natural areas and several ski areas are here, as is the New England Ski Museum in the north. Newfound Lake is in the south. The Appalachian Trail crosses the county northeast to southwest. • Named for English statesman Augustus H. Fitzroy (1735–1811), 3rd Duke of Grafton • Original county; organized 1769 • Blind and deaf-mute student Laura Dewey Bridgman; U.S. Supreme Court justice Nathan Clifford; religious leader Mary Baker Eddy; pathologist George H. Whipple. Explorer and ethnologist Vilhjalmur Stefansson, psychologist Wolfgang Köhler, and writer Nathaniel Hawthorne died here. • Diversified manufacturing; timber, maple sugar; nursery crops, hay, corn, vegetables, apples, poultry, dairying; mica quarrying, sand and gravel, soapstone; resort tourism (skiing); education (Dartmouth College; Plymouth State College) • The Plymouth State Fair is a popular summer event.

HILLSBOROUGH *Nashua* • 380,841 (the most populated county in NH) • 876 • Southern NH, bounded on the south by the MA state line; drained by the Contoocook, Piscataquog, Souhegan, Merrimack, and Nashua rivers. Silver Lakes, Miller, Greenfield, and Clough state parks are here, as is Fox and Sheiling forests and part of Annett Forest. Wapack National Wildlife Refuge is also found in the county. • One of two counties (the other in FL) named directly or indirectly for Wills Hill (1718–93), 1st Earl of Hillsborough, English secretary of state for the colonies. • Original county; organized 1769 • Manchester developed as the result of the construction of one of America's first textile mills in 1805 by Benjamin Prichard. The MacDowell Colony in Petersborough, established by the wife of composer Edward MacDowell, following his death in 1908, attracted many composers and writers. • Astrophysicist C.B. Abbot; poet Robert Guy Choquette; politician Zachariah Chandler; newspaper editor and politician Horace Greeley; President Franklin Pierce (homestead); educator Francis Parker. American Revolution general John Stark died here. • Hillsborough is one of the leading industrial counties in the U.S. Manufactures include textiles, shoes, leather goods, baskets, rubber, automobile accessories, electrical instruments, paper, electronic components, chemicals, office equipment, plastics. Also, granite quarrying; timber; vegetables, corn, beans, hay, apples, cattle, hogs, poultry, dairying; resort tourism; education (Rivier College; Daniel Webster College; Southern NH U.; U. of NH at Manchester; Notre Dame College; St. Anselm College) • A popular county attraction is the Sharon Arts Center, run by the League of New Hampshire Arts and Crafts.

MERRIMACK *Concord* • 136,225 (the third most populated county in NH) • 935 (virtually tied with Carroll for third largest county in NH) • South-central NH; drained by the Merrimack, Contoocook, Suncook, Soucook, and Blackwater rivers. Kearsage Mountain and Low state forests are here, as are Winslow, Rollins, Wadleigh, Bear Brook, and part of Mount Sunapee state parks. Sunapee Lake is on the western border, the New Hampshire Forest Nursery in the center of the county • Named for the Merrimack River • 1823 from Rockingham and Hillsborough • Concord was settled as Pe-

nacook Plantation on a site granted by the Massachusetts Bay Colony in 1725. A bitter jurisdiction dispute with the Province of NJ was not resolved until 1762. NH's peripatetic legislature finally settled here in 1808. The county was a leading carriage-making and granite quarrying center. • Statesman and orator Daniel Webster; composer Amy Beach; politician William E. Chandler; political leader John Adams Dix; educators John Eaton and Caleb Mills; President Franklin Pierce; flour miller Charles Pillsbury. Neurologist and physiologist Walter B. Cannon, secretary of state John Hay, and photographer Lotte Jacobi died here. Teacher-astronaut Christa McAuliffe taught social studies at Concord High School. • Nursery crops, vegetables, corn, apples, sugar maples, hay, cattle, poultry, dairying; granite quarrying, mica mining, sand and gravel; manufacture of textiles, hosiery, staples, pressure valves, saws, leather and plastic products, electronic parts, electric equipment, leather goods, wood products, concrete; printing and publishing; insurance; state government offices; resort tourism; education (NH Technical Institute; New England College; Colby-Sawyer College) • Concord granite was used in the construction of the State House and the Library of Congress in Washington, D.C. Artificial rain was first used to fight a forest fire on October 29, 1947 near Concord.

ROCKINGHAM *Exeter* • 277,359 (the second most populated county in NH) • 695 • Southeastern NH, bounded on the northeast by the Piscataqua River (forming the ME state line), on the east by the Atlantic Ocean, and on the south by the MA state line; drained by the Exeter, Pawtuckaway, Lamprey, and other rivers. The county includes Fort Constitution and Fort Stark historic sites. Also found here are several state parks, especially along the coast, and numerous ponds in the south. Massabesic Lake is on the western boundary. Portsmouth is the only seaport in NH and one of the world's deepest harbors. • One of three counties named for Charles Watson-Wentworth, Marquis of Rockingham (1730–82), British statesman and prime minister largely responsible for repeal of the Stamp Act • Original county; organized 1769 • John Smith reached the Isle of Shoals in 1614. NH's first settlement was made in 1623 near Portsmouth. During Exeter's early years, it was a commonwealth independent of the English colonies; it eventually submitted to the jurisdiction of MA in 1643. Portsmouth was the state capital from 1679 to 1774. Exeter served as capital from 1775 until 1781. NH's first newspaper, the *New Hampshire Gazette*, began publication in Portsmouth in 1756. The city was a major shipbuilding center in the 18th and 19th centuries. The treaty ending the Russo-Japanese war was signed here in 1905 • Naval commander John Paul Jones; Politician Benjamin F. Butler; ornithologist Elliott Coues; author and publisher James T. Fields; sculptor Daniel Chester French; scholar and editor Bliss Perry; architect and writer Ralph A. Cram; Union general Fitz-John Porter; journalist and charity worker Franklin B. Sanborn; American Revolution general John Stark; poet and short story writer Thomas B. Aldrich; astronaut Alan B. Shepard, Jr. Admiral David Farragut died here. • Diversified manufacturing, including hoes, leather, chemicals, electrical products; apples, nursery crops, vegetables, corn, beans; seafood, fish, lobster; cattle, poultry, dairying; shipping; resort tourism. • Rockingham Park in Salem is well known for its horse races. Cincinnati Memorial Hall in Exeter contains personal effects of the George Washington family. The Brattle organ in St. John's Episcopal Church in Portsmouth is considered to be the oldest pipe organ in the U.S.

STRAFFORD *Dover* • 112,233 • 369 (the smallest county in NH) • Southeastern NH, bounded on the east by the ME state line (Salmon Falls and Piscataqua rivers) and on the south-southeast by Great Bay. The county is drained by the Cocheco, Isinglass, Lamprey, and other rivers. Powder Mill Fish Hatchery is in the northwest; Bow Lake is in the southwest. Blue Hills Range, including Blue Job Mountain, is in the west. • Named for Thomas Wentworth (1593–1641), 1st Earl of Strafford and leader of the House of Commons • Original county; organized 1769 • Dover was an independent entity until 1642 when it voluntarily submitted to the jurisdiction of MA. Dover's Quakers were ordered out of town in 1662, an event described in John Greenleaf Whittier's verses, "How the Women Went from Dover." The county's settlements were under continual Indian attack from 1675 until 1725. The worst occurred in June, 1689 in Dover, and in 1694 in Durham, which was burned and had more than 100 of its residents either killed or captured. During the American Revolution, a large supply of gunpowder that had been seized from the British in New Castle was hidden in the Durham Meeting house. • Arctic explorer Charles Francis Hall; abolitionist John P. Hale; theatrical and film designer Robert E. Jones; inventor Robert P. Parrott; Revolutionary War general John Sullivan • Apples, vegetables, corn, hay, nursery crops, cattle, horses, dairying; timber; sand and gravel; manufacture of shoes, textiles, chemicals, plastics, electronic products, printing presses, synthetic rubber, wood and aluminum products, fiberboard, fabricated metal; education (U. of NH) • The Rochester (agricultural) Fair has been held each year since 1875.

SULLIVAN (one of six counties so named) *Newport* • 40,458 (the least populated county in NH) • 537 • Southwestern NH, bounded on the west by the Connecticut River, forming the VT state line; drained by the Sugar, Little Sugar and Cold rivers. Gile State Forest, and Pillsbury and Honey Brook state parks are here. Snow Hill ski area is in the north. The county has several covered bridges. • One of five counties named directly or indirectly for Gen. John Sullivan (1740–95), officer in the Revolutionary War, member of the Continental Congress, and president of NH • 1827 from Cheshire • Clergyman and bishop Philander Chase; politician and Chief Justice of the U.S. Salmon P. Chase; barbed wire inventor Joseph Glidden; anthropologist Horatio Hale. Sculptor Augustus Saint-Gaudens (national historic site). • Apples, corn, hay, nursery crops, maple trees, cattle, poultry; timber; manufacture of mining and mill machinery, woolens, shoes, paper; resort tourism.

NEW JERSEY

Liberty and Prosperity

New Jersey is unique in calling its counties' governing bodies "boards of chosen freeholders." Each of the state's twenty-one counties has a board of from three to nine members. All freeholders are elected to three-year terms.

ATLANTIC *Mays Landing* • 252,552 • 561 (the third largest county in NJ) • Southeastern NJ, bounded on the east by the Atlantic Ocean and on the north in part by the Mullica River; also drained by the Great Egg Harbor River. The county includes many coastal resorts along its island-embroidered shore. Edwin B. Forsythe National Wildlife Refuge is found on the coast north of Atlantic City. Part of Wharton State Forest is in the extreme northwest. Atlantic City is one of the largest seaside resorts in the world, its famed casino-chocked boardwalk stretching 4½ miles along the Atlantic Ocean. • Named for the Atlantic Ocean • 1837 from Gloucester • Painter Jacob Lawrence; corporate executive Dave Thomas; inventor Simon Lake • Truck crops, grain, fruit, (especially blueberries, cranberries, strawberries), poultry; manufacture of textiles, glass-ware, clothing, furniture, bricks, boats, concrete blocks, food products, including saltwater taffy; canneries; timber; fishing; gambling; education (Richard Stockton College of NJ) • The Miss America Pageant has been held in Atlantic City since 1921.

BERGEN *Hackensack* • 884,118 (the most populated county in NJ) • 234 • Extreme northeastern NJ, bounded on the east by the Palisades of the Hudson River, and on the north by the NY state line; drained by the Ramapo, Saddle, Passaic and Hackensack rivers. The county is located in an industrial, retail shopping, and residential area. It includes part of Palisades Interstate Park and Oradell Reservoir. • Named for the village of Bergen, itself named by early Dutch settlers for the town of Bergen-op-zoom, Netherlands • Original county; organized 1683 • Fort Lee fell to the British in November, 1776. Its garrison, led by General Nathanael Greene, joined George Washington who was headquartered in Hackensack during his retreat from New York City. Ridgewood's Old Paramus Reformed Church was the site of the marriage of Aaron Burr and Theodosia Prevost in 1782, and of the court martial of General Charles Lee after his retreat from the Battle of Monmouth in 1778. From 1907 to 1919, Fort Lee was a center for motion picture production; many short westerns were shot among the cliffs and woods of the Palisades, as well as early work by D.W. Griffith and Mary Pickford. (Photographic-film processing remains a major industry in Fort Lee.) • Ornithologist Frank M. Chapman; poet William Carlos Williams; astronaut Walter M.Schirra. Trumpeter Dizzie Gillespie and composer Ulysses Kay died here. • Fabricated metal products, textiles, chemicals, food products, paper goods, concrete products, electrical and electronic equipment, furniture, paint, embroideries, aircraft engines; education (Fairleigh Dickinson U.; Ramapo College of NJ) • The headquarters of six Fortune 1000 corporations are located in the county. The Actors' Fund Home for sick and retired actors was established in Englewood in 1928. The city was also the first in the U.S. to offer customers direct dialing for long-distance calls (1951). East Rutherford is home to the New Jersey Nets and Devils (Continental Airlines Arena). The Jets and Giants play in Giants Stadium (also in East Rutherford).

BURLINGTON *Mount Holly* • 423,394 • 805 (the largest county in NJ) • Western and central NJ, bounded on the northwest by the Delaware River (forming the PA state line); drained by Rancocas Creek and the Bastro, Bass, Wading, and Oswego rivers. The eastern and southeastern parts of the county lie in the pine barrens region, with several state forests located here, including part of the large Wharton State Forest and Lebanon State Forest. Part of McGuire Air Force Base and Fort Dix Military Reservation are in the northeast. • Named for the town of Burlington, NJ • Original county; organized 1694 • Burlington became the capital of West Jersey in 1681. From 1702 until 1790 it served alternately with Perth Amboy as the capital of NJ. In 1776, the Provincial Congress met here to adopt the state constitution. Mount Holly was raided several times by British forces during the American Revolution. The town's Relief Fire Company was one of the oldest volunteer fire companies in the U.S. Clara Barton organized the Clara Barton Schoolhouse in 1851 in Bordentown as one of the nation's first free public schools. Bordentown was also the site of NJ's first railroad shops. • Abolitionist Gamaliel Bailey; novelist James Fenimore Cooper; suffragist Alice Paul; naval captain James Lawrence; Declaration of Independence signer Francis Hopkinson; patriot Tom Paine; Joseph Bonaparte (brother of Napoleon I); steamboat builder Henry Miller Shreve • Manufacture of textiles, shoes, clothing, metal, leather, paper and concrete products, food products, canned goods, lumber, bricks, chemical dyes, metal prod-

ucts, industrial machinery, electronic components; shipbuilding; vegetables, fruit, grain, livestock, dairy products.

CAMDEN (one of four counties so named) *Camden* • 508,932 • 222 • Southwestern NJ, bounded on the northwest by the Delaware River (forming the PA state line); drained by the Great Egg Harbor and Mullica rivers, and Big Timber Creek. The western part of the county is largely urbanized and residential. Part of Wharton State Forest is in the east. • Named for the city of Camden • 1844 from Gloucester • The first meeting of the NJ legislature was held in Haddonfield at the Indian King Tavern. During the American Revolution, Camden was held by the British in conjunction with their occupation of Philadelphia. Campbell Soup Company started marketing condensed soups in Camden in 1897. The Victor Talking Machine Company, founded in 1894, and purchased by RCA in 1929, developed the phonograph here. • Poet Walt Whitman; educator and chemist Joel Hildebrand; heavyweight boxing champion Jersey Joe Walcott • Manufacture of food products, radio and television equipment, textiles, leather, clothing, pens, lumber, metal, rubber, plastic and paper products, chemicals, foundry products; railroad shops, marine terminals; fruit, truck, soybeans, corn, poultry, dairying; education (Rutgers State U., Camden) • Camden is home to the New Jersey State Aquarium. Haddonfield is named for Elizabeth Haddon who settled here in 1701; her romance with a Quaker missionary is told by Henry Wadsworth Longfellow in his *Tales of a Wayside Inn*. The town was a station on the Underground Railroad. The first drive-in theater opened outside Camden on June 6, 1933.

CAPE MAY *Cape May Court House* • 102,326 • 255 • Southern NJ, bounded on the north by the Tuckahoe River and Great Cedar Swamp, on the east by the Atlantic Ocean, and on the west by Delaware Bay; drained by Dennis Creek and Great Cedar Swamp. The county is mostly peninsula with historic beach resorts. Part of Belleplain State Forest and parts of Cape May National Wildlife Refuge are here. Also found in the county are Cape May Point State Park and Natural Area, Corson's Inlet State Park, Cape May Wetlands Natural Area, and Strathmere Natural Area • Named for the Cape May Promontory, itself named for Cornelius J. Mey, Dutch captain who explored the Atlantic coast of North America from Long Island to Cape May in 1612–14 • 1692 from Cumberland • Cape May has been a popular vacation spot since before the Civil War. Once one of the most fashionable resorts on the Atlantic coast, it was visited by several U.S. presidents, including Lincoln and Grant. In the 1850s, the Mount Vernon Hotel, with room for 2,000 guests, was the largest resort hotel in the nation. • Endocrinologist Gregory Pincus; utopian reformer Uriah Smith Stephens; naval hero Richard Somers; economist and banker Paul Volcker • Fishing, oystering; seafaring; farming; beach tourism; manufacture of boats, canvas goods • Cape May is renowned for its many Victorian homes; more than 600 are concentrated within the city. Ocean City is an "alcohol free" seaside resort, catering to religious conventions and family vacations; it maintains a Victorian flavor, many of its mansions having been built by wealthy Philadelphians around the turn of the last century.

CUMBERLAND (one of eight counties so named) *Bridgeton* • 146,438 • 489 (the fifth largest county in NJ) • Southern NJ, bounded on the southwest by Delaware Bay; drained by the Maurice River (a National Scenic and Recreational River) and Cohansey Creek. • One of four counties named for William Augustus, Duke of Cumberland (1721–65), British general and second son of King George II • 1748 from Salem • In 1774, Greenwich staged the "Greenwich Tea Party," in which locals disguised themselves as Indians and burned a cargo of taxed tea from the East Indian Company's brig *Greyhound*. NJ's Liberty Bell, which pealed to bring citizens to hear a reading of the Declaration of Independence, is in the county's courthouse. • Manufacture of fabricated metal products, construction materials, glass, aircraft parts, paper, rubber, plastic products, transportation equipment, machinery, textiles, food products, clothing, chemicals; fish, seafood; poultry, fruit, berries, beans, corn, dairying. Millville is known as "Holly City," for its holly orchard, one of the largest in the U.S. Several state institutions are located at Vineland, including the American Institute for Mental Studies.

ESSEX *Newark* • 793,633 (the second most populated county in NJ) • 126 (one of the fifty smallest counties in the U.S.) • Northeast NJ, bounded on the west, north, and east by the Passaic River, and on the southeast by Newark Bay. Newark is the state's largest city and a major industrial, commercial, and transportation center. • One of five counties named for Essex County in England • Original county; organized 1683 • Thirty Puritan families, traveling from the Connecticut colony in search of cheap farmland, founded Newark in 1666. Bloomfield served as supply point for both sides during the Revolutionary War. The first low-pressure steam engine built in the U.S. was constructed in Belleville and used in 1798 to power an experimental steamboat on the Passaic River. Large quantities of cloth for Union uniforms were produced in Bloomfield during the Civil War. In July, 1967, five days of rioting in Newark left 26 dead and caused 10 to 15 million dollars worth of property damage. An eleven-week teachers' strike in the city, one of the longest in history for a major city, took place here in 1971. • Playwright Amiri Baraka; film director Brian De Palma; President Grover Cleveland; geneticist Joshua Lederberg; opera singer Dorothy Kirsten; author and philosopher Henry Steel Olcott; aircraft designer John Knudsen Northrop; George Inness (many of his paintings at the Montclair Art Museum); professional boxer Mickey Walker; actor Jerry Lewis; songwriter Paul Simon; writer Philip Roth. Poet and novelist Henry C. Bunner, and work efficiency expert Frank B. Gilbreth died here. Thomas Edison lived and worked in West Orange (Edison National Historic Site) from 1887 until his death in 1931, developing the phonograph and movie camera among hundreds of other inventions here. • Diversified manufacturing, including food products, apparel, furniture, paper products, model electric trains, plastics, fabrics, pharmaceutical supplies, chemicals, leather goods, cutlery, metal castings, tools, metal products, industrial machinery, measuring devices, surgical instruments, jewelry, and electronic equipment, aluminum, concrete and metal products, paint, insecticides; insurance; education (Rutgers State U., Newark; Bloomfield College; Seton Hall U.); container shipping (Newark ranks as the nation's largest port for container ships.) • Montclair boasts of the world's smallest park, a six square foot green with a plaque affixed to a boulder, commemorating George Washington's visit to the area.

GLOUCESTER *Woodbury* • 254,673 • 325 • Southwestern NJ, bounded on the west by the Delaware River (forming the PA state line); drained by the Maurice River and Big Timber Creek. • Named for Glouster and/or Gloucestershire, England • Original county; organized 1686 • Glassboro had a thriving glass industry in its early years. Glassboro State College (later Rowan University) was the site of a meeting in June, 1967 between President Lyndon B. Johnson and Soviet premier Aleksei Kosygin in which the two leaders agreed not to let any crisis push them into war. • Captain James Lawrence • Manufacture of food products, apparel, chemicals, plastic products, fabricated metal products, machinery, electronic equipment, cement products, electronic precision parts; printing and publishing; fruit, truck farming; canneries; education (Rowan U.).

HUDSON *Jersey City* • 608,975 (the fifth most populated county in NJ) • 47 (the smallest county in NJ and one of the fifty smallest counties in the U.S.) • Northeastern NJ, bounded on the east in part by the Passaic River and Newark Bay, and on the west by the Hudson River and Upper New York Bay; drained by the Hackensack River. The county is heavily industrialized. It is the site of Liberty State Park, which includes the New Jersey State Science Center. Jersey City is linked to metropolitan New York City as an area commercial and transportation center. • Named for the Hudson River and/or English Navigator Henry Hudson (c.1569–1611) • 1840 from Bergen • The first permanent European settlement in what is now NJ was the village of Bergen (1660) now preserved in present-day Jersey City. The first brewery in what would become the U.S. was built in Hoboken in 1642. "Lighthorse Harry" Lee stormed the town of Jersey City on July 19, 1779, forcing the British to retreat. The world's first steamboat ferry ran from Hoboken to New York City from 1811 to 1813. The first recorded game of baseball was played in Hoboken on June 19, 1846. During World War I, the city was a major point of embarkation for U.S. troops leaving for Europe. • Financiers John Jacob Astor and Hetty Green; writer Washington Irving; poet William Cullen Bryant; songwriter Stephen Foster; mathematician Howard H. Aiken; physicist and futurist Herman Kahn; photographers Dorothea Lange and Alfred Stieglitz; singer and actor Frank Sinatra. • Artist and author George Catlin died here. Highwood, the estate of NY banker James Gore King, was the scene of the July 11, 1804 duel in which

Aaron Burr fatally wounded Alexander Hamilton. • Diversified manufacturing, including textiles, embroidery (at one point more than 90% of the country's embroidery industry was located within five miles of West New York), clothing, soap and perfume, telephone equipment, machinery, truck bodies, chemicals, shoes, varnishes, plastics, linoleum; shipbuilding, ocean shipping; education (New Jersey City U.; St. Peter's College; Steven's Institute of Technology). A center for oil refining, Bayonne is the northern terminus for several pipeline systems, including the Big Inch, traveling 1,476 miles from Longview, TX. • St. Joseph's Roman Catholic Church in Union City presents the Passion Play *Veronica's Veil* during Lent each year.

HUNTERDON *Flemington* • 121,989 • 430 • Western NJ, bounded on the west by the Delaware River (forming the PA state line) and on the northwest by the Musconetcong River; also drained by the south branch of the Raritan River. Musconetcong Mountain is in the west. The county includes several state parks, natural areas, and recreational areas. Round Valley Reservoir is encompassed by Round Valley Recreation Area. The county is rapidly suburbanizing. • Named for Robert Hunter (?–1734), colonial governor of both NJ and NY • 1714 from Burlington • Philippines governor general Francis B. Harrison; American Revolution general Daniel Morgan; mental healer Phineas P. Quimby. Geologist and paleontologist James Hall, modern dancer and choreographer José Limón, and editor and publisher Samuel Putnam died here. Lindbergh baby kidnapper Bruno Hauptmann was tried here. • Poultry, produce, corn, grain, fruit, dairying; manufacture of food products, plastic and metal products, electronic equipment, measuring and controlling devices; paper printing; publishing; chemicals.

MERCER (one of eight counties so named) *Trenton* • 350,761 • 226 • Western NJ, bounded on the west by the Delaware River (forming the PA state line); drained by the Millstone River and Crosswicks Creek. The county is crossed by the Delaware and Raritan Canal. • One of six counties definitively named for General Hugh Mercer (?–1777), Revolutionary War officer and physician • 1838 from Hunterdon and Middlesex • The capital of the U.S. has twice been located in the county; from June 30, 1783 to November 4, 1783 it was in Princeton, and from November 1, 1784 to December 24, 1784, it was in Trenton. On Christmas night, 1776, General George Washington made his famous crossing of the half-frozen Delaware River (commemorated at Washington Crossing State Park) and the next morning launched a victorious attack against Hessian troops quartered in Trenton. The College of New Jersey (now Princeton U.) changed hands three times during the American Revolution. At the Battle of Princeton (state park) on January 3, 1777, Washington's troops defeated a British detachment. Trenton became the capital of NJ in 1790. In 1868, Abram Hewitt introduced the open-hearth process for steel manufacture here. It was also in Trenton that John Roebling manufactured cable for the Brooklyn Bridge.

• Singer, actor and black activist Paul Robeson; U.S. Supreme Court justice Antonin Scalia; military leader Norman Schwartzkopf. Physicist Albert Einstein, art historian Erwin Panofsky, President Grover Cleveland, civil engineer Washington A. Roebling, colonial Presbyterian preacher Samuel Davies, physicist J. Robert Oppenheimer, and television inventor Vladimir K. Zworykin died here. The Princeton Cemetery contains the graves of Vice President Aaron Burr and some members of the Continental Congress. • Manufacture of wire and wire rope, steel, pottery (early in the 20th century, the county was the nation's leading producer, including fine Lenox china), electrical equipment, rubber products, machinery, hardware; poultry, livestock, vegetables, grains, dairy products, fruit; research; printing and publishing; educational testing; governmental offices; education (Princeton U.; Rider U.; The College of NJ).

MIDDLESEX *New Brunswick* • 750,162 (the third most populated county in NJ) • 311 • Eastern NJ, bounded on the east by Raritan Bay and Arthur Kill; drained by the Raritan, Millstone, and South rivers. The county lies in an industrial, agricultural and growing residential area. • One of four counties named for the ancient county of Middlesex in England • Original county; organized in 1683 • From about 1738 to 1790 Perth Amboy served with Burlington as the alternate provincial capital. The first printing press in NJ was established in Woodbridge by James Parker in 1751. New Brunswick served alternately as headquarters for both Continental and British forces during the American Revolution. It was from here that General Washington initiated the campaign that ended in American victory at Yorktown. New Brunswick's port was a base for privateers who preyed upon British ships around Manhattan during the war. On November 6, 1869, Rutgers and Princeton faced off in New Brunswick in the first intercollegiate football game. Perth Amboy is generally regarded as the place where the first black American cast his vote; Thomas Mundt Peterson voted on March 31, 1870. In 1929, the first cloverleaf highway interchange in the U.S. was constructed in Woodbridge Township. • Commander Lawrence Kearny. Writer Mary Eleanor Freeman and manufacturer Robert Wood Johnson died here. Thomas Edison established a laboratory in Menlo Park in 1876. The Edison Memorial Tower marks the spot where the first commercially practical incandescent lamp was made. • Clay deposits, oil refineries, ore smelters and refineries, shipyards, drydocks, diversified manufacturing, including electrical equipment, candy, cookies and crackers, tile and brick, pharmaceuticals, medical supplies, sheet-metal products and house siding, chemicals, plastics, machinery products; also soybeans, fruit, poultry; education (Rutgers State U. of NJ) • New Brunswick Theological Seminary, the oldest theological school in the U.S. (founded 1784), has been in the city since 1810. The headquarters of seven Fortune 1000 corporations are located in the county. St. Peter's Episcopal Church, built in 1722, is home to the oldest Episcopal parish in the state.

MONMOUTH *Freehold* • 615,301 (the fourth most populated county in NJ) • 472 • Eastern NJ, bounded on the east by the Atlantic Ocean, on the north by Raritan and Sandy Hook bays; drained by the Metedeconk, Manasquan and Shark Rivers. The Navesink River and Shrewsbury River estuaries, Navesink Highlands, and Sandy Hook are found here as well. The county is largely residential, with seasonal resort communities along the coast. Allaire State Park is in the south. • Possibly named for Monmouthshire in Wales • Original county; organized in 1683 • The Battle of Monmouth (state park) was fought at Freehold on June 28, 1778, between the troops of generals Washington and Clinton. It was here that Molly Pitcher took her husband's place on the battlefield after he was killed. Asbury Park was planned in 1869 as a haven for temperance advocates; Ocean Grove was formed the same year as a place for religious worship and rest. Religious meetings are still held here. On September 8, 1935, the steamer Morro Castle caught fire and was grounded ashore at Asbury Park, with over 120 deaths. • Actor Jack Nicholson; commercial aviation pioneer Juan T. Trippe; mathematician James W. Alexander; novelist Norman Mailer; singer Bruce Springsteen. Cartoonist John Held, Jr. died here. Long Branch was a summer resort for many prominent Americans, including Lillie Langtry, Lillian Russell, and "Diamond Jim" Brady. Its St. James Chapel was known as the "Church of the Presidents"; Grant, Hayes, Arthur, Benjamin Harrison, McKinley, and Wilson worshiped here while vacationing in the county. (Woodrow Wilson's summer White House, "Shadow Lawn," was in West Long Branch.) President James Garfield was brought to his summer home in Elberon (part of Long Branch) after being shot in Washington, D. C. on July 2, 1881; he died here on September 17, 1881. • Potatoes, other vegetables and fruits, poultry; manufacture of electronic equipment, biochemicals, plastics, rubber products, glass containers, cable television equipment, rugs, textiles, clothing, clay products, food products, chemicals; education (Monmouth U.). The Earle Naval Weapons Station is north of Earle.

MORRIS (one of three counties so named) *Morristown* • 470,212 • 469 • Northern NJ, bounded on the southeast and east by the Passaic River; drained by the Pequannock, Rockaway, Whippany and Musconetong rivers, and branches of the Raritan River. The county is located in a hilly estate and resort area, with many lakes and mountain ridges. It includes Morristown National Historical Park and part of Lake Hopatcong. The eastern half is largely suburbanized with the western half still agricultural but comprising a growing suburban area. • Named for Lewis Morris (1671–1746), jurist and first governor of the colony of NJ • 1739 from Hunterdon • Morristown was quarters for the Continental Army during two critical winters — January, 1777, and the winter of 1779–80. Alfred Vail and Samuel Morse perfected the telegraph at the Speedwell Ironworks in Morristown in 1837. • Publisher and politician Malcolm Steve Forbes; U.S. Supreme Court justice John McLean. Reputed inventor of baseball Abner Doubleday

and Union general Fitz-John Porter died here. • Dairying, fruit, poultry, nurseries; manufacture of electrical, electronic and radar equipment, pharmaceuticals, metal products, machinery, explosives, chemicals, rubber and paper goods, metal products, ribbons, food products, essential oils, batteries, clothing, cosmetics, wood products, telecommunications; research and development; education (Drew U.) Madison, nicknamed "Rose City," is the center of a large greenhouse industry. • The headquarters of seven Fortune 1000 corporations are located in the county. Parsippany has had over fifty different spellings.

OCEAN *Toms River* • 510,916 • 637 (the second largest county in NJ) • Eastern NJ, on Barnegat Bay; drained by the Toms and Metedeconk rivers, and Cedar Creek. Long Beach Island and Island Beach peninsula, with their many summer resorts and fisheries stretch between the bay and the Atlantic Ocean. Island Beach State Park and Natural Area, and Barnegat Lighthouse State Park are here. Units of Edwin Forsythe National Wildlife Refuge are on the coast and at the southern end of Long Beach Island. Part of the county is located in the pine barrens region. Part of Lebanon State Forest and Double Trouble State Park are found in the county. Part of Fort Dix Military Reservation is in the west. The Intracoastal Waterway passes through the bay. • Named for its location on the Atlantic Ocean • 1850 from Monmouth • Harvey Cedars, the oldest town on Long Beach, was settled by whalers after the War of 1812. Lakehurst National Air Station has played a large role in the history of rigid, lighter-than-air craft. Here the *Shenandoah*, the first American airship, made her maiden flight in 1923, and the *Graf Zeppelin* began and ended a twenty-one-day journey around the world. The *Hindenburg* caught fire here while landing on May 6, 1937, resulting in the loss of thirty-six lives, and ending the era of commercial rigid-airship travel. • Abolitionist James G. Birney died here. • Vegetables, fruit, poultry, dairy products; diversified manufacturing; resort tourism • The Barnegat Lighthouse, constructed in 1858, has stood near the scene of more than 200 shipwrecks.

PASSAIC *Paterson* • 489,049 • 185 • Northern NJ, bounded on the north by the NY state line; drained by the Passaic, Rampo and Pequannock rivers. Wanaque Reservoir is here. The county is highly industrialized and residential. It includes part of the Ramapo Mountains and many lakes, including Greenwood Lake. Part of Ringwood State Park is in the northeast. • Named for the Passaic River • 1837 from Bergen and Sussex • The Dey Mansion (national historic site) was George Washington's headquarters in 1780. Paterson was founded by advocates of American industrial independence from Europe who considered the Great Falls of the Passaic the best possible industrial site along the eastern seaboard. Chartered by the NJ legislature in 1791, the Society for Establishing Useful Manufactures facilitated such enterprises as Samuel Colt's Old Gun Mill, where the first Colt revolvers were produced. In 1851, Notch Brook was the scene of a "pearl rush" when mussels here were discovered to contain freshwater pearls. The

Fenian Ram, one of the first successful submarines, sank in the Passaic River in 1881. Once renowned for its manufacture of fine woolen suits and handkerchiefs, Passaic saw a prolonged strike in its woolen and worsted mills in 1926. • Comedian Lou Costello; sociologists William Graham Sumner and Morris Janowitz; actor Lawrence Barrett; physicist Frederick Reines • Manufacture of steel, rugs, clothing, textiles, rubber goods, machinery, food, aircraft parts, communications equipment, explosives, chemicals, pharmaceuticals, electronic equipment, paperboard; poultry, vegetables; education (William Paterson U. of NJ; Felician College) • The U.S. Animal Quarantine Station was founded in Clifton in 1900.

SALEM *Salem* • 64,285 (the least populated county in NJ) • 338 • Southwestern NJ, bounded on the west by the Delaware River (forming the PA state line); drained by the Maurice and Salem rivers, and Oldmans, Alloway's and Stow creeks. The county includes Parvin State Park and Natural Area, and Supawna Meadows National Wildlife Refuge. • Named for the village of New Salem in England's province of West Jersey • Original county; organized 1694 • The Friends Burial Ground in Salem is home to the Salem Oak (a tree possibly more than 500 years old) under which Quaker John Fenwick, Salem founder, signed a treaty with the Lenni Lenape Indians. • Pole vaulter Don Bragg • Manufacture of chemicals, allied products, glass containers, food products, women's clothing, floor coverings, electronic connectors; dairying, fruit, soybeans, poultry • Finn's Point National Cemetery at Fort Mott State Park contains the graves of more than 2,400 Confederate prisoners and 300 Union soldiers.

SOMERSET (one of four counties so named) *Somerville* • 297,490 (24% increase since 1990; the fastest growing county in NJ) • 305 • North-central NJ, bounded on the northeast by the Passaic River; drained by the Millstone River, and the North and South branches of the Raritan River. Appalachian ridges are in the northwest with part of the Watchung Mountains in the northeast. • Possibly named for Somersetshire in England • 1688 from Middlesex • Bound Brook was the scene of an April, 1777 American Revolution battle in which an American garrison was routed by a British force under Lord Cornwallis. General Washington reputedly unfurled the Stars and Stripes, sewn by Betsy Ross, atop one of the hills behind the village. The Knox-Porter Resolution, which officially ended the state of war between the U.S. and Germany, was signed by President Harding on July 2, 1921 at the Somerville estate of Joseph Frelinghuysen. • Poet and novelist Elinor Wylie; George and Martha Washington (who resided in Somerville in 1778 and 1779) • Vegetables, fruit, grain, poultry, dairying; hothouse flowers; manufacture of textiles, plastics, rubber goods, clothing, metal products, chemicals, roofing materials, electrical and electronic equipment, pharmaceuticals; insurance • Rutgers University and the New Brunswick Theological Seminary were both first established in Somerville at the Old Dutch Parsonage (state historic site).

SUSSEX *Newton* • 144,166 • 521 (the fourth largest county in NJ) • Extreme northwestern NJ, bounded on the west by the Delaware River (forming the PA state line) and on the north by the NY state line; drained by the Wallkill, Paulins Kill and other rivers. The county is in a mountain and lake recreational area, which includes Kittatinny Mountain Ridge, site of Stokes State Forest and High Point (state park), at 1,803 feet, the highest point in the state. Delaware Water Gap National Recreation Area is also here. Wawayanda State Park is in the northeast. Lake Hopatcong is on the southern border. There is suburban residential growth in the east. • One of three counties named for the county of Sussex in England • 1688 • Fruit, hay, nursery products, dairy products, livestock; limestone deposits; manufacture of textiles, metal products, mineral wool, pens; tourism (skiing).

UNION (one of eighteen counties so named) *Elizabeth* • 522,541 • 103 (one of the fifty smallest counties in the U.S.) • Northeastern NJ, bounded on the east by Newark Bay and Arthur Kill; drained by the Rahway River, which forms part of its southeastern boundary. • Given this name as an expression of belief in the federal union of the states, and/or for the union of several smaller towns south of Newark in their desire to escape domination by that city. • 1857 from Essex • NJ's first colonial assembly met in Elizabeth (then Elizabethtown) from 1668 to 1682. The county saw several military engagements during the American Revolution. A British force marching on Morristown, NJ was met by 1,000 Continental troops led by General Nathanael Greene on June 23, 1780. The Reverend James Caldwell, Continental chaplain, is said to have torn up hymn books as wadding for the muskets during the battle, shouting, "Give 'em Watts!" The oldest newspaper in NJ, the *Daily Journal*, established in Chatham in 1779, moved to Elizabeth in 1785. The College of New Jersey, now Princeton University, was founded here in 1746, and attended by later political and dueling rivals Alexander Hamilton and Aaron Burr. Roselle was the site of Edison's first electrical generating plant and the first community to have an incandescent electrical street-lighting system. Guglielmo Marconi, inventor of the wireless, established a plant in Roselle Park in 1913. KDY, pioneer commercial radio station, began broadcasts from the city in 1921. • First NJ governor William Livingston; Continental Congress president Elias Boudinot; Cartoonist Charles Addams; educator Nicholas Murray Butler; jazz pianist Bill Evans; geophysicist and oceanographer Robert S. Dietz; photographer Irving Penn; actor Meryl Streep. Clergyman and educator Jonathan Dickson died here. • Manufacture of automobile parts, chemicals, adhesives, pharmaceuticals, metal products, varnish and paint, vacuum cleaners, sewing machines, soap dispensers, clothing, motor vehicles, electronic equipment, transportation equipment, tools, concrete and stone products, plastics, rubber goods, paper products, printing machinery, aircraft parts; education (Kean U.). • The Singer Manufacturing Company in Elizabethport (now Elizabeth) made the first electric sewing machine in 1889.

WARREN *Belvidere* • 102,437 • 358 • Northwestern NJ,

bounded on the west by the Delaware River (forming the PA state line) and on the southeast and east by the Musconetcong River; drained by the Pohatcong and Pequest rivers, and Paulins Kill. Part of the Kittatinny Mountain ridge (cut by the Delaware River to form the Delaware Water Gap) is here. The county includes Jenny Jump Mountain and part of Stephens State Park, as well as state forests and natural areas. Part of Allamuchy Mountain State Park is in the extreme east. • One of fourteen counties named for Joseph Warren (1741–75), the Revolutionary War patriot and member of the Continental Congress who dispatched Paul Revere on his famous ride • 1824 from Sussex • Manufacture of textiles, candy, paper, chemicals, plastic products, iron foundries, industrial machinery, electronic equipment; dairying, vegetables, poultry, fruit, grain; education (Centenary College).

NEW MEXICO

It Grows as It Goes

Thirty-two of New Mexico's thirty-three counties are run by boards of commissioners. Los Alamos County is administered by a city-county council.

BERNALILLO *Albuquerque* • 556,678 (the most populated county in NM) • 1,166 • North-central NM; drained by the Rio Grande and Rio Puerco. The county contains part of Cibola National Forest (its headquarters in Albuquerque), the Sandia Mountains and Manzano Range, parts of Isleta Pueblo and Laguna Pueblo, and part of Navajo Nation Indian Reservation. Petroglyph National Monument preserves more than sixty archeological sites, including a seventeen-mile gallery of more than 15,000 prehistoric Indian and historic Spanish petroglyphs carved by Indian residents between AD 1300 and 1650. Rio Grande Nature Center State Park is also here. • Named for the town of Bernalillo, New Mexico Territory, now in Sandoval County • Original county; organized 1852 (prior to statehood); annexed Santa Ana 1876 • Albuquerque, founded in 1706 by Don Francisco Cuervo y Valdés, governor and captain general of New Mexico, was an important trading center on the Chihuahua Trail from Mexico. Although captured by the Confederates in 1862, the town was loyal to the Union. Since the 1930s, more than 100 federal agencies have been established here. Situated at a high altitude and possessing a warm, dry climate, Albuquerque became known as a center for the treatment of tuberculosis. • Race car drivers Al and Bobby Unser; corporate executive Jeff Bezos; politician Pete Domenici. Teacher and author Henry Roth, poet and playwright Elder Olson, geochemist Harrison Brown, and balloonist Ben Abruzzo all died here. • Cattle, some sheep, dairying, chilies, corn, hay, alfalfa, oats, barley, grapes; limestone, coal; manufacture of truck trailers, gypsum products, lumber, clothing, aerospace components; railroad shops; nuclear, aerospace and solar research; tourism; education (U. of NM; Nazarene Indian Bible College). Kirtland Air Force Base is a large employer. • The New Mexico State Fair is held in Albuquerque each September. The Albuquerque International Balloon Fiesta (held each October) is the world's largest and most photographed balloon event.

CATRON *Reserve* • 3,543 • 6,928 (the largest county in NM and the twenty-ninth largest county in the U.S.) • Western NM, bounded on the west by the AZ state line; watered by the Gila and San Francisco rivers. The county includes part of Gila, Apache, and Cibola national forests. The Tularosa and Mogollon mountains cross in the southwest; the Datil Mountains are in the northeast. The Continental Divide runs through the county. Gila Cliff Dwellings National Monument (the dwellings inhabited from about A.D. 1280 to the early 1300s) is on the southern boundary of the county. Datil Well Bureau of Land Management Recreation Area is also here. • Named for Thomas B. Catron (1840–1921), large landowner, Confederate officer during the Civil War and one of NM's first two U.S. senators • 1921 from Socorro • Cattle, goats, sheep, hay, alfalfa, wheat, oats, barley; gold and silver mining; timber.

CHAVES *Roswell* • 61,382 • 6,071 (the fourth largest county in NM and the thirty-ninth largest county in the U.S.) • Southeastern NM; watered by the Pecos River and Rio Hondo. Two units of Bitter Lake National Wildlife Refuge, Bottomless Lakes State Park, and a small part of Lincoln National Forest are here. The county also includes the northern end of the Guadalupe Mountains in the southwest and Mescalero Sands in the east. • Named for Lt. Col. Jose F. Chaves (1833–1904), a Union officer during the Civil War and delegate to the U.S. Congress from the territory of NM • 1889 from Lincoln (prior to statehood) • Painter Peter Hurd • Cattle, sheep, rye, alfalfa, hay, chilies, some sorghum, melons, pecans, cotton, corn, some wheat, millet, dairying; oil and gas • Roswell is home to the New Mexico Military Institute and the International UFO Museum and Research Center. • Roswell Museum and Art Center houses several of Robert Goddard's experimental rockets.

CIBOLA *Grants* • 25,595 • 4,540 • Western NM, bounded on the west by the AZ state line; drained by the Rio Paraje. The county contains part of the San Mateo Mountains, parts of Cibola National Forest, and part of the Zuni Mountains. It also includes Acoma Pueblo, parts of Laguna Pueblo, and Zuni Indian Reservation; El Morrow National Monument (containing "Inscription Rock" with hundreds of inscriptions and pre-Columbian petroglyphs); El Malpais National Monument and Conservation Area (featuring a seventeen-mile long lava tube system and more than twenty gas and lava spatter cones); La Ventana Natural Arch and Bandera Crater and Ice Caves. Bluewater Lake State Park is on the northern border. The Continental Divide runs through the west-center of the county. • Named for the Cibola National Forest • 1981 from Valencia • El Malpais is believed to have been a point of contact for the Mogollon, Anasazi, Patayan, and Sinauga cultures; many ruins exist here. Pre-Columbian Acoma is one of the oldest continuously occupied settlements in the U.S. It was visited by Coronado's captains in 1540. It became a Spanish mission in 1598, and in 1680 joined the Pueblo Revolt. • Cattle, sheep, hay, alfalfa, triticale, some wheat, oats, barley, rye; mining and processing of uranium (since its discovery here in 1950) and gypsum.

COLFAX *Raton* • 14,189 • 3,757 • Northeastern NM, bounded on the north by the CO state line; drained by the Canadian, Cimarron and Vermejo rivers. The county includes part of the Raton Mountains and the Sangre de Cristo Mountains (its crest forming the county's western boundary). Maxwell National Wildlife Refuge, a small part of Kiowa National Grassland (on the southern boundary), Sugarite and Cimarron Canyon state parks, Eagle Nest Lake reservoir, a small part of Carson National Forest, Angel Fire ski area, and Philmont Boy Scout Ranch. • One of two counties (the other in NE) named for Schuyler Colfax (1823–85), U.S. representative from IN and vice president under Ulysses S. Grant • 1869 from Mora (prior to statehood) • Cattle, sheep, hay, alfalfa, wheat, oats, barley, millet; coal-mining. • Santa Fe Trail Museum is in Springer.

CURRY *Clovis* • 45,044 • 1,406 • Eastern NM, bounded on the east by the TX state line; drained by Blanco Creek and Frio Draw. Cannon Air Force Base is west of Clovis. • Named for Captain George Curry (?–1947), officer in the Spanish American War, NM territorial governor and NM's first U.S. representative • 1909 from Quay and Roosevelt (prior to statehood) • Cattle, dairying, sheep, peanuts, potatoes, cotton, corn, sorghum, hay, alfalfa, wheat, pumpkins, peas, spinach, cabbage, green beans, blue corn, triticale; caliche; railroad repair shops; meat processing.

DE BACA *Fort Sumner* • 2,240 • 2,325 • Eastern NM; watered by the Pecos River. The 5,000-foot-high Conejos Mesa is in the center of the county. Fort Sumner State Monument is in the northeast. Sumner Lake Reservoir and State Park are on the Pecos River on the northern boundary of the county. • Named for Ezequiel C. de Baca (1864–1917), first lieutenant

governor of NM and its second governor • 1917 from Chaves, Guadalupe, and Roosevelt • Gunfighter Billy the Kid died here (gravesite). • Cattle, sheep, sorghum, hay, alfalfa, wheat, oats, barley, millet.

DONA ANA *Las Cruces* • (the second most populated county in NM) • 3,808 • Southern NM, bounded on the south by the TX state line and the Mexican state of Chihuahua; watered by the Rio Grande. The county includes the Organ Mountains in the east and the Sierra de Las Uvas in the northwest. Part of White Sands National Monument is in the northeast (also in Otero County). It contains the world's largest gypsum dune field, which covers nearly 239 square miles, its dunes rising to heights of sixty feet. The county lies within White Sands Missile Range, which includes White Sands Space Harbor, landing site for the space shuttle. Aguirre Springs B.L.M. Recreation Area is also in the county, as are Leasburg Dam State Park and Fort Selden State Monument • Named for the village of Dona Ana, NM Territory • Original county; organized 1852 (prior to statehood); annexed Arizona County 1861 • Mesilla was briefly the Confederate capital of AZ Territory. • Lawman Pat Garrett and astronomer Clyde W. Tombaugh died here. • Cattle, sheep, dairying, chilies, jalapeños, onions, lettuce, pecans, cotton, corn, hay, alfalfa, sorghum, wheat, spinach, triticale, melons, cabbage, fruit, nuts; stone; education (NM State U.)

EDDY (one of two counties so named, the other in ND) *Carlsbad* • 51,658 • 4,182 • Southeastern NM, bounded on the south by the TX state line; watered by the Pecos River (here forming Lake McMillan and Red Bluff reservoirs). Carlsbad Caverns National Park in the southwest is one of the world's largest collections of connected underground chambers, with thirty miles of explored passages. The county also includes part of the Guadalupe Mountains in a unit of Lincoln National Forest. Also here are Living Desert Zoological and Botanical and Brantley Lake state parks. • Named for Charles B. Eddy (1857–?), rancher, promoter of the Carlsbad Irrigation Project and railroad builder • 1889 from Lincoln (prior to statehood) • Cattle, sheep (wool production), dairying, chilies, pecans, cotton, corn, sorghum, hay, alfalfa, wheat, oats, barley, millet, rye; potash mining and refining; salt, petroleum.

GRANT (one of fifteen counties so named) *Silver City* • 31,002 • 3,966 • Southwestern NM, bounded in part on the west by the AZ state line, and in part on the east by the Black Range and Mimbres Mountains; watered by the Gila River. The Continental Divide crosses the county twice. Also here are the Big Burro and part of the Mogollon mountains, and parts of Gila National Forest (its headquarters in Silver City). The county includes the Pinos Altos Mountains, City of Rocks State Park, and the Santa Rita Open Pit Copper Mine. • One of twelve counties named for President Ulysses Simpson Grant • 1868 from Socorro (prior to statehood) • Silver City was a boomtown in the 1880s. The Santa Rita open-pit copper mine has been in operation since the days of primary Indian occupancy.

• Copper, silver, gold, zinc, lead mining; cattle, some sheep, hay, alfalfa, oats, barley, millet; lumbering; tourism; education (Western NM U.) • The Phelps Dodge Corporation has revitalized the ghost town of Tyrone as a copper-mining center. Fort Bayard National Cemetery is east of Silver City.

GUADALUPE (one of two counties so named, the other in TX) *Santa Rosa* • 4,680 • 3,031 • East-central NM; watered by the Pecos River, which forms Sumner Lake reservoir, and by Pintada Arroyo. Santa Rosa Lake State Park and Rock Lake Trout Rearing Station are located here. • Named for Our Lady of Guadalupe (the Virgin Mary), patron saint of Mexico • 1891 from Lincoln and San Miguel (prior to statehood); in 1903 the name was changed to Wood and in 1905 it was changed back to Guadalupe. • Barley, oats, cattle, sheep, hay, alfalfa, some sorghum.

HARDING (one of two counties so named, the other in SD) *Mosquero* • 810 (the least populated county in NM) • 2,126 • Northeastern NM, bounded on the west by the Canadian River (here forming the Canadian River Canyon); drained by Ute, Tequesquite and Carrizo creeks. Part of Kiowa National Grassland is here. • Named for President Warren G. Harding • 1921 from Mora and Union • Hay, some alfalfa, wheat, oats, barley, millet, cattle, some sheep.

HIDALGO (one of two counties so named, the other in TX) *Lordsburg* • 5,932 • 3,446 • Extreme southwestern NM, bounded on the west by the AZ state line, on the south by the Mexican states of Sonora and Chihuahua, and on the east in part by the Mexican state of Chihuahua; watered by the Gila River. The county includes part of Coronado and Gila national forests. The Continental Divide in the south passes through the Animas Mountains and part of the Pyramid Mountains. • Named for either the Treaty of Guadalupe Hidalgo, which ended the Mexican War; or for Miguel Hidalgo y Costilla (1753–1811), leader of the Mexican war for independence from Spain • 1919 from Grant • Cattle, some sheep, chilies, cotton, hay, alfalfa, some sorghum, wheat, oats, barley, Christmas trees; mining of clay, gold, silver, silica. • Numerous ghost towns are scattered throughout the county.

LEA *Lovington* • 55,511 • 4,393 • Extreme southeastern NM, on Llano Estacado, bounded on the south and east by the TX state line. • Named for General Joseph C. Lea (1841–1904), Confederate officer in the Civil War, large landowner, and Roswell's first mayor • 1917 from Chaves and Eddy • Hobbs became a boomtown following the discovery of oil and natural gas here in 1928. From a population of 598, it exploded to more than 25,000 and became NM's petroleum center. • Cattle, sheep, dairying, chilies, corn, sorghum, hay, alfalfa, melons, peas, spinach, pecans, peanuts, cotton, wheat, oats, barley, millet, rye; petroleum, natural gas, potash deposits; manufacture of oil field equipment; education (College of the Southwest) • The Confederate Air Force Flying Museum is west of Hobbs.

LINCOLN (one of twenty-four counties so named) *Carrizozo*

• 19,411 (59% increase since 1990; the second most populated county in NM) • 4,832 • South-central NM; watered by the Rio Hondo, Gallo Arroyo, and Arroyo del Macho. The county includes part of Lincoln and Cibola national forests, ranges of the Sacramento Mountains, Lincoln State Monument, Smokey Bear Historical State Park (where the U.S. Forest Service's original Smokey Bear is buried), Valley of Fires and Fort Stanton B.L.M. national recreation areas, and Ski Apache ski area. Part of White Sands Missile Range is in the southwest. • One of eighteen counties named for Abraham Lincoln • 1869 (prior to statehood) • The county was the scene of the so-called Lincoln County cattle war (1878–1881), fought between the gun-slinging posses of two area cattle barons. Cattle thief and killer Billy the Kid, a participant in the war, was dispatched by Lincoln County sheriff Pat Garrett in 1881. • Sheep, cattle, hay, alfalfa, some wheat, oats.

LOS ALAMOS *Los Alamos* • 18,343 • 109 (the smallest county in NM and one of the fifty smallest counties in the U.S.) • Northern NM, bounded on the southeast by the Rio Grande. The county is largely contained within the Valle Grande Mountains, with part of the Jemez Mountains in the southwest. A small part of Santa Fe National Forest lies along the northern and western boundaries. Pajarito ski area and part of Bandelier National Monument are in the county. • Named for the city of Los Alamos, NM • 1949 from Sandoval and Santa Fe • Because of its comparative isolation and natural facilities, Los Alamos was chosen by the U.S. government in 1942 as the location for the Manhattan Project, directed by J. Robert Oppenheimer, which developed the first nuclear-fission atomic bomb. Following World War II, what was then called the Los Alamos Scientific Laboratory developed the first thermonuclear-fusion, or hydrogen bomb. The city was "opened" in 1957. In 1962, property was transferred from federal to private ownership. • Solar and nuclear research is conducted here by the University of California under contract to the U.S. government.

LUNA *Deming* • 25,016 • 2,965 • Southwestern NM, bounded on the south by the Mexican state of Chihuahua. The Cedar Mountains are in the county, as is part of the Cookes Range of the Mimbres Mountains. The Continental Divide closely parallels the county's western boundary. Rockhound and Pancho Villa State parks are also here. • Named for Solomon Luna, a large sheep rancher and a leader of the Republican party in the state • 1901 from Dona Ana and Grant counties (prior to statehood) • The town of Columbus was raided by Mexican rebels led by Pancho Villa in 1916, leaving sixteen Americans dead. • Cattle, some sheep, melons, grapes, fruit, nuts, jalapeños, chilies, onions, green beans, cabbage, some lettuce, pecans, cotton, corn, sorghum, hay, alfalfa, wheat, oats, barley; mining and smelting of copper, manganese, lead, fluorspar, silver; retirement complexes.

MCKINLEY *Gallup* • 74,798 • 5,449 (the forty-ninth largest county in the U.S.) • Northwestern NM, bounded on the west by the AZ state line; watered by the Rio Puerco. The Continental Divide crosses the county. It also includes part of the Zuni and San Mateo mountains, parts of Cibola National Forest, including Ignacio Chavez Management Area, and parts of Navajo and Zuni Indian reservations. Red Rock State Park is here, as is part of Chaco Culture National Historical Park. • Named for President William McKinley • 1899 from Bernalillo, Valencia, and San Juan • Uranium, molybdenum, copper, coal mines; hay, alfalfa; timber and forest products; cattle, sheep (wool production); Native American crafts, pottery; tourism. • The Inter-tribal Indian Ceremonial is held each August in Gallup. Federal installations in Gallup include the Bureau of Indian Affairs and Fort Wingate Army ordnance depot. A:shiwi A:wan Museum and Heritage Center is located in Zuni Pueblo.

MORA *Mora* • 5,180 • 1,931 • Northeastern NM, bounded on the east by the Canadian River; watered by the Mora River. The county includes part of the Sangre de Cristo Mountains (its crest forming most of the county's western boundary), part of Santa Fe National Forest, Charette Lake, part of Kiowa National Grasslands, and Morphy Lake and Coyote Creek state parks. • Named for the town of Mora, NM Territory • 1860 from San Miguel (prior to statehood) • Fort Union (National Monument) was a key supply point on the Santa Fe Trail and has the largest visible network of ruts along the historic route. • Fruit, hay, alfalfa, wheat, nuts, cattle, some sheep.

OTERO (one of two counties so named, the other in CO) *Alamogordo* • 62,298 • 6,627 (the third largest county in NM and the thirty-second largest county in the U.S.) • Southern NM, bounded on the south by the TX state line. Part of Fort Bliss Military Reserve is in the southwestern part of the county; part of White Sands Missile Range and Holloman Air Force Base are in the northwest. Also here are Mescalero Indian Reservation, Three Rivers Petroglyph B.L.M. National Recreation Site, and Oliver Lee Memorial State Park. The county includes part of the Guadalupe Mountains, parts of Lincoln National Forest (its headquarters in Alamogordo), and part of White Sands National Monument, including Heart of the Sands Nature Center. • Named for Miguel A. Otero II (1859–1944), governor of NM Territory • 1899 from Dona Ana and Lincoln • Physicist Edward Condon • Gold, silver; cattle, sheep, fruit, nuts, pecans, hay, alfalfa, some wheat; timber.

QUAY *Tucumcari* • 10,155 • 2,875 • Eastern NM, bounded on the east by the TX state line; watered by the Canadian River (which forms Ute Lake reservoir) and Tucumcari Creek. Caprock Amphitheater and Ute Lake State Park are in the county. • Named for Matthew S. Quay (1833–1904), U.S. senator from PA who advocated statehood for NM • 1903 (prior to statehood) • Triticale, cotton, sorghum, hay, alfalfa, blue corn, bloom corn, wheat, oats, barley, millet, sheep, cattle, some dairying; tourism; light industries.

RIO ARRIBA *Tierra Amarilla* • 41,190 • 5,858 (the fifth largest county in NM and the forty-fourth largest county in

the U.S.) • Northwestern NM, bounded on the north by the CO state line and on the northwest by the San Juan River, here forming Navajo Lake reservoir; watered by the Rio Grande, Rio Chama (designated a National Wild and Scenic River), and Rio Brazos. The Continental Divide crosses in the west. The county includes part of Santa Fe National Forest, parts of Carson National Forest, and the San Juan Mountains. Vicarilla Apache and a part of Santa Clara Pueblo Indian reservations are here. The county also contains Navajo Lake, Heron Lake, and El Vado Lake state parks. • Named for the area of NM in the upper region of the Rio Grande • Original county; organized 1852 (prior to statehood) • Cattle, sheep, chilies, hay, apples, alfalfa.

ROOSEVELT *Portales* • 18,018 • 2,449 • Eastern NM, on Llano Estacado, bounded on the east by the TX state line. Oasis State Park and Grulla National Wildlife Refuge (on Salt Lake) are in the county. • One of two counties (the other in MT) named for President Theodore Roosevelt • 1903 from Chaves and Guadalupe (prior to statehood) • Triticale, blue corn, peanuts, potatoes, wheat, hay, alfalfa, oats, barley, millet, rye, sorghum, corn, cotton, green beans, pumpkins, melons, cattle, sheep, dairying; education (Eastern NM U.) • Blackwater Draw Archaeological Site Museum exhibits 12,000-year-old artifacts found in adjacent archaeological sites.

SANDOVAL *Bernalillo* • 89,908 (the fifth most populated county in NM) • 3,710 • Northwestern NM; drained by the Rio Grande, Rio Puerco, and Jemez River. The county contains part of Santa Fe and Cibolo national forests, and Bandelier National Monument. It also includes part or all of several Indian reservations: Laguna, Sandia, San Felipe, Santa Domingo, Zia, Jemez, Santa Ana, and Santa Clara pueblos and Jicarilla Apache. The Continental Divide runs through the northwestern part of the county. Ranges of the Rocky Mountains are in the north. Fenton Lake State Park, Jemez and Coronado state monuments, Kasha-Katuwe Tent Rocks National Monument and Cabezon Peak B.L.M. Recreation Area are also here. • Named for the Sandoval family of north-central NM Territory • 1903 from Rio Arriba (prior to statehood) • Approximately 100 square miles were carved out of the county to form Los Alamos County in 1949. • Cattle, sheep, dairying, apples, corn, chilies, hay, alfalfa; Christmas trees; gypsum and pumice.

SAN JUAN (one of four counties so named) *Aztec* • 113,801 (the fourth most populated county in NM) • 5,514 (tied with Yuma County, AZ, for forty-seventh largest county in the U.S.) • Extreme northwestern NM, bounded on the north by the CO state line and on the west by the AZ state line. (The Four Corner Area, the only point common to four states, is in the extreme northwest.) The county is drained by the Animas, Chaco, and San Juan rivers. The San Juan forms Navajo Lake reservoir on the northeastern boundary. Aztec Ruins National Monument and Salmon Ruins and Heritage Park are here. The Chuska Mountains cross the southwest. De-Na-Zin and

Bisti wilderness areas, and Angel Peak, Simon Canyon, and Negro Canyon B.L.M. recreation areas are also in the county. Navajo Lake (reservoir) is on the northeast border. Part of Navajo Nation Indian Reservation occupies more than half of the county in the west. Part of Ute Mountain Indian Reservation is in the north. • Named for the San Juan River • 1887 from Rio Arriba (prior to statehood) • Cattle, sheep, dairying, pumpkins, potatoes, apples, peanuts, blue corn, hay, oil and natural gas, vanadium and uranium; Indian crafts, pottery. • Along with hundreds of smaller ruins, the thirteen major ruins which constitute Chaco Culture National Historic Park represent the zenith of Pueblo pre-Columbian civilization. The many-storied houses of Pueblo Bonito (Ruins) were built by the Anasazi beginning in about A.D. 700.

SAN MIGUEL (one of two counties so named, the other in CO) *Las Vegas* • 30,126 • 4,718 • Northeastern NM; watered by the Canadian, Conchas, and Gallinas rivers. Conchas Lake reservoir is formed at the confluence of the Conchas and Canadian rivers. Part of the Sangre de Cristo Mountains are in the northwest. The county also includes parts of Santa Fe National Forest, Pecos National Historical Park, Las Vegas National Wildlife Refuge, and Conchas Lake, Villanueva, and Storric Lake state parks. • Named for the town of San Miguel del Bado, NM Territory • Original county; organized 1852 (prior to statehood) • Cattle, sheep, hay, alfalfa, corn, peas, oats, barley; gold; education (NM Highlands U.). • The Rough Riders Memorial is in Las Vegas.

SANTA FE *Santa Fe* • 129,292 (the third most populated county in NM) • 1,909 • North-central NM; drained by the Rio Grande. The county includes parts of Santa Fe National Forest, part of the Sangre de Cristo Mountains, part of Bandelier National Monument, Santa Cruz Lake B.L.M. Recreation Area, Hyde Memorial State Park, and part of Glorieta Mesa. Pojoaque, Nambe, Cochiti, and Tesuque pueblos are in the north. • Named for the city of Santa Fe, NM Territory • Original county; organized 1852 (prior to statehood) • Santa Fe served as the terminus of the El Camino Real from Mexico City; the first road established by Europeans in what is now the U.S. began serving as a trade route about 1581. The Palace of the Governors, the oldest government building in the U.S., served Spain for two centuries. Santa Fe has served as the only capital for both the territory and state of New Mexico. The Santa Fe Trail, established in 1821 by William Becknell, extended 700 miles from MO to Santa Fe. In 1949, part of the county was used to form Los Alamos County. • Novelist and essayist Mary Austin, military diplomat Patrick J. Hurley, anthropologist Clyde K. M. Kluckhohn, painter Georgia O'Keeffe, photographer Laura Gilpin, mathematician Stanislaw M. Ulam, naturalist and writer Ernest Thompson Seton, and photographer Eliot Porter all died here. • Livestock, corn, hay, alfalfa, apples, chilies, wheat, oats, barley, millet; pumice, sand and gravel, gypsum, mining of lead, zinc, coal, gold, silver; timber; government offices; education (St. John's College; College of Santa Fe); tourism • The Loretto Chapel,

begun in 1873, features the "Miraculous Staircase," which spirals upward without any center support. San Miguel Mission is North America's oldest church structure. At 7,000 feet above sea level, Santa Fe is the highest state capital.

SIERRA (one of two counties so named, the other in CA) *Truth or Consequences* • 13,270 • 4,181 • Southwestern NM; drained by the Rio Grande (which forms Elephant Butte and Caballo reservoirs) and the Alamosa River. The Continental Divide crosses in the northwest. Part of Gila and Cibola national forests are in the county, as are parts of Black Range and the Mimbres, Caballo, and San Andres mountains. Part of White Sands Missile Range is in the eastern quarter of the county. Also here are Cabblo Lake, Elephant Butte Lake, and Percha Dam state parks, and part of Jornada del Muerto plain. • Named for the Sierra de los Caballos Range or possibly for the Black Mountain Range, or for the fact that the county is mountainous • 1884 from Socorro (prior to statehood) • Cattle, some sheep, dairying, hay, alfalfa, chilies, cabbage, onions, lettuce, pecans, wheat, apples; placer mining for gold; tourism (mineral springs) • In 1950 the citizens of Hot Springs voted to change their city's named to Truth or Consequences after the popular radio quiz show moderated by Ralph Edwards. A Ralph Edwards Fiesta is held every May.

SOCORRO *Socorro* • 18,078 • 6,647 (the second largest county in NM and the thirty-first largest county in the U.S.) • Central NM; watered by the Rio Grande, which flows through Elephant Butte Reservoir on the southern border. The Magdalena Mountains are in the county, as are the San Mateo Mountains, part of the Gallinas Mountains, and parts of Cibola National Forest. Part of White Sands Missile Range is here, including Trinity Site (where the first atomic bomb was exploded, July 16, 1945). The county also includes Fort Craig Historic Site, Bosque del Apache and Sevilleta national wildlife refuges, part of Jornada del Muerto plain, the National Radio Astronomy Observatory VLA Telescope (on the western border), the Gran Quivira unit of Salinas Pueblo Missions National Monument, and Navajo Nation Reservation. • Named for the town of Socorro, NM Territory • Original county; organized 1850 (prior to statehood) • The site that would become Soccoro was first visited by a Spanish expedition led by Juan de Oñate. A mission named Nuestra Señora de Perpetuo Socorro was abandoned during the Pueblo Revolt of 1680. With the discovery of silver in 1867 and arrival of the Santa Fe Railway in 1880, Socorro became the largest city in the NM Territory. • Cattle, sheep, dairying, chilies, corn, hay, alfalfa, wheat, barley, oats; education (NM Inst. of Mining and Tech.); mining; maintenance of White Sands Missile Range.

TAOS *Taos* • 29,979 • 2,203 • Northern NM, bounded on the north by the CO state line; watered by the Rio Grande (designated here a Wild, Scenic and Recreational River). The Sangre de Cristo Mountains extend along the eastern boundary, rising to 13,161+ feet at Wheeler Peak, the highest point in the state. The county includes parts of Carson National Forest (its headquarters in Taos), Picuris Pueblo and Taos Pueblo Indian reservations, Kit Carson Park, Orilla Verde and Wild Rivers B.L.M. recreation areas. Rio Grande Gorge is in the center of the county. Numerous ski areas are also here. • Named for the settlement of Taos in NM Territory • Original county; organized 1852 (prior to statehood) • Taos was the staging area for a 1680 revolt of Taos and other Pueblo Indians against Spanish occupiers of the region. The town has been a resort colony for writers and painters since the early part of the 20th century. • Frontiersman-scout Kit Carson; short and long term residents included D.H. Lawrence, Willa Cather, Robinson Jeffers, Dorothy Brett, and Maurice Sterne. Writer Mabel Dodge Luhan died here. • Grain, cattle, sheep; lumbering; ski resorts • The county is well known for its Indian fiestas and ceremonial dances. The St. Francis of Assisi Mission in Taos is one of the oldest churches in the Southwest. Taos Pueblo, located here, is the nation's largest and possibly oldest pueblo.

TORRANCE *Estancia* • 16,911 (64% increase since 1990; the fastest growing county in NM) • 3,345 • Central NM; watered by Laguna del Perro and Pintada Arroyo. Parts of Cibola National Forest are in the west and south. The county also contains part of Isleta Pueblo Indian Reservation, Manzano Mountains State Park, Abo and Quarai units of Salinas Pueblo Missions National Monument. • Named for Francis J. Torrance, a New Mexico Central Railroad promoter and developer • 1903 (prior to statehood) • Corn, hay, alfalfa, beans, wheat, rye, oats, pumpkins, apples, cattle.

UNION (one of eighteen counties so named) *Clayton* • 4,174 • 3,830 • Extreme northeastern NM, bounded on the north by the CO state line, and on the east by the TX and OK state lines; watered by the Cimarron River and Carrizo and Ute creeks. Most of the county lies on the high plateau of the Great Plains. It includes Capulin Volcano National Monument, a section of Kiowa National Grassland, and Clayton Lake State Park. • The county's name reflects the uniting of the counties that formed it. • 1893 from Colfax, Mora, and San Miguel (prior to statehood) • Cattle, sheep, triticale, sorghum, hay, alfalfa, wheat, oats, corn, barley, millet.

VALENCIA *Los Lunas* • 66,152 (46% increase since 1990; the third fastest growing county in NM) • 1,068 • Central NM; watered by the Rio Grande and Rio Puerco. A small part of Cibola National Forest is in the east in the Manzano Mountains. Part of Isleta Pueblo Indian Reservation lies along its northern border. • Named for the village of Valencia, NM Territory • Original county; organized 1852 (prior to statehood) • Cattle, sheep, dairying, corn, hay, alfalfa, oats, barley, grapes, apples; Christmas trees • Cibola County was created out of a large part of the western corner of the county.

NEW YORK

Ever Upward

Each of New York's sixty-two counties is governed by either a board of supervisors or a county legislature except for the five New York City boroughs, each of which has county status, although they have lost almost all of their functions and officials to the city government.

ALBANY (one of two counties so named, the other in WY) *Albany* • 294,565 • 524 • Eastern NY, bounded on the east by the Hudson River (Albany is the northern terminus of its deep water channel) and partly on the north by the Mohawk River and the New York State Barge Canal. The county includes the Helderbergs and part of the Catkills resort area. Its state parks include Thompson's Lake and John Boyd Thacher. • Named for King James II (1633–1701), formerly Duke of York and Albany • Original county; organized 1683 • In 1609 Henry Hudson anchored his *Halfmoon* in shallows near the future site of Albany while searching for the Northwest Passage. Albany, which has served as capital of NY since 1797, is one of the oldest cities in the U.S.; Dutch settlers established the first white settlement here in 1624. One of the first intercolonial conventions was held in Albany in 1689 to discuss a system of mutual defense. In 1754, the Albany Congress adopted Benjamin Franklin's "Plan of Union." The first informal community of Shakers in America was founded in Watervliet by Ann Lee. The U.S. arsenal at Watervliet has produced arms for wars since the War of 1812. • Political leader Roscoe Conkling; jurist Learned Hand; scientist Joseph Henry; merchant and real-estate promoter Potter Palmer; U.S. Constitution framer and Supreme Court justice William Paterson; microbiologist & pathologist Theobald Smith; explorer and ethnologist Henry Rowe Schoolcraft; political leader Philip John Schuyler; newspaper editor E.G. Squier; painter William Page; writers Bret Harte and William Kennedy • The county has extensive manufacturing and ranks third in the state in numbers employed in industry; manufactures include textiles, electrical appliances, paper, machine tools, felt and metal products, alarm systems; shipbuilding; also dairying, hay, vegetables, horticultural crops, cattle, calves, lambs and sheep; government services; education (Siena College; College of St. Rose; U. of Albany, S.U.N.Y.) • Albany's Dutch heritage is reflected in its annual Tulip Festival.

ALLEGANY (one of two counties so named, the other in MD; one of five counties named Allegany with variant spellings) *Belmont* • 49,927 • 1,030 • Southwestern NY, bounded on the south by the PA state line; drained by the Genessee and Canisteo rivers, and Canaseraga and Angelica creeks. The county includes part of Oil Springs Indian Reservation. Also here are Turnpike State Forest and Swain ski area. • Named for a trail that followed the Allegheny River, with a variant spelling • 1806 from Genesee • Seneca Oil Spring is the site of the first European discovery (1627) of petroleum in North America. • Preacher and inspirational writer Charles Monroe Sheldon • Dairying, sugar beans, corn, livestock, poultry; maple sugar; oil and natural gas; diversified manufacturing; recreational tourism; education (Houghton College; Alfred U.).

BRONX • 1,332,650 • 42 (one of the fifty smallest counties in the U.S.) • The county comprises the southern part of a peninsula bounded on the west by the Hudson River, on the southwest by the Harlem River, on the south by the East River, and on the east by the Long Island Sound. It is coterminous with the New York City borough of the Bronx, each of the city's five boroughs having county status. It is primarily residential, although much of its significant waterfront is used for shipping, warehousing and manufacturing. Pelham Bay and Van Cortlandt Park are in the north. • Named for the Bronx borough in New York City • 1912 from New York County • The area that became Bronx County was called Keskeskeck by the Indians who sold it to the Dutch West India Company in 1639. In 1641, Jonas Bronck, a Scandinavian, purchased 500 acres here. The first European settler north of the Harlem River, he called his farm "Broncksland." Shortly thereafter, New England settlers and religious dissenters moved into the area. South Bronx has been economically blighted over the last thirty years, but is undergoing redevelopment via government incentives to businesses located here. • Long jumper Bob Beamon; fashion designers Ralph Lauren and Calvin Klein; lawyer and baseball team owner Walter O'Malley; theatrical impresario Billy Rose; secretary of state Colin Powell; gangster Dutch Schultz; singer and songwriter Billy Joel; singer and actor Jennifer Lopez • Manufacture of textiles, food products, machinery, paper products; education (Fordham U.; Lehman College [C.U.N.Y.]; College of Mount St. Vincent and others) • The county is best known for the Bronx Zoo and Wildlife Conservation Park, the large New York Botanical Gardens, and the venerable "house that Ruth built," Yankee Stadium. The campus of Bronx Community College of the City University of New York is home to the Hall of Fame, honoring the memory of great Americans. City Island in Long Island Sound resembles a New England village.

BROOME *Binghamton* • 200,536 • 707 • Southern NY, bounded on the south by the PA state line; drained by the Susquehanna, Chenango, Tioughnioga, the West Branch of the Delaware, and Otselic rivers. The county includes Chenango Valley and Oquaga Creek state parks. • Named for John Broome (1738–1810), state legislator and lieutenant governor of NY • 1806 from Tioga • Author and dramatist Rod Serling; children's author Howard R. Garis; philanthropist and businessman Frederick T. Gates; humorist Petroleum Nasby; scholar and author Camille Paglia; heavyweight-boxing champion Jack Sharkey. Baseball player and manager Bill Martin died here. • Dairying, grain, poultry, livestock; maple sugar and syrup; manufacture of business machines, shoes, textiles, photo supplies, machinery, electronic equipment, computers and other high-tech products, cosmetics, foundry products; education (Binghamton U., S.U.N.Y.); ski resorts.

CATTARAUGUS *Little Valley* • 83,955 • 1,310 • Southwestern NY, bounded on the south by the PA state line and on the north by Cattaraugus Creek; intersected by the Allegheny River; drained by Conewango and Ischua creeks. The county includes Allegany, part of Cattaraugus, and part of Oil Springs Indian reservations. Part of Allegany State Park is on the southern boundary. Rock City State Forest and Hidden Valley ski area are also here. • Named for Cattaraugus Creek; the name is probably Seneca for "bad smelling shore" • 1808 from Genesee • Olean was an embarkation point on the Allegheny river for settlers bound for the Ohio River valley in flatboats. The county, along with adjacent Allegany and Chautauqua counties, was important in the late 19th and early 20th century petroleum industry. • Dairying, fruit, hay, potatoes, stock-raising; manufacture of turbines, compressors, electrical components; natural gas and oil wells, sand and gravel pits; education (St. Bonaventure U.).

CAYUGA *Auburn* • 81,963 • 693 • West-central NY, an elongated county bounded on the north by Lake Ontario and extending south into the Finger Lakes region, bounded on the west in part by Cayuga Lake; drained by the Seneca River. The county is crossed by the Erie Canal. There are many summer residences on the Cayuga, Skaneateles and Owasco lakes. Fair Haven Beach and Long Point state parks are here. • Named for the Cayuga Indians, one of the Five Nations of the Iroquois • 1799 from Onondaga • President Millard Fillmore (Fillmore Glen State Park); inventor William S. Burroughs; penologist Thomas Mott Osborne (who as a prison reformer, spent time in Auburn State Prison incognito to study conditions there); secretary of state William H. Seward; abolitionist and former slave Harriet Tubman; Indian chief Logan. • Dairying, hay, corn, grain; manufacture of diesel engines, electrical rectifiers, air conditioners, rope, shoes, plastic products, electronic equipment, rugs; education (Wells College) • Owasco Teyetasta Iroquois Museum is located in Owasco.

CHAUTAUQUA (one of two counties so named, the other in KS) *Mayville* • 139,750 • 1,062 • Extreme southwestern NY, bounded on the south and west by the PA state line and on the northwest by Lake Erie. Part of Cattaraugus Indian Reservation is in the north. Mount Pleasant State Forest is in the southwest. Lake Erie and Chautauqua Lake are resort areas and include Lake Erie and Long Point on Lake Chautauqua state parks. Several ski areas are also here. • Named for Chautauqua Lake • 1808 from Genesee • Chautauqua township is the home of the Chautauqua Institution, a lyceum and amusement series popular in the late 19th and early 20th centuries, begun by John H. Vincent to educate Methodist Sunday School teachers (Chautauqua Institution Historic District). • Journalist and author Samuel Hopkins Adams, actor Lucille Ball; civic and political leader John Bidwell; economist Richard T. Ely; inventor Haywood Harvey; industrialist and inventor George M. Pullman; ornithologist Roger T. Peterson; U.S. Supreme Court justice Robert H. Jackson; chemist and researcher Willis Rodney Whitney • Chautauqua is one of the state's leading agricultural counties, producing poultry, seeds, fruits, especially grapes for viniculture, dairying. Also state fish hatchery; manufacture of washing machines, dryers, tools, bearings, automobile parts, kitchen equipment, metal furniture, voting machines, wooden furniture, radiators and boilers, marine motors, shovels and hoes; education (S.U.N.Y. College of Fredonia); ski resorts • In 1821, Fredonia became one of the first communities in the U.S. to use natural gas for street lighting. The state's first chapter of the National Grange was organized here in 1868. One of the earliest branches of the Women's Christian Temperance Union was founded in Fredonia in 1873.

CHEMUNG *Elmira* • 91,070 • 408 • Southern NY, bounded on the south by the PA state line; cut by the Chemung River; drained by Cayuta, Newtown, and Wynkoop creeks. The county includes Mark Twain State Park. • Named for the Chemung River • 1836 from Tioga • After exterminating the Susquehannas, the Senecas took control of the area, which was then settled by refugee tribes from the southeast. U.S. General John Sullivan defeated Indian and Tory forces led by Sir John Johnson and Chief Joseph Brant here in the Battle of Newtown in 1779, thus clearing the Chemung Valley for white settlement. The Elmira area was inundated by floodwaters in June, 1972; more than 5,000 homes were destroyed. • Playwright Clyde Fitch; composer Charles Griffes; film director Hal Roach; ecologist Victor E. Shelford. Educator and author Catherine E. Beecher and ballet dancer André Eglevsky died here. Mark Twain wrote many books on the Quarry Farm near Elmira and is buried in the city. • Dairying, poultry; sand and gravel pits; manufacture of office machines, electric fuel pumps, glass bottles, fire engines, valves, and hydrants, fabricated structural steel, machine tools, prefabricated homes, sailplanes, crop-dusting planes, processed foods, greeting cards; education (Elmira College — one of the earliest institutions of higher institutions for women in the U.S.) • Elmira's Woodlawn National Cemetery contains the graves of nearly 3,000 Confederate prisoners who died in the prison camp here. Established in 1870, Elmira Reformatory (now Correctional Facility) was a leader in prison reform. Harris Hill has been the site of glider contests since 1930. The National Soaring Museum is here.

CHENANGO *Norwich* • 51,401 •894 • South-central NY, bounded on the east by the Unadilla River; drained by the Susquehanna, Otselic, and Chenango rivers. The county includes Hunts Pond and Bowman Lake state parks and Whaupaunaucau and Long Point state forests. • Named for the Chenango River, Chenango Lake, or an Indian village by this name • 1798 from Herkimer and Tioga • The nation's oldest fish-line factory was established in South Otselic in 1816. • Condensed milk pioneer Gail Borden; diplomat Anson Burlingame; trader and explorer Jedediah Smith • Dairying, general farm crops, poultry; maple sugar; timber; manufacturing. • The county provided so many longshoremen to the New York City waterfront in the late 19th century that the name "Chenangoe" came to mean "longshoreman."

CLINTON (one of nine counties so named) *Plattsburgh* • 79,894 • 1,039 • Extreme northeastern NY, bounded on the north by the Canadian province of Quebec and on the east by Lake Champlain (here forming the VT state line); drained by the Saranac and Great Chazy rivers. The northern Adirondacks rise in the west. The county is situated partly in Adirondack Park and forest preserve. Macomb Reservation State Park is in the south. Point au Roche and Cumberland Bay state parks are found along the shore of Lake Champlain. Ausable Chasm, with its 1.5 miles of eye-catching stone formations, has been called the "Grand Canyon of the East." • One of two counties (the other in OH) named for George Clinton (1739–1812), first governor of NY and vice president of the U.S. • 1788 (prior to statehood) from Washington County • Plattsburg formed the backdrop for an important U.S. victory in the War of 1812, as 14,000 British troops under Sir George Prevost, reaching the town in a joint land and sea operation, were forced to retreat when a 14-ship U.S. naval squadron under Commander Thomas Macdonough decisively defeated the British fleet on September 11, 1814. • Geneticist Calvin B. Bridges • The county is home to the world's largest MacIntosh apple orchard. Also, dairying; recreational tourism; lumbering, paper milling; some manufacturing; education (Plattsburgh State U. S.U.N.Y.) • The Plattsburgh Air Force Base is one of the oldest military installations in the U.S.

COLUMBIA (one of eight counties so named) *Hudson* • 63,094 • 636 • Southeastern NY, bounded on the east by the MA state line and on the west by the Hudson River; drained by Kinderhook Creek. The county includes Beebe Hills State Forest, Lake Taghkanic State Park and part of Taconic State Park. • The county's name is a feminine form of Columbus, a poetic and honorific reference to Christopher Columbus • 1786 (prior to statehood) from Albany • The county was involved in the violent land claim disputes between NY and MA after the American Revolution. In 1804, Alexander Hamilton argued a case in favor of freedom of the press in the Old Hudson County Courthouse in Claverick. (It was a retrial of publisher Harry Roswell, found guilty of libeling President Jefferson.) Hudson was once a whaling and sealing port. It missed becoming the state capital by one vote. • U.S. presidential candidate Samuel J. Tilden;

U.S. President Martin Van Buren (national historic site); painter Frederick Church (Olana State Historic Site); Declaration of Independence co-drafter Robert R. Livingston; lawyer and statesman Edward Livingston • Dairying and beef cattle, fruit, sweet corn, potatoes, hay; sand and gravel, peat and limestone; resort tourism; manufacture of cement, machine tools, textiles. • The Museum of Fire Fighting, the largest of its kind in the U.S., was founded in Hudson in 1925. The four-day Winterhawk Bluegrass Festival is held in Ancram. The largest collection of Shaker handiwork in the U.S. is found in the Shaker Museum and Library outside Old Chatham.

CORTLAND *Cortland* • 48,599 • 500 • Central NY; drained by the Tioughnioga River. Part of Morgan Hill State Forest is in the north. Greek Peak ski area is also here. • Named for Pierre Van Cortlandt, Jr. (1762–1848), NY legislator, U.S. representative, and banker • 1808 from Onondaga • Reformer Amelia Bloomer; Presidential nominee Alton B. Parker; inventor Elmer Ambrose Sperry; educator and diplomat Andrew Dickson White; baseball player and manager John McGraw • Cabbage, sweet corn, potatoes, grain crops, sheep, lambs, hogs, poultry, Holstein and Guernsey dairy cattle; maple sugar; manufacture of screen cloth, wire netting, fishlines, motor trucks, forging and drilling machines, thermocouples, boats, overhead doors, clothing and wood products, sporting equipment; education (S.U.N.Y. College at Cortland); skiing resorts.

DELAWARE (one of six counties so named) *Delhi* • 48,055 • 1,446 (the fifth largest county in NY) • Southern NY, situated in the western Catskills, bounded on the northwest by the Susquehanna River, on the southwest by the Delaware River (here forming the PA state line); drained by Beaver Kill and the Charlotte River. There are many summer residences and second homes spread throughout the county. Murphy Hill and Plattekill state forests are also here. • Named for the Delaware River • 1797 from Ulster and Otsego • The county was once a leading dairy producer in the state, as well as one of NY's top wool producers. Its 1845 Anti-Rent War precipitated the end of the feudal land system in the state. Armed bands roved through the county disguised as Native Americans, preventing the sheriff from collecting rents. • Naturalist John Burroughs; World War II guerrilla Marine officer Evans Carlson; railroad executive and financier Jay Gould; adventurer and writer E.Z.C. Judson • Hay, cauliflower, potatoes, poultry; bluestone quarrying; some lumbering; diversified manufacturing • Fleischmanns, named for Cincinnati yeast- and distilling-magnate Charles F. Fleischmann, was one of the first Jewish enclaves in the Catskills.

DUTCHESS *Poughkeepsie* • 280,150 • 802 • Southeastern NY, bounded on the west by the Hudson River and on the east by the CT state line; drained by Wappinger and Fishkill creeks. The county includes part of the Taconic Mountains (state park here) and part of the highlands of the Hudson River. The Vanderbilt Mansion and Hyde Park (lifelong home and gravesite of President Franklin D. Roosevelt) are national historic sites within the county. • Named for Mary (1658–1718), wife of James, Duke of York and Albany, later James II, king of England; spelling is 17th century variant of duchess • Original county; organized 1683 • The county was originally occupied by Wappingers; a large influx of French Huguenots followed in 1720. Poughkeepsie became the temporary capital of NY in 1777. In 1788, the state legislature met here to ratify the U.S. Constitution. • First U.S. secretary of defense James V. Forrestal; dramatist and novelist James K. Paulding; physician Sara Josephine Baker; inventor Samuel Morse; naturalist and Lutheran minister John Bachman. Industrial chemist Leo H. Baekeland, secretary of the treasury Henry Morgenthau, Jr., poet, dramatist and critic John Jay Chapman, and U.S. vice president Levi Morton died here. Timothy Leary once ran his League for Spiritual Discovery in Millbrook. • Dairying, poultry, fruit, grain, potatoes, other diversified farming; hothouse flowers; horse breeding; sand and gravel, shale (bluestone); diversified manufacturing, including gauges, electronic equipment, business machines, cough drops (made in Poughkeepsie by the Smith Brothers since the 1850s), ball bearings, cream separators; education (Vassar College; Marist College; Bard College; the Culinary Institute of America — the nation's most prestigious cooking school) • Eleanor Roosevelt's home at Val-Kill is the only national historic site dedicated to a president's wife. The Old Rhinebeck Aerodome has about 75 historic planes dating back to the early 1900s.

ERIE (one of three counties so named) *Buffalo* • 950,265 • 1,045 • Western NY; drained by Cattaraugus, Tonawanda, Buffalo, and Cayuga creeks. The county includes parts of Cattaraugus and Tonawanda Indian reservations. Ski areas are in the south. • One of two counties (the other in OH) named for the Erie Indian tribe • 1821 from Niagara • Buffalo was headquarters for U.S. military operations during the War of 1812. The town was burned by an invading force of British and Indians in 1813. It grew rapidly after the opening of the Erie Canal in 1825, subsequently becoming a major transfer point for settlers moving west. Buffalo was the site of the world's first steam-operated grain elevator, constructed in 1843. Wells Fargo Express was formed in the city in 1851. Laurence D. Bell founded his Bell Aircraft company in the city in 1935. • Four U.S. presidents had strong connections to the county. Millard Fillmore lived and died here. Grover Cleveland served as mayor of the city in 1881. President William McKinley was shot by an assassin in Buffalo on September 6, 1901, during a reception at the Pan American Exposition. Upon McKinley's death eight days later, Theodore Roosevelt was sworn in here as president. Other famous residents include Seneca Indian chief Red Jacket; lawyer, soldier and diplomat William J. Donovan; architect Gordon Bunshaft; air conditioner inventor Willis Haviland Carrier; Protestant minister Harry E. Fosdick; and professional baseball player Warren Spahn. Businessman William G. Fargo died here. • Buffalo leads the nation in flour production, averaging one million short tons each year. Dairying, poultry, livestock, field and sweet corn, hay, beans, potatoes, tomatoes, strawberries, grapes; stone and gypsum quarrying; manufacture of steel (Lackawanna was once among the largest producers in the U.S.), chemicals, paper and paper products, electronics, silk, felt, baskets, metal and wood products, automobile cushion springs, abrasives, cement, concrete; bridgeworks, shipyards, railroad shops (Buffalo is one of the nation's largest railroad centers); education (U. of Buffalo, S.U.N.Y.; Buffalo State College; Hilbert College; and others) • Lackawanna's Basilica of Our Lady of Victory is visited by thousands of Roman Catholics each year. About twenty cemeteries are located within the town limits of Cheektowaga. East Aurora (located ninety miles *west* of Aurora) was the home to the earlier incarnation of Roycroft enterprises, known for the excellent craftsmanship of its handicrafts and the printing of *The Philistine* magazine. Buffalo is home to the Buffalo Sabres professional hockey team. The Buffalo Bills play in Orchard Park at Ralph Wilson Stadium.

ESSEX *Elizabethtown* • 38,851 • 1,797 (the second largest county in NY) • Northeastern NY, bounded on the east by Lake Champlain (forming the VT state line); drained by the Hudson River (which rises here and forms part of the county's southwestern boundary), the Ausable River, and various streams. The county includes recreational Lake Placid and other lakes distributed throughout. Situated entirely within Adirondack Park, the county contains some of the highest peaks of the Adirondack range, including the highest in the state, Mount Marcy (5,344 feet). • One of five counties named for Essex County in England • 1799 from Clinton • Essex County figured heavily in the French and Indian Wars, the American Revolution, and the War of 1812. The French garrison at Fort Ticonderoga was repulsed by a British attack in July, 1758. On May 10, 1775, in one of the earliest engagements of the American Revolution, Ethan Allen's Green Mountain Boys overran the fort in a surprise attack. The next day, Allen's forces took Crown Point from the British. Fort Ticonderoga was retaken and briefly held by British General Burgoyne, later to be abandoned after the Battles of Saratoga. Iron manufacturing began in the county in 1801 with the production of anchors at Willsborough Falls. By the mid-1800s, the county's forges, rolling mills, and nail factories were among the most productive in the U.S. Mines in the county once made it the principal source in the U.S. for crystalline graphite. Lake Placid was the site of the third (1932) and thirteenth (1980) Winter Olympic Games. • Abolitionist John Brown is buried near Lake Placid (state historic site). Writer Robert Louis Stevenson came to the county seeking a cure for his tuberculosis; he wrote *Master of Ballantrae* in a cottage here. Librarian Melvil Dewey founded the exclusive Lake Placid Club here in 1895. • Truck farming, apples, potatoes, hay, livestock, dairying; lumbering; Wollatonite, titanium, and garnet deposits; paper and pulp industries; resort tourism • A bobsled run operates on Mount Van Hoevenberg. Ticonderoga is the headquarters of the New York State Historical Association.

FRANKLIN (one of twenty-five counties so named) *Malone* • 51,134 • 1,632 (the fourth largest county in NY) • Northeastern NY, bounded on the north by the Canadian province of Quebec; drained by the Saranac, St. Regis, Salmon, Little Salmon, Chateaugay, and Raquette rivers. The Adirondack Mountains and Adirondack Park are located in the southern two-thirds of the county. Franklin County contains a number of lakes and resorts, including parts of Saranac and Tupper lakes, and Upper and Lower Saranac lakes. Part of St. Regis Mohawk Indian Reservation is in the extreme northwest. • One of twenty-three counties named for Benjamin Franklin • 1808 from Clinton • Saranac Lake became well know for its open-air treatment of tuberculosis following the founding in 1884 of a sanitorium here by Edward L. Trudeau. • U.S. vice president William A. Wheeler. Professional baseball pitcher Christy Mathewson died here. • Field corn, potatoes, hay, cheddar cheese; timber; hunting, fishing; tourism (skiing) • The U.S. Eastern Amateur Ski Association was founded in the village of Saranac Lake (partly in Essex County). A Winter Carnival is held here each February.

FULTON (one of eight counties so named) *Johnstown* • 55,073 • 496 • East-central NY, in the Adirondacks; drained by East Canada Creek and the Sacandaga River. The northern half of the county is located in Adirondack Park and includes part of Great Sacandaga Lake in the east. • One of seven counties named for Robert Fulton (1765–1815), developer of the *Clermont*, the first commercially successful steamboat • 1838 from Montgomery • The county was formerly a major glove-making center, especially in Gloversville and Johnstown, dating back to the colonial era. Johnstown was the scene of a minor battle of the American Revolution on October 25, 1781. • Harness-racing driver and trainer Billy Haughton; pioneer suffragist Elizabeth Cady Stanton • Dairying, poultry, apples, potatoes; manufacture of leather and leather goods, knitting mill products, furniture, baseball and softball bats, clothing.

GENESEE (one of two counties so named, the other in MI) *Batavia* • 60,370 • 494 • Western NY; drained by Tonawanda and Oak Orchard creeks. The county includes part of Tonawanda Indian Reservation. Darien Lake State Park is in the southwest, and part of Iroquois National Wildlife Refuge is on the northwestern border. • Named for the Genesee River valley • 1802 from Ontario • The county originally included most of western New York. Batavia was the center of the Holland Land Purchase, acquired in 1793–1797 by Dutch capitalists. In the summer of 1826 in Batavia, William Morgan, a Mason, published the secrets of Freemasonry and was never seen again. • Chief of the U.S. Federal Detective Police LaFayette Curry Baker • Manufacture of shoes, paper die castings, televisions, transformers, heavy and light machinery, machine parts, mobile homes, fiberglass boats, apparel, processed foods, candy, champagne; dairying, truck farming, poultry, fruit, wheat, beans, sweet corn, field corn, peas, hay; timber; sand and gravel; expanded perlite; natural gas, gypsum. • Ingram University, founded in 1837 but closed in 1902, was one of the first chartered universities for women. Jell-O was invented in Le Roy.

GREENE (one of fourteen counties so named) *Catskill* • 48,195 • 648 • Southeastern NY, situated mostly in the Catskills, bounded on the east by the Hudson River; drained by Schoharie and Catskill creeks. The county includes part of Catskill Park. Many of the Catskills' highest peaks and waterfalls are located here. The Kaaterskill Falls, at 260 feet, are the highest waterfalls in the state. Numerous ski areas are also found here. • One of sixteen counties named for General Nathanael Greene (1742–86), hero of the Revolutionary War • 1800 from Albany and Ulster • First settled by Pieter Bronck in 1661, Coxsackie was the site of the signing of the 1775 Coxsackie Declaration of Independence, precursor of the national Declaration of Independence. In the 1800s and early 1900s, Catskill had thriving knitting factories, brickyards and distilleries. During Prohibition, a lucrative moonshine trade made the city a hangout for New York City gangsters. Athens was once a major ice harvesting center. The icehouses were later converted to indoor mushroom farms. The Catskills were nearly destroyed by the harvesting of hemlock tree bark for tanning. • Painter and leader of the "Hudson River School" movement Thomas Cole (national historic site); inventor and builder James Bogardus; life insurance company founder Henry B. Hyde. Asher Durand, James Fenimore Cooper, and William Cullen Bryant all found creative inspiration from the Catskill Mountains here. • Hay, field and sweet corn, tomatoes, apples, grapes, dairying; some timber; resort tourism; manufacture of women's wear, machinery • The *Catskill Packet*, now today's *Greene County News*, was begun in 1792. It was near Palenville that Rip Van Winkle supposedly fell into his deep 20-year sleep. The Irish resort town of East Durham contains the largest Irish import store in the U.S., Guaranteed Irish.

HAMILTON (one of ten counties so named) *Lake Pleasant* • 5,379 (the least populated county in NY) • 1,721 (the third largest county in NY) • Northeast-central NY; drained by tributaries of the Hudson River (forming part of the eastern border), and the Black and Sacandaga rivers. The county is located entirely within the Adirondack Mountains and Park, and includes the skiing, hunting, and fishing resorts of Indian, Long, Raquette, Piseco and Pleasant lakes, as well as the Fulton Chain of Lakes. The Adirondack Museum is located at Blue Mountain Lake. • One of eight counties named for Alexander Hamilton (?–1804), first U.S. secretary of the treasury • 1816 from Montgomery • Dairying, poultry, livestock, hay, grain; tourism.

HERKIMER *Herkimer* • 64,427 • 1,412 • North-central NY; drained by the Mohawk, Unadilla, Black, and Moose rivers. The northern part of this narrow, elongated county extends into the Adirondack Mountains and Adirondack Park; its southern part reaches into the Mohawk valley. Stillwater Reservoir and part of the Fulton Chain of Lakes are in the north. •

Named for native son General Nicholas Herkimer (1728–77), Revolutionary War officer and patriot, fatally wounded at the Battle of Oriskany • 1791 from Montgomery • The Erie Canal, the first important national waterway built in the U.S., was completed through the county in 1825 and spurred industrial growth here. • Firearms manufacturer and inventor Eliphalet Remington, Jr. (Remington Arms Museum is in Ilion.) • Truck farming, dairying; diversified manufacturing, including guns, ammunition, computers, bicycles, dairy equipment, food, paper, cotton products, dresses; resort tourism • Little Falls is the site of the highest lift lock in the New York State Barge Canal. Remington Industries introduced the first practical typewriter in Ilion in 1873. Its Univac computer line was one of the industry's earliest.

JEFFERSON *Watertown* • 111,738 • 1,272 • Northern NY, bounded on the west by Lake Ontario, on the northwest by the St. Lawrence River; drained by the Black and Indian rivers. The county contains over 188 square miles of military installations, including Fort Drum. There are several recreational areas and state parks on Lake Ontario and in the Thousand Islands region of the St. Lawrence River. Tug Hill State Forest is in the southeast. • One of twenty-six counties named directly or indirectly for Thomas Jefferson • 1805 from Oneida • Early settlers of the county were refugees from the French Revolution, who returned to France, unhappy with the demands of pioneer life. Sackets Harbor (state historic site) played a prominent role in the War of 1812. During a Jefferson County fair in 1878, F. W. Woolworth originated the idea of selling a fixed-price line of dry goods. • Architect Daniel H. Burnham; diplomat and intelligence expert Allen W. Dulles; librarian Melvil Dewey; humorist Marriet Holley; secretary of agriculture J. Sterling Morton • Metallic and non-metallic mineral mining; large-scale dairying; manufacture of machinery, transportation equipment, thermometers, clothing, snowplows, and ski lifts, paper products; tourism.

KINGS (one of two counties so named, the other in CA) • 2,465,326 (the most populated county in NY and the seventh most populated county in the U.S.) • 70 (one of the fifty smallest counties in the U.S.) • Southeastern NY, on western Long Island. The county is coterminous with the New York City borough of Brooklyn, each of the city's five boroughs having county status. It shares Gateway National Recreation Area and Jamaica Bay Wildlife Refuge with Queens County. • Named for Charles II (1630–85), king of England • Original county, organized 1683 • Canarsie Indians were the first inhabitants of the area that would become Kings County. Dutch farmers moved here in 1636. The Battle of Long Island was fought here on August 27, 1776, with remnants of the American army retreating to Brooklyn Heights overlooking the East River. • Attorney Alan Dershowitz; entertainment executive David Geffen; U.S. Supreme Court justice Ruth Bader Ginsburg; gangster Bugsy Siegel; politician Rudolph Giuliani; singer and actor Barbra Streisand; actors Mae West, Mickey Rooney, and Clara Bow; professional football coach Vince

Lombardi; director Woody Allen; publisher Frank Nelson Doubleday • The county is an important port and industrial center. There is diversified manufacturing, mostly along the waterfront, including hardware, plastics, textiles, knitware. Other industries include pharmaceutical preparation, shipbuilding, and ship repair. The county has several institutions of higher learning, including Brooklyn College (C.U.N.Y.), Medgar Evans College (C.U.N.Y.), Pratt University, and Long Island University, Brooklyn Campus.• Two of the county's oldest neighborhoods, Brooklyn Heights and Cobble Hill, have more than 1,000 houses over 100 years old. Bedford-Stuyvesant is the largest African-American neighborhood in New York City. Prospect Park is one of the finest landscaped parks in the U.S. The Brooklyn Bridge, designated a national historic landmark in 1964, links Kings County to New York County. The Verrazano-Narrows Bridge, linking Kings and Richmond counties, is one of the world's longest suspension bridges. Coney Island is the home of New York's Aquarium for Wildlife Conservation. Its beaches and famous boardwalk, though a remnant of its early days as a national amusement center, still attracts thousands of visitors. The Brooklyn Museum, one of the world's largest museums, has extensive Egyptian holdings.

LEWIS (one of seven counties so named) *Lowville* • 26,944 • 1,276 • North-central NY; drained by the Black and Moose rivers. The foothills of the Adirondacks cross in the east; they are separated from the Tug Hill Plateau (a winter recreational area) by the Black River valley. The county includes Whetstone Gulf State Park and The Lesser Wilderness State Forest. A portion of Adirondack Park is on its eastern boundary. Part of Fort Drum Military Reservation is in the north. • Named for Morgan Lewis (1754–1844), officer in the Revolutionary War and the War of 1812, NY legislator, and governor of NY • 1805 from Oneida • The county played a large role in a romantic scheme to settle refugees from the French Revolution. The building of the Black River Canal from Utica to Carthage began in 1836. The canal ceased operation in 1922. • Botanist J.C. Arthur • Paper, wood products, lumbering; food processing; dairying; tourism • Lake Bonaparte was named for Napoleon's brother Joseph, who owned a large tract of land in the area.

LIVINGSTON (one of six counties so named) *Geneseo* • 64,328 • 632 • West-central NY, in the Finger Lakes region, bounded on the southwest by the Genesee River; drained by Canaseraga and Honeoye creeks. The county is bisected by the Genesee River valley and contains Conesus and Hemlock lakes. It includes part of Letchworth State Park on the western border. • One of two counties (the other in KY) definitively named for Robert R. Livingston (1746–1813), NY patriot, statesman, and a drafter of the Declaration of Independence • 1821 from Genesee and Ontario • Botanist and geneticist Albert F. Blakeslee; astrophysicist Jonathan H. Lane; journalist and politician Henry J. Raymond; geologist and ethnologist John Wesley Powell • Dairying, grain, vegetables, hay, poultry; salt mines, gypsum and limestone quarries, diversified manufacturing; horse farms; education (S.U.N.Y. College at Geneseo) • The Genesee Valley Hunt, founded in 1876, is the second oldest hunt in the U.S.

MADISON *Wampsville* • 69,441 • 656 • Central NY, bounded on the northwest in part by Oneida Lake; drained by the Chenango and Unadilla rivers (the latter forming part of the southeastern boundary), and by several creeks. The county includes Green Lakes and Chittenango Falls state parks, and Stoney Pond State Forest. The Oneida Indian Reservation is also here. • One of twenty counties named directly or indirectly for President James Madison • 1806 from Chenango • In 1848, the John Noyes sect established the communistic Oneida Community here. In 1881, it was reorganized as a stock company that has since become know for its silverware. • Dairying, onions, cabbages, grain, poultry; manufacture of copper wire fabricators, dishes, paper products, wood products, burial vaults, dairy equipment, office furniture, plastics, castings and bearings, machine tools; canning; education (Colgate U.; Cazenovia College).

MONROE *Rochester* • 735,343 • 659 • Western NY, bounded on the north by Lake Ontario; drained by the Genesee River, and Honeoye and other creeks, and crossed by the Erie Canal. Hamlin Beach State Park and Irondequoit Bay State Marine Park are in the county. • One of seventeen counties named for President James Monroe • 1821 from Genesee and Ontario • Part of the nation's leading wheat-growing region in the mid-1800s, Rochester became a boom town with the coming of the Erie Canal in 1825, and was known as the "Flour City" for its prosperous milling operations. Later, clothing and shoe industries flourished, as did nursery enterprises (the city pioneering in the field of mail-order seed and shrub sales). Rochester was the home of spiritualists Margaret and Kate Fox, who attracted attention in the 1840s with a series of seances known as the Rochester rappings. Rochester was also a terminus for the Underground Railroad; in 1847 abolitionist Frederick Douglass published his paper *North Star* here. In the 20th century Rochester grew as a science and manufacturing center. George Eastman invented instant photography here in 1887. Other industrialists developed optical and precision equipment. • Physicist Jeremy Bernstein; geologist Grove Karl Gilbert; composer and pianist Gean Harwood; golfer Walter Hagen; lawyer Arthur G. Hays; dance authority Lincoln Kirstein; clergyman and theology professor Walter Rauschenbusch; educator and reformer Frances Willard; poet John Ashbery. Pioneer suffragist Susan B. Anthony died here. • Dairy products, horticultural products, vegetables, grain; extensive manufacture of photographic equipment, photocopy machines, thermometers, machine tools, business machines, dental and electrical equipment, chemicals; science center; education (S.U.N.Y. College at Brockport; Rochester Institute of Technology; U. of Rochester, including the Eastman School of Music; Nazareth College of Rochester; St. John Fisher College). Six Fortune 1000 companies have their corporate headquarters in the county. The Rochester Lilac Time Festival is a popular annual event.

MONTGOMERY (one of eighteen counties so named) *Fonda* • 49,708 • 405 • East-central NY, in the Mohawk River valley; drained by Schoharie Creek. Rural Grove State Forest is here. • One of sixteeen counties named directly or indirectly for General Richard Montgomery (1738–75), Revolutionary War officer • Organized as Tryon County 1772 (prior to statehood) from Albany County; name changed 1784 • Actor Kirk Douglas. Political cartoonist Bernhard Gillam died here. • Dairying; diversified manufacturing, including carpets, electronic equipment, toys • Auriesville is the site of the shrine, Our Lady of Martyrs, which honors the first Roman Catholic martyr saints of the continent. The Schoharie Crossing State Historic Site includes a seven-arched aqueduct constructed in 1842 to carry the water of the Erie Canal over a transverse stream.

NASSAU (one of two counties so named, the other in FL) *Mineola* • 1,334,544 (the fifth most populated county in NY) • 287 • Southeastern NY, on western Long Island, bounded on the south by the Atlantic Ocean and on the north by Long Island Sound. The county is immediately east of New York City (Queens borough and county). It is chiefly residential with a number of shopping centers. Its northern shore is deeply indented; the south shore has bays and marshy islands, sheltered from the Atlantic Ocean by resort barrier beaches. Jones Beach State Park is one of several state parks. • Named for the family name of King William III (1650–1702), derived from the name of a former duchy in Germany • 1898 from Queens • The Presbyterian Society of Hempstead, the oldest such organization in the U.S. was formed here in 1644. Founded in 1869 by Alexander T. Stewart, Garden City was one of the nation's first planned communities. The first airmail flight to Washington, D.C. left from the Belmont Park racetrack on May 15, 1918. Charles A. Lindbergh took off from Roosevelt Field on his historic flight to Paris in 1927. Port Washington, an early seaplane base, was embarkation point for the Pan American Dixie Clipper, one of the world's first transatlantic passenger planes, which left for France on June 28, 1939. Lake Success was the temporary headquarters of the United Nations from 1946 to 1951. Levittown, one of the first planned communities in the U.S. to provide housing for World War II veterans, completed the last of its 17,447 private homes on November 20, 1951; the community became a national symbol for the post World War II building boom. • Astronomer Henry Norris Russell; President Theodore Roosevelt (his summer White House from 1901 to 1908, Sagamore Hill, is in Oyster Bay); Canadian poet Robert Finch; corporation executive Louis Gerstner; historian Doris Kearns Goodwin; writers Thomas Pynchon, Louis Auchincloss, and F. Scott Fitzgerald; poet William Cullen Bryant; entertainer-composers George M. Cohan and John Philip Sousa; finanacier and railroad magnate Edward H. Harriman. Corporation executive Walter P. Chrysler, crime boss Carlo Gambino, painter and

sculptor Max Weber, and Chilean poet Gabriela Mistral died here. • Vestigial shellfishing and agriculture; nurseries, greenhouse horticultural crops; diversified manufacturing, including office supplies, wood products, clothing, electronic devices, plastics, aircraft and space vehicles, scientific instruments, photographic equipment, marine supplies, machinery; printing and publishing; education (Hofstra U.; Adelphi U., Long Island U., C.W. Post Campus) • The headquarters of four Fortune 1000 corporations are located in the county. The Robert Bacon Memorial Children's Library in Westbury is the only independent children's library in the U.S. Uniondale is home to the New York Islanders (Nassau Veterans Memorial Coliseum).

NEW YORK • 1,537,195 (the third most populated county in NY and seventeenth most populated county in the U.S.) • 28 (the smallest county in NY; only three U.S. counties are smaller) • Southeastern NY, coterminous with the New York City borough of Manhattan, each of the city's five boroughs having county status. • Named for King James II, Duke of York and Albany (1633–1701) • Original county, organized 1683 • The area that would become Manhattan was settled by the Dutch in the 1620s. It is here that the trial of John Peter Zenger was held in 1735, the Stamp Act Congress convened in 1765, George Washington took the oath as the first president of the U.S., and the Bill of Rights was adopted in 1789. New York County was the site of the temporary capital of the U.S. from January, 1785 through August, 1790. Thousands of immigrants arrived in Manhattan during the Tammany machine-controlled 1800s, making it one of the most ethnically diverse counties in the U.S. One of the bloodiest riots in U.S. history took place here from July 12 to July 15, 1863 in protest against the first U.S. draft lottery, resulting in as many as 2,000 casualties. Manhattan was the site of the most devastating component of the terrorist attacks on the U.S. on September 11, 2001, through the bombing by hijacked commercial airliners of the twin towers of the World Trade Center. • A list of its famous residents would be far too lengthy to include here. A sampling of the eclectic mix of those who spent their last years here: explorer John C. Frémont; inventor Robert Fulton; financier Jay Gould; editor and politician Horace Greeley; folk composer Woody Guthrie; American Revolutionary hero Nathan Hale; presidents James Monroe, Herbert Hoover, and Richard M. Nixon; ragtime composer Scott Joplin; sculptor and designer Isamu Noguchi; short story writer O. Henry; writer Ayn Rand; Polish statesman Ignacy Paderewski; political pamphleteer Thomas Paine; first lady Eleanor Roosevelt; baseball player Babe Ruth; U.S. secretary of the treasury Alexander Hamilton; poet Dylan Thomas; architect Stanford White; film actor Rudolph Valentino; singer and songwriter John Lennon. President Theodore Roosevelt was born here. President Ulysses S. Grant is buried here (Grant's Tomb, a former tourist destination). • As the heart and nerve center of New York City, Manhattan is one of the world's most important centers for business, culture, trade, and, as the site of the United Nations, world diplomacy. The county is a major finance, publishing, advertising, and insurance center; a theatre and arts mecca (the Metropolitan Museum of Art has one of the largest collections of any U.S. museum), and the garment capital of the U.S. Institutions of higher education here include New York University and Columbia University. The New York Public Library is among the largest research libraries in the world. • The corporate headquarters of sixty-five Fortune 1000 companies are located in the county. Hundreds of architectural landmarks make its skyline the most recognizable in the nation. Among them, the Empire State Building stands tallest. The county is also home to the preeminent Lincoln Center for the Performing Arts, home of the Metropolitan Opera and the New York Philharmonic; Rockefeller Center; the Museum of Modern Art; the American Museum of Natural History, and Central Park, a model of urban park design. With a seating capacity of 5,900, Radio City Music Hall is the world's largest indoor theatre. The New York Knicks and Rangers play at Madison Square Garden.

NIAGARA *Lockport* • 219,846 • 523 • Western NY, bounded on the west by the Canadian province of Ontario (formed by the Niagara River), on the north by Lake Ontario, and on the south by Tonawanda Creek; crossed by the Erie Canal. The county includes the Niagara Falls resort area. Tuscarora Indian Reservation is here. Several state parks are located along the Lake Ontario shoreline. • Named for the Niagara River • 1808 from Genesee • Niagara Falls was mapped by the French as early as 1612, using descriptions from Indians living in the region. The British refused to evacuate Fort Niagara (state historic site) at the close of the Revolutionary War; it was not turned over to the U.S. until 1796. The county suffered destruction by the British during the War of 1812. Development of the Niagara River's hydroelectric potential (ultimately, one of the greatest concentrations of hydroelectric power in the world) began in 1881; within a few years the city's industrial future was assured, its hydroelectric plants now supplying power to much of the state. The Falls View Bridge collapsed in 1938. • Feminist lawyer Belva Ann Lockwood; paleontologist Othniel C. Marsh; novelist and short story writer Joyce Carol Oates; financier John Jakob Raskob; domestic terrorist Timothy McVeigh • The county is a major fruit grower. The Niagara grape and peach originated here. For over a half century the county has been the leading apple producer in the East. Also, dairy products; manufacture of chemicals, abrasives, electronic, electrochemical, and electrometallic products, automobile radiators, air conditioners, alloy steel products, paper and plastic products, chemicals, textiles, flour, canned goods, aircraft equipment, aerospace components, paints, furniture, musical instruments; mining of wollastonite, limestone and sandstone quarrying; oil refining; education (Niagara U.); tourism (visitors to the falls have included thousands of honeymooning couples over the years). • An enlargement of the Erie Canal system at Lockport resulted in one of the widest bridges in the world (409 feet).

ONEIDA (one of three counties so named) *Utica* • 235,469 • 1,213 • Central NY, bounded on the west in part by Oneida Lake; drained by the Mohawk and Black rivers, and by Oneida, Oriskany, and West Canada creeks. The Adirondack Mountains cross in the northeast. The county is traversed by the Erie Canal. It has a number of recreational facilities on its Adirondack lakes. State parks include Verona Beach, Delta Lake, and Pixley Falls. • One of two counties (the other in WI) named for the Oneida Indian tribe • 1798 from Herkimer • Fort Stanwix (national monument) was the site of the treaty of Fort Stanwix with the Iroquois, signed on November 5, 1768. The stand taken by American forces here in the Battle of Oriskany on August 6, 1777 played a large role in repulsing the British invasion from Canada. The completion of the Erie Canal through the county, created an embarkation point here for settlers moving west. Utica, its name drawn from a hat, was an early textile center. F.W. Woolworth opened his first store here in 1879, selling only five-cent merchandise. • Agricultural research chemist Stephen Babcock; geologist James D. Dana; painter and printmaker Arthur B. Davies; camera manufacturer George Eastman; journalist Harold Frederic, botanist Asa Gray; U.S. Supreme Court justice Ward Hunt; portraitist Henry Inman; missionary Gerrit P. Judd; U.S. vice president James Sherman; reformer and philanthropist Gerrit Smith. Founder of U.S. Methodism Philip Embury died here. • Extensive manufacturing, including a variety of industrial wire products, fishing tackle, silverware, ornamental ironwork, tools and dies, road graders, vacuum cleaners, air conditioners, radiators, baskets, furniture, wood products, electronic equipment; livestock, dairying and truck farming; limestone quarries, lime and lime products; education (Hamilton College; Utica College of Syracuse U.; S.U.N.Y. Institute of Tech. at Utica/Rome) • Rome was once known as the "Copper City" for its manufacture of brass, wire, cable and other copper-related products. Utica's annual Eisteddfod festival is sponsored by its citizens of Welsh descent.

ONONDAGA *Syracuse* • 458,336 • 780 • Central NY; in the Finger Lakes region of the state, bounded on the northeast by Oneida Lake; drained by the Seneca and Oswego rivers, and Onondaga and Chittenango creeks; crossed by the Erie Canal. Clark Reservation State Park and Labrador Hollow State Unique Area are here. There are resorts on Oneida and Skaneateles lakes. The county includes Onondaga Indian Reservation. • Named for the Onondaga Indian tribe, one of the Five Nations of the Iroquois • 1794 • The area of the county that would become Syracuse comprised the first territory of the Onondaga Indians and headquarters of the Iroquois League. It was visited by explorers Samuel de Champlain in 1615 and Pierre Esprit Radisson in 1651. Its brine springs became the basis of the county's prosperous salt industry, which, until 1870, supplied most of the country's salt needs. • Businessman William G. Fargo; women's rights advocate Matilda Joslyn Gage; architect Irving John Gill; Roman Catholic priest and educator Theodore M. Hesburgh; Jewish leader Louis Marshall; presidential candidate Horatio Seymour; novelist and banker Edward Noyes Westcott; inventor Sigurd Varian; painter Bradley W. Tomlin; actor Tom Cruise. Civil engineer James Geddes and furniture designer Gustav Stickley died here. • Poultry, corn, potatoes, hay, dairying; manufacture of chinaware, pharmaceuticals, jet engines, electrical machinery, air conditioners, radio, television and electronic equipment; education (Syracuse U.; Le Moyne College; S.U.N.Y. College of Environmental Science and Forestry) Syracuse has been the site of the New York State Fair since 1851.

ONTARIO *Canandaigua* • 100,224 • 644 • West-central NY, in the Finger Lakes region, bounded in part on the east by Seneca Lake; drained by Honeoye, Mud, and Flint creeks, and Canandaigua Outlet. The county includes Canandaigua Lake and Harriet Hollister Spencer State Recreation Area. Bristol Mountain and Hunt Hollow ski areas are also here. • Named for Lake Ontario • 1789 from Montgomery • The Pickering Treaty with the Six Nations of the Iroquois was signed in Canandaigua in 1794. • Author John Bigelow; clergyman Charles E. Cheney; painter Arthur G. Dove; financier Henry M. Flagler; prominent radical and editor Max Eastman; publisher Frank E. Gannett; novelist Joseph Kirkland; zoologist Raymond Pearl; research scientist Ralph W. G. Wycoff. Mormon Church founder Joseph Smith is said to have unearthed the Golden Plates from which he translated the *Book of Mormon* at Hill Cumorah in 1827. In 1849, Elizabeth Blackwell, the first woman physician of modern times, graduated from Geneva Medical College. • Fruit, nurseries, grain, hay, potatoes, dairy products, poultry; diversified manufacturing, including food processing, machinery, steel castings, electronic components, corrugated cartons, fishing tackle, baby furniture, underwear, wines; education (Hobart and William Smith Colleges).

ORANGE (one of eight counties so named) *Goshen* • 341,367 • 816 • Southeastern NY, bounded on the east by the Hudson River, on the southwest by the NJ and PA state lines and the Delaware River; drained by the small Wallkill and Ramapo rivers and by Shawangunk Kill. The county includes parts of the Hudson highlands, the Ramapos, and the Shawangunk range. It shares Harriman and Bear Mountain state parks with Rockland. Other state parks include Goosepond Mountain and Highland Lakes. The Appalachian Trail crosses the county in the southeast. Once an important dairying region, it is now largely suburban. • Named for King William III (1650–1702), titled Prince of Orange • Original county; organized 1683 • It was in the once thriving whaling port and factory town of Newburgh that George Washington spent the last six months of the Revolutionary War and where he announced the end of hostilities on April 19, 1783. • Statesman DeWitt Clinton; U.S. vice president George Clinton; U.S. vice presidential candidate Geraldine Ferraro; "Jesus Loves Me" hymn-writer Anna Warner; painter George Inness; capitalist and railroad promoter David H. Moffat; novelist Gore Vidal. Graduates of the U.S. Military Academy at West Point include a pantheon of

familiar American generals, and military misfits James Whistler and Edgar Allen Poe. Noah Webster taught school in Goshen; William H. Seward studied here. • The county's onion crop is the most successful in the state. Also, fruit, hay, poultry; education (Mount Saint Mary College) • Orange County is second only to the Everglades in its concentration of highly fertile "muck," left here by glacial lakes 10,000 years before. The Storm King Arts Center celebrates the work of nearly every major post-World War II sculptor. Sterling Forest is the site of the popular New York Renaissance Festival. The county is also the birthplace of the tuxedo, first introduced in the exclusive community of Tuxedo Park. Goshen, once a major dairy center, is best known for being the "Cradle of the Trotter" and former home to the most important harness-racing track in the country. Behind the town's Harness Racing Museum and Hall of Fame is the Historic Track, the only sports facility to be named a National Historic Landmark.

ORLEANS (one of three counties so named) *Albion* • 44,171 • 391 • Western NY, bounded on the north by Lake Ontario; crossed by the Erie Canal and drained by Oak Orchard Creek. The county includes Iroquois National Wildlife Refuge on its southern border. Also here are Lakeside Beach State Park and Oak Orchard State Marine Park. • Named for either the royal French house of Orleans or for the French city of Orleans • 1824 from Genesee • Naturalist and explorer Carl Akeley • Diversified manufacturing; vegetables, fruit, dairying.

OSWEGO *Oswego* • 122,377 • 953 • North-central NY, bounded on the northwest by Lake Ontario, on the south by Oneida Lake and the Oneida River; drained by the Oswego and Salmon rivers; crossed by the Erie Canal. Selkirk Shores and Battle Island state parks, and Chateaugay State Forest are all found here. • Named for the Oswego River • 1816 from Oneida and Onondaga • Oswego was visited by Samuel de Champlain about 1616. The surrounding area was settled by the Jesuits about 1654. The area around Oswego River Falls in Fulton, described in several novels by James Fenimore Cooper, was a strategic theatre in the French and Indian War. Forts Oswego and Ontario played roles in the war. The latter, ceded to the U.S. by the British in 1796, was recaptured in the War of 1812. The county benefited commercially for several decades following the opening of the Oswego Canal in 1828. The city became the northern terminus of the Erie (NY State Barge Canal) system in 1917, and a world port with the opening of the St. Lawrence Seaway in 1959, serving as transfer point for shipments by lake, canal, and railroad. • Poet and novelist Henry C. Bunner; geologist and scientific explorer Raphael W. Pumpelly • Dairying, strawberries, hay, potatoes, lettuce, poultry; limited shipping of building cement, fuel oil and limestone; manufacture of frozen food, chocolate candy, cork, plastics, waxed cardboard containers, milk bottle caps, paper mill machinery, textiles, marine engines, clothing, aluminum, copper wire, sheet metals; tourism; education (S.U.N.Y. College at Oswego). The county's major power installations make it an important source of electricity generation for upstate NY. • Oswego is the easternmost U.S. port on the Great Lakes.

OTSEGO (one of two counties so named, the other in MI) *Cooperstown* • 61,676 • 1,003 • Central NY, bounded on the west by the Unadilla River; drained by the Susquehanna River, which issues here from Otsego Lake. Canadarago and Otsego lakes here are the easternmost of the Finger Lakes. Glimmerglass and Gilbert Lake state parks and several state forests are located here. The county is seasonal home to many downstate residents. • Probably named for Otsego Lake • 1791 from Montgomery • A caboose in Oneonta, an historically important railroad center, was the site of the organization of the Brotherhood of Railroad Trainmen in 1883. • Reputed inventor of baseball Abner Doubleday; confirmed inventor of the carpet sweeper Melville R. Bissell; railroad magnate and collector of rare books Henry Huntington; novelist James Fenimore Cooper, who made the county the scene of his *Leatherstocking Tales*. (Otsego Lake is the "Glimmerglass" of his novels.) • Diversified manufacturing, including electronic components, plastics, and clothing; substantial dairying, with livestock, grain, hay; education (Hartwick College; S.U.N.Y. College at Oneonta • The county is home to both the National Baseball Hall of Fame and Museum (in Cooperstown) and the National Soccer Hall of Fame (in Oneonta). Each year an exhibition baseball game is played as part of festivities surrounding the induction of new members into the baseball pantheon. • The Alice Busch Opera Theatre in Cooperstown is home to the Glimmerglass Opera.

PUTNAM (one of nine counties so named) *Carmel* • 95,745 • 232 • Southeastern NY, bounded on the west by the Hudson River and on the east by the CT state line. The county is located in a hilly region with many lakes and New York City water supply reservoirs of the Croton River system. It includes part of the Taconic Mountains, meeting the highlands of the Hudson River here. It is both agricultural and suburban. Clarence Fahnestock State Park has skiing facilities. Several multiple use and unique areas are in the county. • One of eight counties definitively named for Israel Putnam (1718–90), MA general and American commander at the Battle of Bunker Hill • 1812 from Dutchess • Charcoal from trees in the county fired foundries that produced the Parrot guns, locomotives and machinery used by the Union army in the Civil War. Gail Borden began producing condensed milk in Brewster in the 1850s • Railway financier Daniel Drew; hymn writer Fanny Crosby; detective fiction author Rex Stout; jurist James Kent. Inventor Robert P. Parrott died here. • Dairying, poultry; light manufacturing.

QUEENS • 2,229,379 (the second most populated county in NY and the ninth most populated county in the U.S.) • 109 (one of the fifty smallest counties in the U.S.) • Southeastern NY, on Long Island. The county is coterminous with the New York City borough of Queens, each of the city's five boroughs having county status. It is mostly residential except for manufacturing around Long Island City and shipping facilities lining the East River, which bounds the county on the west. New York City's John F. Kennedy International and La Guardia airports are in the county. Queens shares the Gateway National Recreation Area and Jamaica Bay Wildlife Refuge with Kings County • Named for Queen Catharine of Braganza (1638–1705), wife of King Charles II of England • Original county; organized 1683 • The first settlement here was made by the Dutch in 1636 near Flushing Bay. The American motion picture industry spent several years of its infancy here. The Flushing section of Queens was the site of the 1939–40 and 1964–65 New York world's fairs. In 1978, Flushing Meadow-Corona Park became the site of the U.S. Tennis Association's National Tennis Center. • Public speaker pioneer Dale Carnegie; secretary of the treasury Albert Gallatin; discus thrower Al Oerter; financier Carl Icahn; politician Mario Cuomo; politician Geraldine Ferraro; columnist and author Jimmy Breslin; fashion designer Donna Karan; trumpeter Louis Armstrong; baseball player Jackie Robinson; humorist Will Rogers; writer Jack Kerouac; architectural critic Lewis Mumford; film director Martin Scorsese. Helen Keller's teacher Anne Sullivan Macy died here. • Diversified manufacturing; education (several branches of City University of NY; St. John's University) • Queens is perhaps the most ethnically diverse county in the U.S.; it has been said that a regular rider on the county's No. 7 subway train will in short time see a native of every nation on earth. Queens is home to the New York Mets (Shea Stadium).

RENSSELAER *Troy* • 152,538 • 654 • Eastern NY, bounded on the west by the Hudson River, on the east by the MA and VT state lines; drained by the Hoosic River. Part of the Taconic Mountains are in the east. Tomhannock Reservoir is here, as are several small (resort) lakes. Tibbitts State Forest, and Grafton Lakes and Cherry Plain state parks are also in the county. • Named for the van Rensselaer family and their large patroonship here • 1791 from Albany • The county was settled by the Dutch in the 17th century; the most successful patroonships under Kiliaen van Rensselaer were here. Fort Crailo, built about 1642 to protect settlers from the Indians, was reputedly where Dr. Richard Schuckburgh composed "Yankee Doodle." Bennington Battlefield State Historic Site marks the spot of the successful capture of Burgoyne's raiding party on Aug. 16, 1777. During the War of 1812, large contracts for U.S. Army beef were filled by "Uncle Sam" Wilson of Troy, whose name evolved into the popular symbol of the United States. Troy was an early iron and steel center. The Vital Burden Iron Works made the iron plate for the Union's ironclad warship *Monitor* during the Civil War. • Folk painter Grandma Moses; financier and philanthropist George F. Baker; businessman and banker Charles Crocker; dramatist James A. Herne; inventor Isaac Merrit Singer • Dairying, hay, sweet corn, cauliflower, tomatoes, strawberries, apples, potatoes, poultry; manufacture of textiles, chemicals, dyes, leather goods, clothing; auto, electrical and aircraft engineering industries; education (Rensselaer Polytechnic Institute; Russell Sage College).

RICHMOND (one of four counties so named) • 443,728 (17% increase since 1990; the fastest growing county in NY) • 59 (one of the fifty smallest counties in the U.S.) • The county is coterminous with the New York City borough of Staten Island, each of the city's five boroughs having county status. It is the southernmost county in the state. • Named for Charles Lennox (1672–1723), first Duke of Richmond, son of King Charles II of England • Original county; organized 1683 • Settled by the Dutch in the 1660s, the county was a military camp for the British during the Revolutionary War. The only conference to discuss reconciliation and negotiate an end to hostilities took place on September 11, 1776 in the Village of Tottenville and ended in failure; participants included British Vice-Admiral Lord Richard Howe and American delegates Benjamin Franklin, John Adams, and Edward Rutledge. Richmond was largely agricultural until the completion of the Verrazano-Narrows bridge which linked it to Brooklyn (Kings County) in 1964. • Photographer Alice Austin; the Vanderbilt family, including shipping and railroad magnate Cornelius Vanderbilt; ballet choreographer Gerald Arpino; folk singer Joan Baez. Photographer Timothy H. O'Sullivan and U.S. vice president Daniel D. Tompkins died here. The county was home to generations of Mafia bosses. • Diversified manufacturing; shipbuilding; oil refining; metalworking; education (Wagner College; College of Staten Island) • The county is a twenty-five minute ride to Manhattan on the world-famous Staten Island ferry, a journey taken by over three million Staten Islanders and tourists each year. Voorlezer's House, built in 1695, is the oldest existing elementary school in the U.S.

ROCKLAND *New City* • 286,753 • 174 • Southeastern NY, bounded on the east by the Hudson River (widening here into Tappan Zee), and on the southwest and south by the NJ state line; drained by the Hackensack and Ramapo rivers. The county includes the part of the Ramapo Mountains (at nearly 600 million years of age, one of the oldest land masses in North America) that form the border between Rockland and Orange counties. It contains several state parks, most along the Hudson River. Part of the large Harriman State Park is in the west. Many of its cities and towns are bedroom communities of New York City. • Given this name for its rocky terrain • 1798 from Orange • It was in Tappan that George Washington entrusted Benedict Arnold with West Point, and in that same town that Arnold's colleague in espionage British major John André was imprisoned and later hung. Stony Point, a strongly fortified British post, was stormed and captured by General Anthony Wayne's colonial troops in July, 1779. During World War II, 1.3 million troops passed through Camp Shanks, one of the two largest Army ports of embarkation on the East Coast. (Today the site is occupied by Shanks Village, the largest veterans housing complex in the U.S.) • Artists Joseph Cornell and Edward Hopper; writers Ben Hecht, Carson McCullers, Toni Morrison. Actor Helen Hayes and sociologist Charles Wright Mills died here. • Fruit, dairying, hothouse flowers, vegetables; some manufacturing; education

(Nyack College; Dominican College; St. Thomas Aquinas College) • Rockland has the largest non-urban community in the U.S., Spring Valley.

SAINT LAWRENCE *Canton* • 111,931 • 2,686 (the largest county in NY) • Northern NY, bounded on the northwest by the St. Lawrence River (here forming the border with the Canadian province of Ontario); drained by the St. Regis, Indian, Grass, Oswegatchie, and Raquette rivers, all tributaries of the St. Lawrence. Plains along the St. Lawrence rise to the Adirondacks in the southeast. The county has several state parks located along the St. Lawrence River. Greenwood Creek State Forest is in the south. Black, Carry Falls Reservoir, and Cranberry are its largest lakes. Part of Tupper Lake is in the extreme southeast. The southeastern third of the county is occupied by part of the large Adirondack Park. • Named for the Saint Lawrence River • 1802 from Clinton, Montgomery and Herkimer • Ogdensburg was captured by the British during the War of 1812. In August, 1940, President Franklin D. Roosevelt and Canadian Prime Minister W.L. Mackenzie King issued the Ogdensburg Declaration here, a statement of cooperation between the two nations in defense of the North American continent through the creation of a Permanent Joint Board on Defense. • Painter and sculptor Frederic Remington. (The Remington Art Museum in Ogdensburg contains many of his paintings and bronzes.) • A leading U.S. dairying county. Also, general farming, poultry; timber, saw-timber mills; maple-sugar production; lead, limestone, talc deposits; manufacture of paper, shade rollers, office equipment and supplies, aluminum products (Massena, a major production center), drapery hardware, including aluminum smelting and refining; tourism; education (Clarkson U.; S.U.N.Y. College at Potsdam; St. Lawrence U.; Wadhams Hall Seminary College) • The St. Lawrence Seaway Development Corporation Headquarters is located in Massena. The city is the focal point of several Seaway power projects. The Custom House in Ogdensburg (1809–10) was officially designated in 1964 as the oldest U.S. federal government building. Geologists have given the name Potsdamian to Late Cambrian and Early Ordovician rock formations in acknowledgement of the reddish sandstone deposits once quarried here.

SARATOGA *Ballston Spa* • 200,635 • 812 • Eastern NY, bounded on the north in part and on the east by the Hudson River, and on the south by the Mohawk River. The county lies partly in the southern Adirondacks and includes Saratoga National Historic Park and Cemetery, Saratoga Springs State Park, Saratoga Lake, and part of Sacandaga Lake. • The name of the county is of Indian origin, possibly stemming from a Mohawk word meaning "springs from the hillside," or from the Iroquois for "beaver place" • 1791 from Albany • The second battle of Saratoga, fought on October 7, 1777, was a turning point for American forces in the American Revolution (national historic park). The beneficial mineral waters of Saratoga Springs have made the area a health resort since the late eighteenth century. Horse racing began here about 1850, and for many years it was one of the most important thoroughbred racing venues in the U.S. (The National Museum of Racing attests to the city's role in the history of the sport.) • Reputed inventor of baseball Abner Doubleday; playwright Howard Lindsay. President Ulysses S. Grant died here (state historic site). • Dairying, corn, hay, poultry, livestock; manufacture of textiles, electronic components, packaging, plastics, humidifiers, precision instruments, hosiery, yarn, cider and vinegar, mobile homes, wallpaper; education (S.U.N.Y. Empire State College; Skidmore College) • "Yaddo" in Saratoga Springs has been a high-profile retreat for authors and painters since 1926.

SCHENECTADY *Schenectady* • 146,555 • 206 • Eastern NY, bounded on the west by Schoharie Creek; intersected by the Mohawk River (forming part of the eastern boundary) and the Erie Canal. Featherstonhaugh State Forest is here. • Named for the city, itself a Mohawk word meaning "on the other side of the pinelands" • 1809 from Albany • In 1690, the village of Schenectady was virtually destroyed by French and Indians in what became known as the Schenectady Massacre. The establishment of a locomotive works in 1848 and the creation of the General Electric Company here in 1892 led to the slogan, "The city that lights and hauls the world." • Engineer and physical chemist William D. Coolidge; research chemist and meteorologist Vincent Joseph Schaefer. Electrical engineer and television pioneer Ernest F. W. Alexanderson died here. • Dairying, fruits, general farming; manufacture of electrical equipment, sporting goods, wire and cable equipment, chemicals; research; education (Union College).

SCHOHARIE *Schoharie* • 31,582 • 622 • East-central NY; drained by Schoharie Creek and its tributaries, and by Catskill Creek. Recreational facilities and summer homes abound here. There are also several caverns. Max V. Shaul and Mine Kill state parks and Leonard Hill, the Petersburg, and Mount Pisgah state forests are also found in the county. Part of Schoharie Reservoir is on the southern boundary. • Named for the town of Schoharie • 1795 from Albany and Otsego • Dairying, hay, fruit, potatoes, poultry.

SCHUYLER *Watkins Glen* • 19,224 • 329 • South-central NY, in the Finger Lakes region; drained by Cauta and Catherine creeks. The county claims the southern end of Seneca Lake. Watkins Glen State Park, with its scenic waterfalls and gorges, is also here, along with Finger Lakes National Forest. Sugar Hill State Forest is in the southwest. • One of three counties named for General Philip J. Schuyler (1733–1804), an officer in the Revolutionary War, NY legislator, and one of New York's first two U.S. senators • 1854 from Tompkins, Steuben and Chemung • Nurse and educator Jane A. Delano. Inventor Harvey Haywood died here. • Fruit, grain, poultry, livestock, hay, dairy products; diversified manufacturing; salt production • The county was once home to the Watkins Glen Grand Prix automobile race, an annual event until 1981, when the International Auto Sport Federation removed the race from its schedule.

SENECA *Waterloo* • 33,342 • 325 • West-central NY, in the Finger Lakes region, bounded on the east by Cayuga Lake and the Seneca River and on the west in part by Seneca Lake; crossed by the Erie Canal in the northeast. The county includes Montezuma National Wildlife Refuge, and Seneca Lake, Sampson, Cayuga Lake, and Lodi Point state parks. • One of two counties (the other in OH) named for the Seneca native tribe • 1804 from Cayuga • The Seneca Falls Convention for women's rights was held here in 1848 and launched the woman suffrage movement in the U.S. (Women's Rights National Historical Park) • Architect Louise Blanchard Bethune; suffragist Harriot Stanton Blatch; astrophysicist I.S. Bowen; activist Amelia Jenks Bloomer; feminist and abolitionist Elizabeth Cady Stanton • Dairying, fruit, wheat, potatoes, hay, beans; diversified manufacturing, including machinery, electrical and electronic equipment, textiles; tourism • The Women's Hall of Fame is in Seneca Falls.

STEUBEN *Bath* • 98,726 • 1,393 • Southern NY, bounded on the south by the PA state line; drained by the Canisteo, Cohocton, Tioga, and Chemung rivers. The county extends north into the Finger Lakes region and includes part of Keuka Lake. Stony Brook and Pinnacle state parks, and Pigtail Hollow and Birdseye Hollow state forests are here. • One of two counties (the other in IN) named for Baron Friedrich Wilhelm von Steuben (1730–94), Prussian soldier and inspector general of the Continental Army during the American Revolution • 1796 from Ontario • More than 2,000 homes were destroyed in June, 1972 when floodwaters rushed through Corning. • Birth-control movement founder Margaret Sanger; industrialist Thomas J. Watson • Dairying, potatoes, vegetables, grapes, grain, hay; manufacture of flat aerospace products, astronaut suit fabrics, hosiery, ball bearings, ladders, bus bodies, corrugated pipe, wood trimmings, dresses, gloves, home wares, foundry products, air compressors, glass bulbs, tubing, fiber optics (the Corning Glass Works, a leading manufacturer of technical glass, has operated in Corning since 1868); timber; sand and gravel pits • The historical collection of glass at the Corning Glass Center includes the original 200-inch imperfect telescope disk cast in 1934 for the Palomar Observatory in CA. The Museum of Glass displays glass from the ages.

SUFFOLK *Riverhead* • 1,419,369 (the fourth most populated county in NY and the twenty-second most populated county in the U.S.) • 911 • Southeastern NY, on central and eastern Long Island, bounded on the south by the Atlantic Ocean, on the east by Block Island Sound, on the north by Long Island Sound. The county has a number of bays and inlets; the largest is Great Peconic Bay, in the east. It is largely a residential and summer-resort region, with large estates and colorful antique villages. State parks abound throughout the county. • One of two counties (the other in MA) named for Suffolk County in England • Original county; organized 1683 • Patriot-spy Nathan Hale was captured by the British at Huntington Bay. Many of the county's coastal cities were whaling centers from

1785 to 1850, Sag Harbor one of the most active. In 1900–01, Guglielmo Marconi erected the first wireless station in the U.S. at Babylon village. In 1918, Lawrence Sperry experimented with early guided missiles at Amityville. • Poet Walt Whitman; writer Ring Lardner. Painters Jackson Pollock & Willem de Kooning, comic-novelist Sir. P.G. Wodehouse, and advertising designer and photographer Herbert Matter died here. American's first black poet, Jupiter Hammon, was a slave of the Lloyd family in Huntington. • Wineries; manufacture of boats, electrical goods, metal products, electronic instruments, airplane parts, machinery, clothing; a vestigial duck-raising industry; research (Brookhaven National Laboratory); sport and commercial fishing (including shell fish); education (Five Towns College; St. Joseph's College; Stony Brook University S.U.N.Y.; Long Island U., Southampton College) • The headquarters of four Fortune 1000 corporations are located here. The world's largest colony of ospreys are found on Gardiner's Island. The house made famous by John Howard Payne in his "Home, Sweet Home" is maintained by the village of East Hampton. The state's oldest English saltbox house, Halsey Homestead (1648–49), stands in Southampton. Stony Brook's Carriage House Museum has a collection of more than 300-horse-drawn vehicles.

SULLIVAN (one of six counties so named) *Monticello* • 73,966 • 970 • Southeastern NY, bounded on the west and southwest by the Delaware River (here forming the PA state line); drained by the Neversink River, Shawangunk, Beaverkill, and Willowemoc Creek. The county includes parts of the Catskills and Shawangunk ranges, and contains a number of lakes and reservoirs. • One of five counties named directly or indirectly for Gen. John Sullivan (1740–95), Revolutionary War officer, member of the Continental Congress, and president of NH • 1809 from Ulster • The Upper Delaware's only major Revolutionary War battle was fought just west of Barryville on July 22, 1779, after Mohawk chieftain Joseph Brant's Indian and Redcoat alliance burned the settlement of Minisink. The avenging colonial militia was defeated, but heavy casualties were suffered on both sides in what was one of the bloodiest battles of the war. American fly-fishing was developed west of Roscoe where the Willowemoc Creek and Beaverkill meet. (The county's Fly Fishing Center documents its history.) • Methodist layman and evangelist John R. Mott. Bishop Patrick Joseph Hayes died here. • Poultry, dairying; timber; manufacturing; resort tourism • The legendary Woodstock Festival took place near Bethel in August, 1969, and attracted 450,000 rock music devotees. Sullivan County was home to the "Borscht belt" of "mega-resorts" catering to Jewish clientele from New York City, and giving a number of stand up comedians their start. Today the county is a mix of apple farms, ashrams, and Buddhist monasteries. Roebling's Aqueduct is the oldest extant wire suspension bridge in the U.S.

TIOGA *Owego* • 51,784 • 519 • Southern NY, bounded on the south by the PA state line and on the west in part by Cayuta Creek; intersected by the Susquehanna River; drained by Cayuga, Catatonk and Owego creeks. Jenksville State Forest is here. • One of two counties (the other in PA) named for the Tioga River, which no longer flows through the county • 1791 from Montgomery • Politician Thomas C. Platt; industrialist and philanthropist John D. Rockefeller; industrialist and financier William Rockefeller • Dairying, poultry, grain; diversified manufacturing.

TOMPKINS *Ithaca* • 96,501 • 476 • South-central NY. The county includes the southern end of Cayuga Lake. Also here are Taughannock Falls, Robert H. Treman, and Buttermilk Falls state parks, and Allan H. Treman State Marine Park. • Named for Daniel D. Tompkins (1774–1825), associate justice of the NY Supreme Court, governor of NY and U.S. vice president • 1817 from Cayuga and Seneca • Historian Carl Becker, analytical philosopher Max Black, Idealist philosopher James E. Creighton, and physical chemist Peter Debye, all died in the county. • Dairying, grain, fruit, poultry; manufacture of research instruments, shotguns, heat-resistant materials, power drive chains, rayon and cotton underwear, textiles, salt; education (Cornell U.; Ithaca College); tourism • A number of agricultural institutions and agencies, including the NY Artificial Breeders Cooperative and the NY state offices of the Farm Bureau Federation, are in Ithaca. Each August the city hosts the New York State Craft Fair.

ULSTER *Kingston* • 177,749 • 1,127 • Southeastern NY, bounded on the east by the Hudson River; drained by the Wallkill River, and by several creeks. The county lies mainly in the Catskills. It also includes the northern part of the Shawangunk range and part of the highlands of the Hudson River. Minnewaska State Park Preserve is also here. Ashokan Reservoir is an important part of New York City's water supply system. • Named for King James II (1633–1701), titled earl of Ulster • Original county; organized 1683 • After Kingston, the state's first capital and site of the adoption of NY's first constitution, was burned by the British on October 16, 1777, Hurley briefly served as the seat of state government, making the county home to two former state capitals. In the courthouse in Kingston abolitionist and evangelist Sojourner Truth won a lawsuit that saved her son from slavery in AL, the first such case ever won by a black parent. The city was the eastern terminus of the Delaware and Hudson Canal. Saugerties was home to such racing steamers as the *Mary Powell*, the fastest ship on the Hudson River between 1861 and 1885. • Film director Peter Bogdanovich; economist Irving Fisher; painters George Bellows and John Vanderlyn. Printer and typographer Frederic W. Goudy and painters Philip Guston and Yasuo Kuniyoshi died here. • Dairying, fruit, potatoes, poultry; manufacture of computer equipment, machine tools, clothing, furniture; education (S.U.N.Y. at New Paltz); tourism • New Paltz's Huguenot Street is the oldest street in the U.S. with all its original buildings intact to earn National Historic Landmark status. • Woodstock, long a noted artists' colony, gave its name to the music festival that took place in neighboring Sullivan County in 1969 (after residents objected to its being held here).

WARREN *Lake George* • 63,303 • 870 • Eastern NY, in the southern Adirondacks, bounded on the east by Lake George; drained by the Schoon and Hudson rivers (the latter forming part of the southern and southwestern boundary). The county lies entirely within Adirondack Park, a year-round resort region, with lakes, hiking trails and ski resorts. • One of fourteen counties named for Joseph Warren (1741–75), Revolutionary War patriot and member of the Continental Congress who dispatched Paul Revere on his famous ride • 1813 from Washington County • Glens Falls' early industries were built around lumbering, and paper and clothing manufacturing. Author James Fenimore Cooper described the falls here in a graphic scene from his *The Last of the Mohicans* (1826). (Cooper's Cave, where Hawkeye took refuge, is beneath the bridge that links the city with South Glens Falls.) • Agricultural chemist Wilbur O. Atwater; U.S. Chief Justice Charles Evans Hughes; pioneer aviator Floyd Bennett. Clergyman and novelist Edward Eggleston, physician Abraham Jacobi, and social reformer and politician Robert Dale Owen died here. • Tourism; dairying, poultry and livestock; some hay, clover; lumbering; some manufacturing • Glens Falls' Hyde Collection includes notable works of European and American art, including paintings by Picasso, Rembrandt and El Greco.

WASHINGTON *Hudson Falls* • 61,042 • 836 • Eastern NY, bounded on the northwest by Lake Champlain and on the east by the VT state line (partly formed by the southern tip of Lake Champlain and the Mettawee River); drained by Batten Kill, and Poultney, Mettawee, and Hoosic rivers; traversed by the Champlain division of the Erie Canal, which terminates at Whitehall. The Adirondack Mountains and Park, and Whitehall State Heritage Area are in the north. • One of thirty-one counties named for George Washington • Organized as Charlotte 1772 (prior to statehood) from Albany; name changed 1784. • Whitehall is popularly known as the birthplace of the U.S. Navy; ships were constructed here by Benedict Arnold in 1776 to halt the British invasion down Lake Champlain. • Folk painter Grandma Moses • Potatoes, fruit, corn, oats, poultry, dairying; timber; slate, limestone quarries; manufacture of boats, metal products, apparel; railroad shops.

WAYNE (one of sixteen counties so named) *Lyons* • 93,765 • 604 • Western NY, bounded on the north by Lake Ontario; drained by Canandaigua Outlet, the Clyde River and Mud Creek; crossed by the Erie Canal. • One of fifteen counties named for Gen. "Mad Anthony" Wayne (1745–1796), PA soldier in the American Revolution and statesman • 1823 from Ontario and Seneca • Palmyra is closely associated with Joseph Smith, the founder of the Church of Jesus Christ of Latter-Day Saints (the Mormon Church). His first vision supposedly occurred near Sacred Grove in 1823. • Naval officers Bradley Allen Fiske and William T. Sampson; financier and diplomat Myron Taylor • Fruits, including apples, nuts, dairying; diversified manufacturing, including paper boxes, feed, and the processing of vinegar and sauerkraut.

WESTCHESTER *White Plains* • 923,459 • 433 • Southeastern NY, bounded on the west by the Hudson River (here widening into the Tappan Zee), on the southeast by the Long Island Sound and the CT state line, and on the east by the CT state line; drained by the Byram, Mianus, and Rippowam rivers. The county is both urban and affluently suburban, a bedroom county for New York City directly south. It contains Kensico Reservoir in the Bronx River, reservoirs of the Croton River water supply system (which supplies water to New York City), and several lakes. • Named for the former township of Westchester, NY • Original county; organized 1683 • Publisher John Peter Zenger's acquittal in a libel suit in Mount Vernon in 1735 was the first major victory for the principle of freedom of the press in the American colonies. During the American Revolution, allegiances in the county were divided between Americans and British. In the Battle of White Plains in October 1776, General George Washington outmaneuvered the British general Lord Howe. The British spy Major John André was captured in Tarrytown in 1780. Elisha Otis introduced the first "perpendicular stairway" in Yonkers in 1853. • Railroad lawyer and politician Chauncey Depew; First Lady Barbara Bush; playwright Robert E. Sherwood; author James Fenimore Cooper; painters Jasper Francis Cropsey and Albert Bierstadt; first African American millionaire Madame C.J. Walker; financier Jay Gould; philanthropist John D. Rockefeller; general John C. Frémont, financier Cyrus Field; revolutionary author Thomas Paine; U.S. vice president Daniel D. Tompkins; actors Sid Caesar and Mel Gibson. Feminist leader Carrie Chapman Catt, Protestant minister Harry E. Fosdick, and photographer Lewis W. Hine died here. Julius and Ethel Rosenburg were executed at Sing Sing State Prison in Ossining. Washington Irving wrote of the county in his *Sketch Book*. His *The Legend of Sleepy Hollow* was inspired by a Tarrytown tale. Irving, and philanthropists Andrew Carnegie and William Rockefeller are buried in Sleepy Hollow Cemetery. • Apples, pears; manufacture of machinery, electronic and electrical equipment, chemicals, clothing, furniture, plumbing supplies, pharmaceuticals, surgical instruments; education (Marymont College; Mercy College; Concordia College; Sarah Lawrence College; College of New Rochelle; Iona College; State U. of NY at Purchase; and others) • Since 1950 a number of major domestic and multinational corporations have established their headquarters in the county, including eight Fortune 1000 companies. The Union Church in Pocantico Hills contains nine stained glass windows by Marc Chagall and a rose window by Henri Mattise (his final work).

WYOMING (one of three counties so named) *Warsaw* • 43,424 • 593 • Western NY; drained by the Genessee River (forming the southeastern boundary), and Tonawanda and Cattaraugus creeks. The county includes part of Letchworth State Park on the southeastern boundary. Silver Lake State Park is also in the county. • Wyoming is an Indian word meaning "on the broad plain" • 1841 from Genesee • Attica State Correctional Facility was the scene of a prison riot from September 9 to 13, 1971, which led to deaths of forty-three people when some 1,500 state police and other law enforcement officers staged an air and ground assault on the hostage-taking inmates. • Canadian fur trader and explorer Simon Fraser; ichthyologist David Starr Jordan • Dairying, vegetables, grain, fruit; diversified manufacturing.

YATES *Penn Yan* • 24,621 • 338 • West-central NY, situated in the Finger Lakes region, bounded on the east by Seneca Lake; drained by Flint Creek. The county includes parts of Keuka Lake (and state park) on the southern boundary and Canandaiga Lake on the western boundary. • Named for Joseph C. Yates (1768–1837), NY Supreme Court justice and governor of the state at the time of the county's creation • 1823 from Ontario • In 1789, the first wheat crop was raised here and for a time the county sat in the nation's primary wheat-growing region. • Inventor John Wesley Hyatt • Grapes, fruit, wheat, potatoes, hay, dry beans; diversified manufacturing; education (Keuka College).

NORTH CAROLINA

To Be Rather Than to Seem

Each of North Carolina's 100 counties is governed by a board of county commissioners consisting of from three to seven members. Other county officials include the sheriff, register of deeds, county manager, superior court clerk, attorney, finance officer, and tax officials.

ALAMANCE *Graham* • 130,800 • 431 • North-central NC, in the Piedmont; drained and bounded in part on the southeast by the Haw River. Burlington Reservoir is in the north. • Named for the Battle of Alamance • 1849 from Orange • Alamance Battleground State Historic Site commemorates the defeat of the Regulators, a group of dissident colonists, on May 6, 1771 by militia dispatched by the royal governor. • Physician and surgeon Charles R. Drew died here. • Tobacco, grain, dairying; manufacture of furniture, textiles, electronic equipment, chemicals; education (Elon College).

ALEXANDER (one of two counties so named, the other in IL) *Taylorsville* • 33,603 • 260 • West-central NC, in the Piedmont, bounded on the south by the Catawba River (which forms Lookout Shoals reservoir in the southeast and Lake Hickory reservoir in the southwest); drained by the South Fork of the Yadkin River and Fourth Creek. • Probably named for William J. Alexander (1797–1857), NC legislator • 1847 from Iredell, Caldwell and Wilkes • Tobacco, corn, grain, hay, fruit; manufacture of textiles, furniture, electronics; lumber (pine) and sawmilling.

ALLEGHANY (one of two counties named Alleghany, the other in VA; one of five counties named Alleghany with variant spellings) *Sparta* • 10,677 • 235 • Northwestern NC, bounded on the north by the VA state line, and in part on the northwest by the New River (designated a National Scenic River); drained by the North Fork of the New River. The county is in the Blue Ridge Mountains; Blue Ridge (national) Parkway passes along its southern and eastern boundaries. Part of Stone Mountain State Park is located here. • Named for either the Alleghany or the Allegheny River • 1859 from Ashe • Corn, barley, hay, tobacco, poultry, dairying, cattle.

ANSON *Wadesboro* • 25,275 • 532 • Southern NC, bounded on the south by the SC state line, on the east by the Pee Dee River (which forms Blewett Falls Lake reservoir in the northeast), on the north by the Rocky River; drained by Lanes Creek. The county is in the Piedmont region of the state, with sandhills in the southeast. Cason Oil Field and part of Pee Dee National Wildlife Refuge are found here. • Named for George, Lord Anson (1697–1762), British admiral assigned to protect the Carolina coast from pirates • 1749 (prior to statehood) from Bladen • Cotton, corn, hay, fruit, soybeans, sorghum, oats, wheat, sweet potatoes, tobacco, poultry, turkeys, cattle, hogs, dairying; manufacture of cotton textiles (including underwear) and cottonseed products, hosiery, flour, feed; lumber (pine and oak) and sawmilling; sand and gravel.

ASHE *Jefferson* • 24,384 • 426 • Northwestern NC, bounded on the north by the VA state line, on the west by the TN state line; drained by the North and South forks of the New River (designated a National Scenic River here). The county is in the Blue Ridge Mountains; Blue Ridge (national) Parkway passes along its southeastern boundary. New River State Park and Mount Jefferson State Natural Area are found here. • Named for Samuel Ashe (1725–1813), chief justice of NC and governor of the state • 1799 from Wilkes • Tobacco, corn, hay, cattle, dairying; some manufacturing; publishing.

AVERY *Newland* • 17,167 • 247 • Northwestern NC, bounded on the west by the TN state line; drained by the Linville and North Toe rivers. The county is in the Blue Ridge Mountains and is extensively covered by sections of Pisgah National Forest. The Appalachian Trail follows part of the state line in the west. Blue Ridge (national) Parkway crosses the county in the east. Numerous ski resorts are in the north. • Named for Col. Waightstill Avery (1741–1821), Revolutionary War officer, NC legislator, and first attorney general of NC • 1911 from Mitchell, Caldwell and Watauga. (Avery is the youngest county in the state.) • Corn, potatoes, hay, vegetables, apples, cattle; mica, feldspar, kaolin; education (Lees-McRae College).

BEAUFORT (one of two counties so named, the other in SC) *Washington* • 44,958 • 828 • Eastern NC, near the Atlantic coast, bounded on the east in part by the Pungo River estuary. Goose Creek State Park and Historic Bath State Historic Site are here, as is part of East Dismal Swamp. Tidal Pamlico River and the Tar River bisect the county east-west. • Named for Henry Somerset (1684–1714), Duke of Beaufort, a lord proprietor of the colony of SC • About 1712 the name was changed from Pamptecough to Beaufort • Originally the seat of old Bath County (formed 1696), Bath was the colony's first incorporated town (1705) and first official port of entry. It served as refuge for survivors of the Tuscarora (Indian) War (1711–13), and was a base for the pirate Blackbeard. • Secretary of the Navy Josephus Daniels • Fishing; timber; tobacco, wheat, barley, oats, soybeans, sorghum, sweet potatoes, cotton, peanuts, vegetables, cattle, hogs; light manufacturing; mining of phosphates; resort tourism • Washington was one of the first places in the U.S. to be named for George Washington (Dec. 7, 1776).

BERTIE *Windsor* • 19,773 • 699 • Northeastern NC, bounded on the south and southwest by the Roanoke River (two units of Roanoke River National Wildlife Refuge are here) and on the east by the Chowan River and Albemarle Sound; drained by the Cashie River. • Named for James Bertie (1673–1735), or for both James and Henry Bertie (1675–1735), brothers who were lords proprietor of the colony of NC • 1722 (prior to statehood) from Chowan • Tennessee territorial governor William Blount • Peanuts, tobacco, corn, cotton, wheat, oats, soybeans, sorghum, chickens, cattle, hogs; fishing; gum, pine.

BLADEN *Elizabethtown* • 32,278 • 875 (the fourth largest county in NC) • Southeastern NC, bounded on the east by the South and Black rivers, on the west by the Big Swamp River; crossed by the Cape Fear River. The source of the Waccamaw River is in the southeast. There are several lakes in the north and northeast. Singletary Lake and Jones Lake state parks, Turn Bull Creek Educational State Forest, and Bladen Lakes State Forest are found here. • Named for Martin Bladen (1680–1746), British commissioner of trade and plantations • 1734 (prior to statehood) from New Hanover • Supreme Court justice Alfred Moore died here. • Tobacco, corn, peanuts, wheat, oats, soybeans, hay, sweet potatoes, cotton, turkeys, cattle, hogs; timber; sawmilling.

BRUNSWICK (one of two counties so named, the other in VA) *Bolivia* • 73,143 • 855 • Southeastern NC, bounded on the east and northeast by the Cape Fear River, on the south by the Atlantic Ocean, on the southwest by the SC state line, and on the west by the Waccamaw River; drained by Town Creek and Green Swamp. The county includes Smith and Bald Head islands (Cape Fear). The Intracoastal Waterway canal parallels the coast and passes through the Cape Fear River estuary to Carolina Beach inlet. Sunny Point Army Base includes Orton Plantation and Gardens. • Named for the former town of Brunswick, NC. • 1764 (prior to statehood) from New Hanover and Bladen • Southport was burned by the British in 1776; sixty excavated buildings make up the Brunswick Town State Historical Site. • Tobacco, corn, sweet potatoes, cattle, hogs; fishing; timber; beach coast resort tourism; manufacturing.

BUNCOMBE *Asheville* • 206,330 • 656 • Western NC; crossed by the French Broad and Swannanoa rivers. The county is located in the Blue Ridge Mountains, with the Black Mountains in the east. Parts of Pisgah National Forest (including the North Carolina Arboretum) are here. The Blue Ridge (national) Parkway crosses the county southwest-northeast. • Named for Col. Edward Buncombe (1742–1778), a NC officer in the Revolutionary War who died while a prisoner of the British • 1791 from Burke and Rutherford; in 1812 the county annexed Walton, which was formed in 1803 from Indian lands • Painter Kenneth Noland; NC politician Zebulon Vance (birthplace historic site); novelist Thomas Wolfe (state historic site); the graves of Wolfe and short story writer O. Henry are in Riverside Cemetery in Asheville. • Tobacco, corn, hay, chickens, dairying, cattle; timber; sand and gravel; tourism; textiles, furniture, electrical products; education (U. of NC at Asheville; Warren Wilson College; Montreat College) • George Vanderbilt's vast Biltmore estate is located just outside of Asheville. Its 250-room château is the nation's largest private residence.

BURKE (one of three counties so named) *Morganton* • 89,148 • 507 • Western NC, in the Piedmont; drained by the Catawba River (forming Lake James reservoir in the west, Rhodhiss Lake reservoir in the east). Part of Pisgah National Forest is in the west and South Mountain State Park is in the south. • Named for Thomas Burke (?–1783), member of the Continental Congress and NC governor • 1777 (prior to statehood) from Rowan • Senator Sam Ervin • Oats, soybeans, chickens, hogs, hay, corn, wheat; timber; manufacture of furniture, textiles, shoes, chemicals, electronics, clothing • Descendants of a group of Waldenses, religious refugees who moved to the county in 1893 from France and Italy, hold an annual festival in Valdese.

CABARRUS *Concord* • 131,063 • 364 • South-central NC, in the Piedmont; drained by the Rocky River • Named for Stephen Cabarrus (1754–1808), NC legislator and speaker of the NC House of Commons • 1792 from Mecklenburg • For a short time after the discovery of gold here in 1799, Concord was a gold-mining center (Reed Gold Mine State Historic Site located nearby). • Corn, soybeans, sorghum, wheat, hay, cattle, hogs, dairying, poultry; pine and oak; cotton textiles (a number of hosiery mills here); manufacture of cigarettes, foundry

NORTH CAROLINA (Caldwell)

and machine-shop products, soft drinks; education (Barber Scotia College) • Kannapolis, part of which lies in Rowan County, is the largest unincorporated community in NC; it is a company town, owned by textile giant Cannon Mills.

CALDWELL (one of five counties so named) *Lenoir* • 77,415 • 472 • West-central NC, bounded on the south by the Catawba River (which forms Hickory Lake and Rhodhiss Lake reservoirs); drained by the Yadkin River. The county includes part of the Blue Ridge Mountains and part of Pisgah National Forest in in west. Tuttle Educational State Forest is also located here. • Named for Joseph Caldwell (1773–1835), first president of the University of NC at Chapel Hill • 1841 from Burke and Wilkes • Biochemist Kary Mullis • Potatoes, cattle, hogs, chickens, tobacco, corn, wheat, hay, dairying; timber; manufacture of furniture, textiles, and hosiery.

CAMDEN (one of four counties so named) *Camden* • 6,885 • 241 • Northeastern NC, bounded on the north by the VA state line, on the southeast by the North River estuary, on the south by Albemarle Sound, and on the southwest by the Pasquotank River estuary. Much of the county lies in the Great Dismal Swamp, comprising part of the Great Dismal Swamp National Wildlife Refuge; the Dismal Swamp Canal (a branch of the Intracoastal Waterway) crosses the county (its Welcome Center located near the VA state line). • Named for Charles Pratt (1716–94), Earl of Camden, English jurist and political leader who supported the American colonies before the Revolutionary War • 1777 (prior to statehood) from Pasquotank • Pine, gum; corn, soybeans, cotton, wheat, peanuts, potatoes, cattle; duck hunting, fishing.

CARTERET *Beaufort* • 59,383 • 531 • Eastern NC on the Atlantic Ocean, bounded on the south and east by the Atlantic Ocean, on the northeast by Pamlico Sound, on the north in part by Ratton Bay, on the west by the White Oak River, on the south by Bogue Sound, and on the east by Core Sound. The county includes Bogue and Portsmouth islands and other sand barrier islands. The Intracoastal Waterway follows the coast through Bogue Sound, then crosses the county through Beaufort Harbor and canal. The county contains part of Croatan National Forest, Cedar Island National Wildlife Reserve, Cape Lookout National Seashore, Theodore Roosevelt State Nature Area, and Fort Macon State Park. • One of two counties in NC (the other, Granville) named for John Carteret (1690–1763), later Earl Granville, a lord proprietor of the Carolinas • 1722 (prior to statehood) from Craven • Beaufort Harbor was the base for pirate Edward Teach (Blackbeard) and home port for his ship *Queen Anne's Revenge*. The town was occupied by Union troops in 1862 in an attempt to thwart blockade running through the Beaufort Inlet. • Corn, wheat, oats, soybeans, sorghum, potatoes, cotton; manufacture of fish meal; boat building; lumber milling; commercial and sport fishing; resort tourism • Morehead is NC's only deepwater port north of Wilmington. It has one of the world's largest tobacco terminals, and provides accommodation facilities for all variety of watercraft.

CASWELL *Yanceyville* • 23,501 • 426 • Northern NC, in the Piedmont, bounded on the north by the VA state line; drained by the Dan and Hyco rivers. Part of Hyco Lake reservoir is here. • Named for General Richard Caswell (1729–89), Revolutionary War officer and governor of NC • 1777 (prior to statehood) from Orange • Tobacco, corn, wheat, oats, soybeans, sorghum, potatoes, cattle, hogs, hay; pine, oak.

CATAWBA *Newton* • 141,685 • 400 • West-central NC, in the Piedmont, bounded on the north and east by the Catawba River (forming Lake Hickory and Lookout Shoals reservoirs in the north, part of Lake Norman reservoir in the east); drained by the South Fork of the Catawba River and its branches. • Probably named for the Catawba Indians who lived in the area • 1842 from Lincoln • Secretary of the Interior Hoke Smith • Corn, wheat, hay, sorghum, dairying, oats, soybeans, cattle, chickens, hogs; pine, oak; manufacture of furniture, textiles, cordage, electronic and electrical components, hosiery (Hickory is the site of the only exposition and market — held annually since 1960 — devoted entirely to the hosiery business.); education (Lenoir Rhyne College).

CHATHAM *Pittsboro* • 49,329 • 683 • Central NC, in the Piedmont, bounded on the south in part by the Cape Fear and Deep rivers; also drained by the Haw River (joining Deep River on the southern boundary to form the Cape Fear River) and New Hope River. Jordan Lake State Recreation Area is located on B. Everett Jordan Lake reservoir. Part of Harris Lake reservoir is also here. • One of two counties (the other in GA) named for William Pitt (the Elder; 1708–78), 1st Earl of Chatham, known as "the Great Commoner," for his support of the American colonies before the Revolutionary War • 1771 (prior to statehood) from Orange • Tobacco, corn, wheat, soybeans, sorghum, hay, chickens, cattle, hogs, turkeys, dairying; timber; manufacturing.

CHEROKEE (one of eight counties with this name) *Murphy* • 24,298 • 455 • Extreme western NC, bounded on the south by the GA state line, and on the west and northwest by the TN state line; drained by the Hiwassee River (forming Appalachia and Hiwassee Lake reservoirs). The county lies partly in the Blue Ridge Mountains. The Unicoi and Snowbird mountains are in the north. The county is largely occupied by Nantahala National Forest. • Named for the Cherokee Indian tribe • 1839 from Macon • Lumbering (oak, pine); corn, hay, tobacco, apples, cattle, chickens; marble quarrying; some manufacturing.

CHOWAN *Edenton* • 14,526 • 173 (the smallest county in NC) • Northeastern NC, bounded on the west by the Chowan River, on the south by Albemarle Sound. Drummond Point is here. • Named for either the Chowan River or for the Chowanoc Indian tribe • Organized as Shaftsbury Precinct of Albemarle County in 1668 (prior to statehood); name changed about 1681 • Edenton was settled around 1600 and served as the unofficial capital of the colony of North Carolina until 1760. Its busy port exported fish, lumber and plantation products. The anti-British Edenton Tea Party was staged on October 25, 1774 by the women of the town. • Declaration of Independence signers Joseph Hewes and James Wilson. U.S. Supreme Court justice James Iredell died here. • Peanuts, truck crops, cotton, tobacco, corn, hay, sorghum, wheat, oats, soybeans, sweet potatoes, chickens, cattle, hogs; lumbering (pine, gum); fishing; light manufacturing.

CLAY (one of eighteen counties so named) *Hayesville* • 8,775 • 215 • Western NC, bounded on the south by the GA state line and on the northeast in part by the Nantahala River; drained by the Hiwassee River. Part of Chatuge Lake reservoir is located on the southern border. Most of the county is occupied by Nantahala National Forest. The Appalachian Trail crosses the southeast corner. • One of fifteen counties named for Henry Clay (1777–1852), U.S. senator from KY, known as the "Great Pacificator" for his advocacy of compromise to avert national crises • 1861 from Cherokee • Corn, hay, apples, tobacco, cattle, chickens, some dairying; lumbering; resorts.

CLEVELAND (one of three counties so named) *Shelby* • 96,287 • 464 • Southwestern NC, in the Piedmont, bounded on the south by the SC state line; drained by the Broad and First Broad rivers and their affluents. • Named for Col. Benjamin Cleaveland (1738–1806), a hero of the Battle of King's Mountain (1780) • Organized as Cleaveland County in 1841 from Rutherford and Lincoln. The present spelling was adopted in 1887. • Novelist and dramatist Thomas Dixon died here. • Cotton, corn, fruit, wheat, soybeans, hay, sorghum, chickens, turkeys, cattle, hogs, dairying; manufacture of textiles, hosiery, flour and baked goods, lumber; education (Gardner-Webb U.).

COLUMBUS *Whiteville* • 54,749 • 937 (the third largest county in NC) • Southeastern NC, bounded on the southwest by the SC state line, on the northwest by the Lumber River, on the extreme northeast by the Cape Fear River, and on the southeast in part by the Waccamaw River, which also drains the county. Lake Waccamaw and Lumber River state parks are here, as is part of Green Swamp. • Named for Christopher Columbus • 1808 from Bladen and Brunswick • Tobacco, wheat, cotton, peanuts, soybeans, sorghum, hay, corn, sweet potatoes, cattle, hogs; timber.

CRAVEN *New Bern* • 91,436 • 696 • Eastern NC, bounded on the southeast by the Nuese River estuary; drained by the Neuse and Trent rivers. Part of Croatan National Forest is in the south, as is Cherry Point Marine Corps Air Station. The Intracoastal Waterway canal crosses the extreme southeast corner and forms a small part of the county boundary. • Probably named for William (1668–1711), 2nd Earl of Craven. • Organized 1705 (prior to statehood) as Archdale Precinct of Bath District, although there is evidence that an Archdale County had existed since 1696. The name was changed in 1712. • New Bern is the second oldest city in NC. The state's first printing press began operating here in 1749. The state's first tax-supported school (1764) was also located here. The

city served as the colonial and state capital from 1746 to 1792. Tryon Palace, built by the royal governor, William Tryon, from 1767 to 1770, served as its first capitol. The first and second provincial congresses in NC in opposition to the British met here in 1774 and 1775. Until its capture by Federal forces under General Ambrose E. Burnside in 1862, New Bern enjoyed a thriving seaport trade with New England and the West Indies. One of the first public schools for American blacks was established here in 1862. • Tobacco, wheat, oats, barley, soybeans, hay, potatoes, cotton, peanuts, corn, poultry, cattle, hogs; timber; diversified manufacturing; resort tourism. • New Bern is the site of a National Cemetery.

CUMBERLAND (one of eight counties so named) *Fayetteville* • 302,963 (the fifth most populated county in NC) • 653 • South-central NC, bounded on the east by the South River; drained by the Cape Fear River and the Little River (which forms part of its northern boundary). The county is located in the Sandhill region. Pope Air Force Base and part of Fort Bragg Military Reservation are in the northwest. • One of four counties named for William Augustus (1721–65), Duke of Cumberland, British general and second son of George II • 1754 (prior to statehood) from Bladen • On Nov. 21, 1789, Fayetteville was the scene of a second state convention to ratify the U.S. Constitution (after its previous rejection at Hillsboro). In 1831, a fire that spread through the city destroyed more than 600 buildings. Fayetteville was occupied by Union troops under Gen. William T. Sherman in March, 1865. • First black man elected to the U.S. Senate Hiram R. Revels • Cotton, wheat, oats, barley, soybeans, sorghum, hay, potatoes, peanuts, poultry, cattle, hogs, tobacco, corn; timber; manufacture of textiles, lumber and other wood products, machinery, power hand tools; bakery and dairy products; education (Fayetteville State U.; Methodist College).

CURRITUCK *Currituck* • 18,190 • 262 • Extreme northeastern NC, bounded on the north by the VA state line, on the east by the Atlantic Ocean, on the southeast by Currituck Sound, on the south by Albemarle Sound, and on the southwest by the North River estuary. The county is made up of three sections: a mainland section which lies partially in Dismal Swamp, a peninsula located between the North river estuary and Currituck Sound, and a section of the Outer Banks sand barrier. A four-mile portion of the Albemarle and Chesapeake canal crosses the base of the peninsula. The Intracoastal Waterway passes through the canal and the northwestern part of Currituck Sound. Part of Mackey Island National Wildlife Refuge and Currituck National Wildlife Refuge are also in the county. • The derivation of the county name is unclear. It could have been named for an Indian tribe, or might be an Indian word meaning "wild geese." • Organized by 1668 (prior to statehood) as a precinct of Albemarle District • Corn, wheat, peanuts, hogs, sorghum, potatoes, soybeans, cotton; pine.

DARE *Manteo* • 29,967 • 382 • Northeastern NC, bounded on the south and east by the Atlantic Ocean, on the north by

Albemarle Sound, on the west by the Alligator River estuary, and on the southwest by Pamlico Sound. Jockey's Ridge State Park is on the Outer Banks, as is a large part of Cape Hatteras National Seashore. The Intracoastal Waterway passes through the county. Dare County also includes Pea Island and part of Alligator River national wildlife refuges. • Named for Virginia Dare, born 1587 on Roanoke Island, the first child of English parents to be born in the Americas • 1870 from Tyrrell, Hyde and Currituck • The first English settlement in North America was attempted on Roanoke Island from 1585 to 1587 (Fort Raleigh National Historic Site). The fate of Sir Walter Raleigh's "Lost Colony" remains a mystery. On December 7, 1862, Confederate troops under Col. Henry M. Shaw surrendered the island to Union general Ambrose E. Burnside. The first sustained flight in a heavier-than-air machine was made at Kitty Hawk by Wilbur and Orville Wright on December 17, 1903 (national memorial). • Grapes, oats, soybeans; fishing; tourism.

DAVIDSON *Lexington* • 147,246 • 552 • Central NC, in the Piedmont, bounded on the west and southwest by the Yadkin River, forming High Rock Lake and Badin Lake reservoirs; drained by numerous creeks. A small part of Uwharrie National Forest is here, as is Boone's Cave State Park. • One of two counties (the other in TN) named for General William Lee Davidson (?–1781), army officer killed during the Revolutionary War • 1822 from Rowan • The first operating silver mine in the U.S. opened in 1838 near Lexington. • Tobacco, corn, wheat, hay, soybeans, sorghum, chickens, dairying, cattle, hogs; pine, oak, and sawmilling; manufacturing, especially furniture, also textiles, clothing, plastics, and construction materials.

DAVIE *Mocksville* • 34,835 • 265 • Central NC, in the Piedmont, bounded on the east by the Yadkin River, and on the south by the South Fork of the Yadkin River; drained by Hunting Creek. • Named for Gen. William R. Davie (1756–1820), Revolutionary War hero, NC governor, and peace commissioner in France • 1836 from Rowan • Author Hinton Rowan Helper • Tobacco, wheat, corn, soybeans, chickens, dairying, cattle, hogs, hay; timber.

DUPLIN *Kenansville* • 49,063 • 818 • Eastern NC; drained by the Northeast Cape Fear River. The county is located partly in pine gum forest and partly on swampy coastal plain. • Named for Thomas Hay (1710–87), Viscount Dupplin, member of the Board of Trade and Plantations • 1750 (prior to statehood) from New Hanover • Tobacco, corn, cotton, wheat, oats, soybeans, sorghum, hay, cucumbers, peppers, sweet potatoes, poultry, cattle, hogs; timber.

DURHAM *Durham* • 223,314 • 291 • North-central NC, in the Piedmont; drained by the Flat and Eno rivers, which join in the east to form Falls Lake reservoir (Neuse River). The county is largely urbanized as part of the Durham metropolitan area. Part of Falls Lake State Recreation Area and Lake Michie reservoir (Flat River) are located here. • Named for the

city of Durham • 1881 from Orange and Wake • Tobacco has played a leading role in the development of the county's economy, beginning with the efforts of pioneer Robert R. Morris, continuing with the opening of the Duke family factory in 1874, and the successful marketing of John R. Green's Bull Durham blend after the Civil War. On April 26, 1865 at Bennett Place, seventeen days after Lee surrendered to Grant, General Joseph E. Johnston surrendered to Union General William T. Sherman. • Tobacco magnate James B. Duke. Physicist Fritz Wolfgang London died here. • Tobacco, wheat, hay, soybeans, corn, cattle; pine; manufacture of tobacco products, textiles • In large part through the philanthropy of the Duke family, Durham has become an educational, medical and research center. Leading institutions include Duke University, North Carolina Central University, and Durham Technical Institute. Research Triangle Park is southeast of Durham.

EDGECOMBE *Tarboro* • 55,606 • 505 • East-central NC, bounded on the north and drained by Fishing Creek; also drained by the Tar River. • Named for Richard Edgcumbe (1680–1758), later 1st Baron Edgcumbe, English statesman. The state legislature failed to spell the name correctly at the time of its establishment. • 1741 (prior to statehood) from Bertie County, although deeds began in 1732 • Historian John S. Bassett; congressional leader Nathaniel Macon • Pine, gum; peanuts, cotton, corn, wheat, oats, barley, sorghum, hay, soybeans, sweet potatoes, chickens, cattle, hogs, tobacco (growing, manufacturing, and marketing) • The tracks of the Seaboard Coast (railway) Line bisect the main street of Rocky Mount and mark the boundary of Edgecombe and Nash counties.

FORSYTH (one of two counties so named, the other in GA) *Winston-Salem* • 306,067 (the fourth most populated county in NC) • 410 • North-central NC, in the Piedmont, bounded on the west by the Yadkin River. Part of Belews Lake reservoir is in the northeast corner. The county is urbanized around Winston-Salem and in the east. • Named for Col. Benjamin Forsyth (?–1814), NC legislator and army officer killed during the War of 1812 • 1849 from Stokes • Winston-Salem was created in 1913 from two towns originally a mile apart. Salem was laid out in the Wachovia land tract by Moravian colonists in 1766. Winston was founded in 1849 as the county seat. R.J. Reynolds' tobacco company began operation here in 1875. • Senator Sam Ervin died here. • Local industry is dominated by tobacco. (It is one of the world's largest leaf-tobacco markets.) Also, corn, hay, wheat, oats, cattle; timber (pine and oak); manufacture of textiles, beer, rubber, leather, petroleum, men's and boys' knitwear, hosiery, electronic equipment; education (Wake Forest U.; Salem College; Winston-Salem State U.) • Old Salem (a replica of the original settlement here) is the site of the annual Moravian Easter Sunrise Service.

FRANKLIN (one of twenty-five counties so named) *Louisburg* • 47,260 • 492 • North-central NC, bounded on the north in part by Fishing Creek and on the northwest in part by the Tar River (which also drains the county). Perry's Pond is here. •

One of twenty-three counties named for Benjamin Franklin • 1779 (prior to statehood) from Bute County, which was discontinued at that time • Tobacco, corn, wheat, oats, barley, soybeans, sorghum, hay, sweet potatoes, chickens, cattle, hogs; pine; asphalt, crushed stone; manufacture of oil seals, wire harnesses, electronic components, concrete, hardwood flooring; mica processing.

GASTON *Gastonia* • 190,365 • 356 • Southern NC, in the Piedmont, bounded on the south by the SC state line, on the east by the Catawba River, forming Mountain Island and Lake Wylie reservoirs; drained by the South Fork of the Catawba River. Crowders Mountain State Park is here. • Named for William J. Gaston (1778–1844), U.S. representative from NC, and NC Supreme Court justice • 1846 from Lincoln • After the establishment of its first cotton mill in 1848, Gastonia became one of the nation's largest textile-manufacturing centers. In 1929, the city was the scene of a bitter strike of textile workers, which resulted in the deaths of several people, including the chief of police. In the trial that followed, a number of labor organizers were convicted of conspiracy to murder, and sentenced to long prison terms. The strike was the inspiration for the novels *Strike!* (1930) by Mary Heaton Vorse, and *To Make My Bread* (1932) by Grace Lumpkin. • Cotton, wheat, hay, corn, soybeans, sweet potatoes, tobacco, poultry, hogs, cattle, dairying; pine, oak; stone quarrying; sawmilling. The county produces much of the combed cotton yarn made in the U.S. (textile center at Gastonia); also the manufacture of machinery, motor oil filters, electronics, plastics, corrugated boxes goes on here.

GATES *Gatesville* • 10,516 • 341 • Northeastern NC, bounded on the north by the VA state line, on the southwest and west by the Chowan River; drained by Bennetts Creek. Part of Dismal Swamp is in the east. Merchants Millpond State Park and part of Dismal Swamp National Wildlife Refuge are here. • Named for Gen. Horatio Gates (?–1806), Continental Army officer who defeated John Burgoyne at the Battle of Saratoga (1777) • 1779 (prior to statehood) from Chowan, Hertford, and Perquimans • Wheat, barley, sorghum, hay, tobacco, peanuts, cotton, corn, soybeans, chickens, cattle, hogs; gum, cedar, pine, cypress.

GRAHAM (one of three counties so named) *Robbinsville* • 7,993 • 292 • Western NC, bounded on the west by the TN state line, on the north by the Little Tennessee River (Fontana Lake reservoir); drained by the Cheoah River. The county contains the Unicoi and Snowbird mountains, and lies almost entirely within Nantahala National Forest. Joyce Kilmer Memorial Forest and Santeetlah Lake reservoir are also here. The county is crossed by the Appalachian Trail. • Named for William A. Graham (1804–75), U.S. senator from NC, governor of NC, and U.S. secretary of the navy • 1872 from Cherokee • Tobacco, hay, hogs, cattle; timber; resorts; manufacture of paper, textiles, apparel, transportation equipment, fabricated metal products, consumer goods; machining; printing and publishing.

GRANVILLE *Oxford* • 48,498 • 531 • Northern NC, in the Piedmont, bounded on the north by the VA state line; drained by the Tar River. Several arms of Falls Lake Reservoir extend into the southern part of the county, and part of J.H. Kerr Lake reservoir extends into the northwest. • One of two counties in NC (the other, Carteret) named for John Carteret (1690–1763), Earl of Granville, a lord proprietor who owned the district in which the new county was located • 1746 (prior to statehood) from Edgecombe • Tobacco, corn, wheat, oats, soybeans, sorghum, hogs, chickens, cattle, dairying; timber; sawmilling.

GREENE (one of fourteen counties so named) *Snow Hill* • 18,974 • 265 • East-central NC, bounded on the northeast by the Nuese River; drained by Contentnea Creek, forming part of the southern boundary. • One of sixteen counties named for Gen. Nathanael Greene (1742–86), hero of the Revolutionary War, quartermaster general, and commander of the Army of the South • 1799, when Glasgow County was renamed Greene • Tobacco, corn, wheat, oats, soybeans, hay, sweet potatoes, peanuts, cotton, chicken, turkeys, cattle, hogs; pine, gum.

GUILFORD *Greensboro* • 421,048 (the third most populated county in NC) • 650 • North-central NC; drained by the Haw and Deep rivers. • Named for Francis North (1704–90), 1st Earl of Guilford and father of Frederick, Lord North (1732–92), who was the prime minister of England at the time of the American Revolution • 1770 or 1771 (prior to statehood) from Rowan and Orange • The Battle of Guilford Courthouse (national monument), which was fought here on March 15, 1781, opened the campaign that led to Yorktown and the end of the American Revolution. The Civil Rights–related sit-in movement began in Greensboro on Feb. 1, 1960 when four black college students refused to move from a Woolworth lunch counter when denied service. • Politician Joseph G. Cannon; short story writer William Sydney Porter (O. Henry); First Lady Dolley Madison; broadcast journalist Edward R. Murrow • Tobacco, corn, wheat, oats, soybeans, sorghum, hay, dairying, chickens, cattle, hogs; timber (pine and oak); granite quarrying. The county is a major wholesaling and manufacturing center, especially of furniture; also, textiles, apparel, petroleum pumping equipment, chemical and pharmaceutical products, electronic equipment, brick and clay products, tobacco products; petroleum marketing; education (Guilford College; Greensboro College; U. of NC at Greensboro; High Point College; NC Agricultural & Tech. State U.) • Greensboro was the first city in the U.S. to have an ombudsman and to establish a full-time human relations commission with a paid staff. High Point is the site of the Southern Furniture Market, which attracts thousands of furniture buyers to its exhibition complex four times a year. It is also a leader in the manufacture of hosiery. The headquarters of five Fortune 1000 companies are located in the county.

HALIFAX *Halifax* • 57,370 • 725 • Northeastern NC, in the Piedmont, bounded on the north and east by the Roanoke

River (forming Roanoke Rapids Lake and Gaston Lake reservoirs), on the south by Fishing Creek. Its northwest border lies within three miles of the VA state line. Medoc Mountain State Park and Roanoke River National Wildlife Refuge are here. • One of two counties (the other in VA) named for George Montagu Dunk (1716–71), 2nd Earl of Halifax, president of the Board of Trade and Plantations; he was called the "Father of the Colonies" for his strong support of trade with them. • 1758 (prior to statehood) from Edgecombe • Tobacco, peanuts, cotton, corn, wheat, oats, soybeans, sorghum, hay, potatoes, sweet potatoes, chickens, hogs, some dairying; timber; manufacturing.

HARNETT *Lillington* • 91,025 • 595 • Central NC, bounded on the south in part by the Little River; drained by the Cape Fear and South rivers. Raven Rock State Park is here. • Named for Cornelius Harnett (1723–81), patriot and one of the three NC signers of the Articles of Confederation • 1855 from Cumberland • Tobacco, cotton, corn, wheat, sorghum, hay, potatoes, sweet potatoes, peppers, chickens, cattle, hogs; catfish; textile manufacturing; timber; sand and gravel; education (Campbell U.).

HAYWOOD (one of two counties so named, the other in TN) *Waynesville* • 54,033 • 554 • Western NC, bounded on the northwest by the TN state line; drained by the Pigeon River. The county lies partly in the Blue Ridge Mountains. Blue Ridge (national) Parkway follows the county boundary in the southwest and southeast. Parts of Pisgah National Forest, Waterville Lake (Pigeon River) reservoir, and part of Great Smoky Mountains National Park are in the county. The Appalachian Trail follows along the state line in the west. • Named for John Haywood (1755–1827), NC treasurer and an original trustee of the University of NC at Chapel Hill • 1808 from Buncombe • Tobacco, hay, corn, potatoes, cattle, hogs; timber; manufacture of lumber, pulp, paper, and other wood products; resort tourism.

HENDERSON (one of five counties so named) *Hendersonville* • 89,173 • 374 • Southwestern NC, bounded on the south by the SC state line; drained by the upper French Broad and Green rivers. Holmes Educational State Forest is here, as is part of Pisgah National Forest. • Named for Leonard Henderson (1772–1833), chief justice of the NC Supreme Court • 1838 from Buncombe • Poet and author Carl Sandburg (national historic site) • Dairying, cattle, corn, soybeans, hay, tobacco, poultry, apples, pole beans, cabbages and other vegetables; stone quarrying; manufacture of textiles, hosiery, rugs, outdoor lighting equipment, industrial ceramics; resort tourism.

HERTFORD *Winton* • 22,601 • 354 • Northeastern NC, bounded on the north by the VA state line, and on the east by the Chowan River; drained by the Meherrin River (forming the northwest boundary of the county) and Potecasi Creek. • Named for British statesman Francis Seymour Conway (1719–94), Earl (later Marquis) of Hertford • 1750s (prior to statehood) from Chowan, Bertie, and Northampton • Novel-

ist and dramatist William Hill Brown died here. • Peanuts, tobacco, cotton, corn, wheat, sorghum, soybeans, potatoes, chickens, hogs; pine, gum, oak; education (Chowan College).

HOKE *Raeford* • 33,646 (47.2% increase since 1990; the third fastest growing county in NC) • 391 • South-central NC, bounded on the west by Drowning Creek, and on the north by the Little River. Part of large Fort Bragg Military Reservation is here. • Named for General Robert F. Hoke (1837–1912), a Confederate Army officer • 1911 from Cumberland and Robeson • Cotton, tobacco, corn, peaches, wheat, soybeans, hay, peanuts, cattle; timber.

HYDE *Swanquarter* • 5,826 • 613 • Eastern NC, bounded on the southeast by the Atlantic Ocean, on the north in part by the Alligator River estuary, on the west in part by the Pungo River estuary, and on the east by the Long Shoal River estuary; crossed by the Alligator-Pungo Canal. Part of Cape Hatteras National Seashore is on Ocracoke Island across Pamlico Sound. Lake Mattamuskeet and Swanquarter national wildlife refuges on the sound are on the north-south Atlantic flyway of migratory birds. • Named for Edward Hyde (1650–1712), governor of England's colony of NC • 1705 (prior to statehood) as Wickham Precinct of Bath District; name changed in 1712 • Cotton, corn, wheat, soybeans, hogs; timber; fish, crabs, oysters.

IREDELL *Statesville* • 122,660 • 574 • West-central NC, in the Piedmont, bounded on the southwest by the Catawba River (forming Lake Norman reservoir); drained by the South Fork of the Yadkin River, and Hunting and Fourth creeks. Lake Norman State Park is in the southwest. Fort Dobbs State Historical Site is also in the county. • Named for James Iredell (1751–1799) attorney general of NC and U.S. Supreme Court justice • 1788 (prior to statehood) from Rowan • Tobacco, corn, wheat, hay, barley, soybeans, dairying; manufacture of rubber, plastics, metal products, textiles, clothing, furniture, machinery, food products, flour; timber.

JACKSON (one of twenty-four counties so named) *Sylva* • 33,121 • 491 • Western NC, bounded on the south by the SC state line; drained by the Tuckasegee and Chattooga rivers. The county lies in the Blue Ridge Mountains, with Balsam Mountain in the east, and the Cowee Mountains in the west. All but the northern end of the county is occupied by Nantahala National Forest. Thorpe Reservoir is in the county. Blue Ridge (national) Parkway follows the county line in the northeast. Part of Eastern Cherokee Indian Reservation is in the north. • One of twenty-two counties named directly or indirectly for President Andrew Jackson • 1851 from Haywood and Macon • Cattle, apples, tobacco, hay, corn; timber; mica and talc mining; resorts; manufacturing; education (W. Carolina U.).

JOHNSTON (one of two counties so named, the other in OK) *Smithfield* • 121,965 (50% increase since 1990; the fastest growing county in NC) • 792 • Central NC; drained by the Neuse and Little rivers. The source of the South River is in the southwest. Clemmons Educational State Forest is located in the county. • Named for Gabriel Johnston (?–1752), colonial governor of NC • 1746 (prior to statehood) from Craven • Bentonville Battlefield (state historic site) near Smithfield was the scene of one of the last important Civil War battles; on March, 1865, General William T. Sherman's troops defeated the Confederate forces of General Joseph E. Johnston. • Actress Ava Gardner • Tobacco, cotton, corn, wheat, oats, barley, soybeans, hay, potatoes, sweet potatoes, chickens, turkeys, cattle, hogs; lumber (pine, gum); cotton milling; tobacco processing; manufacturing.

JONES (one of six counties so named) *Trenton* • 10,381 • 473 • Eastern NC, bounded on the south in part by the White Oak River; drained by the Trent River. White Oak Swamp, including part of Catfish Lake, is on the eastern boundary. The county includes part of Croatan National Forest and Hofmann Forest. • Named for Willie Jones (1741–1801), American Revolutionary leader and member of the Continental Congress who later opposed the adoption of the Constitution • 1778 or 1779 (prior to statehood) from Craven • Tobacco, corn, cotton, beans, wheat, soybeans, hay, hogs; pine and gum; stone quarrying.

LEE (one of twelve counties so named) *Sanford* • 49,040 • 257 • Central NC, bounded on the northeast by the Cape Fear River and on the northwest by the Deep River. • One of eight counties named for Robert E. Lee (1807–70), American general and commander in chief of the Confederate forces during the Civil War • 1907 from Chatham and Moore • Tobacco, cotton, corn, wheat, oats, soybeans, hay, chickens; timber; manufacture of apparel, electronics, furniture, brick and tile, machinery; sand, stone quarrying.

LENOIR *Kinston* • 59,648 • 400 • East-central NC, bounded on the northeast by Contentnea Creek; drained by the Neuse River. The source of the Trent River is in the south. • Named for General William Lenoir (1751–1839), one of the heroes of the Battle of Kings Mountain during the American Revolution and speaker of the NC Senate • 1791 from Dobbs County, when the county was dissolved and divided between Glasgow and Lenoir • Kinston was the home of the first governor of NC, Richard Caswell (memorial). It was also the construction site of the Confederate ram *Neuse*, an ironclad gunboat scuttled and burned by its crew in 1865 (its salvaged hull now part of a state historic site). The Battle of Wise Forks that year was one of the last Confederate victories of the war. • Tobacco, corn, cotton, wheat, soybeans, hay, sweet potatoes, chickens, turkeys, hogs; manufacture of textiles, chemicals, yarn, lumber products, paper boxes, bricks, molded concrete, processed foods.

LINCOLN (one of twenty-four counties so named) *Lincolnton* • 63,780 • 299 • West-central NC, in the Piedmont, bounded on the east by the Catawba River, which forms Lake Norman reservoir; drained by the South Fork of the Catawba. • One of four counties directly named for Gen. Benjamin Lin-

coln (1733–1810), Revolutionary War officer, U.S. secretary of war, and lieutenant governor of MA • Organized 1779 (prior to statehood) from Tryon County, which was organized in 1768 and abolished in 1779 • Cotton, corn, wheat, hay, oats, barley, soybeans, poultry, cattle, dairying; manufacturing; stone quarrying.

MACON *Franklin* • 29,811 • 516 • Western NC, bounded on the south by the GA state line (its southeast corner is near the junction of NC, GA and SC); drained by the Nantahala River (forming Nantahala Lake reservoir) and the Little Tennessee River. The county lies entirely within Nantahala National Forest. Part of the Blue Ridge Mountains are in the southeast. The Nantahala Mountains cross the county from north to south. The Appalachian Trail crosses through the western part of the county. • One of six counties named for Nathaniel Macon (1758–1837), U.S. representative from NC, U.S. senator and president of the NC Constitutional Convention • 1828 from Haywood • Vegetables, apples, corn, hay, tobacco, cattle, dairying; timber; mica mining; resorts.

MADISON *Marshall* • 19,635 • 449 • Western NC, bounded on the north by the TN state line; drained by the French Broad River. The Bald Mountains are located along its northern border. Part of Pisgah and Cherokee national forests are in the county. The Appalachian Trail follows a portion of the state line here. • One of twenty counties named directly or indirectly for President James Madison • 1851 from Yancey and Buncombe • Tobacco, corn, hay, potatoes, cattle; timber; resorts; some manufacturing; education (Mars Hill College).

MARTIN (1 of 6 counties so named) *Williamston* • 25,593 • 463 • Eastern NC, bounded on the north by the Roanoke River. The county lies partially in East Dismal Swamp. One unit of Roanoke River National Wildlife Refuge and Fort Branch Battlefield State Historical Site are here. • Originally named for Josiah Martin (1737–86), the last royal governor of NC. Although the governor was much despised by the people of the colony, the name was probably retained and reapplied to popular NC governor Alexander Martin. • 1774 (prior to statehood) from Tyrell and Halifax • Corn, wheat, oats, soybeans, cotton, peanuts, tobacco, chickens, hogs; tobacco and peanut processing; pine, gum; fishing.

MCDOWELL (one of two counties so named, the other in WV) *Marion* • 42,151 • 442 • West-central NC, in the Blue Ridge Mountains; drained by the Catawba River (forming Lake James reservoir). Part of Pisgah National Forest and Lake James State Park are located here. The Blue Ridge (national) Parkway follows the county's northwest boundary. • Named for Major Joseph McDowell (1756–1801), a hero of the Battle of Kings Mountain during the Revolutionary War and U.S. representative from NC • 1842 from Burke and Rutherford • Corn, apples, soybeans, hay, chickens, cattle; timber; stone quarrying; resort tourism; manufacturing.

MECKLENBURG *Charlotte* • 695,454 (the most populated county in NC) • 527 • Southern NC, in the Piedmont, bounded on the southwest by the SC state line, on the west by the Catawba River (which forms Lake Wylie reservoir on the SC state line and Mountain Island and Lake Norman reservoirs). Most of the county is highly urbanized, especially around Charlotte in the south and center. The James K. Polk Memorial State Historical Site at Pineville is in the south. • One of three counties (the other two in VA) named for Queen Charlotte Sophia of Mecklenburg–Strelitz (1744–1818), queen consort of King George III • 1762 (prior to statehood) from Anson • Charlotte was settled around 1750. The Mecklenburg Declaration of Independence, signed here on May 20, 1775, declared Mecklenburg citizens free of British rule. Lord Cornwallis received such hostile treatment when he occupied Charlotte in 1780 that he dubbed the town "the hornet's nest," a phrase that became the city's official emblem. Charlotte was the center of gold production in the U.S. until the CA Gold Rush of 1849. A mint was located here from 1837 to 1861 and from 1867 to 1913. The city served the Confederacy as a naval yard during the Civil War. In 1970, the Charlotte-Mecklenburg school system began one of the first large-scale programs to integrate schools by busing. • President James K. Polk; Evangelist Billy Graham; swimmer Don Schollander; painter Romare Bearden. Andrew Jackson received his schooling in Charlotte. • Charlotte is a major wholesale distribution point for the Southeast. Cattle, dairying, corn, oats, barley, hay; banking and insurance; manufacture of textiles, machinery, metal, food products, printed materials; education (U. of NC at Charlotte; Davidson College; Johnson C. Smith U.; Queens College) • Nine Fortune 1000 companies have their corporate headquarters in the county. Charlotte is home to the Carolina Panthers.

MITCHELL (one of five counties so named) *Bakersville* • 15,687 • 221 • Western NC, bounded on the north by the TN state line, on the west by the Nolichucky River, and on the southwest by the Toe River. The Unaka Mountains are in the north, the Blue Ridge Mountains in the south. The county lies largely in Pisgah National Forest. The Appalachian Trail follows part of the state line, and the Blue Ridge Parkway follows the county line in the southeast. • Named for Elisha Mitchell (1793–1857), a professor at the University of North Carolina who was killed while exploring what is now called Mount Mitchell • 1861 from Burke, Caldwell, Yancey, McDowell, and Watauga • Tobacco, corn, apples, hay, cattle; mining of mica, feldspar, quartz, kaolin (Museum of North Carolina Minerals); resorts.

MONTGOMERY (one of eighteen counties so named) *Troy* • 26,822 • 491 • Central NC, in the Piedmont, bounded on the west by the Yadkin River (which forms Badin Lake and Lake Tillery reservoirs), and on the southeast by Drowning Creek; drained by the Uwharrie and Little rivers. Part of Uwharrie National Forest covers most of the county. Town Creek Indian Mound State Historical Site is here. • One of sixteen counties named directly or indirectly for Gen. Richard Montgomery (1738–75), American Revolutionary War officer

who captured Montreal, Canada • 1779 (prior to statehood) from Anson • Wheat, soybeans, hay, sweet potatoes, peaches, cotton, tobacco, corn, chickens, cattle, hogs; some manufacturing.

MOORE (one of three counties so named) *Carthage* • 74,769 • 699 • Central NC, in the Piedmont, bounded on the southeast by the Little River and Fort Bragg Military Reserve, on the southwest by Drowning Creek, and on the northeast in part by the Deep River; drained by the Deep River. House in the Horseshoe State Historical Site is here. The county is also the site of Weymouth Woods (Sandhills Nature Preserve) • Named for Captain Alfred Moore (1755–1810), Revolutionary War officer, attorney general of NC, and U.S. Supreme Court justice • 1784 (prior to statehood) from Cumberland • Politician John Edwards. Journalist and diplomat Walter H. Page died here. • Tobacco, peaches, corn, wheat, oats, barley, soybeans, hay, cattle, hogs; timber, sawmilling; textiles • Pinehurst, a year-round resort, is a center for horse enthusiasts and golfers. The city hosts several golf tournaments. The World Golf Hall of Fame was opened here in 1974.

NASH *Nashville* • 87,420 • 540 • Northeast-central NC, bounded on the northeast by Fishing Creek; drained by the Tar River. • Named for General Francis Nash (?–1777), Revolutionary War officer and NC legislator • 1777 (prior to statehood) from Edgecombe • Tobacco (Rocky Mount has one of the largest bright-leaf tobacco marts in the world.) Also, wheat, oats, soybeans, hay, sweet potatoes, peanuts, cotton, corn, chickens, cattle, hogs; pine; manufacture of textiles, furniture, fabricated metals, chemicals, clothing, glass, clay, concrete, electrical equipment; education (NC Wesleyan College). • The Country Doctor Museum is located in Bailey.

NEW HANOVER *Wilmington* • 160,307 • 199 • Southeastern NC, bounded on the east by the Atlantic Ocean (Onslow Bay), on the west by the Cape Fear River, and on the north and northwest by the Northeast Cape Fear River. The Intracoastal Waterway channel parallels the coast south to Carolina Beach Inlet, continuing south in the Cape Fear River estuary. The county includes Wrightsville, Carolina, and Kure beach resort areas. Also here are Fort Fisher State Recreation Area and Historic Site, the North Carolina Aquarium at Fort Fisher, and Carolina Beach State Park. • Named for the British royal house of Hanover, which began with George I, Duke of Hannover. (Anglicized to Hanover) • 1729 from Craven • Wilmington was the scene of the first armed resistance to the Stamp Act in November, 1765. The Battle of Moore's Creek Bridge in February, 1776 frustrated a British effort to conquer the colonies by division. British general Lord Cornwallis used Wilmington as his headquarters in 1781. During the Civil War, the city was a center for blockade running. It was the last Confederate port to close, holding out until the fall of Fort Fisher in January, 1865. The county suffered severe hurricane damage in the 1950s. • Supreme Court justice Alfred Moore; broadcast journalist David Brinkley; abolitionist David Walker • Truck farming; stone quarrying; shipping; manufacture of textiles, baked goods, chemicals, containers, refrigeration equipment; beach resorts; education (U. of NC at Wilmington) • The USS *North Carolina* Battleship Memorial of WW II is moored in the Cape Fear River at Wilmington. The city is home to a National Cemetery.

NORTHAMPTON (one of three counties so named) *Jackson* • 22,086 • 536 • Northeastern NC, bounded on the north by the VA state line, on the southwest by the Roanoke River (forming Roanoke Rapids Lake and Gaston Lake reservoirs); drained by the Meherrin River, forming part of the northeast boundary, and by Potecasi Creek. • Named for James Compton (1687–1754), Earl of Northampton • 1741 from Bertie • The 75-mile Petersburg Railroad connecting Blakely (which no longer exists) and Petersburg, VA was the first interstate railroad (1833) • Peanuts, cotton, corn, tobacco, wheat, soybeans, sorghum, hay, poultry, hogs; timber.

ONSLOW *Jacksonville* • 150,355 • 767 • Eastern NC, bounded on the south by the Atlantic Ocean, and on the northeast by the White Oak River; drained by the New River and indented by its estuary in the southeast. The county includes Catherine Lake, Hammocks Beach State Park, part of Hoffman Forest, part of Croatan National Forest, and part of Topsail Island beach resort. The Intracoastal Waterway channel parallels the coast in the southeast. • Named for Arthur Onslow (1691–1768), speaker of the House of Commons in England • 1734 (prior to statehood) from New Hanover • Jacksonville was a small hunting and fishing resort until 1942 when the creation of New River Marine Base (now Camp Lejeune) expanded the economy. • Tobacco, corn, wheat, cotton, soybeans, hay, sweet potatoes; some manufacturing; fishing.

ORANGE (one of eight counties so named) *Hillsborough* • 118,227 • 400 • North-central NC, in the Piedmont, bounded by the Haw River in the southwest corner; drained by the Eno River. Eno River State Park is on its eastern boundary. University Lake reservoir is in the south. The North Carolina Botanical Garden is also found in the county. • Named for either William of Orange (1650–1702), who was King William III; or for one of his descendants • 1752 (prior to statehood) from Bladen, Granville, and Johnston • In 1768, Hillsborough (then Hillsboro) was the scene of disturbances by colonials called Regulators, who fought against taxes and legal fees. It served for a brief period as the capital of NC during the American Revolution. The city was also the muster point for troops under Lord Cornwallis prior to the 1781 Battle of Guilford Courthouse. • Politician Thomas Hart Benton. Poet and novelist Randall Jarrell died here. • Tobacco, corn, dairying, wheat, oats, soybeans, hay, cattle, hogs; pine, oak; manufacture of textiles, furniture; timber; stone quarrying; research and education (U. of NC at Chapel Hill; chartered in 1789, it was the first state university in the U.S.) • Chapel Hill's Carolina Playmakers, founded in 1918, is a nationally recognized community theatre. Hillsborough has preserved a number of its colonial buildings, including Heartsease, the home

of Gov. Thomas Burke and the scene of his capture by Loyalists in 1781.

PAMLICO *Bayboro* • 12,934 • 337 • Eastern NC, bounded on the east by the Pamlico Sound and Ratton Bay, in the far northeast by the Pamlico River estuary, and on the south by the Nuese River estuary. The Intracoastal Waterway crosses the Nuese River in the south. • Named for the Pamlico Sound, itself named for the Pamlico Indian tribe • 1872 from Craven and Beaufort • Potatoes, corn, tobacco, wheat, soybeans, cotton, hogs; fish, crabs, shrimp; timber.

PASQUOTANK *Elizabeth City* • 34,897 • 227 • Northeastern NC, bounded on the south by Albemarle Sound, on the east by the Pasquotank River and estuary, and on the southwest in part by the Little River estuary. The county lies partly in Dismal Swamp and includes a portion of Dismal Swamp National Wildlife Refuge. • Named for the Pasquotank Indians • 1668 (prior to statehood) as a precinct of Albemarle County • The first Grand Assembly of Carolina in 1665 took place at Halls Creek near Elizabeth City. Enfield Farm was the scene of Culpeper's Rebellion instigated in 1677 by John Culpeper and others who established a revolutionary government in opposition to proprietorship in what was then part of Albemarle County. Elizabeth City developed as a West Indies trading center with the completion of the Dismal Swamp Canal in 1828. On Feb. 10, 1862, a Union flotilla won a naval victory against the Confederates near the city. • Shipping (Elizabeth City is a port of entry). Diversified industries, including lumberyards, shipyards, textile mills; manufacture of boxes, barrels, baskets, textiles, furniture, candy. Also soybeans, corn, sorghum, wheat, oats, potatoes, cotton, peanuts, hogs; fishing; education (Elizabeth City State U.; Roanoke Bible College) • The International Cup Regatta is an annual event in Elizabeth City.

PENDER *Burgaw* • 41,082 • 871 (the fifth largest county in NC) • Southeastern NC, bounded on the southeast by the Atlantic Ocean, and on the southwest by the Cape Fear River; drained by the Northeast Cape Fear River (forming part of the county's southern boundary) and the Black River (forming part of its western boundary). Holly Shelter Swamp is here, as well as the southwestern part of Topsail Island. The Intracoastal Waterway passes behind Topsail and small islands. • Named for Gen. William D. Pender (1834–63), officer in the Confederate Army killed at the Battle of Gettysburg • 1875 from New Hanover • The revolutionary cause was advanced in the South by a victory of NC patriots over Loyalists at Moores Creek near Currie on Feb. 27, 1776 (national battlefield). • Corn, wheat, soybeans, hay, sweet potatoes, peanuts, tobacco, turkeys, hogs; beach resort tourism; some manufacturing.

PERQUIMANS *Hertford* • 11,368 • 247 • Northeastern NC, bounded on the south by Albemarle Sound and on the east in part by the Little River estuary; drained by the Perquimans River and indented from the southeast by its estuary. The county includes part of Dismal Swamp in the northeast. • Named for the Perquiman Indians • Organized 1679 (prior to statehood) as Berkeley Precinct of Albemarle County • Wheat, soybeans, peanuts, cotton, corn, turkey, hay, chickens, cattle, hogs; fish, crabs.

PERSON *Roxboro* • 35,623 • 392 • Northern NC, bounded on the north by the VA state line; drained by the Hyco and Flat rivers. Part of Hyco Lake reservoir is here. • Named for General Thomas Person (1733–1800), Revolutionary War officer and NC legislator • 1791 from Caswell • Corn, wheat, oats, soybeans, sorghum, hay, tobacco, cattle, hogs; timber.

PITT *Greenville* • 133,798 • 652 • East-central NC, bounded on the southwest by Contentnea Creek, and partly in the extreme south by the Neuse River; drained by the Tar River and Swift Creek. • Named for William Pitt (1708–78), 1st Earl of Chatham, known as "the Great Commoner" for his support of the American colonies before the Revolutionary War • 1760 (prior to statehood) from Beaufort • Tobacco (Greenville is one of the largest bright-leaf tobacco markets in the world). Also, corn, wheat, oats, barley, soybeans, hay, cotton, peanuts, chickens, cattle, hogs; catfish; stone quarrying; diversified manufacturing; education (East Carolina U.).

POLK (one of twelve counties so named) *Columbus* • 18,324 • 238 • Southwestern NC, in the Piedmont, bounded on the south by the SC state line; drained by the Green River (which forms Lake Adger reservoir). • Named for Colonel William Polk (1758–1834), an officer in the American Revolution, NC legislator, and supervisor of internal revenue for NC • 1855 from Rutherford and Henderson • Novelist and dramatist DuBose Heyward died here. • Wheat, hay, peaches, corn, cattle; timber.

RANDOLPH (one of eight counties so named) *Asheboro* • 130,454 • 787 • Central NC, in the Piedmont; drained by the Deep, Little, and Uwharrie rivers. Part of Uwharrie National Forest is in the southwest. • Named for Peyton Randolph (?–1775), speaker of the VA House of Burgesses and first president of the Continental Congress • 1779 (prior to statehood) from Guilford • Race car driver Richard Petty • Tobacco, hay, corn, wheat, oats, soybeans, dairying, poultry, cattle, hogs; manufacture of furniture, upholstery, knitwear, hosiery, lumber and wood products; stone quarrying • The North Carolina Zoological Park and the Seagroves potters' colony are in the county.

RICHMOND (one of four counties so named) *Rockingham* • 46,564 • 474 • Southern NC, bounded on the south by the SC state line, on the west by the Pee Dee River (which forms Blewett Falls Lake reservoir), and on the northeast by Drowning Creek; drained by the Little River. Part of Pee Dee National Wildlife Refuge is here. • One of two counties (the other in GA) named for Charles Lennox (1735–1806), third Duke of Richmond, British secretary of state who favored independence for the American colonies • 1779 (prior to statehood) from Anson • Tobacco, cotton, corn, wheat, soybeans,

hay, sweet potatoes, poultry, cattle, hogs; sand and gravel; timber. • The National Railroad Museum and Hall of Fame is in Hamlet.

ROBESON *Lumberton* • 123,339 • 949 (the largest county in NC) • Southeastern NC, bounded on the southeast by the Lumber River, on the east in part by the Big Swamp River, and on the southwest by the SC state line. Lumber River State Park is in the south. • Named for Col. Thomas Robeson, Jr., (1740–85), an officer in the American Revolution and member of NC's provincial congress • 1786 from Bladen (prior to statehood) • Lumberton was founded in 1787 by Captain John Willis. It started out as a shipping point for lumber and naval supplies destined for Georgetown, SC. • Wheat, oats, soybeans, sorghum, hay, cotton, peanuts, tobacco, poultry, cattle, hogs; lumber; manufacture of textiles, shoes, apparel; education (U. of NC at Pembroke, which began as an Indian education center in 1887).

ROCKINGHAM *Wentworth* • 91,928 • 566 • Northern NC, in the Piedmont, bounded on the north by the VA state line; drained by the Dan and Haw rivers. Part of Belews Lake reservoir is in the southwest corner. • One of three counties named for Charles Watson-Wentworth (1730–82), second Marquis of Rockingham, prime minister of England, and supporter of independence for the American colonies • 1785 (prior to statehood) from Guilford • Tobacco, corn, wheat, oats, soybeans, sorghum, hay, dairying, poultry, cattle, hogs.

ROWAN (one of two counties so named, the other in KY) *Salisbury* • 130,340 • 511 • West-central NC, in the Piedmont, bounded on the east and north by the Yadkin River (which forms High Rock Lake and Baden Lake reservoirs); drained by Fourth Creek. • Named for Matthew Rowan (?–1760), NC colonial legislator and acting governor when the county was established • 1753 (prior to statehood) from Anson • A historical marker in downtown Salisbury designates the spot from which the famous Boone Trail began in 1765. In February, 1781, British general Lord Cornwallis pursued colonial general Nathanael Greene through the town of Salisbury prior to the Battle of Guilford Courthouse. Salisbury was the site of one of the largest Confederate prisons; within the Salisbury National Cemetery are the graves of about 11,700 Union soldiers who died there. • Pioneer Daniel Boone; President Andrew Jackson; senator Elizabeth Dole • Corn, wheat, hay, oats, barley, soybeans, cotton, chickens, cattle, dairying; manufacture of machinery, textiles, furniture, chemicals, paper products, rubber hose, glass, medicines, mobile homes; granite quarrying; sawmilling; education (Catawba College) • Kannapolis, a company town, owned by Cannon Mills, one of the world's largest producers of household textiles, is the largest unincorporated community in the state. (The town lies partly in Cabarrus County.) The annual "Steamfest" celebration, held in October, commemorates the selection of Spencer in 1896 as the largest steam locomotive-servicing center for the Southern Railway Company (state historic site).

RUTHERFORD *Rutherfordton* • 62,899 • 564 • Southern

NC, bounded on the south by the SC state line; drained by the Broad River (forming Lake Lure reservoir). The source of the French Broad River is in the county, as is Chimney Rock Park. • One of two counties (the other in TN) named for General Griffith Rutherford (?–1805), Indian fighter, member of the Provincial Congress, and Revolutionary War officer • 1779 (prior to statehood) from Burke and Tryon counties, the latter organized in 1768 and abolished in 1779 • Cotton, corn, wheat, soybeans, hay, cattle, chickens, turkeys, dairying; textile and lumber mills; resorts; manufacturing.

SAMPSON *Clinton* • 60,161 • 945 (the second largest county in NC) • Southeast-central NC, bounded on the west and southwest by the South River; drained by the Black River, and Great Coharrie, Little Coharrie, and Six Runs creeks. • Named for Col. John Sampson (?–1784), patriot, wealthy land owner and advisor to Josiah Martin, the last royal governor • 1784 (prior to statehood) from Duplin • Wheat, oats, barley, soybeans, peanuts, sorghum, hay, potatoes, sweet potatoes, tobacco, corn, cotton, poultry, hogs, cattle; pine, gum; manufacturing.

SCOTLAND *Laurinburg* • 35,998 • 319 • Southern NC, bounded on the southwest by the SC state line and on the east by Drowning Creek (extension of the Lumber River). • Named for the country, home of many early settlers • 1899 from Richmond • Cotton, tobacco, corn, wheat, soybeans, hay, chickens, hogs; manufacturing; education (St. Andrews Presbyterian College).

STANLY *Albemarle* • 58,100 • 395 • South-central NC, in the Piedmont, bounded on the east by the Yadkin River (forming Baden Lake and Lake Tillery reservoirs), and on the south by the Rocky River. Morrow Mountain State Park is here. • Named for John Stanly (1774–1834), NC legislator and U.S. representative from NC • 1841 from Montgomery • Cotton, corn, wheat, barley, oats, soybeans, hay, chickens, turkeys, cattle; dairying; pine, oak; manufacturing; education (Pfeiffer U.).

STOKES *Danbury* • 44,711 • 452 • Northern NC, in the Piedmont, bounded on the north by the VA state line; drained by the Dan River. Part of Belews Lake reservoir is in the southeast corner. Hanging Rock State Park is also located in the county. • Named for Col. John Stokes (1756–90), hero of the American Revolution, NC legislator, and district judge • 1798 from Surry • Tobacco, corn, wheat, soybeans, hay, cattle; timber.

SURRY (one of two counties so named, the other in VA) *Dobson* • 71,219 • 537 • Northwestern NC, bounded on the north by the VA state line, on the south by the Yadkin River. Pilot Mountain State Park is here, as is Horne Creek Farm State Historic Site. The Blue Ridge Mountains are in the extreme northwest. The Blue Ridge (national) Parkway closely follows the county's western boundary • Named for either an unidentified Lord Surrey, or for Surrey County in England, home of then-incumbent governor, William Tryon. The spelling without the "e" seems to have been a common colonial practice • 1771 (prior to statehood) from Rowan • Actor

Andy Griffith. Conjoined twins Chang and Eng Bunker and poet Carl Sandburg died here. • Tobacco, corn, dairying, wheat, soybeans, hay, chickens, cattle; timber; stone and granite quarrying; manufacturing.

SWAIN *Bryson City* • 12,968 • 528 • Western NC, bounded on the north by the TN state line. The western extension of the county is bounded on the south by the Little Tennessee River (which forms Fontana Lake and Cheoah reservoirs). The county lies largely within Great Smoky Mountains National Park. Authorized by Congress in 1926, the park contains the most extensive virgin hardwood and red spruce forests in the U.S. The county includes part of Eastern Cherokee Indian Reservation (Museum of the Cherokee Indian). The Appalachian Trail follows part of the state line here. The southern part of the county is in Nantahala National Forest. The southwest terminus of the Blue Ridge (national) Parkway is in the east. • Named for David L. Swain (1801–68), NC governor and president of the University of NC • 1871 from Jackson and Macon • Cattle, hay; lumbering; resort tourism.

TRANSYLVANIA *Brevard* • 29,334 • 378 • Western NC, bounded on the south by the SC state line; drained by the French Broad River. The county lies in the Blue Ridge Mountains, with a large part in Pisgah National Forest. It contains Cradle of Forestry National Historic Area and Looking Glass Rock Scenic Area. Sassafras Mountain, at 3,560 feet, the highest point in neighboring SC, is partly in the county. Looking Glass Falls, Toxaway and Rainbow Falls are here, as is Whitewater Falls, the highest falls in the eastern U.S., its upper cascade dropping from 441 feet • The name comes from Latin *trans* plus *sylva* "across the woods." • 1861 from Jacksonville and Henderson • Vegetables, hay, corn, cattle; oak, poplar, chestnut, hemlock; resorts; manufacture of cigarette paper, cellophane, lumber. • The popular Brevard Music Festival is held in the county seat each August.

TYRRELL *Columbia* • 4,149 (the least populated county in NC) • 390 • Northeastern NC, bounded on the north by Albemarle Sound, and on the east and part of the south by the Alligator River estuary. Part of Pettigrew State Park and part of Pocosin Lakes National Wildlife Refuge are located here. The county lies entirely within East Dismal Swamp. The Intracoastal Waterway passes through the Alligator River. • Named for John Tyrrell (1685–1729), a lord proprietor of NC • 1729 (prior to statehood) from Chowan, Bertie, Currituck, and Pasquotank • Wheat, oats, hay, peanuts, potatoes, cotton, soybeans, hogs, corn; fishing.

UNION (one of eighteen counties so named) *Monroe* • 123,677 • 637 • Southern NC, in the Piedmont, bounded on the south and southwest by the SC state line, and on the northeast by the Rocky River; drained by Lanes Creek. The source of the Lynches River is in the south. • The county's name reflects a compromise to a disagreement between Whigs and Democrats as to whether it should be named for Clay or Jackson; it might also have been given this name for the union of the two counties from which it was formed, Mecklenburg and Anson. • 1842 • Senator Jesse Helms • Wheat, oats, soybeans, barley, cotton, corn, hay, chickens, turkeys, cattle, hogs, dairying; timber; manufacturing; education (Wingate U.).

VANCE *Henderson* • 42,954 • 254 • Northern NC, in the Piedmont, bounded on the north by the VA state line and on the south by the Tar River. Several arms of the J.H. Kerr Reservoir extend from VA; Kerr Lake State Recreation Area is located on the south branch. • Named for Zebulon B. Vance (1830–94), NC governor and U.S. senator from NC • 1881 from Franklin, Granville, and Warren • The area around Henderson was settled by Germans, Scots and Scots-Irish in 1713. • Corn, wheat, soybeans, hay, tobacco (with bright-leaf auction market), cattle, dairying; timber; tungsten deposits; manufacture of textiles, processed foods, glass containers, fertilizers, flour, lumber, trucks.

WAKE *Raleigh* • 627,846 (48.3% increase since 1990; the second fastest growing and second most populated county in NC) • 834 • Central NC; drained by the Neuse River, forming Falls Lake reservoir in the north. Part of Harris Lake Reservoir is in the southwest. The county also includes part of Falls Lake State Recreation Area and William B. Umstead State Park. Part of Research Triangle Park is in the northwest. The county is urbanized in the center around Raleigh with development occurring in the northwest toward Durham County. • Named for Margaret Wake (1733–1819), wife of Royal Gov. William Tryon • 1771 (prior to statehood) from Cumberland, Johnston, and Orange • Raleigh has been the state capital since 1792. The first capitol, completed in 1794, burned in 1831 and was replaced by the present building in 1840. • Journalists Walter H. Page and Vermont Royster; President Andrew Johnson. Heavyweight boxer Jack Johnson, novelist Thomas Dixon, singer Kate Smith, and Secretary of the Navy Josephus Daniels all died here. • Tobacco, cotton, corn, wheat, oats, barley, soybeans, sorghum, hay, chickens, cattle, hogs; granite quarrying; manufacture of electronic equipment, computers, processed foods; insurance; state government offices; research and development (especially textiles and chemicals); education (NC State U.; Meredith College; Peace College; Shaw U.) • The NC Museum of Art is in Raleigh. The city is the site of a National Cemetery. Raleigh is home to the Carolina Hurricanes (Raleigh Entertainment and Sports Arena).

WARREN *Warrenton* • 19,972 • 429 • Northern NC, in the Piedmont, bounded on the north by the VA state line; drained by the Roanoke River (which forms Roanoke Rapids Lake reservoir) and Fishing Creek • One of fourteen counties named for Gen. Joseph Warren (1741–75), American Revolutionary War officer who died at the Battle of Bunker Hill • 1779 (prior to statehood) from Bute County, which was discontinued at that time • Confederate officer Braxton Bragg • Corn, wheat, oats, soybeans, sorghum, hay, tobacco, chickens, dairying, cattle, hogs; timber.

WASHINGTON *Plymouth* • 13,723 • 348 • Eastern NC, bounded on the north by Albemarle Sound and on the northwest by the Roanoke River. Part of Phelps Lake is here, as is Pungo Lake (on the southern boundary). Somerset Place State Historic Site and part of Pettigrew State Park are also here. Much of the county lies within East Dismal Swamp. • One of thirty-one counties named for George Washington • 1799 from Tyrrell • Playwright Augustin Daly • Pine, gum; peanuts, tobacco, corn, wheat, oats, soybeans, sorghum, potatoes, cotton, chickens, hogs, cattle; timber; fishing; manufacturing.

WATAUGA *Boone* • 42,695 • 313 • Northwestern NC, bounded on the northwest by the TN state line; drained by the Watauga, Yadkin, South Fork, and New rivers. The county lies in the Blue Ridge Mountains. Blue Ridge (national) Parkway crosses in the south. Part of Pisgah National Forest is here, as are Julian Price Park and several ski areas. • Named for the Watauga River • 1849 from Ashe, Caldwell, Wilkes, and Yancey • The settlement of Boone, nestled at the crest of the Blue Ridge Mountains at an altitude of 3,333 feet, is located on the Daniel Boone Trail at the fork of the Wilderness Road. • Tobacco, vegetables, corn, hay, cattle, dairying; timber; manufacture of electric components, apparel, canned foods; tourism and recreational activities (skiing, fishing, hunting); education (Appalachian State U. has a noted collection of Appalachian artifacts in its Belk Library) • *Horn in the West*, an outdoor pioneer drama by Kermit Hunter, has been produced at the Daniel Boone Theatre each summer since 1952.

WAYNE (one of sixteen counties so named) *Goldsboro* • 113,329 • 553 • East-central NC; crossed by the Neuse river. The source of the Northeast Cape Fear River is in the southeast. Cliffs of the Neuse and Waynesborough state parks are here. Seymour Johnson Air Force Base is located near Goldsboro. • One of fifteen counties named for "Mad Anthony" Wayne (1745–96), PA Revolutionary War general and statesman • 1779 (prior to statehood) from Dobbs • Educator and politician Charles B. Aycock (state historic birthplace site) • Tobacco (principal crop); also, wheat, oats, soybeans, hay, sweet potatoes, chickens, turkeys, dairying, cattle, hogs, cotton, green beans, corn; manufacture of wood products, furniture, textiles, apparel, leather goods, metal products, electrical equipment; education (Mount Olive College).

WILKES *Wilkesboro* • 65,632 • 757 • Northwestern NC; drained by the Yadkin River. The county lies mostly in the Blue Ridge Mountains. The Blue Ridge (national) Parkway follows the northwestern border. Rendezvous Mountain Educational State Forest is in the county, as is Stone Mountain State Park (on the northern border). The county also contains W. Kerr Scott Reservoir. • One of two counties (the other in GA) named for John Wilkes (1727–97), English political leader who supported the American colonies at the time of the Revolutionary War • 1777 (prior to statehood) from Surry • Senator Robert Byrd • Chickens, cattle, dairying, wheat, soybeans, hay, honey, tobacco, cotton, corn; manufacturing; stone quarrying; mountain resorts.

WILSON (one of four counties so named) *Wilson* • 73,814 • 371 • East-central NC; drained by Contentnea Creek. • Named for Louis D. Wilson (1789–1847), member of the NC General Assembly and an officer in the Mexican War • 1855 from Edgecombe, Johnston, Wayne, and Nash • Corn, wheat, hay, sweet potatoes, tobacco (sizable bright-leaf market), cotton, chickens, hogs, dairying; timber; meat packing, cotton milling; manufacture of animal feed, textiles, concrete products, truck and bus bodies, wagons, electronic equipment, agricultural implements, lumber and wood products; education (Barton College). • The annual North Carolina Amateur Golf Tournament is held in Wilson each June.

YADKIN *Yadkinville* • 36,348 • 336 • Northwestern NC, in the Piedmont, bounded on the north and east by the Yadkin River. • Named for the Yadkin River • 1850 from Surry • Tobacco, corn, wheat, oats, barley, soybeans, hay, dairying, cattle; pine, oak • The Yadkin River valley was a neutral zone acknowledged by local Indian tribes. Before battle, women, children, and old men were deposited here, assured of their safety.

YANCEY *Burnsville* • 17,774 • 312 • Western NC, bounded on the northwest by the TN state line and on the northeast by the Nolichucky River; drained by the South Toe and Cape rivers. The county is crossed by the Blue Ridge and Black Mountains, including Mount Mitchell, at 6,684 feet, the highest point east of the Rocky Mountains. The Bald Mountains and Appalachian Trail follow the TN state line, while the Blue Ridge (national) Parkway follows the county line in the south and southeast. The county includes part of Pisgah and part of Cherokee national forests, as wall as Mount Mitchell State Park and Middle Creek Natural Area. • Named for Bartlett Yancey (1785–1828), U.S. representative from NC and presiding officer of the state senate • 1833 from Buncombe and Burke • Tobacco, hay, cattle, corn, livestock; timber; mining of mica, kaolin, and feldspar; resorts.

NORTH DAKOTA

Liberty and Union, Now and Forever, One and Inseparable

Each of the state's fifty-three counties is governed by a board of commissioners, composed of three to five members, elected to four-year terms. Auditor, sheriff, register of deeds, superintendent of schools, and treasurer are other county-wide elective offices.

ADAMS (one of twelve counties so named) *Hettinger* • 2,593 • 988 • Southwestern ND, bounded on the south by the SD state line; drained by Cedar Creek. • Named for John Quincy Adams (1848–1919). Distantly related to the president of the same name, Adams served as land agent for the Chicago, Milwaukee and St. Paul Railroad. • 1907 from Hettinger • Dairying, wheat, cattle; transportation; utilities.

BARNES *Valley City* • 11,775 • 1,492 • Southeastern ND; drained by the Sheyenne River (which forms Lake Ashtabula reservoir). There are two national fish hatcheries near Bald Hill Dam. Hobart Lake National Wildlife Refuge and Wadeson Cabin State Historic Site are located here. • Named for Alanson H. Barnes (1818–90), associate justice of the Supreme Court of Dakota Territory • Organized as Burbank by the 1872–1873 territorial legislature (prior to statehood) from Cass; renamed 1875 • Wheat, oats, barley, potatoes, soybeans, other grains, flax, hogs; flour milling; dairy products; manufacture of electronic equipment, metal stampings; education (Valley City State U.).

BENSON *Minnewaukan* • 6,964 • 1,389 • North-central ND; watered by the Sheyenne River. The county includes numerous lakes, including Devils Lake on its eastern border. Much of Spirit Lake Indian Reservation is in the southeast, and includes Fort Totten State Historic Site, Sullys Hill National Game Preserve, Skyline ski area, and Shelvers Grove and Black Tiger Bay state recreation areas within its boundaries. Part of Buffalo Lake National Wildlife Refuge is in the west. • Named for Bertil W. Benson, a Dakota Territory legislator at the time the county was organized • 1883 (prior to statehood) from Ramsey • Dairy products, wheat, barley, rye, livestock, poultry; textile products.

BILLINGS *Medora* • 888 • 1,151 • Western ND; watered by the Little Missouri River and headwaters of the Green and Knife rivers. The county is located in the North Dakota Badlands and Little Missouri National Grassland. Theodore Roosevelt National Park, South Unit is here, as is the Elkhorn Ranch Unit (containing Roosevelt's ranch). De Mores Historic site and Sully Creek State Recreation Area are in the west. • Named for Frederick Billings (1823–90), president of the Northern Pacific Railroad • 1879 (prior to statehood) from unorganized territory • Oil, some agriculture.

BOTTINEAU *Bottineau* • 7,149 • 1,669 • Northern ND, bounded on the north by the Canadian provinces of Manitoba and Saskatchewan; watered by the Souris River and Cut Bank Creek. The Turtle Mountains, Turtle Mountain State Forest, Lake Metogoshe State Park, Homen State Forest, and Bottineau Winter Park ski area are in the northeast. J. Clark Salyer National Wildlife Refuge lies along the Souris River. • Named for Pierre Bottineau (?–1895), a French-Canadian frontiersman, guide, and land speculator • 1873 (prior to statehood) from unorganized territory • Oil and natural gas deposits; diversified farming, including wheat, dairy, livestock.

BOWMAN *Bowman* • 3,242 • 1,162 • Extreme southwestern ND; watered by the Little Missouri River, Cedar Creek, and the North Fork of the Grand River. Bowman Haley Dam and Lake are here, as is Butte View Campground. Fort Dilts is on the northern boundary. • Named for Edward M. Bowman, a Dakota Territory legislator • Organized 1883 (prior to statehood) from Billings. The county was eliminated in 1903, for lack of settlement; reestablished 1907 • Lignite coal; cattle, wheat, flax.

BURKE (one of three counties so named) *Bowbells* • 2,242 • 1,104 • Northwestern ND, bounded on the north by the Canadian province of Saskatchewan; drained by Des Lacs and White Earth rivers. Part of Des Lacs and Lostwood national wildlife refuges are here. • Named for John Burke (1859–1937), governor of ND, treasurer of the U.S., and justice of the ND Supreme Court • 1910 from Ward • Cattle, wheat, barley, flax; mining. • The ninth hole of the International Golf Course based in Portal, with its tee in Canada and cup in the U.S., allows for the possibility of an "international hole-in-one," which was first achieved by George Wegener in 1934.

BURLEIGH *Bismarck* • 69,416 (the second most populated county in ND) • 1,633 • Central ND, bounded on the west by the Missouri River (which forms Lake Oahe reservoir); drained by Apple Creek. Florence Lake and Canfield Lake national wildlife refuges are here, as are Camp Hancock, Double Ditch Indian Village, and Menoken Indian Village state historic sites. Long Lake and its national wildlife refuge extend into Kidder County in the Southeast. Numerous small lakes are in the northeast. • Named for Walter A. Burleigh (1820–96), attorney, physician, and Dakota Territory delegate to Congress • 1873 (prior to statehood) from Buffalo County, which was discontinued • Bismarck originated as a port in the 1830s called "Crossing the Missouri." In 1872, Camp Greeley (later Camp Hancock) was established here to protect Northern Pacific Railway crews. The town was named for German chancellor Otto von Bismarck in hopes of attracting German investment in the railway. It became an outfitting center for prospectors following the discovery of gold in the Black Hills to the southwest. In 1883, the capital of Dakota Territory was moved here. When the territory was divided into North and South Dakota for admission to the Union in 1889, Bismarck became ND's state capital. • Presbyterian scholar John Gresham Machen • Diversified agricultural crops, including spring wheat; livestock; lignite mines; education (U. of Mary; Bismarck State College) • The first highway bridge across the

Missouri River was constructed at Bismarck. The Dakota Zoo and North Dakota Heritage Center are also both located in the city.

CASS (one of nine counties so named) *Fargo* • 123,138 (19.7% increase since 1990; the fastest growing and most populated county in ND) • 1,766 • Eastern ND, bounded on the east by the Red River of the North (forming the MN border); drained by the Maple, Sheyenne, and Rush rivers. With its population centered around Fargo in the east, it is the most urbanized county in ND. Maple Creek Crossing State Historic Site is in the south. • Named for George W. Cass (1810–88), president of the Northern Pacific Railroad • Original county; organized 1873 (prior to statehood) • Fargo was founded in 1871 by the Northern Pacific Railway as an outfitting post for settlers. • Sculptor John Bernard Flannagan; writer William H. Gass • Cattle, hogs (West Fargo's meat packing plants and stockyards rank among the largest in the U.S.). Also, wheat, soybeans, barley, flax; food processing; manufacture of farm equipment, computer software, construction equipment and materials, chemicals, automobile accessories; agricultural research and education (ND State U.) Fargo is an important regional medical center. • Very little of the film *Fargo* is set here; most of it takes place in Brainerd, MN (Crow Wing County). The Cass County Historical Society Museum and the Forsberg House in Fargo have collections of pioneer relics. Bonanzaville U.S.A. is a reconstruction of a 19th century farming boomtown. Fargo also has a museum dedicated to home run king Roger Maris.

CAVALIER *Langdon* • 4,831 • 1,489 • Northeastern ND, bounded on the north by the Canadian province of Manitoba; drained by the Pembina, Tongue and Park rivers. An agricultural experimental station is at Langdon. Frostfire Mountain ski area, Rush Lake, and part of Tetrault Woods State Forest are also in the county. • Named for Charles T. Cavileer (1818–1902), territorial librarian, collector of customs for the district of MN, and one of the first white settlers in what is now the state of ND. The spelling was changed to make the name seem French. • 1873 (prior to statehood) from Pembina • Langdon claims the title "Durum (wheat) Capital of the World." Also, barley, dairy products, cattle.

DICKEY *Ellendale* • 5,757 • 1,131 • Southeastern ND; drained by the James and Maple rivers. Whitestone Hill Battlefield State Historic Site is in the northwest. • Named for George H. Dickey (1858–1923), a ND territorial legislator • 1881 (prior to statehood) from La Moure • Wheat, barley, rye, dairy products, poultry, cattle, hogs; education (Trinity Bible College).

DIVIDE *Crosby* • 2,283 • 1,259 • Extreme northwestern ND, bounded on the north by the Canadian province of Saskatchewan and on the west by the MT state line; drained by Long Creek. Writing Rock (a five foot-high boulder with incised Indian symbols) State Historic Site is in the southwest. • The county's name reflects the division of its mother county Williams • 1910 • Lignite mines; cattle, wheat, barley.

DUNN (one of two counties so named, the other in WI) *Manning* • 3,600 • 2,010 • West-central ND, bounded on the northeast by the Missouri River (Lake Sakakawea); drained by the Little Missouri (a time zone boundary here; Central north, Mountain south), Knife, and Green rivers, and Spring Creek. Little Missouri State Park, Killdeer Mountain Battlefield Historic Site, Lake Ilo National Wildlife Refuge and part of Fort Berthold Indian Reservation are here. • Named for John P. Dunn (1839–1917), mayor of Bismarck, ND • 1883 (prior to statehood) from Howard County, which was discontinued • Dairying, wheat, oats, cattle.

EDDY (one of two counties so named, the other in NM) *New Rockford* • 2,757 • 632 (the smallest county in ND) • Central ND; drained by the Sheyenne and James rivers. Part of Spirit Lake Indian Reservation is here. Several small lakes are in the east. • Named for Ezra B. Eddy (1829–85), founder of the first National Bank of Fargo • 1885 (prior to statehood) from Foster • Sunflowers, dairying, wheat, rye, flax, poultry, cattle.

EMMONS *Linton* • 4,331 • 1,510 • Southern ND, bounded on the south by the SD state line and on the west by Lake Oahe reservoir of the Missouri River; drained by Beaver, Little Beaver, and Long Lake creeks. • Named for James A. Emmons (1845–1919), steamboat captain, early settler, and merchant • 1879 (prior to statehood) from unorganized territory • Band leader Lawrence Welk • Wheat, barley, cattle, dairying.

FOSTER *Carrington* • 3,759 • 635 • Central ND; drained by the James River and Pipestem Creek. Hawks Nest Ridge and a small portion of Arrowwood National Wildlife Refuge are on the southern boundary. • Named for James S. Foster (1828–1890), first superintendent of public instruction for Dakota Territory and commissioner of immigration • 1873 (prior to statehood) from Pembina • Sunflowers, wheat, barley, flax, cattle, dairying.

GOLDEN VALLEY (one of two counties so named, the other in MT) *Beach* • 1,924 • 1,002 • Western ND, bounded on the west by the MT state line; drained by Beaver Creek. Little Missouri National Grassland covers the eastern portion of the county. • Named for the Golden Valley Land and Cattle Company of St. Paul, MN • 1912 from Billings • Oil fields, lignite mines; cattle, wheat.

GRAND FORKS *Grand Forks* • 66,109 (the third most populated county in ND) • 1,438 • Eastern ND, bounded on the east by the Red River of the North (on the MN border); watered by the Goose, Forest, and Turtle rivers. Turtle River State Park and Kellys Slough National Wildlife Refuge are in the county. • Named for the village of Grand Forks in Dakota Territory • 1873 (prior to statehood) from Pembina • A trading post of the Northwest Company was located in Grand Forks in 1801. Permanent settlement began here in 1871 and expanded with the arrival of the Great Northern Railway in 1880. Grand Forks was devastated by floodwaters from the Red River in the spring of 1997, forcing the evacuation of nearly all of the town's residents. • Grand Forks is the principal trade center for the Red River valley. Wheat, barley, mustard, potatoes, sugar beets, field seeds, cattle, hogs; sugar refining, grain milling, feed milling, potato processing; manufacture of fertilizer; creameries; aerospace science research and education (U. of ND — the state's oldest and largest institute of higher learning). Grand Forks has a lignite research laboratory of the U.S. Bureau of Mines. The county is also home to Grand Forks Air Force Base, a large employer.

GRANT (one of fifteen counties so named) *Carson* • 2,841 • 1,660 • Southern ND, bounded on the south by Cedar Creek and the Cannonball River; watered by the Heart and Cannonball rivers and Antelope Creek. Lake Tschida (Heart River) reservoir is here. Part of Cedar River National Grassland and Cannonball Stage Station State Historic Site are in the south. • One of twelve counties named for President Ulysses S. Grant • 1916 from Morton • Cattle, hogs, dairy products, barley, rye, wheat.

GRIGGS *Cooperstown* • 2,754 • 709 • East-central ND; drained by the Sheyenne River and Bald Hill Creek. The northern part of Lake Ashtabula reservoir is in the southeast corner. Part of Johnson Lake National Wildlife Refuge and Camp Atchison State Historic Site are here. • Named for Alexander Griggs (1838–1903), an early Red River pilot, founder of the city of Grand Forks, and member of the ND Constitutional Convention • 1881 (prior to statehood) from Foster • Wheat, rye, cattle, dairy products.

HETTINGER *Mott* • 2,715 • 1,132 • Southwestern ND; drained by the Cannonball River and Thirtymile Creek. • Named for Mathias Hettinger (1810–1890), by his son-in-law, Erastus A. Williams, Speaker of the House of the Dakota territorial legislature and county founder • 1883 (prior to statehood) from Stark • Wheat, rye, cattle.

KIDDER *Steele* • 2,753 • 1,352 • Central ND; watered by numerous small lakes, including part of Long Lake, which is encompassed by Long Lake National Wildlife Refuge. The county also includes Slade and Lake George national wildlife refuges. • Named for Jefferson P. Kidder (?–1883), VT legislator and lieutenant governor, and associate justice of Dakota Territory Supreme Court • 1873 (prior to statehood) from Buffalo County, which was discontinued • Cattle, wheat, barley, oats, hay, flax, dairying.

LA MOURE *La Moure* • 4,701 • 1,147 • Southeastern ND; drained by the James and Maple rivers and Cottonwood Creek. • Named for Judson La Moure (1839–1918), pioneer and Dakota territorial legislator • 1873 (prior to statehood) from Pembina • Wheat, corn, barley, rye, cattle, hogs, dairy products.

LOGAN (one of ten counties so named) *Napoleon* • 2,308 • 993 • Southern ND; watered by Beaver Creek and numerous lakes, including Rush and Alkali. Beaver Lake State Park is also in the county. • One of five counties named for General John A. Logan (1826–86), officer in the Mexican War and Civil

War and U.S. senator from IL • 1873 (prior to statehood) from Buffalo County, which was discontinued • Cattle, sunflowers, wheat, barley, dairy products.

MCHENRY (one of two counties so named, the other in IL) *Towner* • 5,987 • 1,874 • North-central ND; drained by the Souris River (Mouse River), Wintering River, and Spring Coulee and Cut Bank creeks. Among its several lakes are North, Buffalo Lodge, George, and Smoky. Part of J. Clark Salyer National Wildlife Refuge is here, as are Mouse River State Forest and Denbigh Experimental Forest. • Named for James McHenry, an early settler of Vermillion, SD and a Dakota territorial legislator • 1873 (prior to statehood) from Buffalo County, which was discontinued • Explorer and fur trader David Thompson (state historic site) • Cattle, poultry, dairy products, wheat, rye, barley, hay.

MCINTOSH (one of three counties so named) *Ashley* • 3,390 • 975 • Southern ND, bounded on the south by the SD state line; watered by the South Branch of Beaver Creek. The county includes Doyle Memorial State Park on Green Lake, and Lake Hoskins. • Named for Edward H. McIntosh (?–1901), a Dakota territorial legislator • 1883 (prior to statehood) from Logan • Dairy products, wheat, rye, cattle; manufacture of farm machinery.

MCKENZIE *Watford City* • 5,737 • 2,742 (the largest county in ND) • Western ND, bounded on the west by the MT state line and on the north by the Missouri River (Lake Sakakawea); watered by the Yellowstone and Little Missouri rivers. Little Missouri National Grassland is here, as is the north unit of Theodore Roosevelt National Park. The county also includes part of Fort Berthold Indian Reservation. McKenzie is one of only a few U.S. counties that straddle time zones; the south is in the Mountain time zone and the north is in the Central time zone. • Named for Alexander McKenzie (1851–1922), sheriff of Burleigh County and a powerful political leader responsible for moving the capital of Dakota Territory to Bismarck • Organized 1883 (prior to statehood) from Howard County, which was discontinued. The county was eliminated in 1891 for lack of settlement and reorganized in 1905 • Lignite, oil, natural gas; wheat, sugar beets, cattle. • Three Affiliated Tribes Museum is located in Fort Berthold Indian Reservation.

MCLEAN (one of three counties so named) *Washburn* • 9,311 • 2,110 (the third largest county in ND) • Central ND, bounded on the west and south by the Missouri River (Lake Sakakawea). The county includes Fort Stevenson State Park and part of Fort Berthold Indian Reservation. Audubon, Lake Nettie, and McLean national wildlife refuges are here, as is Indian Hills State Recreation Area. • Named for John A. McLean (1849–1916), early mayor of Bismarck, ND • 1883 (prior to statehood) from Stevens • Lewis and Clark wintered at Fort Mandan (state historic site, interpretive center) during their 1804–05 western trek • Lignite mines; cattle, dairy products, wheat, barley, rye, flax.

MERCER (one of eight counties so named) *Stanton* • 8,644

• 1,045 • Central ND, bounded on the north and east by the Missouri River; drained by the Knife River and Spring Creek. Lake Sakakawea is formed by Garrison Dam, one of the largest earth-fill dams in the U.S. Sakakawea State Park is located at the dam. The county also includes Knife River Indian Village National Historic Site and part of Fort Berthold Indian Reservation. • Named for William H. H. Mercer (1844–1901), an early rancher • 1875 (prior to statehood) from original territory • Lignite mines; wheat, cattle.

MORTON *Mandan* • 25,303 (the fifth most populated county in ND) • 1,926 • Central ND, bounded on the east by the Missouri River (Lake Oahe reservoir) and on the south in part by the Cannonball River; drained by Big Muddy Creek. Fort Rice State Historic Site, Huff Indian Village State Historic Site, On-A-Slant Indian Village, and Huff Hills ski area are here. Fort Abraham Lincoln State Park includes reconstructed blockhouses of the fort commanded by Lt. Colonel George Armstrong Custer prior to his "last stand" at the Battle of Little Bighorn in 1876. Most of the county is in the Mountain time zone. A small section in the northeast is in the Central time zone. • One of two counties (the other in KS) named for Oliver Hazard Perry Throck Morton (1823–77), jurist, governor of IN, and U.S. senator from IN • Organized 1873 (prior to statehood) from parts of Rolette, Bottineau, and McHenry counties and all of De Smet County; annexed part of Church Colony in 1891 • Cattle, hogs, dairying (Mandan is a center for livestock auctions.) Also, wheat, barley, hay; manufacture of food products, building materials; petroleum refining; creameries; lignite deposits • The Northern Great Plains Research Center south of Mandan is one of the largest agricultural research facilities in the U.S.

MOUNTRAIL *Stanley* • 6,631 • 1,824 • Northwest-central ND, bounded on the southwest by the Missouri River (Lake Sakakawea) and on the south by the Van Hook arm of Lake Sakakawea; drained by the White Earth and Little Knife rivers, and Shell Creek. The county contains part of Fort Berthold Indian Reservation, Shell Lake National Wildlife Refuge, part of Lostwood National Wildlife Refuge, and several lakes, including Powers, White, and Lower Lostwood. • It was possibly named for "Savage" Joseph Mountraille, prominent voyageur who carried the mail. • Organized as Mountraille in 1873 (prior to statehood) from Ward County. Eliminated in 1891; reestablished with its present spelling in 1909 • Lignite mines; cattle, dairying, wheat, rye.

NELSON (one of three counties so named) *Lakota* • 3,715 • 982 • East-central ND; watered by the Sheyenne and Goose rivers. Stump Lake is here, as are Stump Lake and part of Johnson Lake national wildlife refuges. • Named for Nelson E. Nelson (1830–1913), a ND territorial legislator at the time of establishment • 1883 (prior to statehood) from Foster and Grand Forks • Dairying, cattle, poultry, wheat, oats, sunflowers.

OLIVER *Center* • 2,065 • 724 • Central ND, bounded on the east by the Missouri River; watered by Square Butte and Otter creeks. The county includes Cross Ranch State Park and Nature Preserve and Fort Clark Historic Site. • Named for Harry S. Oliver (1855–1909), landowner and Dakota Territory legislator • 1885 (prior to statehood) from Mercer • Lignite mines; cattle, wheat, barley, potatoes.

PEMBINA *Cavalier* • 8,585 • 1,119 • Extreme northeastern ND, bounded on the east by the Red River of the North (forming the MN state line), and on the north by the Canadian province of Manitoba; drained by the Tongue and Pembina rivers. Includes Icelandic State Park, Pioneer Heritage Center, and Gingras Trading Post and Walhalla state historic sites. • Named for the earliest European trading post in Dakota Territory. • 1867 (prior to statehood) from Indian lands • The earliest settled county in the state, it was colonized by Scottish and Swiss emigrants from near Winnipeg 1812–13. Thought to be part of Canada, it came under U.S. domain when the boundary was formally set between the two countries in 1818. • Wheat, rye, sugar beets, potatoes, cattle, hogs; manufacture of transportation equipment.

PIERCE (One of five counties so named) *Rugby* • 4,675 • 1,018 • North-central ND, watered by numerous mid-sized lakes. Buffalo Lake National Wildlife Refuge is located here. • Named for Lt. Col. Gilbert A. Pierce (1839–1901), governor of Dakota Territory, and one of the first two U.S. senators from ND • 1887 (prior to statehood) from parts of Rolette, Bottineau, and McHenry and all of De Smet; annexed part of Church in 1891 • Cliff Thompson, at 8'7", one of the tallest men in the world • Dairying, wheat, barley, rye, cattle • The U.S. Geological Survey has determined Rugby to be the geographical center of North America.

RAMSEY *Devils Lake* • 12,066 • 1,186 • Northeast-central ND, bounded on the south by Devils Lake. The county has several lakes, including Sweetwater, Dry, and Alice (encompassed by Lake Alice Wildlife Refuge). Grahams Island State Park is also here. • One of two counties (the other in MN) named for Alexander Ramsey (1815–1903), first governor of MN Territory, U.S. senator from MN, and U.S. secretary of war • 1873 (prior to statehood) from Pembina • Wheat, sunflowers, barley, rye, cattle, dairy products; manufacture of sheet-metal products, flour, farm implements, liquid fertilizer.

RANSOM *Lisbon* • 5,890 • 863 • Southeastern ND; drained by the Sheyenne and Maple rivers. Fort Ransom State Park and Fort Ransom Historic Site are in the northwest, as are Sheyenne State Forest and Bears Den Mountain ski area. Part of Sheyenne National Grassland is in the southeast, including Pigeon Point Preserve and part of H.R. Morgan Nature Preserve. • Named for Fort Ransom in Dakota Territory • 1873 (prior to statehood) from Pembina • Fort Ransom, active as a military post between 1867–72, was established to protect settlers traveling from MN to MT Territory from Indian attacks. • Cattle, hogs, soybeans, dairying, corn, wheat, barley, rye, hay, sunflowers.

RENVILLE (one of two counties so named, the other in MN) *Mohall* • 2,610 • 875 • Northern ND, bounded on the north by the Canadian province of Saskatchewan; drained by the Souris River (Mouse River), encompassed, in part, by a large portion of Upper Souris National Wildlife Refuge. • Named for either Gabriel Renville (?–1892), an early settler, chief of scouts for the U.S. Army and chief of Sisseton and Wahpeton Indian Reservation; or for his uncle Joseph Renville (?–1846), guide and interpreter for Zebulon Pike • 1873 (prior to statehood) from Pembina. Dissolved in 1891 for lack of settlement; present county created 1910 • Cattle, wheat, barley, rye, dairy products.

RICHLAND (one of seven counties so named) *Wahpeton* • 17,998 • 1,437 • Extreme southeastern ND, bounded on the south by the SD state line, on the east by the Bois de Sioux River and Red River on the North (forming the MN state line); watered by the Sheyenne and Wild Rice rivers. Fort Abercrombie State Historic Site is here, as is a small portion of Lake Traverse Indian Reservation. Part of Sheyenne National Grassland, including part of H.R. Morgan Nature Preserve is in the northwest. Chahinkapa Park and Zoo is in Wahpeton. • Named for Morgan T. Rich (1832–98), early Dakota settler and founder of the city of Wahpeton • Original county; organized 1873 (prior to statehood) • Corn, wheat, soybeans, sunflowers, sugar beets, poultry, cattle, hogs, sheep; food processing, manufacture of wood products, metal stampings, industrial machinery, electrical equipment, pottery, sheet iron; printing & binding; education (ND State School of Science).

ROLETTE *Rolla* • 13,674 • 903 • Northern ND, bounded on the north by the Canadian province of Manitoba; drained by Willow, Wolf, and Ox creeks. The Turtle Mountains and Turtle Mountain Indian Reservation (including Turtle Mountain Chippewa Heritage Center) are here, as are numerous lakes. The International Peace Garden and International Music Camp are on the U.S./Canada border. • Named for Joseph Rolette (1820–71), customs official at Pembina and MN territorial legislator • 1873 (prior to statehood) from Buffalo, which was discontinued • Wheat, barley, rye, cattle; manufacture of communications equipment, truck trailers, watch parts.

SARGENT *Forman* • 4,366 • 859 • Southeastern ND; drained by the Wild Rice River. Lake Traverse Indian Reservation is here, as are Tewaukon National Wildlife Refuge on Lake Tewaukon and Storm Lake National Wildlife Refuge. • Named for Gen. Homer E. Sargent (1822–?), general manager of the Northern Pacific Railroad Company and developer of the Red River valley • 1883 (prior to statehood) from Ransom • Wheat, rye, soybeans, cattle, hogs, dairying.

SHERIDAN *McClusky* • 1,710 • 972 • Central ND; watered by the Sheyenne River. The McClusky Canal connects the Sheyenne River to Lake Audubon/Lake Sakakawea (Missouri River). Krueger Lake is here, as is Sheyenne Lake reservoir (Sheyenne River). Florence Lake National Wildlife Refuge and Sheridan Preserve are in the south. • One of five counties named directly or indirectly for Gen. Philip H. Sheridan (1831–88), Union officer during the Civil War and commander in chief of the U.S. Army • 1908 from McLean • Dairy products, wheat, barley, rye, cattle.

SIOUX (one of three counties so named) *Fort Yates* • 4,044 • 1,094 • Southern ND, bounded on the north by Cedar Creek and the Cannonball River, and on the south by the SD state line. Standing Rock Indian Reservation comprises the entire county, its headquarters at Fort Yates. A large part of Cedar River National Grassland is in the southwest. Most of the county lies within the Mountain time zone; the southeast corner is in the Central time zone. • One of five counties named for the Sioux Indians • 1914 from Standing Rock Indian Reservation • Indian Chief Sitting Bull is buried at Fort Yates (historic site) • Cattle, wheat, dairying.

SLOPE *Amidon* • 767 (the least populated county in ND) • 1,218 • Southwestern ND, bounded on the west by the MT state line; drained by the Little Missouri and Cannonball rivers and Deep Creek. The county contains White Butte, at 3,506 feet, the highest point in the state. Little Missouri National Grassland is in the western half. North Dakota Badlands run north/south through the county. Fort Dilts Historic Site, Burning Coal Vein and Columnar Cedars, and Stewart Lake and White Lake national wildlife refuges are here. • Named for the Missouri Slope, a popular name for western ND, especially the area west of the Missouri River • 1915 from Billings • Extensive lignite deposits; cattle, wheat.

STARK (one of three counties so named) *Dickinson* • 22,636 • 1,338 • Western ND; drained by the Heart and Green rivers and Antelope Creek. Edward A. Patterson and Schnell Bureau of Land Management recreation areas are here, as is the Dakota Dinosaur Museum in Dickinson. • Named for George Stark, president of the Northern Pacific Railroad • 1879 (prior to statehood) from unorganized territory • Early settlers to the county were Russian and German. Founded in 1882, Dickinson was later a forwarding point for supplies to the gold fields of the Black Hills. • Cattle, hogs, wheat, barley, hay, dairying; food processing, meat packing; manufacture of wood products, lignite briquettes, furniture, machinery, transportation equipment; steel fabrication; oil, clay; education (Dickinson State U.).

STEELE (one of two counties so named, the other in MN) *Finley* • 2,258 • 712 • Eastern ND; watered by the Maple and Goose rivers. • Probably named for Edward H. Steele (1846–99), secretary of the Red River Land Company, which figured prominently in the establishment of the county • 1883 (prior to statehood) from Traill • Wheat, rye, potatoes, flax, cattle, dairy products.

STUTSMAN *Jamestown* • 21,908 • 2,221 (the second largest county in ND) • Central ND; drained by the James River, and Pipestem and Beaver creeks. The county includes Arrowwood and Chase Lake national wildlife refuges, Fort Seward Historic Site, Jamestown Reservoir (Jim Lake), Arrowwood, Mud, Pipestem, and Chase lakes. • Named for Enos Stutsman (1826–74), Dakota territorial legislator and Federal customs agent • 1873 (prior to statehood) from Pembina • Sunflowers, rye, hay, flax, wheat, dairying, cattle, hogs, sheep; manufacture of food products, machinery, transportation equipment, cement and concrete products; education (Jamestown College) • In 1963, the Northern Wildlife Research Center was established in Jamestown. The Frontier Village and National Buffalo Museum is located in the city.

TOWNER *Cando* • 2,876 • 1,025 • Northern ND, bounded on the north by the Canadian province of Manitoba; watered by creeks and streams. Rock Lake is in the north and a small part of Hurricane Lake is in the extreme southwest corner. • Named for Oscar M. Towner (1842–97), early rancher, land speculator, and Dakota territorial legislator • 1883 (prior to statehood) from Rolette • Politician Richard K. Army • Wheat, barley, cattle.

TRAILL *Hillsboro* • 8,477 • 862 • Eastern ND, bounded on the east by the Red River of the North (forming the MN state line); drained by the Goose and Elm rivers. The Carl Ben Eielsen Memorial Arch is on the northwest boundary. • Named for Walter J.S. Traill (1847–1933) of the Hudson's Bay Company • 1875 (prior to statehood) from Grand Forks • Wheat, corn, barley, soybeans, flax, beans, cattle, hogs; beet-sugar refining; education (Mayville State U.) • At 2,063 feet, The KVLY-TV Tower located between Blanchard and Galesburg, is the world's tallest structure.

WALSH *Grafton* • 12,389 • 1,282 • Northeastern ND, bounded on the east by the Red River of the North (forming the MN state line); drained by the Forest and Park rivers. Lake Ardoch (bordered by Ardoch National Wildlife Refuge) and Homme Lake reservoir are here. • Named for George H. Walsh (1845–1913), newspaper publisher and member of ND's first state legislature. • 1881 (prior to statehood) from Grand Forks and Pembina • Cattle, hogs, wheat, rye, barley, sugar beets, potatoes; beet-sugar refining, manufacture of industrial machinery.

WARD (one of two counties so named, the other in TX) *Minot* • 58,795 (the fourth most populated county in ND) • 2,013 (the fifth largest county in ND) • North-central ND; drained by the Souris and Des Lacs rivers. A small part of Fort Berthold Indian Reservation is in the southwest corner. Part of Des Lacs, and part of Upper Souris national wildlife refuges are also here. • Named for Mark Ward (1844–1902), member of the Dakota Territory legislature when the county was formed • 1885 (prior to statehood) from Renville • Minot is an important shipping point and regional trade center. Cattle, wheat, sunflowers, barley, oats, rye, hay, nurseries, dairying; lignite mines, oil and gas extraction, sand and gravel deposits, marble; manufacture of food products, beverages; millwork, nurseries; railroad shops, large freight classification yard; education (Minot State U.). Minot Air Force Base is also economically important. Minot is a medical center for northwest ND • The city is also the site of the annual ND State Fair.

WELLS (one of two counties so named, the other in IN) *Fessenden* • 5,102 • 1,271 • Central ND; drained by the Sheyenne and James rivers, connected by New Rockford Canal southeast of Harvey. • Named for Edward P. Wells (1847–1936), ND territorial legislator, banker, and developer of the James River valley • Organized as Gingras County in 1873 (prior to statehood) from Sheridan; name changed 1881 • Wheat, barley, flax, rye, hay, sunflowers, poultry, cattle.

WILLIAMS (one of two counties so named, the other in OH) *Williston* • 19,761 • 2,071 (the fourth largest county in ND) • Northwestern ND, bounded on the west by the MT state line, and on the south by the Missouri River (Lake Sakakawea); drained by Little Muddy and Cow creeks. Lewis and Clark State Park is here, as is Fort Buford State Historic Site. Lake Zahl National Wildlife Refuge is also in the county. • Named for Erastus A. Williams (1850–1930), Dakota territorial legislator and ND surveyor general • Created in 1873 by absorbing both Buford and Flannery counties. Originally located south of the Missouri River, near present-day Dunn and Mercer counties; it was established in its present location in 1892 • The county includes the (national historic) site of the Fort Union Trading Post, the principal fur-trading depot in the Upper Missouri River region from 1829 to 1867, serving the Dakotas, Montana, and the Prairie provinces. The discovery of gold in Western MT about 1864 created the town of Williston, which began as a wood refueling stop on the Missouri River for gold field-bound steamboats. The county was ravaged by drought in the 1930s. Oil was discovered in the Williston Basin in 1951 and has had a positive impact on the local economy. • Coal mines, oil wells, natural-gas fields, salt, lignite coal mines; wheat, barley, mustard, hay, cattle, dairy products; oil refining; education (U. of ND, Williston) • Williston's Band Festival each spring brings thousands of visitors into the city.

OHIO

With God, All Things Are Possible

Each of Ohio's eighty-eight counties except for Summit is governed by an elected three-member board of commissioners. Summit is administered by an elected county executive and a seven-member council.

ADAMS (one of twelve counties so named) *West Union* • 27,330 • 584 • Southern OH, bounded on the south by the Ohio River, forming the KY state line; drained by small creeks. In the east are part of Shawnee and part of Brush Creek state forests. The county also includes Robert A. Whipple, Chaparral Prairie, and Davis Memorial state nature preserves, as well as Serpent Mound. (This 1,348-foot-long serpentine embankment is one of the nation's largest effigy mounds.) • One of eight counties named for President John Adams • Original county; organized 1797 (prior to statehood) • Livestock, dairy products, tobacco, corn; manufacture of lumber and wood products, industrial machinery, apparel.

ALLEN (one of five counties so named) *Lima* • 108,473 • 404 • Western OH; intersected by the Ottawa and Auglaize rivers. Kendrick Woods State Nature Preserve is in the west. • Named for Ethan Allen (1738–89), leader of the Green Mountain Boys of VT in the Revolutionary War • 1820 from Mercer • Oil was discovered here in 1885, and within a few years it had become the center of a large, productive oil field, now nearly exhausted. • Cartoonist Al Frueh • Petroleum refining; extensive manufacturing, including petroleum products for industry and agriculture, food products, chemicals, machinery, motor vehicle equipment, aircraft parts, heavy construction equipment, steel castings, electric motors, electric signs, cigars; also livestock, corn, poultry, soybeans; limestone quarries; education (Bluffton College; OH State U. at Lima).

ASHLAND (one of two counties so named, the other in WI) *Ashland* • 52,523 • 424 • North-central OH; drained by the forks of the Mohican River. The county contains Mohican Memorial State Forest and Mohican State Park. • Named for Ashland, home of Henry Clay, at Lexington, KY • 1846 from Huron, Lorain, Richland and Wayne • Politician William B. Allison • Livestock, grain, hay, fruit; gravel pits; manufacture of pipe fittings, pumps, farm tools, automotive supplies, industrial tools, hydraulic cylinders, vinyl and plastic toys, poultry products, insecticides; toy balloons (a large percentage of the toy balloons produced in the U.S. are made in Ashland); education (Ashland U.) • Many of Ashland's original settlers came from New England, and the city maintains a strong New England ambience. Itinerant tree planter John Chapman ("Johnny Appleseed") often passed through the county; he is commemorated through a monument in Ashland City. In 1977, a dugout canoe built about 1600 B.C. was found in a peat bog at the head of the Vermilion River; it is the oldest known watercraft in North America.

ASHTABULA *Jefferson* • 102,728 • 703 (the largest county in OH) • Extreme northeastern OH, bounded on the north by Lake Erie and on the east by the PA state line; intersected by the Grand and Ashtabula rivers, and Conneaut and Pymatuning creeks. The county includes part of Pymatuning Reservoir, Geneva and Pymatuning state parks. • Named for the Ashtabula River • 1807 from Trumbull • Army officer Adna

R. Chaffee; inventor and automobile designer Ransom E. Olds; painter Charles E. Burchfield • Fruit, vegetables, corn, livestock, dairy products; greenhouses, apiaries, wineries; commercial fisheries; railroad shops; manufacture of inorganic pigments, plastics, transportation equipment, electric motors, rubber and rubber foam products, corrugated boxes, leather, fiberglass. The county handles the shipping of large quantities of coal and iron ore. • Ashtabula was a key terminus of the Underground Railroad network of the 1850s. The Conneaut Railroad Museum is noteworthy.

ATHENS *Athens* • 62,223 • 507 • Southeastern OH, bounded on the southeast by the Ohio River, forming the WV state line; intersected by the Hocking and Shade rivers, and Sunday and Federal creeks. The county also includes Burr Oak and Strouds Run state parks, Marie J. Desonier State Nature Perserve, and Gifford State Forest. Sections of Wayne National Forest are in the north. • Named for Athens, Greece • 1805 from Washington • Playwright and novelist Wilson Collison • Livestock, fruit, corn; manufacture of shoes, pens and mechanical pencils, paper products, brick and tile, woodworking products, business machines, tire molds, forged hand and bench tools, midget automobiles and trucks, scooters, building materials; limestone quarries, clay, bituminous-coal mining; education (Ohio University, founded in Athens in 1804, was the first college in the Northwest Territory).

AUGLAIZE *Wapakoneta* • 46,611 • 401 • Western OH; drained by the Auglaize and St. Marys rivers. Part of Grand Lake (St. Marys) is in the west. Grand Lake St. Marys State Park is also here. • Named for the Auglaize River • 1848 from Allen and Mercer • Astronaut Neil Armstrong; writer Jim Tully • Manufacture of mechanical and rubber goods, plastics, fabricated metal products, machinery, consumer goods; sand and gravel, clay pits; livestock, poultry, corn, soybeans, wheat, dairying; hunting and fishing • The Neil Armstrong Air and Space Museum in Wapakoneta contains exhibits that chronicle Ohioans' contributions to the history of flight.

BELMONT *St. Clairsville* • 70,226 • 537 • Eastern OH, bounded on the east by the Ohio River, here forming the WV state line; also drained by Captina, Wheeling, and McMahon creeks. The county includes part of Piedmont Lake reservoir and Barkcamp State Park. • The county's name is French for "beautiful mountain." • 1801 (prior to statehood) from Jefferson • Novelist William Dean Howells; basketball player John Havlicek • Coal mining, limestone quarries; manufacture of apparel, food products, industrial machinery, fabricated metals, castings, ferroalloys, pipe couplings, glass, caskets; cultivation of fruit, corn; dairying; education (Ohio U.–Eastern) • Zane Grey set some of his early novels here.

BROWN (one of nine counties so named) *Georgetown* • 42,285 • 492 • Southwestern OH, bounded on the south by the Ohio River, forming the KY state line; drained by the East Fork of the Little Miami River and White Oak Creek. • One of four counties named for Gen. Jacob J. Brown (1775–1828),

an officer in the War of 1812 and commander of the U.S. Army • 1818 from Adams and Clermont • Ulysses S. Grant's boyhood was spent in Georgetown (historic site). • Livestock, poultry, tobacco, corn, soybeans, dairy products; manufacture of leather products, machinery, medical equipment and supplies • A major stop on the Underground Railroad, the Rankin House (state memorial) in Ripley was immortalized in Harriet Beecher Stowe's *Uncle Tom's Cabin.*

BUTLER (one of eight counties so named) *Hamilton* • 332,807 • 467 • Southwestern OH, bounded on the west by the IN state line; intersected by the Great Miami River and its small tributaries. The county includes the site of Fort Hamilton. • One of three counties named for Major General Richard Butler (?–1791), an officer in the Revolutionary War and Indian commissioner • 1803 from Hamilton • Gen. Anthony Wayne built Fort Hamilton in 1791 as one of a series of forts near the western border of Ohio Territory. • Novelist and playwright Fannie Hurst; seismologist Charles F. Richter • Cattle, hogs, sheep, poultry, dairying, corn; steel mills; manufacture of millwork, furniture, paper products, construction materials, electronic equipment, electric furnaces, automobile bodies, safes and vaults, camping trailers, building materials, baking mixes; limestone quarrying; education (Miami U.) • Middletown was one of the first cities in the U.S. to enclose existing downtown buildings in a climate-controlled mall.

CARROLL (one of thirteen counties so named) *Carrollton* • 28,836 • 395 • Eastern OH; drained by Sandy, Conotton, and Yellow creeks. The county includes part of Atwood Lake Reservoir, Lake Mohawk, and Leesville Lake. • One of twelve counties named for Charles Carroll (1737–1832), a signer of the Declaration of Independence, U.S. senator from MD and founder of the Baltimore and Ohio Railroad • 1833 from Columbiana, Stark, Harrison and Jefferson • Army officer and inventor William Crozier • Livestock, dairy products, corn; manufacture of textiles, fabricated metal products, ceramic wall and floor tile; printing and publishing; fire-clay quarries.

CHAMPAIGN (one of two counties so named, the other in IL) *Urbana* • 38,890 • 429 • West-central OH; intersected by the Mad River, Big Darby, Buck, and Little Darby creeks. It contains Ohio Caverns, Kiser Lake State Park, and Davey Woods, Cedar Bog, and Siegenthaler–Kaestner Esker state nature preserves. • The name is a variation of French champagne "field" or "plain," referring to the flatness of the county • 1805 from Greene and Franklin • General Robert L. Eichelberger; journalist and politician Brand Whitlock; sculptor John Quincy Adams Ward (his "Soldier's Monument stands in Urbana's Monument Square); buried in the county are Indian fighter Simon Kenton and George Washington's valet Richard Stanhope (who is believed to have been 114 years old at the time of his death) • Sheep, cattle, poultry, soybeans, honey, dairy products; manufacture of paper and plastic products, chemicals, polishes, farm machinery, transportation equipment, motor vehicle parts and accessories; sand and gravel pits; education (Urbana U., founded in 1850 on the theology of Emanuel Swedenborg).

CLARK (one of twelve counties so named) *Springfield* • 144,742 • 400 • West-central OH; intersected by the Mad and Little Miami rivers, and by Buck, Beaver, and Honey creeks. The county includes George Rogers Clark Memorial Park and Buck Creek State Park. • One of six counties named for General George Rogers Clark (1752–1818), officer in the Revolutionary War and frontiersman in the Northwest Territory • 1817 from Champaign, Madison and Greene • In 1807, settlers and Indian chiefs, among them Tecumseh, met in Springfield to negotiate a peace for the region; a tablet marks the site of the tavern where the conference took place. • Actor Lillian Gish; photographer Berenice Abbott; soldier Frederick Funston; politician Joseph W. Keifer; botanist and geneticist George H. Shull (who conducted his early hybrid corn experiments in Springfield); painter Worthington Whittredge • Corn, soybeans, dairy products, livestock; manufacture of textiles, plastics, ventilating equipment, generators, hoists, cranes, aircraft components, diesel engines, metal products, funeral supplies, iron and steel products, aluminum products; commercial printing; limestone quarrying, sand and gravel pits; education (Wittenberg U.) • The manufacture of farm equipment in Springfield began in 1855 with the invention of a successful binder by William Whiteley. *Farm and Fireside* was published in the 1880s in Springfield as a periodical of P.J. Mast; this launched the Crowell-Collier publishing business.

CLERMONT *Batavia* • 177,977 • 452 • Southwestern OH, bounded on the southwest by the OH River (forming the KY state line) and on the northwest by the Little Miami River (The Miami Scenic Park Trail follows this National Wild and Scenic River here); intersected by the East Fork of the Little Miami River. The county includes East Fork Lake (encompassed by East Fork State Park), Stonelick State Park, and Crooked Run Memorial Sanctuary. • The name of the county, French for "clear mountain," was possibly given to the county in honor of the province in France from which some of its early settlers came. • Original county; organized 1800 (prior to statehood) • President Ulysses S. Grant (birthplace historic site) • Livestock, corn, soybeans, tobacco, fruit, dairy products; diversified manufacturing; nurseries.

CLINTON (one of nine counties so named) *Wilmington* • 40,543 • 411 • Southwestern OH; drained by forks of the Little Miami River, and Caesar Creek. The county includes a portion of Caesar Creek State Park in the extreme northwest and Cowan Lake State Park. • One of two counties (the other in NY) named for George Clinton (1739–1812), first governor of NY and vice president of the U.S. • 1810 from Highland • Cattle, hogs, corn, soybeans; dairying; manufacture of paper products, hand and edge tools, semiconductors, surgical appliances and supplies; education (Wilmington College).

COLUMBIANA *Lisbon* • 112,075 • 533 • Eastern OH, bounded on the east by the PA state line and on the southeast by the Ohio River; drained by the Ohio River, Little Beaver River (designated a National Scenic River), and Sandy and Yellow creeks. Yellow Creek State Forest, and Guilford Lake and Beaver Creek state parks are here. • The county's name is a variation of Columbus or Columbia, for Christopher Columbus • 1803 from Jefferson and Washington • Salem, a station on the Underground Railway, was also headquarters for the Western Anti-Slavery Society, which published the *Anti-Slavery Bugle*. • Industrialist Harvey Firestone; jurist John H. Clark; businessman and politician Mark Hanna; politician William P. Hepburn; army officer Alexander M. McCook; politician Clement L. Vallandigham • Livestock, dairy products, fruit, corn, vegetables; meat packing; manufacture of plastic products, glass, fabricated metal products, machine parts, household appliances, tools and dies, pumps, optical instruments and lenses; coal mines, oil and gas extraction. • Ceramics has been the economic mainstay of East Liverpool since James Bennett built a one-kiln pottery in 1840 and began making yellow and Rockingham ware. The city has the Museum of Ceramics and holds an annual pottery festival.

COSHOCTON *Coshocton* • 36,655 • 564 • Central OH; drained by the Muskingum, Tuscarawas, and Walhonding rivers. • The county's name is a variation of the name of a local Delaware Indian village. • 1810 from Muskingum • On the site of Coshocton in 1764, a rebellion led by Indian chief Pontiac ended by treaty offered by British officer Henry Bouquet. • Labor leader William Green • Livestock, dairy products, grain; manufacture of cast-iron pipe, stainless steel, laminated plastics, corrugated paper, milk products; coal deposits, sand and gravel pits; oil pools. • The Appalachian area station of the U.S. Dept. of Agriculture's soil and water conservation research division is in the county.

CRAWFORD (one of eleven counties so named) *Bucyrus* • 46,966 • 402 • North-central OH; drained by the Sandusky and Olentangy rivers, and Sycamore Creek. Carmean Woods State Nature Preserve is in the county. • One of three counties named for Col. William Crawford (1732–82), VA officer in the Revolutionary War, Indian fighter, and surveyor • 1820 from old Indian Territory • Livestock, dairy products, corn, soybeans; manufacture of lamps, road and farm machinery, boats, construction machinery, roller bearings, steel and iron stampings, fluorescent lamps, rubber hose; hardwood timber; limestone quarries. • The Lincoln Highway National Museum is located in Galion.

CUYAHOGA *Cleveland* • 1,393,978 (the most populated county in OH and twenty-third most populated county in the U.S.) • 458 • Northern OH, bounded on north by Lake Erie; drained by the Cuyahoga and Rocky rivers. The county is largely urbanized with Cleveland as its metropolitan focus. The Cleveland Hopkins International Airport is in Brook Park. Part of Cuyahoga Valley National Park is in the south; established in 2000, it is among the nation's youngest national parks. • Named for the Cuyahoga River • 1808 from Geauga

• About 1820, a society of Shakers established a colony at present Shaker Heights. In 1908, the Collinwood School fire in Cleveland killed 172 children. In 1944, a gas tank explosion killed 135 people. The Cuyahoga River self-combusted on June 22, 1969. • Football coach John Heisman; actor Paul Newman; baseball team owner George Steinbrenner; President James A. Garfield; philosopher William E. Hocking; zoologist William K. Brooks; inventor Charles F. Brush; chemist William M. Burton; lawyer and philanthropist Leonard Case; writer Charles W. Chesnutt; engineer and metallurgist Alfred H. Cowles; surgeon Harvey W. Cushing; educator Clarence A. Dykstra; journalist and reformer Nathan Cook Meeker; physician Joseph O'Dwyer; historians James F. Rhodes and Constance Mayfield Rourke; painter Archibald M. Willard; writer Sarah C. Woolsey; talk show host Phil Donahue • Vegetables, poultry, dairying; heavy diversified manufacturing, including apparel, wood products, food products, transportation equipment, machinery, fabricated metal products, electronic equipment; sand and gravel pits, salt wells; education (Cleveland State U.; Baldwin-Wallace College; John Carroll U.) • The county is headquarters for 15 Fortune 1000 companies. Cleveland is home to the Rock and Roll Hall of Fame. Elected in 1967, Cleveland politician Carl B. Stokes was the first black mayor of a major U.S. city. Eliot Ness, the famous U.S. Treasury Dept. crime fighter, was defeated in his bid for the office of mayor of Cleveland in 1947. Baldwin-Wallace College has an annual Bach Festival. The Great Lakes Shakespeare Festival takes place in Lakewood. John D. Rockefeller opened an oil refinery in Cleveland in 1863, several years before the discovery of large amounts of oil in western PA. Cleveland is home to the Indians (Jacobs Field), Browns (Cleveland Browns Stadium), and Cavaliers (Gund Arena).

DARKE *Greenville* • 53,309 • 600 • Western Ohio; drained by Greenville Creek, Stillwater and Mississinewa rivers. Fort Jefferson State Memorial is south of Greenville. • Named for General William Darke (1736–1801), Indian fighter and officer in the French and Indian War, and the Revolutionary War • 1809 from Miami • General Anthony Wayne built Fort Greenville here in 1793 as part of a fortified line against the Indians between Cincinnati and Lake Erie. In 1795 he signed the Treaty of Greenville here with the Indians, opening the Northwest Territory to settlers. From 1805 until 1808, the site was occupied by Shawnees, including Chief Tecumseh. • Journalist Lowell Thomas (birthplace historic site); sharpshooter Annie Oakley (birthplace historic site); automobile manufacturer Harry C. Stuz • Poultry, corn, wheat, soybeans, tobacco, tomatoes, fruit; manufacture of textiles, electrical appliances, stoves, tile, plastics, glass, including specialty glass, knit goods, electronic equipment, transportation equipment, machinery; meat packing; clay and gravel pits.

DEFIANCE *Defiance* • 39,500 • 411 • Northwestern OH, bounded on the west by the IN state line; intersected by the Maumee, Auglaize and Tiffin rivers. The county includes Independence Dam State Park. • Named for Fort Defiance •

1845 from Williams, Henry, and Paulding • General Anthony Wayne, in his campaign against the Indians, built Fort Defiance here in 1794. He described it as being so strong that he "defied hell and all her emissaries" to take it. Fort Winchester Memorial Bridge over the Auglaize River commemorates the fort built on this spot in 1812 by General William Henry Harrison. Johnny Appleseed established a nursery in Defiance in 1811. • Indian chief Pontiac • Poultry, hogs, cattle, corn, soybeans; manufacture of screw machine products, hand tools, ferrous castings, glass fiber, food products; education (Defiance College).

DELAWARE (one of six counties so named) *Delaware* • 109,989 (64% increase since 1990; the fastest growing county in OH) • 443 • Central OH; intersected by the Olentangy and Scioto rivers, and Big Walnut and Alum creeks. Olentangy Indian Caverns, Alum Creek and Delaware state parks, and Seymour Woods and Highbanks state nature preserves are located in the county. Numerous reservoirs are also located here. • Named for the Delaware Indians • 1808 from Franklin • President Rutherford B. Hayes; chemist F. Sherwood Rowland • Livestock, dairying, grain, fruit; manufacture of air conditioners, ranges, truck bodies, valves, tools and dies, cranes, building materials, thermostats, chemicals, machine screws, concrete blocks, paints, cans, wood products, chairs; limestone quarries; education (Ohio Wesleyan U., Perkins Observatory) • Since 1946, the Little Brown Jug, a harness-racing classic, has been run at the Delaware County Fair each September in Delaware city.

ERIE (one of three counties so named) *Sandusky* • 79,551 • 255 • Northern Ohio, bounded on the north by Lake Erie; drained by the Huron and Vermilion rivers, and Pipe Creek. The county includes Kelleys Island in Lake Erie. Erie Sand Barrens, Sheldon Marsh and Dupont Marsh state nature preserves are located here. • One of two counties (the other in NY) named for the Erie Indians • 1838 from Huron and Sandusky • Fort Sandusky was burned in 1763 during Pontiac's War. The site served as a supply depot during the War of 1812. It was settled as Portland in 1816 by CT residents who had been awarded the land for losses suffered by British raids during the Revolutionary War. Named Sandusky in 1845, the city served as a terminus of the Underground Railroad network. • Thomas A. Edison (birthplace museum); theatrical manager Charles Frohman; Senator George Norris; banker Jay Cooke; engineer Lester A. Pelton. Union general John Pope died here. • Corn, soybeans, fruits, livestock; food products, including prepared meats, olive processing; manufacture of fluorescent lights, paints, boats, plastics, fertilizers, glues and pastes, chemicals, rubber products, steel products, machinery, vehicular lighting equipment; limestone quarries, sand and gravel; fisheries; wineries; summer resorts. Sandusky is a port of entry and an important shipping point for coal. • Cedar Point boasts more roller coasters than any other amusement park in the U.S.

FAIRFIELD (one of three counties so named) *Lancaster* •

122,759 • 506 • Central OH; drained by the Hocking River and Rush and Walnut creeks. The county includes part of Buckeye Lake. Buckeye Lake State Park, Shallenberger State Nature Preserve, and Wahkeena Nature Preserve are also here. • The county's name is descriptive of the farmland in the area • 1800 (prior to statehood) from Franklin • Lancaster was founded in 1800 by Ebenezer Zane on land granted to him in payment for building the 266-mile wilderness road that bears his name. Many of the first settlers who came over Zane's Trace (which connects Wheeling and present day Maysville, KY) hailed from Lancaster, PA. Completion in 1808 of the Lancaster Lateral Canal connected the city with the Ohio and Erie Canal. • Union general William Tecumseh Sherman; political leader John Sherman; cartoonist Richard F. Outcault • Sheep, hogs, poultry, corn, soybeans, dairying, beef cattle; manufacture of plastic and leather products, glassware, fiberglass, batteries, automobile parts, boiler equipment, industrial machinery; gray and ductile iron foundries; oil wells, sand and gravel pits; timber; education (OH U.–Lancaster). The county is also a retailing headquarters. • The Tarlton Cross Mound State Memorial is the only known Indian earthwork shaped in the form of a cross.

FAYETTE (one of eleven counties so named) *Washington Court House* • 28,433 • 407 • South-central OH; drained by Paint, Sugar and Rattlesnake creeks. Part of Deer Creek State Forest is in the northwest. • One of seventeen counties named for the Marquis de Lafayette (1757–1834), French statesman and soldier who fought with the Americans during the Revolutionary War • 1810 from Ross and Highland • Lawyer and political manager Harry Daugherty • Sheep, dairy products, grain, soybeans, fruit; manufacture of plastic products, fabricated metal products, machinery, medical appliances and supplies • Two famous trails cross the county: Zane's Trace and the Miami Trace. A number of homes in the county served as stations along the Underground Railroad. The Harding Cabin, located on the banks of Deer Creek, was a favorite retreat for President Harding and his "Ohio Gang."

FRANKLIN (one of twenty-five counties so named) *Columbus* • 1,068,978 (the second most populated county in OH) • 540 • Central OH; intersected by the Scioto and Olentangy rivers, and Alum, Big Darby, and Big Walnut creeks. • One of twenty-three counties named for Benjamin Franklin • 1803 from Ross • Columbus has been the capital of OH since 1816. The National Road reached the city in 1833. During the Civil War, Columbus was a large marshalling area for OH soldiers headed south. It was also the site of the Union's largest prisoner-of-war camp. The graves of some 2,260 Confederate soldiers lie in Camp Chase Cemetery. After the war, the city was known for its many buggy factories. A flood in 1913 took over 100 lives. • Professional golfer Jack Nicklaus; WW I flying ace Eddie Rickenbacker; historian Arthur Schlesinger, Jr.; artist George W. Bellows; lawyer and humanitarian Ernest K. Coulter; actor Elsie Janis; army officer Irvin McDowell; writer Donald Ogden Stewart; botanist William S. Sullivant; cartoonist and writer James Thurber; magician Howard Thurston; mathematician John W. Young • Livestock, dairy products, grain, fruit, vegetables; food processing, diversified manufacturing, including machinery, electronic products, pharmaceuticals; sand and gravel pits, limestone pits; state government offices; education (Ohio State U.; Otterbein College; Franklin U.; Ohio Dominican College) • A 20-foot-high bronze statue of Christopher Columbus, located in City Hall Plaza in Columbus, was a gift from the citizens of Genoa, Italy. German Village, a neighborhood in Columbus that thrived from the mid-1800's to the early 20th century, is now a restored historic village. The Battelle Memorial Institute operates the largest scientific research facility in the world for private industry and the U.S. government. The Pontifical College Josephinum is the only seminary in the Western Hemisphere supervised by the Vatican. The corporate headquarters for eleven Fortune 1000 companies are located in the county. Founded in 1839, Westerville was known as the "dry capital of America" from 1909 to 1948, when it was the national headquarters of the Anti-Saloon League. The Ohio State Fair takes place in Columbus each year. Columbus is home to the Bluejackets (Nationwide Arena).

FULTON (one of eight counties so named) *Wauseon* • 42,084 • 407 • Northwestern OH, bounded on the north by the MI state line; drained by the Tiffin River. The county includes Maumee State Forest, Harrison Lake State Park, and Goll Woods State Nature Preserve. • One of seven counties named for Robert Fulton (1765–1815), builder of the *Clermont*, the first commercially successful steamboat • 1850 from Lucas, Henry and Williams • Race-car driver Barney Oldfield • Livestock, soybeans, corn, tomatoes; diversified manufacturing including furniture, plastics, steel pipes and tubes, sporting goods, motor vehicle parts and accessories • The Archbold La-Choy plant is billed as the largest producer of Chinese food in the world.

GALLIA *Gallipolis* • 31,069 • 469 • Southern OH, bounded on the east by the Ohio River, forming the WV state line; intersected by Raccoon, Symmes and Campaign creeks. A portion of Wayne National Forest is in the south. • Named for Gaul, the Latin name for France • 1803 from Washington • Gallipolis is the third oldest European settlement in OH. It was founded in 1790 by the Scioto Company, ostensibly for Royalists fleeing the French Revolution; however, agents for the company deceived purchasers with worthless land certificates. Eventually the company financed a settlement here, and some French immigrants did move here. The city's strategic location on the Ohio River brought Civil War-related economic prosperity. • Cattle, corn, tobacco, fruit; manufacture of motors and generators, motor vehicle parts, stone, clay and glass products; coal, limestone, sand and gravel; education (U. of Rio Grande) • South of Gallipolis a large roller dam raises the navigable depth of the Ohio River for fifty miles and uplifts the Kanawha River for thirty miles.

GEAUGA *Chardon* • 90,895 • 404 • Northeastern OH;

drained by the Cuyahoga, Chagrin, and Grand rivers. The county includes several reservoirs and Punderson State Park. Alpine Valley ski area is in the west. • Geauga is an Indian name for the Grand River and possibly means "raccoon." • 1806 from Trumbull • Wild animal trainer Clyde Beatty • Dairy products, corn, fruit, poultry; manufacture of chemical preparations, furniture, plastic products, construction machinery.

GREENE (one of fourteen counties so named) *Xenia* • 147,886 • 415 • Southwest-central OH; intersected by the Little Miami (designated a National Scenic and Recreational River) and Mad rivers, and Caesar Creek. The county includes the National Afro-American Museum and Culture Center, Williamson Mound, and John Bryan State Park. It also has mineral springs. • One of sixteen counties named for Gen. Nathanael Greene (1742–1786), Revolutionary War officer • 1803 from Hamilton and Ross • Tornadoes destroyed half of Xenia in 1974. • Journalist and diplomat Whitelaw Reid; historian Arthur M. Schlesinger; author Ridgely Torrence. Educator and elocutionist Hallie Quinn Brown died here. • Corn, fruit, soybeans, hogs, cattle, poultry; manufacture of aircraft engines, furniture, cordage, plastics, castings, rubber components, scientific instruments, stained glass; commercial printing; sand and gravel pits; education (Central State U.; Wright State U.; Cedarville U. Antioch College, founded in 1852 with Horace Mann as its first president, now has several campuses elsewhere in the U.S.) • On November 21, 1995, warring former Yugoslav republics signed a peace agreement at Wright-Patterson Air Force Base here. The base is also the site of Huffman Prairie Flying Field, established by the Wright brothers as the first permanent flying school. It represents OH's largest remaining stretch of prairie.

GUERNSEY *Cambridge* • 40,792 • 522 • Eastern OH; drained by Wills Creek. Salt Fork State Park is the largest state park in OH. • The name Guernsey was chosen to honor settlers from the island in the English Channel • 1810 from Belmont • Central to the history of the county is the building of the National Road through Cambridge in 1827. The first bridge authorized in the Northwest Territory was built here. Early in the 1900s, a glass industry flourished in the county; it was known for Mosser Glass and Boyd's Crystal Art Glass. Examples of the "Glass period" can be found in the Glass Museum and Degenhart Paperweight Museum in Cambridge. • Astronaut John Glenn; actor William Boyd (Hopalong Cassidy) • Cattle, poultry, corn, hay; oil and gas extraction, clay mining, limestone quarrying; stone, clay and glass products; computer equipment, machinery • The county has several curving "S" bridges.

HAMILTON (one of ten counties so named) *Cincinnati* • 845,303 (the third most populated county in OH) • 407 • Extreme southwestern OH, bounded on the west by the IN state line, on the south by the Ohio River (forming the KY state line), and on the northeast by the Little Miami River (desig-

nated a Wild and Scenic River); drained by the Great Miami and Whitewater rivers, and by Mill Creek. The county is located entirely within the Cincinnati metropolitan area. • One of eight counties named for Alexander Hamilton (?–1804), first U.S. secretary of the treasury • Original county; organized 1790 (prior to statehood) • Cincinnati was incorporated in 1820. By 1842 it had the largest population of any settlement west of the Alleghenies. Harriet Beecher Stowe's father, Lyman Beecher, helped organize Cincinnati's Underground Railroad network, which served as inspiration for Harriet's novel *Uncle Tom's Cabin*. In 1869, the Cincinnati Red Stockings became the first professional baseball team. In 1999, a tornado leveled a square mile section of the city of Cincinnati. • President William Henry Harrison (state memorial); President William Howard Taft (National Historic Site); newspaper publisher Adolph S. Ochs; actor Tyrone Power; conductor James Levine; journalist Elizabeth Drew; singer and actor Doris Day; television executive Ted Turner; actor Theda Bara; illustrator and outdoorsman Daniel Carter Beard; poets Alice and Phoebe Cary; manufacturer Powell Crosley; architect Henry Mather Green; painter Robert Henri; educator George P. Krapp; politician Nicholas Longworth; jurist Stanley Matthews; physicist John W. Mauchly; sculptor Charles H. Niehaus; journalist Donn Piatt; paleontologist Charles Schuchert; geologist William B. Scott; politician Robert A. Taft; painter John H. Twachtman; social worker Lillian D. Wald; film director and producer Steven Spielberg; fashion and social celebrity Kate Chase Sprague; football quarterback Roger Staubach; bridge builder Joseph B. Strauss • Vegetables, nursery, greenhouse crops, dairying; diversifed manufacturing, including food products, beverages, clothing, plastics, consumer goods (more soap is produced in Cincinnati than anywhere else in the world), metal and electrical products; coal mining, oil and gas extraction; education (U. of Cincinnati; Xavier U.; College of Mount St. Joseph; Cincinnati Bible College) • The John A. Roebling Suspension Bridge in Cincinnati, built in 1867, served as a model for the engineer's famous Brooklyn Bridge. The corporate headquarters of eleven Fortune 1000 companies are located in the county. English novelist Frances Trollope's scathing bestseller *The Domestic Manners of the Americans* was based upon several years of observations she made as a Cincinnati resident in the 1820s. The first public weather forecasting service was started in Cincinnati in 1869. Winston Churchill on a visit to Cincinnati called it America's handsomest inland city. Cincinnati is home to the Reds (Cinergy Field) and Bengals (Paul Brown Stadium).

HANCOCK *Findlay* • 71,295 • 531 • Northwestern OH, intersected by the Blanchard and Portage rivers. Van Buren State Park is in the north. • One of ten counties named for John Hancock (1737–93), noted signer of the Declaration of Independence, statesman and governor of MA • 1820 from Indian lands • Findlay was active in the Underground Railroad. In 1860, using the pen name Petroleum V. Nasby, Findlay *Jeffersonian* editor David Ross Locke published the first of his satirical letters attacking slavery. An economic boom followed the discovery of natural gas in the county in 1884 and the population of Findlay doubled. In 1887, the city vaunted its success in oil and gas production with its "Gas Jubilee," a celebratory "spectacular." • Astronomer William W. Campbell; writer Russell Crouse; pathologist Howard T. Ricketts; physicist Willard H. Bennett • Hogs, sheep, corn, soybeans, vegetables; manufacture of food and plastic products, household appliances, rubber tires, photographic supplies, heavy machinery, laundry equipment, petroleum products, solid-state components; limestone quarries; education (U. of Findlay) • Tell Taylor was inspired to compose the popular song "Down by the Old Mill Stream" while fishing on the Blanchard near old Misamore Mill. Findlay's extensive display of American flags has earned the Congressional designation "Flag City."

HARDIN (one of six counties so named) *Kenton* • 31,945 • 470 • West-central OH; intersected by the Scioto and Blanchard rivers, and Hog Creek. • One of two counties (the other in KY) named for Gen. John Hardin (1753–92), Revolutionary War officer and Indian fighter with George Rogers Clark in the trans-Ohio campaigns • 1820 from Indian lands • Hogs, poultry, wheat, corn, soybeans; manufacture of paper products and transportation equipment; limestone quarries, gravel pits; education (Ohio Northern U.).

HARRISON (one of eight counties so named) *Cadiz* • 15,856 • 404 • Eastern OH; drained by Stillwater and Conotton creeks. The county includes Tappan Lake and Clendening Lake reservoirs and Harrison State Forest. • One of four counties named for President William Henry Harrison • 1813 from Jefferson and Tuscarawas • Baseball player Cy Young; actor Clark Gable; anthropologist William H. Holmes; clergyman Matthew Simpson; general George Custer (monument) • Coal mining, limestone quarries; nursery and greenhouse crops; hogs, grains, soybeans, vegetables; printing and publishing • Built near Freeport in 1921, a sixteen-sided barn is one of only three in the U.S. Several historic trails, including the Moravian Trail and the Buckeye Trail, traverse the county.

HENRY (one of ten counties so named) *Napoleon* • 29,210 • 417 • Northwestern OH, intersected by the Maumee River. • One of ten counties (including Patrick County, VA) named for Patrick Henry (1736–99), patriot, governor of VA and statesman • 1820 from Wood • Corn, wheat, oats, sugar beets, vegetables; manufacture of fabricated metal products, cutlery and tools, transportation equipment; preserved fruits and vegetables.

HIGHLAND (one of two counties so named, the other in VA) *Hillsboro* • 40,875 • 553 • Southwestern Ohio, bounded on the northeast by Paint Creek; drained by the East Fork of the Little Miami River, and White Oak and Rattlesnake creeks. The county includes Rocky Fork and Paint Creek parks. • Named for the highlands between the Scioto River and the Little Miami River • 1805 from Ross, Adams and Clermont • Politician and historian Albert Beveridge; comic-strip

artist Milton Caniff • Nursery and greenhouse crops, tobacco, grains, dairying, hogs; manufacture of textiles, plastic products, transportation equipment; limestone quarries.

HOCKING *Logan* • 28,241 • 423 • South-central Ohio; intersected by the Hocking River and Rush, Salt, and Monday creeks. Part of Wayne National Forest is in the east. The county also includes Hocking State Forest and Hocking Hills State Park, as well as Logan State Park and Rockbridge State Nature Preserve. • Named for the Hocking River • 1818 from Athens and Ross • Nursery and greenhouse crops, cattle, poultry, corn; coal mining, clay and gravel pits.

HOLMES (one of three counties so named) *Millersburg* • 38,943 • 423 • Central Ohio; intersected by Killbuck Creek and the Lake Fork of the Mohican River. • Named for Major Andrew H. Holmes (?–1814), officer in the War of 1812 killed in combat at the Straits of Mackinac • 1824 from Coshocton • Livestock, dairy products, grain, nursery crops; manufacture of rubber, plastic and wood products; coal mines, sandstone quarries, gravel pits.

HURON (one of two counties so named) *Norwalk* • 59,487 • 493 • Northern OH; drained by the West Branch of the Huron and Vermilion rivers. • Named for the Huron Indians • 1809 from Indian lands • The area in and around Norwalk was known as the "Firelands" because it was settled through land grants to former CT residents whose homes were burned by Loyalists during the Revolutionary War. • Inventor Ephraim Shay; baseball organizer Ban Johnson; aviator Paul Wilber, football executive Paul Brown. Future U.S. president Rutherford B. Hayes attended Norwalk Academy, a widely known institution in the 1830s. • Nursery and greenhouse crops, sheep, corn, vegetables; manufacture of household furniture, farm and garden machinery, bakery products, rubber, metal toys, wire products, auto seats, truck cabs, thermostats, furniture, candy; gravel pits; printing.

JACKSON (one of twenty-four counties so named) *Jackson* • 32,641 • 420 • Southern OH; drained by the Little Scioto River, and Symmes and Little Raccoon creeks. The county includes Buckeye Furnace and Leo Petroglyph. Also here are Jackson Lake State Park, Richland Furnace State Forest, Lake Katherine State Nature Preserve, and a small part of Wayne National Forest in the south. • One of twenty-two counties named directly or indirectly for President Andrew Jackson • 1816 from Pike • Poultry, corn; manufacture of food and wood products; coal mining.

JEFFERSON *Steubenville* • 73,894 • 410 • Eastern OH, bounded on the east by the Ohio River, forming the WV state line; drained by Yellow and Cross creeks. Jefferson Lake State Park and Fernwood State Forest are located here, as is Quaker Meeting House State Memorial. • One of twenty-six counties named directly or indirectly for President Thomas Jefferson • Original county; organized 1797 (prior to statehood) • Laid out in 1797, Steubenville is one of the oldest communities in OH. • Astronomer Charles Dillon Perrine; Sculptor Alexander

Doyle; army officer and politician Edward McCook; secretary of war Edwin M. Stanton • Coal mining; manufacture of lumber and wood products, steel and steel products, titanium and ferroalloys, paper and clay products, tin, chemicals; cattle, corn; education (Franciscan U. of Steubenville).

KNOX *Mount Vernon* • 54,500 • 527 • Central OH; drained by the Kokosing and Mohican rivers, and the North Fork of the Licking River. The county includes Knox Woods State Nature Preserve. • One of nine counties named for Gen. Henry Knox (1750–1806), Revolutionary War officer and first U.S. secretary of war • 1808 from Fairfield • In the original settlement of Mount Vernon, which was laid out in 1805, Johnny (Appleseed) Chapman owned several lots. • War nurse Mary Ann Bickerdyke; minstrel show writer Dan Emmett. Poet and critic John Crowe Ransom died here. • Sheep, hogs, cattle, poultry, corn; manufacture of engines, air and gas compressors, motor vehicle equipment and parts, metal foil and leaf, glass and paper products; millwork; oil and gas; education (Mount Vernon Nazarene College; Kenyon College).

LAKE (one of twelve counties so named) *Painesville* • 227,511 • 228 (the smallest county in OH) • Northeastern OH, bounded on the north by Lake Erie; drained by the Grand and Chagrin rivers. The county includes Headlands Beach State Park. • Named for Lake Erie • 1840 from Geauga and Cuyahoga • Religious leader Joseph Smith III; President James A. Garfield (national historic site); psychologist and philosopher George Trumbull Ladd; illustrator and cartoonist Frederick Burr Opper; journalist and explorer Walter Wellman • Nurseries, apples, grapes, poultry; manufacture of paper products, industrial organic chemicals (part of Lake Erie's "Chemical Shore"), metal forgings and stampings, precision measuring devices, computer components, electronic instruments, lift trucks, air conditioners, auto parts, rubber products, patterns, lubricants, tools and cranes; iron and steel foundries; resorts • The Boulevard of 500 Flags in Eastlake is the largest permanent display of American flags in the U.S. At 3,100 acres, Holden Arboretum near Kirtland is the largest arboretum in the U.S. Fairport claims to have had the first woman mayor in the U.S., Amy Kaukonen, elected in 1921.

LAWRENCE (one of eleven counties so named) *Ironton* • 62,319 • 455 • Southern Ohio, bounded on the south by the Ohio river, here forming the KY and WV state lines; drained by the Symmes River. Much of the northern half of the county is covered by a portion of Wayne National Forest, which includes Timber Ridge Recreation Area and Dean State Forest. • One of eight counties named for Capt. James Lawrence (1781–1813), U.S. naval officer in the war with Barbary pirates near Tripoli and commander of the U.S.S. *Chesapeake* in the War of 1812 • 1815 from Gallia • Dairy products, livestock, grain, fruit, tobacco, hay; manufacture of chemicals, fabricated metals, metal castings, plastics, cement, tile, firebrick, coke, steel and iron (Ironton was formerly the center of the famous pig iron industry of southern OH.); limestone quarrying; education (OH U.–Southern Campus).

LICKING *Newark* • 145,491 • 687 (the third largest county in OH) • Central Ohio; drained by the Licking River and Raccoon Creek. Part of Buckeye Lake is in the south. Also here are Morris Woods and Blackhand Gorge state nature preserves, and Newark Earthworks State Memorial. • Named for the Licking River • 1808 from Fairfield • Along the banks of the Licking River are several earthworks constructed by pre-Columbian Mound Builders. • Historian of the American west Hubert H. Bancroft; ethnographer of North American Indians George A. Dorsey; businessmen Edward and John A. Creighton; jurist William B. Woods • Hogs, dairy products, corn, grain, fruit; manufacture of tires, stone, clay and glass products, commercial printing, motor vehicle parts, aluminum, lighting equipment, containers, plastics, missile and electronic components, sports equipment; coal, oil and gas, sand and gravel pits; education (Ohio State U. at Newark; Denison U.).

LOGAN (one of ten 10 counties so named) *Bellefontaine* • 46,005 • 458 • West-central Ohio; drained by the Great Miami and Mad rivers, and Mill and Big Darby creeks. The county includes Indian Lake State Park, Zane Caverns, and Campbell Hill, at 1,549 feet, the state's highest point. • One of two counties (the other in KY) named for Gen. Benjamin Logan (?–1802), VA patriot and soldier active in the West during the Revolutionary War • 1817 from Champaign • Anthropologist Melville J. Herskovits; humorist Frank M. Hubbard • Cattle, hogs, corn, wheat, soybeans, dairy products, grain; manufacture of electric motors and circuit breakers, aluminum extrusions, sleeve bearings, power tools, food products; printing • The first concrete street in the U.S. was laid in Bellefontaine in 1891.

LORAIN *Elyria* • 284,664 • 493 • Northern OH, bounded on the north by Lake Erie; drained by the Vermilion River and the East Branch of the Black River • Named for the province of Lorraine, France, which charmed a local judge who donated money for the courthouse • 1822 from Huron, Cuyahoga, and Medina • Due in large part to abolitionist fervor at Oberlin College, the county was one of the busiest routes of the Underground Railroad. Charles Martin Hall developed the electrolytic process for producing aluminum cheaply in Oberlin in 1886. • Writer Toni Morrison; Admiral Ernest J. King; painter Archibald M. Willard; politician Frank Harris Hitchcock • Grain, fruit, poultry, livestock, dairying; widely diversified manufacturing including shipbuilding, automotive vehicles, automotive and aviation equipment, plastics, electric motors, air conditioners, steel and gypsum products, power shovels and cranes; commercial fishing; lake resorts; sandstone quarries (Findley State Park sits atop the world's thickest deposit); education (established in 1833, Oberlin College was the first coeducational college in the U.S.) • The city of Lorain honors its more than fifty ethnic and nationality groups with an international festival each July. With a collection of art works numbering 14,000, Oberlin's Allen Memorial Art Museum is one of the most complete college art museums in the U.S. Before the introduction of pasteurization, Wellington was known as the cheese center of the U.S.

LUCAS *Toledo* • 455,054 • 340 • Northwestern OH, bounded on the north by the MI state line, on the southeast by the Maumee River, and on the northeast by the western end of Lake Erie. Found here are Maumee Bay State Park, Irwin Prairie State Nature Preserve, Cedar Point National Wildlife Refuge, and part of Ottawa National Wildlife Refuge, including Crane Creek State Park. • One of two counties (the other in IA) named for Col. Robert Lucas (1781–1853), governor of OH and first territorial governor of IA • 1835 from Wood • In the Battle of Fallen Timbers (national historic site), fought here in 1794, General Anthony Wayne defeated a confederacy of Indians, thus ending twenty years of border warfare, and opening OH to large scale European-American settlement. Permanent settlement at the site of Toledo was established at Fort Industry after the War of 1812. The so-called Toledo War of 1835 pitted residents of Toledo who wished to transfer political jurisdiction of the area from MI to OH against those in MI Territory in opposition to the boundary change. Governor Mason of MI Territory sent in troops as did governor Lucas of OH. The dispute was settled by President Jackson in favor of OH. • Feminist Gloria Steinem; pianist Art Tatum; composer and editor David Stanley Smith; civic politician Samuel M. Jones • Corn, vegetables, wheat, agricultural bedding plants; diversified manufacturing, including glassmaking (a world leader in industrial production), paper products, motor vehicles (jeeps) and associated products, plastics, petroleum, weighing machines, furnaces, machinery, tools; education (U. of Toledo; Lourdes College) • Toledo was a major supplier of jeeps to the American army in WW II. The historic West End District of the city is said to have the largest collection (twenty-five square blocks) of extant late-Victorian houses still standing in the U.S.

MADISON *London* • 40,213 • 465 • Central Ohio; drained by Deer, Paint, and Big Darby creeks. Madison Lake State Park, part of Deer Creek State Forest, and two state nature preserves are located here. • One of twenty counties named directly or indirectly for President James Madison • 1810 from Fayette • Livestock, corn, wheat, soybeans, fruit; manufacture of metal products, transportation equipment • The historic "cloverleaf" at the junction of routes 40 and 42 near London represents an early step in the creation of the national highway system. Established in 1983, the Farm Science Review at Molly Caren Farm, is one of the three largest farm equipment expositions in the U.S. London, a crime-fighting mecca, is home to the Bureau of Criminal Investigation, the OH Peace Officers Training Academy, and the London and Madison Correctional Institutions.

MAHONING *Youngstown* • 257,555 • 415 • East Ohio, bounded on the east by the PA state line; intersected by the Mahoning River and Little Beaver Creek. The county includes Lake Milton reservoir and State Park, and part of Berlin Lake reservoir. • Named for the Mahoning River • 1846 from Columbiana and Trumbull • In 1805, Yellow Creek residents James and Daniel Heaton built OH's first furnace for producing iron by reducing ore with charcoal and limestone. Later, locally mined black coal was used directly for iron smelting. By 1920, Youngstown had become one of the largest steel-producing centers in the U.S. The industry has since declined. • Livestock, poultry, grains, dairy products; iron and steel works; manufacture of industrial machinery, aluminum, rubber and paper products, office furniture, aircraft and automotive parts, storm windows and doors, awnings; coal mining, limestone quarries; education (Youngstown State U.).

MARION *Marion* • 66,217 • 404 • Central OH; intersected by the Scioto River; also drained by the Olentangy and Little Scioto rivers, and Tymochtee Creek. • One of seventeen counties named for Gen. Francis Marion (?–1795), SC soldier and legislator, known as "The Swamp Fox" for his tactics in the Carolina swamps during the Revolutionary War • 1820 from Crawford • President Warren G. Harding (house, museum and memorial); reformer and politician Norman Thomas • Livestock, dairy products, grain; limestone quarries, sand and gravel pits; manufacture of processed foods, glass and primary metal products, appliances, machinery; education (OH State U. at Marion). In 1874, the first steam shovel was manufactured in Marion, earning the city the nickname "Shovel City of the World." • The county promotes popcorn through its farms, the Wyandot Popcorn Museum, and an annual popcorn festival.

MEDINA (one of two counties so named, the other in TX) *Medina* • 151,095 • 422 • Northern OH; drained by branches of the Rocky River, the East Branch of the Black River, and Chippewa Creek. The county contains Chippewa Lake and the Ohio Western Reserve National Cemetery. • Named for the city in Saudi Arabia to which Muhammad, founder of Islam, fled from Mecca in 622 • 1812 from Portage • Botanist William Crocker; inventor Aaron French; phonetician John S. Kenyon • Truck farms, fruit, poultry, sheep, corn, vegetables, dairying; manufacture of food products, matches, valves, cardboard containers, salt, shoe soles, rubber and plastic products, fabricated metal products, machinery.

MEIGS (one of two counties so named, the other in TN) *Pomeroy* • 23,072 • 429 • Southeastern OH, bounded on the east and southeast by the Ohio River, forming the WV state line; drained by the Shade River and Leading Creek. The county includes Shade River State Forest and Forked Run State Park. • One of two counties (the other in TN) named for Return Jonathan Meigs (1764–1825), OH governor, U.S. senator from OH, and U.S. postmaster general • 1819 from Gallia and Athens • George Washington surveyed land here in 1770. The July 1863 Battle of Buffington Island (state memorial) at Portland was the only Civil War battle fought in the state of OH or north of the OH River. Attempting to cross the Ohio River, Confederate John Hunt Morgan and his "Raiders" were met by a debilitating force that included two future U.S. presidents, Rutherford B. Hayes and William

McKinley, and possibly a third, James Garfield. • Newspaperman and author Ambrose Bierce; author James E. Campbell;
generals Curtis LeMay and James Hartinger; riverboat captain
Major John B. Downing who trained Mark Twain as a boat
pilot • Commercial greenhouses, vegetables (especially tomatoes), poultry, grain; manufacture of electronic equipment;
coal mines; limestone quarries • The Chester courthouse, constructed in 1822 before the county seat was moved to Pomeroy,
is the oldest courthouse building in the state. The Meigs
County Historical Society in Pomeroy, established in 1876, is
the oldest continuous historical society in OH. In 1836, the
world's first towboat, the *Condor*, was built in Pomeroy.

MERCER (one of eight counties so named) *Celina* • 40,924
• 463 • Western OH, bounded on the west by the IN state
line; drained by the Wabash and St. Marys rivers. Part of
Grand Lake (St. Marys) is in the east. • One of six counties
definitively named for Gen. Hugh Mercer (?–1777), Revolutionary War officer and physician • 1820 from Darke • Fort
Recovery State Museum preserves the history of the Indian
Wars in the county, chronicling General Arthur St. Clair's defeat in 1791 and General Anthony Wayne's "recovery" of the
fort in 1794. • Poultry, sheep, corn, soybeans, meat products;
manufacture of machinery, furniture, bicycles, lawnmowers,
metal products; canning; printing and publishing; limestone
quarries; timber • Located in Maria Stein, the Shrine of the
Holy Relics is the second largest collection of its type in the
U.S. Many unique cross-tipped spire churches, built by German Catholic settlers, have been preserved throughout the
county.

MIAMI *Troy* • 98,868 • 407 • Western OH; intersected by
the Great Miami and Stillwater rivers. The county includes
Greenville Falls State Nature Park and Buckner Nature Center. • One of four counties named in full or in part for the
Miami Indians • 1807 from Montgomery • In 1794, General
Anthony Wayne built Ft. Piqua near the Upper Piqua. From
here Indian chief Tecumseh departed in 1796 for the headwaters of the Whitewater in IN. As early as 1876 many Quakers
settled in the West Milton area as part of a "Quaker Exodus"
from Bush River Meeting, SC. • Engineer Howard E. Coffin;
inventor Talbert Lanston; clergyman and scholar Henry P.
Smith • Livestock, corn, tobacco, wheat; manufacture of furniture, fixtures, rubber and plastic products, newspaper, steel
pipe and tubes, aluminum die-castings, ordnance, vehicle bodies, oil machinery, air vents; sand and gravel pits, stone quarries; nurseries • Piqua, once known as "The Underwear Capital of the World," hosts The Great Outdoor Underwear
Festival each October. The Piqua Historical Area contains a
restored section of the Miami and Erie Canal.

MONROE *Woodsfield* • 15,180 • 456 • Eastern OH, bounded
on the southeast by the Ohio River, forming the WV state
line; also drained by Sunfish Creek and the Little Muskingum
River. Part of Wayne National Forest covers the southern half
of the county. Sunfish Creek State Forest is in the extreme
northeast. • One of seventeen counties named for President

James Monroe • 1813 from Belmont, Washington and
Guernsey • Cattle, dairy products, corn; manufacture of metal
products, aluminum sheet, plate and foil; coal mines, limestone quarries.

MONTGOMERY (one of eighteen counties so named) *Dayton* • 559,062 (the fourth most populated county in OH) •
462 • Western OH; intersected by the Great Miami, Stillwater, and Mad rivers, and by Bear, Wolf, and Twin creeks. Mi-
amisburg Mound State Memorial and Sycamore State Park are
located in the county. • One of sixteen counties named directly
or indirectly for Gen. Richard Montgomery (1738–75), American Revolutionary War officer who captured Montreal,
Canada • 1803 from Hamilton and Ross • The Wright Brothers, Orville and Wilbur, who hail from the county, built the
first wind tunnel in North America here in 1901 to conduct experiments that led to the first successful airplane flight. In
1913, over 300 people died when the Mad, Great Miami, and
Stillwater rivers flooded Dayton. In 1914, Dayton became the
first U.S. city with more than 100,000 people to adopt the
council-manager system of municipal government. • Scholar
and educator Irving Babbitt; army officer George Crook; comedian Frank Albert Daniels; army officer Joseph T. Dickman;
poet Paul Laurence Dunbar; impresario Arthur Leon Judson;
pianist and composer Billy Strayhorn; politician James Baird
Weaver. • Hogs, corn, soybeans, tobacco; extensive diversified
manufacturing, including non-electrical machinery, rubber
and plastic goods, electric motors and generators, automotive
and aircraft accessories, building materials, printed materials,
cash registers; sand and gravel pits; cement plants; education
(U. of Dayton) • Kettering is a major medical center. Located
here are the Kettering College of Medical Arts, the Cox Coro-
nary Heart Institute, and the Charles F. Kettering Memorial
(research) Hospital. Called the "Birthplace of Aviation," Dayton is home to the Aviation Heritage National Historic Park;
its sites include Carillon Historical Park, which displays the
1905 Wright Flyer III, said to be the first craft capable of sustained flight. The 800-year-old Sun Watch Archeological Site
has yielded over one million artifacts for study.

MORGAN (one of eleven counties so named) *McConnelsville*
• 14,897 • 418 • Eastern OH; intersected by the Muskingum
River. Wayne National Forest and Burr Oak Reservoir are in
the west. Island Run Covered Bridge is located near Triadel-
phia. • One of nine counties named for Gen. Daniel Morgan
(1736–1802), an officer in the Revolutionary War • 1817 from
Washington • Illustrator and painter Howard C. Christy;
painter and writer Frederick S. Dellenbaugh • Limestone quarries, coal mines; manufacturing; livestock, dairy products,
corn, wheat, cabbages.

MORROW (one of two counties so named, the other in OR)
Mount Gilead • 31,628 • 406 • Central Ohio; drained by the
Kokosing River, and Alum and Big Walnut creeks. Mount
Gilead State Park is here. • Named for Jeremiah Morrow
(1771–1852), U.S. senator from OH and governor of OH •
1848 from Knox, Marion, Delaware, and Richland • Novel-

ist Dawn Powell • Hogs, cattle, corn; manufacture of machinery, paper products, electric lighting • In 1919, the Barre Quarriers and Manufacturers Association of Barre VT awarded a monument (the Victory Shaft) to Morrow County upon winning a statewide competition for the most Victory bonds purchased. The world's largest gourd show is held the first full weekend in October at the Morrow County Fairgrounds in Mount Gilead.

MUSKINGUM *Zanesville* • 84,585 • 665 (the fourth largest county in OH) • Central OH; intersected by the Muskingum and Licking rivers, and by Wills and Jonathan creeks. The county includes Blue Rock, Dillon, and Muskingum River state parks. Blue Rock State Forest is in the south. • Named for the Muskingum River • 1804 from Washington and Fairfield • Zanesville was founded in 1797 by Ebenezer Zane on land that the U.S. Congress awarded him for clearing a road to Limestone (now Maysville) KY. The city was a noted pottery center after 1890. (It was once heralded as "Pottery Capital of the World" and "Clay City.") Floods to the area in 1913 led to Congressional authorization of a network of fourteen reservoirs in the Muskingum valley, completed in 1938. • Astronaut John Glenn; architect Cass Gilbert; writer Zane Grey; Hebraist and university president William R. Harper; U.S. vice president Thomas A. Hendricks • Hogs, cattle, dairy products, corn, fruit; manufacture of lumber and wood products, stone, clay, and glass products, pottery products, packaged meats and dairy products, hydraulic and farm machinery, engines and other electric equipment; coal mines, limestone quarries, sand, gravel and clay pits; education (OH U.–Zanesville) • A distinctive feature of the county is the Y Bridge which spans the confluence of the Muskingum and Licking rivers and was proclaimed by Ripley's as "the only bridge in the world which you can cross and still be on the same side of the river." The National Road/Zane Grey Museum east of Zanesville displays Zane Grey memorabilia and traces the history of the National (Cumberland) Road.

NOBLE (one of three counties so named) *Caldwell* • 14,058 • 399 • Eastern Ohio; drained by Wills, Duck and Buffalo creeks. The county is bisected in the northeast by Seneca Lake (reservoir). Wolf Run State Park is centrally located. • Probably named for James Noble, an early settler • 1851 from Monroe, Morgan, Guernsey, and Washington • Livestock, grain, tobacco, dairy products; manufacture of lumber and wood products, motor vehicle parts and accessories, electrometallurgical products; coal mines, clay pits, limestone quarries.

OTTAWA *Port Clinton* • 40,985 • 255 • Northern OH, bounded on the northeast by Lake Erie; drained by the Portage River, and Toussaint and Packer creeks. The county includes several islands in Lake Erie, including the resort-chocked Bass Islands. Part of Ottawa National Wildlife Refuge is in the north. State parks in the county include South Bass Island, Catawba Island, and East Harbor. West Sister Island National Wildlife Refuge is in the far north. • One of four counties named for the Ottawa Indians • 1840 from Erie, Sandusky and Lucas • On Sept. 10, 1813, Commodore Oliver Hazard Perry defeated the British fleet in the Battle of Lake Erie, this victory enabling the U.S. to control the lake and invade Canada. (Perry's Victory and International Peace Memorial, designed by Joseph Freeland to commemorate the event, standing at a height of 352 feet, is the world's most massive Doric column.) Johnson's Island in Sandusky Bay was a prison for Confederate officers during the Civil War. • Composer and organist Leo Sowerby died in the county. • Corn, soybeans, hogs; manufacture of rubber, plastic products, machinery; limestone quarries; fisheries; wineries; summer tourism.

PAULDING *Paulding* • 20,293 • 416 • Northwestern OH, bounded on the west by the IN state line; drained by the Maumee and Auglaize rivers, and Flatrock Creek. • One of two counties (the other in GA) named for John Paulding (?–1818), one of three New York militiamen who inadvertently captured British spy John André during the Revolutionary War. OH honored all three by naming counties after them. • 1820 from Indian lands • In 1794, an army led by General "Mad" Anthony Wayne marched through the county en route to the Battle of Fallen Timbers. During the War of 1812, the county was crossed by General James Winchester who fought a running battle across Emerald Township with the British and Indians. • Hogs, cattle, corn, soybeans, wheat; manufacture of glass, plastics, motor vehicle bodies • Formerly a major limestone quarrying area, the county still operates two large quarries. In the 1820s, Johnny Appleseed planted apple seeds, catnip, pennyroyal, and hoarhound in Carryall Township.

PERRY *New Lexington* • 34,078 • 410 • Central OH; drained by Rush, Sunday, Jonathan, and Moxahala creeks. The county includes part of Buckeye Lake in the extreme northwest and part of Wayne National Forest in the South. • One of ten counties named for Oliver Hazard Perry (1785–1819), U.S. naval officer during the War of 1812 • 1817 or 1818 from Washington, Fairfield, and Muskingum • General Philip Sheridan's childhood home is located in Somerset. The county was also home to Thomas L. Lewis, president of the United Mine Workers of America; Adam Humberger, inventor of the forerunner of the colt revolver; and journalist Januarius Aloysius MacGahan. • Livestock, grain, fruit, produce; manufacture of metal products and stone, clay, and glass products; coal mining, fire-clay quarrying • The New Straitsville mine fires have been burning here since 1884; started by miners during a labor dispute, they have destroyed an estimated $100,000,000 in coal. The Ohio Ceramic Center is near Crooksville.

PICKAWAY *Circleville* • 52,727 • 502 • South-central OH; intersected by the Scioto River and by Big Darby, Deer, Salt, and Walnut creeks. Stage's Pond State Nature Preserve, and A.W. Marion and Deer Creek state parks are here. The county includes part of Deer Creek State Forest. • Named for the Piqua Indians, a subtribe of the Shawnees • 1810 from Ross, Fairfield, and Franklin • Hogs, cattle, corn, soybeans; manufacture of food products, plastics, stone, clay and glass products, electric lamps, sand and gravel pits.

PIKE *Waverly* •27,695 • 442 • Southern OH; intersected by the Scioto River, and Sunfish and Beaver creeks. Found here are Lake White and Pike Lake state parks, Pike State Forest, and part of Brush Creek State Forest. Spicy Run Mountain ski area is also here. • One of ten counties named for General Zebulon Montgomery Pike (1779–1813), U.S. army officer and discoverer of Pikes Peak, CO • 1815 from Ross, Highland, and Scioto • Cattle, poultry, corn; hardwood timber, sawmilling; manufacture of wood products, chemicals, transportation equipment, concrete products.

PORTAGE (one of two counties so named, the other in WI) *Ravenna* • 152,061 • 492 • Northeastern OH; intersected by the Cuyahoga River and tributaries of the Mahoning River. The county has many lakes and reservoirs. Also here are West Branch and Tinker's Creek state parks, and Eagle Creek State Nature Preserve. Nelson-Kennedy Ledge State Park is positioned on the mid-continental divide of streams flowing either to the Atlantic Ocean by way of Lake Erie or to the Gulf of Mexico by way of the Ohio River. • Named for the portage of canoes or other craft between the Cuyahoga and Tuscarawas rivers • 1807 from Trumbull and Jackson • On May 4, 1970, at Kent State U., four students were killed when National Guard troops fired at some 600 antiwar demonstrators. • Religious leader Lorenzo Snow; statesman and Supreme Court justice William R. Day; poet Hart Crane; President James A. Garfield; humorist William Thompson • Dairy products, sheep, lambs, fruit, corn; manufacture of rubber and plastic goods, drilling rigs, compressors, nuts and bolts, sports equipment, highway maintenance vehicles, buses, fabricated metal products, machine tools, machinery; printing; sand and gravel pits, coal mines; education (Hiram College; Kent State U.) • Robert Owen was denied permission from the OH Legislature to establish a commune near Ravenna; undeterred, he founded New Harmony in Indiana. Quaker Mills began its flour and oatmeal milling business in Ravenna in 1877 before moving to Akron.

PREBLE *Eaton* • 42,337 • 425 • Western OH, bounded on the west by the IN state line; drained by Twin, Sevenmile, and Fourmile creeks and by the East Fork of the Whitewater River. The county includes Hueston Woods State Park and Fort Saint Clair near Eaton. • Named for Captain Edward Preble (1761–1807), commander of the U.S.S. *Constitution*, which bombarded Tripoli in 1804 during the war with the Barbary pirates. • 1808 from Montgomery and Butler • The county was a stopping place along the Underground Railroad. • Author Sherwood Anderson • Livestock, tobacco, grain, fruit; manufacturing; limestone quarries; timber; nurseries • Roberts Bridge, the oldest covered bridge remaining in OH and the oldest double-barreled bridge still standing in the U.S., is found here.

PUTNAM (one of nine counties so named) *Ottawa* • 34,726 • 484 • Northwestern OH; intersected by the Auglaize, Ottawa, and Blanchard rivers. • One of eight counties definitively named for Gen. Israel Putnam (1718–90), Revolutionary War officer and American commander at the Battle of Bunker Hill • 1820 from Indian Territory • General William Henry Harrison erected Fort Jennings here during the War of 1812. • Livestock, poultry, corn, soybeans, wheat, sugar beets; food processing and light manufacturing; clay pits, limestone quarries.

RICHLAND (one of seven counties so named) *Mansfield* • 128,852 • 497 • North-central OH; drained by forks of the Mohican River. The county has several reservoirs and ski areas, as well as Malabar Farm State Park and Fowler Woods State Nature Preserve. • Given this name for the fertile soil in the area • 1808 from Knox • Novelist and essayist Louis Bromfield (who used the county as backdrop for some of his books); industrialist Charles Kelly King; orchardist Johnny Appleseed (who saved Mansfield in 1812 by racing more than 30 miles through the night to summon troops to defend the town against an Indian attack). • Livestock, grain, fruit, potatoes, dairy products; manufacture of electric appliances, automotive parts, sheet steel, rubber products, brass castings, snowmobiles, plumbing equipment, pumps, thermostats; greenhouses; sand and gravel pits; education (OH State U. at Mansfield). The Ohio State Reformatory is near Mansfield. • A noted winter-sports center, Mansfield holds the Ohio Ski Carnival each year.

ROSS *Chillicothe* • 73,345 • 688 (the second largest county in OH) • Southern OH; bounded on the southwest by Paint Creek State Park; intersected by the Scioto River, and by Paint, Deer, Walnut, and Salt creeks. Tar Hollow and Scioto Trail state forests are here, as are several state parks. Some of OH's best preserved prehistoric Indian burial mounds are in the county, including the Hopewell Culture National Historical Park. • Named for James Ross (1762–1847), U.S. senator from PA • Original county; organized 1798 (prior to statehood) • Chillicothe served as the capital of the Northwest Territory from 1800 to 1803. The city was the state capital from 1803 to 1810 and from 1812 to 1816. The first state constitution was written here. • Businessman Robert G. Dun; writer Martha Finley; Union general William Starke Rosecrans • Corn, soybeans, hogs, cattle, dairying; manufacture of paper, motor vehicle bodies, shoes, aluminum products, floor tile, steel springs; sand and gravel pits; education (OH U.–Chillicothe) • The *Chillicothe Gazette*, established in 1800, is the oldest continuously published newspaper in OH. Adena (state memorial), the home of the sixth governor of OH, Thomas Worthington, is believed to have been designed by Benjamin H. Latrobe.

SANDUSKY *Fremont* • 61,792 • 409 • Northern OH, bounded on the northeast by Sandusky Bay of Lake Erie; intersected by the Sandusky and Portage rivers, and Muddy and Green creeks. • Named for the Sandusky River • 1820 from Huron • President Rutherford B. Hayes (Library and Museum); army officer James Birdseye McPherson • The county is OH's largest producer of sugar beets; also grows corn, soybeans, vegetables; manufactures include plastic foam products, primary nonferrous metals, hand and edge tools, batteries, electrical products, motor vehicle parts and accessories; processing of preserved fruits and vegetables; limestone quarries.

SCIOTO *Portsmouth* • 79,195 • 612 • Southern OH, bounded on the south by the Ohio River, forming the KY state line; intersected by the Scioto and Little Scioto rivers. The county includes parts of Shawnee and Brush Creek state forests in the west and part of Wayne National Forest in the east. Shawnee State Park is also here. Greenup Lock and Dam is on the Ohio River. • Named for the Scioto River • 1803 from Indian Territory • The early growth of Portsmouth, founded in 1803, was propelled by the opening of the Ohio and Erie Canal, making the town a transfer point from canal barges to river packets. The city suffered a disastrous river flood in 1937. A 77-foot floodwall was completed in 1950 for future protection. • Lambs, dairy products, corn, soybeans, fruit; processing of food and beverages; gray and ductile iron foundries, manufacture of steel, industrial organic chemicals, shoes, plastics, chemicals, firebricks; education (Shawnee State U.) Sandstone quarries here have supplied material for notable public structures, including the Canadian Parliament buildings in Ottawa. • The National Outboard Motor Boat Championship Races are held at Portsmouth.

SENECA *Tiffin* • 58,683 • 551 • Northern OH; drained by the Sandusky River and its tributaries. Seneca Caverns is here, as are Springfield Marsh and Collier state nature preserves. • One of two counties (the other in NY) named for the Seneca Indians • 1820 from Sandusky • Livestock, poultry, dairy products, corn, soybeans; limestone quarries, clay pits; mineral springs (resorts); manufacture of furniture and fixtures, pottery, fabricated metal products, transportation equipment, heavy machinery, pipe fittings, grinding wheels, electronics; education (Founded in 1850, Heidelberg was the third co-educational college in the U.S. Also, Tiffin U.) • Tiffin is known for Tiffin glass, manufactured here for many years. Pieces are displayed in the Seneca County Museum.

SHELBY *Sidney* • 47,910 • 409 • Western OH; intersected by the Great Miami River and Loramie Creek. Lake Loramie State Park and Gross Memorial Woods State Nature Preserve are located here. • One of nine counties named directly or indirectly for General Isaac Shelby (1750–1826), officer in the Revolutionary War, NC legislator, and first governor of KY • 1819 from Miami • Cattle, poultry, dairying, corn, soybeans; preserved fruits and vegetables; manufacture of transportation equipment, apparel, plastic products, aluminum products, lathes, compressors, road machinery; metal finishing and fabrication; gravel pits • Sections of the six original locks and aqueduct of the Miami-Erie canal, built in the 1830s and 40s, are located in Lockington.

STARK (one of three counties so named) *Canton* • 378,098 • 576 • East-central OH; intersected by the Tuscarawas River, and by Nimishillen, Sandy, and Sugar creeks. The county includes Quail Hollow State Park. • One of two counties (the other in IL) named for Gen. John Stark (1728–1822), officer in the French and Indian War and the Revolutionary War • 1808 from Indian Territory • Canton, incorporated as a village in 1822, became an early center for the manufacture of agricultural machinery. • President William McKinley (museum and national memorial in Canton); silent film actor Dorothy Gish; industrialist William Henry Hoover; merchant and patron of music Augustus D. Juilliard • Poultry, corn, fruit, dairying; diversified manufacturing, including meat products, millwork, rubber goods, tiles, metal cans, machinery, transportation equipment, fabricated metal products, electrical equipment, consumer goods, nonferrous foundries; clay, coal mining, limestone quarries, sand and gravel pits, oil and gas extraction; petroleum refining; education (Malone College; Walsh U.; Mount Union College) • The National Professional Football Hall of Fame in Canton is housed in a building shaped like a football. The American Professional Football Association was formed in Canton in 1920; Jim Thorpe of the Canton Bulldogs was its first president. The First Ladies National Historic Site is also located here.

SUMMIT (one of three counties so named) *Akron* • 542,899 (the fifth most populated county in OH) • 413 • Northeastern OH; drained by the Cuyahoga and Tuscarawas rivers. The county includes Portage Lakes State Park. Part of Cuyahoga Valley National Park is in the northwest; established in 2000, it is among the nation's youngest national parks. • Named for the high ground that separates the rivers within the county that flow into the Ohio. • 1840 from Portage, Medina, and Stark • Benjamin F. Goodrich moved a small rubber factory to Akron in 1871. With the advent of the automobile and the demand for rubber tires, the city became the "Rubber Capital of the World" and international headquarters for Firestone, General Tire, Goodrich, and Goodyear. • Geologist Walter H. Bucher; race car driver Art Arfons; White House counsel John Dean III. Journalist and publisher John S. Knight died here. • Corn, vegetables, poultry; diversified manufacturing, including lumber and wood products, bakery products, plastic goods, household furniture, laminated and coated paper, chemicals, boilers, composites, computers, tires, stone, clay and glass products, hand and edge tools and hardware, metal stampings, aircraft parts and equipment, bicycles and other sporting goods, industrial machinery; limestone and sandstone quarries, sand, gravel, clay, salt deposits; education (U. of Akron) • O.C. Barber, president of the Diamond Match Company, formerly located in Barberton, invested millions of dollars in a large experimental farm here before his death in 1920. (His company produced the first book matches here in 1896.) The hangar built in Akron by the Goodyear Aerospace Corporation for its blimps is one of the world's largest buildings without interior supports. Derby Downs in Akron is the site of the annual All-American Soap Box Derby.

TRUMBULL *Warren* • 225,116 • 616 • Northeastern OH, bounded on the east by the PA state line; drained by the Mahoning and Grand rivers, and by Mosquito and Pymatuning creeks. The county includes Mosquito Creek Lake (reservoir) bordered by Mosquito Lakes State Park. Suburbs of Youngstown are in the south. • Named for Jonathan Trumbull (1740–1809), aide-de-camp to Gen. George Washington, governor of CT, and speaker of the House of Representatives • 1800 from Jefferson (prior to statehood) • When settled in 1806, Niles was called Heaton's Furnace for James Heaton's blast furnace there. One of his employees was William McKinley, father of the future president. Settled in 1797, Warren was the first and only capital of the Western Reserve. The city's size and prosperity grew with the discovery of coal in the Mahoning Valley and development of the iron industry after 1870. • Painter and critic Kenyon Cox; experimental poet Kenneth Patchen; lawyer and reformer Wayne Bidwell Wheeler; writer Earl Biggers; clergyman and educator Charles G. Finney; President William McKinley (birthplace memorial and museum); actor and playwright John Charles Nugent; engineer and inventor James W. Packard • Cattle, dairying, corn, soybeans; dairy products; manufacture of home furnishings and furniture, motor vehicle parts, aircraft engines and parts, pressed and blown glass, electric lamps, building materials, steel, lathes, tools and dies; sand and gravel pits, oil and gas extraction.

TUSCARAWAS *New Philadelphia* • 90,914 • 568 • Eastern OH; intersected by the Tuscarawas River, and by Stillwater, Sugar, Sandy, and Conotton creeks. Fort Laurens is in the north. The county includes part of Atwood Lake reservoir and Beach City Lake reservoir. • Named for the Tuscarawas River • 1808 from Jefferson • Schoenbrunn was OH's first village (now restored as a state memorial). • Baseball pitcher Cy Young (state memorial) • Poultry, cattle, corn; manufacture of steel, paper products, chemicals, plastics, construction materials and equipment, fabricated metal products, vacuum cleaners, flooring, clothing, textile machinery, ceramics, industrial fans; coal mines, clay pits • The Warther Museum in Dover contains hand-crafted models of steam engines and railroad locomotives. New Philadelphia is the headquarters for OH's major flood-control and recreation project, the Muskingum Watershed Conservancy District.

UNION (one of eighteen counties so named) *Marysville* • 40,909 • 437 • Central OH; drained by Big Darby, Mill, and Rush creeks. The Milton Center Prairie Preserve is in the southwest. • The county was named for the "union" of land taken from the counties that formed it. • 1820 from Franklin, Madison and Logan • Vice President Charles W. Fairbanks; physicist Wallace Sabine • Hogs, cattle, poultry, dairy products, corn, soybeans; manufacture of chemicals, transportation equipment; limestone quarries, sand and gravel pits.

VAN WERT *Van Wert* • 29,659 • 410 • Western OH, bounded on the west by the IN state line; drained by the Little Auglaize and St. Marys rivers. • Named for Isaac Van Wert (?–1828), one of three NY militiamen who inadvertently captured British spy John Andre during the Revolutionary War. OH honored all three by naming counties after them. • 1820

from Indian Territory • Corn, wheat, soybeans, poultry; manufacture of soybean oils, paper boxes, gaskets, packing and sealing devices, metal stampings, vehicle parts and accessories; limestone quarries, clay pits; nurseries.

VINTON *McArthur* • 12,806 (the least populated county in OH) • 414 • Southern OH; drained by Raccoon and Salt creeks. The county includes Zaleski and Waterloo state forests, and Lake Hope and Lake Alma state parks. Part of Wayne National Forest is in the north. • Named for Samuel F. Vinton (1792–1862), U.S. representative from OH • 1850 from Gallia, Athens, Ross, Hocking, Meigs, and Jackson • Outlaw Elzy Lay • Cattle, corn, fruit; manufacture of lumber and wood products, ordnance; limestone quarrying, coal mining (Historically important, abandoned mines have been replaced by new underground and strip mining operations.)

WARREN *Lebanon* • 158,383 (39% increase since 1990; the second fastest growing county in OH) • 400 • Southwestern OH; intersected by the Little Miami River (designated as a National Scenic and Recreational River); also drained by Todd, Caesar, and Turtle creeks. The county includes Fort Ancient State Memorial Park, Caesar Creek State Park, Halls Creek Woods and Caesar Creek Gorge state nature preserves. • One of fourteen counties named for Gen. Joseph Warren (1741–1775), officer in the Revolutionary War who died at the Battle of Bunker Hill • 1803 from Hamilton • Colorado Territory governor John Evans • Sheep, corn, soybeans, fruit, tobacco; manufacture of textiles, folding paperboard boxes and other paper products; sand and gravel pits.

WASHINGTON *Marietta* • 63,251 • 635 (the fifth largest county in OH) • Southeastern OH, bounded on the southeast by the Ohio River, forming the WV state line; intersected by the Muskingum and Little Muskingum rivers, and Duck Creek. Parts of Wayne National Forest are here, as are Boord State Nature Preserve and Ohio River Island National Wildlife Refuge. • One of thirty-one counties named for George Washington • Original county; organized 1788 (prior to statehood). It was the first county created in the Northwest Territory and the oldest county in the state. • The first permanent white settlement in OH (in April, 1788) was established at the site of Marietta by Revolutionary War General Rufus Putnam and his Ohio Company of Associates. General Arthur St. Clair was installed here as the first governor of the Northwest Territory on July 15, 1788. Marietta was the territory's first capital. • Army officer Don Carlos Buell; politician Charles G. Dawes; newspaper publisher Harrison Gray Otis • Livestock, dairy products, fruit, corn; manufacture of office furniture, aluminum products, grindstones, safes, synthetic rubber, plastics, laboratory apparatus and furniture; oil and gas extraction; limestone quarries; education (Marietta College) • In the river opposite Belpre is Blennerhassett Island where Harman Blennerhassett and Aaron Burr conspired against the U.S. government. The first public library in the Northwest Territory was in Marietta.

WAYNE (one of sixteen counties so named) *Wooster* • 111,564 • 555 • North-central OH; intersected by Killbuck, Chippewa and Sugar creeks, and by the Lake Fork of the Mohican River. The county includes Browns Lake Bog and Johnson Woods state nature preserves. There is an agricultural research station near Wooster. • One of fifteen counties named for General "Mad" Anthony Wayne (1745–1796), officer in the Revolutionary War and statesman • 1808 or 1812. The original Wayne County in the Northwest Territory with which this county is sometimes confused was established in 1796 and had ceased to exist by 1805. • Physicists Arthur Holly and Karl Taylor Compton; philanthropist Anna M. Harkness; railroad executives Oris Paxton and Mantis James Van Sweringen • Poultry, corn, fruit, dairy products; manufacture of food products, paper, metal and plastic products, electronics, motor vehicle parts and accessories, consumer goods, hydraulic pumps; iron foundries; sand and gravel pits, oil and gas wells, salt production; education (College of Wooster) • Wooster claims to have had the first Christmas tree in America. It was introduced in 1847 by August Imgard, a German immigrant.

WILLIAMS (one of two counties so named, the other in ND) *Bryan* • 39,188 • 422 • Extreme northwestern OH, bounded on the north by the MI state line, and on the west by the IN state line; intersected by the St. Joseph and Tiffin rivers. • Named for David Williams (1754–1831), one of three New York militiamen who inadvertently captured British spy John Andre during the Revolutionary War. OH honored all three by naming counties after them. • 1820 from Henry • Livestock, poultry, corn, soybeans, wheat; manufacture of furniture, transportation equipment, plastic products, fabricated metal products, machinery, electronic products, consumer goods, airplane parts, lubricating equipment, furnaces; sand and gravel pits.

WOOD (one of four counties so named) *Bowling Green* • 121,065 • 617 • Northwestern OH, bounded on the northwest by the Maumee River; intersected by the Portage River. Mary Jane Thurston State Park is on the western border. • Named for Captain Eleazer D. Wood (?–1814), an officer in the War of 1812 and builder of Fort Meigs in OH. • 1820 from Indian lands • Bowling Green enjoyed a short boom period following the discovery of oil in the area in 1886; glass manufacture was prominent until the wells ran dry. • Corn, soybeans, tomatoes, dairying, wheat, livestock fruit; manufacture of paper products, oils and greases, rubber and plastic goods, flat glass, lime, metal stampings, motor vehicle parts and accessories, surgical and medical instruments, floor-maintenance equipment; processing of vegetables, canned fruits, meat packing; limestone quarries; education (Bowling Green State U.) • Fort Meigs (state memorial), situated along the banks of the Maumee River, is the largest walled fortification in the U.S.

WYANDOT *Upper Sandusky* • 22,908 • 406 • North-central OH; drained by the Sandusky River, and Broken Sword and Tymochtee creeks. • One of two counties (the other, Wyandotte, in KS) named for the Wyandot (or Wyandotte) Indians • 1845 from Marion, Crawford, Hardin, and Hancock • The only incidence of a U.S. army officer being burned at the stake by Indians occurred along the Tymochtee Creek. In one of the last battles of the Revolutionary War, Col. William B. Crawford was captured by the Delaware Indians and so dispatched. The Wyandots were the last organized band of Indians to leave OH; they broke up their homes here and moved to a reservation in KS in 1843. • Livestock, corn, soybeans, wheat, fruit, poultry, dairy products; manufacture of plastic products, electronic equipment, transportation equipment, structural glass products, porcelain products; limestone, dolomite, and other aggregate quarries, gravel pits, brick clay • The first Methodist mission was established here. The Wyandot County Fair is the largest county fair in the state. Upper Sandusky is the site of the annual Wyandot Open Cornhuskers Festival. Indian Trail Caverns is part of the largest cavern area in OH. Newly unearthed chambers have revealed many significant archeological finds.

OKLAHOMA

Labor Conquers All Things

Each of the state's seventy-seven counties has three commissioners, each elected from a separate district.

ADAIR (one of four counties so named) *Stilwell* • 21,038 • 576 • Eastern OK, bounded on the east by the AR state line and on the west by the edge of the Ozark Mountains; drained by the Illinois River, and Barre and Sallisaw creeks. Adair State Park and Ozark Plateau National Wildlife Refuge are here. The county also includes the Boston Mountains in the southeast. • Named for the Adair family, a family of Cherokee Indians; its prominent member was William P. Adair (?–1881), leader of the Southern Cherokee delegation. • 1907 from Cherokee lands • Strawberries, fruits, vegetables, cattle, poultry, dairying; food processing and canning; manufacture of electronic equipment, industrial machinery.

ALFALFA *Cherokee* • 6,105 • 867 • Northern OK, bounded on the north by the KS state line; intersected by the Salt Fork of the Arkansas River, impounded by Great Salt Plains Dam, forming Great Salt Plains Lake; also drained by Medicine Lodge River, and by Turkey and Eagle Chief creeks. The county contains Great Salt Plains National Wildlife Refuge and Great Salt Plains State Park. • One of two counties (the other, Murray County, also in OK) named for William H. "Alfalfa Bill" Murray (1869–1956), U.S. representative from OK and governor of OK • 1907 from Woods • Wheat, alfalfa, oats, hay, cattle, poultry; manufacturing; oil. • The Sod House Museum, featuring a homesteader's sod structure, is located near Aline.

ATOKA *Atoka* •13,879 • 978 • Southeastern OK; drained by Muddy Boggy and Clear Boggy creeks. Boggy Depot State Park is here, as are Atoka Reservoir, McGee Creek Lake, McGee Creek National Scenic and Recreation Area, and McGee Creek State Park. • Named for Charles Atoka, athletic Choctaw leader and member of the Choctaw Council • 1907, from Choctaw lands • Wheat, peanuts, sheep; timber; manufacture of furniture; coal mining, rock quarries. • The Confederate Memorial Museum and Information Center is located in Atoka.

BEAVER (one of three counties so named) *Beaver* • 5,857 • 1,814 (the fifth largest county in OK) • Western OK panhandle (easternmost of the three Panhandle counties), bounded on the north by the KS state line and on the south by the TX state line; intersected by the Beaver and Cimarron rivers, and Kiowa Creek. The county includes Beaver State Park. • Named for the Beaver River • Original county; organized 1890 (prior to statehood) and comprising the entire panhandle. Present Beaver County was organized 1907 from the eastern third of the original county • Wheat, sorghum, corn, cattle; natural-gas and salt deposits, oil • The Beaver River Wildlife Management Area is home to two prairie dog towns. The Gateway to the Panhandle Museum is located in Gate.

BECKHAM *Sayre* • 19,799 • 902 • Western OK, bounded on the west by the TX state line; intersected by the North Fork of the Red River and Elk Creek. • Named for John C. W. Beckham (1869–1940), KY governor and U.S. senator from KY • 1907 from Greer and Roger Mills • Balloonist Maxie Anderson • Cotton, wheat, sorghum, oats, peanuts, cattle, horses; honey; manufacture of cotton-gin equipment, furniture, feed; oil extraction and refining, natural gas wells and gas recycling, salt deposits • Old Town Museum near Elk City is a replica of an early Western town.

BLAINE *Watonga* • 11,976 • 929 • West-central OK; intersected by the North Canadian, Canadian, and Cimarron rivers. Roman Nose State Resort Park is here. • One of four counties named for James G. Blaine (1830–93), Speaker of the House, U.S. senator from ME, and U.S. secretary of state • Original county; organized as "C" County in 1890; renamed in 1892 (prior to statehood) • Wheat, oats, cattle, dairy prod-

ucts; shipping and processing of farm products; gypsum mining and processing; oil and natural gas, salt deposits.

BRYAN (One of two counties so named, the other in GA) *Durant* • 36,534 • 909 • Southern OK, bounded on the south by the Red River (forming the TX state line) and on the west by the Washita Arm of Lake Texoma (Washita River); impounded by Denison Dam; drained by the Blue River. • Named for William Jennings Bryan (1860–1925), U.S. secretary of state and defeated presidential candidate in 1896, 1900 and 1908 • 1907 from Chickasaw lands • Corn, hay, soybeans, peanuts, cotton, cattle, dairy products; manufacture of utility truck bodies, clothing, cement blocks; lumbering; oil and gas; education (Southeastern OK State U.) • Fort Washita (historic site), on the east side of Lake Texoma, was used as a Confederate military post during the Civil War.

CADDO (one of two counties so named, the other in LA) *Anadarko* • 30,150 • 1,278 • West-central OK; intersected by the Washita River; drained by Fort Cobb and Sugar creeks. Red Rock Canyon and Fort Cobb state parks, and Fort Cobb Reservoir are here. • Named for the Caddo Indians • 1907. Originally "I" County of Indian Territory • Cotton, wheat, sorghum, fruits, vegetables, hay, corn, peanuts, cattle, poultry; manufacture of rugs; farm-products processing; sand and gravel • Anadarko reflects its large Indian population through Indian City, U.S.A. (a tourist attraction), the American Indian Exposition held here each year, and the National Hall of Fame for Famous American Indians.

CANADIAN *El Reno* • 87,697 (the fifth most populated county in OK) • 900 • Central OK; drained by the Canadian River (which forms the eastern part of the southern border) and by the North Canadian River. The county is urbanized in the east and center, around Oklahoma City. (The city has annexed into the county in the east and southeast.) Historic Fort Reno is located near the center of the county. • Named for the North and South Canadian rivers • Organized 1890 as County "4" (prior to statehood); name changed in 1907. • Cattle, sheep, hogs, dairying, wheat, barley, oats, corn, hay; manufacture of trailers, metal products, fertilizers; food processing; railroad shops.

CARTER (one of five counties so named) *Ardmore* • 45,621 • 824 • Southern OK; drained by the Washita River and Wildhorse Creek. The county includes a section of the Arbuckle Mountains in the far north and Tucker Tower Nature Center. Part of Lake Murray reservoir and Lake Murray State Resort Park are on the southern boundary. • Named for one of the following: Charles D. Carter (1868–1929), OK's first U.S. representative; Benjamin W. Carter (1837–1894), a Cherokee Indian, soldier in the Confederate army and OK territorial judge; or for the Carter family • 1907 from Chickasaw lands • Ballerina and ballet teacher Rosella Hightower; Bill Dalton (of the Dalton Brothers) who died here. • Horses, cattle, sheep, wheat, hay, vegetables, corn, peanuts, dairying; oil extraction and refining, natural-gas wells; manufacture of leather goods, fiberglass, electronics equipment, concrete, sportswear, roofing material; wholesaling; tourism; education (Carter Seminary for Chickasaw Indian Girls).

CHEROKEE *Tahlequah* • 42,521 (25% increase since 1990; the third fastest growing county in OK) • 751 • Eastern OK, bounded on the west by the Neosho River, here forming Fort Gibson Lake; intersected by the Illinois River (forming Tenkiller Lake reservoir). The county includes Sequoyah, and Cherokee Landing state parks. • One of eight counties named for the Cherokee Indians • 1907 from Indian lands • Laid out on Cherokee council grounds in 1843, the town of Tahlequah served as capital of the Cherokee Nation until 1907. Government buildings still standing from that era are the Capitol (1867–70), the National Prison (1874) and the Supreme Court (1844). • Professional rodeo cowboy Tom Ferguson • Fruit, vegetables, corn, grain, dairying; cattle; manufacture of machine-shop products; lumber; education (Northeastern State U.) • The Cherokee Heritage Center is in Tahlequah.

CHOCTAW *Hugo* • 15,342 • 774 • Southeastern OK, bounded on the south by the Red River, forming the TX state line; drained by Muddy Boggy and Clear Boggy creeks, and by the Kiamichi River. The county includes Fort Towson Historic Site and Raymond Gary State Park. Hugo Lake reservoir is also here. • One of three counties named for the Choctaw Indians • 1907 • TV journalist and author Bill Moyers • Soybeans, vegetables, corn; manufacturing and vegetable processing.

CIMARRON *Boise City* • 3,148 (the least populated county in OK) • 1,835 (the fourth largest county in OK) • Western OK panhandle; drained by the Cimarron and Beaver rivers. Cimarron is the only county in the U.S. to be bounded by four states: CO and KS on the north, NM on the west, and TX on the south. The county includes Black Mesa (elevation 4,973 feet), the highest point in OK (in the northwest corner) and part of Rita Blanca National Grassland in the southwest. Old Sante Fe Trail runs northeast-southwest across the northwestern part of the county. Black Mesa State Park and Nature Preserve is also here. • Named for the Cimarron River • 1907 from Beaver • Livestock, wheat, sorghum • During the Santa Fe Trail Daze in June, visitors can take a guided tour to Autograph Rock, which displays about 200 signatures of travelers from the 1840s.

CLEVELAND (one of three counties so named) *Norman* • 208,016 (the third most populated county in OK) • 536 • Central OK, bounded on the southwest by the Canadian River; drained by the Little River. It is part of the Oklahoma City metropolitan area. (The city has annexed into the county in the north.) Lake Thunderbird State Park is on Lake Thunderbird reservoir (Little River). Lake Stanley Draper reservoir is in the north (in Oklahoma City). • One of two counties (the other in AR) named for President Grover Cleveland • Original county; organized 1890 as "Third" County (prior to statehood) from Cherokee lands; name changed 1907. • Engineer

and radio astronomer Karl Jansky • Alfalfa, fruit, melons, wheat, horses, cattle, dairying; light industry, including the manufacture of srings, mattresses; petroleum refining, oil and gas fields; education (U. of OK) • The OK Museum of Natural History is on the campus of the university.

COAL *Coalgate* • 6,031 • 518 • South-central OK; drained by Clear Boggy and Muddy Boggy creeks. • Named for the chief economic product of the county • 1907 • Coalgate was a former coal-mining town; its last mine closed in 1958. • Corn, sorghum, cattle, hogs, poultry; some manufacturing of apparel.

COMANCHE *Lawton* • 114,996 (the fourth most populated county in OK) • 1,069 • Southwestern OK; drained by East Cache, West Cache, and Beaver creeks. The county includes the Wichita Mountains (on the western part of the northern boundary), which include Wichita Mountains Wildlife Refuge. Lake Lawtonka reservoir is here, as is Lake Ellsworth reservoir on the northern border. • One of three counties named for the Comanche Indians • 1907 from Cherokee lands • The county was originally part of the Choctaw-Chickasaw lands in Indian Territory. The area was settled in 1869 by the Kiowa and Comanche Indians. The town of Lawton grew up around Fort Sill, established to control the Indians. It was named for General Henry W. Lawton, sent to the area to capture the Apache leader Geronimo (who died at the fort in 1909). • Peanuts, wheat, hay, oats, sorghum, cattle, dairying; manufacture of mobile homes, concrete products, frozen and canned foods; limestone quarries; sand and gravel pits, oil wells; education (Cameron U.) • Fort Sill Military Reservation has a military museum and about fifty historic sites, including the Apache prisoner of war cemetery and the Medicine Bluffs, which, for the Comanche and Kiowa, were sacred landmarks.

COTTON *Walters* • 6,614 • 637 • Southern OK, bounded on the south by the Red River, here forming the TX state line; drained by Deep Red, Beaver, and East and West Cache creeks. • Named for the principal agricultural crop of the county. Local citizens submitted a number of names for the county; this is the one that was chosen from the hat. • 1912 from Comanche • Cotton, wheat, oats, cattle, sheep; light manufacturing; oil wells.

CRAIG (one of two counties so named, the other in VA) *Vinita* • 14,950 • 761 • Northeastern OK, bounded on the north by the KS state line and on the extreme northeast by the Neosho River; drained by Cabin Creek. • Named for Granville C. Craig, a local farmer and merchant • 1907 from Cherokee lands • Humorist Will Rogers (who jokingly referred to Vinita where he attended high school, as his "college town.") • Soybeans, hay, corn, cattle, dairy products; oil wells, coal mining; meat packing • The Will Rogers Memorial Rodeo is held in Vinita each year. The town was named for Vinnie Ream, who sculpted the statue of Abraham Lincoln in the Capitol in Washington, D.C.

CREEK *Sapulpa* • 67,367 • 956 • Central OK; drained by the

Cimarron River and the Deep Fork of the Canadian River. Heyburn Lake reservoir is here, as is part of Keystone Lake reservoir (Arkansas and Cimarron rivers) on the northern boundary, with Keystone State Park adjacent. • Named for the Creek Nation • 1907 from Cherokee lands • Grain, peanuts, sorghum, poultry, cattle, horses, dairying; extensive oil and natural gas fields; manufacture of trailers, lingerie, glass, pottery, bricks, furnaces, tanks, tools, dairy products; meat packing.

CUSTER *Arapaho* • 26,142 • 987 • Western OK; drained by the Washita and Canadian rivers, and Deer Creek. Washita National Wildlife Refuge, Foss Lake reservoir, and Foss State Park are in the county. • One of six counties named for General George Armstrong Custer (1839–76), U.S. army officer and Indian fighter • Original county; organized as "G" County in 1891 (prior to statehood); name officially changed in 1907. • Astronaut Thomas P. Stafford • Wheat, cotton, sorghum, barley, peanuts, oats, cattle; manufacturing; oil and gas; education (Southwestern OK State U.) • Oklahoma Route 66 Museum is located near Clinton.

DELAWARE (one of six counties so named) *Jay* • 37,077 (32% increase since 1990; the fastest growing county in OK) • 741 • Northeastern OK, bounded on the east by the AR and MO state lines. Lake Spavinaw and Lake Eucha reservoirs are here, as is part of Grand Lake O' the Cherokees (Neosho River) in the north. Bernice, Honey Creek, Disney Little Blue, Lake Eucha, and Natural Falls state parks are also here. • Named for the Delaware Indians • 1907 from Cherokee lands • Hay, cattle, chickens, dairying; manufacture of food and transportation equipment.

DEWEY (one of two counties so named, the other in SD) *Taloga* • 4,743 • 1,000 • Western OK; intersected by the Canadian and North Canadian rivers. Part of Canton Lake reservoir (North Canadian River) is in the northeast. • Named for George Dewey (1837–1917), who captured Manila during the Spanish-American War and was given the rank of Admiral of the Navy • Original county; organized in 1892 as "D" County (prior to statehood); it was changed to Dewey by locals, and endorsed by the state constitutional convention in 1907. • Wheat, sorghum, cattle; oil and natural gas.

ELLIS (one of three counties so named) *Arnett* • 4,075 • 1,229 • Northwestern OK, bounded on the west by the TX state line and on the south by the Canadian River; drained by the South Canadian River and Wolf Creek. • Named for Albert H. Ellis (1861–1950), Speaker Pro Tem of the OK State House of Representatives • Organized 1907 from Day (which had been the northern part of Roger Mills and then abolished) and Woodward • Barley, sorghum, oats, cattle, dairying; oil and gas • The Shattuck Windmill Museum displays twenty-four restored windmills dating from 1850 to 1950.

GARFIELD *Enid* • 57,813 • 1,059 • Northern OK; drained by Turkey, Skeleton, and Black Bear creeks. Vance Air Force Base is here. • One of six counties named for President James

Abram Garfield • Originally "O" County; name changed in 1894 (prior to statehood) • Enid was founded overnight as a tent city around a U.S. land office when the Cherokee Strip (museum) opened to settlement on September 16, 1893. It later became the commercial and cultural center of northwestern OK. • Wheat, cattle, sheep, dairying; oil and gas wells; manufacture of oil-field equipment; flour and grain milling, meat processing; oil refining; education (Phillips U.) • The Tri-State Music Festival is a popular annual event. The Railroad Museum of Oklahoma is in Enid.

GARVIN *Pauls Valley* • 27,210 • 809 • South-central OK; intersected by the Washita River (forming part of the southeastern boundary) and by Rush and Wildhorse creeks. • Named for Samuel J. Garvin, a leader of the Chickasaw Nation • 1907 from Chickasaw lands • Oats, fruit, corn, hay, peanuts, soybeans, sheep; farm products processing; manufacturing; oil and natural gas, oil refining.

GRADY *Chickasha* • 45,516 • 1,101 • Central OK, bounded on the north by the Canadian River; intersected by the Washita River; drained by Rush Creek. • One of two counties (the other in GA) named for Henry W. Grady (1850–89), orator and editor of the *Atlanta Constitution* newspaper • 1907 from Caddo and Comanche • Wheat, oats, winter hay, watermelons, alfalfa, peanuts, sorghum, corn, honey, cattle, sheep, dairying; manufacturing; oil and natural gas; education (U. of Science and Arts of OK).

GRANT (one of fifteen counties so named) *Medford* • 5,144 • 1,001 • Northern OK, bounded on the north by the KS state line; intersected by the Salt Fork of the Arkansas River; drained by Pond Creek. • One of twelve counties named for President Ulysses S. Grant • Originally "L" County; name change ratified in 1907 • Wheat, cotton, sorghum, cattle; manufacturing; oil and natural-gas wells.

GREER *Mangum* • 6,061 • 639 • Southwestern OK, bounded on the east by the North Fork of the Red River (forming Altus Lake reservoir in the southeast); also drained by the Elm and Salt forks of the Red River. Quartz Mountain State Resort Park is here. • Named for John A. Greer (1802–1855), TX Republic senator and secretary of the treasury • The county was established in TX in 1860. It was subsequently given to OK by the U.S. government. Greer County was re-established in its new state by the OK State Constitutional Convention in 1907. • Peanuts, sheep; granite, clay; manufacturing.

HARMON *Hollis* • 3,283 • 538 • Southwestern OK, bounded on the southwest (Red River) and west by the TX state line; drained by the Salt and Elm forks of the Red River. • Named for Judson C. Harmon (1846–1927), governor of OH and U.S. attorney general who participated in the removal of Greer County from TX • 1909 from Greer • The county was originally claimed by both TX and OK territories • Peanuts, sorghum, cotton, wheat, vegetables, black-eyed peas, cattle; mesquite.

HARPER (one of two counties so named, the other in KS)

Buffalo • 3,562 • 1,039 • Northwestern OK, bounded on the north by the KS state line; intersected by the North Canadian and Cimarron rivers, and Kiowa Creek. • Named for Oscar G. Harper (1874–?), an official at the OK State Constitutional Convention (1906–07) who was criticized in the press for having financially benefited from the selection of Buffalo as county seat. • 1907 • Livestock, wheat, barley.

HASKELL (one of three counties so named) *Stigler* • 11,792 • 577 • Eastern OK, bounded on the north by the Canadian River (Eufaula Dam and Lake on the far northwest corner) and Robert S. Kerr Lake (Arkansas River); drained by Sansbois Creek. The Sansbois Mountains are on the southern boundary. Part of Sequoyah National Wildlife Refuge is in the north. • Named for Charles N. Haskell (1860–1933), first governor of OK • 1907 from Choctaw lands • Barley, hay, soybeans, corn, cattle; timber; coal mines.

HUGHES (one of two counties so named, the other in SD) *Holdenville* • 14,154 • 807 • Central OK, bounded, in part, on the northeast and southwest by the Canadian River; intersected by the Canadian, North Canadian, and Little rivers. • Named for William C. Hughes (1869–1939), delegate to the OK State Constitutional Convention • 1907 from Creek lands • Corn, peanuts, hay, watermelons, peanuts, cattle, hogs; manufacturing; oil and natural gas wells; catfish fishing.

JACKSON (one of twenty-four counties so named) *Altus* • 28,439 • 803 • Southwestern OK, bounded on the south by the Red River (forming the TX state line) and on the east by the North Fork of the Red River; drained by the Salt Fork of the Red River. Altus Air Force Base is here. • Named for either President Andrew Jackson or for Confederate General Thomas J. "Stonewall" Jackson • 1907 from Greer • Cotton (also gins, cottonseed-oil mills), wheat, sorghum, alfalfa, cattle; grain elevators; light manufacturing; greyhound breeding. • The Museum of the Western Prairie is located in Altus.

JEFFERSON *Waurika* • 6,818 • 759 • Southern OK, bounded on the south by the Red River, here forming the TX state line; drained by Beaver and Mud creeks. Part of Waurika Lake is in the northwest. • One of twenty-six counties named directly or indirectly for President Thomas Jefferson • 1907 from Comanche • Grain, corn, cattle; manufacturing; oil. • The Chisholm Trail Historical Museum is located in Waurika.

JOHNSTON (one of two counties so named, the other in NC) *Tishomingo* • 10,513 • 645 • Southern OK, bounded on the south in part by Lake Texoma (arm of the Washita River); drained by the Blue and Washita rivers. Part of Tishomingo National Wildlife Refuge borders the Washita River. • Named for Douglas H. Johnston (1856–1939), last governor of the Chickasaw Nation • 1907 from Chickasaw lands • Cattle, raising, dairying, peanuts; sand and gravel pits.

KAY *Newkirk* • 48,080 • 919 • Northern OK, bounded on the north by the KS state line and on the southeast by the Arkansas River (forming Kaw Lake reservoir in the east); intersected by the Arkansas and Chikaskia rivers, and by the Salt Fork of the Arkansas River. The county includes Lake Ponca in the east. • The name Kay evolved from the letter K. (The first seven counties of OK were originally numbered. The later counties were given letters. All eventually received names except "K" County, which became Kay.) • Original county; organized 1895 (prior to statehood) • Ponca City was founded overnight in 1893 with the opening of the Cherokee Strip. Oil discoveries of the 1920s created a boom era for the county. • Wheat, barley, sorghum, alfalfa, soybeans, dairying, cattle, sheep, poultry; oil and natural gas wells, petroleum refining and research; manufacture of petrochemicals, petroleum equipment, metal products; meat packing; zinc smelting; servicing of diesel engines • Ponca City is the site of the Pioneer Woman Museum, dedicated to the courage of the women who helped to settle the West. Oil magnate E.W. Marland's estate is a major tourist draw.

KINGFISHER *Kingfisher* • 13,926 • 903 • Central OK; intersected by the Cimarron River, and Turkey and Skeleton creeks. • Named for the town of Kingfisher • Original county; organized 1890 as the "Fifth" county (prior to statehood); officially named Kingfisher in 1907 at the state constitutional convention. • Retail magnate Sam Walton • Wheat, alfalfa, barley, oats, cattle, sheep, dairying; manufacture of industrial machinery; oil and natural gas deposits • The Chisholm Trail Museum is located in Kingfisher city.

KIOWA *Hobart* • 10,227 • 1,015 • Southwestern OK, bounded on the west by the North Fork of the Red River (forming Altus Lake reservoir) and on the northeast, in part, by the Washita River; drained by Elk Creek. Part of the Wichita Mountains are in the east. The county includes Great Plains State Park and Tom Steed Lake reservoir. • One of three counties named for the Kiowa Indians • Original county; organized 1891 (prior to statehood) • Wheat, cotton, oats, sorghum, cattle, sheep; manufacture of rubber and plastic products; granite and marble quarrying, oils wells.

LATIMER *Wilburton* • 10,692 • 722 • Southeastern OK; drained by Fourche Maline Creek. The southern half of the county lies in the Jack Fork Mountains, and includes the Sansbois Mountains (an extension of the Ouachitas) on its northern boundary. Robbers Cave State Park and part of Sardis Lake reservoir are also here. • Named for James S. Latimer (1855–1941), member of the OK State Constitutional Convention • 1907 from Choctaw lands • Some agriculture, cattle; lumbering; remnant coal mining; manufacture of apparel, electric motors; oil and natural-gas wells.

LE FLORE *Poteau* • 48,109 • 1,586 • Southeastern OK, bounded on the north by the Arkansas River and on the east by the AR state line; drained by the Poteau and Kiamichi rivers. Several Ouachita mountain ranges, including the Kiamichi and Jack Fork mountains, are here. The county also includes Heavener Runestone, Wister, and Talimena state parks, and Winding Stair Mountain National Recreation Area. Spiro Mounds Archeological Center is in the north. Robert S. Kerr Lock and Dam is on the Arkansas River in the northwest corner of the county. • One of two counties (the other in MS) named for Greenwood Leflore (1800–65), chief of the western district of the Choctaw Indian Nation and MS state legislator • 1907 from Choctaw lands • Corn, fruit, vegetables, hay, soybeans, potatoes, cattle, poultry; oil and natural gas wells; timber.

LINCOLN (one of twenty-four counties so named) *Chandler* • 32,080 • 959 • Central OK; intersected by Deep Fork. The Museum of Pioneer History is near Chandler. • One of eighteen counties named for Abraham Lincoln • Original county; organized in 1891 as County "A"; name changed in 1892 (prior to statehood) • Composer Roy Harris • Cotton, sorghum, castor beans, vegetables, pecans, dairying, livestock, poultry; beekeeping; manufacture of apparel, electronic components; oil and natural gas.

LOGAN (one of ten counties so named) *Guthrie* • 33,924 • 745 • Central OK; intersected by the Cimarron River (forming part of the northeastern boundary) and by Skelton Creek. • One of five counties named for General John A. Logan (1826–86), U.S. senator from IL, Union Army officer, and candidate for U.S. vice president. • Original county; organized as County "One" or "First" county in 1891 (prior to statehood); officially renamed in 1907 • The OK State Constitution was written in Guthrie's city hall. The city was founded and became a populous community all on the same day — April 22, 1889 — as "boomers" rushed in at noon to stake their claim to land purchased from the Indians and opened to settlement by order of the U.S. president. Within two months a water system was operational; within four months streets were lit by electricity. Guthrie served as the capital of OK Territory (museum) from 1890 until 1907, and then as the capital of the state of OK until 1910 when the government was moved to Oklahoma City. • Wheat, fruit, cattle, poultry, dairying; manufacture of oil-field equipment, furniture, fabricated steel; railroad and machine shops; grain elevators; oil and natural gas • Guthrie was an important center of the brotherhood of Freemasons. Its Scottish Rite Masonic Temple is one of the city's most noted buildings. The city has 100 structures on the National Register of Historic Places, this figure representing about 90 percent of the downtown area.

LOVE *Marietta* • 8,831 • 515 • Southern OK, bounded on the south by the Red River, forming the TX state line. The county includes part of Lake Murray in the northeast, and a portion of Lake Texoma in the southeast (Red River). • Named for a prominent Chickasaw family whose best-known member was Overton Love (1820–1907), a district judge of the Chickasaw Nation. • 1907 from Chickasaw lands • Grain, corn, asparagus, other vegetables, watermelons, hay, peanuts, cattle, sheep, hogs, horses; manufacturing.

MAJOR *Fairview* • 7,545 • 957 • Northwestern OK; drained by the Cimarron River (forming the western part of the northern border), the North Canadian River, and Eagle Chief Creek. Glass Mountains Conservation Area is located here. • Named for John C. Major (1863–1937), OK territorial legislator and member of the OK Constitutional Convention • 1907 from Woods • Wheat, oats, soybeans, corn, cattle; oil and natural-gas deposits.

MARSHALL (one of twelve counties so named) *Madill* • 13,184 • 371 (the smallest county in OK) • Southern OK, bounded on the south by Lake Texoma (formed by Denison Dam in the Red River) and on the east by the Washita Arm of Lake Texoma. The county includes Lake Texoma Resort State Park. Part of Tishomingo National Wildlife Refuge is in the northeast. • Named for Elizabeth Ellen Marshall Henshaw, mother of George A. Henshaw, a member of the OK Constitutional Convention • 1907 from Chickasaw lands • Cattle, corn, pecans, barley; tourism.

MAYES *Pryor* • 38,369 • 656 • Northeastern OK; intersected by the Neosho River (impounded near the center by Pensacola Dam), forming Grand Lake O' the Cherokees. Part of Fort Gibson Lake reservoir is in the south. Snowdale, Spavinaw, and Cherokee state parks are in the county. • Probably named for Chief Samuel Houston Mayes (1845–1927), principal leader of the Cherokee Nation • 1907 from Indian lands • Nathaniel Pryor, a scout with explorers Lewis and Clark, established a trading post in 1820 near the present site of the city of Pryor. • Cattle, corn, soybeans, sorghum, wheat, oats, dairying; cotton ginning; manufacture of food products, apparel, chemicals, machinery, paper, gypsum products. An agricultural experiment station is located here.

MCCLAIN *Purcell* • 27,740 • 570 • Central OK, bounded on the northeast by the Canadian River; drained by small creeks. The northwest corner is partially urbanized opposite Oklahoma City and Norman. • Named for Charles M. McClain (1840–1915), a member of the OK Constitutional Convention • 1907 from Chicasaw lands • Cotton, alfalfa, hay, soybeans, vegetables, cattle, dairying; natural-gas wells.

MCCURTAIN *Idabel* • 34,402 • 1,852 (the third largest county in OK) • Extreme southeastern OK, bounded on the east by the AR state line and on the south by the Red River, forming the TX state line; drained by the Little and Glover rivers. The Ouachita Mountains cross in the north. Pine Creek Lake reservoir, separate units of Ouachita National Forest, Broken Bow Lake reservoir, Beavers Bend State Resort Park, Hochatown State Park, and McCurtain County Wilderness Area are in the county, as is Little River National Wildlife Refuge. • Named for Green McCurtain (1848–1910), the last elected chief of the Choctaw Nation. • 1907 from Choctaw lands • Lumbering; corn, alfalfa, hay, soybeans, cattle, poultry; resort tourism.

MCINTOSH (one of three counties so named) *Eufaula* • 19,456 • 620 • Eastern OK, bounded on the south by the Canadian River, forming Eufaula Lake. The lake, impounded by Eufaula Dam, is one of the world's largest manmade lakes, covering 102,500 acres. The county is intersected by the North Canadian River and its Deep Fork (forming arms of Eufaula Lake). Fountainhead State Park is north of the lake. • Named for the McIntosh family, a prominent Creek family, whose best known member was William McIntosh (?–1825), general in the War of 1812 • 1907 from Indian lands • Soybeans, peanuts, cattle, dairying; some manufacturing; timber; tourism • The Eufaula Boarding School for Indian Girls is successor to the Asbury Mission School, which was established in 1849 by the Methodist Episcopal Church under contract to the Creek Indian Council. • OK's oldest newspaper, the *Indian Journal*, which was founded in 1876 as a tribal periodical in Muskogee, is published in Eufaula.

MURRAY (one of three counties so named) *Sulphur* • 12,623 • 418 • Southern OK; intersected by the Washita River (forming part of its border on the north and south). The Arbuckle Mountains are located along the southern border. Also here are Turner Falls Park, Arbuckle Wilderness, and Chickasaw National Recreation Area, which encompasses Arbuckle Reservoir. • One of two counties (the other, Alfalfa County, also in OK) named for William "Alfalfa Bill" Murray (1869–1956), U.S representative from OK and governor of the state • 1907 from Chickasaw lands • Livestock, corn, wheat, poultry, fruit, dairying; manufacturing; oil and gas field machinery; mining of limestone, sand; resort tourism.

MUSKOGEE *Muskogee* • 69,451 • 814 • Eastern OK, bounded on the north, in part, by the Arkansas River and on the southeast by the Canadian River. Fort Gibson Historic Site commemorates the state's first military post, established in 1824. Greenleaf State Park is also in the county, as is part of Sequoyah National Wildlife Refuge. • One of two counties (the other, Muscogee, in GA) named for the Muscogee Creek Indians • 1907 from Cherokee lands • The county's growth was stimulated by the opening of oil and gas fields in the area of Muskogee in 1904. With the opening of Arkansas River navigation in 1970, Muskogee became OK's first port with access to the Gulf of Mexico. • Corn, hay, soybeans, cattle, dairying; manufacture of glass, optical machinery; steel fabrication; food processing; oil and natural-gas fields • Muskogee was the agency headquarters for the Five Civilized Tribes (Cherokee, Chickasaw, Choctaw, Creek and Seminole). Five Tribes Museum examines their history and culture. Merle Haggard was proud to be an "Okie from Muskogee."

NOBLE (one of three counties so named) *Perry* • 11,411 • 732 • Northern OK, bounded on the northeast by the Arkansas River; drained by Black Bear and Red Rock creeks. The county includes Tonkawa and Ponca Otoe Indian national headquarters and tribal lands. Lake McMurtry is here. Sooner Lake reservoir is on the eastern boundary. • Named for General John W. Noble (1831–1912), officer in the Union Army, U.S. district attorney for the eastern district of MO, and U.S. secretary of the interior • Organized as County "P" in 1897 (prior to statehood) from Indian lands; officially renamed in 1907 at the state constitutional convention. • Wheat, oats, barley, cattle; manufacture of metal products, construction machinery; oil and natural gas wells.

NOWATA *Nowata* • 10,569 • 565 • Northeastern OK, bounded on the north by the KS state line; drained by the Verdigris River. Part of Oologah Lake is in the southeast. • Named for the town of Nowata • 1907 from Cherokee lands • Cattle, corn, wheat, oats, sorghum; oil and natural-gas fields; limestone quarries; refineries; manufacturing; timber.

OKFUSKEE *Okemah* • 11,814 • 625 • Central OK, bounded on the southwest, in part, by the North Canadian River; intersected by the North Canadian River and the Deep Fork of the Canadian River. • Named for a Creek town in Cleburne County, AL • 1907 from Creek lands • Folk singer and composer Woody Guthrie • Melons, fruit, grain, pecans, peanuts, cattle, dairying; manufacture of machinery, apparel.

OKLAHOMA *Oklahoma City* • 660,448 (the most populated county in OK) • 709 • Central OK; intersected by the North Canadian River, and by the Deep Fork of the Canadian River. Tinker Air Force Base, the county's largest employer, is in the Oklahoma City metropolitan area. The county is the most urbanized in the state. • Named for Oklahoma Territory • Originally established as County "Two" or "Second" County in 1891 (prior to statehood); officially renamed in 1907 at the state constitutional convention. • Following the purchase of land here from the Creek and Seminole Indians, the area was opened to white settlement; on April 22, 1899, 10,000 settlers "rushed" onto the site that would become Oklahoma City. In 1910, Oklahoma City replaced Guthrie as the state capital. On April 19, 1995, a truck bomb destroyed the Alfred P. Murrah Federal Building killing 168 people, including 19 children — one of the worst acts of domestic terrorism in U.S. history. • Professional baseball player Johnny Bench; writer Ralph Ellison; professional baseball player Paul Waner. Welfare leader Kate Barnard died here. • Dairying, cattle, wheat; diversified manufacturing, including aviation equipment, petroleum products, concrete blocks, automobile assemblies, construction equipment, electronic equipment; processing of agricultural products; oil and natural-gas fields; refineries; sand, granite; education (U. of Central OK: OK City U.; Southern Nazarene U.; others) • The religious enclave of Bethany outlaws pool halls, dance halls, theatres, and alcohol consumption. The West Edmond Field is one of the world's largest oil fields. With permission from officials at Midwest Air Depot (now Tinker Air Force Base) which it serves, Midwest City was built in 1942 by W.P. Atkinson as a model city, with curvilinear street design and spacious parks. The State Capitol, located in a major oil field, had a well on the grounds that drew oil from beneath the capitol until 1986. In 1971, the people of Oklahoma City elected the first woman mayor of a U.S. city of 200,000 or more, Patience C. Latting. The National Softball Hall of Fame and National Cowboy Hall of Fame and Western Heritage Center are located here. The first automatic parking meter in the U.S. was installed in Oklahoma City on July 16, 1935.

OKMULGEE *Okmulgee* • 39,685 • 697 • East-central OK; intersected by the Deep Fork of the Canadian River. Lake Okmulgee reservoir and Okmulgee State Park are here, as is Deep Fork National Wildlife Refuge. • Named for the town of Okmulgee, OK • 1907 from Creek lands • Okmulgee was the capital of the Creek Nation from 1868 until OK became a state in 1907. The city enjoyed a boom period after the discovery of oil in 1904. • Legal scholar Anita Hill • Peanuts, cotton, corn, cattle, dairy products; manufacture of glass containers, oil-field equipment, metal stampings, chemicals; oil and natural-gas fields, coal mining; timber; education (OK State U.–Okmulgee is one of the largest technical colleges in the U.S.) • Still considered the capital of the Creek Indian Nation, Okmulgee city hosts an annual national festival celebrating the culture and history of the tribe.

OSAGE (one of three counties so named) *Pawhuska* • 44,437 • 2,251 (the largest county in OK) • Northern OK, contiguous with the Osage Indian Reservation, bounded on the north by the KS state line and on the southwest by the Arkansas River (forming Kaw and Keystone lakes); drained by the Caney River, and Salt, Hominy, and Bird creeks. The county includes parts of Bartlesville and Tulsa, as well as Walnut Creek, Wah-Sha-She, and Osage Hills state parks, numerous reservoirs, and Tall Grass Prairie Preserve. • Named for the Osage Indian tribe • 1907 from Osage Indian lands • The first buildings in Pawhuska, settled in 1872, were those of the Osage Indian Agency. (Pawhuska is presently the tribal capital of the Osage Nation and the site of the Osage Tribal Museum.) • Ballet dancers Marjorie and Maria Tallchief • Cattle, soybeans, sorghum, hay, cattle, horses; manufacture of apparel, machinery, petroleum, and coal products, oil-field equipment, process control instruments; oil and natural gas; cotton ginning • Locals claim that the Rev. John Mitchell organized the first American Boy Scout troop in Pawhuska in 1909.

OTTAWA *Miami* • 33,194 • 471 • Extreme northeastern OK, bounded on the north by the KS state line, on the northwest, in part, by the Neosho River, and on the east by the MO state line; drained by the Neosho (headwaters of Grand Lake O' the Cherokees) and Spring rivers. The county lies in the Ozark foothills. Spring River Canoe Trails and Twin Bridges state parks are here. • One of four counties named for the Ottawa Indians • 1907 from Indian lands • Lead and zinc mining; livestock, dairying, corn, wheat, hay, sorghum, soybeans; manufacture of particle board, steel springs, furniture, carpeting.

PAWNEE (one of three counties so named) *Pawnee* • 16,612 • 570 • Northern OK, bounded on the northeast by the Arkansas River (forming Keystone Lake reservoir); drained by Black Bear Creek. Part of Sooner Lake reservoir is here. • One of two counties (the other in NE) named for the Pawnee Indians • Organized as County "Q" in 1892 (prior to statehood) from Indian lands; the name was officially changed in 1907 at the state constitutional convention. • Cartoonist Chester Gould • Soybeans, wheat, hay, cattle; some manufacturing; oil and natural-gas wells.

PAYNE *Stillwater* • 68,190 • 686 • North-central OK; intersected by the Cimarron River (forming part of the southwestern boundary; drained by Stillwater Creek, forming Lake Carl Blackwell reservoir. • Named for David L. Payne (1836–84). Nicknamed "the Boomer," he conducted several illegal forays into Indian Territory • Original county; organized as County "Six" or the "Sixth" County in 1890 (prior to statehood). In 1892, voters renamed it; this act was made official in 1907 at the state constitutional convention. • Athlete Jim Thorpe • Cattle, poultry, dairying, grain, corn; manufacture of textiles, transportation equipment, building materials; oil and gas fields; education (OK State U.) • The National Wrestling Hall of Fame is in Stillwater.

PITTSBURG *McAlester* • 43,953 • 1,306 • Southeastern OK, bounded on the north by the Canadian River (forming Eufaula Lake reservoir); drained by Gaines Creek. The Ouachita Mountains (and their extension, the Jack Fork Mountains) are in the southeast. Arrowhead Lake, large arm of Eufaula Lake, is in the northeast, and is bordered by Arrowhead State Park. The county is the site of the McAlester U.S. Army Ammunition Plant. • Named for Pittsburgh, PA. The final "h" was inadvertently omitted. • 1907 • McAlester was built in 1870 by James McAlester, who later became lieutenant governor of the state, at the intersection of the Texas and California trails in Choctaw Territory. • Poet John Berryman • Vegetables, peanuts, soybeans, hay, wheat, oats, cattle; aerospace-aviation and marine industries; manufacture of textiles, apparel, plastic products, machinery, electronic equipment; food processing; natural-gas and oil wells, coal reserves; timber. McAlester is the site of the OK State Penitentiary. • It is also the home of the International Temple of the Order of the Rainbow for Girls.

PONTOTOC (one of two counties so named, the other in MS) *Ada* • 35,143 • 720 • South-central OK, bounded on the north by the Canadian River; drained by Clear Boggy and Muddy Boddy creeks, and the Blue River. • Named for Pontotoc County, Chickasaw Nation • 1907 from Choctaw lands • Ada gained early notoriety for violence, but a mass lynching by irate citizens in 1909 led to tighter law enforcement in the county. • Televangelist Oral Roberts • Wheat, oats, hay, sorghum, cattle, hogs, dairying; manufacture of glass containers, mobile homes, auto parts, farm implements, clothing; oil and natural-gas fields, limestone, shale, silica, clay; education (East Central U.).

POTTAWATOMIE (one of two counties so named, the other in KS) *Shawnee* • 65,521 • 788 • Central OK, bounded on the south by the Canadian River and on the northeast, in part, by the North Canadian River; intersected by the North Canadian, Canadian, and Little rivers. The Oklahoma City metropolitan area extends into the county. Lake Shawnee reservoir is in the northwest. • One of three counties named for the Potawatomi (or Pottawattomie) Indian tribe • Original county; organized as County "B" in 1891 (prior to statehood); name changed in 1892 and officially recognized in 1907 at the state constitutional convention. • Astronaut Gordon Cooper; songwriter ("Home on the Range") Dr. Brewster Higley • Diversified farming, corn, peanuts, cattle, dairying; light manufacturing; oil and natural-gas wells; education (OK Baptist U.).

PUSHMATAHA *Antlers* • 11,667 • 1,397 • Southeastern OK, in the Ouachita Mountains; drained by the Kiamichi and Little rivers. Clayton Lake and Sardis Lake reservoirs are here, as is Clayton Lake State Park. • Named for the Pushmataha district of the Choctaw Nation, itself named for the noted Choctaw chief (?–1824) who served with Andrew Jackson • 1907 from Indian lands • Wheat, corn, livestock; manufacturing; timber. • The Choctaw National Historical Museum is located near Sardis Lake.

ROGER MILLS *Cheyenne* • 3,436 • 1,142 • Western OK, bounded on the west by the TX state line and on the north by the Canadian River; intersected by the Washita River. In the north are the Antelope Hills, located in the bend of the Canadian River. Black Kettle National Grasslands and Washita Battlefield National Historic Site are also found in the county. • Named for Col. Roger Q. Mills (1832–1911), Confederate officer and U.S. representative and senator from TX • Original county; organized as County "F" in 1892; the name was changed the same year and officially recognized in 1907 at the state constitutional convention. • Wheat, oats, dairying, cattle; oil and gas (Anadarko Basin).

ROGERS *Claremore* • 70,641 (28% increase since 1990; the second fastest growing county in OK) • 675 • Northeastern OK, bounded on the southwest, in part, by the Verdigris River; intersected by the Verdigris River (forming Oologah Lake reservoir in the north), Bud Creek, and the Caney River. Suburbs of Tulsa are in the southwest. • Named for Clement V. Rogers (1839–1911) member of the OK Constitutional Convention and father of Will Rogers • 1907 from Cherokee lands • Humorist Will Rogers (birthplace, memorial museum, annual rodeo) • Cattle, hogs, poultry, grain, fruit, corn, soybeans, hay, dairying; light manufacture of industrial machinery, auto parts, chemicals, luggage; coal and shale mining, oil and natural gas; resort tourism (mineral springs) • The J. M. Davis Gun Museum is in Claremore.

SEMINOLE *Wewoka* • 24,894 • 633 • Central OK, bounded on the south by the Canadian River, on the north by the North Canadian River; drained by the Little River. Lake Konawa is on the southwest corner. • One of three counties named for the Seminole Indians • 1907 from Seminole lands • Corn, peanuts, fruit, cattle, poultry; manufacturing; oil and natural gas fields • The Seminole Nation Museum, which honors the history and culture of that tribe, is located near Wewoka.

SEQUOYAH *Sallisaw* • 38,972 • 674 • Eastern OK, bounded on the east by the AR state line and on the south by the Arkansas River, forming Robert S. Kerr Lake reservoir in the southwest; drained by the Illinois River. The county is dominated by the Boston Mountains. Part of Sequoyah National

Wildlife Refuge is here, as is Tenkiller State Park on the southeast shore of Tenkiller Ferry Lake. The county also includes Sallisaw and Brushy Creek state parks. • Name taken from the Sequoyah District of the Cherokee Nation, itself named for the Indian chief Sequoyah (?–1843), who invented the Cherokee alphabet and resided in the county (his home preserved as a state monument) • 1907 from Cherokee lands • Founded in 1828, Dwight Mission, seven miles northeast of Sallisaw, functioned for more than a century as one of the most important education institutions in the Indian Territory prior to the Civil War. • Vegetables, fruit, soybeans, corn, cotton, potatoes, poultry, cattle; food processing; some manufacturing; some oil and gas; limestone quarries.

STEPHENS (one of three counties so named) *Duncan* • 43,182 • 877 • Southern OK; drained by Wildhorse and Mud creeks. The county includes Comanche and Duncan lakes (reservoirs) near the center. Part of Waurika Lake reservoir is here (Beaver Creek in the southwest corner). • Named for John H. Stephens (1847–1924), U.S. representative from TX and strong advocate of OK statehood • 1907 from Comanche • The Chisholm Trail once intersected the county. • Political scientist Jeane Kirkpatrick • Wheat, corn, oats, fruit, melons, cotton, peanuts, pecans, poultry, cattle, dairying; oil and natural gas fields; manufacture of concrete products, machinery, medical supplies, asphalt, oilfield supplies; oil refining • Erle Halliburton's oil-well cementing business in Duncan has grown into an energy company of worldwide prominence.

TEXAS (one of two counties so named, the other in MO) *Guymon* • 20,107 • 2,037 (the second largest county in OK) • Western OK panhandle (the middle of the three Panhandle counties), bounded on the north by the KS state line and on the south by the TX state line; intersected by the Beaver River, and Coldwater, Goff, and Palo Dura creeks. Optima National Wildlife Refuge encompasses Optima Lake reservoir (Beaver River) in the east. • Named for the state of Texas • 1907 from part of the old Beaver County • Wheat, barley, alfalfa, broom corn, sorghum, cattle; some manufacturing of farm machinery and equipment; oil and gas extraction and servicing; education (OK Panhandle State U.) • Pioneer Day of No-Man's Land is celebrated in Guymon each May 2. The date marks the anniversary of the passage of the Organic Act of 1890, which made OK Territory a part of the U.S.

TILLMAN *Frederick* • 9,287 • 872 • Southwestern OK, bounded on the south by the Red River, forming the TX state line, and on the west by its North Fork; also drained by Deep Red Creek (Lake Frederick reservoir). • Named for Benjamin R. Tillman (1847–1918), SC governor and U.S. senator from SC who was active in forming the state of OK • 1907 from Comanche • Cotton, sorghum, vegetables, peanuts, cattle; manufacturing.

TULSA *Tulsa* • 563,299 (the second most populated county in OK) • 570 • Northeastern OK; intersected by the Arkansas River and Bird Creek. The county is highly urbanized in the middle around the city of Tulsa, agricultural in the north and far south. • Named for the town of Tulsa • 1907 • Phenomenal growth in the county followed the discovery of oil in Red Fork in 1901 and in the Glenn Pool in 1905. (More than 800 major oil companies now have plants and offices in Tulsa.) • Scholar and politician Daniel Patrick Moynihan; radio journalist Paul Harvey; singer Garth Brooks; actor Tony Randall • Grain, soybeans, cattle, quarterhorses, sheep; an important oil and gas producing county; oil refining; agricultural chemical production; manufacture of corrugated boxes, oil-field pipe and equipment, fiber glass and stone products, plastics, fabricated metal products, machinery, porcelain and cement products, industrial heaters, winches; petroleum industry administrative center; education (Oral Roberts U.; U. of Tulsa; OK State U.–Tulsa) • Tulsa is the site of the International Petroleum Exposition. The city is national headquarters of the U.S. Jaycees. The Thomas Gilcrease Institute of American History and Art features one of the world's largest collections of works by painters Thomas Moran, Frederick Remington, and Charles M. Russell. The Tulsa State Fairgrounds includes the largest livestock display barn in the world.

WAGONER *Wagoner* • 57,491 • 563 • Eastern OK, bounded on the south by the Arkansas River and on the east by the Neosho River (here forming Fort Gibson Lake reservoir); drained by the Neosho and Verdigris rivers. The far northwestern corner of the county is urbanized as part of the Tulsa metropolitan area. Sequoyah Bay State Park is found in the county. • Named for the town of Wagoner, OK • 1907 from Creek lands • Wheat, corn, soybeans, livestock, dairying; manufacturing; oil and natural gas.

WASHINGTON *Bartlesville* • 48,996 • 417 • Northeastern OK, bounded on the north by the KS state line; drained by the Caney River. Copan Lake reservoir is in the north. • One of thirty-one counties named for George Washington • 1907 from Cherokee lands • Situated in the center of the older section of the Mid-Continent oilfield, Bartlesville completed OK's first commercial oil well (Nellie Johnstone #1) in 1897. • Tom Mix was deputy marshal in Dewey before becoming a silent-screen movie star (museum). • Fruit, wheat, soybeans,

cattle, dairying; metal industries, manufacture of transportation equipment and oil-field equipment, business forms, plastics, inorganic fertilizers; oil and natural gas (extraction and refining), zinc smelting; education (Bartlesville Wesleyan College) A U.S. Bureau of Mines petroleum experimental station is in Bartlesville.

WASHITA *Cordell* • 11,508 • 1,003 • Western OK, bounded on the southeast, in part, by the Washita River; intersected by the Washita River and Elk Creek. Crowder Lake State Park and the Kiowa Tribal Museum are located here. • Named for the Washita River • Organized as County "H" in 1892 (prior to statehood) from Indian lands; name officially changed in 1907. • Wheat, cotton, sorghum, hay, peanuts, cattle, sheep; manufacturing; oil and natural gas.

WOODS *Alva* • 9,089 • 1,287 • Northwestern OK, bounded on the west and south by the Cimarron River and on the north by the KS state line; drained by the Salt Fork of the Arkansas River and Eagle Chief Creek. Little Sahara State Park is located on the Cimarron River in the south. • Named for Samuel N. Wood (1825–1891), abolitionist, KS legislator, and owner of the *Kansas Tribune*. The letter "s" was a clerical error allowed to stand. • Original county; organized as County "M" in 1893 (prior to statehood); name changed later and was made official in 1907 at the state constitutional convention. • Wheat, sorghum, cattle; sand and gravel pits; salt and gypsum deposits; education (Northwestern OK State U.).

WOODWARD *Woodward* • 18,486 • 1,242 • Northwestern OK, bounded on the northeast by the Cimarron River; intersected by the North Canadian River and Wolf Creek (impounded here by Fort Supply Dam). Boiling Springs State Park is in the county, as is Alabaster Caverns State Park, considered to be the largest gypsum cave in the world; it contains pink, white, and rare black alabaster walls. • Named for the city of Woodward, OK • Organized as County "N" in 1893 from Indian lands; the name was made official in 1907 at the state constitutional convention. • Wheat, alfalfa, oats, cattle; manufacturing; oil and natural-gas deposits • The city of Woodward hosts the annual Tri-state All Star football game.

OREGON

She Flies with Her Own Wings

Most of Oregon's thirty-six counties are governed by three- or five-member boards of commissioners. The majority of its members are elected to four-year terms. A 1958 amendment to the Oregon state constitution extended home rule privileges to its counties.

BAKER (one of three counties so named) *Baker City* • 16,741 • 3,068 • Eastern OR, bounded on the east by the Snake River

(forming the ID state boundary) and on the northwest in part by the Powder and North Powder rivers; drained by the Powder River (designated here a National Scenic River), Burnt River and numerous creeks. The Blue Mountains are in the west, the Wallowa Mountains in the northeast. The county also includes Oxbow and Brownlee dams (Snake River), Unity Lake State Recreation Site, Farewell Bend State Recreation Area, part of Hells Canyon National Recreation Area, part of Umatilla National Forest, parts of Wallowa-Whitman National Forest, and part of Malheur National Forest (including Monument Rock Wilderness Area). • Named for Col. Edward D. Baker (1811–61), U.S. representative from IL and U.S. senator from OR • 1862 from Wasco • Timber; gold, silver, copper; barley, oats, potatoes, cattle, sheep, dairy products.

BENTON (one of nine counties so named) *Corvallis* • 78,153 • 677 • Western OR, bounded on the east by the Willamette River and valley. Mountains of the Coast Ranges are in the west. The county also contains William L. Finley National Wildlife Refuge, Washburne Wayside State Park, and part of Siuslaw National Forest (its headquarters in Corvallis). • One of seven counties named for Thomas Hart Benton (1782–1858), U.S. journalist and statesman • Original county; 1847 (prior to statehood) • The OR territorial legislature met for a short time in 1855 in Corvallis. • Truck farming, corn, beans, blueberries, wheat, oats, barley, apples, cherries, pears, plums, grapes, poultry, sheep, cattle, dairying (creameries); wineries; engineering consulting; sawmilling; manufacture of business machines; education (OR State U.) • Horner Museum at Oregon State University houses a Pacific Northwest collection.

CLACKAMAS *Oregon City* • 338,391 (the third most populated county in OR) • 1,868 • Northwestern OR, bounded on the southwest by Butte Creek; drained by the Willamette, Molalla, Sandy, and Clackamas rivers (the last designated a National Scenic and Recreational River). Part of Mount Hood National Forest and mountains of the Cascade Range are in the east; the range includes Mount Hood (11,239 feet), the highest mountain in OR (situated partly in Hood River County). Table Rock Wilderness Area, Milo McIver, Molalla River, Mary S. Young, and part of Tryon Creek state parks are located here. As part of a tri-county metropolitan area anchored by Portland, Clackamas County is heavily populated in the northwest. • Named for the Clackama tribe of Chinook Indians • Original county; 1843 (prior to statehood) • Oregon City was settled in 1829–30 by John McLoughlin of the Hudson's Bay Company on the site of an Indian village. It became the territory's first capital in 1849 and served in this capacity until 1852. It was a flourishing supply point during the California gold rush. The *Oregon Spectator*, one of the first newspapers west of the Mississippi, was published in Oregon City in 1846. • Poet and lecturer Edwin Markham • Apples, cherries, pears, plums, peaches, grapes, berries, wheat, oats, barley, corn, potatoes, dairying, sheep, hogs, cattle; manufacture of batteries, paper and wood pulp, cutlery; food canning; education (Marylhurst College); tourism • A free municipal elevator (built in 1915 and replaced in 1955) lifts pedestrians ninety feet from the business section of Oregon City to its residential cliff section.

CLATSOP *Astoria* • 35,630 • 827 • Northwestern OR, bounded on the north by the Columbia River (forming the WA state line) and on the west by the Pacific Ocean; drained by the Nehalem River. Coast Ranges are in the east. Ecola and Fort Stevens state parks, Saddle Mountain State Natural Area, Lewis and Clark National Wildlife Refuge, and several coastal state recreation sites are in the county, which includes parts of Clatsop and Tillamook state forests. • Named for the Clatsop Indian tribe of Chinook Indians • Original county; 1844 (prior to statehood) from the Tuality district • The Lewis and Clark expedition spent the winter of 1805–1806 near the site of Astoria before heading back to Missouri (Fort Clatsop National Memorial). Fort Astoria was established by John Jacob Astor's Pacific Fur Company in 1811. The first U.S. post office on the Pacific coast was opened in Astoria in 1847. With the establishment of a salmon cannery in 1864, Astoria became the center of a major fishing industry. The city experienced a disastrous fire in 1922. It was not until the completion of the new Astoria Bridge spanning the Columbia River in 1966 that the last gap in U.S. Pacific Highway 101 was completed. • Dance-band leader Jimmie Lunceford died here. • Fur farms; poultry, sheep, cattle; commercial fishing; salmon and tuna canneries; wineries; lumbering; manufacture of aluminum products, dairy products, flour; tourism • The Astor Monument stands 124 feet high and commemorates the settlement of the Pacific Northwest.

COLUMBIA (one of eight counties so named) *Saint Helens* • 43,560 • 657 • Northwestern OR, bounded on the north and east by the Columbia River (forming the WA state line); drained by the Nehalem River. Small units of Clatsop State Forest are in the county. • Named for the Columbia River • 1854 (prior to statehood) from Washington County • Fruit, berries, corn, wheat, oats, poultry, sheep, cattle; dairy products; timber; salmon; manufacturing.

COOS (one of two counties so named, the other in NH) *Coquille* • 62,779 • 1,601 • Southwestern OR, bounded on the west by the Pacific Ocean; indented by Coos Bay and drained by the Coquille River, and its North, South, East, and Middle forks, and the South Fork of the Coos River. Mountains of the Coast Ranges are in the east. The county also contains part of Elliott State Forest, part of Siskiyou National Forest, the southern part of Oregon Dunes National Recreation Area, and several state parks and nature areas. • Named for the Coos Indian tribe • 1853 (prior to statehood) from Umpqua and Jackson • Timber, millwork; cranberries, dairy products, poultry, sheep, cattle; fisheries; canning of sea foods; deposits of coal and other minerals; tourism • Coos Bay is the state's second-ranking port and one of the leading lumber-shipping points in the world.

CROOK *Prineville* • 19,182 • 2,980 • Central OR; drained by the Crooked River (designated here a National Recreational

River) and its North Fork (designated here a National Wild, Scenic, and Recreational River). The county includes parts of Ochoco National Forest, including Mill Creek Wilderness Area. Also here are Prineville Reservoir State Park, Ochoco Lake State Recreation Site, and Ochoco State Scenic Viewpoint. • One of two counties (the other in WY) named for General George Crook (1829–90), Union Army officer and Indian fighter • 1882 from Wasco and Grant • Poultry, sheep, cattle, potatoes, wheat, oats, barley; timber; mercury.

CURRY (one of two counties so named, the other in NM) *Gold Beach* • 21,137 • 1,628 • Southwestern OR, bounded on the west by the Pacific Ocean and on the south by the CA state line; drained by the Rogue River (museum here), Chetco and Illinois rivers (all three designated as National Wild, Scenic and Recreational rivers). The county has several state parks, scenic corridors, and state recreation sites, most of which are located along the coast. Siskiyou National Forest covers most of the county except along the coastal margin and the extreme north and northeast. Wild Rogue, part of Kalmiopsis, and Grassy Knob wilderness areas are located here. • Named for George L. Curry (1820–78), governor of Oregon Territory • 1855 (prior to statehood) from Coos • Processing of salmon, tuna, halibut, urchins, crabs, shrimp; timber; nurseries; poultry, sheep, cattle.

DESCHUTES *Bend* • 115,367 (54% increase since 1990; the fastest growing county in OR) • 3,018 • Central OR; drained by the Deschutes River (designated here a National Scenic and Recreational River). The Pacific Crest National Scenic Trail (in the Cascade Range) forms much of the western boundary. Deschutes National Forest (its headquarters in Bend) covers most of the county, including parts of Three Sisters and Mount Jefferson Wilderness Areas. The county also includes Tumalo, La Pine, and Smith Rock state parks. Cline Falls and Pilot Butte state scenic viewpoints are here. On the slopes of Newberry Volcano at Newberry National Volcanic Monument is found the world's largest forest of lava-cast trees, visible pine bark imprinted by molten lava 6,000 years ago. • Named for the Deschutes River • 1916 from Crook • Potatoes, alfalfa, wheat, oats, barley, poultry, sheep, cattle, dairy products; wineries; recreational tourism; quarrying of diatomite, manganese, lead, and zinc; recreational, resort and park tourism.

DOUGLAS *Roseburg* • 100,399 • 5,037 (the fifth largest county in OR) • Southwestern OR, bounded on the northwest by the Pacific Ocean; crossed by the Umpqua River (its North Fork designated here a National Recreational River). The Pacific Crest National Scenic Trail (in the Cascade Range) forms much of the eastern boundary. Parts of Siuslaw National Forest, part of Umpqua National Forest (its headquarters in Roseburg), and Elliott State Forest are in the county, as are Umpqua State Scenic Corridor and Umpqua Lighthouse State Park. Part of Oregon Dunes National Recreation Area is on the coast and a small portion of Crater Lake National Park extends into the county. • One of twelve counties named for

Stephen A. Douglas (1813–61), U.S. orator and statesman • Organized 1852 (prior to statehood) from Umpqua, itself organized in 1851 and whose remnant, after Coos was broken off in 1855, was annexed to Douglas in 1862 • Apples, cherries, pears, plums, peaches, grapes, poultry, sheep, cattle, dairy products; nurseries, wineries; timber, sawmills, wood industries; fish; nickel mining and smelting • There is a National Cemetery in Roseburg.

GILLIAM *Condon* • 1,915 • 1,204 • Northern OR, bounded on the north by the Columbia River and Lake Umatilla reservoir (forming the WA state line) and on the west by the John Day River (designated here a National Recreational River). Dyer State Wayside and J.S. Burres State Recreational Site are here. • Named for Col. Cornelius Gilliam (1798–1848), veteran of Indian wars and commander of volunteer forces for OR's provisional government • 1885 from Wasco • Wheat, oats, barley, cattle.

GRANT (one of fifteen counties so named) *Canyon City* • 7,935 • 4,529 • East-central OR; drained by the John Day River and its North and South forks (both forks designated national recreational rivers), and by the North Fork of the Malheur River (designated here a National Scenic River). The Blue Mountains are here, as is Clyde Holliday Recreation Site, and John Day Fossil Beds National Monument (Sheep Rock Unit), which offers plant and animal fossils from five epochs, from Eocene to the end of the Pleistocene. Parts of Malheur National Forest (its headquarters in John Day) are in the county, and include Strawberry Mountain Wilderness Area. Also here are parts of the Ochoco, Wallowa-Whitman, and Umatilla national forests, and part of North Fork John Day Wilderness Area. • One of twelve counties named for President Ulysses S. Grant • 1864 • Wheat, oats, barley, poultry sheep, cattle; timber; mercury mining • Relics of the county's gold-mining past are on display at the Herman and Eliza Oliver Historical Museum in John Day.

HARNEY *Burns* • 7,609 • 10,135 (the largest county in OR and the tenth largest county in the U.S.) • Southeast-central OR, bounded on the south by the NV state line; drained by the Silvies River and Donner und Blitzen River (designated a National Wild River), and numerous creeks. The county includes Steens Mountain (ridge) in the southeast. Also in the county are Malheur and Harney lakes, Burns Paiute Indian Colony, units of Malheur National Wildlife Refuge, Alvord Desert, part of Malheur and Ochoco national forests, and Frenchglen Hotel State Heritage Site. • Named for General William S. Harney (1800–89), officer in the Black Hawk War, Seminole War, and Mexican War, and army commander instrumental in opening eastern Oregon for settlement • 1889 from Grant • As capital of a large cattle empire, Burns was the administrative headquarters for grazing lands retained in public ownership until the Taylor Grazing Act of 1934. • Alfalfa, wheat, oats, barley, sheep, cattle; timber.

HOOD RIVER *Hood River* • 20,411 • 522 • Northern OR,

bounded on the north by the Columbia River (here forming Bonneville Reservoir); crossed by the Hood River. Mount Hood, at 11,239 feet, the highest point in the state, is in the Cascade Range on the southwestern boundary (situated partly in Clackamas County). Most of the county is canopied by Mount Hood National Forest. There are several state parks here, all on the Columbia River. Parts of Columbia and Mount Hood wilderness areas are in the west and south. • Named for the Hood River • 1908 from Wasco • Large areas of the county were planted in orchards in the 1890s. The shipment of apples to the eastern U.S. in 1900 launched the profitable fruit industry in this part of the state. • Apples, cherries, pears, grapes, peaches, cattle; timber; wineries; recreation. • Hood River Gorge, with its steady winds, has earned the named "Sailboat Capital of the World."

JACKSON (one of twenty-four counties so named) *Medford* • 181,269 • 2,785 • Southwestern OR, bounded on the south by the CA state line; crossed by the Rogue River (designated here a National Wild and Scenic River). The county includes part of the Siskiyou Mountains, and parts of Rogue River National Forest (its headquarters in Medford), including part of Sky Lakes Wilderness Area in the east. Also here are part of Crater Lake National Park (on the northeastern boundary), a small part of Klamath National Forest, Casey and Tou Velle state recreation sites, Tub Springs State Wayside, Ben Hur Lapman State Scenic Corridor, Valley of the Rogue State Park, and Joseph H. Stewart State Recreation Area. • One of twenty-two counties named for Andrew Jackson • 1852 (prior to statehood) from the original Yamhill and Champoeg districts • Poultry, hogs, sheep, cattle, fruit (especially pears), dairying, nurseries, truck-farm produce; wineries; lumbering; education (Southern OR U.); resort tourism • Jacksonville is the state's best-preserved historic settlement. Its Pioneer Village contains restored villages, covered wagons and antique mining equipment. The United States Hotel and the Hillside Amphitheatre here are sites for the Peter Britt Music and Arts Festival. The Oregon Shakespeare Festival is held each year in Ashland.

JEFFERSON *Madras* • 19,009 • 1,781 • Central OR, bounded on the west by the Pacific Crest National Scenic Trail (in the Cascade Range); drained by the Deschutes and Metolius rivers (both designated national recreation rivers). Part of Warm Springs Indian Reservation is here, including its tribal museum. Crooked River National Grassland, part of Deschutes National Forest, Elliott Corbett Memorial State Recreation Site, and The Cove Palisades State Park are also here. • Named for Mount Jefferson, itself named for President Thomas Jefferson (one of twenty-six counties named directly or indirectly for President Jefferson) • 1914 from Crook • Wheat, barley, oats, potatoes, poultry, sheep, cattle; lumber; mercury.

JOSEPHINE *Grants Pass* • 75,726 • 1,640 • Southwestern OR, bounded on the south by the CA state line; crossed by the Rogue River and Illinois River (each designated a National Wild, Scenic and Recreational River). The Klamath Mountains extend along the western border. Parts of the Siskiyou

National Forest (its headquarters in Grants Pass), including Kalmiopsis Wilderness Area, peaks of the Siskiyou Mountains, Oregon Caves National Monument, and Illinois River Forks State Park are in the county. • Named for Josephine Creek, possibly named for Josephine Rollins, the first white woman to settle in the county • 1856 from Jackson • Wheat, oats, barley, apples, pears, plums, peaches, grapes, poultry, hogs, sheep, cattle; nurseries (especially horticulture bulbs); meat packing; lumbering, manufacture of plywood and other products; gold mining; tourism.

KLAMATH *Klamath Falls* • 63,775 • 5,945 (the fourth largest county in OR and forty-third largest county in the U.S.) • Southern OR, bounded on the south by the CA state line, on the northwest in part by the Pacific Crest National Scenic Trail; drained by the Klamath, Williamson, Sprague, and Lost rivers. The county includes parts of Winema National Forest (its headquarters in Klamath Falls), part of Deschutes, Fremont, and Rogue River national forests, several national wildlife refuges, including Upper Klamath (a pelican sanctuary), Collier Memorial State Park, and Jackson F. Kimball State Recreation Site. Most of Crater Lake National Park is in the county. At a depth of 1,932 feet, the deepest lake in the U.S., it sits atop the caldera of Mount Mazama, which last erupted around 5,700 B.C. • Named for either the Klamath Indians or for the Klamath lakes • 1882 from Lake • Wheat, oats, barley, alfalfa, potatoes, poultry, hogs, sheep, cattle, dairy products; millwork; recreation; education (OR Institute of Technology).

LAKE (one of twelve counties so named) *Lakeview* • 7,422 • 8,136 (the third largest county in OR and the twentieth largest county in the U.S.) • Southern OR, bounded on the south by the CA and NV state lines. This county contains Summer and Abert lakes, and a portion of Goose Lake on the southern border. Abert Rim is one of North America's largest exposed fault scarps. The county also includes Hart Mountain National Antelope Refuge. Warm Valley here is a geyser basin of dry lakes; it includes forty-foot-high Old Perpetual Geyser, which spouts every ninety seconds. Parts of Fremont National Forest (its headquarters in Lakeview), Fort Rock State Natural Area, Chandler State Wayside, and Goose Lake State Recreation Area are all in the county. • Named for the numerous lakes in the county • 1874 from Jackson • Lakeview was destroyed by fire in 1900 but quickly rebuilt. • Wheat, oats, barley, sheep, cattle; clay; lumber; recreational tourism.

LANE (one of two counties so named, the other in KS) *Eugene* • 322,959 (the fourth most populated county in OR) • 4,554 • Western OR, bounded on the west by the Pacific Ocean; crossed by the Willamette (its North Fork/Mid Fork designated a National Wild, Scenic and Recreational River) and Siuslaw rivers. The Pacific Crest National Scenic Trail follows the eastern boundary. The county is located in both the Coast and Cascade ranges. It contains part of Willamette National Forest (its headquarters in Eugene), part of Umpqua and

Siuslaw national forests, and part of Oregon Dunes National Recreation Area in the extreme southwest. Fern Ridge Lake reservoir lies in the center of the county. Lane County has several state parks and state recreation sites. • Named for General Joseph Lane (1801–81), first governor of OR Territory and one of the first senators from the state • 1851 (prior to statehood) from Linn and Benton • Discus-thrower Mac Wilkins • Wheat, barley, oats, corn, brans, seeds, strawberries, blackberries, blueberries, grapes, apples, cherries, pears, plums, peaches, hogs, sheep, cattle; nurseries; wineries; salmon fishing; manufacture of lumber, plywood and other forest products, metal products, trailers, fabricated steel, animal feeds, industrial glues, adhesives; education (U. of OR; Eugene Bible College) • The art museum at the University of Oregon has significant Oriental and Pacific Northwest collections. Downtown Eugene boasts a shopping mall more than seventeen blocks long. Florence hosts the popular Rhododendron Festival each May.

LINCOLN (one of twenty-four counties so named) *Newport* • 44,479 • 980 • Western OR, bounded on the west by the Pacific Ocean; drained by the Alsea, Siletz, and Yaquina rivers. Mountains of the Coast Ranges are in the east. Part of Siuslaw National Forest is here, as are Ellmaker State Wayside and Siletz Bay National Wildlife Refuge. Numerous state parks, state recreation sites, and waysides are located on or near the coast. • One of eighteen counties named for President Abraham Lincoln • 1893 from Benton and Polk • A section of the county in the south was transferred to Benton County in 1949. • Salmon, tuna, halibut, crabs, shrimp, clams; paper products; timber; dairy products, poultry, sheep, cattle.

LINN *Albany* • 103,069 • 2,291 • Western OR, bounded on the west by the Willamette River and on the north in part by the North Santiam River, forming Detroit Lake reservoir in the northeast; drained by the Calapooia and McKenzie rivers (the latter designated a National Scenic River). The Pacific Crest National Scenic Trail closely follows the eastern boundary. Part of Willamette National Forest, including part of Mount Washington and Mount Jefferson wilderness areas are here. The Cascade Range is in the east, with the northeast corner of the county marked by the summit of Mount Jefferson. Also here are Foster Lake and Green Peter Lake reservoirs, and Cascadia and Bower's Rock state parks. • One of four counties named for Lewis F. Linn (1795–1843), U.S. senator from MO and author of the Donation Land Law, which gave free western land to settlers • Original county; organized 1847 (prior to statehood) • Logging; corn, beans, wheat, oats, barley, poultry, hogs, sheep, cattle, dairy products; nurseries; wineries; food processing; manufacture of paper products, rare metals, wood and leather products. The U.S. Bureau of Mines maintains the Albany Metallurgy Research Center here. • Albany is host to the World Championship Timber Carnival each July 4.

MALHEUR *Vale* • 31,615 • 9,888 (the second largest county in OR and the twelfth largest county in the U.S.) • South-eastern OR, bounded on the south by the NV state line and on the east by the ID state line; drained by the Owyhee (a National Wild River) and Malheur rivers, which flow to the Snake River. The county has numerous reservoirs, including Lake Owyhee and Antelope. A small part of Malheur National Forest is here, as are Ontario State Recreation Site, Lake Owyhee State Park, and Succor Creek and Crooked Creek state natural areas. There are lava beds in the center of the county. Part of Fort McDermitt Indian Reservation is on the southern border. Malheur is one of only a few counties in the U.S. that lie in two time zones: the northern four-fifths is in the Mountain time zone, the southern fifth in the Pacific time zone. It is the only county in the state not fully on Pacific time. • Named for the Malheur River • 1887 from Baker • Poet and author Phyllis McGinley • Sugar beets, corn, onions, potatoes, wheat, oats, barley, alfalfa, fruit, seeds, hogs, sheep, cattle, dairying; food processing; tourism.

MARION *Salem* • 284,834 (the fifth most populated county in OR) • 1,185 • Northwestern OR, bounded on the south by the North Santiam River (which forms Detroit Lake reservoir in the southeast), on the east, in part, by the Pacific Crest National Scenic Trail (Cascade Range), and on the north by the Willamette River. Ankeny National Wildlife Refuge, Willamette Mission and Silver Falls state parks, and North Santiam and Detroit Lake state recreation areas are here. Part of Mount Hood and Willamette national forests are in the east, including part of Mount Jefferson and Bull of the Woods wilderness areas. • One of seventeen counties named for "The Swamp Fox," American Revolutionary War Gen. Francis Marion (c.1732–95) • Original county; organized as Champoick in 1843 (prior to statehood); name changed 1849 • Settlers organized the first effective government for the future state of OR in 1843 at a site which is now in the Champoeg State Heritage Area. The sale of home sites in the settlement of Salem, laid out in 1848, financed the Oregon Institute, a religious school for Indians that later became Willamette University, the oldest university in the Pacific Northwest. Salem became the territorial capital in 1851. Following a brief move of the government to Corvallis, Salem became the permanent capital of the state. • Fruit, peas, onions, potatoes, mint, seed crops, hay, wheat, barley, poultry, cattle, dairying; wineries; food processing, manufacture of electronic components, electrical products and batteries, machinery, textiles, wood and concrete products; sand and gravel; government offices, state health and penal institutions; education (West Baptist College) • Salem is the site of the Oregon State Fair.

MORROW (one of two counties so named, the other in OH) *Heppner* • 10,995 (44% increase since 1990; the second fastest growing county in OR) • 2,033 • Northern OR, bounded on the north by the Columbia River (forming the WA state line); drained by Willow Creek. A portion of Umatilla Chemical Depot is on the northeastern boundary and the Boardman Bombing Range is in the north. Part of Umatilla National Wildlife Refuge is also in the north. • Named for Jackson L.

Morrow, member of the first OR state legislature • 1885 from Umatilla • Alfalfa, grapes, corn, wheat, oats, barley, onions, potatoes, sheep, cattle.

MULTNOMAH *Portland* • 660,486 (the most populated county in OR) • 435 (the smallest county in OR) • Northwestern OR, bounded on the north by the Columbia River (forming the WA state line); drained by the Willamette River. The county is urbanized in the west with agricultural areas in the center and extreme northwest. Part of Mount Hood National Forest (its headquarters in Portland) is in the east. It includes Columbia Wilderness Area. The county has several state parks and recreation areas, all of them east of Portland, along the Columbia River. • Named for the Multnomah Indians whose primary village was here • 1854 (prior to statehood) from Clackamas and Washington • Settled in 1829 and laid out in 1844, Portland received its name as the result of a penny toss; it was named for Portland, ME, rather than for Boston, MA. Gold rushes and immigrant traffic along the Oregon Trail stimulated its early growth. Between 1900 and 1910 Portland's population increased from 90,426 to 207,214. The Lewis and Clark Centennial Exposition in 1905 brought three million visitors to the city. Shipbuilding and World War II–related industries in Portland brought in nearly 100,000 additional workers. • Photographer Imogen Cunningham; shoe executive Philip H. Knight; chemist Linus Pauling. Architect Pietro Belluschi, singer Marian Anderson, and composer Ernest Bloch died here. • Wheat, oats, barley, potatoes, corn, berries, apples, cherries, pears, plums, peaches, hops; nurseries; wineries; shipping and diversified manufacturing, including aluminum products, machinery, electronic components, lumber, textiles, chemicals, food products; meat packing; education (Portland State U.; Reed College; U. of Portland; Concordia U.; Warner Pacific College; others) Portland is a financial and medical center for the state. • It is known as the "City of Roses" because of its many public and private rose gardens; its annual rose festival in June is a popular event. Portland's 6,000-acre Forest Park is the largest woodland within a U.S. city. Portland is among the vanguard of environmentally-conscious cities in the nation. The city contains the world's smallest official park. Created on St. Patrick's Day, 1948, as a colony for leprechauns and a site for snail races, Mill Ends Park totals 452 inches in area. It became a city park in 1976. Portland is home to the Trailblazers professional basketball team (Rose Garden).

POLK (one of twelve counties so named) *Dallas* • 62,380 • 741 • Northwestern OR, bounded on the east by the Willamette River. Mountains of the Coast Ranges extend along the western border. The county contains Baskett Slough National Wildlife Refuge, Holman State Wayside and Sara Helmick State Recreation Site. A small part of Salem extends into the county from neighboring Marion County. • One of eleven counties named for President James K. Polk • Original county; organized 1845 (prior to statehood) from the Yamhill district • Grapes, hops, apples, cherries, pears, plums, peaches,

blackberries, corn, brans, wheat, oats, barley, hogs, sheep, cattle; dairy products; timber; nurseries; wineries; education (Western OR U.).

SHERMAN (one of four counties so named) *Moro* • 1,934 • 823 • Northern OR, bounded on the north by the Columbia River (forming the WA state line), on the west by the Deschutes River (designated here a National Scenic and Recreational River), and on the east by the John Day River (designated here a National Recreational River). Part of Deschutes River State Recreation Area is in the county. The Columbia River forms Lake Celilo reservoir up to John Day Dam, which forms Lake Umatilla reservoir. • One of three counties named for Union Gen. William Tecumseh Sherman (1820–91) • 1889 from Wasco • Wheat, oats, barley, poultry, cattle.

TILLAMOOK *Tillamook* • 24,262 • 1,102 • Northwestern OR, bounded on the west by the Pacific Ocean; drained by the Nehalem, Tillamook, Trask, and Nestucca rivers. Much of the county is covered by a large part of Tillamook State Forest; part of Siuslaw National Forest is on the southern border. There are several state parks and recreation sites in the county, all of them along the coast. Cape Meares, Three Arch Rocks, and Nestucca Bay national wildlife refuges are also located on the coast. Several bays are here, the largest of which is Tillamook. • Named for the Tillamook Indians • 1853 (prior to statehood) from Clatsop and Yamhill • The Tillamook Burn, a huge forest fire, swept across the county in 1933, and resulted in the closure of many area sawmills. • Dairy products; logging; fisheries; wineries.

UMATILLA *Pendleton* • 70,548 • 3,215 • Northeastern OR, bounded on the north by the WA state line, on the northwest by the Columbia River (forming part of the WA state line); drained by the Umatilla River. Part of the Blue Mountains are on the southern boundary. The county includes parts of Umatilla Wilderness Area, Umatilla Indian Reservation, Cold Springs and McKay Creek national wildlife refuges, Hat Rock State Park, Emigrant Springs State Heritage Area, and several state scenic corridors. Part of Umatilla Chemical Depot is on the northwest border. Umatilla National Forest (its headquarters in Pendleton) is in the east. • Named for the Umatilla River • 1862 from Wasco • Pendleton was a thriving cattle center in the 1870s and 1880s where herds were assembled to be driven across the mountains into ID, WY, and MT. • Wheat, oats, barley, corn, beans, pears, onions, potatoes, apples, grapes, plums, peaches, livestock; wineries; food processing; lumber and woolen mills (blankets); food canning; manufacture of furniture, leather goods, recreational vehicles. An agricultural experiment station of Oregon State University is here. • The Pendleton Round-Up rodeo has been held every September since 1910.

UNION (one of eighteen counties so named) *La Grande* • 24,530 • 2,037 • Northeastern OR, bounded on the south in part by the Powder (designated a National Scenic River) and North Powder rivers, and by Anthony Creek; crossed by the

Grande Ronde River. The Grande Ronde and Minam rivers closely follow the eastern border. The Blue Mountains are in the west and north; the Wallowa Mountains are in the east. The county includes parts of Wallowa-Whitman and Umatilla national forests, parts of Eagle Cap Wilderness Area, Catherine Creek State Park, Hilgard Junction State Park, and Red Bridge State Wayside. One of the Nez Perce National Historic Park sites (Traditional Homesite) is located here. • Named for the town of Union or for the preservation of the Union • 1864 from Baker • Apples, cherries, potatoes, wheat, oats, barley, hogs, sheep, cattle; timber; education (Eastern OR U.).

WALLOWA *Enterprise* • 7,226 • 3,145 • Extreme northeastern OR, bounded on the north by the WA state line and on the east by the Snake River (forming the ID state line); drained by the Wallowa, Imnaha, Minam and Grande Ronde rivers (all designated as national wild and recreational rivers). The Grande Ronde and Minam rivers closely follow part of the western border. The Wallowa Mountains are here, as is Hells Canyon of the Snake River, which extends along the county's eastern boundary. A large part of Hells Canyon National Recreation Area is in the county, as are parts of Wallowah-Whitman National Forest, part of Umatilla National Forest, Wallowa Lake, and Minam State Recreation Area. The county also includes three sites of the Nez Perce National Historic Park: Joseph Canyon Viewpoint, Dug Bar, and Old Chief Joseph's Gravesite. • Named for the Wallowa Lake and Wallowa River. • 1887 from Union • The Snake and Imnaha River junction was the scene of the 1887 massacre of thirty-one Chinese gold miners. • Potatoes, wheat, oats, barley, hogs, sheep, cattle; timber; silver, gold.

WASCO *The Dalles* • 23,791 • 2,381 • Northern OR, bounded on the north by the Columbia River (forming the WA state line) and on the southeast by the John Day River (a National Recreation River); drained by the Deschutes River (a National Scenic and Recreational River), which forms part of the county's eastern boundary. The Columbia River here forms Bonneville and Lake Celilo (The Dalles Dam) reservoirs. Columbia River Gorge National Scenic Area is here. The county also includes part of Deschutes River State Recreational Area and a sizeable portion of Warm Springs Indian Reservation. Part of Mount Hood National Forest and the Cascade Range are located along the western border. White River Falls, Mayer and Memaloose state parks are also found in the county. • Named for the Wasco Indians • 1854 (prior to statehood), from the original Champoeg district which covered all of Oregon east of the Cascade Range, most of Idaho, and parts of MT and WY • The site of The Dalles (officially, "The City of The Dalles") marked the terminus of the Oregon Trail; travelers continued westward from here down the Columbia River

in rafts. The area's first settlement in 1838 was a Methodist mission. Following the discovery of gold in the 1860s, a federal mint was located here. With the completion in 1957 of The Dalles Dam, the city became the eastern terminal for oceangoing craft from the Pacific Ocean. • Apples, grapes, cherries, oats, barley, wheat, hogs, cattle; timber; aluminum plants; wood-treating; flour milling and baking.

WASHINGTON *Hillsboro* • 445,342 (43% increase since 1990; the third fastest growing and second most populated county in OR) • 724 • Northwestern OR; drained by the Tualatin River. The county is highly urbanized in the east as part of the Portland metropolitan area. It lies in the Coast Ranges. Bald Peak State Scenic Viewpoint is on the southwestern border. Part of Tillamook State Forest is also located here. • One of thirty-one counties named for George Washington • Original county; organized as Tuality, 1843 (prior to statehood); name changed in 1849 • Apples, cherries, pears, plums, peaches, grapes, nuts, berries, corn, brans, onions, potatoes, poultry, hogs, sheep, cattle, dairying; nurseries; wineries; manufacture of electronics, high technology, oscilloscopes; logging; education (Pacific U.).

WHEELER (one of four counties so named) *Fossil* • 1,547 (the least populated county in OR) • 1,715 • North-central OR; crossed by the John Day River (a National Recreational River, which forms the county's northwest border). Both the Clarno and Painted Hills units of John Day Fossil Beds National Monument are in the west. Also in the county are Shelton State Wayside, Clarno State Recreation Site, part of Ochoco and Umatilla national forests, Bridge Creek and part of Black Canyon wilderness areas. • Named for Henry H. Wheeler (1826–1915), stage coach line operator and prominent rancher in what is now Wheeler County • 1899 from Crook, Gilliam, and Grant • Timber; sheep, cattle.

YAMHILL *McMinnville* • 84,992 • 716 • Northwestern OR, bounded on the southeast by the Willamette River, and on the west by the Coast Ranges; drained by the Yamhill River and its North and South forks. Part of Siuslaw National Forest is here, as are Bald Peak State Scenic Viewpoint (on the northeastern boundary), Maud Williamson State Recreation Site, and Erratic Rock State Natural Site. The Grand Ronde Indian Community is in the southwest. • Named for the Yamel Indian tribe • Original county; organized 1843 (prior to statehood) • Newburg was founded in 1869 as the first Quaker settlement in the Pacific Northwest. • President Herbert Hoover was a member of the first graduating class of Friends Pacific Academy, now George Fox University • Dairying, corn, brans, onions, wheat, barley, oats, berries, nuts, pears, plums, cherries, peaches, poultry, sheep, cattle; nurseries; wineries; timber; manufacture of paper and wood products.

PENNSYLVANIA

Virtue, Liberty, and Independence

Sixty-two of Pennsylvania's sixty-seven counties are governed by boards of three commissioners, each member elected to a four-year term. Philadelphia is a consolidated city and county with a mayor and seventeen-member council. Erie, Lehigh, and Northampton elect county executives, who serve four-year terms. Delaware County is administered by five county commissioners, each of whom serves a four-year term.

ADAMS (one of twelve counties so named) *Gettysburg* • 91,292 • 520 • Southern PA, bounded on the south by the MD state line and on the west and northwest by the South Mountains; drained by Conewago Creek and its South Branch, and Rock Creek. The county contains Ski Liberty ski area, part of Michaux State Forest, part of Caledonia State Park, Carbaugh Run Natural Area, and Lake Meade and Lake Heritage reservoirs. • One of eight counties named for President John Adams • 1800 from York • The county was the scene of one of the greatest Civil War battles (national military park). In the Battle of Gettysburg, which raged from July 1 to 3, 1863, the Union Army repulsed the second Confederate invasion of the North. President Lincoln delivered his Gettysburg Address in a dedication ceremony for the cemetery here on November 19, 1863. • President Dwight D. and Mamie Eisenhower (national historic site) • Apples, cherries, grapes, wheat, corn, oats, barley, hay, alfalfa, soybeans, potatoes, chickens, eggs, sheep, hogs, cattle, dairying; limestone; manufacture of elevators, furniture, shoes, clothing, textiles; education (Gettysburg College).

ALLEGHENY (one of five counties named Allegheny with variant spellings) *Pittsburgh* • 1,281,666 (the second most populated county in PA) • 730 • Western PA; drained by the Ohio, Allegheny and Monongahela rivers (which join to form the Ohio River in downtown Pittsburgh, referred to as "three rivers") and by the Youghiogheny River. The county is heavily industrialized. It possesses several regional and county parks. Point State Park is in the center of Pittsburgh at the location of Fort Pitt. • Named for the Allegheny River • 1788 from Westmoreland and Washington • The county benefited greatly from western expansion and from Pittsburgh's location at the eastern end of the large Mississippi River transportation system. The presence of bituminous coal beds led to an early iron manufacturing industry. Braddock was the site of General Edward Braddock's defeat in the first battle of the French and Indian War in which regular British troops took part (1755). The British won control of the area from the French in 1758 and built Fort Pitt at the fork of the Allegheny and Monongahela rivers; the settlement that grew up around it became Pittsburgh. (Previously, Fort Necessity was built and surrendered here by 22-year-old lieutenant colonel George Washington.) The county was at the center of the 1794 anti-tax Whiskey Rebellion. Pittsburgh was a chief supplier of arms and ammunition to the Union Army during the Civil War. The first Carnegie library in the U.S. was established in Braddock in 1889. A strike by workers at the Carnegie Steel Company in Homestead in July, 1892 resulted in violence leading to ten deaths and the inability of unions to organize the steel industry until 1937. Commercial broadcasting in the U.S. was born at station KDKA in Wilkinsburg in 1920. Pittsburgh's Golden Triangle was flooded by the Allegheny and Monongahela rivers in 1936, leaving 45 dead and causing $25 million in damage. During WW II, the county's mills produced more steel than Germany and Japan together. McKeesport was hard hit by the decline of the steel industry in the 1980s. • Playwrights George S. Kaufman and Marc Connelly; dancer and choreographer Martha Graham; singer and actress Lillian Russell; painter John White Alexander; author Hervey Allen; biologist and author Rachel Carson; electrical engineer and inventor Frank Conrad; army officer John Murray Corse; jazz musician Roy Eldridge; actor Gene Kelly, songwriter Stephen Foster; army officer Benjamin Henry Grierson; businessman Henry John Heinz; physician Philip S. Hench; pianist Earl "Fatha: Hines; poet Robertson Jeffers; pianist and composer Oscar Levant; financier Andrew Mellon; novelist Mary Rinehart; painter Mary Cassatt, publisher Stanley M. Rinehart; lawyer George W. Wickersham • The county is a major steel center (providing 10% of all American-made steel). Also, other metal products, food, chemicals, paper, machinery, railroad supplies, industrial safety equipment, glassware, heat-resistant materials, food products (including sausage casings), tools, cement blocks and bricks; coal, natural gas, clay, limestone, sandstone, clay and gravel; also, corn, wheat, oats, barley, hay, alfalfa, apples, sheep, cattle, some hogs, dairying; research (nuclear, steel and coal, software development); education (U. of Pittsburgh; Chatham College; Carnegie Mellon U.; Carlow College; Duquesne U.; Point Park College; Robert Morris U.; others) • The corporate headquarters for eleven Fortune 1000 companies are located in the county. Pittsburgh has over 720 bridges, more than any other American city. An elm in Bayne Memorial Park in Bellevue called "Lone Sentinel" is reputed to be over 350 years old. Kennywood Amusement Park in West Mifflin is one of the nation's largest. Pittsburgh is home to the Pirates (PNC Park), Steelers (Heinz Field), and Penguins (Mellon Arena).

ARMSTRONG (one of two counties so named, the other in

TX) *Kittanning* • 72,392 • 654 • Western PA, bounded on the southwest by the Kiskiminetas River and on the north by the Allegheny River and Redbank Creek; drained by the Allegheny River and Mahoning Creek. • Named for Gen. John Armstrong (1717–1795), officer in the Revolutionary War and delegate to the second and third Continental Congress • 1800 from Allegheny, Lycoming, and Westmoreland • Philosopher Charles Hartshorne • Retail trade and services, diversified manufacturing; corn, wheat, oats, hay, alfalfa, sheep, hogs, cattle, dairying; bituminous coal, clay, limestone, sand.

BEAVER (one of three counties so named) *Beaver* • 181,412 • 434 • Western PA, bounded on the west by the OH state line; drained by the Ohio and Beaver rivers, and by Connoquenessing and Raccoon creeks. The county is urbanized and industrialized along the Ohio River. Ohio River Island National Wildlife Refuge is here, as is Raccoon Creek State Park. • Named for the Beaver River • 1800 from Allegheny and Washington • During 1793–94, General Anthony Wayne recruited and trained a force at Baden that would subsequently defeat 2,000 Indians at the Battle of Fallen Timbers in 1794. • Engineer and chemist Thomas Midgley, Jr.; football quarterback Joe Namath. Ascetic George Rapp died here. • Manufacture of iron and steel, miscellaneous metal products, bridge works, electrical equipment, building materials, vitreous china, mineral wool, plastics; bituminous coal, natural gas, oil, limestone, clay, sand and gravel; corn, wheat, hay, alfalfa, apples, sheep, cattle, dairying; education (Geneva College) • In 1859, the communal Harmony Society purchased nearly the entire site of Beaver Falls at a sheriff's sale for $34,000, adding additional land later.

BEDFORD (one of three counties so named) *Bedford* • 49,984 • 1,015 • Southern PA, bounded on the south by the MD state line and on the east by Rays Hill Ridge (Appalachian Mountains); drained by the Raystown Branch of the Juniata River. Part of the Allegheny Mountains are in the northwest. Wills Mountain Ridge is in the southwest. The county also includes Warriors Path, Blue Knob, and Shawnee state parks. Sections of Buchanan State Forest are also in the county, as are Pine Ridge and Sweet Root natural areas. • Named for either the town of Bedford or for Fort Bedford • 1771 (prior to statehood) from Cumberland • Fort Bedford, built in 1758, was staging area and supply base for the British colonial camp against the French Fort Duquesne. • Writer Dean Koontz. President James Buchanan (summer White House here) • Corn, oats, barley, hay, alfalfa, apples, sheep, hogs, cattle, dairying; bituminous coal, limestone, sand; timber; manufacture of clothing, mining equipment, toys, wood products • Hervey Allen used Bedford as the backdrop for several of his historical novels, including *Bedford Village* and *The Forest and the Fort*.

BERKS *Reading* • 373,638 • 859 • Southeast-central PA, bounded on the northwest by the Blue Mountain ridge; drained by the Schuylkill River, and Maiden and Tulpehocken creeks. The county is urbanized around Reading. Lake Ontelaunee and Blue Marsh Lake (encompassed by Blue Marsh

Lake Park) reservoirs are here, as are Crystal Cave, part of French Creek State Park, and Hawk Mountain Sanctuary. The Appalachian Trail closely follows the county's northwestern boundary. • The name comes from the shortened form for Berkshire, England, which also has a Reading as its county seat; it was the site of large land holdings of the Penn family • 1752 from Chester, Lancaster, and Philadelphia • The county was first settled by Swedes. During the American Revolution, Reading served as a supply depot and manufacturing center for cannons. Iron and steel production was strong in the 19th century. In the 1890s, Reading was a center for safety-bicycle production. • Frontiersman Daniel Boone (homestead); zoologist Spencer F. Baird; Indian agent Conrad Weiser (homestead); novelist and short story writer John Updike; poet Wallace Stevens; combat air commander Carl Spaatz. Bandmaster and composer John Philip Sousa died here. • Corn, wheat, oats, mushrooms, hay, alfalfa, soybeans, potatoes, plums, apples, chickens, sheep, hogs, cattle, dairying; manufacture of stainless steel, other specialty steels, hosiery, automobile body frames, textiles, pretzels, bedding, electronic equipment, paint, railroad equipment, candy; education (Albright College, Alvernia College; Penn State Berks–Lehigh Valley College; Kutztown U. of PA). The county's many outlet stores attract shoppers from all over the northeast. • Pagoda on Mount Penn is one of only two authentic Japanese pagodas in the U.S. The Hopewell Furnace National Historic Site (partly in Chester County) is an example of an early rural iron-making community. The county's Pennsylvania Dutch (German) heritage is reflected in a yearly folk festival in Kutztown and the Pennsylvania Dutch Folk Culture Center near Lenhartsville.

BLAIR *Hollidaysburg* • 129,144 • 526 • Central PA, bounded on the northeast by Bald Eagle Mountain Ridge and on the southeast by Tussey Mountain Ridge; drained by the Frankstown Branch of the Juniata and Little Juniata rivers. The Allegheny Mountains are in the west. Dunning, Loop, Lock, and Brush Mountain ridges are in the south. Canoe Creek State Park and part of Allegheny Portage Railroad National Historical Site are also in the county. • Named for John Blair (?–1832), PA legislator and transportation advocate • 1846 from Huntingdon and Bedford • Fort Roberdeau was built here in 1778 to protect a mine that supplied bullets to the Continental army. Altoona was developed by the Pennsylvania Railroad in 1849 as a switching point for locomotives. During the Civil War, the Altoona Conference of Union Governors showed strong support for Abraham Lincoln's Emancipation Proclamation. In 1864, the first steel rails for a U.S. railroad were laid between Altoona and Pittsburgh. The first steel passenger car was built in Altoona in 1902. • Social activist Harold Ickes; gossip columnist Hedda Hopper; entrepreneur Charles M. Schwab. Chemical engineer Charles B. Dudley died here. • Diversified manufacturing, including silk, clothing, shoes, bearings, candy; limestone, sand, clay, shale, bituminous coal; corn, wheat, hay, alfalfa, apples, sheep, hogs, cattle, dairying; education (Penn. State U. Altoona) • Most of the lead used by George Washington's armies in the American Revolution was mined here. Railroad shops in Altoona are said to be the largest of their kind in the world. Just west of Altoona is Horseshoe Curve, a railroad engineering feat 2,375 feet long and incorporating a curve of slightly more than nine degrees and a rise of ninety-one feet per mile.

BRADFORD (one of two counties so named, the other in FL) *Towanda* • 62,761 • 1,151 (the second largest county in PA) • Northeastern PA, bounded on the north by the NY state line; drained by the Susquehanna River, and Towanda and Schrader creeks. Sections of Tioga State Forest are in the west. Mount Pisgah State Park is also here. • Named for William Bradford (1755–95), associate justice of the PA Supreme Court and second U.S. attorney general • Organized as Ontario County 1810 from Luzerne and Lycoming; name changed 1812 • An important Indian village called Tioga Point occupied the site of Athens before 1778, when American troops burned it in revenge for the Wyoming Massacre. A refuge for French nobles was founded in 1793 at Asylum; it flourished until Napoleon's grant of amnesty in 1802. • Politician Joshua R. Giddings • Corn, hay, alfalfa, soybeans, apples, honey, hogs, cattle, dairying; manufacture of pneumatic tools.

BUCKS *Doylestown* • 597,635 (the fourth most populated county in PA) • 608 • Southeastern PA, bounded on the east and southeast by the Delaware River. The southeastern part of the county lies in a corridor between Philadelphia and Trenton NJ, and is highly urbanized. The county has several state parks. Lake Nockamixon reservoir is here. • The name is a shortened form of Buckingham, named for the English county of Buckinghamshire (also called Bucks); it was the home of the Penn family and many original settlers. • Organized as Buckingham 1682; one of the three original Penn counties • On Christmas night in 1776, General George Washington and 2,400 soldiers crossed the ice-choked Delaware River at the site of what is now Washington Crossing (historic park) in hopes of surprising British and Hessian troops in Trenton, NJ. Bristol's Bath Springs was a popular spa for Philadelphians from 1775 to 1822. • Colonial artisan Thomas Godfrey; painters Rembrant Peale and Joseph Pickett; army officer Jacob Jennings Brown; engineer Charles Ellet; surveyor Andrew Ellicott. Seedsman W. Atlee Burpee and lyricist Oscar Hammerstein died here. • Corn, wheat, alfalfa, soybeans, fruit, vegetables, poultry, hogs, cattle, dairying; limestone, sandstone, granite quarrying; manufacture of clothing, textiles, rubber products, building materials, electronic products, metal products, chemicals, plastics, abrasives, soaps, carpets, woolen yarn, leather goods; education (Delaware Valley College) • Levittown, a mass-produced housing development built by the firm of Levitt and Sons from 1951 to 1955 was modeled after the successful community of Levittown, NY. New Hope is a popular artists' and writers' colony and major county tourist attraction with one of the nation's oldest summer theatres, the Bucks County Playhouse, dating from the 1780s.

BUTLER (one of eight counties so named) *Butler* • 174,083

• 789 • Western PA; drained by Connoquenessing and Slippery Rock creeks. Its southeastern and northeastern corners touch the Allgeheny River. Lake Arthur reservoir in Moraine State Park is in the west. • One of three counties named for Maj. Gen. Richard Butler (?–1791), officer in the American Revolution and Indian commissioner • 1800 from Allegheny • The site of Butler was originally owned by Robert Morris of Philadelphia, leading financier of the Revolutionary War. Harmony was laid out in 1805 by members of the Harmonist Society, or "Rappites" led by George Rapp from Germany. In 1815, the religious-communist group migrated to Indiana where they founded New Harmony. • Civil engineer Washington A. Roebling • Corn, wheat, oats, hay, alfalfa, potatoes, apples, sheep, hogs, cattle, dairying; bituminous coal, oil, natural gas, limestone; manufacture of strip-steel car wheels, plate glass, railroad cars, tubing, oil-well equipment, rubber goods, fishing equipment, fertilizer, clothing, tissue paper, machine tools, exhaust fans; education (Slippery Rock U.).

CAMBRIA *Ebensburg* • 152,598 • 688 • West-central PA, bounded on the south in part by the Stonycreek River and on the southwest by Laurel Hill Ridge; drained by the Conemaugh, Little Conemaugh and Stoneycreek rivers. The Allegheny Mountains are in the east. The West Branch of the Susquehanna River rises in the north. The county is urbanized in the southwest corner around Johnstown. Glendale Lake reservoir is encompassed by Prince Gallitzen State Park. • Named for Cambria township in Somerset County. (Cambria is an ancient, poetic name for Wales.) • 1804 from Somerset, Bedford, and Huntingdon • The county was settled by the Welsh. Johnstown became important as the western terminus of the Allegheny Portage Railroad (national historic site), built 1831–34 as a series of inclined planes to transport Pennsylvania canal barges piggyback on railroad cars for thirty-six miles over the Allegheny Mountains. Johnstown, a major steelmaking center by 1873, developed the first blooming mill (for the breaking down of steel ingots) and produced the first U.S.-made steel rails. 2,209 died here on May 31, 1889 when a poorly maintained earth-hill dam across South Fork (a tributary of the Conemaugh River) was destroyed by the rain-swollen waters of Lake Conemaugh and flooded the town, sweeping away most of its northern half. (Johnstown Flood National Memorial stands at the site of the old dam.) The city was flooded again in 1936 and 1977 with additional loss of life and property. • Composer Charles W. Cadman; jockey Bill Hartack; Arctic explorer Robert Peary. Roman Catholic priest Demetrius S. Gallitzin died here. • Corn, wheat, alfalfa, potatoes, sheep, hogs, cattle, dairying; bituminous coal, clay, limestone; manufacture of clothing, chemicals, furniture, synthetic fuels from coal, fabricated steel plate, wheels, axles, freight cars, wire; education (U. of Pittsburgh Johnstown Campus; St. Francis U.; Mount Aloysius College).

CAMERON (one of three counties so named) *Emporium* • 5,974 • 397 • North-central PA; drained by Sinnemahoning Creek and its Driftwood Branch, Bennett Branch, and First

Fork. Sections of Elk State Forest are found throughout the county. Sinnemahoning and Bucktail state parks and part of Sizerville State Park, as well as several natural areas, are here. • Named for Simon Cameron (1799–1889), U.S. senator from PA, U.S. secretary of war, and U.S. minister to Russia • 1860 from Clinton, Elk, McKean, and Potter • Manufacturing; bituminous coal, sandstone, shale, natural gas; oats, hay, alfalfa, cattle, some dairying; timber.

CARBON (one of four counties so named) *Jim Thorpe* • 58,802 • 383 • Eastern PA, bounded on the northeast in part by Tobyhanna and Tunkhannock creeks; drained by the Lehigh River, which forms part of the northern and northwestern boundary. Blue Mountain Ridge and the Appalachian Trail follow county's southern boundary. Hickory Run, Lehigh Gorge, and Beltzville state parks are here. The Beltzville Lake reservoir is also in the county. • Named for deposits of anthracite coal discovered in the area in 1791. • 1843 from Northampton and Monroe • In 1828, the Lehigh Coal and Navigation Company laid out the site and built the first industrial railroad in the U.S. here, a gravity switchback line that hauled coal to the Lehigh Canal. Coal baron Asa Packer founded Lehigh Valley Railroad to replace the canal in 1855. • Remains of the Indian athlete Jim Thorpe have been interred at the Jim Thorpe Memorial near the city named for him. • Wheat, oats, barley, alfalfa, hay, soybeans, potatoes, sheep, hogs, cattle, dairying; manufacture of textiles, clothing, handbags, furniture.

CENTRE *Bellefonte* • 135,758 • 1,108 • Central PA, bounded on the northwest by the West Branch of the Susquehanna River, and by Moshannon Creek; drained by Bald Eagle Creek. The Allegheny Mountains cross the northwestern part of the county and are paralleled by the Bald Eagle Mountain Ridge in the central part, and by Tussey and Long mountains along its southern border. Parts of Rothrock, Moshannon, and Sproul state forests and Eagle State Forest are here. The county also includes Black Moshannon, Bald Eagle (encompassing Blanchard Lake reservoir), Poe Valley, Poe Paddy, and McCall Dam state parks. • The county was given the name Centre for its location in the geographic center of the state • 1800 from Lycoming, Mifflin, Northumberland, and Huntingdon • Sculptor George Grey Barnard. Farmer and agricultural writer John Lorain died here. • Corn, wheat, oats, hay, alfalfa, soybeans, vegetables, apples, eggs, sheep, hogs, cattle, dairying; manufacturing; limestone, bituminous coal, clay, sandstone; education (PA State U.).

CHESTER (one of three counties so named) *West Chester* • 433,501 • 756 • Southeastern PA, bounded in part on the northeast by the Schuylkill River, on the south by the MD and DE state lines, and on the west by Octoraro and East Octoraro creeks; drained by the Schuylkill River and the West Branch of Brandywine Creek. The county lies in an industrial and agricultural area with 35-mile-long Chester Valley extending west-southwest from the Schuylkill River below Valley Forge. Contained here are part of French Creek State Park,

Marsh Creek reservoir and State Park, White Clay Creek Preserve, and part of Valley Forge National Historical Park. • One of two counties (the other in SC) named for Chester, Cheshire, England, home of many settlers brought to America by William Penn • Original county; organized as Upland, March 10, 1682; name changed shortly thereafter. One of the three original Penn counties. • Phoenixville marks the most westerly penetration of British troops in PA during the Revolutionary War. Settlement of West Chester began in 1762 but was delayed by a prolonged dispute with Chester (now in Delaware County) over the permanent location of the county seat. In the Battle of Brandywine, fought here (and in neighboring Delaware County) on September 11, 1777, Washington's forces were outmaneuvered by the British who then moved unopposed to Philadelphia. It was the largest land battle fought in the American Revolution up to this point. Shortly thereafter, American General Anthony Wayne's forces were routed by the British several miles to the northeast. • Composer Samuel Barber; physician and Arctic explorer Isaac I. Hayes; editor and newspaper publisher Hezekiah Niles; marine officer Smedley D. Butler; frontiersman John Filson; attorney William Maclay; orientalist George Foot Moore; painter Horace Pippin; French economist and statesman Pierre S. du Pont; author Bayard Taylor; outlaw Harry Longabaugh (the Sundance Kid); singer Ethel Waters. Inventor Albert C. Barnes died here. • Corn, wheat, oats, mushrooms, barley, hay, alfalfa, soybeans, potatoes, apples, poultry, eggs, sheep, hogs, cattle, dairying; diversified manufacturing, including steel, automobile parts, apparel, paper boxes, abrasives, rubber products, felt; granite, limestone; education (West Chester U. of PA; Immaculata College; others) • The headquarters of six Fortune 1000 companies are located in the county. Hopewell Furnace National Historic Site (partly in Berks County) is one of the best examples of a rural 19th century iron complex. Founded in 1771 by Mark Bird, the first ironmaster, it operated until 1883.

CLARION *Clarion* • 41,765 • 602 • West-central PA, bounded on the southwest by the Allegheny River (designated a National Recreational River) and on the south by Redbank Creek; drained by the Clarion River. The county lies on the Allegheny Plateau. Part of Cook Forest State Park is in the northeast. • Named for the Clarion River • 1839 from Venango and Armstrong • The county had strong iron, lumber, and oil industries in the 19th century. • Bituminous coal, clay, gas, oil; timber; some manufacturing; corn, wheat, oats, barley, hay, alfalfa, potatoes, apples, sheep, hogs, cattle; dairying; education (Clarion U.).

CLEARFIELD *Clearfield* • 83,382 • 1,147 (the third largest county in PA) • Central PA; drained by the West Branch of the Susquehanna River (forming Curwensville Lake reservoir). The county includes Parker Dam and S.B. Elliott state parks, and parts of Moshannon State Forest. • Named for the "cleared fields" here • 1804 from Lycoming and Huntingdon. In early years it functioned as part of Centre County; its first county commissioners were elected in 1812, courts established in 1822

• Bituminous coal, natural gas, sandstone, clay; diversified manufacturing, including leather goods, school supplies, stainless steel products, electronics equipment, sportswear; dairying, corn, some wheat, oats, barley, hay, alfalfa, sheep, cattle, dairying; recreational tourism.

CLINTON (one of nine counties so named) *Lock Haven* • 37,914 • 891 • North-central PA; drained by the West Branch of the Susquehanna River (forming part of the southwestern boundary), and Kettle and Sinnemahoning creeks. Bald Eagle Mountain is in the southeastern part of the county. Sproul and Tiadaghton state forests cover much of the county. Several state parks, including Hyner Run, Hyner View, and Kettle Creek and numerous natural areas are located here. • One of eight counties named for DeWitt Clinton (1769–1828), governor of New York, and supporter of the Erie Canal. • 1839 from Lycoming and Centre • Metallurgist James Gayley; painter John French Sloan • Clay, bituminous coal, limestone; timber; manufacture of airplanes, paper, textiles, furniture, chemicals; corn, wheat, oats, barley, hay, alfalfa, apples, hogs, cattle, dairying; education (Lock Haven U. of PA).

COLUMBIA (one of eight counties so named) *Bloomsburg* • 64,151 • 486 • East-central PA, bounded on the southwest by the South Branch of Roaring Creek; drained by the Susquehanna River, and Roaring and Fishing creeks. The Muncy Hills are located in the west. Jakey Hollow Natural Area is also here. • Columbia is a feminine form of Columbus, a poetic reference to Christopher Columbus and America • 1813 from Northumberland • During the Civil War, Union troops sought without success to root out an alleged confederacy of draft dodgers in Bloomsburg who had reputedly built a fort in Fishing Creek valley. In the 1870s, the town was the site of one of the murder trials that ended a rampage of violence in PA coalfields carried out by members of the Molly Maguires. • Physiologist Halden K. Hartline • Corn, wheat, oats, barley, hay, alfalfa, soybeans, potatoes, apples, poultry, sheep, hogs, cattle, dairying; manufacture of carpets, silks, clothing, architectural aluminum, electronic products; canned and frozen foods; education (Bloomsburg U. of PA) • The county has more than twenty covered bridges. In 1870, Bloomsburg became the only incorporated town in PA (all other communities being boroughs or cities).

CRAWFORD (one of eleven counties so named) *Meadville* • 90,366 • 1,013 • Northwestern PA, bounded on the west by the OH state line; drained by the Shenango River and French Creek. Pymatuning State Park encompasses Pymatuning Reservoir (Shenango River) in the west. Conneaut Lake, the state's largest natural lake, is also here. Sections of Erie National Wildlife Refuge are in the county. • One of three counties named for Col. William Crawford (1732–82), surveyor, army officer, and Indian fighter • 1800 from Allegheny • Titusville is near the site of the world's first successful oil well (just south in Venango County). The town's survival has been threatened by fires, floods, and explosions over the years. As the center of the struggle by independent oil producers against incursions of the Standard Oil Company, the town was also the scene of violence in the 1870s. • Chemist William Harkins; educator Charles H. Haskins • Manufacture of specialty steel, forgings, crankshafts, heavy oil-well equipment, lumber, wood products, plastic tile, textiles, electronic components, wallpaper, paints, camper bodies; oil, gas, sand and gravel; corn, wheat, oats, barley, hay, alfalfa, soybeans, potatoes, sheep, hogs, cattle, dairying; education (Allegheny College) • Meadville has manufactured zippers since 1923.

CUMBERLAND (one of eight counties so named) *Carlisle* • 213,674 • 550 • Southern PA, bounded on the northeast by the Susquehanna River and on the southeast by Yellow Breeches Creek; drained by Conodoguinet Creek. Blue Mountain Ridge runs along the northern boundary. The northeast section of the county is part of the urbanized Harrisburg metropolitan area. Pine Grove Furnace and Colonel Denning state parks are both here, as is part of Michaux State Forest. The Appalachian Trail crosses the county. • Named for Cumberlandshire, England • 1750 from Lancaster • The county's Cumberland Valley (part of Great Appalachian Valley) was a famous 18th century route to the western territories. Carlisle was a munitions supply point during the Revolutionary War. In 1794, it served as Washington's headquarters during the Whiskey Rebellion. Carlisle Barracks, one of the oldest of U.S. Army posts (established in 1757), was the site of the Carlisle Indian School from 1878 to 1918. The school was famous for its athletes, among them Jim Thorpe. (The Barracks has been occupied since 1951 by the U.S. Army War College.) In June, 1863, Carlisle was briefly occupied by Confederate troops who bombarded it when they retreated. A skirmish was fought at Camp Hill. • Civil engineer James Geddes; army officer and politician John Armstrong; jurist Robert C. Grier; politician Samuel Smith. Early American novelist Hugh H. Brackenridge died here. • Clay, limestone; corn, wheat, hay, alfalfa, soybeans, fruit, poultry, hogs, cattle, dairying, eggs; manufacture of electronic equipment, quartz crystals, rubber products; education (Dickinson College).

DAUPHIN *Harrisburg* • 251,798 • 525 • South-central PA, bounded on the west by the Susquehanna River, on the south by Conewago Creek and on the north by Mahantango Creek; drained by Swatara Creek. The county has undergone some urbanization in the southwest. East-west running mountain ridges include Mahantango, Bear, Peters, Stony, Second and Blue. Parts of Weiser State Forest are in the north. The Appalachian Trail passes along Peters Mountain Ridge. • The county was named after the hereditary title of the eldest son of the king of France, dauphin, in honor of France, ally of the American states in the Revolutionary War. (Louis Joseph [1781–89], son of Louis XVI and Marie Antoinette, was dauphin at the time the county was established.) • 1785 from Lancaster • Harrisburg, capital of PA since 1812, was the scene of the National Tariff Convention of 1827 and the first Whig Convention in 1839, which nominated William Henry Harrison for president. On March 28, 1979, the worst commercial nuclear accident in U.S. history occurred at the Three Mile Island reactor in Middletown, PA, as equipment failures and human mistakes led to a loss of coolant and a partial core meltdown. • Speaker of the House Newt Gingrich; novelist James Boyd; naval officer David Conner; army officer Josiah Gorgas; industrialist Milton S. Hershey. Zoologist Raymond Pearl died here. • Diversified manufacturing, including chocolate and cocoa (the Hershey Plant in Hershey is the world's largest chocolate and confectionery factory), steel, clothing, shoes, electronic equipment, precision and road machinery; corn, wheat, hay, alfalfa, vegetables, soybeans, apples, poultry, sheep, hogs, cattle, dairying; limestone; government operations • Hershey celebrates Dutch Days each year and is also the headquarters of the Antique Automobile Club of America. The 272-foot dome of the capitol in Harrisburg was patterned after St. Peter's in Rome; it was completed in 1906 to replace the first capitol destroyed by fire in 1897.

DELAWARE (one of six counties so named) *Media* • 550,864 (the fifth most populated county in PA) • 184 • Southeastern PA, bounded on the east by Darby and Cobb creeks, on the southeast by the Delaware River (forming the NJ state line), on the south by the DE state line, and on the southwest by Brandywine Creek; drained by Darby, Crum, Ridley and Chester creeks. The county lies in a highly urbanized residential and industrial area between the cities of Philadelphia to the northeast and Wilmington DE to the southwest. Ridley Creek State Park and Springton Reservoir are located here, as is Valley Forge State Forest, on Little Tinincum Island in the Delaware River. Philadelphia International Airport is in the southeast corner. • Named for the Delaware River • 1789 from Chester • The county, the oldest settled area in PA, was originally ruled by Sweden. Darby was settled by Philadelphia Quakers in 1692. In the Battle of Brandywine, fought here (and in neighboring Chester County) on September 11, 1777, Washington's forces were outmaneuvered by the British who then moved unopposed to Philadelphia. It was the largest land battle fought in the American Revolution up to this point. • Shipbuilder and naval architect Joshua Humphreys; Union naval officer David D. Porter; botanist John Bartram; engraver James B. Longacre; writer Christopher D. Morley; patriot John Morton; composer Alex North • Oil refining; shipbuilding, steel mills, locomotive works; manufacture of helicopters, electronic precision instruments, paper products, textiles, chemicals, floor covers; alfalfa, cattle, dairying; education (Widener U.; Swarthmore College; Villanova U., others) • The Caleb Pusey House in Chester is the oldest English-built house in PA (1683). The Old Court House (1724) is the oldest public building in the U.S.

ELK (one of two counties so named, the other in KS) *Ridgway* • 35,112 • 829 • North-central PA; drained by the Clarion River and the Bennett Branch of Sinnemahoning Creek. Located on the forested Allegheny Plateau, much of the county is covered by parts of Allegheny National Forest, and Moshannon and Elk state forests. Bendigo and Elk state parks, several natural areas, and the East Branch Clarion River Lake reservoir are also here. • Named for the elk herds once abundant here • 1843 from Jefferson, Clearfield, and McKean • Reformer Mary Elizabeth Lease • Corn, oats, barley, hay, alfalfa, dairying; bituminous coal, clay, sandstone, limestone; manufacturing.

ERIE (one of three counties so named) *Erie* • 280,843 • 802 • Northwestern PA, bounded on the north by Lake Erie (the only PA county on a Great Lake), on the northeast by the NY state line, and on the west by the OH state line; drained by Elk and French creeks. Sheltered by the seven-mile peninsula of Presque Isle which curves into the lake, Erie's harbor is one of the best anchorages on the Great Lakes. Presque Isle State Park is on the peninsula. • Named for Lake Erie • 1800 from Allegheny • French forts built in 1753 at Presque Isle and Le Boeuf (at Waterford) were occupied in 1760 by the British. Claims to the Erie Triangle were ceded in 1781–85 to the U.S. government by NY and MA, and sold to PA in 1788. Commodore Oliver Hazard Perry's headquarters was in Erie. From here he sailed to the Battle of Lake Erie off Put-in-Bay, OH in 1813. In the early 19th century, Erie was principally engaged in the salt trade. • Baritone and composer Harry T. Burleigh; magician Harry Kellar; ethnographer Frank H. Cushing; author Ida Tarbell. General Anthony Wayne died here. • Grapes, cherries, apples, corn, wheat, oats, barley, potatoes, hay, alfalfa, hogs, dairying; timber; limestone, sand and gravel; manufacture of paper and paper products, plastics, rubber, transportation equipment, electrical machinery, ships, aluminum forgings, clothing, chemicals; education (Gannon U., Edinboro U. of PA; PA State U. at Erie, the Behrend College; Mercyhurst College) • Erie is the site of Millcreek Mall, one of the largest shopping centers in the U.S. The restored hull of Perry's flagship, the USS *Niagara*, is on the Public Dock here.

FAYETTE (one of eleven counties so named) *Uniontown* • 148,644 • 790 • Southwestern PA, bounded on the south by the WV and MD state lines, on the west by the Monongahela River, and on the east by Laurel Hill; drained by the Youghiogheny River, forming Youghiogheny River Lake reservoir on the southeast boundary. Chestnut Ridge crosses diagonally northeast to southwest. The county includes part of Laurel Ridge State Park, Ohiopyle State Park, Forbes State Forest, including Laurel Caverns, and Bear Run Nature Reserve. Other reservoirs are found in the county. Friendship Hill National Historic Site and Searights Toll house National Historic Landmark are in the west. • One of seventeen counties named for the Marquis de Lafayette (1757–1834), French statesman and soldier who fought with the Americans during the Revolutionary War • 1783 from Westmoreland • The county was settled in 1752 by Virginians. The first skirmishing of the French and Indian War occurred at Jumonville Glen on May 28, 1754. The county was the scene of a battle lost by Lt. Col. George Washington on July 3, 1754 (Fort Necessity National Battlefield). The Whiskey Rebellion was put down here in 1794. Cumberland Road passed through the county. • Detective fiction writer John D. Carr; politician Philander C. Knox; religious figure Eliza Maria Gillespie; army officer and statesman George C. Marshall; filmmaker Edwin S. Porter; secretary of the treasury Albert Gallatin; army officer and inventor Isaac Newton Lewis • Corn, wheat, oats, barley, hay, alfalfa, apples, sheep, hogs, cattle, dairying; timber; bituminous coal, natural gas, limestone; some manufacturing. • In 1769, George Washington acquired 234 acres of land near Fort Necessity, which he still owned at the time of his death. Frank Lloyd Wright's Fallingwater at Bear Run (1936–37) is considered one of the premiere houses of the world.

FOREST (one of two counties so named, the other in WI) *Tionesta* • 4,946 (the least populated county in PA) • 428 • Northwestern PA, bounded in part on the south by the Clarion River (designated a National Scenic and Recreational River); drained by the Allegheny River (designated a National Recreational River), the Clarion River, and Tionesta Creek (forming Tionesta Lake reservoir). Located on the Allegheny Plateau, most of the county is covered by Allegheny National Forest. Part of Cook Forest State Park and Clear Creek State Forest are in the south. • The county was given this name by pioneer settler Cyrus Blood because it was thickly forested • 1848 from Jefferson • Forest County was settled by Moravian missionaries. • Corn, oats, hay, alfalfa, cattle, dairying; timber; sand and gravel.

FRANKLIN (one of twenty-five counties so named) *Chambersburg* • 129,313 • 772 • Southern PA, bounded on the south by the MD state line and on the west by the Tuscarora Mountain Ridge; drained by Conodoguinet Creek. Parts of the Cove, South, and Blue mountains are here. Mont Alto and Caledonia state parks and sections of Michaux and Buchanan state forests are also in the county. The Appalachian Trail passes through the southeast. Letterkenny Army Depot is north of Chambersburg. • One of twenty-three counties named for Benjamin Franklin • 1784 from Cumberland • Prior to the end of the American Revolution, the county was the scene of a number of Indian massacres. General Robert E. Lee gathered troops in Chambersburg for the attack on Gettysburg in July, 1863. Chambersburg was raided by Confederate forces on three occasions. The only Northern town burned in the Civil War, it earned this distinction in retaliation for a Union raid into VA after Chambersburg citizens had refused to pay an indemnity of $100,000 in gold. • James Buchanan (Buchanan Birthplace State Park); Revolutionary War heroine Margaret Corbin • Corn, wheat, oats, barley, hay, alfalfa, soybeans, potatoes, apples, peaches, poultry, sheep, hogs, cattle, dairying; sand and gravel; manufacture of clothing, dropforging equipment, power transmission machinery, containers, paper products; education (Wilson College).

FULTON (one of eight counties so named) *McConnellsburg* • 14,261 • 438 • Southern PA, bounded on the south by the MD state line, with Tuscarora Mountain Ridge on the eastern boundary, Town Hill and Ray Hill ridges on the western boundary; drained by Aughwick and Licking creeks. Part of Cowans Gap State Park is here, as is Redbud Valley Nature Center. Sections of Buchanan State Forest are also in the county. • One of seven counties named for Robert Fulton (1765–1815), developer of the *Clermont*, the first commercially successful steamboat • 1850 from Bedford • Meteorologist William Ferrel • Corn, wheat, oats, hay, alfalfa, hogs, cattle, dairying; bituminous coal, limestone; manufacturing.

GREENE (one of fourteen counties so named) *Waynesburg* • 40,672 • 576 • Southwestern PA, bounded on the south and west by the WV state line, on the east by the Monongahela River, on the northwest by the Enlow Fork of Wheeling Creek, and on the northeast corner by Tenmile Creek. Ryerson Station State Park is here. • One of sixteen counties named for Gen. Nathanael Greene (1742–86), hero of the Revolutionary War • 1796 from Washington County • The area was in dispute between PA and VA until 1784. • Clergyman and educator John F. Goucher • Corn, hay, alfalfa, sheep, hogs, cattle, dairying; bituminous coal, gas, oil, limestone, sandstone, clay, shale, sand; education (Waynesburg College). • It almost always rains in Waynesburg on July 29; the town holds a festival to celebrate this fact.

HUNTINGDON (one of two counties so named, the other in IN) *Huntingdon* • 45,586 • 875 • South-central PA; drained by the Juniata River and the Raystown Branch of the Juniata (forming Raystown Lake reservoir). The county is crossed by several ridges, including Bald Eagle Mountain, Tussey Mountain, Jacks Mountain, and Tuscarora Mountain. Parts of Rockroth State Forest are here, as are Lincoln and Indian caverns, and Trough Creek, Greenwood Furnace, and Whipple Dam state parks. • Named for the county seat, itself named for Selina Shirley Hastings (1707–1791), Countess of Huntingdon, who made a large donation to the College and Academy of Philadelphia (now U. of PA) • 1787 from Bedford • Merchant John Purdue • Clay, bituminous coal, glass sand; manufacturing; corn, wheat, oats, hay, alfalfa, poultry, hogs, cattle, dairying; education (Juniata College).

INDIANA *Indiana* • 89,605 • 829 • West-central PA, bounded on the south by the Conemaugh River, forming Conemaugh River Lake reservoir; drained by Blacklick, Two Lick, Mahoning, and Little Mahoning creeks. The county includes Charles F. Lewis Natural Area, Yellow Creek State Park, and Yellow Creek Lake and Two Lick reservoirs. • Possibly named for the Indiana Territory • 1803 from Westmoreland and Lycoming • Film actor James Stewart (museum) • The county is a leading supplier of Christmas trees; also bituminous coal, limestone; corn, wheat, oats, hay, alfalfa, potatoes, poultry, sheep, hogs, cattle, dairying; manufacture of leather goods, men's and boys' apparel, clay products, concrete blocks, aluminum doors and windows, thermostat controls, beverages; education (Indiana U. of PA).

JEFFERSON *Brookville* • 45,932 • 655 • West-central PA, bounded on the north by the Clarion River (designated here a National Scenic and Recreational River); drained by Mahoning and Redbank creeks. Clear Creek State Park and State Forest are in the north. • One of twenty-six counties named directly or indirectly for President Thomas Jefferson • 1804 from Lycoming • Bituminous coal; dairying; manufacturing; clay, sand and gravel; corn, wheat, oats, barley, hay, alfalfa, soybeans, sheep, hogs, cattle, poultry. • Punxsutawney is home to the "official" groundhog; on February 2 of each year townspeople gather for its meteorological prediction.

JUNIATA *Mifflintown* • 22,821 • 392 • Central PA, bounded on the extreme east by the Susquehanna River and on the northeast by Mahantango Creek and its west branch; drained by the Juniata River and Tuscarora Creek. Blacklog Mountain sits on county's southwest border and Shade Mountain on its northwest border. The Tuscarora Mountain Ridge forms the southeastern border of the county. Parts of Tuscarora State Forest are located throughout the county. • Named for the Juniata River • 1831 from Mifflin • Manufacturing; corn, wheat, oats, hay, alfalfa, apples, poultry, sheep, hogs, cattle, dairying; timber.

LACKAWANNA *Scranton* • 213,295 • 459 • Northeastern PA, bounded on the southwest by the Susquehanna River, on the southeast by the Lehigh River; drained by the Lackawanna River. The county includes part of Lackawanna State Forest, Spruce Swamp Natural Area, and Lackawanna and Archbald Pothold state parks. • Named for the Lackawanna River • 1878 from Luzerne; it was the last PA county to be created • Iron smelting from local ores in the 1850s was replaced by a successful anthracite-coal industry (PA Anthracite Heritage Museum is in Scranton), which brought in hundreds of immigrant miners whose wives worked in silk weaving and clothing industries. (Scranton was noted for its production of Nottingham lace.) In June, 1831, the world's first underground anthracite mine was opened in Carbondale. With the decline of the coal industry in the 1950s, Scranton diversified its economy and received national attention for its "Scranton Plan" to provide jobs through industrial expansion. • Labor leader Terence V. Powderly; politician Joe Biden; manufacturer Robert Wood Johnson; cell biologist Daniel Mazia; economist Edwin Walter Kemmerer; playwright Charles MacArthur • Corn, oats, hay, alfalfa, vegetables, fruit, truck farms, cattle, dairying; diversified manufacturing, including automobile parts, electrical and electronic equipment, clothing, textiles, silk mills, metal and wood products; printing and publishing; education (U. of Scranton; Marywood U.) • The Steamtown National Historic Site (the former Delaware, Lackawanna and Western Railroad yard) in Scranton offers the story of early 20th century steam railroading through the remains of a historic roundhouse and other buildings, thirty steam locomotives and seventy-eight cars. The Everhart Museum of Natural History, Science and Art is known for its large bird collection.

LANCASTER (one of four counties so named) *Lancaster* • 470,658 • 949 • Southeastern PA, bounded on the south by the MD state line, on the west and southwest by the Susquehanna River (its dams forming several reservoirs), on the southeast by Octararo Creek and its East Branch, and on the northwest by Conewago Creek. Susquehannock State Park is located on Muddy Run Reservoir. • One of two counties (the other in VA) named for Lancaster, Lancashire, England, former home of John Wright, who worked for the formation of the county. • 1729 from Chester • The county was first settled in 1709 by Swiss and French immigrants, and later by Germans, Welsh, English and Scotch-Irish. Unlike the original three PA counties, which were created as copies of English shires, Lancaster, became the prototype for the sixty-three counties to follow. The conestoga wagon and Kentucky rifle were early products. Following the British invasion of Philadelphia, the city of Lancaster was made the capital of the United States for one day (Sept. 27, 1777). The Supreme Executive Council of PA took refuge here for nine months in 1777–78. Both Columbia and Lancaster were considered by Congress in 1790 as location for the permanent national capital. Lancaster was the capital of PA from 1799 to 1812. • Inventor Robert Fulton; painter Charles Demuth; financier and politician Simon Cameron; American patriot Barbara Frietschie; psychologist James M. Cattell; theologian John W. Nevin; President James Buchanan; abolitionist Thaddeus Stephens; U.S. secretary of state Robert Smith • Corn, wheat, oats, barley, hay, alfalfa, tobacco, soybeans, potatoes, apples, sheep, hogs, cattle, chickens, eggs, dairying; manufacture of clothing, glass, malleable castings, farm machinery, electrical products, linoleum, watches; tourist center (The county's Amish Mennonite community is a major draw.); education (Lancaster Bible College; Franklin and Marshall College; Millersville U. of PA; Elizabethtown College) • F.W. Woolworth opened his first successful "5-and-10-cent store" in Lancaster in 1879–80. The German Seventh Day Baptists in Ephrata were known for their weaving, pottery, and Frakturschriften (calligraphic art). Four generations of the Gorgas family in Ephrata won recognition for their clocks and cabinets. The Clositer Press here printed the Declaration of Independence, as well as Continental money while Philadelphia was occupied by the British.

LAWRENCE (one of eleven counties so named) *New Castle* • 94,643 • 360 • Western PA, bounded on the west by the OH state line; drained by the Shenango, Mahoning, and Beaver rivers, and by Neshannock and Slippery Rock creeks. McConnell's Mill State Park is here. • Named for the *Lawrence*, the flagship of American commander Oliver Hazard Perry in the Battle of Lake Erie (1813) • 1849 from Beaver and Mercer • The county was a major iron center in the mid-19th century. New Castle became the terminus for the Erie Extension Canal in 1833. • Sand, gravel, limestone, iron ore, bituminous coal, fire clay; corn, oats, wheat, hay, alfalfa, apples, sheep, hogs, cattle, dairying; manufacture of steel and allied products, pottery, chemicals, leather goods, pottery, cement; education (Westminster College).

LEBANON *Lebanon* • 120,327 • 362 • Southeastern PA;

drained by Swatara Creek. Part of Fort Indiantown Gap Military Reservation is here (and includes a national cemetery). The Appalachian Trail passes through the northern part of the county along Second Mountain Ridge. The county also contains Memorial Lake and Lake Swatara state parks and part of Middle Creek Management Area. • Named for Lebanon Township or Lebanon Borough • 1813 from Dauphin and Lancaster • Lebanon's location near the Cornwall ore mines and other mineral deposits made the city an iron center before the Revolutionary War. Stiegel glassware was made here in the 18th century. • Corn, wheat, oats, barley, hay, alfalfa, soybeans, sheep, hogs, cattle, chickens, eggs, dairying; manufacture of iron and steel products, pharmaceuticals, shoes, textiles; limestone; education (Lebanon Valley College).

LEHIGH *Allentown* • 312,090 • 347 • Eastern PA, bounded on the northeast and drained by the Lehigh River; also drained by Jordan and Little Lehigh creeks. The Blue Mountain Ridge runs the length of the northwestern boundary. The county is urbanized in the southeast around the twin cities of Allentown and Bethelehem. • Named for the Lehigh River • 1812 from Northampton • Emmaus was settled in 1740 by Moravians who closed the town to members of other denominations from 1758 until 1836. Allentown's location amid rich mineral deposits and productive farmland contributed to its early development as an industrial and market center (established 1762). • Automobile executive Lee Iacocca; Declaration of Independence signer George Taylor; jazz performer and composer Keith Jarrett • Corn, wheat (flour also processed), oats, barley, hay, alfalfa, soybeans, potatoes, apples, chickens, sheep, hogs, cattle, dairying; limestone, slate, sand and gravel; manufacture of textiles, heating and electrical equipment, iron and steel products, cement; printing and publishing; education (seat of five colleges) • The county has five covered bridges on Jordan Creek. The Liberty Bell Shrine in Allentown contains a replica of the original bell, brought to the city during the American Revolution for safekeeping in the Zion Reformed Church.

LUZERNE *Wilkes-Barre* • 319,250 • 891 • East-central PA, bounded on the southeast by the Lehigh River; drained by the Susquehanna River (forming part of the northeast boundary). The Nescopeck Mountain Ridge crosses in the center. Nescopeck, Frances Slocum, and (part of) Ricketts Glen state parks are here, as is part of Lackawanna State Forest. • Named for Anne Cesar, Chevalier de la Luzerne (1741–91), French diplomat who helped raise money for the Continental army. • 1786 from Northumberland • The first permanent settlements in the county were made in the 1750s and 60s by families from CT. Wilkes-Barre was at the center of the Pennamite-Yankee Wars fought from 1769 to 1784 between PA and CT settlers over rival land claims. Conflicts with Loyalists and the Iroquois Indians during the Revolutionary War culminated in the slaughter of settlers in the Wyoming Massacre of July 3, 1778. The punitive expedition of 1779 against the Iroquois was formed by General John Sullivan in Wilkes-Barre. In 1959, the swollen Susquehanna flooded the Knox Mine, killing twelve

and forcing an end to deep mining in the county; to close the huge hole in the river bed, the Lehigh Valley Railroad tracks were diverted and 30 railroad cars and 400 mine cars were pushed into the brink. Widespread property damage resulted from a flooding of the Susquehanna River in 1972 • Artist and author George Catlin; developmental geneticist Edward Lewis; artist Franz Kline; sociologist Robert E. Park; illustrator and author Rose Cecil O'Neill; film producer Joseph Mankiewicz • Corn, wheat, oats, hay, alfalfa, vegetables, potatoes, apples, hogs, cattle, dairying; anthracite coal, sandstone; manufacture of footwear, pencils, glass, boilers, furniture, toys, steel fabrications, airplane parts, electronic equipment; education (Wilkes U.; Kings College; College Misericordia) • Sitting atop Spring Mountain at 1,886 feet, Hazleton has the highest elevation of any city in PA. With the decline of coal mining in Hazleton in the early 1950s, the city used volunteer labor, donated materials and bootstrap determination to create an industrial park that by the late 1960s was filled with over fifty new diversified industries. West Pittson is sometimes known as "The Garden Village" for it spacious homes and lawns.

LYCOMING *Williamsport* • 120,044 • 1,235 (the largest county in PA) • North-central PA; drained by the West Branch of the Susquehanna River and by Lycoming (forming part of the northern boundary), Loyalsock, and Pine creeks. Part of Allenwood Federal Prison Camp is in the southeast. Little Pine, Upper Pine Bottom, and Susquehanna state parks, as well as several natural areas, are here. Parts of Tiadaghton State Forest are located throughout the county. • Named for Lycoming Creek; for many years the creek had been the dividing line between settled and disputed Indian lands • 1795 from Northumberland • Williamsport became a lumbering center in the 1860s. The "Sawdust War" broke out in 1872 as workers sought a 10-hour day, and was put down by the militia. • Painter George B. Luks; propulsion engineer Samuel K. Hoffman • Corn, wheat, oats, barley, hay, alfalfa, soybeans, potatoes, apples, sheep, hogs, cattle, dairying; manufacture of metal and leather products, furniture, textiles; education (Lycoming College; PA College of Tech.) • South Williamsport is the international headquarters for Little League Baseball; its World Series is held here every August.

MCKEAN *Smethport* • 45,936 • 982 • Northern PA, bounded on the north by the NY state line; drained by the Allegheny River. Kinzua Bridge State Park is here, as are Kinzua Bay and Sugar Bay, arms of Allegheny Reservoir. The western third of the county is covered by Allegheny National Forest. • Named for Thomas McKean (1734–1817), signer of the Declaration of Independence, chief justice of PA and PA's second state governor • Organized 1804 from Lycoming, but administered through Centre until 1814, then Potter and Lycoming; fully organized in 1826 • Ten years after the discovery of oil here in 1871 the area around Bradford was producing forty percent of the world's output. • Industrialist J. Howard Pew; opera singer Marilyn Horne • The county is the largest producer of lubricating oils in PA; also, petroleum, natural gas; corn, oats, hay, alfalfa, hogs, cattle, dairying; manufacturing; education (U. of Pittsburgh at Bradford).

MERCER (one of eight counties so named) *Mercer* • 120,293 • 672 • Northwestern PA, bounded on the west by the OH state line; drained by the Shenango River, and Neshannock and Wolf creeks. The county includes Lake Wilhelm and Shenango River Lake reservoirs. Maurice K. Goddard State Park and Brucker Great Blue Heron Sanctuary are here. • One of six counties definitively named for Gen. Hugh Mercer (?–1777), Revolutionary War officer and physician • 1800 from Allegheny • Mercer was settled by veterans of the Revolution. The Sharon Furnace, built following the completion of the Lake Erie extension of the Pennsylvania Canal in 1844, engendered an important early steel industry here. • Corn, wheat, oats, barley, hay, alfalfa, potatoes, hogs, cattle, dairying; bituminous coal, sandstone, limestone; manufacture of steel, electrical equipment; education (Thiel College; Grove City College).

MIFFLIN *Lewistown* • 46,486 • 411 • Central PA, bounded on the northwest by the Stone Mountain Ridge, on the north by Long Mountain Ridge, and on the southeast by Blue Mountain Ridge; bisected by Jacks Mountain Ridge; drained by the Juniata River (forming part of the southwestern boundary) and Kishacoquilla Creek. The county includes Reeds Gap State Park, and parts of Rothrock, Tuscarora and Bald Eagle state forests. • Named for General Thomas Mifflin (1744–1800), member of the Continental Congress, PA legislator, and longest-serving governor of PA • 1789 from Cumberland and Northumberland • Lewistown was one of PA's pioneering iron-manufacturing centers. With the opening of the Pennsylvania Canal in 1829, it became an important shipping point. • Corn, wheat, oats, hay, alfalfa, sheep, hogs, cattle, poultry, eggs, dairying; limestone, sand; manufacture of rayon, electronic equipment, steel, manufacture of farm machinery.

MONROE *Stroudsburg* • 138,687 (45% increase since 1990; the second fastest growing county in PA) • 607 • Eastern PA, bounded on the east by the Delaware River, a National Scenic and Recreational River (forming the NJ state line), and on the northwest by the Lehigh River. The Pocono Mountains are in the west. Part of Delaware Water Gap National Recreation Area is in the northeast. The county also contains part of Delaware State Forest, and Gouldsboro, Tobyhanna, and Big Pocono state parks. The Appalachian Trail follows the southern boundary along the Kittatinny and Blue Mountain ridges. • One of seventeen counties named for President James Monroe • 1836 from Northampton and Pike • The first settlers to the county in 1725 worked in copper mines here. • Corn, wheat, oats, hay, alfalfa, cattle, dairying; resort area; light manufacturing; education (East Stroudsburg U. of PA).

MONTGOMERY (one of eighteen counties so named) *Norristown* • 750,097 (the third most populated county in PA) • 483 • Southeastern PA, bounded on the southeast by Philadelphia; drained by the Schuylkill River (which forms part of the southwest boundary in the west) and Perkiomen Creek (which forms Green Lane Reservoir in the north) and Pennypack Creek. The county is highly urbanized in the southeast and center, and rural in the northwest. It includes part of Valley Forge National Historical Park, and Evansburg and Fort Washington state parks. • One of sixteen counties named directly or indirectly for Gen. Richard Montgomery (1738–1775), Revolutionary War officer and hero • 1784 from Old Philadelphia • The county was first settled by Swedes and Welsh, and later by Germans. The Coventry forge at Pottstown produced the first commercial steel in PA in 1732. The county was the site of the frigid crucible of Valley Forge (partly in Chester County), the Continental Army's encampment during the winter of 1777–78. Canalization of the Schuylkill and Delaware rivers and completion of a railroad link in 1834 to Philadelphia spurred Norristown's development as an industrial center. • Dancer and choreographer William Dollar; minister Washington Gladden; baseball player Reggie Jackson; Librarian of Congress James Billington; preacher Jacob Albright; army officers Winfield S. Hancock and John R. Brooke • Corn, wheat, barley, hay, alfalfa, soybeans, hogs, cattle, dairying; sand and gravel, limestone; manufacture of iron, steel, zinc and aluminum die casting, chemicals, tires, plastics, textiles, cement, pipe fittings; education (Bryn Mawr College; Rosemount College; Penn. State U.; Abington College; others) • Mill Grove, home of artist-ornithologist John James Audubon, has been developed as a wildlife sanctuary. The county is headquarters to six Fortune 1000 companies.

MONTOUR *Danville* • 18,236 • 131 (the smallest county in PA and one of the fifty smallest counties in the U.S.) • Central PA; drained by the Susquehanna River (forming part of its southeast boundary) and Chillisquaque Creek. Lake Chillisquaque reservoir in the Montour Preserve is in the north. The Muncy Hills are in the north, Montour Ridge in the south • Named for either the Montour Mountain Ridge, or for Madame Montour (c. 1684 –1754), an early PA settler and Indian interpreter who dissuaded the Iroquois from attacking the white settlers. • 1850 from Columbia • Corn, wheat, oats, barley, alfalfa, soybeans, sheep, hogs, cattle, poultry, dairying; limestone; manufacturing.

NORTHAMPTON (one of three counties so named) *Easton* • 267,066 • 374 • Eastern PA, bounded on the east by the Delaware River (forming the NJ state line), on the west by the Lehigh River, and on the north by the Blue Mountain and Kittatinny Mountain ridges. The Appalachian Trail follows the county's northern boundary. A small part of Delaware Water Gap National Recreation Area is here. The county also includes Jacobsburg Environmental Education Center. • Named for Northamptonshire, England, home of Thomas Penn's father-in-law, Lord Pomfret • 1752 from Bucks • During the French and Indian Wars, Easton was the scene of several Indian peace councils. It was an outpost during the American Revolution. Wounded colonial soldiers during the war were treated in Bethlehem's old Colonial Hall. The Sun Inn was temporary refuge for members of the Continental Congress. Nazareth was a closed community of Moravians from 1740 to 1865. Adherents to the tenets of Christian socialism, the group was noted for its contributions to education and religious work among the Indians. One of the first pumped waterworks in North America started operations in Bethlehem on June 27, 1755. Bethlehem became a station on the Lehigh Valley Railroad in 1855. • Psychologist James M. Cattell; jurist Joseph Crater; gun maker Henry Deringer; surgeon Samuel D. Gross; lexicographer Francis A. March; army officer Peyton C. March; novelist and poet Stephen Vincent Benét; poet Hilda Doolittle; Declaration of Independence signer George Taylor • Corn, wheat, oats, barley, hay, alfalfa, soybeans, potatoes, apples, sheep, hogs, cattle, poultry, dairying; manufacture of machinery, textiles, paper products, cement, guitars, knit goods, fabricated steel, transportation equipment, furniture, chemicals; slate quarrying; education (Lafayette College) • Easton is the home of Crayola crayons. The Easton Area Public Library has a flag made by the women of the city on the occasion of the reading of the Declaration of Independence on the "Great Square" on July 8, 1776. Bethlehem has enjoyed a national reputation as a music center for over 100 years; the first performance in the U.S. of J.S. Bach's *The Passion According to St. John* was given in 1888. There is a Bach festival here every May. Bethlehem's Christmas festivities include many Moravian traditions.

NORTHUMBERLAND *Sunbury* • 94,556 • 460 • East-central PA, bounded on the southwest by the Susquehanna River, on the northwest by its West Branch, and on the south in part by Mahantango Creek. The Appalachian Mountains run along the county's southern border. Milton and (part of) Shikellamy state parks are also here. • One of two counties (the other in VA) named for Northumberland County in England • 1772 from Lancaster, Bedford, Berks, Northampton, and Cumberland • The world's first three-wire central electric lighting station was put into operation by Thomas Edison in Sunbury in July, 1883. • Indian leader James Logan; electrical engineer Daniel M. Moore. Showman Earl Carroll died here. • Corn, wheat, oats, barley, alfalfa, vegetables, soybeans, potatoes, apples, poultry, sheep, hogs, cattle, dairying; manufacture of textiles, clothing, metal products, machine tools, construction materials; coal mining.

PERRY *New Bloomfield* • 43,602 • 553 • South-central PA, bounded on the east by the Susquehanna River, on the north by the Tuscarora Mountain Ridge, and on the south by the Blue Mountain Ridge; drained by the Juniata River and Sherman Creek. The Appalachian Trail passes through the southeast. The county contains several natural areas, Big Spring, Little Buffalo, and Fowlers Hollow state parks, and parts of Tuscarora State Forest. • One of ten counties named for Oliver Hazard Perry (1785–1819), U.S. Naval officer during the War of 1812 • 1820 from Cumberland • Corn, hay, alfalfa, soybeans, poultry, cattle, dairying; limestone quarrying; some manufacturing.

PHILADELPHIA *Philadelphia* • 1,517,550 (the most populated county in PA and the eighteenth most populated county in the U.S.) • 135 (one of the fifty smallest counties in the U.S.) • The county is coterminous with the city of Philadelphia. (The two were merged in 1854.) It is bounded on the east and south by the NJ state line, formed by the Delaware River; and on the east in part by the Schuylkill River and Cobbs Creek. Pennypack Park flanks Pennypack Creek in the north; the Schuylkill River and its tributary Wissahickon Creek are flanked by Fairmount Park in the east. • Named for the city, itself named by William Penn perhaps for Philadelphia, seat of one of the seven early Christian churches • 1682 (original county) • Philadelphia is the birthplace of the United States. Independence National Historical Park, covering just a few square blocks, includes such historic sites as Carpenter's Hall, where the First Continental Congress convened; Independence Hall, where delegates adopted the Declaration of Independence and the Constitution; and Congress Hall, where both Washington and Adams took their presidential oaths of office. The city was the capital of the American colonies during most of the Revolutionary War, capital of the U.S. from 1790 until 1800, and capital of PA from 1683 to 1799. Swedes established the first settlement here in the 1640s. The city of Philadelphia was founded by English Quaker William Penn in 1682 as a center for religious freedom. (American Quakers still have their headquarters here.) During the early 1700s, Philadelphia became the leading industrial center and busiest port of the colonies. The Library Company of Philadelphia, established in 1731, was the nation's first circulating library. *The American Magazine*, published in 1741, was the first magazine in America. The city was captured by British troops on September 26, 1777 and held until June 18, 1778. In 1793, 5,000 Philadelphians died during a yellow fever epidemic. Founded in 1805, the Pennsylvania Academy of Fine Arts is the oldest art school in the U.S. Riots between native-born protestants and Roman Catholic immigrants left thirty dead in 1844. During the mid-1800s, the city was a center of the abolitionist movement. The 1876 Centennial Exposition was the nation's first successful world's fair. • Benjamin Franklin; seamstress Betsy Ross; photographer and filmmaker Man Ray; physician and political leader Benjamin Rush; contralto Marian Anderson; actors John, Lionel, and Ethel Barrymore; financier Nicholas Biddle; sculptor Alexander Calder; actor and singer Edwin Pearce Christy; poet Florence Coates; diplomat and politician George Mifflin Dallas; newspaperman Richard Harding Davis; painter and sculptor Thomas Eakins; entertainer W.C. Fields (whose epitaph reads, "I would rather be living in Philadelphia"); actors Edwin Forrest, Grace Kelly, and Joseph Jefferson; jazz musician Stan Getz; political leader Francis Hopkinson; cartoonist Walt Kelly; anthropologist Margaret Mead; army officer George B. McClellan; playwright Clifford Odets; politician Boies Penrose; astronomer David Rittenhouse; financiers Robert Morris and Haym Salomon; linguist and activist Noam Chomsky; abolitionist Lucretia Mott; banker Jay Cooke; comedian Bill Cosby • Finance; insurance; health care; manufacture of pharmaceuticals, clothing, industrial chemicals, pesticides, fabricated metal products; food processing; education (Philadelphia U.; La Salle U.; Gratz College; Temple U.; Drexel U.; U. of PA [the sixth oldest university in the U.S.]; Moore College of Art and Design; Curtis Institute of Music; Thomas Jefferson U.; St. Joseph's U.; other institutions of higher learning). The United States Mint here, the nation's largest, produces about $350 million worth of coins each year. • The corporate headquarters for eleven Fortune 1000 companies are located in the county. The Liberty Bell, Philadelphia's most visited site, rang for the last time on Washington's birthday in 1846. The statue of William Penn atop City Hall is the world's largest sculpture on the top of a building. Elfreth's Alley is the nation's oldest street of continuously occupied homes. The Walnut Street Theatre, the oldest active theatre in the U.S., staged its first production in 1809. Opened in 1857, the Academy of Music is the oldest U.S. opera house extant. The Academy of Natural Sciences, Franklin Institute (of science and technology), and the Pennsylvania Academy of Fine Arts were the nation's first museums of their kind. The Philadelphia Museum of Art has a collection of over 500,000 objects of art. 200 pieces by French sculptor Auguste Rodin are displayed in the Rodin Museum here. Philadelphia's New Year's Mummers' Parade attracts thousands to the city each year. Philadalphia is home to the Phillies and Eagles (Veteran's Stadium), Flyers and 76'ers (First Union Center).

PIKE *Milford* • 46,302 (66% increase since 1990; the fastest growing county in PA) • 547 • Northeastern PA, bounded on the northeast (NY state line) and on the southeast (NJ state line) by the Delaware River (designated here a National Scenic and Recreational River). Much of the county is covered by sections of Delaware State Forest. There are numerous small reservoirs and ponds found throughout. Part of Delaware Water Gap National Recreation Area is here, as are Promised Land State Park, part of Tobyhanna State Park, and numerous natural areas. • One of ten counties named for Gen. Zebulon Montgomery Pike (1779–1813), U.S. army officer and discoverer of Pikes Peak, CO • 1814 from Wayne • Hay, cattle, dairying; timber; recreational tourism.

POTTER (one of three counties so named) *Coudersport* • 18,080 • 1,081 (the fifth largest county in PA) • Northern PA, bounded on the north by the NY state line. The source of the Allegheny River is in the county. Streams drain to the Gulf of Mexico by way of Allegheny River; to Chesapeake Bay by way of the Susquehanna River; and to the Gulf of St. Lawrence by way of the Genesee River. Parts of Susquehannock State Forest are in the south. More state parks are located in Potter than in any other county in PA. • Named for General James Potter (1729–89), hero of the Revolutionary War • 1804 from Lycoming • In 1911, the Austin Dam broke, resulting in 89 deaths and the near destruction of the towns of Austin and Costello. • Corn, oats, hay, alfalfa, potatoes, cattle, dairying; timber. Major league baseball bats are fabricated from Potter County trees.

SCHUYLKILL *Pottsville* • 150,336 • 779 • East-central PA; drained by the Schuylkill River. The Appalachian Trail follows the Blue Mountain Ridge along the southern border. Tuscarora and Locust Lake state parks are in the county. Parts of Weiser State Forest are here, as well. • Named for the Schuylkill River • 1811 from Berks and Northampton • Formerly an anthracite coal mining center (museum), Pottsville was the headquarters of the Molly Maguires, a secret miners' society that fought to improve mining conditions, often by employing violence. In 1877 in Pottsville, six society members were hung and a number handed down prison sentences for their activities. • Band leaders Jimmy and Tommy Dorsey; economist Gary S. Becker; novelist John Henry O'Hara (who used Pottsville as the model for Gibbsville in *Appointment in Samarra* and other works) • Corn, wheat, oats, hay, alfalfa, soybeans, potatoes, apples, chickens, hogs, cattle, dairying; anthracite coal, limestone; manufacture of textiles, aluminum, steel products, shoes; education (PA State U.; Schuylkill Campus of the Capital College).

SNYDER *Middleburg* • 37,546 • 331 • Central PA, bounded on the east by the Susquehanna River and on the south in part by the West Branch of Mahantango Creek; drained by Penns and Middle creeks. Jacks Mountain Ridge runs across the northwest. Parts of Bald Eagle State Forest, Shikellamy State Park, and Tall Timbers Natural Area are here. • Named for Simon Snyder (1759–1819), governor of PA • 1855 from Union • Corn, wheat, oats, hay, alfalfa, apples, poultry, cattle, eggs; manufacturing.

SOMERSET (one of four counties so named) *Somerset* • 80,023 • 1,075 • Southwestern PA, bounded on the south by the MD state line, on the southwest by the Youghiogheny River (forming Youghiogheny River Lake reservoir), and on the north in part by the Stonycreek River and Paint Creek; drained by the Casselman River. The Allegheny Mountains are in the east and Laurel Hill is situated along the western border. Mount Davis, at 3,213 feet, is the highest point in PA. The county includes part of Laurel Ridge State Park, and Laurel Hill and Kooser state parks. • Named for the town of Somerset, PA • 1795 from Bedford • Within the county is the site of the 9–11–2001 crash of terrorist-hijacked United Airlines Flight 93, and the Quecreek Mine from which nine miners were rescued on July 28, 2002. • Hotel proprietor Ellsworth M. Statler • Corn, wheat, oats, barley, hay, alfalfa, soybeans, potatoes, sheep, hogs, cattle, dairying; timber; bituminous coal, sand and gravel, limestone; manufacturing.

SULLIVAN (one of six counties so named) *Laporte* • 6,556 • 450 • Northeastern PA; drained by Loyalsock and Muncy creeks. North Mountain and part of Ricketts Glen State Park are in the southeast. Worlds End State Park is also here, as are parts of Wyoming State Forest, and Tamarack Run and Kettle Creek Gorge natural areas. • One of five counties named directly or indirectly for General John Sullivan (1740–95), Revolutionary War officer, member of the Continental Congress, and chief executive of NH • 1847 from Lycoming • Corn, oats, hay, alfalfa, cattle, dairying; anthracite-coal mining.

SUSQUEHANNA *Montrose* • 42,238 • 823 • Northeastern PA, bounded on the north by the NY state line; drained by the West Branch of Susquehanna River. The Lackawanna River rises in the east. The county also contains Salt Spring State Park and Elk Mountain ski area. • Named for the Susquehanna River • 1810 from Luzerne • Corn, oats, hay, alfalfa, hogs, cattle, dairying; some manufacturing.

TIOGA (one of two counties so named, the other in NY) *Wellsboro* • 41,373 • 1,134 (the fourth largest county in PA) • Northern PA, bounded on the north by the NY state line and on the southeastern corner by Lycoming Creek; drained by the Tioga and Cowanesque rivers and Pine Creek. Conwanesque Lake, Hammond, and Tioga reservoirs are here. The county also includes Leonard Harrison, Colton Point, and Hills Creek state parks, several natural areas, and the Grand Canyon of PA. Units of Tioga State Forest are found throughout the county. • Named for the Tioga River • 1804 from Lycoming • Manufacturing; bituminous coal, natural gas; corn, oats, hay, alfalfa, hogs, cattle, dairying; recreation; education (Mansfield U. of PA).

UNION (one of eighteen counties so named) *Lewisburg* • 41,624 • 317 • Central PA, bounded on the east by the West Branch of the Susquehanna River. Lewisburg Federal Penitentiary is in the east. Part of Allenwood Federal Prison Camp is also in the county. The forested western third of the county includes part of Tiadaghton State Forest, part of Bald Eagle State Forest, and several state parks and natural areas. • Named Union in support of the federal union of the states • 1813 from Northumberland • Military commander Tasker Howard Bliss • Corn, wheat, oats, hay, alfalfa, poultry, dairying; manufacturing; limestone; education (Bucknell U.).

VENANGO *Franklin* • 57,565 • 675 • Northwestern PA; drained by the Allegheny River (designated a National Recreational River). Clear Creek State Forest is in the southwest. • Named for either the Venango River (now called French Creek) or for the Indian village at its mouth • 1800 from Allegheny and Lycoming • Franklin was the site of three forts: Machault (French); Venango (British); and Franklin (American). Col. Edwin Drake drilled the world's first commercial oil well here in 1859, launching the modern oil age. (The Drake Well Museum is at the edge of Oil Creek State Park.) When a Franklin blacksmith named James Evans dug a well for water in 1860, he inadvertently produced PA's third oil gusher. Within two years the county had become the hub of an oil region producing more than two million barrels of oil a year. Oil City was a major shipping point for crude oil from the Oil Creek fields; at its high point between 1860 and 1870, riverboats were transporting millions of barrels to Pittsburgh. On June 5, 1892, Oil Creek flooded, wrecking many oil tanks and causing extensive damage. The Venango County oil boom lasted until 1900. • Writer Lee Wilson Dodd; oil magnate John D. Rockefeller. Presidential assassin John Wilkes Booth was owner of an early Franklin oil well. • Corn, hay, alfalfa, hogs, cattle, dairying; oil production, sandstone, natural gas; man-

ufacture of petroleum and gas products, oil-well equipment and supplies, steel products, lumber.

WARREN *Warren* • 43,863 • 883 • Northwestern PA, bounded on the north by the NY state line; drained by the Allegheny River (designated a National Recreational River), which forms Allegheny Reservoir in the northeast (extending into NY) behind Kinzua Dam; also drained by Conewango and Brokenstraw creeks. Chapman State Park and part of Allegheny National Forest are here. • One of fourteen counties named for General Joseph Warren (1741–1775) army officer in the Revolutionary War who died at Bunker Hill • 1800 from Allegheny and Lycoming • The county had a lumber boom in the mid 19th century, followed by an oil boom. • Seneca Indian leader Cornplanter • Oil wells and refineries; corn, oats, hay, alfalfa, potatoes, sheep, hogs, cattle, dairying; manufacture of metal products, oil-field equipment, furniture, plastics • Though heavily logged in the 1800s, the county has a vibrant second growth forest in Anders Run Natural Area that represents the best young stand of white pine and hemlock in western PA.

WASHINGTON *Washington* • 202,897 • 857 • Southwestern PA, bounded on the west by the WV state line and on the east by the Monongahela River. There is urbanization from the Pittsburgh metropolitan area in the northeast. Hillman State Park is here, as are several covered bridges. • One of thirty-one counties named for President George Washington (the first in the U.S. so named) • 1781 from Westmoreland • Indian chief Logan was driven from the area in 1774 by Lord Dunmore, governor of VA. Prior to the American Revolution the county lay at the center of a land dispute with VA. PA's claim was finally validated by the VA constitution of 1776. The county was also at the center of the Whiskey Rebellion (against an excise tax on distilled liquor) by David Bradford in 1794. From October 26 to 31, 1948, Donora was blanketed by a poisonous pollution cloud from the local Donora Zinc Works that killed twenty people and made an additional 5,000 ill. • Politician James G. Blaine • Corn, wheat, oats, barley, hay, alfalfa, apples, sheep, hogs, cattle, dairying; bituminous coal mining; manufacture of steel, glass, mining equipment, paper cartons, beverages, electrical transformers, fabricated metal products, pottery; education (Washington and Jefferson College; California U. of PA) • The Rock Shelter at Meadowcroft Museum of Rural Life, located near Avella, is the earliest documented habitation in the Western Hemisphere, estimated to have been visited by prehistoric man some 40,000 years ago. Each May, the National Road Festival celebrates the history of that early thoroughfare. Many county communities developed here along the road, now called US Route 40; cast iron mile markers are still visible along the route. The first crematory in the U.S. was built in Washington in 1876 by Francis Julius Le Moyne; public opinion of his endeavor was so negative that the building had to be constructed at night.

WAYNE (one of sixteen counties so named) *Honesdale* • 47,722 • 729 • Northeastern PA, bounded on the north and northeast by the NY state line (the northeast border formed by the Delaware River, designated here a National Scenic and Recreational River) and on the southeast in part by Wallenpaupack Creek (forming Lake Wallenpaupack reservoir); drained by the Lackawaxen River. The source of the Lehigh River is in the southwestern corner. Part of the Moosic Mountains lie in the west, part of the Poconos in the south. Undeveloped Prompton State Park is here. • One of fifteen counties named for Revolutionary War Gen. "Mad Anthony" Wayne (1745–1796), PA soldier and statesman • 1798 from Northampton • From 1828 to 1898, Honesdale was the major shipping point for coal carried from the Susquehanna Valley. In 1829, the first locomotive in the U.S. to run on rails, the "Stourbridge Lion" (now in the Smithsonian Institute), was tested between Carbondale to Honesdale, but proved too dangerous to operate. • Physicist Henry August Rowland • Corn, oats, hay, alfalfa, apples, sheep, hogs, cattle, dairying; manufacture of textiles, clothing, furniture; recreation.

WESTMORELAND *Greensburg* • 369,993 • 1,023 • Southwestern PA, bounded on the northeast by the Kiskiminetas and Conemaugh rivers, on the southwest by the Monongahela River, and on the northwest by the Allegheny River; drained by the Youghiogheny River (which forms part of its western border) and Loyalhanna Creek. Chestnut Ridge crosses the center of the county, paralleling Laurel Hill Ridge, which runs along its southeastern border. Urbanization has occurred in the west and central part of the county from the expansion of the Pittsburgh metropolitan area. The county includes numerous reservoirs, state parks, and a portion of Forbes State Forest. • One of two counties (the other in VA) named for the former county of Westmoreland in northwest England • 1773 (prior to statehood) from Bedford • Chief Pontiac was defeated here in 1764. The Revolutionary Rattlesnake Flag originated here in 1775. • Biochemist Christian B. Andinsen; professional football player George Blanda; soldier and politician John White Geary; newspaper proprietor William L. McLean • The county is known for its glass production. Jeannette is sometimes called the "Glass City" because it grew around the glassworks. Also, bituminous coal, iron, limestone, sand and gravel, oil, natural gas; manufacture of aluminum, steel, textiles, fabricated metals, clothing, ceramics, plastics, powerplant equipment, turbines and motors, lighting fixtures; corn, wheat, oats, hay, alfalfa, apples, sheep, hogs, cattle, eggs, dairy-

ing; education (U. of Pittsburgh at Greensburg); research and development centers.

WYOMING (one of three counties so named) *Tunkhannock* • 28,080 • 397 • Northeastern PA; drained by the Susquehanna River and Tunkhannock Creek. Part of Ricketts Glen State Park is in the extreme southwest. • Named for the Wyoming Valley, the northern extent of which is in the county • 1842 from Luzerne • During the last half of the 1700s, several battles between Indians and white settlers occurred here. • Professional baseball pitcher Christy Mathewson • Corn, oats, hay, alfalfa, cattle, dairying; timber; sand and gravel; some manufacturing.

YORK (one of five counties so named) *York* • 381,751 • 905 • Southern PA, bounded on the east by the Susquehanna River and on the south by the MD state line; drained by Conewago, Muddy, and Codorus creeks. The county is urbanized around York and in the northern tip near Harrisburg. It includes Samuel S. Lewis, Codorus (encompassing Lake Marburg reservoir), and Gifford Pinchot state parks. • Named for the town of York, PA • 1749 from Lancaster • York was the capital of the United States from September 30, 1777 to June 27, 1778. It was here that Congress passed the Articles of Confederation and issued the first national thanksgiving proclamation. The Conway Cabal's attempt to oust Gen. Washington was frustrated here by the Marquis de Lafayette's toast to Washington in General Gates' House. York was also the destination of a $1,500,000 silver loan sent from France in 1778. $10,000,000 in Continental money was issued from Benjamin Franklin's printing press here. When Confederate troops under General Jubal Early entered York on June 28, 1863, it became the largest community north of the Mason and Dixon Line to be occupied by Southern forces. • World War II general Jacob L. Devers; virologist J. Michael Bishop; viticulturist John Adlum; army officer William B. Franklin; engraver Christian Gobrecht; explorer and fur trader Andrew Henry; writer John L. Long • Corn, wheat, oats, barley, hay, alfalfa, soybeans, potatoes, grapes, apples, poultry, sheep, hogs, cattle, dairying; limestone; manufacture of refrigerating and air-conditioning equipment, turbines, farm and construction machinery, wire cloth, roofing materials, paper, furniture, textiles; education (York College of PA) • York is known for its markets operated mostly by Mennonite and Dunkard farm families.

RHODE ISLAND

Hope

County government in Rhode Island no longer exists. Counties remain as geographical units within the state but carry no additional functions.

BRISTOL (one of two counties so named, the other in MA) • no county seat • 50,648 (the least populated county in RI) • 25 (only Kalawao County in Hawaii is smaller) • Eastern RI, bounded on the southwest by Narragansett Bay, on the northeast by the MA state line, and on the southeast by Mount Hope Bay; drained by the Barrington, Warren and Kickamuit rivers. Colt and Haines Memorial state parks are here. • Named for Bristol, RI • 1746–47 from Newport • Bristol was an active center for privateering and the Triangular Trade in the 1700s. On October 7, 1775 and again on May 25, 1778, the city of Bristol was attacked by the British and partially destroyed. General Lafayette made his headquarters here during part of the Revolutionary War. The city was once an important whaling and shipbuilding center. • Indian chief Massasoit; Union general Ambrose E. Burnside; monologist Spaulding Gray. Nathanael G. Herreshoff and family built racing yachts in Bristol, including successful America's Cup defenders (marine museum). • Resorts, fishing; manufacture of textiles, plastic goods, food products, machinery, wire and cable, rubber products, luggage; shipbuilding and boat building; dairying, poultry, vegetables; education (Roger Williams U.) • Warren is known for its annual waterfront festival and clambakes.

KENT (one of five counties so named) • no county seat • 167,090 (the second most populated county in RI) • 170 • Western and central RI, bounded on the east by Narragansett Bay and on the west by the CT state line; drained by the Pawtuxet, Moosup, Flat, and Wood rivers. Several wildlife management areas are in the county. • One of two counties (the other in DE) named for Kent County, England. • 1750 from Washington County • The home of Governor William Greene served as capitol for the state during the Revolutionary War. The burning of the British revenue schooner *Gaspee* by RI patriots in 1772 is remembered each year through the Gaspee Day celebration. The voluntary militia, the Independent Company of Kentish Guards (still active), was formed under General James M. Varnum in 1774. • Revolutionary War general Nathanael Greene; Physicist and electrical engineer William A. Anthony • Manufacture of textiles, textile machinery, apparel, silverware, chemicals, food products, printing materials, jewelry; dairying, poultry, corn, potatoes, fruit, mushrooms; fisheries; lumbering; printing and publishing; tourism • Windmill Cottage in East Greenwich was the subject of a poem by Henry Wadsworth Longfellow. Warwick's Musical Theater is one of the largest arena theatres in the world.

NEWPORT • no county seat • 85,433 • 104 (one of the fifty smallest counties in the U.S.) • Southeastern RI, bounded on the east by the MA state line and on the south by the Rhode Island Sound (Atlantic Ocean). It includes Conanicut, Prudence and Rhode Islands (Aquidneck) on Narragansett Bay. The Naval Education and Training Center, and Naval Undersea Warfare Center Division Newport are here. The county has several state parks and wildlife management areas. • Named for Newport, RI • Original county; organized as Rhode Island County 1703; name changed 1729 • Newport and Portsmouth were founded in the 1630s by families from the Massachusetts Bay Colony seeking religious freedom. The Portsmouth Compact established democratic government in that settlement. The Battle of Almy's Pea Field was fought during King Philip's War on July 8, 1675, southwest of Tiverton Four Corners. The burning of the British ship *Liberty* in 1769 was one of the first acts of rebellion by the American colonists. Butts Hill Fort was the scene of a delaying action by colonial forces during the Battle of Rhode Island in 1778. In the colonial era Newport rivaled Boston and New York City as a shipping center and was later known as the summer home of the wealthy, who built palatial mansions that stand as architectural testaments to the nation's Gilded Age. (Perhaps the best known is the Breakers, built by Cornelius Vanderbilt II.) The city served as co-capital of the state with Providence from 1854 to 1900. • Naval captain Robert Gray; Irish philosopher George Berkeley. Architect Richard Morris Hunt, author and lecturer Julia Ward Howe, film director John Huston, poet and scholar Clement Clarke Moore, and geologist and scientific explorer Raphael W. Pumpelly died here. • Tourism; manufacture of textiles, rubber and aluminum products, electronic, computer and data-processing equipment, jewelry; fisheries; boat building and boat repair; education (Salve Regina U.) • The Touro Synagogue, built in 1763, is the oldest synagogue in the U.S. Newport Casino, which now houses the International Tennis Hall of Fame, was the site of the U.S. Tennis Championships from 1881 to 1915.

PROVIDENCE • no county seat • 621,602 (the most populated county in RI) • 413 • Northern RI, bounded on the west by the CT state line and on the north by the MA state line; drained by the Blackstone (here becoming the Seekonk), Providence, Woonasquatucket, Moshassuck, Pawtucket and Ten Mile river systems. The county contains several reservoirs, including Scituate, Smith and Sayles, and Pascoag. Several management areas are in the northwest. State parks are scattered throughout the county. • Named for Providence Plantations, founded by Roger Williams following his forced removal from Massachusetts for his religious beliefs • Original county; organized as the County of Providence Plantations in 1703; name modified 1729 • Roger Williams, who broke from the Massachusetts Puritans because of his liberal theology, established Providence in 1636 as the only haven for religious freedom in the American colonies (national memorial). In 1790, Samuel Slater built the first successful water-powered cotton mill in North America in Pawtucket. Cranston was an early textile center. Providence served as one of several capitals of RI from 1663 until 1900, when it became the state's only capital. • Songwriter and actor George M. Cohan; television journalist James McLaughlin; Writer Cormac McCarthy; Declaration of Independence signer Stephen Hopkins • Dairying, poultry, truck farming; gravel pits, limestone deposits; manufacture of textiles, plastics, rubber products, fiber glass, nuts and bolts, processed foods, pharmaceuticals, toys, scientific instruments, marine equipment, silverware, machinery, metal products, fire extinguishers, chemicals, jewelry (much of the world's costume jewelry is produced here); bleaching and dyeing plants; insurance; government offices; education (Brown U., chartered in 1764, one of the oldest colleges in the U.S.; Bryant College; RI College; Providence College; Johnson and Wales U.; RI School of Design); resort tourism; recreational fisheries. Cranston is the seat of several state adult and juvenile correction institutions. • The headquarters of five Fortune 1000 corporations are located in the county. Woonsocket has a strong Franco-American population, descendants of French Canadians who immigrated to work in the city's textile mills; French is still the second language of the city. The oldest Baptist church in the U.S. is in Providence; it was completed in 1775.

Only St. Peter's Basilica in Rome has a larger unsupported marble dome than the RI State House in Providence.

WASHINGTON • no county seat • 123,546 (12% increase since 1990; the fastest growing county in RI) • 333 • Southwestern RI, bounded on the west by the CT state line, on the south by Block Island Sound, and on the east by Narragansett Bay; drained by the Wood, Hunt, Queen and Pawcatuck rivers. There are resorts on Narragansett Bay, Block Island Sound, and on Block Island (with its high chalk cliffs). The county also contains Narragansett Indian Reservation, and several state parks, beaches, lakes and management areas. • One of thirty-one counties named for President George Washington • Incorporated as King's County 1729 from Newport; name changed in 1781 • King Philip's War all but ended in what is now South Kingston on December 19, 1675 in what was called the Great Swamp Fight. The county was once famous for its granite quarries. (Westerly granite is still used for fine monument work.) • Portrait painter Gilbert Stuart (birthplace); naval officers Matthew C. Perry and Oliver Hazard Perry • Resort tourism; manufacture of textiles, woolen goods, furniture, wood products, food products, fishlines, bleach and dye, printing presses, electronic equipment; printing; turf grass, nursery goods, potatoes, poultry; education (U of RI). • The county is commonly known as South County. The first quonset hut was built at the Quonset Point Naval Air Station near Davisville in 1941. The biennial Block Island Regatta is a popular event. Wickford contains more well-preserved 18th century houses than any other village its size in New England. Its Old Narragansett Church (1707) is the oldest Episcopal church in the North. Davisville has been the home of the Atlantic Seabees since 1942.

SOUTH CAROLINA

While I Breathe, I Hope

Each of South Carolina's forty-six counties has a government headed by a board of county commissioners, a county council or similar local board. County government agencies are often directed by professional administrators appointed by county councils. Officials in South Carolina counties include the auditor, clerk of court, county attorney, treasurer and sheriff.

ABBEVILLE *Abbeville* • 26,167 • 508 • Northwestern SC, bounded on the southwest by the Savannah River (forming Russell Lake reservoir and the GA state line) and on the northeast in part by the Saluda River. The county includes part of Sumter National Forest and Calhoun Falls State Recreation Area. • Named for the town of Abbeville, SC • 1785 from Ninety Six District. (In 1868, all districts were renamed counties.) • The city of Abbeville has been called the "Cradle and Grave of the Confederacy." It was here on November 22, 1860 that a secessionist meeting was held, and here on May 2, 1865 that the Confederate president Jefferson Davis held one of his last Cabinet meetings. • Political leader and U.S. vice president John C. Calhoun • Chickens, eggs, hogs, cattle, wheat, oats, soybeans hay, dairying; manufacture of textiles; education (Erskine College).

AIKEN *Aiken* • 142,552 • 1,073 (the fourth largest county in SC) • Southwestern SC, bounded on the southwest by the Savannah River (forming the GA state line) and on the northeast by the North Fork of the Edisto River; drained by the South Fork of the Edisto. Aiken State Recreation Area and Redcliffe State Historic Site are located here. Part of the U.S. Department of Energy Savannah River Site is in the south. • Named for the town of Aiken, SC • 1871 from Edgefield, Barnwell, Lexington, and Orangeburg • Confederate forces under General Joe Wheeler defeated General Hugh J. Kilpatrick's Union troops in Aiken's main street during the Civil War. Originally a health resort, Aiken became a popular winter colony for wealthy northern tourists, around the turn of the 20th century. The city was known for its equestrian sports. It experienced a boom with the building of the Savannah River Atomic Plant after 1950. • English polo player Thomas Hitchcock, Jr. • Chickens, eggs, hogs, cattle, corn, wheat, rye, oats, soybeans, sorghum, hay, cotton, peaches; manufacture of textiles, glass fiber, electrical equipment; cotton milling; kaolin mining; education (U. of SC–Aiken), resort tourism • Site of the Thoroughbred Hall of Fame, Aiken hosts the annual Aiken Triple Crown, which includes harness racing, trials and steeplechase.

ALLENDALE *Allendale* • 11,211 • 408 • Southern SC, bounded on the west by the Savannah River (forming the GA state line); drained by the Coosawhatchie River. • Named for the county seat • 1919 from Barnwell and Hampton • Hogs, cattle, watermelons, corn, wheat, rye, oats, soybeans, peanuts, cotton, peaches.

ANDERSON (one of five counties so named) *Anderson* • 165,740 • 718 • Northwestern SC, bounded on the southwest by the Tugaloo and Savannah rivers (forming Hartwell Lake reservoir and the GA state line) and on the northeast by the Saluda River; drained by the Seneca and Rocky rivers. Sadler Creek State Recreaton Area is located here. • Named for Col. Robert Anderson (1741–1813), a SC officer in the American Revolution and SC legislator • 1826 from Old Pendleton District, which was abolished at that time • Chickens, eggs, hogs, cattle, dairying, corn, wheat, oats, soybeans, market vegetables, sorghum, hay; manufacture of textiles, textile machinery, fiber glass, fishing tackle; tree farming; education (Anderson College) • One of the earliest cotton mills in the South, built in 1838 (and still operational) is in La France. Anderson is called the "Electric City" because it was among the first in the South to pull power from a local hydroelectric plant.

BAMBERG *Bamberg* • 16,658 • 393 • South-central SC, bounded on the northwest by the South Fork of the Edisto River and on the southwest by the Salkehatchie River; drained by the Little Salkehatchie River. Rivers Bridge State Historic Site is in the south. • Named for the town of Bamberg, SC • 1897 from Barnwell • Hogs, cattle, dairying, corn, wheat, soybeans, sorghum, hay, cotton, watermelons; education (Voorhees College).

BARNWELL *Barnwell* • 23,478 • 548 • Southern SC, bounded on the southwest by the Savannah River (forming the GA state line) and on the northeast by the South Fork of the Edisto River. The county includes most of the U.S. Department of Energy Savannah River Site, which contains Par Pond reservoir. Barnwell State Park is located here. • Probably named for brother legislators John and Robert (1761–1814) Barnwell; John served in the SC state legislature and Robert was U.S. representative from the state. • Organized as Winston District in 1798 from Orangeburg District • Chickens, eggs, hogs, cattle, dairying, corn, wheat, rye, oats, soybeans, peanuts, hay, cotton, watermelons, asparagus, cucumbers, peaches; naval stores.

BEAUFORT *Beaufort* • 120,937 (40% increase since 1990; the fastest growing county in SC) • 587 • Extreme southern SC, bounded on the northeast by the Combahee River and on the southwest by the New River. The county extends along the Atlantic coast from the New River to St. Helena Sound, and is crossed by the Intracoastal Waterway. It includes Port Royal (site of Beaufort), Parris, St. Helena, and Hilton Head sea islands. Hunting Island State Park, Victoria Bluff Heritage Preserve, and Pinckney Island National Wildlife Refuge are also here. • Named for the town of Beaufort, SC • Original county; organized 1768 or 1769 (prior to statehood) • The area now occupied by Beaufort County was first visited by Spaniards in the 1520s. In 1562, the French built Charlesfort on what is now Parris Island. The Spanish fort of San Felipe was constructed here in 1566 to guard Santa Elana, the capital of Spanish Florida. Beaufort was the site of a British post during the Revolutionary War. During the Civil War, Hilton Head housed 50,000 Union soldiers. Since 1915, tens of thousands of U.S. marines have been trained at the U.S. Marine Corps Recruit Depot on Parris Island. • Politician Robert B. Rhett; boxing champion Joe Frazier; African American naval hero and politician Robert Smalls. Journalist and author Samuel H. Adams died here. • Fishing, truck farming, corn, soybeans, tomatoes, cattle, hogs; lumbering; canning, seafood processing; manufacture of apparel; winter resort tourism • The South Atlantic Sailing Regatta is held each July during the Beaufort Water Festival.

BERKELEY (one of two counties so named, the other in WV) *Moncks Corner* • 142,651 • 1,100 (the third largest county in SC) • Southeastern SC, bounded on the northeast by the Santee River. Part of Lake Marion reservoir, formed by Santee Dam, is located on the northwest border; Pinopolis Dam on the Cooper River forms Lake Moultire. Francis Marion National Forest covers much of the county. A unit of Santee National Wildlife Refuge, and Guilliard Lake Scenic Area are also here. • Named for either John Berkeley (?–1678), one of eight original lords proprietor of Carolina, or for his brother Sir William Berkeley (1606–77), lord proprietor and governor of VA; some sources say the county was named for both • 1882 from Charleston • Limestone, sand, gravel, clay; timber; poultry, hogs, sheep, cattle, cotton, corn, wheat, oats, soybeans, tobacco, hay, dairy products.

CALHOUN *Saint Matthews* • 15,185 • 380 • Central SC, bounded on the north by the Congaree River and on the southeast by Lake Marion reservoir. • One of eleven counties named for John C. Calhoun (1782–1850), U.S. statesman and champion of Southern causes • 1908 from Lexington and Orangeburg • Sand, clay, kaolin; cattle, hogs, corn, wheat, rye, oats, soybeans, hay, cotton, pecans, vegetables.

CHARLESTON *Charleston* • 309,969 (the third most populated county in SC) • 917 • Southeastern SC, extending along the Atlantic Coast from the mouth of the South Edisto River (in the southwest) to the mouth of the Santee River (in the northeast). Much of the Intracoastal Waterway passes inland parallel to the coast. The county contains a number of sea islands, including Kiawah, Seabrook, Folly Beach, and Isle of Palms. Fort Sumter National Monument, Fort Moultrie, and Castle Pinckney National Monument are in Charleston Harbor. Part of Francis Marion National Forest is in the northeast. Also in the county are Edisto Beach State Park, Bird Key–Stono Heritage Preserve, Cape Romain National Wildlife Refuge, and Charleston Air Force Base. • Named for the city of Charleston • Original county; 1785 (prior to statehood) • Settlement of South Carolina began with the establishment of Charles Towne by English colonists in 1670 (state historic site). Moved to its present site on the eastern bank of the Ashley River, Charleston was an early commercial center of trade in rice and indigo. Prosperous plantations surrounded the city during the antebellum period. Fort Moultrie was the scene of one of the early defeats of the British in the Revolutionary War (June 28, 1776). The city was held by the British from 1780 to 1782. Charleston served as provincial and state capital from 1670 until 1790. Moultrie's sister Fort Sumter was captured by Confederates on April 12, 1861, a precipitant of the Civil War. The city was blockaded by Union land and sea forces from July 10, 1863 until February 18, 1865. In September, 1989, the county was heavily damaged by Hurricane Hugo. • Politicians Charles Rutledge and James F. Byrnes; diplomat and railroad president James Gadsden; physician John Gorrie; poet and literary leader Hamilton Hayne; novelist and dramatist DuBose Heyward; statesman Henry Laurens; statesmen Charles Pinckney, Charles Cotesworth Pinckney, and Thomas Pinckney. Indian leader Osceola and publisher Joseph Pulitzer died here. • Shipping and diversified manufacturing, including paper and pulp products, metal products, molded rubber products, cigars, clothing; oil refining; shipbuilding; seafood; sweet potatoes, corn, vegetables, hogs, cattle; fisheries, hunting; education (The Citadel; College of Charleston [the nation's first municipal college]; Charleston Southern U.); tourism • Founded in 1773, the Charleston Museum is the oldest museum in the nation. The first musical society in America, the St. Cecilia Society, was established in here in 1762. The Fireproof Building, completed in Charleston in 1826, was the first building of fireproof construction in the U.S. The reformed branch of Judaism in America originated in Charleston with the Reformed Society of Israelites. Established in 1741,

Middleton Place Gardens are the nation's oldest landscaped gardens.

CHEROKEE *Gaffney* • 52,537 • 393 • Northern SC, bounded on the north by the NC state line and on the south by the Pacolet River; drained by the Broad River. Part of Kings Mountain National Military Park is here. • One of eight counties named for the Cherokee Indian tribe. • 1897 from Union, Spartanburg, and York • Brigadier General Daniel Morgan won a decisive Revolutionary War victory over British Lieutenant Colonel Banastre Tarleton at the Battle of Cowpens here on January 17, 1781 (national battlefield site). Gaffney developed in the 1800s as a resort catering to plantation owners seeking therapeutic treatment at local limestone springs. • Author W. J. Cash • Cotton, grain, wheat, soybeans, hay, peaches, turkeys, hogs, dairying; limestone, shale, clay; textile milling, metal working, screen printing; education (Limestone College).

CHESTER (one of three counties so named) *Chester* • 34,068 • 581 • Northern SC, bounded on the west by the Broad River and on the east by the Catawba River, forming Fishing Creek Reservoir. The county includes part of Sumter National Forest along the western border. Chester and Landsford Canal state parks are also located here. • Named for Chester County, Pennsylvania • 1785 from Camden District • Chickens, eggs, turkeys, hogs, cattle, dairying, corn, wheat, sorghum, hay; flour mills, manufacture of textiles.

CHESTERFIELD *Chesterfield* • 42,768 • 799 • Northern SC, bounded on the east by the Pee Dee River, on the west by the Lynches River, on the north by the NC state line. The county includes Cheraw State Recreation Area, Carolina Sandhills National Wildlife Refuge and Sandhills State Forest. • One of two counties (the other in VA) named for Philip Dormer Stanhope (1694–1773), 4th earl of Chesterfield, English statesman and writer • 1785 from Cheraws District • Trumpeter Dizzie Gillespie • Gold, silver, shale, granite, sand, gravel, clay; chickens, eggs, turkeys, hogs, cattle, corn, wheat, rye, tobacco, hay, watermelons, peaches; manufacturing.

CLARENDON *Manning* • 32,502 • 607 • East-central SC, bounded on the south by the Santee River (forming Lake Marion reservoir); drained by the Black and Pocotaligo rivers. Several units of Santee National Wildlife Refuge are located on Lake Marion. Bennett's Bay Heritage Preserve and Woods Bay State Recreation Area are also here. • Named for Edward Hyde (1609–1674), first earl of Clarendon and one of the original eight lords proprietor of Carolina • 1785; organized 1855 from Sumter District • Chickens, eggs, cattle, corn, wheat, rye, tobacco, soybeans, hay, cotton; timber

COLLETON *Walterboro* • 38,264 • 1,056 (the fifth largest county in SC) • Southern SC, bounded on the southeast by the Edisto river, on the west by the Combahee and Salkehatchie rivers, and on the south by St. Helena Sound. The South Edisto River and St. Helena Sound comprise part of the Intracoastal Waterway. One unit of Ace Basin National

Wildlife Refuge and St. Helena Sound Heritage Preserve are located here. • Named for Sir John Colleton (1608–1666), one of the original eight lords proprietor of Carolina • 1795; organized in 1798 from part of the Province of Carolina • Tobacco, hay, watermelons, cotton, truck crops, poultry, eggs, dairy cattle, hogs; manufacture of baskets, laminated plywood boxes, asbestos drier felts, dresses; meatpacking; sawmilling; peat; sand and clay; timber; hunting and fishing, tourism.

DARLINGTON *Darlington* • 67,394 • 562 • Northeastern SC, bounded on the northeast by the Great Pee Dee River. Part of Lake Robinson reservoir is here. • Named for either Darlington, Durham, England, or for a Colonel Darlington in the Revolutionary War • 1785 from Cheraws District • Cattle, dairying, hogs, tobacco, wheat, rye, oats, soybeans, hay, corn; pedigreed seeds; timber; manufacture of electronics, textiles, paper, plastics, steel; education (Coker College). Coker Experimental Seed Farms was designated a national historic landmark in 1964. • Darlington has a large automobile auction market. It is also the home of the Stock Car Hall of Fame and the Darlington Raceway, site of the Rebel 500 and the Southern 500. Kalmia Gardens displays trees and shrubs native to SC.

DILLON *Dillon* • 30,722 • 405 • Northeastern SC, bounded on the northeast by the NC state line, on the extreme southwest by the Pee Dee River, and on the extreme southeast by the Lumber River; drained by the Little Pee Dee River. Little Pee Dee State Park is here. • Named for the county seat • 1910 from Marion • Hogs, cattle, corn, rye, soybeans, hay, cotton.

DORCHESTER (one of two counties so named, the other in MD) *Saint George* • 96,413 • 575 • Southern SC, bounded on the south by the Edisto River. The county includes Old Fort Dorchester State Historic Site (which contains the ruins of Saint George's Parish Church), Givhans Ferry and Colleton state parks. • Named for the town in SC, itself named for Dorchester, MA, former home of the town founders • 1897 from Colleton and Berkeley • The county had many popular health resorts from the early 18th through the mid 20th centuries. • Corn, soybeans, hogs, cattle; timber; manufacture of polypropylene fabric, fuel injectors, portland cement, office supplies, food casings.

EDGEFIELD *Edgefield* • 24,595 (34% increase since 1990; the third fastest growing county in SC) • 502 • Western SC, bounded on the southwest by the Savannah River, forming the GA state line; drained by the South Fork of the Edisto River. The county includes part of Sumter National Forest. • Its name is descriptive of its location on the edge of an Indian battlefield or possibly because it borders the state of GA • 1785 from Ninety Six District. (In 1868, all districts were renamed counties.) • Senator Strom Thurmond; populist politician Benjamin R. Tillman; Confederate officer James Longstreet • Cotton, peaches, chickens, eggs, hogs, cattle, dairying, corn, wheat, rye, oats, soybeans, sorghum, hay; manufacture of textiles.

FAIRFIELD (one of three counties so named) *Winnsboro* • 23,454 • 687 • North-central SC, bounded on the west by the Broad River and on the east by the Catawba River (forming Lake Wateree reservoir). Lake Wateree State Recreation Area and Monticello Reservoir are located here. The county includes part of Sumter National Forest. • The derivation of the county's name is in doubt. Many guesses abound, most having to do with exclamations and pronouncements of its beauty. • 1785 from Camden District • Gold, silver, sand, clay, granite; cattle, corn, hay, cotton; timber • The South Carolina Railroad Museum is located near Winnsboro.

FLORENCE (one of two counties so named, the other in WI) *Florence* • 125,761 • 799 • East-central SC, bounded on the east by the Pee Dee River; drained by the Lynches River (forming part of the southwest border). • Named for the town of Florence, SC • 1888 from Marion, Darlington, Williamsburg, and Clarendon • During the Civil War, Union soldiers were imprisoned south of Florence city; many died of typhoid fever during their incarceration. • Stock-car racing driver Cale Yarborough; Poet laureate of the Confederacy Henry Timrod (his one-room school is in Timrod Park) • Sand and clay; chickens, hogs, corn, wheat, rye, oats, tobacco, pecans, soybeans, sorghum, hay, cotton, vegetables; timber; manufacture of film, electronic components, fabricated steel, welding equipment, furniture, textiles, paper; railroad shops; research and education (Florence-Darlington Technical College; Francis Marion U.; Clemson U.–Pee Dee Experiment Station; U.S. Dept. of Agriculture Boll Weevil Laboratory • A National Civil War Cemetery is near Florence. The Air and Missile Museum is at the Florence Airport.

GEORGETOWN *Georgetown* • 55,797 • 815 • Eastern SC, bounded on the east by the Atlantic Ocean, on the northeast by the Pee Dee River, and on the south by the Santee River; watered by the Waccamaw, Great Pee Dee, Sampit and Black rivers. Tom Yawkey Wildlife Center and Huntington Beach State Park are on the coast. The Intracoastal Waterway crosses along the Waccamaw River • Named for the county seat • Original county; organized 1769 (prior to statehood) • The Spanish settled here in 1526 but abandoned the site because of fever. The first English settlement was made around 1700. The county was formerly the site of sizeable plantations. The Marquis de Lafayette first landed on American soil on June 13, 1777 at North Island. Georgetown was occupied by the British during the Revolutionary War and was attacked several times by American "Swamp Fox" Francis Marion. • First black U.S. representative Joseph H. Rainey • Timber, naval supplies; cattle, corn, rice, indigo, wheat, tobacco, hay; fishing; tourism; sand, clay and limestone; manufacture of paper and pulp; tourism (yachting, fishing). Georgetown's harbor, on the Intracoastal Waterway, has been developed as a deepwater port. • Brookgreen Gardens offers more than 400 pieces of sculpture in the gardens of a former rice and indigo plantation.

GREENVILLE *Greenville* • 379,616 (the most populated county in SC) • 792 • Northwestern SC, bounded on the north by the NC state line and on the west by the Saluda River; drained by the Enoree and Reedy rivers. Part of the Blue Ridge Mountains are in the north. Paris Mountain, Table Rock, Jones Gap and Caesar's Head state parks are located here. • Named for either Revolutionary War general Nathanael Greene (1742–1786); Isaac Green (1762–?), operator of a local mill; or for the verdant appearance of the countryside. • 1786 from Ninety Six District. (In 1868, all districts were renamed counties.) • Greenville strongly opposed nullification in 1832 and secession of SC from the Union in 1860. Editor and later state governor Benjamin F. Perry was prominent among the city's Unionists. • Civil rights leader Jesse Jackson; physicist Charles H. Townes. Detective fiction writer John Dickson Carr died here. • Dairying, hogs, cattle, eggs, tomatoes, corn, wheat, soybeans, sorghum, hay, peaches; granite, sand and gravel; education (Bob Jones U.; Furman U., North Greenville College); manufacture of chemicals, plastic film, machinery, fabricated metals, electronics, aircraft, cotton textiles. Greenville is the site of the biennial Southern Textile Exposition and American Textile Machinery Exhibition-International. The Shriner's Hospital for Crippled Children is in Greenville. • Bob Jones U. has a museum and gallery devoted to religious art. Greenville holds a major arts festival every other year.

GREENWOOD (one of two counties so named, the other in KS) *Greenwood* • 66,271 • 456 • Western SC, bounded on the northeast by the Saluda River, dammed in the southeast by Buzzard Roost Dam to form Lake Greenwood reservoir. The county includes part of Sumter National Forest and Lake Greenwood Recreation Area. • Named for the county seat • 1897 from Abbeville and Edgefield • Ninety Six (national historic site) was a British stronghold during the Revolutionary War and the scene of Nathanael Greene's siege in 1781. Five different railroads converged on Greenwood in the mid-1800s to make it a transportation center. • Shale, sand and granite; cotton, corn, fruit, lespedeza hay, grains, dairying; cotton and synthetic-fiber mills, food processing, meat packing; manufacture of textiles, surgical dressings, garments, wood products, bricks and tiles, tools, mops and handles; education (Lander U.).

HAMPTON *Hampton* • 21,386 • 560 • Southern SC, bounded on the southwest by the Savannah River (forming the GA state line) and on the northeast by the Salkehatchie River; drained by the Coosawhatchie River. Lake Warren State Park is located here. • Named for General Wade Hampton (1818–1902), first post-Reconstruction governor of SC and senator from the state • 1878 from Old Beaufort • Timber; hogs, cattle, corn, wheat, soybeans, peanuts, cotton, watermelons, peaches.

HORRY *Conway* • 196,629 (36% increase since 1990; the second fastest growing county in SC) • 1,134 (the largest county in SC) • Eastern SC, bounded on the west and northwest by the Little Pee Dee River, on the southeast by the Atlantic Ocean, on the northeast by the NC state line, and on the southwest by the Great Pee Dee River; drained by the Wac-

camaw River. The Intracoastal Waterway canal crosses near the coast. Most of the Grand Strand, which stretches from the NC border to Pawleys Island, is in Horry County. Myrtle Beach State Park, and Waccamaw River, Little Pee Dee River, Ervin Dargan, and Cartwheel Bay heritage preserves are located in the county. • Named for Peter Horry, officer in the Revolutionary War and prominent citizen. The county has been referred to by residents as "The Independent Republic of Horry." • 1801 from All Saints Parish • Timber, lumber mills, woodworking plants; tobacco, melons, truck crops, cotton, corn, hogs, cattle, soybeans, oats, wheat; hunting and fishing, resort tourism; education (Coastal Carolina U., Clemson U.–Experiment Station).

JASPER *Ridgeland* • 20,678 • 654 • Extreme southern SC, bounded on the west by the Savannah River (forming the GA border), on the northeast by the Coosawhatchie River, and on the southeast by the New River. Sergeant Jasper State Park, Tillman Sand Ridge Heritage Preserve, and Savannah National Wildlife Refuge are all located here. • One of eight counties named for Sergeant William Jasper (?–1779), heroic American Revolutionary War soldier. • 1912 from Beaufort and Hampton • Cattle, hogs, wheat, soybeans, hay, corn.

KERSHAW *Camden* • 52,647 • 726 • North-central SC, bounded on the east by the Lynches River. The county contains Lake Wateree reservoir and the Wateree River. Savage Bay Heritage Preserve and N.R. Goodale State Park are located here. • Named for Col. Joseph Kershaw, SC army officer during the Revolutionary War and a founding settler of Camden • 1791 from old Craven County • Camden is the oldest inland city in the state. A principal British garrison, it was the site of the August 16, 1780 Battle of Camden, one of the most crushing defeats ever inflicted upon an American army, as forces under American general Horatio Gates were nearly wiped out by troops under Lord Cornwallis. The British halted a second attack on Camden by General Nathanael Green on April 25, 1781 at Hobkirk's Hill. During the Civil War the city served as a Confederate supply base. It was occupied and burned by General Sherman's troops in February, 1865. • Financier Bernard Baruch; labor leader Lane Kirkland. Continental Army officer Johann de Kalb died here. • Peaches, pecans, sweet potatoes, poultry, cattle, corn, rye, hay, cotton; timber; mica, granite, sand, kaolin; manufacture of clothing, chemicals, textile fibers, watches, building stone, lumber products, fabricated steel equipment, cement blocks. • An equestrian sport center, Camden is the site of the Springdale Course, the scene of the annual Caroline Cup and International Colonial Cup steeplechases.

LANCASTER (one of four counties so named) *Lancaster* • 61,351 • 549 • Northern SC, bounded on the west by the Catawba River, on the north by the NC state line, and on the east by the Lynches River. The county includes Fishing Creek and part of Lake Wateree reservoirs. Forty Acre Rock Heritage Preserve is in the east. • Named for the county and city of Lancaster, PA, at the suggestion of settlers from there • 1785 from

Camden District • Lancaster was identified with the Waxhaw Revival, which was part of the Great Revival. Witchcraft was once legally recognized here. • President Andrew Jackson was born in the Waxhaw Settlement on the NC and SC state line; Jackson believed that he was born on the SC side (Andrew Jackson State Park). • Mica, clay, sand, shale, gold, silver; corn, wheat, oats, hay, soybeans, turkeys, cattle; timber; light manufacturing; education (the U. of SC at Lancaster).

LAURENS (one of two counties so named, the other in GA) *Laurens* • 69,567 • 713 • Northwest-central SC, bounded on the southwest by the Saluda River and on the northeast by the Enoree River. Part of Lake Greenwood reservoir is in the south. The county also contains part of Sumter National Forest. • Named for Henry Laurens (1724–92), president of the Continental Congress • 1785 from Ninety Six District (In 1868, all districts were renamed counties.) • President Andrew Johnson (who served as a tailor's apprentice in Laurens in 1824) • Granite, sand, vermiculite; chickens, hogs, cattle, eggs, dairying, corn, wheat, rye, soybeans, sorghum, hay; manufacture of rayon, draperies, clothing, bottles, jars, and other ceramics, trailers; education (Presbyterian College).

LEE (one of twelve counties so named) *Bishopville* • 20,119 • 410 • Northeast-central SC; drained by the Black and Lynches rivers (the latter forming part of the southeastern boundary). The State Penitentiary, Lynchburg Savanna Heritage Preserve, and Lee State Natural Area are here. • One of eight counties named for Robert E. Lee (1807–70), commander of the Confederate forces during the Civil War • 1902 from Darlington, Sumter, and Kershaw • Clay, sand; cotton, peanuts, corn, oats, soybeans, hay, hogs, cattle; timber.

LEXINGTON *Lexington* • 216,014 (the fifth most populated county in SC) • 701 • Central SC, bounded on the southeast by the Congaree River, on the northeast in part by the Saluda River, and on the southwest by the North Fork of the Edisto River; drained by the Saluda River (dammed to form Lake Murray reservoir) in the north. The county is highly urbanized in the east. • Named for the Battle of Lexington, MA, the first conflict in the Revolutionary War • 1785 from Orangeburg District • The Cayce house, built in 1765, was a stronghold for both sides in the American Revolution. • Chickens, hogs, dairying, vegetables, corn, wheat, rye, oats, soybeans, hay, peaches; sand, granite, kaolin; manufacture of cement blocks, crushed granite, processed silica, fabricated steel, iron and brass foundry products, chemicals, plastics, lumber, caskets, dolls, packed meats, salad dressing, jellies, candy.

MARION *Marion* • 35,466 • 489 • Eastern SC, bounded on the west by the Pee Dee River and on the east by the Little Pee Dee River. The rivers join at the southeastern tip of the county to form the Great Pee Dee River. • One of seventeen counties named for the "Swamp Fox," Revolutionary War Gen. Francis Marion (?–1795) • Created as Liberty County in 1785; name changed in 1798, effective in 1800 • Sand, clay; tobacco, corn, oats, sorghum, hay, hogs, cattle.

MARLBORO *Bennettsville* • 28,818 • 480 • Northeastern SC, bounded on the north and northeast by the NC state line and on the southwest by the Pee Dee River. • Named for John Churchill (1650–1722), Duke of Marlborough • 1785 from Cheraws District • Children's rights advocate Marian Wright Edelman • Sand and gravel, clay; hogs, corn, peaches, rye, oats, tobacco, soybeans, hay, cotton, vegetables; some timber; manufacture of yarn and tire fabric, kitchen cabinets, electrical equipment.

MCCORMICK *McCormick* • 9,958 (the least populated county in SC) • 360 (the smallest county in SC) • Western SC, bounded on the southwest by the Savannah River (forming J. Strom Thurmond Lake reservoir and the GA state line). Much of the county is covered by part of Sumter National Forest. Baker Creek State Park and Hamilton Branch State Recreation Area are located in the county, as is Stevens Creek Heritage Preserve. • Named for Cyrus H. McCormick (1809–84), inventor of farm implements and local landowner • 1916 from Edgefield, Greenwood, and Abbeville • Chickens, cattle, hay; timber; textile milling.

NEWBERRY *Newberry* • 36,108 • 631 • Northwest-central SC, bounded on the east by the Broad River, on the south by the Saluda River, and on the north in part by the Enoree River. Part of Lake Murray reservoir is in the southeast. The county contains part of Sumter National Forest, which includes the Broad River Scenic Area. • The derivation of the county's name is uncertain. • 1785 from Ninety Six District • Chickens, turkeys, hogs, cattle, eggs, corn, oats, soybeans, sorghum, hay; timber; granite; manufacturing; education (Newberry College).

OCONEE (one of two counties so named, the other in GA) *Walhalla* • 66,215 • 625 • Extreme northwestern SC, bounded on the northwest by the Chattooga River (designated a National Wild, Scenic and Recreational River, and forming the GA and NC state lines), on the southwest by Tugaloo and Hartwell lakes (both forming the GA state line), and on the east by Lake Keowee and Lake Jocassee reservoirs. The Blue Ridge Mountains (a summer resort area) are found here. Part of Sumter National Forest is here as well. Buzzard Roost and Brasstown Creek heritage preserves, Oconee Station State Historic Site, Devils Fork and Oconee state parks, and Lake Hartwell State Recreation Area are also here. • Named for one of the following: the Oconee Indian tribe, the GA county by this name, or the Oconee River. • 1868 from Pickens • Chickens, eggs, hogs, cattle, dairying, corn, wheat, soybeans, sorghum, hay, apples.

ORANGEBURG *Orangeburg* • 91,582 • 1,106 (second largest county in SC) • South-central SC, bounded on the southwest by the South Fork of the Edisto River and on the northeast by Lake Marion reservoir; drained by the North Fork of the Edisto. The county includes Santee State Park. • Named for the city of Orangeburg, SC • Original district; organized 1769 (prior to statehood) • Orangeburg was established in 1735 by

German, Swiss, and Dutch settlers. The Donald Bruce House on Middlepen Plantation served as the headquarters for Governor John Rutledge, General William Moultrie, and Lord Rawdon during the Revolutionary War. • A leading agricultural county in the South: poultry, hogs, cattle, corn, wheat, rye, tobacco, sorghum, peanuts, pecans, cotton, watermelons, peaches; also sand, clay, limestone; manufacture of textiles, wood products, tools, asphalt, chemicals, cement, concrete, food products, lumber; printing and publishing; education (Claflin University, SC State U.) • The Edisto Memorial Gardens have test sections associated with the American Rose and Camellia societies. Twenty acres of ponds make up the Orangeburg National Fish Hatchery.

PICKENS *Pickens* • 110,757 • 497 • Northwestern SC, bounded on the east by the Saluda River, on the west by Lake Keowee and Lake Jocassee reservoirs (Keowee and Seneca rivers), and on the north by the NC state line. The highest point in the state is Sassafras Mountain (3,560 feet), in the Blue Ridge Mountains in the north. Table Rock State Park and Keowee-Toxaway State Natural Area are here, as are Glassy Mountain Heritage Preserve and part of Sumter National Forest. • One of three counties named for Gen. Andrew Pickens (1739–1817), Revolutionary War hero and U.S. representative from SC • 1826 from Pendleton District, which was abolished at that time • Political leader and vice president John C. Calhoun (Fort Hill home and plantation here) • A summer-resort area; also manufacture of textiles; limestone, granite and sand quarries; cotton, corn, poultry; timber; education (Clemson U., Southern Wesleyan U.).

RICHLAND (one of seven counties so named) *Columbia* • 320,677 (the second most populated county in SC) • 757 • Central SC, bounded on the southwest in part by the Congaree River and on the east by the Wateree River; drained by the Broad River. Part of Lake Murray reservoir is in the west. The county is also the site of Fort Jackson Military Reservation, established during World War I. Congaree Swamp National Monument in the south represents the last significant tract of virgin Southern bottomland hardwoods in the southeastern U.S. • The county's name is possibly descriptive of the fertile farmland along its rivers • 1799 (An earlier county by this name was abolished.) • The move of the state capital from Charleston to Columbia in 1790 resulted in a compromise between Up Country farmers and Low Country plantation owners. A Confederate transportation center and government center, Columbia was occupied and burned by Union troops in 1865. • Philosopher and theoretical psychologist James M. Baldwin; director and choreographer Stanley Donen; President Woodrow Wilson. Politician James F. Byrnes and poet and novelist James Dickey died here. • Eggs, hogs, cattle, cotton, peaches, tobacco, corn, oats, hay; sand, clay, shale, granite, kaolin; manufacture of synthetic fibers, textiles, structural steel, aerospace products; education (U. of SC; Columbia International U.; Columbia College; Benedict College; Allen U.) • The Columbia Museum of Art and Science houses a collection of Italian Renaissance paintings. Columbia is the headquarters for Francis Marion and Sumter national forests.

SALUDA *Saluda* • 19,181 • 451 • West-central SC, bounded on the north by the Saluda River (forming Lake Murray reservoir). The county contains part of Sumter National Forest. • Named for the river • 1896 from Edgefield • Chickens, eggs, turkeys, cattle, corn, wheat, soybeans, sorghum, hay, peaches; timber; manufacturing.

SPARTANBURG *Spartanburg* • 253,791 (the fourth most populated county in SC) • 811 • Northwestern SC, bounded on the north by the NC state line and on the southwest by the Enoree River; drained by numerous rivers and creeks. Croft State Natural Area and Pacolet River Heritage Preserve are here. • Named for the Spartan Regiment of the SC militia, which acquitted itself impressively during the Revolutionary War • 1785 from Ninety Six District. (In 1868, all districts were renamed counties.) • Spartanburg was first established as a courthouse village in 1785. Its growth was accelerated in 1865 by the intersection of three major rail lines here. • Golfer Betsy Rawls • Granite, sand and gravel production, vermiculite; peaches, melons, cotton, wheat, oats, soybeans, sorghum, hay, apples, hogs, chickens, eggs, dairying; manufacture of textiles, apparel, fabricated metal products, office furniture, chemicals, plumbing supplies, rubber and paper products, clothing, ceramics, carpets, motor vehicles; education (Wofford College; Converse College; U. of SC Spartanburg).

SUMTER *Sumter* • 104,646 • 665 • Central SC, bounded on the west by the Wateree River and on the northeast by the Lynches River; drained by the Black River. Part of Lake Marion reservoir is in the south. Poinsett State Park and Manchester State Forest are located here, as are Shaw Air Force Base and the U.S. Air Force Gunnery Range. • One of four counties named for General Thomas Sumter (1734–1832), American Revolutionary officer nicknamed the "Gamecock of the Revolution," U.S. representative and senator from SC • 1798 from Camden District • Molecular geneticist Joseph L. Goldstein • Sand and gravel, clay; lumbering; hogs, cattle, dairying, wheat, rye, oats, tobacco, sorghum, peanuts, soybeans, hay, cotton; food processing, cottonseed oil production; manufacture of furniture, batteries, clothing; wood dyeing and textile printing, fertilizer mixing; education (Morris College) • The Swan Lake Iris Gardens in Sumter city abound in old cypress trees, azaleas, camellias, and irises.

UNION (one of eighteen counties so named) *Union* • 29,881 • 514 • Northern SC, bounded on the north by the Pacolet River, on the south by the Enoree River, and on the east by the Broad River; drained by the Tyger River. Much of the southern half of the county is covered by Sumter National Forest. Rose Hill Plantation State Historic Site, former home of SC Governor William H. Gist, is also here. • Named for the old Union Church, erected in 1765 to serve several different denominations • 1785 from Ninety Six District. (In 1868, all districts were renamed counties.) • When Columbia was burned during the Civil War, Dawkins House in Union, became the provisional Confederate statehouse. • Hay, grains, soybeans, peaches, cattle; manufacture of textiles, hosiery, ropes, fabricated metal products, plastics, medical equipment; printing and publishing; sand, vermiculite; timber.

WILLIAMSBURG *Kingstree* • 37,217 • 934 • East-central SC, bounded on the south by the Santee River; drained by the Black River. • Named for Williamsburg township, SC • 1785 • Dairying, livestock, grains, soybeans, cotton, tobacco, sorghum; timber; hunting and fishing.

YORK (one of five counties so named) *York* • 164,614 • 683 • Northern SC, bounded on the west in part by the Broad River, on the east in part by the Catawba River, and on the north by Lake Wylie reservoir (created by Catawba Dam and forming the NC state line). Part of Kings Mountain National Military Park is here. Kings Mountain State Park is also in the county. • Named for York, PA, former home of early settlers • 1785 from Camden District • The county was the site of two important Revolutionary War victories, the Battle of Huck's Defeat and Kings Mountain (Oct. 7, 1780). The last meeting of the full Confederate Cabinet took place at the White Homestead in Fort Mill. • Manufacture of textiles and wood pulp; mining of granite, sand and gravel; also, poultry, hogs, cattle, dairying, corn, wheat, oats, soybeans, sorghum, hay, peaches; education (Winthrop U.) • Smyrna, occupying one square mile in the west, is the smallest town in the state. The Catawba Cultural Center on the Catawba Indian Reservation holds its annual "Yap Ye Iswa" festival, celebrating its culture and heritage.

SOUTH DAKOTA

Under God the People Rule

Each of the South Dakota's sixty-six counties is governed by a county commission, consisting of a board of three to five members, elected to four-year terms. Other county officials in the state are the state's attorney, auditor, coroner, register of deeds, treasurer, and sheriff.

AURORA *Plankinton* • 3,058 • 708 • Southeast-central SD; watered by Firesteel and Platte creeks. • Named for the Roman goddess of dawn • Created 1879 and organized 1882 (prior to statehood) from land that had been parts of Hanson County (what was later Davison, Jerauld and Cragin counties) • A stratosphere balloon landing site was located here in 1935 in the southwest. • Corn, barley, soybeans, wheat, hogs, cattle, dairy products.

BEADLE *Huron* • 17,023 • 1,259 • East-central SD; drained by the James River, and Pearl, Foster, and Cain creeks. Lake Byron Lakeside Use Area is in the north. • Named for General William H. H. Beadle (1838–1915), Union officer in the Civil War and surveyor general of Dakota Territory • 1879 (prior to statehood) from Spink and Clark • Huron was established in 1879 as a division headquarters for the Chicago and North Western Railway. • U.S. vice president Hubert H. Humphrey • Corn, wheat, cattle, hogs, dairying, poultry, honey; manufacture of textiles, cement products; metal fabrication; meat packing, food processing; tourism; pheasant hunting; education (Huron U.) • The South Dakota State Fair is held in Huron each September.

BENNETT *Martin* • 3,574 • 1,185 • Southern SD, bounded on the south by the NE state line, on the west and north by the Pine Ridge Indian Reservation and on the east by the Rosebud Indian Reservation; drained by the Little White River, and Bear-in-the-Lodge and Pass creeks. Lacreek Lake is in the south, encompassed by Lacreek National Wildlife Refuge. • Named for either Granville G. Bennett (1833–1910), IA legislator, jurist, and Dakota Territory's delegate to the U.S. Congress; or for John E. Bennett, SD Supreme Court judge • 1909 from Indian lands • Wheat, flax, soybeans, hogs, honey.

BON HOMME *Tyndall* • 7,260 • 563 • Southeastern SD, bounded on the south by the Missouri River (forming the NE state line), and on the west by Choteau Creek. Springfield Recreation Area and Tabor Lakeside Use Area are in the southeast, located on Lewis and Clark Lake. • Named for the village of Bonhomme in Dakota Territory • Original county; 1862 (prior to statehood) from unorganized territory • U.S. presidential candidate George McGovern • Corn, wheat, soybeans, dairying, hogs, sheep.

BROOKINGS *Brookings* • 28,220 (the fourth most populated county in SD) • 794 • Eastern SD, bounded on the east by the MN state line; drained by the Big Sioux River and Deer Creek. Oakwood Lakes State Park, Lake Hendricks Land Use Area, and Lake Poinsett Recreation Area are in the north. • Named for Wilmot W. Brookings (1833–85), Dakota territorial legislator and Dakota Territory Supreme Court justice • 1862 (prior to statehood) from unorganized territory • Corn, wheat, soybeans, flax, dairying, cattle, hogs, poultry, honey; processing of hybrid sorghums and seed corn; gravel, concrete; manufacture of aluminum doors and windows, fire fighting equipment, outdoor advertising signs; education (SD State U., the state's only land-grant school).

BROWN (one of nine counties so named) *Aberdeen* • 35,460 (the third most populated county in SD) • 1,713 • Northeastern S.D., bounded on the north by the ND state line; drained by the James River, and Elm, Maple, Mud and Foot creeks. Elm Lake reservoir is in the northwest. Richmond Lake Recreation Area is in the west. The county also includes Mud Lakes and Columbia Road reservoirs. Sand Lake National Wildlife Refuge is in the northeast. • Named for Alfred Brown (1836–1919), member of the Dakota Territory legislature, instrumental in consolidating the then existing counties, earning him the nickname, "Consolidation Brown" • 1879 (prior to statehood) from Beadle • Senator Tom Daschle. Fascinated with the "Wild West," L. Frank Baum moved to Aberdeen in 1888 and became owner/journalist for the *Aberdeen Saturday Pioneer*, the town newspaper. • The county has a strong dairy industry. Also, wheat, corn, flax, soybeans, vegetables, cattle, hogs; manufacture of automotive tools, oxygen, acetylene gas, wood products, farm implements; machine shops; education (Northern State U.; Presentation College).

BRULE *Chamberlain* • 5,364 • 819 • South-central SD, bounded on the west by the Missouri River (Lake Francis Case reservoir); drained by Smith Creek in the north. Red Lake is in the west. • Named for the Brule tribe of the Sioux Indians • 1875 (prior to statehood) from Buffalo • Corn, wheat, cattle, hogs. • Akta Lakota Museum is here.

BUFFALO (one of three counties so named) *Gannvalley* • 2,032 • 471 • Central SD, bounded on the west by the Missouri River (forming Lake Sharpe Reservoir). Crow Creek Indian Reservation is in the western part of the county. • Named for the once plentiful bison in the area • 1864 (prior to statehood) from territorial county • Cattle.

BUTTE (one of three counties so named) *Belle Fourche* • 9,094 • 2,249 • Western SD, bounded on the west by the WY and MT state lines; drained by the Belle Fourche River, the North and South forks of the Moreau River, and Owl, Indian, and Sulphur creeks. Belle Fourche Reservoir on Owl Creek is used for extensive irrigation of surrounding valleys. • Named for buttes found in the region • 1883 (prior to statehood) from Harding; the county was significantly enlarged in 1897 • Since its early days Belle Fourche has been an important market and shipping center for livestock. (Experimental cross-breeding here between buffalo and Brahmin cattle have produced the brahmalo.) Crops include corn, hay, sugar beets (cultivation and refining). Also, dairying, sheep (wool); manufacture of bricks and lumber; bentonite mining and processing • The geographical center of all fifty United States (including AK and HI) is located five miles west of Castle Rock. The popular Black Hills Roundup rodeo has been held in Belle Fourche since 1918.

CAMPBELL (one of five counties so named) *Mound City* • 1,782 • 736 • Northern SD, bounded on the north by the ND state line and on the west by the Missouri River. Pocasse National Wildlife Refuge is on Lake Pocasse in the northwest. • Named for Norman B. Campbell, Dakota territorial legislator • 1873 (prior to statehood) from Buffalo • Dairying, cattle, hogs, wheat, corn, barley.

CHARLES MIX *Lake Andes* • 9,350 • 1,098 • Southern SD, bounded on the west and south by the Missouri River (partially forming the NE state line); watered by Lake Andes. Lake Frances Case reservoir is in the south; Lake Andes reservoir and National Wildlife Refuge are in east-center. Yankton Indian Reservation occupies the southeastern half of the county, with its headquarters at Marty. Snake Creek, Platte Creek, and Pease Creek recreation areas are here. • Named for Charles H. Mix (1833–1909), Indian agent for the Blue Earth Agency and commandant of Fort Abercrombie • Original county; 1862 (prior to statehood) • Corn, wheat, soybeans, sorghum, hay, cattle, hogs, poultry, dairying.

CLARK (one of twelve counties so named) *Clark* • 4,143 • 958 • East-central SD. The county occupies an area of high ground between the Minnesota and James rivers, sources of numerous small creeks. • Named for Newton Clark, pioneer schoolteacher and Dakota territorial legislator • 1873 (prior to statehood) from Hanson • Dairying, poultry, cattle, hogs, corn, wheat, rye, soybeans, oats, hay, potatoes.

CLAY (one of eighteen counties so named) *Vermillion* • 13,537 • 412 (the smallest county in SD) • Southeastern SD, bounded on the south by the Missouri River (forming the NE state line); drained by the Vermillion River. Clay County Land Use Area is in the south on the Missouri River. • One of fifteen counties named for Henry Clay (1777–1852), U.S. senator from KY, known as the "Great Pacificator" for support of compromise to mitigate national crises • Original county; 1862 (prior to statehood) from unorganized territory • A flood in 1881 completely destroyed the city of Vermillion, established in 1859. It was rebuilt higher on the bluffs overlooking the Missouri River. • Corn, soybeans, hay, cattle, hogs, dairy products, truck vegetables, grains; education (U. of SD) • Spirit Mound was constructed by the Mound Builders of the Midwest between A.D. 500 and 1000.

CODINGTON *Watertown* • 25,897 (the fifth most populated county in SD) • 688 • Eastern SD; drained by the Big Sioux River, with numerous lakes. The county lies on the Coteau des Prairies plateau and includes the southern extremity of triangular Lake Traverse Indian Reservation in the north. Pelican Lake and Sandy Shore recreation areas are here. • Named for the Rev. G.S. Codington, clergyman and Dakota Territory legislator • 1877 (prior to statehood) from Indian lands • An earlier settlement on the site of Watertown (1878) was abandoned in 1874 after an invasion of grasshoppers destroyed the crops. • Dairying, corn, flax, wheat, soybeans, turkey, cattle, hogs, sheep; manufacturing; tourism (sport fishing) • The Bramble Park Zoo in Watertown has one of the largest waterfowl and pheasant collections in the U.S.

CORSON *McIntosh* • 4,181 • 2,473 (the fifth largest county in SD) • Northern SD, bounded on the north by the ND state line and on the east by the Missouri River; drained by the Grand River and Oak, Rock and other creeks. The county is coterminous with Standing Rock Indian Reservation, which also includes all of Sioux County, ND to the north. A small unit of Grand River National Grassland is in the southwest. • Named for Dighton Corson (?–1915), WI state legislator, a framer of the SD constitution, and one of the first SD Supreme Court justices • 1909 from Dewey • The grave of the Sioux Indian chief Sitting Bull and a monument to Lewis and Clark's Indian guide Sacajawea can be found at the Missouri River near where the Standing Rock and Cheyenne River Indian reservations merge. • Cattle, wheat, flax, soybeans, hay; lignite mines.

CUSTER *Custer* • 7,275 • 1,558 • Southwestern SD, bounded on the west by the WY state line; watered by the Cheyenne River (forming part of the eastern boundary), and French, Battle, and Bed Canyon creeks. The county includes the southern part of the Black Hills and part of Black Hills National Forest (its headquarters in Custer). Wind Cave National Park and Custer State Park are in the center. Jewel Cave National Monument (the fourth longest cave in the world), and a portion of Buffalo Gap National Grassland are also here. • One of six counties named for General George Armstrong Custer (1839–76), soldier and Indian fighter • 1875 (prior to statehood) from Indian lands • Custer was laid out in 1875 after gold was discovered in French Creek by miners who were accompanying General Custer's reconnaissance expedition. • Dairy products, livestock, poultry, grain; timber; mining and related industries (processing of gold, quartz, beryl, mica, gypsum) • Work continues on the mountain sculpture of Crazy Horse mounted on his horse, designed and started in 1947 by Korczak Ziolkowski (monument). Annual pageants in Custer dramatize the discovery of gold in the county and an 1881 lynching.

DAVISON *Mitchell* • 18,741 • 435 • Southeast-central SD; watered by the James River and Firesteel Creek. • Named for Henry Davison, one of the first settlers in the county • 1873 (prior to statehood) from Hanson • Corn, wheat, hay, cattle, hogs, dairying; light manufacturing; tourism (pheasant hunting); education (Dakota Wesleyan U.) • The Mitchell Corn Palace (built in 1921 to replace the original constructed in 1892) is a unique Byzantine-styled structure with minarets and towers, decorated each year with corn. The Soukup and Thomas International Balloon and Airship Museum in Mitchell chronicles the history and science of gas and hot-air ballooning.

DAY *Webster* • 6,267 • 1,029 • Northeastern SD, on the east slope of Coteau des Prairies; watered by numerous lakes, most of them in the eastern half (the largest being Waubay). Part of Lake Traverse Indian Reservation is in the east. Waubay National Wildlife Refuge, South Blue Dog Land Use Area, and Pickerel Lake State Recreation Area are also in the east. Amsden Lakeside Use Area is in the west. • Named for Merritt H. Day (1844–1900), Dakota Territory legislator • 1879 (prior to statehood) from Clark • TV journalist Tom Brokaw • Corn, flax, soybeans, wheat, dairying, cattle, hogs.

DEUEL (one of two counties so named, the other in NE) *Clear Lake* • 4,498 • 624 • Eastern SD, bounded on the east by the MN state line; watered by Hidewood Creek and the West Fork of Lac qui Parle River. The county has numerous lakes. Lake Cochran Recreation Area and Clear Lake Land Use Area are both in the county. • Named for Jacob S. Deuel (1830–?), member of the first Dakota territorial legislature • 1862 (prior to statehood) from Brookings • Corn, wheat, flax, soybeans, potatoes, dairying, cattle, hogs.

DEWEY (one of two counties so named, the other in OK) *Timber Lake* • 5,972 • 2,303 • North-central SD, bounded on the east by the Missouri River (forming Lake Oahe); drained by the Moreau River. Little Moreau State Recreation Area is here. The county is coterminous with Cheyenne River Indian Reservation (as is neighboring Ziebach County). • Named for William P. Dewey (?–1900), surveyor general of the Dakota Territory • Created as Rusk County in 1873 (prior to statehood); name changed to Dewey in 1883 • Cattle, flax, wheat, dairy, hogs; lignite.

DOUGLAS *Armour* • 3,458 • 434 • Southeastern SD; drained by Choteau Creek. The county includes Corsica Lake. • One of twelve counties named for Stephen A. Douglas (1813–61), U.S. orator and statesman • 1873 (prior to statehood) from Charles Mix • Corn, wheat, soybeans, oats, cattle, hogs, poultry, dairy.

EDMUNDS *Ipswich* • 4,367 • 1,146 • North-central SD; drained by Snake Creek and other creeks. Mina Lake Recreation Area is here, as is Lake Parmley reservoir on the eastern boundary (Snake Creek). • Named for Newton Edmunds (1819–1908), governor of Dakota Territory • 1873 (prior to statehood) from Buffalo • Wheat, flax, barley, dairy, cattle, hogs, poultry.

FALL RIVER *Hot Springs* • 7,453 • 1,740 • Extreme Southwestern SD, bounded on the west by the WY state line and on the south by the NE state line; drained by the Cheyenne River and numerous creeks. Buffalo Gap National Grassland covers much of the county. The southern part of Black Hills National Forest is in the north. Angostura Reservoir Recreation Area and Mammoth Site 23 are also located in the county. Shannon County, which borders on the east, is administered by Fall River. • Named for the Fall River which flows through the county • 1883 (prior to statehood) from Custer • The warm mineral springs here became a popular tourist destination in the 1890s. • Wheat, hay, cattle, sandstone quarries. Evans Plunge is reputedly the world's largest natural indoor warm-water pool.

FAULK *Faulkton* • 2,640 • 1,000 • North-central SD; watered by intermittent streams which branch off the James River. Lake Faulkton Lakeside Use Area is in the south. • Named for Andrew J. Faulk (1814–98), a governor of Dakota Territory • 1873 (prior to statehood) from Buffalo and unorganized territory • Wheat, other grains, livestock • Faulkton is home to SD's only permanent, electrically operated 1925 Parker carousel, the "Happy Times Carousel."

GRANT (one of fifteen counties so named) *Milbank* • 7,847 • 683 • Northeastern SD, bounded on the east by the MN state line; watered by the North Fork of the Whetstone River. Part of Lake Traverse Indian Reservation is in the northwest. • One of twelve counties named for President Ulysses S. Grant • 1878 (prior to statehood) from Codington and Deuel • Established as a division point for the Milwaukee Railroad, which was extended through the city in 1880, Milbank attracted a number of Irish and Dutch railroad workers. • Corn, wheat, sorghum, soybeans, flax, dairying, cattle, hogs; granite quarrying; food processing • Milbank is the birthplace of American Legion Junior League Baseball (1925).

GREGORY *Burke* • 4,792 • 1,016 • Southern SD, bounded on the south by the NE state line and on the northeast by the Missouri River; drained by Ponca Creek. Fort Randall Dam (Missouri River) forms Lake Francis Case reservoir. Buryanek Lakeside Use Area, Burke Lake State Recreation Area, Karl E. Mundt National Wildlife Refuge (the nation's first federal eagle sanctuary), and Randall Historic Site are here. • Named for John S. Gregory (1831–?), member of the first legislature of Dakota Territory • 1862 (prior to statehood) from Yankton • Corn, wheat, soybeans, dairy products, poultry, cattle, hogs • The Dallas water tower, historically a landmark for settlers, is the only water tower located in the middle of a federal highway. Fairfax's Gregory County State Bank, built in 1918, is the only terra-cotta building in the state.

HAAKON *Philip* • 2,196 • 1,813 • Central SD, bounded on the north by the Cheyenne River; drained by the Bad River and Plum Creek. • Named for Haakon VII (1872–1957), king of Norway; on a suggestion by Hugh J. McMahon who wished to gain the votes of the Norwegian immigrants in favor of the division of Stanley County into two new counties • 1914 from Stanley • Wheat, cattle, poultry.

HAMLIN *Hayti* • 5,540 • 511 • Eastern SD; drained by the Big Sioux River. There are several lakes in the south, including part of Lake Poinsett and State Recreation Area. • Named for Hannibal Hamlin (1809–91), Speaker of the House and vice president • 1873 (prior to statehood) from Deuel • Corn, wheat, soybeans, flax, potatoes, cattle, hogs, poultry.

HAND *Miller* • 3,741 • 1,437 • Central SD; watered by Wolf, Turtle, and Sand creeks. Lake Louise Recreation Area and Rosehill Lakeside Use Area are here. • Named for George H. Hand (1837–91), U.S. attorney for Dakota Territory and legislator • 1873 (prior to statehood) from Buffalo • Wheat, oats, rye, barley, corn, dairy products, cattle, hogs.

HANSON *Alexandria* • 3,139 • 435 • Southeastern SD; drained by the James River. • Named for Major Joseph R. Hanson (?–1917), Dakota Territory legislator and Indian affairs official • 1871 (prior to statehood) from Buffalo and Deuel • Dairy products, corn, wheat, poultry, cattle, hogs.

HARDING (one of two counties so named, the other in NM) *Buffalo* • 1,353 • 2,671 (the fourth largest county in SD) • Northwestern SD, bounded on the west by the MT state line and on the north by the ND state line; watered by the Little Missouri River; drained by the North Fork of the Moreau River and the South Fork of the Grand. Crow Butte has limestone ridges in the north, southwest and east. Portions of Custer National Forest are distributed throughout. • Named for John A. Harding, Dakota Territory legislator • Created in 1881 and later absorbed by Butte County; re-established in 1909 • During the Battle of Slim Buttes in 1876, Sioux veterans of the Custer battle were overtaken by the U.S. Cavalry, but escaped into the rugged buttes. • Wheat, sheep; petroleum and large deposits of lignite coal • The Cave Hills section of Custer National Forest served as a popular hideout for bandits and outlaws.

HUGHES (one of two counties so named, the other in OK) *Pierre* • 16,481 • 741 • Central SD, bounded on the south and southwest by the Missouri River; watered by Medicine Knoll Creek and other intermittent streams. Lake Oahe reservoir is formed by Oahe Dam, located north of Pierre. Part of Crow Creek Indian Reservation is in the county. • Named for Alexander Hughes (1846–1907), Dakota Territory and state legislator • 1873 (prior to statehood) from Buffalo • Pierre was founded in 1880 as the terminus of the Chicago and North Western Railway. It became the capital of SD in 1889. • Wheat, corn, barley, hogs, cattle; state government offices; tourism.

HUTCHINSON *Olivet* • 8,075 • 813 • Southeastern SD; drained by the James River and Wolf Creek • Named for John S. Hutchinson (1829–1889), Dakota Territory's first secretary and frequent acting governor • 1862 (prior to statehood) from unorganized territory • Dairy products, corn, wheat, barley, soybeans, oats, cattle, hogs, poultry.

HYDE (one of two counties so named) *Highmore* • 1,671 • 861 • Central SD; drained by Medicine Knoll and Wolf creeks. A bend in the Missouri River (Lake Sharpe Reservoir) forms its southwest border. A portion of Crow Creek Indian Reservation is in the south. • Named for James Hyde (1842–1902), pioneer settler of Clay County and Dakota territorial legislator • 1873 (prior to statehood) from Buffalo • Wheat, dairying, cattle.

JACKSON (one of twenty-four counties so named) *Kadoka* • 2,930 • 1,869 • Southwest-central SD; watered by intermittent streams, and Pass and Potato creeks. Buffalo Gap National Grassland, Prairie Homestead Historic Site (featuring the only original sod building on public display in SD), and part of Badlands National Park are all in its northern half. The southern half is dedicated to the Pine Ridge Indian Reservation. • Named for John R. Jackson, Dakota Territory legislator when the original Jackson County was formed in 1883. A claim for Andrew Jackson seems to be unjustified • 1914 from Stanley; in 1976 it annexed Washabaugh, which was organized 1883 from Indian lands and continued as an Indian reservation. • Hay, soybeans, cattle.

JERAULD *Wessington Springs* • 2,295 • 530 • Southeast-central SD; watered by intermittent streams; drained by Firesteel, Sand, and Smith creeks. Twin Lakes Lakeside Use Area is here. • Named for H. A. Jerauld, Dakota Territory legislator when the county was formed • 1883 from Aurora • Corn, wheat, cattle.

JONES (one of six counties so named) *Murdo* • 1,193 (the least populated county in SD) • 971 • South-central SD, bounded on the south by the White River; drained by the Bad River, and Dry and White Clay creeks. Part of Fort Pierre National Grassland is in the northeast. The Mountain/Central time zone boundary bisects the county down the middle, then follows the White River east. • Named for Jones County, IA, home of early settlers • 1917 from Lyman • Wheat, cattle.

KINGSBURY *De Smet* • 5,815 • 838 • East-central SD. The county is dotted by several lakes in its eastern half, including Whitewood, Henry, Preston, and Thompson (the last attached to Lake Thompson Recreation Area). • Named for George W. Kingsbury (1837–1925), and T. A. Kingsbury, brothers who were active in territorial affairs; George wrote a history of Dakota Territory • 1873 (prior to statehood) from Hanson • Corn, wheat, flax, soybeans, dairying, cattle. The county has an abundance of ducks and pheasants. • The area in and around De Smet figures prominently in the books of Laura Ingalls Wilder, who moved to the area as a young girl in 1879. There are eighteen sites here, including several of the author's childhood homes, that can be toured ("Little Town on the Prairie").

LAKE (one of twelve counties so named) *Madison* • 11,276 • 563 • Eastern SD; drained by the East Fork of the Vermillion River. The county includes Lake Herman State Park and Walkers Point Recreation Area. • Named for the many lakes in the area • 1873 (prior to statehood) from Brookings and Hanson • Corn, soybeans, dairy products, cattle, hogs, poultry, honey; education (Dakota State U.) • Dakota Prairie Village, a living museum of an authentic pioneer town, is the site of the annual Steam Threshing Jamboree and Antique Equipment Show.

LAWRENCE (one of eleven counties so named) *Deadwood* • 21,802 • 800 • Western SD, in the Black Hills, bounded on the west by the WY state line; drained by the Spearfish River, and Whitewood and Elk creeks. Over half of the county is covered by the Black Hills National Forest (its headquarters in Deadwood) except for a pocket around Lead and Deadwood, set aside for mining interests. Terry Peak and Deer Mountain ski areas are here, as is Roughneck Falls. • Named for John Lawrence, Dakota Territory legislator and first trea-

surer of the county • 1875 (prior to statehood) from unorganized territory • The discovery of gold in Deadwood Gulch, in September, 1875, created the brawling mining town of western lore, Deadwood. The development of the county parallels the growth of the Homestake Mining Company in Lead, the chief producer of gold in the U.S. at what is reputedly the largest underground gold mine in the Western Hemisphere. Lead was once the largest city in SD. • Collegiate basketball coach Piggy Lambert. In Mount Moriah cemetery in Deadwood are the graves of residents "Wild Bill" Hickok, "Calamity" Jane, Dr. Flora Hayward Standford (the first woman physician in the region) and "Preacher" Smith, the town's first minister. • Gold, silver, quartz; timber; cattle, dairying, grain, honey; gambling; tourism; education (Black Hills State U.) • The money made by George Hearst as head of the Homestake Mining Company provided for the family fortune inherited by his son William Randolph. In 1929, Potato Creek Johnny found a gold nugget, weighing 7 and ½ troy ounces, in western Lawrence County, one of the largest ever recovered from the Black Hills.

LINCOLN (one of twenty-four counties so named) *Canton* • 24,131 (56% increase since 1990; the fastest growing county in SD) • 578 • Southeastern SD, bounded on the east by the Big Sioux River (forming the IA state line); drained by the East Fork of the Vermillion River. Newton Hills State Park and Lake Alvin Recreation Area are here. The county is growing more urbanized in the north as part of the expanding Sioux Falls metropolitan area. • Understood by the legislature to be named for President Lincoln but, in fact, officially named for Lincoln County, ME • 1862 (prior to statehood) from Minnehaha • Canton was called Commerce City when it was founded in 1860, but its name was changed to Canton in 1867 by settlers who believed that it was diametrically opposite Canton, China. • Physicists Ernest Orlando Lawrence and Merle A. Tuve • Corn, grain, poultry, commercially raised pheasants, dairying, soybeans, cattle, hogs; light industries • Canton, with a large Norwegian community, was used by Ole Rölvaag as a setting for his 1927 novel, *Giants in the Earth*.

LYMAN *Kennebec* • 3,895 • 1,640 • South-central SD, bounded on the south by the White River and on the east by the Missouri River. Lower Brule Indian Reservation is in the north. A portion of Fort Pierre National Grassland is in the northwest corner. • Named for W. P. Lyman, possibly the first white settler in Yankton County and a member of the Dakota territorial legislature • 1873 (prior to statehood) from unorganized territory • In the days of the large cattle outfits, Presho was the "bedding down" place for extensive round-ups. It was once one of the largest hay-baling and shipping points in the U.S. • Corn, wheat, cattle, hogs, poultry, dairy products.

MARSHALL (one of twelve counties so named) *Britton* • 4,576 • 839 • Northeastern SD, bounded on the north by the ND state line. The county has numerous lakes. A portion of Lake Traverse Indian Reservation is in the east. Sica Hollow, Fort Sisseton, and Roy Lake state parks are all found in the county. • Named for Marshall Vincent, purveyor of flour and feed, and Day County commissioner • 1885 (prior to statehood) from Day • Corn, wheat, flax, hay, dairy products, poultry.

MCCOOK *Salem* • 5,832 • 575 • Southeastern SD; drained by the East and West Forks of the Vermillion River. Lake Vermillion Recreation Area is here. • Named for Edwin S. McCook (1837–73), secretary of the Dakota Territory, killed in a political dispute • 1873 (prior to statehood) from Hanson • Corn, soybeans, cattle, hogs.

MCPHERSON *Leola* • 2,904 • 1,137 • Northern SD, bounded on the north by the ND state line; drained by Spring and Foot creeks. • One of three counties named for General James B. McPherson (1828–64), commander of the Union Army of the Tennessee during the Civil War • 1873 (prior to statehood) from Buffalo • Al Neuharth, founder of Gannet Newspapers • Wheat, flax, cattle.

MEADE (one of three counties so named) *Sturgis* • 24,253 • 3,471 (the largest county in SD) • West-central SD, bounded on the east by the Cheyenne River; drained by the Belle Fourche River, and Elk, Sulphur, Alkali, and Cherry creeks. The county includes Bear Butte State Park and a small part of Black Hills National Forest. Ellsworth Air Force Base is on the southern boundary. • Named for Fort Meade, itself named for Gen. George G. Meade (1815–72), Union commander who defeated Gen. Lee at Gettysburg • 1889 from Lawrence • Fort Meade, established in 1878 to protect white settlers, was converted into a Veterans Administration Hospital in 1944. • Gold, manganese, lignite, bentonite, fuller's earth, marble; corn, soybeans, hay, sugar beets, cattle, hogs, sheep, dairying.

MELLETTE *White River* • 2,083 • 1,307 • Southern SD, bounded on the north by the White River; drained by the Little White River and Oak Black Pipe Creek. • Named for Arthur C. Mellette (1842–96), governor of SD Territory and first governor of the state • 1909 from Tripp • Cattle, wheat.

MINER *Howard* • 2,884 • 570 • East central SD; drained by the West Fork of the Vermillion River, and Rock and Redstone creeks. Lake Carthage State Lakeside Use Area is in the north. • Named for Captain Nelson Miner (1827–79), and Ephraim Miner (1833–?), members of the Dakota Territory legislature when the county was formed • 1873 (prior to statehood) from Hanson • Corn, wheat, soybeans, dairy products, cattle, hogs, poultry.

MINNEHAHA *Sioux Falls* • 148,281 (the most populated county in SD) • 809 • Eastern SD, bounded on the east by the MN state line; drained by the Big Sioux River and Pipestone Creek. The county is urbanized around Sioux Falls. • The derivation of this county's name has never been firmly established. It was possibly inspired by the Dakota Indian maiden of Henry Wadsworth Longfellow's popular poem, "The Song of Hiawatha." • 1862 (prior to statehood) from Big Sioux, a territorial county; original county • Sioux Falls was

founded in 1857; altercations with Minnesota Sioux Indians caused it to be abandoned in 1862. Settlers returned with the establishment of Fort Dakota on the site in 1865. After the harnessing of the falls, shipment of Sioux Falls granite (a hard quartzite used in construction) began in 1878. Because of liberal divorce laws, the city earned notoriety as a "divorce mill" in the 1890s and early 1900s. • Sioux Falls' stockyards form one of the largest livestock markets in the U.S. Also, corn, soybeans, hay, dairying, honey; manufacture of farm machinery, electronic components, meat packing, food processing; wood and metal fabrication; education (Augustana College; U. of Sioux Falls) • The U.S Department of the Interior's EROS Data Center for the application of space technology to life on earth is in Sioux Falls. One of the world's first commercial nuclear-power plants is outside of Sioux Falls. According to local legend, Jesse James on horseback jumped Devil's Gulch near Garretson, a twenty-foot-wide, fifty-foot deep chasm, to elude a posse.

MOODY *Flandreau* • 6,595 • 520 • Eastern SD, bounded on the east by the MN state line; drained by the Big Sioux River and Pipestone Creek. Flandreau Indian Reservation is located north of Flandreau. • Named for Col. Gideon C. Moody (1832–1904), one of the first two U.S. senators from SD and justice on the SD Territory Supreme Court • 1873 (prior to statehood) from Brookings and Minnehaha • Flandreau was settled in 1869 by twenty-five Santee Sioux Indians who gave up their tribal rights so that they could legally homestead. • Corn, soybeans, hogs, cattle, sheep, dairying. • The First Presbyterian Church in Flandreau is the oldest continually operated church in the state.

PENNINGTON (one of two counties so named, the other in MN) *Rapid City* • 88,565 (the second most populated county in SD) • 2,776 (the third largest county in SD) • Southwestern SD, bounded on the west by the WY state line; drained by the Cheyenne River (forming its northeast border) and numerous creeks. The Black Hills and Black Hills National Forest are in the west. Other places of interest include Harney Peak (the state's highest point at 7,242 feet), Buffalo Gap National Grassland, and Badlands National Park, which contains numerous fossil beds yielding the remains of such exotic animals as the three-toed horse, camel, sabre-toothed tiger, and rhinoceros. The county's primary tourist draw is Mount Rushmore National Memorial. Designed by sculptor Gutzon Borglum, its four presidential faces took fourteen years to carve from granite. A small portion of Ellsworth Air Force Base is in the north. • Named for John L. Pennington, Dakota Territory governor • 1875 (prior to statehood) from unorganized territory • Rapid City was settled in 1876 during the Black Hills gold rush. A cloudburst over the Black Hills in June, 1972 triggered flash flooding down Rapid Creek that left 235 persons dead. • Wheat, cattle, other livestock; mining of gold, silver, feldspar, gypsum, mica, uranium, granite; timber; tourism; manufacture of computer components, cement, pottery, jewelry; meat processing; education (SD School of

Mines and Technology) • Rapid City's many museums cover the geology of the area, the Sioux Indians, transportation and history. Chapel in the Hills is an exact replica of the 860-year-old Borgund Church in Norway.

PERKINS (one of two counties so named, the other in NE) *Bison* • 3,363 • 2,873 (the second largest county in SD) • Northwestern SD, bounded on the north by the ND state line; drained by the North Fork of the Grand River, the Moreau River, and numerous creeks. Shadehill and Llewellyn Johns Memorial state recreation areas, and Petrified Wood Park are here. The Grand River National Grassland is in the north. • Named for Henry E. Perkins (1864–?), state senator who helped pass the act that established the county • 1909 from Harding and Butte • Lignite deposits and mines; wheat, hay, cattle, sheep • The Hugh Glass Monument marks the area where the hunter was attacked in 1823 by a grizzly bear and left for dead by companions; Glass miraculously crawled 190 miles east to Fort Kiowa.

POTTER (one of three counties so named) *Gettysburg* • 2,693 • 867 • North central SD, bounded on the west by the Missouri River (Lake Oahe reservoir); drained by Swan and Okobojo creeks. West Whitlock Recreation Area and East Whitlock Lakeside Use Area are located on Lake Oahe. • Named for Dr. Joel A. Potter (1825–1895), Dakota territorial legislator and steward of the State Hospital for the Insane in Yankton • Created as Ashmore 1875 (prior to statehood) from Buffalo; name changed 1877 • Dairy products, corn, wheat, rye, oats, barley, cattle, hogs.

ROBERTS (one of two counties so named, the other in TX) *Sisseton* • 10,016 • 1,101 • Northeastern SD, bounded on the north by the ND state line and on the east by Big Stone Lake (Minnesota River) and Lake Traverse (Bois de Sioux River), forming the MN state line. Coteau des Prairies plateau runs north/south. Most of the county is occupied by Lake Traverse Indian Reservation. Hartford Beach State Park and Big Stone Lake Nature Area are in the southeast. • Probably named for Samuel G. Roberts (1943–?), publisher, banker and a member of the Dakota territorial legislature when the county was established • 1883 (prior to statehood) from Grant • Corn, wheat, soybeans, cattle, hogs.

SANBORN *Woonsocket* • 2,675 • 569 • Southeast-central SD; watered by the James River and Sand and Redstone creeks. Twin Lakes Lakeside Use Area is here. • Named for George W. Sanborn (1832–?), a Milwaukee Railroad official • 1883 (prior to statehood) from Miner • Corn, soybeans, dairy, produce, cattle, hogs, poultry, honey.

SHANNON (one of two counties so named, the other in MO) *Hot Springs* (in Fall River County) • 12,466 • 2,094 • Southwestern SD, bounded on the south by the NE state line; drained by the White River and Medicine Rock, Porcupine, Wounded Knee, and White Clay creeks. The entire county, except for a large southern extension of Badlands National Park in the north (containing animal fossils that date back forty million years), is coterminous with the Pine Ridge Indian Reservation. The county is administratively attached to Fall River County to the west. • Named for Peter C. Shannon (1821–1899), Chief Justice of the Dakota Territory Supreme Court • 1875 (prior to statehood) from territorial county. • Wounded Knee (Big Foot Massacre Monument) was the scene of the 1890 massacre of over 250 mostly unarmed Sioux Indians, including women and children, by the U.S. Seventh Cavalry. In 1973, some 200 armed Indians occupied Wounded Knee for over two months to call attention to their grievances. • Grain, cattle; education (Oglala Lakota College) • The Heritage Center at Red Cloud Indian School (operated continually by Jesuit priests and Franciscan nuns since 1888) contains one of the finest collections of American Indian art.

SPINK *Redfield* • 7,454 • 1,504 • Northeast-central SD; drained by the James River, and Snake, Mud, Timber, Turtle, and Wolf creeks. Fisher Grove State Park is here. • Named for Solomon L. Spink (1831–81), Dakota Territory secretary and acting governor, and territorial delegate to Congress • 1873 (prior to statehood) from Hanson and Walworth • Corn, wheat, soybeans, hay, cattle, hogs, sheep, dairy products.

STANLEY *Fort Pierre* • 2,772 • 1,443 • Central SD, bounded on the north by the Cheyenne River (west arm of Lake Oahe reservoir) and on the east by the Missouri River (impounded here to form the reservoir); drained by the Bad River. The county is divided between the Mountain and Central time zones. A small portion of Fort Pierre National Grassland is in the southeast. • Named for General David S. Stanley (1828 - 1902), commander of Fort Sully and director of the U.S. Soldier's Home in Washington, D.C. • 1873 (prior to statehood) from unorganized territory • Fort Pierre, the oldest continuous settlement in SD, was the fur trade capital of the Northwest from 1817 to about 1867. Louis and Francois Vérendrye buried a lead plate in 1743 (discovered here in 1913) claiming the region for France; La Verendrye Monument commemorates the site. • Livestock, wheat, barley, flax, oats, alfalfa • The Oahe Dam, which connects Stanley and Hughes counties, is reportedly the fourth largest rolled-earth dam in the world. The Triple U Buffalo Ranch is grazing ground for the largest buffalo herd in the U.S.

SULLY *Onida* • 1,556 • 1,007 • Central SD, bounded on the west by the Missouri River (Lake Oahe reservoir); drained by Okobojo and Medicine Knoll creeks. • Named for either Fort Sully or for General Alfred Sully (1821–1879) for whom the fort was named • 1873 (prior to statehood) from Potter • Cattle, corn, wheat.

TODD (one of three counties so named) *Winner* (in Tripp County) • 9,050 • 1,388 • Southern SD, bounded on the south by the NE state line; drained by the Little White and Keya Paha rivers. The entire county is coterminous with the Rosebud Indian Reservation (the most populated of the state's reservations) and is administered by Tripp County. • One of two counties (the other in MN) named for General John Blair

Smith Todd (1814–72), officer in the Seminole War and Mexican War, and U.S. congressional delegate from Dakota Territory • 1909 from Indian lands; unorganized; attached to Tripp County for governmental purposes • Olympic Gold Medalist Billy Mills • Grain, cattle; education (Sinte Gleska U.). The Buechel Memorial Lakota Museum is here.

TRIPP *Winner* • 6,430 • 1,614 • Southern SD, bounded on the south by the NE state line and on the north by the White River; drained by the Keya Paha River and Bull, Thunder and Cottonwood creeks. Rahn Lake State Recreation Area is here. The county administers Todd County to the west. • Named for Bartlett Tripp (1842–1911), U.S. minister to Austria-Hungary and Chief Justice of Dakota Territory. • 1873 (prior to statehood) from unorganized territory. • Corn, wheat, sorghum, hay, dairy products, cattle, hogs, sheep, poultry.

TURNER (one of two counties so named, the other in GA) *Parker* • 8,849 • 617 • Southeastern SD; drained by the Vermillion River and its East and West forks, which converge near Parker. • Named for John W. Turner (1800–83), member of the Dakota Territory legislature and Dakota Territory superintendent of public instruction • 1871 (prior to statehood) from Lincoln and part of the now-defunct Jayne • Corn, soybeans, cattle, hogs, sheep, dairy products, honey.

UNION (one of eighteen counties so named) *Elk Point* • 12,584 • 460 • Southeastern SD, bounded on the east by the Sioux River, forming the IA state line, and on the southwest by the Missouri River (designated here a National Scenic River), forming the NE state line. Union County State Park and Adams Homestead and Nature Preserve are here. • Named for support of the Union in the Civil War • Organized as Cole 1862 (prior to statehood) from unorganized territory; name changed 1864 • In 1927, Charles Lindbergh selected North Sioux City as his landing site for the Spirit of Saint Louis. • Dairy products, hay, corn, soybeans, honey, cattle, hogs.

WALWORTH (one of two counties so named, the other in WI) *Selby* • 5,974 • 708 • North-central SD, bounded on the west by the Missouri River (Lake Oahe reservoir); drained by Swan Creek. Lake Hiddenwood State Park and Swan Creek Recreation Area are located here. • Named for Walworth County, Wisconsin, former home of early settlers • 1873 (prior to statehood) from territorial county • Wheat, other grains, dairy products, cattle, hogs • Mobridge's unusual name originated from a telegrapher's combination of the abbreviation "Mo" for Missouri River, and the word "bridge" for the Milwaukee Railroad bridge that crosses here in his reports. The Land of the Sioux Museum in Mobridge displays Indian relics. The Sitting Bull Stampede is an annual rodeo held here.

YANKTON *Yankton* • 21,652 • 522 • Southeastern SD, bounded on the south by the Missouri River (which forms the NE state line); drained by the James River. Lewis and Clark Lake reservoir, impounded by Gavins Point Dam, is one of the largest fish hatcheries in the U.S. Lewis and Clark Recreation Area is in the southwest. • Named for the city of Yankton, itself named for the Indian tribe • 1862 (prior to statehood) from territorial county • From 1861 to 1863 Yankton served as the first capital of Dakota Territory. • Hay, soybeans, corn, fruit, cattle, hogs, dairy products; agricultural product processing and shipping; manufacture of machine tools, crates, sheet-metal products, electronic components; processing of poultry and meat products; marble; education (Mount Marty College).

ZIEBACH *Dupree* • 2,519 • 1,962 • Northwest-central SD, bounded on the south by the Cheyenne River; drained by the Moreau River, and Thunder Butte and Cherry creeks. The county is coterminous with Cheyenne River Indian Reservation (as is neighboring Dewey county) • Named for Frank M. Ziebach (1830–1929), publisher of the first newspaper in Dakota Territory and Dakota Territory legislator • 1911 from Pennington • Sioux leader Chief Hump • Wheat, cattle, hogs.

TENNESSEE

Agriculture and Commerce

Most of Tennessee's ninety-five counties are governed by county commissions, consisting of from nine to twenty-five members. Either a county executive or the chairman of the commission presides over meetings. Other county officials include the sheriff, assessor of property, register of deeds, county clerk, and trustee. Davidson County and Nashville have combined their governments into a single unit governed by a mayor and metropolitan council.

ANDERSON (one of five counties so named) *Clinton* • 71,330 • 338 • Eastern TN, bounded on the northeast by Norris Lake reservoir and on the south in part by Melton Hill Lake reservoir; drained by the Clinch River. The northwestern part of the county is in the Cumberland Mountains. The county includes Norris Dam State Park. It lies partly in the Knoxville metropolitan area. • Named for Major Joseph Anderson (1757–1837), U.S. senator from TN and first comptroller of the U.S. Treasury • 1801 from Knox and Grainger • The site of Oak Ridge was selected in 1942 as the headquarters for the

Manhattan Project, the U.S.'s wartime atomic energy program. The city was built by the U.S. Army Corps of Engineers behind security fences. In 1945 it had a population of 75,000. The Atomic Energy Commission began selling land and homes to the public in 1955. • Coal, clay, oil, gas; lumbering; livestock, dairying, apples, tobacco, corn, hay; some manufacturing, including radioactive pharmaceuticals, electronic instrumentation, machinery, tools; nuclear research and atomic-materials production in Oak Ridge • Oak Ridge is the site of the Atomic Museum of Science and Energy and the Oak Ridge National Laboratory's Graphite Reactor, a national historic landmark. The Museum of Appalachia is near Norris.

BEDFORD (one of three counties so named) *Shelbyville* • 37,586 • 474 • Central TN; drained by the Duck River. • One of two counties (the other in PA) named for Thomas Bedford (1758–1804), captain in the Continental Army and large landowner • 1807 from Rutherford and Indian lands • The county was the scene of a number of skirmishes during the Civil War. • Livestock, especially the Tennessee Walking Horse (breeding and training), dairying, hay, corn, grain; poultry processing; light manufacturing, including textiles, pencils, metal goods, plastics, leather, clothing, truck transmissions; printing • Shelbyville holds the annual Tennessee Walking Horse National Celebration in August.

BENTON (one of nine counties so named) *Camden* • 16,537 • 395 • Western TN, bounded on the east and northwest by arms of Kentucky Lake reservoir (Tennessee River); crossed by the Big Sandy River. The county includes three sections of the Tennessee National Wildlife Refuge, Nathan Bedford Forrest State Park, and part of Natchez Trace State Resort Park and Forest. • Originally named for Thomas Hart Benton; in 1852 the TN legislature changed the name of the honoree to local farmer and magistrate David Benton (1779–1860) • 1835 from Henry and Humphreys • Dairying, livestock, poultry, corn, soybeans, sorghum; gravel pits. • The Tennessee River Fresh Water Farm and Museum is located near Camden.

BLEDSOE *Pikeville* • 12,367 • 406 • Central TN; drained by the Sequatchie River. It is located on the Cumberland Plateau. Bledsoe State Forest is in the northwest. The highest waterfall in the eastern U.S., Fall Creek Falls, is located here. • Probably named for Anthony Bledsoe (1733-1788), surveyor and colonel of the county militia who died in an Indian attack • 1807 from Roane and Indian lands • Timber; dairying, livestock raising; tomatoes, fruit, pumpkins (The self-proclaimed "Pumpkin Capital" of the world, the county holds a fall festival each year to promote the gourd); coal mining • The county is the final resting place for John A. Murrell, known as the "Great Western Land Pirate."

BLOUNT (one of two counties so named, the other in AL) *Maryville* • 105,823 • 559 • Eastern TN, partially bounded on the southwest by Tellico Lake reservoir and the Little Tennessee River, and on the north by Fort Loudoun Lake reservoir; drained by the Little River and Ellejoy, Crooked, Hesse, and Ninemile creeks. The Great Smoky Mountains are in the east and southeast, including part of Great Smoky Mountains National Park (which preserves some of the world's best examples of deciduous forest). • Named for William Blount (1749–1800), the only territorial governor of TN and one of the first two U.S. senators from TN • 1795 from Knox (prior to statehood) • Politician Lamar Alexander. Future Texas Republic president Sam Houston taught school here in 1794. • Lumbering; marble quarrying; livestock, dairying, apples, strawberries, corn, tobacco, hay; aluminum reduction; education (Maryville College) • The city of Alcoa was founded by the Aluminum Company of America, following the purchase by the company of dams on the Little Tennessee River as a power source. A planned industrial center, the community produces a number of aluminum products.

BRADLEY (one of two counties so named, the other in AR) *Cleveland* • 87,965 • 329 • Southeastern TN, bounded on the south by the GA state line and on the north by the Hiwassee River. • Named for Col. Edward Bradley (?–1829), an officer in the War of 1812 and the Southern Indian wars, and TN legislator • 1836 from Indian lands • After the Georgia legislature moved to prevent the Cherokee from assembling for any public purpose in 1832, the Indians moved their capital to Red Clay (state historic park) an ultimately futile legal attempt to retain their land. The Trail of Tears began from here in 1838. During the Civil War, Union generals Ulysses S. Grant and William Tecumseh Sherman had headquarters in Cleveland. • Pine timber; corn, hay, fruit, livestock; manufacture of stoves, furniture, textiles, clothing, chemicals; education (Lee University is operated by the Church of God, which has its national headquarters in Cleveland). Cleveland is the headquarters of Cherokee National Forest to the east.

CAMPBELL (one of five counties so named) *Jacksboro* • 39,854 • 480 • Northeastern TN, bounded on the north by the KY state line and on the southeast by the Clinch River, impounded by Norris Dam to form Lake Norris reservoir. The county is partially located in the Cumberlands (in the northwest). Cove Lake and Indian Mountain state parks are also here. • Named for either George Washington Campbell (1769–1848), U.S. senator from TN, U.S. secretary of the treasury, and ambassador to Russia; or for Arthur Campbell (?–1811), militia commander in the American Revolution and a key participant in the establishment of the state of Franklin • 1806 from Anderson and Claiborne • Bituminous-coal mining, lumbering (hardwoods); livestock, tobacco, corn, hay.

CANNON *Woodbury* • 12,826 • 266 • Central TN; drained by the affluents of the Cumberland and Stones rivers. • Named for Col. Newton Cannon (1781–1841), U.S. representative from TN and governor of TN • 1836 from Rutherford, Warren and Smith • Livestock, dairying, truck farming; lumbering.

CARROLL (one of thirteen counties so named) *Huntingdon* • 29,475 • 599 • Northwestern TN; drained by the Big Sandy River, and the South and Rutherford forks of the Obion River.

Part of Natchez Trace State Resort Park and Forest is here, as is part of Milan Army Ammunition Plant. • Named for General William Carroll (1788–1844), officer in the Battle of New Orleans and TN governor • 1821 from Western District (Indian lands) • Cotton, corn, soybeans, sorghum, livestock, truck farms; hardwood lumber; clay; manufacturing.

CARTER (one of five counties so named) *Elizabethton* • 56,742 • 341 • Northeastern TN, bounded on the south and southeast by the Appalachian Trail, forming the NC state line; drained by the Watauga and Doe rivers. Roan Mountain State Park and Hampton Creek Cove State Natural Area are here. The county also includes parts of Cherokee National Forest and Watauga Lake reservoir. • Named for Col. Landon Carter (1760–1800), officer in the Revolutionary and Indian wars, and secretary of the state of Franklin • Organized as Carteret County in 1796 from Washington County; name changed later • Elizabethton is one of the region's oldest settlements. Its settlers organized an independent, democratic government, the Watauga Association here in 1772. Revolutionary War soldiers gathered at Sycamore Shoals (state historic park) in 1780 to march to the Battle of Kings Mountain in SC. • President Andrew Johnson died here. • Tobacco, grain, livestock, fruit; timber; iron-ore deposits; limestone quarries; manufacture of synthetic yarns, twine, clothing, aluminum products, corrugated boxes, piano strings, furniture; education (Milligan College).

CHEATHAM *Ashland City* • 35,912 • 303 • North-central TN, bounded on the west in part by the Cumberland River and on the southwest by the Harpeth River. The county contains the Cheatham Lake reservoir and Narrows of the Harpeth State Historic Area. • Named for Edwin S. Cheatham (1818–1878), TN legislator and Confederate TN state senator • 1856 from Dickson, Montgomery, Davidson, and Robertson counties • Apples, grain, hay, tobacco, livestock.

CHESTER (one of three counties so named) *Henderson* • 15,540 • 289 • Southwestern TN; drained by the South Fork of the Forked Deer River. The county contains part of Chickasaw State Park and Forest. Pinson Mounds State Archeological Park is northwest of Henderson. • Named for Robert I. Chester (1793–?), TN legislator and U.S. marshal for western TN. Chester donated a bell for the courthouse in gratitude for the county having been named for him. • Created as Wisdom in 1875 from Hardeman, Madison, McNairy, and Henderson; name changed in 1879 • Timber; cotton, sorghum, livestock; education (Freed-Hardeman U.).

CLAIBORNE *Tazewell* • 29,862 • 434 • Northeastern TN, bounded on the north by the KY and VA state lines and on the south by the Clinch River, here forming Norris Lake reservoir; drained by the Powell River. The county is traversed by the Cumberland Mountains in the northwest and includes part of Cumberland Gap National Historical Park. • One of three counties named for William C. C. Claiborne (1775–1817), governor of Mississippi Territory, Orleans Territory, LA's first governor, and U.S. representative from TN • 1801 from Grainger and Hawkins • Oil wells, coal mining; lumbering, woodworking; livestock, corn, hay, apples, tobacco; education (Lincoln Memorial U.).

CLAY (one of eighteen counties so named) *Celina* • 7,976 • 236 • Northern TN, bounded on the north by the KY state line; drained by the Obey and Cumberland rivers. The county includes the Dale Hollow National Fish Hatchery, located on Dale Hollow Lake reservoir. • One of fifteen counties named for Henry Clay (1777–1852), U.S. senator from KY, the "Great Pacificator" • 1870 from Jackson and Overton • Coal mining; lumbering; tobacco, grains, livestock.

COCKE *Newport* • 33,565 • 434 • Eastern TN, bounded on the southeast by the Appalachian Trail, forming the NC state line; drained by the French Broad, Pigeon, and Nolichucky rivers. Great Smoky and Bald Mountain ranges are located along the state border. The county includes sections of Great Smoky Mountains National Park, Cherokee National Forest and Douglas Lake reservoir. • Named for William Cocke (1748–1828), explorer with Daniel Boone, territorial legislator who sponsored a bill for the creation of Blount College, now the University of Tennessee, and one of the first two U.S. senators from TN • 1797 from Jefferson • Barite mines; corn, tobacco, tomatoes, apples, dairying, livestock. • The Folklife Center of the Smokies is in Cosby.

COFFEE (one of three counties so named) *Manchester* • 48,014 • 429 • Central TN, bounded on the southeast by the Elk River; drained by the Duck River. The county is located partly in the Cumberlands. Normand Lake reservoir and old Stone Fort State Archeological Park are here. The Arnold Air Force Base, part of which lies in the county, maintains laboratories and a wind tunnel to test jet aircraft and guided missiles. • One of two counties (the other in AL) named for Gen. John Coffee (1772–1833), surveyor and officer in the Battle of New Orleans in the War of 1812 • 1836 from Franklin, Warren, and Bedford • A large Cherokee Indian camp first occupied the site that would become Tullahoma. The present city started out as a labor camp set up in 1850 to construct a railroad between Nashville and Chattanooga. Tullahoma was captured by Union forces in 1863. • Timber; coal; corn, cotton, hay, soybeans, tobacco, potatoes, livestock, dairying; manufacture of aircraft components, shoes, wood products, baseballs, neon signs; food processing; whiskey distilling • The University of TN Space Institute opened in Tullahoma in 1964.

CROCKETT *Alamo* • 14,532 • 265 • Western TN, bounded in part on the northeast by the Middle Fork, and on the southwest by the South Fork of Forked Deer River. • One of two counties (the other in TX) named for Davy Crockett (1786–1836), soldier, scout, and U.S. representative from TN • 1845 from Dyer, Madison, Gibson, and Haywood; declared unconstitutional in 1846; recreated in either 1870 or 1871 • Cotton, corn, soybeans, sorghum, livestock.

CUMBERLAND (one of eight counties so named) *Crossville* • 46,802 • 682 (the fourth largest county in TN) • East-central TN. The county is located on the Cumberland Plateau and is drained by the Sequatchie River and the Obed River (designated here a National Wild and Scenic River). Cumberland Mountain State Park and Ozone Falls State Nature Area are found here. • Named for the Cumberland Mountains. • 1855 from Bledsoe, Morgan, Roane, White, Putnam, Rhea, Van Buren, and Fentress • Stone quarries, coal deposits; timber; corn, hay, potatoes, tobacco, apples, livestock.

DAVIDSON *Nashville* • 569,891 (the second most populated county in TN) • 502 • North-central TN, bounded on the northwest by the Cumberland River, here forming Old Hickory Lake reservoir; intersected by the Cumberland River. • One of two counties (the other in NC) named for General William L. Davidson (?–1781), officer with the NC militia during the Revolutionary War, killed in battle • 1783 from Washington (prior to statehood) • Union troops occupied Nashville from 1862 until the end of the war, although Confederate General John Hood tried to recapture the city during his assault in 1864. During the latter years of the Civil War in Union-occupied Nashville Andrew Johnson served as military governor from within the heavily defended state capitol. The county merged with the city of Nashville in 1963. • President Andrew Jackson (both Jackson and wife Rachel are buried at his "Hermitage" here). Also, politician John Bell; civil rights leader Julian Bond; journalist and humorist Opie Read; astronomer Edward E. Barnard; Air Force officer Frank M. Andrews; writer and critic Randall Jarrell; adventurer and revolutionary leader William Walker. President James K. Polk and Supreme Court justice Howell E. Jackson died here. • Limestone processing; diversified manufacturing; livestock, small grains, dairying, tobacco, tomatoes, fruit; education (Vanderbilt U., Fisk U., and others). Nashville is a religious publishing center; the Southern Baptist Convention's Sunday School Board produces more Sunday school literature here than is published anywhere in the world. • Called "Music City, U.S.A.," Nashville is home to the Country Music Hall of Fame. The Parthenon in the city's Centennial Park is the world's only full-scale reproduction of the original in Greece. Fisk University was home to the Fisk Jubilee singers, who raised money in the mid-1800s by touring the nation and Europe. "Buddy," the first guide dog for the blind in the U.S., joined her owner Morris Frank in Nashville in 1928. Nashville is home to the Predators (Gaylord Entertainment Center) and Titans (Coliseum).

DECATUR *Decaturville* • 11,731 • 334 • Western TN, bounded on the east and south by the Tennessee River, forming Kentucky Lake reservoir in the northeast; drained by its tributaries. The county includes part of Tennessee National Wildlife Refuge. • One of five counties named for Stephen Decatur (1779–1820), U.S. naval officer during the War of 1812 • 1845 from Perry • Livestock, dairying, cotton, corn, hay.

DE KALB *Smithville* • 17,423 • 305 • Central TN, bounded on the southeast by Center Hill Lake reservoir; drained by the Caney Fork of the Cumberland River. Edgar Evins State Park is here as is the Appalachian Craft Center. • One of six counties named for Johann Baron de Kalb (1721–80), German-born French soldier who fought with the Americans during the Revolutionary War • 1837 from Cannon, Warren, White, Wilson and Jackson • Lumber; livestock, corn, small grains, soybeans, fruit, tobacco, dairying.

DICKSON *Charlotte* • 43,156 • 490 • North-central TN, bounded on the northeast by the Cumberland River, here forming part of Cheatham Lake reservoir, and on the east in part by the Harpeth River. Montgomery Bell State Resort Park is here. • Named for William Dickson (1770–1816), physician, TN legislator, and U.S. representative from TN • 1803 from Montgomery and Robertson • Livestock, dairying, field crops, tobacco; timber; iron-ore deposits; manufacture of fabricated-metal products, wood products, and textiles.

DYER *Dyersburg* • 37,279 • 511 • Northwestern TN, bounded on the west by the Mississippi River and on the southwest by the Forked Deer River; drained by the Obion River. • Named for Robert H. Dyer (?–1826), TN legislator and soldier in the War of 1812 and in the Seminole wars • 1823 from Western District (Indian lands) • Cotton, sorghum, soybeans, corn, wheat, livestock; timber; sand and gravel, clay; manufacture of canned foods, cottonseed oil, textiles, rubber products, electric products.

FAYETTE (one of eleven counties so named) *Somerville* • 28,806 • 705 (the third largest county in TN) • Southwestern TN, bounded on the south by the MS state line; drained by the Loosahatchie River Drainage Canal and Wolf River. • One of seventeen counties named for the Marquis de Lafayette (1757–1834), French statesman and soldier who fought with the Americans during the Revolutionary War • 1824 from Shelby and Hardeman • Cotton, livestock, corn, soybeans, sorghum, pecans, fruit.

FENTRESS *Jamestown* • 16,625 • 499 • Northern TN, bounded on the southeast by the Clear Fork River; drained by forks of the Obey and Cumberland rivers. Located in the Cumberland Mountains, the county also includes part of Big South Fork National River and Recreation Area, Scott State Forest and Colditz Cove State Nature Area. • Named for James Fentress (1763–1843), speaker of the TN House of Representatives • 1823 from Overton, White, and Morgan • World War I hero Alvin C. York (state historic park) • Lumbering (hardwoods); corn, tobacco, fruit, vegetables, dairying, livestock; oil and gas; bituminous-coal mines, dimension sandstone.

FRANKLIN (one of twenty-five counties so named) *Winchester* • 39,270 • 553 • Southern TN, bounded on the south by the AL state line and on the west in part by the Elk River. The Cumberland Mountains here rise to 1,800 feet. Also found here are Tim's Ford State Park and two units of South Cumberland Recreation Area (Sewanee Natural Bridge and Carter Caves). Part of Arnold Air Force Base encompasses Woods Reservoir, which, along with Tims Ford Lake reservoir, bisects the county in the north. • One of twenty-three counties named for Benjamin Franklin • 1807 from Rutherford and Indian lands • Winchester began as a stop on the mail route that ran from Virginia to New Orleans. • Singer Dinah Shore • Livestock, corn, cotton, hay, potatoes; timber; coal, crushed stone; education (U. of the South) • Davy Crockett came to Winchester to sign up for the militia. Winchester was the site of Mary Sharp College, nicknamed, "The Pioneer Female College of the South." Founded in 1850, it was the first women's college in the U.S. whose graduation requirements for women were the same as those set for men.

GIBSON (one of two counties so named, the other in IN) *Trenton* • 48,152 • 603 • Northwestern TN, bounded on the northeast by the South Fork of the Obion River on the southwest by the Middle Fork of the Forked Deer River; drained by the North Fork of the Forked Deer River and the Rutherford Fork of the Obion River. Part of Milan Army Ammunition Plant is in the southeast. • Named for Major John H. Gibson (?–1823), an officer in General Andrew Jackson's Natchez expedition • 1823 from Western District (Indian lands) • Cotton, corn, apples, peaches, soybeans, sorghum, vegetables, livestock; manufacturing; timber; clay pits. • One of Davy Crockett's cabins is located near Rutherford.

GILES *Pulaski* • 29,447 • 611 • Southern TN, bounded on the south by the AL state line; drained by the Elk River and Richland Creek. • One of two counties (the other in VA) named for William B. Giles (1762–1830), governor of, and U.S. senator and representative from VA • 1809 from Maury • Poet and critic John C. Ransom • Dairy products, livestock, hay, cotton, tobacco; phosphate mining; manufacturing. • The Sam Davis Memorial Museum in Pulaski honors the young Confederate spy hanged by Union soldiers here for refusing to divulge his source.

GRAINGER *Rutledge* • 20,659 • 280 • Eastern TN, bounded on the north by the Clinch River (here forming in part an arm of Norris Lake reservoir) and on the east and south by the Holston River (here forming in part Cherokee Lake reservoir). The county is traversed by the Clinch Mountains. • Named for Mary Grainger Blount (?–1802), popular First Lady to territorial Governor William Blount • 1796 from Hawkins • Livestock, dairy products, corn, tobacco; lumbering; marble quarrying; manufacture of mobile homes, furniture; mineral spring resorts • Marble from this county was used to build the National Gallery of Art and the Supreme Court building in Washington, D.C.

GREENE (one of fourteen counties so named) *Greeneville* • 62,909 • 622 • Northeastern TN, bounded on the southeast by the Appalachian Trail, here forming the NC state line; drained by the Nolichucky River and Lick Creek. The county

includes part of the Bald Mountains and Cherokee National Forest along the southeastern border. • One of sixteen counties named for General Nathanael Greene (1742–86), hero of the Revolutionary War • 1783 from Washington (prior to statehood) • From 1785 to 1788 Greeneville was the capital of the short-lived state of Franklin that seceded from NC. • Lawyer and Confederate army officer David M. Key. President Andrew Johnson operated a tailor shop in Greeneville (national historic site). Confederate cavalry raider John H. Morgan was killed here on Sept. 4, 1864. • Tobacco (the county is leader in the state), blueberries, strawberries, corn, wheat, hay, poultry, livestock, dairying; oak and pine lumbering; limestone, natural gas, oil and silica deposits; manufacture of electronic equipment, furniture, shoes, pocketbooks, dairy products • Founded as Greeneville College in 1794, Tusculum College is the oldest institution of higher learning west of the Appalachian Mountains. (Virginia Hall on the campus is one of only three buildings in the south designed by Louis Sullivan.) • The Tobacco Experiment Station of the University of TN is in Greeneville.

GRUNDY *Altamont* • 14,332 • 361 • Southeast-central TN; drained by the Elk, Collins, and Little Sequatchie rivers. Four units of South Cumberland Recreation Area are here, including the Visitor Center, the Savage Gulf Area, Grundy Lakes, and Grundy Forest. • One of four counties named for Felix Grundy (1777–1840), U.S. senator and representative from TN, and U.S. attorney general • 1844 from Franklin and Warren • Coal mining; lumbering; apple growing.

HAMBLEN *Morristown* • 58,128 • 161 • Northeastern TN, bounded on the north by Cherokee Lake reservoir (Holston River) and on the south by the Nolichucky River. The county is in the Great Appalachian Valley region with Bays Mountain on its southeastern border. • Named for Hezekiah Hamblen (1775–1855), wealthy landowner and member of the Hawkins County court • 1869 from Grainger, Hawkins, and Jefferson • A cavalry action known as Gilliam's Stampede was fought here on Nov. 12, 1864. • Frontiersman Davy Crockett • Tobacco, corn, hay, soybeans, potatoes, vegetables, poultry, livestock, dairying; manufacture of nylon, rayon, furniture, radio and television equipment. • Panther Creek State Park is home to rare albino white-tailed deer.

HAMILTON (one of ten counties so named) *Chattanooga* • 307,896 (the fourth most populated county in TN) • 543 • Southeastern TN, bounded on the south by the GA state line, crossed by the Tennessee River. The county includes several state parks and part of Chickamauga Lake reservoir. Walden Ridge is in the west and northwest, with parts of Lookout Mountain, and Chickamauga and Chattanooga National Military Park in the south. • One of eight counties named for Alexander Hamilton (?–1804), first U.S. secretary of the treasury • 1819 from Rhea and Indian lands. In January, 1920, the county annexed James, which was organized 1871 from Hamilton and Bradley counties • A major Confederate victory on Chickamauga Creek in GA, September 19–20, 1863, was answered by Union victories at Lookout Mountain ("the Battle Above the Clouds") and Missionary Ridge in Chattanooga on November 23–25, 1863. • Blues singer Bessie Smith; journalist Ralph McGill. Newspaper publisher Adolph Simon Ochs died here. • Livestock, corn, hay, fruit; coal and iron deposits, gravel, clay; timber. Chattanooga, with over 500 factories, is the primary industrial city in the South; manufactures include chemicals, clay products, clothing, furniture, iron and steel products, kitchenware, machinery, paints, paper, petroleum products, textiles; also education (U. of TN at Chattanooga) • Chickamauga and Chattanooga National Military Park was the first national military park. The world's steepest passenger railway, built in 1895, links Chattanooga with the summit of Lookout Mountain. The Chattanooga National Cemetery contains the graves of over 12,000 soldiers. Moonpies were invented in Chattanooga. The first Coca-Cola bottling franchiser was also in the city. The eighty-five-foot dome of the Chattanooga Choo-Choo, a complex of shops and restaurants, in what was once Chattanooga's Southern Railway, is the highest freestanding structure in the world.

HANCOCK *Sneedville* • 6,786 • 222 • Northeastern TN, bounded on the north by the VA state line; drained by the Clinch and Powell rivers; traversed by the Powell Mountains and other ridges of the Appalachians. • One of ten counties named for John Hancock (1737–93), statesman and signer of the Declaration of Independence • 1844 from Claiborne and Hawkins • Livestock, tobacco, tomatoes.

HARDEMAN *Bolivar* • 28,105 • 668 (the fifth largest county in TN) • Southwestern TN, bounded on the south by the MS state line; drained by the Hatchie River. Part of Chickasaw State Park and Forest is in the extreme northeast. • One of two counties (the other in TX) named in full or in part for Col. Thomas J. Hardeman (1788–1854), TN officer in the War of 1812, later a Texas patriot and legislator • 1823 from Hardin County and Western District (Indian lands) • Cotton, corn, fruit, livestock; timber, some lumbering; fuller's clay. • The National Bird Dog Museum is located in Grand Junction.

HARDIN (one of six counties so named) *Savannah* • 25,578 • 578 • Southwestern TN, bounded on the south by the MS and AL state lines, and on the northeast (and drained) by the Tennessee River. The county includes Pickwick Landing State Resort Park on Pickwick Lake reservoir. • Named for Joseph Hardin (1734–1801), officer of the NC minutemen during the Revolutionary War and speaker of the territorial assembly of the Territory South of the River Ohio • 1819 from Western District (Indian lands) • The county was the scene of the Battle of Shiloh, fought on April 6–7, 1862, which prepared the way for General Ulysses Grant's successful siege of Vicksburg. The Confederates lost more than 10,000 men. More than 13,000 died on the Union side. (Shiloh National Military Park is adjoined by Shiloh National Cemetery with 3,716 interments.) • Timber; livestock, cotton, corn, hay; iron ore, limestone deposits; manufacturing.

HAWKINS *Rogersville* • 53,563 • 487 • Northeastern TN, bounded on the north by the VA state line; crossed by the Clinch and Bay mountains; drained by the Holston River. The county includes part of Cherokee Lake reservoir. • Named for Benjamin Hawkins (1754–?), French interpreter for George Washington, U.S. senator from NC in the first Congress, and Indian agent for all tribes south of the Ohio River • 1786 (prior to statehood) from Sullivan • Hardwood timber; tobacco, corn, fruit, hay, livestock, dairying; industrial sand, marble • Marble from this county was used in the Washington Monument. Erected in 1836, the county courthouse is the oldest continually operating courthouse in TN.

HAYWOOD *Brownsville* • 19,797 • 533 • Western TN, bounded in part on the west by the Hatchie River; drained by the Hatchie River and the South Fork of the Forked Deer River. Hatchie National Wildlife Refuge is in the southeast. • Named for John Haywood (?–1826), NC attorney general and TN Supreme Court justice • 1823 from Western District (Indian lands) • Sea adventure writer Richard Halliburton • Cotton, soybeans, sorghum, tomatoes, corn, livestock; timber.

HENDERSON (one of five counties so named) *Lexington* • 25,522 • 520 • Western TN; drained by the Big Sandy and Middle Fork of the Forked Deer rivers. The county includes part of Natchez Trace State Resort Park and Forest, and numerous reservoirs. • Probably named for James Henderson, an officer under the command of Andrew Jackson in the War of 1812 • 1821 from Western District (Indian lands) • Cotton, corn, soybeans, peaches, vegetables, livestock; lumbering.

HENRY (one of ten counties so named) *Paris* • 31,115 • 562 • Northwestern TN, bounded on the north by the KY state line, on the east by Kentucky Lake reservoir (the Tennessee River receiving the Big Sandy River here); drained by the East Fork of the Clarks River and forks of the Obion. Paris Landing State Resort Park and part of Tennessee National Wildlife Refuge are located here. • One of ten counties (including Patrick County, VA) named for Patrick Henry (1736–99), patriot, governor of VA and statesman • 1821 from Western District (Indian lands) • Supreme Court justice Howell E. Jackson • Corn, cotton, tobacco, sweet potatoes, soybeans, livestock; dairy products; some manufacturing; timber; clay pits. • Located in Paris, the world's largest replica of the Eiffel Tower stands sixty-five feet tall.

HICKMAN *Centerville* • 22,295 • 613 • Central TN; drained by the Duck River and its tributaries. The Natchez Trace closely parallels the southeast boundary. • Named for Edwin Hickman, American surveyor killed by Indians • 1807 from Dickson • Livestock, dairying; diverse agriculture; phosphate mining; lumbering; some manufacturing.

HOUSTON (one of five counties so named) *Erin* • 8,088 • 200 • Northwestern TN, bounded on the west by Kentucky Lake reservoir (the second largest man-made lake in the U.S.), formed here by the Tennessee River). • One of three counties named for Sam Houston (1793–1863), governor of TN, president of the Republic of Texas, U.S. senator from TX and governor of TX • 1871 from Dickson, Montgomery, Stewart and Humphreys • Livestock, dairying, corn, tobacco, sweet potatoes.

HUMPHREYS (one of two counties so named; the other in MS) *Waverly* • 17,929 • 532 • Central TN, bounded on the west by Kentucky Lake reservoir, formed here by the Tennessee River; drained by the Duck and Buffalo rivers. The county includes Johnsonville State Historic Park and part of Tennessee National Wildlife Refuge. • Named for Parry Wayne Humphreys (?–1839), U.S. representative from TN and TN jurist • 1809 from Stewart • Timber; livestock, dairying, corn, soybeans, tomatoes.

JACKSON (one of twenty-four counties so named) *Gainesboro* • 10,984 • 309 • North-central TN; crossed by the Cumberland River, here forming part of Cordell Hull Lake reservoir. • One of twenty-two counties named directly or indirectly for President Andrew Jackson • 1801 from Smith County and Indian lands • Tobacco, livestock, corn, fruit; oil wells; timber.

JEFFERSON *Dandridge* • 44,294 • 274 • Eastern TN, bounded on the northwest by the Holston River; drained by the French Broad River. The county is located in the Great Appalachian Valley. It includes parts of Cherokee Lake and Douglas Lake reservoirs. • One of twenty-six counties named directly or indirectly for President Thomas Jefferson • 1792 (prior to statehood) from Greene and Hawkins • Livestock, dairying, tobacco, fruit, corn, hay; zinc mines, limestone quarries; education (Carson-Newman College) • The County Museum displays the original marriage bond of David Crockett and Polly Findley, dated August 12, 1806. Dandridge was saved from extinction by Eleanor Roosevelt who persuaded her husband to have a dike built around the town before the TVA flooded the area.

JOHNSON (one of twelve counties so named) *Mountain City* • 17,499 • 298 • Extreme northeastern TN, bounded on the north by the VA state line, and on the east and southeast by the NC state line; drained by the Watauga River. The county is traversed by the Iron and Stone mountains. Part of Watauga Lake reservoir and Cherokee National Forest are located here. The Appalachian Trail closely follows the northwestern boundary of the county. • Probably named for Thomas Johnson, prominent citizen of the area and one of its first justices of the peace • 1836 from Carter • Lumbering; tobacco, vegetables, fruit, livestock; granite quarries.

KNOX *Knoxville* • 382,032 (the third most populated county in TN) • 508 • Eastern TN, bounded on the southwest by the Clinch River and on the south in part by Fort Loudon Lake reservoir; drained by the Holston and French Broad rivers, which converge in Knoxville to form the Tennessee River. House Mountain State Nature Area is in the northeast. • One of nine counties named for Gen. Henry Knox (1750–1806), Revolutionary War officer and first U.S. secretary of war •

1792 (prior to statehood) from Greene and Hawkins • Knoxville served as the capital of TN from 1792 to 1812 and in 1817. It was here that the TN state constitution was written. During the Civil War, Union forces led by Major General Ambrose E. Burnside defeated Confederate troops under Gen. James Longstreet here. The 1982 World's Fair was held in Knoxville. • TN's first governor John Sevier; writer James Agee; admiral David Farragut; Supreme Court justice Edward T. Sanford; naturalist and conservationist Joseph Wood Krutch. TN governor William Blount, newspaper editor William G. Brownlow, and singer Hank Williams all died here. Novelist Cormac McCarthy spent many years in Knoxville and set some of his work here. • Dairying, corn, hay, tobacco, fruits; coal mines, limestone and marble quarries, clay pits; manufacture of textiles, clothing, food products; education (U. of TN; Knoxville College) • Blount Mansion, built in 1792 by territorial governor William Blount, is the oldest frame house west of the Appalachians. TVA has its headquarters in Knoxville.

LAKE (one of twelve counties so named) *Tiptonville* • 7,954 • 163 • Extreme northwestern TN, bounded on the north by the KY state line and on the west by the Mississippi River (forming the MO state line). Reelfoot Lake State Resort Park, Lake Isom National Wildlife Refuge, and part of Reelfoot National Wildlife Refuge are here. • Named for Reelfoot Lake on its eastern border • 1870 from Obion • Timber; corn, sorghum, soybeans, alfalfa, cotton, livestock • Reelfoot Lake was formed from the Mississippi River as a result of land shifts during the New Madrid earthquakes of 1811 and 1812.

LAUDERDALE *Ripley* • 27,101 • 470 • Western TN, bounded on the west by the Mississippi River, on the north by the Forked Deer River and on the south by the Hatchie River. Chickasaw National Wildlife Refuge, Sunk Lake State Nature Area, and Fort Pillow State Historic Park are here. • One of three counties named for Col. James Lauderdale (?–1814), commander of troops during the War of 1812 who died in the Battle of New Orleans • 1835 from Dyer, Tipton, and Haywood • Novelists Roark Bradford and Alex Haley (house museum) • Timber; cotton, corn, soybeans, wheat, sorghum, fruit, livestock.

LAWRENCE (one of eleven counties so named) *Lawrenceburg* • 39,926 • 617 • Southern TN, bounded on the south by the AL state line; drained by the Buffalo River and Shoal Creek. David Crockett State Park and David Crockett Cabin and Museum are here. • One of nine counties named for Captain James Lawrence (1781–1813), U.S. Navy commander in the War of 1812 • 1817 from Hickman and Maury • Peanuts, fruit, cotton, corn, livestock, dairy products, especially cheese; timber; phosphate mining; manufacture of clothing. • The Natchez Trace crosses the county in the extreme northwest.

LEWIS (one of seven counties so named) *Hohenwald* • 11,367 • 282 • Central TN; drained by the Buffalo River and Swan Creek. The Meriwether Lewis National Monument near Hohenwald marks the site of the explorer's death. The Natchez Trace crosses the county southwest to northeast. • One of five counties named for Meriwether Lewis (1774–1809), co-leader of the Lewis and Clark Expedition. • 1843 from Hickman, Maury, Wayne, and Lawrence • Lumbering; dairying, livestock, corn, hay, cotton.

LINCOLN (one of twenty-four counties so named) *Fayetteville* • 31,340 • 570 • Southern TN, bounded on the south by the AL state line; crossed by the Elk River. • One of four counties directly named for General Benjamin Lincoln (1733–1810), Revolutionary War officer, U.S. secretary of war • 1809 from Bedford • Timber; livestock, corn, grain, fruits, sweet potatoes, tomatoes, dairying; some manufacturing.

LOUDON *Loudon* • 39,086 • 229 • Eastern TN, bounded on the northwest by the Clinch River and on the northeast in part by Fort Loudon Lake reservoir. The county is located in the Great Appalachian Valley and is crossed by the Tennessee and Little Tennessee rivers. It includes part of Tellico Lake reservoir. • Named for Fort Loudon, itself named for John Campbell (1705–82), 4th earl of Loudoun, commander of British forces during the French and Indian Wars • Organized as Christiana County in 1870 from Blount, Monroe, McMinn, and Roane; the name was changed later that year. • Corn, tobacco, hay, fruit, livestock, dairying; wineries; barite mines; pine oak harvesting; diversified manufacturing.

MACON *Lafayette* • 20,386 • 307 • Northern TN, bounded on the north by the KY state line; drained by affluents of the Barren and Cumberland rivers. • One of six counties named for Nathaniel Macon (1758–1837), NC legislator, Speaker of the House and President Pro Tem of the U.S. senate • 1842 from Smith and Sumner • Nera White, first female player inducted into the National Basketball Hall of Fame • Timber; corn, tobacco, livestock • Its numerous mineral springs and elegant hotels made Red Boiling Springs a 1920s tourist mecca. The Red Boiling Springs Co-Generation Electricity Plant was the world's first sawdust-fired gas turbine plant for producing electricity.

MADISON *Jackson* • 91,837 • 557 • Western TN; drained by the Middle and South forks of Forked Deer River. There are extensive Native American mounds at Pinson Mounds State Archeological Park. • One of twenty counties named directly or indirectly for President James Madison • 1821 from Western District (Indian lands) • A key supply point, Jackson was occupied by both Confederate and Union forces during the Civil War, with both Nathan Bedford Forrest and Ulysses S. Grant quartering troops here. • Railroad engineer Casey Jones; blues singer and harmonica virtuoso Sonny Boy Williams; jurist Ben B. Lindsey • Vegetables, soybeans, strawberries, cotton, livestock; sand pits; manufacture of textiles, tile, wood and paper products, power tools, batteries, offset printing plates, store fixtures, aluminum foil; food processing and soft-drink bottling; education (Union U.; Lambuth College; Lane College). The Tennessee Agricultural Experiment Station is in the county.

MARION *Jasper* • 27,776 • 500 • Southern TN, bounded on the south by the AL and GA state lines; drained by the Tennessee and Sequatichie rivers and Little Sequatchie River. The county is partly located in the Cumberlands. Prentice Cooper and Franklin state forests are here. • One of seventeen counties named for Gen. Francis Marion (?–1795), SC soldier and legislator, known as "The Swamp Fox" for his tactics during the Revolutionary War • 1817 from Western District (Indian lands) • Coal, iron-ore deposits; dairying, livestock, corn, hay, soybeans, cotton.

MARSHALL (one of twelve counties so named) *Lewisburg* • 26,767 • 375 • Central TN; drained by the Duck River and its tributaries. Henry Horton State Resort Park is located here. • One of eight counties named for John Marshall (1755–1835), fourth Chief Justice of the U.S. • 1836 from Giles, Bedford, Lincoln and Maury • Livestock, dairy products, fruit, hay, grain, tobacco; timber; some manufacturing • Lewisburg is the world headquarters of the Tennessee Walking Horse Breeders and Exhibitors Association.

MAURY *Columbia* • 69,498 • 613 • Central TN; drained by the Duck River. The Natchez Trace closely parallels the northwest boundary of the county. Tennessee Wildlife Observation Area–Mansanto Ponds and Southport Saltpepper Cave are also here. • Named for Abram P. Maury, Sr. (1766–1825), TN legislator and one of the commissioners to superintend sales of land acquired from the Cherokee Indians • 1807 from Williamson and Indian lands • Columbia developed as a mule trading center. During the Civil War it was Confederate general Nathan Bedford Forrest's base of operations, and was occupied alternately by Union and Confederate forces. • President James K. Polk • Cattle, mules, dairying, corn, hay, tobacco, wheat, sorghum, pecans; phosphate and phosphate chemicals; manufacture of graphite electrodes, air conditioners, work clothing, hosiery, cellulose sponges, food processing. • The National Tennessee Walking Horse Jubilee is held in Columbia each year.

MCMINN *Athens* • 49,015 • 430 • Southeastern TN, bounded on the southwest by the Hiwassee River. The county lies in the Great Appalachian Valley. Cherokee National Forest lies on its southeastern border. • Named for Joseph McMinn (1758–1824), governor of TN • 1819 from Cherokee Indian lands • Corn, wheat, fruit, tobacco, hay, beef and dairy cattle; limestone, barrite; pine, hardwood; manufacture of textiles, furniture, paper, animal feeds, chemicals, kitchen stoves, electric motors, farm machinery; education (Tennessee Wesleyan College).

MCNAIRY *Selmer* • 24,653 • 560 • Southwestern TN, bounded on the south by the MS state line; drained by tributaries of the South Fork of the Forked Deer, Hatchie and Tennessee rivers. Big Hill Pond State Park is here. • Named for John McNairy (1762–1937), a judge in U.S. District Court for TN • 1823 from Hardin • Sheriff Buford Pusser (home and museum) • Cotton, corn, hay, soybeans, vegetables, livestock; timber; manufacturing.

MEIGS (one of two counties so named; the other in OH) *Decatur* • 11,086 • 195 • Southeastern TN, bounded on the northwest by the Tennessee River, forming Chickamauga Lake and Watts Bar Lake reservoirs; drained by the Hiwassee River. The county is located in the Great Appalachian Valley. • Named for Return Jonathan Meigs (1740–1823), colonel in the Revolutionary War • 1836 from Hamilton, McMinn, Rhea, and Roane • Livestock, tobacco; lumbering, sawmills and planing mills.

MONROE *Madisonville* • 38,961 • 635 • Southeastern TN, bounded on the southeast and east by the NC state line, and on the northeast by the Little Tennessee River; drained by its tributaries. The Unicoi Mountains are found along its southern border. The county includes Fort Loudon State Historic Park and part of Cherokee National Forest. Lost Sea, the largest underground lake in the U.S., is also here. • One of seventeen counties named for President James Monroe • 1819 from Roane (Hiwassee Purchase, Indian lands) • Some gold was mined here in the 19th century. • American Indian scholar Sequoyah (birthplace museum) • Lumbering; livestock, dairying, fruit, tobacco, hay, corn, dairying; barite mines.

MONTGOMERY (one of eighteen counties so named) *Clarksville* • 134,768 • 539 • Northern TN, bounded on the north by the KY state line; drained by the Cumberland and Red rivers. Part of Fort Campbell Military Reservation is located here. Dunbar Cave State Natural Area has a subterranean stream and varicolored rock formations. • Named for John Montgomery (?–1794), captain under George Rogers Clark, planner of Clarksville, TN • Organized 1796 by the division of Tennessee County into Montgomery and Robertson counties. • Clarksville was captured by the Union Army in 1862. • Olympic athlete Wilma Rudolph; columnist Elizabeth M. Gilmer; Supreme Court justice Horace Lurton; pathologist E.W. Goodpasture; federal judge West Hughes Humphreys • Strawberries, dark tobacco (a leading market center), beef and dairy cattle; diversified manufacturing, including snuff, cigars, cheese, rubber, flour, heating and air-conditioning units, clothing, footwear, machine parts; iron ore and limestone deposits; education (Austin Peay State U.) • Dunbar Cave, a famous dance hall during the Big Band period, was purchased by Roy Acuff to showcase Grand Ole Opry performers in the 50s and 60s. Port Royal State Historical Park features one of the few remaining covered bridges in the state.

MOORE (one of three counties so named) *Lynchburg* • 5,740 • 129 (one of the fifty smallest counties in the U.S.) • Southern TN, bounded on the southeast by the Elk River. • Named for General William Moore (1786–1871), officer in the War of 1812 and TN legislator • 1871 from Bedford, Franklin, Lincoln and Coffee • Livestock, grain, tobacco, timber • The Jack Daniels distillery is located here.

MORGAN (one of eleven counties so named) *Wartburg* • 19,757 • 522 • Northeast-central TN, located on the Cumberland Plateau. The county is bounded in part on the northwest by the South Fork of the Cumberland River and drained by the Obed River (designated here a National Wild and Scenic River). A small part of Big South Fork National River and Recreation Area extends into the county. Also here are Frozen Head State Park and Natural Area, and Lone Mountain State Forest. • One of nine counties named for General Daniel Morgan (1736–1802), an officer in the Revolutionary War and U.S. representative from VA • 1817 from Roane; in 1903 the county annexed part of Anderson • Lumbering; corn, hay, tobacco, vegetables, livestock, dairying; coal and gas deposits.

OBION *Union City* • 32,450 • 545 • Northwestern TN, bounded on the north by the KY state line and on the northwest by Reelfoot Lake; drained by the Obion River and its tributaries. The county includes part of Reelfoot National Wildlife Refuge. • Named for the Obion River • 1823 from Western District (Indian lands) • Reelfoot Lake, formed by the earthquakes of 1811–12, was the object of a violent feud between the Tennessee Land Company and local fishermen. Davy Crockett represented the area in Congress. 10,000 Confederate troops were trained at Camp Brown in Union City in preparation for an invasion of KY. Gen. Nathan Bedford Forrest and his troops captured Union forces at Union City in 1864. The first monument erected to the memory of unknown Confederate soldiers was dedicated here in 1869. • Soybeans, grain, corn, cotton, wheat, sorghum, livestock; meat packing; manufacture of textiles, clothing, blinds and awnings, automobile accessories and parts.

OVERTON *Livingston* • 20,118 • 433 • Northern TN; drained by affluents of the Obey and Cumberland rivers. Located in the Cumberlands, the county also includes Standing Stone State Park and Forest. (The park was named after "standing stone," an eight-foot-tall rock that separated two Native American nations.) • Named for John Overton (1766–1833), TN Supreme Court Justice and founder with Andrew Jackson of Memphis, TN • 1806 from Jackson and Indian lands • The first commercial oil well in TN was sunk here in 1866. • Corn, hay, tobacco, fruits, livestock, poultry, dairying; coal mining; lumbering; manufacture of clothing, auto parts • The county is home to the Muddy Pond Mennonite community.

PERRY *Linden* • 7,631 • 415 • West-central TN, bounded on the west by the Tennessee River, here forming the Kentucky Lake reservoir; drained by the Buffalo River. The county includes Mousetail Landing State Park. • One of ten counties named for Oliver Hazard Perry (1785–1819), U.S. naval officer during the War of 1812 • 1821 from Hickman and Humphreys • Livestock, corn, hay, soybeans; timber.

PICKETT *Byrdstown* • 4,945 (the least populated county in TN) • 163 • Northern TN, bounded on the north by the KY state line and on the west by Dale Hollow Lake (reservoir). The county includes part of Pickett State Park and Big South Fork National River and Recreation Area. • Named for Howell L. Pickett (1847–?), a TN legislator instrumental in forming the county • 1879 from Fentress and Overton • American statesman and Nobel Peace prize winner Cordell Hull • Hardwood, pine; bituminous-coal mining; livestock, tobacco, corn.

POLK (one of twelve counties so named) *Benton* • 16,050 • 435 • Southeastern TN, bounded on the east by the NC state line, on the south by the GA state line, and on the northeast by the Unicoi Mountains; drained by the Hiwassee (State Scenic) River and Ocoee (State Recreational) River. The county also includes Rock Creek Gorge, Coker Creek, and Turtletown Creek Falls scenic areas. Most of the county is located in Cherokee National Forest. • One of eleven counties named for President James K. Polk • 1839 from Bradley and McMinn • Beginning in 1843, the copper ore processing industry created a fifty-four-mile swatch of deforested, denuded, and degraded land called the Copper Basin. The TVA and copper industry have recently partnered a reforestation program to fight erosion, but have excluded several hundred acres near Ducktown as a reminder of the devastation • Copper production; pine; oats, corn, hay, soybeans, livestock, dairy products; tourism (whitewater rafting and kayaking).

PUTNAM (one of nine counties so named) *Cookeville* • 62,315 • 401 • Central TN; drained by affluents of the Cumberland River. The county is located on the Cumberland Plateau. It includes part of Center Hill Lake reservoir (Caney Fork River). Burgess Falls State Natural Area is also here. • One of eight counties definitively named for Gen. Israel Putnam (1718–90), American commander at the Battle of Bunker Hill • 1842 from Smith, White, DeKalb, Overton, and Jackson • Small grains, tobacco, corn, apples, hay, poultry, cattle, hogs; lumbering; granite quarrying, oil and gas; diverse manufacturing, including filtration equipment, furniture, heating elements, motor vehicle parts, candy and wood products, marble and granite works; education (TN Tech. U.).

RHEA *Dayton* • 28,400 • 316 • Eastern TN, bounded on the southeast by Chickamauga Lake reservoir and on the northeast by Watts Bar Lake reservoir; drained by the Tennessee River. Stinging Fork, Piney Falls, and Laurel-Snow Pocket Wilderness state nature areas are here. • Named for John Rhea (1753–1832), U.S. representative from TN • 1807 from Roane • The Rhea County Courthouse in Dayton was the scene of the Scopes Trial (July 10–21, 1925) in which William Jennings Bryan prosecuted biology teacher John Thomas Scopes for teaching evolution. Clarence Darrow was defense attorney. Bryan died here five days after the conclusion of the trial. • Fruit, corn, vegetables, hay, dairying, livestock; bituminous-coal mining; manufacture of synthetic yarns, textiles, stone products, gas heating equipment, electrical appliances; education (Bryan College).

ROANE (one of two counties so named; the other in WV) *Kingston* • 51,910 • 361 • Eastern TN, drained by the Clinch River, which enters the Tennessee River north of Watts Bar Lake. Part of Oak Ridge National Laboratory is here. • Named

for Archibald Roane (?–1819), governor of TN and TN Supreme Court justice • 1801 from Knox and Indian lands • Kingston was the state capital for one day: September 21, 1807, during which time the state legislature discussed a treaty with the Cherokee Indians. • Speaker of the House Sam Rayburn • Coal and iron mines; hardwood lumbering; fruit, tobacco, corn, wheat, livestock, dairying; some manufacturing.

ROBERTSON (one of three counties so named) *Springfield* • 54,433 • 477 • Northern TN, bounded on the north by the KY state line; drained by the Red River and its affluents Carr Creek and Sulphur Fork • Named for James Robertson (1742–1814), active supporter of statehood for TN, and founder of present-day Nashville • Organized 1796 by the division of Tennessee County into Montgomery and Robertson. • Banker and public official Jesse H. Jones • Dairying, fruit, tobacco (Springfield is an important tobacco auction, shipping, and manufacturing center), grain, livestock; manufacture of leather boots, shoe heels, golf bags, milling machine blades and cutters, electric ranges, furniture, cushions, pet foods, candy, soft drinks; wild horse and burro adoption; limestone deposits • Adams is known throughout the region as home to the legendary Bell Witch ghost.

RUTHERFORD *Murfreesboro* • 182,023 (53% increase since 1990; the second fastest growing and fifth most populated county in TN) • 619 • Central TN; drained by the Stones River. The county includes part of J. Percy Priest Lake reservoir. • One of two counties (the other in NC) named for General Griffith Rutherford (?–1805), Revolutionary War hero and NC legislator • 1803 from Davidson, Williamson, and Wilson • Murfreesboro served as state capital from 1819 to 1825. It was the scene of a Union offensive to trisect the Confederacy from Dec. 31, 1862 to Jan. 2, 1863 (Stones River National Battlefield) • Economist and educator James M. Buchanan; writer Charles E. Craddock (pseudonym of Mary Noailles Murfree); sports columnist and author Grantland Rice; Confederate spy Samuel Davis • Corn, hay, wheat, cotton, beef cattle, dairying, Tennessee Walking Horses, gaited horses, ponies, racehorses; lumbering, cedar woodenware; limestone quarries; manufacture of motor vehicles, electric motors and heating units, furniture, clothing, silk and rayon goods, hospital equipment; education (Middle TN State U.).

SCOTT (one of eleven counties so named) *Huntsville* • 21,127 • 532 • Northern TN, bounded on the north by the KY state line; drained by the South Fork of the Cumberland River and New River. The county is situated in a rugged region of the Cumberlands. It includes part of Big South Fork National River and Recreation Area. • One of five counties named for Winfield Scott (1786–1866), commander of the Union Army at the beginning of the Civil War • 1849 from Fentriss, Morgan, Anderson, and Campbell • Lumbering; coal and clay, oil fields; corn, tobacco, hay, livestock, vegetables.

SEQUATCHIE *Dunlap* • 11,370 • 266 • Southeast-central TN; drained by the Sequatchie River. The county lies partly in the Cumberland Mountains, with Walden Ridge in the southeast. The Dunlap Coke Ovens Historic Site is also here. • Named for the valley of the Sequatchie River • 1857 from Hamilton (and previously from Bledsoe, Marion, and Grundy) • Coal mining; lumbering; livestock, feed crops, tobacco; some manufacturing.

SEVIER (one of three counties so named) *Sevierville* • 71,170 (39% increase since 1990; the third fastest growing county in TN) • 592 • Eastern TN, bounded on the south and southeast by the Appalachian Trail, forming the NC state line; drained by the French Broad River and Little Pigeon River. Some of the oldest mountains in the world are found in the Great Smoky Mountains (national park), which tower along its southern border. The peak of Clingmans Dome here, at 6,643 feet, is the highest point in the state. The county includes Douglas Dam and part of Douglas Lake reservoir. • Named for John Sevier (1745–1815), only governor of the state of Franklin, later governor of TN, and U.S. representative from TN • 1794 (prior to statehood) from Jefferson • Singer and songwriter Dolly Parton • Lumbering; livestock, fruit, tobacco, corn, hay; manufacturing; a major tourist center. • The Arrowmont School of Arts and Crafts was established in Gatlinburg in 1912 as a settlement school in what was then a poor Appalachian town; the school now serves over 1,500 students each summer.

SHELBY *Memphis* • 897,472 (the most populated county in TN) • 755 (the largest county in TN) • Extreme southwestern TN, bounded on the south by the MS state line and on the west by the AR state line, formed by the Mississippi River; drained by the Loosahatchie and Wolf rivers. The county includes Meeman-Shelby Forest and T.O. Fuller state parks, and the U.S. Naval Air Station. • One of nine counties named directly or indirectly for General Isaac Shelby (1750–1826), officer in the Revolutionary War, and first governor of KY • 1819 from Hardin • Explorer Hernando de Soto first saw the Mississippi River from the bluff that would in 1819 be organized by generals Andrew Jackson and James Winchester and Judge John Overton into the river town of Memphis. Thousands perished in a series of yellow fever epidemics in the 1870s. Civil rights activist Dr. Martin Luther King was assassinated here in 1968. Elvis Presley reigned from Graceland as the king of Rock and Roll until his death in 1977. • Supreme Court justice Abe Fortas; blues singers Aretha Franklin and Alberta Hunter; actor Morgan Freeman; government official Benjamin Hooks. Confederate general Nathan Bedford Forrest died here. • Cotton, pecans, soybeans, wheat, dairying, livestock; commercial, distribution, and manufacturing center of the Midsouth, trading market for hardwood lumber and cotton; music recording; education (U. of Memphis; Rhodes College) • The first Holiday Inn was built in Memphis. The Memphis in May International Festival, held in conjunction with the Cotton Carnival and the International Barbecue Contest is one of the largest annual events in the U.S. Memphis is home to the Grizzlies (The Pyramid).

SMITH (one of four counties so named) *Carthage* • 17,712 • 314 • North-central TN, in the central basin; drained by the Cumberland River and its tributaries. Part of Old Hickory Lake and Cordell Hull Lake reservoirs are here. • Named for Colonel Daniel Smith (1748–1818), officer in the Revolutionary War, secretary of the Territory South of the River Ohio, and U.S. senator from TN • 1799 from Indian lands • Livestock, dairying, tobacco, soybeans, grain, corn; lumbering; zinc mines, limestone quarries.

STEWART (one of two counties so named; the other in GA) *Dover* • 12,370 • 458 • Northwestern TN, bounded on the north by the KY state line and on the west by the Tennessee River (Kentucky Lake reservoir); drained by the Cumberland River, here forming Lake Barkley. The county contains Fort Donelson National Battlefield and Fort Henry, and the southern third of the Land Between the Lakes Recreational Area. Cross Creeks National Wildlife Refuge is also here. • Named for Duncan Stewart (1752–1815), Revolutionary War veteran, wealthy planter and surveyor-general, and TN legislator • 1803 from Montgomery • The first major victory for the Union Army in the Civil War occurred here in February, 1862 under the leadership of General Ulysses S. Grant. • Livestock, dairying, corn, fruit, hay, tobacco.

SULLIVAN (one of six counties so named) *Blountville* • 153,048 • 413 • Northeastern TN, in the Great Appalachian Valley, bounded on the north by the VA state line; drained by the South Fork of the Holston River, forming South Holston Dam. The county includes part of Cherokee National Forest, Warriors' Path State Park, and Bays Mountain Park State Natural Area (a 4,000-acre nature center and animal sanctuary). The Holston Mountain Range and a section of the Appalachian Trail are on the eastern border. • One of five counties named directly or indirectly for General John Sullivan (1740–95), officer in the Revolutionary War and governor of NH • 1779 (prior to statehood) from Washington County • At one time VA claimed ownership of the county over NC, eventually losing it to the state of TN. Fort Patrick Henry was built in Kingsport in 1776 to protect the Wilderness Road, which later facilitated the first great westward migration. In 1909, in an effort to attract industry, a MA city planner was hired by two NY financiers to set up Kingsport as one of the first model cities. • Tobacco, corn, fruit, hay, dairying, livestock; lumbering; limestone, clay, iron-ore deposits; manufacture of structural steel, office machines, lumber, textiles, chemicals, explosives, leather, glass, paper, bricks, cement, fabricated metals, books (Kingsport Press is one of the largest book plants in the U.S.); education (East TN State U.) • Bristol is a dual city. After a bitter boundary dispute, the TN/VA state line was placed down the center of the main thoroughfare in 1903. Elvis Presley played his last concert as an opening act in Kingsport in 1955.

SUMNER (one of two counties so named, the other in KS) *Gallatin* • 130,449 • 529 • Northern TN, bounded on the north by the KY state line and on the south by Old Hickory

Lake reservoir, formed by the Cumberland River; drained by headstreams of the Red River and by Drake Creek. Bledsoe Creek State Park is here. • Named for Jethro Sumner (?–1785), officer in the Revolutionary War and wealthy landowner • Organized 1786 or 1787 (prior to statehood) from Davidson County (NC), becoming part of the Territory South of the River Ohio from its creation in May 1790 until it became the state of TN in 1796 • Livestock, dairying, wheat, hay, tobacco, strawberries, apples, corn. • Wynnewood, built in 1828 as a stagecoach inn, is believed to be the largest log structure ever built in TN.

TIPTON (one of two counties so named, the other in IN) *Covington* • 51,271 • 459 • Western TN, bounded on the west in part by the Mississippi River and on the north by the Hatchie River. • Named for Jacob Tipton (?–1791), soldier killed in a battle with Indians • 1823 from Western District (Indian lands) • Cotton, fruit, livestock; cotton processing, some manufacturing.

TROUSDALE *Hartsville* • 7,259 • 114 (the smallest county in TN and one of the fifty smallest counties in the U.S.) • Northern TN, bounded on the south in part by Old Hickory Lake reservoir, formed by the Cumberland River. • Named for General William Trousdale (1790–1872), TN legislator, governor of TN, and U.S. minister to Brazil • 1870 from Macon, Smith, Wilson, and Sumner • Livestock, tobacco, corn, grain, hay. • The abandoned hull of an enormous concrete cooling tower marks the site of what would have been the largest nuclear reactor plant in the world.

UNICOI *Erwin* • 17,667 • 186 • Northeastern TN, bounded on the southwest and south by the Appalachian Trail, forming the NC state line; drained by the Nolichucky River. The Bald Mountains run partly along the eastern boundary. Much of the county is covered by Cherokee National Forest. • Named for the Unaka Mountains. • 1875 from Washington and Carter • Lumbering, tobacco, fruit, hay, livestock; some manufacturing.

UNION (one of eighteen counties so named) *Maynardville* • 17,808 • 224 • Northeastern TN, bounded on the northwest by the Powell River (here forming one arm of Norris Lake reservoir); crossed by the Clinch River (here forming the other part of Norris Lake reservoir); drained by Bullrun Creek. The county is traversed by ridges of the Appalachians. Part of Chuck Swan State Forest and Big Ridge State Park are here. • Given this name in support of the preservation of the United States or for the union of land taken from several counties to form the county. • 1850 from Anderson, Campbell, Grainger, Claiborne, and Knox • Tobacco, livestock.

VAN BUREN *Spencer* • 5,508 • 273 • Central TN, bounded on the north by the Caney Fork of the Cumberland River. The county is located in the Cumberlands and includes part of Fall Creek Falls State Park and Natural Area, and Big Bone Cave State Natural Area. • One of four counties named for President Martin Van Buren • 1840 from Bledsoe, Warren and White • Coal mines; livestock; some farming; lumbering.

WARREN *McMinnville* • 38,276 • 433 • Central TN; drained by the Collins River. The eastern portion of the county is in the Cumberlands. Cumberland Caverns, one of the largest cave systems in the U.S., is here. The county also contains part of Center Hill Lake reservoir and Great Falls Dam. • One of fourteen counties named for General Joseph Warren (1741–1775), Revolutionary War officer who died in the Battle of Bunker Hill • 1807 from White, Jackson, and Smith counties, and Indian lands • Livestock, peaches, apples; manufacturing; marble and granite quarries; tree nurseries (With over 400 nurseries shipping trees and plants throughout the world, the county has been called the "Nursery Center of the South.")

WASHINGTON *Jonesborough* • 107,198 • 326 • Northeastern TN, bounded on the northeast by the Watauga River; drained by the Nolichucky River. The county is located in the Great Appalachian Valley, with mountain ridges in the south and southeast. It includes part of Cherokee National Forest. • One of thirty-one counties named for President George Washington • 1777; original county (prior to statehood). Washington was the first county in TN formed at the request of the Watauga Association of settlers. • Founded in 1779, Jonesborough (also spelled Jonesboro) is the oldest incorporated town in the state. Here the state of Franklin was organized with the town designated as its capital and John Sevier the interim state's first and only governor. The Franklin General Assembly convened twice in the town before its disintegration. One of the first abolitionist newspapers in the U.S., the *Emancipator*, was published in Jonesborough in 1820. • Frontiersman Davy Crockett (birthplace); President Andrew Jackson (who practiced law in Jonesborough) • Fruit, burley tobacco (cultivation and marketing), corn, hay, alfalfa, dairying, cattle, poultry; iron ore, lead, zinc, manganese, clay, limestone quarries; hardwood timber; manufacture of telephone and electrical and electronic equipment, textiles, hardwood flooring, hospital supplies, chemicals, clothing, furniture, tools, building materials; education (East TN State U.). A Veterans Administration center in the county serves five states. • The National Association for the Preservation and Perpetuation of Storytelling (NAPPS) is headquartered in Jonesborough and hosts the annual National Storytelling Festival here in October.

WAYNE (one of sixteen counties so named) *Waynesboro* • 16,842 • 734 (the second largest county in TN) • Southern TN, bounded on the south by the AL state line; drained by the Buffalo River and tributaries of the Tennessee River. • One of fifteen counties named for "Mad Anthony" Wayne (1745–96), PA Revolutionary War general and statesman • 1817 from Hickman and Humphreys • Timber, lumbering, wood products; limestone, iron ore; corn, cotton, soybeans, livestock.

WEAKLEY *Dresden* • 34,895 • 580 • Northwestern TN,

bounded on the north by the KY state line and on the southwest by the South Fork of the Obion River; drained by the forks of the Obion River. Big Cypress Tree State Nature Area is here. • Named for Robert Weakley (1764–1845), U.S. representative from TN and member of the TN Constitutional Convention • 1823 from Western District (Indian lands) • Tobacco, corn, cotton, hogs, fruit; timber; clay pits; some manufacturing; education (U. of TN at Martin).

WHITE (one of five counties so named) *Sparta* • 23,102 • 377 • Central TN, partly bounded on the south by the Caney Fork, and on the southwest by Center Hill Lake (reservoir). Virgin Falls State Natural Area and Rock Island State Park are here. The county is located on the Cumberland Plateau. • Named for Col. John White, one of the first settlers in the county • 1806 from Jackson and Smith • Coal mining; limestone quarrying; lumbering; livestock, dairying, tobacco, corn, hay, vegetables.

WILLIAMSON (one of two counties so named, the other in TX) *Franklin* • 126,638 (56% increase since 1990; the fastest growing county in TN) • 583 • Central TN; drained by the Harpeth River. The county is urbanizing in the north as part of the Nashville metropolitan area. • Named for Hugh Williamson (1735–1819), surgeon general of NC's troops during the American Revolution and U.S. representative from NC • 1799 from Davidson • A bloody battle, which marked

the failure of Confederate General John B. Hood's Tennessee campaign, was fought here on November 30, 1864. Union troops under General John Schofield sustained 2,500 casualties and retreated to Nashville, but losses for the Confederates amounted to more than 6,000, the Confederate Cemetery in the county, a reminder of the carnage. Six Confederate generals died on the battlefield here. • Corn, livestock, wheat, tobacco, hay, apples, dairy products (especially cheese); phosphate mining; diversified manufacturing; hardwood timber.

WILSON (one of four counties so named) *Lebanon* • 88,809 • 571 • North-central TN, bounded on the north by Old Hickory Lake reservoir (Cumberland River). There are extensive cedar glades (one of the largest stands of virgin cedar in the U.S.) at Cedars of Lebanon State Park and Forest. • Named for Major David Wilson (1752–?), an officer in the Revolutionary War; he later presided over the General Assembly of the Territory South of Ohio River during which time the state of TN was organized • 1799 from Sumner • Before deployment to Europe, General George Patton's tanks performed maneuvers in Lebanon. • TX Republic President Sam Houston practiced law in Lebanon. TN's first native-born governor James Chamberlain was from the county. • Tobacco (most important cash crop), livestock, corn; dairying; manufacture of flour, bedding, clothing, leather and rubber goods, auto parts, furniture, clocks; timber (cedar wood).

TEXAS

Friendship

Each of Texas's 254 counties is governed by a county commissioners court made up of the county judge and four commissioners. Each member is elected to a four-year term. Other county officials include the assessor-collector of taxes, the county attorney, the sheriff, and the treasurer.

ANDERSON (one of five counties so named) *Palestine* • 55,109 • 1,071 • Eastern Texas, bounded on the west by the Trinity River and on the east by the Neches River (forming Lake Palestine reservoir in the northeast corner). Texas State Railroad State Historical Park, which connects Palestine to Rusk (in Cherokee County), is TX's longest and narrowest park (25.5 miles). • Named for Kenneth L. Anderson (1805–45), the last vice president of the Republic of TX • 1846 from Houston • Transportation and processing center; lumber, Christmas trees; oil, natural gas; peaches, blackberries, melons, vegetables, sorghum, grain, hay, beef cattle, dairying, hogs, poultry; hunting and fishing; tourism.

ANDREWS *Andrews* • 13,004 • 1,501 • Western TX, on the southern part of Llano Estacado, bounded on the west by the NM state line; drained in the north by Seminole Draw and

Monument Draw. The county includes Shafter Lake. • Named for Richard Andrews (?–1835), first TX soldier killed in the Texas Revolution • 1876 from Bexar • One of the state's leading oil-producing counties, also natural gas, minerals; cattle, cotton, corn, grain sorghums, hay, fishing, hunting • Each year Andrews holds the Mustang Relays, a major track and field event.

ANGELINA *Lufkin* • 80,130 • 802 • Eastern Texas, bounded on the north and northeast by the Angelina River (which forms Sam Rayburn Reservoir, the largest lake in TX, with over 570 miles of shoreline, and on the west and south by the Neches River. Part of Angelina National Forest is in the east. • Named for the Angelina River • 1846 from Nacogdoches • Forest products, including newsprint, lumber, creosoted wood; manufacture of trailers, oil field machinery; cattle, poultry, horses, peaches, hay, greenhouse and landscape plants; hunting and fishing • The Texas Forestry Museum, in Lufkin, is the only museum in the state devoted to the forestry industry. Lufkin serves as the headquarters for the national forests of TX. The Museum of East Texas is also in Lufkin.

ARANSAS *Rockport* • 22,497 • 252 • Southern TX, on the Gulf coast, indented by Copano and St. Charles bays. Aransas Bay separates the mainland from San Jose Island, a Gulf barrier island. The county is traversed by the Intracoastal Waterway. Most of Aransas National Wildlife Refuge (a wintering ground for the endangered whooping crane) is located here. Goose Island State Park, in the center of the county, contains the "Lamar Oak," the largest coastal live oak in TX. Fulton Mansion State Historical Park and Copano Bay State Fishing Pier are also in the county. • Named for one or more of the following: Aransas Bay, Aransas Pass, or the Aransas River • 1871 from Refugio • Cattle, cotton, sorghum, corn; fisheries, redfish hatchery, seafood (shrimping); oyster shells, sand; some oil and gas; tourism.

ARCHER *Archer City* • 8,854 • 910 • Northern TX; drained by the Little Wichita and Wichita rivers. The county's reservoirs include Lake Kickapoo and Olney Lake, and part of Lake Diversion and Lake Arrowhead. • Named for Dr. Branch T. Archer (?–1856), TX Republic Speaker of the House • 1858 from Fannin • Wheat, dairying, cattle; oil and natural gas fields. • Archer City was the model for the fictional town of Thalia in Larry McMurtry's *The Last Picture Show.*

ARMSTRONG (one of two counties so named, the other in PA) *Claude* • 2,148 • 914 • Extreme northern TX; drained by the Salt Fork of the Red River. The county is located in the high plains of the Panhandle, with part of Caprock Escarpment in the east. Part of Palo Duro Canyon State Park is in the southwest along Prairie Dog Town Fork of the Red River. • Named for a family of pioneers named Armstrong • 1876 from Bexar • Cattle, wheat, cotton, hay; sand and gravel; duck hunting • The Goodnight ranch house, home of Charles Goodnight, one of the first five inductees into the National Cowboy Hall of Fame, is located near the town of Goodnight.

ATASCOSA *Jourdanton* • 38,628 • 1,232 • Southern TX; drained by the Atascosa River • Named for the Atascosa River • 1856 from Bexar • Irrigated agriculture, including peanuts, vegetables, strawberries, sesame, corn, grain sorghums, hay, cattle, dairying; oil, natural-gas wells, clay, lignite, sand deposits.

AUSTIN *Bellville* • 23,590 • 653 • Southeastern TX, bounded on the east by the Brazos River, on the southwest in part by the San Bernard River, and on the north in part by Caney Creek. Stephen F. Austin State Historical Park is on its eastern boundary. • Named for Stephen F. Austin (1793–1836), father of Texas • 1836; original county (prior to statehood) • San Felipe (previously San Felipe de Austin), regarded as the "birthplace of Anglo-American settlement in TX," was founded in 1822 as headquarters for the colony of Stephen F.

Austin. The first English newspaper in TX, the *Gazette,* was published here in 1829. Conventions petitioning for independence from Mexico were held here, as well. At the Consultation of 1835, several Anglo-American town leaders met here to plan a provisional government to organize the TX Revolution. Prior to occupation by General Santa Anna's invading Mexican army, the town was torched by retreating Texans under the command of Captain Mosely Baker. Stephen F. Austin State Historical Park marks the site of the settlement. • Oilfield firefighter Red Adair • Cotton, peanuts, corn, hay, rice, sorghum, cattle, hogs, poultry, dairying; timber; oil, natural-gas wells.

BAILEY *Muleshoe* • 6,594 • 827 • Northwestern TX, bounded on the west by the NM state line. The county is located on Llano Estacado and crossed by intermittent Blackwater Draw. It has several lakes, including Coyote Lake. Muleshoe National Wildlife Refuge, in the southeast, is home to wintering sandhill cranes. Established in 1935, it is the oldest national wildlife refuge in TX. • Named for Private Peter J. Bailey (1812–36), killed at the Alamo • 1876 from Bexar • Coronado is believed to have passed through the county while searching for the golden city of Quivira. • Sorghum, cotton, wheat, corn, vegetables, potatoes, dairying, beef cattle • The National Mule Memorial, a life-size statue of a mule, is located in Muleshoe. The Muleshoe Heritage Center contains the largest muleshoe in the world.

BANDERA *Bandera* • 17,645 • 792 • Central TX; bounded in part on the southeast by Medina Lake; drained by the Sabinal and Medina rivers. The county is located on Edwards Plateau. It is the source of Cibola Creek in the east. Part of Hill Country State Natural Area is here. The only maple forest in TX is located in Lost Maples State Natural Area. • Named for the Bandera Mountains and/or Bandera Pass • 1856 from Uvalde and Bexar • Cattle, sheep, goats, pecans, apples, tourism (dude ranches, lake recreation, hunting, horse racing at Bandera Downs); some timber.

BASTROP *Bastrop* • 57,733 • 888 • South-central TX; drained by the Colorado River. Lake Bastrop and Bastrop state parks are near the center of the county. Buescher State Park is in the east. • Named for Felipe Enrique Neri, Baron de Bastrop (?–1827) who assisted Moses Austin in securing permission to establish an Anglo-American colony in Mexican Texas • 1836 (prior to statehood) • The historic El Camino Real crossed through land that now belongs to the county. Camp Swift, located in Bastrop, served as a German prisoner of war camp during WW II. • Cotton, corn, alfalfa, wheat, sorghum, cattle, emus, ostriches, hogs; clay, lignite mining, oil, natural-gas wells; some timber. • The "Lost Pines" of Bastrop are believed to have been separated from the pine forests of East Texas by a slow moving glacier during the Ice Age. The *Bastrop Advertiser,* begun in 1853, is the oldest continuously published weekly in TX.

BAYLOR *Seymour* • 4,093 • 871 • Northern TX; drained by the Wichita River (which forms Lake Kemp and Diversion Lake reservoirs), the Brazos River, and Millers Creek (which forms Millers Creek reservoir) • Named for Henry W. Baylor (1818–?), Texas military physician • 1858 from Fannin • Cattle, cotton, peanuts, wheat, hay; oil, natural-gas wells.

BEE *Beeville* • 32,359 • 880 • Southern TX, bounded on the northeast by Blanco Creek; drained by the Aransas River, with its source here, and Medio Creek. • Named for Barnard E. Bee (1787–1853), minister from TX to the U.S., who opposed the annexation of TX • 1857 from Goliad, Refugio, Live Oak, San Patricio and Karnes • Corn, grain sorghum, cotton, wheat, cattle, horses; oil, natural gas wells, sand and gravel; hunting and fishing.

BELL (one of two counties so named, the other in KY) *Belton* • 237,974 • 1,059 • Central TX; drained by the Leon and Lampasas rivers which join in the center of the county to form the Little River. Part of Fort Hood is on the northwestern boundary. Part of Belton Lake reservoir and Stillhouse Hollow Lake reservoir are here. • Named for Peter H. Bell (1812–98), governor of TX and U.S. representative • 1850 from Milam • Belton was located on the Chisholm Trail and was a stagecoach stop between Dallas and Austin. During WW II, Gen. George S. Patton, Jr.'s "Hell on Wheels" Second Armored Division was headquartered at Fort Hood in Killeen. • Dancer and choreographer Alvin Ailey; professional football player Sammy Baugh; politicians James "Pa" and Miriam "Ma" Ferguson (first woman governor of TX); editor and publisher Oveta Culp Hobby. Ernie Pyle's "G.I. Joe" was patterned after county native Captain Henry T. Waskow. • Corn, sorghum, soybeans, alfalfa, wheat, cattle, turkeys, exotic fowl; hunting and fishing; oil and gas, clay, lignite, limestone, sand and gravel; manufacture of rock-wool insulation, furniture, farm implements, steel and aluminum products, precision tools, plastic building materials, leather goods, clothing, cottonseed products; education (U. of Mary Hardin-Baylor; Tarleton State U.–Central TX). • The Sanctificationists, a group of women led by Martha McQuirter who abandoned their husbands until the men were "sanctified," lived together in Bell County before moving on to McLennan County and Washington D.C. Temple is the seat of the TX Soil Conservation Service and the Blackhand Experiment Station, as well as the state headquarters for the Farmers Home Administration. It is also one of the largest health care centers in the southwest.

BEXAR *San Antonio* • 1,392,931 (the fourth most populated county in TX and twenty-fourth most populated county in the U.S.) • 1,247 • South-central TX, bounded on the north and northeast by Cibolo Creek; drained by the Medina and San Antonio rivers. Balcones Escarpment divides the hills in the northwest from the prairies. The county is heavily urbanized around San Antonio. Calaveras Lake, Braunig Lake, and Mitchell Lake reservoirs are in the southeast. San Antonio Missions National Historical Park includes four 18th century Spanish missions located along the historic Mission Trail. Several military bases, including Lackland, Brooks, and Randolph

Air Force bases, are in the county, as is Camp Bullis. • The county's name derives from names given at San Antonio, TX, to an early presidio, villa, and municipality • 1836 (prior to statehood) • Established in the early 1700's as a Spanish mission, the Alamo was the site of a thirteen day-stand against the Mexican Army in 1836 in which all 189 colonists lost their lives. Beginning in the 1860s, San Antonio thrived as a stop along cattle trails to KS. With the construction of what is now Fort Sam Houston between 1876 and 1879, the city was established as an important military center. San Antonio hosted HemisFair '68, a world's fair that celebrated the city's 250th anniversary. • Texas patriot Jose Anthonio Navarro (historic site); Astronaut Edward White; actors Joan Crawford and Carol Burnett; former national security aid Oliver North; Shamu the Killer Whale (at Sea World of Texas). Texas Revolution heroes Jim Bowie and Davy Crockett both died here (at the Alamo). President Lyndon B. Johnson, editor and publisher Joseph Medill, Army general Jonathan M. Wainwright, and labor leader Samuel Gompers also died in the county. • Corn, sorghum, wheat, nursery crops, vegetables, beef and dairy cattle; oil, natural-gas wells, limestone, gravel; diversified manufacturing, including aircraft parts, clothing, electronic products, food products, fertilizer, medical supplies, oil field equipment, petroleum products; medical research; education (Trinity; Our Lady of the Lake U.; St. Mary's U. of San Antonio; others) • The headquarters of six Fortune 1000 companies are located here. The Institute of TX Cultures honors over twenty-seven ethnic groups that have contributed to the cultural diversity of the state. The Paseo del Rio, a shopping and restaurant center along the San Antonio River, was a public works project during the Depression, the brainchild of architect Robert H.H. Hugman. Teddy Roosevelt trained his Rough Riders in the county. The San Antonio Zoo has one of the largest bird collections in the world. San Antonio is home to the San Antonio Spurs (SBC Center).

BLANCO *Johnson City* • 8,418 • 711 • South-central TX, on Edwards Plateau; drained by the Pedernales and Blanco rivers. Part of Lyndon B. Johnson National Historical Park is in the center of county. Pedernales Falls and Blanco state parks are also here. • Named for the Blanco River • 1858 from Gillespie, Comal, Hays and Burnet • President Lyndon B. Johnson • Cattle, sheep, goats (mohair wool marketed); hay, peaches, wheat, pecans; hunting, fishing.

BORDEN *Gail* • 729 • 899 • Western TX; drained by the Colorado River. Caprock Escarpment of Llano Estacado runs through the center of the county. Part of Lake J.B. Thomas is in the southeastern corner of the county. • Named for Gail Borden (1801–74), inventor of condensed milk, who also prepared the first topographical map of TX • 1876 from Bexar • Cattle, horses, cotton, wheat, milo, oats, soybeans, pecans; limestone.

BOSQUE *Meridian* • 17,204 • 989 • Central TX, bounded on the northeast and east by the Brazos River, here forming Whitney Lake reservoir; drained by the Bosque River. Meridan State Park is in the center of the county. • Named for the Bosque River • 1854 from McLennan and Milam • Oats, corn, grain sorghums, hay, wheat, pecans, peaches, cattle, sheep, dairying; limestone quarrying; cedar.

BOWIE *Boston* • 89,306 • 888 • Extreme northeastern TX, bounded on the north by the Red River (forming the OK and AR state lines), on the east by the AR state line, and on the south by the Sulphur River (forming Wright Patman Lake reservoir). The Red River Army (ordnance) Depot is here. The county is partly forested. • Named for Alamo hero Col. James A. Bowie (?–1836) • 1840 from Red River • Composer and pianist Scott Joplin; businessman and philanthropist H.Ross Perot; theatrical director and playwright Josh Logan • Pine, oak, gum timber; wheat, milo, rice, corn, vegetables, peanuts, soybeans, blueberries, cattle, dairying; oil and gas, sand and gravel; diversified manufacturing, including paper, steel; state prison unit; education (Texas A and M U.–Texarkana) • Bowie County is inextricably linked to Miller County, AR through the twin cities of Texarkana, the city, county, and state dividing line being State Line Avenue. The line runs through the middle of the shared post office/federal building, the only such anomaly in the country. It is appropriately constructed of Texas pink granite and Arkansas limestone. The two cities have separate municipal governments, but are linked economically and socially. The cities get their names from TEXas, ARKansas, and LouisiaANA (a few miles south).

BRAZORIA *Angleton* • 241,767 • 1,387 • South-eastern TX, bounded on the southeast by the Gulf of Mexico, on the northwest in part by the Brazos River, and on the southwest by Linville Bayou and Cedar Lake Creek; drained by the Brazos and San Bernard rivers. The Gulf Intracoastal Waterway passes along the coast. Christmas Bay State Park and Brazoria and San Bernard national wildlife refuges are in the south. Varner-Hogg Plantation State Historical Park is also in the county. • Named for the Brazos River • 1836; original county (prior to statehood) • The San Luis Peninsula is the reputed landing site of Cabeza de Vaca's expedition in 1528. In 1832, the Brazoria militia prevailed over Mexican forces in the Battle of Velasco near present day Surfside several years before the War for Texas Independence. Velasco (annexed by Freeport in 1957) served as the temporary capital of the TX Republic, and was the site of the signing of the treaty that concluded the TX Revolution in 1836. • Professional baseball player Nolan Ryan. Father of Texas, Stephen F. Austin. • The county is a large oil, sulphur, natural gas, salt, sand and gravel producer; magnesium extracted from sea water; extensive chemical industry; manufacture of plastics, machinery, metal products, fabricated vessels; also rice, sorghum, corn, cotton, hay, soybeans, pecans, cattle; commercial and sport fishing; tourism.

BRAZOS *Bryan* • 152,415 • 586 • East-central TX, bounded on the east by the Navasota River and on the west and southwest by the Brazos River. • Named for the Brazos River • 1841 (prior to statehood) as Navasota, from Washington and

Robertson counties; renamed Brazos in 1842 • Bryan stands on part of the original territory granted to American colonizer of TX, Stephen F. Austin, and was settled by his colonists between 1821 and 1831. • Cotton, corn, wheat, oats, sorghum, pecans, extensive dairying, cattle, hogs, poultry; sand and gravel, lignite, gas and oil; manufacture of aluminum windows, concrete, furniture, chemicals, soft drinks, feeds, fertilizers, shoes; education (Texas A. and M. University — one of the ten largest universities in the U.S.).

BREWSTER *Alpine* • 8,866 • 6,193 (the largest county in TX and the thirty-seventh largest county in the U.S.) • Western Texas. The county is in a rugged mountainous area, and lies within the Big Bend of the Rio Grande (forming the border with the Mexican states of Chihuahua and Coahuila). Big Bend National Park here contains 75 species of mammals, about 400 species of birds, 65 species of amphibians and reptiles, and more than 1000 identified plant specimens, including 60 forms of cacti. The Rio Grande Wild and Scenic River originates in the park and flows into neighboring Terrell County. Part of Big Bend Ranch State Park and Black Gap Wildlife Management Area are also here. The Santiago, Del Norte, Christmas, and Glass Mountains are in the county, as are the Chisos Mountains, and Santa Elena, Mariscal and Boquilla canyons. • Named for Henry P. Brewster (1816–84), Texas Republic secretary of war • 1887 from Presidio • Cattle, sheep, goats, horses; tourism (dude ranches); some irrigated agriculture, including pecans, apples; beekeeping; mercury mines (now inactive), copper, sulphur, bentonite, perlite, fluorspar • Sul Ross State University is headquarters for the Chihuahuan Desert Research Institute; it also hosts an intercollegiate rodeo. Terlingua holds the world's best known chili cook-off.

BRISCOE *Silverton* • 1,790 • 900 • Northwestern TX; drained by Tule Creek (which forms MacKenzie Reservoir on the western border) and the Prairie Dog Town Fork of the Red River. The county, broken by Caprock Escarpment, is located on the southwestern part of Llano Estacado. Caprock Canyons State Park is here. Palo Duro Canyon extends into the county in the north. • Named for Captain Andrew Briscoe (1810–49), who fought at the battle of San Jacinto, and was a supporter of early TX railroad expansion • 1876 from Bexar • Cattle, wheat, grain sorghum, vegetables, melons, cotton; clay products, fuller's earth.

BROOKS (one of two counties so named, the other in GA) *Falfurrias* • 7,976 • 943 • Southern TX; drained by Los Olmos, Palo Blanco and Balaurte creeks. Laguna Salada is southeast of Falfurrias. • Named for James A. Brooks (1855–1944), TX legislator, judge, and long-tenured Texas Ranger • 1911 from Starr, Zapata and Hidalgo • Watermelons, sorghum, corn, cattle, dairying, ostriches, emus; oil and natural gas fields.

BROWN (one of nine counties so named) *Brownwood* • 37,674 • 944 • Central TX, bounded on the south by the Colorado River; drained by Pecan Bayou (with dam impounding Lake Brownwood) and Jim Ned Creek. Lake Brownwood State Park is here. • Named for Henry S. Brown (?–1834), Republic of TX soldier and delegate to the TX convention • 1856 from Comanche and Travis • Peanuts, oats, sorghum, wheat, pecans, vegetables, hay, beef and dairy cattle, sheep, angora goats, hogs; oil, natural gas, clay, glass sand; education (Howard Payne U.) • A Santa Fe railroad depot in Brownwood, constructed in 1909, is one of the few remaining in the nation, and has been preserved along with its Harvey House restaurant. The USDA Pecan Field Station, a research station for the development of pecan varieties, is located in Brownwood. Lake Brownwood State Park boasts a number of limestone rubble structures constructed during WW II by the Civilian Conservation Corps.

BURLESON *Caldwell* • 16,740 • 666 • South-central TX, bounded on the northeast by the Brazos River, on the south by Yegua Creek (which forms Somerville Lake reservoir), and on the southwest by East Yegua Creek. Lake Somerville State Park is here. • Named for Edward Burleson (1798–1851), senator in the first TX congress and vice president of the Republic of TX • 1846 from Milam and Washington • Cotton, corn, grain, sorghum, peanuts, pecans, wheat, oats, soybeans, cattle, hogs, horses; farm product processing; wire and coat hanger production; oil, gas, sand, gravel • The Kolache Festival, held every September in Caldwell, celebrates local Czech heritage and pastry.

BURNET *Burnet* • 34,147 • 995 • Central Texas, bounded on the west and drained by the Colorado River, forming Lake Travis, Marble Falls Lake, Lyndon B. Johnson Lake, Inks Lake, and Lake Buchanan (the last three on the western boundary); also drained by the Lampasas River. The source of the San Gabriel River is in the center of the county. Two state parks in the county are Inks Lake and Longhorn Cavern (the site of TX's oldest public cave). • Named for David G. Burnet (1788–1870), vice president and the first ad interim president of the Republic of TX. • 1852 from Travis, Williamson and Bell • Goats, sheep, cattle, pecans, fruit; cedar; granite, limestone, graphite, sand and gravel, clay; tourism. Operated by the Lower Colorado River Authority, Kingsland Archeological Center houses over 100,000 Indian artifacts, some dating back 10,000 years.

CALDWELL (one of five counties so named) *Lockhart* • 32,194 • 546 • South-central TX, bounded on the southwest by the San Marcos River. Lockhart State Park is in the center of the county. • Named for Captain Mathew Caldwell (?–1842), officer in the War for TX Independence and signer of the TX Declaration of Independence • 1848 from Gonzales and Bastrop • In 1840, a volunteer army of Texans routed some 1,000 Comanches at Plum Creek near Lockhart, pushing the defeated Indians permanently westward. • Cotton, corn, grain sorghum, vegetables, cattle, turkeys; farm products processing; oil and natural gas, sand and gravel.

CALHOUN *Port Lavaca* • 20,647 • 512 • Southern TX, bounded on the southeast by the Gulf of Mexico, indented here by San Antonio Bay (in the southwest) and Lavaca Bay (arm of Matagorda Bay) which splits the county in half, and Matagorda Bay. Espiritu Santo Bay connects the two bays behind Matagorda Island sand barrier paralleling the Gulf Coast and part of the county. Matagorda Island State Park is situated here, as is a small portion of Aransas National Wildlife Refuge. • One of eleven counties named for John C. Calhoun (1782–1850), U.S. statesman and champion of Southern causes • 1846 from Victoria, Jackson and Matagorda • French explorer La Salle landed at what is now Indianola in 1685 and established Fort Saint Louis. Port Lavaca was settled, in part, by refugees from a 1840 raid on nearby Linnville. A seawall was built in Port Lavaca in 1920 to protect the city. • Cotton, corn, sorghums, rice, livestock; crabs, shrimps, crayfish farming; oil, natural gas wells; refineries; manufacture of chemicals, aluminum products; tourism (fishing and duck hunting). Port Lavaca is a deepwater port with oceangoing shipping.

CALLAHAN *Baird* • 12,905 • 899 • Central TX; drained by Pecan Bayou, and Deep and Hubbard creeks. Lake Clyde reservoir is here. • Named for James H. Callahan (1814–1856), soldier and Texas Ranger • 1858 from Milam, Travis, Bexar, and Bosque • Beef cattle, grain sorghum, peanuts, wheat, hay; oil, natural-gas production and processing • Early settlers in Clyde included a group of Portuguese wine growers who elected their own king and had their own government before moving on to CA. In Cross Plains, Robert E. Lee and Ulysses S. Grant camped on the banks of Turkey Creek, now in Treadaway Park. Gorman has the largest peanut shelling plant in the Southwest.

CAMERON (one of three counties so named) *Brownsville* • 335,227 • 906 • Extreme southern TX, bounded on the south by the Rio Grande River (forming the border with the Mexican State of Tamaulipas) and on the east by the Gulf of Mexico; drained by Arroyo Colorado (forming, in part, the northern border). Laguna Madre separates the southern end of Padre Island from the mainland. The county also contains Laguna Atascosa National Wildlife Refuge, Palo Alto National Battlefield Historic Site, Lower Rio Grande Valley National Wildlife Refuge, and Port Isabel Lighthouse State Historic Park. • Named for Capt. Ewen Cameron (1811–43), a Republic of TX soldier, executed by the Mexicans in the black bean lottery on the ill-fated Mier Expedition. • 1848 from Nueces • The first two important battles of the Mexican War fought on American soil, Palo Alto and Resaca de la Palma, took place here on May 8–9, 1846. General Zachary Taylor's victory made invasion of Mexico possible. During the Civil War, Brownsville and Matamoras (specifically the section that later became Brownsville) served as ports of call for blockade runners handling guns and ammunition, and for Confederate cotton. The last battle of the Civil War was fought here on May 12–13, 1865; a Federal force was captured at Palmito Hill by Confederate troops under Gen. Richard Taylor who was unaware that the war had ended a month earlier. Brownsville was the scene of the 1906 Brownsville Affair in which black soldiers were unjustly accused of murdering a white man and wounding another. • Financier and banker James Stillman. Mathematician Leonard E. Dickson died here. • Citrus fruits, winter vegetables, sugar cane, nursery crops, sorghum, cotton (also gins and cottonseed oil mills); processing and shipping of produce; canneries; shrimp processing; oil, natural gas production and refining, clay mining; manufacture of aircraft parts, electronic equipment; tourism (Padre Island is a top spring break destination for Midwestern college students.); education (U. of TX at Brownsville) • The "Confederate Air Force" Museum, with its collection of WW II planes, is in Harlingen. The Gladys Porter Zoo in Brownsville provides habitat for numerous endangered species.

CAMP *Pittsburg* • 11,549 • 198 • Northeastern TX, bounded on the north and east by Big Cypress Creek (here forming Lake Bob Sandlin reservoir on the northwest and Lake O' the Pines reservoir on the southwest. • Named for Col. John L. Camp (?–1891), officer in the Confederate Army, Texas legislator and judge • 1874 from Upshur • Poultry is the largest industry in the county. Also, hay, peaches, blueberries, cattle, dairying; timber, lumber milling; oil and natural gas wells, coal, clay • Pittsburg was the home of the *Ezekiel Airship*, reputed to have flown a year before the Wright brothers.

CARSON *Panhandle* • 6,516 • 923 • Northern TX, in the high plains of the Panhandle; drained by McClellan Creek and tributaries of the Red and Canadian rivers. • Named for Samuel P. Carson (1798–?), signer of the TX Declaration of Independence and secretary of state of the Republic of TX • 1876 from Bexar • The county is underlaid by the Pandhandle natural gas and oil field, one of the world's largest; it sends gas pipelines to several U.S. cities. Agricultural products here include cattle, wheat and hay.

CASS (one of nine counties so named) *Linden* • 30,438 • 937 • Northeastern TX, bounded on the east by the AR and LA state lines, and on the north by the Sulphur River (which forms Wright Patman Lake reservoir). Atlanta State Park is in the north. • One of eight counties named for Gen. Lewis Cass, (1782–1866), U.S. secretary of war, secretary of state, and candidate for U.S. president • 1846 as Cass from Bowie; named changed 1861 to Davis; named changed back 1871. • Timber; vegetables, hay, cattle, chickens; oil, natural gas wells, iron ore; manufacturing.

CASTRO *Dimmitt* • 8,285 • 898 • Northwestern TX, on Llano Estacado; drained by Running Water Draw • Named for Henri Castro (1786–1865), Frenchman who established a colony in the Republic of TX and was consul general to France from the Republic of TX. • 1876 from Wheeler • Cattle, sheep, hogs, wheat, cotton, corn.

CHAMBERS (one of two counties so named, the other in AL) *Anahuac* • 26,031 • 599 • Southeastern TX, bounded on the west by Cedar Bayou and on the south by East Bay; indented by Trinity Bay, an extension of Galveston Bay, which here receives the Trinity River. The county is bounded on the southeast by the Gulf Intracoastal Waterway. Anahuac National Wildlife Refuge is here. • Named for Thomas Jefferson Chambers (1802–65), surveyor general and state attorney of the Mexican state of "Coahuila and Texas" and major general in the Texas Revolution • 1858 from Jefferson and Liberty • Chambers is a leading TX oil producing county. Also, natural gas, sulfur, salt, clay, sand and gravel; rice (the county holds the Texas Rice Festival), soybeans, cattle; varied manufactures; fish processing.

CHEROKEE *Rusk* • 46,659 • 1,052 • Eastern TX, bounded on the west by the Neches River (forming Lake Palestine reservoir in the northwest corner), and partly on the east by the Angelina River. Jacksonville Lake and Striker Creek reservoirs are here. Caddoan Mounds State Historical Park (its excavations revealing occupation of the site since 6,000 BC) and Jim Hogg State Historical Park are also located in the county. Texas State Railroad State Historical Park runs from Rusk west to Palestine in Anderson County. Fairchild State Forest is on the western boundary. • One of eight counties named for the Cherokee Indians • 1846 from Nacogdoches • Tomatoes, vegetables, forage crops, peaches, cattle, dairying, greenhouses; timber, Christmas trees; oil, natural gas wells, iron ore; manufacturing.

CHILDRESS *Childress* • 7,688 • 710 • Northern TX, in the southeastern Panhandle; drained by Prairie Dog Town Fork of the Red River. Lake Childress and Baylor Lake are in the west. • Named for George C. Childress (1804–41), considered to be the author of the TX Declaration of Independence • 1876 from Bexar and Fannin • The county acquired part of Harmon County (OK) in relocation of the 100th meridian in 1930. • Cotton, wheat, grain sorghum, melons, peanuts, goats, ostriches.

CLAY (One of eighteen counties so named) *Henrietta* • 11,006 • 1,098 • Northern TX, bounded on the north by the Red River (forming the OK state line); drained by the Wichita and Little Wichita rivers. Lake Arrowhead (Little Wichita River) reservoir and State Park are on the county's western boundary. • One of fifteen counties named for Henry Clay (1777–1852), U.S. senator from KY; the name was chosen in spite of Clay's opposition to Texas statehood. • 1857 from Cooke • Cattle, horses, dairying, wheat, cotton, pecans, tree nurseries, peaches, mesquite; stone, oil and gas production; some manufacturing.

COCHRAN *Morton* • 3,730 • 775 • Northwestern TX, bounded on the west by the NM state line; drained by Sulphur Draw. The county is located on Llano Estacado. • Named for Robert E. Cochran (1810–1836), a private killed at the Alamo • 1876 from Bexar • Cattle, cotton, grain sorghum, wheat; oil and gas wells.

COKE *Robert Lee* • 3,864 • 899 • Western TX; drained by the Colorado River (forming E.V. Spence Reservoir). The North Concho River passes through the southwest corner.

The county also includes Oak Creek reservoir. • Named for Captain Richard Coke (1829–97), TX governor and U.S. senator • 1889 from Tom Green • Sheep, goats, cattle, wheat, hay, cotton; oil, natural gas.

COLEMAN *Coleman* • 9,235 • 1,273 • Central TX, bounded on the south by the Colorado River (which forms Lake O.H. Ivie reservoir in the southwest); drained by Jim Ned and Hords creeks, and Pecan Bayou. Lake Coleman and Hords Creek Lake reservoirs are in the county. • Named for Col. Robert M. Coleman (1797–1837), one of the signers of the TX Declaration of Independence • 1858 from Travis • Oats, wheat, grain sorghums, cotton, cattle, sheep, goats, horses, hogs; oil, natural gas wells, silica, limestone, clay mining, coal deposits; mesquite; manufacture of glass, saddles, bricks, tile, boots, Western wear; livestock processing, grain elevators, machine shops, iron fabrication; shipping. • The Warbird Museum, located at Coleman Municipal Airport, exhibits vintage WWII and Korean War planes. "Santa Anna's Peak," two large hills located in the county, served as solitary landmarks on the open prairie and were used as look-out points for both the Texas Rangers and the Comanches. Coleman was located on the Western Trail, a cattle trail that ran from Matamoros, Mexico to Dodge City, Kansas.

COLLIN *McKinney* • 491,675 (86% increase since 1990; the fastest growing county in TX) • 848 • Northern TX; drained by the East Fork of the Trinity River. It is urbanized in the southwest as part of the Dallas metropolitan area. Lake Lavon reservoir and headwaters of Lake Ray Hubbard (East Fork of the Trinity River) are here. • Named for Collin McKinney (1766–1861), Republic of TX legislator and signer of the TX Declaration of Independence. (Oddly, Collin McKinney's last name was given to the county seat and his first name to the county.) • 1846 from Fannin • Plano was almost totally destroyed by fire in 1881. Significant population growth began in the 1960s. • Cotton, corn, grain sorghum, wheat, hay, cattle, sheep, horses; stone quarries; diversified manufacturing, including compact discs, printed materials, metals, satellite communication equipment, bakery equipment, electronic equipment.

COLLINGSWORTH *Wellington* • 3,206 • 919 • Northern TX, in the Panhandle, bounded on the east by the OK state line; drained by the Salt Fork of the Red River. • Named for Major James Collinsworth (1806–38), Republic of TX senator and its first chief justice. A clerical spelling error was allowed to stand. • 1876 from Bexar and Fannin • The county gained parts of Beckham and Harmon counties in OK in a 1930 resurvey of the 100th meridian. • Cotton, wheat, peanuts, cattle; oil and gas.

COLORADO *Columbus* • 20,390 • 963 • Southern TX, bounded on the east in part by the San Bernard River and on the far west by the Navidad River; drained by the Colorado River. Eagle Lake is here. The county also contains Attwater Prairie Chicken National Wildlife Refuge. • Named for the

Colorado River • Original county; organized 1836 (prior to statehood) from Old Mexican Municipality • Colorado is a leading rice producing county in TX; also cotton, wheat, corn, grain sorghum, peanuts, soybeans, livestock, dairying. The county has a large gravel- and sand-mining industry; also natural gas, oil, uranium; pine and cedar.

COMAL *New Braunfels* • 78,021 • 561 • South-central TX, bounded on the southwest by Cibolo Creek; drained by the Guadalupe River, here forming Canyon Lake reservoir. The county is crossed by Balcones Escarpment, which separates a broken, hilly area from the prairies in the south and southeast. Part of Guadalupe State Park is here, as are Honey Creek State Natural Area, and Natural Bridge Caverns and Wildlife Ranch. The southern corner of the county is becoming urbanized as part of the San Antonio metropolitan area. • Named for the Comal River (at two and one half miles in length, the shortest river in TX). • 1846 from Bexar and Gonzales • New Braunfels was established in 1845 by a group of German immigrants led by Prince Carl of Solms-Braunfels. The group was sponsored by the Society for the Protection of German Immigrants in Texas. • Cattle, dairying, exotic animals, corn, sorghum, hay; Christmas trees; limestone (quarrying and processing), sand and gravel; varied manufactures; flour and seed mills, leather tanning; tourism • New Braunfels maintains much of its early German heritage and charm. There is a monument to German pioneers here; Sophienburg, former home of Prince Carl, is a museum. Schlitterbahn is considered by many as the best water park in the country.

COMANCHE *Comanche* • 14,026 • 938 • Central TX; drained by the Leon and South Leon rivers, with mountains in the southwest. Proctor Lake reservoir is here. • One of three counties named for the Comanche Indians • 1856 from Bosque and Coryell • Beef and dairy cattle, sheep, goats (wool and mohair marketed), peanuts, pecans, grains, vegetables, hay, fruit; oil, natural gas wells, clay • The state's oldest courthouse, "Old Cora," is located on the town square in Comanche.

CONCHO *Paint Rock* • 3,966 • 992 • West-central TX on the north Edwards Plateau, bounded on the northeast by the Colorado River (which forms Lake O.H. Ivie reservoir); drained by the Concho River, and Brady and Kickapoo creeks. • Named for the Concho River • 1858 from Bexar • Sheep, goats (wool and mohair marketed), cattle, wheat, grain sorghum, cotton; oil and gas, stone • Paint Rock was named for the approximately 1,500 Indian pictographs on a nearby river bluff; the images date from prehistoric times to the appearance of Christian missions in the area.

COOKE *Gainesville* • 36,363 • 874 • Northern TX, bounded on the north by the Red River (forming the OK state line); drained by the Elm Fork of the Trinity River, and Clear Creek. Lake Texoma is in the northeast. The county also includes Hubert H. Moss Lake, Lake Kiowa, and part of Ray Roberts Lake reservoirs. • Named for Captain William G. Cooke (1808–47), senior officer in the Battle of San Jacinto • 1848 from Fannin • Sprinter Charlie Paddock • Peanuts, hay, sorghum, wheat, soybeans, corn, dairying, cattle, hogs, horses; oil, gas, sand, gravel • Gainesville was a stopover on a major southern route to the California gold rush.

CORYELL *Gatesville* • 74,978 • 1,052 • Central TX; drained by the Leon River and House Creek. The county includes Mother Neff State Park, part of Belton Lake reservoir, and part of large Fort Hood Military Reservation. • Named for James Coryell (?–1837), a Texas Ranger killed by Indians • 1854 from Bell and McLennan • Hay, sorghum, pecans, peaches, grapes, cattle, sheep, goats, horses, turkeys; sand and gravel; hunting and fishing.

COTTLE *Paducah* • 1,904 • 901 • Northwestern TX; drained by the North Wichita, and North, Middle, and South Pease rivers. • Named for Private George W. Cottle (1811–1836), killed at the Alamo • 1892 from Childress (although some sources say 1876) • Cotton, grains, alfalfa, cattle, horses.

CRANE *Crane* • 3,966 • 786 • Western TX, on the western edge of Edwards Plateau, bounded on the south by the Pecos River. The county includes Juan Cordona Lake, Lake Soda, and the historic Horsehead Crossing of the Pecos. • Named for William C. Crane (1816–85), Virginian who became president of Baylor University • 1887 from Tom Green • Oil and natural-gas production; cattle, goats, sheep.

CROCKETT *Ozona* • 4,099 • 2,808 • Western TX, on Edwards Plateau, bounded on the west by the Pecos River; drained by Live Oak Creek and Howard, Johnson, and Buckhorn draws. Fort Lancaster, a state historical park, is here. • One of two counties (the other in TN) named for Davy Crockett (1786–1836), frontiersman, TN congressman and fighter for TX Independence, who was killed at the Alamo • 1875 from Bexar • Oil, natural gas; sheep, angora goats, cattle.

CROSBY *Crosbyton* • 7,072 • 900 • Northwestern TX; drained by the White River (here forming White River Lake reservoir) and the North Fork of the Double Mountain Fork of the Brazos River. The county lies on the edge of Llano Estacado, with Caprock Escarpment curving from the southwest to the north. • Named for Stephen Crosby (1808–69), commissioner of the general land office of TX • 1876 from Baylor (some sources say Garza) • Cattle, hogs, sheep, cotton, grain sorghum, wheat, hay • Associated Cotton Growers of Crosbyton runs the world's largest cotton processing plant.

CULBERSON *Van Horn* • 2,975 • 3,813 (the fifth largest county in TX) • Western TX, bounded on the north by the NM state line; drained by Delaware, Salt, and Cottonwood creeks. The county is in a plateau and mountainous region. Guadalupe Peak (8,749 feet) in the Guadalupe Mountains is the highest point in Texas. Several mountain ranges are here, including part of Sierra Diablo, Delaware, Apache, Baylor, and Van Horn. The county includes part of Guadalupe Mountains National Park (which contains portions of the world's most extensive Permian limestone fossil reef). The northwest corner of the county is in the Mountain time zone, the rest in the Central time zone. • Named for Col. David B. Culberson (1830–1900), Confederate Army officer, TX legislator, and U.S. representative • 1911 from El Paso County • Cattle, sheep, goats, vegetables, melons, pecans, cotton; talc, sulfur, marble; tourism.

DALLAM *Dalhart* • 6,222 • 1,505 • Extreme north-western TX, in the high plains of the Panhandle, bounded on the north by the OK state line, and on the west by the NM state line; drained by Carrizo, Rita Blanca and Coldwater creeks. Part of Rita Blanca National Grassland is in the northern half of the county. • Named for James W. Dallam (1818–47), Texas legal writer • 1876 from Bexar • Cattle, sorghum, wheat, pinto beans.

DALLAS (one of five counties so named) *Dallas* • 2,218,899 (the second most populated county in TX and tenth most populated county in the U.S.) • 880 • Northern TX, drained by the Trinity River, here formed by its Elm and West forks. The county, dominated by the city of Dallas, is highly urbanized with most of the remaining agricultural land in the southeast and on the south margin of the county. Numerous reservoirs, including North Lake, Mountain Creek Lake, Joe Pool Lake, and part of Lake Ray Hubbard are here. Cedar Hill State Park is in the southwest. The Dallas-Fort Worth International Airport straddles the western boundary with Tarrant County. • The derivation of this county's name has never been firmly established. • 1846 from Nacogdoches • Sam Houston met with representatives of Indian tribes on Rawhide Creek in Farmers Branch in 1843. Dallas served as the administrative center for the Confederate Army during the Civil War. President John F. Kennedy was assassinated here on November 22, 1963. His accused assailant Lee Harvey Oswald was fatally wounded on November 24. Dallas has been through several booms and busts centered on agriculture, the oil business, insurance, banking, real estate, and high tech industries. • Jazz guitarist Charlie Christian; professional golfer Lee Trevino; Supreme Court justice Tom C. Clark; tennis player Maureen Connolly; retail store executive Stanley Marcus • The county is an important industrial, commercial, and financial center, with widely diversified industries; horticultural crops, hay, cotton (one of the world's leading cotton markets), corn, wheat, beef cattle, breeder cattle, horses; clay; education (several colleges, including Southern Methodist U.; U. of TX–Dallas; U. of Dallas; Dallas Baptist U.; Paul Quinn College; others) • The county is headquarters for over 20 Fortune 1000 companies; more oil firms are headquartered here than in any other U.S. city. Fair Park is the site of the annual Cotton Bowl and the largest state fair in the nation. Mesquite has an annual balloon festival. The Kalita Humphreys Theater at the Dallas Theater Center was designed by Frank Lloyd Wright. Dallas is home to the Mavericks (American Airlines Center). The Dallas Stars play in Duncanville (Dr. Pepper Starcenter), the Cowboys in Irving (Texas Stadium).

DAWSON (one of four counties so named) *Lamesa* • 14,985 • 902 • Western TX, on the high plains, with Caprock Escarpment in the east; drained by intermittent Sulphur Springs Draw and the Colorado River. • Named for Nicholas M. Dawson (1808–42), Republic of TX army officer • 1876 from Bexar District • Wheat, sorghum, cotton, cattle, hogs; oil and natural gas wells; hunting.

DEAF SMITH *Hereford* • 18,561 • 1,497 • Northern TX, in the high plains of the Panhandle, bounded on the west by the NM state line; drained by Palo Duro and Tierra Blanca creeks. • Named for Erastus "Deaf" Smith (1787–1837), Republic of Texas scout and soldier • 1876 from Bexar • A prisoner of war camp, established in Hereford during WWII, was later converted to a migrant work camp, housing thousands of laborers during peak vegetable season. • Deaf Smith is a leading Texas cattle and wheat county. Also, sorghum, oats, barley, corn, cotton, onions, sunflowers • Proclaimed the "Town Without a Toothache," Hereford and its citizens were studied during the 1940s, and a correlation was found between the lack of tooth decay and the high concentration of minerals in the soil and naturally occurring fluorine in the town's drinking water.

DELTA (one of three counties so named) *Cooper* • 5,327 • 277 • Northeastern TX, between the north and south forks of the Sulphur River, which join to form the river at the eastern tip. Cooper Lake State Park and reservoir are on the southern boundary. • Named for its shape, similar to the Greek letter delta • 1870 from Lamar • Cotton, corn, sorghum, hay, wheat, soybeans, dairying, cattle; lumbering.

DENTON *Denton* • 432,976 • 888 • Northern TX, drained by the Elm Fork of the Trinity River and Denton Creek. Lake Lewisville State Park is here, the large reservoir used for flood control. Part of Ray Roberts Lake reservoir (Elm Fork of the Trinity River) and part of Grapevine Lake reservoir are here. Ray Roberts Lake State park is on the northern boundary. • Named for Captain John B. Denton (1806–41), a Texas Ranger killed by Indians • 1846 from Fannin • Cotton, wheat, hay, sorghum, peanuts, beef cattle, horses; natural gas, clay, sand and gravel deposits; manufacture of business forms, bricks, plastics, processed foods; education (TX Woman's U.; U. of North TX; Denton State School for the mentally retarded) • Denton is the site of the first federal regional emergency center, headquarters for civil defense, disaster and preparedness operations. It serves a five-state area.

DEWITT (one of two counties so named, the other in IL) *Cuero* • 20,013 • 909 • Southern Texas, bounded on the southwest by Fifteenmile Creek; drained by the Guadalupe River. • Named for Green C. De Witt (1787–1835), an early colonizer in Mexican Texas • 1846 from Goliad, Gonzales, and Victoria • De Witt is a leading poultry and egg-producing county in TX (Cuero holds a Turkey fest each October). Also, peaches, pecans, corn, grain sorghum, hay, cotton, wheat, beef cattle, hogs, ratites, dairying; oil, natural gas.

DICKENS *Dickens* • 2,762 • 904 • Northwestern TX; drained by the North and South Wichita rivers and by Croton and Duck creeks. Caprock Escarpment of Llano Estacado is in the extreme northwest. • Named for Sergeant James R. Dimpkins (?–1836), Alamo hero whose last name is variously listed as Demkins, Dimpkins, and Dickens • 1876 from Bexar • Cattle, goats, cotton, peanuts; gypsum, caliche, gravel deposits.

DIMMIT *Carrizo Springs* • 10,248 • 1,331 • Southern TX; drained by the Nueces River. The southwest corner of the county is within four miles of the Rio Grande (and Mexican border). • Named for Captain Philip Dimmitt (?–1841), Republic of TX officer who drafted the Goliad Texas Declaration of Independence; the statute creating the county misspelled its namesake's surname. • 1858 from Bexar and Maverick • Vegetables; processing and shipping of onions, carrots, spinach and other vegetables; cotton, hay, pecans, cattle; oil (wells and refining), natural gas.

DONLEY *Clarendon* • 3,828 • 930 • Northern TX, in the Panhandle, traversed by the Salt Fork of the Red River (forming Greenbelt Lake reservoir). • Named for Stockton P. Donley (1821–71), Confederate Army officer and member of the Supreme Court of TX • Created as Wedgefarth in 1873; act repealed in 1876 and Donley established • Wheat, hay, cotton, peanuts, sorghum, cattle, horses, hogs.

DUVAL (one of two counties so named, the other in FL) *San Diego* • 13,120 • 1,793 • Southern TX; drained by San Diego and Los Olmos creeks • Probably named for Burr H. Duval (1809–36), an officer killed at Goliad during the Texas Revolution • 1858 from Live Oak, Starr and Nueces • Natural gas, oil, sand and gravel, uranium; beef cattle, sorghum, cotton, hay, vegetables; hunting.

EASTLAND *Eastland* • 18,297 • 926 • North-central TX; drained by the Leon and Sabana rivers. The county includes Lake Cisco and Lake Leon. • Named for William M. Eastland (1806–43), Texas Revolutionary officer executed by Mexican Gen. Antonio Lopez de Santa Anna • 1858 from Bosque, Coryell and Travis • Peanuts, pecans, hay, vegetables, cattle, dairying, emus, goats, poultry; oil, natural-gas wells, stone, clay, sand and gravel; manufacturing; education (Ranger College) • Eastland's most famous resident, "Old Rip," can be seen lying in state at the Courthouse; this horned toad was placed in the cornerstone of the old courthouse in 1897 and removed alive in 1928 when the building was razed. In 1927, an armed robber disguised as Santa Claus killed several law officers during a bank robbery in Eastland and was later attacked by a mob, earning the town the title: "The Town that Lynched Santa Claus." Conrad Hilton (museum) renovated his first hotel in Cisco.

ECTOR *Odessa* • 121,123 • 901 • Western TX; drained by Monahans Draw. The south Llano Estacado meets Edwards Plateau here. Sand dunes are in the southwest. • Named for General Mathew D. Ector (1822–79), TX legislator and jurist

• 1887 from Tom Green • The city of Odessa was settled by Russian-German colonists. Later organized as a Methodist college town, it was subsequently burned by a group of cowboys. The city expanded rapidly after local oil discoveries in the 1920s. • Oil wells, natural gas, stone, potash deposits; manufacture of oilfield supplies (approximately fifty firms so engaged). Odessa is a major petrochemical distribution-processing-servicing point. Also, cattle, horses, pecans, hay; education (U. of TX of the Permian Basin) • The second largest meteor crater in the U. S. and the third largest in the world is located near Odessa. The Permian Basin Oil Show, held in Odessa, is the largest inland exhibition of oil and gas products and services in the world. Possibly the world's most authentic replica of Shakespeare's original Globe Theatre was built in Odessa during the 1960s. The Presidential Museum, located in Odessa, is the only museum in the U.S. dedicated to the office of the presidency.

EDWARDS (one of three counties so named) *Rocksprings* • 2,162 • 2,120 • Southwestern TX, on Edwards Plateau, bounded in part on the east by the Nueces river; drained by the South Llano and West Nueces rivers. Part of Kickapoo Cavern State Park is on the southern border. • Named for Hayden Edwards, Sr. (1771–1849), founder of a colony at Nacogdoches in Mexican TX • 1858 from Bexar • Edwards is a leading TX county in Angora goat raising. Also, sheep, cattle, horses; pecans; some oil, gas, coal, kaolin; hunting and fishing.

ELLIS (one of three counties so named) *Waxahachie* • 111,360 • 940 • Northern TX, bounded on the east by the Trinity River; drained by Chambers and Waxahachie (forming Bardwell Lake reservoir) creeks. • Named for Richard Ellis (1781–1846), AL jurist, signer of the TX Declaration of Independence, and senator of the Republic • 1849 from Navarro • The Confederate government established a powder mill in Waxahachie, but it was blown up in 1863. During the cotton boom years Ellis was known as the "Banner Cotton County of the World." • Cotton, corn, wheat, milo, cattle, horses; limestone quarrying, oil and gas; manufacture of clothing, furniture, boats, oil well equipment, cottonseed oil, sales books, commercial refrigerators, soft drinks; poultry processing • 170 large gingerbread-trimmed Victorian homes have given Waxahachie the name "Gingerbread City." Ennis hosts the National Polka Festival. The county is the site of the now defunct Super Conducting Super Collider project. 17,000 acres were purchased in 1989; in October 1993, Congress voted to discontinue funding.

EL PASO (one of two counties so named, the other in CO) *El Paso* • 679,622 • 1,013 • Extreme western TX, bounded on the north by the NM state line and on the south by the Rio Grande River (forming the border with the Mexican state of Chihuahua). The county is urbanized in the west around the city of El Paso, with mountains and agrarian land in the east and southeast. Hueco Tanks State Park (with natural rain-collecting rock basins) is here, as well as Franklin Mountains State Park. Across the northern part of the county is Fort Bliss Military Reservation. The Tigua Indian Reservation, located in El Paso city, is the only TX Indian reservation within a city. El Paso is one of only two TX counties lying entirely within the Mountain time zone. • Named for the city of El Paso. • 1850 from Bexar • Some of the oldest communities in TX are here: Ysleta (now part of El Paso city and the oldest town in the state), Socorro and San Elizario. Fort Bliss, located in El Paso, was attacked by a Union force from CA in 1862 and reclaimed as part of the Union. El Paso was a prominent stagecoach station on the Southern Overland Mail and Butterfield Stage routes. Due to changes in the course of the Rio Grande River, some 1000 acres of land between the river and downtown El Paso were in dispute until the Chamizal Treaty of 1963 divided them between the U.S. and Mexico. • TV journalist Sam Donaldson; Supreme Court justice Sandra Day O'Connor; entertainer Debbie Reynolds. Politician Albert Fall and gunslinger John Wesley Hardin died here. • El Paso is a leading cotton-producing county. Also, alfalfa, poultry, dairying, cattle, hogs; limestone, sand and gravel; manufacture of cotton clothing, food processing, leather products, especially Western boots; oil refining, copper and lead smelting and refining; military bases • A small stretch of irrigated land just east of Mission Nuestro Señora del Carmen, the oldest mission in TX, is claimed to be the oldest continuously cultivated plot in the U.S. (originally plowed in 1681). The first Thanksgiving, in what is now the U.S., occurred on the banks of the Rio Grande in El Paso in 1598, when Don Juan de Oñate ordered a feast of thanksgiving for his colonizing expedition after its difficult journey through the Chihuahua Desert. The only jail that Billy the Kid ever broke "into" is located in San Elizario.

ERATH *Stephenville* • 33,001 • 1,086 • North-central TX; drained by the Bosque and Paluxy rivers • Named for George B. Erath (1813–91), Texas Ranger, TX Republic and state legislator • 1856 from Bosque and Coryell • Golfer Ben Hogan • The county is a leading milk producer. Also, peanuts, grain sorghum, horticultural crops, beef cattle, horses; oil, natural gas; education (Tarleton State U.) • The county pays tribute to its large dairy industry with a life-size Holstein statue on the Stephenville town square.

FALLS *Marlin* • 18,576 • 769 • East-central TX; drained by the Brazos River. • Named for the rapids of the Brazos River • 1850 from Limestone and Milam • The county was once in a popular health resort area, with hot artesian wells. • Cotton, corn, grain sorghum, soybeans, cattle, hogs, sheep, goats; oil and natural gas, stone; manufacture of clothing.

FANNIN *Bonham* • 31,242 • 892 • Northeastern TX, bounded on the north by the Red River (forming the OK state line); drained by the South Sulphur and North Sulphur rivers, and Bois d'Arc Creek (forming Lake Bonham reservoir). Several units of Caddo National Grassland are here, as is Bonham State Park. • One of two counties (the other in GA) named for James W. Fannin (1804–1836), GA soldier executed in the Texas War for Independence • 1837 from Red River • Gunslinger John Wesley Hardin; Speaker of the House Sam Rayburn (memorial library) • Corn, wheat, hay, sorghum, peanuts, turf grass, cattle, goats, sheep, hogs, ratites; manufacture of gasoline pumps, lawn mowers, cables, cheese.

FAYETTE (one of eleven counties so named) *La Grange* • 21,804 • 950 • South-central TX; drained by the Colorado River and headwaters of the Navidad River. The county includes Winedale Historic Center. • One of seventeen counties named for the Marquis de Lafayette (1757–1834), French statesman and soldier who fought with the Americans during the Revolutionary War • 1837 from Bastrop and Colorado counties • Monument Hill (and Kreische Brewery State Historical Park) is the burial site for the remains of Texans who died in the Battle of Salado Creek in 1842 and on the Mier Expedition in 1843. The first Protestant and Methodist University in Texas was founded here in 1840. • Cattle, dairying, corn, grain sorghum, hay, wheat, peanuts, pecans; timber; oil wells, gas, sand and gravel • A collection of "painted churches," featuring intricate interior painting, is found near the German and Czech community of Schulenburg.

FISHER *Roby* • 4,344 • 901 • Northwest-central TX; drained by the Double Mountain and Clear forks of the Brazos River. • Named for Samuel R. Fisher (1794–1839), signer of the TX Declaration of Independence and Republic secretary of the navy • 1876 from Bexar • Oil and natural gas, cotton, wheat, hay, alfalfa, beef cattle, hogs, Angora goats; gypsum quarrying.

FLOYD (one of six counties so named) *Floydada* • 7,771 • 992 • Northwestern TX; drained by the White River. Caprock Escarpment of Llano Estacado is in the northwest. • Named for Dolfin W. Floyd (1804–36), private killed at the Alamo • 1876 from Bexar • Geophysicist Maurice Ewing • Grain sorghum, corn, soybeans, sunflowers, pumpkins, cotton, cattle.

FOARD *Crowell* • 1,622 • 707 • Northern TX, bounded in part on the north by the Pease River and in part on the south by the North Wichita River. Pease River Battlefield is here. • Named for Major Robert J. Foard (1831–98), Confederate Army officer and attorney • 1891 from Knox and King • Cattle, wheat, cotton, alfalfa, hay; oil and natural gas, copper deposits.

FORT BEND *Richmond* • 354,452 • 875 • Southeastern TX; drained by the Brazos (forming the southeastern and northwestern boundaries) and San Bernard (forming the southwestern boundary) rivers. Brazos Bend State Park is in the extreme southeast. The county is becoming more urbanized in the northeast as part of the growing Houston metropolitan area. • Named for the fort built at a bend in the Brazos River • 1837 from Austin County • Richmond was the site of the "Jaybird-Woodpecker War" in the late 1880s between white settlers and ex-Confederates ("Jaybirds") and pro-Black reconstructionists ("Woodpeckers"). The showdown resulted in a shootout around the courthouse on August 16, 1889, with

the governor eventually backing the Jaybirds. • Buried in Richmond are Deaf Smith, scout and hero of the War for TX Independence; Mirabeau B. Lamar, the second president of the TX Republic; and Jane Long, called the "Mother of TX." The Nation Hotel in Richmond was owned by Carry Nation and her husband. • Oil, natural gas, sulphur, salt, clay, sand and gravel; cotton, rice, corn, vegetables, soybeans, sorghum, nurseries, cattle, poultry, horses; sugar refining.

FRANKLIN (one of twenty-five counties so named) *Mount Vernon* • 9,458 • 286 • Northeastern TX, bounded on the north by the Sulphur River; drained by White Oak Creek and Cypress Creek (which forms Lake Bob Sandlin and Lake Cypress Springs reservoirs). • Named for Captain Benjamin C. Franklin (1805–73), first judge in the Republic of Texas • 1875 from Titus • Franklin is among the top TX counties in dairy and broiler production. Also, cattle, vegetables, blueberries, peaches, hay, soybeans, sorghum, wheat; Christmas trees; oil, natural-gas wells, lignite.

FREESTONE *Fairfield* • 17,867 • 885 • East-central TX, bounded on the northeast and east by the Trinity River. Fairfield Lake State Park is here. Part of Richland-Chambers Reservoir is in the north. • The county's name is descriptive of a local stone • 1850 from Limestone • Corn, pecans, peaches, melons, vegetables, hay, cattle; timber; gas and oil, lignite, sand; hunting.

FRIO *Pearsall* • 16,252 • 1,133 • Southern TX; drained by the Frio River, and Hondo Creek. • Named for the Frio River • 1858 from Bexar and Uvalde • Frio is a leading peanut producing county in TX. Also, melons, corn, grain sorghum, winter vegetables, hogs, cattle; oil and natural gas wells, stone.

GAINES *Seminole* • 14,467 • 1,502 • Western TX, on Llano Estacado, bounded on the west by the NM state line; drained by Seminole, Monument, and McKenzie draws. Cedar Lake, one of the largest alkali lakes in TX, is in the east. • Named for James Gaines (?–1856), signer of the TX Declaration of Independence and TX Republic legislator • 1876 from Bexar • Oil and some natural gas, sodium sulphate; substantial cotton and peanut production, sorghum, vegetables, grains, hogs, sheep, cattle.

GALVESTON *Galveston* • 250,158 • 399 • Southeastern TX, bounded on the north by Clear Creek and Clear Lake, and on the southeast by the Gulf of Mexico. Its boundary crosses Galveston Bay from San Leon to Smith Point, follows the northern shore of East Bay, and includes part of Bolivar Peninsula and High Island. The boundary crosses West Bay in the southwest to include the southern end of Galveston Island. The northwest is urbanizing as part of the Houston metropolitan area. The Intracoastal Waterway runs the length of the county. Galveston Island State Park, Old Fort San Jacinto, and Pelican Spit Military Reservation are here. • Possibly named for the city of Galveston, Galveston Island, and/or Galveston Bay, each named for Bernardo de Galvez (1746–86),

Spanish colonial leader active along the Gulf of Mexico • 1838 (prior to statehood) from Brazoria • Pirate Jean Lafitte made Galveston Island his base of operations from 1817 to 1821. The deadliest natural disaster in U.S. history struck Galveston in the form of a hurricane in 1900, killing 6,000. Between 1906 and 1914, close to 50,000 immigrants arrived in Galveston, earning it the title "second Ellis Island." In 1947, an explosion of a shipload of ammonium nitrate in the harbor resulted in nearly 600 deaths and destroyed much of Texas City. • Boxer Jack Johnson; dermatologist Isadore Dyer; senator Kay Bailey Hutchinson; film director King Vidor. Confederate general Braxton Bragg and sportswoman Babe Didrikson Zaharias died here. • Oceangoing shipping (Galveston is the oldest deepwater port west of New Orleans); oil, natural gas, clay and gravel; sulphur, chemicals, tin smelting; oil-refining; processing and shipping of cotton, wheat, metals, agricultural products, shipping of petroleum and petroleum products; fisheries, shrimping, oysters, sport fishing; rice, soybeans, sorghum, cotton, pecans, cattle, horses; education (TX A and M University–Galveston) • Galveston is referred to as "Oleander City" for the thirty varieties of the plant, which bloom here between April and October. The *Galveston News* is the earliest extant TX newspaper.

GARZA *Post* • 4,872 • 896 • Northwestern TX, with Caprock Escarpment in the west; drained by the Salt and Double Mountain forks of the Brazos River, and the North Fork of the Double Mountain Fork of the Brazos River. • Named for the family of Geronimo Garza, a colonizer who founded San Antonio • 1876 from Bexar • Cattle, cotton, grains, hay, poultry; oil, natural gas wells.

GILLESPIE *Fredericksburg* • 20,814 • 1,061 • Central TX; drained by the Pedernales River and several creeks. The county lies on Edwards Plateau and includes part of Enchanted Rock State Natural Area on the northern boundary. The Lyndon B. Johnson State Historical Park (LBJ Ranch Unit) is also here. • Named for R. A. Gillespie (?–1846), Texas Ranger killed during the Mexican War • 1848 from Bexar • Fredericksburg was founded by Baron Ottfried Hans von Meusebach who moved his German colonists into Comanche territory in 1846, then negotiated a peace treaty with the tribe. The Germanic heritage of the town is still strong. • President Lyndon B. Johnson; naval commander Chester W. Nimitz (museum and historical center) • Cattle, goat and sheep ranching (wool, mohair), some poultry, wheat, oats, hay, sorghum; hunting, fishing; granite quarrying, gypsum, sand and gravel • The county is the leading peach-producer of TX; its peaches are world-renowned for their succulence.

GLASSCOCK *Garden City* • 1,406 • 901 • Western TX; drained by Mustang Draw and the North Concho River. The county includes Dewey Lake and Currie Reservoir. • Named for George W. Glasscock, Sr. (1810–79), a miller in Austin, TX, and TX state legislator • 1887 from Tom Green • Cattle, goats (Angora wool and milk), sheep, hogs, grain sorghum, hay, wheat, pecans, cotton; some oil and natural gas.

GOLIAD *Goliad* • 6,982 • 854 • Southern TX, bounded on the southwest by the Blanco River and on the northeast by Coleto Creek and Coleto Creek reservoir; drained by the San Antonio River. Goliad State Historical Park is here, as is Fannin Battleground State Historical Site. • Named for the Municipality of Goliad, TX. Goliad is a near-anagram for (H)IDALGO (a Mexican patriot) and served as a symbol of Anti-Mexican sentiment during Texas Revolution. • Original county; organized 1836 (prior to statehood) from Old Mexican Municipality • A Spanish mission and its protective presidio were established here in 1749 on the site of an Aranama Indian village. The fort was occupied briefly in 1812 by a filibustering American expedition, and in 1821 by James Long's invading Mississippians. In December, 1835 the presidio's Mexican garrison was overwhelmed by a Texan force led by George Collingsworth and Ben Milam. On December 20, a preliminary "declaration of independence" was published here. On March 20, 1836, a detachment of 330 American and Texan troops surrendered to superior Mexican forces here after the Battle of Coleto Creek and were executed on March 27 in what came to be known as the Goliad Massacre. A monument near La Bahía Presidio marks the burial site. • Cattle, ranching, corn, grain sorghum, hay; oil, natural gas wells.

GONZALES *Gonzales* •18,628 • 1,068 • South-central TX; drained by the Guadalupe and San Marcos rivers. The county includes Palmetto State Park. • Named for the municipality of Gonzales and the Battle of Gonzales • Original county; organized 1836 (prior to statehood) from Old Mexican Municipality • Gonzales was settled by American immigrants in 1825 when Texas was a department of Mexico. The first battle of the War for Texas Independence was fought here, on October 2, 1835. Responding to Col. William B. Travis's appeal for help, approximately three dozen Gonzales men fought and died during the siege of the Alamo. • Chickens, turkeys, eggs, corn, grain sorghums, cattle; clay and kaolin mining, gravel, oil and gas; mineral spring resort tourism; poultry processing, cold storage plants, cotton and cotton-oil mills, bottling works • The "Come and Take It Cannon," sent to Gonzales in 1831 to protect the citizenry from Indian attacks, and buried in 1835 to keep Mexico from retrieving it, was unearthed 101 years later by a flood.

GRAY (one of two counties so named, the other in KS) *Pampa* • 22,744 • 928 • Northern TX, in the Panhandle high plains, broken by Caprock Escarpment; drained by the North Fork of the Red River and McClellan Creek. McClellan Creek National Grassland is here. • Named for Captain Peter W. Gray (1819–74), TX legislator and justice of the TX Supreme Court • 1876 from Bexar • McLean was built on land donated by English rancher Alfred Rowe who later died on the *Titanic*. • Olympic shotputter Randy Matson • It is one of TX's most productive oil and natural gas counties; refineries; manufacture of oil well equipment and supplies, chemicals, clothing; meat-packing, cattle, wheat, sorghum, corn, forage crops, hay; hunting and fishing • Reputed to be the largest barbed wire display in the world, the Devil's Rope Museum in McLean exhibits the fencing material and notes its place in history. McLean and Alanreed are stops along the historic Route 66. Woody Guthrie's farewell song to Pampa, "So Long, It's Been Good to Know You," includes a reference to the Dust Bowl days of "...the county called Gray."

GRAYSON (one of three counties so named) *Sherman* • 110,595 • 934 • Northern TX, bounded on the north by the Red River and Lake Texoma (forming the OK state line). Eisenhower State Park, Hagerman National Wildlife Refuge, and part of Ray Roberts Lake reservoir are all here. • Named for Peter W. Grayson (1788–1838), Republic of TX attorney general • 1846 from Fannin • In 1858, the county was the entry point in TX for the westbound Overland Mail/Butterfield Trail from St. Louis to San Francisco. Known as the "Athens of Texas," Sherman was home to four private colleges in 1900. In 1873, the nation's westernmost north-south railroads were linked in Denison, this development contributing to the demise of the famed Longhorn cattle drives. In 1930, Texas Rangers were called into Sherman after a mob burned the county courthouse to the ground. • President Dwight D. Eisenhower (birthplace and state historical park) • Cattle, dairying, wheat, peanuts, some citrus, hogs, poultry, horses; some oil and gas, stone; timber; food processing; manufacture of cotton fabrics and apparel, furniture, mattresses, air conditioning equipment, wood products, electronic components, machinery, truck bodies, textiles, surgical supplies, business forms, pharmaceuticals, aluminum, steel, and steel products; education (Austin College) • Lydia McPherson was the first woman newspaper publisher in TX and OK (Whitesboro *Democrat* and the Sherman *Weekly Democrat*). The Munson Viticulture-Enology Center honors T.V. Munson who is credited with helping to save the French wine industry in the mid-1800s and was given the French Legion of Honor award. Each year Sherman hosts the U.S. National Aerobatic competition.

GREGG *Longview* • 111,379 • 274 • Eastern TX, bounded on the north in part by Little Cypress Creek and on the southeast in part by the Sabine River (which also drains the county). Lake Cherokee reservoir is on the southern boundary. The county is characterized by its abundance of oil derricks throughout. • Named for Gen. John Gregg (1828–64), officer in the Confederate Army • 1873 from Rusk and Upshur • Originally a trading center for beef cattle, hogs and horses, with lumber and cotton as additional economic mainstays, the county experienced rapid industrial expansion and population growth with the discovery of oil in the 1930s (East Texas Oil Museum). • Gregg is a leading oil-producing county. Also, natural gas, sand and gravel, clay; timber; racehorses; manufacture of petroleum-related products, aircraft components, industrial machinery, truck beds and trailers, metal cans, lumber and wood products, plumbing fixtures, clothing, breweries, food products, farm and earth-moving equipment, clothing; education (Le Tourneau U.) • Kilgore (junior) College is nationally known for its Rangerette precision drill and dance team.

GRIMES *Anderson* • 23,552 • 794 • East-central TX, bounded on the west by the Navasota and Brazos rivers. Gibbons Creek Reservoir is here, as is Fanthorp Inn State Historical Park • Named for Jesse Grimes (1788–1866), signer of the TX Declaration of Independence and legislator • 1846 from Montgomery County • The county enjoyed significant interracial cooperation in the late 1800s, resulting in the election of a number of black local office holders. • Corn, hay, honey, cattle, dairying; shipment of cotton, pecans, grain; timber; hunting and fishing; cotton gins, oil mills and compresses; lignite coal, oil • Plantersville is the site of the Annual Texas Renaissance Festival.

GUADALUPE (one of two counties so named, the other in NM) *Seguin* • 89,023 • 711 • South-central TX, bounded on the northeast by the San Marcos River and on the southwest by Cibolo Creek; drained by the Guadalupe River. Lake McQueeney reservoir (Guadalupe River) is in the northwest. • Named for the Guadalupe River • 1846 from Bexar and Gonzales • Pecans, cotton, corn, peanuts, grain sorghum, wheat, oats, vegetables, peaches, nursery crops, cattle, horses, hogs, poultry, exotic animals; Christmas trees; greyhound breeding; oil, natural gas, clay mining, sand and gravel; processing of farm products; hunting and fishing • Seguin is known for its many pecan and oak trees. Some of the oaks are estimated to be over 1,000 years old, and are fondly named by the locals. At the courthouse in Seguin sits a half ton metal-and-cement pecan, calling attention to the fact that the county produces more than three million pounds of pecans a year. Seguin was once known as "Cement City" for its more than 100 concrete buildings, made possible by the development of a new formula for concrete by Seguin resident Dr. John E. Park.

HALE (one of two counties so named, the other in AL) *Plainview* • 36,602 • 1,005 • Northwestern TX; drained by the White River, Running Water Draw (continuation of White River), and Blackwater Draw. The county lies on Llano Estacado. • Named for Lt. John C. Hale (?–1836), one of the nine Texans who died in the Battle of San Jacinto • 1876 from Bexar • Grain sorghum, wheat, cotton, alfalfa, corn, vegetables, beef cattle; oil, clay and natural gas deposits; meat packing; hunting (waterfowl); manufacture of irrigation equipment; education (Wayland Baptist U.).

HALL (one of three counties so named) *Memphis* • 3,782 • 903 • Northwestern TX. Located in the plains region below Caprock Escarpment of Llano Estacado. The county is crossed by the Prairie Dog Town Fork of the Red River. • Named for Warren D.C. Hall (1788–1867), adjutant general and secretary of war of the Republic of Texas • 1876 from Bexar • Father of "country swing," Bob Wills • Chiefly cotton; also grain, wheat, peanuts, beef and dairy cattle, hogs.

HAMILTON (one of ten counties so named) *Hamilton* • 8,229 • 836 • Central TX; drained by the Leon, North Bosque and Lampasas rivers, and Cowhouse Creek. Vista Mountain is in the southwest. • Named for General James Hamilton (1786–1857), U.S. representative from SC and SC governor who was diplomatic agent to various European countries for the Republic of TX • 1858, from part of the Milam Land District of TX and developed from parts of Bosque, Lampasas, and Comanche • Cattle, sheep and goats (wool and mohair marketed), dairying, wheat, oats, sorghum, hay; natural gas and oil fields; sand and gravel.

HANSFORD *Spearman* • 5,369 • 920 • Extreme northern TX, in the high plains of the Panhandle, bounded on the north by the OK state line; drained by Coldwater and Palo Duro creeks. Palo Duro reservoir is here. • Named for Gen. John M. Hansford (?–1844), TX jurist and speaker of the TX Republic House of Representatives • 1876 from Bexar • Hansford served as a stage stop for the Dodge City-Tascosa Trail, its trodden path still visible along Palo Duro Creek. • Wheat, grain sorghums, corn, beef cattle, some sheep; natural gas wells, some oil, stone, helium.

HARDEMAN (one of two counties so named, the other in TN) *Quanah* • 4,724 • 695 • Northern TX, bounded in part on the south and drained by the Pease River; bounded on the north by the Red River (forming the OK state line). The county is also drained by Wanderer's Creek, which forms Lake Pauline reservoir. Copper Breaks State Park is here. • Named for brothers Thomas J. Hardeman (1788–1854), TX Republic congressman, and Bailey Hardeman (1795–1836), signer of the TX Declaration of Independence and secretary of the treasury of the TX Republic • 1858 from Fannin • Wheat, cotton (and cotton oil milling), pumpkins, goats, cattle; gypsum mining, some oil and gas production.

HARDIN (one of six counties so named) *Kountze* • 48,073 • 894 • Southeastern TX, bounded on the east by the Neches River. The county is bounded in part on the south and drained by Pine Island Bayou. Village Creek State Park is here, as are several units of Big Thicket National Preserve. • Named for the five Hardin brothers, including Augustine B. Hardin (1797–1871), signer of the TX Declaration of Independence • 1858 from Jefferson and Liberty • Forage crops, cattle, hogs, fruit, rice, honey, egg production; oil, natural gas, sand and gravel; timber.

HARRIS (one of two counties so named, the other in GA) *Houston* • 3,400,578 (the most populated county in TX and the third most populated county in the U.S.) • 1,729 • Eastern TX. The county is a seaport and industrial center on the Gulf Coast plains, bounded on the north by Spring Creek, on the east in part by Cedar Creek, on the south by Clear Creek and Clear Lake, and on the southeast by Galveston Bay; drained by the San Jacinto River (which forms Lake Houston reservoir in the northeast) and its tributaries. The county is forested in the north, and highly urbanized in the south and east as part of the Houston metropolitan area. George Bush Intercontinental Airport is in the north. Battleship Texas State Historic Site, Sheldon State Park, and the Johnson Space Center are also here. • Named for the former community of Harrisburg, itself named for John R. Harris (1790–1829), trading post owner and early settler • Organized as Harrisburg, 1836 (prior to statehood) from Austin and Liberty (Old Mexican Municipality); name shortened 1839 • Mexican forces under Santa Anna were defeated by General Sam Houston in the decisive battle of the War for Texas Independence, fought at San Jacinto (state historic park) in April, 1836. Houston was the capital of Texas from 1837 to 1840. A fire destroyed much of the city in 1859. Houston was a world cotton market in the 19th century. The discovery of petroleum at Spindletop boosted the city's economy and turned it into the oil metropolis it remains today. In the 1960s, the county became the focus of the U.S. Space Program. • Surgeon and educator Denton A. Cooley; baseball player Curt Flood; race car driver A.J. Foyt; politician Jeb Bush; diplomat Edward M. House; industrialist and aviator Howard Hughes. Baseball player Roger Maris, dance-band leader Guy Lombardo, and editor and publisher Oveta Culp Hobby died here. • Large oil and natural gas production; rice, corn, peanuts, vegetables, hay, some nurseries, cattle; timber; manufacture of steel, gypsum products, petrochemicals, fertilizers, insecticides, oil field equipment, scientific instruments, transportation equipment, plastics, synthethic rubber, paper; bay resorts; research (oil); education (U. of Houston; TX Southern U.; Rice U.; U. of St. Thomas; Houston Baptist U.) The Houston Ship Channel, linking the city to the Gulf of Mexico, makes Houston one of the world's major seaports; among U.S. port cities, only New York City and New Orleans handle more cargo than does Houston. • The corporate headquarters of 33 Fortune 1000 companies are located in the county, many in the energy field. Houston is home to the Rockets (Compaq Center), Astros (Minute Maid Field), and Texans (Reliant Stadium).

HARRISON (one of eight counties so named) *Marshall* • 62,110 • 899 • Eastern TX, bounded on the east by the LA state line, on the northeast by Caddo Lake (formed by Big Cypress Creek), and on the southwest by the Sabine River; drained by Little Cypress Bayou (forming part of the northern border). The county includes Starr Family State Historical Park. Caddo Lake State Park is on the southern shore of Caddo Lake. • Named for Jonas Harrison (1777–1836), TX patriot who pushed for TX independence • 1839 (prior to statehood) from Shelby • Marshall served as the temporary Confederate capital of MO during the Civil War; Governor Claiborne F. Jackson, unable to win secession from the Union for his state, moved the official seal and state records to the TX city. • First Lady Lady Bird Johnson; boxer George Foreman • Extensive timber harvesting; nurseries, hay, dairying, vegetables, cattle, hogs, horses; railroad shops; manufacture of petrochemicals, plastics, carbon; clay products industry, oil, natural gas, coal, sand and gravel; education (East TX Baptist U.) • The "Stagecoach Days" festival is held in Marshall each May.

HARTLEY *Channing* • 5,537 • 1,462 • Northern TX, in the high plains of the Panhandle, bounded on the west by the NM state line; drained by Rita Blanca and Punta de Agua creeks. The county includes Lake Rita Blanca State Park. • Named for brothers Oliver C. Hartley (1823–59) and Rufus K. Hartley, attorneys and court reporters of the TX Supreme Court • 1876 from Bexar • Large-scale cattle-ranching operations; wheat, corn, sorghum; natural gas wells.

HASKELL (one of three counties so named) *Haskell* • 6,093 • 903 • Northwest-central TX; drained by the Double Mountain Fork of the Brazos River and Paint Creek, forming Lake Stamford reservoir in the southeast corner. • Named for Charles R. Haskell (1817–36), Republic of Texas soldier killed with Fannin at Goliad • 1858 from Fannin and Milam • Cotton, sorghum, wheat, oats, barley, peanuts, beef cattle; oil and natural gas.

HAYS *San Marcos* • 97,589 • 678 • South-central TX; drained by the San Marcos and Blanco rivers. The county, situated on Edwards Plateau, is crossed by Balcones Escarpment, dividing prairies in the southeast from the hilly north and west. • Named for Captain John C. Hays (1817–83), Texas Ranger, officer in the Mexican War, sheriff of San Francisco County, CA and surveyor general of CA • 1848 from Travis • Special prosecutor Leon Jaworski died here. • Cattle, sheep and goats, (wool and mohair marketed), llamas, exotic deer, cotton, corn, wheat, grain sorghum, oats, hay, fruit, vegetables; limestone, sand and gravel (cement production); meat packing, feed processing; aircraft assembly production, metal stamping; hunting and fishing; tourism; education (Southwest TX State U.) • Camp Ben McCulloch, located near Driftwood, was established in 1896 as the reunion site for the United Confederate Veterans. Ezell Cave in San Marcos is the habitat of the rare Texas blind salamander as well as other species of fauna found only in the underground waters of the cave. Located at the headwaters of the San Marcos River is Aquarena Springs. Its hanging gardens, submarine theatre, and caves make it a popular central TX attraction.

HEMPHILL *Canadian* • 3,351 • 910 • Northern TX, on the high plains of the Panhandle, bounded on the east by the OK state line; drained by the Canadian and Washita rivers. Black Kettle National Grassland is here. • Named for General John Hemphill (1803–62), Chief Justice of the TX Supreme Court and U.S. senator • 1876 from Bexar • Many military encounters of the Red River Wars occurred in the county, including the Buffalo Wallow Fight of 1874, which led to the defeat of the Comanches and Kiowas. A boundary dispute between TX and OK in the 1920s led to a U.S. Supreme Court decision, which expanded Hemphill and four neighboring counties at the expense of four OK counties. Hemphill acquired parts of Ellis and Roger Mills counties in OK through the resulting 1930 resurvey of the 100th meridian. • Cattle, horses, wheat, grain sorghum, hay; oil and natural gas; hunting and fishing • The Canadian Rodeo, an annual event first staged on July 4, 1888, is regarded as the first organized commercial rodeo in the U.S.

HENDERSON (one of five counties so named) *Athens* • 73,277 • 874 • Eastern TX, bounded on the west by the Trinity River and on the east by the Neches River (forming Lake Palestine reservoir). Purtis Creek State Park is here. The county also includes Cedar Creek and Lake Athens reservoirs. • Named for General James P. Henderson (1808–58), the first governor of the state of TX • 1846 from Houston County • The Battle of the Neches, which forced the removal of East Texas Indians to OK Territory, was partially fought within present day boundaries of the county in 1839. • Timber; vegetables, melons, nursery crops, black-eyed peas (Athens, called the "Black-eyed Pea Capital of the World," holds a Black-eyed Pea Jamboree each year), other legumes; cattle, hogs, horses, emus, ostriches, rheas; oil, natural gas, lignite, sulfur, sand and gravel; cotton gins; oil- and gas-processing; manufacture of brick, tile, glass, pottery, television sets, clothing, furniture, hardwood lumber; hunting and fishing.

HIDALGO (one of two counties so named, the other in NM) *Edinburg* • 569,463 • 1,569 • Extreme southern TX, bounded on the south by the Rio Grande River (forming the border with the Mexican state of Tamaulipas). Santa Ana National Wildlife Refuge (located on both the Central and Mississippi flyways) and Bentsen-Rio Grande Valley State Park are both here. • Named for Miguel Hidalgo y Costilla (1753–1811), Mexican priest and hero of the Mexican War for Independence from Spain • 1852 from Cameron • Football coach Tom Landry; politician Lloyd Bentsen • Large agribusiness industry including growing, packing and shipping of citrus. Also, vegetables, sugar cane, grain, cotton, beef and dairy cattle; food processing; oil and natural gas production and refining; stone, sand and gravel; manufacture of textiles, machinery; winter tourism; education (U. of TX–Pan American) • Mission is the site of the annual Texas Citrus Fiesta honoring Texas Ruby Red Grapefruit. The city is also the national headquarters of the American Poinsettia Society. Edinburg operates one of the most scattered school districts in the U.S., covering 945 square miles of fruit groves, ranches and farmland. McAllen, the "City of Palms," is a port of entry for trade with Mexico. Civic development plans in Weslaco have required all the buildings in its business section to be remodeled in Spanish architectural style. The only government-licensed hand-pulled ferry on a U.S. border is located at Los Ebanos.

HILL (one of two counties so named, the other in MT) *Hillsboro* • 32,321 • 962 • North-central TX, bounded on the west by the Brazos River (here forming Whitney Lake reservoir); drained by Aquilla and Nolan creeks. Aquilla Lake and part of Navarro Mills Lake reservoirs are here. Lake Whitney State Park is on the western border. • Named for George W. Hill (1814–60), secretary of war and marine for the Republic of TX • 1853 from Navarro • Athlete Rafer Johnson; Baseball player Tris Speaker • Cotton, corn, wheat, sorghum, hay, beef cattle, dairying and dairy products, horses, hogs; limestone, oil and gas; some manufacturing. • The Audie Murphy Gun Museum is here.

HOCKLEY *Levelland* • 22,716 • 908 • Northwestern TX; drained by intermittent Yellow House Draw. • Named for General George W. Hockley (1802–54), Republic of Texas officer and secretary of war and marine • 1876 • Large oil and gas production; cotton, grain sorghum, beef cattle, hogs, some sheep, horses, mules; processing of agricultural products; manufacture of fertilizers, irrigation and oil-field equipment, sheet metal, plastics products.

HOOD *Granbury* • 41,100 • 422 • North-central TX; drained by the Brazos River. Part of Squaw Creek Lake reservoir is in the south. Granbury Lake reservoir and Acton State Historical Park are also here. • Named for Gen. John B. Hood (1831–79), commander of TX troops in the Confederate Army • 1865 from Johnson • Elizabeth Crockett, wife of Davy, is buried here. • Peanuts, hay, pecans, beef and stocker cattle; oil and gas, stone • J. Frank Dalton is buried in Granbury; many contend that Dalton was Jesse James.

HOPKINS (one of two counties so named, the other in KY) *Sulphur Springs* • 31,960 • 785 • Northeastern TX, bounded on the north by the South Fork of the Sulphur River (forming Cooper Lake reservoir in the northwest); drained by White Oak and Lake Fork creeks. • Named for David Hopkins (1825–?) and members of his pioneer family • 1846 from Lamar and Nacogdoches • Founded in the mid-1850s, Sulphur Springs was known for its mineral baths until the early 1900s. • Hopkins is a leading TX dairy-producing county. Also, hay, silage, corn, rice, cattle, cotton, poultry; timber; oil and natural gas wells, clay mining, lignite; processing of farm products, especially milk; light industry.

HOUSTON (one of five counties so named) *Crockett* • 23,185 • 1,231 • Eastern TX, bounded on the west by the Trinity River and on the east by the Neches River. The county includes part of Davy Crockett National Forest. The county also contains Houston County Lake reservoir and Mission Tejas State Historical Park, which offers a log replica of the first Spanish mission building in East TX. • One of three counties named for Sam Houston (1793–1863), president of the Republic of Texas and one of TX's first two new senators • 1837 from Nacogdoches (prior to statehood). The county was the first created by the Republic of TX. • Trinity College, chartered in 1841, was the first college of the Republic of Texas. Legend has it that Davy Crockett camped here in 1836 on his way to the Alamo. • Hay, cotton, peanuts, watermelons, cattle, hogs, horses; oil, natural gas, sand and gravel; lumber milling, oil refining; produce processing • Crockett is the home of the World's Champion Fiddler's Festival and a Valentine's Day "Lovefest."

HOWARD (one of seven counties so named) *Big Spring* • 33,627 • 903 • Western TX; drained by Beals Creek and Mustang Draw. The county is located on the edge of Llano Estacado, and includes Big Spring State Park • Named for Volney E. Howard (1809–89), U.S. representative from TX • 1876 from Bexar • The site of Big Spring was previously a frontier watering place in dispute by Comanche and Shawnee Indians. With the arrival of the Texas and Pacific Railway in May, 1881, it became a railroad division point, with growth further accelerated by the discovery of oil in the county in 1925. • Beef cattle, cotton, wheat, vegetables, black-eyed peas, sesame; oil, natural gas fields, oil and gas refining, stone, sand and gravel; manufacture of petrochemicals and carbon black. The county is a medical center for the area. • The numerous lakes here provide a winter stopover for migrating cranes; the county celebrates the annual Cranefest in February.

HUDSPETH *Sierra Blanca* • 3,344 • 4,571 (the third largest county in TX) • Extreme western TX, bounded on the north by the NM state line and on the south by the Rio Grande River (forming the border with the Mexican state of Chihuahua). The county is located in a high plateau region, with mountains rising to 7,500 feet, including part of the Sierra Diablo, and the Eagle, Quitman, Finlay, and Hueco mountains. Part of Guadalupe Mountains National Park is located in the Salt Basin. Hudspeth is one of only two TX counties that lie entirely within the Mountain time zone. • Named for Claude B. Hudspeth (1877–1941), U.S. representative • 1917 from El Paso County • Outlaw John Wesley Hardin is buried here. • The salt flats west of the Guadalupe Mountains figured into the Salt War of 1877. • Cotton, alfalfa, vegetables, cattle, hogs; talc, gypsum.

HUNT *Greenville* • 76,596 • 841 • Northeastern TX; drained by the Sabine River (which forms Lake Tawakoni in the southeast corner) and the South Fork of the Sulphur River. Part of Lake Tawakoni State Park is on its southern boundary. • Named for General Menucan Hunt (1807–56), Republic of TX officer and statesman • 1846 from Fannin and Nacogdoches • Aviator Claire L. Chennault • Cotton, hay, nursery crops, wheat, dairying, cattle, horses; some oil and gas production, sand and rock; manufacture of clothing, oil-field equipment, trailers, fertilizers; machine shops, grain elevators, planing mills; education (TX A & M University–Commerce).

HUTCHINSON (one of two counties so named, the other in SD) *Stinnett* • 23,857 • 887 • Northern TX, on the high plains of the Panhandle. The county is broken by the Canadian River Gorge. Part of Lake Meredith National Recreation Area is in the southwest corner; it includes Sanford Dam, which forms the lake (Canadian River). • Named for Anderson Hutchinson (?–1853), Republic of TX district judge and compiler of a code of TX law • 1876 from Bexar • The Battle of Adobe Walls, the last Indian skirmish on the Panhandle plains, occurred here in 1874. The completion of the first oil well in the county in 1926 created an overnight tent and shack boomtown. • The county has one of the world's largest natural gas pumping stations. Also, carbon black and oil refining, petroleum product processing; corn, wheat, sorghum, beef cattle; manufacture of printer's ink, synthetic rubber • Lake Meredith Aquatic and Wildlife Museum is located on the reservoir.

IRION *Mertzon* • 1,771 • 1,052 • Western TX; drained by the Middle Concho River and its tributaries. The county lies on Edwards Plateau. Dove Creek Battlefield is in the southeast. • Named for Robert A. Irion (1806–?), Republic of TX senator and secretary of state for the Republic of TX • 1889 from Tom Green • Sheep, Angora goats (wool and mohair marketing); cattle; milo, cotton; oil and gas.

JACK *Jacksboro* • 8,763 • 917 • Northern TX; drained by the West Fork of the Trinity River. Fort Richardson State Historical Park is here, as is Lost Creek Reservoir. Part of Bridgeport Reservoir is on the eastern boundary. • Named for brothers Patrick C. Jack (1808–1844), and William H. Jack (1806–1844), both TX statesmen and legislators • 1856 from Cooke • Cattle, horses, ostriches, wheat, pecans; wool and mohair marketed; oil and natural gas, gravel; timber.

JACKSON (one of twenty-four counties so named) *Edna* • 14,391 • 830 • South-eastern TX, on the Gulf of Mexico coastal plain, bounded on the southwest by Arenosa Creek; drained by the Lavaca and Navidad rivers. The county is indented by Lavaca and Carancahua bays. Lake Texana reservoir (Navidad River) and State Park are here. • Named for the former municipality of Jackson, TX, itself named for President Andrew Jackson (one of twenty-two counties named directly or indirectly for President Jackson) • Original county; 1836 (prior to statehood) from Old Mexican Municipality • Oil, natural gas; cattle, cotton, rice, grain sorghum, soybeans, corn; sheet and metal fabrication.

JASPER *Jasper* • 35,604 • 937 • Eastern TX, bounded on the west by the Neches River (forming B.A. Steinhagen Lake reservoir). Part of Big Thicket National Preserve follows the course of the Neches River downstream from the reservoir. Part of Sam Rayburn Reservoir (Angelina River) is on the northern boundary. Part of Angelina National Forest and Masterson State Forest are also found in the county. Martin Dies, Jr. State Park borders Steinhagen Lake. • One of eight counties named for Sgt. William Jasper (?–1779), American Revolutionary War hero. (TX is one of five states in which Jasper and Newton counties have been placed adjacent to one another to honor the allied efforts of sergeants William Jasper and John Newton to rescue captive colonial soldiers near Savannah.) • Original county; organized 1836 (prior to statehood) from Old Mexican Municipality • Lumbering is the dominant industry in the county. Also, cattle, hogs, horses, poultry, vegetables, pecans, fruit; oil and gas.

JEFF DAVIS (one of two counties so named, the other in GA) *Fort Davis* • 2,207 • 2,265 • Western TX, touching the Rio Grande River (and Mexican border) in the west. The Davis Mountains are here, including Mount Livermore (at 8,382 feet, the second highest peak in the state), and Davis Mountains State Park. The McDonald Observatory, atop Mount Locke at the center of the county, is considered one of the world's best astronomical observatories. Peaks of the Sierra Vieja are in the west. • One of four counties named for

Jefferson Davis (1808–89), president of the Confederate States of America • 1887 from Presidio • Fort Davis (national historic site) was erected in 1854 to protect travelers who used the San Antonio-El Paso road on the southern transcontinental trail west. Razed by Indians, it was rebuilt and reactivated in 1867, and manned by black infantry and cavalry, called "buffalo soldiers" by the Indians. • Cattle, dairying, goats, hogs, sorghum, cotton, melons, corn, hay, wheat; wine grapes • Situated in the Davis Mountains at an altitude of 5,050 feet, Fort Davis is the highest town in TX. The Overland Trail Museum commemorates the historic trail that passed through the county.

JEFFERSON *Beaumont* • 252,051 • 904 • Southeastern TX, bounded on the east by Sabine Lake (here forming the LA state line), on the northeast by the Neches River, on the north by Pine Island Bayou, and on the south by the Gulf of Mexico; crossed by the Gulf Intracoastal Waterway. Sabine-Neches Waterway offers access from the Gulf to the deep-water ports of Beaumont and Port Arthur. The county includes Texas Point and McFadden national wildlife refuges, Sea Rim State Park, and Sabine Pass Battleground State Historical Park. • Named for the town of Jefferson, itself named for President Thomas Jefferson (one of twenty-six counties named directly or indirectly for President Jefferson) • Original county; organized 1836 (prior to statehood) from Old Mexican Municipality • Spindletop, the first major oil field in TX, was discovered here in 1901. (The strike at the original Lucas Well and the subsequent boom town that sprung up here are commemorated in the Lucas Gusher Monument and reconstructed Gladys City-Spindletop Boomtown.) • Painter and graphic artist Robert Rauschenberg; professional baseball player Frank Robinson; sportswoman Babe Didrikson Zaharias (museum); singer Janis Joplin; astronaut Robert L. Crippen • Oil, natural-gas fields, salt and sulfur domes; cattle, rice, soybeans; fishing, duck hunting; ship building; education (Lamar U.). Beaumont and Port Arthur, along with Orange in neighboring Orange County, form the "Golden Triangle," a petrochemical and industrial complex. • Port Arthur salutes its petroleum heritage each October with its CavOILcade celebration.

JIM HOGG *Hebbronville* • 5,281 • 1,136 • Southern TX; drained by Palo Blanco Creek and Arroyo Baluarte. • Named for James S. Hogg (1851–1906), first TX-born governor of the state • 1913 from Brooks and Duval • Oil and natural gas; cattle, sorghum.

JIM WELLS *Alice* • 39,326 • 865 • Southern TX, bounded on the northeast by the Nueces River (including the dam of Lake Corpus Christi reservoir); drained by Los Olmos and San Diego creeks. • Named for James B. Wells, Jr. (?–1923), lawyer who worked to improve relations between Mexicans and Anglos in the Brownsville area • 1911 from Nueces • Chemist Robert F. Curl, Jr. • Large oil and natural gas production, oil refining, caliche; grain sorghum, wheat, corn, vegetables, cotton, cattle, hogs, dairying; meatpacking, cottonseed-oil milling, sheet-metal working.

JOHNSON (one of twelve counties so named) *Cleburne* • 126,811 • 729 • North-central TX, bounded on the southwest by the Brazos River; drained by the tributaries of the Brazos River. Cleburne State Park is here, as is Lake Pat Cleburne. • Named for Middleton T. Johnson (?–1866), AL legislator, Texas Ranger, and TX Republic legislator • 1854 from McLennan and Navarro • Johnson is a leading dairy county. Also, cotton, wheat, grain sorghum, corn, silage, hay, cattle, hogs, horses; limestone, sand and gravel; railroad shops, diversified manufacturing, including sheet-metal products, furniture, textiles, garments, fiber glass, trailers, air conditioners, electronic appliances, steel • In 1886, the Texas (Farmers) Alliance drew up the "Cleburne Demands," the first document of the Populist movement.

JONES (one of six counties so named) *Anson* • 20,785 • 931 • West-central TX; drained by the Clear Fork of the Brazos River. Lake Fort Phantom Hill reservoir is in the extreme southeast. • Named for Anson Jones (1798–1858), second president of the Republic of Texas. • 1858 from Bexar and Bosque • Cotton, wheat, milo, hay, sesame, peanuts, cattle; oil and gas wells, gypsum, sand and gravel, stone; manufacture of western clothing • "Cowboy Dance," by Jenne Magafan, one of the best preserved examples of Depression-era post office murals, adorns the walls of the Anson Post Office. Near Anson are ruins of Fort Phantom Hill, a military post established in 1851, which was later used as Station 54 for Southerland Overland Mail on the old Butterfield Trail. Stamford is home to the Texas Cowboy Reunion, held annually during the Fourth of July weekend.

KARNES *Karnes City* • 15,446 • 750 • Southern TX; drained by the San Antonio River and Cibolo Creek. • Named for Captain Henry W. Karnes (1812–40), TX Republic officer and military scout • 1854 from Goliad • Corn, wheat, grain sorghum, cattle, dairying; oil, natural gas wells, uranium. • Established in 1854, Panna Maria is the oldest Polish settlement in the U.S.

KAUFMAN *Kaufman* • 71,313 • 786 • Northeastern TX, bounded on the southwest by the Trinity River; drained by its East Fork (which forms Lake Ray Hubbard reservoir) and Cedar Creek. Part of Cedar Creek Reservoir is here. • Named for David S. Kaufman (1813–51), Speaker of the House of the Republic of TX and one of the state's first two U.S. representatives • 1848 from Henderson • Cotton, corn, sorghum, wheat, hay, peaches, nursery products, cattle, horses; timber; manufacturing; oil and gas, stone.

KENDALL (one of two counties so named, the other in IL) *Boerne* • 23,743 • 662 • South-central TX, bounded on the south by Balcones Creek; drained by the Guadalupe and Blanco rivers. The county is located on the southern edge of Edwards Plateau, with caverns (including Cascade Caverns) that attract many visitors. Part of Guadalupe River State Park is here. • Named for George W. Kendall (1809–1867), one of the founders of the *New Orleans Picayune* • 1862 from Kerr and Blanco • Settled by German "free thinkers," escaping religious persecution in their homeland, Comfort and Boerne prohibited the building of churches within their city limits from the 1850s to the 1880s. • Angora-goat ranching, sheep (mohair and wool marketed), beef cattle, grain, wheat, oats; natural gas deposits; tourism • Located in Comfort, the Treue der Union Monument is the only monument south of the Mason-Dixon Line dedicated to Union Soldiers, reflecting the anti-Confederacy sentiments of the county's German settlers. Polo, first played in the U.S. in the Boerne area, was imported by British colonists who came to the county in the 1870s to establish cattle ranches. In 1996, the Boerne Village Band received the Pro Musica-Plakette, Germany's highest musical award; it was the first time the award was ever given to a band outside of Germany. Boerne possesses a rare 1614 Low German Bible, one of six known in the world.

KENEDY *Sarita* • 414 (only three U.S. counties have fewer people) • 1,457 • Southern TX, bounded on the east by the Gulf of Mexico and on the north by Los Olmos Creek and Baffin Bay. Padre Island (National Seashore), a sand barrier island, is separated from the mainland by Laguna Madre and the Intracoastal Waterway. Most of the county is occupied by the large King Ranch (its 1,300 square miles spread over four counties). One of the largest and oldest working cattle and horse ranches in the world, King has pioneered in livestock and agricultural research; its Santa Gertrudis breed, a Brahman-Shorthorn cross, was the first true breed of beef cattle to be developed in the Western Hemisphere. The county has numerous small lakes. • Named for Mifflin Kenedy (1818–95), U.S. Army steam boat captain in the Mexican War and half-owner of the King Ranch • Organized as Willacy County in 1911 from Hidalgo and Cameron; its name was changed in 1921, at which time a new Willacy County was created from Cameron and Hidalgo counties, plus a 1.4 mile strip of Old Willacy • Cattle, horses, watermelons; oil and gas.

KENT (one of five counties so named) *Jayton* • 859 • 902 • Northwestern TX; drained by the Salt and Double Mountain forks of the Brazos River and the White River. • Named for Andrew Kent (?–1836), a private killed at the Alamo • 1876 from Bexar • Cattle, cotton, wheat, sorghum, beekeeping; oil and gas, sand and gravel.

KERR *Kerrville* • 43,653 • 1,106 • Central TX; drained by the Guadalupe River and its forks, which originate in springs here. The county is located on Edwards Plateau, and includes Kerrville-Schreiner State Park. • Named for James Kerr (1790–1850), Republic of TX congressman • 1856 from Bexar • Early in the 1900s, Kerrville was the satrapy of developer Charles A. Schreiner whose company owned more than 600,000 acres of land in the area and held substantial interests in a number of local industries. Schreiner gambled that Angora goats would prosper in the county; subsequently, Schreiner's goats have made Kerrville the mohair center of the world. • Sheep, goats, cattle, hay, pecans, apples; strong tourist industry (hunting, dude ranches, youth camps, health resorts); retirement centers;

education (Schreiner College) • The Cowboy Artists Museum is in the county. Kerrville holds the Texas State Arts and Crafts Fair each year. The Kerrville Folk Festival is also a popular event.

KIMBLE *Junction* • 4,468 • 1,251 • West-central TX; drained by the North Llano and South Llano rivers, which join to form the Llano River at Junction in the center of the county. The South Llano River State Park is here. The Blue Mountains cross in the east. • Named for George C. Kimbell (1803–36), a lieutenant killed at the Alamo • 1858 from Bexar • Goats, sheep (a leading U.S. county in mohair and wool production), cattle, sorghum, pecans; sand and gravel; tourism (fishing and hunting).

KING (one of two counties so named, the other in WA) *Guthrie* • 356 (only two U.S. counties have fewer people) • 912 • Northwestern TX; drained by tributaries of the South and Middle Wichita rivers. Haystack Mountain and Blizzard Peak are in the south. • Named for Private William King (1820–36), youngest soldier killed at the Alamo • 1876 from Fannin • Large-scale cattle ranching, horses, cotton, wheat, sorghum, hay; oil and natural gas wells; lime.

KINNEY *Brackettville* • 3,379 • 1,364 • Southwestern TX, bounded on the southwest by the Rio Grande River (forming the border with the Mexican state of Coahuila); drained by the West Nueces River and the East Fork of Sycamore Creek (which forms part of the western boundary). The county sits on the southern edge of Edwards Plateau and is crossed by Balcones Escarpment. The Anacacho Mountains are in the southeast. Part of Kickapoo Cavern State Park is also here. • Named for Henry L. Kinney, founder of Corpus Christi and Texas state legislator • 1850 from Bexar • Fort Clark, established in 1852 and active until 1946, was used as a prisoner of war camp for German soldiers during both world wars. • Cattle, sheep, goats (wool and mohair marketed); cotton, wheat, sorghum, hunting • A replica of the Alamo, constructed for the film of the same name, is located in Alamo Village near Bracketville.

KLEBERG *Kingsville* • 31,549 • 871 • Southern TX, bounded on the east by the Gulf of Mexico and on the south by Baffin Bay and Los Olmos Creek. The northern part of Padre Island (a national seashore) is separated from the mainland by Laguna Madre, which is a conduit for the Intracoastal Waterway. The county is dominated by the large King Ranch. Alazan Bay and Cayo del Grullo divide the county into three sections. Kingsville Naval Air Station is located here. • Named for Robert J. Kleberg (1803–88), German immigrant and Texas Revolutionary soldier • 1913 from Nueces • Richard King, an early steamboat captain, and his heirs increased an original purchase of 15,500 acres of land in 1853 to nearly one million, spread over four counties, and headquartered here in Kingsville. • Beef cattle, cotton, sorghum, corn, vegetables; oil, natural gas, stone; chemical and plastic production; resort tourism; education (Texas A and M University–Kingsville).

KNOX *Benjamin* • 4,253 • 854 • Northern TX, bounded on the north in part by the North Wichita River; drained by the Salt Fork of the Brazos River, and the North and South forks of the Wichita. Lake Catherine and Lake Davis reservoirs are here. • One of nine counties named for General Henry Knox (1750–1806), first U.S. secretary of war • 1858 from Fannin • Grain sorghum, wheat, vegetables (Texas A and M Vegetable Research Station is in Munday), cattle, horses, dairying; oil and gas • Knox City, hailed as the "Seedless Watermelon Capital of the World," hosts an annual festival on the last Saturday in July.

LAMAR (one of four counties so named) *Paris* • 48,499 • 917 • Northeastern TX, bounded on the north by the Red River (forming the OK state line) and on the south by the North Fork of the Sulphur River. Pat Mayse Lake and Lake Crook reservoirs are here. The Gambill Wildlife Refuge (for Canadian geese) is on Lake Gibbons. • Named for Mirabeau B. Lamar (1798–1859), president of the Republic of TX • 1840 from Red River • Lamar was one of the few TX counties to support Sam Houston's position against seceding from the Union. Paris suffered disastrous fires in 1877 and 1916. • Cattleman John Chisum; Confederate general Samuel Bell Maxey (state historical park) • Cotton, grain, hay, soybeans, wheat, sorghum, corn, peanuts, cattle, timber; manufacture of light bulbs, boilers, food and paper products • Paris is the second largest city in the world with this name.

LAMB *Littlefield* • 14,709 • 1,016 • Northwestern TX; drained by the intermittent Blackwater and Running Water draws. The county is located on Llano Estacado. • Named for Lt. George A. Lamb (1814–1836), one of only nine Texans killed at the Battle of San Jacinto • 1876 from Bexar • The county leads the state in the production of grain sorghum. Also, cattle, sheep, cotton, corn, vegetables, hay, soybeans; oil, natural-gas wells, potash deposits, stone.

LAMPASAS *Lampasas* • 17,762 • 712 • Central TX, bounded on the west by the Colorado River; drained by the Lampasas River. Part of Colorado Bend State Park is on the western boundary. • Named for the Lampasas River • 1856 from Bell and Travis • The Indians used the sulphur springs here for their curative powers long before settlers arrived in the 1850s. The Farmers' Alliance was founded near Lampasas in 1877 to address dire economic conditions facing farmers of the day. The organization grew to more than 3,000, and in 1887 merged with the Farmers' Union. The first state bankers' association in the U.S. was formed in Lampasas in 1885 and called the Texas State Bankers' Association. • Grain sorghum, wheat, hay, oats, pecans, Angora goats, cattle; glass-sand mining, sand and gravel, stone; tourism.

LA SALLE *Cotulla* • 5,866 • 1,489 • Southern TX; drained by the Nueces and Frio rivers. • One of three counties named for Rene Robert Cavelier (1643–87), Sieur de La Salle, French adventurer and explorer • 1858 from Bexar and Webb • Established in 1852, Fort Ewell defended the "Camino Real" from San Antonio to Laredo. • Short story writer O. Henry;

President Lyndon B. Johnson (who held his first teaching job at Welhausen School in Cotulla from 1928 to 1929) • Cattle, peanuts, watermelons, sorghum, corn; oil and natural gas; hunting.

LAVACA *Hallettsville* • 19,210 • 970 • Southern TX; drained by the Lavaca River and the Navidad River, which form the county's northeast border • Named for the Lavaca River • 1846 from Colorado, Victoria and Jackson • Cattle, eggs, poultry, corn, sorghum, rice, hay; oil and natural gas; production of leather goods.

LEE (one of eleven counties so named) *Giddings* • 15,657 • 629 • Central TX, bounded on the northeast by East Yegua Creek and on the southeast in part by Yegua Creek, forming Somerville Lake reservoir in the eastern corner; drained by Middle Yegua and Yegua creeks. Part of Lake Somerville State Park is here. • One of eight counties named for Confederate military leader Robert E. Lee • 1874 from Bastrop, Burleson, Washington and Fayette • Cattle, peanuts, goats, hay; oil and gas, lignite.

LEON (one of two counties so named, the other in FL) *Centerville* • 15,335 • 1,072 • East-central TX, bounded on the west by the Navasota River, forming Lake Limestone reservoir in the northwest, and on the east by the Trinity River. Fort Boggy State Natural Area is here. • The derivation of the county's name is uncertain. There are several conflicting possibilities. • 1846 from Robertson • Musician Lightnin' Hopkins • Cattle, hogs, grain, vegetables, watermelons, hay; timber; oil and gas wells, lignite, iron ore; hunting and fishing.

LIBERTY (one of four counties so named) *Liberty* • 70,154 • 1,160 • Southeastern TX, bounded on the southwest by Cedar Bayou; drained by the Trinity River and San Jacinto River. Part of Big Thicket National Preserve is here, as is Davis Hill State Park and Trinity River National Wildlife Refuge. • Named for the town of Liberty • 1836 from Bexar • The Champ D'Asile, a colony of French Bonapartists, was founded on the Trinity River near present day Liberty in 1818 and lasted a mere six months. During World War II, a German prisoner of war camp was located at the Liberty Fairgrounds. • Rice, soybeans, sorghum, corn, cattle; pine, lumber milling; oil and natural gas wells, oil refining, sulphur production, sand and gravel • The Sam Houston Regional Library and Research Center houses items that document the history of southeast Texas.

LIMESTONE (one of two counties so named, the other in AL) *Groesbeck* • 22,051 • 909 • East-central TX; drained by the Navasota River. The county contains Fort Parker State Park and Old Fort Parker State Historical Park. Confederate Reunion Grounds State Historical Park is here, as is part of Lake Limestone. • Named for Lake Limestone • 1846 from Robertson • Cotton, corn, peaches, hay, vegetables, pecans, nursery crops, dairying, cattle, horses, sheep, goats, exotic animals; oil, natural gas, clay, stone, lignite, sand and gravel.

LIPSCOMB *Lipscomb* • 3,057 • 932 • Extreme northern TX, on the northeast corner of the Panhandle, bounded on the north and east by the OK state line; drained by Kiowa and Wolf creeks. • Named for Abner S. Lipscomb (1789–1858), secretary of state of the Republic of TX and associate justice of the TX Supreme Court • 1876 from Bexar • The county acquired part of Ellis County, OK in a re-survey of the 100th Meridian in 1930. • Wheat, grain sorghum, corn, alfalfa, cattle; oil and gas; quail, wild turkey and deer hunting.

LIVE OAK *George West* • 12,309 • 1,036 • Southern TX; drained by the Frio, Atascosa, and Nueces rivers. Part of Choke Canyon Lake reservoir (Frio River) and State Park (South Shore Unit) is located on the western boundary. Part of Lake Corpus Christi (Nueces River) forms the southeastern corner of the county. • Named for the local live oak trees • 1856 from Nueces • Cattle, hogs, grain sorghum, corn, cotton, hay; oil, natural gas, sand and gravel.

LLANO *Llano* • 17,044 • 935 • Central TX, bounded on the east by the Colorado River (which forms Lake Buchanan, Inks Lake, and Lake Lyndon B. Johnson); drained by the Llano River, and Sandy and Pecan creeks. Enchanted Rock State Natural Area (site of the second largest exposed mass of granite in the U.S.) is also here. • Named for the Llano River • 1856 from Bexar • Founded in 1855 as a farming and ranching community, Llano became a boomtown in the 1880s with the discovery of iron ore in the area. In 1886, the Wakefield Iron and Coal Company of MN moved in to mine the ore. Speculators swelled the population to 10,000. Boom turned to bust in the "Pittsburgh of the West" when no local coal was found with which to turn the iron ore into steel. • Cattle, sheep, goats, hogs, peanuts, pecans, peaches, grapes, grain, hay; granite, stone, vermiculite; deer hunting (Llano calls itself the "Deer Capital of TX") and fishing, rock houndry, tourism • Llano County is part of the 1.5 billion-acre Llano Uplift, offering amethyst, azurite, dolomite, galena, garnet, quartz, serpentine, traces of gold, and Llanite, a type of granite found nowhere else in the world.

LOVING *Mentone* • 67 (the least populated county in the U.S.) • 673 • Western TX, bordered on the north by the NM state line and on the southwest by the Pecos River. Red Bluff Lake reservoir (Pecos River), on the county line in the northwest, is used for irrigation and recreation. • Named for Oliver Loving (?–1867), cattle driver who helped to establish the Goodnight-Loving Trail. • 1887 from Tom Green • Some cattle ranching; oil and natural gas • The county's number one attraction is an automatic flagpole at the courthouse. Loving has one elevator, two stop signs, 674 oil wells, no stoplights, no churches, and no lawyers. County voter turnout is 100 percent.

LUBBOCK *Lubbock* • 242,628 • 900 • Northwestern TX; drained by the intermittent North Fork of the Double Mountain Fork of the Brazos River (which forms Buffalo Springs Lake in the southeast), Yellow House Draw, and Blackwater

Draw. Lubbock Lake Landmark State Historical Park is in Lubbock City. Archeological evidence gathered here dates back 12,000 years to the Clovis Period. • Named for Col. Thomas S. Lubbock (1817–1862), an organizer of Terry's Texas Rangers • 1876 from Bexar • Lubbock's population increased fivefold during its growth spurt from 1940 to 1970. One of the costliest tornadoes in the history of the state hit the city in May, 1970. • Lubbock is one of TX's leading agricultural counties and one of the nation's leading inland cotton markets. Sorghum, wheat, hay, vegetables, sunflowers, soybeans, beef cattle, sheep, hogs, poultry, eggs; oil and gas, stone, sand and gravel; manufacture of petroleum, agricultural and earth-moving equipment, cottonseed oil, engineering products, fire-protection equipment; education (TX Tech U.; Lubbock Christian U.) • The annual Panhandle-South Plains Fair is held in Lubbock each year. The Texas Tech U. Museum has assembled donated ranch buildings from throughout the state to demonstrate the history of ranching in TX.

LYNN *Tahoka* • 6,550 • 892 • Western TX. The county is located on Llano Estacado and includes Tahoka Lake and other intermittently dry lakes. • Named for William Linn (?—1836), a private killed at the Alamo • 1876 from Bexar • Sorghum, cotton, wheat, beef cattle, hogs, sheep; oil and gas, stone.

MADISON *Madisonville* • 12,940 • 470 • East-central TX, bounded on the west by the Navasota River, on the east by the Trinity River, and on the southeast by Bedias Creek. • One of nineteen counties named directly or indirectly for President James Madison • 1853 from Montgomery, Walker, Grimes and Leon • Cattle, hogs, horses, forage crops; timber; oil, gas, gravel. • Survivors of the Battle of Medina were executed on Spanish Bluff near the town of Antioch.

MARION *Jefferson* • 10,941 • 381 • Eastern TX, bounded on the east by the LA state line and on the south by Big Cypress Creek and Little Cypress Bayou, forming Caddo Lake reservoir; drained by Big Cypress Creek. Most of Lake O' the Pines reservoir is on the western boundary. Caddo Lake State Park is also here. • One of seventeen counties named for General Francis Marion (?–1795), SC soldier and legislator, known as "The Swamp Fox" for his tactics during the Revolutionary War • 1860 from Cass and Harrison • Timber; oil, natural gas wells, gravel, lignite; peaches, pecans, vegetables, blueberries, horticulture, hay, cattle, horses, hogs, ratites.

MARTIN (one of six counties so named) *Stanton* • 4,746 • 915 • Western TX; drained by Mustang Draw. The county is located on the southern part of Llano Estacado, with Caprock Escarpment in the northeast. • Named for Wylie Martin (?–1842), TX Republic congressman who worked for TX statehood. • 1876 from Bexar • Cattle, hogs, sheep, goats, grain sorghum; oil and gas production.

MASON (one of six counties so named) *Mason* • 3,738 • 932 • Central TX; drained by the San Saba River, Llano River and its tributaries. The Blue Mountains extend into the southwest. The county is located on Edwards Plateau. • Named for

Fort Mason • 1858 from Bexar • Robert E. Lee served at Fort Mason as a young officer. • Peanuts, watermelons, hay, beef cattle, sheep and goats (marketing of wool and mohair); granite, topaz; tourism (hunting and fishing).

MATAGORDA *Bay City* • 37,957 • 1,115 • South-eastern TX, bounded on the east in part by Linville Bayou and Cedar Lake Creek; drained by the Colorado River. The county borders Matagorda and East Matagorda bays and is sheltered from the Gulf of Mexico by Matagorda Peninsula, a sand barrier running parallel to the coast. The Gulf Intracoastal Waterway also parallels the coast. Big Boggy National Wildlife Refuge and part of San Bernard National Wildlife Refuge are here. • Named for Matagorda Bay and the existing Mexican municipality by that name • Original county; organized 1836 (prior to statehood) from Old Mexican Municipality • Matagorda is a leading cattle-ranching and rice-raising county. Also, cotton, grain, poultry; commercial fishing; oil fields, natural gas, salt; beach tourism; manufacture of petrochemicals; oil refining, welding, sheet-metal working, rice milling, meatpacking.

MAVERICK *Eagle Pass* • 47,297 • 1,280 • Southwestern TX, bounded on the southwest by the Rio Grande (forming the border with the Mexican state of Coahuila) • Named for Samuel A. Maverick (1803–70), Republic of TX patriot, rancher, and legislator, source of the word "maverick" • 1856 from Kenedy • Mexican General Antonio Lopez de Santa Anna crossed through what is now Maverick County in 1836 on his way to the Battle of the Alamo. Camp California, in Eagle Pass, was a staging area for the California 49'ers choosing the "Mexican route" during the Gold Rush. Fort Duncan, established that year by the U.S. Army, remained active until 1900 and was reactivated in 1916 to protect the border during the Mexican Revolution. • Many officers who later became famous were stationed at Fort Duncan, including Phil Sheridan, William R. Shafter, John L. Bullis, Zenas R. Bliss, Terry Allen, James Doolittle, Matthew Ridgeway, and James Van Fleet. • Grain sorghum, oats, wheat, pecans, vegetables, cattle; oil and gas, sand and gravel; border trade; tourism • The last flag to fly over an organized Confederate force was buried in the Rio Grande at Eagle Pass.

MCCULLOCH *Brady* • 8,205 • 1,069 • The geographical center of TX (exact center near Placid), bounded on the north by the Colorado River; drained by the San Saba River and Brady Creek (which forms Brady Creek reservoir). • Named for General Ben McCulloch (1811–62), legislator and Confederate Army officer • 1856 from Bexar • A State Historical Marker, located southwest of Brady near Calf Creek, marks the old Bowie Battleground where, in 1831, Jim Bowie and company fought local Indians. A prisoner of war internment camp was located near Brady during the last half of World War II. • Peanuts, cotton, wheat, hay, cattle, sheep and goats (wool and mohair manufactured); oil and gas; sand and gravel • The longest fenced cattle trail in the world once extended 100 miles from the railhead at Brady to Sonora. The county features a restored Sante Fe depot.

MCLENNAN *Waco* • 213,517 • 1,042 • East-central TX; drained by the Brazos River, Bosque River and its North and Middle branches, and Aquilla and Tradinghouse creeks. The county includes Lake Waco (Bosque River) in the center; Tradinghouse Creek Reservoir is in the east. • Named for Neil McLennan (?–1867), surveyor and pioneer • 1850 from Milam, Robertson and Navarro • A 470-foot suspension bridge over the Brazos River opened in 1870 and was, for a time, the longest single span suspension bridge west of the Mississippi River. It brought the TX section of the Chisholm Trail through Waco. In 1885, Waco pharmacist Charles Curtis Alderton invented Dr. Pepper. In 1911, the first skyscraper in TX was built by the Amicable Life Insurance Company in Waco. One of the deadliest tornadoes in TX history struck the city in 1953, killing 114 people. After a fifty-one-day standoff with federal agents, more than seventy members of the Branch Davidian religious cult perished in a fire at their compound near Waco. • Special prosecutor and lawyer Leon Jaworski; sociologist Charles Wright Mills; advice columnist Heloise; governor Ann Richards; hostess Texas Guinan; physician and cancer researcher E. Donnall Thomas • Oats, wheat, hay, cotton, corn, grain sorghum, pecans, extensive dairying, beef cattle, turkeys; limestone, clay, stone, sand and gravel, oil and gas; manufacture of bomb casings, clothing, machinery, tires, glass; railroad maintenance shops; fishing; education (Baylor U., the largest Baptist university in the world) • The remains of over twenty-two mammoths have been discovered and are being excavated at the Waco Mammoth Site.

MCMULLEN *Tilden* • 851 • 1,113 • Southern TX; drained by the Frio and Nueces rivers. Part of Choke Canyon Lake reservoir (Frio River) is in the northeast; Choke Canyon State Park (Calliham Unit) is on its southern shore, on the county line. • Named for John McMullen (?–1853), an early colonizer • 1858 from Bexar and Live Oak • Cattle, grain sorghum, sunflowers; oil, natural-gas wells, lignite coal, zeolite-kaline; manufacture of kitty litter; tourism.

MEDINA (one of two counties so named, the other in OH) *Hondo* • 39,304 • 1,328 • Southern TX; drained by the Medina River and Hondo Creek, with the source of the Atascosa River in the southeast. The county is crossed by Balcones Escarpment, separating Edwards Plateau (in the north) from plains of the south. Part of Medina Lake reservoir (forming part of the northern boundary) is in the northeast. Landmark Inn State Historical Park is in Castroville, and part of Hill Country State Natural Area is on the county's northern boundary. • Named for the Medina River • 1848 from Bexar • Dinosaur tracks, left by the tyrannosaurus 65 million years ago, have been found near Tarpley. Mission Valley is the site of the first Black settlement in TX. During World War II, the world's largest navigational school was located at Hondo Air Base. • Cattle, sheep and goats (wool and mohair marketed), corn, grain sorghum, peanuts, cotton, vegetables; oil, natural

gas, clay mining, sand and gravel • Erected in 1930, the Hondo welcome sign admonishes, "This is God's country. Please don't drive through it like hell."

MENARD (one of two counties so named, the other in IL) *Menard* • 2,360 • 902 • West-central TX; drained by the San Saba River. The county is located on Edwards Plateau. Fort McKavett (established 1852) State Historical Park is in the west. The Spanish San Saba Presidio is also here. • Named for Michele B. Menard (1805–56), signer of the Texas Declaration of Independence, Republic of TX legislator, and founder of Galveston • 1858 from Bexar • Sheep and goats (wool and mohair marketing), cattle, grains, pecans; oil and natural gas; hunting and fishing, tourism • Jim Bowie Days Celebration is held in Menard every June.

MIDLAND (one of two counties so named, the other in MI) *Midland* • 116,009 • 900 • Western TX; drained by tributaries of the Colorado River. Midland is located on Llano Estacado. • The county was given this name for its location midway on the railway between Fort Worth and El Paso • 1885 from Tom Green • Several pioneer trails crossed the county, including the Chihuahua Trail and the Emigrant Road. Midland entered a boom period following the discovery of oil in the Permian Basin in 1923. • President George H.W. and Barbara Bush; President George W. and Laura Bush • Midland is the hub of a twelve-county ranching region noted for Hereford cattle. Also, horses, cotton, alfalfa, pecans; manufacture of aircraft, fabricated steel, plastics, apparel, chemicals, oil tools; dairy processing; natural gas, anhydrite, salt, potassium, oil. (The county serves as headquarters for many oil companies and is the administrative center for the large Permian Oil Basin.) • Midland, the city that rescued "Baby Jessica" (who fell in a well), sponsors the "Community Spirit Award" in recognition of the good works of other American cities. The fossilized remains of "Midland Minnie," of the late Pleistocene Age, were discovered on the Scharbauer Ranch in 1953. The Confederate Air Force, the world's largest flying museum, with a fleet of 134 WWII aircraft, is based in Midland.

MILAM *Cameron* • 24,238 • 1,017 • Central TX, bounded on the northeast by the Brazos River; drained by the Little and San Gabriel rivers, and East Yegua Creek. • Named for the municipality of Milam, itself named for Benjamin R. Milam (1788—1835), Republic of TX army officer • Original county; organized 1836 (prior to statehood) from Old Mexican Municipality • Cotton, corn, grain sorghum, wheat, hay, melons, peanuts, cattle, poultry, hogs, horses; meat packing; large lignite deposits, oil wells, aluminum processing • A miniature replica of 1940s downtown Cameron took John Johnson over 25 years to build, and is on display in the city.

MILLS (one of two counties so named, the other in IA) *Goldthwaite* • 5,151 • 748 • Central TX, bounded on the southwest by the Colorado River; drained by Pecan Bayou and other tributaries. • Named for John T. Mills (1817–1871), Republic of TX district judge • 1887 from Brown, Comanche,

Lampasas, and Hamilton • Ranching; sheep, goats, beef and dairy cattle, hay, grains, pecans. • Apache and Comanche battle sites are found throughout the county.

MITCHELL (one of five counties so named) *Colorado City* • 9,698 • 910 • Western TX; drained by the Colorado River and Beals Creek. Champion Creek reservoir and Lake Colorado City (State Park) are here. • Named for Asa (?–1865) and Eli Mitchell (?–1876), early settlers of Austin's colony • 1876 from Bexar • Politician Martin Dies. Isaac Ellwood and Joseph Glidden, the inventors of barbed wire, also made Mitchell County their home. • Beef cattle, sheep, cotton, grain sorghum; oil and natural gas wells; shipping; cotton gins and compresses, cottonseed oil mill, oil and asphalt refining • In Colorado City, the Wall of Brands depicts the long history of ranching in the region.

MONTAGUE *Montague* • 19,117 • 931 • Northern TX, bounded on the north by the Red River (forming the OK state line). Found here are the source of the Elm Fork of the Trinity River, and Clear, Denton and Brushy creeks. Farmers Creek reservoir is in the north, on a tributary of the Red River. Lake Amon G. Carter reservoir is in the southwest. • Named for Daniel Montague (1798–1876), surveyor and veteran of the Mexican War • 1857 from Cooke • Socialist Otis Dudley Duncan • Large poultry and dairy operations, also peanuts, wheat, watermelons, canteloupes, cotton; oil, rock, limestone; timber; some manufacturing • Nocona remains only one of two major baseball glove producers in the U.S.

MONTGOMERY (one of eighteen counties so named) *Conroe* • 293,768 • 1,044 • Eastern TX, bounded on the south by Spring Creek; drained by the West Fork of the San Jacinto River (which forms Lake Conroe) and Peach Creek (which forms the northeastern boundary). The county is part of the Houston metropolitan area. It also includes W. G. Jones State Forest and parts of Sam Houston National Forest. • Named for the town of Montgomery, itself named for General Richard Montgomery (1738–75), American Revolutionary War officer who captured Montreal, Canada (one of sixteen counties named directly or indirectly for General Montgomery) • 1837 from Washington County • George W. Strake struck oil here on June 4, 1932 and started the Conroe Field, which is still producing. • Oil, natural gas, sand and gravel; cattle, horses, ratites, fruit, nursery and greenhouse products; timber; hunting and fishing. • In 1997, the 75th Texas Legislature proclaimed the county the "Birthplace of the Lone Star Flag." Dr. Charles Bellinger Stewart, the designer of the Lone Star Flag and State Seal, is buried in the Montgomery Cemetery. The town of Cut and Shoot east of Conroe received its name from the quote "cut around the corner and shoot through the bushes."

MOORE (one of three counties so named) *Dumas* • 20,121 • 900 • Northern TX, on the high plains of the Panhandle; drained by the Canadian River. Part of Lake Meredith reservoir (Canadian River) and Lake Meredith National Recreation Area are in the southeastern corner. • Named for Edwin W. Moore (1810–65), a Republic of Texas naval officer who charted a coastal map of TX • 1876 from Bexar • In 1865, Col. Kit Carson and his troops battled 3,000 Southern Plains Indians to a draw in the southeast part of the county. • Rich oil and natural gas fields, helium production; wheat, corn, sorghum, pinto beans, cattle • Bandleader and songwriter Phil Baxter wrote the 1930s hit "I'm a Ding Dong Daddy from Dumas" after a brief stay in the town.

MORRIS (one of three counties so named) *Daingerfield* • 13,048 • 255 • Northeastern TX, bounded on the north by the Sulphur River and on the south by Cypress Creek and Ellison Creek (Ellison Creek reservoir is in the south). Daingerfield State Park is here. • Probably named for W.W. Morris (1805–1883), who founded Morristown and became a prominent east TX attorney • 1875 from Titus • Peanuts, watermelons, cattle, poultry; iron-ore deposits; pine and hardwood.

MOTLEY *Matador* • 1,426 • 989 • Northwestern TX; drained by the North, South, and Middle Pease rivers. The county is located just below Caprock Escarpment of Llano Estacado. • Named for Junius W. Mottley (1812–36), signer of the TX Declaration of Independence who was one of only nine Texans killed at the Battle of San Jacinto. Clerical spelling error was allowed to stand. • 1876 from Bexar • Cattle, cotton, peanuts, grain sorghum; oil and gas fields, sand and gravel; timber.

NACOGDOCHES *Nacogdoches* • 59,203 • 947 • Eastern TX, bounded on the west and south by the Angelina River and on the east by Attoyac Bayou. The rivers converge in the southeast to form Sam Rayburn Reservoir. The county includes part of Angelina National Forest. Lake Nacogdoches is in the east. • Named for the Mexican department of Nacogdoches, itself named for the Indian tribe • Original county; organized 1836 (prior to statehood) from Old Mexican Municipality. • In 1826, Hayden Edwards declared Texas independent of Mexico and attempted to organize the Republic of Fredonia at Nacogdoches, but he was quickly removed by Mexican authorities. • One of the founders of the Republic of TX, Adolphus Sterne • Lumbering; dairying, poultry, truck crops, beef cattle; feed processing; oil (in 1866, the first oil in TX was discovered here), natural gas, clay; some manufacturing; tourism; education (Stephen F. Austin State U.) • The university campus is the site of the Old Stone Fort, a Spanish trading post built in 1779, torn down in 1902, and reconstructed in 1936.

NAVARRO *Corsicana* • 45,124 • 1,071 • East-central TX, bounded on the northeast by the Trinity River; drained by Richland, Chambers and Waxahachie creeks. Navarro Mills Lake reservoir is in the west (Richland Creek). A large part of Richland-Chambers Reservoirs is in the south. • Named for Jose A. Navarro (1795–1871), Republic of TX patriot and legislator active in promoting statehood • 1846 from Robertson • Cotton, corn, grains, vegetables, sorghum, wheat, herbs, beef and dairy cattle, horses, ratites; oil wells and refining. (The first oil refinery west of the Mississippi River was established in Corsicana in 1896. It represents the largest continuous oil flow in the state.) Also natural gas wells; processing of peanuts, potato and corn products; manufacture of bricks, lumber, clothing, oil-field and farm supplies.

NEWTON (one of six counties so named) *Newton* • 15,072 • 933 • Eastern TX, bounded on the east by the Sabine River (forming the LA state line); drained by its tributaries. The county includes E. O. Siecke State Forest. Toledo Bend Reservoir extends into the northeast corner. • One of five counties named for Sgt. John Newton (?–1780), Revolutionary War hero. (TX is one of five states in which Jasper and Newton counties have been placed adjacent to one another to honor the allied efforts of sergeants William Jasper and John Newton to rescue captive colonial soldiers near Savannah.) • 1846 from Jasper • Lumbering; peaches, vegetables; oil and natural gas.

NOLAN *Sweetwater* • 15,802 • 912 • Western TX; drained by Sweetwater Creek and other tributaries of the Colorado. • Named for Philip Nolan (1771–1801), an American agitator in Spanish-held TX, killed by Spanish soldiers • 1876 from Bexar • The county was struck by a severe blizzard in 1885, which destroyed much of its livestock, and by a disastrous drought in 1886–87. (The desolation that resulted here inspired Dorothy Scarborough's 1925 novel *The Wind*.) Sweetwater revived with the arrival of the Atchison, Topeka and Santa Fe Railway in 1911. • The county is one of the leading centers of the registered Hereford cattle industry in the U.S. Also, sheep, Angora goats (mohair production), hogs, ratites, cotton, sorghum, wheat, hay, dairying, oil and natural gas production; gypsum, stone, sand and gravel, clay; manufacture of apparel and electronic products; meat packing, cotton ginning, cottonseed-oil processing • Sweetwater's Avenger Field was training base for the Women's Air Force Service Pilots (WASPs) during World War II. The World's Largest Rattlesnake Round-Up is held here every March. The snakes are used for snakebite serum and medical research.

NUECES *Corpus Christi* • 313,645 • 836 • Southern TX; bounded on the east by the Gulf of Mexico, on the north in part by the Nueces River, on the northeast by Corpus Christi Bay, and on the southwest by San Fernando Creek. Laguna Madre separates Mustang and Padre islands from the mainland, and is conduit for the Gulf Intracoastal Waterway. Part of Laguna Largo extends into the county on the southern boundary. Also on the southern fringe is the King Ranch. Mustang Island State Park and Lipantitlan State Historical Park are also here. • Named for the Nueces River • 1846 from San Patricio • Henry Lawrence Kinney's small trading post at the site of Corpus Christi became the unofficial capital of southeastern TX around 1838. The Federal Navy blockaded the port in 1862; it was captured by Federal troops two years later. The county was heavily damaged by a hurricane in 1919, but quickly rebuilt. The city of Corpus Christi was economically transformed by the discovery of petroleum and natural gas in the area in the early 20th century. • Nueces is a leading oil and gas-producing county in TX. Corpus Christi ranks as the sixth largest port in the U.S. Sand and gravel; cotton, grain sorghum, goats, hogs, corn, wheat, some citrus, cattle (the county is a leader in production); commercial fishing; oil refining; manufacture of chemicals, stone, clay and glass products, aluminum; processing of farm foods and seafood; resort tourism (sport fishing and water sports); education (Texas A and M University — Corpus Christi; Del Mar College). The large Corpus Christi Naval Air Station and Army Depot make a significant contribution to the local economy. • Life-size replicas of the Niña, the Pinta and the Santa Maria, built by the Spanish government to commemorate the 500th anniversary of Columbus's voyage, are docked in Corpus Christi. The International Kite Museum, which traces the history and uses of kites, is also in Corpus Christi.

OCHILTREE *Perryton* • 9,006 • 918 • Extreme northern TX in the Panhandle high plains, bounded on the north by the OK state line; drained by Wolf and Kiowa creeks, tributaries of the North Canadian River. • Named for Col. William B. Ochiltree (1811–67), Republic of TX secretary of the treasury, TX legislator, and Confederate officer • 1876 from Bexar • Ochiltree is a leading wheat-producing county in the U.S.; also, cattle, ranching, sheep, hogs, horses, cotton, corn, sorghum; oil and gas, sand and gravel, clay, caliche.

OLDHAM (one of two counties so named, the other in KY) *Vega* • 2,185 • 1,501 • Northern TX, in the high plains of the Panhandle, bounded on the west by the NM state line; drained by the Canadian River and Rita Blanca Creek. • Named for Williamson S. Oldham (1813–68), AR Speaker of the House, member of the TX secession convention and TX senator to the Confederate Congress • 1876 from Bexar • Wheat, sorghum, cattle; oil and gas, sand and gravel, stone • Cal Farley's Boys Ranch, a 10,700 acre working ranch for youths established in the 1930s, is the largest employer in the county. Located at the midway point between Chicago and Los Angeles on the historic Route 66, the county once proclaimed "When You're Here, You're Halfway There."

ORANGE (one of eight counties so named) *Orange* • 84,966 • 356 • Eastern TX, bounded on the east by the Sabine River (forming here the LA state line), on the west and southwest by the Neches River, and on the south by Sabine Lake. Part of Big Thicket National Preserve is here. • Named for an orange grove near the Neches River • 1852 from Jefferson • Legend has it that Jean Lafitte used the area that would become Orange County as a repair stop for his pirate ships in the early 1800s. Orange was a boom town during both world wars because of its robust shipbuilding industry. The U.S. Navy's "mothball fleet" was kept here after World War II. • Orange is a deepwater port on the Sabine River (which has been canalized to connect with the Gulf Intracoastal Waterway). It forms the "Golden Triangle" with Beaumont and Port Arthur in Jefferson County. Timber, Christmas trees; cattle, horses, hogs, rice; aquaculture; honey; hunting; oil and natural gas, sand and gravel, clay, salt; steel fabrication; manufacture of chemicals, petrochemicals, synthetic rubber, paper products, portland cement • The Stark Museum has a large collection of the art of the American West. Locals contend that the Lutcher Memorial Church Building (1908–1912) was the first public building in the world to be air-conditioned. The county is a stop for Monarch butterflies in their fall migration to Mexico.

PALO PINTO *Palo Pinto* • 27,026 • 953 • North-central TX; drained by the Brazos River. Part of Possum Kingdom Lake reservoir is here, with Possum Kingdom State Park forming part of its western boundary. The Palo Pinto Mountains are in the west. Lake Palo Pinto reservoir is in the south. • Named for Palo Pinto Creek • 1856 from Navarro • Wheat, hay, cattle, horses; oil and natural gas, clay, sand and gravel; hunting and fishing; juniper (locally called "cedar") fence posts.

PANOLA (one of two counties so named, the other in MS) *Carthage* • 22,756 • 801 • Eastern TX, bounded on the east by the LA state line; drained by the Sabine River (forming part of the northern boundary), and by Martin Creek and Murvau Bayou. Martin Creek Lake State Park is on the western boundary. Lake Murvau reservoir and part of Toledo Bend reservoir are also found in the county. • The name of the county comes from the Choctaw word for cotton • 1846 from Harrison and Shelby • Singers Jim Reeves and Tex Ritter; historian Walter P. Webb • Extensive lumbering of pine, gum, cypress; natural gas, some oil wells, coal deposits; cattle, hogs, poultry (a leading broiler producing county).

PARKER *Weatherford* • 88,495 • 904 • Northern TX; drained by the Brazos River and the Clear Fork of the Trinity River. Lake Mineral Wells State Park and Weatherford Lake reservoir are here. The county is urbanized in the east as part of the Fort Worth metropolitan area. • Probably named for Isaac Parker (1793–1883), Republic of TX patriot and legislator • 1855 from Bosque and Navarro • Singer and actress Mary Martin • Peaches, peanuts, pecans, hay, cattle, dairying, horses; gas and oil, stone, clay, sand and gravel; manufacture of oilfield and electronic equipment; education (Weatherford College) • The Texas Railroad Museum is in Weatherford's old Santa Fe Depot.

PARMER *Farwell* • 10,016 • 882 • Western TX, bounded on the west by the NM state line; drained by Running Water Draw. • Named for Martin Parmer (1778–1850), MO legislator and signer of the TX Declaration of Independence • 1876 from Bexar • Wheat, grain sorghum, hay, barley, sunflowers, cotton, vegetables, sugar beets, beans, corn, cattle, hogs, sheep.

PECOS *Fort Stockton* • 16,809 • 4,764 (second largest county in TX) • Western TX, bounded on the northeast and drained by the Pecos River; also drained by intermittent creeks and draws. The Glass Mountains are in the southwest. The county lies on Stockton Plateau in the east. Imperial Reservoir is here. • Named for the Pecos River • 1871 from Presidio • Zoologist and cytologist Theophilus S. Painter died here. • Extensive ranching of cattle, sheep, goats, also alfalfa, vegetables, pecans,

grapes, cotton; large scale oil and natural gas production; tourism. • A 22,000-year-old mammoth tusk, unearthed near Fort Stockton, is now housed in the Annie Riggs Memorial Museum. A ten-foot-tall, twenty-two-foot-long statue of "Paisano Pete," Fort Stockton's mascot, is the world's largest roadrunner.

POLK (one of twelve counties so named) *Livingston* • 41,133 • 1,057 • Eastern TX, bounded on the southwest by the Trinity River, forming Lake Livingston reservoir, and on the northeast by the Neches River. Alabama and Coushatta Indian Reservation is here. Part of Big Thicket National Preserve is also found in the county. Lake Livingston State Park is in the southwest. • One of eleven counties named for President James K. Polk • 1846 from Liberty • Pine, hardwoods, Christmas trees; oil and natural gas, sand and gravel; peaches, blueberries, vegetables, cattle, hogs, horses; hunting and fishing.

POTTER (one of three counties so named) *Amarillo* • 113,546 • 909 • Northern TX in the high plains of the Panhandle; drained by the Canadian River (which forms Lake Meredith reservoir). Alibates Flint Quarries National Monument, the only national monument located in TX, was the site of more than 10,000 years of Pre-Columbian Native American toolmaking, using agatized dolomite from its quarries. Part of Lake Meredith National Recreation Area is nearby. • Named for Robert Potter (?–1842), U.S. representative from NC, Republic of TX official and naval officer • 1876 from Bexar • In the early 1800s, Amarillo (partly in Randall County) was the world's greatest cattle shipping market, with as many as 50,000 head in the area at times. After the turn of the 20th century, the county grew as part of a major wheat belt. The discovery of petroleum and natural gas deposits in the 1920s led to economic development that was stifled in the 1930s by the Depression and drought. • Amarillo is the commercial and industrial center of the TX Panhandle. The county produces much of the world's supply of helium. Other products include oil and gas, clay, sand and gravel; cattle, sunflower seeds, oats, barley, grains, sorghums, forage. Copper refining; manufacture of ordnance, helicopters; education (Amarillo College) • The world's largest equine registry is located in Amarillo. The city is also the headquarters of the American Quarter Horse Association. Amarillo boasts a six-story stainless steel column constructed in 1968 to commemorate the centennial of the discovery of helium.

PRESIDIO *Marfa* • 7,304 • 3,856 (the fourth largest county in TX) • Western TX, bounded on the west and south by the Rio Grande (forming the border with the Mexican state of Chihuahua); drained by Cibolo and Alamito creeks. The Sierra Vieja are in the northwest and the Chinati Mountains are in the west. The county includes Fort Leaton State Historic Park. Big Bend Ranch State Park in the south, at 265,000 acres, is the largest state park in TX; it provides habitat for six endangered and eleven threatened plant and animal species and is home to a herd of TX Longhorns. Capote Falls here is the highest in the state.• Named for Presidio del Norte, a

395 (Roberts) TEXAS

Spanish military post • 1850 from Bexar • Large-scale ranching of cattle and horses; also onions, vegetables, lettuce, peppers, hay; silver mines, sand and gravel; hunting and tourism. • Since the 1880s, the Marfa Ghost Lights have mystified and delighted observers.

RAINS *Emory* • 9,139 • 232 • Northeastern TX, bounded on the southwest by the Sabine River, forming Lake Tawakoni in the west. One arm of Lake Fork Reservoir is on the eastern boundary. • Named for Emory Rains (1800–78), Republic of TX legislator and surveyor • 1870 from Hopkins, Wood and Hunt • Watermelons, vegetables, sweet potatoes, hay, cattle; gas, oil and coal.

RANDALL *Canyon* • 104,312 • 914 • Northern TX, Panhandle high plains; drained by Tierra Blanca and Palo Duro creeks, here forming the Prairie Dog Town Fork of the Red River. Palo Duro Canyon State Park contains the state's own "Grand Canyon," a 1000-foot deep, 100-mile-long gorge cutting through the plains. Buffalo Lake National Wildlife Refuge in the southwest encompasses Buffalo Lake reservoir. • Named for Col. Horace Randal (1833–64), Confederate Army officer. The misspelling was allowed to stand. • 1876 from Bexar • In the Battle of Palo Duro Canyon, the last great Indian battle in TX (1874), the U.S. cavalry under Col. R. S. Mackenzie routed a camp of Comanches who had left their reservations. • Cattle, horses, sorghum, wheat; tourism; education (West Texas A and M University) • The Panhandle Plains Historical Museum, the oldest and largest state museum, is located in Canyon. Georgia Okeeffe taught at West Texas State Normal College in Canyon from 1916 to 1918. Cadillac Ranch, five miles west of Amarillo, offers ten fin-back-style Cadillacs from 1949 to 1960 buried with their noses at a 40-degree angle in a field. The Canyon Pioneer Amphitheatre stages *Texas*, a musical drama by Paul Green, each summer.

REAGAN *Big Lake* • 3,326 • 1,175 • Western TX; drained by an extension of the Middle Concho River. The county lies at the northern edge of Edwards Plateau. It includes Big Lake in the south. • Named for Col. John H. Reagan (1818–1905), postmaster general of the Confederacy and U.S. representative and senator from TX • 1903 from Tom Green • Sheep, Angora goats, cattle, cotton, grains; oil, natural-gas wells. • Located in the county is the oil well, Santa Rita No. 1, activated in 1923 on University of Texas property.

REAL *Leakey* • 3,047 • 700 • Southwestern TX; drained by the Nueces (forming part of the western boundary) and Frio rivers. The county is located on Edwards Plateau. Part of Lost Maples State Natural Area is on the eastern boundary. • Named for Julius Real (1860–1944), county jurist and TX legislator • 1913 from Bandera and Kerr • Goats (the county is a leader in mohair production), sheep, cattle, pecans; cedar harvesting; hunting, fishing, dude ranch tourism.

RED RIVER *Clarksville* • 14,314 • 1,050 • Northeastern TX, bounded on the north by the Red River (forming the OK state line) and on the south by the Sulphur River. • One of two

counties/parishes (the other in LA) named for the Red River • Original county; organized 1836 (prior to statehood) from Mexican Municipality • U.S. vice president John Nance Garner; "Father of Texas Journalism" Col. Charles DeMorse. Captain William Becknell, founder of the Santa Fe Trail, is buried near Clarksville. • Cotton, soybeans, wheat, corn, cattle, some dairying; lumbering, lumber milling; manufacturing; some oil and gas production • A marker, designating the spot where Sam Houston entered TX, is located in Jonesboro. The city was the Protestant port of entry to Spanish Texas.

REEVES *Pecos* • 13,137 • 2,636 • Western Texas, bounded on the northeast by the Pecos River (forming Red Bluff Lake reservoir) and in the extreme north by the NM state line; drained by Toyah Creek (which forms Lake Toyah in the north). Lake Balmorhea in the south is bordered by Balmorhea State Park. The county's plains slope to the Pecos River from the foothills of the Davis Mountains. • Named for Col. George R. Reeves (1826–82), speaker of the Texas House • 1883 from Pecos • Pecos, a wild frontier town in its infancy, was once known as "the place where the law ended." On July 4, 1883, ranching outfits competed in various contests to determine who had the best cowboys; this competition inadvertently became the world's first rodeo. (The tradition continues each July.) During World War II, Pecos was selected as the site for one of the largest B1-13 Training Centers in the U.S. • Outlaws Billy the Kid and Clay Allison • Cattle, sheep, cotton, cantaloupes, onions, bell peppers, other vegetables; some oil and gas production, gravel; automotive tire proving grounds; sulphur processing; tourism • The county's rolling plains are well populated by javelina and prairie dogs. West of the Pecos Museum is considered one of the finest museums in the country containing old west artifacts.

REFUGIO *Refugio* • 7,828 • 770 • Southern TX, bounded on the north by the San Antonio River, on the southwest by the Aransas River, on the southeast by Copano Bay, and on the northeast by San Antonio Bay; drained by the Mission River and Copano Creek. Small portions of Aransas National Wildlife Refuge extend into the county. • Named for the town of Refugio or Mision Nuestra Señora del Refugio • Original county; organized 1836 (prior to statehood) from Old Mexican Municipality • Professional baseball pitcher Nolan Ryan • Refugio is a leading TX oil- and natural gas-producing county. Also, cattle ranching, cotton, grain sorghum, corn, soybeans, sunflowers; oil refineries, pipelines; hunting.

ROBERTS (one of two counties so named, the other in SD) *Miami* • 887 • 924 • Northern TX, on the Panhandle high plains; drained by the Canadian River and its tributaries. The source of the Washita River is in the east. • Named for John S. Roberts (1796–1871), a signer of the TX Declaration of Independence, and/or for Oran M. Roberts (1815–1898), TX governor • 1876 from Bexar • Cattle, hogs, wheat, milo, corn, hay; oil and gas • Miami has hosted the National Cow Calling Contest every June since 1949. It is the only town in the county.

ROBERTSON (one of three counties so named) *Franklin* • 16,000 • 855 • East-central TX, bounded on the west by the Brazos River and on the east by the Navasota River. Lake Limestone reservoir is here, as is Twin Oaks Reservoir. • Named for Sterling C. Robertson (1785–1842), signer of the TX Declaration of Independence and Republic of TX legislator • 1837 (prior to statehood) from Bexar • Los Angeles mayor Tom Bradley • Cotton, sorghum, grain, hay, cattle, hogs, poultry, dairying; oil, natural gas, lignite coal; brick manufacturing.

ROCKWALL *Rockwall* • 43,080 (68% increase since 1990; the third fastest growing county in TX) • 129 (the smallest county in TX and one of the fifty smallest counties in the U.S.) • Northeastern TX; drained by the East Fork of the Trinity River. The western part of the county is becoming urbanized as part of the expanding Dallas-Fort Worth metropolitan area. Lake Ray Hubbard reservoir is on the western border. • Named for the city of Rockwall, itself named for a subterranean wall or dike that thrusts up in various parts of the county • 1873 from Kaufman • Wheat, hay, sorghum, cattle, horses; some timber.

RUNNELS *Ballinger* • 11,495 • 1,054 • West-central TX; drained by the Colorado River and numerous creeks. An arm of Lake O.H. Ivey reservoir (Colorado River) extends into the extreme southeast corner. • The derivation of the county's named is uncertain. It may have been named for Hardin R. Runnels (1820–73), TX governor; or for Hiram G. Runnels (1796–1857), TX state senator • 1858 from Coleman • Cotton, wheat, grain sorghum, cattle, goats, sheep (wool marketing); oil and natural-gas wells, sand and gravel • The Z. I. Hale Museum in Winters has a permanent exhibit on native son Rogers Hornsby who was born here. Ballinger lays claim to the largest courthouse square in TX. A monument erected here in 1919 honors Charles Noyes and all Texas cowboys.

RUSK *Henderson* • 47,372 • 924 • Eastern TX, bounded on the extreme northeast by the Sabine River and on the southeast by Attoyac Bayou. Lake Cherokee reservoir and part of Striker Creek reservoir are here. Martin Creek Lake reservoir and State Park are on the northeast border. • Named for General Thomas J. Rusk (1803–57), Chief Justice of the Republic of TX Supreme Court, signer of the TX Declaration of Independence, and one of TX's first two U.S. senators • 1843 from Nacogdoches • A school explosion in New London in 1937 killed 293 students and teachers. • Rusk is a leading petroleum county in TX. Also natural gas, clay, lignite deposits; vegetables, watermelons, nursery crops, cotton (including processing), dairying, beef cattle, poultry, horses; manufacture of lumber, clothing.

SABINE (one of two counties so named, the other in LA) *Hemphill* • 10,469 • 490 • Eastern TX, bounded on the east by the Sabine River (Toledo Bend Reservoir forming the LA state line). Most of the county is in Sabine National Forest; about three quarters of the county is now occupied by reservoir or national forest. One arm of Sam Rayburn Reservoir extends into the southwest corner. • Named for the former municipality of Sabine • Original county; organized 1836 (prior to statehood) from Old Mexican Municipality. • Timber, lumber milling; vegetables, fruit, cattle, poultry; hunting and fishing; glauconite.

SAN AUGUSTINE *San Augustine* • 8,946 • 528 • Eastern TX, bounded on the west by Attoyac Bayou and the Attoyac Arm of Sam Rayburn Reservoir, and on the southwest by the Angelina River (Sam Rayburn Reservoir). The county includes part of Angelina National Forest and part of Sabine National Forest. • Named for the municipality of San Augustine • Original county; organized 1836 (prior to statehood) from Old Mexican Municipality • Pine, hardwoods harvesting; corn, vegetables, watermelons, beef cattle, horses, poultry; hunting, fishing.

SAN JACINTO *Coldspring* • 22,246 • 571 • Eastern TX, bounded on the north and east by the Trinity River, forming Lake Livingston reservoir, and on the southwest by Peach Creek; drained by the West Fork of the San Jacinto River. The county is contained within Sam Houston National Forest, except for its eastern and northern ends. • Named for the Battle of San Jacinto • 1870 from Liberty • Timber; cattle, hogs, horses, hay; oil and gas wells, iron ore; hunting and fishing.

SAN PATRICIO *Sinton* • 67,138 • 692 • Southern TX, bounded on the southeast by Redfish Bay, on the south by the Nueces River and Nueces and Corpus Christi bays, and on the northeast by the Aransas River. The Intracoastal Waterway follows the mainland shore in Redfish Bay. The county includes part of Lake Corpus Christi and Lake Corpus Christi State Park. Welder Wildlife Foundation Refuge is the largest privately endowed wildlife refuge in the world. • Named for the town of San Patricio • Original county; organized 1836 (prior to statehood) from Old Mexican Municipality • It is a leading TX oil- and natural-gas-producing county (also petroleum and gas processing), stone, clay, caliche; cotton, grain sorghum, corn, fruit, flax, livestock; resort area beaches; fishing, shrimping • Sinton has three sites that have been accepted for inclusion in the Great Texas Birding Trail.

SAN SABA *San Saba* • 6,186 • 1,135 • Central TX, on Edwards Plateau, bounded on the north and east by the Colorado River, with part of Lake Buchanan in the southeast; drained by the San Saba River and Brady Creek. Colorado Bend State Park is in the county. • Named for the San Saba River • 1856 from Bexar • The Comanche Indian Treaty, signed here in 1847 between Comanche chiefs and German colonists, was never broken. • Cattle, sheep, goats, peanuts, wheat; hunting and fishing; stone quarrying; some manufacturing. Edmond Risien, an amateur horticulturist arriving here in the early 1870s, successfully cross-pollinated the indigenous paper shell pecan to obtain several varieties, earning San Saba the title "Pecan Capital of the World." • Beveridge Bridge, one of the few remaining swinging bridges in TX, spans the San Saba River northwest of San Saba.

SCHLEICHER *Eldorado* • 2,935 • 1,311 • Western TX, on the edge of Edwards Plateau; drained by the South Concho River, Buckhorn Draw, and branches of the Devils's River. • Named for Gustave Schleicher (1823–79), TX legislator, captain of engineers in the Confederate Army, and U.S. representative • 1887 from Crockett • Sheep and goats (shipping of wool and mohair), cattle, hay, milo, oats, wheat, cotton; oil, natural gas; hunting. • Eldorado's local playhouse is called "Way Off Broadway."

SCURRY *Snyder* • 16,361 • 903 • Northwest-central TX; drained by the Colorado River, forming Lake J.B. Thomas on its western boundary. • Named for General William R. Scurry (1821–64), Confederate Army officer • 1876 from Bexar • It is a leading U.S. oil producing county; also natural gas, limestone; dairying, cattle, cotton, grain sorghum, wheat, hay, silage, pecans, sheep, hogs, poultry. • Indian pictographs can be found in Sandstone Canyon.

SHACKELFORD *Albany* • 3,302 • 914 • North-central TX; drained by the Clear Fork of the Brazos River and Hubbard Creek. Fort Griffin State Historical Park is here. • Named for John Shackelford (1790–1857), AL physician and legislator who fought for TX independence • 1858 from Bosque • Cattle, horses, hogs, sheep, wheat, cotton, grain sorghum; mesquite; oil, natural-gas wells • Fort Griffin is home to part of the official State of Texas Longhorn Herd. Local citizens erected the Georgia Monument in Albany to honor the Georgia volunteers who gave their lives for Texas Independence.

SHELBY (one of nine counties so named) *Center* • 25,224 • 794 • Eastern TX, bounded on the east by the Sabine River (Toledo Bend Reservoir) and here forming the LA state line; and on the west by Attoyac Bayou. The county includes part of Sabine National Forest. • Named for the municipality of Shelby, itself named for General Isaac Shelby (1750–1826), officer in the Revolutionary War, NC legislator, and first governor of KY (one of nine counties named directly or indirectly for the general) • Original county; organized 1836 (prior to statehood) from Old Mexican Municipality • A boundary dispute between the U.S. and Spain over TX and LA following the Louisiana Purchase left an area of "neutral territory" comprising what is now part of Shelby County, and an opportunity for outlaws to roam unfettered. Law and order were not restored until 1821. • Shelby leads in broiler and egg production in TX. Also, beef and dairy cattle, vegetables, watermelons; hardwood; natural gas wells, oil; hunting and fishing • The National Hall of Fame Cemetery of Foxhounds is in Boles Field.

SHERMAN (one of four counties so named) *Stratford* • 3,186 • 923 • Extreme northern TX, bounded on the north by the OK state line; drained by the North Fork of the Canadian River, and intermittent Coldwater and Frisco creeks. • Named for General Sidney Sherman (1805–73), officer in the Republic of TX Army and TX legislator • 1876 from Bexar • Beef cattle, silage, corn, sorghum, wheat, pinto beans; natural-gas wells, some oil.

SMITH (one of four counties so named) *Tyler* • 174,706 • 928 • Eastern TX, bounded on the north by the Sabine River and on the west by the Neches River, forming Lake Palestine reservoir in the southwest. Tyler State Park is in the north. • Named for General James Smith (1792–1855), officer in the War of 1812 and the War for TX Independence, and TX legislator • 1846 from Nacogdoches • Camp Ford, the largest Confederate Civil War prison camp west of the Mississippi River was located near Tyler. During the war Tyler supplied arms to the Confederacy. • Smith is a leading rose-growing county in TX. (Tyler claims the title "Rose Capital of the World.") Also, watermelons, vegetables, pecans, cattle; oil (as the center of the East TX oil fields, Tyler is administrative headquarters for many oil companies), natural gas, clay, stone, sand and gravel; timber; oil refining; manufacture of cast iron, heating and cooling equipment, ceramics, pre-fabricated houses, clothing, furniture, plastics; education (U. of TX at Tyler) • To celebrate its flower industry, Tyler holds a Texas Rose Festival each October and sponsors Azalea and Spring Flower trails. The East Texas Agricultural Fair is held in Tyler in September.

SOMERVELL *Glen Rose* • 6,809 • 187 • North-central TX; drained by the Brazos and Paluxy rivers, and Squaw Creek. The county includes Dinosaur Valley State Park (known for its dinosaur fossils) and Fossil Rim Wildlife Center. Part of Squaw Creek Lake reservoir is on the northern boundary. • Named for General Alexander Somervell (1796–1854), Republic of TX secretary of war, and commander of the 1842 Somervell expedition to Mexico • 1875 from Hood • Grains, peanuts, hay, cattle, dairying; sand and gravel; resort tourism.

STARR *Rio Grande City* • 53,597 • 1,223 • Extreme southern TX, bounded on the south and southwest by the Rio Grande (forming the border with the Mexican state of Tamaulipas). Part of Falcon State Park and International Falcon Reservoir are in the western corner of the county. • Named for James H. Starr (1809–90), Republic of Texas secretary of the treasury and TX promoter • 1848 from Nueces • General Zachary Taylor established Fort Ringgold after the Mexican War, as one in a line of forts built every 100 miles along the border to protect citizens from Indians and bandits. • Vegetables, cotton, sorghum, cattle; oil, natural gas wells, sand and gravel • Starr has the largest percentage of Hispanics of any county in the U.S. (98%). Much of downtown Roma is designated a National Historic District; a number of structures built by German stone mason Heinrich Portscheller in the late 1800s survive today.

STEPHENS (one of three counties so named) *Breckenridge* • 9,674 • 895 • North-central TX; drained by the Clear Fork of the Brazos River, and Sandy, Hubbard, and Cedar creeks. Part of Possum Kingdom Lake and Possum Kingdom State Park are on the eastern border. The county also includes Hubbard Creek Lake and Daniel reservoirs. • One of two counties (the other in GA) named for Alexander Hamilton Stephens, vice president of the Confederate government • Established as Buchanan in 1858 from Bosque; name changed in 1861 • Wheat, oats, grain sorghum, peanuts, pecans, cotton, cattle, goats, sheep, hogs, horses; oil, natural-gas wells, stone; timber; manufacture of mobile homes, aircraft parts.

STERLING *Sterling City* • 1,393 • 923 • Western TX; drained by the North Concho River and its tributaries. • Named for W.S. Sterling, Indian fighter, rancher, and buffalo hunter • 1891 from Tom Green • Sheep and goats (wool and mohair marketed); beef cattle; oil and natural gas.

STONEWALL *Aspermont* • 1,693 • 919 • Northwest-central TX; drained by the Salt and Double Mountain forks of the Brazos River, joining in the northeast to form the river. The county lies below Caprock Escarpment. The Double Mountains are in the southwest. • Named for General Thomas J. "Stonewall" Jackson (1824–63), Confederate Army officer • 1876 from Fannin • Cattle, peanuts, cotton, wheat, hay, sheep, hogs, goats; oil and natural-gas wells, gypsum.

SUTTON *Sonora* • 4,077 • 1,454 • Western TX, on Edwards Plateau; drained by the Devils and North Llano rivers. The Caverns of Sonora are located here. • Named for Lt. Col. John S. Sutton (1821–62), Confederate Army officer who also participated in the Mier Expedition (museum) • 1887 from Wood • Sheep and goats (Sutton is a leading county in the shipment of wool and mohair, and holds a goat cookoff each year.) Also, beef cattle; oil and natural gas; hunting.

SWISHER *Tulia* • 8,378 • 900 • Northwestern TX, on Llano Estacado; drained by Tule Creek and its forks. Caprock Escarpment in the east is broken by Tule Canyon. Part of MacKenzie Reservoir (Tule Creek) is on the eastern boundary. • Named for Captain James G. Swisher (1794–1864), Republic of TX soldier and a signer of the TX Declaration of Independence • 1876 from Bexar • Wheat, cattle, grain sorghum, corn, cotton.

TARRANT *Fort Worth* • 1,446,219 (the third most populated county in TX and the twentieth most populated county in the U.S.) • 863 • Northern TX; drained by the West and Clear forks of the Trinity River. The county is highly urbanized in the center and east, growing from Fort Worth, the smaller member in the Dallas-Fort Worth metropolitan partnership. It includes Worth and Eagle Mountain lakes. Dallas-Fort Worth International Airport straddles the Tarrant and Dallas boundary. Part of Grapevine Lake and Grapevine Recreation Area are in the northeast corner. Forth Worth Nature Center and Refuge is in the northwest, south of Eagle Mountain Lake. The county also includes Benbrook Lake, Lake Arlington, and part of Joe Pool Lake. Naval Air Station Fort Worth Joint Reserve Base is in the west. • Named for General Edward H. Tarrant (1796–1858), TX Ranger and legislator • 1849 from Navarro • Fort Worth was established in 1849 as an Army post to protect settlers from Indian attacks. Nicknamed "Cow-

town," Fort Worth had a long history as a cattle-shipping center. Hell's Half Acre, a Fort Worth neighborhood with a high concentration of saloons and brothels, was the hangout for Butch Cassidy and the Sundance Kid. During World War I, the Canadian government constructed three airfields near the city to train members of the British Army's Royal Flying Corps. The first round-the-world nonstop airplane flight (beginning on February 26 and ending March 2, 1949) originated from Carswell Air Force Base in Fort Worth. • Pianist Van Cliburn; biochemist and educator Bruce Merrifield. Dancer Vernon Castle died here. • Dairying, grains, cotton, pecans, sorghum, vegetables, nursery crops, cattle, poultry, horses, emus, ostriches; natural gas, sand and gravel, stone; oil refining, meat packing, grain milling; shipping; manufacture of aircraft and aircraft parts, helicopters, automobiles, rubber and paper products, trailers, machinery, chemicals, food products, mobile homes, oil-well equipment, shipping containers; insurance; education (TX Wesleyan U.; TX Christian U.; U. of TX–Arlington) • The Van Cliburn International Piano Competition, held every four years, is the premier piano competition in the U.S. The Cattleman's Museum traces the history of Texas cattle ranching through interactive exhibits and artifacts. Fort Worth's annual Southwestern Exposition and Livestock Show is one of the largest livestock shows in the U.S. The Kimbell Art Museum includes a large collection of European paintings. Arlington is home to the Texas Rangers (The Ballpark at Arlington).

TAYLOR (one of seven counties so named) *Abilene* • 126,555 • 916 • West-central TX; drained by Elm Creek and other tributaries of the Brazos River, and by tributaries of the Colorado River. Lake Abilene reservoir and Abilene State Park (containing 4,000 native pecan trees and part of the official TX Longhorn herd) are southwest of Abilene. • The derivation of the county's name is uncertain. In March, 1954, the TX State Legislature passed a bill assigning the name to the three Taylor brothers who died at the Alamo • 1858 from Bexar • Abilene was founded in 1881 as the new railhead for the overland TX cattle drives, taking business from its namesake, Abilene, KS. During World War II, Camp Barkeley housed over 60,000 men, and was a prisoner of war facility. • Educator Hyder E. Rollins • Cotton, grain sorghum, sesame, wheat, hay, cattle, sheep, goats; oil, natural gas wells, stone, clay, caliche, sand and gravel; manufacture of light machinery, aerospace structures, band instruments. Three church-affiliated universities are located in Abilene: Hardin Simmons, Abilene Christian, and McMurry. • Abilene holds the West Texas Fair and annual rodeos and livestock shows. Buffalo Gap Historic Village includes the county's original courthouse and jail. Dyess Air Force Base is the training center for crews of the B-1 Bomber. An Air Combat Command wing is stationed here with two B-1B and C-130 Squadrons attached.

TERRELL (one of two counties so named, the other in GA) *Sanderson* • 1,081 • 2,358 • Western TX, bounded on the south by the Rio Grande (forming the border with the Mexican state of Coahuila and designated here a National Wild and Scenic River) and on the east in part by the Pecos River. The county lies on Stockton Plateau and is carved by numerous creek canyons. • Named for Col. Alexander W. Terrell (1827–1912), TX legislator and U.S. minister to Turkey • 1905 from Pecos • Sheep, goats, cattle, alfalfa; hunting; natural gas and oil, limestone.

TERRY *Brownfield* • 12,761 • 890 • Western TX, on Llano Estacado, crossed by intermittent Sulphur Springs Draw. Sulphur Draw Mound Lake is on the eastern boundary. • Named for Col. Benjamin F. Terry (1821–61), a Confederate Army officer who organized Terry's TX Rangers • 1876 from Bexar • Grain sorghum, wheat, peanuts, cotton, vegetables, cattle; oil, natural gas wells, sodium sulfate; manufacture of agricultural implements, chemical fertilizers, insecticides, feeds, processed meats, ready-mixed concrete and cottonseed-oil mill products.

THROCKMORTON *Throckmorton* • 1,850 • 912 • Northern TX; drained by the Brazos River and its Clear Fork. Part of Millers Creek Reservoir is in the northwest. • Probably named for William E. Throckmorton (1795–1843), early pioneer in northern TX and father of Gov. James W. Throckmorton • 1858 from Bosque • Wheat, cotton, grain sorghums, oats, cattle, sheep, horses; mesquite; oil and gas wells. • The county has several historic sites, including Camp Cooper, Camp Wilson, and the site of a former Comanche reservation.

TITUS *Mount Pleasant* • 28,118 • 411 • Northeastern TX, bounded on the north by the Sulphur River, on the south by Big Cypress Creek; drained by White Oak Bayou. Monticello Reservoir is in the southwest, An arm of Lake Bob Sandlin is on the southern boundary, with Bob Sandlin State Park on its northern shore. • Named for Andrew J. Titus (?–1855), an early settler who helped establish the first road and stagecoach line linking Jefferson with the Red River • 1846 from Red River • Grain sorghum, watermelons, hay, dairying, cattle, poultry (a leading county in broiler production); large oil production, natural gas, lignite; oil refining, farm product processing.

TOM GREEN *San Angelo* • 104,010 • 1,522 • Western TX; drained by the North, Middle and South Concho rivers, here joining to form the Concho River. The county is located on Edwards Plateau. O.C. Fisher Lake (North Concho), Twin Buttes and Lake Nasworthy reservoirs are found here. San Angelo State Park is also in the county. • Named for General Thomas Green (1814–64), officer in the War for Texas Independence, the Mexican War, and the Civil War (Confederacy) • 1874 from Bexar • The Goodnight-Loving (cattle) Trail passed through what would become Tom Green County. • Sheep and goats (one of the nation's foremost markets for wool and mohair), cattle, cotton, oats, wheat, sesame, grain sorghum, hay; oil and gas wells; limestone; hunting and fishing; manufacture of petroleum products, meat and dairy products, cottonseed products, shoes, boots, saddles, Western-

style jewelry, metal products, stone, clay and glass products; printing and binding; education (Angelo State U.) Goodfellow Air Force Base helps to diversify the county's economy. • Fort Honcho National Historic Landmark, a restored military outpost, is in San Angelo.

TRAVIS *Austin* • 812,280 (the fifth most populated county in TX) • 989 • South-central TX, crossed from southwest to northeast by Balcones Escarpment; drained by the Colorado River. The Highland Lakes, including Austin Lake and Lake Travis, are recreational. Balcones Canyonlands National Wildlife Refuge is in the north. • Named for Lt. Col. William B. Travis (1809–36), commanding officer at the Alamo • 1840 (prior to statehood) from Bastrop • In the fall of 1838, the vice president of the recently formed Republic of Texas, Mirabeau B. Lamar, impressed by the run of buffalo near his friend Jake Harrell's log stockade, "Waterloo," proclaimed that "this should be the seat of a future empire." A year later Waterloo became Austin and shortly thereafter Austin became the new capital of the Republic. When Mexican invasion threatened Texas in 1842, the government moved to Houston, but the Travis County citizenry, determined to keep Austin the capital, staged the Archives War, and forcibly retained the government records. Austin became the permanent capital of TX in 1845. • Political scientist Vladimer Orlando Key, Jr.; short story writer O. Henry; sculptor Elizabeth Ney; President George W. Bush; singer-songwriter Willie Nelson. • Cotton, grain sorghum, pecans, dairying, hogs, horses, cattle, goats, sheep (mohair and wool marketed); lime, sand and gravel, stone, oil, gas; high tech industry; manufacture of computer components; government operations; research and education (U. of TX; TX State School for the Deaf; St. Edward's U.; Concordia U.; Huston-Tillotson College) • Archives and documents of Lyndon B. Johnson's presidency are kept at the Johnson Library at the University of Texas. Late each afternoon hundreds of Austinites gather at the Congress Avenue Bridge to watch the downtown bat population take their ritual flight. Mercury vapor lamps that have sat atop twenty-seven tall towers for over 100 years cast a blue glow over the city of Austin. Austin boasts the largest and tallest state capitol in the nation. The world's first photograph (by Joseph Niepce, 1826) is housed in the University of Texas's Harry Ransom Humanities Research Center.

TRINITY (one of two counties so named, the other in CA) • *Groveton* • 13,779 • 693 • Eastern TX, bounded on the southwest by the Trinity River and on the northeast by the Neches River. The county includes part of Davy Crockett National Forest in its northeastern half. Lake Livingston reservoir is on the southwestern boundary. • Named for the Trinity River • 1850 from Houston • Timber; cattle, hogs, poultry, hay, vegetables, peaches, pecans; oil and natural gas, lignite, sand and gravel, clay.

TYLER (one of two counties so named, the other in WV) *Woodville* • 20,871 • 923 • Eastern TX, bounded on the north and east by the Neches River, which forms B. A. Steinhagen

Lake reservoir. Units of Big Thicket National Preserve are here, as is J.H. Kirby Memorial State Forest. • Named for President John Tyler • 1846 from Liberty • Pine, hardwoods, Christmas trees; cattle, vegetables, goats, emus, ostriches; oil and natural gas; hunting and fishing.

UPSHUR *Gilmer* • 35,291 • 588 • Northeastern TX, bounded on the southwest by the Sabine River and on the northeast by Big Cypress Creek, forming Lake O' the Pines reservoir; drained by Little Cypress Creek, which also forms part of the southeastern border. Lake Gladewater reservoir is in the south. • One of two counties (the other in WV) named for Abel P. Upshur (1791–1844), judge in VA courts, U.S. secretary of the navy, and U.S. secretary of state • 1846 from Harrison and Nacogdoches • Pine lumbering; large oil production, also natural gas, sand and gravel; hay, vegetables, peaches, sweet potatoes, cattle, poultry, dairying.

UPTON *Rankin* • 3,404 • 1,242 • Western TX; drained by an extension of the Middle Concho River. The county lies on the edge of Edwards Plateau. Castle and King mountains are in the southwest. • Named for Confederate heroes Lt. Col. John C. Upton (1828–62), and his brother Lt. Col. William F. Upton (1832–1887) • 1887 from Tom Green • Sheep, some goats, cattle, cotton, pecans; oil, natural-gas wells. • The Mendoza Trail Museum is located here.

UVALDE *Uvalde* • 25,926 • 1,557 • Southern TX, crossed by Balcones Escarpment, dividing the hilly north (which is part of Edwards Plateau) from the southern plains; drained by the Nueces, West Nueces, Frio, Leona, and Sabine rivers. Garner State Park is in the north. • Named for Uvalde Canyon • 1850 from Bexar • U.S. vice president John Nance Garner (museum). According to locals, lawman Pat Garrett is buried at Pioneer Park in Uvalde. • Hogs, goats (mohair), sheep (wool), cattle, extensive beekeeping (honey), vegetables, wheat, corn, oats, grain sorghum, hay, cotton, fruit; asphalt mines, sand and gravel, stone; manufacture of animal feed; tourism.

VAL VERDE *Del Rio* • 44,856 • 3,171 • Southwestern TX, lying partly on Edwards Plateau, bounded on the southwest and south by the Rio Grande (forming the border with the Mexican state of Coahuila) and on the southeast by Sycamore Canyon; drained by the Pecos and Devils rivers. Devils River State Natural Area and Seminole Canyon State Historical Park (containing some of North America's oldest pictographs) are here. The Rio Grande forms International Amistad Reservoir on the southern border. Its Devils River Arm extends northeast, encompassed by Amistad National Recreation Area, including its Mexican counterpart. • Named for the Civil War skirmish at Valverde, NM Territory • 1885 from Kinney and Pecos • The present community of Del Rio was founded in 1872. Remnants of an old canal system, which carried water from San Felipe Springs, can be found here. • Val Verde was the colorful Judge Roy Bean's bailiwick. The "Law West of the Pecos" ruled with a six-shooter, and worshipped English music hall performer Lillie Langtry from afar, even naming a town

here after her. • Val Verde is one of the largest wool- and lamb-producing counties in the U.S. Also, cattle, horses, grapes. Del Rio is a port of entry, with a strong tourism component. Laughlin Air Force Base contributes to the local economy.

VAN ZANDT *Canton* • 48,140 • 849 • Northeastern TX, bounded on the northeast by the Sabine River and partly on the east by the Neches River (its source in the southeast). The Sabine River forms Lake Tawakoni reservoir in the northwestern corner of the county. Lake Tawakoni State Park is also here. Part of Purtis Creek State Park is on the southern boundary. • Named for Isaac Van Zandt (1813–47), Republic of Texas legislator who drafted the state's constitution • 1848 from Henderson • Pilot Wiley Post • Oil, salt, natural-gas production, iron ore, clay; cotton, vegetables, sweet potatoes, hay, grains, rose nurseries, extensive dairying, cattle; timber.

VICTORIA *Victoria* • 84,088 • 883 • Southern TX, bounded on the northeast by Arenosa Creek and on the south in part by the San Antonio River; drained by the Guadalupe River and Coleto Creek (forming part of the western border of the county). The county touches Lavaca Bay in the extreme southeast. Coleto Creek reservoir is on the western boundary. • Named for the municipality of Victoria, TX • Original county; organized 1836 (prior to statehood) from Old Mexican Municipality • Fort St. Louis, established by La Salle in 1685, is reputed to have been located here on Garcitas Creek. Victoria was actively involved in the TX Revolution, and was incorporated in 1839 as a city in the Republic of TX. In the 1840s, many Germans moved to the county. Developing as a cattle center, it was a rendezvous point for trail drivers moving northward. Completion in the 1960s of the 35-mile long Victoria Barge Canal to the Gulf Intracoastal Waterway stimulated the county's industrial growth • Dairying, corn, rice, cotton, sorghum, soybeans; oil, natural gas wells; sand and gravel deposits; diversified manufacturing, including petrochemicals; education (U. of Houston–Victoria; Victoria College) • The Texas Continental Meat Company, established in Victoria in 1883, pioneered new techniques in meatpacking, and was the first company to use refrigerated freight cars and to manufacture oleomargarine and gelatin from animal fats. The state's second oldest daily newspaper still in existence, the *Victoria Advocate*, was established in 1846.

WALKER (one of three counties so named) *Huntsville* • 61,758 • 788 • East-central TX, bounded on the northeast by the Trinity River and Lake Livingston reservoir, and on the northwest by Bedias Creek; drained by tributaries of the Trinity and the West Fork of the San Jacinto River. The county includes part of Sam Houston National Forest across much of the south. Huntsville State Park is here. Part of Lake Conroe reservoir is on the southern boundary. • Originally named for Robert J. Walker (1801–69), U.S. senator who introduced the resolution to annex TX to the U.S. The honor was rescinded in 1863 and given to Samuel H. Walker (?–1847), co-developer of the Walker-Colt revolver • 1846 from Montgomery •

Texas Republic president Sam Houston (museum, grave and monument here) • Pine, hardwood timber, Christmas trees; sand and gravel, stone, clay mining, some gas and oil; cattle, horses, hay; hunting and fishing; education (Sam Houston State U.) • Huntsville, headquarters of the TX Department of Corrections, is the site of the oldest prison in Texas. Visitors to the Texas Prison Museum can see "Old Sparky," the electric chair used to electrocute death-row inmates from 1924 to 1964. The two-block long street to Oakwood Cemetery in Huntsville, Spur 94, constitutes the shortest highway in the state. The Sam Houston Folk Festival and Huntsville Prison Rodeo are popular annual events in the county.

WALLER *Hempstead* • 32,663 • 514 • Southeastern TX, bounded on the west by the Brazos River and on the east in part by Spring Creek; also drained by tributaries of the San Jacinto River. • Named for Edwin Waller (1800–81), signer of the TX Declaration of Independence • 1873 from Austin • Corn, rice, hay, cattle, hogs, sheep, goats; timber; natural gas, oil wells, sand and gravel; education (Prairie View A and M University).

WARD (one of two counties so named, the other in ND) *Monahans* • 10,909 • 836 • Western TX, in the Pecos Valley, bounded on the west and south by the Pecos River. Part of Monahans Sandhills State Park is in the extreme northeast. • Named for Thomas W. "Peg Leg" Ward (?–1872), commissioner of the general office for the Republic of TX • 1891 from Tom Green (some sources say 1887) • Oil and natural gas, sand and gravel; cattle, horses, hogs, goats, cotton, alfalfa, grain sorghums, pecans, hay. • Pyote is home to the Rattlesnake Museum.

WASHINGTON *Brenham* • 30,373 • 609 • South-central TX, bounded on the north and east by the Brazos River, on the north in part by Yegua Creek, and on the west by Cedar Creek. Yegua Creek forms Somerville Lake reservoir in the northwest. • Named for the municipality of Washington-on-the-Brazos • 1836 (prior to statehood) from TX Municipality • The county is the site of the birthplace of the TX Republic. The TX Declaration of Independence was issued from a convention held in Washington-on-the-Brazos on March 2, 1836, and a constitution was adopted on March 17. David G. Burnet was inaugurated as provisional president and Sam Houston was made commander in chief of the TX Army. The town served as capital from 1842 until 1845. (Washington-on-the-Brazos State Historical Park is the site of restored buildings that played key roles in the establishment of the republic.) Brenham was partly burned during the Reconstruction era after the Civil War. • Last president of the TX Republic Anson Jones • Cotton, corn, grains, nursery plants, beef cattle, hogs, horses, poultry, dairying (especially creameries); oil, natural gas wells, stone; manufacturing.

WEBB *Laredo* • 193,117 • 3,357 • Southern TX, bounded on the west and southwest by the Rio Grande (forming the border with the Mexican states of Coahuila, Nuevo Léon, and Tamaulipas). Lake Casa Blanca International State Park is in the southwest. • Named for James Webb (1792–1856), Republic of TX secretary of state and attorney general • 1848 from Bexar • Established as a ferry crossing in 1755, Laredo endured more than 200 years of lawlessness, and was a no-man's land following the TX revolt against Mexico in 1836. It was the seat of the short-lived Republic of the Rio Grande from 1839 to 1841. During the Mexican War, Laredo was occupied first by the Texas Rangers in 1846, then by Texas volunteers under Gen. Mirabeau Lamar in 1847. Seven national flags have flown over the city. • Laredo is a chief port of entry from Mexico. Citrus fruits, vegetables, melons, some cotton, grain sorghums, cattle; meat packing; oil, natural-gas wells, caliche, stone, sand and gravel, coal deposits; considerable export-import trade; manufacture of bricks, clothing, electronic components, machine tools, medical goods, mattresses, furniture, glass specialties, leather products; smelting; tourism; education (Texas A and M International U.).

WHARTON *Wharton* • 41,188 • 1,090 • Southeastern TX, on the Gulf coastal plains, bounded on the northeast by the San Bernard River; drained by the Colorado River. • Named for two brothers John A. Wharton (1806–1838), TX Republic secretary of war; and William H. Wharton (1802–39), minister to the U.S. from the Republic of TX and Republic senator • 1846 from Colorado and Jackson • Broadcast journalist Dan Rather; playwright Horton Foote • A leading sulphur-producing county in the U.S. Also oil and natural gas; rice (Wharton is a leading rice-producing county), cotton, corn, sorghum, cattle; alfalfa dehydration; meat packing, poultry and rice processing; manufacture of fertilizer; hunting and fishing.

WHEELER (one of four counties so named) *Wheeler* • 5,284 • 914 • Northern TX in the Panhandle, bounded on the east by the OK state line; drained by the North Fork of the Red River and Sweetwater Creek. • Named for Royal T. Wheeler (1810–64), Chief Justice of the TX State Supreme Court • 1876 from Bexar • Astronaut Alan Bean • Oil and natural gas; grain sorghum, wheat, cotton, cattle, horses, hogs, ostriches. • The Pioneer West Museum is located in Shamrock.

WICHITA (one of two counties so named, the other in KS) *Wichita Falls* • 131,664 • 628 • Northern TX, bounded on the north by the Red River (forming the OK state line); drained by the Wichita River and small creeks. The county includes Lake Wichita and North Fork Buffalo Creek reservoirs. • Named for the Wichita River • 1858 from Fannin • Burkburnett was a boom town following the discovery of oil here in 1911. A tornado that touched down in the county in April, 1964, devastated Wichita Falls and collapsed a hangar at Sheppard Air Force Base. Another destructive tornado struck in April 1979, killing forty-two and injuring 1,700. (Between 1950 and 1995, there were forty-five tornadoes in the county.) • Writer Larry McMurtry • It is a leading TX oil-producing county. Also, natural gas, stone, sand and gravel; wheat, cotton, cattle, horses; manufacture of fiberglass products, clothing, electronic components; education (Midwestern State U.) Sheppard Air Force Base/Wichita Falls is an economic factor in the county. • Each August the county hosts the Hotter 'N Hell Hundred bicycle race, regarded as the largest bike race in the U.S.

WILBARGER *Vernon* • 14,676 • 971 • Northern TX; bounded on the north by the Red River (forming the OK state line); drained by the Pease River and Beaver Creek (which forms Santa Rosa Lake). • Named for brothers Josiah P. Wilbarger (1801–45), and Mathias Wilbarger, surveyors and early settlers • 1858 from Bexar • Musician Jack Teagarden • Large-scale cattle ranching, cotton, wheat, peanuts, watermelons, alfalfa, hogs, horses; extensive oil production and natural gas; clay mining; manufacture of clothing, meat products, stock feed, athletic equipment, metal goods • The W.T. Waggoner estate ranch, incorporating 500,000 acres of southern Wilbarger and neighboring counties is headquartered in Vernon. Annual events in the county include the Santa Rosa Rodeo and Quarter Horse Show held on the Waggoner ranch.

WILLACY *Raymondville* • 20,082 • 597 • Extreme southern TX, bounded on the east by the Gulf of Mexico and on the southeast by the Arroyo Colorado. Laguna Madre separates Padre Island from the mainland, with the Intracoastal Waterway passing through the channel. The northern edge of the county is occupied by part of the large King Ranch. A small part of Padre Island National Seashore is in the northeast. • Named for John G. Willacy (?–1943), TX legislator • 1911 from Cameron and Hidalgo • Cotton, sorghum, sugar cane, corn, vegetables, beef and dairy cattle, horses, hogs, poultry, Spanish goats; oil wells, natural gas; commercial fishing; food processing (especially shrimp); manufacture of clothing; winter tourism.

WILLIAMSON (one of three counties so named) *Georgetown* • 249,967 (79% increase since 1990; the second fastest growing county in TX) • 1,124 • Central TX; drained by the San Gabriel River and its North and South forks, and Brushy Creek. Inner Space Caverns is located here. The northern fringe of the Austin metropolitan area extends into the southern part of the county. Lake Georgetown and Granger Lake reservoirs are here. • Named for Major Robert M. Williamson (?–1859), Republic of TX Army officer, editor, and legislator • 1848 from Milam • Georgetown, established in 1848, was a staging area for large cattle drives north. Round Rock was the scene of a shootout in 1878 that fatally wounded the outlaw Sam Bass (who is buried in the old cemetery). In 1933, Bartlett (partially in Bell County) received the first rural electrification in the U.S. • Cattle, cotton, corn, wheat, sorghum, sheep, goats; cedar, oak; limestone quarries, sand and gravel, some oil; manufacture of computer components, bedding, furniture, clothing; woodworking, food processing; hunting, fishing; education (Southwestern U.) • Georgetown's County Courthouse Square is a beautiful and tidy example of a Victorian era business district.

WILSON (one of four counties so named) *Floresville* • 32,408

• 807 • Southern TX; drained by the San Antonio River and Cibolo Creek • Named for James C. Wilson (1816–61), Republic of TX soldier and Mier Expedition survivor, and legislator • 1860 from Bexar • Peanuts, watermelons (Stockdale holds an annual watermelon festival), grain sorghums, corn, sunflowers, fruit, cattle, hogs, poultry; some oil and gas, clay mining. • The ruins of Mission Las Cabras are located southeast of Floresville.

WINKLER *Kermit* • 7,173 • 841 • Western TX, indented in the northwest by the southwest corner of NM. Part of Monahans Sandhills State Park is in the extreme southeast. • Named for Lt. Col. Clinton M. Winkler (1821–82), TX legislator, and civil appeals court judge • 1887 from Tom Green • Oil, natural-gas fields; cattle (cow-calf production), horses.

WISE (one of two counties so named, the other in VA) *Decatur* • 48,793 • 905 • Northern TX; drained by the West Fork of the Trinity River, forming Bridgeport Reservoir in the west, and by Big Sandy and Denton creeks. LBJ National Grassland covers much of the northern half of the county. • Named for Brig. Gen. Henry A. Wise (1806–76), governor of VA • 1856 from Cooke • Wheat, oats, peanuts, pecans, hay, cattle, horses, sheep, ratites, poultry, dairying; clay mining, limestone quarrying, sand and gravel, gas and oil; manufacturing.

WOOD (one of four counties so named) *Quitman* • 36,752 • 650 • Northeastern TX, bounded on the southwest and south by the Sabine River; drained by its tributaries, including Lake Fork and Big Sandy creeks. Governor Hogg Shrine State Historical Site is here. The county contains several reservoirs, including Lake Quitman, Lake Winnsboro, Lake Fork, Holbrook Lake, and Lake Hawkins. • Named for George T. Wood (1795–1858), TX legislator and governor of TX • 1850 from Van Zandt • San Francisco mayor Willie Brown • Wood is a leading petroleum-producing county. Also, natural gas, sand and gravel, clay; vegetables, grain, corn, hay, dairying, poultry, cattle, hogs, horses; timber, Christmas trees; hunting and fishing.

YOAKUM *Plains* • 7,322 • 800 • Western TX, located on Llano Estacado, bounded on the west by the NM state line; drained by Sulphur Springs. • Named for Col. Henderson K. Yoakum (1810–56), army officer in the Mexican War and TX historian • 1876 from Bexar • Cattle; production and refinement of oil and natural gas, salt; grains, sorghum, peanuts, cotton.

YOUNG *Graham* • 17,943 • 922 • Northern TX; drained by the Brazos River, here receiving its Clear Fork and tributary creeks. The headwaters of Possum Kingdom Lake reservoir (Brazos River) are in the county's southeastern corner. • Named for Col. William C. Young (1812–62), TX sheriff and district attorney, and Confederate Army officer • 1856 from Bosque • Wheat, cotton, pecans, hay, nurseries, cattle; oil and natural-gas fields, sand and gravel; manufacture of oil products, aluminum honeycomb products, cement, flour, stockfeed, saddles, dresses, sportswear, soft drinks; resorts • Olney stages a one-arm dove hunt. The Fort Belknap restoration is located near Newcastle. A plaque on an oak tree marks the site in Graham where local ranchers formed the predecessor to the Texas and Southwestern Cattle Raisers Association.

ZAPATA *Zapata* • 12,182 • 997 • Southern TX, bounded on the west by the Rio Grande (here forming the border with the Mexican state of Tamaulipas and Falcon International Reservoir); drained by its many tributaries. Part of Falcon State Park is on the southern boundary. • Named for Col. Antonio Zapata (?–1840), Mexican revolutionary • 1858 from Starr and Webb • Cattle, sheep, vegetables, cantaloupes, melons, some

dairying; oil, natural gas. The county exports gas to Mexico by pipeline.

ZAVALA *Crystal City* • 11,600 • 1,299 • Southern TX; drained by the Nueces and Leona rivers. • Named for Manuel Lorenzo Justiniano de Zavala (1789–1836), vice president of the Republic of TX, and signer of the Texas Declaration of Independence • 1858 from Uvalde and Maverick • Spinach, onions, peppers, tomatoes, grain sorghums, corn, cotton, pecans, cattle, hogs, sheep, goats; oil and gas; hunting • Spinach is so important to the county's economy that Crystal City in 1937 erected a statue of spinach-friendly Popeye in its city square.

UTAH

Industry

Three-member boards of county commissioners manage most of Utah's twenty-nine counties. Two of the members of each board are elected to four-year terms. The remaining member is elected to a two-year term. The board supervises county departments and officers. Utah county officials include the assessor, attorney, auditor, clerk, recorder, surveyor, treasurer, and sheriff.

BEAVER (one of three counties so named) *Beaver* • 6,005 • 2,590 • Southwestern UT, bounded on the west by the NV state line; drained by the Beaver River. Indian Peak and Pahvant ranges and the Wahwah and San Francisco mountains cross the county. Also here are Elk Meadows ski area, Minersville Reservoir and State Park, and part of Fishlake National Forest. • Named for the Beaver River • 1856 from Iron (prior to statehood) • Opened in 1858, the Lincoln Mine near Minersville was possibly the first mine in UT. The famous Horn Silver Mine, located near Frisco (now a ghost town), attracted J. P. Morgan as an investor. Fort Cameron was established in Beaver City in 1873 to quell Indian hostilities and to aid in the prosecution of the participants of the Mountain Meadows Massacre. The two trials of John D. Lee, implicated in the massacre, were held in Beaver. • Outlaw Butch Cassidy; television pioneer Philo T. Farnsworth • Alfalfa, barley, potatoes, dairying, cattle; lead, sulphur.

BOX ELDER *Brigham City* • 42,745 • 5,724 (the fourth largest county in UT and the forty-fifth largest county in the U.S.) • Northwestern UT, bounded on the west by the NV state line and on the north by the ID state line. Most of the northern half of Great Salt Lake is situated in the southeast and is entered by the Bear River. Great Salt Lake Desert and part of the Newfoundland Evaporation Basin (which receives flood overflow from Great Salt Lake) are in the southwest. The western ninety percent of the county is nearly uninhabited. The county includes Willard Bay State Park, part of Utah

Test and Training Range North, Bear River Migratory Bird Refuge, and a part of Caribou and Sawtooth national forests. • Named for the abundant box elder (North American maple) trees in the area • 1856 from Weber (prior to statehood) • The Treaty of Box Elder, which ended hostilities between Indians and settlers, was signed in Brigham City in 1863. The Golden Spike National Historic Site commemorates the 1869 completion of the transcontinental line which linked the Central Pacific and the Union Pacific railroads. The feisty residents of Corinne founded the Liberal party here in 1870 as an opposition voice to the Mormons' People's party. • Dancer/choreographers Harold Lew and William Christensen • Sugar beets, peaches, cherries (the growing and shipping of peaches and other fruits is the county's chief economic activity), wheat, barley, alfalfa, cattle, sheep; salt, magnesium; manufacture of woolen goods, canned goods, beet sugar; education (Intermountain School, boarding school for Indians). It also produces solid-fuel rocket propellants. • Morton-Thiokol, the largest employer in the county, builds the Minuteman missile and the space shuttle booster rockets. Peach Days Harvest Festival has been held in Brigham every year since 1904.

CACHE *Logan* • 91,391 (the fifth most populated county in UT) • 1,165 • Northern UT, bounded on the north by the ID state line; drained by the Bear River. The county includes the fertile Cache Valley (extending north to south) in the northwest. Bear River of the Wasatch Range is found along the eastern boundary. Several ski areas are here, including Beaver and Powder mountains. The eastern half of the county is covered by part of Cache National Forest, with a small Section of Caribou National Forest in the northwest. Hyrum State park is also here. • Named for Cache Valley • 1856 from unorganized territory (prior to statehood) • Wheat, barley, alfalfa, hay, sugar beets, vegetables, raspberries, cheese, cattle; some manufacture of hardware, pianos and organs, textiles, farm equipment; education (UT State U., Logan).

CARBON (one of four counties so named) *Price* • 20,422 • 1,479 • Central UT, bounded on the east by the Green River; drained by the Price River. The county rests in large part on West Tavaputs Plateau. Scofield Reservoir and State Park, and Price Canyon B.L.M. Recreation Area are here, as is part of Manti-La Sal National Forest (its headquarters in Price) which runs the length of the western border. • Named for the abundant coal deposits in the area • 1894 from Emery (prior to statehood) • Attracting many eastern European and Japanese laborers to work on railroad gangs and in mines, Helper came to be known as the town of "57 Varieties." Mine explosions killed 200 near Scofield in 1900, and in 1924, killed 172 near Castle Gate. • Coal; hay, sugar beets, grains, cattle • The College of Eastern UT maintains the Prehistoric Museum, with its noted dinosaur display. The collection includes an Allosaurus found in nearby Cleveland Lloyd Quarry (located in Emery County). The "Head Hunter" rock art panel, located near Gordon Creek, is evidence of the influence of the Fremont Indian culture in the area.

DAGGETT *Manila* • 921 (the least populated county in UT) • 698 • Northeastern UT, bounded on the north by the WY state line and on the east by the CO state line; crossed by the Green River. The Uinta Mountains and Ashley National Forest extend throughout most of the county. Flaming Gorge Dam forms Flaming Gorge Reservoir (and provides hydroelectric power for UT and surrounding states); Flaming Gorge National Recreation Area is here. Browns Park National Wildlife Refuge is on the eastern boundary. • Named for Ellsworth Daggett (1845–1923), first surveyor-general of UT Territory and developer of irrigation projects throughout the state • 1918 from Uintah • John Wesley Powell journeyed through parts of the county from 1869 to 1871 as he floated down the Green and Colorado Rivers. The town of Dutch John was built near Flaming Gorge to provide housing for those working at the dam. • Sheep; tourism • Sheep Creek Canyon offers visitors a million-year survey of geology within its boundaries.

DAVIS (one of two counties so named, the other in IA) *Farmington* • 238,994 (the third most populated county in UT) • 304 (the smallest county in UT) • Northern UT. The county includes part of southeastern Great Salt Lake (including Antelope Island and Antelope Island State Park) and part of the Wasatch Range, with Wasatch National Forest in the east. Hill Air Force Base is in the north. Farmington Bay Management Area is on the shore of Great Salt Lake. It is a highly urban-

ized county with numerous communities springing up since the 1970s. • Named for Daniel C. Davis (1804–50), commander of the Mormon batallion in the Mexican War • 1850 (organized prior to statehood); original county • Bountiful (1847) is the second oldest Mormon settlement in UT. • Apples, alfalfa, wheat, barley, hay, sugar beets, cherries, peaches, berries, apricots, vegetables, cattle, sheep, poultry; food processing (food and vegetable canneries); gravel, coal, salt.

DUCHESNE *Duchesne* • 14,371 • 3,238 • Northeastern UT. The county is served by irrigation projects on the Strawberry and Duchesne rivers and Lake Fork. Kings Peak, at 13,528 feet, the highest point in UT, is on the northern edge of the county in the Uinta Mountains. Part of Uintah and Ouray Indian Reservation is also in the county. A small part of Wasatch National Forest, Starvation Reservoir and State Park, and parts of Ashley National Forest are here. Bad Land Cliffs lie along the southern boundary. • Named for the Duchesne River • 1913 from Wasatch • Unique in the state, Duchesne County was settled by individuals who obtained land grants under the federal Homestead Act rather than by direction of the Mormon Church. In 1861, President Lincoln created the Uintah Reservation for the Uintah and Whitewater Utes. • Wheat, barley, alfalfa, sugar beets, dairy products, cattle, sheep • The Ute Indian tribe owns and controls most of the county.

EMERY *Castle Dale* • 10,860 • 4,452 • Central UT, bounded on the east by the Green River; drained by the Price and San Rafael rivers, and Muddy Creek. Part of the Wasatch Plateau and Manti-La Sal National Forest are in the northwest. The county also contains four state parks: Huntington, Millsite, Goblin Valley, and part of Green River. The San Rafael Desert is in the southeast. • Named for George W. Emery (1830–1909), governor of Utah Territory • 1880 (prior to statehood) from Sanpete and Sevier • Numerous pictographs and petroglyphs from the Fremont Culture (500 AD-1300 AD) are found in Temple Mountain Wash, Muddy Creek, Ferron Box, Black Dragon Canyon, and Buckhorn Wash. The Old Spanish Trail, frequented by Spanish traders and American fur trappers, cuts through present day Emery County. A bronze statue of a coal miner, located on the grounds of the county courthouse, honors the memory of twenty-seven coal miners who died in the Wilberg Mine Fire on December 19, 1984—the most deadly coal-mine fire in the state's history. • Alfalfa, peaches, melons, cattle; coal. • Forty-five Allosaurus skeletons have been discovered at the active Cleveland Lloyd Dinosaur Quarry. The John Wesley Powell River History Museum is located in Green River.

GARFIELD *Panguitch* • 4,735 • 5,175 (the fifth largest county in UT) • Southern UT, bounded on the east by the Colorado River, here forming an arm of Lake Powell reservoir (Glen Canyon National Recreation Area extending along its banks); drained by the Escalante River, and the Sevier River and its East Fork. The Henry Mountains cross in the east; the Sevier and Paunsaugunt plateaus are in the west. Much of the county is covered by Dixie National Forest. It also contains sections of three national parks: a small piece of Canyonlands in the extreme northeast, the lower portion of Capitol Reef in the center, and the northern half of Bryce in the east. Part of Grand Staircase–Escalante National Monument is in the south. • One of six counties named for President James A. Garfield • 1882 from Iron (prior to statehood) • Alfalfa, barley, cattle; timber; tourism; antimony mining • In the mid 1930's, the CCC constructed a road to Boulder, which had previously been considered the most isolated town in Utah.

GRAND (one of two counties so named, the other in CO) *Moab* • 8,485 • 3,682 • Eastern UT, bounded on the west by the Green River and on the east by the CO state line; drained by the Colorado River. The county includes part of Uintah and Ouray Indian Reservation, most of East Tavaputs Plateau, and Book and Roan Cliffs in the north. A small portion of Manti-La Sal National Forest extends into the southwest corner. Arches National Park is found in the county, as are Green River State Park and Sego Canyon Petroglyphs. • The county's name reflects the original name given to the Colorado River (changed in 1921). • 1890 (prior to statehood) • Spanish explorers, the first Europeans to journey through the area, crossed the Colorado River near present day Moab. Moab found itself in the middle of a "uranium rush" when rich deposits were found nearby in 1952. • Cattle, sheep; oil, natural gas, salt, potassium, vanadium, uranium, copper; tourism • Moab is the hub of southern UT's tourist industry, serving as the center for river rafting, mountain biking, four-wheel drive recreation, and ballooning. At 291 feet, Landscape Arch, in Arches National Park, is the longest natural rock bridge in the world.

IRON (one of four counties so named) *Parowan* • 33,779 (62% increase since 1990; the third fastest growing county in UT) • 3,299 • Southwestern UT, bounded on the west by the NV state line. Indian Peak Range and Escalante Desert are in the west. Cedar Breaks National Monument (resembling a miniature Bryce Canyon) is also in the county, as are parts of Dixie National Forest (its headquarters in Cedar City) on Markagunt Plateau. The county also includes Parowan Gap Petroglyphs, Old Irontown Ruins, a small part of Fishlake National Forest, and a small section of Zion National Park. • Named for the county's mines and iron deposits • Organized as Little Salt Lake County in 1850 (prior to statehood) from unorganized territory; named changed later that year • In 1776, the Dominguez-Escalante expedition journeyed through the area in its search for a route to central California. Cedar City's Iron Mission State Park is the site of the first blast furnace west of the Mississippi. • Alfalfa, barley, dairying (creameries), cattle; lumbering; brick making, canning, meatpacking; education (Southern UT U.); coal, iron ore • Cedar City serves as the tribal reservation headquarters for the Southern Paiute Indians. The Utah Shakespearean Festival is held every summer at Southern Utah University. Several rare pioneer log homes and English two-bay log barns are located about the county.

JUAB *Nephi* • 8,238 • 3,392 • Western UT, bounded on the west by the NV state line; watered by the Sevier River. The county includes part of Goshute Indian Reservation, which borders the Deep Creek Range in the northwest corner; Fish Springs National Wildlife Refuge; part of Fishlake National Forest; and parts of Uinta National Forest, including a portion of Mount Nebo Wilderness Area. Mona Reservoir is also in the county, as is Yuba State Park in the extreme southeast. • The county's name is an Indian word for level plain • 1852; original county (prior to statehood) • Nephi Mounds, one of the most important Fremont Culture agricultural sites in the eastern Great Basin, is located near Nephi. Government surveyors John Gunnison and J.H. Simpson explored the area during the 1850s, with Simpson establishing the route later used by the Pony Express and the transcontinental telegraph. Producing nearly $35,000,000 in mineral wealth between 1870 and 1899, the Tintic Mining District (museum) was one of the foremost mining areas in the U.S. • Wheat, barley, alfalfa, cattle; silver, gold • The highest peak in the Wasatch Range, Mount Nebo (elevation 11,928 feet) is located within the county. Sand dunes found at the Little Sahara B.L.M. Recreation Area shift about eighteen inches a year.

KANE (one of two counties so named; the other in IL) *Kanab* • 6,046 • 3,992 • Southern UT, bounded on the south by the AZ state line and on the east and southeast by the Colorado River, here forming Powell Lake reservoir (Glen Canyon National Recreation Area extending along the entire shoreline); drained by the Virgin, Escalante, and Paria rivers, and Kanab Creek. The Kaiparowits Plateau is on the east, and the White and Vermillion Cliffs cross in the center. Grand Staircase–Escalante National Monument covers a large portion of the county. Also here are part of Bryce and a small part of Zion national parks, as well as Coral Pink Sand Dunes and Kodachrome Basin state parks. • Named for General Thomas L. Kane (1822–83), Union Army officer and political intermediary between Mormons and non-Mormons • 1864 from Washington (prior to statehood) • Apples, cattle, grain, alfalfa; timber; terra-cotta; tourism • Kodachrome Basin State Park's most prominent feature is Grosvenor Arch, a natural double arch. Popular as a film location during the 1930's, Kanab was referred to as "Hollywood's backyard." A brief resident of Kanab, Zane Grey used the county's canyons, dunes, and flatlands as backdrops for his *Riders of the Purple Sage* (1912). Best Friends Animal Sanctuary in Kanab is one of the nation's largest no-kill animal shelters.

MILLARD *Fillmore* • 12,405 • 6,590 (the third largest county in UT and the thirty-third largest county in the U.S.) • Western UT, bounded on the west by the NV state line; watered by the Sevier River, which flows into intermittent Sevier Lake in the Sevier Desert. The Confusion and House ranges and Wahwah Mountains cross in the west; the Pahvant Range forms the eastern border. Desert Range Experimental Station and part of Fishlake National Forest are here. • One of three counties named for President Millard Fillmore (1800–74), thirteenth U.S. president, who signed the act creating the Territory of Utah • 1851 from Juab (prior to statehood) • Chosen by Brigham Young as the site of UT's first territorial capitol (state park), Fillmore served as the official, but not actual capital until the city gave up its position to Salt Lake City in 1856. (The unfinished red sandstone statehouse here is now a state historic monument.) The Gunnison Massacre site, where in 1853, seven members of a transcontinental railroad survey team led by Lieutenant John Gunnison were killed by Indians, is located near Delta. The county was the site of the Topaz Relocation Camp, a WW II Japanese-American internment camp. • Alfalfa seed (75% of the state's yield grown here), wheat, sugar beets, potatoes, barley, dairying, livestock; mountain mushrooms processing; beryllium ore mining, limestone, precious metals.

MORGAN (one of eleven counties so named) *Morgan* • 7,129 • 609 • Northern UT; watered by the Weber River. The county is located in the heart of the Wasatch Range, with Wasatch-Cache National Forest in the north and west. Lost Creek Reservoir and State Park, and East Canyon Reservoir and State Park are also here. • Named for Jedediah Morgan Grant (1816–56), prominent Mormon churchman • 1862 from Davis and Summit (prior to statehood) • In 1825, fur trappers from the British Hudson's Bay Company squared off against American trappers near present-day Mountain Green. Between 1860 and 1875, Hardscrabble Canyon provided much of the timber for the production of railroad ties for the Union Pacific Railroad. • Alfalfa, barley, sugar beets, vegetables, dairying, cattle, sheep • The county has more privately owned land than any other in UT.

PIUTE *Junction* • 1,435 • 758 • Southwest-central UT; drained by the Sevier River and its East Fork, and Otter Creek. The Sevier Plateau dominates in the west. Piute Reservoir and State Park, parts of Fishlake National Forest, Otter Creek Reservoir and State Park, and a small part of Dixie National Forest are in the county. • Named for the Paiute Indians • 1865 from Beaver (prior to statehood) • Cattle, sheep, alfalfa, vegetables, dairying; gold, silver, antimony • Big Rock Candy Mountain, immortalized in the song of the same name, is located here. The caves of Kingston Canyon offer evidence of prehistoric inhabitants, the predecessors of the local Paiute Indians.

RICH *Randolph* • 1,961 • 1,029 • Northern UT, bounded on the north by the ID state line, and on the east by the WY state line; drained by the Bear River. Part of Wasatch-Cache National Forest and the Bear River Range of the Wasatch Mountains are located along the western border. Also found in the county are the southern half of Bear Lake and Bear Lake State Park. • Named for Charles C. Rich (1808–1883), a Mormon apostle who fathered fifty-one children • Created as Richland in 1864; name changed in 1868 • In 1827 and 1828, the annual trappers' rendezvous was held on the south shore of Bear Lake, now a part of Bear Lake (Rendezvous Beach) State Park. • Alfalfa, barley, wheat, cattle, sheep.

SALT LAKE *Salt Lake City* • 898,387 (the most populated county in UT) • 737 • North-central UT, bounded on the northwest by Great Salt Lake; drained by the Jordan River. The county is highly urbanized from Salt Lake City south through the Jordan Valley. It includes part of Camp Williams military reservation, Great Salt Lake (south shore), Jordan River, This is the Place, and Veterans Memorial state parks, part of Wasatch-Cache and Vinta national forests, and several ski areas in the Wasatch Range. • Named for the Great Salt Lake • Original county; organized as Great Salt Lake County in 1849 (prior to statehood); name changed in 1868 • Salt Lake City, the capital of Utah Territory since 1856 and subsequently the state capital, was founded in 1847 by Mormons fleeing persecution. The Seagull Monument was erected by grateful pioneers to honor the birds that ate hordes of crop-destroying grasshoppers in 1848. An all Black "buffalo soldiers" battalion was stationed at Fort Douglas located near Salt Lake City. The first transcontinental telegraph line in the U.S. was completed at Salt Lake City on October 24, 1861. • Director Frank Borzage; labor leader Bill Haywood; cartoonist and illustrator John Held, Jr.; engineer Simon Ramo; actor Roseanne. Television pioneer Philo T. Farnsworth and songwriter/union organizer Joe Hill both died here. • Diversified manufacturing; copper, salt, sand and gravel, limestone, magnesium, salt; cattle, sheep, wheat, barley, alfalfa, sugar beets, fruit, vegetables, ski resort tourism • Kennecott Corporation open-cut copper mine is the largest in the world. Salt Lake City is the world headquarters of The Church of Jesus of Christ of Latter Day Saints (the Mormons). The Mormon Tabernacle, famous for its choir, features an 11,623-pipe organ. Salt Lake City is home to the Utah Jazz (Delta Center).

SAN JUAN (one of four counties so named) *Monticello* • 14,413 • 7,821 (the largest county in UT and the twenty-fourth largest county in the U.S.) • Southeastern UT, bounded on the east by the CO state line, on the south by the AZ state line, and on the west by the Colorado River, here forming Lake Powell reservoir; crossed by the San Juan River. (Glen Canyon National Recreation Area extends along both arms of the reservoir.) Navajo Nation Indian Reservation dominates the southern quarter of the county and includes Four Corners Monument (the only point common to four states) and Navajo Tribal Park, part of Hovenweep National Monument, Goosenecks State Park, and part of Monument Valley. Most of Canyonlands National Park is in the northwest and units of Manti-La Sal National Forest are located throughout. The county also includes Canyon Rims B.L.M. Recreation Area, Edge of the Cedars and Dead Horse Point state parks, and Natural Bridges National Monument. • Named for the San Juan River • 1880 (prior to statehood) from Kane, Iron, Sevier, and Piute • Timber; oil, natural gas, uranium mining; wheat, cattle • Rainbow Bridge National Monument features a 290-feet high arch, the largest known natural bridge.

SANPETE *Manti* • 22,763 • 1,588 • Central UT, crossed north-south by Wasatch Plateau; watered by the Sevier and

San Pitch rivers. The county includes the irrigated Sanpete Valley, part of Manti-La Sal National Forest, part of Uinta National Forest, part of Sevier Bridge Reservoir, and Palisade State Park. • Its name is a corruption of San Pitch Valley, Creek, and/or Mountains • 1852; original county (prior to statehood) • The county served as the winter base for the wide-ranging Ute Indians. • Cattle, sheep, poultry, hogs, alfalfa, barley, wheat, sugar beets, fruit, vegetables; rock salt, gypsum, sand and gravel; timber • Developed during the Great Depression, the turkey industry in Sanpete places the county among the top ten producers in the U.S.

SEVIER (one of three counties so named) *Richfield* • 18,842 • 1,910 • Central UT. The county is crossed by the Sevier River. The Pahvant Range extends along the western border. Fishlake National Forest covers half the county. The Utah State Fish Hatchery is here, as are Fremont Indian State Park, a small part of Capitol Reef National Park (in the extreme southeast), Fish Lake and John Reservoir. • Named for the Sevier River • 1865 from Sanpete (prior to statehood) • The oldest known time record in Utah east of the Wasatch, BC 5080 to AD 1900, is found at Sudden Shelter, a prehistoric Indian site. Fremont State Park features 500 panels of petroglyphs and the remains of a Fremont Culture prehistoric village. All Sevier settlements were abandoned in 1867 due to confrontations with the Utes during the Black Hawk War. • Cattle, alfalfa, barley, hay, sugar beets, fruit, vegetables, dairying; gypsum (the state's leading producer), coal • The epicenters of numerous earthquakes have been located along the Sevier Fault in the southern part of the county.

SUMMIT (one of three counties so named) *Coalville* • 29,736 (92% increase since 1990; the fastest growing county in UT) • 1,871 • Northeastern UT, bounded on the north by the WY state line; drained by the Weber River. The county includes Wasatch-Cache National Forest and the Uinta Mountains in the east. Most of its population resides in the west in Weber Valley. Also here are Echo Reservoir, Rockport Reservoir and State Park, the Wasatch Range (along the southwest boundary), and a small part of Ashley National Forest. • Named for its location on the summit of the divide between the Green River Valley and Salt Lake Valley • 1854 from Green River Valley (prior to statehood) • Vegetables, alfalfa, dairying; timber; oil, natural gas; ski resorts • On the verge of becoming a ghost town during the 1950s, the old mining town of Park City was revitalized by the ski industry. The Sundance Film Festival is held every winter in venues in and around Park City.

TOOELE *Tooele* • 40,735 • 6,946 (the second largest county in UT and the twenty-seventh largest county in the U.S.) • Northwestern UT, bounded on the west by the NV state line and on the northeast by Great Salt Lake. The Deep Creek Range and Silver Island Mountains cross the county in the west. Great Salt Lake Desert (including part of Newfoundland Evaporation Basin and Bonneville Salt Flats) is also here. Lakeside Mountain and two units of Wasatch-Cache National Forest are in the east. Much of the county is reserved for military use and includes the South Unit and part of the North Unit of the Utah Test and Training Range, Dugway Proving Ground, Tooele Army Depot (a chemical storage facility), and Deseret Chemical Depot. Skull Valley Indian Reservation is also here. • Named for the Tooele Valley • Original county; organized as Tuilla, 1850 (prior to statehood); spelling changed 1852 • Cattle, poultry, alfalfa, wheat, barley; copper, lead, zinc, silver, salt, magnesium, gold (The old mining town of Mercur is currently the largest source of gold in UT.) • The extremely level, smooth flats that comprise the Bonneville Speedway have seen the establishment of several world automobile and motorcycle speed and endurance records since 1935.

UINTAH *Vernal* • 25,224 • 4,477 • Northeastern UT, crossed and bounded on the west in part by the Green River and on the east by the CO state line; drained by the White and Duchesne rivers and Bitter Creek. The Uinta Mountains cross along the northern border. The county includes Ouray National Wildlife Refuge, Red Fleet Reservoir and State Park, Steinaker Reservoir and State Park, part of Dinosaur National Monument, and part of Ashley National Forest (its headquarters in Vernal). A portion of the Uintah and Ouray Indian Reservation, established by President Lincoln in 1861, occupies the southern two-thirds of the county. • Named for the Uinta Ute Indians • 1880 • The Dominguez-Escalante expedition explored the Uintah Basin in 1776. • General farming, cattle, sheep; lumbering; oil, oil shale, natural gas, phosphate rock, asphalt, Gilsonite; tourism • Fort Duchesne, which operated from 1886 to 1913 as a military post, now serves as headquarters for the Ute Indians. The Outlaw Festival, a month-long event held every summer in Vernal, celebrates the "wild west" tradition of the area. Dinosaur Quarry, part of Dinosaur National Monument, reveals the well-preserved bones of the Stegosauras, Apatosauras, and Allosauras. Vernal lies at the heart of UT's "Dinosaurland," and is the site of the Utah Field House of Natural History (state park). It hosts a summer art festival and the Dinosaur Roundup Rodeo in July.

UTAH *Provo* • 368,536 (the second most populated county in UT) • 1,998 • North-central UT; drained by Utah Lake and tributaries, Provo, American Fork and Spanish Fork rivers. Utah Lake (the state's largest freshwater lake) is drained by the Jordan River. Part of the Wasatch Range is in the east and includes Mount Timpanogos and Timpanogos Cave National Monument. Part of Camp Williams Military Reservation is here, as are Powell Slough Waterfowl Management Area, and Camp Floyd/Stagecoach Inn and Utah Lake state parks, part of Uinta National Forest (its headquarters in Provo), part of Manti-La Sal National Forest, and a small part of Ashley National Forest. • Named for the Ute Indians • Original county; 1852 (prior to statehood); absorbed Cedar County, which was abolished in 1862 • Physicist Harvey Fletcher • Vegetables, berries, orchard fruits; mining of copper, silver, lead, zinc, limestone, clay, calcite iron; manufacture of steel (Provo ranks among the leading centers of iron and steel production in the west.), electrical components, ski equipment; tomato canning; resort tourism; education (Brigham Young U.; UT Valley State College). • The Geneva Steel Plant was constructed here during WW II as backup in the event that coastal steel plants were destroyed by the enemy.

WASATCH *Heber City* • 15,215 • 1,181 • North-central UT; drained by the Strawberry Reservoir in the south and the Provo River, which forms Jordanelle and Deer Creek reservoirs. Also in the county are Deer Creek State Park, parts of Uinta National Forest, small parts of Ashley and Wasatch-Cache national forests, and part of the Uinta Mountains. • Named for the Wasatch Mountains • 1862 from Summit (prior to statehood) • The Dominguez-Escalante expedition, the first white men in the county, explored the area in 1776. Heber Valley served as the summer hunting grounds for the Timpanogos Utes. • Barley, oats, alfalfa, sugar beets, vegetables, fruit, dairying, cattle, sheep; sand and gravel, lead, silver, zinc. • Heber Valley is called "Utah's Switzerland" because of the rugged Wasatch Mountains and the Swiss heritage of the town of Midway.

WASHINGTON *Saint George* • 90,354 (86% increase since 1990; the second fastest growing county in UT) • 2,427 • Southwestern UT, bounded on the west by the NV state line, and on the south by the AZ state line; drained by the Virgin River. Most of Zion National Park is here, including the Kolob Canyons North Unit. Dixie National Forest covers much of the county. It also includes Gunlock, Snow Canyon, and Quail Creek state parks, and Joshua Tree Natural National Landmark. The Pauite Indian Reservation is in the southwest. • One of thirty-one counties named for George Washington • 1852, from unorganized territory (prior to statehood) • The county was the scene of the notorious Meadow Mountain Massacre in September, 1857, in which a band of AR emigrants on their way to CA were attacked by Paiute Indians and Mormon settlers led by John Doyle Lee. Tribal lands were restored to the Shivwits branch of the Southern Paiutes in 1980. • Cattle, poultry, fruit, vegetables, alfalfa, barley, potatoes, cotton, timber; tourism • Zion National Park, established here in 1909, is one of the state's top tourist attractions. St. George, founded in 1861, was called "Dixie" because of its southern location and cotton production. The first Mormon temple to be erected in the state was completed in St. George in 1877. The Brigham Young Winter Home (1873) is in the county.

WAYNE (one of sixteen counties so named) *Loa* • 2,509 • 2,460 • South-central UT, bounded on the east by the Green and Colorado rivers; drained by the Fremont and Dirty Devil rivers. Part of Canyonlands National Park borders the Green and Colorado rivers, with the separate Horseshoe Canyon Unit of the park located just to the northeast. The upper portion of Capitol Reef National Park divides the county, separating the Awapa Plateau in the west from the San Rafael Reefs and Desert. Glen Canyon Recreation Area is also here. • Named for Wayne C. Robison, deceased son of Willis Eugene Robison, member of the Territorial legislature • 1892 from Piute (prior to statehood) • The CCC operated three camps in the county during the Depression, building several roads and campsites. • Alfalfa, barley, cattle; tourism.

WEBER *Ogden* • 196,533 (the fourth most populated county in UT) • 576 • Northern UT; drained by the Weber and Ogden rivers. The county captures a small wedge of Great Salt Lake (including Fremont Island). Fort Buenaventura State Park, Ogden Bay Waterfowl Management Area, and part of the Wasatch Range are in the county. Wasatch-Cache National Forest covers most of its eastern half. • Named for the Weber River • 1850; original county (prior to statehood) • After the arrival of the Union Pacific Railroad in 1869, Ogden, founded by Brigham Young in 1850, became a distribution point for the agricultural produce of the intermountain region • The Osmonds (family of entertainers). Novelist and historian Bernard De Voto and novelist Herman Bang died here. • Cattle, sheep, alfalfa, barley, wheat, sugar beets, fruit, vegetables; manufacture of aerospace components, pharmaceuticals, clothing, transportation equipment, clothing, wet-cell batteries and battery cases, stone, clay and glass products; canning of fruits, vegetables, and dog food; shipping; railroads; ski resorts; income-tax processing; education (Weber State U.) With Ogden Arsenal, Hill Air Force Base, the Utah General Depot, and the Naval Supply Depot located here, Ogden has become a major military supply center. • Browning Firearms Museum in Ogden exhibits the inventions, including the single shot rifle, of Ogden native John M. Browning.

VERMONT

Freedom and Unity

Vermont has fourteen counties. Local needs of the state are mainly served at the town level. The powers of county governments are limited chiefly to judicial matters and administration.

ADDISON *Middlebury* • 35,974 • 770 • Western VT, bounded on the west by Lake Champlain and rising to the Green Mountains in the east; drained by Otter Creek, and the New Haven and White rivers. The county includes lake and mountain resorts. Green Mountain National Forest dominates the eastern half of the county. State parks include Kingsland Bay, D.A.R., Branbury, and Button Bay. Moss Glen Falls Natural Area is in the east. • Named for the town of Addison, NH • 1785 from Rutland (prior to statehood) • The state's marble-quarrying industry began in the county in 1803. • Physicist Louis W. Austin; U. S. vice president Levi Morton. • Dairying, fruit; poultry; manufacture of wood products; tourism; education (Middlebury College, noted for its summer writers' conference) • The famous Morgan horses are bred at a farm near Middlebury, managed by the University of Vermont.

BENNINGTON *Bennington and Manchester* • 36,994 • 676 • Southwestern VT, bounded on the south by the MA state line and on the west by the NY state line; drained by Batten Kill, Deerfield, Hoosic, Walloomsac and Mettawee rivers. The county lies in the Green Mountains and Green Mountain National Forest. Emerald Lake, Lake Shaftsbury, and Woodford state parks are here. The Appalachian Trail passes through the county. • Named for the town of Bennington • 1779 (prior to statehood; VT's oldest county) • Ethan Allen and his Green Mountain Boys, headquartered in Bennington, successfully resisted claims to Bennington lands made by absentee New York landlords, thus establishing the independence of Vermont. Americans defeated the British in the Battle of Bennington on August 16, 1777. • Author and moralist William E. Channing; financier James Fisk; painter and printmaker Reginald Marsh; lawyer and editor Myra Colby Bradwell. Robert Frost is buried in Bennington's Old Burying Ground. • Dairying, apples, maple sugar, poultry; manufacture of paper and wood products, batteries, lubricating equipment, electronic capacitors, lithographic products, furniture, plastics; summer and winter resort tourism; education (Bennington College; Southern VT College) • The Bennington Museum has the oldest stars and stripes in existence and a number of works by Grandma Moses.

CALEDONIA *Saint Johnsbury* • 29,702 • 651 • Northeastern VT, bounded on the east by the Connecticut River (forming the NH state line); drained by the Passumpsic, Moose, Lamoille, and Wells rivers. The county has both winter and summer resorts. Mathewson and part of Willoughby state forests are in the north; part of Groton and L.R. Jones state forests are in the south. Also located in the county are several state parks. • Given the ancient name of Scotland • 1792 from Chittenden and Orange • Manufacture of platform scales, modular homes, tools, gloves, cattle feed, machinery, paper and wood products; dairying; lumber; granite quarrying; maple sugar (Saint Johnsbury has become well known for its maple sugar industry); education (Lyndon State College) • Engineer and manufacturer Henry M. Leland; Radical Republican congressional leader Thaddeus Stevens • St. Johnsbury Athenaeum Art Gallery has a strong collection of Hudson River paintings. Fairbanks Museum and Planetarium and Maple Grove Maple Museum are also in Johnsbury.

CHITTENDEN *Burlington* • 146,571 (the most populated county in VT) • 539 • Northwestern VT, bounded on the west by Lake Champlain; drained by the Winooski and Lamoille rivers. The Green Mountains are in the east. The county contains lake and mountain resorts. Several state parks are here, including Mount Philo, Law Island, Underhill, and Camel's Hump. Ethan Allen Firing Range is in the east. • Named for Thomas Chittenden (1730–97), first governor of VT • 1787 from Addison (prior to statehood) • Burlington was an American naval base in the War of 1812. During the war, Battery Park saw several engagements between land batteries and British warships on Lake Champlain. Fort Ethan Allen was used as a military reservation during the Spanish-American War, and both world wars. Winooski was a major textile manufacturing center in the 1800s. • Philosopher and educator John Dewey; soldier and frontiersman Ethan Allen. Medical missionary Sir Wilfred Grenfell and Union officer Oliver O. Howard died here. • Dairying, maple products, fruit; granite; lake and mountain resorts; manufacture of brush fibers, ovens, airplane parts, structural steel, clothing, machine parts, furniture, food and beverages, computer components; woodworking; tool and die industries; meat packing; shipping; education (U. of VT; Burlington College; Champlain College; St. Michael's College) • The State Health Department and Laboratory, and the Medical Center of VT are in Burlington. The Unitarian Church in Burlington has a bell cast by Paul Revere.

ESSEX *Guildhall* • 6,459 (the least populated county in VT) • 665 • Northeastern VT, bounded on the north by the Canadian province of Quebec and on the east by the Connecticut River (forming the NH state line); drained by the Moose, Nulhegan, and Clyde rivers. Brighton and Maidstone state parks are here. Victory State Forest is in the east. The county encompasses most of Vermont's "Northeast Kingdom." • One of five counties named for the county of Essex in England • 1792 from Chittenden and Orange • Singer Rudy Vallee • Lumber, paper and wood products; dairying; hunting and fishing. • The Concord Academy, which opened in 1823, was the first teacher's training school.

FRANKLIN (one of twenty-five counties so named) *Saint Albans* • 45,417 (the fifth most populated county in VT) • 637 • Northwestern VT, bounded on the north by the Canadian province of Quebec and on the west by Lake Champlain. The county rises to the Green Mountains in the east and is drained by the Missisquoi and Lamoille rivers. There are a number of state parks in and around Lake Champlain. Lake Carmi State Park is in the north. • One of twenty-three counties named for Benjamin Franklin • 1792 from Chittenden • St. Albans' location near the Canadian border made it a smuggling base from 1807 to 1812. It was also a station on the Underground Railroad. The city was the scene of an attack by Confederate Lieutenant Bennett H. Young and twenty armed, mounted men on October 19, 1864; in their wake, the raiders left several dead and wounded, and local banks bereft of $200,000. In 1866, St. Albans served as headquarters for an ultimately abortive attempt by the (Irish nationalist) Fenians to invade Canada. • President Chester Alan Arthur (state historic site); anesthetist and inventor Gardner Q. Colton • Manufacture of farm machinery, textiles equipment, paper and wood products, flashlights, pharmaceuticals; dairying, hay; maple sugar; railroad shops; resorts.

GRAND ISLE *North Hero* • 6,901 (30% increase since 1990; the fastest growing county in VT) • 83 (the smallest county in VT and one of the fifty smallest counties in the U.S.) • Northwestern VT, on a peninsula and several islands in Lake Champlain. The county includes North Hero Island, South Hero Island, and Isle La Motte. • Named for the largest of the islands comprising the county • 1802 from Franklin and Chittenden • Isle La Motte is the site of the state's first European settlement (c. 1665) • Dairying, apples; lumber; resorts.

LAMOILLE *Hyde Park* • 23,233 • 461 • North-central VT; drained by the Lamoille River. The Green Mountains are in the west. Mount Mansfield, at 4,392 feet, the highest point in the state, is a popular winter resort spot. Long Trail passes through the north. Found here are Elmore and Smugglers Notch state parks, Morristown Bog and Moss Glen Falls natural areas, and Smugglers' Notch and Stowe ski areas. • Named for the Lamoille River • 1835 from Orleans, Franklin, Washington and Chittenden • Maria Trapp and the Trapp family singers • Dairying; maple sugar; manufacture of machinery, wood products and textiles; talc, asbestos; lumber; education (Johnson State College); tourism.

ORANGE (one of eight counties so named) *Chelsea* • 28,226 • 689 • Central and eastern VT, bounded on the east by the Connecticut River (forming the NH state line); drained by the White, Waits and Ompompanoosuc rivers. Washington State Forest, and Allis and Thetford Hill state parks are here. • The county was possibly named for a town in CT or MA, or for Orange County NY • 1781 from the former Cumberland County (prior to statehood) • Inventor Thomas Davenport; pioneer American expressman Henry Wells; politician Justin Smith Morrill (homestead) • Dairying, lumbering; manufacture of machinery, wood products and paper; maple sugar; winter and summer resorts; education (VT Tech. College).

ORLEANS (one of three counties so named) *Newport* • 26,277 • 697 • Northern VT, bounded on the north by Quebec; drained by the Barton, Missisquoi, Black, and Clyde rivers. There are resorts on Lake Memphremagog (shared with Canada), Lake Willoughby, Seymour Lake and smaller lakes. Big Falls of the Missisquoi and Hazen's Notch natural areas are here, as are Crystal Lake State Park and Jay State Forest. Part of Lake Willoughby State Forest is in the east. • Probably named for the city of Orleans in France or for Louis Philippe Joseph (1747–93), Duke of Orleans, a friend of the Marquis de Lafayette • 1792 from Chittenden and Orange • Dairying; maple sugar; lumbering; manufacture of furniture and wood products; winter sport tourism.

RUTLAND *Rutland* • 63,400 (the second most populated county in VT) • 932 (the second largest county in VT) • Western VT, bounded on the west in part by Lake Champlain (forming the NY state line in the north) and by the NY state line alone in the south; drained by Otter Creek, and the Castleton, Poultney, and Clarendon rivers. The Green Mountains are in the east, with separate units of Green Mountain National Forest (its headquarters in Rutland) in the northeast and southeast. Pico and Killington ski areas are in the east. State parks here include Lake St. Catherine, Half Moon, Bomoseen, and Gifford Woods. The Appalachian and Long trails pass through the county. • Named for the town of Rutland, NH • 1781 from Bennington (prior to statehood) • In 1759, Rutland was an outpost on the military road built by British general Sir Jeffrey Amherst across VT, which connected forts on Lake Champlain with the Connecticut River valley. Rutland served as capital of VT from 1784 to 1804. • Political leader Stephen A. Douglas; inventor and agricultural implements manufacturer John Deere; educator and philosopher Ralph B. Perry; senator James Jeffords • Dairying, fruit, poultry; manufacture of scales, castings, plywood products, textiles, tools, machinery (especially for stone-working), airplane parts; lumber; maple sugar; winter resort tourism; education (Castleton State College; Green Mountain College) • Rutland is known as "Marble City" for its nearby marble quarries. The *Rutland Daily Herald*, published continuously since 1794, is the oldest newspaper in the state. The Vermont Marble Exhibit in Proctor displays 100 different kinds of marble and granite. The New England Maple Museum is north.

WASHINGTON *Montpelier* • 58,039 (the third most populated county in VT) • 689 • Central VT; drained by the Winooski and Mad rivers. The county includes part of Green

Mountains National Forest. Camels Hump, one of the highest peaks of the Green Mountains, is in the west. Part of Groton State Forest is in the east. Mount Mansfield State Forest is in the northwest. Also found in the county are Mad River Glen and Sugarbush ski areas, and Little River and Waterbury Center state parks. • One of thirty-one counties named for George Washington • Organized as Jefferson in 1810 from Addison, Caledonia, Chittenden and Orange; name changed 1814 • Montpelier was named state capital in 1805. It subsequently defeated several attempts by Burlington and other towns to become capital, especially after its statehouse was gutted by fire in 1857. • Philosopher and educator John Dewey • The county is in the granite-quarrying center of the state (Barre is said to be the largest granite center in the world); also dairy products (especially ice cream); manufacture of textiles, wood products, machinery, electrical equipment; maple sugar; winter tourism; government offices; printing; education (Norwich U.; Goddard College) • A granite statue of Scottish poet Robert Burns in Barre is an area attraction. The state capitol in Montpelier was constructed with Vermont granite. Montpelier is the least populated state capital (pop. 8,035).

WINDHAM (one of two counties so named, the other in CT) *Newfane* • 44,216 (the third largest county in VT) • 789 • Southeastern VT, bounded on the east by the Connecticut River (forming the NH state line) and on the south by the MA state line; drained by the West and Deerfield rivers. The county rises to the Green Mountains in the west. Part of Green Mountain National Park is here. Grafton State Forest and several state parks and ski areas are also found in the county. • Possibly named for both the town and county of Windham in CT, former home of early settlers • 1781 from the former Cumberland County (prior to statehood) • Fort Drummer was established as one of VT's first white settlements in 1724. It was built by MA pioneers to protect the colony's western settlements from French and Indian raids. • Explorer and documentary filmmaker Robert Flaherty; architect Richard Morris Hunt; Oneida Community founder John H. Noyes; Antiland mine activist Jody Williams; author Rudyard Kipling. Pianist Rudolf Serkin and Contract Bridge authority Ely Culbertson died here. • Dairying; manufacture of paper and wood products, textiles, paper machinery, shoes, sports equipment, handbags, optical goods, feed; resorts; education (Marlboro College) • Brattleboro Retreat is one of the largest private psychiatric hospitals in the U.S. The Holstein-Friesian (cattle) Association is in the town.

WINDSOR *Woodstock* • 57,418 (the fourth most populated county in VT) • 971 (the largest county in VT) • Eastern VT, bounded on the east by the Connecticut River (forming the NH state line); drained by the Ottauquechee, White, Black and Williams rivers. The county has several state parks and forests. Part of Green Mountain National Forest is in the southwest. • Named for the town of Windsor, NH • 1781 from the former Cumberland County (prior to statehood) • Called the "birthplace of Vermont," Windsor was the site of the July 8, 1777 convention to adopt a constitution for the independent republic of Vermont. • Chemist Donald J. Cram; astronomer and archaeologist Andrew E. Douglass; sculptor Hiram Powers; Mormon founder Joseph Smith; President Calvin Coolidge (state historic site; he took his presidential oath on August 3, 1923 in the family homestead in Plymouth Notch); biologist and geneticist Nettie Maria Stevens; diplomat and scholar George Perkins Marsh • Manufacture of machinery, tools, textiles, wood and metal products, sports equipment; lumber; dairying; maple sugar; seasonal resort tourism (including several ski areas) • During the 19th century, the sewing machine, hydraulic pump and coffee percolator were invented in Windsor. Springfield became a gathering place for amateur astronomers in the 1920s. Governor James Hartness built an observatory here, as well as a laboratory to make and test telescopes.

VIRGINIA

Thus Always to Tyrants

Each of Virginia's ninety-five counties, except Arlington, is governed by a board of supervisors. Arlington is administered by a county board. Most of the state's counties have a treasurer, sheriff, commonwealth's attorney, county clerk, and commissioner of revenue. All county officials are elected to four-year terms except for the clerk, who serves eight years. A few Virginia counties have a county-manager or county-executive form of government. Virginia has forty independent cities, which are legally separate from the counties in which they are located.

ACCOMACK *Accomac* • 38,305 • 455 • Eastern VA on the Delmarva peninsula, bounded on the north by the MD state line, on the west by Chesapeake Bay, and on the east by the Atlantic Ocean. Off the coast to the east lie the barrier islands of Chincoteague, Assateague, Assawoman, Metompkin, and Cedar. Included in the county are Tangier Island, and part of Smith Island Group to the west. Chincoteague National Wildlife Refuge, with its wild ponies, is part of Assateague Island National Seashore in the northeast. Assateague Island is on the main Atlantic flyway and includes a large population of resident and migratory birds. Parker Marsh Natural Area is also here. NASA Wallops Flight Facility, in the north, tracks spacecraft and satellites. • Named for the Accomac Indians • 1663 from Northampton • Tangier Island, discovered by Captain John Smith in 1608, is an isolated enclave with some residents who still speak with an Elizabethan English accent. The county was the refuge of Governor William Berkeley during Bacon's Rebellion in 1675–76. • Poultry raising and processing, potatoes, sweet potatoes, tomatoes, fruit, corn, barley, wheat, soybeans, hogs, cattle; fish, oysters, clams; pine timber; tourism, game fishing.

ALBEMARLE *Charlottesville* • 79,236 • 723 • North-central VA, bounded on the southwest in part by the Rockfish River and on the south by the James River; drained by the Rivanna and Hardware rivers. The western part of the county lies in the Piedmont and rises to the Blue Ridge. The county includes part of Shenandoah National Park in the northwest. The Appalachian Trail and Blue Ridge (national) Parkway follow the western boundary, the latter becoming Skyline Drive in Shenandoah Park. Though serving as the seat for the county, Charlottesville is otherwise independent. • Named for William Anne Keppel (1702–54), 2nd Earl of Albemarle, absentee governor of the colony of VA • 1744 from Goochland • President Thomas Jefferson (Monticello); President James Monroe (Ashlawn-Highland); frontier military leader George Rogers Clark; explorer Meriwether Lewis • Wheat, apples, peaches, corn, hay, alfalfa, cattle, sheep, horses, poultry, dairying; timber; limestone, stone • Jefferson's design for Monticello, one of the architectural masterpieces of the 18th century, was influenced by the 16th century Italian Palladian style, rather than the popular Georgian architecture of the day.

ALLEGHANY (one of two counties so named, the other in NC; one of five counties named Allegany with variant spellings) *Covington* • 12,926 • 446 • Western VA, bounded on the west by the WV state line; drained by the Jackson and James rivers. The county is located in the Allegheny Mountains, with Peters Mountain Ridge on the southeast boundary. It includes part of Jefferson National Forest in the south and part of George Washington National Forest in the north. Though serving as the seat for the county, Covington is otherwise independent. The city of Clifton Forge is also independent. • Named for the Allegheny Mountains, with a variant spelling • 1822 from Bath and Botetourt counties, VA; and Monroe County (now in WV) • Corn, hay, alfalfa, apples, peaches, cattle; iron and coal mining, limestone quarrying; some manufacturing.

AMELIA *Amelia Court House* • 11,400 • 357 • Central VA, bounded on the north and northeast by the Appomattox River (forming Lake Chesdin) and on the southeast by Namozinc Creek. Sailor's Creek Battlefield Historic State Park is in the southwest. • Named for Princess Amelia Sophia (1711–86), second daughter of George II of England • 1734 from

Brunswick and Prince George • Soil chemist Edmund Ruffin died here • Tobacco, corn, barley, wheat, hay, alfalfa, soybeans, cattle, dairying; timber; feldspar, mica, pegmatite deposits.

AMHERST *Amherst* • 31,894 • 475 • West-central VA, bounded on the southwest, south and southeast by the James River. The county lies mainly in the Piedmont, rising northwest to the Blue Ridge, and traversed by Blue Ridge Parkway and the Appalachian Trail. Part of George Washington National Forest is here. • Named for Lord Jeffrey Amherst (1717–97), commander of British forces in North America during the French and Indian Wars • 1761 from Albemarle • Western trader William Becknell; merchant Clarence Saunders • Corn, hay, apples, peaches, cattle; titanium ore deposits; education (Sweet Briar College).

APPOMATTOX *Appomattox* • 13,705 • 334 • Central VA, bounded on the northwest by the James River. Holliday Lake State Park and part of Appomattox-Buckingham State Forest are in the county. • Named for the Appomattox River, which runs through the county • 1845 from Buckingham, Campbell, Charlotte, and Prince Edward • At Appomattox Court House (national historic park) on April 9, 1865, General Robert E. Lee surrendered the Confederacy's largest field army to Lt. General Ulysses S. Grant, effectively ending the Civil War. • Tobacco, hay, wheat, corn, soybeans, cattle, dairying; timber.

ARLINGTON *Arlington* • 189,453 (the fifth most populated county in VA) • 26 (the smallest county in VA; only two U.S. counties are smaller) • Northern VA, across the Potomac River from Washington, D.C., immediately north of Alexandria. The county and the unincorporated city of Arlington are coterminous. Arlington, a residential and commercial suburb of Washington, D.C., which borders it on the north, contains Arlington National Cemetery (America's national burial ground), Arlington House, the Robert E. Lee Memorial, the Pentagon, Fort Myer Military Reservation, the Office of Naval Research, the Federal Highway Administration Research Station, CIA headquarters and Reagan National Airport. Northern Virginia Regional Park is in the north, Glen Carlyn Park in the southwest. The county contains major office and housing developments. • Named for the home of George Washington Parke Custis, grandson of Martha Washington, itself possibly named for the Custis family estate in Gloucester, England • Formerly called Alexandria, it was ceded to the Federal Government in 1790 to form part of the District of Columbia. It was returned to VA by the U.S. Congress in 1846 and renamed in 1920. • The area that would later become Arlington County was occupied by Union troops during the Civil War; a number of forts were built here as part of the defenses surrounding Washington, D.C. The Pentagon was one of the targets of the September 11, 2001 terrorist attack on the U.S.; in addition to killing all those aboard American Airlines Flight 77, 125 others perished on the ground. • Naval officer and engineer Hyman G. Rickover. • Printing and publishing; shipbuilding; manufacture of apparel, bakery products, radar systems electric components, scientific instruments, machinery; education (Marymount U.) • A number of famous Americans are buried in Arlington National Cemetery, including U.S. presidents William Howard Taft and John F. Kennedy. The list also includes a number of U.S. Supreme Court justices, generals John J. Pershing, Jonathan Wainwright, and George C. Marshall, polar explorers Admiral Richard E. Byrd and Robert E. Peary, Robert Todd Lincoln, architect Major Pierre-Charles L'Enfant, William Jennings Bryan, Joe Louis, and Robert F. Kennedy. Pianist and Polish statesman Ignacy Paderewski is also buried here.

AUGUSTA *Staunton* • 65,615 • 973 (the largest county in VA) • Northwestern VA; drained by the Middle and South rivers (headstreams of the Shenandoah River) and Calfpasture River. The county is located mostly in the Shenandoah Valley, with the Shenandoah Mountains in the west and northwest, and the Blue Ridge in the southeast and east. The county contains part of Shenandoah National Park and George Washington National Forest. The Appalachian Trail and Blue Ridge Parkway follow the southeastern boundary. Though serving as seat for the county, Staunton is otherwise independent. The city of Waynesboro is also independent. • Named for Princess Augusta of Saxe-Coburg-Gotha (1719?–72), mother of George III of England • 1738 from Orange • Clergyman and missionary to the Cherokee Indians Gideon Blackburn; U.S. Supreme Court justice Robert Trimble • Apples, peaches, wheat, corn, hay, barley, soybeans, alfalfa, cattle, hogs, sheep, poultry, dairying; timber; manganese mining, rock quarrying • At the Cyrus McCormick farm and birthplace, exhibits include a model of his invention, the first reaper. (The house sits squarely on the boundary line between Augusta and Rockbridge counties.)

BATH (one of two counties so named, the other in KY) *Warm Springs* • 5,048 • 532 • Western VA, in the Allegheny Mountains, bounded on the west by the WV state line; drained by the Jackson and Cowpasture rivers. The county is located entirely within George Washington National Forest and includes Lake Moomaw Recreation Area, Douthat State Park, and the Homestead ski area. It has several notable mineral springs. • Named Bath for its springs • 1790 from Augusta and Botetourt in VA, and Greenbrier, now in WV • Hot Springs has a been therapeutic resort destination since its first inn was built in 1765; some of its famous visitors include several U.S. presidents. • Sheep, cattle, horses, hay; timber; hunting, fishing, tourism.

BEDFORD (one of three counties so named) *Bedford* • 60,371 • 755 (the fifth largest county in VA) • Central VA, bounded on the southwest by the Roanoke River (forming Leesville Lake and Smith Mountain Lake reservoir in the south) and on the northeast by the James River; drained by the Big Otter River and Goose Creek. The county is partially located in the Piedmont with Blue Ridge in the northwest. Part of Jefferson National Forest is also in the northwest and includes the Appalachian Trail and Blue Ridge Parkway, which follow part of the county boundary. Also here is Smith Mountain Lake State Park. Though serving as the seat for the county, Bedford is independent. • Named for John Russell (1710–71), 4th Duke of Bedford, British statesman who negotiated an end to the French and Indian Wars (Russell's other namesake county in PA) • 1753 from Albemarle and Lunenberg • Tobacco, barley, corn, wheat, tomatoes, peaches, apples, cattle, sheep, dairying; timber; feldspar mining • Thomas Jefferson's retreat home and final architectural work, Poplar Forest (national historic landmark), is in the process of being restored.

BLAND *Bland* • 6,871 • 359 • Southwestern VA, bounded on the north by the WV state line; drained by Wolf and Walker creeks. Located in a scenic region of the Allegheny Mountains, most of the county lies within Jefferson National Forest and includes Falls of Dismal on the eastern border. The Appalachian Trail passes through the middle of the county. • Named for Richard Bland (1710–76), member of the Continental Congress • 1861 from Giles, Tazewell and Wythe • Corn, hay, alfalfa, tobacco, cattle, sheep, dairying; timber; limestone quarrying, manganese.

BOTETOURT *Fincastle* • 30,496 • 543 • West-central VA; drained by the James River and Craig Creek. The county, located mainly in the Great Appalachian Valley, is traversed by ridges, with the Blue Ridge and the Appalachian Trail along its southeastern boundary. It contains part of Jefferson National Forest in the west and east, and George Washington National Forest in the north. Apple Orchard Falls is also here. • Named for Norborne Berkeley (?–1770), Baron de Botetourt, the penultimate English governor of VA • 1769 from Augusta • Tomatoes, wheat, corn, hay, alfalfa, soybeans, potatoes, apples, peaches, cattle, sheep, dairying; timber; limestone quarrying; resort tourism.

BRUNSWICK (one of two counties so named; the other in NC) *Lawrenceville* • 18,419 • 566 • Southern VA, bounded on the south by the NC state line and on the north by the Nottoway River; drained by the Meherrin River and Fontaine Creek. Part of Fort Pickett Military Reservation is here. The northern arms of Lake Gaston reservoir (Roanoke River) are in the south. • Named for the British House of Brunswick • 1720 from Prince George, Isle of Wight, and Surry • Tobacco, wheat, corn, soybeans, cotton, hay, sweet potatoes, peanuts, some dairying, cattle, hogs, poultry; some manufacturing; education (St. Paul's College).

BUCHANAN *Grundy* • *26,978* • *504* • Southwestern VA, bounded on the northwest by the KY state line, on the northeast by the WV state line (the Tug Fork forming the boundary in the far north), and on the southwest in part by Russell Fork; drained by the Levisa Fork of the Big Sandy River. • One of three counties named for President James Buchanan • 1858 from Tazewell and Russell • Hay, potatoes, sweet potatoes, tobacco, poultry, cattle; timber; bituminous-coal mining.

BUCKINGHAM *Buckingham* • 15,623 • 581 • Central VA, bounded on the northwest and north by the James River and on the south by the Appomattox River; drained by the Slate and Willis rivers. Part of Appomattox-Buckingham State Forest is in the southwest. James River State Park is in the west. • Possibly named for Buckinghamshire, England • 1761 from Albemarle • Predominantly lumbering and tobacco; also hay, wheat, corn, apples, peaches, cattle; slate quarrying, sand, kyanite.

CAMPBELL (one of five counties so named) *Rustburg* • 51,078 • 504 • South-central VA, bounded on the north by the James River and on the south by the Roanoke River (forming Leesville Lake reservoir in the southwestern corner); drained by the Falling and Big Otter rivers. The city of Lynchburg is independent of the county. • Named for General William Campbell (1745–81), officer in the American Revolution • 1781 from Bedford • Tobacco, corn, hay, wheat, alfalfa, barley, soybeans, cattle, poultry, dairying; some manufacturing.

CAROLINE (one of two counties so named, the other in MD) *Bowling Green* • 22,121 • 533 • Northeastern VA, bounded on the northeast by the Rappahannock River, on the southwest by the North Anna River, and on the south by the Pamunkey River; drained by the Mattaponi River. Fort A.P. Hill Military Reservation is here. • Named for Princess Caroline of Anspach (1683–1737), influential wife of George II of England • 1727 from Essex, King and Queen, and King William • Explorer William Clark; patriot Edmund Pendleton; Liberal agrarian political scientist John Taylor • Hay, barley, wheat, corn, soybeans, tobacco, sweet and white potatoes, cattle; timber; stone quarrying. • The Stonewall Jackson Shrine is in the west.

CARROLL (one of thirteen counties so named) *Hillsville* • 29,245 • 476 • Southwestern VA, bounded on the south by the NC state line; drained by the New River. The county is in the Blue Ridge (Blue Ridge Parkway passes through) and includes part of Mount Rogers National Recreation Area. New River Trail State Park is in the northwest. The city of Galax is independent of the county. • One of twelve counties named for Charles Carroll (1737–1832), signer of the Declaration of Independence, U.S. senator from MD and founder of the Baltimore and Ohio Railroad • 1842 from Grayson • Hay, alfalfa, corn, clover, cabbage, apples, peaches, cattle, dairying; timber; limestone quarrying.

CHARLES CITY *Charles City* • 6,926 • 182 • Eastern VA, bounded on the south by the James River and on the north and east by the Chickahominy River, which enters James River in the southeastern corner. The county is located in the Tidewater region. It contains some of the state's oldest and most historic plantation estates, including Westover, Greenway, Berkeley, Evelynton, and Shirley. Berkeley was the ancestral home of Benjamin Harrison, signer of the Declaration of Independence and primogenitor of two presidents, William Henry Harrison and Benjamin Harrison. The first Thanks-

giving was claimed to have been observed here on December 4, 1619. In 1862, Berkeley served as headquarters for Union General McClellan. While quartered there, Major General Daniel Butterfield composed the bugle call "Taps." • Named for one of VA's earliest settlements, itself named for Charles I (1600–49), king of Great Britain • 1634 (original county) • Both candidates at the top of the Whig ticket in the 1840 national election were from Charles City County, and both ultimately became president: William Henry Harrison and his vice president John Tyler (Greenway Plantation) who, upon Harrison's death thirty-one days into his administration, ascended to the presidency. Robert E. Lee's mother was born here. • Hay, barley, wheat, corn, soybeans, poultry, cattle; timber • The carved walnut staircase at Shirley ascends three stories with no visible means of support, the only one of its kind in the U.S.

CHARLOTTE (one of two counties so named, the other in FL) *Charlotte Court House* • 12,472 • 475 • Southern VA, bounded on the west and south by the Roanoke (Staunton) River • Named for Charlotte Sophia, Princess of Mecklenburg-Strelitz (1744–1818), wife of George III of England • 1764 from Lunenburg • Tobacco, corn, hay, wheat, soybeans, cattle, dairying; timber • The sixty-four-foot high Osage Orange Tree, located at Red Hill-Patrick Henry National Memorial, is listed in the American Forestry Hall of Fame.

CHESTERFIELD *Chesterfield* • 259,903 (the fourth most populated county in VA) • 426 • East-central VA, bounded on the south by the Appomattox River (which forms Lake Chesdin reservoir in the south) and on the north and northeast in part by the James River. The county excludes the independent cities of Richmond and Colonial Heights. Pocahontas State Park, Presquile National Wildlife Refuge, and Swift Creek reservoir are here. Civil War battle sites are located in the villages of Bermuda Hundred in the southeast and Drewry's Bluff in the northeast (Richmond National Battlefield Park). • One of two counties (the other in SC) named for English statesman and writer, Philip Dormer Stanhope (1694–1773), 4th Earl of Chesterfield • 1749 from Henrico • Wheat, corn, tobacco, hay, soybeans, cattle, poultry; education (VA State U.)

CLARKE *Berryville* • 12,652 • 177 • Northern VA, bounded on the northeast by the WV state line and on the west by Opequon Creek; drained by the Shenandoah River and Opequon Creek. The county is located in the northern Shenandoah Valley, with the Blue Ridge in the southeast. The Appalachian Trail follows the southeastern border. The State Arboretum of Virginia and part of Sky Meadows State Park are here. • One of six counties named for George Rogers Clark (1752–1818), general in the American Revolution and frontiersman in the Northwest Territory • 1836 from Frederick and Warren • Apples, peaches, corn, wheat, barley, soybeans, hay, alfalfa, horses.

CRAIG (one of two counties so named, the other in OK) *New Castle* • 5,091 • 330 • Southwestern VA, bounded on the west by the WV state line; drained by Craig Creek. The county is located in the Allegheny Mountains with most of the county in Jefferson National Forest. The Appalachian Trail passes through its southern edge. • Named for Robert Craig (1792–1852), U.S. representative from VA • 1851 from Botetourt, Roanoake, Giles and Monroe • Grain, hay, cattle, sheep; timber; iron-ore deposits, sand and gravel; resort and mineral spring tourism.

CULPEPER *Culpeper* • 34,262 • 381 • Northern VA, in the Piedmont, bounded on the south by the Rapidan River and on the east and northeast by the Rappahannock River, with the two rivers meeting in the southeastern corner of the county; drained by the Hazel River. • Named for Lord Thomas Culpeper (1635–89), colonial governor of VA. • 1748 from Orange • Confederate general A.P. Hill; U.S. Supreme Court justice John McKinley • Apples, peaches, barley, wheat, corn, soybeans, hay, alfalfa, cattle, sheep, poultry, dairying.

CUMBERLAND (one of eight counties so named) *Cumberland* • 9,017 • 298 • Central VA, bounded on the south and southeast by the Appomattox River and on the northeast by the James River; drained by the Willis River. Bear Creek Lake State Park and Cumberland State Forest are here. • One of four counties named for William Augustus, Duke of Cumberland (1721–65), British general and second son of George II of England • 1749 from Goochland • Predominantly tobacco; also wheat, corn, hay, alfalfa, dairying, cattle; timber.

DICKENSON *Clintwood* • 16,395 • 333 • Southwestern VA, bounded on the northwest by the KY state line; drained by the Russell Fork (forming part of the southeastern border) and the Pound River (forming John W. Flannagan Reservoir). The Cumberland Mountains and part of Jefferson National Forest are in the northwest and include Breaks Interstate Park. • Named for William J. Dickenson (1828–1907), lawyer and state legislator • 1880 from Buchanan, Russell, and Wise • Hay, potatoes, tobacco, cattle; timber; bituminous-coal mining.

DINWIDDIE *Dinwiddie* • 24,533 • 504 • Southeast-central VA, bounded on the north by the Appomattox River and on the southwest by the Nottoway River; drained by Stoney Creek. Part of Fort Pickett Military Reservation is here, as is Poplar Grove National Cemetery. Petersburg lies within county boundaries but is independent. • Named for Robert Dinwiddie (?–1770), lieutenant governor of VA • 1752 from Prince George • Battles at Five Forks and in the Petersburg vicinity to the northeast were among the last struggles (April 1865) of the Civil War. • Tobacco, barley, wheat, corn, soybeans, peanuts, cotton, hay, hogs, cattle, dairying; lumber milling; granite quarrying • Pamplin Historic Park, where Grant's troops broke through the Confederate line to end the siege of Petersburg, contains some of the best preserved examples of Confederate earthen fortifications. The National Museum of the Civil War Soldier is located here.

ESSEX *Tappahannock* • 9,989 • 258 • Eastern VA, bounded on the northeast and east by the Rappahannock River. The county is located in the Tidewater region. • One of five counties named for Essex County in England • 1692 from Old Rappahannock County, which was organized in 1656 from Lancaster County and abolished in 1692 • Barley, wheat, soybeans, corn, hay, cattle.

FAIRFAX *Fairfax* • 969,749 (the most populated county in VA) • 396 • Northern VA, bounded on the southwest by Bull Run Creek and the Occoquan River, and on the east (in part) and northeast by the Potomac River (forming the MD state line). The county excludes the independent cities of Alexandria and Falls Church. Though serving as seat for the county, Fairfax city is also otherwise independent. Fairfax County is chiefly residential with some agriculture. Since the 1960s it has become largely urbanized, comprising part of the Washington, D.C. metropolitan area. Mount Vernon and Gunston Hall historical sites are in the southeast. Wolf Trap Farm Park for the Performing Arts (a national park unit) is in north-center. Mason Neck State Park, George Washington's Grist Mill State Historical Park, and Mason Neck National Wildlife Refuge are also here. Fort Belvoir Military Reservation is in the southeast. • Named for Thomas Fairfax, Baron Fairfax of Cameron (1692–1782), Lord proprietor of VA • 1742 from Prince William • Reston, founded in 1961 by Robert E. Simon, was an early planned community, with dwellings in its many villages placed within a half-mile radius of "town centers" offering all necessary services. • Martha and President George Washington • Cattle, poultry, hay, nursery stock; manufacture of asphalt, fabricated steel; education (George Mason U.) • The headquarters of six Fortune 1000 corporations are in the county. The U.S. Geological Survey is located in Reston, which is also home to the annual Northern Virginia Fine Arts Festival. Part of Washington Dulles International Airport occupies most of the 3,000 acres which comprised the original Sully Plantation, built in 1794 by Richard Bland Lee.

FAUQUIER *Warrenton* • 55,139 • 650 • Northern VA, bounded on the south and southwest by the Rappahannock River; drained by the Little River. The county is mainly located in the Piedmont with part of the Blue Ridge in the northwest. The Appalachian Trail follows the northwestern boundary. Sky Meadows State Park and Whitney State Forest are here. The county also includes part of Quantico U.S. Marine Corps Base. • Named for Francis Fauquier (?–1768), lieutenant governor of the colony of VA • 1759 from Prince William • Father of statesman Richard Henry Lee, Thomas Lee • The county is noted for Thoroughbred horse raising; also wheat, barley, corn, soybeans, hay, alfalfa, apples, peaches, cattle, hogs, dairying; oak, hickory, pine • Warrenton is known for its fox-hunting events.

FLOYD (one of six counties so named) *Floyd* • 13,874 • 381 • Southwestern VA; drained by the Little River (forming part of the northwestern boundary). The county is in the Blue Ridge, with the Blue Ridge Parkway following the eastern and southeastern boundary. • Named for General John Floyd

(1783–1837), U.S. representative and governor of VA • 1831 from Montgomery and Franklin • Corn, apples, livestock, dairying; timber.

FLUVANNA *Palmyra* • 20,047 • 287 • Central VA, bounded on the south by the James River; drained by the Rivanna and Hardware rivers. Lake Monticello reservoir is in the northwest. • Fluvanna is the name by which the upper James River was known until the Civil War; from Latin fluvius "river," and anna for Queen Anne (1776–1714) of England • 1777 from Albemarle • Tobacco, hay, alfalfa, wheat, corn, cattle; some timber; slate quarrying.

FRANKLIN (one of twenty-five counties so named) *Rocky Mount* • 47,286 • 692 • Southern VA, bounded on the northeast by the Roanoke River, here forming Smith Mountain Lake reservoir; drained by the Blackwater and Pigg rivers. The county is partly located in the Piedmont, rising to the Blue Ridge in the northwest. The Blue Ridge Parkway follows the northwestern boundary. Philpott Reservoir is on the southern boundary. • One of twenty-three counties named for Benjamin Franklin • 1784 from Bedford, Henry, and Patrick • Educator Booker T. Washington (national monument) • Confederate general Jubal Early died here. • Tobacco, hay, alfalfa, barley, wheat, corn, apples, peaches, cattle; timber; mica mining; manufacturing; education (Ferrum College).

FREDERICK (one of two counties so named, the other in MD) *Winchester* • 59,209 • 415 • Northern VA, bounded on the west and northeast by the WV state line. The county lies mainly in the Shenandoah Valley, with the Appalachian Mountains in the west. Though serving as seat for the county, Winchester is otherwise independent. • Named for Frederick Louis (1707–51), Prince of Wales, son of George II and father of George III of England • 1738 from Orange • U.S. Supreme Court justice Noah H. Swayne • Frederick is a leading apple-growing county in VA. Also, wheat, corn, hay, alfalfa, cattle, sheep, hogs, dairying; limestone, sand and gravel.

GILES *Pearisburg* • 16,657 • 358 • Southwestern VA, bounded on the northwest by the WV state line; drained by the New River, and Sinking, Walker, and Wolf creeks. The county lies in the Allegheny Mountains, with parts of Jefferson National Forest in the west and north. The Appalachian Trail crosses the northern part of the county. Mountain Lake Scenic Area, White Rocks, and Cascade Falls recreation areas are here. • One of two counties (the other in TN) named for William B. Giles (1762–1830), U.S. senator from VA and governor of VA (the other county in TN) • 1806 from Montgomery and Tazewell in VA; and Monroe, now in WV • Hay, alfalfa, apples, cattle, poultry; timber; some coal mining; manufacturing.

GLOUCESTER *Gloucester* • 34,780 • 217 • Eastern VA, bounded on the west and south by the York River estuary and on the east by Mobjack Bay, the arms of the Chesapeake, and its many tidal inlets. • Named for either Gloucestershire in England, or for Henry, Duke of Gloucester (1640–60), brother

of Charles II and James II • 1651 from York • Barley, wheat, corn, hay, soybeans, some cattle, bulb growing; fisheries; some manufacturing.

GOOCHLAND *Goochland* • 16,863 • 284 • Central VA, bounded on the south by the James River. The county contains historic estates and state penal farms. • Named for Sir William Gooch (1681–1751), lieutenant and acting governor of the colony of VA • 1727 from Henrico • Politician Edward Bates • Barley, wheat, corn, soybeans, hay, some dairying, cattle; timber.

GRAYSON (one of three counties so named) *Independence* • 17,917 • 443 • Southwestern VA, bounded on the south by the NC state line; drained by the New River. The Iron Mountains are in the west and include White Top Mountain and Mount Rogers (standing partially in Smyth County), the highest peak in VA (5,729 feet). Part of the Blue Ridge is in the southeast corner. The county includes Mount Rogers National Recreation Area in the west and north. The Appalachian Trail passes through the western part of the county. Grayson Highlands State Park is also here. The city of Galax is independent of the county. • One of two counties (the other in KY) named for Col. William Grayson (?–1790), officer in the Revolutionary War, member of the Continental Congress, and one of VA's first U.S. senators • 1792 from Wythe • Tobacco, corn, hay, alfalfa, cattle, sheep, poultry, dairying; timber; manufacturing.

GREENE (one of fourteen counties so named) *Stanardsville* • 15,244 • 157 • North-central VA, bounded on the northwest by the Blue Ridge and on the northeast by the Rapidan River, and its Conway River branch. Part of Shenandoah National Park (including sections of the Appalachian Trail and Skyline Drive) follows the northwest county line. • One of sixteen counties named for Gen. Nathanael Greene (1742–86), hero of the Revolutionary War and commander of the Army of the South • 1838 from Orange • Corn, alfalfa, hay, tobacco, fruit, cattle, hogs, sheep, poultry, dairying; oak, pine.

GREENSVILLE *Emporia* • 11,560 • 295 • Southern VA, bounded on the south by the NC state line and on the north by the Nottoway river; drained by the Meherrin river (forming part of the eastern boundary), and Fontaine Creek. Though serving as the seat, Emporia is otherwise independent of the county. • The derivation of this county's name has never been firmly established. It was possibly named for General Nathanael Greene (1742–86), hero of the American Revolution • 1780 from Brunswick • Peanuts, cotton, tobacco, hay, wheat, corn, soybeans, melons, eggs, cattle, hogs, poultry; timber.

HALIFAX *Halifax* • 37,355 (the fourth largest county in VA) • 819 • Southern VA, bounded on the south by the NC state line and on the north and east by the Roanoke (Staunton) River; drained by the Dan, Banister, and Hyco rivers. An arm of John H. Kerr Reservoir extends into the county in the east.

Staunton River and part of Staunton River Battlefield state parks are here. South Boston reverted from Independent City to town in 1995. • One of two counties (the other in NC) named for George Montagu Dunk (1716–71), 2nd Earl of Halifax, English statesman and a strong supporter of trade with the American colonies • 1752 from Lunenburg • Tobacco (a leading VA county); also wheat, corn, hay, soybeans, cattle; manufacturing.

HANOVER *Hanover* • 86,320 • 473 • East-central VA, partly in the Piedmont region, bounded on the northeast by the North Anna and Pamunkey rivers and on the south by the Chickahominy River; drained by the South Anna River. • Named for King George I (1660–1727), member of the British royal House of Hanover • 1720 from New Kent, prior to statehood • The county was the site of several Civil War battles, including Cold Harbor, Gaines's Mill and Mechanicsville (all three units of Richmond National Battlefield Park). Over 7,000 Union soldiers suffered casualties at Cold Harbor within only thirty minutes. • Statesman Henry Clay; American Revolutionary patriots Patrick Henry (who argued cases in the Hanover County Courthouse) and Thomas Sumter • Tobacco, soybeans, barley, wheat, corn, peanuts, hay, cattle, poultry, dairying; education (Randolph Macon College).

HENRICO *Richmond* • 262,300 (the third most populated county in VA) • 238 • East-central VA, bounded on the south in part by the James River and on the north and northeast by the Chickahominy River. The western part of the county lies in the Piedmont region. Most of the county is urbanized, especially in the center around Richmond, which, though the county seat, is otherwise independent of the county. Civil War battlefields in the county are included in sections of Richmond National Battlefield Park in the south. Glendale National Cemetery is in the southeast. • Named for an early settlement in colonial VA • 1634 (original county) • Hay, barley, wheat, corn, soybeans, poultry, beef cattle.

HENRY (one of ten counties so named) *Martinsville* • 57,930 • 382 • Southern VA, in the Piedmont, bounded on the south by the NC state line; drained by the Smith River. Part of Fairy Stone State Park and Philpott Reservoir are in the northwest. Though serving as the seat for the county, Martinsville is otherwise independent. • One of ten counties (including Patrick County, VA) named for Patrick Henry (1736–99), patriot, governor of VA and statesman. (The two counties in the state named for Henry sit side by side; in combination, they present his name on VA state maps.) • 1776 from Pittsylvania • Tobacco, hay, cattle, poultry, honey; timber; manufacture of furniture products.

HIGHLAND (one of two counties so named, the other in OH) *Monterey* • 2,536 (the least populated county in VA) • 416 • Northwestern VA, bounded on the west and north by the WV state line; drained by the Jackson, Bullpasture, and Cowpasture rivers, the South Branch of the Potomac River, and Back Creek. The Allegheny Mountains are in the west.

The Shenandoah Mountains extend along the county's eastern boundary. Part of George Washington National Forest is also here. • Named for the mountainous terrain of the county • 1847 from Bath in VA, and Pendleton (now in WV) • Hay, alfalfa, potatoes, cattle, sheep; sugar maples; timber; trout • The county has the highest mean altitude of any of VA's counties.

ISLE OF WIGHT *Isle of Wight* • 29,728 • 316 • Southeastern VA, in the Tidewater region, bounded on the west by the Blackwater River and on the northeast by the James estuary. • Named for the Isle of Wight in the English Channel • Organized as Warrascoyack (one of several alternate spellings); name changed in 1637 • Peanuts, corn, hay, soybeans, melons, barley, wheat, cotton, hogs, cattle; timber • St. Luke's Church, one of the oldest churches in America, is at Benn's Church.

JAMES CITY *Williamsburg* • 48,102 • 143 (one of the fifty smallest counties in the U.S.) • Southeastern VA, in the Tidewater region, bounded on the northeast by the York River, on the west in part by the Chickahominy River, and on the south by the James River. York River State Park is in the northeast. Though serving as seat for the county, Williamsburg is otherwise independent. • Named for the town of Jamestown, VA, itself named for King James I (1566–1625) • 1634 (original county) • The county includes Jamestown Island, site of the first permanent English settlement in America (1607). Jamestown was burned to the ground in 1676 during Bacon's Rebellion against Governor William Berkeley. • Hay, barley, wheat, soybeans, tobacco, corn, potatoes, fruit, cattle, dairying; fish, oysters, crabs • Near the Jamestown settlement site are reproductions of the three ships, the *Susan Constant*, *Godspeed*, and *Discovery*, which transported the first colonists to VA.

KING AND QUEEN *King and Queen Court House* • 6,630 • 316 • Eastern VA, in the Tidewater region, bounded on the southwest by the Mattaponi and York rivers. Part of Zoar State Forest is here. • Named for joint sovereigns King William III (1650–1702) and Queen Mary II (1662–94) of England • 1691 from New Kent • U.S. Supreme Court justice Thomas Todd • Tomatoes, barley, hay, soybeans, corn, wheat, legumes, cattle; oysters.

KING GEORGE *King George* • 16,803 • 180 • Eastern VA, at the base of the Northern Neck peninsula, bounded on the north and northeast by the Potomac River (the shore forming the MD border), and on the south by the Rappahannock River. The county includes Dahlgren Division of the Naval Surface Warfare Center. Caledon Natural Area is in the north. • Named for King George I of England (1660–1727) • 1720 from Richmond and Westmoreland • Dairying, corn, barley, wheat, hay, soybeans, alfalfa, cattle, hogs; commercial fishing.

KING WILLIAM *King William* • 13,146 • 275 • Eastern VA, in the Tidewater region, bounded on the southwest by the Pamunkey river, on the northeast by the Mattaponi River. The two rivers join at the southeastern tip of the county to form York River estuary, an arm of Chesapeake Bay. Pamunkey and Mattaponi Indian reservations are here, as is part of Zoar State Forest. • Named for William III of England (1650–1702) • 1701 from King and Queen • In 1691, the state General Assembly designated West Point as a point of entry and in 1705 as a free borough. George Washington often stopped in the town on his way to Williamsburg from Mount Vernon. During the Civil War, West Point, lying at the head of navigation on the York River and positioned at the terminus of the Richmond and York River Railroad, was of strategic importance. The immediate area was the scene of an engagement on May 7, 1862 between Union and Confederate troops. • Manufacture of pulp and paper; corn, barley, wheat, soybeans, hay, legumes, cattle, dairying; timber; fish and shellfish industries.

LANCASTER (one of four counties so named) *Lancaster* • 11,567 • 133 (one of the fifty smallest counties in the U.S.) • Eastern VA, on Northern Neck peninsula, bounded on the west and south by the Rappahannock River estuary, on the southeast by Chesapeake Bay (estuary entering the bay at the southeastern tip of the county). The county's shores are indented by many inlets. Belle Isle State Park is in the northwest. • One of two counties (the other in PA) named for the city and/or county in England • 1652 from York and Northumberland • Tomatoes, vegetables, barley, wheat, corn, soybeans, poultry, cattle; pine; fish, oysters, crabs; resort tourism.

LEE (one of twelve counties so named) *Jonesville* • 23,589 • 437 • Extreme southwestern VA, bounded on the northwest by the KY state line and on the south by the TN state line; drained by the Powell River. The Cumberland Mountains follow the KY state line. The Cumberland Gap passes at the southwest tip and comprises part of Cumberland Gap National Historic Park. The county includes part of Jefferson National Forest and Wilderness Road State Park. • Named for Henry "Lighthorse Harry" Lee (1756–1818), VA soldier, statesman, governor, and father of Robert E. Lee • 1792 from Russell • The Wilderness Road, a main artery of the great trans-Allegheny migration to settle the "Old West," passed through the county. During the 1780s, over 300,000 settlers followed explorer Daniel Boone through the Cumberland Gap, the mountain pass on the road, which was also an important objective in the Civil War. • Tobacco, corn, hay, alfalfa, cattle; timber; extensive bituminous-coal mining, limestone quarrying and caves.

LOUDOUN *Leesburg* • 169,599 (97% increase since 1990; the fastest growing county in VA) • 520 • Northern VA, in the Piedmont, rising to the Blue Ridge in the west, bounded on the northeast by the WV state line and on the north and northeast by the Potomac River (forming the MD state line); drained by the Little River and Goose Creek. Part of Harpers Ferry National Historic Park is in the west. Part of Dulles International Airport is also here. The Appalachian Trail parallels the county's western boundary. • Named for John Campbell (1705–82), 4th Earl of Loudoun, commander in chief of British forces during the French and Indian Wars and non-resident governor-general of the colony of VA • 1757 from Fairfax • Columnist Russell Baker • The county has many country estates with horse and cattle breeding, fox hunting; wheat, corn, barley, hay, soybeans, alfalfa, tobacco, apples, cattle, sheep, poultry, dairying; timber; limestone • Leesburg, the epicenter of "hunt country," is home to the Museum of Hounds and Hunting.

LOUISA (one of two counties so named, the other in IA) *Louisa* • 25,627 • 497 • Central VA, bounded on the north and northeast by the North Anna River (here forming Lake Anna reservoir); drained by the South Anna River. • Named for Princess Louise, (1724–51), daughter of George II of England, who later became queen consort of Denmark and Norway • 1742 from Hanover • Marine architect David Watson Taylor • Tobacco, barley, wheat, corn, soybeans, hay, cattle; timber.

LUNENBURG *Lunenburg* • 13,146 • 432 • Southern VA, bounded on the south in part by the Meherrin River and on the north by the Nottaway River • Named for King George II (1683–1760), who was Duke of Brunswick-Luneburg • 1746 from Brunswick • Manufacturing; tobacco, hay, wheat, barley, soybeans, cattle; pine, oak, lumber milling.

MADISON *Madison* • 12,520 • 321 • Northern VA, in the northern Piedmont, rising in the northwest to the Blue Ridge, bounded on the southwest and south by the Rapidan River; drained by the Robinson River. The county includes part of Shenandoah National Park. Blue Ridge (national) Parkway and the Appalachian Trail follow its northwestern border. • One of twenty counties named directly or indirectly for President James Madison • 1792 or 1793 from Culpeper • Barley, wheat, corn, alfalfa, soybeans, hay, apples, peaches, cattle, sheep, hogs, dairying; timber; trout fishing.

MATHEWS *Mathews* • 9,207 • 86 (one of the fifty smallest counties in the U.S.) • Eastern VA, in the Tidewater region, bounded on the east by the Chesapeake Bay, on the north by the Piankatank River estuary, and on the south by Mobjack Bay. The county has many seasonal homes. • Named for either Thomas Mathews, American Revolutionary patriot and speaker of the VA house of delegates, or for George Mathews (1739–1812), American Revolution army officer and governor of GA • 1790 or 1791 from Gloucester • Only woman commissioned in the Confederate army, humanitarian and hospital administrator Sally Louisa • Corn, soybeans, vegetables, melons, bulbs, poultry; fish, crabs, oysters; waterfowl hunting.

MECKLENBURG *Boydton* • 32,380 • 624 • Southern VA, bounded on the south by the NC state line and on the north by the Meherrin River; drained by the Roanoke River (here forming John H. Kerr Reservoir and Lake Gaston reservoir). Occoneechee State Park is here, as is part of Staunton River State Park (both on the western boundary and both on Kerr Reservoir). • One of three counties (including Charlotte in

VA) named for Queen Charlotte Sophia of Mecklenburg-Strelitz (1744–1818), wife of George III of England • 1764 from Lunenburg • Tobacco, wheat, barley, corn, soybeans, cotton, hay, alfalfa, peanuts, cattle, hogs, poultry, dairying; some timber; resort tourism.

MIDDLESEX *Saluda* • 9,932 • 130 (one of the fifty smallest counties in the U.S.) • Eastern VA, in the Tidewater region, bounded on the north by the Rappahannock River, on the south in part by the Piankatank River, and on the east by Chesapeake Bay. • One of four counties named for the ancient county of Middlesex in England • 1667–75 from Lancaster • Diplomat Arthur Lee died here. • Hay, barley, wheat, soybeans, tobacco, corn, melons, cattle, hogs, poultry; pine, oak; fish, oysters; resort tourism.

MONTGOMERY (one of eighteen counties so named) *Christiansburg* • 83,629 • 388 • Southwestern VA, mainly in the Great Appalachian Valley, bounded on the west by the New River, and on the south and southwest by the Little and Roanoke rivers. The Allegheny Mountains are in the northwest and the Blue Ridge is in the southeast. The county includes part of Jefferson National Forest. The Appalachian Trail passes through the north corner. The city of Radford is independent of the county. • One of sixteen counties named directly or indirectly for Gen. Richard Montgomery (1738–75), American Revolutionary War officer • 1776 from Fincastle (organized 1772 from Botetourt and abolished 1777), Botetourt and Pulaski counties • Politician John B. Floyd • Corn, alfalfa, hay, apples, cattle, sheep, dairying; some bituminous-coal mining, stone quarrying; manufacturing; education (VA Polytechnic Institute and State U.).

NELSON (one of three counties so named) *Lovingston* • 14,445 • 472 • Central VA, in the Piedmont region, with the Blue Ridge in the west, bounded on the southeast by the James River; drained by the Rockfish River. The Blue Ridge Parkway follows the northwestern border. The Appalachian Trail crosses the county in the northwest. Part of Washington National Forest is also here. Crabtree Falls, a series of cascades 1,200 feet high, constitutes the highest waterfall in VA. • One of two counties (the other in KY) named for Thomas Nelson (1738–89), signer of the Declaration of Independence and governor of VA • 1807 from Amherst • Political leader William H. Crawford • Apples, hay, alfalfa, corn, cattle; mining of titanium ores, apatite, stone quarrying.

NEW KENT *New Kent* • 13,462 • 210 • Eastern VA, in the Tidewater region, bounded on the south by the Chickahominy River, on the north by the Pamunkey River, and on the northeast by the York River estuary. Cumberland Marsh Preserve is here. • Named for Kent County, England and/or Kent Island, MD • 1654 from York • Hay, barley, wheat, corn, soybeans, sweet and white potatoes, poultry; timber.

NORTHAMPTON (one of three counties so named) *Eastville* • 13,093 • 207 • Eastern VA, at the southern end of the Eastern Shore (Delmarva) peninsula, bounded on the east by the Atlantic Ocean and on the west by Chesapeake Bay. The county has many barrier and bay islands off the Atlantic coast. Kiptopeke State Park, Wreck Island Natural Area Preserve, and Fisherman's Island National Wildlife Refuge are all here. The Intracoastal Waterway passes through the bay to the west. • Named for either Spencer Compton (1601–43), 2nd Earl of Northampton or for Northamptonshire, England • 1634 as Accawmack (with alternate spellings); name changed 1642 or 1643 • Canneries, processing of seafood and farm produce; white and sweet potatoes, strawberries, corn, barley, wheat, soybeans, poultry, hogs; pine; limestone; crabs, oysters.

NORTHUMBERLAND *Heathsville* • 12,259 • 192 • Eastern VA, on the northeastern part of Northern Neck peninsula, bounded on the northeast by the Potomac River estuary and on the east by the Chesapeake Bay. The coast has many bays and inlets and is indented by the Great Wicomico River estuary. Bush Mill Stream and Hughlett Point natural area preserves are here. • One of two counties (the other in PA) named for Northumberland County in England • 1648 from Chicacoun Indian District • Fish processing; hay, barley, wheat, corn, soybeans, tomatoes, cattle, poultry; oysters, crabs, herring; resort tourism (fishing, bathing) • The Reedville Fisherman's Museum honors the menhaden, a small, toothless fish valuable only for its byproducts, and the basis for the area's economic stability.

NOTTOWAY *Nottoway* • 15,725 • 315 • South-central VA, bounded on the south by the Nottoway River, with the source of Stony Creek in the southeast. Part of Fort Pickett Military Reservation is here. • Named for the Nottoway River and/or Nottoway Indian tribe • 1788 or 1789 from Amelia • Manufacturing; tobacco, fruit, hay, barley, wheat, corn, soybeans, cattle, sheep, poultry, dairying; timber; granite quarrying.

ORANGE (one of eight counties so named) *Orange* • 25,881 • 342 • North-central VA, in the Piedmont, bounded on the north by the Rapidan River and on the south by the North Anna River. The county contains many historic estates, including Madison's "Montpelier." • Named for William IV, Prince of Orange (1711–51) • 1734 from Spotsylvania • President James and Dolley Madison • Barley, wheat, corn, soybeans, grapes, fruit, legumes, sweet potatoes, tobacco, hay, alfalfa, cattle, sheep, poultry, dairying; oak.

PAGE (one of two counties so named, the other in IA) *Luray* • 23,177 • 311 • Northern VA, in the Shenandoah Valley, bounded on the east by the Blue Ridge; drained by the South Fork of the Shenandoah River. Massanutten ski area is in the west. The county includes part of Shenandoah National Park. Also here are Luray Caverns (with its unique sound system produced through the electronic manipulation of its stalactites) and part of George Washington National Forest. The Appalachian Trail closely parallels the eastern boundary. • Named for John Page (1743–1808), U.S. representative from VA and governor of the state • 1831 from Rockingham and Shenandoah • Corn, barley, wheat, alfalfa, hay, apples, peaches, poultry, cattle, hogs, dairying; timber.

PATRICK *Stuart* • 19,407 • 483 • Southern VA, lying partly in the Piedmont and rising to the Blue Ridge in the west and northwest, bounded on the south by the NC state line; drained by the Smith and Dan rivers. Fairy Stone Mountain (in Fairy Stone State Park) is in the northeast. The county also includes Philpott Reservoir (Smith River). The Blue Ridge Parkway follows the northwestern border of the county. • One of ten counties named for Patrick Henry (1736–99), patriot, statesman and governor of VA (the only one named Patrick). The two counties named for Henry sit side by side; in combination, they present his name on VA state maps. • 1790 or 1791 from Henry • Confederate cavalry officer Jeb Stuart • Corn, hay, alfalfa, soybeans, tobacco, apples, peaches, cattle, dairying; timber.

PITTSYLVANIA *Chatham* • 61,745 • 971 (the second largest county in VA) • Southern VA, in the Piedmont, bounded on the south by the NC state line and on the north by the Roanoke River (forming Leesville Lake and Smith Mountain Lake reservoirs); drained by the Dan, Banister, Pigg and Sandy rivers. The city of Danville is independent of the county. • Named for William Pitt (the Elder, 1708–78), 1st Earl of Chatham, prime minister of England and supporter of the American colonies • 1766 or 1767 from Halifax • Manufacturing, tobacco, hay, alfalfa, barley, wheat, soybeans, corn, cattle, dairying; timber.

POWHATAN *Powhatan* • 22,377 • 261 • Central VA, bounded on the north by the James River and on the south in part by the Appomattox River. • Named for chief Powhatan (?–1618), the leader of a confederacy of thirty-two tribes • 1777 from Cumberland and Chesterfield • Congressman and fur trader William Henry Ashley • Tobacco, corn, barley, wheat, hay, alfalfa, soybeans, cattle, dairying.

PRINCE EDWARD *Farmville* • 19,720 • 353 • Central VA, bounded on the north by the Appomattox River and on the south in part by the Nottoway River. Twin Lakes State Park and Prince Edward-Gallion State Forest are located in the county. • Named for Prince Edward Augustus (1739–1767), grandson of King George II • 1752, 1753, or 1754 from Amelia • Physician and amateur astronomer Henry Draper; MO governor and Confederate general Sterling Price; senator Blanche K. Bruce • Wheat, barley, tobacco, hay, corn, hogs, dairying; some timber; education (Hampden-Sydney College; Longwood College).

PRINCE GEORGE *Prince George* • 33,047 • 266 • Eastern VA, in the Tidewater region; bounded on the northwest by the Appomattox River and on the north by the James River; drained by the Blackwater River. Fort Lee Military Reservation is here. The cities of Hopewell and Petersburg are independent of the county. • One of two counties (the other, Prince George's, in MD) named for George of Denmark (1653–1708), husband of Queen Anne of England • Probably 1703 from Charles City • Petersburg National Battlefield, lying partly in the county, was the site of the Union Army's ten-month campaign in 1864–65 to seize the town of Petersburg, center of the railroads supplying Richmond and General Robert E. Lee's Army. • Political leader John Randolph • Peanuts, corn, wheat, barley, hay, soybeans, cotton, melons, poultry, cattle, hogs. • The Softball Hall of Fame is located here.

PRINCE WILLIAM *Manassas* • 280,813 (the second most populated county in VA) • 338 • Northern VA, bounded on the east by the Potomac River and on the northeast and north by the Occoquan and Bull Run rivers. Though serving as seat for the county, Manassas is otherwise independent. Manassas Park is also independent of the county. Prince William is becoming more urbanized as part of the Washington D.C. metropolitan area. It is the site of Potomac Mills, one of the largest shopping centers in the U.S. Manassas National Battlefield is in the north. Prince William Forest Park, a unit of the National Capital Parks system, is in the southeast. The county also contains Leesylvania State Park and part of Quantico U.S. Marine Corps Base. • Named for Prince William Augustus (1721–65), Duke of Cumberland, son of George II of England • 1730 or 1731 from King George and Stafford • During the American Revolution, colonial vessels were serviced in Quantico. The Civil War battles of First and Second Manassas were fought in the county on July 21, 1861, and Aug. 28–30, 1862, the 1861 battle a first test of military prowess for both sides. Here, Confederate Brigadier General Thomas J. Jackson acquired his nickname "Stonewall." • Senator Blanche K. Bruce • Corn, wheat, barley, hay, alfalfa, soybeans, tobacco, cattle, sheep, hogs, dairying.

PULASKI *Pulaski* • 35,127 • 320 • Southwestern VA, in the Great Appalachian Valley; drained by the New River, here dammed to form Claytor Lake. The county is traversed by ridges and has mineral springs. It includes Jefferson National Forest, and New River Trail and Claytor Lake state parks. The city of Radford is independent of the county. • One of seven counties named for Count Casimir Pulaski (1748–79), Polish soldier who fought for America during the Revolutionary War • 1839 from Montgomery and Wythe • Manufacturing; hay, alfalfa, corn, cattle, sheep, dairying; timber; anthracite coal, iron and zinc mining.

RAPPAHANNOCK *Washington* • 6,983 • 267 • Northern VA, in the Piedmont, rising to the Blue Ridge in the west and northwest, bounded on the northeast by the Rappahannock River; drained by the Thornton and Hughes rivers. The county includes part of Shenandoah National Park. The Appalachian Trail follows the county's northwest boundary. • Named for the Rappahannock River • 1833 from Culpeper County (not to be confused with Old Rappahannock County, with county seat at Lancaster organized 1656 from Lancaster County and abolished 1692) • Hay, alfalfa, apples, peaches, cattle.

RICHMOND (one of four counties so named) *Warsaw* • 8,809 • 191 • Eastern VA, on the Northern Neck peninsula, bounded on the southwest by the Rappahannock River. Rappahannock National Wildlife Refuge is here. • Named for either Richmond, England, or for Charles Lennox, Duke of Richmond (1672–1723) • 1691 or 1692 from Old Rappahannock County, which was organized in 1656 from Lancaster County and abolished in 1692 • Capitalist & railroad builder Mark Hopkins • Barley, wheat, hay, corn, soybeans, cattle; pine; fish and shellfish industries.

ROANOKE *Salem* • 85,778 • 251 • Southwestern VA, in the Great Appalachian Valley; drained by the Roanoke River. The Brush Mountain Ridge is in the northwest and the Blue Ridge is in the southeast. The county includes part of Jefferson National Forest, Poor Mountain Natural Area Preserve, Havens State Wildlife Management Area, and Dixie Caverns. The Blue Ridge Parkway passes through the southeast. The Appalachian Trail also crosses the county. The city of Roanoke is independent of the county. Salem, though serving as county seat, is also independent. • Named for the Roanoke River • 1838 from Botetourt and Montgomery • Hay, alfalfa, apples, peaches, cattle, poultry; diversified industries; education (Hollins U.) • Vinton, known as the "Dogwood Capital of VA," holds a special celebration each spring at the peak of the blossoms.

ROCKBRIDGE *Lexington* • 20,808 • 600 • Central VA; drained by the Maury and Calfpasture rivers. The northern section of the county is at the southern end of the Shenandoah Valley, with the Allegheny Mountains in the northwest and the Blue Ridge in the southeast. The county includes parts of the George Washington National Forest. It also contains mineral springs. Natural Bridge and Caverns of Natural Bridge are in the south. Goshen Pass Natural Area is on the Calfpasture River. The city of Buena Vista is independent of the county. Though serving as seat for the county, Lexington is also independent. • Named for the natural rock bridge over Cedar Creek • 1778 from Augusta and Botetourt • TX Republic president Sam Houston; industrialist and inventor Cyrus Hall McCormick (His farm and birthplace exhibits include a model of his invention, the first reaper; the house sits squarely on the boundary line between Augusta and Rockbridge counties.) • Manufacturing; hay, alfalfa, corn, soybeans, apples, peaches, cattle, sheep, hogs, horses, dairying; timber; limestone quarrying • As a surveyor, young George Washington carved his initials on the natural rock bridge here. In 1774, Thomas Jefferson purchased it.

ROCKINGHAM *Harrisonburg* • 67,725 • 851 (the third largest county in VA) • Northwestern VA, bounded on the northwest and northeast in part by the WV state line; drained by the North River, which joins the South River to form the South Fork of the Shenandoah River. The county lies partly in the central Shenandoah Valley. The Allegheny Mountains are in the west and northwest. The Massanutten Mountain Ridge and Blue Ridge are also here. The county includes End-

less Caverns, Paul State Forest and parts of George Washington National Forest. Part of Shenandoah National Park lies along the southeastern border as do the Appalachian Trail and Skyline Drive. Though serving as seat for the county, Harrisonburg is otherwise independent. • One of three counties named for Charles Watson-Wentworth (1730–82), 2nd Marquess of Rockingham, prime minister of England who was largely responsible for the repeal of the Stamp Act • 1778 from Augusta • Manufacturing; hay, alfalfa, wheat, corn, soybeans, apples, peaches, poultry, cattle, sheep, hogs, dairying; timber; limestone quarrying; trout; education (Bridgewater College).

RUSSELL (one of four counties so named) *Lebanon* • 30,308 • 475 • Southwestern VA, in the Allegheny Mountains, bounded on the southeastern border by Clinch Mountain; drained by the Clinch River (forming part of the southwestern boundary) and Copper Creek. Part of Jefferson National Forest is in the southeast. Pinnacle Natural Area Preserve is also in the county. • One of two counties (the other in KY) named for William Russell (1758–1825), VA officer in the Revolutionary War, and VA and KY legislator • 1786 from Washington • Sociologist and social psychologist W.I. Thomas • Cattle, sheep, tobacco, hay, alfalfa, corn, dairying; mining of bituminous coal, some lead and zinc.

SCOTT (one of eleven counties so named) *Gate City* • 23,403 • 537 • Southwestern VA, partly in the Allegheny Mountains, bounded on the south by the TN state line; drained by the Clinch River, the North Fork of the Holston River, and by Copper Creek. The county is crossed by parts of the Clinch Mountain and Powell Mountain ridges. Found here are Natural Tunnel State Park (which includes an 850-foot-long tunnel cut by an underground river) and part of Jefferson National Forest, including Falls of Little Stony. • One of five counties named for General Winfield Scott (1786–1866), officer during the War of 1812 and the Mexican War; general in chief of the U.S. Army and commander of the Union armies at the beginning of the Civil War • 1814 from Lee, Russell, and Washington • Tobacco, corn, hay, alfalfa, cattle, sheep, dairying; timber; bituminous-coal mining.

SHENANDOAH *Woodstock* • 35,075 • 512 • Northwestern VA, in the Shenandoah Valley, bounded on the northwest by the WV state line and the Allegheny Mountains, and on the southeast by the Massanutten Mountain Ridge; drained by the North Fork of the Shenandoah River and Cedar Creek. The county has mineral springs. Parts of George Washington National Forest are here, as is Shenandoah Caverns. • Named for the Shenandoah River • Organized as Dunmore in 1772 from Frederick; name changed 1777 • New Market Battlefield Park was the site of a May 15, 1864 Civil War battle in which boy-cadets from the Virginia Military Institute under Confederate General Scott Schipp distinguished themselves against the seasoned forces of Union Franz Sigel. After a train raid in Martinsburg, WV, General Stonewall Jackson rolled the Union locomotives into the train station at Strasburg, now a museum. Shenvalee, a historic plantation house, held Italian detainees with diplomatic rank during World War II. • First governor of TN John Sevier • Manufacturing; wheat, corn, barley, alfalfa, soybeans, hay, apples, peaches, poultry, dairy and beef cattle, sheep, hogs; timber; limestone quarrying; resort tourism.

SMYTH *Marion* • 33,081 • 452 • Southwestern VA, in the Great Appalachian Valley; drained by the North, Middle, and South forks of the Holston River. Walker Mountain is in the north. Peaks of the Iron Mountains are in the south, including Mount Rogers on the county border with Grayson; at 5,729 feet, it is the highest mountain in VA. The county includes Hungry Mother State Park, parts of Jefferson National Forest, and part of Mount Rogers National Recreation Area. The county is crossed in the southeast by the Appalachian Trail. • Named for General Alexander Smyth (1765–1830), U.S. representative from VA • 1832 from Washington and Wythe • Tobacco, hay, alfalfa, corn, vegetables, fruit, cattle, sheep, dairying; timber; salt and gypsum mining; limestone quarrying; manufacturing.

SOUTHAMPTON *Courtland* • 17,482 • 600 • Southeastern VA, in the Tidewater region, bounded on the south by the NC state line, on the west by the Meherrin River, and on the east by the Blackwater River; drained by the Nottoway River. The Independent city of Franklin in the east is separate from the county. • Named for the Southampton Hundred, a political subdivision in VA • 1748 or 1749 from Isle of Wight and Nansemond • The county was the site of Nat Turner's Rebellion. During the 1831 revolt, more whites were killed by Turner and his fellow slaves than during any other slave revolt in U.S. history. • Hay, peanuts, wheat, cotton, corn, soybeans, melons, cattle, hogs; timber.

SPOTSYLVANIA *Spotsylvania* • 90,395 • 401 • Northeastern VA, bounded on the northeast by the Rappahannock and Rapidan rivers and on the south by the North Anna River (forming Lake Anna reservoir); drained by the Mattaponi River. Lake Anna State Park is on Lake Anna reservoir. The city of Fredericksburg is independent of the county. • Named for Alexander Spotswood (1676–1740), lieutenant governor of the colony of VA and postmaster general for the American colonies • 1720 or 1721 from Essex, King William, and King and Queen • The county was formerly part of the estate of Alexander Spotswood, VA Colonial governor. It was the scene of several Civil War engagements, including the battles of the Wilderness, Chancellorsville, and Spotsylvania Courthouse (sites which are now part of Fredericksburg and Spotsylvania National Military Park). • Pioneer hydrographer Matthew F. Maury; Methodist Episcopal bishop Francis Asbury died here. • Soybeans, wheat, corn, hay, alfalfa, barley, cattle, dairying; light manufacturing.

STAFFORD (one of two counties so named, the other in KS) *Stafford* • 92,446 • 270 • Northeastern VA, bounded on the east by the Potomac River (forming the MD state line), and on the southwest and south by the Rappahannock River;

drained by Aquia Creek. Part of Fredericksburg and Spotsylvania National Military Park is in the south. A large part of Quantico U.S. Marine Corps Base is in the north. Established in 1917, the base still provides Marine Corps officers with basic training. • Named for Staffordshire, England • 1664 or 1666 from Westmoreland • Gold was formerly mined in the county. • Physician Kate Barrett; abolitionist Moncure D. Conway; U.S. Supreme Court justice Peter V. Daniel • Wheat, corn, soybeans, hay, tobacco, cattle, poultry.

SURRY (one of two counties so named, the other in NC) *Surry* • 6,829 • 279 • Southeastern VA, in the Tidewater region, bounded on the north and northeast by the James River and on the south in part by the Blackwater River. The county contains Chippokes Plantation State Park. • Named for Surrey County, England; the spelling is a clerical error • 1652 from James City • Peanuts, corn, wheat, soybeans, melons, cattle, hogs, dairying; timber.

SUSSEX *Sussex* • 12,504 • 491 • Southeastern VA, in the Tidewater region, bounded on the northeast in part by the Blackwater River; drained by the Nottoway River (which forms part of the southwestern boundary) and Stony Creek. • One of three counties named for Sussex County in England • 1753 or 1754 from Surry • Peanuts, wheat, soybeans, corn, tobacco, melons, hogs, cattle, poultry; timber.

TAZEWELL (one of two counties so named, the other in IL) *Tazewell* • 44,598 • 520 • Southwestern VA, in the Allegheny Mountains, bounded on the north by the WV state line; drained by the Clinch River. The county includes parts of Jefferson National Forest in the south and east. The Appalachian Trail follows part of the southeastern boundary. • Named for Henry Tazewell (1753–99), jurist and U.S. senator from VA • 1799 from Russell and Wythe • Corn, tobacco, hay, alfalfa, cattle, sheep, hogs, dairying; timber; limestone quarrying, bituminous-coal mining; manufacturing.

WARREN *Front Royal* • 31,584 •214 • Northern VA, in the Shenandoah Valley. The Blue Ridge is in the east; part of Massanutten Mountain is in the west. The county includes part of Shenandoah National Park (including the northern part of Skyline Drive). The north and south forks of the Shenandoah River join in the north to form the river. Part of George Washington National Forest is here and includes Raymond "Andy" Guest Shenandoah River State Park. The Appalachian Trail follows the eastern boundary of the county. • One of fourteen counties named for Gen. Joseph Warren (1741–75), Revolutionary War patriot and member of the Committee of Safety who sent Paul Revere on his famous ride • 1836 from Frederick and Shenandoah • The Belle Boyd Cottage in Front Royal was the home of the Confederate spy whose pillow talk with Union lovers led to a surprise victory for the South at the Battle of Front Royal in 1862. • Dairying, apples, peaches, corn, wheat, hay, alfalfa; limestone quarrying; manufacturing; tourism; education (Christendom College) • Skyline Caverns features anthodites, unique rock formations that grow only one inch every 7,000 years.

WASHINGTON *Abingdon* • 51,103 • 564 • Southwestern VA, bounded on the south by the TN state line; drained by the North, Middle, and South forks of the Holston River. Part of South Holston Reservoir is in the south. The county is in the Great Appalachian Valley and includes parts of Clinch Mountain, Walker Mountain, and the Iron Mountains. It includes part of Jefferson National Forest and a section of the Appalachian Trail in the Mount Rogers National Recreation Area. The city of Bristol is independent of the county. • One of thirty-one counties named for George Washington • 1776 from Fincastle (organized 1772 from Botetourt and abolished 1777) and Montgomery counties • Blacks Fort, built in 1776, was attacked by Indians in the late 18th century. The town of Abingdon was burned by Union troops in 1864. The county lay at the center of a boundary dispute with TN, resulting in the placement of the state line down the center of the main thoroughfare of the dual city of Bristol in 1903. • Politician John B. Floyd died here. • Cattle, sheep, poultry, dairying, tobacco, hay, alfalfa, corn; limestone, gypsum mining • The Barter Theatre in Abingdon (1933), a well known regional theatre, accepted farm produce for admission during the Depression.

WESTMORELAND *Montross* • 16,718 • 229 • Eastern VA, in the northern part of the Northern Neck peninsula, bounded on the northeast by the Potomac River estuary (the shore forming the MD boundary), and on the southwest in part by the Rappahannock River. Westmoreland State Park is here. • One of two counties (the other in PA) named for Westmoreland County in England • 1653 from Northumberland • President George Washington (George Washington Birthplace National Monument); Confederate General Robert E. Lee (Stratford Hall Plantation); President James Monroe; colonial landowner and feminist Margaret Brent; diplomat Arthur Lee • Fish, oysters, crabs; seafood canning; barley, wheat, corn, soybeans, tomatoes, tobacco, hay, cattle, poultry • The great hall of Stratford Hall Plantation is one of the best examples of colonial design to have survived to present day.

WISE (one of two counties so named, the other in TX) *Wise* • 40,123 • 403 • Southwestern VA, bounded on the northwest by the KY state line and on the south in part by the Clinch River; drained by the North Fork of the Pound River, and Powell and Clinch rivers. The county lies in the Cumberland Mountains. The city of Norton is independent of the county.

Much of the county is in Jefferson National Forest and includes High Knob Recreation Area. • Named for General Henry A. Wise (1806–76), U.S. representative from VA, governor of VA, and officer in the Army of Confederacy • 1856 from Lee, Russell and Scott • Hay, tobacco, cattle; timber; limestone, bituminous-coal fields, iron mines; education (U. of VA College at Wise) • Harry W. Meador, Jr. Coal Museum in Big Stone Gap explains the industry, which has supported the local economy for over a century.

WYTHE *Wytheville* • 27,599 • 463 • Southwestern VA; drained by the New River. The county lies partly in the Great Appalachian Valley with the Allegheny Mountains in the north and northwest. Part of the Iron Mountains are in the south. The county includes part of Jefferson National Forest and part of Mount Rogers National Recreational Area. The Appalachian Trail crosses in the northwest. Shot Tower Historic State Park in the east features a circa 1807 stone tower used for the production of lead round shot; the lead was mined from nearby Austinville, birthplace of Texas colonizer Stephen F. Austin. • Named for George Wythe (1726–1806), first law professor in the U.S. and signer of the Declaration of Independence • 1789 or 1790 from Montgomery • Newspaper editor William G. Brownlow. Confederate general William J. Hardee died here • Cabbage, corn, hay, alfalfa, potatoes, cattle, sheep, hogs, dairying; timber; lead, zinc mines, limestone.

YORK (one of five counties so named) *Yorktown* • 56,297 • 106 (one of the fifty smallest counties in the U.S.) • Southeastern VA, in the Tidewater region, bounded on the northeast by the York River estuary and on the east by Chesapeake Bay. Yorktown is part of Colonial National Historical Park, which includes the Colonial Parkway to Williamsburg and Jamestown. • Named for either King James II (1633–1701), born Duke of York, or for Yorkshire, England • Organized as Charles River County 1634; name changed 1643 • Yorktown's Colonial Custom House (1706) is regarded as the cradle of the American tariff system. Yorktown was the site of the last decisive battle of the Revolutionary War, culminating in the surrender of General Charles Cornwallis on October 19, 1781. Articles of capitulation between Cornwallis and General Washington were negotiated the day before in the Moore House. Congress authorized the ninety-five-foot-high Yorktown Victory Monument overlooking the York River that same year. Yorktown was captured by Union General George B. McClellan on his drive toward Richmond in 1862. • Live-

WASHINGTON

By and By

Most of Washington's thirty-nine counties have three-member boards of commissioners with both executive and legislative powers, each member commissioner elected to a four-year term. Other county officials are the prosecuting attorney, superintendent of schools, sheriff, treasurer, and clerk. King County has a council-manager government with a county executive and nine-member county council.

ADAMS (one of twelve counties so named) *Ritzville* • 16,428 • 1,925 • Southeastern WA, bounded on the southeast by the Palouse River; drained by Cow Creek, which forms Sprague Lake. Part of Columbia National Wildlife Refuge is in the southwest. • One of eight counties named for President John Adams • 1883 from Whitman (prior to statehood) • Onions, asparagus, peppermint, potatoes, beans, alfalfa, hay, cattle, hogs, corn, wheat, oats, fruit, dairying.

ASOTIN *Asotin* • 20,551 • 636 • Extreme southeastern WA, bounded on the south by the OR state line and on the east by the ID state line (formed by the Snake River); watered by the Grande Ronde River and by Joseph and Asotin creeks. The Blue Mountains cross in the southwest. Part of Umatilla National Forest extends along its western border. Fields Spring State Park is in the south. • Named for the town of Assotin City, Washington Territory • 1883 from Garfield (prior to statehood); in 1886 the spelling was changed for both the county and the city. • Alfalfa, hay, fruit, wheat, barley; timber.

BENTON (one of nine counties so named) *Prosser* • 142,475 • 1,703 • Southern WA, bounded on the north, east, and south by the Columbia River (forming the OR state line in the south); bisected by the Yakima River, which merges with the Columbia River in the east. Horse Heaven and Rattlesnake hills extend into the county from the west. Umatillo National Wildlife Refuge and Crow Butte State Park border Lake Umatillo reservoir in the southwest. The county also includes part of Hanford Reach National Monument. • One of seven counties named for Thomas Hart Benton (1782–1858), U.S. journalist and statesman • 1905 from Yakima and Klickitat • Apples, pears, peaches, grapes, cherries, hops, corn, beans, sugar beets, onions, carrots, asparagus, potatoes, alfalfa, hay, wheat, cattle, sheep; food processing and shipping; manufacture of chemicals, printed materials, pulp paper; education (WA State U. Tri–Cities) • A large part of the U.S. Department of Energy Hanford Site is here. A major atomic energy facility, it was established in 1944 as a development point for the atomic bomb. Constructed by E.I. de Pont de Nemours, Inc., it was taken over by the Atomic Energy Commission in 1947. The burial and above-ground storage of atomic by-products in the county is an ongoing controversy.

CHELAN *Wenatchee* • 66,616 • 2,922 (the third largest county in WA) • Central WA, bounded on the southeast by the Columbia River (here forming Lake Entiat reservoir); drained by numerous creeks and rivers. The Cascade Range dominates in the west. The Pacific Crest National Scenic Trail closely parallels part of the western border. Wenatchee National Forest (its headquarters in Wenatchee) covers most of the county. It also contains parts of Glacier Peak and Lake Chelan-Sawtooth wilderness areas, Lincoln Rock and Wenatchee Confluence state parks, Chelan National Recreation Area and part of the southern unit of North Cascades National Park. The county includes Squilchuck, Lake Chelan, Lake Wenatchee, Peshastin Pinnacles, and Twenty-five Mile Creek state parks. • Named for Lake Chelan • 1899 from Kittitas and Okanogan • Aviator Clyde Pangborn • Apples, pears, alfalfa, hay, wheat, barley, livestock; lumber; gold; resort tourism; aluminum reduction; education (Wenatchee Valley College, Washington State University's Tree Fruit Experiment Station) • Wenatchee claims the title, "Apple Capital of the World" and hosts the Washington State Apple Blossom Festival every spring. The U.S. Public Health Service Toxicology Laboratory is in Wenatchee, as is the North Central Regional Library, which serves readers over a 15,000 square mile area.

CLALLAM *Port Angeles* • 64,525 • 1,745 • Northwestern WA, bounded on the west by the Pacific Ocean, and on the north by the Strait of Juan de Fuca, forming the U.S.–Canada (British Columbia) border; drained by the Elwha, Bogachiel, and Sol Duc (Soleduck) rivers. The county contains part of Olympic National Forest; Flattery Rocks, Dungeness, and Protection Island national wildlife refuges; and Sequim Bay and Bogachiel state parks. Indian reservations in the county include Makah, Ozette, Jamestown S'Kallam, and Lower Elwha. Cape Flattery is on the northwest tip of the county. The Olympic Mountains rise in the south. The county includes parts of Olympic National Park (its headquarters in Port Angeles), the world's finest remnant of Pacific Northwest rain forest. • Named for the Clallam Indian tribe • Organized as Clalm County in 1854 (prior to statehood) from Jefferson County; spelling changed soon thereafter • Commercial fishing; timber; dairying; paper and pulp mills; resorts • Port Angeles is known for its annual Salmon Derby.

CLARK (one of twelve counties so named) *Vancouver* • 345,238 (45% increase since 1990; the fastest growing and fifth most populated county in WA) • 628 • Southwestern

WA; bounded on the south and west by the Columbia River (forming the OR state line), on the north by the Lewis River, which forms Lake Merwin reservoir in the north, and Yale Lake reservoir in the northeast. Ridgefield National Wildlife Refuge is in the west on the Columbia River. A small part of Gifford Pinchot National Forest (its headquarters in Vancouver) is on the eastern border. Also in the county are Steigerwald Lake National Wildlife Refuge, and Battle Ground Lake and Paradise Point state parks. • One of three counties named for William Clark (1770–1838), explorer and co-leader of the Lewis and Clark expedition • Original county, organized as Vancouver County 1845; name changed to Clark in 1849 • From 1825 to 1849 Fort Vancouver (national historic site) was the western headquarters for the Hudson's Bay Company's fur trading operations. It became the center of political, cultural, commercial, and manufacturing activities in the Pacific Northwest. The first steamboat (*SS Beaver*) to operate on the Pacific north of San Francisco made Vancouver its home port in 1836. The city was a U.S. military reservation (Vancouver Barracks) in 1848. • Blueberries, raspberries, lettuce, potatoes, alfalfa, hay, barley, oats, dairying, poultry; lumbering; port operations (including the shipment of grain, lumber, paper, cable, and canned foods); education (Clark College; state schools for the deaf and blind) • Vancouver is a distribution center for hydroelectric power produced in the Columbia Basin.

COLUMBIA (one of eight counties so named) *Dayton* • 4,064 • 869 • Southeastern WA, bounded on the south by the OR state line and on the north by the Snake River (Little Goose dam forming Lake Herbert G. West); drained by the Tucannon River. Part of Umatilla National Forest is here, as are some of the Blue Mountains, which cross in the southeast. Lewis and Clark Trail State Park and Ski Bluewood ski area are also in the county. • Named for the Columbia River • 1875 (prior to statehood) from Walla Walla. Original legislation was passed naming the new county "Ping," but the governor vetoed the bill. • Wheat, barley, oats, peas, alfalfa, hay, apples, hogs, cattle; timber.

COWLITZ *Kelso* • 92,948 • 1,139 • Southwestern WA, bounded on the southwest by the Columbia River (forming the OR state line) and on the south by the Lewis River (forming Lake Merwin and Yale Lake reservoirs); watered by the Toutle, Kalama and Coweeman rivers. The foothills of the Cascade Range are in the east. Part of Mount Saint Helens National Volcanic Monument is also in the east. Part of Gifford Pinchot National Forest is here. Seaquest State Park is on the shore of Silver Lake reservoir. • Named for either the Cowlitz River or for the Cowlitz Indians • 1854 (prior to statehood) from Lewis County • Longview, one of the first planned cities in the U.S., was designed by the Long-Bell Lumber Company to resemble Washington, D.C. One of the world's great lumber centers, it was founded in 1922 on the site of old Monticello, where a convention met to seek creation of Washington Territory in 1852. • Peas, carrots, hay, dairying, poultry; limestone; timber; salmon; paper, wood, aluminum, paint; food

processing industries; education (Lower Columbia College) • Longview is the largest port on the Columbia River.

DOUGLAS *Waterville* • 32,603 • 1,821 • Central WA, bounded on the north and west by the Columbia River, forming Lake Entiat reservoir in the northwest and Rufus Woods Lake reservoir in the north. The east-boundary zigzags along the northwest side of Grand Coulee, touching Banks Lake reservoir at several points. The county includes Wenatchee Confluence, Lincoln Rock, and Daroga state parks. Grand Coulee Dam (often referred to as the "Eighth Wonder of the World') stands one mile beyond the northeast boundary, virtually where Douglas, Grant, and Okanogan counties meet. Part of Coulee Dam National Recreation Area is here, including Crown Point Overlook. Douglas Creek B.L.M. Recreation Site is in the county. • One of twelve counties named for Stephen Arnold Douglas (1813–61), U.S. orator and statesman • 1883 (prior to statehood) from Lincoln, just four days after Lincoln County was formed • Alfalfa, hay, wheat, barley, oats, rye, cattle, sheep • The town of Mansfield is known for its "Roving Parking Meter," which mysteriously moves around town.

FERRY *Republic* • 7,260 • 2,204 • Northeastern WA, bounded on the north by the Canadian province of British Columbia and on the south and east by the Columbia River (forming Franklin D. Roosevelt Lake reservoir); watered by the Sanpoil and Kettle rivers. The Kettle River forms part of the eastern boundary in the north. Lake Roosevelt National Recreation Area extends along the entire length of the reservoir. The Kettle River Range crosses north-south in the center. Part of Colville Indian Reservation dominates the southern half of the county. Parts of Colville National Forest are found throughout the northern half. Curlew Lake reservoir and State Park are in the northwest-center. • Named for Elisha P. Ferry (1825–95), first governor of the state of WA • Organized as Eureka from Stevens in 1899; name changed to Ferry that same year • Timber; gold, silver; hay, alfalfa, barley, oats, dairying, cattle.

FRANKLIN (one of twenty-five counties so named) *Pasco* • 49,347 • 1,242 • Southeastern WA, bounded on the west by the Columbia River (here forming Lake Wallala reservoir), on the southeast by the Snake River (here forming Lake Sacajawea reservoir), and on the extreme northeast by the Palouse River. Part of Hanford Reach National Monument is in the northwest. The county also contains Lyons Ferry and Sacajawea state parks, and part of Palouse Falls State Park. • One of twenty-three counties named for Benjamin Franklin • 1883 (prior to statehood) from Whitman • Wheat, alfalfa, hay, barley, oats, corn, onions, carrots, asparagus, potatoes, beans, sheep, hogs.

GARFIELD *Pomeroy* • 2,397 (the least populated county in WA) • 711 • Southeastern WA, in the Palouse region, bounded on the south by the OR state line and on the north by the

Snake River (forming Lower Granite Lake reservoir in the northeast). Part of Umatilla National Forest is in the south. Chief Timothy State Park adjoins the Snake River. • One of six counties named for President James Garfield • 1881 (prior to statehood) from Columbia • Apples, wheat, hay, alfalfa, barley, oats, hogs.

GRANT (one of fifteen counties so named) *Ephrata* • 74,698 • 2,676 (the fourth largest county in WA) • East-central WA, bounded on the south and southwest by the Columbia River. The northwestern border closely follows the Grand Coulee, touching Banks Lake and Lenore Lake reservoirs at several points. The Grand Coulee Dam (often called the "Eighth Wonder of the World") is located here near the convergence of three counties. The Saddle Mountains cross in the south. The county includes Lake Lenore Caves and Steamboat Rock, Sun Lakes, Summer Falls, and Moses Lake state parks. Potholes Reservoir dominates the southeast and adjoins Potholes State Park on its western shore. Several units of Columbia National Wildlife Refuge are also here. Part of Hanford Reach National Monument is on the southern border. • One of twelve counties name for President Ulysses S. Grant • 1909 from Douglas • Wheat, barley, oats, alfalfa, hay, sugar beets, potatoes, beans, corn, onions, peas, carrots, asparagus, peppermint, spearmint, cattle, sheep, hogs; food processing; tourism; diversified industry.

GRAYS HARBOR *Montesano* • 67,194 • 1,917 • Western WA, bounded on the west by the Pacific Ocean; drained by the Chehalis, Wynoochee, Humptulips, Quinault, and North rivers, and the West Fork of the Satsop River. Grays Harbor, an inlet of the Pacific, is in the southwest. The county includes parts of Olympic National Forest, Lower Chehalis State Forest and part of Capitol State Forest, Quinault Indian Reservation, and several state parks, most on the Pacific coast. Copalis National Wildlife Refuge is in the northwest. A small part of Olympic National Park borders Lake Quinault in the north. • Named for Grays Harbor, itself named for its discoverer Robert Gray (1755–1806) • Organized as Chehalis 1854 (prior to statehood); name changed 1915 • Pharmacologist George H. Hitchings; painter Robert Motherwell; physicist Douglas D. Osheroff • Peas, hay, cranberries, dairying; lumber; fishing, seafood, including oysters, clams, salmon; manufacture of metal products, wood products and pulp paper, fish byproducts; canning • The American tree farm system began in Montesano when the Weyerhaeuser Company built a 130,000-acre timber farm here in 1941. Washington State's largest tree, a western red cedar and the world's largest Sitka spruce are found in the Quinault Rain Forest. The coastal waters off Gray's Harbor are home to the gray whale.

ISLAND *Coupeville* • 71,558 • 209 • Northwestern WA. The county consists of Whidley Island and Camano Island in Puget Sound, and Smith Island in the Strait of Juan de Fuca. It is bounded by Skagit Bay, Davis Slough, and Port Susan Bay on the east, and by the main channel of Puget Sound on the southwest. Saratoga Passage separates the two northern is-

lands. Ebey's Landing, Camano Island, Deception Pass, Joseph Whidbey, and Fort Ebey state parks are in the county. • Given the name Island for the islands in Puget Sound • 1853 (prior to statehood) from either King or Thurston • Alfalfa, hay, berries, vegetables; fishing; summer resort tourism.

JEFFERSON *Port Townsend* • 25, 953 • 1,809 • Western WA, bounded on the west by the Pacific Ocean, on the east by Hood Canal and Puget Sound, and on the far northeast by the Strait of Juan de Fuca. It includes Hoh Indian Reservation and part of Quinault Indian Reservation. The lower half of Olympic National Park and the Olympic Mount. is (including Mount Olympus) divide the county, isolating the western part along the Pacific Coast from the eastern part on Puget Sound. Located in the county are Protection Island and Quillayute national wildlife refuges, and the southern part of the coastal section of Olympic National Park. The county has numerous state parks in the east. Parts of Olympic National Forest are here. It also includes Marrowstone and Indian islands in the northeast. • One of twenty-six counties named directly or indirectly for President Thomas Jefferson • Original county; organized 1852 (prior to statehood) • Timber, wood pulp; fish; cattle, dairying.

KING (one of two counties so named, the other in TX) *Seattle* • 1,737,034 (the most populated county in WA and the twelfth most populated county in the U.S.) • 2,126 • West-central WA, bounded on the west by Puget Sound and Colvos Passage, on the east by the crest of the Cascade Range, and on the south in part by the White River. Muckleshoot Indian Reservation is in the south. The county is part of a rapidly-expanding urban area, with strong growth in the west between the mountains and the Sound, around Seattle, and south toward Tacoma (just southwest of the county line). It includes part of Mount Baker-Snoqualmie National Forest and Alpine Lake Wilderness. State parks are distributed throughout. The county includes Vashon and Maury islands near Kitsap Peninsula in Puget Sound. • Originally for William Rufus King (1786–1853), U.S. senator from AL and vice president. In 1986 it was decided the name would honor Martin Luther King, Jr. (1929–68), slain civil rights leader • 1852 (prior to statehood) from Thurston • In 1889, an unattended glue pot ignited a fire, burning most of Seattle to the ground. The Klondike Gold Rush National Historic Park highlights the extensive preparation undertaken by gold seekers before leaving Seattle, a city that profited by an estimated $25,000,000 from outfitting prospectors. In 1889, city streets were raised eight to thirty-two inches above sidewalks and building entrances in an effort to escape mud and sewage, forcing citizens to climb ladders until the city relocated up to the new street level some five years later. Seattle held Century 21, a world's fair, in 1962. The first municipal monorail service in the U.S. began operating here that same year, connecting the fairgrounds to downtown Seattle. • Computer programmer and businessman William H. Gates; guitarist Jimi Hendrix; dancer and choreographer Robert Joffrey; striptease artist Gypsy Rose Lee; actor Carol

Channing • Truck farms, strawberries, lettuce, hay, dairying, poultry; lumber; clays, coal; high tech and internet industries; diversified manufacturing, including aircraft, aircraft parts, aerospace and spacecraft equipment (the Boeing Company produced the booster rocket for the Apollo/Saturn 5 moon landing of 1969 and the Lunar Rover), electric and electronic equipment, railroad cars, plastics, clay and ceramic industries, furniture, woodenware, glass, fishing tackle, telephone and switchboard equipment, fruit and vegetable canneries, cold-storage plants, greenhouses; commercial fishing • The county is headquarters for fourteen Fortune 1000 companies. • The Will Rogers Memorial recalls the origination in Renton of the last leg of Rogers' ill-fated flight around the world. • The Federal Aviation Administration air traffic control center in Auburn serves ID, AK, and WA. The city is also a regional General Services Administration distribution point for overseas shipment. Seattle is home to the Supersonics (Key-Arena at Seattle Center), Mariners (Safeco Field), and Seahawks (Seahawks Stadium).

KITSAP *Port Orchard* • 231,969 • 396 • Western WA, occupying the northern part of Kitsap peninsula, bounded on the west by Hood Canal and on the east by Puget Sound; deeply indented by Sinclair and Dyes inlets and Liberty Bay. Bainbridge Island is separated from the mainland by Port Orchard passage. Puget Sound Navy Yard, home to the U.S. Pacific Fleet, is in the county, as is the U.S. Naval Station at Bangor, which has Trident ballistic missile submarines. Also found here are Illahee, Scenic Beach, Fay Bainbridge, and Fort Ward state parks, Blake Island State Marine Park, and Port Madison Indian Reservation. • Named for a local Indian chief and medicine man • Organized as Slaughter County (prior to statehood) from Jefferson and King 1857; name changed later that year • Truck gardening; dairying, fruits, nuts, poultry, fish, crabs, oysters, clams; lumber; naval shops and dry docks • The battleship USS *Missouri*, upon which Japan surrendered to the U.S. and its allies (September 2, 1945), thus ending World War II, is anchored adjacent to Puget Sound Naval Yard in Bremerton.

KITTITAS *Ellensburg* • 33,362 • 2,297 • Central WA, bounded on the southwest by the Naches and Little Naches rivers, and on the east by the Columbia River (forming Wanapum Lake reservoir); drained by the Yakima River. The Wenatchee Mountains extend along the northeast border and the Saddle Mountains cross in the southeast. Part of Mount Baker-Snoqualmie and Wenatchee national forests cover much of the western half of the county. Wanapum, Olmstead Place, Lake Easton, and Iron Horse state parks are here. The county includes Kachess, Cle Elum, and Priest Rapids Lake reservoirs. Several ski areas are also here. Part of U.S. Military Reservation Yakima Training Center is in the southeast. • Kittitas is an Indian word, its meaning uncertain • 1883 (prior to statehood) from Yakima • Potatoes, alfalfa, hay, wheat, barley, oats, peas, cattle, sheep, dairying; lumber; coal, gold, silica; education (Central WA U.); tourism (dude ranches); meat-

packing, canning • Ellensburg is the site of the state's major rodeo • Ginkgo Petrified Forest State Park, at 7,184 acres, is one of the world's largest petrified forests, with numerous species of agatized wood.

KLICKITAT *Goldendale* • 19,161 • 1,872 • Southern WA, bounded on the southwest by the Columbia River (forming the OR state line); drained by the Klickitat River (designated here a National Recreational River) and White Salmon River (forming part of the western boundary). The county includes part of Yakima Indian Reservation along its northern boundary. The Columbia River Gorge National Scenic Area extends along the southern boundary. Also here are Conboy Lake National Wildlife Refuge and several state parks. • Named for the Klikitat Indians • Created in 1859 as Clickitat prior to statehood (original county); present spelling came into use in 1869 • Lumbering; carrots, potatoes, alfalfa, hay, wheat, oats, grapes, pears, apples, cattle • The Goldendale Observatory (state park) is the site of the nation's largest telescope available for public use. • As a memorial to slain World War I soldiers of the county, Samuel Hill built a reproduction of Stonehenge near Goldendale. • The Maryhill Museum of Art contains one of the country's most outstanding collections of Native American basketry.

LEWIS (one of seven counties so named) *Chehalis* • 68,600 • 2,408 • Southwestern WA; drained by the Cowlitz and Chehalis rivers. The Pacific Crest national Scenic Trail closely parallels the eastern border. Riffa Lake (Mossyrock Dam) and Mayfield Lake (Mayfield Dam) reservoirs are here. The county includes parts of Mount Baker-Snoqualmie and Gifford Pinchot national forests and part of Mount Rainier National Park. Also in the county are Tatoosh Wilderness Area and parts of Goat Rocks and William O. Douglas wilderness areas. Lewis and Clark and Ike Kinswa state parks are in the center of the county, Rainbow Falls State Park in the west. • One of five counties named for Meriwether Lewis (1774–1809), co-leader of the Lewis and Clark expedition (1804–06) • 1845 prior to statehood (original county) • In the mid 19th century, the site that would become Centralia was a stopover point for stagecoaches. In 1919, four American Legionnaires were killed and one member of the Industrial Workers of the World lynched, after a Legion parade was fired upon in front of the IWW hall. • Dancer and choreographer Merce Cunningham • Peas, alfalfa, hay, oats, vegetables, berries, dairying, poultry; quicksilver; lumber; food processing; manufacture of wood products, gloves, cement products, abrasives; forestry research.

LINCOLN (one of twenty-four counties so named) *Davenport* • 10,184 • 2,311 • Eastern WA, bounded on the north by the Spokane and Columbia rivers (the latter forming Franklin D. Roosevelt Lake reservoir). Little Falls and Long Lake dams impound the Spokane River here. Lake Roosevelt National Recreation Area extends along much of the northern boundary. • One of eighteen counties named for President Abraham Lincoln • 1883 (prior to statehood) from Spokane • Potatoes, wheat, alfalfa, hay, barley, oats, rye.

MASON (one of six counties so named) *Shelton* • 49,405 • 961 • Western WA, indented in the northeast by Hood Canal. Olympic National Park dips into the county in the extreme northwest. Also in the northwest is part of Olympic National Forest. Tahuya State Forest is in the northeast. Several state parks are here. • Named for Charles H. Mason (1830–1859), secretary and sometimes acting governor of WA Territory • Organized as Sawamish in 1854 from Thurston; name changed 1864 • Timber; fish, clams, oysters; hay, dairying, poultry.

OKANOGAN *Okanogan* • 39,564 • 5,268 (the largest county in WA) • Northern WA, bounded on the north by Canada (British Columbia) and on the south by the Columbia River, forming Lake Entiat and Rufus Woods Lake; drained by numerous rivers, including the Okanogan and Methow. The Cascade Mountains are in the west. The county includes part of Colville National Forest, Loomis and Loup Loup state forests, and several state parks. Nearly all of the largest unit of Okanogan National Forest is in the west, including Pasayten and part of Lake Chelan-Sawtooth wilderness areas. Several smaller sections of Okanogan National Forest are in the northeast. Roughly half of Colville Indian Reservation is in the southeast. • Okanogan is an Indian word with its meaning unclear • 1888 (prior to statehood) from Stevens • Timber; apples, barley, oats, alfalfa, wheat, cattle, sheep; gold, silver, copper; recreational tourism, ski resorts. • The county includes the final site of the Nez Perce National Historic Park (Chief Joseph Memorial).

PACIFIC *South Bend* • 20,984 • 975 • Southwestern WA, bounded on the west by the Pacific Ocean, and on the south by the Columbia River, forming the OR state line. The county includes Grayland Beach, Leadbetter Point, Pacific Pines, Loomis Lake, Fort Canby, and Fort Columbia state parks, and Shoalwater Bay Indian Reservation. Willapa Bay, arm of the Pacific, is in the west, separated from the ocean by the North Beach Peninsula, its entrance in the northwest. Willapa National Wildlife Refuge is on Long Island at the southern end of the bay, and on Leadbetter Point. • Named for the Pacific Ocean • 1851 prior to statehood (original county) • Timber; dairying, hay; fish, shellfish, crabs, oysters • The county includes an area known locally as "Washaway Beach," which is considered the fastest eroding area in America, losing almost three miles of land in the last 100 years. Willapa Bay is considered one of the cleanest estuaries in the lower forty-eight states, and grows about one sixth of the oysters harvested in the U.S. The World Kite Museum is located on North Beach Peninsula.

PEND OREILLE *Newport* • 11,732 • 1,400 • Northeastern WA, bounded on the east by the ID state line and on the north by the Canadian province of British Columbia; drained by the Pend Oreille River. The Selkirk Mountains cross in the northwest. Parts of Colville and Kaniksu national forests cover over three-quarters of the county. Crawford State Park and Boundary Dam B.L.M. Recreation Site are on the northern border. • Named for the Pend d'Oreille Indians • 1911 from Stevens •

Alfalfa, hay, oats, dairying; gold, silver, copper, lead • Pend Oreille boasts Roosevelt Grove of Ancient Cedars, an extensive stand of massive cedar trees. Osprey nesting sites are found along the Pend Oreille River in the southern part of the county. The caves of Manresa Grotto, on Kalispel Indian Reservation, were used for ceremonies by Indians and early white settlers. A winter feeding station for big horn sheep is found at the southern end of Sullivan Lake.

PIERCE (One of five counties so named) *Tacoma* • 700,820 (the second most populated county in WA) • 1,676 • West-central WA, bounded on the east by the crest of the Cascade Range; drained by the White (forming part of the northern boundary), Puyallup, Nisqually (forming most of the southern and southwestern boundary), and Carbon rivers. There is urbanization around Tacoma and along Puget Sound. The Pacific Crest National Scenic Trail closely parallels the county's eastern border. Fort Lewis Military Reservation and McChord Air Force Base are here. The county includes the southeastern part of Kitsap Peninsula, separated from the rest of the county by Puget Sound. It also includes McNeil, Fox, and Anderson islands in Puget Sound, Kopachuck, Federation Forest, and Penrose Point state parks, Crystal Mountain Ski Resort, part of Mount Baker-Snoqualmie National Forest, and Clearwater and part of Norse Peak wilderness areas. Most of Mount Rainier National Park is in the county. At 14,410 feet, the mountain's summit is the highest point in WA. • One of four counties named for President Franklin Pierce • 1852 prior to statehood (original county) • Physical chemist Philip H. Abelson; singer Bing Crosby; presidential assistant John D. Ehrlichman • Lumber and lumber processing; berries, lettuce, hay, daffodil bulbs, fresh flowers, dairying, poultry, cattle; education (U. of Puget Sound; Pacific Lutheran U.); shipyards, smelters, foundries, food processing, electrochemical plants • Tacoma Narrows Bridge (1950) connecting Tacoma to the Olympic Peninsula replaces the original, which collapsed in 1940. A replica of the Hudson's Bay Company's 1833 Fort Nisqually is in Tacoma, as is the Washington State Historical Society. The greatest snowfall ever recorded in one season took place at Rainier Paradise Ranger Station from July 1971 through June 1972. A total of 1,122 inches of snow fell here.

SAN JUAN (one of four counties so named) *Friday Harbor* • 14,077 (40% increase since 1990; the second fastest growing county in WA) • 175 (the smallest county in WA) • Northwestern WA, bounded on the north by the Strait of Georgia, on the east by Rosario Strait, on the south by the Strait of Juan de Fuca, on the west by Haro Strait, and on the north and west by the Canadian province of British Columbia. The county includes the main islands (San Juan, Lopez and Orcas) of the San Juan Islands, an archipelago at the northern end of Puget Sound. It has seventeen state parks, including Moran, Lime Kiln Point and Spencer Spit. All others are marine parks on small offshore islands. Parts of San Juan Islands National Wildlife Refuge are found throughout the group of islands.

Jones Island National Wildlife and Migratory Bird Refuge is also here. • Named for San Juan Island • 1873 from Whatcom (prior to statehood) • San Juan was the scene of the so-called Pig War of 1859 and other events from 1853 to 1872 connected with final settlement of Oregon Territory's northern boundary (San Juan National Historic Park). • Hay, dairying, cattle; fish, oysters, crabs, prawns; lime.

SKAGIT *Mount Vernon* • 102,979 • 1,735 • Northwestern WA, bounded on the west by Rosario Strait, on the southwest by Skagit Bay (Puget Sound), and on the east by the crest of the Cascade Range; drained by the Skagit (designated here a National Recreational and Scenic River), Sauk, and Cascade rivers and South Fork of the Nooksack River. The Pacific Crest National Scenic Trail parallels the northeast border. The county also includes parts of Mount Baker-Snoqualmie National Forest, Lower Baker Dam on the Baker River, part of North Cascades National Park, and several state parks, including Rockport, Rasar, and Bay View. Numerous islands in the bay are also part of the county. • Named for either the Indian tribe or for the bay, river, delta, island, and/or mountain range with this name • 1883 from Whatcom (prior to statehood) • Berries, peas, carrots, potatoes, wheat, barley, oats, barley, hay, tulips, dairying, cattle, poultry; fish, oysters; deepwater shipping; oil refining; manufacture of chemicals, wood pulp, plywood, hardwood; fish-canning.

SKAMANIA *Stevenson* • 9,872 • 1657 • Southwestern WA, bounded on the south by the Columbia River (forming Bonneville reservoir and the OR state line); watered by the Lewis and Cispus rivers. The Cascade Range and the Pacific Crest National Scenic Trail cross from the southwest to the northeast. Part of Gifford Pinchot National Forest dominates the county. Indian Heaven and Trapper Creek Wilderness Area, Franz Lake and Pierce national wildlife refuges, Beacon Rock State Park, part of Mount Saint Helens National Volcanic Monument, Spirit Lake (the lake's elevation was raised by 200 feet after the landslide from the volcanic eruption swept through the area), and Swift Creek reservoir (Lewis River) are all in the county. • Skamania is an Indian word meaning "swift waters" • 1854 from Clark (prior to statehood) • Mount Saint Helens erupted on May 18, 25, and June 12, 1980, and transformed the surrounding landscape; the blast left fifty-seven dead. • Lumber; cattle, dairying, fruit, nuts.

SNOHOMISH *Everett* • 606,024 (the third most populated county in WA) • 2,090 • Northwestern WA, bounded on the east by the crest of the Cascade Range and on the west by Puget and Possession sounds, Port Susan and Skagit bays; drained by Skykomish, Sauk, Stillaguamish, and Snoqualmie rivers. The county is largely urbanized in the southwest as an extension of the Seattle metropolitan area. Glacier Peak is in the northeast. Mukeltio and Wenberg state parks are in the west. Also in the county are Wallace Falls and Mount Pilchuck state parks, Sultan-Pilchuck State Forest, Boulder River Wilderness Area, parts of Glacier Peak and Henry M. Jackson Wilderness Area, and Tulalip Indian Reservation. The eastern

part of the county is in Mount Baker-Snoqualmie National Forest. The Pacific Crest National Scenic Trail parallels part of the eastern border. • Named for the Snohomish Indians • 1861 from Island (prior to statehood) • Timber; gold, silver, copper, nickel, granite quarrying; strawberries, peas, hay, dairying, cattle, poultry; salmon, crabs, oysters, herring, prawns; boats, aircraft, finished lumber, plywood, pulp and paper products; foundries, machine shops; canning, frozen food packing. Covering more than 98 acres, Boeing's manufacturing plant in Everett is the world's largest building.

SPOKANE *Spokane* • 417,939 (the fourth most populated county in WA) • 1,764 • Eastern WA, bounded on the east by the ID state line and on the northwest by the Spokane River, here forming Long Lake reservoir; drained by the Spokane River and Hangman Creek. Mount Spokane State Park and ski area are here, as are Turnbull National Wildlife Refuge and Fairchild Air Force Base. Spokane Plains Battlefield is in the west. • Named for the Spokane Indians • Created in 1858 from Stevens (prior to statehood); its boundaries changed in 1859 and it was later abolished; recreated around 1864. • After incorporation in 1881, Spokane became known as the "Inland Empire" for its abundant waterpower and rich natural resources, and served as a trade and shipping point for eastern WA, northern ID, northeastern OR, western MT, and southern British Columbia. A large fire destroyed much of the city in 1889. It was rebuilt and reincorporated. Its Riverfront Park was the site of EXPO '74, a world's fair. • Timber; lettuce, alfalfa, hay, barley, oats, dairying, sheep, hogs; mining of gypsum, limestone, gold, silver, uranium, copper; processing of metal and food; aluminum reduction and rolling mills; education (Gonzaga U.; Whitworth College; Eastern WA U.) • Spokane is the birthplace of Father's Day, originated here by Sonora Louise Smart Dodd on June 19, 1910.

STEVENS (one of three counties so named) *Colville* • 40,066 • 2,478 (the fifth largest county in WA) • Northeastern WA, bounded on the north by the Canadian province of British Columbia, on the west by the Kettle River and the Columbia River, here forming Franklin D. Roosevelt Reservoir (Lake Roosevelt National Recreation Area extending along the entire length of the reservoir), and on the south by the Spokane River; watered by the Columbia and Colville rivers. The Selkirk Mountains cross in the east. The county includes Forty-Nine Degrees North ski area, a small part of Kaniksa National Forest, Little Pend Oreille National Wildlife Refuge, Crystal Falls State Park, parts of Colville National Forest, and Spokane Indian Reservation. • One of two counties (the other in MN) named for Gen. Isaac I. Stevens (1818–62), first governor of WA Territory • 1863 prior to statehood (original county) • Copper, gold, silver, zinc, marble, magnesium mining, stone quarries; alfalfa, hay, wheat, barley, oats, hogs, dairying; magnesite and cement processing.

THURSTON (one of two counties so named, the other in NE) *Olympia* • 207,355 • 727 • Western WA, bounded on the northeast by the Nisqually River (forming Alder Lake reservoir) and on the north by Puget Sound; drained by the Skookumchuck, Deschutes, and Black rivers. The county includes part of Capitol State Forest and a small part of Mount Baker-Snowqualmie National Forest. The county also contains part of Fort Lewis Military Reservation, Nisqually National Wildlife Refuge, Tolmie and Millersylvania state parks, and Mima Mounds National Archeological Park. It is indented by Eld, Budd, and Henderson inlets. • Named for Samuel R. Thurston (1816–1851), first delegate to Congress from the Oregon territory • 1852 from Lewis, prior to statehood • Lumber; coal; oysters; livestock, blueberries, carrots, hay, nuts, dairying, poultry; brewing; manufacture of plastics, mobile homes, foodstuffs; government operations; education (Evergreen State College). Olympia is an anchorage for the U.S. Maritime Administration fleet. • Olympia oysters are found only in Puget Sound. Every September and October salmon may be seen going up fish ladders at Capitol Lake and the Deschutes River. The deep-sea port of Olympia has served as the only capital of both the territory and state of WA and is headquarters for Olympic National Forest.

WAHKIAKUM *Cathlamet* • 3,824 • 264 • Southwestern WA, bounded on the south by the Columbia River (forming the OR state line). The county includes Puget Island in the Columbia River. Julia Butler Hansen National Wildlife Refuge is in the south. • Named for the Wahkiakum Indians, Chief Wahkiakum, and one of their villages • 1854 from Lewis, prior to statehood • Cattle, dairying, hay, potatoes; salmon and other fish; timber.

WALLA WALLA *Walla Walla* • 55,180 • 1,271 • Southeastern WA, bounded on the south by the OR state line, on the north and northwest by the Snake River (forming Lake Sacajawea reservoir and Lake Herbert G. West reservoir) and on the west by the Columbia River (forming Lake Wallula reservoir); drained by the Touchet and Walla rivers. A small part of Umatilla National Forest is in the county. • Walla Walla is an Indian word for water(s) • 1854 prior to statehood (original county) • In 1836, Marcus and Narcissa Whitman established a medical mission and way station on the Oregon Trail at what would become Walla Walla. They and eleven others were killed by the Cayuse in 1847 (Whitman Mission National Historic Site). The Idaho gold rush of 1861 brought pioneers to the area who turned to ranching and agriculture. • Army general Jonathan M. Wainwright • Truck farming, wheat, fruit, peanuts, peas, asparagus, potatoes, hay, alfalfa, corn, hogs; timber; food processing; port facilities for Columbia River barges; education (Whitman College; Walla Walla College). Walla Walla city is a district headquarters for the U.S. Army Corps of Engineers, and site of WA State Penitentiary.

WHATCOM *Bellingham* • 166,814 • 2,120 • Northwestern WA, bounded on the north by the Canadian province of British Columbia and on the west by Puget Sound; drained by the Baker, Nooksack, and Skagit rivers. The Pacific Coast National Scenic Trail parallels part of the county's eastern border. In the west are Lummi Island and Point Roberts. Mount

Baker stands in the center of the county, with Mount Baker National Recreation Area on its southern slopes. Baker Lake is formed by Upper Baker Dam. Also in the county are Birch Bay and Larrabee state parks, parts of North Cascades National Park, Diablo Dam and Lake, and Ross Dam and Lake, both in Ross National Recreation Area. • Whatcom is an Indian word for "noisy water," probably referring to Whatcom Falls, in what is now the city of Bellingham.• 1854 from Island County prior to statehood • Bellingham Bay was a temporary "staging area" for the Fraser River gold rush of 1857–58. • Confederate general George E. Pickett • Dairying, truck farming, fruit, especially berries, tulips, grain, vegetables, cattle, poultry; salmon, oysters, crabs, clams; lumber; gold, silver, coal; manufacture of lumber and wood products, paper and pulp, processed foods, pleasure boats; salmon canneries; education (Western WA U.) • Peace Arch State Park at Blaine on the Canadian border, commemorates many years of peace between U.S. and Canada. In 1846 when the US and Britain, acting for Canada, agreed to extend the 49th parallel for the boundary between the two countries, no one noticed Point Roberts at the end of a peninsula extending below the parallel. It is part of Whatcom County but can only be reached overland through Canada.

WHITMAN *Colfax* • 40,740 • 2,159 • Southeastern WA, bounded on the east by the ID state line and on the south by the Snake River (forming Lake Herbert G. West, Little Goose Reservoir, and Lower Granite Lake reservoir); drained by the Palouse River (forming part of the western border), and Pine, Rock and Union Flat creeks. The county occupies an area referred to as the Palouse. Occasional buttes here rise over 3,000 feet. It includes a part of Palouse Falls State Park, part of Lyons Ferry State Park, Steptoe Butte and Central Ferry state parks, and Steptoe Memorial Battlefield. • Named for Dr. Marcus Whitman (1802–47), massacred leader of a missionary colony • 1871 from Stevens, prior to statehood • Pullman suffered a disastrous fire in 1890. • Peas, lentils, wheat, barley, oats, alfalfa, hay, cattle, sheep, hogs; education (Washington State U.).

YAKIMA *Yakima* • 222,581 • 4,296 (the second largest county in WA) • Southern WA, bounded on the northeast corner by the Columbia River (forming Priest Rapids Lake); drained by the Naches and Yakima rivers. The Pacific Crest National Scenic Trail closely parallels the western boundary. Yakima Indian Reservation dominates the southern half of the county, which includes Fort Simcoe State Park and Toppenish National Wildlife Refuge, Rimrock Lake and Bumping Lake reservoirs, part of Gifford Pinchot National Forest, and part of Mount Baker–Snoqualmie National Forest. Part of the U.S. Military Reservation–Yakima Training Center (an important training center for both desert and mountain warfare) is in the northeast. The Cascade Range extends along the western border, and the Horse Heaven and Rattlesnake hills cross in the southeast. • Named for the Yakima Indians • 1865 from Indian Territory, prior to statehood • Economist Robert E.

Lucas, Jr. • Corn, alfalfa, hay, onions, asparagus, peppermint, spearmint, wheat, barley, oats, grapes, apples, sugar beets, hops, cattle, sheep, poultry, dairying; lumbering; manufacture of plastic products, paper, chemicals, aircraft parts, malt, wine,

flour, cider, clay products, clothing, machinery, small arms, agricultural equipment, construction materials; meat processing; printing and publishing. • The Yakima Nation Cultural Center is located here.

WEST VIRGINIA

Mountaineers Are Always Free

Each of West Virginia's fifty-five counties elects three county commissioners except for Jefferson County, which elects five. All of these county officials serve six-year terms. Other county officials include the circuit clerk, county clerk, surveyor, prosecuting attorney, sheriff, and assessor.

BARBOUR (one of two counties so named, the other in AL) *Philippi* • 15,557 • 341 • Northern WV; drained by the Tygart River. The county sits on the Allegheny Plateau and includes parts of the following: Laurel Ridge, Tygart Lake reservoir, Tygart Lake State Park, and Audra State Park. The county also contains Teter Creek Wildlife Management Area. • Named for Philip P. Barbour (1783–1841), U.S. representative from VA, Speaker of the House, and U.S. Supreme Court justice • 1843 from Harrison, Lewis and Randolph • The first land battle of the Civil War took place at Philippi on June 3, 1861 (and is annually re-enacted there). It is locally referred to as the "Philippi Races," due to the fast retreat of Confederate troops under Col. George A. Porterfield as they were routed by Union forces under the command of Col. B.F. Kelley. • Coal mining, gas and oil wells; honey, corn, alfalfa, hay, cattle, hogs, poultry, sheep, dairying; timber; natural gas and oil wells; some manufacturing; education (Alderson-Broaddus College) • The Philippi Covered Bridge, erected in 1852, is the longest two-lane covered bridge still in use on a federal highway.

BERKELEY (one of two counties so named, the other in SC) *Martinsburg* • 75,905 (28% increase since 1990; the fastest growing county in WV) • 321 • Northeastern WV in the eastern panhandle, bounded on the northeast by the Potomac River (which forms the MD state line) and on the southwest by the VA state line; drained by Opequon and Back creeks, short tributaries of the Potomac River. The county lies partly in the Great Appalachian Valley. Part of Sleepy Creek Wildlife Management Area is in the county. • Named for Norborne Berkeley, Baron de Botetourt (?–1770), royal governor of VA, popular with the colonists • 1772 (prior to statehood) from Frederick (in VA) • Martinsburg was occupied by both sides during the Civil War. When, in 1861, a Confederate raid de-

stroyed the Baltimore and Ohio Railroad line into the city, engines were hauled by horses over muddy roads from Martinsburg to Winchester, VA. A strike and threat of riot by railroad firemen was put down by federal troops in 1877. This act marked the first time in American history that the U.S. army was used for such purpose. • Confederate spy Belle Boyd; U.S. secretary of war Newton D. Baker • Grains, soybeans, hay, alfalfa, sorghum, vegetables, apples, peaches, poultry, dairying; limestone quarrying; manufacture of glassware, hosiery, auto parts, paper products; mineral springs (at Berkeley Springs) • Bunker Hill village near Martinsburg is one of the oldest recorded European settlements in WV (c.1729).

BOONE (one of eight counties so named) *Madison* • 25,535 • 503 • West-central WV; drained by the Big Coal and Little Coal rivers, and Cabin Creek. The county sits on the Allegheny Plateau and includes Fork Creek Wildlife Management Area. • One of seven counties named for Daniel Boone, onetime resident of the nearby Kanawha Valley • 1847 from Kanawha, Cabell, and Logan • Bituminous-coal mining, natural gas and oil fields; honey, tobacco; timber.

BRAXTON *Sutton* • 14,702 • 514 • Central WV; drained by the Elk, Little Kanawha and Birch rivers. The county is located on the Allegheny Plateau. Burnsville Lake reservoir (Little Kanawha River) is in Burnsville Lake Wildlife Management Area. Sutton Lake reservoir (Elk River) is in Elk River Wildlife Management Area. • Named for Carter Braxton (1736–97), signer of the Declaration of Independence • 1836 from Kanawha, Lewis and Randolph • Honey, corn, alfalfa, fruit, poultry; oil and natural-gas wells, coal mines; timber; manufacture of glass, fabricated metal products, rebuilt aircraft engines, aircraft ground-support equipment, military systems; machining; meat processing.

BROOKE *Wellsburg* • 25,447 • 89 (one of the fifty smallest counties in the U.S.) • Northern WV in the northern panhandle, bounded on the west by the Ohio River (which forms the OH state line) and on the east by the PA state line; drained by Cross and Buffalo creeks. Part of Castleman Run Wildlife Management Area is in the southeast. • Named for Robert Brooke (1761–1800), governor of VA and its attorney general • 1796 from Ohio (County) • Settled during the American Revolution, Weirton (also in Hancock County) was an early iron-making center. Iron ore smelting began here in the 1790s, and by the time of the War of 1812, cannonballs were being supplied for use in Oliver Hazard Perry's assault against the British in the Battle of Lake Erie. Until 1947 Weirton was one of the nation's largest unincorporated "company towns" (Weirton Steel Company). It now stretches across the narrow seven-mile panhandle between PA and OH. WV's first glass plant was built in Wellsburg in 1813. • Founder of the Disciples of Christ Alexander Campbell • Coal mines, natural-gas and oil wells; grain, alfalfa, hay, apples, cattle, dairying; manufacture of paper, glass products, cement, tin cans, chemicals, steel; education (West Liberty State College; Bethany College) • Until a 1937 law was passed mandating a three-day waiting period, Wellsburg was widely regarded as the place to go for a "quickie" wedding.

CABELL *Huntington* • 96,784 (the second most populated county in WV) • 282 • Western WV, bounded on the northwest by the Ohio River (forming the OH state line); drained by the Guyandotte and Mud rivers. Part of Beech Fork State Park is in southwest. The county also includes Greenbottom Wildlife Management Area. • Named for William H. Cabell (1772–1853), governor of VA • 1809 from Kanawha • Lawyer and statesman Dwight W. Morrow • Corn, tobacco, alfalfa, nursery crops, hay, cattle, poultry; natural gas and oil wells, bituminous-coal mining (Huntington is a principal trading center and shipping port for southwestern WV and eastern coal fields); extensive railroad shops; manufacture of chemicals, electrical products, nickel and other metal products, wood products, paints and dyes, glass products (especially hand-blown and handcrafted glassware); education (Marshall U.) • Huntington Galleries is the principal art gallery of the Appalachian region. Huntington is protected from the Ohio River by an eleven-mile floodwall.

CALHOUN *Grantsville* • 7,582 • 281 • Central WV; drained by the Little Kanawha River. The county lies on the Allegheny Plateau. • One of eleven counties named for John C. Calhoun (1782–1850), U.S. statesman and champion of Southern causes • 1856 from Gilmer • Corn, potatoes, alfalfa, hay, cattle, poultry; oil and natural gas wells.

CLAY (one of eighteen counties so named) *Clay* • 10,330 • 342 • Central WV; drained by the Elk River. The county rests on the Allegheny Plateau. Part of B.J. Taylor and Wallback wildlife management areas are found here. • One of fifteen counties named for Henry Clay (1777–1852), statesman and presidential candidate • 1858 from Braxton and Nicholas • Alfalfa, hay, cattle; timber; coal mines.

DODDRIDGE *West Union* • 7,403 • 320 • Northern WV; drained by Middle Island Creek, McElroy Creek and the South Fork of the Hughes River. The county is located on the Allegheny Plateau. North Bend Rail Trail passes east-west through the center of the county. • Named for Philip Doddridge (?–1832), member of the VA house of delegates, U.S. representative from VA, and advocate of the rights of western Virginians • 1845 from Harrison, Tyler, Ritchie and Lewis • Potatoes, alfalfa, hay, apples, cattle, poultry; some bituminous coal; timber.

FAYETTE (one of eleven counties so named) *Fayetteville* • 47,579 • 664 • South-central WV, bounded on the south, in part, by the New River; drained by the Kanawha River and the Gauley River (which forms part of the northern border). The county is bounded on the northeast by the Meadow River. It sits on the Allegheny Plateau. Part of New River Gorge National River is here, as is Gauley River National Recreation Area. Babcock and Hawks Nest state parks are in the county. Plum Orchard Wildlife Management Area is located here as well. • One of seventeen counties named for the Marquis de Lafayette (1757–1834), French statesman and Revolutionary War soldier • 1831 from Kanawha, Greenbrier, Nicholas and Logan • Dancer and ballet director Lawrence Rhodes • Bituminous-coal mining; corn, oats, alfalfa, hay, cattle, sheep; timber; some manufacturing • The county has the world's highest arch span bridge, the New River Gorge Bridge. "Bridge Day" is one of the top 100 festivals in North America. The New River is considered one of the world's oldest rivers. The county is the site of the only legal BASE (Building, Antenna, Span, Earth) parachute jump in North America.

GILMER (one of two counties so named, the other in GA) *Glenville* • 7,160 • 340 • Central WV; drained by the Little Kanawha River and its tributaries. The county is located on the Allegheny Plateau. Cedar Creek State Park is in the south. • Named for Thomas W. Gilmer (1802–44), U.S. representative from VA and secretary of the Navy • 1845 from Lewis and Kanawha • Oil and gas wells; coal mines; corn, alfalfa, hay, cattle, poultry, sheep; timber; education (Glenville State College).

GRANT (one of fifteen counties so named) *Petersburg* • 11,299 • 477 • In eastern WV, in the eastern panhandle, bounded on the northwest by the North Branch of the Potomac River (forming the MD state line); drained by the South Branch of the Potomac River and Patterson Creek. The county is traversed by the Allegheny Front (in the west), Knobly Mountain Ridge (in the center) and Patterson Creek Mountain Ridge (on the northeastern border). It contains part of Monongahela National Forest, as well as Smoke Hole Caverns, Mount Storm Lake and Stony River reservoirs. Fairfax Stone Historic Monument State Park (featuring a land grant marker located at the junction of three counties) is on the western corner. • One of twelve counties named for President Ulysses S. Grant • 1866 from Hardy. Grant is one of the few WV counties established after the state's secession from VA. • Corn, grains, hay, alfalfa, honey, nursery crops, poultry; coal mining; some manufacturing, including wood products and space industry products.

GREENBRIER *Lewisburg* • 34,453 • 1,021 (the second largest county in WV) • Southeastern WV, bounded on the east by the VA state line and on the west in part by the Meadow River; also drained by the Greenbrier River. The county lies partially on the Allegheny Plateau. The Alleghenies run along the southeastern border. Grassy Knob and other summits are in the northwest. Parts of Monongahela National Forest, part of Beartown State Park, Greenbrier State Forest, and Meadow River Wildlife Management Area are all here. Also found in the county are Blue Bend Recreation Area, Lost World Caverns, and Organ Cave. The southern part of Greenbrier Trail is east-center. • Named for the Greenbrier River • 1777 from Montgomery and Botetourt (in VA) • Settlement at Lewisburg developed after 1769 around Camp Union, a rendezvous point for the VA militiamen serving under Gen. Andrew Lewis prior to their successful campaign against Indian forces under Shawnee chief Cornstalk. (The campaign culminated in the Oct. 10, 1774 Battle of Point Pleasant.) Several Civil War battles were fought in the area, including Lewisburg in May, 1862, and White Sulphur Springs in August, 1863. Organ Cave was used by Gen. Robert E. Lee as a refuge. • Coal mining, limestone quarrying; honey, corn, oats, tobacco, potatoes, alfalfa, hay, apples, nursery crops, livestock, dairying; diversified manufacturing; resort tourism (mineral springs) • The Old Stone Presbyterian Church, built in 1796, is the oldest church in continual use west of the Alleghenies. The President's Cottage has served as a summer White House since 1816; among the chief executives who have stayed here are Martin Van Buren, John Tyler, and Millard Fillmore. German, Italian, and Japanese diplomats were interned in White Sulphur Springs during WW II. The national Sam Snead Golf Festival is held in White Sulphur Springs each May. Fairlea is the site of the WV State Fair.

HAMPSHIRE (one of two counties so named, the other in MA) *Romney* • 20,203 (22% increase since 1990; the third fastest growing county in WV) • 642 • Northeastern WV, in the eastern panhandle, bounded on the north, in part, by the Potomac River (forming the MD state line) in the east by the VA state line; drained by the South Branch of the Potomac, and the Cacapon and North rivers. The county is traversed by valleys and ridges of the Appalachian Mountains. A small part of George Washington National Forest is in the southeast. Several wildlife management areas are also located here. • Named for Hampshire County in England • 1754 from Frederick and Augusta (in VA); it is the oldest county in what is now WV. • Rising from the settlement of Pearsall's Flats in 1738, Romney shares claim with Shepherdstown in Jefferson County to being the state's oldest incorporated town. Because of its strategic position near the Baltimore and Ohio Railroad, the town of Romney changed hands fifty-six times during the Civil War. Some of the best-preserved trenches in the coun-

try were dug in 1861 and 1862 by Union soldiers at nearby Fort Mill Ridge. The county was strongly pro-south during the war. • Corn, hay, alfalfa, grains, potatoes, sorghum, honey, fruit, cattle, poultry; some manufacturing; limestone quarrying; timber; hunting (wild turkey, deer, small game) • Located near Slanesville, Ice Mountain once supplied Indians, tourists, and locals with ice year-round.

HANCOCK *New Cumberland* • 32,667 • 83 (the smallest county in WV and one of the fifty smallest counties in the U.S.) • Northern WV at the tip of the northern panhandle, bounded on the north and west by the Ohio River (forming the OH state line) and on the east by the PA state line. The county contains Tomlinson Run State Park and Hillcrest Wildlife Management Area. • One of ten counties named for John Hancock (1737–93), statesman and signer of the Declaration of Independence • 1848 from Brooke • The area around Weirton became one of the first iron-making centers west of the Allegheny Mountains when a blast furnace was built here in the late 1790s. Weirton supplied cannonballs for Oliver Hazard Perry's battle against the British on Lake Erie. • Clay and glass-sand pits; corn, wheat, oats, alfalfa, nursery crops; manufacture of steel, chemicals, cement products.

HARDY *Moorefield* • 12,669 • 583 • Northeastern WV in the eastern panhandle, bounded on the east and south by the VA state line; drained by the South Branch of the Potomac River and its South Fork, and by the Cacapon and Lost rivers. The county is traversed by ridges (including the North and Shenandoah mountains) and valleys of the Allegheny Mountains. It contains Lost River State Park and part of George Washington National Forest in the east. • Named for Samuel Hardy (1758–85), member of the Continental Congress and lieutenant governor of VA • 1785 from Hampshire • Corn, oats, grains, soybeans, potatoes, alfalfa, sorghum, poultry, dairying; limestone and marble quarrying; poultry processing.

HARRISON (one of eight counties so named) *Clarksburg* • 68,652 • 416 • Northern WV; drained by the West Fork River, and Simpson and Tenmile creeks. The county is located on the Allegheny Plateau. Watters Smith Memorial State Park is here, as is the eastern part of North Bend Rail Trail. • Named for Benjamin Harrison (1726–91), a signer of the Declaration of Independence, governor of VA, father of President William Henry Harrison and great grandfather of President Benjamin Harrison • 1784 from Monongalia, Randolph and Ohio • Quakers from New Jersey established the town of Shinn's Run on the West Fork River in 1818. Clarksburg was an important Union supply base during the Civil War and the headquarters of Gen. George B. McClellan who was charged with holding what was then western VA for the Union. • Statesman Cyrus Vance; Confederate general Thomas J. "Stonewall" Jackson; U.S. presidential candidate John W. Davis; filmmaker Pare Lorentz • Corn, alfalfa, hay, nursery crops, livestock, poultry, dairying; natural gas, oil wells, bituminous-coal mines; manufacture of glass products, chemicals, coffins, machinery, brick and tile, evaporated milk, marbles; education (Salem International U.) • Clarksburg is home to the popular West Virginia Italian Heritage Festival.

JACKSON (one of twenty-four counties so named) *Ripley* • 28,000 • 466 • Western WV, bounded on the northwest by the Ohio River (forming the OH state line); drained by Mill Creek. Frozen Camp and Woodrum wildlife management areas are here. The county also includes Cedar Lake State Camp. • One of twenty-two counties named directly or indirectly for President Andrew Jackson • 1831 from Kanawha, Mason and Wood • Corn, wheat, oats, tobacco, potatoes, alfalfa, hay, nursery crops, cattle, some dairying; some manufacturing.

JEFFERSON *Charles Town* • 42,190 • 210 • Northeastern WV at the end of the eastern panhandle, bounded on the northeast by the Potomac River (forming the MD state line) and on the southeast and southwest by the VA state line; drained by the Shenandoah River which joins the Potomac at Harpers Ferry, and by Opequon Creek. The county is located in the southern part of the Great Appalachian Valley. The Blue Ridge and the Appalachian National Scenic Trail are found along the southeastern border. Shannondale Springs Wildlife Management Area is also located in the county. • One of twenty-six counties named directly or indirectly for President Thomas Jefferson • 1801 from Berkeley • First chartered in 1762 as Mecklenburg, Shepherdstown was considered by George Washington as the site of the nation's capital in 1790. Also that year, WV's first newspaper, the *Potomac Guardian*, was first published here by Nathaniel Willis. The town was also the site of the successful demonstration of James Rumsey's steamboat on the Potomac in 1787 (state historic monument). The famous raid by John Brown on the U.S. arsenal at Harpers Ferry (its site chosen by President Washington in 1796) took place in October, 1859 (national historic park here). Brown was tried and hanged in Charles Town later that year. During the Civil War, the town's strategic location made it a prize of both the Union and the Confederacy and it changed hands several times. In September, 1862, its capture by the Confederates following a heated engagement paved the way for General Robert E. Lee's invasion of MD, culminating in the Battle of Antietam. • Poet, novelist and critic John Peale Bishop • Corn, wheat, oats, barley, soybeans, potatoes, alfalfa, hay, sorghum, apples, cattle, horses, poultry, dairying; limestone and dolomite quarrying; diversifed manufacturing; education (Shepherd College) • Dolley Payne Todd and James Madison were married at Harewood in Charles Town.

KANAWHA *Charleston* • 200,073 (the most populated county in WV) • 903 (the fourth largest county in WV) • West-central WV, bounded on the west in part by the Big Coal River; drained by the Kanawha, Elk, and Pocatalico rivers. The county sits on the Allegheny Plateau. Kanawha State Forest is in the southwest; part of Wallback Wildlife Management Area is in the northeast corner. • Named for the Kanawha River • 1788 from Greenbrier (WV) and Montgomery (in VA) • Charleston was an early trans-shipment point and by 1823,

with the arrival of the first steamboat, an important salt center. The city was occupied by Union troops after the Battle of Charleston on September 13, 1862. It served as the capital of WV from 1870 to 1875, and became the state's permanent capital in 1885. • Composer George Crumb; frontiersmen Daniel Boone and Simon Kenton • Bituminous coal, natural gas, oil wells, salt; large scale manufacture of chemicals (Nylon and Lucite originated in the Kanawha River valley), also wire products, glass; vegetables, corn, tobacco, alfalfa, hay, cattle, poultry; dairying; state government operations; education (U. of Charleston; WV State College) • The National Track and Field Hall of Fame is in Charleston. 10,080 hand-cut Czechoslovakian crystals make up the large chandelier that hangs in the golden dome of the state capitol.

LEWIS (one of seven counties so named) *Weston* • 16,919 • 389 • Central WV; drained by the West Fork River (a headstream of the Monongahela river). The county is located on the Allegheny Plateau. Stonewall Jackson State Park and Wildlife Management Area encompasses Stonewall Jackson Lake. Jackson's Mill historic site and state 4-H camp and part of Stonecoal Lake reservoir and Wildlife Management Area are also in the county. • Named for Charles Lewis (?–1774), Indian fighter and member of the VA house of burgesses • 1816 from Harrison and Randolph • Corn, potatoes, alfalfa, hay, cattle, sheep; manufacturing; natural-gas and oil wells; timber.

LINCOLN (one of twenty-four counties so named) • *Hamlin* • 22,108 • 437 • Western WV, bounded on the northeast by the Coal River; drained by the Guyandotte and Mud rivers. The county is located on the Allegheny Plateau. Big Ugly and Hilbert wildlife management areas are here. • One of eighteen counties named for President Abraham Lincoln • 1867 from Boone, Cabell, and Kanawha. Lincoln is one of the few WV counties established after the state's secession from VA. • Corn, potatoes, alfalfa, hay, nursery crops, tobacco, cattle, honey; oil and natural gas, bituminous coal.

LOGAN (one of ten counties so named) *Logan* • 37,710 • 454 • Southwestern WV; drained by the Guyandotte River. The county is situated on the Allegheny Plateau. Chief Logan State Park is here. • Named for John Logan (?–1780), a Mingo Indian chief who was friend and later foe of white settlers • 1824 from Cabell and Kanawha (WV); Giles and Tazewell (VA) • The county was made famous by the mountain-family feud between the Hatfields (of Logan County) and the McCoys (of Pike County, KY). It was also the scene of a 1972 coal-mining related disaster in which coal mine waste waters burst a makeshift dam on Buffalo Creek and flooded local mining communities, leaving 188 people dead. • Bituminous-coal mining, natural gas field; tobacco; manufacture of mining equipment.

MARION *Fairmont* • 56,598 • 310 • Northern WV. The county is situated on the Allegheny Plateau. Tygart and West Fork rivers join at Fairmont to form the Monongahela River.

Prickett's Fort State Park is here, as is part of Valley Falls State Park. • One of seventeen counties named for the "Swamp Fox" Gen. Francis Marion (?–1795), SC soldier and legislator • 1842 from Harrison and Monongalia • The county was the site of the first commercial Monongahela Valley bituminous-coal mine. In 1907, a disastrous mine explosion at Monongah killed 359. • Writer John Knowles • Coal mining (which has been in recent rapid decline), gas and oil fields, aluminum and iron industries; manufacture of coal-mining machinery, glass, aluminum products, fluorescent lamps; corn, alfalfa, hay, apples, cattle, poultry, sheep; education (Fairmont State College).

MARSHALL (one of twelve counties so named) *Moundsville* • 35,519 • 307 • Northern WV, the southernmost county in the northern panhandle, bounded on the west by the Ohio River (forming the OH state line), and on the east by the PA state line; drained by Wheeling, Fish, and Grave creeks. Grave Creek Mound Historic Site contains one of the nation's largest conical Indian mounds. Numerous relics dating from 800 B.C. have been recovered since excavations began in two burial chambers here in 1838. Burches Run Wildlife Management Area is also in the county. • One of eight counties named for John Marshall (1755–1835), fourth Chief Justice of the United States • 1835 from Ohio (County) • In 1852, the last spike joining the Baltimore and Ohio Railroad was driven at Rosby's Rock. • Timber; coal, natural gas, oil, glass-sand, clay, and related industry; honey, corn, potatoes, alfalfa, hay, nursery crops, cattle, hogs, sheep, poultry. Moundsville has one of the largest handmade-glass factories in the U.S. A state penitentiary is also located here.

MASON (one of six counties so named) *Point Pleasant* • 25,957 • 432 • Western WV, bounded on the north and west by the Ohio River (forming the OH state line); drained by the Kanawha River, which joins the Ohio here. Chief Cornstalk and Clifton F. McClintic wildlife management areas are in the county. • One of two counties (the other in KY) named for George Mason (?–1792), VA statesman and author of the VA Declaration of Rights • 1804 from Kanawha • At the confluence of the Ohio and Kanawha rivers on October 10, 1774, a band of VA frontiersmen under Gen. Andrew Lewis defeated allied Indian nations under the command of Chief Cornstalk. The victory was recognized by the U.S. Senate in 1908 as the first battle of the American Revolution, since the Indians were supposedly incited by the British (Point Pleasant Battle Monument State Park). • The county contains the graves of Chief Cornstalk and celebrated frontierswoman Ann Bailey. • Bituminous-coal mines, some natural-gas wells; honey, corn, wheat, oats, tobacco, potatoes, alfalfa, hay, vegetables, nursery crops, cattle, hogs, sheep, dairying; manufacture of iron products, textiles. • The West Virginia State Farm Museum is near Point Pleasant.

MCDOWELL (one of two counties so named, the other in NC) *Welch* • 27,329 • 535 • Southern WV, bounded on the west, south and southeast by the VA state line; drained by Tug Fork and Dry Fork rivers (which are head streams of the

Big Sandy River). The county is located on the Allegheny Plateau. Panther State Forest, and Berwind Lake and Anawalt wildlife management areas are here. • Named for James McDowell (1795–1851), VA governor and U.S. representative from VA • 1858 from Tazewell (VA) • Timber; apples; some natural gas, extensive semi-bituminous-coal mining (Welch is the service center for the area that includes the profitable Pocahontas field, source of "Black Diamond" coal.) • Premier Cut is reputed to be the deepest highway defile in the world.

MERCER (one of eight counties so named) *Princeton* • 62,980 • 420 • Southern WV, bounded on the south by the VA state line; drained by the Bluestone River. The county is situated on the Allegheny Plateau. Camp Creek State Forest and State Park are here, as is Pinnacle Rock State Park. • One of six counties definitively named for Hugh Mercer (?–1777), Revolutionary War officer and physician • 1837 from Giles and Tazewell (in VA) • Journalist and publisher John S. Knight • Semi–bituminous-coal mining (Pocahontas coal field), silica, limestone deposits; timber; railroad shops; manufacture of mining machinery, furniture, caskets, clothing; corn, oats, tobacco, potatoes, alfalfa, hay, nursery crops, cattle, sheep; education (Bluefield State College; Concord College) • Situated at the foot of East River Mountain, Bluefield is, at 3,480 feet, one of the highest cities in the U.S. east of the Rocky Mountains.

MINERAL (one of four counties so named) *Keyser* • 27,078 • 328 • Northeastern WV, in the eastern panhandle, bounded on the north and northwest by the North Branch of the Potomac River (forming the MD state line, with Jennings Randolph Lake reservoir in the west); drained by Patterson Creek. The county is traversed by Knobly and Patterson Creek Mountain ridges (on the western boundary) and other ridges. Nancy Hanks Memorial marks the site where the mother of Abraham Lincoln was born. Parts of Springfield Wildlife Management Area are also in the county. • Named for its mineral resources, particularly coal • 1866 from Hampshire • Fort Ashby, completed in 1775, is the only remaining fort out of a chain of sixty-nine established by Gen. George Washington to protect the VA frontier from Indians. • Scholar Henry Louis Gates, Jr. • Coal mines; timber; corn, wheat, oats, barley, rye, tobacco, alfalfa, hay, cattle, hogs, sheep, poultry; manufacturing.

MINGO *Williamson* • 28,253 • 423 • Southwestern WV, bounded on the southwest by the Tug Fork River (forming the KY state line). The county includes Laurel Creek Wildlife Management Area and part of R.D. Bailey Lake (reservoir) Wildlife Management Area. • Named for the Mingo Indians • 1895 from Logan; it is one of the few WV counties established after the state's secession from VA. • Extensive bituminous-coal fields (one of the southern WV counties that sit atop the "Billion Dollar Coal Field"); natural-gas and oil wells; timber; some agriculture; machine armature plants • Williamson's chamber of commerce, called the "Coal House," has walls made from coal blocks.

MONONGALIA *Morgantown* • 81,866 (the fourth most populated county in WV) • 361 • Northern WV, bounded on the north by the PA state line; drained by the Monongahela and Cheat rivers. The county is situated on the Allegheny Plateau. Part of Chestnut Ridge Park and part of Coopers Rock State Forest are in the northeast. • The county employs a variant spelling for the Monongahela River • 1776 from District of West Augusta • Coal mining, gas and oil fields, limestone quarries, sand pits; manufacture of wood, glass, and metal products, chemicals, plumbing supplies; honey, corn, oats, alfalfa, hay, strawberries, nursery crops, cattle, poultry, sheep; education (WV U., which maintains experimental farms and forests in the county) • The U.S. Bureau of Mines oversees the Morgantown Energy Research Center. The Appalachian Laboratory for occupational health and respiratory diseases is also in Morgantown.

MONROE *Union* • 14,583 • 473 • Southeastern WV, bounded on the southeast and southwest by the VA state line; drained by Indian and Potts creeks. Peters Mountain stands on the VA state line and summits of the Allegheny Mountains (including Bickett Knob) are in the west. Moncove Lake State Park and Wildlife Management Area is here, as is part of Jefferson National Forest. The Appalachian Trail follows part of the VA state line in the south. • One of seventeen counties named for President James Monroe • 1779 from Greenbrier (WV) and Botetourt (in VA) • Corn, oats, barley, rye, alfalfa, hay, cattle, dairying, hogs, poultry, sheep; limestone and iron-ore deposits, some natural gas; aircraft parts manufacturing.

MORGAN (one of eleven counties so named) *Berkeley Springs* • 14,943 (23% increase since 1990; the second fastest growing county in WV) • 229 • Northeastern WV in the eastern panhandle, bounded on the north and west by the Potomac River (forming the MD state line) and on the south in part by the VA state line; drained by the Cacapon River. Cacapon Resort State Park and Berkeley Springs State Park are located here. Part of Sleepy Creek Wildlife Management Area is also here. • One of nine counties named for Daniel Morgan (1736–1802), Revolutionary War general • 1820 from Berkeley and Hampshire • The colonial owner of the site that would become Berkeley Springs, Lord Fairfax, gave the springs to the people of VA in 1756. • Honey, corn, wheat, oats, barley, alfalfa, hay, apples, cattle, poultry; furniture manufacture; glass-sand pits; timber; tourism (health resorts and mineral springs).

NICHOLAS (one of two counties so named, the other in KY) *Summersville* • 26,562 • 649 • Central WV, bounded on the southwest by the Gauley and Meadow rivers; drained by the Gauley, Cranberry, Cherry, and Birch rivers. Part of Monongahela National Forest and part of Gauley River National Recreation Area are found in the county. It also contains Summersville Lake reservoir (Gauley River) and Wildlife Management Area. • Named for Wilson C. Nicholas (1761–1820), U.S. senator and representative from VA, and governor of VA • 1818 from Greenbrier, Kanawha, and Randolph • In July, 1861, Confederate spy Nancy Hart led an attack upon Summersville, burning most of its buildings and capturing a Union force. On September 10, 1861, Union troops under General William S. Rosecrans defeated forces under Brig. General John B. Floyd at Carnifex Ferry (state park) and moved western VA toward statehood. • Corn, potatoes, alfalfa, hay, apples, cattle, poultry, dairying, corn; bituminous-coal mining; lumbering, sawmilling • Richwood is known as the "Ramp Capital" of the world; for over sixty years the town has celebrated the "Feast of the Ramson," a weekend of digging and cooking this relative of the wild leek.

OHIO (one of three counties so named) *Wheeling* • 47,427 • 106 (one of the fifty smallest counties in the U.S.) • In the northern panhandle of WV, bounded on the west by the Ohio River (forming the OH state line) and on the east by the PA state line; drained by Wheeling Creek. Oglebay Park is here, as is Bear Rocks Lakes Wildlife Management Area. Part of Castleman Run Wildlife Management Area is also found in the county. • Named for the Ohio River • 1776 from Augusta • One of the last skirmishes of the Revolutionary War was fought in Wheeling September 11–13, 1782. (Zane Grey's novel *Betty Zane* depicts the bravery of his ancestor during the siege.) Wheeling was designated the "Gateway to the West" on the National Road. It is the only city in the U.S. to serve as the capital of two state governments (restored government of VA in 1861 and capital of WV, 1863–70 and 1875–85). The Wheeling Conventions of 1861–62 led to the formation of the State of WV. • Labor leader Walter P. Reuther; oilman Harry F. Sinclair • Coal mines, natural-gas wells; iron, steel and metal-working industries, manufacture of sheet metal, tin-plate, glass, tobacco, pottery, textiles; corn, wheat, oats, barley, hay, cattle, dairying, hogs; education (Wheeling Jesuit U.) • Jamboree USA is the second oldest live radio broadcast in the U.S. Wheeling's American Legion Post No. 1 was the first of its kind in the nation.

PENDLETON *Franklin* • 8,196 • 698 (the fifth largest county in WV) • Eastern WV in the eastern panhandle, bounded on the east, south, and southwest by the VA state line; drained by the South Branch of the Potomac River and its North and South forks. The Allegheny Mountains traverse the county in the west. Spruce Knob (4,861 feet high) is the highest point in WV. Shenandoah Mountain is on the VA state line in the east. The county includes Seneca Caverns and Seneca Rocks. Parts of George Washington and Monongahela national forests are also here. Spruce Knob-Seneca Rocks National Recreation Area is in the west. • One of two counties (the other in KY) named for Edmund Pendleton (1721–1803), member of the VA House of Burgesses and VA House of Delegates • 1787 from Hardy (WV); and Augusta and Rockingham (in VA) • Corn, potatoes, alfalfa, hay, livestock, cattle, hogs, poultry, sheep; timber; manufacturing; resort tourism.

PLEASANTS *St. Marys* • 7,514 • 131 (one of the fifty smallest counties in the U.S.) • Northwestern WV, bounded on the northwest by the Ohio River (forming the OH state line); drained by Middle Island Creek. • Named for James Pleasants

(1769–1836), U.S. senator and representative from VA, and governor of VA • 1851 from Ritchie, Tyler, and Wood • Corn, wheat, alfalfa, hay, cattle; coal mines, gas and oil wells.

POCAHONTAS *Marlinton* • 9,131 • 940 (the third largest county in WV) • Eastern WV, bounded on the east by the Allegheny Mountains which form the VA state line; drained by the Greenbrier, Gauley, Cranberry, and Shavers Fork rivers. Cass Scenic Railroad State Park, Calvin Price and Seneca state forests, and Greenbrier River Trail are all here. The county also includes Watoga State Park. Most of the county lies in Monongahela National Forest. Cranberry Glades Botanical Area and Falls of Hills Creek Scenic Area are in the southwest. Numerous recreation areas are also here. • One of two counties (the other in IA) named for Indian Princess Pocahontas • 1821 from Pendleton, Randolph, and Greenbrier (WV); and Bath (VA) • The last serious Southern resistance in the state was ended on Nov. 6, 1863 when Union forces under Gen. William Averell defeated troops under the command of Gen. John Echols at Droop Mountain, three miles south of Hillsboro (state park). • Author Pearl S. Buck (museum) • Corn, oats, potatoes, alfalfa, hay, fruit (especially apples), cattle, poultry, sheep, dairying; timber; some manufacturing; ski resort tourism. • The National Radio Astronomy Observatory is located here.

PRESTON *Kingwood* • 29,334 • 648 • Northern WV, bounded on the north by the PA state line, and on the east by the MD state line; drained by the Cheat River. The county is situated on the Allegheny Plateau, and includes part of Laurel Ridge and other mountains. It contains a small part of Monongahela National Forest, as well as Cathedral State Park (home to the largest virgin forest in the eastern U.S.) and part of Coopers Rock State Forest. • Named for James P. Preston (1774–1843), VA legislator and governor of VA • 1818 from Monongalia and Randolph • Honey, corn, wheat, oats, barley, potatoes, alfalfa, hay, vegetables, apples, grapes, nursery crops, dairying, poultry, cattle, hogs, sheep; coal mining, limestone quarrying; timber • Our Lady of the Pines, located in Horse Shoe Run, is the smallest church in the forty-eight contiguous states; it seats twelve worshippers. Arthurdale, established 1933–34, served as the first of several model planned communities under FDR's Federal Homestead Act.

PUTNAM (one of nine counties so named) *Winfield* • 51,589 • 346 • Western WV; drained by the Kanawha and Pocatalico rivers. • One of eight counties definitively named for Israel Putnam (1718–90), Revolutionary War general • 1848 from Kanawha, Mason, and Cabell • Bituminous-coal mines, some natural-gas and oil wells; corn, potatoes, alfalfa, hay, tobacco, vegetables, nursery crops, cattle, poultry; diversified manufacturing.

RALEIGH *Beckley* • 79,220 (the fifth most populated county in WV) • 607 • Southern WV, bounded on the east by the New River (New River Gorge National River); drained by the Big Coal and Guyandotte rivers. The county is located on the Allegheny Plateau. Also located here are Tamarack State Crafts Center, Little Beaver State Park and Stephens Lake reservoir. The county includes several mining communities. • Named for Sir Walter Ralegh (Raleigh) (?–1618), British naval commander and promoter of colonization of VA • 1850 from Fayette • The growth of Beckley dates from 1890 when the first commercial smokeless coal shipment was made from mines in the area. With the opening of the Winding Gulf coalfield in 1907, the population of the city grew sharply. During the Civil War, the town was occupied by both Union and Confederate troops. • Extensive mining of semi-bituminous coal; gas fields; corn, oats, alfalfa, hay, nursery crops, cattle; light manufacturing, including mining machinery, electronic devices, processed foods; lumber; education (Appalachian Bible College; Mountain State U.) • Beckley Exhibition Coal Mine in River City Park attracts visitors to the county.

RANDOLPH (one of eight counties so named) *Elkins* • 28,262 • 1,040 (the largest county in WV) • East-central WV, at the base of the eastern panhandle; drained by the Elk and Tygart rivers, Shavers and Laurel forks of the Cheat River, and by Gandy Creek. The county is located on the Allegheny Plateau, and is traversed north–south by the Allegheny Mountains (on the eastern border), Rich Mountain, Cheat Mountain, Shaver's Mountain, and other ridges. Kumbrabow State Forest is here. Monongahela National Forest (its headquarters in Elkins) dominates the eastern half of the county. Rich Mountain Battlefield is near Elkins. • One of two counties (the other in IL), named for Edmund Jennings Randolph (1753–1813), governor of VA, first U.S. attorney general, and U.S. secretary of state • 1786 from Harrison • The Battle of Rich Mountain, decisive in McClellan's Northwest Virginia campaign, was fought here on July 11, 1861. In a surprise attack, General W. S. Rosecrans defeated Confederate forces led by Captain J.A. deLagnel. • Corn, oats, soybeans, potatoes, alfalfa, hay, cattle, hogs, poultry, sheep, dairying; coal mining, limestone quarries; timber; light manufacturing; education (Davis and Elkins College) • The Mountain State Forest Festival is held in Elkins each October.

RITCHIE *Harrisville* • 10,343 • 454 • Northwestern WV; drained by the North and South forks of the Hughes River. North Bend State Park is here. North Bend Rail Trail passes through the west. The county also includes Ritchie Mines and part of Hughes River wildlife management areas. • Named for Thomas Ritchie (1778–1854), owner and editor of the *Richmond Enquirer* • 1843 from Harrison, Lewis and Wood • Corn, alfalfa, hay, cattle, poultry, sheep; oil and natural-gas wells; manufacturing.

ROANE (one of two counties so named, the other in TN) *Spencer* • 15,446 • 484 • Western WV; drained by the Pocatalico River, and Sandy, Reedy, and Mill creeks. Parts of Wallback and B.J. Taylor wildlife management areas are in the south. • Named for Spencer Roane (1762–1822), justice of the VA Supreme Court of Appeals and son-in-law of Patrick

Henry • 1856 from Kanawha, Jackson, and Gilmer • Timber; corn, tobacco, potatoes, alfalfa, hay, cattle, poultry, sheep; some manufacturing.

SUMMERS *Hinton* • 12,999 • 361 • Southern WV; drained by the New River and its branches, and by the Greenbrier and Bluestone rivers. The county is situated on the Allegheny Plateau. Bluestone Lake reservoir in the south is encompassed by part of Bluestone State Park and Wildlife Management Area. Bluestone National Scenic River and part of Pipestem Resort State Park are in the southwest. • Named for George W. Summers (1804–68), U.S. representative from VA and jurist • 1871 from Greenbrier, Monroe, and Mercer; it is one of the few WV counties established after the state's secession from VA. • Corn, oats, potatoes, alfalfa, hay, nursery crops, cattle, sheep; timber; some natural gas • A statue honoring the legendary John Henry is located near Big Bend Tunnel where, in 1873, Henry reputedly died after competing with a steam-powered drill.

TAYLOR (one of seven counties so named) *Grafton* • 16,089 • 173 • Northern WV; drained by the Tygart River. The county is situated on the Allegheny Plateau and includes part of Tygart Lake reservoir and Tygart Lake State Park. Part of Valley Falls State Park is also located here, as is Pleasant Creek Wildlife Management Area. • Probably named for Col. John Taylor (?–1824), officer in the Revolutionary War and U.S. senator from VA • 1844 from Harrison, Barbour, and Marion • Alfalfa, hay, cattle; timber; natural-gas field; manufacturing.

TUCKER *Parsons* • 7,321 • 419 • Northeastern WV; drained by the Cheat, Laurel Fork, Shavers Fork and Blackwater rivers. The county is located on the Allegheny Plateau at the base of the eastern panhandle. Laurel Ridge runs along its western border. Most of the county is in Monongahela National Forest, here including Fernow Experimental Forest. Blackwater Falls State Park and Fairfax Stone Historic State Monument are here, as are Canaan Valley Resort State Park and National Wildlife Refuge. • Named for Henry St. George Tucker (1780–1848), U.S. representative from VA, and jurist • 1856 from Randolph • Coal-mining, limestone quarrying; timber; corn, oats, potatoes, alfalfa, hay, cattle, poultry; manufacturing.

TYLER (one of two counties so named, the other in TX) *Middlebourne* • 9,592 • 258 • Northwestern WV, bounded on the northwest by the Ohio River (forming the OH state line); drained by Middle Island and McElroy creeks. The Jug, Public, and Conaway Run wildlife management areas are here. • Named for John Tyler (1747–1813), jurist, VA governor, and father of U.S. president John Tyler • 1814 from Ohio County • Oil and natural-gas wells; corn, alfalfa, hay, nursery crops, cattle, sheep, dairying; some manufacturing, including petroleum processing.

UPSHUR *Buckhannon* • 23,404 • 355 • Central WV; drained by the Buckhannon River. The county is located on the Allegheny Plateau. It includes part of Audra State Park and Stonecoal Lake Wildlife Management Area. West Virginia State Wildlife Center is also here. • One of two counties (the other in TX) named for Abel Parker Upshur (1791–1844), U.S. secretary of the navy and U.S. secretary of state • 1851 from Randolph, Barbour, and Lewis • Buckhannon was settled in 1770, its site platted in 1815 by Colonel Edward Jackson, grandfather of General Thomas J. "Stonewall" Jackson. • Potatoes, buckwheat, alfalfa, hay, apples, nursery crops, cattle, poultry, strawberries (the state strawberry festival is held each June in Buckhannon); bituminous-coal mines, natural-gas wells; timber; manufacture of wood products, business forms, men's clothing; education (WV Wesleyan College).

WAYNE (one of sixteen counties so named) *Wayne* • 42,903 • 506 • Western WV, bounded on the west by the Tug Fork and Big Sandy rivers (forming the KY state line) and on the north by the Ohio River (forming the OH state line); drained by Twelvepole Creek. The county is situated on the Allegheny Plateau. Beech Fork State Park and Beech Fork Lake (reservoir)Wildlife Management Area are here, as is Cabwaylingo State Forest. • One of fifteen counties named for Gen. "Mad" Anthony Wayne (1745–96), Revolutionary War soldier and statesman • 1842 from Cabell • Corn, tobacco, alfalfa, hay, nursery crops, cattle; bituminous-coal mines, oil- and natural-gas wells, sand and gravel pits; timber; manufacturing.

WEBSTER *Webster Springs* • 9,719 • 556 • Central WV; drained by the Elk, Gauley, Williams, and Cranberry rivers. The county is located on the Allegheny Plateau. Part of Monongahela National Forest is in the southeast. Holly River State Park and Big Ditch Wildlife Management Area are also in the county. • One of eight counties named for Daniel Webster (1782–1852), U.S. statesman and orator from MA • 1860 from Braxton, Nicholas, and Randolph • Bituminous-coal mining; timber; potatoes, alfalfa, hay, cattle; hunting and fishing.

WETZEL *New Martinsville* • 17,693 • 359 • Northern WV, bounded on the west by the OH River (forming the OH state line) and on the north in part by the PA state line; drained by Fish and Fishing creeks. Lewis Wetzel Wildlife Management Area is here. Hannibal Locks and Dam, and Lock and Dam No. 15 are on the Ohio River. • Named for Lewis Wetzel (1763–1808), an Indian fighter and scout • 1846 from Tyler • Oil and natural-gas wells, sand and gravel pits; corn, potatoes, hay, cattle, poultry, sheep; manufacturing.

WIRT *Elizabeth* • 5,873 (the least populated county in WV) • 233 • Western WV; drained by the Little Kanawha and Hughes rivers. Palestine State Fish Hatchery and Hughes River Wildlife Management Area are here. • Named for William Wirt (1774–1838), army officer in the War of 1812 and U.S. attorney general who, in 1807, prosecuted the case against Aaron Burr • 1848 from Wood and Jackson • Soldier Jessica Lynch • Corn, tobacco, potatoes, alfalfa, hay, nursery crops, cattle, poultry, some dairying.

WOOD (one of four counties so named) *Parkersburg* • 87,986 (the third most populated county in WV) • 367 • Northwestern WV, bounded on the west by the Ohio River (forming the OH state line); drained by the Little Kanawha River. The western part of North Bend Rail Trail is in the east. Lock and Dam Number 17 is on the Ohio River. • Named for General James Wood (?–1813) Indian fighter, officer in the Revolutionary War, and governor of VA • 1798 from Harrison and Kanawha • George Washington visited the area in 1770 when he was searching for lands awarded to him for his military service. Blennerhassett Island (historic state park) in the Ohio River was the site of Harman Blennerhassett's alleged plot with Aaron Burr to seize the Southwest and create a separate empire. Growth was stimulated in Parkersburg by the discovery of oil in 1860 in nearby Burning Springs. • Oil and natural-gas wells; bituminous coal, clay; corn, wheat, tobacco, soybeans, alfalfa, hay, nursery crops, cattle, hogs, poultry, sheep; manufacture of glassware (the county is the glass marble manufacturing center of the U.S., making most of the nation's glass marbles), ferrous metals, chemicals, plastics, laboratory equipment, paper, rayon, synthetic rubber; railroad shops. • The Parkersburg Art Center houses reproductions of paintings in the National Gallery in Washington D.C.

WYOMING (one of three counties so named) *Pineville* • 25,708 • 501 • Southern WV on the Allegheny Plateau; drained by the Guyandotte River and its Clear Fork. Twin Falls Resort State Park is here, as are parts of R.D. Bailey Lake reservoir (Guyandotte River) and Wildlife Management Area. • The derivation of the county's name has never been firmly established. It was possibly named for the Wyoming Indians or for PA's Wyoming Valley • 1850 from Logan • An important bituminous- and semi–bituminous-coal-producing county; also timber; natural gas; corn, potatoes, cattle.

WISCONSIN

Forward

Each of Wisconsin's seventy-two counties is governed by a board of elected supervisors. The head of each board is selected by its members. Other county officials in the state are the district attorney, treasurer, clerk, register of deeds, clerk of circuit court, and sheriff. Nine Wisconsin counties elect a county executive.

ADAMS (one of twelve counties so named) *Friendship* • 18,643 • 648 • Central WI, bounded on the west by the Wisconsin River (forming Petenwell Lake and Castle Rock Lake reservoirs); drained by tributaries of the Wisconsin River. The county includes Rocky Arbor and Roche-a-Cri state parks. • One of eight counties named for President John Adams • 1848 from Portage • Dairying, corn, soybeans, peas, beans, potatoes; timber; railroad repair shops; manufacture of shipping containers, modular housing.

ASHLAND (one of two counties so named, the other in OH) *Ashland* • 16,866 • 1,044 • Northern WI, bounded on the north by Lake Superior; drained by the Bad River and the East Fork of the Chippewa River. The county includes the Apostle Islands just north of Chequamegon Bay (comprising most of Apostle Islands National Lakeshore, and Madeline). Part of the Gogebic Iron Range can be found in the county. The Bad River Indian Reservation is in the north; a smaller unit is on the eastern end of Madeline Island. Copper Falls and Big Bay state parks, and part of Chequamegon National Forest are also in the county. • Named for the village of Ashland, WI, which was itself named for the KY estate of Henry Clay • 1860 (from unorganized territory) • In 1877, Ashland became the terminus of the first railroad of northern WI. • Barley; lumbering; iron, coal, black granite; education (Northland College).

BARRON *Barron* • 44,963 • 863 • Northwestern WI; drained by the Red Cedar and Hay rivers. The county contains many lakes, most notably Red Cedar and Lake Chetek. A section of Tuscobia State Trail is in the northeast. • Named for Henry D. Barron (1833–1882), Speaker of the WI House of Representatives and jurist • Organized as Dallas, 1859; name changed 1869 • Dairying, cattle, hogs, sheep, turkeys, potatoes, barley, oats, wheat, corn, peas, alfalfa.

BAYFIELD *Washburn* • 15,013 • 1,476 (the second largest county in WV) • Extreme northern WI, bounded on the north by Lake Superior (Chequamegon Bay to the northeast); drained by the Namekagon River (which here constitutes the East Branch of St. Croix National Scenic Riverway). A large portion of the county rests on a wide peninsula. It is generally wooded, with some cutover farm land and several resort lakes. The western end of the Gogebic Iron Range crosses the county. Red Cliff Indian Reservation is in the north. A large section of Chequamegon National Forest is found in the county, as well. Telemark and Mount Ashwabay ski areas are also here. The mainland shore unit and three islands of Apostle Islands National Lakeshore are in the extreme northeast. • Named for the town of Bayfield, itself named for Henry W. Bayfield (1795–1885), admiral in the British navy • Organized as La Pointe in 1845 (prior to statehood) from Ashland; name changed 1866 • Barley, sheep, poultry; lumbering; fishing; some manufacturing; tourism.

BROWN (one of nine counties so named) *Green Bay* • 226,778 (the fourth most populated county in WI) • 529 • Eastern WI, bounded on the north by Green Bay of Lake Michigan; drained by the Fox River. The northeastern part of the county extends onto the Door Peninsula. Green Bay urbanizes the center of the county. Heritage Hill State Park is at Allouez. Part of Oneida Indian Reservation is in the west. • One of four counties named for General Jacob Jennings Brown (1775–1828), officer in the War of 1812 and commander of the U.S. Army • 1818 (prior to statehood) from a territorial county; part of Shawano and Oconto annexed in 1919 • Jacques Marquette and Claude-Jean Allouez were active at the French missionary settlement and fur trading post established at the site of Green Bay in 1634 by Jean Nicolet, the first explorer to enter Wisconsin. WI's first newspaper, the *Green Bay Intelligencer*, was established in 1833. The WI state constitution was drafted at Hazlewood House in Green Bay. • Sports columnist Red Smith; football coach Curly Lambeau • Green Bay is a port of entry for oceangoing vessels using the St. Lawrence Seaway to the Great Lakes. Dairying, barley, oats, wheat, corn, peas, beans, alfalfa, hay, cattle, sheep; timber; manufacture of paper and paper products, machinery, machine parts; grain elevators; cheese processing, food canning; education (U. of WI–Green Bay; St. Norbert College; Northeast WI Technical Institute) • Green Bay has supported its professional football team, the Packers, since its organization in 1919 (Lambeau Field). • The National Railroad Museum in Ashwaubenon exhibits a large collection of locomotives and railroad equipment.

BUFFALO (one of three counties so named) *Alma* • 13,804 • 684 • Western WI, bounded on the northwest by the Chippewa River, on the west and southwest by the Mississippi River (forming the MN state line), and on the southeast by the Trempealeau River; drained by the Buffalo river. Part of the Upper Mississippi River National Wildlife and Fish Refuge is on the Mississippi River. A section of Buffalo River State Trail is in the northwest. Merrick State Park is also located here. • Named for the Buffalo River • 1853 • Psychologist and pediatrician Arnold Gesell • Dairying, cattle, hogs, sheep, alfalfa, hay; timber.

BURNETT *Siren* • 15,674 • 822 • Northwestern WI, bounded on the northwest by the St. Croix River (forming the MN state line) and on the northeast by the Namekagon River. The county is largely wooded, with numerous lakes. St. Croix National Scenic Riverway defines the St. Croix and Namekagon rivers. Governor Knowles (St. Croix) State Forest is in the west. Units of the St. Croix Indian Reservation are in the southeast. Fort Folle Avoine Historical Park is also here. • Named for Thomas P. Burnett (1800–1846), WI territorial legislator • 1856 from Polk • Sheep; timber.

CALUMET *Chilton* • 40,631 • 320 • Eastern WI, bounded on the west by Lake Winnebago; drained by the Manitowoc River. High Cliff State Park is in the northwest on Lake Winnebago. The county is urbanized in the north as part of the Appleton metropolitan area. • Named for a Menominee village that was located here, itself named for the Indian smoking pipe • 1836 from a territorial county • Dairying, barley, oats, corn, peas, hay; cattle, sheep; diversified manufacturing.

CHIPPEWA (one of three counties so named) *Chippewa Falls* • 55,195 • 1,010 • West-central WI; drained by the Chippewa and Yellow rivers. The county contains several small lakes, the largest being Lake Wissota, the state's largest artificial lake; Lake Wissota State Park is on its eastern shore. Brunet Island State Park, Chippewa Morraine State Recreation Area, and old Abe State Trail are here. • One of two counties (the other in MN) named for the Chippewa River • 1845 (prior to statehood) from Crawford (A former county of the same name existed at the time of the 1830 census, covering much of what is now Douglas, Bayfield, Ashland, Iron and Vilas counties) • Electronics engineer Seymour R. Cray • Dairying with creameries producing high-grade butter, barley, oats, soybeans, brans, alfalfa, hay, cattle, sheep, poultry; manufacture of computer parts, electronic components, hydraulic pumps, fishing lures, plastics, shoes, doors, sashes; beer, bottled spring water, packed meats.

CLARK (one of twelve counties so named) *Neillsville* • 33,557 • 1,216 • Central WI, drained by the Black and Eau Claire rivers. Bruce Mound ski area is in the southwest. • One of six counties named for General George Rogers Clark (1752–1818), officer in the Revolutionary War and frontiersman in the Northwest Territory • 1853 from Marathon • Principally dairying (especially cheese), also hogs, sheep, poultry, barley, oats, corn, alfalfa, hay, cranberries; vegetable canning, lumbering.

COLUMBIA (one of eight counties so named) *Portage* • 52,468 • 774 • South-central WI; drained by the Fox, Crawfish, Baraboo and Wisconsin rivers (the last forming part of the northwest and southwest boundary). The county contains resort lakes, notably Lake Wisconsin, and part of the Baraboo Range in the west. Wisconsin Dells, a dramatic and unusual canyon feature carved by the Wisconsin River, is a popular tourist area in the northwest. Cascade Mountain ski area is also here. • Named for the town of Columbus, WI • 1846 (prior to statehood) from Portage, Brown and Crawford • The 1.5-mile portage between the Wisconsin and Fox rivers at the site of the city of Portage was first crossed by Louis Joliet and Jacques Marquette in 1683. This vital link between the Great Lakes and the Mississippi River is now maintained by the Portage Canal. • Historian Frederick Jackson Turner. The city of Portage was the setting for many of the early short stories of native novelist and playwright Zona Gale. • Barley, oats, wheat, soybeans, peas, beans, tobacco, hogs, sheep, poultry, cattle, dairying; vegetable canning; manufacture of mobile homes, plastics, hosiery; tourism • The Indian Ceremonial (a dance) takes place at the natural Standing Rock amphitheater at the Wisconsin Dells each summer.

CRAWFORD (one of eleven counties so named) *Prairie du*

Chien • 17,243 • 573 • Southwestern WI, bounded on the west by the Mississippi River (here forming the IA state line) and on the southeast by the Wisconsin River, which enters the Mississippi River at the southeastern corner of the county; drained by the Kickapoo River. Lock and Dam No. 9 is north of Prairie du Chien. Part of the Upper Mississippi National Wildlife and Fish Refuge extends along the western border. • Named for Fort Crawford, itself named for William Harris Crawford (1772–1834), U.S. senator from GA, U.S. secretary of war and U.S. secretary of the treasury (one of six counties named directly or indirectly for the secretary) • 1818 from a territorial county • Long a rendezvous point for explorers, missionaries and traders as the western terminus of the Fox-Wisconsin river route to the Mississippi River, Prairie du Chien is the second oldest white settlement in WI after Green Bay. It was first the site of British and French forts and trading posts before becoming Fort Shelby during the War of 1812, and Fort Crawford in 1816. In 1820, it became the depot for the American Fur Company. The company's factor, Hercules Dousman, is considered WI's first millionaire. • Neurologist and physiologist Walter B. Cannon • Dairying, corn, alfalfa, hay, tobacco, cattle, hogs, sheep; cheese-making, processing of other farm products, other light manufacturing. • The Fort Crawford Medical Museum is located in a restored military hospital at Fort Crawford. It was here that William Beaumont continued his experiments with the human digestive system.

DANE *Madison* • 426,526 (the second most populated county in WI) • 1,202 • Southern WI, bounded on the northwest by the Wisconsin River; drained by the Yahara and Sugar rivers, and by Waterloo and Koshkonong creeks. The county is urbanized at its center around Madison. It includes several large lakes, notably the Four Lakes (Mendota, Monona, Waubesa, Kegonsa). Blue Mound State Park is on its western border. The western part of Glacial Drumlin State Trail is in the east; the eastern half of Military Ridge State Trail is in the southwest. Lake Kegonsa State Park is in the southeast; Governor Nelson State Park is on the northern shore of Lake Mendota. • Named for Nathan Dane (1752–1835), U.S. representative from MA who proposed the Ordinance of 1787 establishing the Northwest Territory • 1836 from Iowa County • Madison became the permanent capital of WI Territory in 1838 following strong advocacy by James Duane Doty in the midst of frenetic land speculation in the newly formed territory. The capitol rose in an uninhabited wooded site on a narrow isthmus between lakes Monona and Mendota. The territorial legislature held its first session here even before the building was completed. Madison was headquarters for the Progressive Party in the 1920s, led by the La Follette family. • Olympic skater Eric Heiden; physician William P. Murphy; painter Georgia O'Keeffe; novelist and playwright Thornton Wilder. Agricultural research chemist Stephen Babcock and Xhosa novelist and educator A. C. Jordan both died here. • Dairying prominent, also barley, oats, wheat, corn, soybeans, peas, beans, alfalfa, hay, cattle, hogs, sheep, poultry; meat packing; manu-facture of batteries, dairy equipment, hospital supplies; finance, insurance; research and education (U. of WI–Madison; Edgewood College) government offices. Federal agencies here include the U.S. Forest Products Laboratory.

DODGE (one of four counties so named) *Juneau* • 85,897 • 882 • South-eastern WI; drained by the Rock River and its tributaries, including the Crawfish River. The county includes Beaver Dam, Fox and Sinissippi lakes. Horicon National Wildlife Refuge and Horicon Marsh Wildlife Area are in the north. • One of three counties named for General Henry Dodge (1782–1867), officer in the War of 1812 and Black Hawk War, first governor of WI Territory and U.S. senator from WI • 1836 (prior to statehood) from territorial county • The county's first settlers arrived in 1838, attracted by the beauty and fertility of the Rock River valley. • Dairying (especially cheese production), barley, oats, soybeans, peas, beans, alfalfa, hay, cherries, cattle, hogs, sheep, poultry; processing of farm products, including the canning of peas, corn, and beans; manufacture of stoves, shoes, cement blocks, metal products; iron mining.

DOOR *Sturgeon Bay* • 27,961 • 483 • Northeastern WI, on the northern end of the Door Peninsula, bounded on the east by Lake Michigan, on the west by Green Bay (of Lake Michigan). The county includes Washington and Chamber islands. A resort area, the county contains Peninsula, Potawatomi, Newport, Whitefish Dunes, and Rock Island state parks. National wildlife refuges here include Gravel Island and two units of Green Bay. • Named for Porte des Morts Strait, which translates, "Death's Door" • 1851 from Brown • Football coach Curly Lambeau died here. • Fishing; dairying, barley, oats, wheat, peas, beans, cherries, cranberries, apples; quarrying; shipbuilding; tourism • A ship canal, constructed across the Door peninsula in 1878, connects Green Bay with the rest of Lake Michigan, and is maintained by the federal government.

DOUGLAS *Superior* • 43,287 • 1,309 (the fourth largest county in WI) • Extreme northwestern WI, bounded on the west by the MN state line and on the north by the St. Louis River (forming the MN state line) and Lake Superior; drained by the Eau Claire, Amnicon, Bois Brule, and Black rivers. Pattison State Park (containing Big Manitou Falls, the largest in the state) Mont Du Lac ski area, Amnicon Falls State Park, Brule River State Forest, and part of St. Croix National Scenic Riverway are all in the county. Saunders and Wild Rivers state trails are also here. • One of twelve counties named for Stephen A. Douglas (1813–61), U.S. orator and statesman • 1854 from unorganized territory • Senator Douglas was a member of the company that developed the site of Superior. The city's growth was stimulated by the discovery of Gogebic Range iron ore deposits in 1883. • Cattle, poultry; limited farming on cutover forest land; manufacture of briquets, hardboard, flour, dairy products, ships, heavy equipment; wood conversion; flour milling; oil refining; tourism; education (U. of WI–Superior). The port of Superior, WI–Duluth, MN (across the St. Louis River) is the western terminus of the St. Lawrence Seaway and one of the largest ports in the U.S. in cargo tonnage handled. Crude oil arrives here from western Canada via a 1,127-mile pipeline. Superior tranships grain, iron ore, taconite, limestone, and coal from rail to water conveyances.

DUNN (one of two counties so named, the other in ND) *Menomonie* • 39,858 • 852 • Western WI; drained by the Red Cedar and Chippewa rivers. Hoffman Hills State Recreation Area is here. Red Cedar and Chippewa River state trails are also in the county. • Named for Charles Dunn (1799–1872), WI state senator and first Chief Justice of WI territory • 1854 from Chippewa • Dairying, barley, oats, corn, soybeans, beans, alfalfa, hay, cattle, hogs, sheep, poultry; lumbering; manufacturing; education (U. of WI–Stout).

EAU CLAIRE *Eau Claire* • 93,142 • 638 • West-central WI; drained by the Chippewa and Eau Claire rivers. Lake Eau Claire Reservoir is here. The county includes a section of Buffalo River State Trail. • Named for the Eau Claire River • 1856 from Clark • Dairying is the most important industry; also cattle, barley, corn, oats, soybeans, peas; with diversified manufacturing, including rubber tires, culverts, machineshop products, paper; meat packing, brewing, food processing; printing; education (U. of WI–Eau Claire) • Eau Claire's Carson Park contains the Chippewa Valley Museum and the Paul Bunyan Logging Camp (a replica of an early lumber camp).

FLORENCE (one of two counties so named, the other in SC) *Florence* • 5,088 • 488 • Northeastern WI, bounded on the north by the Brule River and on the east by the Menominee River (together forming the MI state line); drained by the Pine River. The county contains a section of Nicolet National Forest and Keyes Park ski area. Lakes are scattered throughout. • Named for the Florence Mine and the town of Florence, WI, which were both named for the wife of Nelson P. Hulst, geologist and mining engineer who developed the mine • 1882 from Marinette and Oconto • Lumbering; dairying, potatoes.

FOND DU LAC *Fond du Lac* • 97,296 • 723 • Eastern WI; drained by the Milwaukee, Rock, Sheboygan, and Fond du Lac rivers. The southern tip of Lake Winnebago is in the northeast. The northern section of Horicon National Wildlife Refuge, Wild Goose State Trail, and part of Kettle Moraine State Forest (north unit), including Ice Age National Science Reserve, are also here. • Named for the city of Fond du Lac, WI • 1836 (prior to statehood) from territorial county • The site of Ripon was first a communal settlement organized by a group of Fourierites (followers of the French socialist philosopher Charles Fourier) in 1844. The city was a stronghold of the abolitionist movement. It is considered the birthplace of the Republican Party; organizational meetings attended by disaffected Whigs, anti-Nebraska Democrats, and Free Soilers were held here in February and March, 1854 (Little White School House shrine). • Feminist leader Carrie Chapman Catt; inventor and manufacturer King Camp Gillette; London merchant Harry Gordon Selfridge • Barley, oats, wheat, soybeans, peas, alfalfa, hay, cattle, hogs, sheep; vegetable canning, processing of dairy products, animal feed production; manufacture of dairy-processing equipment, machine tools, outboard motors, snowmobiles, ignition parts, fuel pumps, structural steel products, washing machines and dryers, microscope slides; education (Ripon College; Marian College) • St. Paul's Episcopal Cathedral in Fond du Lac has stained glass windows and wood carvings from Oberammergau, Germany.

FOREST (one of two counties so named, the other in PA) *Crandon* • 10,024 • 1,014 • Northeastern WI, bounded on the north in part by the Brule River (forming the MI state line); drained by the Pine and Peshtigo rivers. Most of the county is covered by Nicolet National Forest. Many resort lakes are found here, as well as Sokaogon Chippewa and Forest County Potawatomi Indian communities. • Named for the forests in the area • 1885 from Langlade and Oconto • Some dairying, potatoes; tourism; lumbering.

GRANT (one of fifteen counties so named) *Lancaster* • 49,597 • 1,148 • Extreme southwestern WI, bounded on the south by the IL state line, on the north by the Wisconsin River, and on the west by the Mississippi River, here forming the IA state line; drained by the Platte and Blue rivers. Wyalusing and Nelson Dewey state parks are here, as is the western end of Pecatonica State Trail, which terminates at Platteville. Lock and Dam numbers 10 and 11 are on the Mississippi River. • Probably named for the Grant River • 1836 from Iowa County • Physiologist Herbert S. Gassner; reformer William Simon U'Ren • Barley, oats, corn, soybeans, alfalfa, hay, cattle, hogs, sheep, poultry; zinc, lead; some manufacturing; education (U. of WI–Platteville).

GREEN (one of two counties so named) *Monroe* • 33,647 • 584 • Southern WI, bounded on the south by the IL state line; drained by the Sugar and Pecatonica rivers. The county includes New Glarus Woods State Park and Sugar River State Trail. Also located here is Browntown-Cadiz Springs State Recreation Area. • One of sixteen counties named for General Nathanael Greene (1742–86), Revolutionary War officer and quartermaster general. (The missing e is not explained.) • 1836 from Iowa County • New Glarus was established as a semi-commune in 1845 by immigrants driven from their canton of Glarus in Switzerland by famine. • Air Force officer Nathan F. Twining • Dairying center (especially Swiss cheese), barley, oats, wheat, corn, soybeans, beans, alfalfa, hay, hogs, sheep, poultry; manufacture of wood products, feed, hardware, Swiss-style embroidery • The town of New Glarus preserves its Swiss heritage through Swiss Historical Village, which includes replicas of buildings constructed by its early settlers. The Heidi Festival is held in June, a Swiss Volksfest takes place in August, and Schiller's drama *Wilhelm Tell* is presented each September.

GREEN LAKE *Green Lake* • 19,105 • 354 • Central WI;

drained by the Fox and Grand rivers. Green Lake and Puckaway Lake are here. • Named for Green Lake • 1858 from Marquette District • In the early 20th century Green Lake was a popular vacation resort for wealthy Chicagoans. • Vegetables, wheat, corn, soybeans, peas, hogs, poultry, sheep; canning; creameries; fur farms; tourism.

IOWA (one of two counties so named, the other in IA) *Dodgeville* • 22,780 • 763 • Southern WI, bounded on the north by the Wisconsin River; drained by the Pecatonica and Blue rivers. The county includes Tower Hill, Blue Mound, and Governor Dodge state parks. The western part of Military Ridge State Trail runs through the center of the county, terminating at Dodgeville. • Named for either the Iowa River or the Iowa Indians • 1829 (prior to statehood) from a territorial county • Dairy-products processing; barley, oats, corn, soybeans, cattle, hogs, sheep, poultry; lead and zinc deposits • Frank Lloyd Wright's Taliesin (East), including Wright's first architectural school for apprentices, is located here. The House on the Rock, designed by Wright's disciple Alexander Jordan, is a few miles south.

IRON (one of four counties so named) *Hurley* • 6,861 • 757 • Northern WI, bounded partly on the north by Lake Superior and the Montreal River (here forming the MI state line) and on the northeast by the MI state line; drained by tributaries of the Bad River and by the Montreal River. The Gogebic Iron Range extends across the southern half of the county. (Mining operations here began in 1884 when the railroad extended its line to the district.) The county is mostly wooded with resort lakes. Whitecap Mountain ski area is here, as well as Turtle-Flambeau Flowage Reservoir. Part of Northern Highland American Legion State Forest and Lac Du Flambeau Indian Reservation are on the southeast. • Named for the Gogebic Iron Range • 1893 from Ashland and Oneida • Iron mining is its principal industry.

JACKSON (one of twenty-four counties so named) *Black River Falls* • 19,100 • 987 • West-central WI; intersected by the Black, Buffalo, and Trempealeau rivers. The county includes Ho-Chunk Indian Reservation. Black River State Forest is prominent in the center of the county. • One of twenty-two counties named directly or indirectly for President Andrew Jackson • 1853 from Crawford • Dairying, potatoes, barley, corn, soybeans, peas, brans, cranberries, cattle, hogs, sheep, poultry.

JEFFERSON *Jefferson* • 74,021 • 557 • Southern WI; drained by the Rock, Bark and Crawfish rivers. The county includes Aztalan State Park. Lake Koshkonong is in the southwest, with Glacial Drumlin State Trail passing through the center of the county. A small part of Kettle Moraine State Forest is also here. • One of twenty-six counties named directly or indirectly for President Thomas Jefferson • 1836 from Dodge and Waukesha • Dairying is predominant; wheat, corn, soybeans, potatoes, cattle, hogs, sheep, poultry; diversified manufacturing. • The first kindergarten in the U.S. was opened in Watertown (in the section of town that falls within Jefferson County) in 1856 by Mrs. Carl Schurz.

JUNEAU *Mauston* • 24,316 • 768 • Central WI, bounded on the east by the Wisconsin River (forming Castle Rock and Pentenwell lakes); drained by the Yellow, Lemonweir and Baraboo rivers. The county contains part of the Wisconsin Dells. Necedah National Wildlife Refuge is in the northwest. Also here are Buckhorn State Park and sections of La Crosse River and Elroy-Sparta state trails. Volk Field ANG Base is located at Camp Douglas. • Named for Solomon Juneau (1793–1856), early French trader and "Father of Milwaukee" • 1856 from Adams • Botanist Bernard O. Dodge • Dairy products; potatoes, beans, corn, soybeans, cattle, hogs, sheep, poultry.

KENOSHA *Kenosha* • 149,577 • 273 • Extreme southeastern WI, bounded on the east by Lake Michigan and on the south by the IL state line; drained by the Des Plaines and Fox rivers. The county includes Bong State Recreation Area and Wilmot Mountain ski area. • Named for the city of Kenosha, WI • 1850 from Racine • The first public school in WI was opened in Kenosha in 1849. • Dairying, wheat, corn, soybeans, hogs, sheep; manufacture of automobiles, musical instruments, tools, textiles, wire rope, underwear, brass rods, plumbing fixtures, commercial fertilizer, fire apparatus, cranberry products, equipment for food and dairy processing, furniture, apparel; education (Carthage College; U. of WI–Parkside) • Kenosha's Harmony Hall is headquarters for the Society for the Preservation and Encouragement of Barber Shop Quartet Singing in America, Inc. Kenosha owns most of its Lake Michigan frontage and has developed parkland here.

KEWAUNEE *Kewaunee* • 20,187 • 343 • Eastern WI, bounded on the east by Lake Michigan and on the northwest by Green Bay (of Lake Michigan); drained by the Kewaunee River and several small streams. The county is located near the base of Door Peninsula. A section of Ahnapee State Trail is in the north. • Named for the Kewaunee River • 1852 from Manitowoc • Plant pathologist Elvin C. Stakman • Dairying, barley, oats, wheat, corn, peas, beans, hay, cattle, hogs; lumbering, woodworking.

LA CROSSE *La Crosse* • 107,120 • 453 • Western WI, bounded on the west by the Mississippi River; drained by the La Crosse and Black rivers (the latter forming the county's northwestern boundary). Part of the Upper Mississippi National Wildlife and Fish Refuge follows the river. La Crosse River and Great River state trails traverse the county. Mount La Crosse ski area is also located here. • Named for the city of La Crosse, WI • 1851 from unorganized territory • La Crosse was the site of neutral ground established by local Indian tribes to socialize and play Indian games, including lacrosse. • Author Hamlin Garland; film director Nicholas Ray; film director Joseph Losey • Corn, soybeans, cattle, hogs, sheep, dairying; lumber milling; manufacture of heating and cooling equipment, aircraft parts, clothing, rubber footwear, beer and carbonated beverages, plastic products, sausage; education (U.

of WI at La Crosse; Viterbo College) • La Crosse's popular Oktoberfest attracts numerous visitors to the county.

LAFAYETTE (one of six counties so named) *Darlington* • 16,137 • 634 • Southern WI, bounded on the south by the IL state line; drained by the Pecatonica and Galena rivers. The eastern section of Pecatonica State Trail is located here, as is Yellowstone Lake State Park. • One of seventeen counties named for the Marquis de Lafayette (1757–1834), French statesman and soldier who fought with the Americans during the Revolutionary War • 1846 (prior to statehood) from Iowa County • Belmont was the first capital of WI territory; the first legislature met here for forty-two days in 1836 in one of four hastily constructed frame buildings. The area formerly had a large lead-mining industry. • Barley, oats, wheat, corn, soybeans, cattle, hogs, sheep; zinc mining.

LANGLADE *Antigo* • 20,740 • 873 • Northeastern WI; drained by the Wolf (a National Scenic River) and Eau Claire rivers. The county has numerous lakes. Part of Nicolet National Forest is in the east. Kettlebowl Hill ski area is also here. • Named for Charles-Michel Mouet de Langlade, an Indian leader who established a trading post at Green Bay in 1764. • 1879 as New County from Oconto; name changed in 1880 • Communications theorist Jeffrey Heinle • Predominantly lumbering; also potatoes, barley, oats, wheat, corn, beans, poultry.

LINCOLN (one of twenty-four counties so named) *Merrill* • 29,641 • 883 • North-central WI; drained by the Wisconsin River. The county includes Council Grounds State Park. Also here is the southern terminus of Bearskin-Hiawatha State Trail. • One of eighteen counties named for President Abraham Lincoln • 1874 from Marathon • Dairying, barley; paper milling; diversified manufacturing.

MANITOWOC *Manitowoc* • 82,887 • 592 • Eastern WI, bounded on the east by Lake Michigan; drained by the Manitowoc River. The county contains Point Beach State Forest and Hidden Valley ski area. • Named for the Manitowoc River • 1836 (prior to statehood) from a territorial county • Manitowoc has been a shipbuilding center since the 1840s. Hundreds of ships, including World War II submarines, have been constructed over the years. • Senator Thomas J. Walsh • Barley, oats, wheat, corn, soybeans, peas, brans, alfalfa, hay, poultry, cattle, dairying; marble and stone; diversified manufacturing, including aluminum products, electrical machinery; vegetable canning; processing of malt products; shipbuilding; education (Silver Lake College) • The Hamilton Wood Type and Printing Museum is in Two Rivers. The Wisconsin Maritime Museum in Manitowoc displays ship models and equipment.

MARATHON *Wausau* • 125,834 • 1,545 (the largest county in WI) • Central WI; drained by the Wisconsin River and its tributaries (Eau Claire, Big and Little Eau Pleine), Big Rib and Placer rivers, and DuBay and Big Eau Pleine reservoirs. Rib Mountain State Park is a winter sports center. Mountain-Bay State Trail is also found here. • Named for the site of the famous battle in Greece (490 B.C.) • 1850 from Portage • Major cheese producer, other dairy products; lumbering, and manufacture of wood and paper products; oats, barley, corn, potatoes, alfalfa, hay, ginseng, cranberries, cattle, sheep, hogs, poultry; manufacture of electric motors, construction equipment, plastics; insurance • Wausau is headquarters of the Wisconsin Valley Improvement Company, a state-regulated enterprise that stores and releases water to factories.

MARINETTE *Marinette* • 43,384 • 1,402 (the third largest county in WI) • Northeastern WI, bounded on the east by the Menominee River (forming the MI state line) and on the southeast by Green Bay; drained by the Peshtigo River. • Named for the city of Marinette, WI, itself named for Marguerite "Marinette" Chevalier (1793–1865), a successful female fur trader • 1879 from Oconto • On October 8, 1871, the same day as the more famous Chicago fire, winds delivered flames from the forest fires in the county to the city of Peshtigo. 1,152 are known to have died. The whole city was leveled and more than 1,200,000 acres of forest were destroyed (Peshtigo Fire Museum). Logging was the primary industry of the county until about 1900. • Lumbering; wheat, corn, beans, dairying; some manufacturing, including chemicals, wood and paper products, auto parts, boats; tourism, smelt fishing.

MARQUETTE *Montello* • 15,832 (28% increase since 1990; the fastest growing county in WI) • 455 • South-central WI; drained by the Fox River and its tributaries. The county contains several lakes, including Buffalo and part of Puckaway. Fox River National Wildlife Refuge is also here. • One of two counties (the other in MI) named for Jacques Marquette (1637–75), French missionary explorer (with Louis Joliet) of the Wisconsin and Mississippi Rivers • 1836 (prior to statehood) from Marquette District • Corn, soybeans, hogs, sheep; dairy product processing; granite quarries.

MENOMINEE (one of two counties so named, the other in MI) • *Keshena* • 4,562 (the least populated county in WI) • 358 • East-central WI; drained by the Wolf (a National Scenic River) and Red rivers. The county consists entirely of the Menominee Indian Reservation; Indians own ninety-nine percent of the land here. • Named for the Menominee Indians, the name probably meaning "wild rice people" • 1961 from Shawano and Oconto • In the 1950s, the Menominee tribe won a $9.5 million judgment against the U.S. government for mismanagement of its tribal affairs. • Wild rice (harvested with traditional Indian techniques), barley, oats, alfalfa, cattle, hogs, sheep, dairying; lumber.

MILWAUKEE *Milwaukee* • 940,164 (the most populated county in WI) • 242 • Southeastern WI, bounded on the east by Lake Michigan; drained by the Milwaukee, Menomonee, and Root rivers. The county is highly urbanized and industrialized around the city of Milwaukee. There are small areas of remnant agriculture mostly in the far south. • Named for the Milwaukee River • 1834 (prior to statehood) • German, Irish, and Polish immigrants have played an important role in the cultural, economic, and political development of the county. In 1910, Milwaukee became the first major city in the U.S. to elect a Socialist mayor (Emil Seidel). Milwaukee was the scene of Civil rights-related marches and riots during the 1960s. • Poet and critic Horace Gregory; Chief Justice of the U.S. William H. Rehnquist; publisher and philanthropist Walter H. Annenberg; architect Benjamin Church; aviation pioneer Billy Mitchell • Manufacture of beer, automobile parts, industrial and farming machinery; spark plugs, electronic equipment, malleable castings, electrical appliances, excavating and garden machinery, industrial cranes, conveyor belts, malt, high-tech biomedical supplies, tile, wood, metal, plastic, and leather products; wheat, soybeans; insurance; education (Marquette U.; Mount Mary College; Alverno College; U. of WI–Milwaukee; Cardinal Stritch U.; Milwaukee School of Engineering, WI Conservatory of Music; WI Lutheran College) • The corporate headquarters of seven Fortune 1000 companies are located in the county. One of Frank Lloyd Wright's last major works, the Annunciation Greek Orthodox Church, was completed in 1961. Marquette University's Joan of Arc Chapel was built in France during the 1400s and reassembled on the campus in the 1960s; it is the only medieval structure in the Western Hemisphere where Mass is said regularly. Grant Park in South Milwaukee is the scene of the annual Spectacle of Music. Milwaukee is often called "Cream City" for its many old cream-colored brick buildings. The Wisconsin State Fair is held each August in West Allis. The first practical typewriter was invented in Milwaukee in 1867 by Christopher Latham Sholes. Milwaukee is home to the Milwaukee Brewers (Miller Park) and Bucks (Bradley Center).

MONROE *Sparta* • 40,899 • 901 • West-central WI; drained by the Lemonweir, Black, La Crosse and Kickapoo rivers. The county contains Fort McCoy Military Reserve. Mill Bluff State Park is on the eastern boundary. A section of La Crosse River State Trail traverses the county; Elroy-Sparta State Trail crosses from the southeast and terminates at Sparta. • One of seventeen counties named for President James Monroe • 1854 from unorganized territory • Dairying, tobacco, cranberries (Cranberry Expo in the northeast), corn, soybeans, alfalfa, hay, cattle; timber; lumber; processing of dairy products.

OCONTO *Oconto* • 35,634 • 998 • Northeastern WI, bounded on the east by Green Bay; drained by the Oconto River. A large section of Nicolet National Forest is here, as is Copper Culture State Park. • Named for the Oconto River • 1851 from unorganized territory • Oconto city was the site of a mission established by Jesuit Claude-Jean Allouez in 1669. The world's first Christian Science Church was erected here in 1886. • Lumbering and paper manufacture; dairying, barley, oats, wheat, brans, hay, cattle, hogs, poultry; manufacture of small boats, gloves; food processing (especially pickles); resort tourism.

ONEIDA (one of three counties so named) *Rhinelander* •

36,776 • 1,125 • Northern WI; drained by the Wisconsin River. The county has numerous lakes with attached resorts. It includes part of Northern Highland American Legion State Forest and a section of Nicolet National Forest. The northern terminus of Bearskin-Hiawatha State Trail is here; the trail crosses into Lincoln County to the south. • One of two counties (the other in NY) named for the Oneida Indians • 1885 from Lincoln • Oneida was an early logging county. • Lumbering; dairying, potatoes, cranberries, brans; manufacture of paper (glassine and wax paper), high speed drills; tourism • The Rhinelander Logging Museum includes a mock-up of a pioneer lumber camp. Also on display here is a replica of a "hodag," an animal revealed to be a photographic hoax.

OUTAGAMIE *Appleton* • 160,971 • 640 • Eastern WI; drained by the Wolf, Fox, and Embarrass rivers. The county is urbanized in the south along the Fox River. Part of Oneida Indian Reservation is here. • Outagamie is the Ojibway name for the Fox Indian tribe • 1851 from Brown • America's first hydroelectric power station opened in Appleton in September, 1882. The Hearthstone was the first home in the world lit by hydroelectric power. • Dairying; paper milling; some cattle, hogs, sheep, poultry, also barley, oats, wheat, corn, soybeans, peas, beans, alfalfa, hay; manufacture of paper-mill machinery and equipment; education (Lawrence U.) • The Institute of Paper Chemistry affiliated with Lawrence University is home to the Dard Hunter Paper Museum.

OZAUKEE *Port Washington* • 82,317 • 232 (tied with Pepin for smallest county in WI) • Eastern WI, bounded on the east by Lake Michigan; drained by the Milwaukee River. The southern part of the county has been urbanized as part of the Milwaukee metropolitan area. Huntington Beach State Park is on Lake Michigan. • Ozaukee is the proper name of the Sauk Indian tribe • 1853 from Milwaukee • Geologist and paleontologist Amadeus William Grabau • Dairying and dairy-product processing, livestock, poultry, vegetables, barley, wheat, soybeans, peas; diversified manufacturing; fisheries; education (Concordia U. WI).

PEPIN *Durand* • 7,213 • 232 (tied with Ozaukee for smallest county in WI) • Western WI, bounded on the southwest by Lake Pepin (enlargement of the Mississippi River formed by a natural dam composed of silt from the Chippewa River); drained by the Chippewa River (forming the southeastern boundary) • Named for Lake Pepin • 1858 from Chippewa • Educator Helen Parkhurst • Corn, soybeans, hogs, dairying; fishing and resort tourism.

PIERCE (One of five counties so named) *Ellsworth* • 38,804 • 576 • Western WI, bounded on the west by the St. Croix River (St. Croix National Scenic Riverway) and on the southwest and south by the Mississippi River (creating Lake Pepin in the south) all forming the MN state line. Lock and Dam No. 3 on the Mississippi River is here. Kinnickinnic State Park is in the northwest. • One of four counties named for President Franklin Pierce • 1853 from Saint Croix • Dairying, cattle, hogs, sheep, barley, oats, corn, soybeans, hay, poultry; lumbering; manufacturing; education (U. of WI–River Falls).

POLK (one of twelve counties so named) *Balsam Lake* • 41,319 • 917 • Northwestern WI, bounded on the west by the St. Croix River, forming the MN state line. Part of the St. Croix National Scenic Riverway is here. The county includes Interstate State Park, part of Knowles State Forest, Trollhaugen ski area, St. Croix Falls, and Gandy Dancer State Trail. • One of eleven counties named for President James K. Polk • 1853 from Saint Croix • Furniture designer Gustav Stickley • Dairying, barley, wheat, corn, soybeans, beans, alfalfa, hay, cattle, hogs, sheep.

PORTAGE (one of two counties so named, the other in OH) *Stevens Point* • 67,182 • 806 • Central WI; intersected by the Wisconsin River (impounded by Du Bay Dam near the northern border); drained by the Plover and Waupaca rivers. The county contains Standing Rocks ski area and a section of Tomorrow River State Trail. • Named for the portage of canoes or other craft between the Fox and Wisconsin rivers, previously located in this county but now in Columbia County. • 1836 from territorial county (prior to statehood) • The county's cultural development was influenced by a large number of Polish immigrants. • Corn, peas, potatoes, cattle, hogs, sheep, poultry, dairying; manufacture of pulp and paper products, furniture, sports and fishing equipment, beer, plastics; insurance; education (U. of WI — Stevens Point).

PRICE *Phillips* • 15,822 • 1,253 • Northern WI; drained by the Flambeau and Jump rivers. The county includes a section of Chequamegon National Forest, a small part of Flambeau River State Forest, a section of Tuscobia State Trail, and several resort lakes. Timms Hill, at 1,951 feet, is the highest point in WI. • Named for William T. Price (1824–86), WI state senator and U.S. representative from WI • 1879 from Chippewa and Lincoln • Phillips was destroyed by fire in 1894. • Dairying, barley; lumbering • The world's largest collection of concrete art is found in Wisconsin Concrete Park in Phillips.

RACINE *Racine* • 188,831 (the fifth most populated county in WI) • 333 • Southeastern WI, bounded on the east by Lake Michigan; drained by the Fox and Root rivers. The county is urbanized in the east. There are small lakes in the west. • Named for the town of Racine, WI • 1836 from territorial county (prior to statehood) • Jerome I. Case's threshing-machine plant, established in Racine in 1842, was the first agricultural-machinery factory in what was then considered the American West. • Actor Frederic March • Wheat, corn, oats, soybeans, hogs, sheep; recreation; extensive manufacture of chemicals, waxes and polishes, farm machinery, metal casings, electrical equipment, automotive and hydraulic products, processed foods; publishing • Racine is the site of the S.C. Johnson Wax administration and research complex, one of the most important commercial and industrial designs of architect Frank Lloyd Wright. Malted milk was invented in Racine in 1887 by William Horlick.

RICHLAND (one of seven counties so named) *Richland Center* • 17,924 • 586 • South-central WI, bounded on the south by the Wisconsin River; drained by the Pine and Kickapoo rivers. • Richland originated as a promotional name chosen at a meeting of locals to draw more settlers to the county • 1842 from Crawford, Sauk, and Iowa counties (prior to statehood) • Architect Frank Lloyd Wright • Dairying, corn, apples, alfalfa, hay, cattle, hogs, sheep; maple syrup.

ROCK (one of three counties so named) *Janesville* • 152,307 • 720 • Southern WI, bounded on the south by the IL state line; drained by the Rock and Sugar rivers, and Turtle Creek. A small part of Lake Koshkonong is on the northeast border. • Probably named for the Rock River, although some sources say it was named for a large rock used as landmark on the north side of the river. • 1836 from territorial county (prior to statehood) • Naturalist and author Roy Chapman Andrews; astronomer Harold D. Babcock; educator and reformer Frances E. Willard; poet Ella Wheeler Wilcox; composer Carrie Jacobs Bond (who wrote "I Love You Truly" in Janesville) • Wheat, corn, soybeans, peas, beans, cattle, sheep, hogs, tobacco, dairying; manufacture of automobiles, auto bodies, fountain pens, organs, folding doors, insulation, electronic equipment, woodworking machinery, paper; resort tourism; education (Beloit College) • The Wisconsin State School for the Visually Handicapped is the oldest of the state's welfare institutions.

RUSK (one of two counties so named, the other in TX) *Ladysmith* • 15,347 • 913 • Northern WI; drained by the Thornapple, Chippewa and Flambeau rivers. Part of Flambeau River State Forest is here, as is Christie Mountain ski area. • Named for Col. Jeremiah M. Rusk (1830–93), governor of WI and U.S. secretary of agriculture • 1901 as Gates from Chippewa; name changed in 1905 • Barley, sheep; lumbering; education (Mt. Senario College).

SAINT CROIX *Hudson* • 63,155 (26% increase since 1990; the second fastest growing county in WI) • 722 • Western WI, bounded on the west by the St. Croix River, forming the MN state line; drained by the Eau Galle and Apple rivers. St. Croix Nation Scenic Riverway defines the St. Croix. The county includes Willow River State Park, Lake George reservoir (on the southern boundary) and many small lakes. • Named for the river • 1840 from territorial county, prior to statehood • Dairying, barley, oats, wheat, corn, soybeans, beans, alfalfa, hay, cattle, sheep, hogs, poultry; manufacture of wood products.

SAUK *Baraboo* • 55,225 • 838 • South-central WI, bounded on the northeast and south by the Wisconsin River (here forming Lake Wisconsin), with Wisconsin Dells in the northeast; drained by the Baraboo River and tributaries of the Wisconsin River. The county has several lake resorts. It also includes Devils Lake, Natural Bridge, Mirror Lake, and Rocky Arbor state parks. Christmas Mountain and Devils Head ski areas are also in the county. • Named for a large village of Sauk Indians located here • 1840 from territorial county (prior to statehood) • From 1884 to 1938 Baraboo served as the winter headquarters for the Barnum and Bailey Circus. It was the home of other smaller circuses, as well. (The county is now the home of Circus World Museum.) • Circus founder John Ringling and his brothers (The county is the birthplace of their circus.) • Dairying, grains, peas, beans, soybeans, alfalfa, hay, livestock, poultry; lumbering; manufacture of textiles; processing of canned foods. • The Mid-Continent Railway Museum in Baraboo displays steam locomotives and a restored 1894 depot. Spring Green is best known for its association with Frank Lloyd Wright. (His Taliesin [East] is just south in Iowa County.)

SAWYER *Hayward* • 16,196 • 1,256 (the fifth largest county in WI) • Northern WI; drained by the Chippewa, Namekagon, Thornapple, and Flambeau rivers. The county is largely forested, with many lakes; the largest is Lake Chippewa. It includes Lac Court Oreilles Indian Reservation, part of Chequamegon National Forest, and part of Flambeau River State Forest, including part of Little Falls-Slough Gundy Scenic Area. St. Croix National Scenic Waterway defines the Namekagon River in the northwest. A section of Tuscobia State Trail crosses the county. • Named for Philetus Sawyer (1816–1900), U.S. representative and senator from WI • 1883 from Ashland and Chippewa • Lumbering; tourism • The National Freshwater Fishing Hall of Fame is in Hayward.

SHAWANO *Shawano* • 40,664 • 893 • East-central WI; drained by the Wolf (a National Scenic River) and Embarrass rivers. Stockbridge-Munsee Indian Community is here. Shawano is the largest of several lakes in the county. • Probably named for Shawano Lake • 1853 from Oconto • Sawmills; barley, oats, corn, beans, potatoes, alfalfa, hay, cattle, sheep, hogs; granite and marble.

SHEBOYGAN *Sheboygan* • 112,646 • 514 • Eastern WI, bounded on the east by Lake Michigan; drained by the Sheboygan and Onion rivers. The county includes Kohler-Andrae State Park and a part of the northern unit of Kettle Moraine State Forest. • Named for the Sheboygan River • 1836 from territorial county (prior to statehood) • Sheboygan Indian Mound Park, a state historic site in the city, contains 18 effigy burial mounds (500–750 AD) of the Woodland Indians. German immigrants played a strong role in the cultural and economic development of Sheboygan city. • One of the leading dairying and one of the largest cheese-exporting counties in the U.S.; also barley, oats, wheat, soybeans, peas, alfalfa, hay, cattle, hogs, poultry; manufacture of enamelware, porcelain and wood products, furniture, plastics, clothing, mirror plate, stainless steel, leather goods, food products (especially sausage); education (Lakeland College).

TAYLOR (one of seven counties so named) *Medford* • 19,680 • 975 • North-central WI; drained by the Black, Yellow, Jump, and Rib rivers. The county includes Miller Dam Flowage (reservoir) and part of Chequamegon National Forest. • Named for William Robert Taylor (?–1909), Grange activist and "farmer governor" of WI • 1875 from Clark and Lincoln • Dairying, barley, hay, livestock; sawmilling.

TREMPEALEAU *Whitehall* • 27,010 • 734 • Western WI, bounded on the west in part by the Trempealeau River, on the southwest by the Mississippi River (forming the MN state line), and on the southeast by the Black River; drained by the Buffalo, Black and Trempealeau rivers. The Upper Mississippi River National Wildlife and Fish Refuge follows the southwestern boundary. The county contains Perrot State Park and Great River State Trail in the south, on the Mississippi River. A section of Buffalo River State Trail is in the north. The county also includes Trempealeau National Wildlife Refuge. • Named for the Trempealeau River • 1854 from Chippewa • Dairying, barley, oats, corn, soybeans, alfalfa, hay, tobacco, cattle, hogs, sheep, poultry; timber; processing of farm products.

VERNON (one of three counties so named) *Viroqua* • 28,056 • 795 • Southwestern WI, bounded on the west by the Mississippi River (here forming the IA and MN state lines); drained by the Kickapoo, Bad Axe, and Baraboo rivers. Wildcat Mountain State Park and part of the Upper Mississippi National Wildlife and Fish Refuge are here. Lock and Dam No. 8 on the Mississippi is at Genoa. • Named for George Washington's Mount Vernon • Organized as Bad Ax County in 1851 from Richland and Crawford; name changed 1862 • On August 2, 1832, U.S. Army troops routed Sauk Indians here at the Battle of Bad Axe. • World War II naval officer Marc. A. Mitscher • Dairying, barley, corn, alfalfa, hay, cattle, hogs, sheep, poultry, tobacco growing and processing.

VILAS *Eagle River* • 21,033 • 873 • Northern WI, bounded on the north by the MI state line; drained by the Wisconsin and Manitowish rivers. The county lies in a wooded resort area with many lakes (including Lac Vieux Desert and Trout). It includes part of Nicolet National Forest, a large part of Northern Highland American Legion State Forest, and part of Lac du Flambeau Indian Reservation, site of G.W. Brown, Jr. Ojibwe Museum and Cultural Center. • Named for Col. William F. Vilas (1840–1908), Union officer, cabinet secretary, and U.S. senator from WI • 1893 from Oneida • Lumbering; resort tourism.

WALWORTH (one of two counties so named; the other in SD) *Elkhorn* • 93,759 • 555 • Southeastern WI, bounded on the south by the IL state line; drained by Turtle Creek and several other small streams. The county serves as a resort and recreation area for metropolitan Milwaukee. The southern part of Kettle Moraine State Forest is in the northwest. Big Foot Beach State Park is on Lake Geneva, a popular area for retirement and seasonal homes. • Named for Col. Reuben H. Walworth (1788–1867), officer in the War of 1812, jurist, and U.S. representative from NY • 1836 from territorial county (prior to statehood) • Fontana, at the western end of Lake Geneva, is the site of the Potawatomi village of Chief Big Toe (or Big Foot), which flourished in the 1830s. • Astronomer Edward E. Barnard died here. • Dairying, wheat, corn, soybeans, peas, potatoes, cattle, hogs, sheep, poultry; some manufacturing; food processing; education (U. of WI–Whitewater) • The University of Chicago's Yerkes Astronomical Observatory is in Williams Bay on Lake Geneva.

WASHBURN *Shell Lake* • 16,036 • 810 • Northwestern WI; drained by the Namekagon and Yellow rivers. The St. Croix National Scenic Riverway (Namekagon River) flows through the center of the county. • Named for Cadwallader C. Washburn (1818–82), U.S. representative from WI and governor of WI • 1883 from Burnett • Beans, cattle, sheep; resort tourism. • The Wisconsin Great Northern Railroad Excursion Train is located in Spooner.

WASHINGTON *West Bend* • 117,493 • 431 • Eastern WI; drained by the Milwaukee, Menomonee, and Rubicon rivers. Part of Kettle Moraine State Forest (northern unit) is in the north. The county also includes Sunburst ski area and Pike Lake State Park. The southeast is urbanized as part of the expanding Milwaukee metropolitan area. • One of thirty-one counties named for President George Washington • 1836 from territorial county (prior to statehood) • Dairying, barley, oats, wheat, corn, soybeans, peas, hogs, sheep, poultry; processing of dairy products, canning of fruit and vegetables; other industry; resort tourism.

WAUKESHA *Waukesha* • 360,767 (the third most populated county in WI) • 556 • Southeastern WI; drained by the Fox and Bark rivers. The county is urbanized in the east as an extension of the Milwaukee metropolitan area. Part of the southern unit of Kettle Moraine State Forest is in the southwest. The eastern part of Glacial Drumlin State Trail crosses the county, terminating here. • Named for the Fox River and the Fox Indian tribe, from Pottawattomi "wakusheg" meaning "foxes" • 1846 from Milwaukee (prior to statehood) • Waukesha was a major center for abolitionist activity before the Civil War; a station on the Underground Railroad, it also published the anti-slavery periodical *American Freeman*. • Union naval officer William B. Cusher and mail order merchant R.W. Sears both died here. • Diversified manufacturing, including paper products, hospital and scientific equipment, machinery; machine

shops, foundries; processing of dairy products; wheat, corn, soybeans, potatoes, hogs, sheep; limestone quarries; education (Carroll College) • Four Fortune 1000 corporations have their headquarters in the county.

WAUPACA *Waupaca* • 51,731 • 751 • Central WI; drained by the Wolf and Embarrass rivers. Hartman Creek State Park is on the western boundary. • Named for the Waupaca River, a short tributary of the Wolf River • 1851 from Winnebago and Brown • Dairying, wheat, corn, soybeans, peas, beans, potatoes, hay, cattle, hogs, sheep, poultry; some manufacturing.

WAUSHARA *Wautoma* • 23,154 • 626 • Central WI; drained by the White and Pine rivers, and Willow Creek. There are resorts at the western end of Lake Poygan. Nordic Mountain ski area and part of Mascoutin Valley State Trail are also here. • Waushara is a contrived or pseudo-Indian name • 1851 from Marquette • Dairying, corn, soybeans, peas, beans, potatoes, sheep, timber.

WINNEBAGO (one of three counties so named) *Oshkosh* • 156,763 • 439 • East-central WI, bounded on the east by Lake Winnebago; drained by the Wolf and Fox rivers. The county includes Poygan, Wenneconne, and Butte des Morts lakes (on the Wolf River) and Rush Lake. A section of Wiouwash State Trail is also here. • Named for either the Winnebago Indians or for Lake Winnebago • 1840 from Brown (prior to statehood) • Photographer Lewis W. Hine • Dairying (especially cheese), barley, oats, wheat, corn, soybeans, peas, hogs, sheep, poultry; manufacture of paper (among the nation's leading counties) and other wood products, machine-shop products, knit goods, transportation equipment, electronic components, industrial machinery, paints, tools, concrete blocks, pumps, plastic packaging; education (U. of WI–Oshkosh) • The Experimental Aircraft Association, headquartered in Oshkosh, hosts the EAA Fly-In Convention here each summer, and maintains the EAA AirVenture Museum.

WOOD (one of four counties so named) *Wisconsin Rapids* • 75,555 • 793 • Central WI; drained by the Wisconsin and Yellow rivers. The State Nursery is in the southeast. Powers Bluff ski area is in the center of the county. • Named for Joseph Wood (1811–1890), WI state legislator, county judge, and commissioner of state lands • 1856 from Portage • Barley, corn, soybeans, beans, potatoes, hay, cattle, sheep, cranberries; manufacturing.

WYOMING

Equal Rights

Each of the state's twenty-three counties is governed by a board composed of three or five commissioners, each elected to a four-year term.

ALBANY (one of two counties so named; the other in NY) *Laramie* • 32,014 • 4,274 • Southeastern WY, bounded on the south by the CO state line; watered by the Laramie River (forming Wheatland Reservoir No. 2). A portion of Medicine Bow National Forest (its headquarters in Laramie) is here, as is Hutton Lake and Bamforth national wildlife refuges. Part of Medicine Bow and Laramie mountain ranges are also in the county. Snowy Range ski area is here, as is Como Bluff, a dinosaur fossil bed. A few miles southeast of Laramie is the highest point on Transcontinental I-80 (elevation 8,640 feet) • Named for Albany, NY, former home of Charles D. Bradley, member of the WY legislature • 1868 from Laramie • Laramie was founded in 1868 as a tent and shanty town during construction of the Union Pacific Railroad. It was the site of the first "mixed" jury trial in 1870. • Humorist Edgar Wilson (Bill) Nye. (The *Laramie Boomerang*, which he helped found in 1881, is still published.) • Hay, alfalfa, cattle, sheep; timber, lumber; oil, natural gas, mining of gold, silver, coal; manufacture of cabinets, food products, toys, electronic teaching aids, portland cement, bricks, tile: education (U. of WY); tourism • The world's largest bronze bust, a likeness of Abraham Lincoln, is located near Laramie; it is twelve feet tall and rests on a stone base thirty feet high.

BIG HORN (one of two counties so named; the other in MT) *Basin* • 11,461 • 3,137 • Northern WY, bounded on the north by the MT state line; watered by the Bighorn River. Part of Bighorn National Forest and the Bighorn Mountains are situated along the eastern boundary of the county. Bighorn Lake (formed by the Bighorn River) and part of Bighorn Canyon National Recreation Area are here, as are Medicine Lodge State Archaeological Site, Medicine Wheel National Historic Landmark, and Pryor Mountain Wild Horse Range. • Named for the Bighorn River and the Bighorn Mountains • 1890 from Fremont and Johnson • Lovell was laid out in 1900 by Mormons. • Natural gas, oil (extraction and refining), coal; sugar beets, oats, barley, beans, hay, alfalfa, cattle, sheep; timber; manufacture of flour, concrete, steel products, gypsum products; tourism (skiing).

CAMPBELL (one of five counties so named) *Gillette* • 33,698 (the fifth most populated county in WY) • 4,797 • Northeastern WY, bounded on the north by the MT state line; watered by the Little Powder and Belle Fourche rivers. A portion of Thunder Basin National Grassland is in the southeast, with a separate smaller unit in the northeast. The county also contains Pumpkin Buttes. • Probably named for either General John A. Campbell (1835–80), first territorial governor of WY; or for Robert Campbell (1804–1879), fur trader and Indian commissioner • 1911 from Crook and Weston • Coal, natural gas, uranium; wheat, oats, sheep, cattle.

CARBON (one of four counties so named) *Rawlins* • 15,639 • 7,897 (the third largest county in WY and the twenty-third largest county in the U.S.) • Southern WY, bounded on the south by the CO state line; watered by the North Platte, Little Snake, and Medicine Bow rivers. The county includes Pathfinder Reservoir, part of Pathfinder National Wildlife Refuge, Pathfinder Bird Refuge, Seminoe Reservoir, Seminoe State Park, parts of Medicine Bow National Forest, the Sierra Madres, and the Medicine Bow Mountains. The Continental Divide forks in the west, forming part of the Great Divide Basin along the northwestern border. • Named for the coal deposits in the area • 1868 from Laramie • In 1874, "Rawlins Red" pigment from local paint mines was sent to New York City to be used on the Brooklyn Bridge. Rawlins became an important shipping point for uranium from the Gas Hills area north of the city. • Alfalfa, hay, cattle, sheep; coal mining, oil, natural gas, uranium; lumbering; tourism. The state penitentiary is in Rawlins.

CONVERSE *Douglas* • 12,052 • 4,255 • Eastern WY; drained by the North Platte River. Part of the Laramie Mountains and Medicine Bow National Forest are in the south. The county also contains Fort Fetterman State Historic Site and Ayers Park and Natural Bridge, a 100-foot arch spanning La Prele Creek. Part of Thunder Basin National Grassland is in the northeast. • Named for Amasa R. Converse (1842–85), banker, cattleman and treasurer of WY Territory • 1888 from Albany • Near Orpha is the site of the most notorious gambling resort and saloon in 1882, the "Hog Ranch." • Alfalfa, hay, sheep, cattle; coal, oil • The Wyoming State Fair is held in Converse each year.

CROOK *Sundance* • 5,887 • 2,859 • Northeastern WY, bounded on the east by the SD state line, and on the north by the MT state line; watered by the Belle Fourche (forming Keyhold Reservoir) and Little Missouri rivers. Devils Tower National Monument was the nation's first national monument; the popularity of this 865-foot tower of columnar rock was enhanced by its prominent role in the film *Close Encounters of the Third Kind*. The county also contains Keyhole State Park and Missouri Buttes. The Bear Lodge Mountains are in the center, part of Black Hills are in the south, and parts of Black Hills National Forest are also in the county. • One of two counties (the other in OR) named for General George Crook (1829–90), Union officer in the Civil War and Indian fighter • 1875 • Grain, wheat, hay, alfalfa, oats, sheep, cattle; timber; coal mines; oil refining.

FREMONT *Lander* • 35,804 (the fourth most populated county in WY) • 9,183 (the second largest county in WY; the sixteenth largest county in the U.S.) • West-central WY; watered by the Sweetwater, Popo Agie, Wind, and Bighorn rivers. The Wind River Mountains are in the west; the Green and Granite mountains are in the south. The Bighorn River forms Boysen Reservoir in the north. Castle Gardens and Gas Hills uranium mining districts are in the east. The Continental Divide passes through the southwest and northwest corners of the county and forms most of the county's western boundary. Fremont County includes parts of Shoshone and Bridger-Teton national forests, Sinks Canyon and Boysen state parks, and most of Wind River Indian Reservation. • One of four counties named for John C. Frémont (1813–90), soldier, politician and western explorer • 1884 from Sweetwater • South Pass, a national historic landmark in the southwest, was a major feature of the Oregon Trail and was used by thousands of westward emigrants during the mid 1800s. • Shoshone chief Washakie died here. Shoshone Indian guide of the Lewis and Clark expedition Sacajawea is buried at the Wind River Indian Reservation. • Grain, sugar beets, hay, barley, alfalfa, corn, beans, cattle, sheep; timber; coal, iron ore, and uranium mining, oil and natural gas; sulfuric acid plants, manufacture of railroad cross ties, fence posts • Lander sponsors the One-Shot Antelope Hunt each year.

GOSHEN *Torrington* • 12,538 • 2,225 • Southeastern WY, bounded on the east by the NE state line; watered by the North Platte River. Fort Laramie National Historic Site, and Hawk Springs Reservoir and State Recreation Area are here. • Possibly Named for Goshen Hole Valley • 1911 from Platte and Laramie • On August 19, 1854, Lt. John Grattan left Fort Laramie to arrest a Sioux tribal member for killing a cow. A shot was fired, panic resulted, and Grattan's entire force was killed. The incident touched off a series of retaliations on both sides. The resulting Plains Indian Wars continued until the Indians were removed to reservations later in the century. Torrington was on the Pony Express route and on both the Texas and Oregon trails. • Beans, oats, corn, hay, sugar beets, alfalfa, wheat, cattle; mining of uranium and coal; livestock auctions; food processing (especially beet-sugar refining).

HOT SPRINGS (the only county so named, although there is a Hot Spring County in AR) *Thermopolis* • 4,882 • 2,004 (the smallest county in WY) • North-central WY; drained by the Bighorn River. Parts of the Absaroka Range, Shoshone National Forest, and Wind River Indian Reservation are here. The Owl Creek Mountains are located in the south. Big Horn Hot Spring in Hot Springs State Park is one of the largest hot mineral springs in the world. The Wyoming State Buffalo Herd roams in hills near the park. Legend Rock State Petroglyph Site is near Hamilton Dome. • Named for the hot springs near Thermopolis • 1911 from Fremont, Johnson, and Big Horn • Natural gas and oil, coal mining; alfalfa, sugar beets, some cattle; manufacture of hand guns.

JOHNSON (one of twelve counties so named) *Buffalo* • 7,075 • 4,166 • North-central WY; watered by the Powder River, and Clear and Crazy Woman creeks. The county includes parts of Bighorn National Forest, Cloud Peak Wilderness Area, and the Big Horn Mountains. Lake De Smet reservoir is also here. • Named for Edward P. Johnson (1842–1879), U.S. attorney for WY Territory and WY territorial legislator • Created as Pease County in 1875; named changed in 1879 • The county experienced much conflict between farmers and cattlemen, and was the scene of the Johnson County Cattle War in 1892, which culminated in a battle between locals and the hired guns of the cattle barons. (The war is dramatized in Owen Wister's *The Virginian*.) Many Indian battles were fought in the county, two of which occurred at Fort Phil Kearny, now a State Historic Site. In the southwest is the site of the "Dull Knife" battle, in which Col. Mackenzie fought the Cheyenne Indians on November 25, 1876. • Sugar beets, hay, alfalfa, sheep, cattle; timber; sand and gravel; oil, uranium and coal • Johnson County contains the site of the mysterious "Lost Cabin Mine" where, in 1865, seven Swedish miners from the Black Hills, five of whom were later killed while being routed by Indians, mined $7,000 worth of placer gold in three days. Hole-in-the-Wall, the most famous hideout for Butch Cassidy and his gang, is near the southern border.

LARAMIE *Cheyenne* • 81,607 (the most populated county in WY) • 2,686 • Southeastern WY, bounded on the south by the CO state line and on the east by the NE state line; watered by Chugwater, Horse, North Bear, Little Bear, and Lodgepole creeks. The foothills of the Laramie Mountains are in the west. Curt Gowdy State Park is in the southwest. • Named for Jacques La Ramee (?–1821), French-Canadian trapper. • First county in WY, created in 1867 • Squatters arriving in the county in 1867 just ahead of the Union Pacific Railroad were removed by federal troops. Cheyenne, capital of WY Territory and later the state capital, was also the outfitting point for the Black Hills gold fields and a major shipping point for cattle from TX. It became known for its wealthy cattle barons and Hereford herds. The city was at the center of the war between cattlemen and sheepmen and populated by gunmen, gamblers and transients. It was here in Cheyenne that Nellie Tayloe Ross became, in 1925, the first woman governor in the U.S. • Wheat, sugar beets, hay, alfalfa, corn, beans, oats, cattle, sheep, dairying; timber; oil; manufacture of chemicals, plastics; government offices. • The Francis E. Warren Air Force Base was designated in 1957 as headquarters for the nation's first Atlas intercontinental ballistic missile base. Cheyenne holds Frontier Days each July, a six-day celebration, featuring one of the oldest and largest rodeos in the U.S.

LINCOLN (one of twenty-four counties so named) *Kemmerer* • 14,573 • 4,069 • Western WY, bounded on the west by the UT and ID state lines; drained by the Green, Greys and Salt rivers. The Green River forms Fontenelle Reservoir in the east. The Salt River Range, Bridger-Teton National Forest, and Pine Creek ski area are here, as is the Grand Canyon of the Snake River. Fossil Butte National Monument preserves within its fifty-five-million-year-old rock layers the most noteworthy record of freshwater fossil fish ever found in the U.S. • One of eighteen counties named for Abraham Lincoln • 1911 from Uinta • Barley, hay, alfalfa, sheep, cattle, dairying; coal, oil and phosphate; some manufacturing • The J.C. Penney Mother Store (opened in 1902), the first in the nation-wide chain, is located in Kemmerer, and still operating.

NATRONA *Casper* • 66,533 (the second most populated county in WY) • 5,340 (the fifth largest county in WY) • Central WY; watered by the North Platte and Sweetwater rivers, and the headstreams of the Powder River. Alcova Reservoir and part of Pathfinder Reservoir are in the south. The northern end of the Laramie Mountains is in the southeastern corner and the southern end of Bighorn Mountains is in the northwest corner. Hogadon ski area, Edness K. Wilkins State Park, and Pathfinder National Wildlife Refuge are located here. • Named for the mineral natron, a sodium carbonate, found in the county • 1888 from Carbon • Fort Caspar, built in 1863, served as a Pony Express depot and offered protection to travelers on the Oregon Trail. Casper, founded in 1888 as a tent town prior to the arrival of the Chicago and Western Railway, became an oil town with the exploitation of the Salt Creek Oil Field just north. The oil fields at Teapot Dome were at the center of the scandal that darkened the administration of President Warren G. Harding in 1922. • Hay, alfalfa, cattle, sheep; oil extraction (large fields here) and refining, coal, bentonite, and uranium mining; education (Casper College); manufacture of oil field equipment • The Central WY Fair and Rodeo is held each August. Independence Rock (state historic site) in the southwest is called the "Register of the Desert." More than 5,000 pioneers have carved their names on the large granite boulder, some as long ago as the early 1800s.

NIOBRARA *Lusk* • 2,407 (the least populated county in WY) • 2,626 • Eastern WY, bounded on the east by the SD and NE state lines; watered by the South Fork of the Cheyenne River and its branches. A small part of Thunder Basin Grassland is near the north boundary. Lost Creek Fossil Area is in the center. • Named for the Niobrara River which rises within the county • 1911 from Converse • Silver and radium were once mined here. The population of Lusk briefly swelled to 10,000 during the oil boom of 1918. • Wheat, oats, cattle, sheep; petroleum, natural gas • Lusk refers to itself as the seat of the least populated county in the least populated state.

PARK (one of three counties so named) *Cody* • 25,786 • 6,943 (the fourth largest county in WY and the twenty-eighth largest county in the U.S.) • Northwestern WY, bounded on the north and west by the MT state line; watered by the Yellowstone, Shoshone and Greybull rivers. The northwestern part of the county now includes the northern half and southeast-

ern corner of Yellowstone National Park (which was formerly independent of any county), home to 10,000 geysers and hot springs and constituting the world's greatest geyser area. Shoshone National Forest (its headquarters in Cody) was the first national forest in the U.S.; it was created on March 30, 1891 by President Benjamin Harrison. North Absaroka Wilderness Area, part of the Absaroka Range, and Buffalo Bill Reservoir (Shoshone River) and State Park are located here. The eastern shore of Yellowstone Lake forms part of the county's western boundary. Gallatin Range is in the northwest corner. • Named for Yellowstone National Park • 1909 from Sweetwater, Fremont, and Big Horn • Painter Jackson Pollock • Oats, barley, hay, sugar beets, alfalfa, corn, brans, beans, sheep, cattle; oil extracting and refining, coal mining, limestone; manufacture of gypsum-board; tourism (dude ranches) • Attractions in Cody include the Buffalo Bill Museum and the William Cody House. Buffalo Bill's boyhood home was moved here from Le Claire, IA. Cody is the site of the three-day Cody Stampede rodeo in early July. Camp Monaco, in the north, was the scene of Buffalo Bill's last big game hunt in September, 1913; Prince Albert I of Monaco was a member of one of the illustrious hunter's many celebrated hunting parties.

PLATTE (one of three counties so named) *Wheatland* • 8,807 • 2,085 • Southeastern WY; watered by Chugwater Creek, the North Platte (forming Guernsey and Glendo reservoirs in the north) and Laramie rivers. Part of the Laramie Mountains and a small part of Medicine Bow National Forest are in the west. Guernsey and Glendo state parks are also in the county. Grayrocks Reservoir is near Wheatland. The Oregon Trail Ruts and Register Cliff is here. • Named for the North Platte River • 1911 from Laramie • Corn, oats, wheat, hay, sugar beets, alfalfa, beans, cattle; manufacture of marble products, stone, fabricated metal products, consumer goods; logging; mica quarrying.

SHERIDAN *Sheridan* • 26,560 • 2,523 • Northern WY, bounded on the north by the MT state line; watered by the Little Bighorn (its source in the northwest corner), Tongue, and Powder rivers. Part of Bighorn National Forest and the Bighorn Mountains are here. Connor Battlefield and Trail End state historic sites are also located in the county. Massacre Hill marks the spot of the historic 1866 Fetterman Fight. • Named for the county's major town and county seat, itself named for Union General Philip Henry Sheridan (1831–88); one of five counties named directly or indirectly for the general • 1888 from Johnson • Geochemist Harrison Brown • Barley, oats, alfalfa, corn, wheat, sugar beets, beans, cattle; coal mining; diversified manufacturing, milling; tourism (dude ranches, fishing, big game hunting) • Sheridan celebrates All American Indian Days each August.

SUBLETTE *Pinedale* • 5,920 • 4,882 • Western WY, bounded on the northeast by the Continental Divide; watered by the Green River (with the headwaters of Fontenelle Reservoir in the west). Parts of Bridger-Teton National Forest, including part of the Wind River Mountains and Shoshone National Forest are here. Gannett Peak (13,804 feet), the highest point in the state, is also found in the county. Big Sandy Reservoir is on the southern boundary. Boulder Lake B.L.M. Recreation Site and White Pine ski area are in the east. • Named for William L. Sublette (1799–1845), fur trader and explorer of the Rocky Mountain region. His trading post grew to become Fort Laramie. • 1921 from Fremont • Sheep, cattle, hay; timber • One mile east of Daniel is a monument dedicated to the memory of Father De Smet at the site of the first Holy Mass offered in WY (July 25, 1840).

SWEETWATER *Green River* • 37,613 (the third most populated county in WY) • 10,426 (the largest county in WY and the eighth largest county in the U.S.) • Southwestern WY, bounded on the south by the UT and CO state lines; watered by the Green River (forming Flaming Gorge Reservoir in the south) and Sandy Creek. The northeastern part of the county is dominated by the Great Divide Basin of the Continental Divide. Killpecker Sand Dunes, Big Sandy State Recreation Area, part of Flaming Gorge National Recreation Area, and Seedskadee National Wildlife Refuge are here. • Named for the Sweetwater River, which flows through Fremont County, at that time still a part of Sweetwater County • Created as Carter County 1867 from Laramie; name changed 1869 • In 1885 Federal troops were called to Rock Springs to quell riots against Chinese mine workers; the troops remained there until 1898. • Coal, oil, natural gas, and trona (source of soda ash), sand and gravel; manufacturing; alfalfa, oats, cattle. • The site of the town of Green River marked the starting point for John Wesley Powell's historic 1869 expedition into the Grand Canyon. Point of Rocks contains the remains of old Rock Point Stage Station, a relay point for the 1862 Ben Holliday Overland Trail Stages. The outlaw Butch Cassidy earned his nickname when he worked in a butcher's shop in Rock Springs.

TETON (one of three counties so named) *Jackson* • 18,251 (63% increase since 1990; the fastest growing county in WY) • 4,008 • Northwestern WY, bounded on the west by the MT and ID state lines; watered by the Snake River and Jackson Lake. Jackson Hole Valley runs through the center of the county. It also includes the National Elk Refuge (established in 1912 as the nation's first big-game refuge and home to the largest elk herd in the U.S.), Grand Teton National Park, Gros Ventre Range, part of Bridger-Teton National Forest, and part of Targhee National Forest. The Continental Divide runs through the northeastern part of the county. Part of Yellowstone National Park is in the north. Old Faithful and some 10,000 other geysers and hot springs make this the greatest geyser area on earth. Established in 1872, it was the world's first national park. • Named for the Teton Mountains • 1921 from Lincoln • The Yellowstone area was explored in 1808 by John Colter, a member of the 1804–06 Lewis and Clark Expedition, and the first white American to enter WY. Massive fires in Yellowstone Park consumed over 700,000 acres in 1988. • Photography critic and editor Nancy Newhall • Alfalfa, barley; tourism (Jackson is a popular resort destination for visitors.)

UINTA *Evanston* • 19,742 • 2,082 • Southwestern WY, bounded on the south and west by the UT state line; watered by the Black Forks of the Green River and Bear River. The foothills of the Uinta Mountains and the Bear River Divide range are located here. A small part of Wasatch National Forest is on the southern border. Bear River State Park and Fort Bridger State Historic Site are also in the county. • Named for either the Uinta Mountains or for the Uintah Ute Indian tribe • 1869 (original county) • Fort Bridger offered protection and supplies to thousands of pioneers crossing the state in covered wagons. • Sheep, grain, hay, alfalfa; coal, oil, natural gas; manufacture of lumber, petroleum products, concrete, wire harnesses; printing.

WASHAKIE *Worland* • 8,289 • 2,240 • North-central WY; watered by the Bighorn River, and Nowood, Nowater, and Gooseberry creeks. Part of the Bighorn Mountains are in the east. A small portion of Bighorn National Forest, which includes Powder Pass ski area, is in the northeast corner. • Named for Washakie (?–1900), Shoshone Indian chief • 1911 from Big Horn and Johnson • Beans, grain, barley, sugar beets, hay, alfalfa, sheep; meat processing; manufacture of dairy products, soft drinks, aluminum products; printing and publishing; timber.

WESTON *Newcastle* • 6,644 • 2,398 • Northeastern WY, bounded on the east by the SD state line; drained by the South Fork of the Cheyenne River, and Beaver and Black Thunder creeks. A large portion of Thunder Basin National Grassland is here, as is part of the Black Hills and Black Hills National Forest. • The derivation of the county's name is uncertain. It was possibly named for one of two men with the surname Weston, one a banker in Beatrice, the other a geologist and surveyor. • 1890 from Crook • Oats, cattle; timber; oil, natural gas, clay, bentonite mining; manufacture of lumber, petroleum products.

Appendix I
Independent Cities

There are forty-three independent cities in the United States. They are legally separate from the counties in which they are located or to which they lie adjacent. Each is listed below with figures for population (based on the 2000 census) and area in square miles.

MARYLAND

Baltimore (651,154) (81)

MISSOURI

St. Louis (348,189) (62)

NEVADA

Carson City (52,457) (143)

VIRGINIA

Alexandria (128,283) (15)
Bedford (6,299) (7)
Bristol (17,367) (13)
Buena Vista (6,349) (7)
Charlottesville (45,049) (10)
Chesapeake (199,184) (341)
Clifton Forge (4,289) (3)
Colonial Heights (16,897) (7)
Covington (6,303) (6)
Danville (48,411) (43)
Emporia (5,665) (7)
Fairfax (21,498) (6)
Falls Church (10,377) (2)
Franklin (8,346) (8)
Fredericksburg (19,279) (11)
Galax (6,837) (8)
Hampton (146,437) (52)
Harrisonburg (40,468) (18)
Hopewell (22,354) (10)
Lexington (6,867) (2)
Lynchburg (65,269) (49)
Manassas (35,135) (10)
Manassas Park (10,290) (2)
Martinsville (15,416) (11)
Newport News (180,150) (68)
Norfolk (234,403) (54)
Norton (3,904) (8)
Petersburg (33,740) (23)
Poquoson (11,566) (16)
Portsmouth (100,565) (33)
Radford (15,859) (10)
Richmond (197,790) (60)
Roanoke (94,911) (43)
Salem (24,747) (15)
Staunton (23,853) (20)
Suffolk (63,677) (400)
Virginia Beach (425,257) (248)
Waynesboro (19,520) (15)
Williamsburg (11,998) (9)
Winchester (23,585) (9)

Appendix II

Alaskan Boroughs and Census Areas

The state of Alaska has no counties. It is divided into local government units called organized boroughs. The rest of the state is referred to as the unorganized borough. Each organized borough and census area is listed below, along with population (based on the 2000 census) and area in square miles.

Aleutians East Borough   (2,697)   (6,988)
Aleutians West Census Area   (5,465)   (4,397)
Anchorage Borough   (260,283)   (1,697)
Bethel Census Area   (16,006)   (40,633)
Bristol Bay Borough   (1,258)   (505)
Denali Borough   (1,893)   (12,750)
Dillingham Census Area   (4,922)   (18,675)
Fairbanks North Star Borough   (82,840)   (7,366)
Haines Borough   (2,392)   (2,344)
Juneau Borough   (30,711)   (2,717)
Kenai Peninsula Borough   (49,691)   (16,013)
Ketchikan Gateway Borough   (14,070)   (1,233)
Kodiak Island Borough   (13,913)   (6,560)
Lake and Peninsula Borough   (1,823)   (23,782)

Matanuska-Susitna Borough   (59,322)   (24,682)
Nome Census Area   (9,196)   (23,001)
North Slope Borough   (7,385)   (88,817)
Northwest Arctic Borough   (7,208)   (35,898)
Prince of Wales–Outer Ketchikan Census Area   (6,146)   (7,411)
Sitka Borough   (8,835)   (2,874)
Skagway-Hoonah-Angoon Census Area   (3,436)   (7,896)
Southeast Fairbanks Census Area   (6,174)   (24,815)
Valdez-Cordova Census Area   (10,195)   (34,319)
Wade Hampton Census Area   (7,028)   (17,194)
Wrangell-Petersburg Census Area   (6,684)   (5,835)
Yakutat Borough   (808)   (7,650)
Yukon-Koyukuk Census Area   (6,551)   (145,900)

Appendix III

State Abbreviations

Alabama	AL	Louisiana	LA	Ohio	OH
Alaska	AK	Maine	ME	Oklahoma	OK
Arizona	AZ	Maryland	MD	Oregon	OR
Arkansas	AR	Massachusetts	MA	Pennsylvania	PA
California	CA	Michigan	MI	Rhode Island	RI
Colorado	CO	Minnesota	MN	South Carolina	SC
Connecticut	CT	Mississippi	MS	South Dakota	SD
Delaware	DE	Missouri	MO	Tennessee	TN
Florida	FL	Montana	MT	Texas	TX
Georgia	GA	Nebraska	NE	Utah	UT
Hawaii	HI	Nevada	NV	Vermont	VT
Idaho	ID	New Hampshire	NH	Virginia	VA
Illinois	IL	New Jersey	NJ	Washington	WA
Indiana	IN	New Mexico	NM	West Virginia	WV
Iowa	IA	New York	NY	Wisconsin	WI
Kansas	KS	North Carolina	NC	Wyoming	WY
Kentucky	KY	North Dakota	ND		

Index